T5-CCJ-867

CASES AND COMMENTARY ON INTERNATIONAL LAW

By

Mark W. Janis
Sometime William F. Starr Professor of Law
University of Connecticut
Reader in Law & Fellow of Exeter College
University of Oxford

John E. Noyes
Professor of Law & Director,
International Legal Studies Program
California Western School of Law

AMERICAN CASEBOOK SERIES®

WEST PUBLISHING CO.
ST. PAUL, MINN., 1997

610 Opperman Drive
P.O. Box 64526
St. Paul, MN 55164–0526
1–800–328–9352

Library of Congress Cataloging-in-Publication Data

Janis, Mark W.
Cases and commentary on international law / by Mark W. Janis and John E. Noyes.
p. cm. — (American casebook series)
Includes index.
ISBN 0–314–21129–2 (hardcover)
1. International law—Cases. I. Noyes, John E., 1951– . II. Title. III. Series.
JX68.J36 1997
341—dc21 97–1881
CIP

ISBN 0–314–21129–2

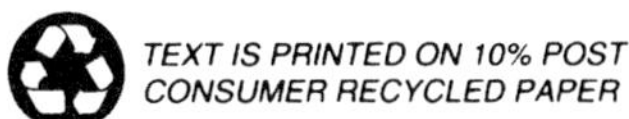

To Janet, Matthew, Robert, Philip, and Edward
—MWJ

To Barbara, Sarah, and Ellen
—JEN

*

Preface

> A comprehensive and scientific knowledge of international law is highly necessary, not only to lawyers practicing in our commercial ports, but to every [one] who is animated by liberal views, and a generous ambition to assume stations of high public trust. It would be exceedingly to the discredit of any person who should be called to take a share in the councils of the nation, if [that person] should be found deficient in the great leading principles of this law; and I think I cannot be mistaken in considering the elementary learning of the law of nations, as not only an essential part of the education of an American lawyer, but as proper to be academically taught.—James Kent, 1 *Commentaries on American Law* 20 (2d ed. 1832).

The teaching of international law in the American law school goes back at least as far as the Columbia lectures of Chancellor James Kent (1763–1847) and the four volumes of his *Commentaries on American Law* (1826–1830), the first great U.S. legal treatise. Kent's *Commentaries* begin with 200 pages devoted to the law of nations. The tradition of an American casebook on international law also dates to the last century. In 1893, Freeman Snow's *Cases and Opinions on International Law* made its appearance, followed in 1906 by a greatly developed and very influential revision, *Cases on International Law* by James Brown Scott.

Our new casebook builds on this by now long-standing tradition, but it departs from some of its immediate predecessors by providing an intellectual consolidation of what may have become a too-great proliferation of topics, issues, and cases. Our ambition here is simply to teach, to give law professors and law students the cases and commentary necessary to achieve a first-class professional education in the fundamentals of international law. No matter what international law specialty a student may go on to study or to practice—international corporate law, international environmental law, international litigation, international human rights, etc.—we mean to lay the foundation for that study and practice in the pages that follow.

We believe that the order of our chapters constitutes a sensible organization for most courses in international law. Chapter 1 introduces international law, looking briefly at the subject's history and presenting and discussing two sample, albeit well-known, cases to illuminate the nature of international legal rules and international legal process. Chapters 2 and 3 examine the sources of international law in greater depth, showing the student how lawyers, judges, and jurists draw international legal rules from a variety of sources, *e.g.,* treaties, custom, general principles, *jus cogens,* and equity. Chapters 4 and 5 return to international legal process, exploring the ways in which international law is applied first in municipal courts and second in international tribunals. We then turn to the relationship between international law and the actors in international relations: individuals in Chapter 6, states in Chapter 7, and international organizations in Chapter 8. Finally, we address two areas of great practical importance in modern international law: regimes and common spaces in Chapter 9 and international conflict of laws in Chapter 10.

Most chapters deserve six hours of class, *i.e.,* about two weeks. Only Chapters 1, 2, and 7 are shorter, each calling for about three or four hours. So, even though this casebook is a great deal briefer than most, there is still about 17 or 18 weeks of material between the covers; in most courses some pruning will need be done. Ordinarily, we expect that teachers will choose to teach Chapters 1 through 5 in about seven or eight weeks and then choose from among Chapters 6 to 10 for an additional six or seven weeks. We have tried to make the later five chapters free-standing so that any of them can be taught in any order after the first five chapters are completed.

For students who wish to go beyond the casebook, quite a number of textbooks are available, including Ian Brownlie, *Principles of Public International Law* (Oxford 4th ed. 1990), Mark W. Janis, *An Introduction to International Law* (Little Brown 2d ed. 1993), and *Oppenheim's International Law* (Longman 9th ed. by Robert Jennings & Arthur Watts 1992). There are thousands of other books, articles, cases, and treaties cited below. However, footnotes and string citations from excerpted materials have ordinarily been omitted; when footnotes have been retained in the materials, the original's numbering has been used; three asterisks mark other omissions.

Chapters 1, 2, 3, 4, 5, 6, and 10 were originally prepared by Mark Janis and Chapters 7, 8, and 9 by John Noyes, but the two of us have used these materials over quite a number of years and, by now, have traded many ideas and much wording on most pages. We have also been fortunate in the assistance of others, and at risk of inadvertently leaving out some names, let us mention those who have helped along the way: William Alford, David Bederman, Howard Berman, Phillip Blumberg, Anthony Bradley, John Bridge, Ian Brownlie, Thomas Buergenthal, Arthur Campbell, Michael Dessent, James Friedberg, Christine Gray, Richard Kay, Chin Kim, David Kennedy, Harold Koh, Robert Lutz, William Lynch, Hugh Macgill, Phyllis Marion, Diane May, Samuel Menefee, Michael Reisman, John Ryan, Philippe Sands, Henry Schermers, Stephen Schwebel, Steven Smith, Louis Sohn, Kenneth Vandevelde, and Carol Weisbrod. Several students and librarians at California Western School of Law, the University of Connecticut School of Law, the University of Oxford, and Roger Williams University School of Law also provided able research support: Rachel Smith Alsop, Daniel Bender, Todd Dressel, Stephanie Edwards, Darlene Glenn, Barbara Glennan, Edward Johnson, Kenneth Naide, Loretta Nelms–Reyes, Jane Petitmermet, Risto Vahimets, Tara Velez, Linda Weathers, Katherine Young, and Teodora

Ziamou. The technical assistance of Elizabeth Johnson, Cheryl Meegan, Sandra Michalik, Sandra Murray, Anita Simons, Sonia Smith, and Donna Vella was indispensable.

MARK W. JANIS
Oxford

JOHN E. NOYES
San Diego

January 1997

*

Acknowledgments

Excerpts from the following books, articles, cases, and treaties appear with the kind permission of the copyright holders.

—, An Agenda for Peace 1995 (2d ed. 1995). Copyright © 1995 by the United Nations.

Alvarez, Jose E., The Once and Future Security Council, 18 The Washington Quarterly No. 2 (Spring 1995). Copyright © 1995 by The Center for Strategic and International Studies and the Massachusetts Institute of Technology. Reprinted by permission of The Center for Strategic and International Studies, the Massachusetts Institute of Technology, and Professor Jose E. Alvarez of the University of Michigan Law School.

American Law Institute, Foreign Relations Law of the United States. Copyright © 1988 by the American Law Institute. Reprinted with permission.

—, AM&S Europe Ltd. v. EC Commission, Common Market Law Reports (1982). Copyright © 1982 by Sweet & Maxwell Limited.

—, The Antarctic Treaty, No. 5778, 402 U.N.T.S. 71. Copyright © 1962 by the United Nations.

—, Arbitration Between Great Britain and Costa Rica. Reproduced with permission from 18 AJIL 147 (1924), © The American Society of International Law.

Bederman, David J., "The Souls of International Organizations: Legal Personality and the Lighthouse at Cape Spartel," 36 Va. J. Int'l L. 275 (1996). Copyright © 1996 by Virginia Journal of International Law.

Caron, David D., Protection of the Stratospheric Ozone Layer and the Structure of International Environmental Lawmaking. Copyright © 1991 by University of California, Hastings College of Law. Reprinted from Hastings International and Comparative Law Review, Vol. 14, No. 4, pp. 755, 758–76, by permission.

—, Case Concerning the Barcelona Traction, Light and Power Co., Ltd., Second Phase *(Belgium v. Spain),* I.C.J. 3 (1970). Copyright © 1970 by the United Nations.

—, Case Concerning Military and Paramilitary Activities In and Against Nicaragua *(Nicaragua v. United States),* I.C.J. 14 (1986). Copyright © 1986 by the United Nations.

—, Case Concerning Questions of Interpretation and Application of the 1971 Montreal Convention Arising from the Aerial Incident at Lockerbie *(Libya v. United States),* I.C.J. 114 (1992). Copyright © 1992 by the United Nations.

—, Cession of Alaska (1867), 134 Consolidated Treaty Series 331 (1969). Copyright © 1969 by Oceana Publications, Inc.

Committee of the Inquiry into Shipping, Report 51 (1970). Copyright © 1970 by Crown, HMSO Publications Centre. Reprinted by permission.

Conference for Peace in Yugoslavia, Arbitration Commission. Reproduced with permission from 30 I.L.M. 550 (1991), © The American Society of International Law.

Conference on Security and Cooperation in Europe, Final Act. Reproduced with permission from 14 I.L.M. 1292 (1975), © The American Society of International Law.

—, Convention on the Continental Shelf, No. 7302, 499 U.N.T.S. 311. Copyright © 1964 by the United Nations.

—, Convention on Rights and Duties of States, 165 L.N.T.S. 19 (1929). Copyright © 1929 by the League of Nations. Reprinted by permission of the United Nations.

—, Corfu Channel Case *(United Kingdom v. Albania)* (Merits), I.C.J. Rep. 4 (1949). Copyright © 1949 by the United Nations.

D'Amato, Anthony, International Law: Process and Prospect (2d ed. 1995). Copyright © 1995 by Transnational Publishers, Inc.

—, The Diplomatic and Consular Staff Case *(United States v. Iran),* I.C.J. 3 (1980). Copyright © 1980 by the United Nations.

—, The Dogger Bank Case *(Great Britain v. Russia),* Report of February 26, 1905, The Hague Court Rep. Copyright © 1916 by the Carnegie Endowment for International Peace.

—, The Eastern Greenland Case, P.C.I.J., Series A/B, No. 53 (1933), 3 World Court Reports 151 (1969). Copyright © 1969 by Oceana Publications, Inc.

—, The ELSI Case *(United States v. Italy),* I.C.J. 15 (1989). Copyright © 1989 by the United Nations.

European Community, Declaration on Yugoslavia and on the Guidelines on the Recognition of New States. Reproduced with permission from 31 I.L.M. 1485 (1992), © The American Society of International Law.

Feldman, Mark B., The United States Foreign Sovereign Immunities Act of 1976 in Perspective: A Founder's View. This article is reproduced from (1986) 35 I.C.L.Q. 302 with permission from the publishers The

British Institute of International and Comparative Law, 17 Russell Square, London WC1B 5DR.

—, Fisheries Jurisdiction Case *(United Kingdom of Great Britain and North Ireland v. Iceland)* (Merits), I.C.J. 3 (1974). Copyright © 1974 by the United Nations.

Franck, Thomas M. and Faiza Patel, UN Police Action in Lieu of War: "The Old Order Changeth." Reproduced with permission from 85 AJIL 63 (1991), © 1991 The American Society of International Law. Reprinted by permission.

—, The Golder Case. Copyright © The Round Hall Press. Reprinted with permission from Berger, Case Law of the European Court of Human Rights: Vol. I, 1979 (The Round Hall Press, Dublin, Ireland, 1979).

Grotius, Hugo, The Freedom of the Seas. Copyright © 1916 by the Carnegie Endowment for International Peace.

Guruswamy, Laksham D. et al., International Environmental Law and World Order. Copyright © 1994 by West Publishing Co.

Henkin, Louis, "Use of Force: Law and U.S. Policy," Right v. Might: International Law and the Use of Force. Copyright © 1989 by Council on Foreign Relations Press. Reprinted with permission.

Henkin, Louis, Will the U.S. Supreme Court Fail International Law? Reproduced with permission from ASIL Newsletter, August-September 1992, © The American Society of International Law.

International Arbitral Tribunal (Texaco/Libya Arbitration). Reproduced with permission from 17 I.L.M. 1 (1978), © The American Society of International Law.

ITU Broadcasting Satellite Conference, Doc. No. 81–E (Jan. 17, 1977), Annex 4, in 2 Manual on Space Law 383 (Jasentuliyana, Nandasiri & Roy S.K. Lee, eds. 1979). Copyright © 1979 by Oceana Publications, Inc.

Janis, Mark W., The Doctrine of Forum Non Conveniens and the Bhopal Case, XXXIV NILR 192, 193–204 (1987). Copyright © 1987 by Martinus Nijhoff Publishers/Dordrect. Reprinted by permission of Kluwer Academic Publishers.

Janis, Mark W., An Introduction to International Law. Copyright © 1993 by Little, Brown and Company.

Janis, Mark W., Sea Power and the Law of the Sea. Copyright © Mark W. Janis.

Janis, Mark W., Somber Reflections on the Compulsory Jurisdiction of the International Court. Reproduced with permission from 81 AJIL 144 (1987), © The American Society of International Law.

Janis, Mark W., Individuals as Subjects of International Law, 17 Cornell Int'l L.J. 61 (1984). Copyright © 1984 by Cornell International Law Journal. Reprinted by permission of Cornell International Law Journal and Fred B. Rothman & Co.

Joyner, Christopher C., "Antarctic Treaty Diplomacy: Problems, Prospects, and Policy Implications," The Diplomatic Record 1989–1990. Copyright © 1991 by the Institute for the Study of Diplomacy, School of Foreign Service, Georgetown University, Washington, D.C.

—, The Kellogg-Briand Pact (1928), Renunciation of War as an Instrument of National Policy, 94 L.N.T.S. 57 (1929). Copyright © 1929 by the League of Nations. Reprinted by permission of the United Nations.

League of Nations, Report of the International Committee of Jurists entrusted by the Council of the League of Nations with the Task of Giving an Advisory Opinion upon the Legal Aspects of the Aaland Islands Question, League of Nations Official Journal, Special Supp. No. 3 (1920). Copyright © 1920 by the League of Nations. Reprinted by permission of the United Nations.

Lebow, Richard Ned, Accidents and Crises: The Dogger Bank Affair, 31(1) Naval War College Rev., at 66 (Summer 1978). Reprinted by permission of U.S. Naval War College.

—, Legal Consequences for States of the Continued Presence of South Africa in Namibia (Southwest Africa) Notwithstanding Security Council Resolution 276 (1970), Advisory Opinion, I.C.J. 16 (1971). Copyright © 1971 by the United Nations.

—, The Lotus Case *(France v. Turkey),* P.C.I.J. Rep., Ser. A., No. 10 (1927). Copyright © 1927 by the League of Nations. Reprinted by permission of the United Nations.

Lowenfeld, Andreas F., International Litigation and Arbitration. Copyright © 1993 by West Publishing Co.

I Maccabees 8. Scripture quotation found on pp. 22–23 from I Maccabees 8 is taken from Today's English Version Deuterocanonicals/Apocrypha. Copyright © 1979, 1992 American Bible Society. Used by permission.

Mann, F.A., Contempt of Court in the House of Lords and the European Court of Human Rights, 95 Law Quarterly Review 348, 348–49 (1979). Copyright © 1979 by Steven and Sons Limited. Reprinted by permission of Sweet & Maxwell.

Mazzola, Maria A., Note, Forum Non Conveniens and Foreign Plaintiffs: Addressing the Unanswered Questions of Reyno, 6 Fordham Int'l L.J. 577 (1983). Copyright © 1983 by Fordham International Law Journal.

—, The Meuse Case, P.C.I.J. Rep., Ser. A/B, No. 70 (1937). Copyright © 1937 by the League of Nations. Reprinted by permission of the United Nations.

—, The Miniquiers and Ecrehos Case *(Great Britain v. France),* I.C.J. 47 (1953). Copyright © 1953 by the United Nations.

—, The Nottebohm Case *(Liechtenstein v. Guatemala),* I.C.J. 4 (1955). Copyright © 1955 by the United Nations.

—, North Sea Continental Shelf Cases *(Federal Republic of Germany v. Denmark; Federal Republic of Germany v. The Netherlands),* I.C.J. 4 (1969). Copyright © 1969 by the United Nations.

Noyes, John E., The Functions of Compromissory Clauses in U.S. Treaties, 34 Va. J. Int'l L. 831 (1994). Copyright © 1994 by Virginia Journal of International Law.

Noyes, John E., An Introduction to the Law of Piracy, 21 Calif. Western Int'l L.J. 105 (1990). Copyright © 1990 by California Western International Law Journal.

Noyes, John E. and Brian D. Smith, State Responsibility and the Principle of Joint and Several Liability, 13 Yale J. Int'l L. 225. Copyright © 1988 by Yale Journal of International Law.

—, Peace of Westphalia (1648), 1 Consolidated Treaty Series 198 (1969). Copyright © 1969 by Oceana Publications, Inc.

Price, A. Grenfell, The Winning of Australian Antarctica: Mawson's B.A.N.Z.A.R.E. Voyages 1929–31. Copyright © 1962 by Collins/Angus & Robertson, Ltd.

—, Rainbow Warrior *(N.Z. v. France),* 82 Int'l L.Rep. 559 (1990). Copyright © 1990 by Cambridge University Press.

Reisman, W. Michael, Criteria for the Lawful Use of Force in International Law, 10 Yale J.Int'l Law 279 (1985). Copyright © 1985 by Yale Journal of International Law.

—, Reparation for Injuries Suffered in the Service of the United Nations Advisory Opinion, I.C.J. 174 (1949). Copyright © 1949 by the United Nations.

—, Reservations to the Genocide Convention, Advisory Opinion, I.C.J. 15 (1951). Copyright © 1951 by the United Nations.

Riesenfeld, Stefan, Sovereign Immunity in Perspective, 19 Vand.J. Transnat'l L. 1 (1986). Copyright © 1986 by The Vanderbilt Journal of Transnational Law.

Rostow, Eugene V., Until What? Enforcement Action or Collective Self-Defense? Reproduced with permission from 85 AJIL 506 (1991), © The American Society of International Law.

—, Safer Ships, Cleaner Seas, Report of Lord Donaldson's Inquiry (1994). Crown copyright is reproduced with the permission of HMSO.

—, The Soering Case. Copyright © The Round Hall Press. Reprinted with permission from Berger, Case Law of the European Court of Human Rights: Vol. II, 1989 (The Round Hall Press, Dublin, Ireland, 1989).

—, South West Africa Cases *(Ethiopia v. South Africa; Liberia v. South Africa),* I.C.J. 4 (1966). Copyright © 1966 by the United Nations.

—, The Sunday Times Case. Copyright © The Round Hall Press. Reprinted with permission from Berger, Case Law of the European Court of Human Rights: Vol. I, 1979 (The Round Hall Press, Dublin, Ireland, 1979).

—, Trail Smelter Case *(United States v. Canada),* Arbitral Tribunal, 1941, U.N.Rep.Int'l Arb. Awards 1905 (1949). Copyright © 1949 by the United Nations.

—, Treaty of Paris (1783), 48 Consolidated Treaty Series 487 (1969). Copyright © 1969 by Oceana Publications, Inc.

—, Treaty of Principles Governing the Activities of States in the Exploration and Use of Outer Space Including the Moon and Other Celestial Bodies. Reproduced with permission from 6 I.L.M. 386 (1967), © The American Society of International Law.

—, United Nations Convention on the Law of the Sea. Copyright © 1982 by the United Nations.

Vagts, Detlev F., An Introduction to International Civil Practice, 17 Vand.J.Transnat'l L. 1 (1984). Copyright © 1984 by The Vanderbilt Journal of Transnational Law.

Verdross, Alfred von, Forbidden Treaties in International Law. Reproduced with permission from 31 AJIL 571 (1937), © The American Society of International Law.

Watt, Donald C., First Steps in Enclosure of the Oceans: The Origins of Truman's Proclamation on the Resources of the Continental Shelf, 28 September 1945, 3 Marine Policy 212 (1979). Copyright © 1979 by Butterworth-Heinemann. Reprinted by permission of the publishers, Butterworth-Heinemann Ltd. © and Professor Emeritus Donald Cameron Watt.

—, Western Sahara, Advisory Opinion, I.C.J. 12 (1975). Copyright © 1975 by the United Nations.

Wilson, Julian, Editorial, US exports in anti-trust: the primacy of economic muscle over international law, International Litigation News, July 1995, at 3. Copyright © 1995 by the International Bar Association.

Summary of Contents

Table of Contents

Page

*

Table of Cases

The principal cases are in bold type. Cases cited or discussed in the text are roman type. References are to pages. Cases cited in principal cases and within other quoted materials are not included.

*

CASES AND COMMENTARY ON
INTERNATIONAL LAW

*

Chapter 1

THE NATURE OF INTERNATIONAL LAW

International law is sometimes compared unfavorably with other kinds of law, especially the law of nation states. At first glance, international law seems to lack an effective legislature, a generally competent judiciary, and a powerful executive. Yet, whatever its theoretical ambiguities, international law has been practiced by lawyers for centuries. This chapter explains the nature of international law by introducing the history of the discipline and by exploring two sample international law cases. These two cases, *Golder* and *Filartiga*, begin to show how international law is in fact, in the real world, legislated, adjudicated, and enforced.

A. THE HISTORY OF INTERNATIONAL LAW

MARK W. JANIS, AN INTRODUCTION TO INTERNATIONAL LAW

1–4 (2d ed. 1993).

The roots of international law run deep in history. In early religious and secular writings, there are many evidences of what we now know as international law; there are, for example, the detailed peace treaties and alliances concluded between the Jews and the Romans, Syrians, and Spartans. The Romans knew of a *jus gentium*, a law of nations, which Gaius, in the second century, saw as a law "common to all men," a universal law that could be applied by Roman courts to foreigners when the specific law of their own nation was unknown and when Roman law was inapposite. In the seventeenth century, the Dutch jurist Hugo Grotius argued that the law of nations also established legal rules that bound the sovereign states of Europe, then just emerging from medieval society, in their relations with one another. Grotius' classic of 1625, *The Law of War and Peace*, is widely acknowledged, more than any other work, as founding the modern discipline of the law of nations, a subject that, in 1789, the English philosopher Jeremy Bentham renamed "international law." Nowadays, the terms *the law of nations* and *international law* are used interchangeably.

At least since the end of the Thirty Years War in 1648, world politics has principally involved the relations of more or less independent sovereign states. An important part of international law has consequently had to do with the establishment of a set of mutually agreed-upon rules respecting the nature of these states and their fundamental rights and obligations inter se. If there is a single international legal principle underlying the modern state system, it probably is the one neatly framed by Montesquieu in 1748 and offered to Napoleon in 1806 by Talleyrand: "that nations ought to do to one another in peace, the most good, and in war, the least evil possible."

International law is sometimes conceived to be divided into public and private parts, the first concerning the legal relations of states, the second involving the law governing the foreign transactions of individuals and corporations. However, the public-private division of international law can be misleading. Many of the laws and processes traditionally within the ambit of public international law actually concern private, not public, parties, while much of the domain of private international law covers the transactions of public entities. Nonetheless, the terms *public* and *private* international law are highly popular and, in a rough kind of way, do compartmentalize legal rules addressing two problem areas: public international law mostly concerns the political interactions of states; private international law relates to legal aspects of the international economy and conflicts and cooperation among national legal systems.

Few deny that the rules of international law actually influence state behavior. Even international law's most famous jurisprudential critic, John Austin, acknowledged in 1832 that international legal rules were effective. At the same time, however, he argued that, because there was no international sovereign to enforce it, international law could not be the same sort of positive law as that enacted by sovereign states for internal application:

> [T]he law obtaining between nations is not positive law: for every positive law is set by a given sovereign to a person or persons in a state of subjection to its author. As I have already intimated, the law obtaining between nations is law (improperly so called) set by general opinion. The duties which it imposes are enforced by moral sanctions: by fear on the part of nations, or by fear on the part of sovereigns, of provoking general hostility, and incurring its probable evils, in case they shall violate maxims generally received and respected.

Just a few years later, in 1836, the United States diplomat Henry Wheaton, in the first great Anglo–American treatise on international law, was already grappling with Austin's characterization of the rules governing international politics as being a form of mere "morality." Wheaton accepted Austin's view that international law's principal sanction was "the hazard of provoking the hostility of other communities," but contended that "[e]xperience shows that these motives, even in the worst times, do really afford a considerable security for the observance of justice between States, if they do not furnish the perfect sanction annexed by the lawgiver to the observance of the municipal code of any particular State." Unlike Austin, Wheaton found international law sufficiently law-like to justify calling it "law," a definitional outcome reached by generations of subsequent international lawyers.

Whether the international rules regulating interstate behavior are to be properly termed "legal" or "moral" is in truth a question that can only be answered after one has made more or less arbitrary definitions of what really constitutes "law" and "morality," a sometimes sterile exercise.[12] Suffice it to say at this early stage of our own discussion that there are a great many rules regulating international politics commonly referred to as "international law" and that these rules are usually, for one reason or another, observed in international practice. Moreover, there is no doubt that the norms of international law are frequently applied as rules of decision by law courts, domestic as well as international.

B. AN INTERNATIONAL LAW SAMPLER

The two cases that follow explore some of the different ways in which international law is actually made and applied. The *Golder Case* illustrates an international legal rule made by a treaty, adjudicated by an international court, and enforced by a regional international legal system. The *Filartiga Case* shows a customary or perhaps fundamental international legal norm adjudicated by a municipal—*i.e.*, a domestic—court and enforced (or not) by the ordinary mechanisms of that domestic legal system. The Notes and Questions that follow introduce several of the central issues about the rules and process of international law, issues that occupy us throughout the book.

THE GOLDER CASE

European Court of Human Rights
Judgment of 21 February 1975, Series A, No. 18.

1. The Golder case was referred to the Court by the Government of the United Kingdom of Great Britain and Northern Ireland (hereinafter called "the Government"). The case has its origin in an application against the United Kingdom lodged with the European Commission of Human Rights (hereinafter called "the Commission") under Article 25 of the Convention for the Protection of Human Rights and Fundamental Freedoms (hereinafter referred to as "the Convention"), by a United Kingdom citizen, Mr. Sidney Elmer Golder. * * *

9. The facts of the case may be summarized as follows.

12. "The only intelligent way to deal with a verbal question like that concerning the definition of the word 'law' is to give up thinking and arguing about it." Williams, "International Law and the Controversy Concerning the Word 'Law,'" 22 *British Yearbook of International Law* 146, 163 (1945).

10. In 1965, Mr. Sidney Elmer Golder, a United Kingdom citizen born in 1923, was convicted in the United Kingdom of robbery with violence and was sentenced to 15 years' imprisonment. In 1969, Golder was serving his sentence in Parkhurst Prison on the Isle of Wight.

11. On the evening of 24 October 1969, a serious disturbance occurred in a recreation area of the prison where Golder happened to be.

On 25 October, a prison officer, Mr. Laird, who had taken part and been injured in quelling the disturbance, made a statement identifying his assailants, in the course of which he declared: "Frazer was screaming . . . and Frape, Noonan and another prisoner whom I know by sight, I think his name is Golder . . . were swinging vicious blows at me."

12. On 26 October Golder, together with other prisoners suspected of having participated in the disturbance, was segregated from the main body of prisoners. On 28 and 30 October, Golder was interviewed by police officers. At the second of these interviews he was informed that it had been alleged that he had assaulted a prison officer; he was warned that "the facts would be reported in order that consideration could be given whether or not he would be prosecuted for assaulting a prison officer causing bodily harm."

13. Golder wrote to his Member of Parliament on 25 October and 1 November, and to a Chief Constable on 4 November 1969, about the disturbance of 24 October and the ensuing hardships it had entailed for him; the prison governor stopped these letters since Golder had failed to raise the subject-matter thereof through the authorized channels beforehand.

14. In a second statement, made on 5 November 1969, Laird qualified as follows what he had said earlier:

> "When I mentioned the prisoner Golder, I said 'I think it was Golder', who was present with Frazer, Frape and Noonan, when the three latter were attacking me.
>
> "If it was Golder and I certainly remember seeing him in the immediate group who were screaming abuse and generally making a nuisance of themselves, I am not certain that he made an attack on me.
>
> "Later when Noonan and Frape grabbed me, Frazer was also present but I cannot remember who the other inmate was, but there were several there one of whom stood out in particular but I cannot put a name to him."

On 7 November, another prison officer reported that:

> ". . . during the riot of that night I spent the majority of the time in the T.V. room with the prisoners who were not participating in the disturbance.
>
> 740007, Golder was in this room with me and to the best of my knowledge took no part in the riot.

His presence with me can be borne out by officer ... who observed us both from the outside."

Golder was returned to his ordinary cell the same day.

15. Meanwhile, the prison authorities had been considering the various statements, and on 10 November prepared a list of charges which might be preferred against prisoners, including Golder, for offenses against prison discipline. Entries relating thereto were made in Golder's prison record. No such charge was eventually preferred against him and the entries in his prison record were marked "charges not proceeded with." Those entries were expunged from the prison record in 1971 during the examination of the applicant's case by the Commission.

16. On 20 March 1970, Golder addressed a petition to the Secretary of State for the Home Department, that is, the Home Secretary. He requested a transfer to some other prison and added:

"I understand that a statement wrongly accusing me of participation in the events of 24th October last, made by Officer Laird, is lodged in my prison record. I suspect that it is this wrong statement that has recently prevented my being recommended by the local parole board for parole.

"I would respectfully request permission to consult a solicitor with a view to taking civil action for libel in respect of this statement.... Alternatively, I would request that an independent examination of my record be allowed by Mrs. G.M. Bishop who is a magistrate. I would accept her assurance that this statement is not part of my record and be willing to accept then that the libel against me has not materially harmed me except for the two weeks I spent in the separate cells and so civil action would not be then necessary, providing that an apology was given to me for the libel...."

17. In England the matter of contacts of convicted prisoners with persons outside their place of detention is governed by the Prison Act 1952, as amended, and subordinate legislation made under that Act.

Section 47, sub-section 1, of the Prison Act provides that "the Secretary of State may make rules for the regulation and management of prisoners ... and for the ... treatment ... discipline and control of persons required to be detained...."

The rules made by the Home Secretary in the exercise of this power are the Prison Rules 1964, which were laid before Parliament and have the status of a Statutory Instrument. The relevant provisions concerning communications between prisoners and persons outside prison are contained in Rules 33, 34 and 37 as follows:

"*Letters and visits generally*

Rule 33

(1) The Secretary of State may, with a view to securing discipline and good order or the prevention of crime or in the interests of any

persons, impose restrictions, either generally or in a particular case, upon the communications to be permitted between a prisoner and other persons.

(2) Except as provided by statute or these Rules, a prisoner shall not be permitted to communicate with any outside person, or that person with him, without the leave of the Secretary of State.

. . .

Personal letters and visits

Rule 34

. . .

(8) A prisoner shall not be entitled under this Rule to communicate with any person in connection with any legal or other business, or with any person other than a relative or friend, except with the leave of the Secretary of State.

. . .

Legal advisers

Rule 37

(1) The legal adviser of a prisoner in any legal proceedings, civil or criminal, to which the prisoner is a party shall be afforded reasonable facilities for interviewing him in connection with those proceedings, and may do so out of hearing but in sight of an officer.

(2) A prisoner's legal adviser may, with the leave of the Secretary of State, interview the prisoner in connection with any other legal business in the sight and hearing of an officer."

18. On 6 April 1970, the Home Office directed the prison governor to notify Golder of the reply to his petition of 20 March as follows:

"The Secretary of State has fully considered your petition but is not prepared to grant your request for transfer, nor can he find grounds for taking any action in regard to the other matters raised in your petition."

19. Before the Commission, Golder submitted two complaints relating respectively to the stopping of his letters (as mentioned above at paragraph 13) and to the refusal of the Home Secretary to permit him to consult a solicitor. On 30 March 1971, the Commission declared the first complaint inadmissible, as all domestic remedies had not been exhausted, but accepted the second for consideration of the merits under Articles 6 § 1 and 8 of the Convention.

20. Golder was released from prison on parole on 12 July 1972.

* * *

23. Paragraphs 73, 99 and 110 of the Commission's report indicate that the Commission consider unanimously that there was a violation of Article 6 § 1. The Government disagree with this opinion.

24. Article 6 § 1 provides:

"In the determination of his civil rights and obligations or of any criminal charge against him, everyone is entitled to a fair and public hearing within a reasonable time by an independent and impartial tribunal established by law. Judgment shall be pronounced publicly but the press and public may be excluded from all or part of the trial in the interests of morals, public order or national security in a democratic society, where the interests of juveniles or the protection of the private life of the parties so require, or to the extent strictly necessary in the opinion of the court in special circumstances where publicity would prejudice the interests of justice." * * *

32. * * *

The Government have submitted that the expressions "fair and public hearing" and "within a reasonable time", the second sentence in paragraph 1 ("judgment", "trial"), and paragraph 3 of Article 6 clearly presuppose proceedings pending before a court.

While the right to a fair, public and expeditious judicial procedure can assuredly apply only to proceedings in being, it does not, however, necessarily follow that a right to the very institution of such proceedings is thereby excluded; the Delegates of the Commission rightly underlined this at paragraph 21 of their memorial. Besides, in criminal matters, the "reasonable time" may start to run from a date prior to the seisin of the trial court, of the "tribunal" competent for the "determination ... of (the) criminal charge" (Wemhoff judgment of 27 June 1968, Series A no. 7, pp. 26–27, § 19; Neumeister judgment of 27 June 1968, Series A no. 8, p. 41, § 18; Ringeisen judgment of 16 July 1971, Series A no. 13, p. 45, § 110). It is conceivable also that in civil matters the reasonable time may begin to run, in certain circumstances, even before the issue of the writ commencing proceedings before the court to which the plaintiff submits the dispute. * * *

35. * * *

Were Article 6 § 1 to be understood as concerning exclusively the conduct of an action which had already been initiated before a court, a Contracting State could, without acting in breach of that text, do away with its courts, or take away their jurisdiction to determine certain classes of civil actions and entrust it to organs dependent on the Government. Such assumptions, indissociable from a danger of arbitrary power, would have serious consequences which are repugnant to the aforementioned principles and which the Court cannot overlook (Lawless judgment of 1 July 1961, Series A no. 3, p. 52, and Delcourt judgment of 17 January 1970, Series A no. 11, pp. 14–15).

It would be inconceivable, in the opinion of the Court, that Article 6 § 1 should describe in detail the procedural guarantees afforded to parties in a pending lawsuit and should not first protect that which alone makes it in fact possible to benefit from such guarantees, that is, access to a court. The fair, public and expeditious characteristics of judicial proceedings are of no value at all if there are no judicial proceedings.

36. Taking all the preceding considerations together, it follows that the right of access constitutes an element which is inherent in the right stated by Article 6 § 1. * * *

40. * * *

In these circumstances, Golder could justifiably wish to consult a solicitor with a view to instituting legal proceedings. It was not for the Home Secretary himself to appraise the prospects of the action contemplated; it was for an independent and impartial court to rule on any claim that might be brought. In declining to accord the leave which had been requested, the Home Secretary failed to respect, in the person of Golder, the right to go before a court as guaranteed by Article 6 § 1. * * *

41. In the opinion of the majority of the Commission (paragraph 123 of the report) "the same facts which constitute a violation of Article 6 § 1 constitute also a violation of Article 8." The Government disagree with this opinion.

42. Article 8 of the Convention reads as follows:

> "1. Everyone has the right to respect for his private and family life, his home and his correspondence.
>
> 2. There shall be no interference by a public authority with the exercise of this right except such as is in accordance with the law and is necessary in a democratic society in the interests of national security, public safety or the economic well-being of the country, for the prevention of disorder or crime, for the protection of health or morals, or for the protection of the rights and freedoms of others."

43. The Home Secretary's refusal of the petition of 20 March 1970 had the direct and immediate effect of preventing Golder from contacting a solicitor by any means whatever, including that which in the ordinary way he would have used to begin with, correspondence. While there was certainly neither stopping nor censorship of any message, such as a letter, which Golder would have written to a solicitor—or vice-versa—and which would have been a piece of correspondence within the meaning of paragraph 1 of Article 8, it would be wrong to conclude therefrom, as do the Government, that this text is inapplicable. Impeding someone from even initiating correspondence constitutes the most far-reaching form of "interference" (paragraph 2 of Article 8) with the exercise of the "right to respect for correspondence"; it is inconceivable that that should fall outside the scope of Article 8 while mere supervision indisputably falls within it. In any event, if Golder had attempted to write a solicitor notwithstanding the Home Secretary's decision or without requesting the required permission, that correspondence would have been stopped and he could have invoked Article 8; one would arrive at a paradoxical and hardly equitable result, if it were considered that in complying with the requirements of the Prison Rules 1964 he lost the benefit of the protection of Article 8. * * *

46. Article 50 of the Convention provides that if the Court finds, as in the present case, "that a decision ... taken" by some authority of a Contracting State "is completely or partially in conflict with the obligations arising from the ... Convention, and if the internal law of (that State) allows only partial reparation to be made for the consequences of this decision", the Court "shall, if necessary, afford just satisfaction to the injured party." * * *

The Court considers accordingly that the above question, which was duly raised by the Court, is ready for decision and should therefore be decided without further delay. The Court is of opinion that in the circumstances of the case it is not necessary to afford to the applicant any just satisfaction other than that resulting from the finding of a violation of his rights.

FOR THESE REASONS, THE COURT

1. *Holds* by nine votes to three that there has been a breach of Article 6 § 1;
2. *Holds* unanimously that there has been a breach of Article 8;
3. *Holds* unanimously that the preceding findings amount in themselves to adequate just satisfaction under Article 50.

Notes and Questions

1. *European Human Rights Law.* The European Court of Human Rights in Strasbourg, France, can be described as an "international court" in at least two ways. Constitutionally, the Court is established by an international agreement: the 1950 European Convention for the Protection of Human Rights and Fundamental Freedoms, 213 U.N.T.S. 221 (1953)(signed at Rome November 4, 1950; entered into force September 3, 1953). More about international adjudication in general is found in Chapter 5. Substantively, the rules the Court applies are international law: human rights made and protected by the same European Human Rights Convention. As of June 1996, some 34 European countries were parties to the European Human Rights Convention and subject to the European Human Rights Court's jurisdiction. The structure and substance of European human rights law are more fully explored in Chapter 6. Also see Mark W. Janis, Richard S. Kay & Anthony W. Bradley, *European Human Rights Law* (2d ed. 1995); Ralph Beddard, *Human Rights and Europe* (3d ed. 1993); P. van Dijk & G.J.H. van Hoof, *Theory and Practice of the European Convention on Human Rights* (2d ed. 1990).

2. *The Nature of Treaties.* In *Golder*, the European Court of Human Rights applies two substantive rules drawn from the 1950 European Human Rights Convention: Article 6(1) protecting fair trial and Article 8 protecting private and family life, home, and correspondence. The ordinary theory explaining the legally binding effect of an international agreement is that a sovereign state may exercise its sovereignty not only by making domestic law but also by making international law. Hence, Articles 6(1) and 8 oblige the U.K. in international law because of the U.K.'s own consent. Chapter 2 more fully explores treaties.

If, in this way, the European Convention on Human Rights resembles an international contract among states, the Convention may also be said to resemble an international statute in that it provides a generally applicable set of rules for all its member-states. This helps explain why states are considered to be not only the legislators of international law but also subjects of international law. We consider the nature of the sovereign state in Chapter 7.

3. *The Efficacy of International Law*. After *Golder,* Britain changed its prison rules to comply with the Court's decision. What "sanction" could have been applied against the U.K. if the government had failed to comply with the ruling? Why should a sovereign state like the United Kingdom voluntarily comply with an international court judgment like *Golder*? What would the U.K. lose if it were to be expelled from the Council of Europe for failure to comply with decisions of the European Court of Human Rights? Could the U.K. expect other states to comply with the Convention if it repudiated the Court's judgment? Would repudiation spoil the U.K.'s reputation and make it more difficult for the government to conclude treaties in the future?

The many European countries that are parties to the European Convention on Human Rights have their own domestic legal rules and processes protecting human rights. Why should they also enter into an international legal system establishing European rules about human rights and setting up European institutions to enforce those rules? How close are the European Court of Human Rights and European human rights law in form and substance to the U.S. Supreme Court and U.S. constitutional law, especially the Bill of Rights?

FILARTIGA v. PENA–IRALA

630 F.2d 876 (2d Cir.1980).

Irving R. Kaufman, Circuit Judge:

Upon ratification of the Constitution, the thirteen former colonies were fused into a single nation, one which, in its relations with foreign states, is bound both to observe and construe the accepted norms of international law, formerly known as the law of nations. Under the Articles of Confederation, the several states had interpreted and applied this body of doctrine as a part of their common law, but with the founding of the "more perfect Union" of 1789, the law of nations became preeminently a federal concern.

Implementing the constitutional mandate for national control over foreign relations, the First Congress established original district court jurisdiction over "all causes where an alien sues for a tort only [committed] in violation of the law of nations." Judiciary Act of 1789, ch. 20, § 9(b), 1 Stat. 73, 77 (1789), *codified at* 28 U.S.C. § 1350. Construing this rarely-invoked provision, we hold that deliberate torture perpetrated under color of official authority violates universally accepted norms of the international law of human rights, regardless of the nationality of the parties. Thus, whenever an alleged torturer is found and served with process by an alien within our borders, § 1350 provides federal jurisdiction. Accordingly, we reverse the judgment of the district court dismissing the complaint for want of federal jurisdiction.

I

The appellants, plaintiffs below, are citizens of the Republic of Paraguay. Dr. Joel Filartiga, a physician, describes himself as a long-standing opponent of the government of President Alfredo Stroessner, which has held power in Paraguay since 1954. His daughter, Dolly Filartiga, arrived in the United States in 1978 under a visitor's visa, and has since applied for permanent political asylum. The Filartigas brought this action in the Eastern District of New York against Americo Norberto Pena–Irala (Pena), also a citizen of Paraguay, for wrongfully causing the death of Dr. Filartiga's seventeen-year old son, Joelito. Because the district court dismissed the action for want of subject matter jurisdiction, we must accept as true the allegations contained in the Filartigas' complaint and affidavits for purposes of this appeal.

The appellants contend that on March 29, 1978, Joelito Filartiga was kidnapped and tortured to death by Pena, who was then Inspector General of Police in Asuncion, Paraguay. Later that day, the police brought Dolly Filartiga to Pena's home where she was confronted with the body of her brother, which evidenced marks of severe torture. As she fled, horrified, from the house, Pena followed after her shouting, "Here you have what you have been looking for so long and what you deserve. Now shut up." The Filartigas claim that Joelito was tortured and killed in retaliation for his father's political activities and beliefs.

Shortly thereafter, Dr. Filartiga commenced a criminal action in the Paraguayan courts against Pena and the police for the murder of his son. As a result, Dr. Filartiga's attorney was arrested and brought to police headquarters where, shackled to a wall, Pena threatened him with death. This attorney, it is alleged, has since been disbarred without just cause.

During the course of the Paraguayan criminal proceeding, which is apparently still pending after four years, another man, Hugo Duarte, confessed to the murder. Duarte, who was a member of the Pena household, claimed that he had discovered his wife and Joelito *in flagrante delicto*, and that the crime was one of passion. The Filartigas have submitted a photograph of Joelito's corpse showing injuries they believe refute this claim. Dolly Filartiga, moreover, has stated that she will offer evidence of three independent autopsies demonstrating that her brother's death "was the result of professional methods of torture." Despite his confession, Duarte, we are told, has never been convicted or sentenced in connection with the crime.

In July of 1978, Pena sold his house in Paraguay and entered the United States under a visitor's visa. He was accompanied by Juana Bautista Fernandez Villalba, who had lived with him in Paraguay. The couple remained in the United States beyond the term of their visas, and were living in Brooklyn, New York, when Dolly Filartiga, who was then living in Washington, D.C., learned of their presence. Acting on information provided by Dolly the Immigration and Naturalization Service arrested Pena and his companion, both of whom were subsequently ordered deported on April 5, 1979 following a hearing. They had then resided in the United States for more than nine months.

Almost immediately, Dolly caused Pena to be served with a summons and civil complaint at the Brooklyn Navy Yard, where he was being held pending deportation. The complaint alleged that Pena had wrongfully caused Joelito's death by torture and sought compensatory and punitive damages of $10,000,000. The Filartigas also sought to enjoin Pena's deportation to ensure his availability for testimony at trial. The cause of action is stated as arising under "wrongful death statutes; the U.N. Charter, the Universal Declaration on Human Rights; the U.N. Declaration Against Torture; the American Declaration of the Rights and Duties of Man; and other pertinent declarations, documents and practices constituting the customary international law of human rights and the law of nations," as well as 28 U.S.C. § 1350, Article II, sec. 2 and the Supremacy Clause of the U.S. Constitution. Jurisdiction is claimed under the general federal question provision, 28 U.S.C. § 1331 and, principally on this appeal, under the Alien Tort Statute, 28 U.S.C. § 1350.

* * * The Filartigas submitted the affidavits of a number of distinguished international legal scholars, who stated unanimously that the law of nations prohibits absolutely the use of torture as alleged in the complaint.[4] Pena, in support of his motion to dismiss on the ground of *forum non conveniens*, submitted the affidavit of his Paraguayan counsel, Jose Emilio Gorostiaga, who averred that Paraguayan law provides a full and adequate civil remedy for the wrong alleged. Dr. Filartiga has not commenced such an action, however, believing that further resort to the courts of his own country would be futile. * * *

The district court continued the stay of deportation for forty-eight hours while appellants applied for further stays. These applications were denied by a panel of this Court on May 22, 1979, and by the Supreme Court two days later. Shortly thereafter, Pena and his companion returned to Paraguay.

4. Richard Falk, the Albert G. Milbank Professor of International Law and Practice at Princeton University, and a former Vice President of the American Society of International Law, avers that, in his judgment, "it is now beyond reasonable doubt that torture of a person held in detention that results in severe harm or death is a violation of the law of nations." Thomas Franck, professor of international law at New York University and Director of the New York University Center for International Studies offers his opinion that torture has now been rejected by virtually all nations, although it was once commonly used to extract confessions. Richard Lillich, the Howard W. Smith Professor of Law at the University of Virginia School of Law, concludes, after a lengthy review of the authorities, that officially perpetrated torture is "a violation of international law (formerly called the law of nations)." Finally, Myres MacDougal, a former Sterling Professor of Law at the Yale Law School, and a past President of the American Society of International Law, states that torture is an offense against the law of nations, and that "it has long been recognized that such offenses vitally affect relations between states."

II

Appellants rest their principal argument in support of federal jurisdiction upon the Alien Tort Statute, 28 U.S.C. § 1350, which provides: "The district courts shall have original jurisdiction of any civil action by an alien for a tort only, committed in violation of the law of nations or a treaty of the United States." Since appellants do not contend that their action arises directly under a treaty of the United States, a threshold question on the jurisdictional issue is whether the conduct alleged violates the law of nations. In light of the universal condemnation of torture in numerous international agreements, and the renunciation of torture as an instrument of official policy by virtually all of the nations of the world (in principle if not in practice), we find that an act of torture committed by a state official against one held in detention violates established norms of the international law of human rights, and hence the law of nations.

The Supreme Court has enumerated the appropriate sources of international law. The law of nations "may be ascertained by consulting the works of jurists, writing professedly on public law; or by the general usage and practice of nations; or by judicial decisions recognizing and enforcing that law." *United States v. Smith*, 18 U.S. (5 Wheat.) 153, 160–61, 5 L.Ed. 57 (1820); *Lopes v. Reederei Richard Schroder*, 225 F.Supp. 292, 295 (E.D.Pa.1963). In *Smith*, a statute proscribing "the crime of piracy [on the high seas] as defined by the law of nations," 3 Stat. 510(a) (1819), was held sufficiently determinate in meaning to afford the basis for a death sentence. The *Smith* Court discovered among the works of Lord Bacon, Grotius, Bochard and other commentators a genuine consensus that rendered the crime "sufficiently and constitutionally defined." *Smith, supra*, 18 U.S. (5 Wheat.) at 162, 5 L.Ed. 57.

The Paquete Habana, 175 U.S. 677, 20 S.Ct. 290, 44 L.Ed. 320 (1900), reaffirmed that

> where there is no treaty, and no controlling executive or legislative act or judicial decision, resort must be had to the customs and usages of civilized nations; and, as evidence of these, to the works of jurists and commentators, who by years of labor, research and experience, have made themselves peculiarly well acquainted with the subjects of which they treat. Such works are resorted to by judicial tribunals, not for the speculations of their authors concerning what the law ought to be, but for trustworthy evidence of what the law really is.

Id. at 700, 20 S.Ct. at 299. Modern international sources confirm the propriety of this approach. * * *

The United Nations Charter (a treaty of the United States, *see* 59 Stat. 1033 (1945)) makes it clear that in this modern age a state's treatment of its own citizens is a matter of international concern. It provides:

> With a view to the creation of conditions of stability and well-being which are necessary for peaceful and friendly relations among nations ... the United Nations shall promote ... universal respect for, and observance of, human rights and fundamental freedoms for all without distinctions as to race, sex, language or religion.

Id. Art. 55. And further:

> All members pledge themselves to take joint and separate action in cooperation with the Organization for the achievement of the purposes set forth in Article 55.

Id. Art. 56.

While this broad mandate has been held not to be wholly self-executing, *Hitai v. Immigration and Naturalization Service*, 343 F.2d 466, 468 (2d Cir.1965), this observation alone does not end our inquiry. For although there is no universal agreement as to the precise extent of the "human rights and fundamental freedoms" guaranteed to all by the Charter, there is at present no dissent from the view that the guaranties include, at a bare minimum, the right to be free from torture. This prohibition has become part of customary international law, as evidenced and defined by the Universal Declaration of Human Rights, General Assembly Resolution 217 (III)(A)(Dec. 10, 1948) which states, in the plainest of terms, "no one shall be subjected to torture."[10] The General Assembly has declared that the Charter precepts embodied in this Universal Declaration "constitute basic principles of international law." G.A.Res. 2625 (XXV) (Oct. 24, 1970).

Particularly relevant is the Declaration on the Protection of All Persons from Being Subjected to Torture, General Assembly Resolution 3452, 30 U.N. GAOR Supp. (No. 34) 91, U.N.Doc. A/1034 (1975) * * *. The Declaration expressly prohibits any state from permitting the dastardly and totally inhuman act of torture. Torture, in turn, is defined as "any act by which severe pain and suffering, whether physical or mental, is intentionally inflicted by or at the instigation of a public official on a person for such purposes as ... intimidating him or other persons." The Declaration goes on to provide that "[w]here it is proved that an act of torture or other cruel, inhuman or degrading treatment or punishment has been committed by or at the instigation of a public official, the victim shall be afforded redress and compensation, in accordance with national law." This Declaration, like the Declaration of Human Rights before it, was adopted without dissent by the General Assembly. Nayar, "Human Rights: The United Nations and United States Foreign Policy," 19 *Harv. Int'l L.J.* 813, 816 n.18 (1978).

These U.N. declarations are significant because they specify with great precision the obligations of member nations under the Charter. Since their adoption, "[m]embers can no longer contend that they do not know what human rights they promised in the Charter to promote."

10. Eighteen nations have incorporated the Universal Declaration into their own constitutions. 48 *Revue Internationale de Droit Penal* Nos. 3 & 4, at 211 (1977).

Sohn, "A Short History of United Nations Documents on Human Rights," in *"The United Nations and Human Rights," 18th Report of the Commission* (Commission to Study the Organization of Peace ed. 1968). Moreover, a U.N. Declaration is, according to one authoritative definition, "a formal and solemn instrument, suitable for rare occasions when principles of great and lasting importance are being enunciated." 34 U.N. ESCOR, Supp. (No. 8) 15, U.N. Doc. E/cn.4/1/610 (1962)(memorandum of Office of Legal Affairs, U.N. Secretariat). Accordingly, it has been observed that the Universal Declaration of Human Rights "no longer fits into the dichotomy of 'binding treaty' against 'nonbinding pronouncement,' but is rather an authoritative statement of the international community." *E. Schwelb, Human Rights and the International Community* 70 (1964). Thus, a Declaration creates an expectation of adherence, and "insofar as the expectation is gradually justified by State practice, a declaration may by custom become recognized as laying down rules binding upon the States." 34 U.N. ESCOR, *supra.* Indeed, several commentators have concluded that the Universal Declaration has become, *in toto*, a part of binding, customary international law. Nayar, *supra*, at 816–17; Waldlock, "Human Rights in Contemporary International Law and the Significance of the European Convention," *Int'l & Comp. L.Q.*, Supp. Publ. No. 11 at 15 (1965).

Turning to the act of torture, we have little difficulty discerning its universal renunciation in the modern usage and practice of nations. *Smith*, *supra*, 18 U.S. (5 Wheat.) at 160–61, 5 L.Ed. 57. The international consensus surrounding torture has found expression in numerous international treaties and accords. *E.g.*, *American Convention on Human Rights*, Art. 5, OAS Treaty Series No. 36 at 1, OAS Off. Rec. OEA/Ser 4 v/II 23, doc. 21, rev. 2 (English ed., 1975)("No one shall be subjected to torture or to cruel, inhuman or degrading punishment or treatment"); International Covenant on Civil and Political Rights, U.N. General Assembly Res. 2200 (XXI)A, U.N. Doc. A/6316 (Dec. 16, 1966)(identical language); European Convention for the Protection of Human Rights and Fundamental Freedoms, Art. 3, Council of Europe, European Treaty Series No. 5 (1968), 213 U.N.T.S. 211 (*semble*). The substance of these international agreements is reflected in modern municipal—*i.e.* national—law as well. Although torture was once a routine concomitant of criminal interrogations in many nations, during the modern and hopefully more enlightened era it has been universally renounced. According to one survey, torture is prohibited, expressly or implicitly, by the constitutions of over fifty-five nations, including both the United States and Paraguay. Our State Department reports a general recognition of this principle:

> There now exists an international consensus that recognizes basic human rights and obligations owed by all governments to their citizens.... There is no doubt that these rights are often violated; but virtually all governments acknowledge their validity.

Department of State, *Country Reports on Human Rights for 1979*, published as Joint Comm. Print, House Comm. on Foreign Affairs, and

Senate Comm. on Foreign Relations, 96th Cong. 2d Sess. (Feb. 4, 1980), Introduction at 1. We have been directed to no assertion by any contemporary state of a right to torture its own or another nation's citizens. Indeed, United States diplomatic contacts confirm the universal abhorrence with which torture is viewed:

> In exchanges between United States embassies and all foreign states with which the United States maintains relations, it has been the Department of State's general experience that no government has asserted a right to torture its own nationals. Where reports of torture elicit some credence, a state usually responds by denial or, less frequently, by asserting that the conduct was unauthorized or constituted rough treatment short of torture.[15]

Memorandum of the United States as *Amicus Curiae* at 16 n.34.

Having examined the sources from which customary international law is derived—the usage of nations, judicial opinions and the works of jurists[16]—we conclude that official torture is now prohibited by the law of nations. The prohibition is clear and unambiguous, and admits of no distinction between treatment of aliens and citizens. Accordingly, we must conclude that the dictum in *Dreyfus v. von Finck*, [534 F.2d 24, 31 (2d Cir.), *cert. denied,* 429 U.S. 835, 97 S.Ct. 102, 50 L.Ed.2d 101 (1976)], to the effect that "violations of international law do not occur when the aggrieved parties are nationals of the acting state," is clearly out of tune with the current usage and practice of international law. The treaties and accords cited above, as well as the express foreign policy of our own government, all make it clear that international law confers fundamental rights upon all people vis-a-vis their own governments. While the ultimate scope of those rights will be a subject for continuing refinement and elaboration, we hold that the right to be free from torture is now among them. * * *

IV * * *

In the twentieth century the international community has come to recognize the common danger posed by the flagrant disregard of basic human rights and particularly the right to be free of torture. Spurred first by the Great War, and then the Second, civilized nations have banded together to prescribe acceptable norms of international behavior. From the ashes of the Second World War arose the United Nations

15. The fact that the prohibition of torture is often honored in the breach does not diminish its binding effect as a norm of international law. As one commentator has put it, "The best evidence for the existence of international law is that every actual State recognizes that it does exist and that it is itself under an obligation to observe it. States often violate international law, just as individuals often violate municipal law; but no more than individuals do States defend their violations by claiming that they are above the law." J. Brierly, *The Outlook for International Law* 4–5 (Oxford 1944).

16. *See also Ireland v. United Kingdom,* Judgment of Jan. 18, 1978 (European Court of Human Rights), *summarized in* [1978] Yearbook, European Convention on Human Rights 602 (Council of Europe)(holding that Britain's subjection of prisoners to sleep deprivation, hooding, exposure to hissing noise, reduced diet and standing against a wall for hours was "inhuman and degrading," but not "torture" within meaning of European Convention on Human Rights).

Organization, amid hopes that an era of peace and cooperation had at last begun. Though many of these aspirations have remained elusive goals, that circumstance cannot diminish the true progress that has been made. In the modern age, humanitarian and practical considerations have combined to lead the nations of the world to recognize that respect for fundamental human rights is in their individual and collective interest. Among the rights universally proclaimed by all nations, as we have noted, is the right to be free of physical torture. Indeed, for purposes of civil liability, the torturer has become—like the pirate and slave trader before him—*hostis humani generis*, an enemy of all mankind. Our holding today, giving effect to a jurisdictional provision enacted by our First Congress, is a small but important step in the fulfillment of the ageless dream to free all people from brutal violence.

Notes and Questions

1. *Individuals as Subjects of International Law. Filartiga* involved international human rights claims of Paraguayan citizens against an official of the government of Paraguay. *Golder* concerned an Englishman's international human rights claim against his own government. Why in principle and practice should either the Paraguayan or U.K. government be subject to international law rules or process with respect to complaints by their own citizens?

J.L. Brierly in his classic British introduction to international law defined the discipline "as the body of rules and principles of action which are binding upon civilized states in their relations with one another." J.L. Brierly, *The Law of Nations* 1 (4th ed. 1949). How well does Brierly's definition describe the law the rules of which were actually applied in *Filartiga* and *Golder*? How might this definition be reformulated in the light of these two cases where individual rights in international law are in issue? More about individual rights under international law is in Chapter 6.

2. *States as Subjects of International Legal Process.* In *Golder*, the United Kingdom was subject to the jurisdiction of the European Court of Human Rights because it had signed and ratified an international convention formally and explicitly accepting the jurisdiction of the Court. Furthermore, in accordance with the terms of the treaty the U.K. government had itself submitted the dispute to the Court for judgment. In *Filartiga* why should Paraguayan government officials be subject to the jurisdiction of United States federal courts in New York? If it appeared unlikely that the government of Paraguay would permit the Filartigas to sue in Paraguayan courts would it be likely that that government would respect or enforce a U.S. judgment in favor of the Filartigas?

3. *Litigating International Human Rights Law.* Why did the Filartigas bring the case in a U.S. court? Why did U.S. lawyers volunteer to prosecute the action without the prospect of compensation? One of the goals of both the Filartigas and their lawyers could have been to publicize the human rights abuses of the Paraguayan government in particular and of other regimes in general. Judge Kaufman himself authored an article on *Filartiga* in which he wrote that "the decision breaks new ground in the body of law governing torture." Irving R. Kaufman, "A Legal Remedy for International

Torture?," *New York Times Magazine*, Nov. 9, 1980, at 44, 44. Several years later he chose *Filartiga* to conclude an article about his judicial career. Irving R. Kaufman, "The Anatomy of Decisionmaking," 53 *Fordham Law Review* 1, 20–22 (1984). The *Filartiga* judgment continues to evoke controversy. See the debate between Steven R. Schneebaum and Richard A. Hibey et al., the defense team for Ferdinand Marcos, in "At Issue: International Law: Should U.S. courts decide international human rights violations?," *ABA Journal*, Feb. 1990, at 34.

The lawyers who brought the *Filartiga* case explain that they turned to the Alien Tort Claims Act, "a little-used 200–year old statute," in their search for a way to give lawyers "the opportunity to establish that officials who violate the rights of their own citizens could be brought to justice in U.S. courts." After *Filartiga* their goal "was to bring more cases, obtain more circuit court opinions in our favor and make the *Filartiga* principle unassailable." They plainly acknowledge that they are "political lawyers, [wanting] to use the *Filartiga* precedent to fight those who were violating human rights." Michael Ratner & Beth Stephens, "The Center for Constitutional Rights: Using Law and the *Filartiga* Principle in the Fight for Human Rights," in American Civil Liberties Union, *International Civil Liberties Report*, Dec. 1993, at 29. In general, for the relation between municipal courts and international law, see Chapter 4.

4. *The Nature of Customary International Law.* In theory, at least, customary international law is developed as a result of the actual practice of states. If the Paraguayan government and other governments do actually torture their own citizens, how can there be a rule of customary international law proscribing such practice? Is the court in *Filartiga* truly applying customary international law, or is it perhaps finding and applying rules drawn from some sort of fundamental international law, an international human rights law analogous to municipal constitutional guarantees of human rights?

Note the diverse evidences of international law employed by the *Filartiga* court in deciding that international law prohibits torture. Does the court give any one kind of evidence primacy over the others? Do some evidences seem more or less persuasive? Does the judgment demonstrate that Paraguay has consented to the rule prohibiting torture or only that the community of nations generally supports such a rule? Chapter 3 further explores customary international law and the various non-consensual sources of international law, such as *jus cogens*.

5. *The Efficacy of International Law.* Although one might assume that national courts, like the United States federal courts, are usually more efficacious than international courts, here the expectation is reversed. Though the decision of the international court in *Golder* was respected, the decisions of the national courts in *Filartiga* were not. On remand, the district court imposed a judgment for $10,385,364 against Pena–Irala in order "to reflect adherence to the world community's proscription of torture and to attempt to deter its practice," 577 F.Supp. 860, 867 (E.D.N.Y.1984), but these damages were never paid.

6. *The Organization of the Book.* The international rules and processes introduced in *Golder* and *Filartiga* are explored in more depth below.

Chapter 2 examines treaties. Chapter 3 turns to customary international law and other sources of international law such as general principles of law, natural law, *jus cogens*, and equity. Chapter 4 considers the role of national courts in applying international law. Chapter 5 discusses public international arbitration and the International Court of Justice. The later chapters in the book deal with a variety of the actors involved with and the substantive issues addressed by international law: Chapter 6 the protection of individuals (including European human rights law); Chapter 7 the rights, duties, and relations of sovereign states; Chapter 8 war and peace and the United Nations; Chapter 9 international regimes and common spaces, *e.g.*, Antarctica, the sea, and the environment; and Chapter 10 international conflict of laws.

Chapter 2

TREATIES

A. THE SOURCES OF INTERNATIONAL LAW

The term "sources" can be used in at least two ways when referring to the sources of international law. One way is to think of a *material source* of an international rule: the place one looks to actually read a rule of international law. So, for example, any given treaty may prescribe a specific legal obligation, *e.g.*, the United Nations Charter provides in Article 2(4) that "All Members shall refrain in their international relations from the threat or use of force against the territorial integrity or political independence of any State, or in any other manner inconsistent with the Purposes of the United Nations."

A second way to think about a source of international law is to think about a *formal source* of international law, that is, a fashion in which international lawyers, judges, and jurists agree that international law may be made. The notion of a formal source of international law is related to ideas in the philosophy of law about rules of recognition and validating norms. For any legal system to function effectively in practice, the participants in that system must agree upon what counts as a legal rule and what does not. An ordinary starting point for international lawyers from most any part of the globe when thinking about the formal sources of international law is Article 38 of the Statute of the International Court of Justice.

STATUTE OF THE INTERNATIONAL COURT OF JUSTICE, ARTICLE 38

June 26, 1945, 59 Stat. 1031, T.S. No. 993.

1. The Court, whose function is to decide in accordance with international law such disputes as are submitted to it, shall apply:

(a) international conventions, whether general or particular, establishing rules expressly recognized by the contesting States;

(b) international custom, as evidence of a general practice accepted as law;

(c) the general principles of law recognized by civilized nations;

(d) subject to the provisions of Article 59, judicial decisions and the teachings of the most highly qualified publicists of the various nations, as subsidiary means for the determination of rules of law.

2. This provision shall not prejudice the power of the Court to decide a case *ex aequo et bono*, if the parties agree thereto.

Notes and Questions

1. *Sources Not Listed in Article 38.* Article 38 of the ICJ Statute is often taken to be a listing of the sources of international law, but note the following reservations. First, Article 38 nowhere mentions "sources." Strictly speaking, Article 38 is an instruction only to the judges of the International Court; it does not by its terms apply to other international courts or lawyers. Second, in practice, judges on other tribunals (and even sometimes those on the ICJ itself) and other practicing international lawyers do use other sources of international law than those listed in Article 38, *e.g.*, natural law, equity, *jus cogens*, the resolutions of international organizations. These other sources of international law are considered alongside customary law and the general principles of law in Chapter 3.

2. *Judicial Decisions as Sources of International Law.* Article 38(1)(d) refers to Article 59, which reads: "The decision of the Court has no binding force except between the parties and in respect of that particular case." This seems to be meant to limit any inference that the reference to "judicial decisions" allows judicial precedent itself to be a source of international law. Although judicial precedent is quite an ordinary source of law in common law legal systems like those in the United States and England, many civil law legal systems formally restrict the judicial role to merely applying the law. As we shall see in Chapter 3 and throughout the book, Article 59 has, however, not prevented the International Court from relying heavily on its own past decisions as a guide in finding customary international law.

3. Ex Aequo et Bono. Article 38(2) allows the Court to decide *ex aequo et bono*, by what is equal and good, if the parties agree, but there has never been such agreement. Neither the International Court of Justice nor its predecessor, the Permanent Court of International Justice, has ever played an *ex aequo et bono* role in more than 75 years. Article 38(2) has, however, caused problems for the Court's use of equity, a topic also explored in Chapter 3.

4. *The Hierarchy of the Sources of International Law.* Are treaties the primary source of international law? Partly because "international conventions" are listed first in Article 38(1), the judges of the ICJ and other international lawyers have often given treaties pride of place among the sources of international law. There are other reasons too for thinking of treaties as primary among the rules of international law. Treaties ordinarily clearly show the legal rule because they are in written form. Moreover, treaties are subject to the explicit acceptance of states. Treaties therefore can often be clearer in their terms and more certain in their acceptance than other sorts of international law sources. Furthermore, since the 19th century treaties have been widely used by states. Many areas that used to be the province of customary international law, *e.g.*, the law of the sea and the law of treaties, have now been put into conventions. However, as we

shall see here and in Chapter 3, treaties do not cover all topics in international law, nor do they include all states as parties. Sometimes treaties may even be trumped by other forms of international law, especially natural law or *jus cogens*, and they always need to be interpreted in practice by judges or commentators who will use other sources of international law in their interpretations.

B. A TREATY SAMPLER

The conclusion of treaties between nations is a natural feature of human society. For as long as there have been written records, there have been international compacts. The five sample agreements excerpted below span more than two thousand years. Among other things, they demonstrate the permanence of treaties as part of the human experience. They also introduce treaties as vehicles for (1) military and political alliances, (2) peace-making, (3) the creation of new states, (4) the exchange of territory, and (5) the control of international violence. Today, as before, treaties constitute the most frequent sort of international law made in practice. The treaties below give students an idea of the actual "feel" and nature of international agreements, rather than leaving them to read about treaties second hand in court cases.

THE TREATY BETWEEN THE JEWS AND THE ROMANS (CIRCA 160 B.C.)

1 Maccabees 8:1–29 (*Good News Bible with Deuterocanonicals/Apocrypha*).

Judas had heard about the Romans and their reputation as a military power. He knew that they welcomed all those who joined them as allies and that those who came to them could be sure of the friendship of Rome. People had told him about the wars the Romans had fought and their heroic acts among the Gauls, whom they had conquered and forced to pay taxes. He had been told what they had done in Spain when they captured the silver mines and the gold mines there. By careful planning and persistence, they had conquered the whole country, even though it was far from Rome. They had overcome the kings from distant lands who had fought against them; they had defeated them so badly that the survivors had to pay annual taxes. They had fought and conquered Philip and Perseus, kings of Macedonia, and all who had joined them against Rome. They had even defeated Antiochus the Great, king of Syria, who had attacked them with 120 elephants, cavalry, chariots, and a powerful army. They took him alive and forced him and his successors to pay heavy taxes, to give hostages, and to surrender India, Media, Lydia, and some of their best lands. They took these and gave them to King Eumenes.

When the Greeks made plans to attack and destroy them, the Romans learned of the plans and sent a general to fight against them. The Romans killed many of the Greeks, took their wives and children captive, plundered their possessions, occupied their land, tore down their fortresses, and made them slaves, as they are today. They also destroyed or made slaves of other kingdoms, the islands, and everyone who had ever fought against them. But they maintained their friendship with their allies and those who relied on them for protection. They conquered kings near and far, and everyone who heard of their reputation was afraid of them. They helped some men to become kings, while they deposed others; they had become a world power. In spite of all this, no Roman ever tried to advance his own position by wearing a crown or putting on royal robes. They created a senate, and each day 320 senators came together to deliberate about the affairs of the people and their well-being. Each year they entrusted to one man the responsibility of governing them and controlling their whole territory. Everyone obeyed this one man, and there was no envy or jealousy among them.

Judas chose Eupolemus, the son of John and grandson of Accos, and Jason son of Eleazar and sent them to Rome to make a treaty of friendship and alliance with the Romans. He did this to eliminate Syrian oppression, since the Jews clearly saw that they were being reduced to slavery. After a long and difficult journey, Eupolemus and Jason reached Rome and entered the Senate. They addressed the assembly in these terms: "Judas Maccabeus, his brothers, and the Jewish people have sent us here to make a mutual defense treaty with you, so that we may be officially recorded as your friends and allies."

The Romans accepted the proposal, and what follows is a copy of the letter which was engraved on bronze tablets and sent to Jerusalem to remain there as a record of the treaty:

> May things go well forever for the Romans and for the Jewish nation on land and sea! May they never have enemies, and may they never go to war! But if war is declared first against Rome or any of her allies anywhere, the Jewish nation will come to her aid with whole-hearted support, as the situation may require. And to those at war with her, the Jews shall not give or supply food, arms, money, or ships, as was agreed in Rome. The Jews must carry out their obligations without receiving anything in return.
>
> In the same way, if war is declared first against the Jewish nation, the Romans will come to their aid with hearty support, as the situation may require. And to their enemies there shall not be given or supplied food, arms, money, or ships, as was agreed in Rome. The Romans must carry out their obligations without deception.
>
> These are the terms of the treaty that the Romans have made with the Jewish people.

Notes and Questions

1. *The Historical Permanence of Treaties.* The Treaty Between the Jews and the Romans we have from the Bible. Despite its antiquity, this treaty of peace and alliance has quite a modern ring to it and is not all that dissimilar in language or purpose from many treaties, like that of the North Atlantic Treaty Organization, still in force today.

2. *Reciprocity and Good Faith.* The first part of the extract is more or less its legislative history. What does it tell us about the reasons why the Jews sought a treaty? What were the reasons the Romans consented? How was the treaty to be enforced? If the Romans had not had such a good record of respecting their treaty commitments, would the Jews have been as eager to enter into an alliance with them? Reciprocal good faith always seems to have been one of the key components in ensuring the obligatory force of treaties.

3. *In Written Form.* Why was it important that the Jewish–Roman treaty be in writing? Was it to make sure the terms were clear? Would it help ensure the continuing efficacy of the treaty after those who negotiated the agreement had passed from the scene? What could have been the disadvantages of an unwritten agreement?

4. *Religion and International Law.* The so-called "father" of international law, Hugo Grotius, relied heavily on the Bible for his evidences of the law of nations in his seminal treatise of 1625, *De Jure Belli Ac Pacis, The Law of War and Peace.* Grotius cited a great number of treaties that were made between the Jews and their neighbors as proof for the proposition that treaties with non-believers were permitted. His other principal evidences were drawn from the great Greek and Roman classical authors. Mark W. Janis, "Religion and the Literature of International Law: Some Standard Texts," in *The Influence of Religion on the Development of International Law* 61, 64 (Mark W. Janis ed. 1991).

5. *The Inter-temporal Problem.* On the face of it, does the Treaty between the Jews and the Romans look to be part of "international law" as we now understand the concept? Would the Jews and the Romans have thought of the Treaty as creating "legal" obligations? How possible is it for people in one time or place to use terms and concepts common to peoples from other times and places? Questions like this are sometimes thought of as part of the "inter-temporal" problem of international law.

THE PEACE OF WESTPHALIA (1648)

1 Consolidated Treaty Series 198.

A Treaty of Peace between the Empire *and* Sweden, *concluded and sign'd at* Osnabrug *the 24th of* October, 1648. *The King of* France *was comprehended in this Treaty as an Ally of* Sweden.

Be it known to all and singular whom it does concern, or whom it may in any manner concern, That after the Differences and Troubles which began several years ago in the *Roman* Empire, had come to such a height, that not only all *Germany*, but likewise some neighbouring Kingdoms, especially *Sweden* and *France*, found themselves so involv'd in them, that from thence there arose a long and cruel War; * * *. At last it fell out by an Effect of the Divine Bounty, that both sides turn'd their Thoughts towards the means of making Peace, and that by a mutual Agreement made at *Hamburg* the 25th of *December* N.S. or the 15th O.S. 1641. between the Parties, the 11th N.S. or the 1st O.S. 1643. was by common Consent appointed for beginning the Assembly or

Congress of Plenipotentiaries at *Osnabrug*, and at *Munster* in *Westphalia*.

* * * After having invok'd the Assistance of God, and reciprocally exchang'd the Originals of their respective full Powers, they transacted and agreed among themselves, to the Glory of God, and Safety of the Christian World (the Electors, Princes and States of the Sacred *Roman* Empire being present, approving and consenting) the Articles of Peace and Amity, whereof the Tenour follows.

THE RE-ESTABLISHMENT OF PEACE AND AMITY.

I. That there be a Christian, universal and perpetual Peace, and a true and sincere Friendship and Amity between his Sacred Imperial Majesty, the House of *Austria*, and all his Allies and Adherents, and the Heirs and Successors of each of them, chiefly the King of *Spain*, and the Electors, Princes and States of the Empire, of the one side; and her Sacred Royal Majesty, and the Kingdom of *Sweden*, her Allies and Adherents, and the Heirs and Successors of each of them, especially the most Christian King, the respective Electors, Princes and States of the Empire, of the other side; and that this Peace be observ'd and cultivated sincerely and seriously, so that each Party may procure the Benefit, Honour and Advantage of one another, and thereby the Fruits of this Peace and Amity may be seen to grow up and flourish anew, by a sure and reciprocal maintaining of a good and faithful Neighbourhood between the *Roman* Empire and the Kingdom of *Sweden* reciprocally.

AN AMNESTY FROM ALL HOSTILITY.

II. That there be on both sides a perpetual Oblivion and Amnesty of all that has been done since the beginning of these Troubles, in what Place or in what Manner soever Hostilities may have been exercis'd by the one or the other Party; so that neither for any of those things, nor upon any other Account or Pretext whatsoever, any Act of Hostility or Enmity, Vexation or Hindrance shall be exercis'd or suffer'd, or caus'd to be exercis'd, either as to Persons, Conditions, Goods or Security, either by one's self or by others, in private, or openly, directly or indirectly, under form of Right or Law, or by open Deed, either within, or in any Place whatsoever without the Empire, notwithstanding all former Compacts to the contrary; but that all Injuries, Violences, Hostilities and Damages, and all Expences that either side has been oblig'd to be at, as well before as during the War, and all Libels by Words or Writing shall be entirely forgotten, without any regard to Persons or Things; so that whatever might be demanded or pretended by one against the other upon this account, shall be bury'd in perpetual Oblivion. * * *

POINT OF ECCLESIASTICAL GRIEVANCES, OR OF RELIGION.

V. Now whereas the Grievances of the one and the other Religion, which were debated amongst the Electors, Princes and States of the Empire, have been partly the Cause and Occasion of the present War, it has been agreed and transacted in the following manner.

1. * * * That there be an exact and reciprocal Equality amongst all the Electors, Princes and States of both Religions * * *. * * *

LIBERTY OF CONSCIENCE.

28. It has moreover been found good, that those of the Confession of *Augsburg* [Protestants], who are Subjects of the Catholicks, and the Catholick Subjects of the States of the Confession of *Augsburg*, who had not the public or private Exercise of their religion in any time of the year 1624 and who after the Publication of the Peace shall possess and embrace a Religion different from that of the Lord of the Territory, shall in consequence of the said Peace be patiently suffer'd and tolerated, without any Hindrance or Impediment to attend their Devotions in their Houses and in private, with all Liberty of Conscience, and without any Inquisition or Trouble, and even to assist in their Neighbourhood, as often as they have a mind, at the publick Exercise of their Religion, or send their children to foreign Schools of their Religion, or have them instructed in their Families by private Masters; provided the said Vassals and Subjects do their Duty in all other things, and hold themselves in due Obedience and Subjection, without giving occasion to any Disturbance or Commotion. In like manner Subjects, whether they be Catholicks, or of the Confession of *Augsburg*, shall not be despis'd any where upon account of their Religion, nor excluded from the Community of Merchants, Artizans or Companies, nor depriv'd of Successions, Legacies, Hospitals, Lazar–Houses, or Alms–Houses, and other Privileges or Rights, and far less of Church-yards, and the Honour of Burial; nor shall any more be exacted of them for the Expence of their Funerals, than the Dues usually paid for Burying–Places in Parish–Churches: so that in these and all other the like things they shall be treated in the same manner as Brethren and Sisters, with equal Justice and Protection. * * *

THE RE–ESTABLISHMENT OF THE ESTATES OF THE EMPIRE TO THEIR ANCIENT RIGHTS.

VIII. And in order to prevent for the future all Differences in the Political State, all and every the Electors, Princes, and States of the *Roman* Empire shall be so establish'd and confirm'd in their ancient Rights, Prerogatives, Liberties, Privileges, free Exercise of their Territorial Right, as well in Spirituals and Temporals, Seigneuries, Regalian Rights, and in the possession of all these things, by virtue of the present Transaction, that they may not be molested at any time in any manner, under any pretext whatsoever.

1. That they enjoy without contradiction the Right of Suffrage in all Deliberations touching the Affairs of the Empire, especially in the manner of interpreting Laws, resolving upon a War, imposing Taxes, ordering Levies and quartering of Soldiers, building for the publick Use new Fortresses in the Lands of the States, and reinforcing old Garisons, making of Peace and Alliances, and treating of other such-like Affairs; so that none of those or the like things shall be done or receiv'd afterwards, without the Advice and Consent of a free Assembly of all the

States of the Empire: That, above all, each of the Estates of the Empire shall freely and for ever enjoy the Right of making Alliances among themselves, or with Foreigners, for the Preservation and Security of every one of them: provided nevertheless that these Alliances be neither against the Emperor nor the Empire, nor the publick Peace, nor against this Transaction especially; and that they be made without prejudice in every respect to the Oath whereby every one of them is bound to the Emperor and the Empire.

Notes and Questions

1. *The Peace of Westphalia.* This excerpt is from the Treaty of Osnabruck between Sweden and the Holy Roman Empire. The Peace of Westphalia also included a second agreement, the Treaty of Munster, between France and the Empire. The Peace of Westphalia brought to a close the bloody Thirty Years War. One of the central issues of the War was the right of princes and peoples to choose to be Catholic or Protestant. Besides the Treaty's general provisions respecting amity and amnesty, some of the clauses about religious liberty have been reproduced above.

The Peace of Westphalia is for many historians and lawyers the real beginning of the era of "modern international relations" and hence of "modern international law." Yet, the Peace itself was drafted by Europeans well familiar with international compacts, who probably had little idea that others would view their newly crafted Peace as an innovation. What makes the Peace of Westphalia so compelling as a "starting point"? Besides ending the Thirty Years War, the Peace of Westphalia in Article VIII "re-established" the "electors, princes, and states of the Roman Empire" to "their ancient Rights." Were these "ancient Rights," described as protecting the German states from any "molestation," a kind of state sovereignty that became the fundamental building block for modern international politics?

2. *Sovereignty and International Law.* Note how ironic it is that states had to agree in a treaty to limit their sovereignty in order to assure their sovereignty. The success of international law as a political and intellectual discipline over the past four centuries has had much to do with international law's utility in regulating and cementing a world political system based on more or less sovereign states.

It should be no surprise that the modern intellectual constructs of state sovereignty and international law both emerged at the same time as the Thirty Years War. A principal craftsman of the notion of the sovereign state was the English philosopher, Thomas Hobbes, who published his celebration of the sovereign state, *Leviathan*, in 1651. Hobbes argued that all humankind required "a Common Power, to keep them in awe, and to direct their actions to the Common Benefit." Meantime, the Dutch jurist, Hugo de Groot (or Grotius) fashioned a legal system in *De Jure Belli Ac Pacis* (1625) that explained that no sovereign state was so powerful as not to need the advantages of laws based on natural law and positive consent. It is this powerful combination of Hobbes's sovereign state and Grotius's international law that have defined much of international relations for more than three centuries ever since. See Mark W. Janis, "Sovereignty and International

Law: Hobbes and Grotius," in *Essays in Honour of Wang Tieya* 391 (Ronald St. John Macdonald ed. 1994).

THE TREATY OF PARIS (1783)

United States and Great Britain
12 Bevans 8, 48 Consolidated Treaty Series 487.

Concluded at Paris September 3, 1783; ratified by Congress January 14, 1784; proclaimed January 14, 1784.

In the name of the Most Holy and Undivided Trinity.

It having pleased the Divine Providence to dispose the hearts of the Most Serene and Most Potent Prince George the Third, by the grace of God King of Great Britain, France, and Ireland, Defender of the Faith, Duke of Brunswick and Lunenburg, Arch–Treasurer and Prince Elector of the Holy Roman Empire, &c. and of the United States of America, to forget all past misunderstandings and differences that have unhappily interrupted the good correspondence and friendship which they mutually wish to restore; and to establish such a beneficial and satisfactory intercourse between the two countries, upon the ground of reciprocal advantages and mutual convenience, as may promote and secure to both perpetual peace and harmony; and having for this desirable end already laid the foundation of peace and reconciliation, by the provisional articles signed at Paris, on the 30th of November, 1782, by the Commissioners empowered on each part; which articles were agreed to be inserted in, and to constitute the treaty of peace proposed to be concluded between the Crown of Great Britain and the said United States, but which treaty was not to be concluded until terms of peace should be agreed upon between Great Britain and France, and His Britannick Majesty should be ready to conclude such treaty accordingly; and the treaty between Great Britain and France having since been concluded, His Britannick Majesty and the United States of America, in order to carry into effect the provisional articles above mentioned, according to the tenor thereof, have constituted and appointed, that is to say, his Britannick Majesty, on his part, David Hartley, Esq., Member of the Parliament of Great Britain: and the said United States, on their part, John Adams, Esq., late a Commissioner of the United States of America at the Court of Versailles, late Delegate in Congress from the State of Massachusets, and Chief Justice of the said State, and Minister Plenipotentiary of the said United States to their High Mightinesses the States General of the United Netherlands; Benjamin Franklin, Esq., late Delegate in Congress from the State of Pennsylvania, President of the Convention of the said State, and Minister Plenipotentiary from the United States of America at the Court of Versailles; John Jay, Esq., late President of Congress, and Chief Justice of the State of New York, and Minister Plenipotentiary from the said United States at the Court of Madrid; to be the Plenipotentiaries for the concluding and signing the present definitive treaty: who, after having reciprocally communicated their respective full powers, have agreed upon and confirmed the following articles:

Article I. His Britannick Majesty acknowledges the said United States, viz. New Hampshire, Massachusets Bay, Rhode Island and Providence Plantations, Connecticut, New York, New Jersey, Pennsylvania, Delaware, Maryland, Virginia, North Carolina, South Carolina, and Georgia, to be Free, Sovereign and Independent States; that he treats with them as such; and for himself, his heirs and successors, relinquishes all claims to the government, propriety, and territorial rights of the same, and every part thereof.

II. And that all disputes which might arise in future on the subject of the boundaries of the said United States may be prevented, it is hereby agreed and declared, that the following are, and shall be, their boundaries, viz. From the north-west angle of Nova Scotia, viz. that angle which is formed by a line drawn due north from the source of Saint Croix river to the Highlands, along the said Highlands which divide those rivers that empty themselves into the river St. Lawrence, from those which fall into the Atlantic ocean, to the north-westernmost head of Connecticut river; thence down along the middle of that river to the forty-fifth degree of north latitude; from thence, by a line due west on said latitude until it strikes the river Iroquois or Cataraquy; thence along the middle of said river into Lake Ontario; through the middle of said lake, until it strikes the communication by water between that lake and lake Erie; thence along the middle of said communication into lake Erie; through the middle of said lake until it arrives at the water communication between that lake and lake Huron; thence along the middle of said water communication into the lake Huron; thence through the middle of said lake to the water communication between that lake and lake Superior; thence through lake Superior, northward of the Isles Royal and Phelipeaux, to the Long Lake; thence through the middle of said Long Lake, and the water communication between it and the Lake of the Woods, to the said Lake of the Woods; thence through the said lake to the most north-western point thereof, and from thence on a due west course to the river Mississippi; thence by a line to be drawn along the middle of the said river Mississippi, until it shall intersect the northernmost part of the thirty-first degree of north latitude:—South, by a line to be drawn due east from the determination of the line last mentioned, in the latitude of thirty-one degrees north of the equator, to the middle of the river Apalachicola or Catahouche; thence along the middle thereof to its junction with the Flint river; thence strait to the head of St. Mary's river, and thence down along the middle of St. Mary's River to the Atlantic ocean:—East, by a line to be drawn along the middle of the river St. Croix, from its mouth in the bay of Fundy, to its source; and from its source directly north to the aforesaid Highlands, which divide the rivers that fall into the Atlantic ocean from those which fall into the river St. Lawrence: comprehending all islands within twenty leagues of any part of the shores of the United States, and lying between lines to be drawn due east from the points where the aforesaid boundaries between Nova Scotia on the one part, and East Florida on the other, shall respectively touch the bay of Fundy, and the Atlantic ocean; excepting such islands as now are, or heretofore have been, within the limits of the said province of Nova Scotia.

III. It is agreed, that the people of the United States shall continue to enjoy, unmolested, the right to take fish of every kind of the grand bank and on all the other banks of Newfoundland: also in the gulph of Saint Lawrence, and at all other places in the sea where the inhabitants of both countries used at any time heretofore to fish. And also that the inhabitants of the United States shall have liberty to take fish of every kind on such part of the coast of Newfoundland as British fishermen shall use, (but not to dry or cure the same on that island) and also on the coasts, bays, and creeks of all other of His Britannick Majesty's dominions in America; and that the American fishermen shall have liberty to dry and cure fish in any of the unsettled bays, harbours, and creeks of Nova Scotia, Magdalen Islands, and Labrador, so long as the same shall remain unsettled; but so soon as the same, or either of them, shall be settled, it shall not be lawful for the said fishermen to dry or cure fish at such settlement without a previous agreement for that purpose with the inhabitants, proprietors, or possessors of the ground.

IV. It is agreed, that creditors on either side shall meet with no lawful impediment to the recovery of the full value, in sterling money, of all *bona fide* debts heretofore contracted.

V. It is agreed, that the Congress shall earnestly recommend it to the legislatures of the respective states, to provide for the restitution of all estates, rights, and properties, which have been confiscated, belonging to real British subjects: and also of the estates, rights, and properties, of persons resident in districts in the possession of his Majesty's arms, and who have not borne arms against the said United States: and that persons of any other description shall have free liberty to go to any part or parts of any of the Thirteen United States, and therein to remain twelve months unmolested in their endeavours to obtain the restitution of such of their estates, rights, and properties, as may have been confiscated: and that Congress shall also earnestly recommend to the several states, a reconsideration and revision of all acts or laws regarding the premises, so as to render the said laws or acts perfectly consistent not only with justice and equity, but with that spirit of conciliation which, on the return of the blessings of peace, should universally prevail. And that Congress shall also earnestly recommend to the several states, that the estates, rights, and properties, of such last-mentioned persons shall be restored to them, they refunding to any persons who may be now in possession the *bona fide* price (where any has been given) which such persons may have paid on purchasing any of the said lands, rights, or properties, since the confiscation.

And it is agreed, that all persons who have any interest in confiscated lands, either by debts, marriage settlements or otherwise, shall meet with no lawful impediment in the prosecution of their just rights.

VI. That there shall be no future confiscations made, nor any prosecutions commenced against any person or persons, for or by reason of the part which he or they may have taken in the present war; and that no person shall, on that account, suffer any future loss or damage either in his person, liberty, or property; and that those who may be in confinement on such charges at the time of the ratification of the treaty in America, shall be immediately set at liberty, and the prosecutions so commenced be discontinued.

VII. There shall be a firm and perpetual peace between His Britannick Majesty and the said States, and between the subjects of the one and the citizens of the other, wherefore, all hostilities, both by sea and land, shall from henceforth cease: all prisoners on both sides shall be set at liberty, and his Britannick Majesty shall, with all convenient speed, and without causing any destruction, or carrying away any negroes, or other property of the American inhabitants, withdraw all his armies, garrisons, and fleets, from the said United States, and from every port, place, and harbour within the same; leaving in all fortifications the American artillery that may be therein: and shall also order and cause all archives, records, deeds, and papers, belonging to any of the said States, or their citizens, which in the course of the war may have fallen into the hands of his officers, to be forthwith restored and delivered to the proper states and persons to whom they belong.

VIII. The navigation of the river Mississippi, from its source to the ocean, shall for ever remain free and open to the subjects of Great Britain, and the citizens of the United States.

IX. In case it should so happen, that any place or territory belonging to Great Britain, or to the United States, should have been conquered by the arms of either from the other, before the arrival of the said provisional articles in America, it is agreed, that the same shall be restored without difficulty, and without requiring any compensation.

X. The solemn ratifications of the present treaty, expedited in good and due form, shall be exchanged between the contracting parties in the space of six months, or sooner if possible, to be computed from the day of the signature of the present treaty.

In witness whereof, we the under-signed, their Ministers Plenipotentiary, have, in their name, and in virtue of our full powers, signed with our hands the present definitive treaty, and caused the seals of our arms to be affixed thereto.

Done at Paris, this third day of September, in the year of our Lord one thousand seven hundred and eighty-three.

D. HARTLEY
JOHN ADAMS
B. FRANKLIN
JOHN JAY

Notes and Questions

1. *Recognition of the United States.* Did Article I of the 1783 Peace of Paris merely declare Britain's formal recognition of the sovereignty of the

United States as it had been already objectively established in 1776 by the United States itself in the Declaration of Independence? Or did the Peace of Paris itself constitute the sovereignty of the United States as of January 14, 1784, when the Treaty came into force? This alternative reflects the theoretical distinction in international law between the so-called "declaratory" and "constitutive" theories of recognition, a topic to which we return in Chapter 7.

U.S. Supreme Court Justice Chase wrote in 1795:

> I have ever considered it as the established doctrine of the United States, that their independence originated from, and commenced with, the declaration of congress, on the 4th of July, 1776; and that no other period can be fixed on for its commencement; and that all laws made by the legislatures of the several states, after the declaration of independence, were the laws of sovereign and independent governments.

Ware v. Hylton, 3 U.S. (3 Dall.) 199, 224, 1 L.Ed. 568, 579 (1796).

2. *Effect of Treaties on Third Parties.* Does Article II delimiting the boundaries of the United States in 1783 legally bind any nation except the United States and the United Kingdom? What would be the effect at international law if France or Spain had protested the U.S.–U.K. territorial delimitation? See Articles 34–38 of the Vienna Convention on the Law of Treaties, reproduced in the Appendix, and the discussion of customary international law in Chapter 3.

3. *Maritime Issues.* Article III concerns fishing off the shores of the United States and Canada. Fishing disputes between the two countries have continued into the present day. In 1984, the International Court of Justice decided the *Gulf of Maine Case* and again divided fishing rights between the United States and Canada in the area. Definition of the Maritime Boundary in the Gulf of Maine Area, 1984 I.C.J. 246.

4. *The Peace of Paris and the U.S. Constitution.* The inability or unwillingness of state courts to protect the rights of British subjects detailed in Articles IV, V, and VI, led Britain to remain in occupation of much of what was then the Northwest Territory (later the states of Illinois, Indiana, Michigan, Ohio, and Wisconsin). This in turn was one impetus to the calling of the Constitutional Convention in 1787, to the establishment of U.S. federal courts in 1789 under the new U.S. Constitution, and to the mention of treaties in the Constitution's supremacy clause. See Chapter 4.

On balance, the Peace of Paris was a diplomatic triumph for the new United States:

> This Peace of Paris certainly gives the lie to the epigram that 'America never lost a war, or won a peace conference.' Considering that the British still held New York, Charleston, Savannah, Detroit, and several other posts in the Northwest, that Washington's army was almost incapable of further effort, and that the British navy had recovered command of the sea, it is surprising what wide boundaries and favorable terms the United States obtained.

Samuel Eliot Morison, Henry Steele Commager & William E. Leuchtenberg, 1 *The Growth of the American Republic* 204 (7th ed. 1980).

THE CESSION OF ALASKA (1867)

11 Bevans 1216, 15 Stat. 539, Treaty Series 301,
134 Consolidated Treaty Series 331.

Convention signed at Washington March 30, 1867

Senate advice and consent to ratification April 9, 1867

Ratified by Russia May 3, 1867

Ratified by the President of the United States May 28, 1867

Ratifications exchanged at Washington June 20, 1867

Entered into force June 20, 1867

Proclaimed by the President of the United States June 20, 1867

The United States of America and His Majesty the Emperor of all the Russias, being desirous of strengthening, if possible, the good understanding which exists between them, have, for that purpose, appointed as their Plenipotentiaries: the President of the United States, William H. Seward, Secretary of State; and His Majesty the Emperor of all the Russias, the Privy Counsellor Edward de Stoeckl, his Envoy Extraordinary and Minister Plenipotentiary to the United States.

And the said Plenipotentiaries, having exchanged their full powers, which were found to be in due form, have agreed upon and signed the following articles:

Article I.

His Majesty the Emperor of all the Russias agrees to cede to the United States, by this convention, immediately upon the exchange of the ratifications thereof, all the territory and dominion now possessed by his said Majesty on the continent of America and in the adjacent islands, the same being contained within the geographical limits herein set forth, to wit: The eastern limit is the line of demarcation between the Russian and the British possessions in North America, as established by the convention between Russia and Great Britain, of February 28–16, 1825, and described in Articles III and IV of said convention, in the following terms:

"Commencing from the southernmost point of the island called Prince of Wales Island, which point lies in the parallel of 54 degrees 40 minutes north latitude, and between the 131st and the 133d degree of west longitude, (meridian of Greenwich,) the said line shall ascend to the north along the channel called Portland channel, as far as the point of the continent where it strikes the 56th degree of north latitude; from this last mentioned point, the line of demarcation shall follow the summit of the mountains situated parallel to the coast as far as the point of intersection of the 141st degree of west longitude, (the same meridian;) and finally, from the said point of intersection, the said meridian line of the 141st degree, in its prolongation as far as the Frozen ocean.

"IV. With reference to the line of demarcation laid down in the preceding article, it is understood—

"1st. That the island called Prince of Wales Island shall belong wholly to Russia," (now, by this cession, to the United States.)

"2d. That whenever the summit of the mountains which extend in a direction parallel to the coast from the 56th degree of north latitude to the point of intersection of the 141st degree of west longitude shall prove to be at the distance of more than ten marine leagues from the ocean, the limit between the British possessions and the line of coast which is to belong to Russia as above mentioned (that is to say, the limit to the possessions ceded by this convention) shall be formed by a line parallel to the winding of the coast, and which shall never exceed the distance of ten marine leagues therefrom."

The western limit within which the territories and dominion conveyed, are contained, passes through a point in Behring's straits on the parallel of 65 degrees 30 minutes north latitude, at its intersection by the meridian which passes midway between the islands of Krusenstern, or Ignalook, and the island of Ratmanoff, or Noonarbook, and proceeds due north, without limitation, into the same Frozen Ocean. The same western limit, beginning at the same initial point, proceeds thence in a course nearly southwest, through Behring's straits and Behring's sea, so as to pass midway between the northwest point of the island of St. Lawrence and the southeast point of Cape Choukotski, to the meridian of 172 west longitude; thence, from the intersection of that meridian, in a southwesterly direction, so as to pass midway between the island of Attou and the Copper island of the Kormandorski couplet or group, in the North Pacific ocean, to the meridian of 193 degrees west longitude, so as to include in the territory conveyed the whole of the Aleutian islands east of that meridian.

Article II.

In the cession of territory and dominion made by the preceding article, are included the right of property in all public lots and squares, vacant lands, and all public buildings, fortifications, barracks, and other edifices which are not private individual property. It is, however, understood and agreed, that the churches which have been built in the ceded territory by the Russian government, shall remain the property of such members of the Greek Oriental Church resident in the territory, as may choose to worship therein. Any government archives, papers, and documents relative to the territory and dominion aforesaid, which may be now existing there, will be left in the possession of the agent of the United States; but an authenticated copy of such of them as may be required, will be, at all times, given by the United States to the Russian government or to such Russian officers or subjects, as they may apply for.

Article III.

The inhabitants of the ceded territory, according to their choice, reserving their natural allegiance, may return to Russia within three years; but if they should prefer to remain in the ceded territory, they, with the exception of uncivilized native tribes, shall be admitted to the enjoyment of all the rights, advantages and immunities of citizens of the United States, and shall be maintained and protected in the free enjoyment of their liberty, property and religion. The uncivilized tribes will be subject to such laws and regulations as the United States, may from time to time, adopt in regard to aboriginal tribes of that country.

Article IV.

His Majesty, the Emperor of all the Russias shall appoint, with convenient despatch, an agent or agents for the purpose of formally delivering to a similar agent or agents appointed on behalf of the United States, the territory, dominion, property, dependencies and appurtenances which are ceded as above, and for doing any other act which may be necessary in regard thereto. But the cession, with the right of immediate possession, is nevertheless to be deemed complete and absolute on the exchange of ratifications, without waiting for such formal delivery.

Article V.

Immediately after the exchange of the ratifications of this convention, any fortifications or military posts which may be in the ceded territory, shall be delivered to the agent of the United States, and any Russian troops which may be in the Territory shall be withdrawn as soon as may be reasonably and conveniently practicable.

Article VI.

In consideration of the cession aforesaid, the United States agree to pay at the Treasury in Washington, within ten months after the exchange of the ratifications of this convention, to the diplomatic representative or other agent of his Majesty the Emperor of all the Russias, duly authorized to receive the same, seven million two hundred thousand dollars in gold. The cession of territory and dominion herein made is hereby declared to be free and unincumbered by any reservations, privileges, franchises, grants, or possessions, by any associated companies, whether corporate or incorporate, Russian or any other, or by any parties, except merely private individual property holders; and the cession hereby made, conveys all the rights, franchises, and privileges now belonging to Russia in the said territory or dominion, and appurtenances thereto.

Article VII.

When this Convention shall have been duly ratified by the President of the United States, by and with the advice and consent of the Senate, on the one part, and on the other by His Majesty the Emperor of all the Russias, the ratification shall be exchanged at Washington within three months from the date hereof, or sooner, if possible.

In faith whereof, the respective plenipotentiaries have signed this convention, and thereto affixed the seals of their arms.

Done at Washington, the thirtieth day of March in the year of our Lord one thousand eight hundred and sixty-seven.

William H. Seward
Edouard De Stoeckl

THE KELLOGG–BRIAND PACT (1928)

Renunciation of War as an Instrument of National Policy
2 Bevans 732, 46 Stat. 2343, Treaty Series 796, 94 L.N.T.S. 57.

Treaty signed at Paris August 27, 1928

Senate advice and consent to ratification January 15, 1929

Ratified by the President of the United States January 17, 1929

Ratifications deposited at Washington March 2, 1929

Entered into force July 24, 1929

Proclaimed by the President of the United States July 24, 1929

The President of the German Reich, the President of the United States of America, His Majesty the King of the Belgians, the President of the French Republic, His Majesty the King of Great Britain, Ireland and the British Dominions Beyond the Seas, Emperor of India, His Majesty the King of Italy, His Majesty the Emperor of Japan, the President of the Republic of Poland, the President of the Czechoslovak Republic,

Deeply sensible of their solemn duty to promote the welfare of mankind;

Persuaded that the time has come when a frank renunciation of war as an instrument of national policy should be made to the end that the peaceful and friendly relations now existing between their peoples may be perpetuated;

Convinced that all changes in their relations with one another should be sought only by pacific means and be the result of a peaceful and orderly process, and that any signatory Power which shall hereafter seek to promote its national interests by resort to war should be denied the benefits furnished by this Treaty;

Hopeful that, encouraged by their example, all the other nations of the world will join in this humane endeavor and by adhering to the present Treaty as soon as it comes into force bring their peoples within the scope of its beneficent provisions, thus uniting the civilized nations of the world in a common renunciation of war as an instrument of their national policy;

Have decided to conclude a Treaty and for that purpose have appointed * * * Plenipotentiaries * * * who, having communicated to one another their full powers found in good and due form have agreed upon the following articles:

Article I

The High Contracting Parties solemnly declare in the names of their respective peoples that they condemn recourse to war for the solution of international controversies, and renounce it as an instrument of national policy in their relations with one another.

ARTICLE II

The High Contracting Parties agree that the settlement or solution of all disputes or conflicts of whatever nature or of whatever origin they may be, which may arise among them, shall never be sought except by pacific means.

ARTICLE III

The present Treaty shall be ratified by the High Contracting Parties named in the Preamble in accordance with their respective constitutional requirements, and shall take effect as between them as soon as all their several instruments of ratification shall have been deposited at Washington.

This Treaty shall, when it has come into effect as prescribed in the preceding paragraph, remain open as long as may be necessary for adherence by all the other Powers of the world. Every instrument evidencing the adherence of a Power shall be deposited at Washington and the Treaty shall immediately upon such deposit become effective as between the Power thus adhering and the other Powers parties hereto.

It shall be the duty of the Government of the United States to furnish each Government named in the Preamble and every Government subsequently adhering to this Treaty with a certified copy of the Treaty and of every instrument of ratification or adherence. It shall also be the duty of the Government of the United States telegraphically to notify such Governments immediately upon the deposit with it of each instrument of ratification or adherence.

IN FAITH WHEREOF the respective Plenipotentiaries have signed this Treaty in the French and English languages both texts having equal force, and hereunto affix their seals.

DONE at Paris, the twenty-seventh day of August in the year one thousand nine hundred and twenty-eight.

[For Germany:]
Gustav Stresemann

[For the United States:]
Frank B. Kellogg

[For the United Kingdom:]
Cushendun

[For the Dominion of Canada:]
W. L. Mackenzie King

[For the Commonwealth of Australia:]
A. J. McLachlan

[For the Dominion of New Zealand:]
C. J. Parr

[For the Union of South Africa:]
J. S. Smit

[For Belgium:]
Paul Hymans

[For France:]
Ari Briand

[For India:]
Cushendun

[For Italy:]
G. Manzoni

[For Japan:]
Uchida

[For Poland:]
August Zaleski

[For Czechoslovakia:]
Dr. Eduard Benes

[For the Irish Free State:]
Liam T. MacCosgair

Notes and Questions

1. *The Efficacy of International Law.* The Cession of Alaska and the Kellogg–Briand Pact make a nice contrast when discussing the efficacy of international law. It is easy to see how the 1867 Cession of Alaska "worked"—Russia ceded the Alaska Territory to the United States and the United States paid the Tsar $7,200,000 in gold. After the conclusion of the treaty, Russian officials left Alaska, U.S. officials arrived, and money changed hands. It is much more difficult to see how the 1928 Kellogg–Briand Pact "worked." What good were "solemn" renunciations of war, especially in light of the developments in world politics in the 1930's and 1940's: the participation of Germany and the Soviet Union in the Spanish Civil War, the invasion of Ethiopia by Italy, the invasion of Manchuria by Japan, the invasion of Czechoslovakia by Germany, the invasion of Poland by Germany and the Soviet Union, the invasion of the Baltic States and Finland by the Soviet Union, the invasion of France, the Netherlands, Belgium, Denmark, Norway, and the Soviet Union by Germany, the German attack on the United Kingdom, the Japanese invasion of China, Malaya, Indonesia, and the Phillipines, and the Japanese attack on the United States? If the Treaty of Cession of Alaska shows treaties at their most efficacious, does not the Kellogg–Briand Pact show them at their least efficacious?

2. *"Hard" and "Soft" International Law.* Are both the Cession of Alaska and the Kellogg–Briand Pact the same sort of "international law"? Some international lawyers distinguish between "hard" and "soft" international law, that is, between rules meant to be followed and rules meant merely to set out a preferred outcome. Are these two treaties examples of the distinction?

Is it fair to conclude that the Kellogg–Briand Pact was only aspirational? If so, was it wrong then to try and execute individuals for the violation of its principles as was done at the Nuremberg trial of Nazi war criminals? See Chapter 6.

3. *Bilateral and Multilateral Treaties.* It is conceptually possible for issues addressed in a multilateral treaty such as the Kellogg–Briand Pact to be dealt with in a series of bilateral agreements. Why was the Kellogg–Briand Pact drawn up as a multilateral treaty? Would the conclusion of a series of bilateral agreements have been too cumbersome? Was the subject matter of the Kellogg–Briand Pact also particularly appropriate for multilateral treatment? Is it more likely that the rules established in a multilateral treaty will pass into customary international law? Use of multilateral treaties increased significantly in the twentieth century.

C. THE LAW OF TREATIES

This section briefly introduces a detailed and complex area of international law, the law of treaties. The law of treaties plays roughly the same role in international law as the law of contracts plays in municipal law: it establishes rules about the making and interpretation of agreements, their observation, modification, and termination. We look first at a sample treaty negotiation and then at two cases before the International Court about the law of treaties.

CORDELL HULL, 1 THE MEMOIRS OF CORDELL HULL

831–843 (1948).

New decisions confronted us in the summer of 1940 as Great Britain's plight on the high seas grew acute. Contrasted with the period before we entered the First World War, it was perilous. A quarter of a century before, Britain had the assistance of the French and Italian fleets in the Atlantic and Mediterranean, and of the Japanese fleet in the Pacific. Now the French fleet lay immobile, German submarines operated out of French ports, the Italian Navy was an enemy and the Japanese Navy a potential enemy. Britain's shipping losses were rising dangerously. If she were to survive, it was necessary for her not only to purchase huge quantities of war supplies in this country, but also to get them safely to the United Kingdom.

British Ambassador Lord Lothian came in to see me on August 4, the day before my departure for White Sulphur Springs, and expressed his Government's "urgent desire" to purchase from us a number of older type destroyers. Britain, he said, needed them to bridge over what he described as her "present emergency situation." * * *

When Lothian came to my office on August 4 I could appreciate Britain's dangers as fully as he could depict them. He said Britain had lost five destroyers during the previous week alone. Destroyers, he pointed out, were vitally important in combating submarine activities and other enemy action in the English Channel where large warships could not be used to advantage.

He said he had already discussed the question with the President while I was at Havana, and now desired to lay the situation before me in the hope that something might be done within the next few weeks. He added that Britain would be willing to make available to us facilities for naval and air bases in certain British islands adjacent to Central and South America and in Bermuda, as well as for aircraft bases in Newfoundland. He said he would give us later in the day a memorandum indicating the bases and facilities Britain had in mind.

I first explained to Lothian that such facilities would, of course, be for the benefit of all the American Republics. "In keeping with the understandings reached at Havana and at prior conferences," I said, "any action taken by the United States would be in cooperation with the other American Republics."

I also pointed out the legal difficulties in the way of our selling the destroyers. The United States Code forbade the departure of vessels from American waters outfitted for cruising against a foreign nation with which we were at peace. Also, the National Defense Act, approved

June 28, 1940, forbade the sale of naval equipment without the approval of the Chief of Naval Operations, and military equipment without the approval of the Chief of Staff of the Army.

"To meet the wishes of your Government," I said, "an amendment to these provisions of law may be necessary, and you well know that such procedures move slowly. Members of Congress are extremely sensitive to representations by constituents who for one reason or another may oppose legislation of this kind."

Britain's dangers, however, were a fact, as it was also a fact that the menace from the dictator who was devouring Europe like a mad dog was ultimately a menace to us. I said to Lothian that we were giving the matter attentive consideration. * * *

During my three weeks rest at White Sulphur Springs I had a private telephone line into my apartment there and received daily pouches from the State Department, hence closely followed and participated in the destroyers-bases negotiations in the hands of the President and Welles. A few hours after I returned to Washington on August 23, I went to the White House to attend a Cabinet meeting.

There the President said to me: "Our negotiations with Britain on the bases and destroyers have bogged down. Please see what you can do."

In talking over the bases with the President, I found he had an amazing personal knowledge of almost all of them. He had either cruised, swum, or fished in those harbors. He knew how many feet deep and wide they were and how many ships they would take.

He also knew the penurious condition of the native populations of most of the islands, and consequently did not want to assume the burden of administering those populations. Therefore he had changed, during my absence from Washington, from his original idea of outright purchase of the bases to that of 99–year leases. I had originally favored outright cession, but was willing to agree to leases instead.

I thereupon undertook the negotiations, determined to push them to completion as quickly as possible. The fact of the negotiations being public property, I felt that to drag them on much longer would be to prejudice the excellent psychological reaction to be expected in Europe when the arrangement went through.

Moreover, Britain vitally needed the destroyers at that very moment, to cover a period of low strength in smaller types of warships until a number of such ships she now had on the ways could be ready in the first part of 1941. As Churchill said in a message to the President on August 15: "The worth of every destroyer that you can spare to us is measured in rubies."

On the following day, as I was reviewing the negotiations to date, the White House informed me that the British Ambassador had an appointment with the President the next evening, a Sunday, and Mr. Roosevelt would like to have me present. * * *

That evening I met Lothian at the White House and, while we sat together awaiting our appointment with the President, I again emphasized to him that the President had no authority to give away Government property.

When the President received us, however, Lothian to my surprise, seemingly ignoring my statement that the President legally could not make a gift of public property, proceeded to present the British proposal. He said he had prepared this himself, in the form of three draft notes, which he handed to the President and me. The first was from himself to me, the second was my reply, and the third was the British acknowledgment of my reply. Lothian said he had sent these to his Government for its approval.

Although Mr. Churchill had suggested that he should define some of the facilities he was prepared to turn over to us, Lothian proposed that a joint Anglo–American body immediately proceed to agree on what the facilities, naval and air, were to be. He thought that Churchill's suggestion would lead to delay and dispute.

In presenting his views, Lothian handed me a personal letter from himself which began: "I understand that all the papers about this awkward destroyer question have been handed over to you. It seems to me that Washington and London are in danger of getting at loggerheads, which if the fact were disclosed might have deplorable effects on public opinion in both countries, largely through a misunderstanding which it is difficult to resolve by telegraph or transatlantic telephone."

Lothian argued in his letter that, if the transaction were treated as a bargain, Mr. Churchill did not feel that he could give us, in return for fifty "oldish destroyers," the right to get whatever air and naval bases in Newfoundland, Bermuda, the Bahamas, Jamaica, St. Lucia, Trinidad, and British Guiana we might choose to ask for, "because the British Government might incur the charge of defaulting on its share of the bargain if it created difficulties about any particular thing the United States Government wanted."

"I think," he said, "Mr. Churchill feels that British public opinion would not support a bargain of this kind if it was presented as a contract and that it would in practice lead to the most dangerous controversies between the United States and Great Britain.... In point of fact there is and can be no parallel between the two halves of the transaction, and to try to make it a bargain is to spoil what would otherwise be a demonstration of mutual good will between our two countries in which the question of the relative consideration on each side has no place."

In general, Lothian argued to the President and me that there should not be cold commercial bargaining but a friendly interest between the two Governments. This would afford a basis for gifts back and forth which would be voluntary and apparently without definite understanding in advance.

After Lothian had finished his arguments, I said for the third time to the Ambassador, and for the first time to the President, that the latter had no authority whatever to make a gift of public property to any Government or individual. Mr. Roosevelt at once agreed with me. I said, and he agreed, that a different arrangement would be necessary to achieve our objectives.

The President thereupon left it to me to work out a solution with Lothian.

The following morning I called to my office Green H. Hackworth, Legal Adviser of the State Department, whose advice was always invaluable to me, and Judge Townsend of the Department of Justice, to try to find a way out. After some discussion, Hackworth suddenly suggested that there might be a compromise after all between Churchill's desire for reciprocal gifts and our own legal position that the President could not give away the destroyers but had to get something in return.

Since the British had not stated precisely what bases they intended to lease to us, why not divide them into two parcels? The first would comprise the bases in Newfoundland and Bermuda. These Britain could lease us as an outright gift. The second would comprise the bases around the Caribbean, strategically more valuable to us because of their nearness to the Panama Canal. These could be leased to us in consideration of the cession of the 50 destroyers.

I saw at once that here was the formula for which we had been looking.

We thereupon set to work to redraft the proposals. Leaving Hackworth and Townsend to complete the drafting, I telephoned the President, told him Hackworth had offered a solution, and asked if I could send Hackworth to outline it to him. That afternoon Hackworth and Townsend saw the President, who agreed to the compromise.

As finished, our draft began with an assurance from the British Government that, if the waters surrounding the British Isles became untenable for British warships, "the British fleet would in no event be surrendered or sunk, but would be sent to other ports of the Empire for continued defense of the Empire."

Mr. Churchill had already given such assurances in his speech to Parliament on June 4, but I wanted a formal repetition because of our transfer of the destroyers to Britain. Basically I was confident that Britain could hold out; but it was obvious that Hitler was now about to unleash a full-scale attack on Britain, first probably by air, then, if that did not bring surrender, an all-out invasion by sea and air.

If my confidence was misplaced and the British fleet were surrendered, the position of the United States would be perilous in the extreme. But if the surrendered fleet included the 50 former American destroyers, our position would be rendered yet more dangerous, and the fire of the isolationists who were opposing the Administration on selling the destroyers would be turned on the White House. * * *

Meantime Lord Lothian sent me on the same day a long cable from Churchill to the President. Churchill, signing himself "Former naval person," approved the proposal previously submitted by Lothian, which, making the leases to all the British bases out to be outright gifts, had not been acceptable to us.

Churchill also was ready to give assurances that the British fleet would not be scuttled or surrendered. This would be in the form of a separate exchange of letters between Lothian and me. According to Churchill's draft he would merely refer to and confirm the statements he made on this subject in his addresses on June 4 and August 20.

With his usual indomitable spirit, he said he did not wish this latter exchange to be published because "I think it is much more likely that the German Government will be the one to surrender or scuttle its fleet or what is left of it. In this, as you are aware, they have already had some practice. You will remember that I said some months ago in one of my private cables to you that any such action on our part would be a dastardly act, and that this is the opinion of everyone of us."

Churchill had already stated his objection to publicity concerning these assurances in a cable he sent the President on August 15, when he said: "You will please bear in mind the disastrous effect from our point of view, and perhaps also from yours, of allowing any impression to grow that we regard the conquest of the British Islands and its naval bases as any other than an impossible contingency. The spirit of our people is splendid."

The Prime Minister now urged immediate action on the destroyers-bases transaction, saying it had become especially urgent in view of Mussolini's menace to Greece. (The Italian invasion of Greece occurred on October 28, 1940.) "If our business," he said, "is put through on bilateral lines and in the highest spirit of good will, it might even now save that small historic country from invasion and conquest. Even the next 48 hours are important."

Lothian having cabled to London the location of the bases the President had in mind, Churchill agreed and himself added the island of Antigua, in the Caribbean, which he said might be useful as a base for flying boats.

That steaming night of August 27, Lothian, Knox, and Stark all appeared at my apartment at about ten-thirty. For more than an hour we four went over the draft I had given Stark. Lothian at first had a few suggestions for revision, but eventually seemed quite satisfied and said he would send the note to his Government.

The negotiations now remained in abeyance for two days, until Lothian could hear from his Government. On August 29 I handed the Ambassador an informal memorandum from myself to argue further our idea that the destroyers and bases should not be dealt with as outright gifts. I said that our proposal whereby Britain would give us leases to bases in Newfoundland and Bermuda and would exchange leases to the other bases for 50 of our destroyers "in the main speaks for itself. It would be unfortunate if the arrangement should be made to appear in any other light, such as that all the bases were to be turned over to the United States as an unqualified gift with no thought or expectation of receiving 50 destroyers. The fact is that the destroyers have been in the mind of the British Government throughout and prior to the beginning of the discussions regarding bases. If the British Government desires to drop the idea of acquiring the destroyers and to turn over the bases as an unqualified gift, a different situation would be presented."

That night at seven o'clock Lord Lothian called at my apartment and left with me his Government's counterproposal. I called Admirals Stark and Woodson and also Green Hackworth to my apartment, and we went over it carefully. We found that Lothian's draft differed in only a few details from my proposal, and added the island of Antigua, which was quite agreeable to us. We made a few changes in the text, and I then telephoned Lothian, who came back to my apartment at ten-thirty. He agreed to our changes.

The following day, August 30, I telephoned the changes to the President at Hyde Park and received his approval.

We drafted at the State Department a message for the President to send to Congress along with the exchange of notes between Lothian and myself. I sent all three documents to the President at Hyde Park on August 31. It was understood that the notes should be signed and exchanged on Monday September 2. The President gave his approval to the three documents, making only a slight change in the message, and handed them to me when I met him at the Union Station in Washington Sunday afternoon September 1.

The President also handed me a letter from himself, which said: "I have carefully read the note from the British Ambassador and your reply thereto as Secretary of State of the United States.

"I give my full and cordial approval to both of these notes." He signed his full name.

Lord Lothian, who had spent the week end in Boston, returned to Washington Monday afternoon, and came to my apartment at seven o'clock that evening. There we signed and exchanged the notes confirming the destroyers-bases transactions.

Lothian also handed me his reply to an *aide-mémoire* I had previously given him requesting assurances concerning the disposition of the British fleet. My *aide-mémoire* had referred to the June 4 speech of the Prime Minister in which he said that if the waters surrounding the British Isles became untenable for British warships, the British fleet would in no event be surrendered or sunk but would be sent overseas for the defense of other parts of the Empire. It then asked "whether the foregoing statement represents the settled policy of the British Government."

Lothian stated in his reply: "His Majesty's Ambassador is instructed by the Prime Minister to inform Mr. Secretary Hull that this statement certainly does represent the settled policy of His Majesty's Government. Mr. Churchill must however observe that these hypothetical contingencies seem more likely to concern the German fleet or what is left of it than the British fleet."

The last sentence was Churchill's own addition. The Prime Minister now agreed to having the exchange of *aides-mémoire* published on condition that the main notes regarding the bases and destroyers should be made public first.

The following morning, September 3, I sent to the White House the President's message to Congress, which he had signed and handed to me; the destroyers-bases notes, and an opinion of Attorney General Robert H. Jackson declaring the transaction legal. All these were for communication to Congress. The President was en route to the Capital, after dedicating Chickamauga Dam, when the documents were published.

Thus were concluded within a week negotiations among the most momentous in our history. As the President said in his message to Congress: "This is the most important action in the reinforcement of our national defense that has been taken since the Louisiana Purchase. Then as now, considerations of safety from overseas attack were fundamental."

Mention of the Louisiana Purchase was not without significance because it, too, had been made without authorization from Congress and, though the reaction to the destroyers-bases exchange throughout the nation was, in general, wholeheartedly favorable, some opponents objected that Congress should have given its approval.

We based our stand, however, on the necessity for defense. "Preparation for defense," said the President's message, "is an inalienable prerogative of a sovereign state. Under present circumstances this exercise of sovereign right is essential to the maintenance of our peace and safety."

The President pointed out that the exchange was not inconsistent in any sense with our status of peace. He put the value of the new bases to the Western Hemisphere as "beyond calculation." They were essential, he said, to the protection of the Panama Canal, Central America, the northern portion of South America, the Antilles, Canada, Mexico, and our Eastern and Gulf seaboards.

In conformity with the thought I had expressed to Lord Lothian when he first broached the subject of bases and destroyers with me on August 4—namely, that any bases we obtained in this hemisphere must be for the benefit of all the American Republics—I sent instructions on September 6 to our diplomatic missions in those countries. I requested them to notify those Governments that we had acquired leases to British bases not only for our own defense but also for more effective cooperation with the other American Republics in the common defense of the hemisphere. "The resulting facilities at these bases," I added, "will, of course, be made available alike to all American Republics on the fullest cooperative basis for the common defense of the hemisphere and in entire harmony with the spirit of the pronouncements made and the understandings reached at the conferences of Lima, Panama, and Havana."

A few international lawyers might have argued that we had violated the Hague Convention of 1907 in that we, a neutral, had sold warships to a belligerent. However, that convention started off with the proposition that "belligerents are bound to respect the sovereign rights of neutral Powers." Neutrals like Poland, Norway, Denmark, The Netherlands, Luxemburg, and Belgium, could testify that the principles of the Hague Convention had not protected them. The convention laid down rights and duties of neutrals and belligerents alike, and the Axis dictators, who had wrecked the convention and alone would have a motive for questioning our transaction, were estopped, by every rule of reason and law, from raising the question. It would be absurd to contend that the convention, which represented a compromise between rights and duties of belligerents on the one hand and neutrals on the other, should bind only the neutrals.

The destroyers-bases transaction went into effect with great speed. The destroyers, reconditioned and stocked with food and munitions, were turned over to Britain at once. Experts of both Governments met and agreed on the exact sites of the eight bases we had acquired, extending along four thousand miles of Atlantic seaboard.

To judge from the many cables I received from our diplomatic missions abroad in the days that followed, the effect of the destroyers-bases deal went far beyond the physical fact that Britain now had 50 more destroyers and we had eight more bases. It was a demonstration to the world that this Government believed that Britain had a real chance to hold fast against all Hitler's might. It showed that we were willing to go beyond ordinary methods and to find new means to aid the major democracy fighting Nazism.

The transaction enheartened the democracies then under the heel of the Prussian boot. The Axis dictators sought to make propaganda that, by acquiring the bases, we were seeking the break up of the British Empire, but in their calculations they had to recognize a new factor, the prospect of ever more American assistance to Britain. Hitler could no longer hope that his offer of peace to Britain, naturally on his own terms, would be accepted. Mussolini realized by now that what he thought an easy chance for booty had turned into a dangerous gamble. Japan, awaiting a British collapse before moving toward the South Sea area, paused and took stock. * * *

The Hull-Lothian Agreement

54 Stat. 2405, 12 Bevans 551.

The British Ambassador (Lothian) to the U.S. Secretary of State (Hull):

British Embassy
Washington, D.C.,
September 2nd, 1940

Sir,

I have the honour under instructions from His Majesty's Principal Secretary of State for Foreign Affairs to inform you that in view of the friendly and sympathetic interest of His Majesty's Government in the United Kingdom in the national security of the United States and their desire to strengthen the ability of the United States to cooperate effectively with the other nations of the Americas in the defence of the Western Hemisphere, His Majesty's Government will secure the grant to the Government of the United States, freely and without consideration, of the lease for immediate establishment and use of naval and air bases and facilities for entrance thereto and the operation and protection thereof, on the Avalon Peninsula and on the southern coast of Newfoundland, and on the east coast and on the Great Bay of Bermuda.

Furthermore, in view of the above and in view of the desire of the United States to acquire additional air and naval bases in the Caribbean and in British Guiana, and without endeavouring to place a monetary or commercial value upon the many tangible and intangible rights and properties involved, His Majesty's Government will make available to the United States for immediate establishment and use naval and air bases and facilities for entrance thereto and the operation and protection thereof, on the eastern side of the Bahamas, the southern coast of Jamaica, the western coast of St. Lucia, the west coast of Trinidad in the Gulf of Paria, in the island of Antigua and in British Guiana within fifty miles of Georgetown, in exchange for naval and military equipment and material which the United States Government will transfer to His Majesty's Government.

All the bases and facilities referred to in the preceding paragraphs will be leased to the United States for a period of ninety-nine years, free from all rent and charges other than such compensation to be mutually agreed on to be paid by the United States in order to compensate the owners of private property for loss by expropriation or damage arising out of the establishment of the bases and facilities in question.

His Majesty's Government, in the leases to be agreed upon, will grant to the United States for the period of the leases all the rights, power, and authority within the bases leased, and within the limits of the territorial waters and air spaces adjacent to or in the vicinity of such bases, necessary to provide access to and defence of such bases, and appropriate provisions for their control.

Without prejudice to the above-mentioned rights of the United States authorities and their jurisdiction within the leased areas, the adjustment and reconciliation between the jurisdiction of the authorities of the United States within these areas and the jurisdiction of the authorities of the territories in which these areas are situated, shall be determined by common agreement.

The exact location and bounds of the aforesaid bases, the necessary seaward, coast and anti-aircraft defenses, the location of sufficient military garrisons, stores and other necessary auxiliary facilities shall be determined by common agreement.

His Majesty's Government are prepared to designate immediately experts to meet with experts of the United States for these purposes. Should these experts be unable to agree in any particular situation, except in the case of Newfoundland and Bermuda, the matter shall be settled by the Secretary of State of the United States and His Majesty's Secretary of State for Foreign Affairs.

I have the honour to be, with the highest consideration, Sir,

Your most obedient, humble servant,

LOTHIAN

The U.S. Secretary of State (Hull) to the British Ambassador (Lothian):

DEPARTMENT OF STATE
WASHINGTON
SEPTEMBER 2, 1940.

EXCELLENCY:

I have received your note of September 2, 1940, of which the text is as follows:

[Here the text of the preceding letter is quoted verbatim.]

I am directed by the President to reply to your note as follows:

The Government of the United States appreciates the declarations and the generous action of His Majesty's Government as contained in your communication which are destined to enhance the national security of the United States and greatly to strengthen its ability to cooperate effectively with the other nations of the Americas in the defense of the Western Hemisphere. It therefore gladly accepts the proposals.

The Government of the United States will immediately designate experts to meet with experts designated by His Majesty's Government to determine upon the exact location of the naval and air bases mentioned in your communication under acknowledgment.

In consideration of the declarations above quoted, the Government of the United States will immediately transfer to His Majesty's Government fifty United States Navy destroyers generally referred to as the twelve hundred-ton type.

Accept, Excellency, the renewed assurances of my highest consideration.

CORDELL HULL

Notes and Questions

1. *Bilateral v. Multilateral Treaty Negotiations.* Contrast the intimate bilateral negotiations leading up to the Hull–Lothian Agreement with the enormous multilateral context of some modern treaty-drafting conferences. The 1982 United Nations Convention on the Law of the Sea, for example, was the result of more than fifteen years of multilateral negotiation, first during 1968–1973 in Committees of the United Nations and then during 1974–1982 in the Third United Nations Conference on the Law of the Sea (UNCLOS III). Altogether, thousands of diplomats from more than 150 states met hundreds of times. The negotiating agenda was complex, encompassing virtually every issue relating to use of and control over the oceans and ocean resources. States with common initial negotiating positions on one issue often found themselves at odds concerning other issues. Excellent studies of the UNCLOS III negotiations are found in: Tommy T.B. Koh & Shanmugam Jayakumar, "The Negotiating Process of the Third United Nations Conference on the Law of the Sea," in 1 *United Nations Convention on the Law of the Sea 1982: A Commentary* 29 (Myron H. Nordquist ed. 1985); Clyde Sanger, *Ordering the Oceans: The Making of the Law of the Sea* (1987); and William Wertenbaker, "The Law of the Sea," *The New Yorker*, Aug. 1, 1983, at 38 (Part I), Aug. 8, 1983, at 56 (Part II). Portions of the Law of the Sea Convention are reproduced in the Appendix, and more on the law of the sea is found in Chapter 9.

2. *Treaties as International Contracts or International Statutes.* Can it be said that the domestic legal analogy to the Hull–Lothian negotiations is the drafting of a contract while the municipal analogy to the U.N. Law of the Sea Conference is the meeting of a legislative assembly? Does that make some treaties rather like contracts and others more like statutes?

3. *Domestic Interests in Treaty Negotiations.* Note that the drafting of the Hull–Lothian Agreement involved the U.S. State Department, including Secretary of State Hull and Legal Advisor Hackworth, the Justice Department, and President Roosevelt. At the U.N. Law of the Sea Conference, the U.S. delegation often numbered more than a hundred persons. This permitted various U.S. "interests" to be represented, including the departments of State, Defense, Interior, Commerce, and Justice. Altogether some twenty U.S. government agencies participated in the U.S. Inter-agency Task Force that "coordinated" U.S. law of the sea negotiations. As Ann Hollick, a long-time commentator on U.S. law of the sea politics, has written, the U.S. delegation "was usually the scene of more intense negotiations than was UNCLOS itself," leading to important problems in making and executing U.S. policy, to "discontent and suspicion" among delegates from other countries, and impatience in Congress. Ann L. Hollick, *U.S. Foreign Policy and the Law of the Sea* 35 (1981). Ultimately, the Reagan administration repudiated the core positions of the Nixon, Ford, and Carter administrations and refused to sign, much less to promote the ratification of, the 1982 Law of the Sea Treaty. See Chapter 9.

4. *The Constitutionality of Executive Agreements.* The Hull–Lothian Agreement was an "international executive agreement" (of which more in Chapter 4), but was it legal at U.S. law? Did the Hull–Lothian Agreement violate federal law prohibiting the departure, much less the sale, of warships to a combatant when the U.S. was a neutral in a war? Did it violate the 1907 Hague Convention, a multilateral treaty accepted by the United States that prohibited sales of warships by a neutral country to a belligerent? Could the President constitutionally make the Hull–Lothian Agreement without a two-thirds vote of the Senate expressing its advice and consent? On the last point, Attorney General Jackson opined to President Roosevelt on August 27, 1940:

> The President's power over foreign relations while "delicate, plenary and exclusive" is not unlimited. Some negotiations involve commitments as to the future which would carry an obligation to exercise powers vested in the Congress. Such Presidential arrangements are customarily submitted for ratification by a two-thirds vote of the Senate before the future legislative power of the country is committed. However, the acquisitions which you are proposing to accept are without express or implied promises on the part of the United States to be performed in the future. * * * The Executive Agreement obtains an opportunity to establish naval and air bases for the protection of our coastline but it imposes no obligation upon the Congress to appropriate money to improve the opportunity. It is not necessary for the Senate to ratify an opportunity that entails no obligation.

G.H. Hackworth, 5 *Digest of International Law* 405–06 (1943). Is Jackson's statement persuasive? Do you think Cordell Hull was effectively kept out of some of the negotiations because it was feared he had a legalistic attitude? A critical view of the Hull–Lothian Agreement is to be found in Robert Shogan, *Hard Bargain* (1995).

5. *Dualism.* How do the problems of the "legality" of the Hull–Lothian Agreement differ at U.S and international law? Regardless of the possible illegality of the Hull–Lothian Agreement in U.S. law, the U.S. was still bound in international law to honor its treaty obligation to the U.K. The International Court has ruled: "It is a generally accepted principle of international law that in the relations between powers who are contracting parties to a treaty, the provisions of municipal law cannot prevail over those in a treaty." Greco–Bulgarian Communities Case, 1930 P.C.I.J., Ser. B, No. 17, at 32. The principle is reaffirmed in Article 27 of the Vienna Convention on the Law of Treaties, which is reproduced in the Appendix. That there are separate spheres of municipal and international law is sometimes referred to as "dualism." See Chapter 4.

THE RESERVATIONS TO THE GENOCIDE CONVENTION CASE

1951 I.C.J. 15, 31, 1951 WL 3.

On November 16th, 1950, the General Assembly of the United Nations adopted the following resolution:

"The General Assembly,

Having examined the report of the Secretary–General regarding reservations to multilateral conventions,

Considering that certain reservations to the Convention on the Prevention and Punishment of the Crime of Genocide have been objected to by some States,

Considering that the International Law Commission is studying the whole subject of the law of treaties, including the question of reservations,

Considering that different views regarding reservations have been expressed during the fifth session of the General Assembly, and particularly in the Sixth Committee,

I. Requests the International Court of Justice to give an Advisory Opinion on the following questions:

In so far as concerns the Convention on the Prevention and Punishment of the Crime of Genocide in the event of a State ratifying or acceding to the Convention subject to a reservation made either on ratification or on accession, or on signature followed by ratification:

I. Can the reserving State be regarded as being a party to the Convention while still maintaining its reservation if the reservation is objected to by one or more of the parties to the Convention but not by others?

II. If the answer to Question I is in the affirmative, what is the effect of the reservation as between the reserving State and:

(a) The parties which object to the reservation?

(b) Those which accept it?

III. What would be the legal effect as regards the answer to Question I if an objection to a reservation is made:

(a) By a signatory which has not yet ratified?

(b) By a State entitled to sign or accede but which has not yet done so? * * *." * * *

The three questions are purely abstract in character. They refer neither to the reservations which have, in fact, been made to the Convention by certain States, nor to the objections which have been made to such reservations by other States. They do not even refer to the reservations which may in future be made in respect of any particular article; nor do they refer to the objections to which these reservations might give rise.

Question I is framed in the following terms:

"Can the reserving State be regarded as being a party to the Convention while still maintaining its reservation if the reservation is objected to by one or more of the parties to the Convention but not by others?"

The Court observes that this question refers, not to the possibility of making reservations to the Genocide Convention, but solely to the question whether a contracting State which has made a reservation can, while still maintaining it, be regarded as being a party to the Convention, when there is a divergence of views between the contracting parties concerning this reservation, some accepting the reservation, others refusing to accept it.

It is well established that in its treaty relations a State cannot be bound without its consent, and that consequently, no reservation can be effective against any State, without its agreement thereto. It is also a generally recognized principle that a multilateral convention is the result of an agreement freely concluded upon its clauses and that consequently none of the contracting parties is entitled to frustrate or impair, by means of unilateral decisions or particular agreements, the purpose and *raison d'être* of the convention. To this principle was linked the notion of the integrity of the convention as adopted, a notion which in its traditional concept involved the proposition that no reservation was valid unless it was accepted by all the contracting parties without exception, as would have been the case if it had been stated during the negotiations.

This concept, which is directly inspired by the notion of contract, is of undisputed value as a principle. However, as regards the Genocide Convention, it is proper to refer to a variety of circumstances which would lead to a more flexible application of this principle. Among these circumstances may be noted the clearly universal character of the United Nations under whose auspices the Convention was concluded, and the very wide degree of participation envisaged by Article XI of the Convention. Extensive participation in conventions of this type has already given rise to greater flexibility in the international practice concerning multilateral conventions. More general resort to reservations, very great allowance made for tacit assent to reservations, the existence of practices which go so far as to admit that the author of reservations which have been rejected by certain contracting parties is nevertheless to be regarded as a party to the convention in relation to those contracting parties that have accepted the reservations—all these factors are manifestations of a new need for flexibility in the operation of multilateral conventions.

It must also be pointed out that although the Genocide Convention was finally approved unanimously, it is nevertheless the result of a series of majority votes. The majority principle, while facilitating the conclusion of multilateral conventions, may also make it necessary for certain States to make reservations. This observation is confirmed by the great number of reservations which have been made of recent years to multilateral conventions.

In this state of international practice, it could certainly not be inferred from the absence of an article providing for reservations in a multilateral convention that the contracting States are prohibited from making certain reservations. Account should also be taken of the fact that the absence of such an article or even the decision not to insert such an article can be explained by the desire not to invite a multiplicity of reservations. The character of a multilateral convention, its purpose, provisions, mode of preparation and adoption, are factors which must be considered in determining, in the absence of any express provision on the subject, the possibility of making reservations, as well as their validity and effect. * * *

The Court recognizes that an understanding was reached within the General Assembly on the faculty to make reservations to the Genocide Convention and that it is permitted to conclude therefrom that States becoming parties to the Convention gave their assent thereto. It must now determine what kind of reservations may be made and what kind of objections may be taken to them.

The solution of these problems must be found in the special characteristics of the Genocide Convention. The origins and character of that Convention, the objects pursued by the General Assembly and the contracting parties, the relations which exist between the provisions of the Convention, *inter se,* and between those provisions and these objects, furnish elements of interpretation of the will of the General Assembly and the parties. The origins of the Convention show that it was the intention of the United Nations to condemn and punish genocide as "a crime under international law" involving a denial of the right of existence of entire human groups, a denial which shocks the conscience of mankind and results in great losses to humanity, and which is contrary to moral law and to the spirit and aims of the United Nations (Resolution 96(I) of the General Assembly, December 11th, 1946). The first consequence arising from this conception is that the principles underlying the Convention are principles which are recognized by civilized nations as binding on States, even without any conventional obligation. A second consequence is the universal character both of the condemnation of genocide and of the co-operation required "in order to liberate mankind from such an odious scourge" (Preamble to the Convention). The Genocide Convention was therefore intended by the General Assembly and by the contracting parties to be definitely universal in scope. It was in fact approved on December 9th, 1948, by a resolution which was unanimously adopted by 56 States.

The objects of such a convention must also be considered. The Convention was manifestly adopted for a purely humanitarian and civilizing purpose. It is indeed difficult to imagine a convention that might have this dual character to a greater degree, since its object on the one hand is to safeguard the very existence of certain human groups and on the other to confirm and endorse the most elementary principles of morality. In such a convention the contracting States do not have any interests of their own; they merely have, one and all, a common interest, namely, the accomplishment of those high purposes which are the *raison d'être* of the convention. Consequently, in a convention of this type one cannot speak of individual advantages or disadvantages to States, or of the maintenance of a perfect contractual balance between rights and duties. The high ideals which inspired the Convention provide, by virtue of the common will of the parties, the foundation and measure of all its provisions.

The foregoing considerations, when applied to the question of reservations, and more particularly to the effects of objections to reservations, lead to the following conclusions.

The object and purpose of the Genocide Convention imply that it was the intention of the General Assembly and of the States which adopted it that as many States as possible should participate. The complete exclusion from the Convention of one or more States would not only restrict the scope of its application, but would detract from the authority of the moral and humanitarian principles which are its basis. It is inconceivable that the contracting parties readily contemplated that an objection to a minor reservation should produce such a result. But even less could the contracting parties have intended to sacrifice the very object of the Convention in favour of a vain desire to secure as many participants as possible. The object and purpose of the Convention thus limit both the freedom of making reservations and that of objecting to them. It follows that it is the compatibility of a reservation with the object and purpose of the Convention that must furnish the criterion for the attitude of a State in making the reservation on accession as well as for the appraisal by a State in objecting to the reservation. Such is the rule of conduct which must guide every State in the appraisal which it must make, individually and from its own standpoint, of the admissibility of any reservation.

Any other view would lead either to the acceptance of reservations which frustrate the purposes which the General Assembly and the contracting parties had in mind, or to recognition that the parties to the Convention have the power of excluding from it the author of a reservation, even a minor one, which may be quite compatible with those purposes. * * *

It results from the foregoing considerations that Question I, on account of its abstract character, cannot be given an absolute answer. The appraisal of a reservation and the effect of objections that might be made to it depend upon the particular circumstances of each individual case.

Having replied to Question I, the Court will now examine Question II, which is framed as follows:

> "If the answer to Question I is in the affirmative, what is the effect of the reservation as between the reserving State and:
>
> *(a)* the parties which object to the reservation?
>
> *(b)* those which accept it?"

The considerations which form the basis of the Court's reply to Question I are to a large extent equally applicable here. As has been pointed out above, each State which is a party to the Convention is entitled to appraise the validity of the reservation, and it exercises this right individually and from its own standpoint. As no State can be bound by a reservation to which it has not consented, it necessarily follows that each State objecting to it will or will not, on the basis of its individual appraisal within the limits of the criterion of the object and purpose stated above, consider the reserving State to be a party to the Convention. In the ordinary course of events, such a decision will only affect the relationship between the State making the reservation and the objecting State; on the other hand, as will be pointed out later, such a decision might aim at the complete exclusion from the Convention in a case where it was expressed by the adoption of a position on the jurisdictional plane. * * *

Question III is framed in the following terms:

> "What would be the legal effect as regards the answer to Question I if an objection to a reservation is made:
>
> *(a)* By a signatory which has not yet ratified?
>
> *(b)* By a State entitled to sign or accede but which has not yet done so?"

The Court notes that the terms of this question link it to Question I. This link is regarded by certain States as presupposing a negative reply to Question I.

The Court considers, however, that Question III could arise in any case. Even should the reply to Question I not tend to exclude, from being a party to the Convention, a State which has made a reservation to which another State has objected, the fact remains that the Convention does not enter into force as between the reserving State and the objecting State. Even if the objection has this reduced legal effect, the question would still arise whether the States mentioned under *(a)* and *(b)* of Question III are entitled to bring about such a result by their objection.

An extreme view of the right of such States would appear to be that these two categories of States have a *right to become* parties to the Convention, and that by virtue of this right they may object to reservations in the same way as any State which is a party to the Convention with full legal effect, i.e. the exclusion from the Convention of the reserving State. By denying them this right, it is said, they would be obliged either to renounce entirely their right of participating in the Convention, or to become a party to what is, in fact, a different convention. The dilemma does not correspond to reality, as the States concerned have always a right to be parties to the Convention in their relations with other contracting States.

From the date when the Genocide Convention was opened for signature, any Member of the United Nations and any non-member State to which an invitation to sign had been addressed by the General Assembly, had the *right to be a party* to the Convention. Two courses of action were possible to this end: either signature, from December 9th,

1948, until December 31st, 1949, followed by ratification, or accession as from January 1st, 1950 (Article XI of the Convention). The Court would point out that the right to become a party to the Convention does not express any very clear notion. It is inconceivable that a State, even if it has participated in the preparation of the Convention, could, before taking one or the other of the two courses of action provided for becoming a party to the Convention, exclude another State. Possessing no rights which derive from the Convention, that State cannot claim such a right from its status as a Member of the United Nations or from the invitation to sign which has been addressed to it by the General Assembly.

The case of a signatory State is different. Without going into the question of the legal effect of signing an international convention, which necessarily varies in individual cases, the Court considers that signature constitutes a first step to participation in the Convention.

It is evident that without ratification, signature does not make the signatory State a party to the Convention; nevertheless, it establishes a provisional status in favour of that State. This status may decrease in value and importance after the Convention enters into force. But, both before and after the entry into force, this status would justify more favourable treatment being meted out to signatory States in respect of objections than to States which have neither signed nor acceded.

As distinct from the latter States, signatory States have taken certain of the steps necessary for the exercise of the right of being a party. Pending ratification, the provisional status created by signature confers upon the signatory a right to formulate as a precautionary measure objections which have themselves a provisional character. These would disappear if the signature were not followed by ratification, or they would become effective on ratification.

Until this ratification is made, the objection of a signatory State can therefore not have an immediate legal effect in regard to the reserving State. It would merely express and proclaim the eventual attitude of the signatory State when it becomes a party to the Convention.

The legal interest of a signatory State in objecting to a reservation would thus be amply safeguarded. The reserving State would be given notice that as soon as the constitutional or other processes, which cause the lapse of time before ratification, have been completed, it would be confronted with a valid objection which carries full legal effect and consequently, it would have to decide, when the objection is stated, whether it wishes to maintain or withdraw its reservation. In the circumstances, it is of little importance whether the ratification occurs within a more or less long time-limit. The resulting situation will always be that of a ratification accompanied by an objection to the reservation. In the event of no ratification occurring, the notice would merely have been in vain.

For these reasons,

THE COURT IS OF OPINION,

In so far as concerns the Convention on the Prevention and Punishment of the Crime of Genocide, in the event of a State ratifying or acceding to the Convention subject to a reservation made either on ratification or on accession, or on signature followed by ratification,

On Question I:

by seven votes to five,

that a State which has made and maintained a reservation which has been objected to by one or more of the parties to the Convention but not by others, can be regarded as being a party to the Convention if the reservation is compatible with the object and purpose of the Convention; otherwise, that State cannot be regarded as being a party to the Convention.

On Question II:

by seven votes to five,

(a) that if a party to the Convention objects to a reservation which it considers to be incompatible with the object and purpose of the Convention, it can in fact consider that the reserving State is not a party to the Convention;

(b) that if, on the other hand, a party accepts the reservation as being compatible with the object and purpose of the Convention, it can in fact consider that the reserving State is a party to the Convention;

On Question III:

by seven votes to five,

(a) that an objection to a reservation made by a signatory State which has not yet ratified the Convention can have the legal effect indicated in the reply to Question I only upon ratification. Until that moment it merely serves as a notice to the other State of the eventual attitude of the signatory State;

(b) that an objection to a reservation made by a State which is entitled to sign or accede but which has not yet done so, is without legal effect. * * *

DISSENTING OPINION OF JUDGES GUERRERO,
SIR ARNOLD MCNAIR, READ, HSU MO

We regret that we are unable to concur in the Opinion of the Court, while agreeing that the Court has competence to give an opinion. * * *

The three questions are described in the majority Opinion as "purely abstract." They are abstract in the sense that they do not mention any particular States or any particular reservations. We consider, however, that it will make our examination of the problem more realistic if we state that before the end of 1950 the Secretary-General had received notice of eighteen reservations, proposed, some by one State, some by another, the total number of States being eight, and that those reservations relate to Article IV (removal of any jurisdictional immunities of "constitutionally responsible rulers, public officials or private individuals"), Article VI (jurisdiction of municipal tribunals), Article VII (extradition), Article IX (the compulsory jurisdiction of the International Court of Justice), and Article XII (the "colonial clause"). Every one of the eight reserving States has made a reservation against, or in regard to, Article IX. * * *

We believe that the integrity of the terms of the Convention is of greater importance than mere universality in its acceptance. While it is undoubtedly true that the representatives of the governments, in drafting and adopting the Genocide Convention, wished to see as many States become parties to it as possible, it was certainly not their intention to achieve universality at any price. There is no evidence to show that they desired to secure wide acceptance of the Convention even at the expense of the integrity or uniformity of its terms, irrespective of the wishes of those States which have accepted all the obligations under it.

It is an undeniable fact that the tendency of all international activities in recent times has been towards the promotion of the common welfare of the international community with a corresponding restriction of the sovereign power of individual States. So, when a common effort is made to promote a great humanitarian object, as in the case of the Genocide Convention, every interested State naturally expects every other interested State not to seek any individual advantage or convenience, but to carry out the measures resolved upon by common accord. Hence, each party must be given the right to judge the acceptability of a reservation and to decide whether or not to exclude the reserving State from the Convention, and we are not aware of any case in which this right has been abused. It is therefore not universality at any price that forms the first consideration. It is rather the acceptance of common obligations—keeping step with like-minded States—in order to attain a high objective for all humanity, that is of paramount importance. Such being the case, the conclusion is irresistible that it is necessary to apply to the Genocide Convention with even greater exactitude than ever the existing rule which requires the consent of all parties to any reservation to a multilateral convention. In the interests of the international community, it would be better to lose as a party to the Convention a State which insists in face of objections on a modification of the terms of the Convention, than to permit it to become a party against the wish of a State or States which have irrevocably and unconditionally accepted all the obligations of the Convention.

The Opinion of the Court seeks to limit the operation of the new rule to the Genocide Convention. We foresee difficulty in finding a criterion which will establish the uniqueness of this Convention and will differentiate it from the other humanitarian conventions which have been, or will be, negotiated under the auspices of the United Nations or its Specialized Agencies and adopted by them. But if the Genocide Convention is in any way unique, its uniqueness consists in the importance of regarding it as a whole and maintaining the integrity and indivisibility of its text, whereas it seems to us that the new rule propounded by the majority will encourage the making of reservations.

In conclusion, the enormity of the crime of genocide can hardly be exaggerated, and any treaty for its repression deserves the most generous interpretation; but the Genocide Convention is an instrument which is intended to produce legal effects by creating legal obligations between the parties to it, and we have therefore felt it necessary to examine it against the background of law.

Notes and Questions

1. *ICJ Advisory Opinions*. The International Court of Justice at The Hague is permitted to give advisory opinions by properly authorized international organizations including, as here, the General Assembly of the United Nations. Although ICJ advisory opinions have great persuasive and precedential value, they are not legally binding and are simply intended to give international institutions helpful legal advice. See Chapter 5.

2. *Treaties as International Contracts*. The majority and dissenting opinions in the *Reservations to the Genocide Convention Case* reflect differing views about the contractual nature of treaties. The majority decision presumes that states have a great deal of discretion to bind themselves or not to the provisions of international agreements. The dissenting opinion takes, if you will, a more statutory approach towards treaties, paying rather more attention to the will of the international community. In a multilateral treaty of this kind, with a significant moral mission, should community sentiment play a larger role than in a more transactional bilateral agreement, say the Cession of Alaska?

3. *Effects on Treaty Negotiations*. How does the position of the majority in the *Genocide Case*, which is reflected in Articles 19–23 of the Vienna Convention on the Law of Treaties (see Appendix), affect the conduct of multilateral treaty negotiations? Some multilateral treaties—for example, the 1982 U.N. Convention on the Law of the Sea, which addresses a wide range of oceans issues—expressly prohibit reservations. See Article 309, Convention on the Law of the Sea, which is reproduced in the Appendix. Why do some multilateral treaties permit reservations, while other treaties prohibit them?

THE EASTERN GREENLAND CASE

1933 P.C.I.J., Ser. A/B, No. 53, 3 *World Court Reports* 151 (Manley O. Hudson ed., reprinted 1969).

By an Application instituting proceedings, filed with the Registry of the Court on July 12th, 1931, in accordance with Article 40 of the Statute and Article 35 of the Rules of Court, the Royal Danish Government, relying on the optional clause of Article 36, paragraph 2, of the Statute, brought before the Permanent Court of International Justice a suit against the Royal Norwegian Government on the ground that the latter Government had, on July 10th, 1931, published a proclamation declaring that it had proceeded to occupy certain territories in Eastern Greenland, which, in the contention of the Danish Government, were subject to the sovereignty of the Crown of Denmark. The Application, after thus indicating the subject of the dispute, proceeds, subject to the subsequent presentation of any cases, counter-cases and any other documents or evidence, to formulate the claim by asking the Court for judgment to the effect that "the promulgation of the above-mentioned declaration of occupation and any steps taken in this respect by the Norwegian Government constitute a violation of the existing legal situation and are accordingly unlawful and invalid." * * *

At the beginning of the present century, opinion again began to be manifested in favour of the more effective occupation of the uncolonized areas in Greenland, in order that the risk of foreign settlement might be obviated.

During the Great War of 1914 to 1918, Denmark by treaty ceded to the United States of America her West Indian Islands—the Danish Antilles—and, during the negotiations for the conclusion of the treaty, broached to the American Secretary of State—at first in conversation and subsequently, on December 27th, 1915, by a written communication—the question of the extension of Danish activities throughout all Greenland. As the result, the United States signed on August 4th, 1916, the same day as the treaty for cession of the Antilles, a declaration to the effect that the United States would not object to the Danish Government extending their political and economic interests to the whole of Greenland.

On July 12th, 1919, the Danish Minister of Foreign Affairs instructed the Danish Minister at Christiania that a Committee had just been constituted at the Peace Conference "for the purpose of considering the claims that may be put forward by different countries to Spitzbergen," and that the Danish Government would be prepared to renew before this Committee the unofficial assurance already given (on April 2nd, 1919) to the Norwegian Government, according to which Denmark, having no special interests at stake in Spitzbergen, would raise no objection to Norway's claims upon that archipelago. In making this statement to the Norwegian Minister for Foreign Affairs, the Danish Minister was to point out "that the Danish Government had been anxious for some years past to obtain the recognition by all the interested Powers of Denmark's sovereignty over the whole of Greenland, and that she intended to place that question before the above-mentioned Committee;" and, further, that the Danish Government felt confident that the extension of its political and economic interests to the whole of Greenland "would not encounter any difficulties on the part of the Norwegian Government."

On July 14th, 1919, the Danish Minister saw M. Ihlen, the Norwegian Minister of Foreign Affairs, who merely replied on this occasion "that the question would be considered." The Norwegian Minister recorded his conversation with the Danish representative in a minute, the accuracy of which has not been disputed by the Danish Government.

On July 22nd following, M. Ihlen made a statement to the Danish Minister to the effect "that the Norwegian Government would not make any difficulties in the settlement of this question" (i.e. the question raised on July 14th by the Danish Government). These are the words recorded in the minute by M. Ihlen himself. According to the report made by the Danish Minister to his own Government, M. Ihlen's words were that "the plans of the Royal [Danish] Government respecting Danish sovereignty over the whole of Greenland . . . would meet with no difficulties on the part of Norway." It is this statement by the Norwegian Minister for Foreign Affairs which is described in this judgment as the "Ihlen declaration." * * *

This declaration by M. Ihlen has been relied on by Counsel for Denmark as a recognition of an existing Danish sovereignty in Greenland. The Court is unable to accept this point of view. A careful examination of the words used and of the circumstances in which they were used, as well as of the subsequent developments, shows that M. Ihlen cannot have meant to be giving then and there a definitive recognition of Danish sovereignty over Greenland, and shows also that he cannot have been understood by the Danish Government at the time as having done so. In the text of M. Ihlen's minute, submitted by the Norwegian Government, which has not been disputed by the Danish Government, the phrase used by M. Ihlen is couched in the future tense: "*ne fera pas de difficultés*"; he had been informed that it was at the Peace Conference that the Danish Government intended to bring up the question: and two years later—when assurances had been received from the Principal Allied Powers—the Danish Government made a further application to the Norwegian Government to obtain the recognition which they desired of Danish sovereignty over all Greenland.

Nevertheless, the point which must now be considered is whether the Ihlen declaration—even if not constituting a definitive recognition of Danish sovereignty—did not constitute an engagement obliging Norway to refrain from occupying any part of Greenland.

The Danish request and M. Ihlen's reply were recorded by him in a minute, worded as follows:

> I. The Danish Minister informed me to-day that his Government has heard from Paris that the question of Spitzbergen will be examined by a Commission of four members (American, British, French, Italian). If the Danish Government is questioned by this Commission, it is prepared to reply that Denmark has no interests in Spitzbergen, and that it has no reason to oppose the wishes of Norway in regard to the settlement of this question.
>
> Furthermore, the Danish Minister made the following statement:
>
> The Danish Government has for some years past been anxious to obtain the recognition of all the interested Powers of Denmark's sovereignty over the whole of Greenland, and it proposes to place this question before the above-mentioned Committee at the same

time. During the negotiations with the U.S.A. over the cession of the Danish West Indies, the Danish Government raised this question in so far as concerns recognition by the Government of the U.S.A., and it succeeded in inducing the latter to agree that, concurrently with the conclusion of a convention regarding the cession of the said islands, it would make a declaration to the effect that the Government of the U.S.A. would not object to the Danish Government extending their political and economic interests to the whole of Greenland.

The Danish Government is confident (he added) that the Norwegian Government will not make any difficulties in the settlement of this question.

I replied that the question would be examined.

14/7–19 Ih.

II. To-day I informed the Danish Minister that the Norwegian Government would not make any difficulties in the settlement of this question.

22/7–19 Ih.

The incident has, therefore, reference, first to the attitude to be observed by Denmark before the Committee of the Peace Conference at Paris in regard to Spitzbergen, this attitude being that Denmark would not "oppose the wishes of Norway in regard to the settlement of this question"; as is known, these wishes related to the sovereignty over Spitzbergen. Secondly, the request showed that "the Danish Government was confident that the Norwegian Government would not make any difficulty" in the settlement of the Greenland question; the aims that Denmark had in view in regard to the last-named island were to secure the "recognition by all the Powers concerned of Danish sovereignty over the whole of Greenland," and that there should be no opposition "to the Danish Government extending their political and economic interests to the whole of Greenland." It is clear from the relevant Danish documents which preceded the Danish Minister's *démarche* at Christiania on July 14th, 1919, that the Danish attitude in the Spitzbergen question and the Norwegian attitude in the Greenland question were regarded in Denmark as interdependent, and this interdependence appears to be reflected also in M. Ihlen's minute of the interview. Even if this interdependence—which, in view of the affirmative reply of the Norwegian Government, in whose name the Minister for Foreign Affairs was speaking, would have created a bilateral engagement—is not held to have been established, it can hardly be denied that what Denmark was asking of Norway ("not to make any difficulties in the settlement of the [Greenland] question") was equivalent to what she was indicating her readiness to concede in the Spitzbergen question (to refrain from opposing "the wishes of Norway in regard to the settlement of this question"). What Denmark desired to obtain from Norway was that the latter should do nothing to obstruct the Danish plans in regard to Greenland. The declaration which the Minister for Foreign Affairs gave on July 22nd,

1919, on behalf of the Norwegian Government, was definitely affirmative: "I told the Danish Minister to-day that the Norwegian Government would not make any difficulty in the settlement of this question."

The Court considers it beyond all dispute that a reply of this nature given by the Minister for Foreign Affairs on behalf of his Government in response to a request by the diplomatic representative of a foreign Power, in regard to a question falling within his province, is binding upon the country to which the Minister belongs. * * *

The Court readily understands that Norway should feel concern for the interests of the Norwegian hunters and fishermen on the East coast of Greenland; but it cannot forget, in this connection, that as early as December 1921, Denmark announced her willingness to do everything in her power to make arrangements to safeguard Norwegian subjects against any loss they might incur as a result of the Decree of May 10th, 1921 (letter from the Danish Minister at Christiania dated December 19th, 1921, to the Norwegian Minister for Foreign Affairs). The Convention of July 9th, 1924, was a confirmation of Denmark's friendly disposition in respect of these Norwegian hunting and fishing interests.

What the Court cannot regard as being in accordance with the undertaking of July 22nd, 1919, is the endeavour to replace an unconditional and definitive undertaking by one which was subject to reservations: and what it is even more difficult for the Court to admit is that, notwithstanding the undertaking of July 22nd, 1919, by which she promised to refrain from making difficulties in the settlement of the Greenland question, Norway should have stipulated that "Eastern Greenland must be Norwegian." This pretension was already apparent at the end of a letter of January 12th, 1923, from the Norwegian Minister at Copenhagen to the Danish Minister for Foreign Affairs; and it was enunciated very definitely on September 28th, 1923, in the minutes of the sixth meeting of the Conference which drew up the Convention of July 9th, 1924, and again in the Protocol signed on January 28th, 1924, referred to above.

The Court is unable to read into the words of the Ihlen declaration "in the settlement of this question" (i.e. the Greenland question) a condition which would render the promise to refrain from making any difficulties inoperative should a settlement not be reached. The promise was unconditional and definitive. It was so understood by the Norwegian Minister for Foreign Affairs when he told the Danish Minister at Christiania on November 7th, 1919, that "it was a pleasure to Norway to recognize Danish sovereignty over Greenland" (dispatch from the Danish Minister at Christiania to the Danish Minister for Foreign Affairs of November 8th, 1919). It was also in the same sense that the Danish Minister at Christiania had understood the Ihlen declaration, when he informed the Danish Minister for Foreign Affairs on July 22nd, 1919, that M. Ihlen had told him "that the plans of the Royal Government in regard to the sovereignty of Denmark over the whole of Greenland would not encounter any difficulties on the part of Norway."

It follows that, as a result of the undertaking involved in the Ihlen declaration of July 22nd, 1919, Norway is under an obligation to refrain from contesting Danish sovereignty over Greenland as a whole, and *a fortiori* to refrain from occupying a part of Greenland.

Notes and Questions

1. *Unwritten Treaties.* Did the Court decide that there was a "treaty" between Norway and Denmark trading Norwegian claims to Greenland for Danish claims to Spitzbergen? May a treaty be unwritten? How was the Ihlen Declaration enough to commit Norway in international law? Would a like assurance be binding in the domestic law of contract?

What does the case say to states and diplomats about the possible legal effects of their negotiating behavior? Here are some observations of Dean Rusk, U.S. Secretary of State in the Kennedy and Johnson administrations between 1961 and 1969, that show that the lesson of *Eastern Greenland* has not been entirely forgotten.

> One evening, after a highball or two, I suggested to [the Foreign Minister of Honduras] that we toss a coin for these islands [the Swan Islands in the Caribbean claimed by both Honduras and the U.S.]. Fortunately, he refused because the International Court of Justice seemed to say in the *Greenland* case that a government has a right to rely upon the statement of a Foreign Minister with respect to a territorial matter. If there is anything clear about our Constitution, it is that the Secretary of State cannot go around the world tossing coins for American territory.

Dean Rusk, "The Role and Problems of Arbitration with Respect to Political Disputes," in *Resolving Transnational Disputes Through International Arbitration* 15, 18 (Thomas E. Carbonneau ed. 1984).

2. *The Validity of Treaties Made in Violation of Municipal Constitutional Requirements.* Should it make any difference that Norwegian constitutional law required Parliamentary assent to the making of treaties? Should Denmark have been on notice about this Norwegian municipal rule? Should Denmark have reasonably expected that the Norwegian Foreign Minister (or the Danish Foreign Minister) would be able to legally bind the state with simply a verbal statement? Does Article 46 of the Vienna Convention on the Law of Treaties, reproduced in the Appendix, satisfactorily treat the issue of compliance with municipal procedures for treaty-making?

3. *"Bargains" in International Relations.* Was there a "bargain" struck at the 1919 Paris Conference whereby Denmark traded its claims to Spitzbergen for Norway's claims to Greenland? Was there also a bargain made in 1916 between Denmark and the United States when Denmark ceded the Danish Antilles in the West Indies to the U.S.? The U.S. declared it "would not object to the Danish Government extending their political and economic interests to the whole of Greenland." Compared to Norway, would the United States be just as or more committed to respect Danish sovereignty over all of Greenland? After all, the U.S. declaration was made in writing, and Denmark legally ceded territories to which it had undisputed title.

Could the legal commitment found by the Court to have been made by Norway be something quite different from a treaty? Could it, for example, be seen as a consummated transaction, a bargain made by the two states, with the Court simply enforcing good faith respect for the status quo? Or might the Ihlen Declaration be looked upon as an act of state in customary international law, binding Norway because of the reasonable expectations of Denmark? Or was the Ihlen Declaration simply a unilateral promise enforceable at international law?

Chapter 3

CUSTOM AND THE NON-CONSENSUAL SOURCES OF INTERNATIONAL LAW

At first glance, one might think that treaties provide all that international law needs by way of rules. Nowadays, there are tens of thousands of international agreements, most all of which offer the distinct advantages of explicitly expressing international norms and the consent of sovereign states. However, other sorts of international law remain just as important as before. This is so for at least two reasons. First, all treaty provisions need to be interpreted and, if treaty interpretation is not to be pure discretion, some guidance from other forms of law is called for. Second, treaties never bind all states, and there needs to be some rules of more general application. In the pages of this chapter that follow, we explore first custom, often conceived as constituting an implicit sort of international agreement, and then the non-consensual sources of international law, where the pretense that international law is always based on the consent of states is finally abandoned.

A. CUSTOMARY INTERNATIONAL LAW

THE PAQUETE HABANA

175 U.S. 677, 20 S.Ct. 290, 44 L.Ed. 320 (1900).

MR. JUSTICE GRAY delivered the opinion of the court.

These are two appeals from decrees of the District Court of the United States for the Southern District of Florida, condemning two fishing vessels and their cargoes as prize of war.

Each vessel was a fishing smack, running in and out of Havana, and regularly engaged in fishing on the coast of Cuba; sailed under the Spanish flag; was owned by a Spanish subject of Cuban birth, living in the city of Havana; was commanded by a subject of Spain, also residing in Havana; and her master and crew had no interest in the vessel, but were entitled to shares, amounting in all to two thirds, of her catch, the other third belonging to her owner. Her cargo consisted of fresh fish, caught by her crew from the sea, put on board as they were caught, and kept and sold alive. Until stopped by the blockading squadron, she had no knowledge of the existence of the war, or of any blockade. She had no arms or ammunition on board, and made no attempt to run the blockade after she knew of its existence, nor any resistance at the time of the capture. * * *

Both the fishing vessels were brought by their captors into Key West. A libel for the condemnation of each vessel and her cargo as prize of war was there filed on April 27, 1898; a claim was interposed by her master, on behalf of himself and the other members of the crew, and of her owner; evidence was taken, showing the facts above stated; and on May 30, 1898, a final decree of condemnation and sale was entered, "the court not being satisfied that as a matter of law, without ordinance, treaty or proclamation, fishing vessels of this class are exempt from seizure."

Each vessel was thereupon sold by auction; the Paquete Habana for the sum of $490; and the Lola for the sum of $800. There was no other evidence in the record of the value of either vessel or of her cargo. * * *

We are then brought to the consideration of the question whether, upon the facts appearing in these records, the fishing smacks were subject to capture by the armed vessels of the United States during the recent war with Spain.

By an ancient usage among civilized nations, beginning centuries ago, and gradually ripening into a rule of international law, coast fishing vessels, pursuing their vocation of catching and bringing in fresh fish, have been recognized as exempt, with their cargoes and crews, from capture as prize of war.

This doctrine, however, has been earnestly contested at the bar; and no complete collection of the instances illustrating it is to be found, so far as we are aware, in a single published work, although many are referred to and discussed by the writers on international law, notably in 2 Ortolan, Règles Internationales et Diplomatie de la Mer, (4th ed.) lib. 3, c. 2, pp. 51–56; in 4 Calvo, Droit International, (5th ed.) §§ 2367–2373; in De Boeck, Propriété Privée Ennemie sous Pavillon Ennemi, §§ 191–196; and in Hall, International Law, (4th ed.) § 148. It is therefore worth the while to trace the history of the rule, from the earliest accessible sources, through the increasing recognition of it, with occasional setbacks, to what we may now justly consider as its final establishment in our own country and generally throughout the civilized world.

The earliest acts of any government on the subject, mentioned in the books, either emanated from, or were approved by, a King of England.

In 1403 and 1406, Henry IV issued orders to his admirals and other officers, entitled "Concerning Safety for Fisherman—*De Securitate pro Piscatoribus*." By an order of October 26, 1403, reciting that it was made pursuant to a treaty between himself and the King of France; and for the greater safety of the fishermen of either country, and so that they could be, and carry on their industry, the more safely on the sea, and deal with each other in peace; and that the French King had consented that English fishermen should be treated likewise; it was ordained that French fishermen might, during the then pending season for the herring fishery, safely fish for herrings and all other fish, from the harbor of Gravelines and the island of Thanet to the mouth of the Seine and the harbor of Hautoune. And by an order of October 5, 1406, he took into his safe conduct, and under his special protection, guardianship and defense, all and singular the fishermen of France, Flanders and Brittany, with their fishing vessels and boats, everywhere on the sea, through and within his dominions, jurisdictions and territories, in regard to their fishery, while sailing, coming and going, and, at their pleasure, freely and lawfully fishing, delaying or proceeding, and returning homeward with their catch of fish, without any molestation or hindrance whatever; and also their fish, nets, and other property and goods soever; and it was therefore ordered that such fishermen should not be interfered with, provided they should comport themselves well and properly, and should not, by color of these presents, do or attempt, or presume to do or attempt, anything that could prejudice the King, or his kingdom of England, or his subjects. 8 Rymer's Foedera, 336, 451.

The treaty made October 2, 1521, between the Emperor Charles V and Francis I of France, through their ambassadors, recited that a great and fierce war had arisen between them, because of which there had been, both by land and by sea, frequent depredations and incursions on either side, to the grave detriment and intolerable injury of the innocent subjects of each; and that a suitable time for the herring fishery was at hand, and, by reason of the sea being beset by the enemy, the fishermen did not dare to go out, whereby the subject of their industry, bestowed by heaven to allay the hunger of the poor, would wholly fail for the year, unless it were otherwise provided—*quo fit, ut piscaturæ commoditas, ad pauperum levandam famem a cœrlesti numine concessa, cessare hoc anno omnino debeat, nisi aliter provideatur*. And it was therefore agreed that the subjects of each sovereign, fishing in the sea, or exercising the calling of fishermen, could and might, until the end of the next January, without incurring any attack, depredation, molestation, trouble or hindrance soever, safely and freely, everywhere in the sea, take herrings and every other kind of fish, the existing war by land and sea notwithstanding; and further that, during the time aforesaid, no subject of either sovereign should commit, or attempt or presume to commit, any depredation, force, violence, molestation or vexation, to or upon such fishermen, or their vessels, supplies, equipments, nets and fish, or other goods soever truly appertaining to fishing. * * *

The herring fishery was permitted, in time of war, by French and Dutch edicts in 1536. Bynkershoek Quæstiones Juris Publicæ, lib. 1, c. 3; 1 Emerigon des Assurances, c. 4, sect. 9; c. 12, sect. 19, § 8.

France, from remote times, set the example of alleviating the evils of war in favor of all coast fishermen. In the compilation entitled Us et

Coutumes de la Mer, published by Cleirac in 1661, and in the third part thereof, containing "Maritime or Admiralty Jurisdiction—*la Jurisdiction de la Marine ou d'Admirauté*—as well in time of peace as in time of war," article 80 is as follows: "The admiral may in time of war accord fishing truces—*tresves pescheresses*—to the enemy and to his subjects; provided that the enemy will likewise accord them to Frenchmen." Cleirac, 544. Under this article, reference is made to articles 49 and 79 respectively of the French ordinances concerning the Admiralty in 1543 and 1584, of which it is but a reproduction. 4 Pardessus, Collection de Lois Maritimes, 319; 2 Ortolan, 51. And Cleirac adds, in a note, this quotation from Froissart's Chronicles: "Fishermen on the sea, whatever war there were in France and England, never did harm to one another; so they are friends, and help one another at need—*Pescheurs sur mer, quelque guerre qui soit en France et Angleterre, jamais ne se firent mal l'un à l'autre; ainçois sont amis, et s'aydent l'un à l'autre au besoin.*"

The same custom would seem to have prevailed in France until towards the end of the seventeenth century. For example, in 1675, Louis XIV and the States General of Holland, by mutual agreement, granted to Dutch and French fishermen the liberty, undisturbed by their vessels of war, of fishing along the coasts of France, Holland and England. D'Hauterive et De Cussy, Traités de Commerce, pt. 1, vol. 2, p. 278. But by the ordinances of 1681 and 1692 the practice was discontinued, because, Valin says, of the faithless conduct of the enemies of France, who, abusing the good faith with which she had always observed the treaties, habitually carried off her fishermen, while their own fished in safety. 2 Valin sur l'Ordonnance de la Marine, (1776) 689, 690; 2 Ortolan, 52; De Boeck, § 192.

The doctrine which exempts coast fishermen with their vessels and cargoes from capture as prize of war has been familiar to the United States from the time of the War of Independence.

On June 5, 1779, Louis XVI, our ally in that war, addressed a letter to his admiral, informing him that the wish he had always had of alleviating, as far as he could, the hardships of war, had directed his attention to that class of his subjects which devoted itself to the trade of fishing, and had no other means of livelihood; that he had thought that the example which he should give to his enemies, and which could have no other source than the sentiments of humanity which inspired him, would determine them to allow to fishermen the same facilities which he should consent to grant; and that he had therefore given orders to the commanders of all his ships not to disturb English fishermen, nor to arrest their vessels laden with fresh fish, even if not caught by those vessels; provided they had no offensive arms, and were not proved to have made any signals creating a suspicion of intelligence with the enemy; and the admiral was directed to communicate the King's intentions to all officers under his control. By a royal order in council of November 6, 1780, the former orders were confirmed; and the capture and ransom, by a French cruiser, of *The John and Sarah*, an English vessel, coming from Holland, laden with fresh fish, were pronounced to be illegal. 2 Code des Prises, (ed. 1784) 721, 901, 903.

Among the standing orders made by Sir James Marriott, Judge of the English High Court of Admiralty, was one of April 11, 1780, by which it was "ordered, that all causes of prize of fishing boats or vessels taken from the enemy may be consolidated in one monition, and one sentence or interlocutory, if under 50 tons burden, and not more than six in number." Marriott's Formulary, 4. But by the statements of his successor, and of both French and English writers, it appears that England, as well as France, during the American Revolutionary War, abstained from interfering with the coast fisheries. *The Young Jacob and Johanna*, 1 C. Rob. 20; 2 Ortolan, 53; Hall, § 148.

In the treaty of 1785 between the United States and Prussia, article 23, (which was proposed by the American Commissioners, John Adams, Benjamin Franklin and Thomas Jefferson, and is said to have been drawn up by Franklin,) provided that, if war should arise between the contracting parties, "all women and children, scholars of every faculty, cultivators of the earth, artisans, manufacturers and fishermen, unarmed and inhabiting unfortified towns, villages or places, and in general all others whose occupations are for the common subsistence and benefit of mankind, shall be allowed to continue their respective employments, and shall not be molested in their persons; nor shall their houses or goods be burnt or otherwise destroyed, nor their fields wasted, by the armed force of the enemy, into whose power, by the events of war, they may happen to fall; but if anything is necessary to be taken from them for the use of such armed force, the same shall be paid for at a reasonable price." 8 Stat. 96; 1 Kent Com. 91 note; Wheaton's History of the Law of Nations, 306, 308. Here was the clearest exemption from hostile molestation or seizure of the persons, occupations, houses and goods of unarmed fishermen inhabiting unfortified places. The article was repeated in the later treaties between the United States and Prussia of 1799 and 1828. 8 Stat. 174, 384. And Dana, in a note to his edition of Wheaton's International Law, says: "In many treaties and decrees, fishermen catching fish as an article of food are added to the class of persons whose occupation is not to be disturbed in war." Wheaton's International Law, (8th ed.) § 345, note 168. * * *

In the war with Mexico in 1846, the United States recognized the exemption of coast fishing boats from capture. In proof of this, counsel have referred to records of the Navy Department, which this court is clearly authorized to consult upon such a question. *Jones v. United States*, 137 U.S. 202; *Underhill v. Hernandez*, 168 U.S. 250, 253.

By those records it appears that Commodore Conner, commanding the Home Squadron blockading the east coast of Mexico, on May 14, 1846, wrote a letter from the ship Cumberland, off Brazos Santiago, near the southern point of Texas, to Mr. Bancroft, the Secretary of the Navy, enclosing a copy of the commodore's "instructions to the commanders of the vessels of the Home Squadron, showing the principles to be observed in the blockade of the Mexican ports," one of which was that "Mexican boats engaged in fishing on any part of the coast will be allowed to pursue their labors unmolested"; and that on June 10, 1846, those instructions were approved by the Navy Department * * *. * * *

International law is part of our law, and must be ascertained and administered by the courts of justice of appropriate jurisdiction, as often as questions of right depending upon it are duly presented for their determination. For this purpose, where there is no treaty, and no controlling executive or legislative act or judicial decision, resort must be had to the customs and usages of civilized nations; and, as evidence of these, to the works of jurists and commentators, who by years of labor, research and experience, have made themselves peculiarly well acquainted with the subjects of which they treat. Such works are resorted to by judicial tribunals, not for the speculations of their authors concerning what the law ought to be, but for trustworthy evidence of what the law really is. *Hilton v. Guyot*, 159 U.S. 113, 163, 164, 214, 215.

Wheaton places, among the principal sources of international law, "Text-writers of authority, showing what is the approved usage of nations, or the general opinion respecting their mutual conduct, with the definitions and modifications introduced by general consent." As to these he forcibly observes: "Without wishing to exaggerate the importance of these writers, or to substitute, in any case, their authority for the principles of reason, it may be affirmed that they are generally impartial in their judgment. They are witnesses of the sentiments and usages of civilized nations, and the weight of their testimony increases every time that their authority is invoked by statesmen, and every year that passes without the rules laid down in their works being impugned by the avowal of contrary principles." Wheaton's International Law, (8th ed.) § 15.

Chancellor Kent says: "In the absence of higher and more authoritative sanctions, the ordinances of foreign States, the opinions of eminent statesmen, and the writings of distinguished jurists, are regarded as of great consideration on questions not settled by conventional law. In cases where the principal jurists agree, the presumption will be very great in favor of the solidity of their maxims; and no civilized nation, that does not arrogantly set all ordinary law and justice at defiance, will venture to disregard the uniform sense of the established writers on international law." 1 Kent Com. 18.

It will be convenient, in the first place, to refer to some leading French treatises on international law, which deal with the question now before us, not as one of the law of France only, but as one determined by the general consent of civilized nations.

"Enemy ships," say Pistoye and Duverdy, in their Treatise on Maritime Prizes, published in 1855, "are good prize. Not all, however; for it results from the unanimous accord of the maritime powers that an exception should be made in favor of coast fishermen. Such fishermen are respected by the enemy, so long as they devote themselves exclusively to fishing." 1 Pistoye et Duverdy, tit. 6, c. 1, p. 314.

[The Court cites other jurists.]

This review of the precedents and authorities on the subject appears to us abundantly to demonstrate that at the present day, by the general consent of the civilized nations of the world, and independently of any express treaty or other public act, it is an established rule of international law, founded on considerations of humanity to a poor and industrious order of men, and of the mutual convenience of belligerent States, that coast fishing vessels, with their implements and supplies, cargoes and crews, unarmed, and honestly pursuing their peaceful calling of catching and bringing in fresh fish, are exempt from capture as prize of war.

The exemption, of course, does not apply to coast fishermen or their vessels, if employed for a warlike purpose, or in such a way as to give aid or information to the enemy; nor when military or naval operations create a necessity to which all private interests must give way.

Nor has the exemption been extended to ships or vessels employed on the high sea in taking whales or seals, or cod or other fish which are not brought fresh to market, but are salted or otherwise cured and made a regular article of commerce.

This rule of international law is one which prize courts, administering the law of nations are bound to take judicial notice of, and to give effect to, in the absence of any treaty or other public act of their own government in relation to the matter. * * *

To this subject, in more than one aspect, are singularly applicable the words uttered by Mr. Justice Strong, speaking for this court: "Undoubtedly, no single nation can change the law of the sea. That law is of universal obligation, and no statute of one or two nations can create obligations for the world. Like all the laws of nations, it rests upon the common consent of civilized communities. It is of force, not because it was prescribed by any superior power, but because it has been generally accepted as a rule of conduct. Whatever may have been its origin, whether in the usages of navigation, or in the ordinances of maritime States, or in both, it has become the law of the sea only by the concurrent sanction of those nations who may be said to constitute the commercial world. Many of the usages which prevail, and which have the force of law, doubtless originated in the positive prescriptions of some single State, which were at first of limited effect, but which, when generally accepted, became of universal obligation." "This is not giving to the statutes of any nation extra-territorial effect. It is not treating them as general maritime laws; but it is recognition of the historical fact that by common consent of mankind these rules have been acquiesced in as of general obligation. Of that fact, we think, we may take judicial note. Foreign municipal laws must indeed be proved as facts, but it is not so with the law of nations." *The Scotia*, 14 Wall. 170, 187, 188.

The position taken by the United States during the recent war with Spain was quite in accord with the rule of international law, now generally recognized by civilized nations, in regard to coast fishing vessels.

On April 21, 1898, the Secretary of the Navy gave instructions to Admiral Sampson, commanding the North Atlantic Squadron, to "immediately institute a blockade of the north coast of Cuba, extending from Cardenas on the east to Bahia Honda on the west." Bureau of Navigation Report of 1898, appx. 175. The blockade was immediately instituted accordingly. On April 22, the President issued a proclamation, declaring that the United States had instituted and would maintain that blockade, "in pursuance of the laws of the United States, and the law of nations applicable to such cases." 30 Stat. 1769. And by the act of Congress of April 25, 1898, c. 189, it was declared that the war between the United States and Spain existed on that day, and had existed since and including April 21. 30 Stat. 364.

On April 26, 1898, the President issued another proclamation, which, after reciting the existence of the war, as declared by Congress, contained this further recital: "It being desirable that such war should be conducted upon principles in harmony with the present views of nations and sanctioned by their recent practice." This recital was followed by specific declarations of certain rules for the conduct of the war by sea, making no mention of fishing vessels. 30 Stat. 1770. But the proclamation clearly manifests the general policy of the Government to conduct the war in accordance with the principles of international law sanctioned by the recent practice of nations.

On April 28, 1898, (after the capture of the two fishing vessels now in question,) Admiral Sampson telegraphed to the Secretary of the Navy as follows: "I find that a large number of fishing schooners are attempting to get into Havana from their fishing grounds near the Florida reefs and coasts. They are generally manned by excellent seamen, belonging to the maritime inscription of Spain, who have already served in the Spanish navy, and who are liable to further service. As these trained men are naval reserves, have a semi-military character, and would be most valuable to the Spaniards as artillerymen, either afloat or ashore, I recommend that they should be detained prisoners of war, and that I should be authorized to deliver them to the commanding officer of the army at Key West." To that communication the Secretary of the Navy, on April 30, 1898, guardedly answered: "Spanish fishing vessels attempting to violate blockade are subject, with crew, to capture, and any such vessel or crew considered likely to aid enemy may be detained." Bureau of Navigation Report of 1898, appx. 178. The Admiral's despatch assumed that he was not authorized, without express order, to arrest coast fishermen peaceably pursuing their calling; and the necessary implication and evident intent of the response of the Navy Department were that Spanish coast fishing vessels and their crews should not be interfered with, so long as they neither attempted to violate the blockade, nor were considered likely to aid the enemy.

The Paquete Habana, as the record shows, was a fishing sloop of 25 tons burden, sailing under the Spanish flag, running in and out of Havana, and regularly engaged in fishing on the coast of Cuba. Her crew consisted of but three men, including the master, and, according to a common usage in coast fisheries, had no interest in the vessel, but were entitled to two thirds of her catch; the other third belonging to her Spanish owner who, as well as the crew, resided in Havana. On her last voyage, she sailed from Havana along the coast of Cuba about 200 miles and fished for 25 days off the cape at the west end of the island within the territorial waters of Spain and was going back to Havana with her cargo of live fish, when she was captured by one of the blockading squadron on April 25, 1898. She had no arms or ammunition on board; she had no knowledge of the blockade or even of the war until she was stopped by a blockading vessel; she made no attempt to run the blockade and no resistance at the time of the capture; nor was there any evidence whatever of likelihood that she or her crew would aid the enemy.

In the case of the Lola, the only differences in the facts were that she was a schooner of 35 tons burden and had a crew of six men, including the master; that after leaving Havana and proceeding some 200 miles along the coast of Cuba, she went on about 100 miles farther to the coast of Yucatan, and there fished for eight days; and that, on her return, when near Bahia Honda on the coast of Cuba, she was captured with her cargo of live fish on April 27, 1898. These differences afford no ground for distinguishing the two cases.

Each vessel was of a moderate size, such as is not unusual in coast fishing smacks, and was regularly engaged in fishing on the coast of Cuba. The crew of each were few in number, had no interest in the vessel, and received, in return for their toil and enterprise, two thirds of her catch; the other third going to her owner by way of compensation for her use. Each vessel went out from Havana to her fishing ground and was captured when returning along the coast of Cuba. The cargo of each consisted of fresh fish caught by her crew from the sea and kept alive on board. Although one of the vessels extended her fishing trip across the Yucatan Channel and fished on the coast of Yucatan, we cannot doubt that each was engaged in the coast fishery and not in a commercial adventure within the rule of international law.

The two vessels and their cargoes were condemned by the District Court as prize of war; the vessels were sold under its decrees; and it does not appear what became of the fresh fish of which their cargoes consisted.

Upon the facts proved in either case, it is the duty of this court, sitting as the highest prize court of the United States, and administering the law of nations, to declare and adjudge that the capture was unlawful, and without probable cause; and it is therefore, in each case,

Ordered, that the decree of the District Court be reversed, and the proceeds of the sale of the vessel, together with the proceeds of any sale of her cargo, be restored to the claimant, with damages and costs.

Notes and Questions

1. The Paquete Habana. The 1900 judgment of the U.S. Supreme Court in *The Paquete Habana* is probably the best-known decision of a U.S. court finding and applying customary international law. The case is frequently cited with respect to at least three issues: (1) the manner of determining rules of customary international law; (2) the way in which customary international law is incorporated into the municipal law of the United States; and (3) the proper relationship between the U.S. courts and the executive branch in legal matters touching on international relations. At this point, we are especially interested in the first issue.

2. *Usages as Law.* Justice Gray opines that the rule providing for the exemption of coastal fishing vessels from capture as prizes of war began as "an ancient usage among civilized nations" and then "gradually ripened into a rule of international law." Regardless of what proof of the rule might be offered, why should such a transformative proposition be valid? Why should or how can the "usages" of states "ripen" into legal rules? Why should states or municipal courts give such "ripened usages" the force of law and apply them as rules of decision in cases before them? Are there any analogies in municipal law to the notion of usages ripening into obligatory rules of law?

3. *Evidences of Law.* Turning to his proof, what does Justice Gray employ as factual evidences "to trace the history of the rule"? Beginning with the first recitations, the orders of Henry IV in 1403 and 1406, in what sense are these evidences "international" usages? Is the next bit of proof, the 1521 treaty between Emperor Charles V and Francis I of France, any more "international"? Of all the evidences and usages shown, are some more persuasive as forms of proof than others?

4. *Contradictory Practice.* When can it be said that a usage "ripens" into a rule of customary international law? What about contradictory practice? For example, the 1675 agreement between Louis XIV and the States General of Holland had to be discontinued in 1681 and 1692 because the enemies of the French monarch "habitually carried off his fishermen, while their own fished in safety." Does such contradictory practice prevent the rule from ripening? Does one know if the rule has ripened by merely weighing the cited bits of practice? Or must the record of practice be overwhelmingly conclusive before the rule ripens?

5. Opinio Juris. Ordinarily, it is said that customary international law is based on state practice and *opinio juris*, a state's belief that it is acting in a certain way because it is legally bound to do so. Is there any proof of *opinio juris* in *Paquete Habana*? *Opinio juris* is vital if custom is to be perceived as the implicit agreement of states. If *opinio juris* is often a legal fiction, what is the real nature of customary international law? Does state practice without clear *opinio juris* still constitute a consensual source of international law?

6. *Custom and Municipal Law.* Note briefly here the other two "lessons" of *Paquete Habana* mentioned in Note 1. First, the Supreme Court holds that "international law is part of our law," an important proposition about the incorporation of customary international law into U.S. municipal law. Second, the Supreme Court notes that it was "the general policy of the Government to conduct the war in accordance with the principles of international law." Does this satisfactorily establish why the Supreme Court has the constitutional authority to trump an executive decision with customary international law? Did both the President and the Court agree that the actions of the Executive ought in any case be subject to customary international law? See Jordan Paust, "*Paquete* and the President: Rediscovering the Brief for the United States," 34 *Virginia Journal of International Law* 981 (1994). We return to the incorporation of customary international law and to the balance of powers in foreign relations among the President, the Congress, and U.S. courts in Chapter 4.

THE LOTUS CASE

France v. Turkey
1927 P.C.I.J., Ser. A, No. 10.

By a special agreement signed at Geneva on October 12th, 1926, between the Governments of the French and Turkish Republics and filed with the Registry of the Court, in accordance with Article 40 of the Statute and Article 35 of the Rules of Court, on January 4th, 1927, by the diplomatic representatives at The Hague of the aforesaid Governments, the latter have submitted to the Permanent Court of International Justice the question of jurisdiction which has arisen between them following upon the collision which occurred on August 2nd, 1926, between the steamships *Boz-Kourt* and *Lotus*.

According to the special agreement, the Court has to decide the following questions:

"(1) Has Turkey, contrary to Article 15 of the Convention of Lausanne of July 24th, 1923, respecting conditions of residence and business and jurisdiction, acted in conflict with the principles of international law—and if so, what principles—by instituting, following the collision which occurred on August 2nd, 1926, on the high seas between the French steamer *Lotus* and the Turkish steamer *Boz-Kourt* and upon the arrival of the French steamer at Constantinople—as well as against the captain of the Turkish steamship—joint criminal proceedings in pursuance of Turkish law against M. Demons, officer of the watch on board the *Lotus* at the time of the collision, in consequence of the loss of the *Boz-Kourt* having involved the death of eight Turkish sailors and passengers?

"(2) Should the reply be in the affirmative, what pecuniary reparation is due to M. Demons, provided, according to the principles of international law, reparation should be made in similar cases?" * * *

THE FACTS. * * *

On August 2nd, 1926, just before midnight, a collision occurred between the French mail steamer *Lotus*, proceeding to Constantinople, and the Turkish collier *Boz-Kourt*, between five and six nautical miles to the north of Cape Sigri (Mitylene). The *Boz-Kourt*, which was cut in two, sank and eight Turkish nationals who were on board perished. After having done everything possible to succour the shipwrecked persons, of whom ten were able to be saved, the *Lotus* continued on its course to Constantinople, where it arrived on August 3rd.

At the time of the collision, the officer of the watch on board the *Lotus* was Monsieur Demons, a French citizen, lieutenant in the merchant service and first officer of the ship, whilst the movements of the *Boz-Kourt* were directed by its captain, Hassan Bey, who was one of those saved from the wreck.

As early as August 3rd the Turkish police proceeded to hold an enquiry into the collision on board the *Lotus*; and on the following day, August 4th, the captain of the *Lotus* handed in his master's report at the French Consulate–General, transmitting a copy to the harbour master.

On August 5th, Lieutenant Demons was requested by the Turkish authorities to go ashore to give evidence. The examination, the length of which incidentally resulted in delaying the departure of the *Lotus*, led to the placing under arrest of Lieutenant Demons—without previous notice being given to the French Consul–General—and Hassan Bey, amongst others. This arrest, which has been characterized by the Turkish Agent as arrest pending trial (*arrestation préventive*), was effected in order to ensure that the criminal prosecution instituted against the two officers, on a charge of manslaughter, by the Public Prosecutor of Stamboul, on the complaint of the families of the victims of the collision, should follow its normal course.

The case was first heard by the Criminal Court of Stamboul on August 28th. On that occasion, Lieutenant Demons submitted that the Turkish Courts had no jurisdiction; the Court, however, overruled his objection. When the proceedings were resumed on September 11th, Lieutenant Demons demanded his release on bail: this request was complied with on September 13th, the bail being fixed at 6,000 Turkish pounds.

On September 15th, the Criminal Court delivered its judgment, the terms of which have not been communicated to the Court by the Parties. It is, however, common ground, that it sentenced Lieutenant Demons to 80 days' imprisonment and a fine of 22 pounds, Hassan Bey being sentenced to a slightly more severe penalty.

It is also common ground between the Parties that the Public Prosecutor of the Turkish Republic entered an appeal against this decision, which had the effect of suspending its execution until a decision upon the appeal had been given; that such decision has not yet been given; but that the special agreement of October 12th, 1926, did not have the effect of suspending "the criminal proceedings .... now in progress in Turkey."

The action of the Turkish judicial authorities with regard to Lieutenant Demons at once gave rise to many diplomatic representations and other steps on the part of the French Government or its representatives in Turkey, either protesting against the arrest of Lieutenant Demons or demanding his release, or with a view to obtaining the transfer of the case from the Turkish Courts to the French Courts.

As a result of these representations, the Government of the Turkish Republic declared on September 2nd, 1926, that "it would have no objection to the reference of the conflict of jurisdiction to the Court at The Hague."

The French Government having, on the 6th of the same month, given "its full consent to the proposed solution," the two Governments appointed their plenipotentiaries with a view to the drawing up of the special agreement to be submitted to the Court; this special agreement was signed at Geneva on October 12th, 1926, as stated above, and the ratifications were deposited on December 27th, 1926.

THE LAW.

I.

Before approaching the consideration of the principles of international law contrary to which Turkey is alleged to have acted—thereby infringing the terms of Article 15 of the Convention of Lausanne of July 24th, 1923, respecting conditions of residence and business and jurisdiction—, it is necessary to define, in the light of the written and oral proceedings, the position resulting from the special agreement. For, the Court having obtained cognizance of the present case by notification of a special agreement concluded between the Parties in the case, it is rather to the terms of this agreement than to the submissions of the Parties that the Court must have recourse in establishing the precise points which it has to decide. In this respect the following observations should be made:

1.—The collision which occurred on August 2nd, 1926, between the S.S. *Lotus*, flying the French flag, and the S.S. *Boz-Kourt*, flying the Turkish flag, took place on the high seas: the territorial jurisdiction of any State other than France and Turkey therefore does not enter into account.

2.—The violation, if any, of the principles of international law would have consisted in the taking of criminal proceedings against Lieutenant Demons. It is not therefore a question relating to any particular step in these proceedings—such as his being put to trial, his arrest, his detention pending trial or the judgment given by the Criminal Court of Stamboul—but of the very fact of the Turkish Courts exercising criminal jurisdiction. That is why the arguments put forward by the Parties in both phases of the proceedings relate exclusively to the question whether Turkey has or has not, according to the principles of international law, jurisdiction to prosecute in this case. * * *

Article 6 of the Turkish Penal Code, Law No. 765 of March 1st, 1926 (Official Gazette No. 320 of March 13th, 1926), runs as follows:

[*Translation.*]

> "Any foreigner who, apart from the cases contemplated by Article 4, commits an offence abroad to the prejudice of Turkey or of a Turkish subject, for which offence Turkish law prescribes a penalty involving loss of freedom for a minimum period of not less than one year, shall be punished in accordance with the Turkish Penal Code provided that he is arrested in Turkey. The penalty shall however be reduced by one third and instead of the death penalty, 20 years of penal servitude shall be awarded.
>
> "Nevertheless, in such cases, the prosecution will only be instituted at the request of the Minister of Justice or on the complaint of the injured Party.
>
> "If the offence committed injures another foreigner, the guilty person shall be punished at the request of the Minister of Justice, in accordance with the provisions set out in the first paragraph of this article, provided however that:
>
> "(1) the article in question is one for which Turkish law prescribes a penalty involving loss of freedom for a minimum period of three years;
>
> "(2) there is no extradition treaty or that extradition has not been accepted either by the government of the locality where the guilty person has committed the offence or by the government of his own country."

Even if the Court must hold that the Turkish authorities had seen fit to base the prosecution of Lieutenant Demons upon the above-mentioned Article 6, the question submitted to the Court is not whether that article is compatible with the principles of international law; it is more general. The Court is asked to state whether or not the principles of international law prevent Turkey from instituting criminal proceedings against Lieutenant Demons under Turkish law. Neither the conformity of Article 6 in itself with the principles of international law nor the application of that article by the Turkish authorities constitutes the point at issue; it is the very fact of the institution of proceedings which is held by France to be contrary to those principles. * * *

II.

Having determined the position resulting from the terms of the special agreement, the Court must now ascertain which were the principles of international law that the prosecution of Lieutenant Demons could conceivably be said to contravene.

It is Article 15 of the Convention of Lausanne of July 24th, 1923, respecting conditions of residence and business and jurisdiction, which refers the contracting Parties to the principles of international law as regards the delimitation of their respective jurisdiction.

This clause is as follows:

> "Subject to the provisions of Article 16, all questions of jurisdiction shall, as between Turkey and the other contracting Powers, be decided in accordance with the principles of international law."

The French Government maintains that the meaning of the expression "principles of international law" in this article should be sought in the light of the evolution of the Convention. Thus it states that during the preparatory work, the Turkish Government, by means of an amendment to the relevant article of a draft for the Convention, sought to extend its jurisdiction to crimes committed in the territory of a third State, provided that, under Turkish law, such crimes were within the jurisdiction of Turkish Courts. This amendment, in regard to which the representatives of France and Italy made reservations, was definitely rejected by the British representative; and the question having been subsequently referred to the Drafting Committee, the latter confined itself in its version of the draft to a declaration to the effect that questions of jurisdiction should be decided in accordance with the principles of international law. The French Government deduces from these facts that the prosecution of Demons is contrary to the intention which guided the preparation of the Convention of Lausanne.

The Court must recall in this connection what it has said in some of its preceding judgments and opinions, namely, that there is no occasion to have regard to preparatory work if the text of a convention is sufficiently clear in itself. Now the Court considers that the words "principles of international law," as ordinarily used, can only mean international law as it is applied between all nations belonging to the community of States. * * *

III.

The Court, having to consider whether there are any rules of international law which may have been violated by the prosecution in pursuance of Turkish law of Lieutenant Demons, is confronted in the first place by a question of principle which, in the written and oral arguments of the two Parties, has proved to be a fundamental one. The French Government contends that the Turkish Courts, in order to have jurisdiction, should be able to point to some title to jurisdiction recognized by international law in favour of Turkey. On the other hand, the Turkish Government takes the view that Article 15 allows Turkey jurisdiction whenever such jurisdiction does not come into conflict with a principle of international law.

The latter view seems to be in conformity with the special agreement itself, No. 1 of which asks the Court to say whether Turkey has acted contrary to the principles of international law and, if so, what principles. According to the special agreement, therefore, it is not a question of stating principles which would permit Turkey to take criminal proceedings, but of formulating the principles, if any, which might have been violated by such proceedings.

This way of stating the question is also dictated by the very nature and existing conditions of international law.

International law governs relations between independent States. The rules of law binding upon States therefore emanate from their own free will as expressed in conventions or by usages generally accepted as expressing principles of law and established in order to regulate the relations between these co-existing independent communities or with a view to the achievement of common aims. Restrictions upon the independence of States cannot therefore be presumed.

Now the first and foremost restriction imposed by international law upon a State is that—failing the existence of a permissive rule to the contrary—it may not exercise its power in any form in the territory of another State. In this sense jurisdiction is certainly territorial; it cannot be exercised by a State outside its territory except by virtue of a permissive rule derived from international custom or from a convention.

It does not, however, follow that international law prohibits a State from exercising jurisdiction in its own territory, in respect of any case which relates to acts which have taken place abroad, and in which it cannot rely on some permissive rule of international law. Such a view would only be tenable if international law contained a general prohibition to States to extend the application of their laws and the jurisdiction of their courts to persons, property and acts outside their territory, and if, as an exception to this general prohibition, it allowed States to do so in certain specific cases. But this is certainly not the case under international law as it stands at present. Far from laying down a general prohibition to the effect that States may not extend the application of their laws and the jurisdiction of their courts to persons, property and acts outside their territory, it leaves them in this respect a wide measure of discretion which is only limited in certain cases by prohibitive rules; as regards other cases, every State remains free to adopt the principles which it regards as best and most suitable. * * *

In these circumstances, all that can be required of a State is that it should not overstep the limits which international law places upon its jurisdiction; within these limits, its title to exercise jurisdiction rests in its sovereignty.

It follows from the foregoing that the contention of the French Government to the effect that Turkey must in each case be able to cite a rule of international law authorizing her to exercise jurisdiction, is opposed to the generally accepted international law to which Article 15 of the Convention of Lausanne refers. * * *

IV.

The Court will now proceed to ascertain whether general international law, to which Article 15 of the Convention of Lausanne refers, contains a rule prohibiting Turkey from prosecuting Lieutenant Demons.

For this purpose, it will in the first place examine the value of the arguments advanced by the French Government, without however omitting to take into account other possible aspects of the problem, which might show the existence of a restrictive rule applicable in this case.

The arguments advanced by the French Government, other than those considered above, are, in substance, the three following:

(1) International law does not allow a State to take proceedings with regard to offenses committed by foreigners abroad, simply by reason of the nationality of the victim; and such is the situation in the present case because the offence must be regarded as having been committed on board the French vessel.

(2) International law recognizes the exclusive jurisdiction of the State whose flag is flown as regards everything which occurs on board a ship on the high seas.

(3) Lastly, this principle is especially applicable in a collision case.

As regards the first argument, the Court feels obliged in the first place to recall that its examination is strictly confined to the specific situation in the present case, for it is only in regard to this situation that its decision is asked for.

As has already been observed, the characteristic features of the situation of fact are as follows: there has been a collision on the high seas between two vessels flying different flags, on one of which was one of the persons alleged to be guilty of the offence, whilst the victims were on board the other.

This being so, the Court does not think it necessary to consider the contention that a State cannot punish offences committed abroad by a foreigner simply by reason of the nationality of the victim. For this contention only relates to the case where the nationality of the victim is the only criterion on which the criminal jurisdiction of the State is based. Even if that argument were correct generally speaking—and in regard to this the Court reserves its opinion—it could only be used in the present case if international law forbade Turkey to take into consideration the fact that the offence produced its effects on the Turkish vessel and consequently in a place assimilated to Turkish territory in which the application of Turkish criminal law cannot be challenged, even in regard to offenses committed there by foreigners. But no such rule of international law exists. No argument has come to the knowledge of the Court from which it could be deduced that States recognize themselves to be under an obligation towards each other only to have regard to the place where the author of the offence happens to be at the time of the offence. On the contrary, it is certain that the courts of many countries, even of countries which have given their criminal legislation a strictly territorial character, interpret criminal law in the sense that offences, the authors of which at the moment of commission are in the territory of another State, are nevertheless to be regarded as having been committed in the national territory, if one of the constituent elements of the offence, and more especially its effects, have taken place there. French courts have, in regard to a variety of situations, given decisions sanctioning this way of interpreting the territorial principle. Again, the Court does not know of any cases in which governments have protested against the fact that the criminal law of some country contained a rule to this effect or that the courts of a country construed their criminal law in this sense. Consequently, once it is admitted that the effects of the offence were produced on the Turkish vessel, it becomes impossible to hold that there is a rule of international law which prohibits Turkey from prosecuting Lieutenant Demons because of the fact that the author of the offence was on board the French ship. * * *

The second argument put forward by the French Government is the principle that the State whose flag is flown has exclusive jurisdiction over everything which occurs on board a merchant ship on the high seas.

It is certainly true that—apart from certain special cases which are defined by international law—vessels on the high seas are subject to no authority except that of the State whose flag they fly. In virtue of the principle of the freedom of the seas, that is to say, the absence of any territorial sovereignty upon the high seas, no State may exercise any kind of jurisdiction over foreign vessels upon them. Thus, if a war vessel, happening to be at the spot where a collision occurs between a vessel flying its flag and a foreign vessel, were to send on board the latter an officer to make investigations or to take evidence, such an act would undoubtedly be contrary to international law.

But it by no means follows that a State can never in its own territory exercise jurisdiction over acts which have occurred on board a foreign ship on the high seas. A corollary of the principle of the freedom of the seas is that a ship on the high seas is assimilated to the territory of the State the flag of which it flies, for, just as in its own territory, that State exercises its authority upon it, and no other State may do so. All that can be said is that by virtue of the principle of the freedom of the seas, a ship is placed in the same position as national territory; but there is nothing to support the claim according to which the rights of the State under whose flag the vessel sails may go farther than the rights which it exercises within its territory properly so called. It follows that what occurs on board a vessel on the high seas must be regarded as if it occurred on the territory of the State whose flag the ship flies. If, therefore, a guilty act committed on the high seas produces its effects on a vessel flying another flag or in foreign territory, the same principles must be applied as if the territories of two different States were concerned, and the conclusion must therefore be drawn that there is no rule of international law prohibiting the State to which the ship on which the effects of the offence have taken place belongs, from regarding the offence as having been committed in its territory and prosecuting, accordingly, the delinquent.

This conclusion could only be overcome if it were shown that there was a rule of customary international law which, going further than the principle stated above, established the exclusive jurisdiction of the State whose flag was flown. The French Government has endeavored to prove the existence of such a rule, having recourse for this purpose to the teachings of publicists, to decisions of municipal and international tribunals, and especially to conventions which, whilst creating exceptions to the principle of the freedom of the seas by permitting the war and police vessels of a State to exercise a more or less extensive control over the merchant vessels of another State, reserve jurisdiction to the courts of the country whose flag is flown by the vessel proceeded against.

In the Court's opinion, the existence of such a rule has not been conclusively proved.

In the first place, as regards teachings of publicists, and apart from the question as to what their value may be from the point of view of establishing the existence of a rule of customary law, it is no doubt true that all or nearly all writers teach that ships on the high seas are subject exclusively to the jurisdiction of the State whose flag they fly. But the important point is the significance attached by them to this principle; now it does not appear that in general, writers bestow upon this principle a scope differing from or wider than that explained above and which is equivalent to saying that the jurisdiction of a State over vessels on the high seas is the same in extent as its jurisdiction in its own territory. On the other hand, there is no lack of writers who, upon a close study of the special question whether a State can prosecute for offences committed on board a foreign ship on the high seas, definitely come to the conclusion that such offences must be regarded as if they had been committed in the territory of the State whose flag the ship flies, and that consequently the general rules of each legal system in regard to offences committed abroad are applicable.

In regard to precedents, it should first be observed that, leaving aside the collision cases which will be alluded to later, none of them relates to offences affecting two ships flying the flags of two different countries, and that consequently they are not of much importance in the case before the Court. The case of the *Costa Rica Packet* is no exception, for the prauw on which the alleged depredations took place was adrift without flag or crew, and this circumstance certainly influenced, perhaps decisively, the conclusion arrived at by the arbitrator.

On the other hand, there is no lack of cases in which a State has claimed a right to prosecute for an offence, committed on board a foreign ship, which it regarded as punishable under its legislation. Thus Great Britain refused the request of the United States for the extradition of John Anderson, a British seaman who had committed homicide on board an American vessel, stating that she did not dispute the jurisdiction of the United States but that she was entitled to exercise hers concurrently. This case, to which others might be added, is relevant in spite of Anderson's British nationality, in order to show that the principle of the exclusive jurisdiction of the country whose flag the vessel flies is not universally accepted. * * *

Finally, as regards conventions expressly reserving jurisdiction exclusively to the State whose flag is flown, it is not absolutely certain that this stipulation is to be regarded as expressing a general principle of law rather than as corresponding to the extraordinary jurisdiction which these conventions confer on the state-owned ships of a particular country in respect of ships of another country on the high seas. Apart from that, it should be observed that these conventions relate to matters of a particular kind, closely connected with the policing of the seas, such as the slave trade, damage to submarine cables, fisheries, etc., and not to common-law offences. Above all it should be pointed out that the offences contemplated by the conventions in question only concern a single ship; it is impossible therefore to make any deduction from them in regard to matters which concern two ships and consequently the jurisdiction of two different States.

The Court therefore has arrived at the conclusion that the second argument put forward by the French Government does not, any more than the first, establish the existence of a rule of international law prohibiting Turkey from prosecuting Lieutenant Demons.

It only remains to examine the third argument advanced by the French Government and to ascertain whether a rule specially applying to collision cases has grown up, according to which criminal proceedings regarding such cases come exclusively within the jurisdiction of the State whose flag is flown.

In this connection, the Agent for the French Government has drawn the Court's attention to the fact that questions of jurisdiction in collision cases, which frequently arise before civil courts, are but rarely encountered in the practice of criminal courts. He deduces from this that, in practice, prosecutions only occur before the courts of the State whose flag is flown and that circumstance is proof of a tacit consent on the part of States and, consequently, shows what positive international law is in collision cases.

In the Court's opinion, this conclusion is not warranted. Even if the rarity of the judicial decisions to be found among the reported cases were sufficient to prove in point of fact the circumstance alleged by the Agent for the French Government, it would merely show that States had often, in practice, abstained from instituting criminal proceedings, and not that they recognized themselves as being obliged to do so; for only if such abstention were based on their being conscious of having a duty to abstain would it be possible to speak of an international custom. The alleged fact does not allow one to infer that States have been conscious of having such a duty; on the other hand, as will presently be seen, there are other circumstances calculated to show that the contrary is true.

So far as the Court is aware there are no decisions of international tribunals in this matter; but some decisions of municipal courts have been cited. Without pausing to consider the value to be attributed to the judgments of municipal courts in connection with the establishment of the existence of a rule of international law, it will suffice to observe that the decisions quoted sometimes support one view and sometimes the other. Whilst the French Government have been able to cite the *Ortigia–Oncle–Joseph* case before the Court of Aix and the *Franconia–Strathclyde* case before the British Court for Crown Cases Reserved, as being in favour of the exclusive jurisdiction of the state whose flag is flown, on the other hand the *Ortigia–Oncle–Joseph* case before the Italian Courts and the *Ekbatana–West–Hinder* case before the Belgian Courts have been cited in support of the opposing contention.

Lengthy discussions have taken place between the Parties as to the importance of each of these decisions as regards the details of which the Court confines itself to a reference to the Cases and Counter–Cases of the Parties. The Court does not think it necessary to stop to consider them. It will suffice to observe that, as municipal jurisprudence is thus divided, it is hardly possible to see in it an indication of the existence of the restrictive rule of international law which alone could serve as a basis for the contention of the French Government. * * *

The Court, having arrived at the conclusion that the arguments advanced by the French Government either are irrelevant to the issue or do not establish the existence of a principle of international law precluding Turkey from instituting the prosecution which was in fact brought against Lieutenant Demons, observes that in the fulfilment of its task of itself ascertaining what the international law is, it has not confined itself to a consideration of the arguments put forward, but has included in its researches all precedents, teachings and facts to which it had access and which might possibly have revealed the existence of one of the principles of international law contemplated in the special argument. The result of these researches has not been to establish the existence of any such principle. It must therefore be held that there is no principle of international law, within the meaning of Article 15 of the Convention of Lausanne of July 24th, 1923, which precludes the institution of the criminal proceedings under consideration. Consequently, Turkey, by instituting, in virtue of the discretion which international law leaves to every sovereign State, the criminal proceedings in question, has not, in the absence of such principles, acted in a manner contrary to the principles of international law within the meaning of the special agreement. * * *

V.

Having thus answered the first question submitted by the special agreement in the negative, the Court need not consider the second question, regarding the pecuniary reparation which might have been due to Lieutenant Demons.

FOR THESE REASONS,

The Court,

having heard both Parties,

gives by the President's casting vote—the votes being equally divided—, judgment to the effect

(1) that, following the collision which occurred on August 2nd, 1926, on the high seas between the French steamship *Lotus* and the Turkish steamship *Boz-Kourt*, and upon the arrival of the French ship at Stamboul, and in consequence of the loss of the *Boz-Kourt* having involved the death of eight Turkish nationals, Turkey, by instituting criminal proceedings in pursuance of Turkish law against Lieutenant Demons, officer of the watch on board the *Lotus* at the time of the collision, has not acted in conflict with the principles of international law, contrary to Article 15 of the Convention of Lausanne of July 24th, 1923, respecting conditions of residence and business and jurisdiction;

(2) that, consequently, there is no occasion to give judgment on the question of the pecuniary reparation which might have been due to Lieutenant Demons if Turkey, by prosecuting him as above stated, had acted in a manner contrary to the principles of international law.

Notes and Questions

1. *Positivism and the Nature of International Law. Lotus* involved a narrow, albeit interesting, jurisdictional issue in international conflict of laws, but the PCIJ sought to teach a far broader lesson. The judgment in *Lotus* has become one of the most usually cited positivist opinions about the nature of international law, because it argued in part III that the "rules of law binding upon States therefore emanate from their own free will as expressed in conventions or by usages generally accepted as expressing principles of law." The ruling half of an evenly divided Court in *Lotus* maintained that all international legal rules are based on state consent: "Restrictions upon the independence of States cannot therefore be presumed." No room was given to general principles, fundamental norms, natural law, or equity as sources of international law; state sovereignty was seen as the fundamental principle of international law from which all other international legal principles and rules are derived. Looking at other cases involving customary international law (*e.g.*, *Filartiga* and *Paquete Habana*), is the strict positivism of the *Lotus* judgment too restrictive?

2. *The Burden of Proof.* In the context of the case, the positivist presumption means that the Court puts the burden of proof on France rather than Turkey. The Court rules that France has to prove that there is a rule of customary international law restricting Turkish independence rather than making Turkey prove that its prosecution of Lieutenant Demons is sanctioned by international law. Given the uncertainty of the evidence of customary international law, was not this allocation of the burden of proof crucial to the outcome of the case? Would a less positivist position have enabled the Court to rely less heavily on the burden of proof as a way of deciding the case?

3. *Reversal of the Rule in* Lotus. As a matter of maritime law, some observers strongly disagreed with the *Lotus* decision, feeling that it exposed shipboard officers to double prosecution. In the High Seas Convention of 1958, Article 11(1) provides that in cases involving collisions on the high seas, only the flag state or the national state of the accused may prosecute the officer in a case of a collision on the high seas. The same anti-*Lotus* rule

has resurfaced in Article 97(1) of the 1982 U.N. Convention on the Law of the Sea, which is reproduced in the Appendix.

4. *Treaty Interpretation*. Note that in *Lotus* two treaties were involved as well as customary international law. The first treaty, the special agreement of October 12, 1926, provided authority for the Permanent Court of International Justice to hear the case and set the questions that the Court was to address. The second treaty was the 1923 Convention of Lausanne, Article 15 of which referred to "principles of international law." The PCIJ took that phrase to refer to customary international law. Was the Court's reluctance to examine the *travaux préparatoires* of Article 15 appropriate? Compare the approach toward treaty interpretation taken in Articles 31–32 of the Vienna Convention on the Law of Treaties (see Appendix).

THE TEXACO/LIBYA ARBITRATION

Award of 19 January 1977, 17 *International Legal Materials* 1 (1978).

Acting in his capacity as Sole Arbitrator, pursuant to the appointment made on 18 December 1974 by the President of the International Court of Justice, of an arbitration between, on the one hand, the Government of the Libyan Arab Republic and, on the other, California Asiatic Oil Company and Texaco Overseas Petroleum Company,

The undersigned Sole Arbitrator has rendered the following award on the merits:

I. The Facts

1. The present arbitration arises out of 14 Deeds of Concession concluded between the competent Libyan Authorities (Petroleum Commission or Petroleum Ministry, depending on the date of the contracts) and the above-mentioned companies * * *. * * *

3. Among the provisions which are contained in the model contract annexed to the Petroleum Law of 1955 and reproduced in the contracts concluded by the concessionaire companies, Clause 16 is worth, at this time, special mention. * * *

The final version of Clause 16 * * * reads as follows:

> "The Government of Libya will take all steps necessary to ensure that the Company enjoys all the rights conferred by this Concession. The contractual rights expressly created by this concession shall not be altered except by mutual consent of the parties.
>
> This Concession shall throughout the period of its validity be construed in accordance with the Petroleum Law and the Regulations in force on the date of execution of the agreement of amendment by which this paragraph (2) was incorporated into this concession agreement. Any amendment to or repeal of such Regulations shall not affect the contractual rights of the Company without its consent." * * *

7. Law No. 11 of 1974 (the Decree of Nationalization of 11 February 1974) nationalized the totality of the properties, rights, assets and

interests of California Asiatic Oil Company and Texaco Overseas Petroleum Company arising out of the 14 Deeds of Concession held by those companies. The more important aspects of this second text may be summarized as follows:

—it was directed against only the plaintiff companies, to the exclusion of any other company or enterprise;

—the text provided for the nationalization of all the properties and interests, rights and assets of California Asiatic Oil Company and Texaco Overseas Petroleum Company;

—the provisions relating to possible compensation (Article 2) were nothing more than a repetition of those which were already contained in Law No. 66 of 1973 (Article 2);

—the transfer of all the properties, rights and assets to N.O.C. [the Libyan National Oil Company] was confirmed (Article 6);

—finally, Article 7 effected a fundamental change in Amoseas, a company governed by foreign law; it was changed into a non-profit company, the assets of which were completely owned by N.O.C. Amoseas lost its name and was renamed the "Om el Jawabi Company."

II. THE PROCEDURE

8. The Tribunal should now, on the one hand, recall and complete the indications already given in its Preliminary Award of 27 November 1975 relating to the arbitration procedure and, on the other, pronounce on the law applicable to the arbitration of which it has been seized.

A. The Development of the Procedure:

9. —by two separate letters, dated 2 September 1973, California Asiatic Oil Company and Texaco Overseas Petroleum Company notified the Government of the Libyan Arab Republic that, pursuant to Article 20(1) of the Law on Petroleum of 1955 and to Clause 28 of the Deeds of Concession, they intended to submit to arbitration the dispute between them and the Government and advised the Government that they had appointed as arbitrator a member of the New York Bar, Mr. Fowler Hamilton.

—during the time which was allowed it by Clause 28 of the Deeds of Concession (and which expired on 1 December 1973), the Government of the Libyan Arab Republic did not appoint its arbitrator and, by a circular letter of 8 December 1973, it declared that it rejected the request for arbitration;

—the Libyan Government's failure and refusal to appoint an arbitrator led the companies to use the provision of Clause 28 of the Deeds of Concession which allows the concessionaires to request that the President of the International Court of Justice appoint a Sole Arbitrator: this was the purpose of the joint letter which the two companies sent on 3 April 1974 to the President of the International Court of Justice * * *.
* * *

III. THE MERITS

17. In their final submissions, those which were stated both at the close of their Memorial on the Merits and at the close of the oral hearings, the plaintiffs requested that the Arbitral Tribunal rule:

"A. Finding in favor of the Companies as follows:

(1) that the Deeds of Concession are binding on the Parties;

(2) that Libya, in adopting the Decrees of 1973 and 1974 and by its subsequent action pursuant thereto, breached its obligations under the Deeds of Concession;

(3) that Libya be held to perform the Deeds of Concession and fulfill their terms; and

(4) that Libya have 90 days after the award, being from the time of the declaration of the award or from the date fixed by the Sole Arbitrator, to inform the Arbitral Tribunal of the measures which it has taken in order to comply with and to execute the award." * * *

SECTION I: Concerning the Binding Nature of the Deeds of Concession * * *

B. How did the parties to these Deeds of Concession deal with the question of the applicable law? * * *

23. What was the law applicable to these contracts? It is this particular question that the parties intended to resolve in adopting Clause 28 of the Deeds of Concession in a form which must be recalled here:

"This concession shall be governed by and interpreted in accordance with the principles of the law of Libya common to the principles of international law and in the absence of such common principles then by and in accordance with the general principles of law, including such of those principles as may have been applied by international tribunals."

Thus, a complex system to determine the law applicable or the "choice of law" has been provided by the contracting parties involving a two-tier system:

—the principles of Libyan law were applicable to the extent that such principles were common to principles of international law;

—alternatively, in the absence of such conformity, reference was made to general principles of law. * * *

1. First question: Did the parties have the right to choose the law or the system of law which was to govern their contract? * * *

32. For the time being, it will suffice to note that the evolution which has occurred in the old case law of the Permanent Court of International Justice is due to the fact that, while the old case law viewed the contract as something which could not come under international law because it could not be regarded as a treaty between States,

under the new concept treaties are not the only type of agreements governed by such law. And it should be added that, although they are not to be confused with treaties, contracts between States and private persons can, under certain conditions, come within the ambit of a particular and new branch of international law: the international law of contracts. * * *

Section II: Did the Libyan Government, in adopting the nationalization measures of 1973 and 1974, breach its obligations under the contracts?

53. The Tribunal must now rule on the point whether, in adopting nationalization measures in 1973 and 1974, the defendant Government has, or has not, breached its obligations arising from the contracts it executed. For this purpose, this Tribunal should examine the various reasons which could be envisaged in order to justify the defendant Government's behavior and which, if established, would constitute reasons for freeing or exonerating it from the obligation which it had assumed and from its related responsibilities.

Three types of reasons could be put forward in order to justify, or attempt to justify, the behavior of the defendant government:

—the first reason could be based on the nature of the contracts under dispute: if they were administrative contracts, they could give rise, under certain conditions, to amendments or even to abrogation on the part of the contracting State; in relation to concession contracts, the nationalization measures would then be analyzed as being decisions bringing about, at least implicitly, abrogation;

—the second reason could be based on the concept of sovereignty and on the very nature of measures of nationalization;

—the third reason, lastly, could be deduced from the present status of international law, and in particular from certain resolutions concerning natural resources and wealth as adopted, in the last few years, by the United Nations. * * *

C. The present state of international law and the resolutions concerning natural resources and wealth adopted by the United Nations

80. This Tribunal has stated that it intends to rule on the basis of positive law, but now it is necessary to determine precisely the content of positive law and to ascertain the place which resolutions by the General Assembly of the United Nations could occupy therein.

In its Preliminary Award of 27 November 1975, this Tribunal postponed the examination of the objection raised by the Libyan Government in its Memorandum of 26 July 1974 according to which:

> "Nationalization is an act related to the sovereignty of the State. This fact has been recognized by the consecutive Resolutions of the United Nations on the sovereignty of States over their natural resources, the last being Resolution No. 3171 of the United Nations

General Assembly adopted on December 13, 1973, as well as paragraph (4/E) of Resolution No. 3201 (S–VI) adopted on 1 May, 1974. The said Resolutions confirm that every State maintains complete right to exercise full sovereignty over its natural resources and recognize Nationalization as being a legitimate and internationally recognized method to ensure the sovereignty of the State upon such resources. Nationalization, being related to the sovereignty of the State, is not subject to foreign jurisdiction. Provisions of the International Law do not permit a dispute with a State to be referred to any Jurisdiction other than its national Jurisdiction. In affirmance of this principle, Resolutions of the General Assembly provide that any dispute related to Nationalization or its consequences should be settled in accordance with provisions of domestic law of the State."

81. * * *

The practice of the United Nations, referred to in the Libyan Government's Memorandum, does not contradict in any way the status of international law as indicated above. This Tribunal wishes first to recall the relevant passages for this case of Resolution 1803 (XVII) entitled "Permanent Sovereignty over Natural Resources," as adopted by the General Assembly on 14 December 1962:

"3. In cases where authorization is granted, the capital imported and the earnings on that capital shall be governed by the terms thereof, by the national legislation in force, and by international law....

4. Nationalization, expropriation or requisitioning shall be based on grounds or reasons of public utility, security or the national interest which are recognized as overriding purely individual or private interests, both domestic and foreign. In such cases the owner shall be paid appropriate compensation, in accordance with the rules in force in the State taking such measures in the exercise of its sovereignty and in accordance with international law...."

82. The Memorandum of the Libyan Government which has just been quoted relies, however, on more recent Resolutions of the General Assembly (3171 and 3201 (S–VI), in particular) which, according to this Government would as a practical matter rule out any recourse to international law and would confer an exclusive and unlimited competence upon the legislation and courts of the host country.

Although not quoted in the Libyan Memorandum, since subsequent to the date of 26 July 1974, Resolution 3281 (XXIX), proclaimed under the title "Charter of Economic Rights and Duties of the States" and adopted by the General Assembly on 12 December 1974, should also be mentioned with the two Resolutions in support of the contention made by the Libyan Government. Two portions of such Resolutions are of particular interest in the present case:

—Resolution 3201 (S–VI) adopted by the General Assembly on 1 May 1974 under the title "Declaration on the Establishment of a New International Economic Order," Article 4, paragraph (e):

> "Full permanent sovereignty of every State over its natural resources and all economic activities. In order to safeguard these resources, each State is entitled to exercise effective control over them and their exploitation with means suitable to its own situation, including the right to nationalization or transfer of ownership to its nationals, this right being an expression of the full permanent sovereignty of the State. No State may be subjected to economic, political or any other type of coercion to prevent the free and full exercise of this inalienable right."

—Article 2 of Resolution 3281 (XXIX):

> "1. Every State has and shall freely exercise full permanent sovereignty, including possession, use and disposal, over all its wealth, natural resources and economic activities.
>
> 2. Each State has the right . . .
>
> . . .
>
> c) To nationalize, expropriate or transfer ownership of foreign property, in which case appropriate compensation should be paid by the State adopting such measures, taking into account its relevant laws and regulations and all circumstances that the State considers pertinent. In any case where the question of compensation gives rise to a controversy, it shall be settled under the domestic law of the nationalizing State and by its tribunals, unless it is freely and mutually agreed by all States concerned that other peaceful means be sought on the basis of the sovereign equality of States and in accordance with the principal [*sic*] of free choice of means."

Substantial differences thus exist between Resolution 1803 (XVII) and the subsequent Resolutions as regards the role of international law in the exercise of permanent sovereignty over natural resources. This aspect of the matter is directly related to the instant case under consideration; this Tribunal is obligated to consider the legal validity of the above-mentioned Resolutions and the possible existence of a custom resulting therefrom.

83. The general question of the legal validity of the Resolutions of the United Nations has been widely discussed by the writers. This Tribunal will recall first that, under Article 10 of the U.N. Charter, the General Assembly only issues "recommendations," which have long appeared to be texts having no binding force and carrying no obligations for the Member States (see Sloan, "The Binding Force of a 'Recommendation' of the General Assembly of the United Nations," 25 Brit.Y.B. Int'l L. 1 *et seq.* (1948); Fitzmaurice, "The Law and Procedure of the International Court of Justice, 1951–4: Questions of Jurisdiction, Competence and Procedure," 34 Brit.Y.B. Int'l L. 1 *et seq.* (1958); Virally,

"La Valeur Juridique des Recommendations des Organisations Internationales," 2 Annuaire Français de Droit International ("A.F.D.I.") 66 *et seq.* (1956); Vallat, "The Competence of the United Nations General Assembly," 97 R.C.A.D.I. 203 *et seq.* (1959); Galino, "Las Resoluciones de la Asemblea General de las Naciones Unidas y su Fuerza Legal," Revista Española de Derecho Internacional 96 *et seq.* (1958); Johnson, "The Effect of Resolutions of the General Assembly of the United Nations," 32 Brit.Y.B. Int'l L. 97 *et seq.* (1955)).

Refusal to recognize any legal validity of United Nations Resolutions must, however, be qualified according to the various texts enacted by the United Nations. These are very different and have varying legal value, but it is impossible to deny that the United Nations' activities have had a significant influence on the content of contemporary international law. In appraising the legal validity of the above-mentioned Resolutions, this Tribunal will take account of the criteria usually taken into consideration, *i.e.*, the examination of voting conditions and the analysis of the provisions concerned.

84. (1) With respect to the first point, Resolution 1803 (XVII) of 14 December 1962 was passed by the General Assembly by 87 votes to 2, with 12 abstentions. It is particularly important to note that the majority voted for this text, including many States of the Third World, but also several Western developed countries with market economies, including the most important one, the United States. The principles stated in this Resolution were therefore assented to by a great many States representing not only all geographical areas but also all economic systems.

From this point of view, this Tribunal notes that the affirmative vote of several developed countries with a market economy was made possible in particular by the inclusion in the Resolution of two references to international law, and one passage relating to the importance of international cooperation for economic development. According to the representative of Tunisia:

> " . . . the result of the debate on this question was that the balance of the original draft resolution was improved—a balance between, on the one hand, the unequivocal affirmation of the inalienable right of States to exercise sovereignty over their natural resources and, on the other hand, the reconciliation or adaptation of this sovereignty to international law, equity and the principles of international cooperation." (17 U.N. GAOR 1122, U.N. Doc. A/PV.1193 (1962).)

The reference to international law, in particular in the field of nationalization, was therefore an essential factor in the support given by several Western countries to Resolution 1803 (XVII).

85. On the contrary, it appears to this Tribunal that the conditions under which Resolutions 3171 (XXVII), 3201 (S–VI) and 3281 (XXIX)(Charter of the Economic Rights and Duties of States) were notably different:

—Resolution 3171 (XXVII) was adopted by a recorded vote of 108 votes to 1, with 16 abstentions, but this Tribunal notes that a separate vote was requested with respect to the paragraph in the operative part mentioned in the Libyan Government's Memorandum whereby the General Assembly stated that the application of the principle according to which nationalizations effected by States as the expression of their sovereignty implied that it is within the right of each State to determine the amount of possible compensation and the means of their payment, and that any dispute which might arise should be settled in conformity with the national law of each State instituting measures of this kind. As a consequence of a roll-call, this paragraph was adopted by 86 votes to 11 (Federal Republic of Germany, Belgium, Spain, United States, France, Israel, Italy, Japan, The Netherlands, Portugal, United Kingdom), with 28 abstentions (South Africa, Australia, Austria, Barbados, Canada, Ivory Coast, Denmark, Finland, Ghana, Greece, Haiti, India, Indonesia, Ireland, Luxembourg, Malawi, Malaysia, Nepal, Nicaragua, Norway, New Zealand, Philippines, Rwanda, Singapore, Sri Lanka, Sweden, Thailand, Turkey).

This specific paragraph concerning nationalizations, disregarding the role of international law, not only was not consented to by the most important Western countries, but caused a number of the developing countries to abstain.

—Resolution 3201 (S–VI) was adopted without a vote by the General Assembly, but the statements made by 38 delegates showed clearly and explicitly what was the position of each main group of countries. The Tribunal should therefore note that the most important Western countries were opposed to abandoning the compromise solution contained in Resolution 1803 (XVII).

—The conditions under which Resolution 3281 (XXIX), proclaiming the Charter of Economic Rights and Duties of States, was adopted also show unambiguously that there was no general consensus of the States with respect to the most important provisions and in particular those concerning nationalization. Having been the subject matter of a roll-call vote, the Charter was adopted by 118 votes to 6, with 10 abstentions. The analysis of votes on specific sections of the Charter is most significant insofar as the present case is concerned. From this point of view, paragraph 2(c) of Article 2 of the Charter, which limits consideration of the characteristics of compensation to the State and does not refer to international law, was voted by 104 to 16, with 6 abstentions, all of the industrialized countries with market economies having abstained or having voted against it.

86. * * * As this Tribunal has already indicated, the legal value of the resolutions which are relevant to the present case can be determined on the basis of circumstances under which they were adopted and by analysis of the principles which they state:

—With respect to the first point, the absence of any binding force of the resolutions of the General Assembly of the United Nations implies that such resolutions must be accepted by the members of the United Nations in order to be legally binding. In this respect, the Tribunal notes that only Resolution 1803 (XVII) of 14 December 1962 was supported by a majority of Member States representing all of the various groups. By contrast, the other Resolutions mentioned above, and in particular those referred to in the Libyan Memorandum, were supported by a majority of States but not by any of the developed countries with market economies which carry on the largest part of international trade.

87. (2) With respect to the second point, to wit the appraisal of the legal value on the basis of the principles stated, it appears essential to this Tribunal to distinguish between those provisions stating the existence of a right on which the generality of the States has expressed agreement and those provisions introducing new principles which were rejected by certain representative groups of States and having nothing more than a *de lege ferenda* value only in the eyes of the States which have adopted them; as far as the others are concerned, the rejection of these same principles implies that they consider them as being *contra legem*. With respect to the former, which proclaim rules recognized by the community of nations, they do not create a custom but confirm one by formulating it and specifying its scope, thereby making it possible to determine whether or not one is confronted with a legal rule. As has been noted by Ambassador Castañeda, "[such resolutions] do not create the law; they have a declaratory nature of noting what does exist" (129 R.C.A.D.I. 204 (1970), at 315).

On the basis of the circumstances of adoption mentioned above and by expressing an *opinio juris communis*, Resolution 1803 (XVII) seems to this Tribunal to reflect the state of customary law existing in this field. Indeed, on the occasion of the vote on a resolution finding the existence of a customary rule, the States concerned clearly express their views. The consensus by a majority of States belonging to the various representative groups indicates without the slightest doubt universal recognition of the rules therein incorporated, *i.e.*, with respect to nationalization and compensation of the use of the rules in force in the nationalizing State, but all this in conformity with international law.

88. While Resolution 1803 (XVII) appears to a large extent as the expression of a real general will, this is not at all the case with respect to the other Resolutions mentioned above, which has been demonstrated previously by analysis of the circumstances of adoption. In particular, as regards the Charter of Economic Rights and Duties of States, several factors contribute to denying legal value to those provisions of the document which are of interest in the instant case.

—In the first place, Article 2 of this Charter must be analyzed as a political rather than as a legal declaration concerned with the ideological strategy of development and, as such, supported only by non-industrialized States.

—In the second place, this Tribunal notes that in the draft submitted by the Group of 77 to the Second Commission, the General Assembly was invited to adopt the Charter "as a first measure of codification and progressive development" within the field of the international law of development. However, because of the opposition of several States, this description was deleted from the text submitted to the vote of the Assembly. * * *

89. Such an attitude is further reinforced by an examination of the general practice of relations between States with respect to investments. This practice is in conformity, not with the provisions of Article 2(c) of the above-mentioned Charter conferring exclusive jurisdiction on domestic legislation and courts, but with the exception stated at the end of this paragraph. Thus a great many investment agreements entered into between industrial States or their nationals, on the one hand, and developing countries, on the other, state, in an objective way, the standards of compensation and further provide, in case of dispute regarding the level of such compensation, the possibility of resorting to an international tribunal. In this respect, it is particularly significant in the eyes of this Tribunal that no fewer than 65 States, as of 31 October 1974, had ratified the Convention on the Settlement of Investment Disputes between States and Nationals of other States, dated March 18, 1965. * * *

Section V. Operative part:

For These Reasons,

The undersigned Sole Arbitrator

1. pronounces and decides that the Deeds of Concession in dispute are binding upon the parties;

2. pronounces and decides that the Libyan Government, the defendant, in adopting measures of nationalization in 1973 and 1974, breached its obligations arising from the said Deeds of Concession;

3. pronounces and decides that the Libyan Government, the defendant, is legally bound to perform these contracts and to give them full effect * * *.

Notes and Questions

1. *"Mixed" International Arbitrations.* One of the advantages of international arbitration is that it can be tailor-made to fit specific cases. Here the Deeds of Concession between the U.S. oil companies and the Libyan government provided that an aggrieved party could request the President of the International Court of Justice to appoint a sole arbitrator if the other party refused to make an appointment to a three-judge panel. Appointment by the President of the International Court did not, of course, make this an ICJ proceeding. Here, because both private and public parties were involved, the procedure was a "mixed" form of international arbitration. Why would the parties drafting the Deeds of Concession have chosen international arbitration to settle their disputes? Why would Libya renege on its promise to arbitrate?

2. *Individuals and International Law.* The excerpts from the case focus on the question of the legal effect of United Nations General Assembly resolutions and only touch on a variety of other interesting issues in international law raised by the opinion. Paragraph 23 quotes the choice of law provision in Clause 28 of the Deeds of Concession which refers to Libyan law, international law, and the general principles of law. In his opinion, the Arbitrator reviews and rejects the positivist doctrine of the 19th and early 20th centuries that held that international law could only bind states. Neither the classical law of nations of the 17th and 18th centuries nor the modern international law of the later 20th century have held such a restrictive view. Both permit individuals, including private corporations, as well as states to be subjects of international law. The Arbitrator finds that under modern international law, contracts may be "delocalized" from municipal law and "internationalized." Paragraph 32 sums up this analysis. More on individuals as subjects of international law is to be found in Chapter 6.

3. *The Role of U.N. General Assembly Resolutions in Making Customary International Law.* The large part of the *Texaco/Libya Case* excerpted concerns Libya's contention that international law permitted the Government to nationalize foreign investments without reference to any standards of foreign or international law. The Libyan argument rested on the foundations of the 1973 and 1974 U.N. General Assembly resolutions proclaiming a New International Economic Order ("NIEO"). The legal question for the Arbitrator was whether these NIEO resolutions had any legal force especially in the light of U.N. General Assembly Resolution 1803 (XVII) of 1962 which recited that in the case of nationalization "the owner shall be paid appropriate compensation, in accordance with the rules in force in the State taking such measures in the exercise of its sovereignty, and in accordance with international law." The NIEO resolutions seem to leave such compensation questions simply to the law of the nationalizing state. As the Arbitrator writes, there are "substantial differences" between the rules in the 1962 and NIEO resolutions. The Arbitrator feels obliged "to consider the legal validity of the above-mentioned Resolutions and the possible existence of a custom resulting therefrom." Though U.N. General Assembly resolutions are formally only "recommendations," the Arbitrator needs to explore whether they could nonetheless pass into customary international law. What theory justifies treating some General Assembly resolutions as customary international law? What is the state practice? The *opinio juris*? As a matter of law-finding, what are the advantages and disadvantages of resolutions vis-à-vis other possible forms of customary international law? Since Article 10 of the U.N. Charter deems General Assembly resolutions "recommendations," does it violate the spirit as well as the letter of the Charter to give resolutions, by any logic, the force of law? Contrarily, given the absence of any general international legislative organ, is there good reason to try to "elevate" the status of General Assembly resolutions?

4. *Evaluating General Assembly Resolutions.* In looking at General Assembly voting, is the Arbitrator right in disregarding majority voting and relying instead on consensus? Is the Arbitrator right in putting great weight on the fact that the 1962 Resolution was "assented to by a great many states representing not only all geographical areas but also all econom-

ic systems"? Even if only such a consensus could elevate a resolution from a recommendation to a custom, did not the voting for the NIEO resolutions at least demonstrate that most states no longer supported the 1962 rule? Is it possible that the General Assembly actions in 1973–1974 destroyed the old customary rule but failed to establish a new rule? Would this leave a *Lotus*-like gap in international law?

In looking to the votes of states on General Assembly resolutions, should the votes of some states be given proportionately greater weight? This could be based on population, economic or political power, or their contributions to the U.N. budget.

5. *The Efficacy of the Arbitral Award.* On September 25, 1977, Libya agreed to pay Texaco and Standard Oil of California $76 million in crude oil to compensate them for the nationalization of their subsidiaries. The agreement effectively terminated the international arbitral proceedings. "Libya to Compensate Two U.S. Companies," *New York Times*, Sept. 26, 1977, at 55. What were the inducements for Libya finally to compensate the American oil companies? What difference might the arbitral award have made? Would Libya be looking to reassure potential new foreign investors? Was there fear of diplomatic pressure? Was Libya afraid of recognition and enforcement actions brought on the basis of the arbitral judgment in third countries? The New York Convention on the Recognition and Enforcement of Foreign Arbitral Awards, June 10, 1958, 330 U.N.T.S. 38 (in force for 107 states as of January 1, 1996), in fact does provide for the recognition and enforcement of many foreign arbitral awards, and is widely used in commercial cases. See A.J. van den Berg, *The New York Arbitration Convention of 1958* (1981).

B. GENERAL PRINCIPLES OF LAW

Sometimes neither treaties nor custom provide a rule to decide a case involving international law. Then the judge or other seeker may look outside the theoretically consensual sources to non-consensual sources. The first we examine is general principles of law.

THE AM&S CASE

Australian Mining & Smelting Europe Ltd. v. E.C. Commission
[1982] 2 Common Market Law Reports 264.

Second Opinion of the Advocate General (Sir Gordon Slynn)

In February 1979, officials of the [European Community's] Commission required the applicants to make available documents which they wished to see in connection with an investigation being conducted pursuant to Article 14(1) of Council Regulation 17 of 6 February 1962. This was said to be an investigation of competitive conditions concerning the production and distribution of zinc metal and its alloys and zinc concentrates in order to verify that there is no infringement of Articles 85 and 86 of the EEC Treaty [relating to the European Community's competition law]. The applicants produced copies of most of the documents. Some, however, were not produced; so far as relevant, on the basis that they were covered by legal confidentiality, which entitled the applicants to withhold them. * * *

The parties were invited to state at the re-opened oral hearing their views on the law as to, and legal opinions relating to, the existence and extent of the protection granted in investigative proceedings instituted by public authorities for the purpose of detecting offenses of an economic nature, especially in the field of competition, to correspondence passing between

(a) two lawyers,

(b) an independent lawyer and his client,

(c) an undertaking and a lawyer in a permanent contractual relationship, or who is an employee of the undertaking,

(d) a legal adviser to, and an employee of, an undertaking or an employee of an associated undertaking,

(e) employees of an undertaking, or different but associated undertakings, where the correspondence mentions legal advice given by an independent lawyer or legal adviser serving one of the undertakings or other undertakings in the same group. * * *

The Commission's investigative powers for the purpose of carrying out the duties assigned to it by Article 89 of the EEC Treaty, and provisions adopted under Article 87 of the Treaty, are so far as relevant conferred by Article 14 of Regulation 17. It may 'undertake all necessary investigations into undertakings and associations of undertakings' and, to that end, its authorised officials are empowered to examine books and business records, to take copies of them, and to ask for oral explanations. There is no reference to any exemption or protection which may be claimed on the basis of legal confidence. Is that silence conclusive that no such protection is capable of applying in any form and in any situation? In my view it is not. The essential enquiry is, first, whether there is a principle of Community law existing independently of the regulation, and, secondly, whether the regulation does on a proper construction restrict the application of that principle. The question is not whether a principle of Community law derogates from Article 14, but whether Article 14 excludes the application of a principle of Community law. * * *

That general principles which have not been expressly stated in the Treaty or in subordinate legislation may exist as part of Community law, the observance of which the Court is required to ensure, needs no emphasis. This was made clear in an article by Judge Pescatore to be found in *Les Cahiers de Droit Européen*. It does not seem to me that the principle is limited to 'fundamental rights' which are more particularly dealt with in the article. It has a broader base. Such indeed appears to be accepted by both parties to this application. The Commission argue that there has to be a consensus among the laws of all the member–

States, and that the Court cannot establish a principle which goes beyond that accepted by any one of the member–States.

It cited no specific authority for that proposition, nor indicated what is the necessary level or degree of consensus required to establish the existence of a general principle. The CCBE [Consultative Committee of the Bars and Law Societies of the European Community], whose views broadly on the point were adopted by the applicants, submits that the aim of Community law is to find the best solution in qualitative terms, having regard to the spirit, orientation and general tendency of the national laws. * * *

That national law may be looked at on a comparative basis as an aid to consideration of what is Community law is shown in many cases * * *. Such a course is followed not to import national laws as such into Community law, but to use it as a means of discovering an *unwritten* principle of Community law. The suggestions made at times in this case, implicitly if not explicitly, that the applicants were trying to force into an unreceptive mould a purely local rule of the common law seems to me unfair to the argument of the applicants, who were seeking, like the CCBE and the United Kingdom Government, to distil a principle which is part of Community law by reference to national laws and which, in its detailed application, required adaptation to Community procedures.

In looking at national laws it does not seem to me that it can be a pre-condition of the existence of a rule of Community law that the principle should be expressed identically, or should be applied in identical form, in all of the member–States. Unanimity, as to a subject which is relevant to a Community law problem, may well be a strong indication of the existence of a rule of Community law. Total unanimity of expression and application is not, however, necessary. It is at best unlikely, not least as the Community grows in size. It seems to me highly probable that there are differences in the various member–States in the application of the principles of '*la bonne administration de la justice*,' rejection of '*un deni de justice*' and in the '*principe de proportionalité*.' Yet such differences do not prevent such principles from being part of Community law. * * *

The Court has been provided with extracts from legislation, case decisions and the opinions of academic authors and a welter of case references. Rather than set those out *in extenso* I propose to summarise what seems to me to be the relevant features for present purposes, fully conscious of the risks that a summary may oversimplify and is incomplete. I deal first with the general position as to the protection of legal confidence and then consider the position in relation to competition law.

In Belgium, it seems that confidential communications between lawyer and client are protected and cannot be seized or used as evidence. Although the basis of the rule may have been that information confided to the lawyer must be protected, it seems from the opinion of Monsieur l'Auditeur Huberlant and the decision of the Counseil d'Etat of 8 June

1961, that it also covers confidential advice given to the client. There exists also a more general principle which protects the privacy of correspondence—see Articles 10 and 22 of the Constitution.

In Denmark, the rule of the professional secret prevents lawyers from giving evidence of confidential information confided to them in their professional capacity and a lawyer can refuse to produce documents covered by professional secrecy. Communications between an accused person and his lawyer are protected in the hands of the accused under section 786 of the Code of Procedure. This rule seems to apply also in civil proceedings.

In Germany, confidential communications to a lawyer are protected in his hands, and breach of the professional confidentiality by a lawyer is a criminal offence. Thus such documents in the hands of the lawyer cannot be seized (section 97 of the Code of Criminal Procedure). Documents in the hands of the client can, it appears, be seized unless they come into existence after the commencement of criminal proceedings.

In France, breach of the rule of professional secrecy is a criminal offence, and although it seems that documents may be seized in some circumstances even in the hands of the lawyer, the importance of the rule is stressed in Lemaire '*Les règles de la profession de l'avocat*' which has been provided for the Court. This rule appears to be closely linked with the right to a fair trial (*les droits de la défense*).

The principle of the '*droits de la défense*' appears to cover confidential documents passing in both directions between lawyer and client and includes protection from seizure of legal advice given to the client before commencement of proceedings and found in his possession or in the possession of a person associated with him. There is also it seems a wider protection for confidential letters than exists under the common law systems. * * *

In Greece it seems that confidential communications in the hands of lawyers are protected in investigative proceedings instituted by judicial or administrative authorities. Documents in the hands of the client are covered by the general principle of privacy defined in Article 9 of the Constitution. The power to search the client's premises is circumscribed by sections 253 *et seq.* of the Code of Criminal Procedure.

In Ireland and the United Kingdom, although there may be differences in detail, broadly the law of the two member-States is the same and it is set out more fully in the opinion of Warner A. G. It should be repeated, however, that it covers both (a) communications between a person and his lawyer for the purpose of obtaining or giving legal advice whether or not in connexion with pending or contemplated legal proceedings and (b) communications between a person and his lawyer and other persons for the dominant purpose of preparing for pending or contemplated legal proceedings.

In Italy, as in most of the member-States, the law forbids lawyers from giving evidence of the information confided in them by their clients and entitles them to withhold documents covered by the doctrine of professional secrecy. On the other hand, it seems that, in the case of criminal investigations, documents held by a lawyer may be seized unless they have been entrusted to him for the preparation of his client's defence. Protection is wider in civil proceedings but it does not, in any case, appear to extend to documents in the hands of the client. It seems that, in the case of lawyers, professional secrecy is a reflection of the right to a fair trial guaranteed by Article 24 of the Constitution.

In Luxembourg, rules of professional secrecy and '*les droits de la défense,*' it would seem, protect legal confidences in the hands of the lawyer, and of the client after proceedings have begun, but little case law has been produced showing the application of these rules in practice.

Dutch law forbids the revelation of confidences by persons exercising a profession, such as lawyers. Coupled with this there is a right to refuse to give evidence on matters covered by professional secrecy. These matters include not only the information revealed by the client but also, in the case of lawyers, the legal advice they have given. Section 98 of the Code of Criminal Procedure provides that, when the premises of someone bound by professional secrecy are searched, the doctrine of professional secrecy must be observed and documents covered by it cannot be seized. There appears to be no authority holding or denying that legal correspondence found in the hands of the client is protected.

This summary is substantially, if not entirely, accepted by the Commission, the applicants and the body representing the Bars of all the member–States as being a fair and acceptable statement of the laws of the member–States.

It seems to me significant that they were able to reach agreement as to the existence of the principles which are set out in the document which they prepared to read to the Court.

From this it is plain, as indeed seems inevitable, that the position in all the member–States is not identical. It is to my mind equally plain that there exists in all the member–States a recognition that the public interest and the proper administration of justice demand as a general rule that a client should be able to speak freely, frankly and fully to his lawyer. * * * Whether it is described as the right of the client or the duty of the lawyer, this principle has nothing to do with the protection or privilege of the lawyer. It springs essentially from the basic need of a man in a civilised society to be able to turn to his lawyer for advice and help, and if proceedings begin, for representation; it springs no less from the advantages to a society which evolves complex law reaching into all the business affairs of persons, real and legal, that they should be able to know what they can do under the law, what is forbidden, where they must tread circumspectly, where they run risks. * * *

Judgment

By application lodged at the Court Registry on 4 October 1979 Australian Mining & Smelting Europe Limited (hereinafter referred to as 'AM & S Europe') which is based in the United Kingdom, instituted proceedings pursuant to the second paragraph of Article 173 of the EEC Treaty to have Article 1 (b) of an individual decision notified to it, namely Commission Decision 79/760/EEC of 6 July 1979 declared void. That provision required the applicant to produce for examination by officers of the Commission charged with carrying out an investigation of all the documents for which legal privilege was claimed, as listed in the appendix to AM & S Europe's letter of 26 March 1979 to the Commission.

The application is based on the submission that in all the member-States written communications between lawyer and client are protected by virtue of a principle common to all those States, although the scope of that protection and the means of securing it vary from one country to another. According to the applicant, it follows from that principle which, in its view, also applies 'within possible limits' in Community law, that the Commission may not when undertaking an investigation pursuant to Article 14 (3) of Council Regulation 17 of 6 February 1962, claim production, at least in their entirety, of written communications between lawyer and client if the undertaking claims protection and takes 'reasonable steps to satisfy the Commission that the protection is properly claimed' on the ground that the documents in question are in fact covered by legal privilege. * * *

The contested decision, based on the principle that it is for the Commission to determine whether a given document should be used or not, requires AM & S Europe to allow the Commission's authorised inspectors to examine the documents in question in their entirety. Claiming that those documents satisfy the conditions for legal protection as described above, the applicant has requested the Court to declare Article 1 (b) of the above-mentioned decision void, or, alternatively, to declare it void in so far as it requires the disclosures to the Commission's inspector of the whole of each of the documents for which the applicant claims protection on the grounds of legal confidence. * * *

(a) *The interpretation of Article 14 of Regulation 17*

The purpose of Council Regulation 17 which was adopted pursuant to the first subparagraph of Article 87 (1) of the Treaty, is, according to paragraph (2)(a) and (b) of that Article, 'to ensure compliance with the prohibitions laid down in Article 85 (1) and in Article 86' of the Treaty and 'to lay down detailed rules for the application of Article 85 (3).' The regulation is thus intended to ensure that the aim stated in Article 3 (f) of the Treaty is achieved. To that end it confers on the Commission wide powers of investigation and of obtaining information by providing in the eighth recital in its preamble that the Commission must be empowered, throughout the Common Market, to require such information to be supplied and to undertake such investigations 'as are necessary' to bring to light infringements of Articles 85 and 86 of the Treaty.

In Articles 11 and 14 of the regulation, therefore, it is provided that the Commission may obtain 'information' and undertake the 'necessary' investigations, for the purpose of proceedings in respect of infringements of the rules governing competition. Article 14 (1) in particular empowers the Commission to require production of business records, that is to say, documents concerning the market activities of the undertaking, in particular as regards compliance with those rules. Written communications between lawyer and client fall, in so far as they have a bearing on such activities, within the category of documents referred to in Articles 11 and 14.

Furthermore, since the documents which the Commission may demand are, as Article 14 (1) confirms, those whose disclosure it considers 'necessary' in order that it may bring to light an infringement of the Treaty rules on competition, it is in principle for the Commission itself, and not the undertaking concerned or a third party, whether an expert or an arbitrator, to decide whether or not a document must be produced to it.

(b) *Applicability of the protection of confidentiality in Community law*

However, the above rules do not exclude the possibility of recognising, subject to certain conditions, that certain business records are of a confidential nature. Community law, which derives from not only the economic but also the legal interpenetration of the member–States, must take into account the principles and concepts common to the laws of those States concerning the observance of confidentiality, in particular, as regards certain communications between lawyer and client. That confidentiality serves the requirement, the importance of which is recognised in all of the member–States, that any person must be able, without constraint, to consult a lawyer whose profession entails the giving of independent legal advice to all those in need of it.

As far as the protection of written communications between lawyer and client is concerned, it is apparent from the legal systems of the member–States that, although the principle of such protection is generally recognised, its scope and the criteria for applying it vary, as has, indeed, been conceded both by the applicant and by the parties who have intervened in support of its conclusions.

Whilst in some of the member–States the protection against disclosure afforded to written communications between lawyer and client is based principally on a recognition of the very nature of the legal profession, inasmuch as it contributes towards the maintenance of the rule of law, in other member–States the same protection is justified by the more specific requirement (which, moreover, is also recognised in the first-mentioned States) that the rights of the defence must be respected.

Apart from these differences, however, there are to be found in the national laws of the member–States common criteria inasmuch as those laws protect, in similar circumstances, the confidentiality of written communications between lawyer and client provided that, on the one hand, such communications are made for the purposes and in the interests of the client's rights of defence and, on the other hand, they emanate from independent lawyers, that is to say, lawyers who are not bound to the client by relationship of employment.

Viewed in that context Regulation 17 must be interpreted as protecting, in its turn, the confidentiality of written communications between lawyer and client subject to those two conditions, and thus incorporating such elements of that protection as are common to the laws of the member–States. * * *

In view of all these factors it must therefore be concluded that although Regulation 17, and in particular Article 14 thereof, interpreted in the light of its wording, structure and aims, and having regard to the laws of the member–States, empowers the Commission to require, in course of an investigation within the meaning of that Article, production of the business documents the disclosure of which it considers necessary, including written communications between lawyer and client, for proceedings in respect of any infringements of Articles 85 and 86 of the Treaty, that power is, however, subject to a restriction imposed by the need to protect confidentiality, on the conditions defined above, and provided that the communications in question are exchanged between an independent lawyer, that is to say one who is not bound to his client by a relationship of employment, and his client. * * *

(d) *The confidential nature of the documents at issue*

It is apparent from the documents which the applicant lodged at the Court on 9 March 1981 that almost all the communications which they include were made or are connected with legal opinions which were given towards the end of 1972 and during the first half of 1973.

It appears that the communications in question were drawn up during the period preceding, and immediately following, the accession of the United Kingdom to the Community, and that they are principally concerned with how far it might be possible to avoid conflict between the applicant and the Community authorities on the applicant's position, in particular with regard to the Community provisions on competition. In spite of the time which elapsed between the said communications and the initiation of a procedure, those circumstances are sufficient to justify considering the communications as falling within the context of the rights of the defence and the lawyer's specific duties in that connection. They must therefore be protected from disclosure.

In view of that relationship and in the light of the foregoing considerations the written communications at issue must accordingly be considered, in so far as they emanate from an independent lawyer entitled to practise his profession in a member–State, as confidential and on that ground beyond the Commission's power of investigation under Article 14 of Regulation 17.

Notes and Questions

1. *EC Competition Law.* The European Community (now the European Union) has a comprehensive system of competition (antitrust) law and procedure. The EC Commission has the power to investigate and to prosecute possible monopolistic and anti-competitive economic activities. In *AM & S*, since the U.K. had just joined the Common Market, what kinds of questions about their on-going activities and EC competition law would a company like AM & S probably have asked their lawyers? How would the answers to these questions have helped the investigations of the Commission?

2. *The Advocate General.* The reading begins with the opinion of Sir Gordon Slynn, one of the EC's Advocates General. The Advocate General is a position unknown to the United States but is somewhat akin to an official *amicus* or friend of the court in U.S. practice. In European Court of Justice cases the opinions of the Advocates General ordinarily are published both because they amplify ECJ opinions and because they have some persuasive value of their own.

3. *Gaps in the Law.* EC competition law is, of course, a form of international law. It is constituted fundamentally by treaty rules like Articles 85–89 of the Treaty of Rome and partly by rules like Council Regulation 17 generated by delegated powers given to the institutions making up the EC, a regional international organization. The legal question in this case is what to do when there is a gap (a *lacuna*) in international law. Here neither the Rome Treaty nor the rules made by the EC institutions say whether there is a right to lawyer-client confidentiality in EC law, and if there is such a right how it is defined. Should international courts like the ECJ be more or less reluctant than municipal courts to fill gaps when formal sources are silent? Should it make a difference that some municipal legal systems (often in the common law tradition) are more willing than others (often in the civil law tradition) to let courts fill gaps in law?

4. *General Principles of Law.* In *AM & S,* the European Court of Justice turns to general principles of law to fill a gap. Does the fact that municipal legal systems use certain similar rules make it plain that states have consented to establishing a rule in international law? What are other consensual arguments justifying the use of general principles to find or develop rules of international law? Non-consensual arguments? Is the Advocate General seeking to avoid the gap problem when he presumes that looking at national laws means "not to import national laws as such into Community law," but to use the search "as a means of discovering an *unwritten* principle of Community Law"? Is this "discovery" really just a justification for a form of judicial discretion and law-making?

5. *The ECJ Judgment.* The ECJ masks any judicial dissent with a single judgment that never discloses the individual votes or opinions of the panel. Does the judgment in *AM & S* show signs of being a compromise? Is it more or less well reasoned than the opinion of the Advocate General? Is it more or less formal, *i.e.*, apparently based on the words of the Treaty of Rome and Council Regulation No. 17? Do the judges adequately explain why communications with independent (out-of-house) counsel are to be protected by privilege but not those with in-house counsel?

6. *"Civilized Nations."* General principles of law are included among the sources of international that the International Court of Justice is permitted to apply. Article 38(1)(c) of the ICJ Statute authorizes the Court to use "the general principles of law recognized by civilized nations." When the clause was originally drafted for the Permanent Court of International Justice in 1920, the term "civilized nations" was meant to exclude most non-European nations; nowadays the term has been rejected by commentators and judges alike. See Gerrit W. Gong, *The Standard of "Civilization" in International Society* (1984).

7. *The Comparative Law Search.* Of course, *AM & S* is a case before the European Court of Justice, not the ICJ, and accordingly the ECJ need only compare the domestic practices of the nine states then members of the European Community. The basic theory behind general principles of law is that some legal principles are so general or fundamental that they are to be found in all or nearly all legal systems. In *AM & S* the presumption is that if rules protecting lawyer-client communication can be found in every municipal legal system within the European Community, then such rules are to be presumed to be included within the body of EC law. In a case before the ICJ, should that Court be obliged to look to the municipal legal systems of all of its nearly 200 member states to discern a general principle?

8. *The Problem of In-house and Foreign Lawyers.* Notice that the search for common legal rules in *AM & S* was conducted on the assumption that only the minimum content of rules found in all relevant European municipal legal systems would be presumed to exist in EC law. This "lowest common denominator" approach thus excluded communications with certain kinds of lawyers. Most notably, the *AM & S* decision refused to protect the communications of both in-house counsel and foreign lawyers not accredited by an EC member nation. For the difficulties that this has caused, see Joseph P. Griffin, Book Review, 79 *American Journal of International Law* 834 (1985)(reviewing C.S. Kerse, *EEC Antitrust Procedure, Supplement 1984*).

C. NATURAL LAW AND *JUS COGENS*

ALFRED VON VERDROSS, "FORBIDDEN TREATIES IN INTERNATIONAL LAW"

31 *American Journal of International Law* 571 (1937).

I. The Principle

James Wilford Garner has given us a profound, detailed and highly valuable Report on The Law of Treaties. This report contains, it is true, a rule concerning the validity of a treaty which is in conflict with an earlier treaty. On the other hand, there is no consideration, as far as this writer can see, of treaties which are in conflict with general international law, a problem which has been discussed many times.

But as there is no settled opinion on this problem, it is necessary, in this writer's view, to unroll this problem once more. Our starting-point is the uncontested rule that, as a matter of principle, states are free to conclude treaties on any subject whatsoever. All we have to investigate, therefore, is whether this rule does or does not admit certain exceptions. The answer to this question depends on the preliminary question, whether general international law contains rules which have the character of *jus cogens*. For it is obvious that if general international law consists *exclusively* of noncompulsory norms, states are always free to agree on treaty norms which deviate from general international law, without by doing so, violating general international law. If, on the other hand, general international law does contain also norms which have the character of *jus cogens*, things are very different. For it is the quintessence of norms of this character that they prescribe a certain, positive or negative behavior unconditionally; norms of this character, therefore, cannot be derogated from by the will of the contracting parties.

The existence of such norms in general international law is particularly contested by those authors who base the whole international law on the agreement of the *wills* of the states; consequently, they know no other international law but treaty law. But they overlook the fact that each treaty presupposes a number of norms necessary for the very coming into existence of an international treaty. These are the norms determining which persons are endowed with the capacity to act in international law, what intrinsic and extrinsic conditions must be fulfilled that an international treaty may come into existence, what juridical consequences are attached to the conclusion of an international treaty. These principles concerning the conditions of the validity of treaties cannot be regarded as having been agreed upon by treaty; they must be regarded as valid independently of the will of the contracting parties. That is the reason why the *possibility* of norms of general international law, norms determining the limits of the freedom of the parties to conclude treaties, cannot be denied *a priori*.

But this reasoning does not decide the problem whether such compulsory norms concerning the contents of international treaties do exist in fact. A careful investigation, however, reveals the existence of such norms. Two groups of these norms can be distinguished. The first group consists of different, single, compulsory norms of customary international law. General international law requires states, for instance, not to disturb each other in the use of the high seas. An international treaty between two or among more states tending to exclude other states from the use of the high seas, would be in contradiction to a compulsory principle of general international law. International law authorizes states to occupy and to annex *terra nullius*. In consequence, an international treaty by which two states would bind themselves to prevent other states from making such acquisitions of territory would be violative of general international law. In the same way, a treaty binding the contracting parties to prevent third states from the exercise of other rights of sovereignty acknowledged by general international law, such as passage through the territorial waters of other states, would be in contradiction to international law.

But apart from these and other positive norms of general international law, there is a second group which constitutes *jus cogens*. This second group consists of the general principle prohibiting states from concluding treaties *contra bonos mores*. This prohibition, common to the juridical orders of all civilized states, is the consequence of the fact that every juridical order regulates the rational and moral coexistence of the members of a community. No juridical order can, therefore, admit treaties between juridical subjects, which are obviously in contradiction to the ethics of a certain community.

This principle is valid also in international law because the general principles of law recognized by civilized nations are also binding between the states, as the history of international arbitration as well as Article 38, point 3, of the Statute of the Permanent Court of International Justice incontestably prove. It may even be said that no other principle of law is so universally recognized as this one. It follows that its validity in international law is free from doubt as soon as it is admitted that the general principles of law recognized by civilized nations are valid in international law.

It could be objected against this argument, it is true, that the general principles of law have only a subsidiary validity in international law and are, therefore, only applicable if there are no contradictory customary or treaty norms. On the strength of this reasoning, Balladore Pallieri, *e.g.*, is of the opinion that there can be no conflict between the general principles of law and the other sources of international law. For the general principles of law cannot be resorted to if there are customary or treaty norms on this subject. But this argument does not take into consideration that the principle of merely subsidiary validity of the general principles of law cannot be true without exception. It is only reasonable as far as it applies to noncompulsory norms. But a compulsory norm cannot be derogated either by customary or by treaty law; if that were not so, compulsory norms could never be applied in international law. In this case the most essential and indispensable principles of law would be excluded from the realm of international law, a situation which necessarily leads to absurd results. A treaty norm, violative of a compulsory general principle of law, is, therefore, void; on the other hand, a general norm of customary international law in contradiction to a general principle of law cannot even come into existence because customary law must be formed by constant custom based on a general juridical conviction.

II. The Different Kinds of International Treaties *Contra Bonos Mores*

The application in international law of the general principle, according to which treaties *contra bonos mores* are void, is not free from difficulties. These difficulties are the consequence of the fact that the ethics of the international community are much less developed than the ethics of national communities; further, the international community embraces different juridical systems, built upon different moral conceptions. But, on the other hand, these difficulties must not be overestimated. For, as we shall show, there are between the subjects of international law far-reaching agreements concerning many single values notwithstanding different basic conceptions.

In order to advance the solution of our problem, it is necessary to see what treaties are regarded as being *contra bonos mores* by the law of civilized nations. To this problem the decisions of the courts of civilized nations give an unequivocal answer. The analysis of these decisions shows that everywhere such treaties are regarded as being *contra bonos mores* which *restrict the liberty of one contracting party in an excessive or unworthy manner or which endanger its most important rights.*

This and similar formulas prove that the law of civilized states starts with the idea which demands the establishment of a juridical order guaranteeing the rational and moral coexistence of the members. It follows that all those norms of treaties which are incompatible with this goal of all positive law—a goal which is implicitly presupposed—must be regarded as void.

This general principle is not disproved by the fact that different states have different conceptions as to the position of the members of the community. There is, *e.g.*, a different conception as to the position of men toward the community under a democratic, fascist or socialistic régime. But everywhere treaties are regarded as immoral which force one contracting party into a situation which is in contradiction to the ethics of the community.

In order to know what international treaties are immoral, we must ask what are the moral tasks states have to accomplish in the international community. In doing so, we must restrict ourselves to find those principles which correspond to the universal ethics of the international community. We must, so to speak, try to find the *ethical minimum* recognized by all the states of the international community, and must leave aside those particular tasks of the state represented only by particular régimes.

Using the utmost prudence, we can say that the following tasks most certainly devolve upon a state recognized by the modern international community: *maintenance of law and order within the state, defense against external attacks, care for the bodily and spiritual welfare of citizens at home, protection of citizens abroad.* A treaty norm, therefore, which prevents a state from fulfilling one of these essential tasks must be regarded as immoral.

On this basis the following international treaties are immoral and, consequently, void:

1. An international treaty binding a state to reduce its police or its organization of courts in such a way that it is no longer able to protect at all or in an adequate manner, the life, the liberty, the honor or the property of men on its territory. Such a treaty would, however, also be violative of positive international law, if the state were prevented from protecting the above-named rights of *aliens*, because international law

obliges states to protect aliens in ways common to civilized nations (principle of the international minimum standard).

2. An international treaty binding a state to reduce its army in such a way as to render it defenseless against external attacks. It is immoral to keep a state as a sovereign community and to forbid it at the same time to defend its existence.

The situation is different if a state is placed under the protectorate of another state, because in this case the defense of the protected state against external attacks is the duty of the protecting state. The same is true if the existence of a state is effectively guaranteed by one or more Powers, because in this case the defense is the duty of the guarantor. But it would be immoral to oblige a state to remain defenseless.

3. An international treaty binding a state to close its hospitals or schools, to extradite or sterilize its women, to kill its children, to close its factories, to leave its fields unploughed, or in other ways to expose its population to distress. * * *

III. The Determination of the Immorality of Treaties

As the conclusion of immoral treaties is forbidden by general international law, no valid obligation can come into existence concerning the immoral contents of a treaty. Therefore, every arbitration tribunal or the Permanent Court, to which a conflict is submitted in which such a treaty is involved, is under a duty to take judicial notice that such treaties are void, even if there be no demand by a party to this effect. This principle follows from the consideration that all organs of international law have to apply international law. They cannot, therefore, order a state to do something forbidden by international law. The statement that the contents of a treaty are immoral has, therefore, no constitutive, but simply a declaratory character; it states that no obligation with such contents has ever come into existence.

In consequence, a formal voidance of immoral contents of treaties is not necessary. The burdened state has the right simply to refuse the fulfillment of such an obligation. If the other party contests the immorality and if agreement cannot be reached by diplomatic means, the conflict has to be submitted to an arbitral or judicial procedure, as it is certainly a legal dispute.

If, however, there is no obligation of this kind between the parties, and if they do not agree to submit the dispute in question to an arbitral or judicial procedure *ad hoc*, the Council of the League of Nations has jurisdiction, provided that both the parties to the dispute are members of the League. If this is not the case, two solutions are possible: either one state submits to the refusal of the other contracting party to fulfill the treaty, or it resorts to self-help in order to enforce its alleged right. In this case another immoral treaty may be made, which again would be void in international law. For never can the immoral contents of a treaty really become law no matter how often it may borrow the external form of the law.

IV. PROPOSALS

In consequence of the above deductions, this writer ventures to propose to amend Professor Garner's report by an Article 22a, to the following effect:

A treaty norm is void if it is either in violation of a compulsory norm of general international law or *contra bonos mores*.

A treaty norm is *contra bonos mores* if a state is prevented by an international treaty from fulfilling the universally recognized tasks of a civilized state.

Such tasks are: the maintenance of the public order, the defense of the state against external attacks, the care for the bodily and spiritual welfare of its citizens at home and the protection of nationals abroad.

If the immorality of a treaty norm is contested, the dispute has to be submitted to the decision of an arbitration tribunal or of the Permanent Court of International Justice.

Notes and Questions

1. *The Challenge to Legal Positivism.* This 1937 article by Vienna's Professor Alfred von Verdross has been singled out as an important step in the development of Article 53 of the Vienna Convention on the Law of the Treaties concerning peremptory norms of international law. E. Jimenez de Arechaga, *El Derecho Internacional Contemporaneo* 79 (1980). Verdross's article is an affirmative answer to the question of whether there may ever be rules of international law not made by state consent. As such, it challenges the notions of legal positivists who read moral and natural law out of municipal and international law, a formalistic position that became increasingly uncomfortable as totalitarian parties captured the machineries of state power in twentieth century Europe. To what extent do beliefs in legal positivism and that states alone are legitimate sources of legal rules depend on an unrealistic expectation that governments will always act responsibly?

2. *Kinds of* Jus Cogens. Verdross's first category of *jus cogens* contains rules drawn from general international law that constrain state behavior. How certain must a rule of general international law be before it can trump a contrary treaty? How many states must agree in a treaty before such a rule can be upset? Compare the formulation in Articles 53 and 66(a) of the Vienna Convention on the Law of Treaties, which are in the Appendix. Two of Verdross's three examples concern the purported illegality of treaty restraints on uses of the oceans. How true might such assertions be today, after recent developments in the law of the sea? See Chapter 9.

Verdross's second category of *jus cogens* contains rules drawn prohibiting treaties *contra bonos mores*, a category he justifies as stemming from the general principles of law recognized by civilized nations. Such norms trump both conventional and customary law. Does it make sense to treat such norms as general principles à la 38(1)(c) of the ICJ Statute? Why not simply accept them as a form of natural or fundamental law? If they are not viewed as natural or fundamental law, how are they different from natural law?

3. *An "Ethical Minimum" to the Law.* Verdross grants that the ethics of democratic, fascist, and socialist regimes are different, but he argues that there is at least an "ethical minimum" to them all. Given the record of World War II, should a *jus cogens* norm need meet even such an "ethical minimum"?

4. *Individuals and* Jus Cogens. Are Verdross's four sorts of immoral treaties too oriented to the protection of weak states and too little directed to the protection of even weaker individuals? Should there be (are there) such fundamental norms of international law? What should they be? How can they be justified as "real" international law?

THE SOUTH WEST AFRICA CASES

Ethiopia v. South Africa; Liberia v. South Africa, 1966 I.C.J. 4, 325, 1966 WL 2.

1. In the present proceedings the two applicant States, the Empire of Ethiopia and the Republic of Liberia (whose cases are identical and will for present purposes be treated as one case), acting in the capacity of States which were members of the former League of Nations, put forward various allegations of contraventions of the League of Nations Mandate for South West Africa, said to have been committed by the respondent State, the Republic of South Africa, as the administering authority.

2. * * * The Court, by its Judgment of 21 December 1962, * * * found that it had "jurisdiction to adjudicate upon the merits of the dispute."

3. In the course of the proceedings on the merits, the Parties put forward various contentions on such matters as whether the Mandate for South West Africa was still in force,—and if so, whether the Mandatory's obligation under Article 6 of the Mandate to furnish annual reports to the Council of the former League of Nations concerning its administration of the mandated territory had become transformed by one means or another into an obligation to furnish such reports to the General Assembly of the United Nations, or had, on the other hand, lapsed entirely;—whether there had been any contravention by the Respondent of the second paragraph of Article 2 of the Mandate which required the Mandatory to "promote to the utmost the material and moral well-being and the social progress of the inhabitants of the territory,"—whether there had been any contravention of Article 4 of the Mandate, prohibiting (except for police and local defence purposes) the "military training of the natives," and forbidding the establishment of military or naval bases, or the erection of fortifications in the territory. The Applicants also alleged that the Respondent had contravened paragraph 1 of Article 7 of the Mandate (which provides that the Mandate can only be modified with the consent of the Council of the League of Nations) by attempting to modify the Mandate without the consent of the General Assembly of the United Nations which, so it was contended, had replaced the Council of the League for this and other purposes. * * *

4. * * * In this connection, there was one matter that appertained to the merits of the case but which had an antecedent character, namely the question of the Applicants' standing in the present phase of the proceedings,—not, that is to say, of their standing before the Court itself, which was the subject of the Court's decision in 1962, but the question, as a matter of the merits of the case, of their legal right or interest regarding the subject-matter of their claim, as set out in their final submission. * * *

10. The mandates system, as is well known, was formally instituted by Article 22 of the Covenant of the League of Nations. As there indicated, there were to be three categories of mandates, designated as 'A', 'B' and 'C' mandates respectively, the Mandate for South West Africa being one of the 'C' category. The differences between these categories lay in the nature and geographical situation of the territories concerned, the state of development of their peoples, and the powers accordingly to be vested in the administering authority, or mandatory, for each territory placed under mandate. But although it was by Article 22 of the League Covenant that the system as such was established, the precise terms of each mandate, covering the rights and obligations of the mandatory, of the League and its organs, and of the individual members of the League, in relation to each mandated territory, were set out in separate instruments of mandate which, with one exception to be noted later, took the form of resolutions of the Council of the League.

11. These instruments, whatever the differences between certain of their terms, had various features in common as regards their structure. For present purposes, their substantive provisions may be regarded as falling into two categories. On the one hand, and of course as the principal element of each instrument, there were the articles defining the mandatory's powers, and its obligations in respect of the inhabitants of the territory and towards the League and its organs. These provisions, relating to the carrying out of the mandates as mandates, will hereinafter be referred to as "conduct of the mandate," or simply "conduct" provisions. On the other hand, there were articles conferring in different degrees, according to the particular mandate or category of mandate, certain rights relative to the mandated territory, directly upon the members of the League as individual States, or in favour of their nationals. Many of these rights were of the same kind as are to be found in certain provisions of ordinary treaties of commerce, establishment and navigation concluded between States. Rights of this kind will hereinafter be referred to as "special interests" rights, embodied in the "special interests" provisions of the mandates. As regards the * * * 'C' mandates * * * they were confined to provisions for freedom for missionaries ("nationals of any State Member of the League of Nations") to "enter into, travel and reside in the territory for the purpose of prosecuting their calling"—(Mandate for South West Africa, Article 5). In the present case, the dispute between the Parties relates exclusively to the former of these two categories of provisions, and not to the latter. * * *

13. In addition to the classes of provisions so far noticed, every instrument of mandate contained a jurisdictional clause which * * * provided for a reference of disputes to the Permanent Court of International Justice and, so the Court found in the first phase of the case, as already mentioned, this reference was now, by virtue of Article 37 of the Court's Statute, to be construed as a reference to the present Court.

14. * * * [T]he question is whether the various mandatories had any direct obligation towards the other members of the League individually, as regards the carrying out of the "conduct" provisions of the mandates. * * *

33. * * * [E]ven as members of the League when that organization still existed, the Applicants did not, in their individual capacity as States, possess any separate self-contained right which they could assert, independently of, or additionally to, the right of the League, in the pursuit of its collective, institutional activity, to require the due performance of the Mandate in discharge of the "sacred trust." This right was vested exclusively in the League, and was exercised through its competent organs. Each member of the League could share in its collective, institutional exercise by the League, through their participation in the work of its organs, and to the extent that these organs themselves were empowered under the mandates system to act. By their right to activate these organs (of which they made full use), they could procure consideration of mandates questions as of other matters within the sphere of action of the League. But no right was reserved to them, individually as States, and independently of their participation in the institutional activities of the League, as component parts of it, to claim in their own name,—still less as agents authorized to represent the League,—the right to invigilate the sacred trust,—to set themselves up as separate custodians of the various mandates. This was the role of the League organs.

34. To put this conclusion in another way, the position was that under the mandates system, and within the general framework of the League system, the various mandatories were responsible for their conduct of the mandates solely to the League—in particular to its Council—and were not additionally and separately responsible to each and every individual State member of the League. If the latter had been given a legal right or interest on an individual "State" basis, this would have meant that each member of the League, independently of the Council or other competent League organ, could have addressed itself directly to every mandatory, for the purpose of calling for explanations or justifications of its administration, and generally to exact from the mandatory the due performance of its mandate, according to the view which that State might individually take as to what was required for the purpose.

35. Clearly no such right existed under the mandates system as contemplated by any of the relevant instruments. It would have involved a position of accountability by the mandatories to each and every

member of the League separately, for otherwise there would have been nothing additional to the normal faculty of participating in the collective work of the League respecting mandates. The existence of such an additional right could not however be reconciled with the way in which the obligation of the mandatories, both under Article 22 of the League Covenant, and (in the case of South West Africa) Article 6 of the instrument of Mandate, was limited to reporting to the League Council, and to its satisfaction alone. * * *

43. * * * [I]t has been pointed out that there is nothing unprecedented in a situation in which the supervision of a certain matter is, on the political plane, entrusted to a given body or organ, but where certain individual States—not all of them necessarily actual parties to the instruments concerned—have parallel legal rights in regard to the same matter, which they can assert in specified ways. This is true but irrelevant, since for the present purposes the question is not whether such rights could be, but whether they were in fact conferred. In various instances cited by way of example, not only was the intention to confer the right and its special purpose quite clear,—it was also restricted to a small group of States, members, either permanent or elected, of the supervisory organ concerned. In such a case, the right granted was, in effect, part of the institutional or conventional machinery of control, and its existence could occasion no difficulty or confusion. This type of case * * * is not the same as the present one. * * *

49. The Court must now turn to certain questions of a wider character. Throughout this case it has been suggested, directly or indirectly, that humanitarian considerations are sufficient in themselves to generate legal rights and obligations, and that the Court can and should proceed accordingly. The Court does not think so. It is a court of law, and can take account of moral principles only in so far as these are given a sufficient expression in legal form. Law exists, it is said, to serve a social need; but precisely for that reason it can do so only through and within the limits of its own discipline. Otherwise, it is not a legal service that would be rendered. * * *

51. * * * [T]he Court must examine what is perhaps the most important contention of a general character that has been advanced in connection with this aspect of the case, namely the contention by which it is sought to derive a legal right or interest in the conduct of the mandate from the simple existence, or principle, of the "sacred trust." The sacred trust, it is said, is a "sacred trust of civilization." Hence all civilized nations have an interest in seeing that it is carried out. An interest, no doubt;—but in order that this interest may take on a specifically legal character, the sacred trust itself must be or become something more than a moral or humanitarian ideal. In order to generate legal rights and obligations, it must be given juridical expression and be clothed in legal form. One such form might be the United Nations trusteeship system,—another, as contained in Chapter XI of the Charter concerning non-self-governing territories, which makes express reference to "a sacred trust." In each case the legal rights and obli-

gations are those, and only those, provided for by the relevant texts, whatever these may be. * * *

60. It is * * * contended that, even if the Judgment of 1962 was * * * not preclusive of the issue of the Applicants' legal right or interest, it did in essence determine that issue because it decided that the Applicants were entitled to invoke the jurisdictional clause of the Mandate, and that if they had a sufficient interest to do that, they must also have a sufficient interest in the subject-matter of the claim. This view is not well-founded. The faculty of invoking a jurisdictional clause depends upon what tests or conditions of the right to do so are laid down by the clause itself. To hold that the parties in any given case belong to the category of State specified in the clause,—that the dispute has the specified character,—and that the forum is the one specified,—is not the same thing as finding the existence of a legal right or interest relative to the merits of the claim. The jurisdictional clause of the Mandate for South West Africa (Article 7, paragraph 2), which appeared in all mandates, reads as follows:

> "The Mandatory agrees that, if any dispute whatever should arise between the Mandatory and another Member of the League of Nations relating to the interpretation or the application of the provisions of the Mandate, such dispute, if it cannot be settled by negotiation, shall be submitted to the Permanent Court of International Justice provided for by Article 14 of the Covenant of the League of Nations." * * *

65. * * * Jurisdictional clauses do not determine whether parties have substantive rights, but only whether, if they have them, they can vindicate them by recourse to a tribunal.

66. Such rights may be derived from participation in an international instrument by a State which has signed and ratified, or has acceded, or has in some other manner become a party to it; and which in consequence, and subject to any exceptions expressly indicated, is entitled to enjoy rights under all the provisions of the instrument concerned. Since the Applicants cannot bring themselves under this head, they must show that the "conduct" provisions of the mandates conferred rights in terms on members of the League as individual States, in the same way that the "special interests" provisions did. It is however contended that there is a third possibility, and that on the basis of the jurisdictional clause alone, the Applicants, as members of the League, were part of the institutional machinery of control relative to the mandates, and that in this capacity they had a right of action of the same kind as, for instance, members of the League Council had under the jurisdictional clauses of the minorities treaties of that period, for the protection of minority rights. On this footing the essence of the contention is that the Applicants do not need to show the existence of any substantive rights outside the jurisdictional clause, and that they had—that all members of the League had—what was in effect a policing function under the mandates and by virtue of the jurisdictional clause.

67. The Court has examined this contention, but does not think that the two cases are in any way comparable. When States intend to create a right of action of this kind they adopt a different method. * * * The intention to confer it must be quite clear; and the Court holds that * * * there was never any intention to confer an invigilatory function of this kind on each and every member of the League. * * *

69. * * * [A]s regards the mandates, the jurisdictional clause was intended to give the individual members of the League the means which might not otherwise be available to them through League channels, of protecting their "special interests" relative to the mandated territories. In the minorities case, the right of action of the members of the Council under the jurisdictional clause was only intended for the protection of minority populations. No other purpose in conferring a right of action on members of the League Council would have been possible in that case. * * *

99. In the light of these various considerations, the Court finds that the Applicants cannot be considered to have established any legal right or interest appertaining to them in the subject-matter of the present claims, and that, accordingly, the Court must decline to give effect to them.

100. For these reasons,

THE COURT

by the President's casting vote—the votes being equally divided,

decides to reject the claims of the Empire of Ethiopia and the Republic of Liberia. * * *

DISSENTING OPINION OF JUDGE JESSUP

Having very great respect for the Court, it is for me a matter of profound regret to find it necessary to record the fact that I consider the Judgment which the Court has just rendered by the casting vote of the President in the *South West Africa* case, completely unfounded in law. In my opinion, the Court is not legally justified in stopping at the threshold of the case, avoiding a decision on the fundamental question whether the policy and practice of apartheid in the mandated territory of South West Africa is compatible with the discharge of the "sacred trust" confided to the Republic of South Africa as Mandatory. * * *

The Court now * * * *on a theory not advanced by the Respondent in its final submissions of 5 November 1965,* decides that the claim must be rejected on the ground that the Applicants have no legal right or interest.

The Applicants have not asked for an award of damages or for any other material amend for the own individual benefit. They have in effect and in part, asked for a declaratory judgment interpreting certain provisions of the Mandate for South West Africa. The Court having decided in 1962 that they had standing *(locus standi)* to bring the action, they are now entitled to a declaratory judgment without any further showing of interest. * * *

My separate opinion in 1962 also called attention to the fact that in more recent times, the same general appreciation of a right to turn to the International Court of Justice for interpretation, application or fulfillment of a treaty having a broad humanitarian interest, is recognized in—

> "the Genocide Convention, which came into force on 12 January 1951 on the deposit of the twentieth ratification. [It] provides in Article IX:
>
> > 'Disputes between the Contracting Parties relating to the interpretation, application or fulfilment of the present Convention, including those relating to the responsibility of a State for genocide or for any of the other acts enumerated in article III, shall be submitted to the International Court of Justice at the request of any of the parties to the dispute.'
>
> As this Court said of the Genocide Convention: 'In such a convention the contracting States do not have any interests of their own; they merely have, one and all, a common interest, namely the accomplishment of those high purposes which are the *raison d'être* of the convention. Consequently, in a convention of this type one cannot speak of individual advantages or disadvantages to States, or of the maintenance of a perfect contractual balance between rights and duties. The high ideals which inspired the Convention provide, by virtue of the common will of the parties, the foundation and measure of all its provisions.' (*I.C.J. Reports 1951,* at p. 23)" * * *

The standing of Applicants in the present cases rests squarely on the right recognized in paragraph 2 of Article 7 of the Mandate for South West Africa, which is a right appertaining to many States. But it must also be recognized that Applicants as African States, do in addition have a special interest in the present and future of the mandated territory of South West Africa and its inhabitants. This special interest is perhaps even greater than that of some maritime State in the right of passage through the Kiel Canal. "Geographical contiguity" is recognized in paragraph 6 of Article 22 of the Covenant of the League as one of the bases for the allocation of the 'C' mandates. It is trite to refer to the shrinkage of territorial space by modern means of transportation and communication, but in a very real sense all African States south of the Sahara are contiguous to each other, and their interrelated interests—geographical and other—cannot be denied. * * *

The Judgment of the Court rests upon the assertion that even though—as the Court decided in 1962—the Applicants had *locus standi* to institute the actions in this case, this does not mean that they have the legal interest which would entitle them to a judgment on the merits. No authority is produced in support of this assertion which suggests a procedure of utter futility. Why should any State institute any proceeding if it lacked standing to have judgment rendered in its favour if it succeeded in establishing its legal or factual contentions on the merits? Why would the Court tolerate a situation in which the parties would be put to great trouble and expense to explore all the details of the merits and only thereafter be told that the Court would pay no heed to all their arguments and evidence because the case was dismissed on a preliminary ground which precluded any investigation of the merits? * * *

Notes and Questions

1. *Standing to Litigate.* Is the International Court's attempt to distinguish its 1962 ruling on standing persuasive? Judge Philip Jessup, whom the United States had nominated to the ICJ, thinks the Court refuses to decide the merits of Ethiopia's and Liberia's claim on grounds—lack of standing—that were decided in their favor in 1962. Was the Court in 1966 reluctant to find that Ethiopia and Liberia had standing because it feared that South Africa would not respect an adverse ruling on the merits? On concerns about the efficacy of the ICJ, see Chapter 5.

2. Jus Cogens *and Obligations* Erga Omnes *in Practice.* Compare the reluctance of the Court to permit Ethiopia and Liberia to protect a "sacred trust" in Southwest Africa with Professor Verdross's insistence on the role of *jus cogens* in international law. The ICJ has moved closer to the positions advanced by Professor Verdross and Judge Jessup. In 1970, in paragraphs 33 and 34 of the *Barcelona Traction Case*, reproduced in Chapter 6, the Court recognized the concept of "obligations *erga omnes*"—"the obligations of a State toward the international community as a whole." The Court cited, as examples, the international legal proscriptions against inter-state aggression, genocide, slavery, and racial discrimination. Does this mean that the ICJ would now allow a state to pursue a judicial action in the common interest with regard to such issues? What would be the implications for the Court if it did so? Note that the content of obligations *erga omnes* has been debated. The International Law Commission, for example, has endorsed both the concept and the list in *Barcelona Traction*. U.N. GAOR, 31st Sess., Supp. No. 10, at 170, U.N. Doc. A/31/10 (1976), art. 19(3), *reprinted in* 2 *Yearbook of the International Law Commission* 73, U.N. Doc. A/CN.4/Ser.A/1976/Add.1 (1976). The Commission added obligations based on the prohibition of colonial domination by force and obligations essential to preserve the human environment, such as those prohibiting massive pollution of the seas or the atmosphere.

How close are the concepts of *jus cogens* and obligations *erga omnes*? Are they both forms of natural law? The ICJ has held that the principles underlying the Genocide Convention are peremptory (*i.e., jus cogens*) norms. Reservations to the Genocide Case, 1951 I.C.J. 15, 1951 WL 3, excerpted in Chapter 2.

3. *Comparing Customary International Law and Fundamental Norms.* It may sometimes be difficult to determine whether an international legal claim is made on the grounds of a violation of customary international law or on the basis of a breach of a fundamental norm. Read Judge Kaufman's opinion in *Filartiga* in Chapter 1 again. Does he make clear whether official torture is prohibited by custom or *jus cogens* (or both)? See the debate in

Mark Janis, Phillippe Sands & Ellen Turpel, "Colloquy: Jus Cogens," 3 *Connecticut Journal of International Law* 359 (1988).

D. EQUITY

THE CAYUGA INDIANS CASE

American and British Claims Arbitration, *Nielsen Reports* 203, 307 (1926).

This is a claim of Great Britain, on behalf of the Cayuga Indians in Canada, against the United States by virtue of certain treaties between the State of New York and the Cayuga Nation in 1789, 1790, and 1795, and the Treaty of 1814 between the United States and Great Britain, known as the Treaty of Ghent.

At the time of the American Revolution, the Cayugas, a tribe of the Six Nations or Iroquois, occupied that part of Central New York lying about Cayuga Lake. During the Revolution, the Cayugas took the side of Great Britain, and as a result their territory was invaded and laid waste by Continental troops. Thereupon the greater part of the tribe removed to Buffalo Creek, and after 1784 a considerable portion removed thence to the Grand River in Canada. By 1790 the majority of the tribe were probably in Canada. In 1789 the State of New York entered into a treaty with the Cayugas who remained at Cayuga Lake, recognized as the Cayuga Nation, whereby the latter ceded the lands formerly occupied by the Tribe to New York and the latter covenanted to pay an annuity of $500 to the nation. In this treaty a reservation at Cayuga Lake was provided for. As there was much dissatisfaction with this treaty on the part of the Indians, who asserted that they were not properly represented, it was confirmed by a subsequent treaty in 1790 and finally by one in 1795, executed by the principal chiefs and warriors both from Buffalo Creek and from the Grand River. By the terms of the latter treaty, in which, as we hold, the covenants of the prior treaties were merged, the State covenanted, among other things, with the "Cayuga Nation" to pay to the said "Cayuga Nation" 1800 dollars a year forever thereafter, at Canandaigua, in Ontario County, the money to be paid to "the Agent of Indian Affairs under the United States for the time being, residing within this State" and, if there was no such agent, then to a person to be appointed by the Governor. Such agent or person appointed by the Governor was to pay the money to the "Cayuga Nation," taking the receipt of the nation and also a receipt on the counterpart of the treaty, left in the possession of the Indians, according to a prescribed form. By this treaty the reservation provided for in the Treaty of 1789 was sold to the State.

There are receipts upon the counterpart of the Treaty of 1795 down to and including 1809, and these receipts and the receipt for 1810, retained by New York, show that the only persons who can be identified among those to whom the money was paid, and the only persons who can be shown to have held prominent positions in the tribe, were then living in Canada. In 1811 an entire change appears. From that time a new set of names, of quite different character, appear on the receipts retained by New York. From that time there are no receipts upon the counterpart. Since that time, it is conceded, no part of the moneys paid under the treaty has come in any way to the Cayugas in Canada, but the whole has been paid to Cayugas in the United States, and since 1829 in accordance with treaties in which the Canadian Cayugas had no part or in accordance with legislation of New York. The claim is: (1) That the Cayugas in Canada, who assert that they have kept up their tribal organization and undoubtedly have included in their number the principal personages of the tribe according to its original organization, are the "Cayuga Nation," covenantees in the Treaty of 1795, and that as such they, or Great Britain on their behalf, should receive the whole amount of the annuity from 1810 to the present. In this connection it is argued that the covenant could only be discharged by payment to those in possession of the counterpart of the treaty and indorsement of a receipt thereon, as in the treaty prescribed. (2) In the alternative, that the Canadian Cayugas, as a part of the posterity of the original nation, and numerically the greater part, have a proportion of the annuity for the future and a proportion of the payments since 1810, to be ascertained by reference to the relative numbers in the United States and in Canada for the time being.

As the occasion of the change that took place in and after 1811 was the division of the tribe at the time of the War of 1812, those in the United States and those in Canada taking the part of the United States and of Great Britain, respectively, Great Britain invokes Article IX of the Treaty of Ghent, by which the United States agreed to restore to the Indians with whom that Government had been a war "all the possessions, rights, and privileges which they may have enjoyed or been entitled to" in 1811 before the war. * * *

It can not be doubted that until the Cayugas permanently divided, all the sachems and warriors, wherever they lived, whether at Cayuga Lake, Buffalo Creek, or the Grand River in Canada, were regarded as entitled to and did share in the money paid on the annuity. Indeed it is reasonably certain that the larger number and the more important of those who signed the Treaty of 1795 were then, or were soon thereafter, permanently established in Canada. It is clear that the greater number and more important of those who signed the annuity receipts from the date of the treaty until 1810 were Canadian Cayugas. We find the person through whom, by the terms of the treaty, the money was to be paid, writing to the Governor of New York in 1797 that the Canadian Cayugas had not received their fair proportion in a previous payment and proposing to make the sum up to them at the next payment. Everything indicates that down to the division the money was regarded as payable to and was paid to and divided among the Cayugas as a people. The claim of the Canadian Cayugas, who are in fact the greater part of that people, is founded in the elementary principle of justice that requires us to look at the substance and not stick in the bark of the legal form.

But there are special circumstances making the equitable claim of the Canadian Cayugas especially strong.

In the first place, the Cayuga Nation had no international status. As has been said, it existed as a legal unit only by New York law. It was a *de facto* unit, but *de jure* was only what Great Britain chose to recognize as to the Cayugas who moved to Canada and what New York recognized as to the Cayugas in New York or in their relations with New York. As to the annuities, therefore, the Cayugas were a unit of New York law, so far as New York law chose to make them one. When the tribe divided, this anomalous and hard situation gave rise to obvious claims according to universally recognized principles of justice.

In the second place, we must bear in mind the dependent legal position of the individual Cayugas. Legally they could do nothing except under the guardianship of some sovereign. They could not determine what should be the nation, nor even whether there should be a nation legally. New York continued to deal with the New York Cayugas as a "nation." Great Britain dealt with the Canadian Cayugas as individuals. The very language of the treaty was in this sense imposed on them. What to them was a covenant with the people of the tribe and its posterity had to be put into legal terms of a covenant with a legal unit that might and did come to be but a fraction of the whole. American Courts have agreed from the beginning in pronouncing the position of the Indians an anomalous one. Miller J., in *United States v. Kagama*, 118 U.S. 375, 381. When a situation legally so anomalous is presented, recourse must be had to generally recognized principles of justice and fair dealing in order to determine the rights of the individuals involved. The same considerations of equity that have repeatedly been invoked by the courts where strict regard to the legal personality of a corporation would lead to inequitable results or to results contrary to legal policy, may be invoked here. In such cases courts have not hesitated to look behind the legal person and consider the human individuals who were the real beneficiaries. Those considerations are even more cogent where we are dealing with Indians in a state of pupilage toward the sovereign with whom they were treating.

There is the more warrant for so doing under the terms of the treaty by virtue of which we are sitting. It provides that decision shall be made in accordance with principles of international law and of equity. Merignhac considers that an arbitral tribunal is justified in reaching a decision on universally recognized principles of justice where the terms of submission are silent as to the grounds of decision and even where the grounds of decision are expressed to be the "principles of international law." He considers, however, that the appropriate formula is that "international law is to be applied with equity." *Traité théorique et pratique de l'arbitrage international*, § 303. It is significant that the present treaty uses the phrase "principles of international law and equity." When used in a general arbitration treaty, this can only mean to provide for the possibility of anomalous cases such as the present.

An examination of the provisions of arbitration treaties shows a recognition that something more than the strict law must be used in the grounds of decision of arbitral tribunals in certain cases; that there are cases in which—like the courts of the land—these tribunals must find the grounds of decision, must find the right and the law, in general considerations of justice, equity, and right dealing guided by legal analogies and by the spirit and received principles of international law. * * *

* * * Our conclusion on this branch of the cause is that, according to general and universally recognized principles of justice and the analogy of the way in which English and American courts, on proper occasions, look behind what in such cases they call "the corporate fiction" in the interests of justice or of the policy of the law (Daimler Company, Ltd., *v.* Continental Tyre and Rubber Company, Ltd. [1916] 2 A.C. 307, 315–316, 338 ff.; 1 Cook (Corporations, 8 ed. § 2)), on the division of the Cayuga Nation the Cayuga Indians permanently settled in Canada became entitled to their proportionate share of the annuity and that such share ought to have been paid to them from 1810 to the present time.

Notes and Questions

1. *The Definition of the "Cayuga Nation."* In the *Cayuga Indians Case* how is the "Cayuga Nation" defined? Are there different definitions of it made in U.S. law, in British law, and in international law? Were the agreements of 1789, 1790, and 1795 between the United States and the Cayuga Nation governed by U.S. or international law? What about the 1814 Treaty of Ghent between the United States and Great Britain?

2. *Individual and Group Rights in International Law.* Notice how the arbitral panel looks behind the "legal person" of the Cayuga Nation so it can protect "human individuals who were the real beneficiaries" of the treaties. How much deference should international law show to other "legal persons"? Is the peculiarity here that the Cayuga Nation was a "nation" but was not a "state" and thus unable to vindicate its own international legal rights? Questions about the relationship of individuals to international law and their international legal rights and obligations vis-à-vis their own and other states are raised in Chapter 6, and questions about the group rights of "peoples" are addressed in Chapter 7.

3. *The Varieties of Equity.* The treaty providing for the resolution of the *Cayuga Indians* dispute explicitly called for the application of "the principles of international law and of equity." Therefore, the arbitral tribunal is not concerned that its use of equity necessarily be within the rules of international law, *i.e.*, that it be equity *intra legem*. The tribunal had a warrant to apply equity at least in place of the law, *i.e.*, equity *praeter legem,* and perhaps even against the law, *i.e.*, equity *contra legem*. Does the *Cayuga Indians* tribunal really venture beyond equity *intra legem*? Can it really be said that the tribunal moved to fill gaps in international law or to reverse international law?

The arbitral tribunal was persuaded that "as a matter of justice" the Canadian Cayugas had a good claim against the United States: "The claim of the Canadian Cayugas, who are in fact the greater part of that people, is founded in the elementary principle of justice that requires us to look at the substance and not stick in the bark of the legal form." Should international law be more or less able than municipal law "to look at the substance" of disputes and "not stick in the bark of the legal form"? On the one hand, formal agreements among sovereign states may deserve special respect. On the other hand, without municipal-type legislative organs, international law may become especially rigid.

THE MEUSE CASE

Judge Hudson's Opinion
1937 P.C.I.J., Ser. A/B, No. 70, at 73.

The Netherlands Government has asked the Court to say that the alimentation of certain canals by the Neerhaeren Lock with water taken from the Meuse elsewhere than at Maestricht is contrary to the Treaty of 1863, and to order that Belgium should discontinue that alimentation. On the other hand, the Belgian Government has asked the Court to say that the alimentation of these canals has not become contrary to the Treaty of 1863 by reason of the fact that lock-water discharged by the *bona fide* operation for the passage of boats of the Neerhaeren Lock, which cannot be treated more unfavourably than the Bosscheveld Lock, is confused with water of the Meuse taken by the *prise d'eau* at Maestricht. In its submissions the Belgian Government does not ask the Court to say that the operation of the Bosscheveld Lock results in an alimentation of the canals which constitutes a violation of the Treaty; but the Belgian Agent contends (Counter–Memorial, p. 17) that if the Court should decide that the functioning of the Belgian lock at Neerhaeren is in opposition to the Treaty of 1863, it ought to admit *a fortiori* that the functioning of the Netherlands lock of Bosscheveld is not more regular (*n'est pas non plus régulier*). A further submission of the Belgian Government, offered alternatively (*trés subsidiairement*), asks the Court to say that by the construction of works contrary to the provisions of the Treaty the Netherlands has lost the right to invoke the Treaty against Belgium.

On this presentation of the case, the Court must consider the functioning of the Bosscheveld Lock in connection with that of the Neerhaeren Lock. The first question is, therefore, whether the two locks are to be placed on the same footing. * * *

It must be concluded that, in law as well as in fact, the Bosscheveld Lock and the Neerhaeren Lock are in the same position. The latter cannot be treated more unfavourably than the former. If the discharge of lock-water into the Zuid–Willemsvaart by one of these locks is in accordance with the Treaty, it is equally so with respect to the other lock; if such discharge is a violation of the Treaty as to one lock, it is a violation also as to the other lock.

The question arises, therefore, whether in this case the Court must pronounce upon the legality or the illegality of the alimentation which results from the operation of either the Neerhaeren Lock or the Bosscheveld Lock. If the operation of both locks were thought to be in conformity with the Treaty of 1863, the submissions of the Netherlands Government as to the Neerhaeren Lock would of course be rejected. It remains to be considered whether that result would be reached if the operation of both locks were thought to be in violation of the Treaty of 1863.

There can be no question here as to the good faith of either Party. Each Party has proceeded on its own view of the Treaty of 1863. Each has taken action which has led to the same result, in fact and in law. If the Court were called upon to give judgment on the action of both of the Parties, it could do so with due regard to the equal positions of the Parties; but here it is asked by one Party to condemn the action taken by the other. Aside from the fact that the moving Party is the one whose action preceded that of the other, that the Bosscheveld Lock was put into service in 1931 and the Neerhaeren Lock only in 1934, is this a case in which affirmative relief should be given by the Court? Or should it be said, in the terms of the alternative Belgian submission, that the Netherlands has in some measure *perdu le droit d'invoquer* the Treaty against Belgium?

What are widely known as principles of equity have long been considered to constitute a part of international law, and as such they have often been applied by international tribunals. Mérignhac, *Traité théorique et pratique de l'Arbitrage international* (1895), p. 295; Ralston, *Law and Procedure of International Tribunals* (new ed., 1926), pp. 53–57. A sharp division between law and equity, such as prevails in the administration of justice in some States, should find no place in international jurisprudence; even in some national legal systems, there has been a strong tendency towards the fusion of law and equity. Some international tribunals are expressly directed by the *compromis* which control them to apply "law and equity." See the Cayuga Indians Case, Nielsen's Report of the United States–British Claims Arbitration (1926), p. 307. Of such a provision, a special tribunal of the Permanent Court of Arbitration said in 1922 that "the majority of international lawyers seem to agree that these words are to be understood to mean general principles of justice as distinguished from any particular systems of jurisprudence." Proceedings of the United States–Norwegian Tribunal (1922), p. 141. Numerous arbitration treaties have been concluded in recent years which apply to differences "which are justiciable in their nature by reason of being susceptible of decision by the application of the principles of law or equity." Whether the reference in an arbitration treaty is to the application of "law and equity" or to justiciability dependent on the possibility of applying "law or equity," it would seem to envisage equity as a part of law.

The Court has not been expressly authorized by its Statute to apply equity as distinguished from law. Nor, indeed, does the Statute expressly direct its application of international law, though as has been said on several occasions the Court is "a tribunal of international law." Series A, No. 7, p. 19; Series A, Nos. 20/21, p. 124. Article 38 of the Statute expressly directs the application of "general principles of law recognized by civilized nations," and in more than one nation principles of equity have an established place in the legal system. The Court's recognition of equity as a part of international law is in no way restricted by the special power conferred upon it "to decide a case *ex æquo et bono*, if the parties agree thereto." * * *

It would seem to be an important principle of equity that where two parties have assumed an identical or a reciprocal obligation, one party which is engaged in a continuing non-performance of that obligation should not be permitted to take advantage of a similar non-performance of that obligation by the other party. The principle finds expression in the so-called maxims of equity which exercised great influence in the creative period of the development of the Anglo–American law. Some of these maxims are, "Equality is equity"; "He who seeks equity must do equity." It is in line with such maxims that "a court of equity refuses relief to a plaintiff whose conduct in regard to the subject-matter of the litigation has been improper." 13 Halsbury's *Laws of England* (2nd ed., 1934), p. 87. A very similar principle was received into Roman Law. The obligations of a vendor and a vendee being concurrent, "neither could compel the other to perform unless he had done, or tendered, his own part." Buckland, *Text Book of Roman Law* (2nd ed., 1932), p. 493. The *exceptio non adimpleti contractus* required a claimant to prove that he had performed or offered to perform his obligation. Girard, *Droit romain* (8th ed., 1929), p. 567; Saleilles, in 6 *Annales de Droit commercial*, (1892), p. 287, and 7 *id.* (1893), pp. 24, 97 and 175. This conception was the basis of Articles 320 and 322 of the German Civil Code, and even where a code is silent on the point Planiol states the general principle that "dans tout rapport synallagmatique, chacune des deux parties ne peut exiger la prestation qui lui est due que si elle-offre elle-même d'exécuter son obligation." Planiol, *Droit civil*, Vol. 2 (6th ed., 1912), p. 320. * * *

One result of applying the principle will be that even if the Court should be of the opinion that the Belgian action with regard to the functioning of the Neerhaeren Lock is contrary to the Treaty of 1863, it should nevertheless refuse in this case to order Belgium to discontinue that action. In equity, the Netherlands is not in a position to have such relief decreed to her. Belgium cannot be ordered to discontinue the operation of the Neerhaeren Lock when the Netherlands is left free to continue the operation of the Bosscheveld Lock.

Notes and Questions

1. *Justifying Hudson's Recourse to Equity.* Unlike the arbitrators in the *Cayuga Indians Case*, Judge Hudson in the *Meuse Case* had no explicit charge from the states involved to apply equity as well as law to the dispute. How then does Hudson justify his use of equity? If the principles of equity

are part of international law, does any kind of equity exist outside international law? Given Hudson's reasoning, is an "international law and equity" authorization à la *Cayuga Indians* simply redundant?

2. *Searching for General Principles.* Hudson notes that equity could be a type of "general principle" which the Court is authorized to apply under Article 38(1)(c) of its Statute. How thorough a search of municipal law does Judge Hudson make in search of his general principle? How does it compare to Advocate General Slynn's search of municipal law in the *AM & S Case*? Is Hudson's search meant to be universal? If so, does it succeed?

3. *The Effect of Applying Equity.* What is the effect of Judge Hudson's application of equity to the facts of the *Meuse Case*? What are the parties supposed to do if they accept Hudson's decision?

4. *Ex Æquo et Bono.* By Article 38(2) of its Statute, the International Court of Justice may decide a case *ex æquo et bono,* but only if the states party to the dispute specifically authorize it to do so. The Court has never been so authorized. What in practice is the difference between applying equitable principles pursuant to Article 38(1)(c) and deciding *ex æquo et bono* pursuant to Article 38(2)?

THE NORTH SEA CONTINENTAL SHELF CASES

Federal Republic of Germany v. Denmark; Federal Republic of Germany v. Netherlands, 1969 I.C.J. 3, 1969 WL 1.

By a letter of 16 February 1967, received in the Registry on 20 February 1967, the Minister for Foreign Affairs of the Netherlands transmitted to the Registrar:

(*a*) an original copy, signed at Bonn on 2 February 1967 for the Governments of Denmark and the Federal Republic of Germany, of a Special Agreement for the submission to the Court of a difference between those two States concerning the delimitation, as between them, of the continental shelf in the North Sea;

(*b*) an original copy, signed at Bonn on 2 February 1967 for the Governments of the Federal Republic of Germany and the Netherlands, of a Special Agreement for the submission to the Court of a difference between those two States concerning the delimitation, as between them, of the continental shelf in the North Sea;

(*c*) an original copy, signed at Bonn on 2 February 1967 for the three Governments aforementioned, of a Protocol relating to certain procedural questions arising from the above-mentioned Special Agreements.

Articles 1 to 3 of the Special Agreement between the Governments of Denmark and the Federal Republic of Germany [and between the Governments of the Netherlands and the Federal Republic of Germany are] as follows:

"ARTICLE 1

(1) The International Court of Justice is requested to decide the following question:

> What principles and rules of international law are applicable to the delimitation as between the Parties of the areas of the continental shelf in the North Sea which appertain to each of them beyond the partial boundary determined by the abovementioned Convention of 9 June 1965?

(2) The Governments of the Kingdom of Denmark and of the Federal Republic of Germany [and of the Netherlands] shall delimit the continental shelf in the North Sea as between their countries by agreement in pursuance of the decision requested from the International Court of Justice. * * *." * * *

3. As described in Article 4 of the North Sea Policing of Fisheries Convention of 6 May 1882, the North Sea, which lies between continental Europe and Great Britain in the east-west direction, is roughly oval in shape and stretches from the straits of Dover northwards to a parallel drawn between a point immediately north of the Shetland Islands and the mouth of the Sogne Fiord in Norway, about 75 kilometres above Bergen, beyond which is the North Atlantic Ocean. In the extreme northwest, it is bounded by a line connecting the Orkney and Shetland island groups; while on its north-eastern side, the line separating it from the entrances to the Baltic Sea lies between Hanstholm at the northwest point of Denmark, and Lindesnes at the southern tip of Norway. Eastward of this line the Skagerrak begins. Thus, the North Sea has to some extent the general look of an enclosed sea without actually being one. Round its shores are situated, on its eastern side and starting from the north, Norway, Denmark, the Federal Republic of Germany, the Netherlands, Belgium and France; while the whole western side is taken up by Great Britain, together with the island groups of the Orkneys and Shetlands. From this it will be seen that the continental shelf of the Federal Republic is situated between those of Denmark and the Netherlands.

4. The waters of the North Sea are shallow, and the whole seabed consists of continental shelf at a depth of less than 200 metres, except for the formation known as the Norwegian Trough, a belt of water 200–650 metres deep, fringing the southern and south-western coasts of Norway to a width averaging about 80–100 kilometres. Much the greater part of this continental shelf has already been the subject of delimitation by a series of agreements concluded between the United Kingdom (which, as stated, lies along the whole western side of it) and certain of the States on the eastern side, namely Norway, Denmark and the Netherlands. These three delimitations were carried out by the drawing of what are known as "median lines" which, for immediate present purposes, may be described as boundaries drawn between the continental shelf areas of "opposite" States, dividing the intervening spaces equally between them. * * *

5. In addition to the partial boundary lines Federal Republic/Denmark and Federal Republic/Netherlands, which * * * were respectively established by the agreements of 9 June 1965 and 1 December 1964, and

which are shown as lines A–B and C–D on Map 3 * * * another line has been drawn in this area, namely that represented by the line E–F on that map. This line, which divides areas respectively claimed (to the north of it) by Denmark, and (to the south of it) by the Netherlands, is the outcome of an agreement between those two countries dated 31 March 1966, reflecting the view taken by them as to what are the correct boundary lines between their respective continental shelf areas and that of the Federal Republic, beyond the partial boundaries A–B and C–D already drawn. These further and unagreed boundaries to seaward, are shown on Map 3 by means of the dotted lines B–E and D–E. They are the lines, the correctness of which in law the Court is in effect, though indirectly, called upon to determine. Also shown on Map 3 are the two pecked lines B–F and D–F, representing approximately the boundaries which the Federal Republic would have wished to obtain in the course of the negotiations that took place between the Federal Republic and the other two Parties prior to the submission of the matter to the Court. The nature of these negotiations must now be described.

6. Under the agreements of December 1964 and June 1965, already mentioned, the partial boundaries represented by the map lines A–B and C–D had, according to the information furnished to the Court by the Parties, been drawn mainly by application of the principle of equidistance, using that term as denoting the abstract concept of equidistance. A line so drawn, known as an "equidistance line," may be described as one which leaves to each of the parties concerned all those portions of the continental shelf that are nearer to a point on its own coast than they are to any point on the coast of the other party. An equidistance line may consist either of a "median" line between "opposite" States, or of a "lateral" line between "adjacent" States. In certain geographical configurations of which the Parties furnished examples, a given equidistance line may partake in varying degree of the nature both of a median and of a lateral line. There exists nevertheless a distinction to be drawn between the two, which will be mentioned in its place.

7. The further negotiations between the Parties for the prolongation of the partial boundaries broke down mainly because Denmark and the Netherlands respectively wished this prolongation also to be effected on the basis of the equidistance principle,—and this would have resulted in the dotted lines B–E and D–E, shown on Map 3; whereas the Federal Republic considered that such an outcome would be inequitable because it would unduly curtail what the Republic believed should be its proper share of continental shelf area, on the basis of proportionality to the length of its North Sea coastline. It will be observed that neither of the lines in question, taken by itself, would produce this effect, but only both of them together—an element regarded by Denmark and the Netherlands as irrelevant to what they viewed as being two separate and self-contained delimitations, each of which should be carried out without reference to the other.

8. The reason for the result that would be produced by the two lines B–E and D–E, taken conjointly, is that in the case of a concave or

recessing coast such as that of the Federal Republic on the North Sea, the effect of the use of the equidistance method is to pull the line of the boundary inwards, in the direction of the concavity. Consequently, where two such lines are drawn at different points on a concave coast, they will, if the curvature is pronounced, inevitably meet at a relatively short distance from the coast, thus causing the continental shelf area they enclose, to take the form approximately of a triangle with its apex to seaward and, as it was put on behalf of the Federal Republic, "cutting off" the coastal State from the further areas of the continental shelf outside of and beyond this triangle. The effect of concavity could of course equally be produced for a country with a straight coastline if the coasts of adjacent countries protruded immediately on either side of it. In contrast to this, the effect of coastal projections, or of convex or outwardly curving coasts such as are, to a moderate extent, those of Denmark and the Netherlands, is to cause boundary lines drawn on an equidistance basis to leave the coast on divergent courses, thus having a widening tendency on the area of continental shelf off that coast. These two distinct effects, which are shown in sketches I–III * * *, are directly attributable to the use of the equidistance method of delimiting continental shelf boundaries off recessing or projecting coasts. It goes without saying that on these types of coasts the equidistance method produces exactly similar effects in the delimitation of the lateral boundaries of the territorial sea of the States concerned. However, owing to the very close proximity of such waters to the coasts concerned, these effects are much less marked and may be very slight,—and there are other aspects involved, which will be considered in their place. It will suffice to mention here that, for instance, a deviation from a line drawn perpendicular to the general direction of the coast, of only 5 kilometres, at a distance of about 5 kilometres from that coast, will grow into one of over 30 at a distance of over 100 kilometres.

9. After the negotiations, separately held between the Federal Republic and the other two Parties respectively, had in each case, for the reasons given in the two preceding paragraphs, failed to result in any agreement about the delimitation of the boundary extending beyond the partial one already agreed, tripartite talks between all the Parties took place in The Hague in February–March 1966, in Bonn in May and again in Copenhagen in August. These also proving fruitless, it was then decided to submit the matter to the Court. * * *

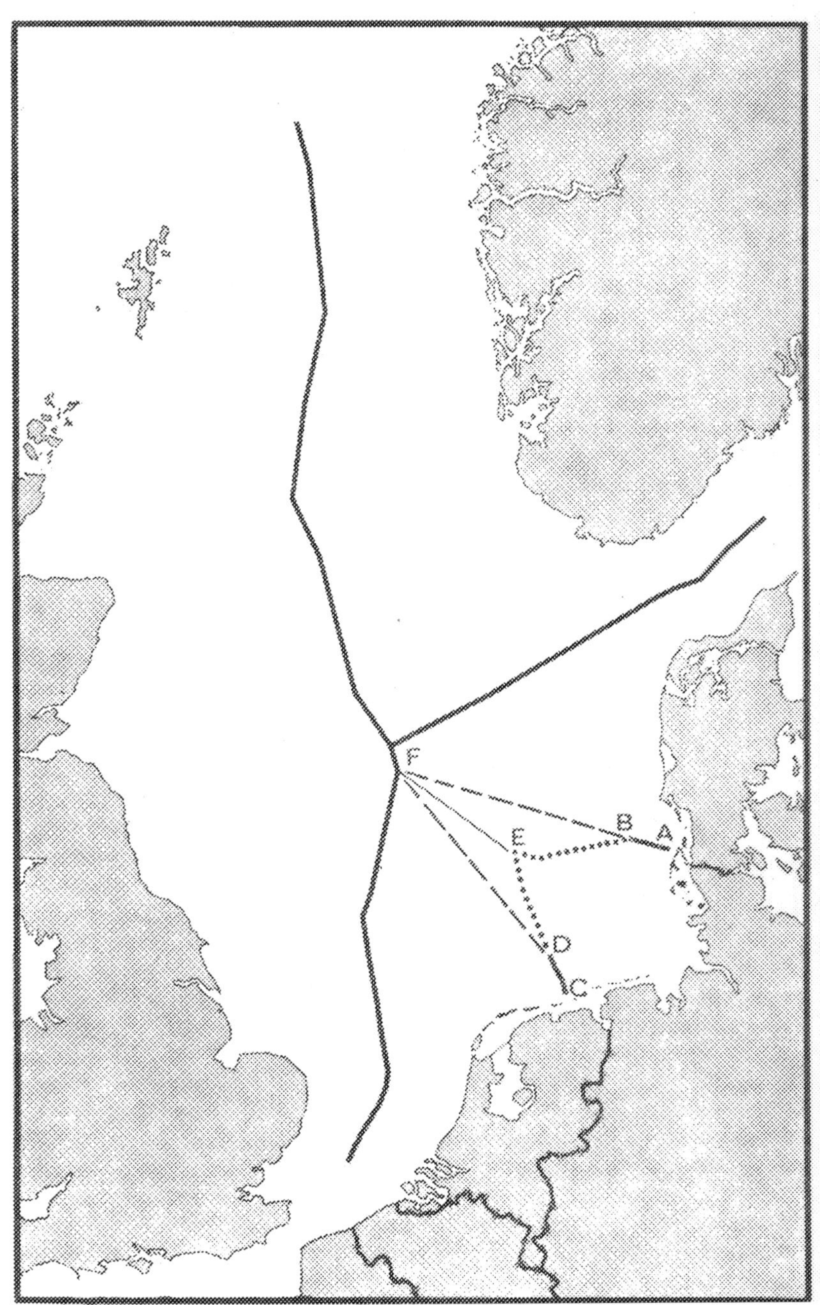

Map 3
(See paragraphs 5-9)

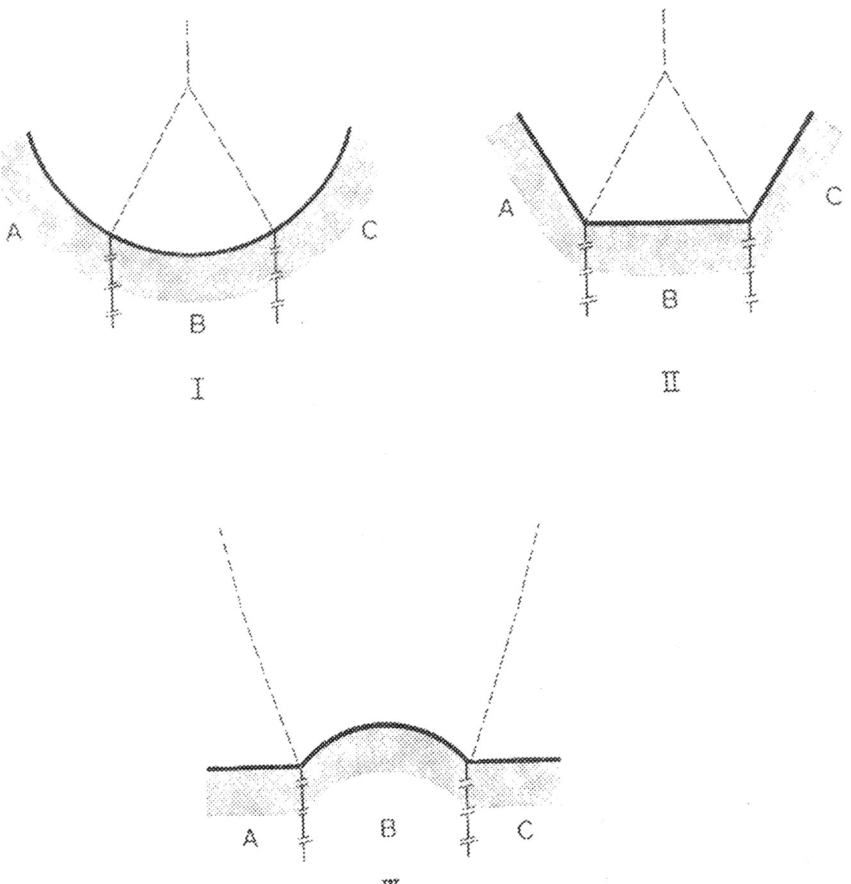

Sketches illustrating the geographical situations described in paragraph 8 of the Judgment

25. The Court now turns to the legal position regarding the equidistance method. The first question to be considered is whether the 1958 Geneva Convention on the Continental Shelf is binding for all the Parties in this case—that is to say whether, as contended by Denmark and the Netherlands, the use of this method is rendered obligatory for the present delimitations by virtue of the delimitations provision (Article 6) of that instrument, according to the conditions laid down in it.

Clearly, if this is so, then the provisions of the Convention will prevail in the relations between the Parties, and would take precedence of any rules having a more general character, or derived from another source. On that basis the Court's reply to the question put to it in the Special Agreements would necessarily be to the effect that as between the Parties the relevant provisions of the Convention represented the applicable rules of law—that is to say constituted the law for the Parties—and its sole remaining task would be to interpret those provisions, in so far as their meaning was disputed or appeared to be uncertain, and to apply them to the particular circumstances involved.

26. The relevant provisions of Article 6 of the Geneva Convention, paragraph 2 of which Denmark and the Netherlands contend not only to be applicable as a conventional rule, but also to represent the accepted rule of general international law on the subject of continental shelf delimitation, as it exists independently of the Convention, read as follows:

> "1. Where the same continental shelf is adjacent to the territories of two or more States whose coasts are opposite each other, the boundary of the continental shelf appertaining to such States shall be determined by agreement between them. In the absence of agreement, and unless another boundary line is justified by special circumstances, the boundary is the median line, every point of which is equidistant from the nearest point of the baselines from which the breadth of the territorial sea of each State is measured.
>
> 2. Where the same continental shelf is adjacent to the territories of two adjacent States, the boundary of the continental shelf shall be determined by agreement between them. In the absence of agreement, and unless another boundary line is justified by special circumstances, the boundary shall be determined by application of the principle of equidistance from the nearest points of the baselines from which the breadth of the territorial sea of each State is measured."

The Convention received 46 signatures and, up-to-date, there have been 39 ratifications or accessions. It came into force on 10 June 1964, having received the 22 ratifications or accessions required for that purpose (Article 11), and was therefore in force at the time when the various delimitations of continental shelf boundaries described earlier (paragraphs 1 and 5) took place between the Parties. But, under the formal provisions of the Convention, it is in force for any individual State only in so far as, having signed it within the time-limit provided for that purpose, that State has also subsequently ratified it; or, not having signed within that time-limit, has subsequently acceded to the

Convention. Denmark and the Netherlands have both signed and ratified the Convention, and are parties to it, the former since 10 June 1964, the latter since 20 March 1966. The Federal Republic was one of the signatories of the Convention, but has never ratified it, and is consequently not a party.

27. It is admitted on behalf of Denmark and the Netherlands that in these circumstances the Convention cannot, as such, be binding on the Federal Republic, in the sense of the Republic being contractually bound by it. But it is contended that the Convention, or the régime of the Convention, and in particular of Article 6, has become binding on the Federal Republic in another way,—namely because, by conduct, by public statements and proclamations, and in other ways, the Republic has unilaterally assumed the obligations of the Convention; or has manifested its acceptance of the conventional régime; or has recognized it as being generally applicable to the delimitation of continental shelf areas. * * *

28. As regards these contentions, it is clear that only a very definite, very consistent course of conduct on the part of a State in the situation of the Federal Republic could justify the Court in upholding them; and, if this had existed—that is to say if there had been a real intention to manifest acceptance or recognition of the applicability of the conventional régime—then it must be asked why it was that the Federal Republic did not take the obvious step of giving expression to this readiness by simply ratifying the Convention. In principle, when a number of States, including the one whose conduct is invoked, and those invoking it, have drawn up a convention specifically providing for a particular method by which the intention to become bound by the régime of the convention is to be manifested—namely by the carrying out of certain prescribed formalities (ratification, accession), it is not lightly to be presumed that a State which has not carried out these formalities, though at all times fully able and entitled to do so, has nevertheless somehow become bound in another way. Indeed if it were a question not of obligation but of rights,—if, that is to say, a State which, though entitled to do so, had not ratified or acceded, attempted to claim rights under the convention, on the basis of a declared willingness to be bound by it, or of conduct evincing acceptance of the conventional régime, it would simply be told that, not having become a party to the convention it could not claim any rights under it until the professed willingness and acceptance had been manifested in the prescribed form.

29. A further point, not in itself conclusive, but to be noted, is that if the Federal Republic had ratified the Geneva Convention, it could have entered—and could, if it ratified now, enter—a reservation to Article 6, by reason of the faculty to do so conferred by Article 12 of the Convention. This faculty would remain, whatever the previous conduct of the Federal Republic might have been—a fact which at least adds to the difficulties involved by the Danish–Netherlands contention.

30. Having regard to these considerations of principle, it appears to the Court that only the existence of a situation of estoppel could suffice to lend substance to this contention,—that is to say if the Federal Republic were now precluded from denying the applicability of the conventional régime, by reason of past conduct, declarations, etc., which not only clearly and consistently evinced acceptance of that régime, but also had caused Denmark or the Netherlands, in reliance on such conduct, detrimentally to change position or suffer some prejudice. Of this there is no evidence whatever in the present case. * * *

37. It is maintained by Denmark and the Netherlands that the Federal Republic, whatever its position may be in relation to the Geneva Convention, considered as such, is in any event bound to accept delimitation on an equidistance-special circumstances basis, because the use of this method is not in the nature of a merely conventional obligation, but is, or must now be regarded as involving, a rule that is part of the *corpus* of general international law;—and, like other rules of general or customary international law, is binding on the Federal Republic automatically and independently of any specific assent, direct or indirect, given by the latter. This contention has both a positive law and a more fundamentalist aspect. As a matter of positive law, it is based on the work done in this field by international legal bodies, on State practice and on the influence attributed to the Geneva Convention itself,—the claim being that these various factors have cumulatively evidenced or been creative of the *opinio juris sive necessitatis*, requisite for the formation of new rules of customary international law. In its fundamentalist aspect, the view put forward derives from what might be called the natural law of the continental shelf, in the sense that the equidistance principle is seen as a necessary expression in the field of delimitation of the accepted doctrine of the exclusive appurtenance of the continental shelf to the nearby coastal State, and therefore as having an *a priori* character of so to speak juristic inevitability.

[The Court first analyzes and rejects the *a priori* argument, concluding:]

55. In the light of this history, and of the record generally, it is clear that at no time was the notion of equidistance as an inherent necessity of continental shelf doctrine entertained. Quite a different outlook was indeed manifested from the start in current legal thinking. It was, and it really remained to the end, governed by two beliefs;—namely, first, that no one single method of delimitation was likely to prove satisfactory in all circumstances, and that delimitation should, therefore, be carried out by agreement (or by reference to arbitration); and secondly, that it should be effected on equitable principles. It was in pursuance of the first of these beliefs that in the draft that emerged as Article 6 of the Geneva Convention, the Commission gave priority to delimitation by agreement,—and in pursuance of the second that it introduced the exception in favour of "special circumstances." Yet the record shows that, even with these mitigations, doubts persisted, partic-

ularly as to whether the equidistance principle would in all cases prove equitable.

56. In these circumstances, it seems to the Court that the inherency contention as now put forward by Denmark and the Netherlands inverts the true order of things in point of time and that, so far from an equidistance rule having been generated by an antecedent principle of proximity inherent in the whole concept of continental shelf appurtenance, the latter is rather a rationalization of the former—an *ex post facto* construct directed to providing a logical juristic basis for a method of delimitation propounded largely for different reasons, cartographical and other. Given also that * * * the theory cannot be said to be endowed with any quality of logical necessity either, the Court is unable to accept it. * * *

60. The conclusions so far reached leave open, and still to be considered, the question whether on some basis other than that of an *a priori* logical necessity, i.e., through positive law processes, the equidistance principle has come to be regarded as a rule of customary international law, so that it would be obligatory for the Federal Republic in that way, even though Article 6 of the Geneva Convention is not, as such, opposable to it. For this purpose it is necessary to examine the status of the principle as it stood when the Convention was drawn up, as it resulted from the effect of the Convention, and in the light of State practice subsequent to the Convention; but it should be clearly understood that in the pronouncements the Court makes on these matters it has in view solely the delimitation provisions (Article 6) of the Convention, not other parts of it, nor the Convention as such.

61. The first of these questions can conveniently be considered in the form suggested on behalf of Denmark and the Netherlands themselves in the course of the oral hearing, when it was stated that they had not in fact contended that the delimitation article (Article 6) of the Convention "embodied already received rules of customary law in the sense that the Convention was merely declaratory of existing rules." Their contention was, rather, that although prior to the Conference, continental shelf law was only in the formative stage, and State practice lacked uniformity, yet "the process of the definition and consolidation of the emerging customary law took place through the work of the International Law Commission, the reaction of governments to that work and the proceedings of the Geneva Conference"; and this emerging customary law became "crystallized in the adoption of the Continental Shelf Convention by the Conference."

62. Whatever validity this contention may have in respect of at least certain parts of the Convention, the Court cannot accept it as regards the delimitation provision (Article 6), the relevant parts of which were adopted almost unchanged from the draft of the International Law Commission that formed the basis of discussion at the Conference. The status of the rule in the Convention therefore depends mainly on the processes that led the Commission to propose it. These processes have

already been reviewed in connection with the Danish–Netherlands contention of an *a priori* necessity for equidistance, and the Court considers this review sufficient for present purposes also, in order to show that the principle of equidistance, as it now figures in Article 6 of the Convention, was proposed by the Commission with considerable hesitation, somewhat on an experimental basis, at most *de lege ferenda*, and not at all *de lege lata* or as an emerging rule of customary international law. This is clearly not the sort of foundation on which Article 6 of the Convention could be said to have reflected or crystallized such a rule.

63. The foregoing conclusion receives significant confirmation from the fact that Article 6 is one of those in respect of which, under the reservations article of the Convention (Article 12) reservations may be made by any State on signing, ratifying or acceding,—for, speaking generally, it is a characteristic of purely conventional rules and obligations that, in regard to them, some faculty of making unilateral reservations may, within certain limits, be admitted;—whereas this cannot be so in the case of general or customary law rules and obligations which, by their very nature, must have equal force for all members of the international community, and cannot therefore be the subject of any right of unilateral exclusion exercisable at will by any one of them in its own favour. Consequently, it is to be expected that when, for whatever reason, rules or obligations of this order are embodied, or are intended to be reflected in certain provisions of a convention, such provisions will figure amongst those in respect of which a right of unilateral reservation is not conferred, or is excluded. This expectation is, in principle, fulfilled by Article 12 of the Geneva Continental Shelf Convention, which permits reservations to be made to all the articles of the Convention "other than to Articles 1 to 3 inclusive"—these three Articles being the ones which, it is clear, were then regarded as reflecting, or as crystallizing, received or at least emergent rules of customary international law relative to the continental shelf, amongst them the question of the seaward extent of the shelf; the juridical character of the coastal State's entitlement; the nature of the rights exercisable; the kind of natural resources to which these relate; and the preservation intact of the legal status as high seas of the waters over the shelf, and the legal status of the superjacent air-space.

64. The normal inference would therefore be that any articles that do not figure among those excluded from the faculty of reservation under Article 12, were not regarded as declaratory of previously existing or emergent rules of law; and this is the inference the Court in fact draws in respect of Article 6 (delimitation), having regard also to the attitude of the International Law Commission to this provision, as already described in general terms. Naturally this would not of itself prevent this provision from eventually passing into the general *corpus* of customary international law by one of the processes considered in paragraphs 70–81 below. But that is not here the issue. What is now under consideration is whether it originally figured in the Convention as such a rule. * * *

69. In the light of these various considerations, the Court reaches the conclusion that the Geneva Convention did not embody or crystallize any pre-existing or emergent rule of customary law, according to which the delimitation of continental shelf areas between adjacent States must, unless the Parties otherwise agree, be carried out on a equidistance-special circumstances basis. A rule was of course embodied in Article 6 of the Convention, but as a purely conventional rule. Whether it has since acquired a broader basis remains to be seen: *qua* conventional rule however, as has already been concluded, it is not opposable to the Federal Republic.

70. The Court must now proceed to the last stage in the argument put forward on behalf of Denmark and the Netherlands. This is to the effect that even if there was at the date of the Geneva Convention no rule of customary international law in favour of the equidistance principle, and no such rule was crystallized in Article 6 of the Convention, nevertheless such a rule has come into being since the Convention, partly because of its own impact, partly on the basis of subsequent State practice,—and that this rule, being now a rule of customary international law binding on all States, including therefore the Federal Republic, should be declared applicable to the delimitation of the boundaries between the Parties' respective continental shelf areas in the North Sea.

71. In so far as this contention is based on the view that Article 6 of the Convention has had the influence, and has produced the effect, described, it clearly involves treating that Article as a norm-creating provision which has constituted the foundation of, or has generated a rule which, while only conventional or contractual in its origin, has since passed into the general *corpus* of international law, and is now accepted as such by the *opinio juris*, so as to have become binding even for countries which have never, and do not, become parties to the Convention. There is no doubt that this process is a perfectly possible one and does from time to time occur: it constitutes indeed one of the recognized methods by which new rules of customary international law may be formed. At the same time this result is not lightly to be regarded as having been attained. * * *

75. The Court must now consider whether State practice in the matter of continental shelf delimitation has, subsequent to the Geneva Convention, been of such a kind as to satisfy this requirement. Leaving aside cases which, for various reasons, the Court does not consider to be reliable guides as precedents, such as delimitations effected between the present Parties themselves, or not relating to international boundaries, some 15 cases have been cited in the course of the present proceedings, occurring mostly since the signature of the 1958 Geneva Convention, in which continental shelf boundaries have been delimited according to the equidistance principle—in the majority of the cases by agreement, in a few others unilaterally—or else the delimitation was foreshadowed but has not yet been carried out. Amongst these 15 are the four North Sea delimitations United Kingdom/Norway–Denmark–Netherlands, and Norway/Denmark already mentioned in paragraph 4 of this Judgment. But

even if these various cases constituted more than a very small proportion of those potentially calling for delimitation in the world as a whole, the Court would not think it necessary to enumerate or evaluate them separately, since there are, *a priori*, several grounds which deprive them of weight as precedents in the present context.

76. To begin with, over half the States concerned, whether acting unilaterally or conjointly, were or shortly became parties to the Geneva Convention, and were therefore presumably, so far as they were concerned, acting actually or potentially in the application of the Convention. From their action no inference could legitimately be drawn as to the existence of a rule of customary international law in favour of the equidistance principle. As regards those States, on the other hand, which were not, and have not become parties to the Convention, the basis of their action can only be problematical and must remain entirely speculative. Clearly, they were not applying the Convention. But from that no inference could justifiably be drawn that they believed themselves to be applying a mandatory rule of customary international law. There is not a shred of evidence that they did and * * * there is no lack of other reasons for using the equidistance method, so that acting, or agreeing to act in a certain way, does not of itself demonstrate anything of a juridical nature. * * *

81. The Court accordingly concludes that if the Geneva Convention was not in its origins or inception declaratory of a mandatory rule of customary international law enjoining the use of the equidistance principle for the delimitation of continental shelf areas between adjacent States, neither has its subsequent effect been constitutive of such a rule; and that State practice up-to-date has equally been insufficient for the purpose. * * *

83. The legal situation therefore is that the Parties are under no obligation to apply either the 1958 Convention, which is not opposable to the Federal Republic, or the equidistance method as a mandatory rule of customary law, which it is not. But as between States faced with an issue concerning the lateral delimitation of adjacent continental shelves, there are still rules and principles of law to be applied; and in the present case it is not the fact either that rules are lacking, or that the situation is one for the unfettered appreciation of the Parties. Equally, it is not the case that if the equidistance principle is not a rule of law, there has to be as an alternative some other single equivalent rule.

84. As already indicated, the Court is not called upon itself to delimit the areas of continental shelf appertaining respectively to each Party, and in consequence is not bound to prescribe the methods to be employed for the purposes of such a delimitation. The Court has to indicate to the Parties the principles and rules of law in the light of which the methods for eventually effecting the delimitation will have to be chosen. The Court will discharge this task in such a way as to provide the Parties with the requisite directions, without substituting itself for them by means of a detailed indication of the methods to be

followed and the factors to be taken into account for the purposes of a delimitation the carrying out of which the Parties have expressly reserved to themselves.

85. It emerges from the history of the development of the legal régime of the continental shelf, which has been reviewed earlier, that the essential reason why the equidistance method is not to be regarded as a rule of law is that, if it were to be compulsorily applied in all situations, this would not be consonant with certain basic legal notions which, as has been observed in paragraphs 48 and 55, have from the beginning reflected the *opinio juris* in the matter of delimitation; those principles being that delimitation must be the object of agreement between the States concerned, and that such agreement must be arrived at in accordance with equitable principles. On a foundation of very general precepts of justice and good faith, actual rules of law are here involved which govern the delimitation of adjacent continental shelves—that is to say, rules binding upon State for all delimitations;—in short, it is not a question of applying equity simply as a matter of abstract justice, but of applying a rule of law which itself requires the application of equitable principles, in accordance with the ideas which have always underlain the development of the legal régime of the continental shelf in this field, namely:

(*a*) the parties are under an obligation to enter into negotiations with a view to arriving at an agreement, and not merely to go through a formal process of negotiation as a sort of prior condition for the automatic application of a certain method of delimitation in the absence of agreement; they are under an obligation so to conduct themselves that the negotiations are meaningful, which will not be the case when either of them insists upon its own position without contemplating any modification of it;

(*b*) the parties are under an obligation to act in such a way that, in the particular case, and taking all the circumstances into account, equitable principles are applied,—for this purpose the equidistance method can be used, but other methods exist and may be employed, alone or in combination, according to the areas involved;

(*c*) * * * the continental shelf of any State must be the natural prolongation of its land territory and must not encroach upon what is the natural prolongation of the territory of another State. * * *

88. The Court comes next to the rule of equity. The legal basis of that rule in the particular case of the delimitation of the continental shelf as between adjoining States has already been stated. It must however be noted that the rule rests also on a broader basis. Whatever the legal reasoning of a court of justice, its decisions must by definition be just, and therefore in that sense equitable. Nevertheless, when mention is made of a court dispensing justice or declaring the law, what is meant is that the decision finds its objective justification in considerations lying not outside but within the rules, and in this field it is precisely a rule of law that calls for the application of equitable princi-

ples. There is consequently no question in this case of any decision *ex aequo et bono*, such as would only be possible under the conditions prescribed by Article 38, paragraph 2, of the Court's Statute. * * *

89. It must next be observed that, in certain geographical circumstances which are quite frequently met with, the equidistance method, despite its known advantages, leads unquestionably to inequity, in the following sense:

(*a*) The slightest irregularity in a coastline is automatically magnified by the equidistance line as regards the consequences for the delimitation of the continental shelf. Thus it has been seen in the case of concave or convex coastlines that if the equidistance method is employed, then the greater the irregularity and the further from the coastline the area to be delimited, the more unreasonable are the results produced. So great an exaggeration of the consequences of a natural geographical feature must be remedied or compensated for as far as possible, being of itself creative of inequity.

(*b*) In the case of the North Sea in particular, where there is no outer boundary to the continental shelf, it happens that the claims of several States converge, meet and intercross in localities where, despite their distance from the coast, the bed of the sea still unquestionably consists of continental shelf. A study of these convergences, as revealed by the maps, shows how inequitable would be the apparent simplification brought about by a delimitation which, ignoring such geographical circumstances, was based solely on the equidistance method. * * *

91. Equity does not necessarily imply equality. There can never be any question of completely refashioning nature, and equity does not require that a State without access to the sea should be allotted an area of continental shelf, any more than there could be a question of rendering the situation of a State with an extensive coastline similar to that of a State with a restricted coastline. Equality is to be reckoned within the same plane, and it is not such natural inequalities as these that equity could remedy. But in the present case there are three States whose North Sea coastlines are in fact comparable in length and which, therefore, have been given broadly equal treatment by nature except that the configuration of one of the coastlines would, if the equidistance method is used, deny to one of these States treatment equal or comparable to that given the other two. Here indeed is a case where, in a theoretical situation of equality within the same order, an inequity is created. What is unacceptable in this instance is that a State should enjoy continental shelf rights considerably different from those of its neighbours merely because in the one case the coastline is roughly convex in form and in the other it is markedly concave, although those coastlines are comparable in length. It is therefore not a question of totally refashioning geography whatever the facts of the situation but, given a geographical situation of quasi-equality as between a number of

States, of abating the effects of an incidental special feature from which an unjustifiable difference of treatment could result. * * *

101. For these reasons,

THE COURT,

by eleven votes to six,

finds that, in each case,

(A) the use of the equidistance method of delimitation not being obligatory as between the Parties; and

(B) there being no other single method of delimitation the use of which is in all circumstances obligatory;

(C) the principles and rules of international law applicable to the delimitation as between the Parties of the areas of the continental shelf in the North Sea which appertain to each of them beyond the partial boundary determined by the agreements of 1 December 1964 and 9 June 1965, respectively, are as follows:

(1) delimitation is to be effected by agreement in accordance with equitable principles, and taking account of all the relevant circumstances, in such a way as to leave as much as possible to each Party all those parts of the continental shelf that constitute a natural prolongation of its land territory into and under the sea, without encroachment on the natural prolongation of the land territory of the other;

(2) if, in the application of the proceeding sub-paragraph, the delimitation leaves to the Parties areas that overlap, these are to be divided between them in agreed proportions or, failing agreement, equally, unless they decide on a régime of joint jurisdiction, user, or exploitation for the zones of overlap or any part of them;

(D) in the course of the negotiations, the factors to be taken into account are to include:

(1) the general configuration of the coasts of the Parties, as well as the presence of any special or unusual features;

(2) so far as known or readily ascertainable, the physical and geological structure, and natural resources, of the continental shelf areas involved;

(3) the element of a reasonable degree of proportionality, which a delimitation carried out in accordance with equitable principles ought to bring about between the extent of the continental shelf areas appertaining to the coastal State and the length of its coast measured in the general direction of the coastline, account being taken for this purpose of the effects, actual or prospective, of any other continental shelf delimitations between adjacent States in the same region.

Notes and Questions

1. *A Hierarchy of Sources?* The *North Sea* judgment provides an excellent resume of the sources of international law, beginning with treaties, moving to custom, and finishing with general principles of law and equity. Does the ICJ's ordering of the sources reflect a necessary hierarchy of the sources of international law, *i.e.*, do treaties necessarily "trump" custom which in turn "trumps" general principles and equity?

Pay special attention to the Court's detailed analysis of the ways in which customary international law might relate to Article 6(2) of the 1958 Continental Shelf Convention. The three-step process goes: the Convention might (1) "embody" or codify the custom, (2) "crystallize" the custom, or (3) contribute to the subsequent development of the custom. Is the Court's rejection of possibility (3) as persuasive as its rejection of (1) and (2)?

2. *The Gap Problem.* What are the perils if the ICJ simply comes up empty handed in its search for an applicable rule? Is the Court willing to rule that there is no guidance that international law can provide Germany, Denmark, and the Netherlands? Would such a finding of a *lacuna* or gap fulfill the expectations of the three countries when they entrusted the dispute to the Court?

3. *The Recourse to Equity in* North Sea. Compare the source of equitable principles to the source of such principles in *Meuse. North Sea* shows no borrowing from municipal legal systems. Where then does the equitable rule come from? Does it really come from customary international law, as the Court seems to suggest by its reference to *opinio juris* in paragraph 85? Does the Court cite sufficient evidence of state practice?

Note that the ICJ was asked to decide what "principles and rules of international law" were applicable to the delimitation of continental shelf between West Germany and Denmark, and between West Germany and the Netherlands. Could the parties have asked the Court to decide the case *ex æquo et bono* pursuant to Article 38(2) of the ICJ Statute? What extra power would the Court have had in *North Sea* if it had an *ex æquo et bono* authorization?

4. *Article 38(1)(d) of the ICJ Statute.* Once rendered, the *North Sea* judgment becomes part of the corpus of evidence of international law. Can other courts deciding continental shelf cases rely on *North Sea* as a subsidiary source of international law per Article 38(1)(d)? How does a subsequent delimitation case differ then from *North Sea*, especially if the countries affected by the judgment adopt it without protest? Can the ICJ's exercise of discretion be a doubtful exercise yet still provide a sound foundation for subsequent practice?

5. *The Content of Equitable Principles in* North Sea. What principles of equity does the Court use? If it would be inequitable to give comparable coastlines different allotments of continental shelf, why is it equitable to deprive land-locked countries of all continental shelf belonging to their continent? Why is this a better kind of equity than one based on equidistance or on population, economic need, or use?

6. *The Need to Delimit the Continental Shelf.* Note the geographical elements of the problem as sketched in Map 3. Because of the indentation

of the German shore, delimitation by the equidistance method bent the line along the route D–E–B. Germany prefers D–F–B. Why had it not been important to delimit the shelf prior to the 1960's? See Chapter 9 for further discussion of the continental shelf.

7. *The Parties' Choice of Tribunal.* Why did the three states choose to come to the Court? What did they expect the ICJ to contribute to the resolution of the dispute? Why could there have been any hope that the Court might help in ways that diplomatic negotiations had not?

8. *Different Meanings of Equity.* Note the use of equity in the Charter of Economic Rights and Duties of States considered by Professor Dupuy in the *Texaco/Libya Arbitration.* There are at least 12 references to equity in the Charter: "the development of international economic relations on a just and equitable basis," "a new system of international economic relations based on equity, sovereign equality, and interdependence of the interests of developed and developing countries," a "new international economic order, based on equity," "equitable benefits for all peace-loving states," "a just and equitable economic and social order," "more rational and equitable international economic relations," "mutual and equitable benefit" (twice), "remunerative and equitable prices," "equitable development of the world economy," "share equitably," and "stable, equitable and remunerative prices for primary products." What do these references to equity mean? Are the meanings all the same? Compare the use of "equity" in promoting the New International Economic Order with its use in international arbitral and judicial decisions like *Cayuga Indians*, *Meuse*, and *North Sea.*

Chapter 4

INTERNATIONAL LAW AND MUNICIPAL LAW

In most instances, when international legal rules are applied in practice, they are applied by municipal courts. Decisions about whether to incorporate international law into domestic legal process are ordinarily made by municipal legal systems. Those decisions are generally governed by the municipal legal system's own constitutional law.

In this chapter, we look only at the rules governing the incorporation of international law into U.S. law. Such rules about incorporation are easily grouped into those involving treaties and those concerning all other forms of international law, a category traditionally called, in England and America, "the law of nations."

A. TREATIES IN MUNICIPAL LAW

The most important U.S. constitutional law decision concerning the relationship of international law and U.S. municipal law is *Foster & Elam* where Chief Justice Marshall introduces the concept, though not the exact term, of "self-executing treaties." Besides noting how and why Chief Justice Marshall employs the concept of self-executing treaties, pay particular attention to why the litigants and the Court in *Foster & Elam* need to know whether the treaty provision in question can serve as a rule of decision.

FOSTER & ELAM v. NEILSON

27 U.S. (2 Pet.) 253, 7 L.Ed. 415 (1829).

MR. CHIEF JUSTICE MARSHALL delivered the opinion of the Court.

This suit was brought by the plaintiffs in error, in the court of the United States for the eastern district of Louisiana, to recover a tract of land lying in that district, about 30 miles east of the Mississippi, and in the possession of the defendant. The plaintiffs claimed under a grant for 40,000 arpents of land, made by the Spanish governor, on the 2d of January 1804, to Jayme Joydra, and ratified by the king of Spain on the 29th of May 1804. The petition and order of survey are dated in

September 1803, and the return of the survey itself was made on the 27 of October in the same year. The defendant excepted to the petition of the plaintiffs, alleging that it does not show a title on which they can recover; that the territory within which the land claimed is situated, had been ceded, before the grant, to France, and by France to the United States; and that the grant is void, being made by persons who had no authority to make it. The court sustained the exception, and dismissed the petition. The cause is brought before this court by writ of error.

The case presents this very intricate, and, at one time, very interesting question: To whom did the country between the Iberville and the Perdido rightfully belong, when the title now asserted by the plaintiffs was acquired? This question has been repeatedly discussed, with great talent and research, by the government of the United States and that of Spain. The United States have perseveringly and earnestly insisted, that by the treaty of St. Ildefonso, made on the 1st of October, in the year 1800, Spain ceded the disputed territory, as part of Louisiana, to France; and that France, by the treaty of Paris, signed on the 30th of April 1803, and ratified on the 21st of October, in the same year, ceded it to the United States. Spain has, with equal perseverance and earnestness, maintained, that her cession to France comprehended that territory only which was, at that time, denominated Louisiana, consisting of the island of New Orleans, and the country she received from France, west of the Mississippi. * * *

[Marshall introduces and discusses the complicated and disputed negotiations among France, Spain, Great Britain, and the United States over the territory before deciding that the Court does not actually have to answer the question about ownership].

A "treaty of amity, settlement and limits, between the United States of America and the king of Spain," was signed at Washington, on the 22d day of February 1819. By the second article, "his Catholic majesty cedes to the United States, in full property and sovereignty, all the territories which belong to him, situated to the eastward of the Mississippi, known by the name of East and West Florida." The eighth article stipulates, "that all the grants of land made before the 24th of January 1818, by his Catholic majesty, or by his lawful authorities, in the said territories ceded by his majesty to the United States, shall be ratified and confirmed to the persons in possession of the lands, to the same extent that the same grants would be valid, if the territories had remained under the dominion of his Catholic majesty."

The court will not attempt to conceal the difficulty which is created by these articles. * * *

Whatever difference may exist respecting the effect of the ratification, in whatever sense it may be understood, we think, the sound construction of the eighth article will not enable this court to apply its provisions to the present case. The words of the article are, that "all the grants of land, made before the 24 of January 1818, by his Catholic majesty, & c., shall be ratified and confirmed to the persons in possession of the lands, to the same extent that the same grants would be valid, if the territories had remained under the dominion of his Catholic majesty." Do these words act directly on the grants, so as to give validity to those not otherwise valid? Or do they pledge the faith of the United States to pass acts which shall ratify and confirm them?

A treaty is, in its nature, a contract between two nations, not a legislative act. It does not generally effect, of itself, the object to be accomplished; especially, so far as its operation is infra-territorial; but is carried into execution by the sovereign power of the respective parties to the instrument.

In the United States, a different principle is established. Our constitution declares a treaty to be the law of the land. It is, consequently, to be regarded in courts of justice as equivalent to an act of the legislature, whenever it operates of itself, without the aid of any legislative provision. But when the terms of the stipulation import a contract—when either of the parties engages to perform a particular act, the treaty addresses itself to the political, not the judicial department; and the legislature must execute the contract before it can become a rule for the court.

The article under consideration does not declare that all the grants made by his Catholic majesty, before the 24th of January 1818, shall be valid, to the same extent as if the ceded territories had remained under his dominion. It does not say, that those grants are hereby confirmed. Had such been its language, it would have acted directly on the subject, and would have repealed those acts of congress which were repugnant to it; but its language is, that those grants shall be ratified and confirmed to the persons in possession, &c. By whom shall they be ratified and confirmed? This seems to be the language of contract; and if it is, the ratification and confirmation which are promised must be the act of the legislature. Until such act shall be passed, the court is not at liberty to disregard the existing laws on the subject. * * *

Notes and Questions

1. *The Application of International Law in Municipal Courts.* We now move from the legislative problems of international law—how to find and make international legal rules—to the discipline's enforcement problems—who applies the rules of international law and how such decisions are made effective. We begin with municipal courts. The great majority of international law cases that are settled by formal judicial process are decided by municipal not by international courts. For most lawyers practicing international law, domestic law courts are the usual fora foreseen in negotiations and employed in litigation. Here for reasons of space and audience we look only at the municipal practice of the United States. *American International Law Cases* publishes cases in which U.S. state and federal courts have used international law. The first 50 volumes of the third series of *American International Law Cases* contain over 2000 such cases, just from the years 1990–1993.

2. *The Self-executing Treaty Doctrine.* The overwhelming majority of U.S. court cases involving international law concern treaties of which the most important is *Foster & Elam v. Neilson.* Not only does the case establish the proposition of the "self-executing" treaty rule in U.S. law, but it introduces the notion into international law generally, making *Foster & Elam* one of the most significant U.S. contributions to the discipline.

3. *Dualism and Monism.* Note that in *Foster & Elam* Marshall's approach to the nature of international law is fundamentally "dualistic," *i.e.*, he sees international law and municipal law not as parts of an integrated "monistic" legal system but each as a separate and discrete legal system. Accordingly, rules from one system must be specially incorporated into the other in order that they be applied there. Does Marshall justify this presumption? Does his justification depend either on the idea that treaties are contracts between nations or on the deference that Marshall accords the sovereign power of states within their own territory?

4. *Treaties and the Supremacy Clause.* Although Chief Justice Marshall does not find the 1819 Treaty of Amity to be self-executing, he does establish the doctrine of self-executing treaties in U.S. law by relying on Article VI(2) of the Constitution, the Supremacy Clause: "This Constitution, and the laws of the United States which shall be made in Pursuance thereof; and all Treaties made, or which shall be made, under the Authority of the United States, shall be the supreme law of the land; and the Judges in every State shall be bound thereby, any thing in the Constitution or Laws of any State to the contrary notwithstanding." Note that the wording of the Supremacy Clause hints that the Founders' central concern was to bind the judges of the states to uphold the U.S. Constitution, federal laws, and U.S. treaties vis-à-vis state laws and constitutions. *Foster & Elam* involves, but avoids, a potential clash between federal law and a U.S. treaty. For discussion of various uses of the self-executing treaty doctrine in U.S. courts, see Carlos Manuel Vázquez, "The Four Doctrines of Self–Executing Treaties," 89 *American Journal of International Law* 695 (1995).

5. *The Self-executing Nature of the 1819 Treaty of Amity.* That Marshall's approach in *Foster & Elam* is formal, looking at the literal language of the 1819 Treaty of Amity, is confirmed in United States v. Percheman, 32 U.S. (7 Pet.) 51, 8 L.Ed. 604 (1833). In *Percheman*, when Marshall examines the Spanish-language version of the Treaty, he holds that the selfsame Article 8 of the 1819 Treaty is in truth self-executing.

ASAKURA v. CITY OF SEATTLE

265 U.S. 332, 44 S.Ct. 515, 68 L.Ed. 1041 (1924).

MR. JUSTICE BUTLER delivered the opinion of the Court.

Plaintiff in error is a subject of the Emperor of Japan, and, since 1904, has resided in Seattle, Washington. Since July, 1915, he has been engaged in business there as a pawnbroker. The city passed an ordinance, which took effect July 2, 1921, regulating the business of pawnbroker and repealing former ordinances on the same subject. It makes it unlawful for any person to engage in the business unless he shall have a license, and the ordinance provides "that no such license shall be granted unless the applicant be a citizen of the United States." Violations of the ordinance are punishable by fine or imprisonment or both. Plaintiff in error brought this suit in the Superior Court of King County, Washington, against the city, its Comptroller and its Chief of Police to restrain them from enforcing the ordinance against him. He attacked the ordinance on the ground that it violates the treaty between the United States and the Empire of Japan, proclaimed April 5, 1911, 37 Stat. 1504; violates the constitution of the State of Washington, and also the due process and equal protection clauses of the Fourteenth Amendment of the Constitution of the United States. He declared his willingness to comply with any valid ordinance related to the business of pawnbroker. It was shown that he had about $5,000 invested in his business, which would be broken up and destroyed by the enforcement of the ordinance. The Superior Court granted the relief prayed. On appeal, the Supreme Court of the State held the ordinance valid and reversed the decree. The case is here on writ of error under § 237 of the Judicial Code.

Does the ordinance violate the treaty? Plaintiff in error invokes and relies upon the following provisions: "The citizens or subjects of each of the High Contracting Parties shall have liberty to enter, travel and reside in the territories of the other to carry on trade, wholesale and retail, to own or lease and occupy houses, manufactories, warehouses and shops, to employ agents of their choice, to lease land for residential and commercial purposes, and generally to do anything incident to or necessary for trade upon the same terms as native citizens or subjects, submitting themselves to the laws and regulations there established.... The citizens or subjects of each ... shall receive, in the territories of the other, the most constant protection and security for their persons and property...."

A treaty made under the authority of the United States "shall be the supreme law of the land; and the judges in every State shall be bound thereby, any thing in the constitution or laws of any State to the contrary notwithstanding." Constitution, Art. VI, § 2.

The treaty-making power of the United States is not limited by any express provision of the Constitution, and, though it does not extend "so far as to authorize what the Constitution forbids," it does extend to all proper subjects of negotiation between our government and other nations. The treaty was made to strengthen friendly relations between the two nations. As to the things covered by it, the provision quoted establishes the rule of equality between Japanese subjects while in this country and native citizens. Treaties for the protection of citizens of one country residing in the territory of another are numerous, and make for good understanding between nations. The treaty is binding within the State of Washington. The rule of equality established by it cannot be rendered nugatory in any part of the United States by municipal ordinances or state laws. It stands on the same footing of supremacy as do the provisions of the Constitution and laws of the United States. It operates of itself without the aid of any legislation, state or national; and it will be applied and given authoritative effect by the courts.

The purpose of the ordinance complained of is to regulate, not to prohibit, the business of pawnbroker. But it makes it impossible for aliens to carry on the business. It need not be considered whether the State, if it sees fit, may forbid and destroy the business generally. Such a law would apply equally to aliens and citizens, and no question of conflict with the treaty would arise. The grievance here alleged is that plaintiff in error, in violation of the treaty, is denied equal opportunity. * * *

By definition contained in the ordinance, pawnbrokers are regarded as carrying on a "business." A feature of it is the lending of money upon the pledge or pawn of personal property which, in case of default, may be sold to pay the debt. While the amounts of the loans made in that business are relatively small and the character of property pledged as security is different, the transactions are similar to loans made by banks on collateral security. * * * We have found no state legislation abolishing or forbidding the business. Most, if not all, of the States provide for licensing pawnbrokers and authorize regulation by municipalities. While regulation has been found necessary in the public interest, the business is not on that account to be excluded from the trade and commerce referred to in the treaty. Many worthy occupations and lines of legitimate business are regulated by state and federal laws for the protection of the public against fraudulent and dishonest practices. There is nothing in the character of the business of pawnbroker which requires it to be excluded from the field covered by the above quoted provision, and it must be held that such business is "trade" within the meaning of the treaty. The ordinance violates the treaty. The question in the present case relates solely to Japanese subjects who have been admitted to this country. We do not pass upon the right of admission or the construction of the treaty in this respect, as that question is not before us and would require consideration of other matters with which it is not now necessary to deal. We need not consider other grounds upon which the ordinance is attacked.

Decree reversed.

Notes and Questions

1. *Treaties and State Law. Asakura* is an example of a state law being "trumped" by a U.S. treaty rule. The case cites *Foster & Elam* and others for the proposition that a treaty "operates of itself without the aid of any legislation, state or national; and it will be applied and given authoritative effect by the Courts." But does the *Asakura* court analyze the problem of self-execution? Is it plain that the treaty norm applied in *Asakura* is self-executing by the test set out in *Foster & Elam*? What arguments might be made for and against it being self-executing?

2. *The* Asakura Case *and U.S.–Japanese Relations. Asakura* was decided at a time when U.S. politics were increasingly hostile to Japanese immigration to the United States. Despite opposition from Japan and from

the U.S. State Department, the House and Senate overwhelmingly passed legislation in 1924 that barred Japanese nationals from settling in the United States. The anti-Japanese bill passed the House 326–71 and the Senate 62–6. The Japanese Ambassador warned that the bill "would seriously wound the proper susceptibilities of the Japanese nation" and could endanger "the otherwise happy and mutually advantageous relations existing between our two countries." "Immigration Bill Is Passed Intact, Barring Japanese," *New York Times*, Apr. 13, 1924, at 1; "Immigration Bill Passes the Senate by Vote of 62 to 6," *New York Times*, Apr. 19, 1924, at 1. U.S.-Japanese relations of course did not improve over the next few decades. Another case involving anti-Japanese acts, *Sei Fujii*, decided after the Second World War, follows.

SEI FUJII v. CALIFORNIA

38 Cal.2d 718, 242 P.2d 617 (1952).

GIBSON, CHIEF JUSTICE.

Plaintiff, an alien Japanese who is ineligible to citizenship under our naturalization laws, appeals from a judgment declaring that certain land purchased by him in 1948 had escheated to the state. There is no treaty between this country and Japan which confers upon plaintiff the right to own land, and the sole question presented on this appeal is the validity of the California alien land law.

UNITED NATIONS CHARTER

It is first contended that the land law has been invalidated and superseded by the provisions of the United Nations Charter pledging the member nations to promote the observance of human rights and fundamental freedoms without distinction as to race. Plaintiff relies on statements in the preamble and in articles 1, 55 and 56 of the Charter.

It is not disputed that the charter is a treaty, and our federal Constitution provides that treaties made under the authority of the United States are part of the supreme law of the land and that the judges in every state are bound thereby. U.S. Const., art. VI. A treaty, however, does not automatically supersede local laws which are inconsistent with it unless the treaty provisions are self-executing. In the words of Chief Justice Marshall: A treaty is "to be regarded in courts of justice as equivalent to an act of the Legislature, whenever it operates of itself, without the aid of any legislative provision. But when the terms of the stipulation import a contract—when either of the parties engages to perform a particular act, the treaty addresses itself to the political, not the judicial department; and the Legislature must execute the contract, before it can become a rule for the court." Foster v. Neilson, 1829, 2 Pet. (U.S.) 253, 314, 7 L.Ed. 415.

In determining whether a treaty is self-executing courts look to the intent of the signatory parties as manifested by the language of the instrument, and, if the instrument is uncertain, recourse may be had to the circumstances surrounding its execution. * * *

In order for a treaty provision to be operative without the aid of implementing legislation and to have the force and effect of a statute, it must appear that the framers of the treaty intended to prescribe a rule that, standing alone, would be enforceable in the courts. * * *

It is clear that the provisions of the preamble and of Article 1 of the charter which are claimed to be in conflict with the alien land law are not self-executing. They state general purposes and objectives of the United Nations Organization and do not purport to impose legal obligations on the individual member nations or to create rights in private persons. It is equally clear that none of the other provisions relied on by plaintiff is self-executing. Article 55 declares that the United Nations "shall promote: * * * universal respect for, and observance of, human rights and fundamental freedoms for all without distinction as to race, sex, language, or religion," and in Article 56, the member nations "pledge themselves to take joint and separate action in cooperation with the Organization for the achievement of the purposes set forth in Article 55." Although the member nations have obligated themselves to cooperate with the international organization in promoting respect for, and observance of, human rights, it is plain that it was contemplated that future legislative action by the several nations would be required to accomplish the declared objectives, and there is nothing to indicate that these provisions were intended to become rules of law for the courts of this county upon the ratification of the charter.

The language used in articles 55 and 56 is not the type customarily employed in treaties which have been held to be self-executing and to create rights and duties in individuals. For example, the treaty involved in Clark v. Allen, 331 U.S. 503, 507–508, 67 S.Ct. 1431, 1434, 91 L.Ed. 1633, relating to the rights of a national of one country to inherit real property located in another country, specifically provided that "such national shall be allowed a term of three years in which to sell the [property] ... and withdraw the proceeds ..." free from any discriminatory taxation. In Nielsen v. Johnson, 279 U.S. 47, 50, 49 S.Ct. 223, 73 L.Ed. 607, the provision treated as being self-executing was equally definite. There each of the signatory parties agreed that "no higher or other duties, charges, or taxes of any kind, shall be levied" by one country on removal of property therefrom by citizens of the other country "than are or shall be payable in each state, upon the same, when removed by a citizen or subject of such state respectively." In other instances treaty provisions were enforced without implementing legislation where they prescribed in detail the rules governing rights and obligations of individuals or specifically provided that citizens of one nation shall have the same rights while in the other country as are enjoyed by that country's own citizens. * * * *Asakura v. Seattle*, 265 U.S. 332, 340, 44 S.Ct. 515, 516, 68 L.Ed. 1041; * * *.

It is significant to note that when the framers of the charter intended to make certain provisions effective without the aid of implementing legislation they employed language which is clear and definite and manifests that intention. For example, Article 104 provides: "The

Organization shall enjoy in the territory of each of its Members such legal capacity as may be necessary for the exercise of its functions and the fulfillment of its purposes." Article 105 provides: "1. The Organization shall enjoy in the territory of each of its Members such privileges and immunities as are necessary for the fulfillment of its purposes. 2. Representatives of the Members of the United Nations and officials of the Organization shall similarly enjoy such privileges and immunities as are necessary for the independent exercise of their functions in connection with the Organization." In Curran v. City of New York, 191 Misc. 229, 77 N.Y.S.2d 206, 212, these articles were treated as being self-executory.

The provisions in the charter pledging cooperation in promoting observance of fundamental freedoms lack the mandatory quality and definiteness which would indicate an intent to create justiciable rights in private persons immediately upon ratification. Instead, they are framed as a promise of future action by the member nations. Secretary of State Stettinius, Chairman of the United States delegation at the San Francisco Conference where the charter was drafted, stated in his report to President Truman that Article 56 "pledges the various countries to cooperate with the organization by joint and separate action in the achievement of the economic and social objectives of the organization without infringing upon their right to order their national affairs according to their own best ability, in their own way, and in accordance with their own political and economic institutions and processes." * * *

The humane and enlightened objectives of the United Nations Charter are, of course, entitled to respectful consideration by the courts and legislatures of every member nation, since that document expresses the universal desire of thinking men for peace and for equality of rights and opportunities. The charter represents a moral commitment of foremost importance, and we must not permit the spirit of our pledge to be compromised or disparaged in either our domestic or foreign affairs. We are satisfied, however, that the charter provisions relied on by plaintiff were not intended to supersede existing domestic legislation, and we cannot hold that they operate to invalidate the alien land law.

[The court concludes, however, that the California Alien Land Law is invalid, because it violates the 14th Amendment to the U.S. Constitution.]

Notes and Questions

1. *The California Alien Land Law.* The 1920 California Alien Land Law had originally aimed at preventing the ownership of land by Asian nationals. By 1952, however, it affected principally Japanese aliens, since by then nationals of the Philippines, China, and India could effectively seek U.S. naturalization. See Lawrence E. Davies, "California's Law on Land is Upset," *New York Times*, Apr. 18, 1952, at 7.

2. *The Self-executing Treaty Doctrine and the U.N. Charter.* Is it self-evident that the *Sei Fujii* court is correct in holding the U.N. Charter

provisions not to be self-executing? The District Court of Appeal of California found the Charter provisions self-executing in *Sei Fujii*. See Sei Fujii v. State, 217 P.2d 481 (Cal.App.1950), *rehearing denied,* 218 P.2d 595 (Cal.App. 1950). When treaty provisions concerning individual rights conflict with state legislation, does a better case exist for finding the treaty to be self executing than when a treaty conflicts with Congressional action? Quincy Wright has noted that Article 56 of the U.N. Charter imposes obligations on the United States as a party, and that Charter provisions do not prevent U.S. courts from interpreting and enforcing the obligations. Quincy Wright, "National Courts and Human Rights—The Fujii Case," 45 *American Journal of International Law* 62 (1951). The critical question then becomes, in Wright's view, whether U.S. obligations under Article 56 are of a character that U.S. courts "can apply." "[C]ommon sense suggests that 'separate action in cooperation with the organization' implies, as a minimum, abstention from separate action, such as enforcement of racially discriminating land laws, which would oppose the purposes of the organization." *Id.* at 72. Wright concludes:

> National courts may not always give a sound interpretation to treaty obligations in respect to human rights, but they are more likely to be guided by general principles than are local legislatures. * * * There is no fundamental reason why the function of incorporating international law into municipal law should be regarded as a legislative rather than a judicial function.

Id. at 80–81. See also Richard Lillich, "Invoking International Human Rights Law in Domestic Courts," 54 *University of Cincinnati Law Review* 367 (1985).

Professor Lockwood has surveyed the use of the United Nations Charter in state and federal courts from 1946 to 1955. He believes that "the Charter played a significant role in helping American courts find the United States Constitution—to redefine the due process and equal protection clauses of the 14th Amendment and the due process clause of the Fifth Amendment to reflect antiracial discrimination norms central to the Charter." Bert B. Lockwood, Jr., "The United Nations Charter and United States Civil Rights Litigation: 1946–1955," 69 *Iowa Law Review* 901, 902 (1984). Lockwood examines *Sei Fujii* and the seminal U.S. Supreme Court civil rights cases, in which human rights provisions of the Charter were raised but not addressed by the Court, and concludes that the Charter was "an important influence on the judiciary, *sub silentio*." *Id.* at 949.

3. *Applying the Self-executing Treaty Rule.* If the 1911 treaty analyzed in *Asakura* had been still in force in 1948, would it have conferred upon Sei Fujii the right to own land? Why is the *Sei Fujii* court more concerned than the *Asakura* court to analyze whether a treaty rule, in this case the U.N. Charter, is self-executing? Should a U.S. court presume that a treaty provision is or is not self-executing? Is the court under any special obligation to try to give effect to treaty purposes if the language of the treaty can be read both ways? Should the positions of other countries be taken into account in determining the incorporation of a treaty into U.S. municipal law?

4. *Treaties and State Law.* Though a federal treaty may always "trump" state law, it may only do so when the treaty provision is incorporated in U.S. law either because it is self-executing or because it has been implemented by congressional legislation. In *Missouri v. Holland* which follows, the Supreme Court does not need to address the self-executing treaty doctrine because Congress has passed a statute implementing the treaty at issue.

MISSOURI v. HOLLAND

252 U.S. 416, 40 S.Ct. 382, 64 L.Ed. 641 (1920).

MR. JUSTICE HOLMES delivered the opinion of the court.

This is a bill in equity brought by the State of Missouri to prevent a game warden of the United States from attempting to enforce the Migratory Bird Treaty Act of July 3, 1918, c. 128, 40 Stat. 755, and the regulations made by the Secretary of Agriculture in pursuance of the same. The ground of the bill is that the statute is an unconstitutional interference with the rights reserved to the States by the Tenth Amendment, and that the acts of the defendant done and threatened under that authority invade the sovereign right of the State and contravene its will manifested in statutes. * * *

On December 8, 1916, a treaty between the United States and Great Britain was proclaimed by the President. It recited that many species of birds in their annual migrations traversed certain parts of the United States and of Canada, that they were of great value as a source of food and in destroying insects injurious to vegetation, but were in danger of extermination through lack of adequate protection. It therefore provided for specified close seasons and protection in other forms, and agreed that the two powers would take or propose to their law-making bodies the necessary measures for carrying the treaty out. The above mentioned Act of July 3, 1918, entitled an act to give effect to the convention, prohibited the killing, capturing or selling any of the migratory birds included in the terms of the treaty except as permitted by regulations compatible with those terms, to be made by the Secretary of Agriculture. Regulations were proclaimed on July 31, and October 25, 1918. It is unnecessary to go into any details, because, as we have said, the question raised is the general one whether the treaty and statute are void as an interference with the rights reserved to the States.

To answer this question it is not enough to refer to the Tenth Amendment, reserving the powers not delegated to the United States because by Article II, § 2, the power to make treaties is delegated expressly, and by Article VI treaties made under the authority of the United States, along with the Constitution and laws of the United States made in pursuance thereof, are declared the supreme law of the land. If the treaty is valid there can be no dispute about the validity of the statute under Article I, § 8, as a necessary and proper means to execute the powers of the Government. The language of the Constitution as to the supremacy of treaties being general, the question before us is narrowed to an inquiry into the ground upon which the present supposed exception is placed.

It is said that a treaty cannot be valid if it infringes the Constitution, that there are limits, therefore, to the treaty-making power, and that one such limit is that what an act of Congress could not do unaided, in derogation of the powers reserved to the States, a treaty cannot do. An earlier act of Congress [of March 4, 1913] that attempted by itself and not in pursuance of a treaty to regulate the killing of migratory birds within the States had been held bad in the District Court. *United States v. Shauver*, 214 Fed. Rep. 154. *United States v. McCullagh*, 221 Fed. Rep. 288. Those decisions were supported by arguments that migratory birds were owned by the States in their sovereign capacity for the benefit of their people, and that under cases like *Geer v. Connecticut*, 161 U.S. 519, this control was one that Congress had no power to displace. The same argument is supposed to apply now with equal force.

Whether the two cases cited were decided rightly or not they cannot be accepted as a test of the treaty power. Acts of Congress are the supreme law of the land only when made in pursuance of the Constitution, while treaties are declared to be so when made under the authority of the United States. It is open to question whether the authority of the United States means more than the formal acts prescribed to make the convention. We do not mean to imply that there are no qualifications to the treaty-making power; but they must be ascertained in different way. It is obvious that there may be matters of the sharpest exigency for the national well being that an act of Congress could not deal with but that a treaty followed by such an act could, and it is not lightly to be assumed that, in matters requiring national action, "a power which must belong to and somewhere reside in every civilized government" is not be found. What was said in that case with regard to the powers of the States applies with equal force to the powers of the nation in cases where the States individually are incompetent to act. We are not yet discussing the particular case before us but only are considering the validity of the test proposed. With regard to that we may add that when we are dealing with words that also are a constituent act, like the Constitution of the United States, we must realize that they have called into life a being the development of which could not have been foreseen completely by the most gifted of its begetters. It was enough for them to realize or to hope that they had created an organism; it has taken a century and has cost their successors much sweat and blood to prove that they created a nation. The case before us must be considered in the light of our whole experience and not merely in that of what was said 100 years ago. The treaty in question does not contravene any prohibitory words to be found in the Constitution. The only question is whether it is forbidden by some invisible radiation from the general terms of the Tenth Amendment. We must consider what this country has become in deciding what that Amendment has reserved.

The State as we have intimated founds its claim of exclusive authority upon an assertion of title to migratory birds, an assertion that is embodied in statute. No doubt it is true that as between a State and its inhabitants the State may regulate the killing and sale of such birds, but it does not follow that its authority is exclusive of paramount powers. To put the claim of the State upon title is to lean upon a slender reed. Wild birds are not in the possession of anyone; and possession is the beginning of ownership. The whole foundation of the State's rights is the presence within their jurisdiction of birds that yesterday had not arrived, tomorrow may be in another State and in a week a thousand miles away. If we are to be accurate we cannot put the case of the State upon higher ground than that the treaty deals with creatures that for the moment are within the state borders, that it must be carried out by officers of the United States within the same territory, and that but for the treaty the State would be free to regulate this subject itself.

As most of the laws of the United States are carried out within the States and as many of them deal with matters which in the silence of such laws the State might regulate, such general grounds are not enough to support Missouri's claim. Valid treaties of course "are as binding within the territorial limits of the States as they are elsewhere throughout the dominion of the United States." No doubt the great body of private relations usually fall within the control of the State, but a treaty may override its power. We do not have to invoke the later developments of constitutional law for this proposition; it was recognized as early as *Hopkirk v. Bell*, 3 Cranch, 454, with regard to statutes of limitation, and even earlier, as to confiscation, in *Ware v. Hylton*, 3 Dall. 199. It was assumed by Chief Justice Marshall with regard to the escheat of land to the State in *Chirac v. Chirac*, 2 Wheat. 259, 275. So as to a limited jurisdiction of foreign consuls within a State. *Wildenhus's Case*, 120 U.S. 1. Further illustration seems unnecessary, and it only remains to consider the application of established rules to the present case.

Here a national interest of very nearly the first magnitude is involved. It can be protected only by national action in concert with that of another power. The subject matter is only transitorily within the State and has no permanent habitat therein. But for the treaty and the statute there soon might be no birds for any powers to deal with. We see nothing in the Constitution that compels the Government to sit by while a food supply is cut off and the protectors of our forests and our crops are destroyed. It is not sufficient to rely upon the States. The reliance is vain, and were it otherwise, the question is whether the United States is forbidden to act. We are of opinion that the treaty and statute must be upheld.

Decree affirmed.

Notes and Questions

1. *Constitution-based Limitations to the Treaty-making Power.* Mr. Justice Holmes writes that "we do not mean to imply that there are no qualifications to the treaty-making power; but they must be ascertained in a

different way." How well does he explicate that way? Is the problem here that Missouri's alleged constitutional prohibition is via "some invisible radiation from the general terms of the Tenth Amendment"? Would a specific constitutional prohibition, *e.g.*, respecting rights to a jury trial in criminal cases, suffice as a qualification on or a limitation to the treaty-making power? In *Reid v. Covert*, 354 U.S. 1, 77 S.Ct. 1222, 1 L.Ed.2d 1148 (1957), which concerned rights to a jury trial under Article III and the Fifth and Sixth Amendments, the Supreme Court held that "no agreement with a foreign nation can confer power on the Congress, or on any other branch of Government, which is free from the restraints of the Constitution." *Id.* at 16, 77 S.Ct. at 1230, 1 L.Ed.2d at 1163.

Mr. Justice Holmes in *Missouri v. Holland* justifies the Supreme Court's decision in part because "a national interest of very nearly the first magnitude is involved." The Treaty was commended in the press as "probably the most important movement for the protection of birds ever instituted in this country or the Dominion." "Safety for the Birds," *New York Times*, Dec. 5, 1916, at 10. Would Missouri's authority to regulate migratory birds have been greater if the national need had been less?

In *Missouri*, questions about the scope of the treaty-making power are posed starkly because a federal statute regulating migratory birds, passed before the 1916 treaty was concluded, had been struck down. Does Holmes mean to say that the Federal Government can achieve ends by way of treaty-making when it cannot do so by simple legislation? How great must a national interest be to outweigh a state interest? May that state interest vary in weight too?

2. *The Historical Context.* Note Holmes's language about Americans' cost in "sweat and blood to prove that they created a nation." Holmes had fought and been wounded in the Civil War. Many of his classmates had been killed. Would the Court have been inclined before 1861 to so subordinate state to federal interests?

WHITNEY v. ROBERTSON

124 U.S. 190, 8 S.Ct. 456, 31 L.Ed. 386 (1888).

MR. JUSTICE FIELD delivered the opinion of the court.

The plaintiffs are merchants, doing business in the city of New York, and in August, 1882, they imported a large quantity of "centrifugal and molasses sugars," the produce and manufacture of the island of San Domingo. These goods were similar in kind to sugars produced in the Hawaiian Islands, which are admitted free of duty under the treaty with the king of those islands, and the act of Congress, passed to carry the treaty into effect. They were duly entered at the custom house at the port of New York, the plaintiffs claiming that by the treaty with the Republic of San Domingo the goods should be admitted on the same terms, that is, free of duty, as similar articles, the produce and manufacture of the Hawaiian Islands. The defendant, who was at the time collector of the port, refused to allow this claim, treated the goods as dutiable articles under the acts of Congress, and exacted duties on them to the amount of $21,936. The plaintiffs appealed from the collector's decision to the Secretary of the Treasury, by whom the appeal was denied. They then paid under protest the duties exacted, and brought the present action to recover the amount. * * *

The treaty with the king of the Hawaiian Islands [of January 30, 1875] provides for the importation into the United States, free of duty, of various articles, the produce and manufacture of those islands, in consideration, among other things, of like exemption from duty, on the importation into that country, of sundry specified articles which are the produce and manufacture of the United States. 19 Stat. 625. The language of the first two articles of the treaty, which recite the reciprocal engagements of the two countries, declares that they are made in consideration "of the rights and privileges" and "as an equivalent therefor," which one concedes to the other.

The plaintiffs rely for a like exemption of the sugars imported by them from San Domingo upon the 9th article of the treaty with the Dominican Republic [of February 8, 1867], which is as follows: "No higher or other duty shall be imposed on the importation into the United States of any article the growth, produce, or manufacture of the Dominican Republic, or of her fisheries; and no higher or other duty shall be imposed on the importation into the Dominican Republic of any article the growth, produce, or manufacture of the United States, or their fisheries, than are or shall be payable on the like articles the growth, produce, or manufacture of any other foreign country, or its fisheries." 15 Stat. 473, 478. * * *

* * * By the Constitution a treaty is placed on the same footing, and made of like obligation, with an act of legislation. Both are declared by that instrument to be the supreme law of the land, and no superior efficacy is given to either over the other. When the two relate to the same subject, the courts will always endeavor to construe them so as to give effect to both, if that can be done without violating the language of either; but if the two are inconsistent, the one last in date will control the other, provided always the stipulation of the treaty on the subject is self-executing. If the country with which the treaty is made is dissatisfied with the action of the legislative department, it may present its complaint to the executive head of the government, and take such other measures as it may deem essential for the protection of its interests. The courts can afford no redress. Whether the complaining nation has just cause of complaint, or our country was justified in its legislation, are not matters for judicial cognizance. * * *

* * * The duty of the courts is to construe and give effect to the latest expression of the sovereign will. In *Head Money Cases*, 112 U.S. 580, it was objected to an act of Congress that it violated provisions contained in treaties with foreign nations, but the court replied that so far as the provisions of the act were in conflict with any treaty, they must prevail in all the courts of the country; and, after a full and elaborate consideration of the subject, it held that "so far as a treaty

made by the United States with any foreign nation can be the subject of judicial cognizance in the courts of this country, it is subject to such acts as Congress may pass for its enforcement, modification, or repeal."

Judgment affirmed.

Notes and Questions

1. *The Last-in-time Rule.* Though the Court in *Whitney* refuses to enforce a U.S. treaty promising to provide most favored nation treatment to imports from San Domingo (the present day Dominican Republic), it makes the general proposition that in case of a conflict between a federal statute and a treaty, "the one last in date will control," a proposition favorable to the status of international agreements. Does Article VI(2) of the Constitution, the Supremacy Clause, itself prescribe any rule as to the relationship between federal law and treaties? Is any other solution preferable to the last-in-time rule? How far should the courts go as they "always endeavor to construe" treaties and federal statutes "so as to give effect to both"? See the *PLO Case* and *Alvarez-Machain* following.

2. *Dualism, Treaties, and the Role of Courts.* Note that the Supreme Court takes a dualistic view of the relationship between international law and municipal law: "If the country with which the treaty is made is dissatisfied with the action of the legislative department, it may present its complaint to the executive head of the government, and take such other measures as it may deem essential for the protection of its interests." In Great Britain, where no treaty is considered self-executing, the courts have made comparable observations about the dualistic nature of international law and municipal law. For example, in *The Parlement Belge* the British court refused to incorporate a treaty provision that gave immunity to a Belgian packet-boat conveying mails because the immunity had not been enacted into statutory form by the British Parliament. (1878–79) 4 P.D. 129. Responding to an objection that this was too unfair to Belgium, the judge wrote: "I acknowledge the hardship, but the remedy, in my opinion, is not to be found in depriving the British subject without his consent, direct or implied, or his right of action against a wrong-doer, but by the agency of diplomacy, and proper measures of compensation arrangement, between the Governments of Great Britain and Belgium." *Id.* at 155. Where, then, in the *Whitney Case* should the government of San Domingo complain about the actions of the United States?

UNITED STATES v. BELMONT

301 U.S. 324, 57 S.Ct. 758, 81 L.Ed. 1134 (1937).

MR. JUSTICE SUTHERLAND delivered the opinion of the Court.

This is an action at law brought by petitioner against respondents in a federal district court to recover a sum of money deposited by a Russian corporation (Petrograd Metal Works) with August Belmont, a private banker doing business in New York City under the name of August Belmont & Co. August Belmont died in 1924; and respondents are the duly-appointed executors of his will. A motion to dismiss the complaint for failure to state facts sufficient to constitute a cause of action was sustained by the district court, and its judgment was affirmed by the court below. 85 F. (2d) 542. The facts alleged, so far as necessary to be stated, follow.

The corporation had deposited with Belmont, prior to 1918, the sum of money which petitioner seeks to recover. In 1918, the Soviet Government duly enacted a decree by which it dissolved, terminated and liquidated the corporation (together with others), and nationalized and appropriated all of its property and assets of every kind and wherever situated, including the deposit account with Belmont. As a result, the deposit became the property of the Soviet Government, and so remained until November 16, 1933, at which time the Soviet Government released and assigned to petitioner all amounts due to that government from American nationals, including the deposit account of the corporation with Belmont. Respondents failed and refused to pay the amount upon demand duly made by petitioner.

The assignment was effected by an exchange of diplomatic correspondence between the Soviet Government and the United States. The purpose was to bring about a final settlement of the claims and counterclaims between the Soviet Government and the United States; and it was agreed that the Soviet Government would take no steps to enforce claims against American nationals; but all such claims were released and assigned to the United States, with the understanding that the Soviet Government was to be duly notified of all amounts realized by the United States from such release and assignment. The assignment and requirement for notice are parts of the larger plan to bring about a settlement of the rival claims of the high contracting parties. The continuing and definite interest of the Soviet Government in the collection of assigned claims is evident; and the case, therefore, presents a question of public concern, the determination of which well might involve the good faith of the United States in the eyes of a foreign government. The court below held that the assignment thus effected embraced the claim here in question; and with that we agree.

That court, however, took the view that the situs of the bank deposit was within the State of New York; that in no sense could it be regarded as an intangible property right within Soviet territory; and that the nationalization decree, if enforced, would put into effect an act of confiscation. And it held that a judgment for the United States could not be had, because, in view of that result, it would be contrary to the controlling public policy of the State of New York. The further contention is made by respondents that the public policy of the United States would likewise be infringed by such a judgment. The two questions thus presented are the only ones necessary to be considered.

First. We do not pause to inquire whether in fact there was any policy of the State of New York to be infringed, since we are of opinion that no state policy can prevail against the international compact here involved. * * *

We take judicial notice of the fact that coincident with the assignment set forth in the complaint, the President recognized the Soviet Government, and normal diplomatic relations were established between that government and the Government of the United States, followed by an exchange of ambassadors. The effect of this was to validate, so far as this country is concerned, all acts of the Soviet Government here involved from the commencement of its existence. The recognition, establishment of diplomatic relations, the assignment, and agreements with respect thereto, were all parts of one transaction, resulting in an international compact between the two governments. That the negotiations, acceptance of the assignment and agreements and understandings in respect thereof were within the competence of the President may not be doubted. Governmental power over internal affairs is distributed between the national government and the several states. Governmental power over external affairs is not distributed, but is vested exclusively in the national government. And in respect of what was done here, the Executive had authority to speak as the sole organ of that government. The assignment and the agreements in connection therewith did not, as in the case of treaties, as that term is used in the treaty making clause of the Constitution (Art. II, § 2), require the advice and consent of the Senate.

A treaty signifies "a compact made between two or more independent nations with a view to the public welfare." *Altman & Co. v. United States*, 224 U.S. 583, 600. But an international compact, as this was, is not always a treaty which requires the participation of the Senate. There are many such compacts, of which a protocol, a modus vivendi, a postal convention, and agreements like that now under consideration are illustrations. * * * [A]lthough this might not be a treaty requiring ratification by the Senate, it was a compact negotiated and proclaimed under the authority of the President, and as such was a "treaty" within the meaning of the Circuit Court of Appeals Act, the construction of which might be reviewed upon direct appeal to this court.

Plainly, the external powers of the United States are to be exercised without regard to state laws or policies. The supremacy of a treaty in this respect has been recognized from the beginning. Mr. Madison, in the Virginia Convention, said that if a treaty does not supersede existing state laws, as far as they contravene its operation, the treaty would be ineffective. "To counteract it by the supremacy of the state laws, would bring on the Union the just charge of national perfidy, and involve us in war." 3 Elliot's Debates 515. And see *Ware v. Hylton*, 3 Dall. 199, 236–237. And while this rule in respect of treaties is established by the express language of cl. 2, Art. VI, of the Constitution, the same rule would result in the case of all international compacts and agreements from the very fact that complete power over international affairs is in the national government and is not and cannot be subject to any curtailment of interference on the part of the several states. Compare *United States v. Curtiss–Wright Export Corp.*, 299 U.S. 304, 316, et seq. In respect of all international negotiations and compacts, and in respect of our foreign relations generally, state lines disappear. As to such purposes the State of New York does not exist. Within the field of its powers, whatever the United States rightfully undertakes, it necessarily has warrant to consummate. And when judicial authority is invoked in aid of such consummation, state constitutions, state laws, and state policies are irrelevant to the inquiry and decision. It is inconceivable that any of them can be interposed as an obstacle to the effective operation of a federal constitutional power. Cf. *Missouri v. Holland*, 252 U.S. 416; *Asakura v. Seattle*, 265 U.S. 332, 341.

Notes and Questions

1. *The Roosevelt–Litvinoff Agreement.* The *Belmont Case* validates the Roosevelt–Litvinoff agreement, a matter of some importance in U.S.–U.S.S.R. relations. At the time of the Supreme Court's decision there were some 15 similar law suits in the U.S. courts involving more than $8,000,000. The Petrograd/Metal Works deposit with August Belmont & Co. was itself only $25,438. "Pact with Soviet on Claims Upheld," *New York Times*, May 4, 1937, at 14.

2. *Executive Agreements and the Constitution.* Is it plain that the Constitution meant to give all international agreements supremacy over state laws or only those which had been favorably reviewed by the Senate? As a result of cases like *Belmont*, the term "treaty" really has two meanings in the U.S. Constitution. First, there is the "treaty" in Article II(2) that requires the "advice and consent" of the Senate. Second, there is the "treaty" in Article VI(2) that, along with the Constitution and U.S. law, is given supremacy.

UNITED STATES v. CURTISS–WRIGHT

299 U.S. 304, 57 S.Ct. 216, 81 L.Ed. 255 (1936).

MR. JUSTICE SUTHERLAND delivered the opinion of the Court.

On January 27, 1936, an indictment was returned in the court below, the first count of which charges that appellees, beginning with the 29th day of May, 1934, conspired to sell in the United States certain arms of war, namely 15 machine guns, to Bolivia, a country then engaged in armed conflict in the Chaco, in violation of the Joint Resolution of Congress approved May 28, 1934, and the provisions of a proclamation issued on the same day by the President of the United States pursuant to authority conferred by § 1 of the resolution. In pursuance of the conspiracy, the commission of certain overt acts was alleged, details of which need not be stated. The Joint Resolution (c. 365, 48 Stat. 811) follows:

Resolved by the Senate and House of Representatives of the United States of America in Congress assembled, That if the President finds that the prohibition of the sale of arms and munitions of war in the United States to those countries now engaged in armed conflict in the Chaco may contribute to the reestablishment of peace between those countries, and if after consultation with the governments of other American

Republics and with their cooperation, as well as that of such other governments as he may deem necessary, he makes proclamation to that effect, it shall be unlawful to sell, except under such limitations and exceptions as the President prescribes, any arms or munitions of war in any place in the United States to the countries now engaged in that armed conflict, or to any person, company, or association acting in the interest of either country, until otherwise ordered by the President or by Congress. * * *

First. It is contended that by the Joint Resolution, the going into effect and continued operation of the resolution was conditioned (a) upon the President's judgment as to its beneficial effect upon the reestablishment of peace between the countries engaged in armed conflict in the Chaco; (b) upon the making of a proclamation, which was left to his unfettered discretion, thus constituting an attempted substitution of the President's will for that of Congress; (c) upon the making of a proclamation putting an end to the operation of the resolution, which again was left to the President's unfettered discretion; and (d) further, that the extent of its operation in particular cases was subject to limitation and exception by the President, controlled by no standard. In each of these particulars, appellees urge that Congress abdicated its essential functions and delegated them to the Executive.

Whether, if the Joint Resolution had related solely to internal affairs it would be open to the challenge that it constituted an unlawful delegation of legislative power to the Executive, we find it unnecessary to determine. The whole aim of the resolution is to affect a situation entirely external to the United States, and falling within the category of foreign affairs. The determination which we are called to make, therefore, is whether the Joint Resolution, as applied to that situation, is vulnerable to attack under the rule that forbids a delegation of the lawmaking power. In other words, assuming (but not deciding) that the challenged delegation, if it were confined to internal affairs, would be invalid, may it nevertheless be sustained on the ground that its exclusive aim is to afford a remedy for a hurtful condition within foreign territory?

It will contribute to the elucidation of the question if we first consider the differences between the powers of the federal government in respect of foreign or external affairs and those in respect of domestic or internal affairs. That there are differences between them, and that these differences are fundamental, may not be doubted.

The two classes of powers are different, both in respect of their origin and their nature. The broad statement that the federal government can exercise no powers except those specifically enumerated in the Constitution, and such implied powers as are necessary and proper to carry into effect the enumerated powers, is categorically true only in respect of our internal affairs. In that field, the primary purpose of the Constitution was to carve from the general mass of legislative powers *then possessed by the states* such portions as it was thought desirable to vest in the federal government, leaving those not included in the enumeration still in the states. *Carter v. Carter Coal Co.*, 298 U.S. 238, 294. That this doctrine applies only to powers which the states had, is self evident. And since the states severally never possessed international powers, such powers could not have been carved from the mass of state powers but obviously were transmitted to the United States from some other source. During the colonial period, those powers were possessed exclusively by and were entirely under the control of the Crown. By the Declaration of Independence, "the Representatives of the United States of America" declared the United [not the several] Colonies to be free and independent states, and as such to have "full Power to levy War, conclude Peace, contract Alliances, establish Commerce and to do all other Acts and Things which Independent States may of right do."

As a result of the separation from Great Britain by the colonies acting as a unit, the powers of external sovereignty passed from the Crown not to the colonies severally, but to the colonies in their collective and corporate capacity as the United States of America. Even before the Declaration, the colonies were a unit in foreign affairs, acting through a common agency—namely the Continental Congress, composed of delegates from the 13 colonies. That agency exercised the powers of war and peace, raised an army, created a navy, and finally adopted the Declaration of Independence. Rulers come and go; governments end and forms of government change; but sovereignty survives. A political society cannot endure without a supreme will somewhere. Sovereignty is never held in suspense. When, therefore, the external sovereignty of Great Britain in respect of the colonies ceased, it immediately passed to the Union. That fact was given practical application almost at once. The treaty of peace, made on September 23, 1783, was concluded between his Brittanic Majesty and the "United States of America."

The Union existed before the Constitution, which was ordained and established among other things to form "a more perfect Union." Prior to that event, it is clear that the Union, declared by the Articles of Confederation to be "perpetual," was the sole possessor of external sovereignty and in the Union it remained without change save in so far as the Constitution in express terms qualified its exercise. The Framers' Convention was called and exerted its powers upon the irrefutable postulate that though the states were several their people in respect of foreign affairs were one. In that convention, the entire absence of state power to deal with those affairs was thus forcefully stated by Rufus King:

"The states were not 'sovereigns' in the sense contended for by some. They did not possess the peculiar features of sovereignty,—they could not make war, nor peace, nor alliances, nor treaties. Considering them as political beings, they were dumb, for they could not speak to any foreign sovereign whatever. They were deaf, for they could not hear any propositions from such sovereign. They had not even the organs or facilities of defence or offence, for they could not of themselves raise troops, or equip vessels, for war."

It results that the investment of the federal government with the powers of external sovereignty did not depend upon the affirmative grants of the Constitution. The powers to declare and wage war, to conclude peace, to make treaties, to maintain diplomatic relations with other sovereignties, if they had never been mentioned in the Constitution, would have vested in the federal government as necessary concomitants of nationality. Neither the Constitution nor the laws passed in pursuance of it have any force in foreign territory unless in respect of our own citizens; and operations of the nation in such territory must be governed by treaties, international understandings and compacts, and the principles of international law. As a member of the family of nations, the right and power of the United States in that field are equal to the right and power of the other members of the international family. Otherwise, the United States is not completely sovereign. The power to acquire territory by discovery and occupation, the power to expel undesirable aliens, the power to make such international agreements as do not constitute treaties in the constitutional sense, none of which is expressly affirmed by the Constitution, nevertheless exist as inherently inseparable from the conception of nationality. This the court recognized, and in each of the cases cited found the warrant for its conclusions not in the provisions of the Constitution, but in the law of nations.

In *Burnet v. Brooks*, 288 U.S. 378, 396, we said, "As a nation with all the attributes of sovereignty, the United States is vested with all the powers of government necessary to maintain an effective control of international relations."

Not only, as we have shown, is the federal power over external affairs in origin and essential character different from that over internal affairs, but participation in the exercise of the power is significantly limited. In this vast external realm, with its important, complicated, delicate and manifold problems, the President alone has the power to speak or listen as a representative of the nation. He *makes* treaties with the advice and consent of the Senate; but he alone negotiates. Into the field of negotiation the Senate cannot intrude; and Congress itself is powerless to invade it. As Marshall said in his great argument of March 7, 1800, in the House of Representatives: "The President is the sole organ of the nation in its external relations, and its sole representative with foreign nations." The Senate Committee on Foreign Relations at a very early day in our history (February 15, 1816), reported to the Senate, among other things, as follows:

"The President is the constitutional representative of the United States with regard to foreign nations. He manages our concerns with foreign nations and must necessarily be most competent to determine when, how, and upon what subjects negotiation may be urged with the greatest prospect of success. For his conduct he is responsible to the Constitution. The committee consider this responsibility the surest pledge for the faithful discharge of his duty. They think the interference of the Senate in the direction of foreign negotiations calculated to diminish that responsibility and thereby to impair the best security for the national safety. The nature of transactions with foreign nations, moreover, requires caution and unity of design, and their success frequently depends on secrecy and dispatch."

It is important to bear in mind that we are here dealing not alone with an authority vested in the President by an exertion of legislative power, but with such an authority plus the very delicate, plenary and exclusive power of the President as the sole organ of the federal government in the field of international relations—a power which does not require as a basis for its exercise an act of Congress, but which, of course, like every other governmental power, must be exercised in subordination to the applicable provisions of the Constitution. It is quite apparent that if, in the maintenance of our international relations, embarrassment—perhaps serious embarrassment—is to be avoided and success for our aims achieved, congressional legislation which is to be made effective through negotiation and inquiry within the international field must often accord to the President a degree of discretion and freedom from statutory restriction which would not be admissible were domestic affairs alone involved. Moreover, he, not Congress, has the better opportunity of knowing the conditions which prevail in foreign countries, and especially is this true in time of war. He has his confidential sources of information. He has his agents in the form of diplomatic, consular and other officials. Secrecy in respect of information gathered by them may be highly necessary, and the premature disclosure of it productive of harmful results. Indeed, so clearly is this true that the first President refused to accede to a request to lay before the House of Representatives the instructions, correspondence and documents relating to the negotiation of the Jay Treaty—a refusal the wisdom of which was recognized by the House itself and has never since been doubted. In his reply to the request, President Washington said:

"The nature of foreign negotiations requires caution, and their success must often depend on secrecy; and even when brought to a conclusion a full disclosure of all the measures, demands, or eventual concessions which may have been proposed or contemplated would be extremely impolitic; for this might have a pernicious influence on future negotiations, or produce immediate inconveniences, perhaps danger and mischief, in relation to other powers. The necessity of such caution and secrecy was one cogent reason for vesting the power of making treaties in the President, with the advice and consent of the Senate, the principle on which that body was formed confining it to a small number of members. To admit, then, a right in the House of Representatives to demand and to have as a matter of course all the papers respecting a negotiation with a foreign power would be to establish a dangerous precedent." * * *

In the light of the foregoing observations, it is evident that this court should not be in haste to apply a general rule which will have the effect of condemning legislation like that under review as constituting an unlawful delegation of legislative power. The principles which justify such legislation find overwhelming support in the unbroken legislative practice which has prevailed almost from the inception of the national government to the present day. * * *

Practically every volume of the United States Statutes contains one or more acts or joint resolutions of Congress authorizing action by the President in respect of subjects affecting foreign relations, which either leave the exercise of the power to his unrestricted judgment, or provide a standard far more general than that which has always been considered requisite with regard to domestic affairs. * * *

The uniform, long-continued and undisputed legislative practice just disclosed rests upon an admissible view of the Constitution which, even if the practice found far less support in principle than we think it does, we should not feel at liberty at this late day to disturb.

We deem it unnecessary to consider, *seriatim*, the several clauses which are said to evidence the unconstitutionality of the Joint Resolution as involving an unlawful delegation of legislative power. It is enough to summarize by saying that, both upon principle and in accordance with precedent, we conclude there is sufficient warrant for the broad discretion vested in the President to determine whether the enforcement of the statute will have a beneficial effect upon the reestablishment of peace in the affected countries; whether he shall make proclamation to bring the resolution into operation; whether and when the resolution shall cease to operate and to make proclamation accordingly; and to prescribe limitations and exceptions to which the enforcement of the resolution shall be subject.

Notes and Questions

1. *The Historical Context. Curtiss–Wright* was politically significant. When three companies and four individuals were indicted for running machine guns to Bolivia in its Chaco War against Paraguay, the indictment was front-page news. "Gun–Running Laid to Aircraft Heads," *New York Times*, Jan. 28, 1936, at 1. After a federal district judge held that the President had no power to outlaw shipments of arms to belligerent nations, the case went to the U.S. Supreme Court where in oral argument there was sharp questioning by judges well-experienced in foreign affairs, *e.g.*, by Chief Justice Hughes, who had been Secretary of State, and Justice Sutherland, who had been a member of the Senate Foreign Relations Committee. "Presidential Ban on Arms Held Void," *New York Times*, Mar. 26, 1936, at 15; "Embargo Argued in Supreme Court," *New York Times*, Nov. 20, 1936, at 10. The 7–1 opinion in *Curtiss–Wright* in favor of the President was again first-page news. "High Court Backs Neutrality Power Held by President," *New York Times*, Dec. 22, 1936, at 1. *Curtiss–Wright* was thought to be a significant contribution to President Roosevelt's attempts to keep all of the Americas out of the impending war in Europe. Delbert Clark, "Monroe Doctrine 'Expanded': American Republics' Joint Policy on Peace Removes Old 'Unilateral' Stigma," *New York Times*, Dec. 27, 1936, at E5.

2. *Executive Lawmaking.* In *Curtiss–Wright,* Justice Sutherland is at pains to distinguish executive lawmaking in the international realm from that sort of executive lawmaking that the Supreme Court had struck down

in a series of judgments limiting the President's domestic power. See, for example, the Court's judgments in A.L.A. Schechter Poultry Corp. v. United States, 295 U.S. 495, 55 S.Ct. 837, 79 L.Ed. 1570 (1935), and Carter v. Carter Coal Co., 298 U.S. 238, 56 S.Ct. 855, 80 L.Ed. 1160 (1936). In a few months the Court would retreat even on the domestic front. See NLRB v. Jones & Laughlin Steel Corp., 301 U.S. 1, 57 S.Ct. 615, 81 L.Ed. 893 (1937).

3. *The Source of Foreign Affairs Powers.* Does the judgment in *Curtiss–Wright* mean that some Presidential powers in international affairs are extra-constitutional? In *Missouri v. Holland*, Justice Holmes looked at the wording of Article VI(2) of the Constitution and noted that "Acts of Congress are the supreme law of the land only when made in pursuance of the Constitution, while treaties are declared to be so when made under the authority of the United States." Does the wording of the Supremacy Clause advance the notion that the federal government possesses powers in foreign affairs that go beyond the Constitution? Justice Sutherland writes in *Curtiss–Wright*: "A political society cannot endure without a supreme will somewhere. Sovereignty is never held in suspense."

4. *The History of the Foreign Relations Powers.* Did foreign relations powers pass directly to the United States during the American Revolution? Justice Chase in *Ware v. Hylton* in 1795 was much nearer the event than the Court in *Curtiss–Wright* when he wrote:

> In June 1776, the convention of Virginia formally declared, that Virginia was a free, sovereign, and independent state; and on the 4th of July, 1776, following, the United States, in congress assembled, declared the 13 united colonies free and independent states; and that, as such, they had full power to levy war, conclude peace, &c. I consider this as a declaration, not that the united colonies jointly, in a collective capacity, were independent states, &c. but that each of them was a sovereign and independent state, that is, that each of them had a right to govern itself by its own authority and its own laws, without any control from any other power upon earth.

Ware v. Hylton, 3 U.S. (3 Dall.) 199, 224, 1 L.Ed. 568, 579 (1796). Later in his opinion Justice Chase proves willing to acknowledge that Congress had some necessary powers even before the ratification of the Articles of Confederation in 1781:

> The powers of congress [between 1774 and 1781] originated from necessity, and arose out of, and were only limited by events; or, in other words, they were revolutionary in their very nature. Their extent depended on the exigencies and necessities of public affairs. It was absolutely and indispensably necessary that congress should possess the power of conducting the war against Great Britain, and therefore, if not expressly given by all (as it was by some of the states), I do not hesitate to say, that congress did rightfully possess such power. The authority to make war, of necessity, implies the power to make peace; or the war must be perpetual. I entertain this general idea, that the several states retained all internal sovereignty; and that congress properly possessed the great rights of external sovereignty * * *.

Id. at 232, 1 L.Ed. at 582.

5. *The Balance of Foreign Relations Powers Among the Different Branches*. Note that even if one concludes that the federal government has special powers in the field of foreign relations, it is still unclear as to what the balance of foreign relations powers are among the Congress, the President, and the federal courts. Although Justice Sutherland's opinion in *Curtiss–Wright* is a strong endorsement of Presidential powers, the executive acts in question were based on a congressional resolution. The next case, *Dames & Moore*, explains more about setting a proper balance among the three branches of the federal government in matters concerning foreign affairs.

DAMES & MOORE v. REGAN

453 U.S. 654, 101 S.Ct. 2972, 69 L.Ed.2d 918 (1981).

JUSTICE REHNQUIST delivered the opinion of the Court.

The questions presented by this case touch fundamentally upon the manner in which our Republic is to be governed. Throughout the nearly two centuries of our Nation's existence under the Constitution, this subject has generated considerable debate. We have had the benefit of commentators such as John Jay, Alexander Hamilton, and James Madison writing in The Federalist Papers at the Nation's very inception, the benefit of astute foreign observers of our system such as Alexis de Tocqueville and James Bryce writing during the first century of the Nation's existence, and the benefit of many other treatises as well as more than 400 volumes of reports of decisions of this Court. As these writings reveal it is doubtless both futile and perhaps dangerous to find any epigrammatical explanation of how this country has been governed. * * *

* * * We are confined to a resolution of the dispute presented to us. That dispute involves various Executive Orders and regulations by which the President nullified attachments and liens on Iranian assets in the United States, directed that these assets be transferred to Iran, and suspended claims against Iran that may be presented to an International Claims Tribunal. This action was taken in an effort to comply with an Executive Agreement between the United States and Iran. We granted certiorari before judgment in this case, and set an expedited briefing and argument schedule, because lower courts had reached conflicting conclusions on the validity of the President's actions and, as the Solicitor General informed us, unless the Government acted by July 19, 1981, Iran could consider the United States to be in breach of the Executive Agreement. * * *

* * * [T]he decisions of the Court in this area have been rare, episodic, and afford little precedential value for subsequent cases. The tensions present in any exercise of executive power under the tripartite system of Federal Government established by the Constitution have been reflected in opinions by Members of this Court more than once. The Court stated in *United States* v. *Curtiss–Wright Export Corp.*, 299 U.S. 304, 319–320 (1936):

> "[W]e are here dealing not alone with an authority vested in the President by an exertion of legislative power, but with such an authority plus the very delicate, plenary and exclusive power of the President as the sole organ of the federal government in the field of international relations—a power which does not require as a basis for its exercise an act of Congress, but which, of course, like every other governmental power, must be exercised in subordination to the applicable provisions of the Constitution."

And yet 16 years later, Justice Jackson in his concurring opinion in *Youngstown* [*Sheet & Tube Co.* v. *Sawyer*, 343 U.S. 579, 72 S.Ct. 863, 96 L.Ed. 1153 (1952)], which both parties agree brings together as much combination of analysis and common sense as there is in this area, focused not on the "plenary and exclusive power of the President" but rather responded to a claim of virtually unlimited powers for the Executive by noting:

> "The example of such unlimited executive power that must have most impressed the forefathers was the prerogative exercised by George III, and the description of its evils in the Declaration of Independence leads me to doubt that they were creating their new Executive in his image."

As we now turn to the factual and legal issues in this case, we freely confess that we are obviously deciding only one more episode in the never-ending tension between the President exercising the executive authority in a world that presents each day some new challenge with which he must deal and the Constitution under which we all live and which no one disputes embodies some sort of system of checks and balances.

I

On November 4, 1979, the American Embassy in Tehran was seized and our diplomatic personnel were captured and held hostage. In response to that crisis, President Carter, acting pursuant to the International Emergency Economic Powers Act, 91 Stat. 1626, 50 U.S.C. §§ 1701–1706 (1976 ed., Supp. III)(hereinafter IEEPA), declared a national emergency on November 14, 1979, and blocked the removal or transfer of "all property and interests in property of the Government of Iran, its instrumentalities and controlled entities and the Central Bank of Iran which are or become subject to the jurisdiction of the United States...." Exec. Order No. 12170, 3 CFR 457 (1980), note following 50 U.S.C. § 1701 (1976 ed., Supp. III). President Carter authorized the Secretary of the Treasury to promulgate regulations carrying out the blocking order. On November 15, 1979, the Treasury Department's Office of Foreign Assets Control issued a regulation providing that "[u]nless licensed or authorized ... any attachment, judgment, decree, lien, execution, garnishment, or other judicial process is null and void with respect to any property in which on or since [November 14, 1979,] there existed an interest of Iran." 31 CFR § 535.203(e)(1980). The regulations also made clear that any licenses or authorizations granted could be "amended, modified, or revoked at any time." § 535.805.

On November 26, 1979, the President granted a general license authorizing certain judicial proceedings against Iran but which did not allow the "entry of any judgment or of any decree or order of similar or analogous effect...." § 535.504(a). On December 19, 1979, a clarifying regulation was issued stating that "the general authorization for judicial proceedings contained in § 535.504(a) includes pre-judgment attachment." § 535.418.

On December 19, 1979, petitioner Dames & Moore filed suit in the United States District Court for the Central District of California against the Government of Iran, the Atomic Energy Organization of Iran, and a number of Iranian banks. In its complaint, petitioner alleged that its wholly owned subsidiary, Dames & Moore International, S. R. L., was a party to a written contract with the Atomic Energy Organization, and that the subsidiary's entire interest in the contract had been assigned to petitioner. Under the contract, the subsidiary was to conduct site studies for a proposed nuclear power plant in Iran. As provided in the terms of the contract, the Atomic Energy Organization terminated the agreement for its own convenience on June 30, 1979. Petitioner contended, however, that it was owed $3,436,694.30 plus interest for services performed under the contract prior to the date of termination. The District Court issued orders of attachment directed against property of the defendants, and the property of certain Iranian banks was then attached to secure any judgment that might be entered against them.

On January 20, 1981, the Americans held hostage were released by Iran pursuant to an Agreement entered into the day before and embodied in two Declarations of the Democratic and Popular Republic of Algeria. The Agreement stated that "[i]t is the purpose of [the United States and Iran] ... to terminate all litigation as between the Government of each party and the nationals of the other, and to bring about the settlement and termination of all such claims through binding arbitration." In furtherance of this goal, the Agreement called for the establishment of an Iran–United States Claims Tribunal which would arbitrate any claims not settled within six months. Awards of the Claims Tribunal are to be "final and binding" and "enforceable ... in the courts of any nation in accordance with its laws." Under the Agreement, the United States is obligated

> "to terminate all legal proceedings in United States courts involving claims of United States persons and institutions against Iran and its state enterprises, to nullify all attachments and judgments obtained therein, to prohibit all further litigation based on such claims, and to bring about the termination of such claims through binding arbitration."

In addition, the United States must "act to bring about the transfer" by July 19, 1981, of all Iranian assets held in this country by American banks. One billion dollars of these assets will be deposited in a security account in the Bank of England, to the account of the Algerian Central Bank, and used to satisfy awards rendered against Iran by the Claims Tribunal.

On January 19, 1981, President Carter issued a series of Executive Orders implementing the terms of the agreement. Exec. Orders Nos. 12276–12285, 46 Fed. Reg. 7913–7932. These Orders revoked all licenses permitting the exercise of "any right, power, or privilege" with regard to Iranian funds, securities, or deposits; "nullified" all non–Iranian interests in such assets acquired subsequent to the blocking order of November 14, 1979; and required those banks holding Iranian assets to transfer them "to the Federal Reserve Bank of New York, to be held or transferred as directed by the Secretary of the Treasury." Exec. Order No. 12294, 46 Fed. Reg. 7919.

On February 24, 1981, President Reagan issued an Executive Order in which he "ratified" the January 19th Executive Orders. Exec. Order No. 12294, 46 Fed. Reg. 14111. Moreover, he "suspended" all "claims which may be presented to the ... Tribunal" and provided that such claims "shall have no legal effect in any action now pending in any court of the United States." *Ibid.* The suspension of any particular claim terminates if the Claims Tribunal determines that it has no jurisdiction over that claim; claims are discharged for all purposes when the Claims Tribunal either awards some recovery and that amount is paid, or determines that no recovery is due. *Ibid.*

Meanwhile, on January 27, 1981, petitioner moved for summary judgment in the District Court against the Government of Iran and the Atomic Energy Organization, but not against the Iranian banks. The District Court granted petitioner's motion and awarded petitioner the amount claimed under the contract plus interest. Thereafter, petitioner attempted to execute the judgment by obtaining writs of garnishment and execution in state court in the State of Washington, and a sheriff's sale of Iranian property in Washington was noticed to satisfy the judgment. However, by order of May 28, 1981, as amended by order of June 8, the District Court stayed execution of its judgment pending appeal by the Government of Iran and the Atomic Energy Organization. The District Court also ordered that all prejudgment attachments obtained against the Iranian defendants be vacated and that further proceedings against the bank defendants be stayed in light of the Executive Orders discussed above.

On April 28, 1981, petitioner filed this action in the District Court for declaratory and injunctive relief against the United States and the Secretary of the Treasury, seeking to prevent enforcement of the Executive Orders and Treasury Department regulations implementing the Agreement with Iran. * * *

II

The parties and the lower courts, confronted with the instant questions, have all agreed that much relevant analysis is contained in *Youngstown Sheet & Tube Co. v. Sawyer*, 343 U.S. 579 (1952). Justice

Black's opinion for the Court in that case, involving the validity of President Truman's effort to seize the country's steel mills in the wake of a nationwide strike, recognized that "[t]he President's power, if any, to issue the order must stem either from an act of Congress or from the Constitution itself." Justice Jackson's concurring opinion elaborated in a general way the consequences of different types of interaction between the two democratic branches in assessing Presidential authority to act in any given case. When the President acts pursuant to an express or implied authorization for Congress, he exercises not only his powers but also those delegated by Congress. In such a case the executive action "would be supported by the strongest of presumptions and the widest latitude of judicial interpretation, and the burden of persuasion would rest heavily upon any who might attack it." When the President acts in the absence of congressional authorization he may enter "a zone of twilight in which he and Congress may have concurrent authority, or in which its distribution is uncertain." In such a case the analysis becomes more complicated, and the validity of the President's action, at least so far as separation-of-powers principles are concerned, hinges on a consideration of all the circumstances which might shed light on the views of the Legislative Branch toward such action, including "congressional inertia, indifference or quiescence." Finally, when the President acts in contravention of the will of Congress, "his power is at its lowest ebb," and the Court can sustain his actions "only by disabling the Congress from acting upon the subject." * * *

III

In nullifying post-November 14, 1979, attachments and directing those persons holding blocked Iranian funds and securities to transfer them to the Federal Reserve Bank of New York for ultimate transfer to Iran, President Carter cited five sources of express or inherent power. The Government, however, has principally relied on § 1702(a)(1)(1976 ed., Supp. III) [of the IEPPA], as authorization for these actions. Section 1702(a)(1) provides in part:

> "At the times and to the extent specified in section 1701 of this title, the President may, under such regulations as he may prescribe, by means of instructions, licensed, or otherwise—
>
> "(A) investigate, regulate, or prohibit—
>
> "(i) any transactions in foreign exchange,
>
> "(ii) transfers of credit or payments between, by, through, or to any banking institution, to the extent that such transfers or payments involve any interest of any foreign country or a national thereof,
>
> "(iii) the importing or exporting of currency or securities, and
>
> "(B) investigate, regulate, direct and compel, nullify, void, prevent or prohibit, any acquisition, holding, withholding, use, transfer, withdrawal, transportation, importation or exportation of, or dealing in, or exercising any right, power, or privilege with respect to, or

transactions involving, any property in which any foreign country or a national thereof has any interest;

"by any person, or with respect to any property, subject to the jurisdiction of the United States." * * *

[Justice Rehnquist concludes that these provisions of the IEEPA explicitly authorized the President to nullify the attachments and transfer the assets.]

Because the President's action in nullifying the attachments and ordering the transfer of the assets was taken pursuant to specific congressional authorization, it is "supported by the strongest of presumptions and the widest latitude of judicial interpretation, and the burden of persuasion would rest heavily upon any who might attack it." *Youngstown,* 343 U.S., at 637 (Jackson, J., concurring). Under the circumstances of this case, we cannot say that petitioner has sustained that heavy burden. A contrary ruling would mean that the Federal Government as a whole lacked the power exercised by the President, and that we are not prepared to say.

IV

Although we have concluded that the IEEPA constitutes specific congressional authorization to the President to nullify the attachments and order the transfer of Iranian assets, there remains the question of the President's authority to suspend claims pending in American courts. Such claims have, of course, an existence apart from the attachments which accompanied them. In terminating these claims through Executive Order No. 12294, the President purported to act under authority of both the IEEPA and 22 U.S.C. § 1732, the so-called "Hostage Act." 48 Fed. Reg. 14111 (1981).

We conclude that although the IEEPA authorized the nullification of the attachments, it cannot be read to authorize the suspension of the claims. The claims of American citizens against Iran are not in themselves transactions involving Iranian property or efforts to exercise any rights with respect to such property. An *in personam* lawsuit, although it might eventually be reduced to judgment and that judgment might be executed upon, is an effort to establish liability and fix damages and does not focus on any particular property within the jurisdiction. The terms of the IEEPA therefore do not authorize the President to suspend claims in American courts.

[Similarly, the Hostage Act does not authorize the President to suspend the claims].

Although we have declined to conclude that the IEEPA or the Hostage Act directly authorizes the President's suspension of claims for the reasons noted, we cannot ignore the general tenor of Congress' legislation in this area in trying to determine whether the President is acting alone or at least with the acceptance of Congress. As we have noted, Congress cannot anticipate and legislate with regard to every possible action the President may find it necessary to take or every possible situation in which he might act. * * *

Not infrequently in affairs between nations, outstanding claims by nationals of one country against the government of another country are "sources of friction" between the two sovereigns. *United States v. Pink,* 315 U.S. 203, 225 (1942). To resolve these difficulties, nations have often entered into agreements settling the claims of their respective nationals. As one treatise writer puts it, international agreements settling claims by nationals of one state against the government of another "are established international practice reflecting traditional international theory." L. Henkin, Foreign Affairs and the Constitution 262 (1972). Consistent with that principle, the United States has repeatedly exercised its sovereign authority to settle the claims of its nationals against foreign countries. Though those settlements have sometimes been made by treaty, there has also been a longstanding practice of settling such claims by executive agreement without the advice and consent of the Senate. Under such agreements, the President has agreed to renounce or extinguish claims of United States nations against foreign governments in return for lump-sum payments or the establishment of arbitration procedures. * * * It is clear that the practice of settling claims continues today. Since 1952, the President has entered into at least 10 binding settlements with foreign nations, including an $80 million settlement with the Peoples Republic of China.

Crucial to our decision today is the conclusion that Congress has implicitly approved the practice of claim settlement by executive agreement. This is best demonstrated by Congress' enactment of the International Claims Settlement Act of 1949, 64 Stat. 13, as amended, 22 U.S.C. § 1621 *et seq*. (1976 ed. and Supp. IV). * * * By creating a procedure to implement future settlement agreements, Congress placed its stamp of approval on such agreements. * * *

In addition to congressional acquiescence in the President's power to settle claims, prior cases of this Court have also recognized that the President does have some measure of power to enter into executive agreements without obtaining the advice and consent of the Senate. In *United States v. Pink*, 315 U.S. 203 (1942), for example, the Court upheld the validity of the Litvinov Assignment, which was part of an Executive Agreement whereby the Soviet Union assigned to the United States amounts owed to it by American nationals so that outstanding claims of other American nationals could be paid. The Court explained that the resolution of such claims was integrally connected with normalizing United States relations with a foreign state:

> "Power to remove such obstacles to full recognition as settlement of claims of our nationals ... certainly is a modest implied power of the President.... No such obstacle can be placed in the way of rehabilitation of relations between this country and another nation, unless the historic conception of the powers and responsibilities ... is to be drastically revised."

Similarly, Judge Learned Hand recognized:

> "The constitutional power of the President extends to the settlement of mutual claims between a foreign government and the United States, at least when it is an incident to the recognition of that government; and it would be unreasonable to circumscribe it to such controversies. The continued mutual amity between the nation and other powers again and again depends upon a satisfactory compromise of mutual claims; the necessary power to make such compromises has existed from the earliest times and been exercised by the foreign offices of all civilized nations." *Ozanic v. United States*, 188 F.2d 228, 231 (CA2 1951). * * *

In light of all of the foregoing—the inferences to be drawn from the character of the legislation Congress has enacted in the area, such as the IEEPA and the Hostage Act, and from the history of acquiescence in executive claims settlement—we conclude that the President was authorized to suspend pending claims pursuant to Executive Order No. 12294. As Justice Frankfurter pointed out in *Youngstown*, 343 U.S., at 610–611, "a systematic, unbroken, executive practice, long pursued to the knowledge of the Congress and never before questioned . . . may be treated as a gloss on 'Executive Power' vested in the President by § 1 of Art. II." Past practice does not, by itself, create power, but "long-continued practice, known to and acquiesced in by Congress, would raise a presumption that the [action] had been [taken] in pursuance of its consent. . . ." *United States v. Midwest Oil Co.*, 236 U.S. 459, 474 (1915). Such practice is present here and such a presumption is also appropriate. In light of the fact that Congress may be considered to have consented to the President's action in suspending claims, we cannot say that action exceeded the President's powers.

Notes and Questions

1. *The* Youngstown *Test.* The test articulated by Justice Jackson in Youngstown Sheet & Tube Co. v. Sawyer, 343 U.S. 579, 72 S.Ct. 863, 96 L.Ed. 1153 (1952), is used quite effectively by Justice Rehnquist in *Dames & Moore*. In *Youngstown*, the test was employed to invalidate President Truman's seizure of steel mills during the Korean War because the Presidential act conflicted with Congressional intent. However, in *Dames & Moore*, the test is used to validate the acts of Presidents Carter and Reagan to end the Iranian hostage crisis. The Presidential acts easier to validate were those nullifying attachments of Iranian property and transferring the assets to the Federal Reserve Bank. Here it seems that the President acted well within the specific authorization of Congress in the International Emergency Economic Powers Act. More difficult for the Court are the Presidential acts suspending U.S. litigation in favor of claims arbitration before an international tribunal in The Hague. How persuasive need evidence be that suspension of claims was an ordinary feature of U.S. international practice? The "10 binding settlements with foreign nations" noted by the Court can be distinguished from the suspension of claims in *Dames & Moore*, *e.g.*, because made pursuant to powers specifically delegated to the President in peace treaties or because they involved lump sum payments to the United

States for distribution to claimants. See "Supreme Court, 1980 Term," 95 *Harvard Law Review* 91, 192–98 (1981). But even if there is sufficient relevant evidence that suspension of claims was customary, how does that custom make the suspension constitutional?

2. *The Continuing Relevance of* Curtiss–Wright. How does *Dames & Moore* treat the broad language of *Curtiss–Wright*? Does Justice Rehnquist mean to incorporate *Curtiss–Wright's* apparent endorsement of executive powers free from foundation in an act of Congress? Or does he mean to limit such powers with the three-tier analysis of *Youngstown*? If the role of the executive vis-à-vis the Congress in the realm of foreign affairs is left somewhat ambiguous after *Curtiss–Wright* and *Dames & Moore*, is that a desirable or undesirable state of affairs?

3. *The Hostages Crisis. Dames & Moore* grew out of the 1979–1981 hostages crisis. We look again at the U.S.–Iran conflict when we read the *Diplomatic and Consular Staff Case* in Chapter 5. Why did President Carter block all Iranian assets in the United States? Why did he initially permit private suits against Iran like that brought by *Dames & Moore*? Did the executive branch "use" private litigants to further the goals of American foreign policy? On President Carter's attempt to end the hostages crisis before he left office, see Jimmy Carter, *Keeping Faith: Memoirs of a President* 580–95 (1982). President Carter wrote that the "release of the American hostages had almost become an obsession with me." *Id.* at 594.

4. *The Constitution and U.S. International Legal Obligations.* If the Supreme Court had found that the executive branch could not lawfully terminate the legal suits against Iran in United States courts, would this have affected the international legal obligations of the United States? What would have been the practical effect? The possibility that the United States might not be able to honor its international legal commitment to Iran persuaded the Supreme Court to hold a rare special session to decide the case. Linda Greenhouse, "High Court Hears Iran Assets Case," *New York Times*, June 25, 1981, at D3.

UNITED STATES v. PALESTINE LIBERATION ORGANIZATION

695 F.Supp. 1456 (S.D.N.Y.1988).

PALMIERI, DISTRICT JUDGE.

The Anti-terrorism Act of 1987 (the "ATA"), is the focal point of this lawsuit. At the center of controversy is the right of the Palestine Liberation Organization (the "PLO") to maintain its office in conjunction with its work as a Permanent Observer to the United Nations. The case comes before the court on the government's motion for an injunction closing this office and on the defendants' motions to dismiss.

I

Background

The United Nations' Headquarters in New York were established as an international enclave by the *Agreement Between the United States and the United Nations Regarding the Headquarters of the United Nations* (the "Headquarters Agreement"). This agreement followed an invitation extended to the United Nations by the United States, one of its principal founders, to establish its seat within the United States.

As a meeting place and forum for all nations, the United Nations, according to its charter, was formed to:

> maintain international peace and security . . .; to develop friendly relations among nations, based on the principle of equal rights and self-determination of peoples . . .; to achieve international cooperation in solving international problems of an economic, social, cultural or humanitarian character . . .; and be a centre for harmonizing the actions of nations in the attainment of these common ends.

U.N. Charter art. 1. Today, 159 of the United Nations' members maintain missions to the U.N. in New York. In addition, the United Nations has, from its incipiency, welcomed various non-member observers to participate in its proceedings. Of these, several non-member nations,[4] intergovernmental organizations,[5] and other organizations[6] currently maintain "Permanent Observer Missions" in New York.

The PLO falls into the last of these categories and is present at the United Nations as its invitee. The PLO has none of the usual attributes of sovereignty. It is not accredited to the United States and does not have the benefits of diplomatic immunity. There is no recognized state it claims to govern. It purports to serve as the sole political representative of the Palestinian people. The PLO nevertheless considers itself to be the representative of a state, entitled to recognition in its relations with other governments, and is said to have diplomatic relations with approximately 100 countries throughout the world.

In 1974, the United Nations invited the PLO to become an observer at the U.N., to "participate in the sessions and the work of the General Assembly in the capacity of observer." The right of its representatives to admission to the United States as well as access to the U.N. was immediately challenged under American law. Judge Costantino rejected that challenge in *Anti–Defamation League of B'nai B'rith v. Kissinger,* Civil Action No. 74 C 1545 (E.D.N.Y. November 1, 1974). The court upheld the presence of a PLO representative in New York with access to the United Nations, albeit under certain entrance visa restrictions which limited PLO personnel movements to a radius of 25 miles from Columbus Circle in Manhattan. It stated from the bench:

> This problem must be viewed in the context of the special responsibility which the United States has to provide access to the United Nations under the Headquarters Agreement. It is important to

4. The Democratic People's Republic of Korea, the Holy See, Monaco, the Republic of Korea, San Marino and Switzerland.

5. The Asian–African Legal Consultative Committee, the Council for Mutual Assistance, the European Economic Community, the League of Arab States, the Organization of African Unity, and the Islamic Conference.

6. The PLO and the South West African Peoples' Organization (SWAPO).

note for the purposes of this case that a primary goal of the United Nations is to provide a forum where peaceful discussions may displace violence as a means of resolving disputed issues. At times our responsibility to the United Nations may require us to issue visas to persons who are objectionable to certain segments of our society.

Since 1974, the PLO has continued to function without interruption as a permanent observer and has maintained its Mission to the United Nations without trammel, largely because of the Headquarters Agreement, which we discuss below.

II

The Anti–Terrorism Act

In October 1986, members of Congress requested the United States Department of State to close the PLO offices located in the United States. That request proved unsuccessful, and proponents of the request introduced legislation with the explicit purpose of doing so.

The result was the ATA, 22 U.S.C. §§ 5201–5203. It is of a unique nature. We have been unable to find any comparable statute in the long history of Congressional enactments. The PLO is stated to be "a terrorist organization and a threat to the interests of the United States, its allies, and to international law and should not benefit from operating in the United States." The ATA was added, without committee hearings, as a rider to the Foreign Relations Authorization Act for Fiscal Years 1988–89, which provided funds for the operation of the State Department, including the operation of the United States Mission to the United Nations. The bill also authorized payments to the United Nations for maintenance and operation.

The ATA, which became effective on March 21, 1988, forbids the establishment or maintenance of "an office, headquarters, premises, or other facilities or establishments within the jurisdiction of the United States at the behest or direction of, or with funds provided by" the PLO, if the purpose is to further the PLO's interests. The ATA also forbids spending the PLO's funds or receiving anything of value except informational material from the PLO, with the same *mens rea* requirement.

Ten days before the effective date, the Attorney General wrote the Chief of the PLO Observer Mission to the United Nations that "maintaining a PLO Observer Mission to the United Nations will be unlawful," and advised him that upon failure of compliance, the Department of Justice would take action in federal court. * * *

The United States commenced this lawsuit the day the ATA took effect, seeking injunctive relief to accomplish the closure of the Mission. The United States Attorney for this District has personally represented that no action would be taken to enforce the ATA pending resolution of the litigation in this court.

There are now four individual defendants in addition to the PLO itself. Defendant Zuhdi Labib Terzi, who possesses an Algerian passport but whose citizenship is not divulged, has served as the Permanent Observer of the PLO to the United Nations since 1975. Defendant Riyad H. Mansour, a citizen of the United States, has been the Deputy Permanent Observer of the PLO to the United Nations since 1983. Defendant Nasser Al–Kidwa, a citizen of Iraq, is the Alternate Permanent Observer of the PLO to the United Nations. And defendant Veronica Kanaan Pugh, a citizen of Great Britain, is charged with administrative duties at the Observer Mission. These defendants contend that this court may not adjudicate the ATA's applicability to the Mission because such an adjudication would violate the United States' obligation under Section 21 of the Headquarters Agreement to arbitrate any dispute with the United Nations. Apart from that, they argue, application of the ATA to the PLO Mission would violate the United States' commitments under the Headquarters Agreement. They assert that the court lacks subject matter and personal jurisdiction over them and that they lack the capacity to be sued. Defendant Riyad H. Mansour additionally moves to dismiss for failure to state a claim upon which relief can be granted. Plaintiff, the United States, moves for summary judgment.

III

Personal Jurisdiction Over the Defendants

The PLO maintains an office in New York. The PLO pays for the maintenance and expenses of that office. It maintains a telephone listing in New York. The individuals employed at the PLO's Mission to the United Nations maintain a continuous presence in New York. There can be little question that it is within the bounds of fair play and substantial justice to hail them into court in New York. *International Shoe Co. v. Washington,* 326 U.S. 310, 320, 66 S.Ct. 154, 160, 90 L.Ed. 95 (1945). The limitations that the due process clause places on the exercise of personal jurisdiction are the only ones applicable to the statute in these circumstances. The PLO does not argue that it or its employees are the beneficiaries of any diplomatic immunity due to its presence as an invitee of the United Nations. We have no difficulty in concluding that the court has personal jurisdiction over the PLO and the individual defendants.

IV

The Duty to Arbitrate

Counsel for the PLO and for the United Nations and the Association of the Bar of the City of New York, as *amici curiae,* have suggested that the court defer to an advisory opinion of the International Court of Justice. *Applicability of the Obligation to Arbitrate Under Section 21 of the United Nations Headquarters Agreement of 26 June 1947,* 1988 I.C.J. 12 (April 26, 1988)(*U.N. v. U.S.*). That decision holds that the United States is bound by Section 21 of the Headquarters Agreement to submit to binding arbitration of a dispute precipitated by the passage of the ATA. Indeed, it is the PLO's position that this alleged duty to arbitrate deprives the court of subject matter jurisdiction over this litigation.

In June 1947, the United States subscribed to the Headquarters Agreement, defining the privileges and immunities of the United Nations' Headquarters in New York City, thereby becoming the "Host Country"—a descriptive title that has followed it through many United Nations proceedings. The Headquarters Agreement was brought into effect under United States law, with an annex, by a Joint Resolution of Congress approved by the President on August 4, 1947. The PLO rests its argument, as do the *amici,* on Section 21(a) of the Headquarters Agreement, which provides for arbitration in the case of any dispute between the United Nations and the United States concerning the interpretation or application of the Headquarters Agreement. Because interpretation of the ATA requires an interpretation of the Headquarters Agreement, they argue, this court must await the decision of an arbitral tribunal yet to be appointed before making its decision.

Section 21(a) of the Headquarters Agreement provides, in part:

> "Any dispute *between the United Nations and the United States* concerning the interpretation or application of this agreement or of any supplemental agreement, which is not settled by negotiation or other agreed mode of settlement, shall be referred for final decision to a tribunal of three arbitrators...."

61 Stat. at 764 (22 U.S.C. § 287 note)(emphasis supplied). Because these proceedings are not in any way directed to settling any dispute, ripe or not, between the United Nations and the United States, Section 21, is, by its terms, inapplicable.[18] The fact that the Headquarters Agreement was adopted by a majority of both Houses of Congress and approved by the President might lead to the conclusion that it provides a rule of decision requiring arbitration any time the interpretation of the Headquarters Agreement is at issue in the United States Courts. That conclusion would be wrong for two reasons.

First, this court cannot direct the United States to submit to arbitration without exceeding the scope of its Article III powers. What sets this case apart from the usual situation in which two parties have agreed to binding arbitration for the settlement of any future disputes, requiring the court to stay its proceedings, is that we are here involved with matters of international policy. This is an area in which the courts are generally unable to participate. These questions do not lend themselves to resolution by adjudication under our jurisprudence. *See generally Baker v. Carr,* 369 U.S. 186, 211–13, 82 S.Ct. 691, 707–08, 7 L.Ed.2d 663 (1962). The restrictions imposed upon the courts forbidding them to resolve such questions (often termed "political questions") derive not only from the limitations which inhere in the judicial process but also

18. The United Nations has explicitly refrained from becoming a party to this litigation. The International Court of Justice makes a persuasive statement that the proceedings before this court "cannot be an 'agreed mode of settlement' within the meaning of section 21 of the Headquarters Agreement. The purpose of these proceedings is to enforce the Anti–Terrorism Act of 1987; it is not directed to settling the [alleged] dispute, concerning the application of the Headquarters Agreement." *U.N. v. U.S. supra,* 1988 I.C.J. 12, ¶ 14, at 34.

from those imposed by Article III of the Constitution. *Marbury v. Madison,* 5 U.S. (1 Cranch) 137, 170, 2 L.Ed. 60 (1803)(Marshall, C.J.)("The province of the court is, solely, to decide on the right of individuals, not to inquire how the executive, or executive officers, perform duties in which they have a discretion. Questions in their nature political, or which are, by the constitution and laws, submitted to the executive can never be made in this Court."). The decision in *Marbury* has never been disturbed.

The conduct of the foreign relations of our Government is committed by the Constitution to the executive and legislative—the "political"—departments of the government. As the Supreme Court noted in *Baker v. Carr,* not all questions touching upon international relations are automatically political questions. Nonetheless, were the court to order the United States to submit to arbitration, it would violate several of the tenets to which the Supreme Court gave voice in *Baker v. Carr.* Resolution of the question whether the United States will arbitrate requires "an initial policy determination of a kind clearly for nonjudicial discretion"; deciding whether the United States will or ought to submit to arbitration, in the face of a determination not to do so by the executive,[21] would be impossible without the court "expressing lack of the respect due coordinate branches of government"; and such a decision would raise not only the "potentiality" but the reality of "embarrassment from multifarious pronouncements by various departments on one question." It is for these reasons that the ultimate decision as to how the United States should honor its treaty obligations with the international community is one which has, for at least 100 years, been left to the executive to decide. *Goldwater v. Carter,* 444 U.S. 996, 996–97 (1979)(vacating, with instructions to dismiss, an attack on the President's action in terminating a treaty with Taiwan); *Clark v. Allen,* 331 U.S. 503, 509 (1947)("President and Senate may denounce a treaty and thus terminate its life")(*quoting Techt v. Hughes,* 229 N.Y. 222, 243 (Cardozo, J.), *cert. denied,* 254 U.S. 643 (1920)); *Oetjen v. Central Leather Co.,* 246 U.S. 297, 302 (1918)(redress for violation of international accord must be sought via executive); *Chae Chan Ping v. United States (The Chinese Exclusion Case),* 130 U.S. 581, 602 ("the question whether our government is justified in disregarding its engagements with another nation is not one for the determination of the courts")(1889); *accord Whitney v. Robertson,* 124 U.S. 190, 194–95 (1888). Consequently the question whether the United States should submit to the jurisdiction of an international tribunal is a question of policy not for the courts but for the political branches to decide.

21. It is important to note that we may not inquire into the executive's reasons for refraining from arbitration, and in fact those reasons are not before us. *See* Press Conference, Assistant Attorney General Charles Cooper, 16 (March 11, 1988)("I would not describe any of the deliberations that went into that decision."); *see also* Letter of Assistant Attorney General John R. Bolton to Judge Edmund L. Palmieri (May 12, 1988)(docketed at the request of government counsel in 88 Civ. 1962 and 88 Civ. 2005)("arbitration would not be appropriate or timely").

Section 21 of the Headquarters Agreement cannot provide a rule of decision regarding the interpretation of that agreement for another reason: treating it as doing so would require the courts to refrain from undertaking their constitutionally mandated function. The task of the court in this case is to interpret the ATA in resolving this dispute between numerous parties and the United States. Interpretation of the ATA, as a matter of domestic law, falls to the United States courts. In interpreting the ATA, the effect of the United States' international obligations—the United Nations Charter and the Headquarters Agreement in particular—must be considered. As a matter of domestic law, the interpretation of these international obligations and their reconciliation, if possible, with the ATA is for the courts. It is, as Chief Justice Marshall said, "emphatically the province and duty of the judicial department to say what the law is." *Marbury v. Madison*, 5 U.S. (1 Cranch) 137, 177 (1803). That duty will not be resolved without independent adjudication of the effect of the ATA on the Headquarters Agreement. Awaiting the decision of an arbitral tribunal would be a repudiation of that duty.

Interpreting Section 21 as a rule of decision would, at a minimum, raise serious constitutional questions. We do not interpret it in that manner. It would not be consonant with the court's duties for it to await the interpretation of the Headquarters Agreement by an arbitral tribunal, not yet constituted, before undertaking the limited task of interpreting the ATA with a view to resolving the actual dispute before it.

In view of the foregoing, the court finds that it is not deprived of subject matter jurisdiction by Section 21 of the Headquarters Agreement and that any interpretation of the Headquarters Agreement incident to an interpretation of the ATA must be done by the court.

V

The Anti–Terrorism Act and the Headquarters Agreement

If the ATA were construed as the government suggests, it would be tantamount to a direction to the PLO Observer Mission at the United Nations that it close its doors and cease its operations *instanter*. Such an interpretation would fly in the face of the Headquarters Agreement, a prior treaty between the United Nations and the United States, and would abruptly terminate the functions the Mission has performed for many years. This conflict requires the court to seek out a reconciliation between the two.

Under our constitutional system, statutes and treaties are both the supreme law of the land, and the Constitution sets forth no order of precedence to differentiate between them. U.S. Const. art. VI, cl. 2. Wherever possible, both are to be given effect. *E.g. Trans World Airlines, Inc. v. Franklin Mint Corp.*, 466 U.S. 243, 252, 104 S.Ct. 1776, 1783, 80 L.Ed.2d 243 (1984). Only where a treaty is irreconcilable with a later enacted statute and Congress has clearly evinced an intent to supersede a treaty by enacting a statute does the later enacted statute take precedence. *E.g. The Chinese Exclusion Case,* 130 U.S. at 599–602, 9 S.Ct. at 627–38 (finding clear intent to supersede). * * *

The long standing and well-established position of the Mission at the United Nations, sustained by international agreement, when considered along with the text of the ATA and its legislative history, fails to disclose any clear legislative intent that Congress was directing the Attorney General, the State Department or this Court to act in contravention of the Headquarters Agreement. This court acknowledges the validity of the government's position that Congress *has the power* to enact statutes abrogating prior treaties or international obligations entered into by the United States. *Whitney v. Robertson,* 124 U.S. at 193–95, 8 S.Ct. at 457–58; *The Head Money Cases,* 112 U.S. at 597–99, 5 S.Ct. at 253–54. However, unless this power is clearly and unequivocally exercised, this court is under a duty to interpret statutes in a manner consonant with existing treaty obligations. This is a rule of statutory construction sustained by an unbroken line of authority for over a century and a half. * * *

The American Law Institute's recently revised *Restatement (Third) Foreign Relations Law of the United States* (1988) reflects this unbroken line of authority:

> § 115. Inconsistency Between International Law or Agreement and Domestic Law: Law of the United States.
>
> (1)(a) An Act of Congress supersedes an earlier rule of international law or a provision of an international agreement as law of the United States *if the purpose of the act to supersede the earlier rule or provision is clear* and if the act and the earlier rule or provision cannot be fairly reconciled.

(emphasis supplied).

We believe the ATA and the Headquarters Agreement cannot be reconciled except by finding the ATA inapplicable to the PLO Observer Mission.

A. The Obligations of the United States under the Headquarters Agreement.

The obligation of the United States to allow transit, entry and access stems not only from the language of the Headquarters Agreement but also from 40 years of practice under it. Section 11 of the Headquarters Agreement reads, in part,

> The federal, state or local authorities of the United States shall not impose any impediments to transit to or from the headquarters district of: (1) representatives of Members . . ., (5) other persons invited to the headquarters district by the United Nations . . . on official business.

61 Stat. at 761 (22 U.S.C. § 287 note). These rights could not be effectively exercised without the use of offices. The ability to effectively organize and carry out one's work, especially as a liaison to an interna-

tional organization, would not be possible otherwise. * * * The exemptions of Section 13 are not limited to members, but extend to invitees as well.

In addition, there can be no dispute that over the 40 years since the United States entered into the Headquarters Agreement it has taken a number of actions consistent with its recognition of a duty to refrain from impeding the functions of observer missions to the United Nations. It has, since the early days of the U.N.'s presence in New York, acquiesced in the presence of observer missions to the U.N. in New York.

After the United Nations invited the PLO to participate as a permanent observer, the Department of State took the position that it was required to provide access to the U.N. for the PLO. The State Department at no time disputed the notion that the rights of entry, access and residence guaranteed to invitees include the right to maintain offices.

The view that under the Headquarters Agreement the United States must allow PLO representatives access to and presence in the vicinity of the United Nations was adopted by the court in *Anti-Defamation League of B'nai B'rith v. Kissinger* [Civil Action No. 74 C 1545 (E.D.N.Y. Nov. 1, 1974)]; see also Harvard Law School Forum v. Shultz, 633 F.Supp. 525, 526–27 (D.Mass.1986). The United States has, for 14 years, acted in a manner consistent with a recognition of the PLO's rights in the Headquarters Agreement. This course of conduct under the Headquarters Agreement is important evidence of its meaning. *O'Connor v. United States,* 479 U.S. 27, 33, 107 S.Ct. 347, 351, 93 L.Ed.2d 206, 214 (1986).

Throughout 1987, when Congress was considering the ATA, the Department of State elaborated its view that the Headquarters Agreement contained such a requirement. Perhaps the most unequivocal elaboration of the State Department's interpretation was the letter of J. Edward Fox, Assistant Secretary for Legislative Affairs, to Dante Fascell, Chairman of the House Committee on Foreign Affairs (November 5, 1987):

> The United States has acknowledged that [the invitations to the PLO to become a permanent observer] give rise to United States obligations to accord PLO observers the rights set forth in sections 11–13 of the Headquarters Agreement. *See, e.g., 1976 Digest of United States Practice in International Law* 74–75. The proposed legislation would effectively require the United States to deny PLO observers the entry, transit, and residence rights required by sections 11–13 and, as a later enacted statute, would supersede the Headquarters Agreement in this regard as a matter of domestic law.
>
> The proposed legislation would also .... break a 40-year practice regarding observer missions by nations hosting U.N. bodies and could legitimately be viewed as inconsistent with our responsibilities under sections 11–13 of the United Nations Headquarters Agreement.

Shortly before the adoption of the ATA, during consideration of a report of the Committee on Relations with the Host Country by the General Assembly of the United Nations, the United States' representative noted "that the United States Secretary of State had stated that the closing of the mission would constitute a violation of United States obligation under the Headquarters Agreement." He had previously stated that "closing the mission, in our view, and I emphasize this is the executive branch, is not consistent with our international legal obligations under the Headquarters Agreement." And the day after the ATA was passed, State Department spokeswoman Phyllis Oakley told reporters that the ATA, "if implemented, would be contrary to our international legal obligations under the Headquarters Agreement [so the administration intends] ... to engage in consultations with the Congress in an effort to resolve this matter."

It seemed clear to those in the executive branch that closing the PLO mission would be a departure from the United States' practice in regard to observer missions, and they made their views known to members of Congress who were instrumental in the passage of the ATA. In addition, United States representatives to the United Nations made repeated efforts to allay the concerns of the U.N. Secretariat by reiterating and reaffirming the obligations of the United States under the Headquarters Agreement. A chronological record of their efforts is set forth in the advisory opinion of the International Court of Justice, *U.N. v. U.S., supra,* 1988 I.C.J. 12 ¶¶ 11–22, at 16–22 (April 26, 1988). The U.N. Secretariat considered it necessary to request that opinion in order to protect what it considered to be the U.N.'s rights under the Headquarters Agreement. The United Nations' position that the Headquarters Agreement applies to the PLO Mission is not new. 1979 U.N.Jurid.Y.B. 169–70; *see* 1980 U.N.Jurid.Y.B. 188 ¶ 3.

"Although not conclusive, the meaning attributed to treaty provisions by the Government agencies charged with their negotiation and enforcement is entitled to great weight." *Sumitomo Shoji America, Inc. v. Avagliano,* 457 U.S. 176, 184–85, 102 S.Ct. 2374, 2379, 72 L.Ed.2d 765 (1982). The interpretive statements of the United Nations also carry some weight, especially because they are in harmony with the interpretation given to the Headquarters Agreement by the Department of State. *O'Connor,* 479 U.S. at 32–33, 107 S.Ct. at 351, 96 L.Ed.2d at 214.

Thus the language, application and interpretation of the Headquarters Agreement lead us to the conclusion that it requires the United States to refrain from interference with the PLO Observer Mission in the discharge of its functions at the United Nations.

B. Reconciliation of the ATA and the Headquarters Agreement.

The lengths to which our courts have sometimes gone in construing domestic statutes so as to avoid conflict with international agreements are suggested by a passage from Justice Field's dissent in *Chew Heong,* 112 U.S. at 560, 560–61, 67 S.Ct. at 267, 267 (1884):

> I am unable to agree with my associates in their construction of the act ... restricting the immigration into this country of Chinese laborers. That construction appears to me to be in conflict with the language of that act, and to require the elimination of entire clauses and the interpolation of new ones. It renders nugatory whole provisions which were inserted with sedulous care. The change thus produced in the operation of the act is justified on the theory that to give it any other construction would bring it into conflict with the treaty; and that we are not at liberty to suppose that Congress intended by its legislation to disregard any treaty stipulations.

Chew Heong concerned the interplay of legislation regarding Chinese laborers with treaties on the same subject. During the passage of the statute at issue in *Chew Heong,* "it was objected to the legislation sought that the treaty of 1868 stood in the way, and that while it remained unmodified, such legislation would be a breach of faith to China...." In spite of that, and over Justice Field's dissent, the Court, in Justice Field's words, "narrow[ed] the meaning of the act so as measurably to frustrate its intended operation." Four years after the decision in *Chew Heong,* Congress amended the act in question to nullify that decision. With the amended statute, there could be no question as to Congress' intent to supersede the treaties, and it was the later enacted statute which took precedence. *The Chinese Exclusion Case,* 130 U.S. at 598–99, 9 S.Ct. at 627 (1889).

The principles enunciated and applied in *Chew Heong* and its progeny, *e.g. Trans World Airlines,* 466 U.S. at 252, 104 S.Ct. at 1783, require the clearest of expressions on the part of Congress. We are constrained by these decisions to stress the lack of clarity in Congress' action in this instance. Congress' failure to speak with one clear voice on this subject requires us to interpret the ATA as inapplicable to the Headquarters Agreement. This is so, in short, for the reasons which follow.

First, neither the Mission nor the Headquarters Agreement is mentioned in the ATA itself. Such an inclusion would have left no doubt as to Congress' intent on a matter which had been raised repeatedly with respect to this act, and its absence here reflects equivocation and avoidance, leaving the court without clear interpretive guidance in the language of the act. Second, while the section of the ATA prohibiting the maintenance of an office applies "notwithstanding any provision of law to the contrary," it does not purport to apply notwithstanding any *treaty*. The absence of that interpretive instruction is especially relevant because elsewhere in the same legislation Congress expressly referred to "United States law (including any treaty.)" Thus Congress failed, in the text of the ATA, to provide guidance for the interpretation of the act, where it became repeatedly apparent before its passage that the prospect of an interpretive problem was inevitable. Third, no member of Congress expressed a clear and unequivocal intent to supersede the Headquarters Agreement by passage of the ATA. In contrast, most who addressed the subject of conflict denied that there would be a conflict: in their view, the Headquarters Agreement did not provide the PLO with any right to maintain an office. Here again, Congress provided no guidance for the interpretation of the ATA in the event of a conflict which was clearly foreseeable. And Senator Clairborne Pell, Chairman of the Senate Foreign Relations Committee, who voted for the bill, raised the possibility that the Headquarters Agreement would take precedence over the ATA in the event of a conflict between the two. His suggestion was neither opposed nor debated, even though it came in the final minutes before passage of the ATA.

A more complete explanation begins, of course, with the statute's language. The ATA reads, in part:

> It shall be unlawful, if the purpose be to further the interests of the PLO * * *
>
> (3) notwithstanding any provision of law to the contrary, to establish or maintain an office, headquarters, premises, or other facilities or establishments within the jurisdiction of the United States at the behest or direction of or with funds provided by the PLO * * *.

The Permanent Observer Mission to the United Nations is nowhere mentioned *in haec verba* in this act, as we have already observed. It is nevertheless contended by the United States that the foregoing provision requires the closing of the Mission, and this in spite of possibly inconsistent international obligations. According to the government, the act is so clear that this possibility is nonexistent. The government argues that its position is supported by the provision that the ATA would take effect "notwithstanding any provision of law to the contrary," suggesting that Congress thereby swept away any inconsistent international obligations of the United States. In effect, the government urges literal application of the maxim that in the event of conflict between two laws, the one of later date will prevail: *leges posteriores priores contrarias abrogant.*

We cannot agree. The proponents of the ATA were, at an early stage and throughout its consideration, forewarned that the ATA would present a potential conflict with the Headquarters Agreement. It was especially important in those circumstances for Congress to give clear, indeed unequivocal guidance, as to how an interpreter of the ATA was to resolve the conflict. Yet there was no reference to the Mission in the text of the ATA, despite extensive discussion of the Mission in the floor debates. Nor was there reference to the Headquarters Agreement, or to any treaty, in the ATA or in its "notwithstanding" clause, despite the textual expression of intent to supersede treaty obligations in other sections of the Foreign Relations Authorization Act, of which the ATA formed a part. Thus Congress failed to provide unequivocal interpretive guidance in the text of the ATA, leaving open the possibility that the ATA could be viewed as a law of general application and enforced as such, without encroaching on the position of the Mission at the United Nations.

That interpretation would present no inconsistency with what little legislative history exists. There were conflicting voices both in Congress and in the executive branch before the enactment of the ATA. Indeed, there is only one matter with respect to which there was unanimity—the condemnation of terrorism. This, however, is extraneous to the legal issues involved here. At oral argument, the United States Attorney conceded that there was no evidence before the court that the Mission had misused its position at the United Nations or engaged in any covert actions in furtherance of terrorism. If the PLO is benefiting from operating in the United States, as the ATA implies, the enforcement of its provisions outside the context of the United Nations can effectively curtail that benefit.

The record contains voices of congressmen and senators forceful in their condemnation of terrorism and of the PLO and supporting the notion that the legislation would close the mission. There are other voices, less certain of the validity of the proposed congressional action and preoccupied by problems of constitutional dimension. And there are voices of Congressmen uncertain of the legal issues presented but desirous nonetheless of making a "political statement." During the discussions which preceded and followed the passage of the ATA, the Secretary of State and the legal Adviser to the Department of State, a former member of this Court, voiced their opinions to the effect that the ATA presented a conflict with the Headquarters Agreement.

Yet no member of Congress, at any point, explicitly stated that the ATA was intended to override any international obligation of the United States.

The only debate on this issue focused not on whether the ATA would do so, but on whether the United States in fact had an obligation to provide access to the PLO. Indeed, every proponent of the ATA who spoke to the matter argued that the United States did not have such an obligation. For instance, Senator Grassley, after arguing that the United States had no obligation relating to the PLO Mission under the Headquarters Agreement, noted in passing that Congress had the *power* to modify treaty obligations. But even there, Senator Grassley did not argue that the ATA would supersede the Headquarters Agreement in the event of a conflict. This disinclination to face the prospect of an actual conflict was again manifest two weeks later, when Senator Grassley explained, "as I detailed earlier ..., the United States has *no international legal obligation* that would preclude it from closing the PLO Observer Mission." As the Congressional Record reveals, at the time of the ATA's passage (on December 15 in the House and December 16 in the Senate), its proponents were operating under a misapprehension of what the United States' treaty obligation entailed. 133 Cong.Rec. S 18,190 (daily ed. December 16, 1987)(statement of Sen. Helms)(closing the Mission would be "entirely within our Nation's obligations under international law"); 133 Cong.Rec. H 11,425 (daily ed. December 15, 1988)(statement of Rep. Burton)(observer missions have "no—zero—rights in the Headquarters Agreement").

In sum, the language of the Headquarters Agreement, the long-standing practice under it, and the interpretation given it by the parties to it leave no doubt that it places an obligation upon the United States to refrain from impairing the function of the PLO Observer Mission to the United Nations. The ATA and its legislative history do not manifest Congress' intent to abrogate this obligation. We are therefore constrained to interpret the ATA as failing to supersede the Headquarters Agreement and inapplicable to the Mission.

Notes and Questions

1. *The Decision Not to Appeal.* The Reagan Administration was split in the aftermath of the *PLO Case.* A high Justice Department official told the *New York Times* that "[t]here is a unanimous belief in this department that the decision should be appealed," but the State Department's Legal Adviser, Abraham Sofaer, countered: "It was a grave mistake for Congress to attempt to close the P.L.O. office. It would violate the United Nations Headquarters Agreement." Clovis Maksoud, the representative of the Arab League in the United States, stated that an appeal "would erode the credibility of the United States in the Middle East." Robert Pear, "U.S. Officials Split Over Whether to Appeal Ruling on P.L.O.," *New York Times*, Aug. 28, 1988, § 1, at 5.

Finally, President Reagan himself had to resolve the dispute between Justice and State. He decided not to appeal the District Court's judgment. On August 29, 1988, the Justice Department issued the following statement: "It is the Administration's normal policy to appeal adverse District Court decisions of this kind. But it was decided, in light of foreign policy considerations, including the U.S. role as host to the United Nations organization, not to appeal in this instance." Robert Pear, "U.S. Will Allow P.L.O. to Maintain Its Office at U.N.," *New York Times*, Aug. 30, 1988, § A, at 1.

2. *The Judicial Reasoning of the* PLO Case. Professor Rosalyn Higgins, now a judge on the International Court of Justice, called the *PLO Case* "a remarkable piece of judicial reasoning, at once admirably purpose-oriented but unpersuasive." Rosalyn Higgins, *Problems and Process: International Law and How We Use It* 215 (1994). Is this a fair critique? After all, the court had to reconcile two competing principles of interpretation in applying international law. One was the rule in *Whitney* that in a conflict between a treaty and a statute "the one last in date will control the other." The other was also enunciated in *Whitney*, *i.e.*, "the courts will always endeavor to construe [a competing treaty and federal statute] so as to give effect to both," a proposition elaborated in *Chew Heong* and *Trans World Airlines,* both discussed in the *PLO Case.* Is the fact that neither the President nor the Congress sought to disturb the District Court's ruling dispositive of whether the judge got the legislative intent of the statute right or not? Or did the President and the Congress simply want to say one thing in the statute and do another in practice?

3. *The Duty to Arbitrate.* Is Judge Palmieri persuasive in refusing to order arbitration between the United States and the United Nations under Section 21(a) of the U.N. Headquarters Agreement? The judge suggests that, even if Section 21(a) did apply, a U.S. court would not order arbitra-

tion. Why not? If the other branches of government have already accepted a treaty obligating the United States to arbitrate certain international disputes, why should a court not order compliance with the legal obligation to arbitrate?

UNITED STATES v. ALVAREZ-MACHAIN

504 U.S. 655, 112 S.Ct. 2188, 119 L.Ed.2d 441 (1992).

CHIEF JUSTICE REHNQUIST delivered the opinion of the Court.

The issue in this case is whether a criminal defendant, abducted to the United States from a nation with which it has an extradition treaty, thereby acquires a defense to the jurisdiction of this country's courts. We hold that he does not, and that he may be tried in federal district court for violations of the criminal law of the United States.

Respondent, Humberto Alvarez–Machain, is a citizen and resident of Mexico. He was indicted for participating in the kidnap and murder of United States Drug Enforcement Administration (DEA) special agent Enrique Camarena–Salazar and a Mexican pilot working with Camarena, Alfredo Zavala–Avelar. The DEA believes that respondent, a medical doctor, participated in the murder by prolonging Agent Camarena's life so that others could further torture and interrogate him. On April 2, 1990, respondent was forcibly kidnapped from his medical office in Guadalajara, Mexico, to be flown by private plane to El Paso, Texas, where he was arrested by DEA officials. The District Court concluded that DEA agents were responsible for respondent's abduction, although they were not personally involved in it. *United States v. Caro-Quintero*, 745 F.Supp. 599, 602–604, 609 (C.D.Cal.1990).[2]

Respondent moved to dismiss the indictment, claiming that his abduction constituted outrageous governmental conduct, and that the District Court lacked jurisdiction to try him because he was abducted in violation of the extradition treaty between the United States and Mexico. Extradition Treaty, May 4, 1978, [1979] United States–United Mexican States, 31 U.S.T. 5059, T.I.A.S. No. 9656 (Extradition Treaty or Treaty). The District Court rejected the outrageous governmental conduct claim, but held that it lacked jurisdiction to try respondent because his abduction violated the Extradition Treaty. The District Court discharged respondent and ordered that he be repatriated to Mexico.

The Court of Appeals affirmed the dismissal of the indictment and the repatriation of respondent * * *. * * *

* * * We granted certiorari, and now reverse.

Although we have never before addressed the precise issue raised in the present case, we have previously considered proceedings in claimed violation of an extradition treaty and proceedings against a defendant

2. Apparently, DEA officials had attempted to gain respondent's presence in the United States through informal negotiations with Mexican officials, but were unsuccessful. DEA officials then, through a contact in Mexico, offered to pay a reward and expenses in return for the delivery of respondent to the United States.

brought before a court by means of a forcible abduction. We addressed the former issue in *United States v. Rauscher,* 119 U.S. 407 (1886); more precisely, the issue of whether the Webster–Ashburton Treaty of 1842, 8 Stat. 576, which governed extraditions between England and the United States, prohibited the prosecution of defendant Rauscher for a crime other than the crime for which he had been extradited. Whether this prohibition, known as the doctrine of specialty, was an intended part of the treaty had been disputed between the two nations for some time. Justice Miller delivered the opinion of the Court, which carefully examined the terms and history of the treaty; the practice of nations in regards to extradition treaties; the case law from the States; and the writings of commentators, and reached the following conclusion:

> "[A] person who has been brought within the jurisdiction of the court by *virtue of proceedings under an extradition treaty,* can only be tried for one of the offences described in that treaty, and for the offence with which he is charged in the proceedings for his extradition, until a reasonable time and opportunity have been given him, after his release or trial upon such charge, to return to the country from whose asylum he had been forcibly taken under those proceedings."

In addition, Justice Miller's opinion noted that any doubt as to this interpretation was put to rest by two federal statutes which imposed the doctrine of specialty upon extradition treaties to which the United States was a party. Unlike the case before us today, the defendant in *Rauscher* had been brought to the United States by way of an extradition treaty; there was no issue of a forcible abduction.

In *Ker v. Illinois*, 119 U.S. 436 (1886), also written by Justice Miller and decided the same day as *Rauscher,* we addressed the issue of a defendant brought before the court by way of a forcible abduction. Frederick Ker had been tried and convicted in an Illinois court for larceny; his presence before the court was procured by means of forcible abduction from Peru. A messenger was sent to Lima with the proper warrant to demand Ker by virtue of the extradition treaty between Peru and the United States. The messenger, however, disdained reliance on the treaty processes, and instead forcibly kidnapped Ker and brought him to the United States. We distinguished Ker's case from *Rauscher,* on the basis that Ker was not brought into the United States by virtue of the extradition treaty between the United States and Peru, and rejected Ker's argument that he had a right under the extradition treaty to be returned to this country only in accordance with its terms. We rejected Ker's due process argument more broadly, holding in line with "the highest authorities" that "such forcible abduction is no sufficient reason why the party should not answer when brought within the jurisdiction of the court which has the right to try him for such an offence, and presents no valid objection to his trial in such court." * * *

The only differences between *Ker* and the present case are that *Ker* was decided on the premise that there was no governmental involvement in the abduction; and Peru, from which Ker was abducted, did not object to his prosecution. Respondent finds these differences to be dispositive, * * * contending that they show that respondent's prosecution, like the prosecution of Rauscher, violates the implied terms of a valid extradition treaty. * * * Therefore, our first inquiry must be whether the abduction of respondent from Mexico violated the extradition treaty between the United States and Mexico. If we conclude that the Treaty does not prohibit respondent's abduction, the rule in *Ker* applies, and the court need not inquire as to how respondent came before it.

In construing a treaty, as in construing a statute, we first look to its terms to determine its meaning. *Air France v. Saks*, 470 U.S. 392, 397 (1985); *Valentine v. United States ex. rel. Neidecker,* 299 U.S. 5, 11 (1936). The Treaty says nothing about the obligations of the United States and Mexico to refrain from forcible abductions of people from the territory of the other nation, or the consequences under the Treaty if such an abduction occurs. Respondent submits that Article 22(1) of the Treaty which states that it "shall apply to offenses specified in Article 2 [including murder] committed before and after this Treaty enters into force," evidences an intent to make application of the Treaty mandatory for those offenses. However, the more natural conclusion is that Article 22 was included to ensure that the Treaty was applied to extraditions requested after the Treaty went into force, regardless of when the crime of extradition occurred.

More critical to respondent's argument is Article 9 of the Treaty which provides:

> "1. Neither Contracting Party shall be bound to deliver up its own nationals, but the executive authority of the requested Party shall, if not prevented by the laws of that Party, have the power to deliver them up if, in its discretion, it be deemed proper to do so.
>
> "2. If extradition is not granted pursuant to paragraph 1 of this Article, the requested Party shall submit the case to its competent authorities for the purpose of prosecution, provided that Party has jurisdiction over the offense."

According to respondent, Article 9 embodies the terms of the bargain which the United States struck: if the United States wishes to prosecute a Mexican national, it may request that individual's extradition. Upon a request from the United States, Mexico may either extradite the individual, or submit the case to the proper authorities for prosecution in Mexico. In this way, respondent reasons, each nation preserved its right to choose whether its nationals would be tried in its own courts or by the courts of the other nation. This preservation of rights would be frustrated if either nation were free to abduct nationals of the other nation for the purposes of prosecution. More broadly, respondent reasons, as did the Court of Appeals, that all the processes and restrictions on the obligation to extradite established by the Treaty would make no sense if either nation were free to resort to forcible kidnapping to gain the presence of an individual for prosecution in a manner not contemplated by the Treaty.

We do not read the Treaty in such a fashion. Article 9 does not purport to specify the only way in which one country may gain custody of a national of the other country for the purposes of prosecution. In the absence of an extradition treaty, nations are under no obligation to surrender those in their country to foreign authorities for prosecution. Extradition treaties exist so as to impose mutual obligations to surrender individuals in certain defined sets of circumstances, following established procedures. See 1 J. Moore, A Treatise on Extradition and Interstate Rendition, § 72 (1891). The Treaty thus provides a mechanism which would not otherwise exist, requiring, under certain circumstances, the United States and Mexico to extradite individuals to the other country, and establishing the procedures to be followed when the Treaty is invoked.

The history of negotiation and practice under the Treaty also fails to show that abductions outside of the Treaty constitute a violation of the Treaty. As the Solicitor General notes, the Mexican government was made aware, as early as 1906, of the *Ker* doctrine, and the United States position that it applied to forcible abductions made outside of the terms of the United States–Mexico Extradition Treaty. Nonetheless, the current version of the Treaty, signed in 1978, does not attempt to establish a rule that would in any way curtail the effect of *Ker*. Moreover, although language which would grant individuals exactly the right sought by respondent had been considered and drafted as early as 1935 by a prominent group of legal scholars sponsored by the faculty of Harvard Law School, no such clause appears in the current treaty.[13]

Thus, the language of the Treaty, in the context of its history, does not support the proposition that the Treaty prohibits abductions outside of its terms. The remaining question, therefore, is whether the Treaty should be interpreted so as to include an implied term prohibiting prosecution where the defendant's presence is obtained by means other than those established by the Treaty.

Respondent contends that the Treaty must be interpreted against the backdrop of customary international law, and that international abductions are "so clearly prohibited in international law" that there was no reason to include such a clause in the Treaty itself. The international censure of international abductions is further evidenced, according to respondent, by the United Nations Charter and the Charter of the Organization of American States. Respondent does not argue that

13. In Article 16 of the Draft Convention on Jurisdiction with Respect to Crime, the Advisory Committee of the Research in International Law proposed:

"In exercising jurisdiction under this Convention, no State shall prosecute or punish any person who has been brought within its territory or a place subject to its authority by recourse to measures in violation of international law or international convention without first obtaining the consent of the State or States whose rights have been violated by such measures." Harvard Research in International Law, 29 Am. J. Int'l L. 442 (Supp. 1935).

these sources of international law provide an independent basis for the right respondent asserts not to be tried in the United States, but rather that they should inform the interpretation of the Treaty terms. * * *

Respondent and his *amici* may be correct that respondent's abduction was "shocking," and that it may be in violation of general international law principles. Mexico has protested the abduction of respondent through diplomatic notes, and the decision of whether respondent should be returned to Mexico, as a matter outside of the Treaty, is a matter for the Executive Branch. We conclude, however, that respondent's abduction was not in violation of the Extradition Treaty between the United States and Mexico, and therefore the rule of *Ker v. Illinois* is fully applicable to this case. The fact of respondent's forcible abduction does not therefore prohibit his trial in a court in the United States for violations of the criminal laws of the United States.

The judgment of the Court of Appeals is therefore reversed, and the case is remanded for further proceedings consistent with this opinion.

So ordered.

JUSTICE STEVENS, with whom JUSTICE BLACKMUN and JUSTICE O'CONNOR join, dissenting.

The Court correctly observes that this case raises a question of first impression. The case is unique for several reasons. It does not involve an ordinary abduction by a private kidnaper, or bounty hunter, as in *Ker v. Illinois,* 119 U.S. 436 (1886); nor does it involve the apprehension of an American fugitive who committed a crime in one State and sought asylum in another, as in *Frisbie v. Collins,* 342 U.S. 519 (1952). Rather, it involves this country's abduction of another country's citizen; it also involves a violation of the territorial integrity of that other country, with which this country has signed an extradition treaty.

A Mexican citizen was kidnaped in Mexico and charged with a crime committed in Mexico; his offense allegedly violated both Mexican and American law. Mexico has formally demanded on at least two separate occasions[1] that he be returned to Mexico and has represented that he will be prosecuted and, if convicted, punished for his alleged offense.[2] It is clear that Mexico's demand must be honored if this official abduction

1. The abduction of respondent occurred on April 2, 1990. Mexico responded quickly and unequivocally. On April 18, 1990, Mexico requested an official report on the role of the United States in the abduction, and on May 16, 1990, and July 19, 1990, it sent diplomatic notes of protest from the Embassy of Mexico to the United States Department of State. See Brief for United Mexican States as *Amicus Curiae* (Mexican *Amicus*) 5–6; App. to Mexican *Amicus* 1a–24a. In the May 16th note, Mexico said that it believed that the abduction was "carried out with the knowledge of persons working for the U.S. government, in violation of the procedure established in the extradition treaty in force between the two countries," and in the July 19th note, it requested the provisional arrest and extradition of the law enforcement agents allegedly involved in the abduction.

2. Mexico has already tried a number of members involved in the conspiracy that resulted in the murder of the DEA agent. For example, Rafael Caro–Quintero, a co-conspirator of Alvarez–Machain in this case, has already been imprisoned in Mexico on a 40–year sentence. See Brief for Lawyers Committee for Human Rights as *Amicus Curiae* 4.

violated the 1978 Extradition Treaty between the United States and Mexico. In my opinion, a fair reading of the treaty in light of our decision in *United States v. Rauscher,* 119 U.S. 407 (1886), and applicable principles of international law, leads inexorably to the conclusion that the District Court, *United States v. Caro–Quintero,* 745 F.Supp. 599 (C.D.Cal.1990), and the Court of Appeals for the Ninth Circuit, 946 F.2d 1466 (1991)*(per curiam),* correctly construed that instrument.

I

The extradition treaty with Mexico is a comprehensive document containing 23 articles and an appendix listing the extraditable offenses covered by the agreement. The parties announced their purpose in the preamble: The two Governments desire "to cooperate more closely in the fight against crime and, to this end, to mutually render better assistance in matters of extradition." From the preamble, through the description of the parties' obligations with respect to offenses committed within as well as beyond the territory of a requesting party, the delineation of the procedures and evidentiary requirements for extradition, the special provisions for political offenses and capital punishment, and other details, the Treaty appears to have been designed to cover the entire subject of extradition. Thus, Article 22, entitled "Scope of Application" states that the "Treaty shall apply to offenses specified in Article 2 committed before and after this Treaty enters into force," and Article 2 directs that "[e]xtradition shall take place, subject to this Treaty, for willful acts which fall within any of [the extraditable offenses listed in] the clauses of the Appendix." Moreover, as noted by the Court, Article 9 expressly provides that neither Contracting Party is bound to deliver up its own nationals, although it may do so in its discretion, but if it does not do so, it "shall submit the case to its competent authorities for purposes of prosecution."

Petitioner's claim that the Treaty is not exclusive, but permits forcible governmental kidnaping, would transform these, and other, provisions into little more than verbiage. For example, provisions requiring "sufficient" evidence to grant extradition (Art. 3), withholding extradition for political or military offenses (Art. 5), withholding extradition when the person sought has already been tried (Art. 6), withholding extradition when the statute of limitations for the crime has lapsed (Art. 7), and granting the requested State discretion to refuse to extradite an individual who would face the death penalty in the requesting country (Art. 8), would serve little purpose if the requesting country could simply kidnap the person. As the Court of Appeals for the Ninth Circuit recognized in a related case, "[e]ach of these provisions would be utterly frustrated if a kidnapping were held to be a permissible course of governmental conduct." *United States v. Verdugo–Urquidez,* 939 F.2d 1341, 1349 (1991). In addition, all of these provisions "only make sense if they are understood as *requiring* each treaty signatory to comply with those procedures whenever it wishes to obtain jurisdiction over an individual who is located in another treaty nation."

It is true, as the Court notes, that there is no express promise by either party to refrain from forcible abductions in the territory of the other Nation. Relying on that omission, the Court, in effect, concludes that the Treaty merely creates an optional method of obtaining jurisdiction over alleged offenders, and that the parties silently reserved the right to resort to self help whenever they deem force more expeditious than legal process.[11] If the United States, for example, thought it more expedient to torture or simply to execute a person rather than to attempt extradition, these options would be equally available because they, too, were not explicitly prohibited by the Treaty.[12] That, however, is a highly improbable interpretation of a consensual agreement, which on its face appears to have been intended to set forth comprehensive and exclusive rules concerning the subject of extradition.[14] In my opinion, "the manifest scope and object of the treaty itself," *Rauscher,* 119 U.S., at 422, plainly imply a mutual undertaking to respect the territorial integrity of the other contracting party. That opinion is confirmed by a consideration of the "legal context" in which the Treaty was negotiated.[15] *Cannon v. University of Chicago*, 441 U.S. 677, 699 (1979).

II

In *Rauscher,* the Court construed an extradition treaty that was far less comprehensive than the 1978 Treaty with Mexico. The 1842 Treaty with Great Britain determined the boundary between the United States and Canada, provided for the suppression of the African slave trade, and also contained one paragraph authorizing the extradition of fugitives "in certain cases." In Article X, each Nation agreed to "deliver up to justice all persons" properly charged with any one of seven specific crimes, including murder. After Rauscher had been extradited for murder, he was charged with the lesser offense of inflicting cruel and unusual punishment on a member of the crew of a vessel on the high seas.

11. To make the point more starkly, the Court has, in effect, written into Article 9 a new provision, which says: "Notwithstanding paragraphs 1 and 2 of this Article, either Contracting Party can, without the consent of the other, abduct nationals from the territory of one Party to be tried in the territory of the other."

12. It is ironic that the United States has attempted to justify its unilateral action based on the kidnaping, torture, and murder of a federal agent by authorizing the kidnaping of respondent, for which the American law enforcement agents who participated have now been charged by Mexico. This goes to my earlier point, that extradition treaties promote harmonious relations by providing for the orderly surrender of a person by one State to another, and without such treaties, resort to force often followed.

14. Mexico's understanding is that "[t]he extradition treaty governs comprehensively the delivery of all persons for trial in the requesting state 'for an offense committed outside the territory of the requesting Party.'" And Canada, with whom the United States also shares a large border and with whom the United States also has an extradition treaty, understands the treaty to be "the exclusive means for a requesting government to obtain ... a removal" of a person from its territory, unless a Nation otherwise gives its consent.

15. The United States has offered no evidence from the negotiating record, ratification process, or later communications with Mexico to support the suggestion that a different understanding with Mexico was reached. See M. Bassiouni, International Extradition: United States Law and Practice Ch. 2, § 4.3, at p. 82 ("Negotiations, preparatory works, and diplomatic correspondence are an integral part of th[e] surrounding circumstances, and [are] often relied on by courts in ascertaining the intentions of the parties")(footnote omitted).

Although the treaty did not purport to place any limit on the jurisdiction of the demanding State after acquiring custody of the fugitive, this Court held that he could not be tried for any offense other than murder. Thus, the treaty constituted the exclusive means by which the United States could obtain jurisdiction over a defendant within the territorial jurisdiction of Great Britain.

The Court noted that the treaty included several specific provisions, such as the crimes for which one could be extradited, the process by which the extradition was to be carried out, and even the evidence that was to be produced, and concluded that "the fair purpose of the treaty is, that the person shall be delivered up to be tried for that offence and for no other." The Court reasoned that it did not make sense for the treaty to provide such specifics only to have the person "pas[s] into the hands of the country which charges him with the offence, free from all the positive requirements and just implications of the treaty under which the transfer of his person takes place." To interpret the treaty in a contrary way would mean that a country could request extradition of a person for one of the seven crimes covered by the treaty, and then try the person for another crime, such as a political crime, which was clearly not covered by the treaty; this result, the Court concluded, was clearly contrary to the intent of the parties and the purpose of the treaty.

Rejecting an argument that the sole purpose of Article X was to provide a procedure for the transfer of an individual from the jurisdiction of one sovereign to another, the Court stated:

> "No such view of solemn public treaties between the great nations of the earth can be sustained by a tribunal called upon to give judicial construction to them.
>
> "The opposite view has been attempted to be maintained in this country upon the ground that there is no express limitation in the treaty of the right of the country in which the offence was committed to try the person for the crime alone for which he was extradited, and that once being within the jurisdiction of that country, no matter by what contrivance or fraud or by what pretence of establishing a charge provided for by the extradition treaty he may have been brought within the jurisdiction, he is, when here, liable to be tried for any offence against the laws as though arrested here originally. This proposition of the absence of express restriction in the treaty of the right to try him for other offenses than that for which he was extradited, is met by the manifest scope and object of the treaty itself."

Thus, the Extradition Treaty, as understood in the context of cases that have addressed similar issues, suffices to protect the defendant from prosecution despite the absence of any express language in the Treaty itself purporting to limit this Nation's power to prosecute a defendant over whom it had lawfully acquired jurisdiction.

Although the Court's conclusion in *Rauscher* was supported by a number of judicial precedents, the holdings in these cases were not nearly as uniform as the consensus of international opinion that condemns one Nation's violation of the territorial integrity of a friendly neighbor.[20] It is shocking that a party to an extradition treaty might believe that it has secretly reserved the right to make seizures of citizens in the other party's territory.[21] Justice Story found it shocking enough that the United States would attempt to justify an American seizure of a foreign vessel in a Spanish port:

> "But, even supposing, for a moment, that our laws had required an entry of The Apollon, in her transit, does it follow that the power to arrest her was meant to be given, after she had passed into the exclusive territory of a foreign nation? We think not. *It would be monstrous* to suppose that our revenue officers were authorized to enter into foreign ports and territories, for the purpose of seizing vessels which had offended against our laws. It cannot be presumed that Congress would voluntarily justify such a clear violation of the laws of nations." *The Apollon,* 9 Wheat. 362, 370–371 (1824)(emphasis added).[22]

The law of Nations, as understood by Justice Story in 1824, has not changed. Thus, a leading treatise explains:

> "A State must not perform acts of sovereignty in the territory of another State.

20. This principle is embodied in Article 17 of the Charter of the Organization of American States, Apr. 30, 1948, 2 U.S.T. 2394, T.I.A.S. No. 2361, as amended by the Protocol of Buenos Aires, Feb. 27, 1967, 21 U.S.T. 607, T.I.A.S. No. 6847, as well as numerous provisions of the United Nations Charter, June 26, 1945, 59 Stat. 1031, T.S. No. 993 (to which both the United States and Mexico are signatories). See generally Mann, Reflections on the Prosecution of Persons Abducted in Breach of International Law, in International Law at a Time of Perplexity 407 (Y. Dinstein and M. Tabory eds. 1989).

21. When Abraham Sofaer, Legal Adviser of the State Department, was questioned at a congressional hearing, he resisted the notion that such seizures were acceptable: " 'Can you imagine us going into Paris and seizing some person we regard as a terrorist ...? [H]ow would we feel if some foreign nation—let us take the United Kingdom—came over here and seized some terrorist suspect in New York City, or Boston, or Philadelphia, ... because we refused through the normal channels of international, legal communications, to extradite that individual?' " Bill To Authorize Prosecution of Terrorists and Others Who Attack U.S. Government Employees and Citizens Abroad: Hearing before the Subcommittee on Security and Terrorism of the Senate Committee on the Judiciary, 99th Cong., 1st Sess., 63 (1985).

22. Justice Story's opinion continued: "The arrest of the offending vessel must, therefore, be restrained to places where our jurisdiction is complete, to our own waters, or to the ocean, the common highway of all nations. It is said, that there is a revenue jurisdiction, which is distinct from the ordinary maritime jurisdiction over waters within the range of a [cannon] shot from our shores. And the provisions in the Collection Act of 1799, which authorize a visitation of vessels within four leagues of our coasts, are referred to in proof of the assertion. But where is that right of visitation to be exercised? In a foreign territory, in the exclusive jurisdiction of another sovereign? Certainly not; for the very terms of the act confine it to the ocean, where all nations have a common right, and exercise a common sovereignty. And over what vessels is this right of visitation to be exercised? By the very words of the act, over our own vessels, and over foreign vessels bound to our ports, and over no others. To have gone beyond this, would have been an usurpation of exclusive sovereignty on the ocean, and an exercise of an universal right of search, a right which has never yet been acknowledged by other nations, and would be resisted by none with more pertinacity than by the American."

> "It is ... a breach of International Law for a State to send its agents to the territory of another State to apprehend persons accused of having committed a crime. Apart from other satisfaction, the first duty of the offending State is to hand over the person in question to the State in whose territory he was apprehended." 1 Oppenheim's International Law 295, and n. 1 (H. Lauterpacht 8th ed. 1955).

Commenting on the precise issue raised by this case, the chief reporter for the American Law Institute's Restatement of Foreign Relations used language reminiscent of Justice Story's characterization of an official seizure in a foreign jurisdiction as "monstrous":

> "When done without consent of the foreign government, abducting a person from a foreign country is a gross violation of international law and gross disrespect for a norm high in the opinion of mankind. It is a blatant violation of the territorial integrity of another state; it eviscerates the extradition system (established by a comprehensive network of treaties involving virtually all states)."

In the *Rauscher* case, the legal background that supported the decision to imply a covenant not to prosecute for an offense different from that for which extradition had been granted was far less clear than the rule against invading the territorial integrity of a treaty partner that supports Mexico's position in this case. If *Rauscher* was correctly decided—and I am convinced that it was—its rationale clearly dictates a comparable result in this case.

III

A critical flaw pervades the Court's entire opinion. It fails to differentiate between the conduct of private citizens, which does not violate any treaty obligation, and conduct expressly authorized by the Executive Branch of the Government, which unquestionably constitutes a flagrant violation of international law, and in my opinion, also constitutes a breach of our Treaty obligations. Thus, at the outset of its opinion, the Court states the issue as "whether a criminal defendant, abducted to the United States from a nation with which it has an extradition treaty, thereby acquires a defense to the jurisdiction of this country's courts." That, of course, is the question decided in *Ker v. Illinois,* 119 U.S. 436 (1886); it is not, however, the question presented for decision today. * * *

IV

As the Court observes at the outset of its opinion, there is reason to believe that respondent participated in an especially brutal murder of an American law enforcement agent. That fact, if true, may explain the Executive's intense interest in punishing respondent in our courts. Such an explanation, however, provides no justification for disregarding the Rule of Law that this Court has a duty to uphold.[33] That the

33. As Justice Brandeis so wisely urged: "In a government of laws, existence of the government will be imperilled if it fails to observe the law scrupulously. Our Govern-

Executive may wish to reinterpret[34] the Treaty to allow for an action that the Treaty in no way authorizes should not influence this Court's interpretation. Indeed, the desire for revenge exerts "a kind of hydraulic pressure ... before which even well settled principles of law will bend," *Northern Securities Co. v. United States,* 193 U.S. 197, 401 (1904)(Holmes, J., dissenting), but it is precisely at such moments that we should remember and be guided by our duty "to render judgment evenly and dispassionately according to law, as each is given understanding to ascertain and apply it." *United States v. Mine Workers*, 330 U.S. 258, 342 (1947)(Rutledge, J., dissenting). The way that we perform that duty in a case of this kind sets an example that other tribunals in other countries are sure to emulate.

The significance of this Court's precedents is illustrated by a recent decision of the Court of Appeal of the Republic of South Africa. Based largely on its understanding of the import of this Court's cases—including our decision in *Ker v. Illinois*—that court held that the prosecution of a defendant kidnaped by agents of South Africa in another country must be dismissed. *S v. Ebrahim*, S. Afr. L. Rep. (Apr.-June 1991).[36] The Court of Appeal of South Africa—indeed, I suspect most courts throughout the civilized world—will be deeply disturbed by the "monstrous" decision the Court announces today. For every Nation that has an interest in preserving the Rule of Law is affected, directly or indirectly, by a decision of this character. As Thomas Paine warned, an "avidity to punish is always dangerous to liberty" because it leads a nation "to stretch, to misinterpret, and to misapply even the best of laws." To counter that tendency, he reminds us:

> "He that would make his own liberty secure must guard even his enemy from oppression; for if he violates this duty he establishes a precedent that will reach to himself."

I respectfully dissent.

ment is the potent, the omnipresent teacher. For good or for ill, it teaches the whole people by its example. Crime is contagious. If the Government becomes a lawbreaker, it breeds contempt for law; it invites every man to become a law unto himself; it invites anarchy. To declare that in the administration of the criminal law the end justifies the means—to declare that the Government may commit crimes in order to secure the conviction of a private criminal—would bring terrible retribution. Against that pernicious doctrine this Court should resolutely set its face." *Olmstead v. United States*, 277 U.S. 438, 485 (1928)(Brandeis, J., dissenting).

34. Certainly, the Executive's view has changed over time. At one point, the Office of Legal Counsel advised the Administration that such seizures were contrary to international law because they compromised the territorial integrity of the other Nation and were only to be undertaken with the consent of that Nation. 4B Op. Off. Legal Counsel 549, 556 (1980). More recently, that opinion was revised, and the new opinion concluded that the President did have the authority to override customary international law. Hearing before the Subcommittee on Civil and Constitutional Rights of the House Committee on the Judiciary, 101st Cong., 1st Sess., 4–5 (1989)(statement of William P. Barr, Assistant Attorney General, Office of Legal Counsel, U.S. Department of Justice).

36. The South African court agreed with appellant that an "abduction represents a violation of the applicable rules of international law, that these rules are part of [South African] law, and that this violation of the law deprives the Court ... of its competence to hear [appellant's] case...."

Notes and Questions

1. *The Aftermath of* Alvarez–Machain. Mexico declared its outrage with the *Alvarez–Machain* decision. Tim Golden, "After Court Ruling, Mexico Tells U.S. Drug Agents to Halt Activity," *New York Times*, June 16, 1992, at 19. Political leaders in the Caribbean, Latin America, Canada, Australia, and Europe also objected to the decision. See Jonathan A. Bush, "How Did We Get Here? Foreign Abduction After *Alvarez–Machain*," 45 *Stanford Law Review* 939, 941–42 & nn.11–15 (1993). The Supreme Court's judgment appeared all the more preposterous when the trial judge ultimately acquitted the Mexican doctor on the grounds that the U.S. government's evidence against him "had been based on 'hunches' and the 'wildest speculation' and had failed to support the charges that he had participated in the torture of the drug agent." Seth Mydans, "Judge Clears Mexican in Agent's Killing," *New York Times*, Dec. 15, 1992, at A20. President-elect Bill Clinton condemned *Alvarez–Machain*: "I think that in the absence of some evidence the [Mexican] government was actually taking a dive or trying to thwart us that the principle the Supreme Court articulated was way too broad." Frank J. Murray, "Clinton Hits Court's Kidnapping Decision," *The Washington Times*, Dec. 16, 1992, at A4. The *Washington Post* opined that "the U.S. government's performance was both embarrassing and badly misguided." "The Collapse of the Alvarez Case," *Washington Post*, Dec. 17, 1992, at A22. As President, Mr. Clinton promised Mexico that the United States government would not conduct any cross-border kidnapping. Steven A. Holmes, "U.S. Gives Mexico Abduction Pledge," *New York Times*, June 22, 1993, at A11. The *Alvarez–Machain* decision reportedly contributed directly to Mexico's rejection of U.S. assistance in combatting the illegal drug industry, and Mexico's drug arrests dropped to 9,728 in 1995, from 27,369 in 1992. Molly Moore & John Ward Anderson, "Drugs Flow as Policing is 'Mexicanized': Diminished U.S. Role Below Border Plays Into Traffickers' Hands," *Washington Post*, Sept. 8, 1996, at A1.

Following the dismissal of U.S. criminal charges against him, Dr. Alvarez–Machain filed a civil claim for damages against the U.S. government. Patrick J. McDonnell, "Doctor Kidnaped by DEA Files $20–million Claim," *Los Angeles Times*, July 10, 1993, at A21; Patrick J. McDonnell, "Scars of an Abduction," *Los Angeles Times*, Feb. 10, 1995, Metro, Pt. B, at 1. On September 24, 1996, the U.S. Court of Appeals for the Ninth Circuit ruled, *inter alia*, that Dr. Alvarez–Machain could pursue his tort claims, his claims alleging that U.S. officials violated his constitutional rights by conduct occurring in the United States, and his claims under the U.S. Torture Victim Protection Act. Alvarez–Machain v. United States, 96 F.3d 1246 (9th Cir.1996).

2. Alvarez–Machain *and International Law*. International lawyers generally condemned the *Alvarez–Machain* judgment. Professor Louis Henkin, the President of the American Society of International Law, wrote:

> During its past term, the U.S. Supreme Court had one of its infrequent opportunities to take international law seriously and to assure that the Executive Branch takes international law seriously. The Supreme Court failed. The Attorney General was "gratified."

> * * * [T]he "victory" for the Department of Justice may prove to be pyrrhic. The judicial-executive distortion of standard extradition treaties is remediable, and our treaty partners will no doubt find their remedies. In reaction to general outrage, the United States will—at the least—have to disown that interpretation if it is to maintain its network of extradition treaties, as important to the United States as to any state in the world.
>
> The larger, longer question is whether the Government of the United States—all branches—is prepared to commit itself to taking international law seriously. * * *
>
> If the Attorney General continues to refuse to take international law seriously, if the Supreme Court refuses to compel the Department of Justice to take international law seriously, it is up to the President of the United States. * * *
>
> If the President will not act, it will be up to Congress. The Constitution put international law in the special care of Congress when it gave to that branch the power to define offenses against the Law of Nations. * * *

Louis Henkin, "Will the U.S. Supreme Court Fail International Law?," *Newsletter of the American Society of International Law*, Aug.–Sept. 1992, at 1–2. Should Congress respond to *Alvarez–Machain* by making it a federal crime for any U.S. official to kidnap any person in violation of international law? Under Article I, § 8 of the U.S. Constitution (see Appendix), Congress has the power to "define and punish * * * Offences against the Law of Nations."

3. *The Reconciliation of Treaty and Municipal Acts.* Is *Alvarez–Machain* an example of stretching the possible interpretation of an international agreement so far to avoid conflict with a local law or act that the interpretation exceeds the limits of plausibility? Arguably, the Court's justification for its strained interpretation is to reconcile U.S. acts with U.S. international obligations. Would it be better to acknowledge that they conflict, and then choose to defer either to international law or to executive action, *e.g.*, on the grounds of judicial deference to the executive in matters of international relations?

B. CUSTOMARY INTERNATIONAL LAW IN MUNICIPAL LAW

RESPUBLICA v. DE LONGCHAMPS

Court of Oyer and Terminer at Philadelphia
1 U.S. (1 Dall.) 111, 1 L.Ed. 59 (1784).

CHARLES JULIAN DE LONGCHAMPS, commonly called the *Chevalier de Longchamps*, was indicted, that "he, on the 17th of May 1784, in the dwelling-house of his excellency the French minister plenipotentiary, in the presence of Francis Barbe Marbois, unlawfully and insolently did threaten and menace bodily harm and violence to the person of the said Francis Barbe Marbois, he being consul-general of France to the United

States, consul for the state of Pennsylvania, Secretary of the French legation &c. resident in the house aforesaid, and under the protection of the law of nations and this commonwealth." And that "afterwards, to wit on the 19th of May, in the public street, &c., he, said Charles Julian de Longchamps, unlawfully, premeditatedly and violently, in and upon the person of the said Francis Barbe Marbois, under the protection of the laws of the nations, and in the peace of this commonwealth, then and there being, an assault did make, and him, the said Francis Barbe Marbois unlawfully and violently did strike and otherwise, &c., in violation of the laws of nations, against the peace and dignity of the United States and of the commonwealth of Pennsylvania."—To these charges, the defendant pleaded not guilty.

The evidence in support of the first count, was, that on the 17th of May, de Longchamps went to the house of the minister of France, and after some conversation with Monsieur Marbois, was heard to exclaim in a loud and menacing tone, "*Je vous deshonnerera, Policon, Coquin,*" addressing himself to that gentleman. That the noise being heard by the minister, he repaired to the room from which it issued, and that, in his presence, the defendant repeated the insult offered to Monsieur Marbois, in nearly the same terms.

In support of the second count, it appeared, that de Longchamps and Monsieur Marbois, having met in Market street, near the coffee-house, entered into a long conversation, in the course of which, the latter said, that he would complain to the civil authority, and the former replied, "you are a blackguard." The witnesses generally deposed, that de Longchamps struck the cane of Monsieur Marbois, before that gentleman used any violent gestures, or even appeared incensed; but that as soon as the stroke was given, Monsieur Marbois employed his stick with great severity, until the spectators interfered and separated the parties. One of the witnesses, indeed, said, that previously to engaging with their canes, he observed the two gentlemen, at the same instant, lay their hands on each others shoulders, in a manner so gentle, that he, who had heard it was customary among the French to part with mutual salutations, imagined a ceremony of that kind was about to take place, and was surprised to see de Longchamps step back, and strike the cane of Monsieur Marbois.

On the part of the defendant, evidence was produced of his having served with honour in the French armies, and his commission of sub-brigadier in the dragoons of Noailles, was read. It appeared, that the occasion of his calling on Monsieur Marbois, was to obtain authentications of these, and some other papers relative to his family, his rank in France, and his military promotions, in order to refute several publications, which had been made in the newspapers, injurious to his character and pretensions. The refusal of Monsieur Marbois to grant the authentications required, was the ground of de Longchamps' resentment, and the immediate cause of his menaces at the minister's house. * * *

McKEAN, CHIEF JUSTICE.—This is a case of the first impression in the United States. It must be determined on the principles of the laws of nations, which form a part of the municipal law of Pennsylvania; and, if the offenses charged in the indictment have been committed, there can be no doubt, that those laws have been violated. The words used in the minister's house (which is to be considered as a foreign domicil, where the minister resides in full representation of his sovereign, and where the laws of the state do not extend), may be compared to the same words applied to the Judges in a court of justice, where they sit in representation of the majesty of the people of Pennsylvania. In that case, the offender would be immediately committed to jail, without the preliminary process of an indictment by a grand jury; and, in the case before us, if the offender is convicted, he may certainly be punished by fine and imprisonment.

In actions of slander, words were formerly construed in the mildest sense they would admit; but reason has superceded such forced interpretations, and words are now to be taken according to their ordinary import and meaning. Those expressed by the defendant are evidently of a tendency so opprobrious and violent, that they cannot fail to aggravate the outrage which has been committed.

As to the assault, this is, perhaps, one of that kind, in which the insult is more to be considered, than the actual damage; for, though no great bodily pain is suffered by a blow on the palm of the hand, or the skirt of the coat, yet these are clearly within the legal definition of assault and battery, and among gentlemen, too often, induce duelling, and terminate in murder. As, therefore, anything attached to the person, partakes of its inviolability; de Longchamps' striking Monsieur Marbois' cane, is a sufficient justification of that gentleman's subsequent conduct. * * *

Charles Julian de Longchamps: You have been indicted for unlawfully and violently threatening and menacing bodily harm and violence to the person of the Honorable Francis Barbe de Marbois, secretary to the legation from France, and consul-general of France to the United States of America, in the mansion-house of the minister plenipotentiary of France; and for an assault and battery committed upon the said secretary and consul, in a public street in the City of Philadelphia. To this Indictment you have pleaded, that you were not guilty, and for trial put yourself upon the country; an unbiased jury, upon a fair trial, and clear evidence, have found you guilty.

These offenses having been thus legally ascertained and fixed upon you, his Excellency the President, and the Honorable the Supreme Executive Council, attentive to the honor and interest of this state, were pleased to inform the judges of this court, as they had frequently done before, that the minister of France had earnestly repeated a demand, that you, having appeared in his house in the uniform of a French regiment, and having called yourself an officer in the troops of his Majesty, should be delivered up to him for these outrages, as a Frenchman to be sent to France; and wished us in this stage of your prosecution, to take into mature consideration, and in the most solemn manner to determine:—

1. Whether you could be legally delivered up by council, according to the claim made by the late minister of France?

2. If you could not be thus legally delivered up, whether your offenses in violation of the law of nations, being now ascertained and verified according to the laws of this commonwealth, you ought not to be imprisoned, until his most Christian Majesty shall declare, that the reparation is satisfactory?

3. If you can be imprisoned, whether any legal act can be done by council, for causing you to be so imprisoned?

To these questions we have given the following answers in writing:—* * *

"1. And as to the first question, we answer, That it is our opinion, that, in this case, Charles Julian de Longchamps cannot be legally delivered up by council, according to the claim made by the minister of France. Though, we think, cases may occur, where council could, *pro bono publico*, and to prevent atrocious offenders evading punishment, deliver them up to the justice of the country to which they belong, or where the offenses were committed.

"2. Punishments must be inflicted in the same county where the criminals were tried and convicted, unless the record of the attainder be removed into the supreme court, which may award execution in the county where it sits; they must be such as the laws expressly prescribe; or where no stated or fixed judgment is directed, according to the legal discretion of the court; but judgments must be certain and definite in all respects. Therefore, we conclude, that the defendant cannot be imprisoned, until his most Christian Majesty shall declare that the reparation is satisfactory.

"3. The answer to the last question is rendered unnecessary by the above answer to the second question."

The foregoing answers having been given, it only remains for the court to pronounce sentence upon you. This sentence must be governed by a due consideration of the enormity and dangerous tendency of the offenses you have committed, of the willfulness, deliberation, and malice, wherewith they were done, of the quality and degree of the offended and offender, the provocation given, and all other circumstances which may any way aggravate or extenuate the guilt.

The first crime in the indictment is an infraction of the law of nations. This law, in its full extent, is part of the law of this state, and is to be collected from the practice of different nations, and the authority of writers. The person of a public minister is sacred and inviolable. Whoever offers any violence to him, not only affronts the sovereign he represents, but also hurts the common safety and well-being of nations—he is guilty of a crime against the whole world.

All the reasons, which establish the independency and inviolability of the person of a minister, apply likewise to secure the immunities of his house. It is to be defended from all outrage; it is under a peculiar protection of the laws; to invade its freedom, is a crime against the state and all other nations.

The *comites* of a minister, or those of his train, partake also of his inviolability. The independency of a minister extends to all his household; these are so connected with him, that they enjoy his privileges and follow his fate. The secretary to the embassy has his commission from the sovereign himself; he is the most distinguished character in the suite of a public minister, and is in some instances considered as a kind of public minister himself. Is it not, then, an extraordinary insult, to use threats of bodily harm to his person, in the domicil of the minister plenipotentiary? If this is tolerated, his freedom of conduct is taken away, the business of his sovereign cannot be transacted, and his dignity and grandeur will be tarnished.

You then have been guilty of an atrocious violation of the law of nations; you have grossly insulted gentlemen, the peculiar objects of this law (gentlemen of amiable characters, and highly esteemed by the government of this state), in a most wanton and unprovoked manner: and it is now the interest as well as duty of the government, to animadvert upon your conduct with a becoming severity—such a severity as may tend to reform yourself, to deter others from the commission of the like crime, preserve the honor of the state, and maintain peace with our great and good ally, and the whole world. * * *

Upon the whole THE COURT, after a most attentive consideration of every circumstance in this case, do award, and direct me to pronounce the following sentence:—

That you pay a fine of 100 French crowns to the commonwealth; that you be imprisoned until the 4th day of July 1786, which will make a little more than two years imprisonment in the whole; that you then give good security to keep the peace, and be of good behaviour to all public ministers, secretaries to embassies, and consuls, as well as to all the liege people of Pennsylvania, for the space of seven years, by entering into a recognisance, yourself in a thousand pounds, and two securities in 500 pounds each: that you pay the costs of this prosecution, and remain committed until this sentence be complied with.

Notes and Questions

1. *The Law of Nations in Municipal Law.* The *de Longchamps Case* preceded the establishment of the federal judiciary. McKean, Chief Justice of Pennsylvania, recites Blackstone's familiar eighteenth-century formula of the English common law: "the law of nations * * * forms a part of the municipal law." The doctrine of the incorporation of the law of nations into the common law predated the Constitution and the Supremacy Clause of Article VI. What are we to make of the fact that the Supremacy Clause

mentions treaties but not the law of nations? Was or is the law of nations the same as customary international law?

2. *The Political Context.* Would American sovereignty have been imperilled if the new United States had delivered up de Longchamps to be shipped off to France as was sought by the French Minister? Or if the United States had imprisoned de Longchamps for so long as the French King should dictate? Was it politically useful to rely upon the law of nations in refusing the French requests? The Marbois-de Longchamps affair was a cause of concern among leading Americans, including Benjamin Franklin, George Washington, Thomas Jefferson, James Madison, John Adams, James Monroe, John Jay, Benjamin Harrison, and Charles Pinckney. See William R. Casto, "The Federal Courts' Protective Jurisdiction Over Torts Committed in Violation of the Law of Nations," 18 *Connecticut Law Review* 467, 492 n.143 (1986). A little over a week after de Longchamps assaulted Marbois, Thomas Jefferson wrote to James Madison to complain that Pennsylvania was "so indecisive" in taking steps with respect to the case: "They have not yet declared what they can or will do.... The affair is represented to Congress who will have the will but not the power to interpose. It will probably go next to France and bring on serious consequences." Letter of May 25, 1784, *quoted in id.* at 493 n.146. The *de Longchamps Case* provided ammunition for those favoring the creation of a federal judiciary under the U.S. Constitution with jurisdiction to hear cases involving foreign citizens.

3. *Crimes in Violation of the Law of Nations.* Was it fair to de Longchamps that he should be subjected to a fine of 100 French crowns and more than two years' imprisonment for an infraction of the law of nations, a law "collected from the practice of different nations, and the authority of writers"? How certain was that law? Should the law have been found in some specific statute of the United States or Pennsylvania? After *United States v. Hudson & Goodwin*, 11 U.S. (7 Cranch) 32, 3 L.Ed. 259 (1812), and *United States v. Coolidge*, 14 U.S. (1 Wheat.) 415, 4 L.Ed. 124 (1816), the doctrine of "common law crimes" lost favor. Defendants today are prosecuted in the United States only for violations of criminal statutes.

A criminal statute, however, may define a crime by explicitly incorporating the law of nations. For example, 18 U.S.C. § 1651 applies to anyone who, "on the high seas, commits the crime of piracy as defined by the law of nations, and is afterwards brought into or found in the United States." In United States v. Smith, 18 U.S. (5 Wheat.) 153, 5 L.Ed. 57 (1820), Justice Story found this statute sufficiently definite to support the conviction of, and death sentences for, several men. Would section 1651 support a criminal conviction today?

> * * * One widely shared judicial preconception is that a criminal statute under which a conviction is sought must appear to provide the defendant with fair notice about wrongful conduct. * * * Judges may also be concerned that loosely worded statutes [could] invite discriminatory or arbitrary enforcement, and they might well prefer, in the criminal law area, that judicial discretion be limited or constrained by legislative intent. * * * In light of the indefiniteness of * * * contemporary international law rules governing piracy * * * and perhaps in light of a general preconception that international law is by its nature

amorphous, a U.S. judge * * * might conclude that the language of section 1651 is unconstitutionally vague.

Cutting in favor of a conviction under section 1651 of a defendant who has committed acts of depredation on the high seas for private gain, however, is the claim that there is a core meaning of piracy that encompasses just such acts. The Congress that enacted the Act of March 3, 1819, from which section 1651 directly descended, likely intended that at least robbery on the high seas committed by those on board one ship against those on board another be punished. U.S. courts also have some Supreme Court precedent that construes section 1651 as providing standards sufficiently certain to support a conviction. Justice Story found in *Smith* that writers on the law of nations, to whom Story looked for evidence of the content of the law of nations, "allude to piracy as a crime of a settled and determinate nature" and "concur in holding, that robbery, or forcible depredations upon the sea, *animo furandi,* is piracy." A U.S. judge thus need not to be left entirely to unfamiliar international sources in seeking to give specific content to section 1651's proscription of "piracy as defined by the law of nations." * * * Some modern U.S. Supreme Court decisions [such as Parker v. Levy, 417 U.S. 733, 94 S.Ct. 2547, 41 L.Ed.2d 439 (1974) (upholding conviction for, *inter alia,* "conduct unbecoming an officer and a gentleman" under Article 133 of the Uniform Code of Military Justice)] have found some very general statutory language not to be void for vagueness. [According to Smith v. Goguen, 415 U.S. 566, 578, 94 S.Ct. 1242, 39 L.Ed.2d 605 (1974),] [c]riminal statutes which "by their terms or as authoritatively construed apply without question to certain activities, but whose application to other behavior is uncertain" may satisfy due process requirements.

John E. Noyes, "An Introduction to the International Law of Piracy," 21 *California Western International Law Journal* 105, 117–18 (1990).

AMERADA HESS v. ARGENTINE REPUBLIC

830 F.2d 421 (2d Cir.1987), *reversed on other grounds,*
488 U.S. 428, 109 S.Ct. 683, 102 L.Ed.2d 818 (1989).

[The issue before the court was whether a federal district court could exercise subject matter jurisdiction over Argentina under the Alien Tort Statute, which establishes district court jurisdiction over "any civil action by an alien for a tort only, committed in violation of the law of nations or a treaty of the United States." Argentina argued that the U.S. Foreign Sovereign Immunities Act [FSIA] was the only statute that could be used to establish jurisdiction over a foreign government.]

Feinberg, Chief Judge: * * *

I. Background

Because the district court dismissed [the] complaint for lack of jurisdiction, we must accept appellants' allegations as true. In 1977,

Amerada [Hess Shipping Corporation] entered a long-term time-charter agreement with United [Carriers, Inc.] for use of the oil tanker HERCULES. Amerada used HERCULES to carry oil from Alaska, around the southern tip of South America, to its refinery in the United States Virgin Islands. This route took HERCULES near the area in the South Atlantic where, in April 1982, an armed conflict began between Argentina and the United Kingdom that became known in this country as the Falklands War.

On May 25, 1982, HERCULES embarked from the Virgin Islands, without cargo but fully fueled, headed for Alaska. On June 3, in an effort to protect United States interest ships, the United States Maritime Administration telexed to both the United Kingdom and Argentina a list of United States flag vessels and United States interest Liberian tankers (like HERCULES) that would be traversing the South Atlantic, to ensure that these neutral vessels would not be attacked. The list included HERCULES.

By June 8, HERCULES was about 600 nautical miles off the Argentine coast and nearly 500 miles from the Falkland Islands, in international waters, well outside the "exclusion zones" declared by the warring parties. That afternoon, HERCULES was attacked without warning in three different strikes by Argentine aircraft using bombs and air-to-surface rockets.

Following these attacks, HERCULES, damaged but not destroyed, headed for safe refuge in the port of Rio de Janeiro, Brazil. Although HERCULES arrived safely in Brazil, her deck and hull had both suffered extensive damage, and a bomb that had penetrated her side remained undetonated in one of her tanks. Following an investigation by the Brazilian navy, United determined that it would be unreasonably hazardous to attempt removal of the undetonated bomb. Accordingly, on July 20, 1982, approximately 250 miles off the Brazilian coast, HERCULES was scuttled. United's loss on the sunken ship is claimed at $10,000,000 and Amerada's loss on the fuel that went down with the ship is claimed at $1,901,259.07.

Following a series of unsuccessful attempts to receive a hearing of their claims by the Argentine government or to retain Argentine attorneys to prosecute their claims in the courts of that country, appellants filed their suits in the district court. The district court found that a "foreign state is subject to jurisdiction in the courts of this nation if, and only if, an FSIA exception empowers the court to hear the case." Concluding that no FSIA exception covered these facts, the district court dismissed the suits for lack of jurisdiction. This consolidated appeal followed.

II. Violation of International Law

The facts alleged by appellants, if proven, would constitute a clear violation of international law. * * *

International treaties and conventions dating at least as far back as the last century recognize the right of a neutral ship to free passage on the high seas. Broad international recognition of the rights of neutrals can be found in paragraph 3 of The Declaration of Paris of 1856: "Neutral goods, with the exception of contraband of war, are not liable to capture under enemy's flag."

A more contemporary statement of the international concern and accord on this issue may be found in The Geneva Convention on the High Seas of 1958 (Convention on the High Seas), to which both Argentina and the United States were signatories. The Convention on the High Seas maps the general usage and practice of nations with regard to the rights of neutral ships in time of war. Article 22 of that treaty states that a warship encountering a foreign merchant vessel on the high seas may not board her without grounds for suspecting her of engaging in piracy, or the slave trade, or traveling under false colors. Even when there are grounds for such suspicion, the proper course is to investigate by sending an officer to inspect the ship's documents or even to board her, not to commence an attack. If such inspection fails to support the suspicions, the merchant vessel shall "be compensated for any loss or damage that may have been sustained." Article 23 of the Convention on the High Seas makes similar provisions for aircraft that have grounds to suspect a neutral vessel. Clearly, Argentina's alleged conduct in this case, bombing HERCULES and refusing compensation, violates the Convention on the High Seas. More recently, the Law of the Sea Convention of 1982 explicitly incorporated these provisions into its text. Argentina is a signatory to the Law of the Sea Convention and the United States has endorsed the relevant sections of it.

Other international accords adopted by the United States supporting a similar view of the rights of neutral ships include The London Naval Conference of 1909, the International Convention Concerning the Rights and Duties of Neutral Powers in Naval War (Hague Convention, 1907) and the Pan–American Convention Relating to Maritime Neutrality of 1928, to which Argentina was a signatory. No agreement has been called to our attention that would cast doubt on this line of authority.

As to "judicial decisions recognizing or enforcing" the rights of neutral ships on the high seas, federal courts have recognized in a variety of contexts that attacking a merchant ship without warning or seizing a neutral's goods on the high seas requires restitution. See, e.g., *Talbot v. Jansen,* 3 U.S. (3 Dall.) 133, 161, 1 L.Ed. 540 (1795); *The Lusitania*, 251 F.715, 732–36 (S.D.N.Y.1918)(dictum); cf. The I'm Alone (Canada v. United States), 3 U.N. Rep.Int.Arb.Awards 1609 (1933). Similarly, the academic literature on the rights of neutrals is of one voice with regard to a neutral's right of passage. See, e.g., Rappaport, "Freedom of the Seas," 2 Encyclopedia of Amer.For.Policy 387 (1978); Restatement of Foreign Relations Law of the United States (Revised) § 521 reporters' note 1, § 522 (Tent.Draft No. 6 1985).

In short, it is beyond controversy that attacking a neutral ship in international waters, without proper cause for suspicion or investigation, violates international law. Indeed, the relative paucity of cases regarding this customary rule of international law underscores the longstanding nature of this aspect of freedom of the high seas. Where the attacker has refused to compensate the neutral, such action is analogous to piracy, one of the earliest recognized violations of international law. See 4 W. Blackstone, Commentaries 68, 72. Argentina has cited no contrary authority.

[The court goes on to examine the Alien Tort Statute and the Foreign Sovereign Immunities Act, concluding that both statutes provided grounds for subject matter jurisdiction over Argentina.]

Notes and Questions

1. *The Foreign Sovereign Immunities Act and the Supreme Court's Reversal.* The Supreme Court overruled the decision of the Second Circuit in *Amerada Hess*, holding that the Foreign Sovereign Immunities Act of 1976 provides the sole basis for suing foreign government and that no exception in the FSIA gives Amerada Hess and United Carriers the right to sue Argentina in this case. 488 U.S. 428, 109 S.Ct. 683, 102 L.Ed.2d 818 (1989). The Supreme Court, however, did not need to rule and did not rule on the alleged violation of international law by Argentina. Accordingly, the Second Circuit's reasoning on the laws of war was not reviewed by the high court. The Supreme Court's opinion appears in Chapter 10.

2. *A Proper Forum?* The Second Circuit seems concerned that Amerada Hess and United Carriers have some forum to hear their claim. It was alleged that Argentine lawyers refused to bring the claim in Argentine courts for fear of reprisal and that the U.S. government for political reasons chose not to prosecute the claim diplomatically against Argentina, especially after the United States sided with the United Kingdom in the Falklands War. If U.S. courts, as well as Argentine courts and U.S. diplomacy, are closed to plaintiffs, where else can they pursue their action?

As a matter of policy, are U.S. courts the proper fora for this dispute? Plaintiffs here were Liberian subsidiaries of U.S. corporations. Should the U.S. have been more or less responsible for providing a forum for the claims if the plaintiffs had been themselves U.S. corporations? Did it matter in *de Longchamps* that neither plaintiff nor defendant was a U.S. citizen?

3. *The Role of Customary International Law in U.S. Municipal Law.* The relationship between customary international law and U.S. municipal law was also explored in two cases already considered, Filartiga v. Pena–Irala, 630 F.2d 876 (2d Cir.1980)(in Chapter 1), and The Paquete Habana, 175 U.S. 677, 20 S.Ct. 290, 44 L.Ed. 320 (1900)(in Chapter 3). In *Filartiga*, as in the Second Circuit's opinion in *Amerada Hess*, the court looked to customary international law because it was construing a U.S. statute that expressly referred to the "law of nations." In *The Paquete Habana*, the Supreme Court derived the rule of decision directly from customary international law, even though no U.S. statute referred to it. It is *The Paquete Habana* where the famous quote, "International law is part of our law," appears. How should U.S. courts today use customary international law

when no statute expressly requires its application? The doctrine that the law of nations or customary international law is part of the common law of the United States is discussed in Mark W. Janis, *An Introduction to International Law* 99–102 (2d ed. 1993), Louis Henkin, "International Law as Law in the United States," 82 *Michigan Law Review* 1555 (1984), and Harold G. Maier, "The Authoritative Sources of Customary International Law in the United States," 10 *Michigan Journal of International Law* 450 (1989). Note that U.S. courts have long maintained that they should seek to interpret U.S. statutes in ways consistent with the United States' international obligations. See Murray v. The Charming Betsy, 6 U.S. (2 Cranch) 64, 2 L.Ed. 208 (1804).

4. *Foreign Relations Law.* Rules affecting relations among states or among nationals of different states come under a variety of different names. In English, "international law" is the most ordinary term, but "the law of nations," "transnational law," "universal law," "the common law of mankind," and "the law of the world public order" also appear. Yet another appellation is "foreign relations law," the term adopted by the American Law Institute.

The 1988 ALI *Restatement of the Foreign Relations Law of the United States* defines "foreign relations law" as

> (a) international law as it applies to the United States in its relations with other states; and
>
> (b) domestic law that has substantial significance for the foreign relations of the United States or has other substantial international consequences.

The first part of the ALI definition treats international law in a more or less traditional sense, albeit limited to rules applicable to the United States. The second part has to do, *inter alia*, with the incorporation of treaties and customary international law into U.S. law, but it also concerns the separation of foreign relations power among the three branches of the federal government. Professors Franck and Glennon define "the law of foreign relations" as having for its subject "the conduct of United States foreign relations and the constitutional distribution of powers, prerogatives and rights within the nation." Thomas M. Franck & Michael J. Glennon, *Foreign Relations and National Security Law* v (2d ed. 1993). Sometimes, cases involving international relations are deemed "political questions," *i.e.*, left to the discretion of the President and Congress and avoided by the courts. For discussion of the foundations of the political question doctrine, see Louis Henkin, *Foreign Affairs and the Constitution* 210–16 (1972).

Chapter 5

INTERNATIONAL DISPUTE SETTLEMENT

The process of interpreting, applying, and enforcing international law involves not only municipal courts but occasionally various forms of international dispute settlement procedures. In this chapter, we introduce both public international arbitration and the one more or less universal international court, the International Court of Justice (the "ICJ"), and its predecessors. Our story begins with the Permanent Court of Arbitration (the "PCA"), established in 1899 in The Hague. The PCA was followed by the Permanent Court of International Justice (the "PCIJ") in 1921, and the ICJ in 1945. The ICJ and its predecessors have never had a heavy caseload: two, three, or four adjudicated cases a year have been typical. However, these decided cases have been a very influential source of international law in the 20th century.

While reading the cases excerpted below, keep in mind the question: when and why do states agree to submit disputes to international arbitration or adjudication? As infrequent as such submissions are, there is no doubt that governments sometimes do wish for their disagreements to be settled by international arbiters or judges. What makes an international dispute "court-friendly" or "court-unfriendly"? An intelligent answer to this question might help us determine not only what international disputes are likely to go to formal international dispute settlement procedures but also which international decisions once rendered will be respected in practice.

A. PUBLIC INTERNATIONAL ARBITRATION

RICHARD NED LEBOW, "ACCIDENTS AND CRISES: THE DOGGER BANK AFFAIR"

31 *Naval War College Review*, No. 1, at 66 (Summer 1978).

Russian expansion into Manchuria in the latter part of the 19th century brought her into conflict with Japan. Russian penetration of Korea, which directly challenged Japan's economic and political primacy in that country, brought the conflict to a head. St. Petersburg's intransigence made a mockery of negotiations and Japan broke relations with Russia on 8 February 1904.

That very morning Japanese torpedo boats and destroyers launched a daring surprise attack against the Russian Pacific Squadron in its moorings at Port Arthur. The attack was followed up the next day by a long-range naval bombardment of the Russian anchorage. When the smoke had cleared the Japanese Navy was supreme in the Far East. They inflicted a further defeat upon the Russians at Chemulpo in August. On land, the Japanese were equally successful. Their army moved into Manchuria and forced the Russians to retreat down the Liaotung Peninsula. By 14 May they had invested Port Arthur.

The relief of Port Arthur became Moscow's most urgent objective. General Kuropatkin, the Russian Commander–in–Chief, ordered the navy to ready its idle Baltic Fleet for service in the Pacific. Departure of the armada awaited completion of four new battleships, during which time the Baltic Fleet, considered to be the least seaworthy component of the navy, received special training. The deteriorating military situation in the Far East forced Admiral Rozhestvensky to cut his training exercises short and on 14 October 1904 the 42 ships of the hastily assembled Second Pacific Squadron departed the Baltic port of Libau for the 10,000 mile journey to Port Arthur.

As the fleet steamed through the Baltic it was warned to be on the lookout for Japanese torpedo boats disguised as trawlers which were planning an ambush somewhere between The Skaw and English Channel. This far-fetched notion had gained credence in St. Petersburg because of the reports of a Captain Hartling, sent to Copenhagen sometime earlier to organize a Russian counterintelligence network. Hartling's agents, anxious to justify their expense, had reported the existence of suspicious vessels in isolated Danish and Norwegian harbors. Rumors of a Japanese "suicide squadron" had also been picked up by the European press which speculated about the effect of Britain's assumed collusion with her Japanese ally upon Anglo–Russian relations.

According to all reports the prospect of a torpedo attack reduced Admiral Rozhestvensky, a man with no command experience, to a state of extreme anxiety. He doubled all watches, arranged to have searchlights sweep the surrounding sea at night and instructed guncrews to remain by their stations around the clock. The admiral ordered that "No vessel of any sort whatsoever must be allowed to get in amongst the fleet." Approaching merchantmen were warned away, often by a shot across their bows. Tension rose on the evening of 20 October, following receipt of a warning that unidentified torpedo boats had departed from secret bases in Norway. Later that night, *Navarin* reported sighting enemy reconnaissance balloons.

The expected attack failed to materialize and as morning broke the fleet steamed into the North Sea, ominously shrouded by fog. More alarming intelligence came in during the day warning of floating mines and trawlers with torpedo tubes preparing to attack the fleet. At dusk, the cruiser *Kamchatka*, which had become separated from the main body of the fleet, reported that it was under attack by eight torpedo boats and was returning fire. Ninety minutes later action stations were sounded abroad the flagship *Suvorov* in response to two flares sighted from the bridge. Shortly thereafter the order to engage the enemy was flashed down the line as searchlights revealed ships barely a half mile away. Battleships and cruisers opened fire and kept up an intensive barrage for 20 minutes until the admiral could discern only a few battered trawlers bobbing hopelessly in the water. The fleet steamed off concluding that the torpedo boats had fled from the scene.

The "enemy" engaged by Russian gunners was the Gamecock fleet of fishing boats which had left Hull for the Dogger Bank 2 days before and was then 200 miles northeast of the Spurn. They were identifiable as trawlers by their sails and red, white and green lights. These lights were probably the flares sighted on the bridge of *Suvorov*. When the firing began, one of the deckhands, illuminated by the searchlights, held up a plaice while his mate displayed a large haddock in the hope of signaling their peaceful intent. Their efforts were unsuccessful and when the barrage finally ceased one trawler had been sent to the bottom and five damaged. Two seamen were dead and six seriously wounded. Fortunately for the fishermen Russian gunnery had proven extremely inaccurate.

News of the incident reached London on Monday, 23 October. The next day the M.P. from Hull brought a deputation of fishermen to the Foreign Office where they produced shell splinters to substantiate their story. The Wednesday morning papers carried a more detailed account of the incident and public opinion was so incensed that the Russian Ambassador needed a police escort to leave his Embassy. Trafalgar Square was filled with protesters and the evening papers demanded strong action. The *Standard* raised the question that was on everybody's mind: was the "wretched Baltic fleet with its inefficient commanders, its drafts of raw landsmen, its blundering navigators and incompetent engineers" to be permitted to continue on its journey? The czarist regime was unpopular in England and as more details were released to the press public sentiment was adamant in favor of going after the Russian Fleet. Valentine Chirol, foreign editor of *The Times*, warned the foreign office that "the feeling in this country is such that no government can trifle with it."

The Balfour government, about to face an election, was particularly susceptible to popular pressure. However, the Cabinet did not act solely in response to public opinion. The majority were hostile to Russia and quite prepared to retaliate against her fleet. The Earl of Selbourne, First Lord of the Admiralty, was the most bellicose but Walter Long and Gerald Balfour, neither of whom normally displayed any interest in foreign affairs, also urged military action unless the Russians put into port and removed the officers responsible for the outrage. Admiral Fisher, who had recently been promoted to First Sea Lord, thought it a superb opportunity to destroy the Russian Fleet. It "is ours," he informed Selbourne, "whenever we like to take it." The King himself referred to the incident as "a most dastardly outrage" and urged a military response although he later moderated his position, fearing that war with Russia would only be in Germany's interest.

Lord Lansdowne, the Foreign Secretary, would have had support for any action against Russia he proposed. But he was an advocate of détente with Russia and was intent on resolving the incident peaceably. Lansdowne was nevertheless as outraged as his colleagues and thought Rozhestvensky's failure to stop and search for survivors particularly reprehensible. He was not convinced of the accidental nature of the incident, attributing it instead to the Russian propensity to "shoot first and ask questions later." In his opinion this trigger happy policy made a mockery of maritime law which Britain more than any other nation was dependent upon for her survival. Lansdowne believed that such incidents were likely to recur unless Russia was compelled to adhere to the established rules and customs that governed maritime behavior. Like other members of the Cabinet he also believed that Britain's reputation as a great power was at stake. * * *

* * * Unwilling to let the hostage fleet escape the prime minister and foreign secretary agreed that Russia must be sent an ultimatum demanding that Rozhestvensky call at the Spanish port of Vigo and put ashore the officers responsible for the incident along with witnesses. The Russians were also to give satisfaction that the investigation of the incident would be complete and impartial. * * *

The Royal Navy had already begun preparations for a showdown. Six battleships of the Home Fleet had been ordered to Gibraltar and the reserve fleet of six battleships was being readied for action. Cruisers were sent to shadow the Russian Fleet, Gibraltar was put on a war footing, and the powerful Mediterranean Fleet was hurriedly recalled from the Austrian and Italian ports it was visiting. By the evening of 26 October, 28 battleships, 44 cruisers and their supporting vessels stood poised off Gibraltar ready to intercept the Russian Fleet which in the graphic words of First Sea Lord Fisher had become the "ham of a strategic sandwich."

On 27 October, [Russian Foreign Minister] Lamsdorff called on Hardinge [the British Minister in St. Petersburg] to warn that "he considered the general purport [of the ultimatum] to be humiliating and unacceptable to a Great Power." Lansdowne and Balfour, in receipt of Hardinge's report that afternoon, were pessimistic about the chances for peace. Their hopes plummeted in response to a second cable from St. Petersburg containing Rozhestvensky's account of the incident. The Russian admiral claimed that his fleet had been set upon by two torpedo boats but that he had tried to avoid firing on the trawlers even though they were in apparent complicity with the torpedo boats. Lansdowne told the Russian Ambassador that the admiral's version "seemed to bristle with improbabilities" and did not alter the situation.

Lansdowne and [Russian Ambassador] Benckendorff conferred at length exploring possible ways out of the crisis. Paul Cambon, the French Ambassador, also participated in these talks. As the representative of France, Russia's ally, and the architect of the Anglo–French Entente, Cambon shared the trust of both sides. He acted as translator, as Benckendorff spoke Russian and French but Lansdowne knew only English, and attempted to bridge the gap between the two men created by their uncomplementary personalities. "Benckendorff is too vague, Lansdowne too reserved," he confided to his son, "and when I am not between them, they inhabit different planets."

The main impediment to a solution was the British demand for an inquiry in which British officers would participate. This was seen as humiliating by the Russians. Cambon nevertheless urged acceptance as did the French Foreign Minister in Paris. On the 27th, the three men agreed that an inquiry conducted by some august international body might be more palatable to the Czar as he had urged the creation of boards of arbitration at the Hague Conference. The suggestion, attributed by Benckendoff to Cambon, was cabled to Lamsdorff who cleverly presented it to the Czar as his own idea in order to secure the autocrat's approval.

No word had been received from St. Petersburg when it came time for Balfour to depart for Southampton on the morning of the 28th. The mood at the Foreign Office was gloomy and remained so until a cable arrived from Hardinge reporting that the Czar approved of an international court of inquiry. A second cable contained the welcome news that Rozhestvensky had received orders to send the ships involved in the attack on the fishing boats to Vigo, that the guilty parties, as determined by the international board of inquiry, would be punished by Russian courts and that measures would be implemented to prevent further incidents. In return Lamsdorff requested that Balfour give credit to Russia in his speech for having expressed its prompt regrets and offering to pay proper compensation.

Upon his arrival at Southampton Balfour was handed a telegram reporting the Russian capitulation. Much relieved, the Prime Minister deleted those parts of his speech which were the equivalent to a declaration of war and told the good news to the cheering crowd. The Royal Navy remained on a war footing until her cruisers had "escorted" Rozhestvensky's fleet half way down the coast of Africa.

THE DOGGER BANK CASE

Great Britain v. Russia, Report of February 26, 1905,
The Hague Court Reports 403 (James Brown Scott ed. 1916).

1. The commissioners [five admirals from Britain, Russia, the United States, France and Austria], after a minute and prolonged examination of the whole of the facts brought to their knowledge in regard to the incident submitted to them for inquiry by the declaration of St. Petersburg of the 12th (25th) November, 1904, have proceeded to make, in this report, an analysis of these facts in their logical sequence.

By making known the prevailing opinion of the commission on each important or decisive point of this summary, they consider that they have made sufficiently clear the causes and the consequences of the incident in question, as well as the deductions which are to be drawn from them with regard to the question of responsibility. * * *

9. Toward 1 o'clock in the morning of 9th (22d) October, 1904, the night was rather dark, a slight, low fog partly clouding the air. The moon only showed intermittently between the clouds. A moderate wind blew from the southeast, raising a long swell, which gave the ships a roll of 5° on each side.

The course followed by the squadron toward the southwest would have taken the last two divisions, as the event proved, close past the usual fishing ground of the fleet of Hull trawlers, which was composed of some thirty of these small steamboats, and was spread over an area of several miles.

It appears from the concordant testimony of the British witnesses that all these boats carried their proper lights, and were trawling in accordance with their usual rules, under the direction of their "admiral," and in obedience to the signals given by the conventional rockets.

10. Judging from the communications received by wireless telegraphy, the divisions which preceded that of Admiral Rojdestvensky across these waters had signaled nothing unusual.

It became known afterward, in particular, that Admiral Folkersam, having been led to pass round the fishing fleet on the north, threw his electric searchlight on the nearest trawlers at close quarters, and, having seen them to be harmless vessels, quietly continued his voyage.

11. A short time afterwards the last division of the squadron, led by the *Souvoroff* flying Admiral Rojdestvensky's flag, arrived in its run close to the spot where the trawlers were fishing.

The direction in which this division was sailing led it nearly toward the main body of the fleet of trawlers, round which and to the south of which it would therefore be obliged to sail, when the attention of the officers of the watch on the bridges of the *Souvoroff* was attracted by a green rocket, which put them on their guard. This rocket, sent up by the "admiral" of the fishing fleet, indicated in reality, according to regulation, that the trawlers were to trawl on the starboard tack.

Almost immediately after this first alarm, and as shown by the evidence, the lookout men, who, from the bridges of the *Souvoroff*, were scanning the horizon with their night glasses, discovered "on the crest of the waves on the starboard bow, at an approximate distance of 18 to 20 cables," a vessel which aroused their suspicions because they saw no light, and because she appeared to be bearing down upon them.

When the suspicious-looking vessel was shown up by the searchlight, the lookout men thought they recognized a torpedo boat proceeding at great speed.

It was on account of these appearances that Admiral Rojdestvensky ordered fire to be opened on this unknown vessel.

The majority of the commissioners express the opinion, on this subject, that the responsibility for this action and the results of the fire to which the fishing fleet was exposed are to be attributed to Admiral Rojdestvensky.

12. Almost immediately after fire was opened to starboard, the *Souvoroff* caught sight of a little boat on her bow barring the way, and was obliged to turn sharply to the left to avoid running it down. This boat, however, on being lit up by the searchlight, was seen to be a trawler.

To prevent the fire of the ships being directed against this harmless vessel, the searchlight was immediately thrown up at an angle of 45°.

The admiral then made the signal to the squadron "not to fire on the trawlers."

But at the same time that the searchlight had lit up this fishing vessel, according to the evidence of witnesses, the lookout men on board the *Souvoroff* perceived to port another vessel, which appeared suspicious from the fact of its presenting the same features as were presented by the object of their fire to starboard.

Fire was immediately opened on this second object, and was, therefore, being kept up on both sides of the ship, the line of ships having resumed their original course by a correcting movement without changing speed.

13. According to the standing orders of the fleet, the Admiral indicated the objects against which the fire should be directed by throwing his searchlight upon them; but as each vessel swept the horizon in every direction with her own searchlights to avoid being taken by surprise, it was difficult to prevent confusion.

The fire, which lasted from ten to twelve minutes, caused great loss to the trawlers. Two men were killed and six others wounded; the *Crane* sank; the *Snipe*, the *Mino*, the *Moulmein*, the *Gull*, and the *Majestic* were more or less damaged.

On the other hand, the cruiser *Aurora* was hit by several shots.

The majority of the commissioners observe that they have not sufficiently precise details to determine what was the object fired on by the vessels; but the commissioners recognize unanimously that the vessels of the fishing fleet did not commit any hostile act; and, the majority of the commissioners being of opinion that there were no torpedo boats either among the trawlers nor anywhere near, the opening of the fire by Admiral Rojdestvensky was not justifiable.

The Russian commissioner, not considering himself justified in sharing this opinion, expresses the conviction that it was precisely the suspicious-looking vessels approaching the squadron with hostile intent which provoked the fire.

Notes and Questions

1. *Incentives to Arbitrate.* Looking at Lebow's account of the Dogger Bank Affair, what were the inducements for England to go to international arbitration? Why was Russia willing to accept an international inquiry into the activities of her Navy? Why did France seek to bring the two sides together? What role did public opinion in England play in building up war fever? In facilitating an arbitral solution to the conflict?

2. *The Composition of the Arbitral Panel.* Note that the arbitral panel in *Dogger Bank* was composed not of lawyers or judges but of naval officers. What would be the advantages and disadvantages of employing admirals instead of jurists as arbitrators? Would it have been probably England or Russia who would have preferred admirals rather than international lawyers on the panel?

3. *Compensation.* James Brown Scott, the editor of the *Reports* of the Permanent Court of Arbitration, notes that "Russia accepted the decision and paid damages to the extent of about $300,000." *Hague Court Reports* 403 (James Brown Scott ed. 1916). Were Russia's misgivings about permitting the arbitration justified? Would Russia have been better off if she had simply paid damages at the outset? Or did the lapse of time and the decision of an arbitral panel make the payment of damages more palatable to the Russians?

Dogger Bank was the kind of dispute 19th-century international arbitration enthusiasts hoped would be settled by courts rather than by war. As Merrills observes, "The *Dogger Bank* episode furnishes a striking example of the value of the international inquiry commission as an instrument of dispute settlement. Had the issue been investigated by two national inquiries, it is almost certain that * * * they would have exacerbated matters by coming to opposite conclusions." J.G. Merrills, *International Dispute Settlement* 46 (2d ed.1991). Did the availability of international arbitral machinery at The Hague make it more likely that the parties would go to arbitration? What might be done to make it even more likely that states use a form of international arbitration in a time of crisis?

4. *The Permanent Court of Arbitration.* Although the Permanent Court of Arbitration still formally exists, it has been rarely used since the establishment of the International Court in 1921. The PCA continues to share the Peace Palace in The Hague with the ICJ. It is just a little mysterious why the PCA still exists, although there have been proposals from time to time for its revitalization. Perhaps it is the hope that some more good may yet come of it that keeps the PCA alive in form if not very often in function.

5. *Public International Arbitration Outside the PCA.* Despite the atrophy of the PCA after 1921, public international arbitration continues to flourish, albeit outside the halls of the Peace Palace. A good example of modern public international arbitration is the *Rainbow Warrior Case* below. Of course, private or commercial international arbitration (between private litigants) and mixed international arbitration (between a state and a private litigant) are even more healthy nowadays. There are many hundreds of such cases a year. We have already seen one, the *Texaco/Libya Case*, in

Chapter 3, in the context of our discussion of the determination of customary international law.

The *Rainbow Warrior Case* contains an interesting discussion of state responsibility, a topic to which we return in Chapter 6. For now, ask, along with the Tribunal, what kind of satisfaction France ought to give New Zealand for its breach of its treaty obligations.

THE RAINBOW WARRIOR CASE

New Zealand v. France
France–New Zealand Arbitration Tribunal,
82 *International Law Reports* 500 (1990).

[In July 1985, French secret service agents affixed mines that sank the *Rainbow Warrior*, a ship belonging to the international nongovernmental organization, Greenpeace International, while the *Rainbow Warrior* was in harbor in New Zealand. A crew member on the vessel, Fernando Pereira, died as a result. Two of the French agents, Major Mafart and Captain Prieur, were arrested in New Zealand, pleaded guilty to criminal charges, and were each sentenced to ten years in jail. At the diplomatic level, France demanded the release of its agents; New Zealand sought compensation for the incident, and complained about French threats to disrupt trade between Europe and New Zealand should New Zealand not release Mafart and Prieur. France and New Zealand asked the Secretary–General of the United Nations to mediate the dispute; they agreed in advance to accept the Secretary–General's ruling. In 1986 the Secretary–General decided that France should pay $7 million to New Zealand and agree not to take certain steps that would injure New Zealand's trade with Europe. 74 Int'l L. Rep. 241. In addition, the ruling also contained provisions concerning the release of the two French agents. France and New Zealand implemented the ruling in a 1986 agreement, which required that Major Mafart and Captain Prieur be transferred to a French military base on Hao, an island in the Pacific, "for a period of not less than three years," and that they be "prohibited from leaving the island for any reason, except with the mutual consent of the two governments."

The 1990 arbitration below involves France's decision to evacuate Major Mafart and Captain Prieur from Hao to France before the three-year period had run. France sought New Zealand's consent to Major Mafart's transfer on December 11, 1987, for urgent health-related reasons. New Zealand asked that its doctors examine Mafart, but France refused to permit a New Zealand military plane carrying New Zealand doctors to land in Hao. Mafart left Hao for France on December 14, 1987, without New Zealand's consent, and France allowed Mafart to remain in France after his treatment, despite New Zealand doctors' conclusions that he could be safely returned to Hao. Captain Prieur left Hao for France in May 1988 after France sought New Zealand's consent on the ground that she was pregnant. France agreed to an independent examination of Prieur in Hao by New Zealand doctors, but Prieur left the day before the doctors arrived, France claiming that her father was dying. Captain Prieur also never returned to Hao.

This 1990 arbitration was authorized under a provision of the 1986 France–New Zealand agreement providing for arbitration of disputes arising out of that accord. New Zealand invoked the provision. On February 14, 1989, the two states concluded a Supplemental Agreement designating three arbitrators (one appointed by each state and one appointed jointly by both states). The Supplemental Agreement also specified the procedures that the Tribunal was to follow, and stated that the Tribunal's decisions would be based on the 1986 agreement between France and New Zealand and on "applicable rules and principles of international law."]

75. * * * [F]or the decision of the present case, both the customary Law of Treaties and the customary Law of State Responsibility are relevant and applicable. The customary Law of Treaties, as codified in the Vienna Convention proclaimed in Article 26, under the title "*Pacta sunt servanda*" that

> "Every treaty in force is binding upon the parties to it and must be performed by them in good faith."

This fundamental provision is applicable to the determination whether there have been violations of that principle and in particular, whether material breaches of treaty obligations have been committed.

Moreover, certain specific provisions of customary law in the Vienna Convention are relevant in this case such as Article 60 which gives a precise definition of the concept of a material breach of a treaty, and Article 70, which deals with the legal consequences of the expiry of a treaty.

On the other hand, the legal consequences of a breach of a treaty, including the determination of the circumstances that may exclude wrongfulness (and render the breach only apparent) and the appropriate remedies for breach, are subjects that belong to the customary Law of State Responsibility.

The reason is that the general principles of International Law concerning State responsibility are equally applicable in the case of breach of treaty obligation, since in the international law field there is no distinction between contractual and tortious responsibility, so that any violation by a State of any obligation, of whatever origin, gives rise to State responsibility and consequently, to the duty of reparation. * * *

76. Under the title "Circumstances Precluding Wrongfulness" the International Law Commission proposed in Articles 29 to 35 a set of rules which include three provisions on *force majeure* and fortuitous event (Article 31), distress (Article 32), and state of necessity (Article 33), which may be relevant to the decision on this case. * * *

77. * * * New Zealand is right in asserting that the excuse of *force majeure* is not of relevance in this case because the test of its applicabili-

ty is of absolute and material impossibility, and because a circumstance rendering performance more difficult or burdensome does not constitute a case of *force majeure*. Consequently, this excuse is of no relevance in the present case.

78. Article 32 of the Articles drafted by the International Law Commission deals with another circumstance which may preclude wrongfulness in international law, namely, that of the "distress" of the author of the conduct which constitutes the act of State whose wrongfulness is in question. * * *

The question therefore is to determine whether the circumstances of distress in a case of extreme urgency involving elementary humanitarian considerations affecting the acting organs of the State may exclude wrongfulness in this case.

79. In accordance with the previous legal considerations, three conditions would be required to justify the conduct followed by France in respect to Major Mafart and Captain Prieur:

1) the existence of very exceptional circumstances of extreme urgency involving medical or other considerations of an elementary nature, provided always that a prompt recognition of the existence of those exceptional circumstances is subsequently obtained from the other interested party or is clearly demonstrated.

2) The reestablishment of the original situation of compliance with the assignment in Hao as soon as the reasons of emergency invoked to justify the repatriation had disappeared.

3) The existence of a good faith effort to try to obtain the consent of New Zealand in terms of the 1986 Agreement.

THE CASE OF MAJOR MAFART

80. The New Zealand reaction to the French initiative for the removal of Major Mafart appears to have been conducted in conformity with the above considerations.

The decision to send urgently a medical doctor to Hao in order to verify the existence of the invoked ground of serious risk to life clearly implied that if the alleged conditions were confirmed, then the requested consent would be forthcoming.

Unfortunately, it proved impossible to proceed with that verification while Major Mafart was still on the island. * * * [N]one of the parties is to blame for the failure in carrying out the very difficult task of verifying *in situ* Major Mafart's health during that weekend.

81. * * * [H]aving accepted the offer to verify whether Major Mafart had required an urgent sanitary evacuation, subsequent consent to that measure would necessarily be implied unless there was an immediate and formal denial by New Zealand of the existence of the medical conditions which had determined Major Mafart's urgent removal, accompanied by a formal request by New Zealand authorities for his

immediate return to Hao, or at least to Papeete. And this did not occur. * * *

88. * * * [T]he Tribunal:

by a majority declares that the French Republic did not breach its obligations to New Zealand by removing Major Mafart from the island of Hao on 13 December 1987;

declares that the French Republic committed a material and continuing breach of its obligations to New Zealand by failing to order the return of Major Mafart to the island of Hao as from 12 February 1988. * * *

THE CASE OF CAPTAIN PRIEUR

93. The facts * * * show that New Zealand would not oppose Captain Prieur's departure, if that became necessary because of special care which might be required by her pregnancy. They also indicated that France and New Zealand agreed that Captain Prieur would be examined by Dr. Brenner, a New Zealand physician, before returning to Paris. * * *

94. * * * [I]t appears that during the day of 5 May the French Government suddenly decided to present the New Zealand Government with the *fait accompli* of Captain Prieur's hasty return for a new reason, the health of Mrs. Prieur's father, who was seriously ill, hospitalized for cancer. Indisputably the health of Mrs. Prieur's father, who unfortunately would die on 16 May, and the concern for allowing Mrs. Prieur to visit her dying father constitute humanitarian reasons worthy of consideration by both Governments under the 1986 Agreement. But the events of 5 May (French date) prove that the French Republic did not make efforts in good faith to obtain New Zealand's consent. First of all, it must be remembered that France and New Zealand agreed that Captain Prieur would be examined in Hao on 6 May, which would allow her to return to France immediately. For France, in this case, it was only a question of gaining 24 or 36 hours. Of course, the health of Mrs. Prieur's father, who had been hospitalized for several months, could serve as grounds for such acute and sudden urgency: but, in this case, New Zealand would have had to be informed very precisely and completely, and not be presented with a decision that had already been made. * * *

* * * New Zealand was really not asked for its approval, as compliance with France's obligations required even under extremely urgent circumstances: it was indeed demanded so firmly that it was bound to provoke a strong reaction from New Zealand.

101. * * * [T]he Tribunal:

declares that the French Republic committed a material breach of its obligations to New Zealand by not endeavoring in good faith to obtain on 5 May 1988 New Zealand's consent to Captain Prieur's leaving the island of Hao;

declares that as a consequence the French Republic committed a material breach of its obligations by removing Captain Prieur from the island of Hao on 5 and 6 May 1988;

declares that the French Republic committed a material and continuing breach of its obligations to New Zealand by failing to order the return of Captain Prieur to the island of Hao. * * *

110. In the present case the Tribunal must find that the infringement of the special regime designed by the Secretary–General to reconcile the conflicting views of the Parties has provoked indignation and public outrage in New Zealand and caused a new, additional non-material damage. This damage is of a moral, political and legal nature, resulting from the affront to the dignity and prestige not only of New Zealand as such, but of its highest judicial and executive authorities as well.

111. It follows from the foregoing findings that New Zealand is entitled to appropriate remedies. It claims certain declarations, to the effect that France has breached the First Agreement. But New Zealand seeks as well an order for the return of the agents. * * *

112. For its part, the French Republic maintains that adequate reparation for moral or legal damage can only take the form of satisfaction, generally considered as the remedy *par excellence* in cases of non-material damage. Invoking the decisions of the International Court of Justice, France maintains that whenever the damage suffered amounts to no more than a breach of the law, a declaration by the judge of this breach constitutes appropriate satisfaction. France points out, moreover, that, rather than *restitutio*, what New Zealand is demanding is the cessation of the denounced behaviour * * *. * * *

114. * * * The recent jurisprudence of the International Court of Justice confirms that an offer for the cessation or discontinuance of wrongful acts or omissions is only justified in case of continuing breaches of international obligations which are still in force at the time the judicial order is issued (*The United States Diplomatic and Consular Staff in Teheran Case,* I.C.J. Reports, 1979, p. 21, para. 38 to 41, and 1980, para. 95, No. 1; *The Case Concerning Military and Paramilitary Activities in and Against Nicaragua*, I.C.J. Reports, 1984, p. 187, and 1986, para. 292, p. 149). * * *

It would be * * * illogical to issue the order requested by New Zealand, which is really an order for the cessation or discontinuance of a certain French conduct, rather than a *restitutio*. The reason is that this conduct, namely to keep the two agents in Paris, is not longer unlawful, since the international obligation expired on 22 July 1989. Today, France is no longer obliged to return the two agents to Hao and submit them to the special regime. * * *

115. On the other hand, the French contention that satisfaction is the only appropriate remedy for non-material damage is also not justified in the circumstances of the present case.

The granting of a form of reparation other than satisfaction has been recognized and admitted in the relations between the parties by the Ruling of the Secretary–General of 9 July 1986, which has been accepted and implemented by both Parties to this case.

In the Memorandum presented to the Secretary–General, the New Zealand Government requested compensation for non-material damage, stating that it was "entitled to compensation for the violation of sovereignty and the affront and insult that involved."

The French Government opposed this claim, contending that the compensation "could concern only the material damage suffered by New Zealand, the moral damage being compensated by the offer of apologies."

But the Secretary–General did not make any distinction, ruling instead that the French Government "should pay the sum of U.S. dollars 7 million to the Government of New Zealand as *compensation for all the damage it has suffered.*" * * *

* * * [T]he compensation constituted a reparation not just for material damage—such as the cost of the police investigation—but for non-material damage as well, regardless of material injury and independent therefrom. * * *

119. New Zealand has not however requested the award of monetary compensation—even as a last resort should the Tribunal not make the declarations and orders for the return of the agents.

120. * * * [T]he Tribunal has decided not to make an order for monetary compensation. * * *

122. There is a long established practice of States and international Courts and Tribunals of using satisfaction as a remedy or form of reparation (in the wide sense) for the breach of an international obligation. This practice relates particularly to the case of moral or legal damage done directly to the State, especially as opposed to the case of damage to persons involving international responsibilities. * * *

Satisfaction in this sense can take and has taken various forms. Arangio–Ruiz [in his 1989 report for the International Law Commission on state responsibility] mentions regrets, punishment of the responsible individuals, safeguards against repetition, the payment of symbolic or nominal damages or of compensation on a broader basis, and a decision of an international tribunal declaring the unlawfulness of the State's conduct.

123. It is to the last of these forms of satisfaction for an international wrong that the Tribunal now turns. * * * The Tribunal accordingly decides to make four declarations of material breach of its obligations by France and further decides in compliance with Article 8 of the Agreement of 14 February 1989 to make public the text of its Award. For the foregoing reasons the Tribunal:

declares that the condemnation of the French Republic for its breaches of its treaty obligations to New Zealand, made public by the decision of the Tribunal, constitutes in the circumstances appropriate satisfaction for the legal and moral damage caused to New Zealand. * * *

126. Th[e] important relationship [between New Zealand and France], the nature of the decisions made by the Tribunal, and the earlier discussion of monetary compensation lead the Tribunal to make a recommendation. The recommendation, addressed to the two Governments, is intended to assist them in putting an end to the present unhappy affair. * * *

128. The power of an arbitral tribunal to address recommendations to the parties to a dispute, in addition to the formal finding and obligatory decisions contained in the award, has been recognized in previous arbitral decisions. * * *

For the foregoing reasons the Tribunal:

in light of the above decisions, recommends that the Governments of the French Republic and of New Zealand set up a fund to promote close and friendly relations between the citizens of the two countries, and that the Government of the French Republic make an initial contribution equivalent to US Dollars 2 million to that fund.

Notes and Questions

1. *The Political Context.* France's sinking of the *Rainbow Warrior* was prompted by Greenpeace's protests against French atmospheric nuclear testing in the South Pacific. France's nuclear testing program had begun well before the Rainbow Warrior was sunk in July 1985. Indeed, New Zealand and Australia had challenged the legality of France's nuclear testing before the International Court of Justice in 1973. France refused to appear in the cases, but its public statements that its 1974 series of atmospheric tests would be its last persuaded the Court to dismiss the cases. The Court concluded that "the objective of the Applicant has in effect been accomplished, inasmuch as the Court finds that France has undertaken the obligation to hold no further nuclear tests in the South Pacific." Nuclear Test Cases (New Zealand v. France), 1974 I.C.J. 457, 475 ¶ 55, 1974 WL 4; Nuclear Tests Case (Australia v. France), 1974 I.C.J. 253, 270 ¶ 52, 1974 WL 3. France subsequently withdrew its acceptance of the compulsory jurisdiction of the ICJ and resumed nuclear testing.

France conducted a nuclear test at Morurua atoll in the South Pacific just two months before the sinking of the *Rainbow Warrior*. Greenpeace was planning to sail the vessel to the French nuclear testing area in protest later in 1985. France admitted the attack. On September 22, 1985, the French Prime Minister confirmed that agents of the French secret service had acted on official orders and had sunk the vessel. French officials at the time expressed regret and indicated France's readiness to make reparations to New Zealand.

2. *Compensating the Victims of the Attack.* France paid 2.3 million French francs to the widow, children, and parents of Fernando Pereira, the crew member killed aboard the *Rainbow Warrior*. France also agreed to a

separate arbitration with Greenpeace after negotiations with that organization failed to reach a settlement. On October 3, 1987, that arbitral tribunal ordered France to pay Greenpeace $8.1 million. Philip Shabecoff, "France Must Pay Greenpeace $8 Million in Sinking of Ship," *New York Times*, Oct. 3, 1987, at A2.

3. *The Decisions to Arbitrate.* What motivated New Zealand and France to agree to the 1986 arbitration? Why did the states believe that recourse to arbitration was desirable, rather than continuing with diplomatic negotiations? Why did France and New Zealand ask the Secretary–General of the United Nations to issue a ruling concerning the scope of France's responsibility for the sinking? The agreement to submit the dispute to the Secretary–General asked for an "equitable and principled" ruling, and the two states agreed to abide by it. France and New Zealand in fact negotiated most of the provisions of the Secretary–General's ruling behind the scenes, and the Secretary–General endorsed them. As noted in paragraph 115 of the 1990 arbitration, the Secretary–General's 1986 ruling included compensation for non-material damage; compensation was one item the Secretary–General decided for himself. See Lakshman Guruswamy, Geoffrey Palmer & Burns Weston, *International Environmental Law and World Order* 163 (1994).

Because of a provision in the 1986 bilateral agreement between France and New Zealand, New Zealand could institute the 1990 arbitration unilaterally. Had France and New Zealand not concluded the 1990 Supplemental Agreement designating the arbitrators, or had the two states had not agreed on the third member of the tribunal, the 1986 agreement authorized the Secretary–General of the United Nations to make the necessary appointments. What did New Zealand hope to gain by the 1990 arbitration?

4. *The Variety of Arbitral Functions.* How do the role and functions of the tribunal in the 1990 *Rainbow Warrior* arbitration compare with the role and functions of the tribunal in the *Dogger Bank* dispute?

5. *Satisfaction.* France complied almost immediately with the arbitral tribunal's recommendation to contribute $2 million to a fund to promote friendly relations. J. Scott Davidson, "The Rainbow Warrior Arbitration Concerning the Treatment of the French Agents Mafart and Prieur," 40 *International and Comparative Law Quarterly* 446, 456 (1991). Michael Rocard, the French Prime Minister, also visited New Zealand in May 1991 and formally apologized for the 1985 bombing. Nevertheless, tensions continued. France resumed its nuclear testing in the South Pacific, and New Zealand expressed outrage when, in July 1991, France awarded Alain Mafart a medal for distinguished service. Richard Long, "New Zealand Disgust as France Honours Bomber," *The Times (London)*, July 6, 1991, at 9. A new round of French nuclear testing in 1995 led New Zealand and other Pacific states to protest anew. New Zealand complained to the International Court that the testing was contrary to the *Nuclear Test Cases* described in Note 1. The Court disagreed, however, noting that those cases concerned atmospheric testing, whereas the more recent French testing was non-atmospheric. See Request for an Examination of the Situation in Accordance with Paragraph 63 of the Court's Judgment of 20 December

1974 in the Nuclear Tests (New Zealand v. France) Case, 1995 I.C.J. 288, 1995 WL 805134.

6. *Compromissory Clauses in Treaties.* The Case Concerning the Air Services Agreement of 27 March 1946, United States v. France, 54 Int'l L. Rep. 304 (1978), concerned the interpretation of the 1946 U.S.–France Air Services Agreement. The Agreement contained a clause, known as a compromissory clause, that authorized a panel of arbitrators to hear disputes concerning the interpretation or application of the Agreement, but arbitration was actually conducted pursuant a separate *compromis.* The arbitral tribunal held, *inter alia,* that in some circumstances a state may take counter-measures even while an international arbitration is on-going. See Marian Lloyd Nash, *Digest of United States Practice in International Law* 770 (1978), and Elizabeth Zoller, *Peacetime Unilateral Remedies* 135 (1984).

A separate *compromis* to arbitrate has been employed in virtually every modern interstate arbitration, even when compromissory clauses—which are found in many different types of treaties—authorize the submission of disputes arising under treaties to arbitral tribunals. See Christine Gray & Benedict Kingsbury, "Inter–State Arbitration Since 1945: Overview and Evaluation," in *International Courts for the Twenty–First Century* 55, 61 (Mark W. Janis ed. 1992). Why should states conclude such separate *compromis* when there already are compromissory clauses? What functions do compromissory clauses serve, other than providing the basis for consent to arbitral proceedings?

> * * * [C]ompromissory clauses may well serve different and even multiple functions, depending on the nature and subject matters of the treaties in which they are found. * * *
>
> One potential function of compromissory clauses in U.S. treaties is in fact to promote binding third-party dispute resolution, as a way to help settle interstate disputes or to provide a forum in which details affecting ongoing relations may be worked out. * * *
>
> The "dispute settlement" function * * * overlaps with the function of strengthening and reaffirming treaty rules. Under the [World Trade Organization system,] for example, the United States often may perceive an advantage to the prompt resolution of issues in order to provide guidelines for future action, under which affected industries and states may plan their future conduct. The establishment of such guidelines may be the paramount achievement of a third-party proceeding. Furthermore, where compromissory clauses appear in a series of bilateral agreements that functionally substitute for a multilateral treaty regime, as is the case with bilateral investment treaties and air transport agreements, a tribunal decision can establish or affirm a norm that will be applied in many situations beyond the one involving the particular parties to the dispute. For these reasons, the United States may occasionally prefer to seek actual adjudication or arbitration of a dispute. * * *
>
> [In addition,] compromissory clauses may well help to create a sense that particular treaty norms are legitimate, and thereby promote a psychological willingness to abide by them relatively closely, even with-

out any proceedings. * * * [W]hen states find close adherence to certain intended treaty standards to be particularly beneficial, they may employ a variety of mechanisms, including compromissory clauses, to promote attitudes of expected compliance on the part of treaty partners.

John E. Noyes, "The Functions of Compromissory Clauses in U.S. Treaties," 34 *Virginia Journal of International Law* 831, 898–900 (1994).

B. THE INTERNATIONAL COURT

1. THE JURISDICTION OF THE INTERNATIONAL COURT

The contentious jurisdiction of the International Court of Justice is based on Article 36 of the Court's Statute, which is an integral part of the United Nations Charter. The Court also may render advisory opinions in accordance with Article 65 of its Statute and Article 96 of the U.N. Charter.

STATUTE OF THE INTERNATIONAL COURT OF JUSTICE, ARTICLES 36, 65

June 26, 1945, 59 Stat. 1031, T.S. No. 993.

ARTICLE 36

1. The jurisdiction of the Court comprises all cases which the parties refer to it and all matters specially provided for in the Charter of the United Nations or in treaties and conventions in force.

2. The states parties to the present Statute may at any time declare that they recognize as compulsory *ipso facto* and without special agreement, in relation to any other state accepting the same obligation, the jurisdiction of the Court in all legal disputes concerning:

a. the interpretation of a treaty;

b. any question of international law;

c. the existence of any fact which, if established, would constitute a breach of an international obligation;

d. the nature or extent of the reparation to be made for the breach of an international obligation.

3. The declarations referred to above may be made unconditionally or on condition of reciprocity on the part of several or certain states, or for a certain time.

4. Such declarations shall be deposited with the Secretary–General of the United Nations, who shall transmit copies thereof to the parties to the Statute and to the Registrar of the Court.

5. Declarations made under Article 36 of the Statute of the Permanent Court of International Justice and which are still in force shall be deemed, as between the parties to the present Statute, to be acceptances of the compulsory jurisdiction of the International Court of Justice for

the period which they still have to run and in accordance with their terms.

6. In the event of a dispute as to whether the Court has jurisdiction, the matter shall be settled by the decision of the Court.

Article 65

1. The Court may give an advisory opinion on any legal question at the request of whatever body may be authorized by or in accordance with the Charter of the United Nations to make such a request.

2. Questions upon which the advisory opinion of the Court is asked shall be laid before the Court by means of a written request containing an exact statement of the question upon which an opinion is required, and accompanied by all documents likely to throw light upon the question.

CHARTER OF THE UNITED NATIONS, ARTICLE 96

June 26, 1945, 59 Stat. 1031, T.S. No. 993.

Article 96

1. The General Assembly or the Security Council may request the International Court of Justice to give an advisory opinion on any legal question.

2. Other organs of the United Nations and specialized agencies, which may at any time be so authorized by the General Assembly, may also request advisory opinions of the Court on legal questions arising within the scope of their activities.

2. CONTENTIOUS CASES AT THE INTERNATIONAL COURT

THE MINQUIERS AND ECREHOS CASE

France v. United Kingdom, 1953 I.C.J. 47, 1953 WL 7.

By a letter dated December 5th, 1951, the British Ambassador to the Netherlands transmitted to the Registry on behalf of his Government a certified copy of a Special Agreement concluded between the Government of the United Kingdom of Great Britain and Northern Ireland and the Government of the French Republic, signed on December 29th, 1950, the instruments of ratification in respect of which were exchanged at Paris on September 24th, 1951. * * *

By Article I of the Special Agreement, signed on December 29th, 1950, the Court is requested

> "to determine whether the sovereignty over the islets and rocks (in so far as they are capable of appropriation) of the Minquiers and Ecrehos groups respectively belongs to the United Kingdom or the French Republic."

Having thus been requested to decide whether these groups belong either to France or to the United Kingdom, the Court has to determine which of the Parties has produced the more convincing proof of title to one or the other of these groups, or to both of them. By the formulation of Article I the Parties have excluded the status of *res nullius* as well as that of *condominium*. * * *

By the Special Agreement the Court is requested to determine the sovereignty over the islets and rocks in so far as they are capable of appropriation. These words must be considered as relating to islets and rocks which are physically capable of appropriation. The Court is requested to decide in general to which Party sovereignty over each group as a whole belongs, without determining in detail the facts relating to the particular units of which the groups consist.

These groups lie between the British Channel Island of Jersey and the coast of France and consist each of two or three habitable islets, many smaller islets and a great number of rocks. The Ecrehos group lies north-east of Jersey, 3.9 sea-miles from that island, measured from the rock nearest thereto and permanently above water, and 6.6 sea-miles from the coast of France, measured in the same way. The Minquiers group lies south of Jersey, 9.8 sea-miles therefrom and 16.2 sea-miles from the French mainland, measured in the same way. This group lies 8 sea-miles from the Chausey Islands which belong to France.

Both Parties contend that they have respectively an ancient or original title to the Ecrehos and the Minquiers, and that their title has always been maintained and was never lost. The present case does not therefore present the characteristics of a dispute concerning the acquisition of sovereignty over *terra nullius*.

The United Kingdom Government derives the ancient title invoked by it from the conquest of England in 1066 by William Duke of Normandy. By this conquest England became united within the Duchy of Normandy, including the Channel Islands, and this union lasted until 1204 when King Philip Augustus of France drove the Anglo–Norman forces out of Continental Normandy. But his attempts to occupy also the Islands were not successful, except for brief periods when some of them were taken by French forces. On this ground the United Kingdom Government submits the view that all of the Channel Islands, including the Ecrehos and the Minquiers, remained, as before, united with England and that this situation of fact was placed on a legal basis by subsequent Treaties concluded between the English and French Kings.

The French Government does not dispute that the Islands of Jersey, Guernsey, Alderney, Sark, Herm and Jethou continued to be held by the King of England; but it denies that the Ecrehos and Minquiers groups were held by him after the dismemberment of the Duchy of Normandy in 1204. After that event, these two groups were, it is asserted, held by the King of France together with some other islands close to the continent, and reference is made to the same medieval Treaties as those which are invoked by the United Kingdom Government.

In such circumstances it must be examined whether these Treaties, invoked by both Parties, contain anything which might throw light upon the status of the Ecrehos and the Minquiers.

The Treaty of Lambeth of 1217, to which the Parties have referred, cannot be said to contain anything which might elucidate this question. The Treaty of Paris of 1259, which appears to be the principal Treaty on which the Parties rely, enumerates in Article 4 all the lands which the King of England should hold in fee of the King of France in Saintonge beyond the river Charente as well as Bordeaux, Bayonne and Gascony and "all the land which he holds on this side of the Sea of England in fee and in demesne and the islands, if any there be, which the king of England holds which are of the realm of france, and he shall hold of us as peer of france and duke of Aquitaine." These terms seem to refer to islands which the King of England held as Duke of Aquitaine, and not to the Channel Islands. But even assuming that these Islands were also included, the article refers in any case only to islands, if any there be, which are held by the English King. It does not say which islands were at that time held by him. [Similarly, the Court finds that neither the Treaty of Calcais of 1360 nor the Treaty of Tropes of 1420 refers specifically to the Minquiers and Ecrehos.]

There are, however, other documents which provide some indication as to the possession of the islets in dispute.

By a Charter of January 14th, 1200, King John of England granted to one of his Barons, Piers des Préaux, the Islands of Jersey, Guernsey and Alderney "to have and to hold of us by service of three knights' fees." Three years later, by a Charter of 1203, Piers des Préaux granted to the Abbey of Val-Richer "the island of Escrehou in entirety," stating that the King of England "gave me the islands" (*insulas mihi dedit*). This shows that he treated the Ecrehos as an integral part of the fief of the Islands which he had received from the King. In an Order from the English King of July 5th, 1258, the Sub-Warden of the Islands was ordered "to guard the islands of Gernere and Geresey, and the king's other islands in his keeping." In Letters Patent of the English King, dated June 28th, 1360, it was provided that the "keeper of the islands of Gernseye, Jerseye, Serk and Aurneye, and the other islands adjacent thereto" may have the keeping for a further period. The Truce of London of 1471 provided in Article 3 that the King of France would not make any hostile act against the Kingdom of England and other lands specially mentioned, including the Islands "of guernsey, Jersey and alderney [and] other territories, islands, lands and lordships, which are, or will be, held and possessed by the said lord King of England or by his subjects." A Papal Bull of January 20th, 1500, transferring the Channel Islands from the Diocese of Coutances to the Diocese of Winchester, mentioned "the islands of Jersey and Guernsey, Chausey, Alderney, Herm and Sark," while two commercial Treaties of 1606 and 1655 mentioned only Jersey and Guernsey.

[The Court reviews the political history of the Channel Islands and concludes:] What is of decisive importance, in the opinion of the Court, is not indirect presumptions deduced from events in the Middle Ages, but the evidence which relates directly to the possession of the Ecrehos and Minquiers groups.

[The Court turns first to the Ecrehos.]

It has already been mentioned that the Charter of 1200 of the English King, whereby he granted the fief of the Channel Islands to Piers des Préaux, and the Charter of 1203, whereby the latter in turn granted the Ecrehos to the Abbey of Val–Richer, show that the Ecrehos were treated by him as an integral part of his fief.

The grant of the Ecrehos was in frankalmoin. The French Government contends that such a grant had the effect of severing the feudal link between Piers des Préaux and the Abbey, so that the Ecrehos no longer formed a part of the fief of the Channel Islands. The view submitted by that Government is that the Ecrehos remained subject to the Duke of Normandy through the intermediary of the Abbey of Val–Richer, which was situated on the French mainland, and that, when the King of France succeeded to the rights of the Duke after the occupation of Continental Normandy in 1204, the Abbey "passed under his protection, as did the Ecrehos, whose overlord he became."

This contention renders it necessary to consider the Charter of 1203 more closely. It provided the following: * * *

> ". . . . Know ye all that I, having regard to the mercy of God, have granted and given and by my present charter have confirmed to God and to the church of St. Mary of Val–Richer and to the monks there serving God, for the salvation of the soul of John, illustrious king of England, who gave me the islands, and for the salvation of the souls of myself and of my father and mother and of all my ancestors, the island of Escrehou in entirety, for the building there of a church in honour of God and of the blessed Mary, so that the divine mysteries be daily celebrated there, to have and possess [it] and whatever in the same island they shall be able to increase and build, freely and quietly, fully and honourably, in free pure and perpetual alms. I have further granted to the aforesaid monks whatever by my men of Jersey, and of Guernsey, and of Alderney, having regard to charity, shall be reasonably given to them, saving my right."

It appears clearly from the *Grand Coutumier de Normandie* of the thirteenth century, chapters XXVIII and XXXII (de Gruchy edition, 1881, pp. 90–91 and 98), that land held in frankalmoin was a tenure, and that such a grant in frankalmoin to an ecclesiastical institution did not have the effect of severing feudal ties. The text of the first part of Chapter XXXII is as follows:

[*Translation*]

"They are said to hold by alms who hold lands given in pure alms to God and his servants, wherein the donors retain nothing to themselves or their heirs save only the patronal domain; and they hold from them by alms only, as from patrons. None can make alms out of any land, save only that which is his own therein. Wherefore note that neither the duke, nor barons, nor anyone, ought to sustain any detriment if their men make alms of the lands which they hold of them; and their lords shall exercise their justice and levy their rights in the lands so put in alms, notwithstanding."

This text shows that the grantor retained the "patronal domain" (*dominium patronale*). According to this ancient Norman custom, Piers des Préaux did not by his grant drop out of the feudal chain as far as the Ecrehos was concerned. He continued to hold the Ecrehos as a part of his fief of the Channel Islands, with the Abbot of Val-Richer as his vassal and the King of England as his overlord, and the King continued to exercise his justice and levy his rights in the land so put in alms. By granting the Ecrehos in frankalmoin to the Abbey, Piers des Préaux did not, and could not, alienate the island from the fief of the Channel Islands; it remained a part of that fief.

This view is contested by the French Government on the ground that Piers des Préaux had not in the Charter reserved any feudal service and that he therefore had not created any feudal tenure. It seems that no such condition for the creation of a "*teneure par omosne*," or frankalmoin, was required by the ancient Norman custom, as described in the *Coutumier*. But even assuming that a condition or reservation was required, the grant to the Abbey did contain such a condition or reservation. As is seen from the text of the Charter, the Abbey was to build a church in the Ecrehos "so that the divine mysteries be daily celebrated there," and when the grant was said to be given "for the salvation of the soul of John, illustrious king of England . . . and for the salvation of the souls of myself and of my father and mother and all my ancestors," this could, in view of the custom at that time, only mean that a service of prayers was reserved in the Charter. That this must also have been the view of the Abbot himself and of his successors is seen from the records of certain *Quo Warranto* proceedings held in Jersey in 1309 before the King's itinerant Justices. The Assize Rolls show that a chapel had in fact been built in the Ecrehos, and that the Prior of that chapel, appearing before the Justices, gave evidence that he and his fellow monk, dwelling in the chapel throughout the whole year, "always celebrate for the lord the King and his progenitors." These records show that the Prior himself as well as the Justices called the grant a *tenura*.

Shortly after his grant of 1203 Piers de Préaux forfeited the fief of the Channel Islands, which thereupon reverted to the English King and were administered by Wardens appointed by that King, except for certain periods in the thirteenth and the beginning of the fourteenth century, when the Islands were again granted in fee. Up to 1309, there is no indication that any change had occurred as to the connection of the Ecrehos with the Channel Islands.

The object of the *Quo Warranto* proceedings of 1309 mentioned above was to enquire into the property and revenue of the English King. These proceedings, which were numerous, took the form of calling upon persons to justify their possession of property. The Abbot of Val–Richer was summoned before the King's Justices to answer regarding a mill and the *advocatio* of the Priory of the Ecrehos as well as a rent. * * * When therefore the Abbot of Val–Richer was summoned before the King's Justices in Jersey to answer for this *advocatio*, it must have been on the ground that the Ecrehos, to which the *advocatio* was attached, was within the domain of the English King. And when the Prior of the Ecrehos appeared as the Abbot's attorney in answer to the summons, jurisdiction in respect of the Ecrehos was exercised by the Justices, who decided that "it is permitted to the said Prior to hold the *premissa* as he holds them as long as it shall please the lord the King."

The Prior of the Ecrehos became involved in three other legal proceedings in Jersey in the years 1323 and 1331. As they concerned events which occurred in Jersey, they do not throw any light upon the status of the Ecrehos, but they show that there was a close relationship between the Ecrehos and Jersey at that time. Further evidence of this relationship is given by Letters of Protection, which, on August 18th, 1337, shortly before the outbreak of the Hundred Years War between England and France, were granted by the English King to ten Priors of Jersey and Guernsey, including the Prior of the Ecrehos, who was described as "*Prior de Acrehowe de Insula de Iereseye.*" Such protection was apparently accorded to him because the Priory was under the authority of the English King.

[The Court reviews more of the history of the Priory and finds that later in the Middle Ages, the Priory "was abandoned and the chapel fell into ruins. The close relationship between the Ecrehos and Jersey ceased and for a considerable period thereafter the islets were only occasionally visited by Jerseymen for the purpose of fishing and collecting seaweed." From the sixteenth to the eighteenth century, the Ecrehos were more or less abandoned.]

From the beginning of the nineteenth century the connection between the Ecrehos and Jersey became closer again because of the growing importance of the oyster fishery in the waters surrounding the islets, and Jersey authorities took, during the subsequent period, action in many ways in respect of the islets. Of the manifold facts invoked by the United Kingdom Government, the Court attaches, in particular, probative value to the acts which relate to the exercise of jurisdiction and local administration and to legislation.

In 1826 criminal proceedings were instituted before the Royal Court in Jersey against a Jerseyman for having shot at a person on the Ecrehos. Similar judicial proceedings in Jersey in respect of criminal offences committed on the Ecrehos took place in 1881, 1883, 1891, 1913 and 1921. On the evidence produced the Court is satisfied that the Courts of Jersey, in criminal cases such as these, have no jurisdiction in the matter of a criminal offence committed outside the Bailiwick of Jersey, even though the offence be committed by a British subject resident in Jersey, and that Jersey authorities took action in these cases because the Ecrehos were considered to be within the Bailiwick. These facts show therefore that Jersey courts have exercised criminal jurisdiction in respect of the Ecrehos during nearly a hundred years.

Evidence produced shows that the law of Jersey has for centuries required the holding of an inquest on corpses found within the Bailiwick where it was not clear that death was due to natural causes. Such inquests on corpses found at the Ecrehos were held in 1859, 1917 and 1948 and are additional evidence of the exercise of jurisdiction in respect of these islets.

Since about 1820, and probably earlier, persons from Jersey have erected and maintained some habitable houses or huts on the islets of the Ecrehos, where they have stayed during the fishing season. Some of these houses or huts have, for the purpose of parochial rates, been included in the records of the Parish of St. Martin in Jersey, which have been kept since 1889, and they have been assessed for the levying of local taxes. Rating schedules for 1889 and 1950 were produced in evidence.

A register of fishing boats for the port of Jersey shows that the fishing boat belonging to a Jersey fisherman, who lived permanently on an islet of the Ecrehos for more than forty years, was entered in that register in 1872, the port or place of the boat being indicated as "Ecrehos Rocks," and that the licence of that boat was cancelled in 1882. According to a letter of June, 1876, from the Principal Customs Officer of Jersey, an official of that Island visited occasionally the Ecrehos for the purpose of endorsing the licence of that boat.

It is established that contracts of sale relating to real property on the Ecrehos islets have been passed before the competent authorities of Jersey and registered in the public registry of deeds of that island. Examples of such registration of contracts are produced for 1863, 1881, 1884 and some later years.

In 1884, a custom-house was established in the Ecrehos by Jersey customs authorities. The islets have been included by Jersey authorities within the scope of their census enumerations, and in 1901 an official enumerator visited the islets for the purpose of taking the census.

These various facts show that Jersey authorities have in several ways exercised ordinary local administration in respect of the Ecrehos during a long period of time.

By a British Treasury Warrant of 1875, constituting Jersey as a Port of the Channel Islands, the "Ecrehou Rocks" were included within the limits of that port. This legislative Act was a clear manifestation of British sovereignty over the Ecrehos at a time when a dispute as to such sovereignty had not yet arisen. The French Government protested in 1876 on the ground that this Act derogated from the Fishery Convention of 1839. But this protest could not deprive the Act of its character as a manifestation of sovereignty.

Of other facts which throw light upon the dispute, it should be mentioned that Jersey authorities have made periodical official visits to the Ecrehos since 1885, and that they have carried out various works and constructions there, such as a slipway in 1895, a signal post in 1910 and the placing of a mooring buoy in 1939.

The French Government, in addition to the alleged original feudal title considered above, has invoked the fact that the States of Jersey in 1646 prohibited the inhabitants of Jersey from fishing without special permission at the Ecrehos and the Chausey Islands, and that they restricted visits to the Ecrehos in 1692 because of the war between England and France. This shows, it is contended, that the Ecrehos were not considered as British territory. But the Court does not consider that this is the necessary or natural inference to be drawn from these facts.

In the course of the diplomatic exchanges between the two Governments in the beginning of the nineteenth century concerning fisheries off the coast of Cotentin, the French Ambassador in London addressed to the Foreign Office a Note, dated June 12th, 1820, attaching two charts sent from the French Ministry of Marine to the French Ministry of Foreign Affairs purporting to delimit the areas within which the fishermen of each country were entitled to exclusive rights of fishery. In these charts a blue line marking territorial waters was drawn along the coast of the French mainland and round the Chausey Islands, which were indicated as French, and a red line marking territorial waters was drawn round Jersey, Alderney, Sark and the Minquiers, which were indicated as British. No line of territorial waters was drawn round the Ecrehos group, one part of which was included in the red line for Jersey and consequently marked as belonging to Great Britain and the other part apparently treated as *res nullius*. When the French Government in 1876 protested against the British Treasury Warrant of 1875 and challenged British sovereignty over the Ecrehos, it did not itself claim sovereignty, but continued to treat the Ecrehos as *res nullius*. In a letter of March 26th, 1884, from the French Ministry of Foreign Affairs to the French Minister of Marine, it was stated that the British Government had not ceased to claim the Ecrehos as a dependency to the Channel Islands, and it was suggested that French fishermen should be prohibited access to the Ecrehos. It does not appear that any such measure was taken, and subsequently, in a Note to the Foreign Office of December 15th, 1886, the French Government claimed for the first time sovereignty over the Ecrehos "*à la lumière des nouvelles données historiques et géologiques.*"

The Court being now called upon to appraise the relative strength of the opposing claims to sovereignty over the Ecrehos in the light of the facts considered above, finds that the Ecrehos group in the beginning of the thirteenth century was considered and treated as an integral part of the fief of the Channel Islands which were held by the English King, and that the group continued to be under the dominion of that King, who in the beginning of the 14th century exercised jurisdiction in respect thereof. The Court further finds that British authorities during the greater part of the nineteenth century and in the twentieth century have exercised State functions in respect of the group. The French Government, on the other hand, has not produced evidence showing that it has any valid title to the group. In such circumstances it must be concluded that the sovereignty over the Ecrehos belongs to the United Kingdom.

[The Court examines the claims to the Minquiers in similar detail.]

THE COURT,

unanimously,

finds that the sovereignty over the islets and rocks of the Ecrehos and Minquiers groups, in so far as these islets and rocks are capable of appropriation, belongs to the United Kingdom.

Notes and Questions

1. *The Decision to Adjudicate.* What made the Minquiers and Ecrehos dispute susceptible to resolution by the International Court? What did the governments of the United Kingdom and France gain and lose by suspending diplomatic negotiations while the Court heard the case? Would France or Britain believe it had the better claim? Does hope of success or fear of failure affect a state's attitude?

Why choose the International Court rather than an *ad hoc* panel of international arbitrators? In delimiting the continental shelf a quarter century later, the same two countries appointed an arbitral tribunal unrelated to the ICJ. See the "Arbitration between the United Kingdom of Great Britain and Northern Ireland and the French Republic on the Delimitation of the Continental Shelf, Decisions of the Court of Arbitration, June 30, 1977, March 14, 1978," 18 I.L.M. 397 (1979).

2. *Territorial Dispute Settlement.* Territorial disputes seem a favorite kind of issue for international adjudication whether by the ICJ or by another sort of forum. For example, five-judge chambers of the ICJ, authorized under Article 26 of the Court's Statute, have been constituted to hear territorial delimitation cases between the Canada and United States, 1984 I.C.J. 246, 1984 WL 499, and between Burkino Faso and Mali, 1985 I.C.J. 6, 1985 WL 136. Are territorial disputes especially amenable to legal argument and judicial settlement? In *Minquiers and Ecrehos*, what kind of proof do the lawyers need to collect and argue? How does the Court weigh the evidence and apply legal rules to reach its judgment?

3. *Compliance With ICJ Decisions.* Why are states likely to comply with ICJ decisions like those in *Minquiers and Ecrehos*? Did both states mean to comply with any eventual judgment when they consented to the *compromis*? Note how France and the United Kingdom formulated the question the Court was authorized to decide. By minimizing the possibility that the Court would find the islets to be either *terra nullius* or subject to a

joint condominium regime, the parties seemingly maximized the possibility that the Court would rule that only one or the other state had sovereignty over the islets. If either France or the U.K. ran a significant risk of losing the case in the ICJ, was this risk worth running because it would be easier politically for the government to give up the islets in a court case than in diplomatic negotiations? Does the ICJ sometimes serve a "scapegoat function"?

4. *The Norman Invasion.* On July 10, 1994, the Ecrehos were "invaded" by 150 French citizens from Normandy who sought to reopen the dispute about the ownership of the islets because Jersey was seeking to extend its territorial waters from three to 12 miles. Despite assurances from the government of Jersey that traditional French fishing rights would not be impaired, the Norman party came to the Ecrehos to protest. They were restrained from tearing down the Union Jack, but Jersey authorities permitted them to hold a mass and to plant a Norman flag of two yellow lions rampant on a red ground beside a temporary altar. Marcus Binney & Michael Hornsby, "Jersey Police Outwit Norman Invasion," *The Times (London)*, July 11, 1994, at 5.

THE DIPLOMATIC AND CONSULAR STAFF CASE

United States v. Iran
1980 I.C.J. 3.

1. On 29 November 1979, the Legal Adviser of the Department of State of the United States of America handed to the Registrar an Application instituting proceedings against the Islamic Republic of Iran in respect of a dispute concerning the seizure and holding as hostages of members of the United States diplomatic and consular staff and certain other United States nationals. * * *

[The United States also applied for an interim order to protect the hostages. Iran refused to plead or argue before the International Court. In December 1979, the ICJ delivered an order instructing Iran to release the hostages immediately, 1979 I.C.J. 7, but Iran failed to comply. The case went forward on the merits.]

10. No pleadings were filed by the Government of Iran, which also was not represented at the oral proceedings, and no submissions were therefore presented on its behalf. The position of that Government was, however, defined in two communications addressed to the Court by the Minister for Foreign Affairs of Iran; the first of these was a letter dated 9 December 1979 and transmitted by telegram the same day [the text of which was set out in full in the Court's Order of 15 December 1979], the second was a letter transmitted by telex dated 16 March 1980 and received on 17 March 1980, the text of which followed closely that of the letter of 9 December 1979 and reads as follows:

[*Translation from French*]

> "I have the honour to acknowledge receipt of the telegram concerning the meeting of the International Court of Justice to be held on 17 March 1980 at the request of the Government of the

United States of America, and to set forth to you below, once again, the position of the Government of the Islamic Republic of Iran in that respect:

The Government of the Islamic Republic of Iran wishes to express its respect for the International Court of Justice, and for its distinguished Members, for what they have achieved in the quest for a just and equitable solution to legal conflicts between States, and respectfully draws the attention of the Court to the deep-rootedness and the essential character of the Islamic Revolution of Iran, a revolution of a whole oppressed nation against its oppressors and their masters, the examination of whose numerous repercussions is essentially and directly a matter within the national sovereignty of Iran.

The Government of the Islamic Republic of Iran considers that the Court cannot and should not take cognizance of the case which the Government of the United States of America has submitted to it, and in the most significant fashion, a case confined to what is called the question of the 'hostages of the American Embassy in Tehran.'

For this question only represents a marginal and secondary aspect of an overall problem, one such that it cannot be studied separately, and which involves, *inter alia*, more than 25 years of continual interference by the United States in the internal affairs of Iran, the shameless exploitation of our country, and numerous crimes perpetrated against the Iranian people, contrary to and in conflict with all international and humanitarian norms.

The problem involved in the conflict between Iran and the United States is thus not one of the interpretation and the application of the treaties upon which the American Application is based, but results from an overall situation containing much more fundamental and more complex elements. Consequently, the Court cannot examine the American Application divorced from its proper context, namely the whole political dossier of the relations between Iran and the United States over the last 25 years.

With regard to the request for provisional measures, as formulated by the United States, it in fact implies that the Court should have passed judgment on the actual substance of the case submitted to it, which the Court cannot do without breach of the norms governing its jurisdiction. Furthermore, since provisional measures are by definition intended to protect the interest of the parties, they cannot be unilateral, as they are in the request submitted by the American Government."

[Despite Iran's refusal to participate, the Court rules it has enough information to decide the case. The Court then examines the factual background respecting the seizure of the hostages.]

17. At approximately 10:30 a.m. on 4 November 1979, during the course of a demonstration of approximately 3,000 persons, the United

States Embassy compound in Tehran was overrun by a strong armed group of several hundred people. The Iranian security personnel are reported to have simply disappeared from the scene; at all events it is established that they made no apparent effort to deter or prevent the demonstrators from seizing the Embassy's premises. The invading group (who subsequently described themselves as "Muslim Student Followers of the Imam's Policy," and who will hereafter be referred to as "the militants") gained access by force to the compound and to the ground floor of the Chancery building. Over two hours after the beginning of the attack, and after the militants had attempted to set fire to the Chancery building and to cut through the upstairs steel doors with a torch, they gained entry to the upper floor; one hour later they gained control of the main vault. The militants also seized the other buildings, including the various residences, on the Embassy compound. In the course of the attack, all the diplomatic and consular personnel and other persons present in the premises were seized as hostages, and detained in the Embassy compound; subsequently other United States personnel and one United States private citizen seized elsewhere in Tehran were brought to the compound and added to the number of hostages.

18. During the three hours or more of the assault, repeated calls for help were made from the Embassy to the Iranian Foreign Ministry, and repeated efforts to secure help from the Iranian authorities were also made through direct discussions by the United States Chargé d'affaires, who was at the Foreign Ministry at the time, together with two other members of the mission. From there he made contact with the Prime Minister's Office and the Foreign Ministry officials. A request was also made to the Iranian Chargé d'affaires in Washington for assistance in putting an end to the seizure of the Embassy. Despite these repeated requests, no Iranian security forces were sent in time to provide relief and protection to the Embassy. In fact when Revolutionary Guards ultimately arrived on the scene, despatched by the Government "to prevent clashes," they considered that their task was merely to "protect the safety of both the hostages and the students," according to statements subsequently made by the Iranian Government's spokesman, and by the operations commander of the Guards. No attempt was made by the Iranian Government to clear the Embassy premises, to rescue the persons held hostage, or to persuade the militants to terminate their action against the Embassy. * * *

21. The premises of the United States Embassy in Tehran have remained in the hands of the militants; and the same appears to be the case with the Consulates at Tabriz and Shiraz. Of the total number of United States citizens seized and held as hostages, 13 were released on 18–20 November 1979, but the remainder have continued to be held up to the present time. The release of the 13 hostages was effected pursuant to a decree by the Ayatollah Khomeini addressed to the militants dated 17 November 1979, in which he called upon the militants to "hand over the blacks and the women, if it is proven they did not spy,

to the Ministry of Foreign Affairs so that they may be immediately expelled from Iran."

22. The persons still held hostage in Iran include, according to the information furnished to the Court by the United States, at least 28 persons having the status, duly recognized by the Government of Iran, of "member of the diplomatic staff" within the meaning of the Vienna Convention on Diplomatic Relations of 1961; at least 20 persons having the status, similarly recognized, of "member of the administrative and technical staff" within the meaning of that Convention; and two other persons of United States nationality not possessing either diplomatic or consular status. Of the persons with the status of member of the diplomatic staff, four are members of the Consular Section of the Mission.

23. Allegations have been made by the Government of the United States of inhumane treatment of hostages; the militants and Iranian authorities have asserted that the hostages have been well treated, and have allowed special visits to the hostages by religious personalities and by representatives of the International Committee of the Red Cross. The specific allegations of ill-treatment have not however been refuted. Examples of such allegations, which are mentioned in some of the sworn declarations of hostages released in November 1979, are as follows: at the outset of the occupation of the Embassy some were paraded bound and blindfolded before hostile and chanting crowds; at least during the initial period of their captivity, hostages were kept bound, and frequently blindfolded, denied mail or any communication with their government or with each other, subjected to interrogation, threatened with weapons.

24. Those archives and documents of the United States Embassy which were not destroyed by the staff during the attack on 4 November have been ransacked by the militants. Documents purporting to come from this source have been disseminated by the militants and by the Government-controlled media. * * *

28. * * * On 25 November 1979, the Secretary–General of the United Nations addressed a letter to the President of the Security Council referring to the seizure of the United States Embassy in Tehran and the detention of its diplomatic personnel, and requesting an urgent meeting of the Security Council "in an effort to seek a peaceful solution to the problem." The Security Council met on 27 November and 4 December 1979; on the latter occasion, no representative of Iran was present, but the Council took note of a letter of 13 November 1979 from the Supervisor of the Iranian Foreign Ministry to the Secretary–General. The Security Council then adopted resolution 457 (1979), calling on Iran to release the personnel of the Embassy immediately, to provide them with protection and to allow them to leave the country. The resolution also called on the two Governments to take steps to resolve peacefully the remaining issues between them, and requested the Secretary–General to lend his good offices for the immediate implementation of the resolution, and to take all appropriate measures to that end. It further

stated that the Council would "remain actively seized of the matter" and requested the Secretary–General to report to it urgently on any developments with regard to his efforts. * * *

33. It is to be regretted that the Iranian Government has not appeared before the Court in order to put forward its arguments on the questions of law and of fact which arise in the present case; and that, in consequence, the Court has not had the assistance it might have derived from such arguments or from any evidence adduced in support of them. Nevertheless, in accordance with its settled jurisprudence, the Court, in applying Article 53 of its Statute, must first take up, *proprio motu*, any preliminary question, whether of admissibility or of jurisdiction, that appears from the information before it to arise in the case and the decision of which might constitute a bar to any further examination of the merits of the Applicant's case. The Court will, therefore, first address itself to the considerations put forward by the Iranian Government in its letters of 9 December 1979 and 16 March 1980, on the basis of which it maintains that the Court ought not to take cognizance of the present case.

34. The Iranian Government in its letter of 9 December 1979 drew attention to what it referred to as the "deep rootedness and the essential character of the Islamic Revolution of Iran, a revolution of a whole oppressed nation against its oppressors and their masters." The examination of the "numerous repercussions" of the revolution, it added, is "a matter essentially and directly within the national sovereignty of Iran." However, as the Court pointed out in its Order of 15 December 1979,

> "a dispute which concerns diplomatic and consular premises and the detention of internationally protected persons, and involves the interpretation or application of multilateral conventions codifying the international law governing diplomatic and consular relations, is one which by its very nature falls within international jurisdiction."

36. The Court * * * in its Order of 15 December 1979, made it clear that the seizure of the United States Embassy and Consulates and the detention of internationally protected persons as hostages cannot be considered as something "secondary" or "marginal," having regard to the importance of the legal principles involved. It also referred to a statement of the Secretary–General of the United Nations, and to Security Council resolution 457 (1979), as evidencing the importance attached by the international community as a whole to the observance of those principles in the present case as well as its concern at the dangerous level of tension between Iran and the United States. The Court, at the same time, pointed out that no provision of the Statute or Rules contemplates that the Court should decline to take cognizance of one aspect of a dispute merely because that dispute has other aspects, however important. It further underlined that, if the Iranian Government considered the alleged activities of the United States in Iran legally to have a close connection with the subject-matter of the United States' Application, it was open to that Government to present its own argu-

ments regarding those activities to the Court either by way of defence in a Counter–Memorial or by way of a counter-claim.

37. The Iranian Government, notwithstanding the terms of the Court's Order, did not file any pleadings and did not appear before the Court. By its own choice, therefore, it has forgone the opportunities offered to it under the Statute and Rules of Court to submit evidence and arguments in support of its contention in regard to the "overall problem." Even in its later letter of 16 March 1980, the Government of Iran confined itself to repeating what it had said in its letter of 9 December 1979, without offering any explanations in regard to the points to which the Court had drawn attention in its Order of 15 December 1979. It has provided no explanation of the reasons why it considers that the violations of diplomatic and consular law alleged in the United States' Application cannot be examined by the Court separately from what it describes as the "overall problem" involving "more than 25 years of continual interference by the United States in the internal affairs of Iran." Nor has it made any attempt to explain, still less define, what connection, legal or factual, there may be between the "overall problem" of its general grievances against the United States and the particular events that gave rise to the United States' claims in the present case which, in its view, precludes the separate examination of those claims by the Court. This was the more necessary because legal disputes between sovereign States by their very nature are likely to occur in political contexts, and often form only one element in a wider and long-standing political dispute between the States concerned. Yet never has the view been put forward before that, because a legal dispute submitted to the Court is only one aspect of a political dispute, the Court should decline to resolve for the parties the legal questions at issue between them. Nor can any basis for such a view of the Court's functions or jurisdiction be found in the Charter or the Statute of the Court; if the Court were, contrary to its settled jurisprudence, to adopt such a view, it would impose a far-reaching and unwarranted restriction upon the role of the Court in the peaceful solution of international disputes.

38. It follows that the considerations and arguments put forward in the Iranian Government's letters of 9 December 1979 and 16 March 1980 do not, in the opinion of the Court, disclose any ground on which it should conclude that it cannot or ought not to take cognizance of the present case. * * *

45. Article 53 of the Statute requires the Court, before deciding in favour of an Applicant's claim, to satisfy itself that it has jurisdiction, in accordance with Articles 36 and 37, empowering it to do so. In the present case the principal claims of the United States relate essentially to alleged violations by Iran of its obligations to the United States under the Vienna Conventions of 1961 on Diplomatic Relations and of 1963 on Consular Relations. With regard to these claims the United States has invoked as the basis for the Court's jurisdiction Article I of the Optional Protocols concerning the Compulsory Settlement of Disputes which

accompany these Conventions. The United Nations publication *Multilateral Treaties in respect of which the Secretary-General Performs Depository Functions* lists both Iran and the United States as parties to the Vienna Conventions of 1961 and 1963, as also to their accompanying Protocols concerning the Compulsory Settlement of Disputes, and in each case without any reservation to the instrument in question. The Vienna Conventions, which codify the law of diplomatic and consular relations, state principles and rules essential for the maintenance of peaceful relations between States and accepted throughout the world by nations of all creeds, cultures and political complexions. Moreover, the Iranian Government has not maintained in its communications to the Court that the two Vienna Conventions and Protocols are not in force as between Iran and the United States. Accordingly, as indicated in the Court's Order of 15 December 1979, the Optional Protocols manifestly provide a possible basis for the Court's jurisdiction, with respect to the United States' claims under the Vienna Conventions of 1961 and 1963. It only remains, therefore, to consider whether the present dispute in fact falls within the scope of their provisions.

46. The terms of Article I, which are the same in the two Protocols, provide:

> "Disputes arising out of the interpretation or application of the Convention shall lie within the compulsory jurisdiction of the International Court of Justice and may accordingly be brought before the Court by an application made by any party to the dispute being a Party to the present Protocol."

The United States' claims here in question concern alleged violations by Iran of its obligations under several articles of the Vienna Conventions of 1961 and 1963 with respect to the privileges and immunities of the personnel, the inviolability of the premises and archives, and the provision of facilities for the performance of the functions of the United States Embassy and Consulates in Iran. In so far as its claims relate to two private individuals held hostage in the Embassy, the situation of these individuals falls under the provisions of the Vienna Convention of 1961 guaranteeing the inviolability of the premises of embassies, and of Article 5 of the 1963 Convention concerning the consular functions of assisting nationals and protecting and safeguarding their interests. By their very nature all these claims concern the interpretation or application of one or other of the two Vienna Conventions. * * *

50. However, the United States also presents claims in respect of alleged violations by Iran of Articles II, paragraph 4, XIII, XVIII and XIX of the Treaty of Amity, Economic Relations, and Consular Rights of 1955 between the United States and Iran, which entered into force on 16 June 1957. With regard to these claims the United States has invoked paragraph 2 of Article XXI of the Treaty as the basis for the Court's jurisdiction. The claims of the United States under this Treaty overlap in considerable measure with its claims under the two Vienna Conventions and more especially the Convention of 1963. * * *

54. No suggestion has been made by Iran that the 1955 Treaty was not in force on 4 November 1979 when the United States Embassy was overrun and its nationals taken hostage, or on 29 November when the United States submitted the dispute to the Court. The very purpose of a treaty of amity, and indeed of a treaty of establishment, is to promote friendly relations between the two countries concerned, and between their two peoples, more especially by mutual undertakings to ensure the protection and security of their nationals in each other's territory. It is precisely when difficulties arise that the treaty assumes its greatest importance, and the whole object of Article XXI, paragraph 2, of the 1955 Treaty was to establish the means for arriving at a friendly settlement of such difficulties by the Court or by other peaceful means. It would, therefore, be incompatible with the whole purpose of the 1955 Treaty if recourse to the Court under Article XXI, paragraph 2, were now to be found not to be open to the parties precisely at the moment when such recourse was most needed. Furthermore, although the machinery for the effective operation of the 1955 Treaty has, no doubt, now been impaired by reason of diplomatic relations between the two countries having been broken off by the United States, its provisions remain part of the corpus of law applicable between the United States and Iran. * * *

56. * * * The events which are the subject of the United States' claims fall into two phases which it will be convenient to examine separately.

57. The first of these phases covers the armed attack on the United States Embassy by militants on 4 November 1979, the overrunning of its premises, the seizure of its inmates as hostages, the appropriation of its property and archives and the conduct of the Iranian authorities in the face of those occurrences. The attack and the subsequent overrunning, bit by bit, of the whole Embassy premises, was an operation which continued over a period of some three hours without any body of police, any military unit or any Iranian official intervening to try to stop or impede it from being carried through to its completion. The result of the attack was considerable damage to the Embassy premises and property, the forcible opening and seizure of its archives, the confiscation of the archives and other documents found in the Embassy and, most grave of all, the seizure by force of its diplomatic and consular personnel as hostages, together with two United States nationals.

58. No suggestion has been made that the militants, when they executed their attack on the Embassy, had any form of official status as recognized "agents" or organs of the Iranian State. Their conduct in mounting the attack, overrunning the Embassy and seizing its inmates as hostages cannot, therefore, be regarded as imputable to that State on that basis. Their conduct might be considered as itself directly imputable to the Iranian State only if it were established that, in fact, on the occasion in question the militants acted on behalf of the State, having been charged by some competent organ of the Iranian State to carry out a specific operation. The information before the Court does not, howev-

er, suffice to establish with the requisite certainty the existence at that time of such a link between the militants and any competent organ of the State.

59. Previously, it is true, the religious leader of the country, the Ayatollah Khomeini, had made several public declarations inveighing against the United States as responsible for all his country's problems. In so doing, it would appear, the Ayatollah Khomeini was giving utterance to the general resentment felt by supporters of the revolution at the admission of the former Shah to the United States. The information before the Court also indicates that a spokesman for the militants, in explaining their action afterwards, did expressly refer to a message issued by the Ayatollah Khomeini, on 1 November 1979. In that message the Ayatollah Khomeini had declared that it was "up to the dear pupils, students and theological students to expand with all their might their attacks against the United States and Israel, so they may force the United States to return the deposed and criminal shah, and to condemn this great plot" (that is, a plot to stir up dissension between the main streams of Islamic thought). In the view of the Court, however, it would be going too far to interpret such general declarations of the Ayatollah Khomeini to the people or students of Iran as amounting to an authorization from the State to undertake the specific operation of invading and seizing the United States Embassy. To do so would, indeed, conflict with the assertions of the militants themselves who are reported to have claimed credit for having devised and carried out the plan to occupy the Embassy. Again, congratulations after the event, such as those reportedly telephoned to the militants by the Ayatollah Khomeini on the actual evening of the attack, and other subsequent statements of official approval, though highly significant in another context shortly to be considered, do not alter the initially independent and unofficial character of the militants' attack on the Embassy.

60. The first phase, here under examination, of the events complained of also includes the attacks on the United States Consulates at Tabriz and Shiraz. Like the attack of the Embassy, they appear to have been executed by militants not having an official character, and successful because of lack of sufficient protection.

61. The conclusion just reached by the Court, that the initiation of the attack on the United States Embassy on 4 November 1979, and of the attacks on the Consulates at Tabriz and Shiraz the following day, cannot be considered as in itself imputable to the Iranian State does not mean that Iran is, in consequence, free of any responsibility in regard to those attacks; for its own conduct was in conflict with its international obligations. By a number of provisions of the Vienna Conventions of 1961 and 1963, Iran was placed under the most categorical obligations, as a receiving State, to take appropriate steps to ensure the protection of the United States Embassy and Consulates, their staffs, their archives, their means of communication and the freedom of movement of the members of their staffs.

62. Thus, after solemnly proclaiming the inviolability of the premises of a diplomatic mission, Article 22 of the 1961 Convention continues in paragraph 2:

> "*The receiving State is under a special duty to take all appropriate steps to protect the premises of the mission against any* intrusion or damage and to prevent any disturbance of the peace of the mission or impairment of its dignity." (Emphasis added.)

So, too, after proclaiming that the person of a diplomatic agent shall be inviolable, and that he shall not be liable to any form of arrest or detention, Article 29 provides:

> "The receiving State shall treat him with due respect and *shall take all appropriate steps to prevent any attack on his person, freedom or dignity*." (Emphasis added.)

The obligation of a receiving State to protect the inviolability of the archives and documents of a diplomatic mission is laid down in Article 24, which specifically provides that they are to be "inviolable at any time and wherever they may be." Under Article 25 it is required to "accord full facilities for the performance of the functions of the mission," under Article 26 to "ensure to all members of the mission freedom of movement and travel in its territory," and under Article 27 to "permit and protect free communication on the part of the mission for all official purposes." Analogous provisions are to be found in the 1963 Convention regarding the privileges and immunities and consular missions and their staffs (Art. 31, para. 3, Arts. 40, 33, 28, 34 and 35). In the view of the Court, the obligations of the Iranian Government here in question are not merely contractual obligations established by the Vienna Conventions of 1961 and 1963, but also obligations under general international law.

63. The facts * * * establish to the satisfaction of the Court that on 4 November 1979 the Iranian Government failed altogether to take any "appropriate steps" to protect the premises, staff and archives of the United States' mission against attack by the militants, and to take any steps either to prevent this attack or to stop it before it reached its completion. They also show that on 5 November 1979 the Iranian Government similarly failed to take appropriate steps for the protection of the United States Consulates at Tabriz and Shiraz. In addition they show, in the opinion of the Court, that the failure of the Iranian Government to take such steps was due to more than mere negligence or lack of appropriate means. * * *

67. This inaction of the Iranian Government by itself constituted clear and serious violation of Iran's obligations to the United States under the provisions of Article 22, paragraph 2, and Articles 24, 25, 26, 27 and 29 of the 1961 Vienna Convention on Diplomatic Relations, and Articles 5 and 36 of the 1963 Vienna Convention on Consular Relations. Similarly, with respect to the attacks on the Consulates at Tabriz and Shiraz, the inaction of the Iranian authorities entailed clear and serious breaches of its obligations under the provisions of several further articles

of the 1963 Convention on Consular Relations. So far as concerns the two private United States nationals seized as hostages by the invading militants, that inaction entailed, albeit incidentally, a breach of its obligations under Article II, paragraph 4, of the 1955 Treaty of Amity, Economic Relations, and Consular Rights which, in addition to the obligations of Iran existing under general international law, requires the parties to ensure "the most constant protection and security" to each other's nationals in their respective territories. * * *

69. The second phase of the events which are the subject of the United States' claims comprises the whole series of facts which occurred following the completion of the occupation of the United States Embassy by the militants, and the seizure of the Consulates at Tabriz and Shiraz. The occupation having taken place and the diplomatic and consular personnel of the United States' mission having been taken hostage, the action required of the Iranian Government by the Vienna Conventions and by general international law was manifest. Its plain duty was at once to make every effort, and to take every appropriate step, to bring these flagrant infringements of the inviolability of the premises, archives and diplomatic and consular staff of the United States Embassy to a speedy end, to restore the Consulates at Tabriz and Shiraz to United States control, and in general to re-establish the status quo and to offer reparation for the damage.

70. No such step was, however, taken by the Iranian authorities. At a press conference on 5 November the Foreign Minister, Mr. Yazdi, conceded that "according to international regulations the Iranian Government is dutybound to safeguard the life and property of foreign nationals." But he made no mention of Iran's obligation to safeguard the inviolability of foreign embassies and diplomats; and he ended by announcing that the action of the students "enjoys the endorsement and support of the government, because America herself is responsible for this incident." As to the Prime Minister, Mr. Bazargan, he does not appear to have made any statement on the matter before resigning his office on 5 November. * * *

73. The seal of official government approval was finally set on this situation by a decree issued on 17 November 1979 by the Ayatollah Khomeini. His decree began with the assertion that the American Embassy was "a centre of espionage and conspiracy" and that "those people who hatched plots against our Islamic movement in that place do not enjoy international diplomatic respect." He went on expressly to declare that the premises of the Embassy and the hostages would remain as they were until the United States had handed over the former Shah for trial and returned his property to Iran. This statement of policy the Ayatollah qualified only to the extent of requesting the militants holding the hostages to "hand over the blacks and the women, if it is proven that they did not spy, to the Ministry of Foreign Affairs so that they may be immediately expelled from Iran." As to the rest of the hostages, he made the Iranian Government's intentions all too clear:

"The noble Iranian nation will not give permission for the release of the rest of them. Therefore, the rest of them will be under arrest until the American Government acts according to the wish of the nation." * * *

79. The Court moreover cannot conclude its observations on the series of acts which it has found to be imputable to the Iranian State and to be patently inconsistent with its international obligations under the Vienna Conventions of 1961 and 1963 without mention also of another fact. This is that judicial authorities of the Islamic Republic of Iran and the Minister of Foreign Affairs have frequently voiced or associated themselves with, a threat first announced by the militants, of having some of the hostages submitted to trial before a court or some other body. These threats may at present merely be acts in contemplation. But the Court considers it necessary here and now to stress that, if the intention to submit the hostages to any form of criminal trial or investigation were to be put into effect, that would constitute a grave breach by Iran of its obligations under Article 31, paragraph 1, of the 1961 Vienna Convention. This paragraph states in the most express terms: "A diplomatic agent shall enjoy immunity from the criminal jurisdiction of the receiving State." Again, if there were an attempt to compel the hostages to bear witness, a suggestion renewed at the time of the visit to Iran of the Secretary–General's Commission, Iran would without question be violating paragraph 2 of that same Article of the 1961 Vienna Convention which provides that: "A diplomatic agent is not obliged to give evidence as a witness."

80. The facts of the present case, viewed in the light of the applicable rules of law, thus speak loudly and clearly of successive and still continuing breaches by Iran of its obligations to the United States under the Vienna Conventions of 1961 and 1963, as well as under the Treaty of 1955. * * *

90. On the basis of the foregoing detailed examination of the merits of the case, the Court finds that Iran, by committing successive and continuing breaches of the obligations laid upon it by the Vienna Conventions of 1961 and 1963 on Diplomatic and Consular Relations, the Treaty of Amity, Economic Relations, and Consular Rights of 1955, and the applicable rules of general international law, has incurred responsibility towards the United States. As to the consequences of this finding, it clearly entails an obligation on the part of the Iranian State to make reparation for the injury thereby caused to the United States. Since however Iran's breaches of its obligations are still continuing, the form and amount of such reparation cannot be determined at the present date.

91. At the same time the Court finds itself obliged to stress the cumulative effect of Iran's breaches of its obligations when taken together. A marked escalation of these breaches can be seen to have occurred in the transition from the failure on the part of the Iranian authorities to oppose the armed attack by the militants on 4 November 1979 and

their seizure of the Embassy premises and staff, to the almost immediate endorsement by those authorities of the situation thus created, and then to their maintaining deliberately for many months the occupation of the Embassy and detention of its staff by a group of armed militants acting on behalf of the State for the purpose of forcing the United States to bow to certain demands. Wrongfully to deprive human beings of their freedom and to subject them to physical constraint in conditions of hardship is in itself manifestly incompatible with the principles of the Charter of the United Nations, as well as with the fundamental principles enunciated in the Universal Declaration of Human Rights. But what has above all to be emphasized is the extent and seriousness of the conflict between the conduct of the Iranian State and its obligations under the whole corpus of the international rules of which diplomatic and consular law is comprised, rules the fundamental character of which the Court must here again strongly affirm. In its Order of 15 December 1979, the Court made a point of stressing that the obligations laid on States by the two Vienna Conventions are of cardinal importance for the maintenance of good relations between States in the interdependent world of today. "There is no more fundamental prerequisite for the conduct of relations between States," the Court there said, "than the inviolability of diplomatic envoys and embassies, so that throughout history nations of all creeds and cultures have observed reciprocal obligations for that purpose." The institution of diplomacy, the Court continued, has proved to be "an instrument essential for effective co-operation in the international community, and for enabling States, irrespective of their differing constitutional and social systems, to achieve mutual understanding and to resolve their differences by peaceful means."

92. It is a matter of deep regret that the situation which occasioned those observations has not been rectified since they were made. Having regard to their importance the Court considers it essential to reiterate them in the present Judgment. The frequency with which at the present time the principles of international law governing diplomatic and consular relations are set at naught by individuals or groups of individuals is already deplorable. But this case is unique and of very particular gravity because here it is not only private individuals or groups of individuals that have disregarded and set at naught the inviolability of a foreign embassy, but the government of the receiving State itself. Therefore in recalling yet again the extreme importance of the principles of law which it is called upon to apply in the present case, the Court considers it to be its duty to draw the attention of the entire international community, of which Iran itself has been a member since time immemorial, to the irreparable harm that may be caused by events of the kind now before the Court. Such events cannot fail to undermine the edifice of law carefully constructed by mankind over a period of centuries, the maintenance of which is vital for the security and well-being of the complex international community of the present day, to which it is more essential than ever that the rules developed to ensure

the ordered progress of relations between its members should be constantly and scrupulously respected.

93. Before drawing the appropriate conclusions from its findings on the merits in this case, the Court considers that it cannot let pass without comment the incursion into the territory of Iran made by the United States military units on 24–25 April 1980 * * *. No doubt the United States Government may have had understandable preoccupations with respect to the well-being of its nationals held hostage in its Embassy for over five months. No doubt also the United States Government may have had understandable feelings of frustration at Iran's long-continued detention of the hostages, notwithstanding two resolutions of the Security Council as well as the Court's own Order of 15 December 1979 calling expressly for their immediate release. Nevertheless, in the circumstances of the present proceedings, the Court cannot fail to express its concern in regard to the United States' incursion into Iran. When, as previously recalled, this case had become ready for hearing on 19 February 1980, the United States Agent requested the Court, owing to the delicate stage of certain negotiations, to defer setting a date for the hearings. Subsequently, on 11 March, the Agent informed the Court of the United States Government's anxiety to obtain an early judgment on the merits of the case. The hearings were accordingly held on 18, 19 and 20 March, and the Court was in course of preparing the present judgment adjudicating upon the claims of the United States against Iran when the operation of 24 April 1980 took place. The Court therefore feels bound to observe that an operation undertaken in those circumstances, from whatever motive, is of a kind calculated to undermine respect for the judicial process in international relations; and to recall that in * * * its Order of 15 December 1979 the Court had indicated that no action was to be taken by either party which might aggravate the tension between the two countries.

94. At the same time, however, the Court must point out that neither the question of the legality of the operation of 24 April 1980, under the Charter of the United Nations and under general international law, nor any possible question of responsibility flowing from it, is before the Court. It must also point out that this question can have no bearing on the evaluation of the conduct of the Iranian Government over six months earlier, on 4 November 1979, which is the subject-matter of the United States' Application. It follows that the findings reached by the Court in this Judgment are not affected by that operation.

95. For these reasons,

THE COURT,

1. By thirteen votes to two,

Decides that the Islamic Republic of Iran, by the conduct which the Court has set out in this Judgment, has violated in several respects, and is still violating, obligations owed by it to the United States of America under international conventions in force between the two countries, as well as under long-established rules of general international law;

IN FAVOUR: *President* Sir Humphrey Waldock; *Vice-President* Elias; *Judges* Forster, Gros, Lachs, Nagendra Singh, Ruda, Mosler, Oda, Ago, El–Erian, Sette–Camara and Baxter.

AGAINST: *Judges* Morozov and Tarazi

2. By thirteen votes to two,

Decides that the violations of these obligations engage the responsibility of the Islamic Republic of Iran towards the United States of America under international law;

IN FAVOUR: *President* Sir Humphrey Waldock; *Vice-President* Elias; *Judges* Forster, Gros, Lachs, Nagendra Singh, Ruda, Mosler, Oda, Ago, El–Erian, Sette–Camara and Baxter.

AGAINST: *Judges* Morozov and Tarazi.

3. Unanimously,

Decides that the Government of the Islamic Republic of Iran must immediately take all steps to redress the situation resulting from the events of 4 November 1979 and what followed from these events, and to that end:

(*a*) must immediately terminate the unlawful detention of the United States Chargé d'affaires and other diplomatic and consular staff and other United States nationals now held hostage in Iran, and must immediately release each and every one and entrust them to the protecting Power (Article 45 of the 1961 Vienna Convention on Diplomatic Relations);

(*b*) must ensure that all the said persons have the necessary means of leaving Iranian territory, including means of transport;

(*c*) must immediately place in the hands of the protecting Power the premises, property, archives and documents of the United States Embassy in Tehran and of its Consulates in Iran;

4. Unanimously,

Decides that no member of the United States diplomatic or consular staff may be kept in Iran to be subjected to any form of judicial proceedings or to participate in them as a witness;

5. By twelve votes to three,

Decides that the Government of the Islamic Republic of Iran is under an obligation to make reparation to the Government of the United States of America for the injury caused to the latter by the events of 4 November 1979 and what followed from these events;

IN FAVOUR: *President* Sir Humphrey Waldock; *Vice-President* Elias; *Judges* Forster, Gros, Nagendra Singh, Ruda, Mosler, Oda, Ago, El–Erian, Sette–Camara and Baxter.

AGAINST: *Judges* Lachs, Morozov and Tarazi.

6. By fourteen votes to one,

Decides that the form and amount of such reparation, failing agreement between the Parties, shall be settled by the Court, and reserves for this purpose the subsequent procedure in the case.

IN FAVOUR: *President* Sir Humphrey Waldock; *Vice-President* Elias; *Judges* Forster, Gros, Lachs, Nagendra Singh, Ruda, Mosler, Tarazi, Oda, Ago, El–Erian, Sette–Camara and Baxter.

AGAINST: *Judge* Morozov.

MARK W. JANIS, "SOMBER REFLECTIONS ON THE COMPULSORY JURISDICTION OF THE INTERNATIONAL COURT"

81 *American Journal of International Law* 144 (1987).

The *Military and Paramilitary Activities* case [Military and Paramilitary Activities In and Against Nicaragua (Nicaragua v. United States), Merits, 1986 I.C.J. 14, 1986 WL 522 (1986)] deepens the gloom already surrounding the two forms of the International Court's compulsory jurisdiction. Neither Article 36(2) of the ICJ Statute, which confers general compulsory jurisdiction upon the Court in cases of reciprocal state declarations, nor that part of Article 36(1) which vests jurisdiction when treaties so provide has been particularly successful in recent practice. No one denies that the ICJ has served a useful, if occasional, role when it has heard and decided cases voluntarily submitted by then-willing states pursuant to the specially conferred provision of Article 36(1). What is in question is the utility of the all too many recent cases where the Court has taken jurisdiction pursuant to the compulsory provisions of its Statute and then has been, to one degree or another, disregarded.

Since 1966, when the ICJ did a volte-face and declined to decide the *South West Africa* case, a moment Professor Leo Gross thought the "nadir" of the Court's fortunes, the ICJ has been considerably more courageous. However, its courage, at least in compulsory jurisdiction cases, has been shown in the face of considerable opposition by states. In the 1970s and 1980s, the Court's compulsory jurisdiction cases have been beset with nonappearing defendants: Iceland in the *Fisheries Jurisdiction* cases, France in the *Nuclear Tests Cases*, Turkey in the *Aegean Sea Continental Shelf* case, Iran in the *Diplomatic and Consular Staff* case, and now the United States in the merits phase of the *Military and Paramilitary Activities* case.

Albeit Article 94(1) of the Charter of the United Nations obliges every state "to comply with the decision of the International Court of Justice in any case to which it is a party," in practice since 1945 states haled into the ICJ by way of compulsory jurisdiction too often have failed to obey adverse court rulings. Albania refused to pay reparations to Great Britain in *Corfu Channel*, Iran disregarded the Court's order to refrain from nationalizing a British corporation pending a final judgment of the Court or agreement between the parties in *Anglo–Iranian Oil Co.*,

Iceland refused to obey an order not to enforce a 50–mile fishing zone until the Court ruled on suits brought by West Germany and the United Kingdom in *Fisheries Jurisdiction*, Iran rejected the Court's Order and Judgment that it release the American hostages in *Diplomatic and Consular Staff*, and the United States has now declared that it will ignore the Court's ruling in *Military and Paramilitary Activities*. There is always the theoretical possibility of enforcing an ICJ judgment against a recalcitrant state by having the Security Council take action, but in practice this has not occurred. What gain is there in disregarded compulsory jurisdiction cases?

Almost three decades ago, Sir Hersch Lauterpacht concluded that the Court was much more useful as a vehicle for developing the rules of international law than it was as a means of maintaining international peace. Certainly, there is grist for many legal mills in the language of even ineffective compulsory jurisdiction cases, *Military and Paramilitary Activities* being no exception. The majority opinion alone has new and very illuminating language about, inter alia, nonappearing parties, the proof of facts in international law, the relationship of treaty law and customary international law, and aggression and self-defense.

There may also be some public relations value in otherwise ineffective compulsory jurisdiction cases. The United States, for example, sought to use the *Diplomatic and Consular Staff* case as a means of maintaining "support for the American position by the vast majority of nations on earth," although it is doubtful the ICJ was ultimately so useful in freeing the hostages as were the economic sanctions taken against Iran. In the *Military and Paramilitary Activities* case, it is far too early to tell whether Nicaragua will be any more successful in its attempt to use the Court's Judgment to sway public opinion in the United States and in other states.

Against such gains must be weighed the loss in respect for the ICJ when it acts like a court in name but not in deed. These cases of compulsory jurisdiction display the Court in its weakest and least effectual role. In these circumstances, the ICJ does not truly adjudicate disputes, if "adjudication" has anything to do with a decision that actually settles a matter.

Plainly, much of the blame for the loss in respect for the Court rests on the shoulders of noncomplying defendant states that are failing to observe Article 94(1) of the Charter. Some fault, too, lies with applicant states that use the Court as a public forum when they know that the ICJ has little practical chance of effectively resolving a dispute. Realistically, it may be time for us to recognize that, given the present context of world politics, the compulsory jurisdiction provisions of the ICJ Statute are simply overoptimistic and that the surer and better role for the Court is in the adjudication of cases jointly submitted by willing states. It may be time, too, for the ICJ to contemplate a strategic retreat and in cases of compulsory jurisdiction to be willing to contemplate a doctrine of judicial restraint when it seems unlikely that its decisions will be respected in practice.

Notes and Questions

1. *The Decision to Litigate.* Why does the United States bring the *Diplomatic and Consular Staff* case to the International Court? Was it likely that Iran would comply with an adverse judgment? Was the legal issue in much doubt? What could the United States gain if Iran disregarded the judgment? What could the U.S. lose? Compare the motivations of Nicaragua in its case against the U.S. Portions of the *Nicaragua Case* are reproduced in Chapter 8.

2. *The Role of Public Opinion.* What exactly is the "public" which is being swayed by the court proceedings in *Diplomatic and Consular Staff*? Is it U.S. public opinion that is being shown that something is being done to free the hostages? Is it public or governmental opinion in third states? Is there a hope in the *Nicaragua Case* that the United States, this time the defendant government, will be affected by adverse public opinion?

3. *The ICJ as a Public Forum.* Should the Court be concerned if it is being used as a forum in which to appeal to and influence public opinion? Should the Court turn away cases where it seems likely that a state will refuse to appear and to comply with the orders of the Court? If the Court is used as a public forum, can it still serve a judicial role? Is it enough to say that, whatever the circumstances, the Court can usefully add the words of a new judgment to the corpus of international law doctrine?

4. *The Problem of the Non-appearing Respondent.* Why should Iceland, France, Turkey, Iran, and the United States refuse to argue before the Court in cases in which the Court finds that it has been vested with jurisdiction by mutual party consent to a form of compulsory jurisdiction? What is left of any sort of ICJ compulsory jurisdiction in the light of the pattern of non-appearing states in the 1970s and 1980s?

5. *Resolving the Hostages Crisis.* Efforts to resolve the hostages crisis proceeded through diplomatic channels, at the U.N. Security Council, before the ICJ, by a failed U.S. helicopter rescue mission, and by the freezing of Iranian assets in the United States and abroad. Ultimately, in January 1981, a U.S.–Iranian treaty, negotiated through the good offices of Algeria, resulted in the release of the U.S. hostages, the unfreezing of Iranian assets, and the establishment of the Iran–U.S. Claims Tribunal to decide disputes among Iran, the United States, and nationals of those countries. The *Dames & Moore Case*, a U.S. case related to the creation of the Iran–U.S. Claims Tribunal and the unfreezing of Iranian assets, appears in Chapter 4. More on the nature of state responsibility is found in Chapter 6, and the succession of the international obligations of a state following a radical change in its government, such as had occurred in Iran, is discussed in Chapter 7.

3. ADVISORY OPINIONS AT THE INTERNATIONAL COURT

ADVISORY OPINION ON THE WESTERN SAHARA

1975 I.C.J. 12, 1975 WL 5.

1. The questions upon which the advisory opinion of the Court has been asked were laid before the Court by a letter dated 17 December 1974, filed in the Registry on 21 December 1974, addressed by the Secretary–General of the United Nations to the President of the Court. In his letter the Secretary–General informed the Court that, by resolution 3292 (XXIX) adopted on 13 December 1974, the General Assembly of the United Nations had decided to request the Court to give an advisory opinion at an early date on the questions set out in the resolution. The text of that resolution is as follows:

"*The General Assembly,*

Recalling its resolution 1514 (XV) of 14 December 1960 containing the Declaration on the Granting of Independence to Colonial Countries and Peoples,

Recalling also its resolutions 2072 (XX) of 16 December 1965, 2229 (XXI) of 20 December 1966, 2354 (XXII) of 19 December 1967, 2428 (XXIII) of 18 December 1968, 2591 (XXIV) of 16 December 1969, 2711 (XXV) of 14 December 1970, 2983 (XXVII) of 14 December 1972 and 3162 (XXVIII) of 14 December 1973,

Reaffirming the right of the population of the Spanish Sahara to self-determination in accordance with resolution 1514 (XV),

Considering that the persistence of a colonial situation in Western Sahara jeopardizes stability and harmony in the north-west African region,

Taking into account the statements made in the General Assembly on 30 September and 2 October 1974 by the Ministers of Foreign Affairs of the Kingdom of Morocco and of the Islamic Republic of Mauritania,

Taking note of the statements made in the Fourth Committee by the representatives of Morocco and Mauritania, in which the two countries acknowledged that they were both interested in the future of the Territory,

Having heard the statements by the representative of Algeria,

Having heard the statements by the representative of Spain,

Noting that during the discussion a legal controversy arose over the status of the said territory at the time of its colonization by Spain,

Considering, therefore, that it is highly desirable that the General Assembly, in order to continue the discussion of this question at its thirtieth session, should receive an advisory opinion on some important legal aspects of the problem,

Bearing in mind Article 96 of the Charter of the United Nations and Article 65 of the Statute of the International Court of Justice,

1. *Decides* to request the International Court of Justice, without prejudice to the application of the principles embodied in General Assembly resolution 1514 (XV), to give an advisory opinion at an early date on the following questions:

I. Was Western Sahara (Río de Oro and Sakiet El Hamra) at the time of colonization by Spain a territory belonging to no one (*terra nullius*)?

If the answer to the first question is in the negative,

II. What were the legal ties between this territory and the Kingdom of Morocco and the Mauritanian entity?;

2. *Calls upon* Spain, in its capacity as administering Power in particular, as well as Morocco and Mauritania, in their capacity as interested parties, to submit to the International Court of Justice all such information and documents as may be needed to clarify those questions;

3. *Urges* the administering Power to postpone the referendum it contemplated holding in Western Sahara until the General Assembly decides on the policy to be followed in order to accelerate the decolonization process in the territory, in accordance with resolution 1514 (XV), in the best possible conditions, in the light of the advisory opinion to be given by the International Court of Justice";
* * *

14. Under Article 65, paragraph 1, of the Statute:

"The Court may give an advisory opinion on any legal question at the request of whatever body may be authorized by or in accordance with the Charter of the United Nations to make such a request."

The present request has been made pursuant to Article 96, paragraph 1, of the Charter of the United Nations, under which the General Assembly may seek the Court's advisory opinion on any legal question. * * *

16. It has been suggested that the questions posed by the General Assembly are not legal, but are either factual or are questions of a purely historical or academic character.

17. It is true that, in order to reply to the questions, the Court will have to determine certain facts, before being able to assess their legal significance.

However, a mixed question of law and fact is none the less a legal question within the meaning of Article 96, paragraph 1, of the Charter and Article 65, paragraph 1, of the Statute. As the Court observed in its Opinion concerning the *Legal Consequences for States of the Continued Presence of South Africa in Namibia (South West Africa) notwithstanding Security Council Resolution 276 (1970)*:

"In the view of the Court, the contingency that there may be factual issues underlying the question posed does not alter its character as a 'legal question' as envisaged in Article 96 of the Charter. The reference in this provision to legal questions cannot be interpreted as opposing legal to factual issues. Normally, to enable a court to pronounce on legal questions, it must also be acquainted with, take into account and, if necessary, make findings as to the relevant factual issues." * * *

23. Article 65, paragraph 1, of the Statute, which establishes the power of the Court to give an advisory opinion, is permissive and, under it, that power is of a discretionary character. In exercising this discretion, the International Court of Justice, like the Permanent Court of International Justice, has always been guided by the principle that, as a judicial body, it is bound to remain faithful to the requirements of its judicial character even in giving advisory opinions. If the question is a legal one which the Court is undoubtedly competent to answer, it may none the less decline to do so. As this Court has said in previous Opinions, the permissive character of Article 65, paragraph 1, gives it the power to examine whether the circumstances of the case are of such a character as should lead it to decline to answer the request. It has also said that the reply of the Court, itself an organ of the United Nations, represents its participation in the activities of the Organization and, in principle, should not be refused. By lending its assistance in the solution of a problem confronting the General Assembly, the Court would discharge its functions as the principal judicial organ of the United Nations. The Court has further said that only "compelling reasons" should lead it to refuse to give a requested advisory opinion.

24. Spain has put forward a series of objections which in its view would render the giving of an opinion in the present case incompatible with the Court's judicial character. Certain of these are based on the consequences said to follow from the absence of Spain's consent to the adjudication of the questions referred to the Court. Another relates to the alleged academic nature, irrelevance or lack of object of those questions. Spain has asked the Court to give priority to the examination of the latter. The Court will, however, deal with the objections founded on the lack of Spain's consent to adjudication of the questions, before turning to the objection which concerns the subject-matter of the questions themselves.

25. Spain has made a number of observations relating to the lack of its consent to the proceedings, which, it considers, should lead the Court to decline to give an opinion. These observations may be summarized as follows:

(*a*) In the present case the advisory jurisdiction is being used to circumvent the principle that jurisdiction to settle a dispute requires the consent of the parties.

(*b*) The questions, as formulated, raise issues concerning the attribution of territorial sovereignty over Western Sahara.

(*c*) The Court does not possess the necessary information concerning the relevant facts to enable it to pronounce judicially on the questions submitted to it.

26. The first of the above observations is based on the fact that on 23 September 1974 the Minister for Foreign Affairs of Morocco addressed a communication to the Minister of Foreign Affairs of Spain recalling the terms of a statement by which His Majesty King Hassan II had on 17 September 1974 proposed the joint submission to the International Court of Justice of an issue expressed in the following terms:

> "You, the Spanish Government, claim that the Sahara was *res nullius*. You claim that it was a territory or property left uninherited, you claim that no power and no administration had been established over the Sahara: Morocco claims the contrary. Let us request the arbitration of the International Court of Justice at The Hague.... It will state the law on the basis of the titles submitted...."

Spain has stated before the Court that it did not consent and does not consent now to the submission of this issue to the jurisdiction of the Court.

27. Spain considers that the subject of the dispute which Morocco invited it to submit jointly to the Court for decision in contentious proceedings, and the subject of the questions on which the advisory opinion is requested, are substantially identical; thus the advisory procedure is said to have been used as an alternative after the failure of an attempt to make use of the contentious jurisdiction with regard to the same question. Consequently, to give a reply would, according to Spain, be to allow the advisory procedure to be used as a means of bypassing the consent of a State, which constitutes the basis of the Court's jurisdiction. If the Court were to countenance such a use of its advisory jurisdiction, the outcome would be to obliterate the distinction between the two spheres of the Court's jurisdiction, and the fundamental principle of the independence of States would be affected, for States would find their disputes with other States being submitted to the Court, by this indirect means, without their consent; this might result in compulsory jurisdiction being achieved by majority vote in a political organ. Such circumvention of the well-established principle of consent for the exercise of international jurisdiction would constitute, according to this view, a compelling reason for declining to answer the request. * * *

29. It is clear that Spain has not consented to the adjudication of the questions formulated in resolution 3292 (XXIX). It did not agree to Morocco's proposal for the joint submission to the Court of the issue raised in the communication of 23 September 1974. Spain made no reply to the letter setting out the proposal, and this was properly understood by Morocco as signifying its rejection by Spain. As to the request for an advisory opinion, the records of the discussions in the Fourth Committee and in the plenary of the General Assembly confirm that Spain raised objections to the Court's being asked for an opinion on

the basis of the two questions formulated in the present request. The Spanish delegation stated that it was prepared to join in the request only if the questions put were supplemented by another question establishing a satisfactory balance between the historical and legal exposition of the matter and the current situation viewed in the light of the Charter of the United Nations and the relevant General Assembly resolution on the decolonization of the territory. In view of Spain's persistent objections to the questions formulated in resolution 3292 (XXIX), the fact that it abstained and did not vote against the resolution cannot be interpreted as implying its consent to the adjudication of those questions by the Court. Moreover, its participation in the Court's proceedings cannot be understood as implying that it has consented to the adjudication of the questions posed in resolution 3292 (XXIX), for it has persistently maintained its objections throughout.

[The Court reviews other cases where it declined to give an advisory opinion because of the opposition of an interested state.]

33. In certain circumstances, therefore, the lack of consent of an interested State may render the giving of an advisory opinion incompatible with the Court's judicial character. An instance of this would be when the circumstances disclose that to give a reply would have the effect of circumventing the principle that a State is not obliged to allow its disputes to be submitted to judicial settlement without its consent. If such a situation should arise, the powers of the Court under the discretion given to it by Article 65, paragraph 1, of the Statute, would afford sufficient legal means to ensure respect for the fundamental principle of consent to jurisdiction.

34. The situation existing in the present case is not, however, the one envisaged above. There is in this case a legal controversy, but one which arose during the proceedings of the General Assembly and in relation to matters with which it was dealing. It did not arise independently in bilateral relations. In a communication addressed on 10 November 1958 to the Secretary–General of the United Nations, the Spanish Government stated: "Spain possesses no non-self-governing territories, since the territories subject to its sovereignty in Africa are, in accordance with the legislation now in force, considered to be and classified as provinces of Spain." This gave rise to the "most explicit reservations" of the Government of Morocco, which, in a communication to the Secretary–General of 20 November 1958, stated that it "claim[ed] certain African territories at present under Spanish control as an integral part of Moroccan national territory." * * *

39. * * * The object of the General Assembly has not been to bring before the Court, by way of a request for advisory opinion, a dispute or legal controversy, in order that it may later, on the basis of the Court's opinion, exercise its powers and functions for the peaceful settlement of that dispute or controversy. The object of the request is an entirely different one: to obtain from the Court an opinion which the General

Assembly deems of assistance to it for the proper exercise of its functions concerning the decolonization of the territory.

40. The General Assembly, as appears from paragraph 3 of resolution 3292 (XXIX), has asked the Court for an opinion so as to be in a position to decide "on the policy to be followed in order to accelerate the decolonization process in the territory ... in the best possible conditions, in the light of the advisory opinion ...." The true object of the request is also stressed in the preamble of resolution 3292 (XXIX), where it is stated "that it is highly desirable that the General Assembly, in order to continue the discussion of this question at its thirtieth session, should receive an advisory opinion on some important legal aspects of the problem."

41. What the Court said in a similar context, in its Advisory Opinion on *Reservations to the Convention on the Prevention and Punishment of the Crime of Genocide*, applies also to the present case: "The object of this request for an Opinion is to guide the United Nations in respect of its own action." The legitimate interest of the General Assembly in obtaining an opinion from the Court in respect of its own future action cannot be affected or prejudiced by the fact that Morocco made a proposal, not accepted by Spain, to submit for adjudication by the Court a dispute raising issues related to those contained in the request. * * *

42. Furthermore, the origin and scope of the dispute, as above described, are important in appreciating, from the point of view of the exercise of the Court's discretion, the real significance in this case of the lack of Spain's consent. The issue between Morocco and Spain regarding Western Sahara is not one as to the legal status of the territory today, but one as to the rights of Morocco over it at the time of colonization. The settlement of this issue will not affect the rights of Spain today as the administering Power, but will assist the General Assembly in deciding on the policy to be followed in order to accelerate the decolonization process in the territory. It follows that the legal position of the State which has refused its consent to the present proceedings is not "in any way compromised by the answers that the Court may give to the questions put to it." * * *

75. Having established that it is seised of a request for advisory opinion which it is competent to entertain and that it should comply with that request, the Court will now examine the two questions which have been referred to it by General Assembly resolution 3292 (XXIX). These questions are so formulated that an answer to the second is called for only if the answer to the first is in the negative:

"I. Was Western Sahara (Río de Oro and Sakiet El Hamra) at the time of colonization by Spain a territory belonging to no one (*terra nullius*)?

If the answer to the first question is in the negative,

II. What were the legal ties between this territory and the Kingdom of Morocco and the Mauritanian entity?" * * *

79. Turning to Question I, the Court observes that the request specifically locates the question in the context of "the time of colonization by Spain," and it therefore seems clear that the words "Was Western Sahara ... a territory belonging to no one (*terra nullius*)?" have to be interpreted by reference to the law in force at that period. The expression "*terra nullius*" was a legal term of art employed in connection with "occupation" as one of the accepted legal methods of acquiring sovereignty over territory. "Occupation" being legally an original means of peaceably acquiring sovereignty over territory otherwise than by cession or succession, it was a cardinal condition of a valid "occupation" that the territory should be terra nullius—a territory belonging to no-one—at the time of the act alleged to constitute the "occupation." In the view of the Court, therefore, a determination that Western Sahara was a "*terra nullius*" at the time of colonization by Spain would be possible only if it were established that at the time the territory belonged to no-one in the sense that it was then open to acquisition through the legal process of "occupation."

80. Whatever differences of opinion there may have been among jurists, the State practice of the relevant period indicates that territories inhabited by tribes or peoples having a social and political organization were not regarded as *terrae nullius*. It shows that in the case of such territories the acquisition of sovereignty was not generally considered as effected unilaterally through "occupation" of *terra nullius* by original title but through agreements concluded with local rulers. On occasion, it is true, the word "occupation" was used in a non-technical sense denoting simply acquisition of sovereignty; but that did not signify that the acquisition of sovereignty through such agreements with authorities of the country was regarded as an "occupation" of a "*terra nullius*" in the proper sense of these terms. On the contrary, such agreements with local rulers, whether or not considered as an actual "cession" of the territory, were regarded as derivative roots of title, and not original titles obtained by occupation of *terrae nullius*.

81. In the present instance, the information furnished to the Court shows that at the time of colonization Western Sahara was inhabited by peoples which, if nomadic, were socially and politically organized in tribes and under chiefs competent to represent them. It also shows that, in colonizing Western Sahara, Spain did not proceed on the basis that it was establishing its sovereignty over *terrae nullius*. In its Royal Order of 26 December 1884, far from treating the case as one of occupation of *terra nullius*, Spain proclaimed that the King was taking the Río de Oro under his protection on the basis of agreements which had been entered into with the chiefs of the local tribes: the Order referred expressly to "the documents which the independent tribes of this part of the coast" had "signed with the representative of the Sociedad Española de Africanistas," and announced that the King had confirmed "the deeds of adherence" to Spain. Likewise, in negotiating

with France concerning the limits of Spanish territory to the north of the Río de Oro, that is, in the Sakiet El Hamra area, Spain did not rely upon any claim to the acquisition of sovereignty over a *terra nullius*.

82. Before the Court, differing views were expressed concerning the nature and legal value of agreements between a State and local chiefs. But the Court is not asked by Question I to pronounce upon the legal character or the legality of the titles which led to Spain becoming the administering Power of Western Sahara. It is asked only to state whether Western Sahara (Río de Oro and Sakiet El Hamra) at the time of colonization by Spain was "a territory belonging to no one (*terra nullius*)." As to this question, the Court is satisfied that, for the reasons which it has given, its answer must be in the negative. Accordingly, the Court does not find it necessary first to pronounce upon the correctness or otherwise of Morocco's view that the territory was not *terra nullius* at the time because the local tribes, so it maintains, were then subject to the sovereignty of the Sultan of Morocco; nor upon Mauritania's corresponding proposition that the territory was not *terra nullius* because the local tribes, in its view, then formed part of the "Bilad Shinguitti" or Mauritanian entity. Any conclusions that the Court may reach with respect to either of these points of view cannot change the negative character of the answer which, for other reasons already set out, it has found that it must give to Question I.

83. The Court's answer to Question I is, therefore, in the negative and, in accordance with the terms of the request, it will now turn to Question II.

84. Question II asks the Court to state "what were the legal ties between this territory"—that is, Western Sahara—"and the Kingdom of Morocco and the Mauritanian entity." The scope of this question depends upon the meaning to be attached to the expression "legal ties" in the context of the time of the colonization of the territory by Spain. That expression, however, unlike "*terra nullius*" in Question I, was not a term having in itself a very precise meaning. Accordingly, in the view of the Court, the meaning of the expression "legal ties" in Question II has to be found rather in the object and purpose of General Assembly resolution 3292 (XXIX), by which it was decided to request the present advisory opinion of the Court.

85. Analysis of this resolution, as the Court has already pointed out, shows that the two questions contained in the request have been put to the Court in the context of proceedings in the General Assembly directed to the decolonization of Western Sahara in conformity with resolution 1514 (XV) of 14 December 1960. During the discussion of this item, according to resolution 3292 (XXIX), a legal controversy arose over the status of Western Sahara at the time of its colonization by Spain; and the records of the proceedings make it plain that the "legal controversy" in question concerned pretensions put forward, on the one hand, by Morocco that the territory was then a part of the Sherifian State and, on the other, by Mauritania that the territory then formed

part of the Bilad Shinguitti or Mauritanian entity. Accordingly, it appears to the Court that in Question II the words "legal ties between this territory and the Kingdom of Morocco and the Mauritanian entity" must be understood as referring to such "legal ties" as may affect the policy to be followed in the decolonization of Western Sahara. In this connection, the Court cannot accept the view that the legal ties the General Assembly had in mind in framing Question II were limited to ties established directly with the territory and without reference to the people who may be found in it. Such an interpretation would unduly restrict the scope of the question, since legal ties are normally established in relation to people.

86. The Court further observes that, inasmuch as Question II had its origin in the contentions of Morocco and Mauritania, it was for them to satisfy the Court in the present proceedings that legal ties existed between Western Sahara and the Kingdom of Morocco or the Mauritanian entity at the time of the colonization of the territory by Spain.

87. Western Sahara (Río de Oro and Sakiet El Hamra) is a territory having very special characteristics which, at the time of colonization by Spain, largely determined the way of life and social and political organization of the people inhabiting it. In consequence, the legal régime of Western Sahara, including its legal relations with neighbouring territories, cannot properly be appreciated without reference to these special characteristics. The territory forms part of the great Sahara desert which extends from the Atlantic coast of Africa to Egypt and the Sudan. At the time of its colonization by Spain, the area of this desert with which the Court is concerned was being exploited, because of its low and spasmodic rainfall, almost exclusively by nomads, pasturing their animals or growing crops as and where conditions were favourable. It may be said that the territory, at the time of its colonization, had a sparse population that, for the most part, consisted of nomadic tribes the members of which traversed the desert on more or less regular routes dictated by the seasons and the wells or water-holes available to them. In general, the Court was informed, the right of pasture was enjoyed in common by these tribes; some areas suitable for cultivation, on the other hand, were subject to a greater degree to separate rights. Perennial water-holes were in principle considered the property of the tribe which put them into commission, though their use also was open to all, subject to certain customs as to priorities and the amount of water taken. Similarly, many tribes were said to have their recognized burial grounds, which constituted a rallying point for themselves and for allied tribes. Another feature of life in the region, according to the information before the Court, was that inter-tribal conflict was not infrequent.

88. These various points of attraction of a tribe to particular localities were reflected in its nomadic routes. But what is important for present purposes is the fact that the sparsity of the resources and the spasmodic character of the rainfall compelled all those nomadic tribes to traverse very wide areas of the desert. In consequence, the nomadic routes of none of them were confined to Western Sahara; some passed

also through areas of southern Morocco, or of present-day Mauritania or Algeria, and some even through further countries. All the tribes were of the Islamic faith and the whole territory lay within the Dar al–Islam. In general, authority in the tribe was vested in a sheikh, subject to the assent of the "Juma'a," that is, of an assembly of its leading members, and the tribe had its own customary law applicable in conjunction with the Koranic law. Not infrequently one tribe had ties with another, either of dependence or of alliance, which were essentially tribal rather than territorial, ties of allegiance or vassalage. * * *

90. Morocco's claim to "legal ties" with Western Sahara at the time of colonization by Spain has been put to the Court as a claim to ties of sovereignty on the ground of an alleged immemorial possession of the territory. This immemorial possession, it maintains, was based not on an isolated act of occupation but on the public display of sovereignty, uninterrupted and uncontested, for centuries.

91. In support of this claim Morocco refers to a series of events stretching back to the Arab conquest of North Africa in the seventh century A.D., the evidence of which is, understandably, for the most part taken from historical works. The far-flung, spasmodic and often transitory character of many of these events renders the historical material somewhat equivocal as evidence of possession of the territory now in question. Morocco, however, invokes *inter alia* the decision of the Permanent Court of International Justice in the *Legal Status of Eastern Greenland* case (*P.C.I.J., Series A/B, No. 53*). Stressing that during a long period Morocco was the only independent State which existed in the north-west of Africa, it points to the geographical contiguity of Western Sahara to Morocco and the desert character of the territory. In the light of these considerations, it maintains that the historical material suffices to establish Morocco's claim to a title based "upon continued display of authority" on the same principles as those applied by the Permanent Court in upholding Denmark's claim to possession of the whole of Greenland.

92. This method of formulating Morocco's claims to ties of sovereignty with Western Sahara encounters certain difficulties. As the Permanent Court stated in the case concerning the *Legal Status of Eastern Greenland*, a claim to sovereignty based upon continued display of authority involves "two elements each of which must be shown to exist: the intention and will to act as sovereign, and some actual exercise or display of such authority." True, the Permanent Court recognized that in the case of claims to sovereignty over areas in thinly populated or unsettled countries, "very little in the way of actual exercise of sovereign rights" might be sufficient in the absence of a competing claim. But, in the present instance, Western Sahara, if somewhat sparsely populated, was a territory across which socially and politically organized tribes were in constant movement and where armed incidents between these tribes were frequent. In the particular circumstances outlined in paragraphs 87 and 88 above, the paucity of evidence of actual display of authority unambiguously relating to Western Sahara

renders it difficult to consider the Moroccan claim as on all fours with that of Denmark in the *Eastern Greenland* case. Nor is the difficulty cured by introducing the argument of geographical unity or contiguity. In fact, the information before the Court shows that the geographical unity of Western Sahara with Morocco is somewhat debatable, which also militates against giving effect to the concept of contiguity. Even if the geographical contiguity of Western Sahara with Morocco could be taken into account in the present connection, it would only make the paucity of evidence of unambiguous display of authority with respect to Western Sahara more difficult to reconcile with Morocco's claim to immemorial possession. * * *

94. Morocco requests that, in appreciating the evidence, the Court should take account of the special structure of the Sherifian State. No rule of international law, in the view of the Court, requires the structure of a State to follow any particular pattern, as is evident from the diversity of the forms of State found in the world today. Morocco's request is therefore justified. At the same time, where sovereignty over territory is claimed, the particular structure of a State may be a relevant element in appreciating the reality or otherwise of a display of State activity adduced as evidence of that sovereignty.

95. That the Sherifian State at the time of the Spanish colonization of Western Sahara was a State of a special character is certain. Its special character consisted in the fact that it was founded on the common religious bond of Islam existing among the peoples and on the allegiance of various tribes to the Sultan, through their caids or sheikhs, rather than on the notion of territory. Common religious links have, of course, existed in many parts of the world without signifying a legal tie of sovereignty or subordination to a ruler. Even the Dar al–Islam, as Morocco itself pointed out in its oral statement, knows and then knew separate States within the common religious bond of Islam. Political ties of allegiance to a ruler, on the other hand, have frequently formed a major element in the composition of a State. Such an allegiance, however, if it is to afford indications of the ruler's sovereignty, must clearly be real and manifested in acts evidencing acceptance of his political authority. Otherwise, there will be no genuine display or exercise of State authority. It follows that the special character of the Moroccan State and the special forms in which its exercise of sovereignty may, in consequence, have expressed itself, do not dispense the Court from appreciating whether at the relevant time Moroccan sovereignty was effectively exercised or displayed in Western Sahara. * * *

98. As evidence of its display of sovereignty in Western Sahara, Morocco has invoked alleged acts of internal display of Moroccan authority and also certain international acts said to constitute recognition by other States of its sovereignty over the whole or part of the territory.

99. The principal indications of "internal" display of authority invoked by Morocco consist of evidence alleged to show the allegiance of Saharan caids to the Sultan, including dahirs and other documents

concerning the appointment of caids, the alleged imposition of Koranic and other taxes, and what were referred to as "military decisions" said to constitute acts of resistance to foreign penetration of the territory. In particular, the allegiance is claimed of the confederation of Tekna tribes, together with its allies, one part of which was stated to be established in the Noun and another part to lead a nomadic life the route of which traversed areas of Western Sahara: through Tekna caids, Morocco claims, the Sultan's authority and influence were exercised on the nomad tribes pasturing in Western Sahara. Moreover, Morocco alleges that, after the marabout Ma ul-'Aineen established himself at Smara in the Sakiet El Hamra in the late 1890s, much of the territory came under the direct authority of this sheikh, and that he himself was the personal representative of the Sultan. Emphasis is also placed by Morocco on two visits of Sultan Hassan I in person to the southern area of the Souss in 1882 and 1886 to maintain and strengthen his authority in the southern part of his realm, and on the despatch of arms by the Sultan to Ma ul-'Aineen and others in the south to reinforce their resistance to foreign penetration. In general, it is urged that Western Sahara has always been linked to the interior of Morocco by common ethnological, cultural and religious ties, and that the Sakiet El Hamra was artificially separated from the Moroccan territory of the Noun by colonization.

100. Spain, on the other hand, maintains that there is a striking absence of any documentary evidence or other traces of a display or political authority by Morocco with respect to Western Sahara. The acts of appointment of caids produced by Morocco, whether dahirs or official correspondence, do not in Spain's view relate to Western Sahara but to areas within southern Morocco such as the Noun and the Dra'a; nor has any document of acceptance by the recipients been adduced. Furthermore, according to Spain, these alleged appointments as caid were conferred on sheikhs already elected by their own tribes and were, in truth, only titles of honour bestowed on existing and *de facto* independent local rulers. As to the Tekna confederation, its two parts are said to have been in quite different relations to the Sultan: only the settled Tekna, established in southern Morocco, acknowledged their political allegiance to the Sultan, while the nomadic septs of the tribe who traversed the Western Sahara were "free" Tekna, autonomous and independent of the Sultan. Nor was Ma ul-'Aineen, according to Spain, at any time the personal representative of the Sultan's authority in Western Sahara; on the contrary, he exercised his authority to the south of the Dra'a in complete independence of the Sultan; his relations with the Sultan were based on mutual respect and a common interest in resisting French expansion from the south; they were relations of equality, not political ties of allegiance or of sovereignty.

101. Further, Spain invokes the absence of any evidence of the payment of taxes by tribes of Western Sahara and denies all possibility of such evidence being adduced; according to Spain, it was a characteristic even of the Bled Siba that the tribes refused to be taxed, and in Western Sahara there was no question of taxes having been paid to the Makhzen.

As to the Sultan's expeditions of 1882 and 1886, these, according to Spain, are shown by the historical evidence never to have reached Western Sahara or even the Dra'a, but only the Souss and the Noun; nor did they succeed in completely subjecting even those areas; and they cannot therefore constitute evidence of display of authority with respect to Western Sahara. Their purpose, Spain maintains, was to prevent commerce between Europeans and the tribes of the Souss and Noun, and this purpose was unrelated to Western Sahara. Again, the alleged acts of resistance in Western Sahara to foreign penetration are said by Spain to have been nothing more than occasional raids to obtain booty or hostages for ransom and to have nothing to do with display of Moroccan authority. In general, both on geographical and on other grounds, Spain questions the unity of the Saharan region with the regions of southern Morocco. * * *

103. The Court does not overlook the position of the Sultan of Morocco as a religious leader. In the view of the Court, however, the information and arguments invoked by Morocco cannot, for the most part, be considered as disposing of the difficulties in the way of its claim to have exercised effectively internal sovereignty over Western Sahara. The material before the Court appears to support the view that almost all the dahirs and other acts concerning caids relate to areas situated within present-day Morocco itself and do not in themselves provide evidence of effective display of Moroccan authority in Western Sahara. Nor can the information furnished by Morocco be said to provide convincing evidence of the imposition or levying of Moroccan taxes with respect to the territory. As to Sheikh Ma ul–'Aineen, the complexities of his career may leave doubts as to the precise nature of his relations with the Sultan, and different interpretations have been put upon them. The material before the Court, taken as a whole, does not suffice to convince it that the activities of this sheikh should be considered as having constituted a display of the Sultan's authority in Western Sahara at the time of its colonization.

[The Court reviews other evidence relating to possible acts of sovereignty relating to the Western Sahara.]

150. In the light of the above considerations, the Court must conclude that at the time of colonization by Spain there did not exist between the territory of Western Sahara and the Mauritanian entity any tie of sovereignty, or of allegiance of tribes, or of "simple inclusion" in the same legal entity. * * *

162. The materials and information presented to the Court show the existence, at the time of Spanish colonization, of legal ties of allegiance between the Sultan of Morocco and some of the tribes living in the territory of Western Sahara. They equally show the existence of rights, including some rights relating to the land, which constituted legal ties between the Mauritanian entity, as understood by the Court, and the territory of Western Sahara. On the other hand, the Court's conclusion is that the materials and information presented to it do not

establish any tie of territorial sovereignty between the territory of Western Sahara and the Kingdom of Morocco or the Muaritanian entity. Thus the Court has not found legal ties of such a nature as might affect the application of resolution 1514 (XV) in the decolonization of Western Sahara and, in particular, of the principle of self-determination through the free and genuine expression of the will of the peoples of the Territory * * *.

163. For these reasons,

THE COURT DECIDES,

with regard to Question I,

by 13 votes to 3,

and with regard to Question II,

by 14 votes to 2,

to comply with the request for an advisory opinion;

THE COURT IS OF OPINION,

with regard to Question I,

unanimously,

that Western Sahara (Río de Oro and Sakiet El Hamra) at the time of colonization by Spain was not a territory belonging to no-one (*terra nullius*);

with regard to Question II,

by 14 votes to 2,

that there were legal ties between this territory and the Kingdom of Morocco of the kinds indicated in paragraph 162 of this Opinion;

by 15 votes to 1,

that there were legal ties between this territory and the Mauritanian entity of the kinds indicated in paragraph 162 of this Opinion.

Notes and Questions

1. *A Contentious Case?* Is the Court's advisory opinion in *Western Sahara* really a contentious case submitted to the ICJ via the General Assembly after Spain refused Morocco's request to accept judicial settlement of the dispute? Why did Morocco want to go to the Court? Note that Morocco would have formulated the question on which an advisory opinion was sought differently from the way the General Assembly eventually phrased the question; Morocco proposed that the question to be resolved was whether the Western Sahara had, at the time of colonization, been *terra nullius* or under Moroccan sovereignty. See Malcolm Shaw, "The *Western Sahara* Case," 49 *British Yearbook of International Law* 119, 124 (1978). Does the ICJ adequately justify its decision to render an advisory opinion?

2. *Answering the Referendum Question.* Why does the ICJ answer the "unasked question," *i.e.*, whether the peoples of the Western Sahara are entitled to a referendum about their future? Does the Court stress the need

for a referendum because it takes account of its role as an organ of the United Nations? Or because it anticipates that Morocco will greet its opinion as a victory for Morocco and invade the Western Sahara?

3. *The Political Aftermath.* Morocco indeed did invade the Western Sahara in November 1975. By the mid–1980's, Morocco was spending some $17 million a day to prosecute its war efforts against the nationalist Polisario Front there. Morocco built a 1243–mile–long wall in the Western Sahara costing billions of dollars and equipped with radar and alarm systems, to keep the Polisario away from valuable land and Moroccan fishing boats. See Louise Lief, "Saudi King Intervenes in Western Sahara in Bid to Stem Conflict," *The Christian Science Monitor*, May 8, 1987, at 11. Following a cease-fire, a United Nations peace-keeping force entered the Western Sahara in 1991, charged with implementing a referendum as suggested by the ICJ. Yet, the dispute in the Western Sahara carries on. In 1995, Morocco was blamed for attempting to block the U.N.–sponsored referendum on sovereignty in the territory. Chris Hedges, "Morocco, Defending Claim in the Desert, Exerts a Hand on Neighbor's Vote," *New York Times,* Mar. 5, 1995, § 1, at 5.

4. *Respecting Advisory Opinions.* How similar is an advisory opinion like that in *Western Sahara* to a judgment in a contentious case like *Hostages*? Neither case was particularly well-respected in practice. Is the Court's prestige less damaged by a disregarded advisory opinion, where there is no legal obligation to obey the opinion, than by a disregarded judgment in a contentious case? Do both serve the same marshalling of public opinion and generation of law functions?

4. CHAMBERS AT THE INTERNATIONAL COURT

STATUTE OF THE INTERNATIONAL COURT OF JUSTICE, ARTICLE 26

June 26, 1945, 59 Stat. 1031, T.S. No. 993.

1. The Court may from time to time form one or more chambers, composed of three or more judges as the Court may determine, for dealing with particular categories of cases; for example, labor cases and cases relating to transit and communications.

2. The Court may at any time form a chamber for dealing with a particular case. The number of judges to constitute such a chamber shall be determined by the Court with the approval of the parties.

3. Cases shall be heard and determined by the chambers provided for in this Article if the parties so request.

THE ELSI CASE

United States v. Italy
1989 I.C.J. 15, 1989 WL 139016.

1. By a letter dated 6 February 1987, filed in the Registry of the Court the same day, the Secretary of State of the United States of America transmitted to the Court an Application instituting proceedings

against the Republic of Italy in respect of a dispute arising out of the requisition by the Government of Italy of the plant and related assets of Raytheon–Elsi S.p.A., previously known as Elettronica Sicula S.p.A. (ELSI), an Italian company which was stated to have been 100 per cent owned by two United States corporations. By the same letter, the Secretary of State informed the Court that the Government of the United States requested, pursuant to Article 26 of the Statute of the Court, that the dispute be resolved by a Chamber of the Court.

2. Pursuant to Article 40, paragraph 2, of the Statute, the Application was at once communicated to the Government of the Republic of Italy. In accordance with paragraph 3 of that Article, all other States entitled to appear before the Court were notified of the Application.

3. By a telegram dated 13 February 1987 the Minister for Foreign Affairs of Italy informed the Court that his Government accepted the proposal put forward by the Government of the United States that the case be heard by a Chamber composed in accordance with Article 26 of the Statute; this acceptance was confirmed by a letter dated 13 February 1987 from the Agent of Italy.

4. By an Order dated 2 March 1987, the Court, after recalling the request for a Chamber and reciting that the Parties had been duly consulted as to the composition of the proposed Chamber in accordance with Article 26, paragraph 2, of the Statute and Article 17, paragraph 2, of the Rules of Court, decided to accede to the request of the Governments of the United States of America and Italy to form a special Chamber of five judges to deal with the case, declared that at an election held on that day President Nagendra Singh and Judges Oda, Ago, Schwebel and Sir Robert Jennings had been elected to the Chamber, and declared a Chamber to deal with the case to have been duly constituted by the Order, with the composition indicated. * * *

6. On 11 December 1988 Judge Nagendra Singh, President of the Chamber, died. Following further consultations with the Parties with regard to the composition of the Chamber in accordance with Article 17, paragraph 2, of the Rules of Court, the Court, by Order dated 20 December 1988, declared that Judge Ruda, President of the Court, had that day been elected a Member of the Chamber to fill the vacancy left by the death of Judge Nagendra Singh. In accordance with Article 18, paragraph 2, of the Rules of Court, President Ruda became President of the Chamber. * * *

12. The claim of the United States in the present case is that Italy has violated the international legal obligations which it undertook by the Treaty of Friendship, Commerce and Navigation between the two countries concluded on 2 February 1948 ("the FCN Treaty") and the Supplementary Agreement thereto concluded on 26 September 1951, by reason of its acts and omissions in relation to, and its treatment of, two United States corporations, the Raytheon Company ("Raytheon") and The Machlett Laboratories Incorporated ("Machlett"), in relation to the Italian corporation Raytheon–Elsi S.p.A. (previously Elettronica Sicula

S.p.A. (ELSI)), which was wholly owned by the two United States corporations. Italy contests certain of the facts alleged by the United States, denies that there has been any violation of the FCN Treaty, and contends, on a subsidiary and alternative basis, that if there was any such violation, no injury was caused for which payment of any indemnity would be justified.

13. In 1955, Raytheon (then known as Raytheon Manufacturing Company) agreed to subscribe for 14 per cent of the shares in Elettronica Sicula S.p.A. Over the period 1956–1967, Raytheon successively increased its holding of ELSI shares (as well as investing capital in the company in other ways) to a total holding of 99.16 per cent of its shares. In April 1963 the name of the company was changed from Elettronica Sicula S.p.A. to "Raytheon–Elsi S.p.A."; it will however be referred to hereafter as "ELSI." The remaining shares (0.84 per cent) in ELSI were acquired in April 1967 by Machlett, which was a wholly-owned subsidiary of Raytheon. ELSI was established in Palermo, Sicily, where it had a plant for the production of electronic components; in 1967 it had a workforce of slightly under 900 employees. Its five major product lines were microwave tubes, cathode-ray tubes, semiconductor rectifiers, X-ray tubes and surge arresters.

14. During the fiscal years 1964 to 1966 inclusive, ELSI made an operating profit, but this profit was insufficient to offset its debt expense or accumulated losses, and no dividends were ever paid to its shareholders. In June 1964, the accumulated losses exceeded one-third of the company's share capital, and ELSI was thus required by Article 2446 of the Italian Civil Code to reduce its equity from 4,300 million lire to 2,000 million lire. The capital stock was therefore devalued by 2,300 million lire and recapitalized by an equal amount subscribed by Raytheon. A similar operation was necessary in March 1967. In February 1967, according to the United States, Raytheon began taking steps to endeavour to make ELSI self-sufficient. Raytheon and Machlett designated a number of highly-qualified personnel to provide financial, managerial and technical expertise, and Raytheon provided a total of over 4,000 million lire in recapitalization and guaranteed credit. By December 1967, according to the United States, major steps had been taken to upgrade plant facilities and operations. * * *

16. The management of ELSI took the view that one of the reasons for its lack of success was that it had trained and was employing an excessively large labour force. In June 1967 it was decided to dismiss some 300 employees; under an Italian union agreement this involved a procedure of notifications and negotiations. * * * [A]n alternative plan was agreed to whereby 168 workers would be suspended from 10 July 1967, with limited pay by ELSI for a period not exceeding six weeks. After a training programme during which the workers were paid by the Sicilian Government, it was contemplated that ELSI would endeavor to reemploy the suspended employees. The necessary additional business to make this possible was not forthcoming, and the suspended employees were dismissed early in March 1968. A number of random strikes had

occurred in early 1968, and as a result of the dismissals a complete strike of the plant occurred on 4 March 1968. According to the Government of Italy, this strike also involved an occupation of the plant by the work-force, which occupation was still continuing when the plant was requisitioned on 1 April 1968 (paragraph 30 below). The United States claims however that strikes and "sit-ins" prior to the requisition were only sporadic and that only after the filing of a petition in bankruptcy on 26 April 1968 * * * did the workers actually occupy the plant for a sustained period.

17. When it became apparent that the discussions with Italian officials and companies were unlikely to lead to a mutually satisfactory arrangement to resolve ELSI's difficulties, Raytheon and Machlett, as shareholders in ELSI, began seriously to plan to close and liquidate ELSI to minimize their losses. General planning for the potential liquidation of ELSI began in the latter part of 1967, and in early 1968 detailed plans were made for a shut-down and liquidation at any time after 16 March 1968. * * *

25. In the view of ELSI's legal counsel at the time * * * and of Italian lawyers consulted by the United States, ELSI was in March 1968 entitled to engage in orderly liquidation of its assets, was under no obligation to file a petition in bankruptcy, and was never in jeopardy of compulsory dissolution under Article 2447 of the Italian Civil Code, and was at all times in compliance with Article 2446 of the Code. It has however been contended by Italy that ELSI was in March 1968 unable to pay its debts, and its capital of 4,000 million lire was completely lost; accordingly, an orderly liquidation was not available to it, but as an insolvent debtor it was under an obligation to file a petition in bankruptcy. * * *

30. On 1 April 1968 the Mayor of Palermo issued an order, effective immediately, requisitioning ELSI's plant and related assets for a period of six months. The text of this order, in the translation supplied by the United States, was as follows:

> "*The Mayor of the Municipality of Palermo,*
>
> *Taking into consideration* that Raytheon–Elsi of Palermo has decided to close its plant located in this city at Via Villagrazia, 79, because of market difficulties and lack of orders;
>
> *That* the company has furthermore decided to send dismissal letters to the personnel consisting of about 1,000 persons;
>
> *Taking notice* that ELSI's actions, besides provoking the reaction of the workers and of the unions giving rise to strikes (both general and sectional) has caused a wide and general movement of solidarity of all public opinion which has strongly stigmatized the action taken considering that about 1,000 families are suddenly destituted;
>
> *That*, considering the fact that ELSI is the second firm in order of importance in the District, because of the shutdown of the plant a

serious damage will be caused to the District, which has been so severely tried by the earthquakes had during the month of January 1968;

Considering also that the local press is taking a great interest in the situation and that the press is being very critical toward the authorities and is accusing them of indifference to this serious civic problem;

That, furthermore, the present situation is particularly touchy and unforeseeable disturbances of public order could take place;

Taking into consideration that in this particular instance there is sufficient ground for holding that there is a grave public necessity and urgency to protect the general economic public interest (already seriously compromised) and public order, and that these reasons justify requisitioning the plant and all equipment owned by Raytheon–Elsi located here at Via Villagrazia 79; * * *

ORDERS

the requisition, with immediate effect and for the duration of six months, except as may be necessary to extend such period, and without prejudice for the rights of the parties and of third parties, of the plant and relative equipment owned by Raytheon–Elsi of Palermo.

With a subsequent decree, the indemnification to be paid to said company for the requisition will be established."

The order was served on the company on 2 April 1968.

31. On 6 April 1968 the Mayor issued an order entrusting the management of the requisitioned plant to Mr. Aldo Profumo, the Managing Director of ELSI, for the purpose, *inter alia*, of "avoiding any damage to the equipment and machinery due to the abandoning of all activity, including maintenance." Mr. Profumo declined to accept this appointment, and on 16 April 1968 the Mayor wrote to Mr. Silvio Laurin, the senior director, appointing him temporarily to replace Mr. Profumo "in the same capacity, with the same powers, functions and limitations," and Mr. Laurin accepted this appointment. The company management requested another of its directors, Mr. Rico Merluzzo, to stay at the plant night and day "to preclude local authorities from somehow asserting that the plant had been 'abandoned' by ELSI."

32. On 9 April 1968 ELSI addressed a telegram to the Mayor of Palermo, with copies to other Government authorities, claiming *(inter alia)* that the requisition was illegal and expressing the company's intention to take all legal steps to have it revoked and to claim damages. On 12 April 1968 the company served on the Mayor a formal document dated 11 April 1968 inviting him to revoke the requisition order. The Mayor did not respond and the order was not revoked, and on 19 April 1968 ELSI brought an administrative appeal against it to the Prefect of Palermo, who was empowered to hear appeals against decisions by local

governmental officials. The decision on that appeal was not given until 22 August 1969 * * * ; in the meantime however the requisition was not formally prolonged, and therefore ceased to have legal effect after six months, more than four months after the bankruptcy of ELSI had been declared * * *. * * *

44. In the bankruptcy proceedings, creditors presented claims against ELSI totalling some 13,000 million lire; these did not include amounts due to Raytheon and Raytheon Service Company * * *. The bankruptcy proceedings closed in November 1985. According to the bankruptcy reports, the bankruptcy realized only some 6,370 million lire for ELSI's assets, as compared with the minimum liquidation value estimated by ELSI's management in March 1968 at 10,840 million lire. Of the amount realized, some 6,080 million lire went to pay banks, employees, and other creditors. The remainder went to pay bankruptcy administration, tax, registry, and customs charges. All of the secured and preferred creditors who filed claims in the bankruptcy were paid in full. The unsecured creditors received less than one per cent of their claims; accordingly no surplus remained for distribution to the shareholders, Raytheon and Machlett.

45. Raytheon had guaranteed the indebtedness of ELSI to a number of banks, and on the bankruptcy of ELSI it was accordingly liable for, and paid, the sum of 5,787.6 million lire to the banks in accordance with the terms of the guarantees. Five of the seven banks which had also made unguaranteed loans to ELSI brought proceedings in the Italian courts seeking payment of these loans by Raytheon, on the basis primarily of Article 2362 of the Italian Civil Code, which renders a sole shareholder liable for the debts of the company. It was argued that Raytheon was in effect sole shareholder, since Machlett was its wholly-owned subsidiary. Three of these cases were ultimately resolved by the Italian Court of Cassation in favour of Raytheon, and two were discontinued by the plaintiffs.

46. On 7 February 1974, the Embassy in Rome of the United States transmitted to the Italian Ministry of Foreign Affairs a note enclosing the "claim of the Government of the United States of America on behalf of Raytheon Company and Machlett Laboratories, Incorporated." That claim, which was based not only on the FCN Treaty but also on customary international law, incorporated a Memorandum of Law, Chapter VI of which was devoted to "Exhaustion of Local Remedies." It was there noted that it was "generally recognized that local remedies must be exhausted before a claim may be formally espoused under principles of international law"; an account was given of the relevant litigation in Italy (some of which was at the time still pending) and, in the light of annexed opinions of two Italian legal experts, it was concluded that "Raytheon and Machlett have exhausted every meaningful legal remedy available to them in Italy." At the time this claim was submitted, the Court of Appeal of Palermo had ruled on the action by the trustee in bankruptcy, but the case was thereafter brought before the Court of Cassation * * * ; it is recognized by both Parties that any other

action arising out of the requisition would by then have been barred by limitation of time. It appears that the United States received no formal response from Italy to the claim until 13 June 1978, when Italy denied the claim in a written aide-mémoire, the text of which has been supplied to the Chamber. The aide-mémoire contained no suggestion that local remedies had not been exhausted, and indeed stated that "the claim is juridically groundless, both from the international and domestic point of view." During the oral proceedings in the present case, counsel for Italy asserted that at an unspecified date prior to the institution of the present proceedings the Italian Government "had made it clear to the United States Government that as a Respondent it would raise the objection of non-exhaustion of local remedies in judicial proceedings." No evidence to that effect has however been supplied to the Chamber. * * *

48. It is common ground between the Parties that the Court has jurisdiction in the present case, under Article 36, paragraph 1, of its Statute, and Article XXVI of the Treaty of Friendship, Commerce and Navigation, of 2 June 1948 ("the FCN Treaty"), between Italy and the United States; which Article reads:

> "Any dispute between the High Contracting Parties as to the interpretation or the application of this Treaty, which the High Contracting Parties shall not satisfactorily adjust by diplomacy, shall be submitted to the International Court of Justice, unless the High Contracting Parties shall agree to settlement by some other pacific means." * * *

56. The damage claimed in this case to have been caused to Raytheon and Machlett is said to have resulted from the "losses incurred by ELSI's owners as a result of the involuntary change in the manner of disposing of ELSI's assets": and it is the requisition order that is said to have caused this change, and which is therefore at the core of the United States complaint. * * *

65. The acts of the Respondent which are thus alleged to violate its treaty obligations were described by the Applicant's counsel in terms which it is convenient to cite here:

> "First, the Respondent violated its legal obligations when it unlawfully requisitioned the ELSI plant on 1 April 1968 which denied the ELSI stockholders their direct right to liquidate the ELSI assets in an orderly fashion. Second, the Respondent violated its obligations when it allowed ELSI workers to occupy the plant. Third, the Respondent violated its obligations when it unreasonably delayed ruling on the lawfulness of the requisition for 16 months until immediately after the ELSI plant, equipment and work-in-process had all been acquired by ELTEL. Fourth and finally, the Respondent violated its obligations when it interfered with the ELSI bankruptcy proceedings, which allowed the Respondent to realize its previously expressed intention of acquiring ELSI for a price far less than its fair market value."

66. The most important of these acts of the Respondent which the Applicant claims to have been in violation of the FCN Treaty is the requisition of the ELSI plant by the Mayor of Palermo on 1 April 1968, which is claimed to have frustrated the plan for what the Applicant terms an "orderly liquidation" of the company as set out in paragraphs 22–25 above. It is fair to describe the other impugned acts of the Respondent * * * as ancillary to this core claim based on the requisition and its effects.

67. The Chamber is faced with a situation of mixed fact and law of considerable complexity, wherein several different strands of fact and law have to be examined both separately and for their effect on each other: the meaning and effect of the relevant Articles of the FCN Treaty and Supplementary Agreement; the legal status of the Mayor's requisition of ELSI's plant and assets; and the legal and practical significance of the financial position of ELSI at material times, and its effect, if any, upon ELSI's plan for orderly liquidation of the company. It will be convenient to begin by examining these considerations in relation to the Applicant's claim that the requisition order was a violation of Article III of the FCN Treaty.

68. Article III of the FCN Treaty is in two paragraphs. Paragraph 1 provides for rights of participation of nationals of one High Contracting Party, in corporations and associations of the other High Contracting Party, and for the exercise by such corporations and associations of their functions. Since there is no allegation of treatment less favourable than is required according to the standards set by this paragraph, it need not detain the Chamber. Paragraph 2 of Article III is however important for the Applicant's claim; it provides:

> "The nationals, corporations and associations of either High Contracting Party shall be permitted, in conformity with the applicable laws and regulations within the territories of the other High Contracting Party, to organize, control and manage corporations and associations of such other High Contracting Party for engaging in commercial, manufacturing, processing, mining, educational, philanthropic, religious and scientific activities. Corporations and associations, controlled by nationals, corporations and associations of either High Contracting Party and created or organized under the applicable laws and regulations within the territories of the other High Contracting Party, shall be permitted to engage in the aforementioned activities therein, in conformity with the applicable laws and regulations, upon terms no less favorable than those now or hereafter accorded to corporations and associations of such other High Contracting Party controlled by its own nationals, corporations and associations."

Again there is no allegation of treatment of ELSI according to standards less favourable than those laid down in the second sentence of the paragraph: the allegation by the United States of a violation of this paragraph by Italy relates to the first sentence.

69. In terms of the present case, the effect of the first sentence of this paragraph is that Raytheon and Machlett are to be permitted, in conformity with the applicable laws and regulations within the territory of Italy, to organize, control and manage ELSI. The claim of the United States focuses on the right to "control and manage"; the right to "organize," apparently in the sense of the creation of a corporation, is not in question in this case. Is there, then, a violation of this Article if, as the United States alleges, the requisition had the effect of depriving ELSI of both the right and practical possibility of selling off its plant and assets for satisfaction of its liabilities to its creditors and satisfaction of its shareholders? * * *

85. Did ELSI, in this precarious position at the end of March 1968, still have the practical possibility to proceed with an orderly liquidation plan? The successful implementation of a plan of orderly liquidation would have depended upon a number of factors not under the control of ELSI's management. Since the company's coffers were dangerously low, funds had to be forthcoming to maintain the cash flow necessary while the plan was being carried out. Evidence has been produced by the Applicant that Raytheon was prepared to supply cash flow and other assistance necessary to effect the orderly liquidation, and the Chamber sees no reason to question that Raytheon had entered or was ready to enter into such a commitment. Other factors governing the matter however give rise to some doubt.

86. First, for the success of the plan it was necessary that the major creditors (i.e., the banks) would be willing to wait for payment of their claims until the sale of the assets released funds to settle them: and this applied not only to the capital sums outstanding, which may not at the time have yet been legally due for repayment, but also the agreed payments of interest or installments of capital. Though the Chamber has been given no specific information on the point, this is of the essence of such a liquidation plan: the creditors had to be asked to give the company time. If ELSI had been confident of continuing to meet all its obligations promptly and regularly while seeking a buyer for its assets, no negotiations with creditors, and no elaborate calculations of division of the proceeds, on different hypotheses, such as have been produced to the Chamber, would have been needed.

87. Secondly, the management were by no means certain that the sale of the assets would realize enough to pay all creditors in full; in fact, the existence of the calculation of a "quick-sale value" suggests perhaps more than uncertainty. Thus the creditors had to be asked to give time in return for an assurance, not that 100 per cent would be paid, but that a minimum of 50 per cent would be paid. While in general it might be in the creditors' interest to agree to such a proposal, this does not mean in this case that ELSI could count on such agreement. * * *

88. Nor should it be overlooked that the dismissed employees of ELSI ranked as preferential creditors for such sums as might be due to

them for severance pay or arrears. In this respect Italy has drawn attention to the Sicilian regional law of 13 May 1968, providing for the payment

> "for the months of March, April and May 1968, to the dismissed employees of Raytheon–Elsi of Palermo of a special monthly indemnity equal to the actual monthly pay received until the month of February 1968."

From this it could be inferred, said Italy, that ELSI did not pay its employees for the month of March 1968. Further it was conceded by the former Chairman of ELSI, when he appeared as a witness and was cross-examined, that the cash available at 31 March 1968 ("22 million in the kitty"), would have been insufficient to meet the payroll of the full staff even for the first week of April ("at least 25 million"). The suggestion that ELSI did not meet its March 1968 payroll was not put to the witness; and counsel for the United States later stated that the assertion that "ELSI could not make its March payroll," was "simply wrong." It is in any event certain that when the company ceased activity there were still severance payments due to the dismissed staff; those, the Applicant suggested, would have been covered by funds to be provided by Raytheon * * *. They could not have been met from the money still remaining in ELSI's coffers at the time.

89. Thirdly, the plan as formulated by ELSI's management involved a potential inequality among creditors: unless enough was realized to cover the liabilities fully, the major creditors were to be content with some 50 per cent of their claims; but the smaller creditors were still to be paid in full. * * * [This] was an additional factor which might have caused a major creditor to hesitate to agree. According to the evidence, when in late March 1968 ELSI started using funds made available by Raytheon to pay off the small creditors in full, "the banks intervened and said that they did not want that to happen as that was showing preference." Once the banks adopted this attitude, the whole orderly liquidation plan was jeopardized, because a purpose of the settlement with small creditors was, according to the 1974 diplomatic claim, "to eliminate the risk that a small irresponsible creditor would take precipitous action which would raise formidable obstacles in the way of orderly liquidation."

90. Fourthly, the assets of the company had to be sold with the minimum delay and at the best price obtainable—desiderata which are often in practice irreconcilable. The United States has emphasized the damaging effect of the requisition on attempts to realize the assets; after the requisition it was no longer possible for prospective buyers to view the plant, nor to assure them that if they bought they would obtain immediate possession. It is however not at all certain that the company could have counted on unfettered access to its premises and plant, and the opportunity of showing it to buyers without disturbance, even if the requisition had not been made. There has been argument between the Parties on the question whether and to what extent the plant was

occupied by employees of ELSI both before and after the requisition; but what is clear is that the company was expecting trouble at the plant when its closure plans became known: the books had been removed to Milan, according to the evidence given at the hearings, "so that if we did have problems we could at least control the books" and "we had moved quite a lot of inventory [to Milan] so that we could sell it from there if we had to."

91. Fifthly, there was the attitude of the Sicilian administration: the company was well aware that the administration was strongly opposed to a closure of the plant, or more specifically, to a dismissal of the workers. True, the measure used to try to prevent this—the requisition order—was found by the Prefect to have lacked the "juridical cause which might justify it and make it operative" * * *. But ELSI's management in March 1968 could not have been certain that the hostility of the local authorities to their plan of closure and dismissals would not take practical form in a legal manner. The company's management had been told before the staff dismissal letters were sent out that such dismissals would lead to a requisition of the plant.

92. All these factors point towards a conclusion that the feasibility at 31 March 1968 of a plan of orderly liquidation, an essential link in the chain of reasoning upon the United States claim rests, has not been sufficiently established. * * *

137. For these reasons,

THE CHAMBER, * * *

(2) By four votes to one,

Finds that the Italian Republic has not committed any of the breaches, alleged in the said Application, of the Treaty of Friendship, Commerce and Navigation between the Parties signed at Rome on 2 February 1948, or of the Agreement Supplementing that Treaty signed by the Parties at Washington on 26 September 1951.

IN FAVOUR: *President* Ruda; *Judges* Oda, Ago and Sir Robert Jennings;

AGAINST: *Judge* Schwebel. * * *

SEPARATE OPINION OF JUDGE ODA * * *

To recapitulate, ELSI (an Italian company) and, later, its trustee in bankruptcy, brought municipal legal proceedings to challenge the requisition order of the Mayor of Palermo. It took its case to the highest court in Italy and is accordingly considered to have exhausted all available municipal remedies. Thus the United States could have espoused the cause of ELSI on the grounds of "denial of justice" *if* the judgment of the domestic court of Italy at the highest level had been found to be "manifestly unjust" in its application of the FCN Treaty.

Neither ELSI, nor its trustee in bankruptcy acting on its behalf, so much as invoked the FCN Treaty in those municipal proceedings. (The assertion that the FCN Treaty is non-self-executing could not have been used by ELSI as an excuse for failure to invoke it before the municipal courts of Italy, since enabling legislation had been enacted in that country.) Nor has evidence been brought by the Applicant to show that, as a consequence of the requisition order of 1 April 1968, ELSI received less favourable treatment than any other Italian corporation controlled by nationals of any third country in exercising its functions, or less favourable treatment than that afforded any Italian corporation controlled by Italians; again, supposing that the present case relates to an enterprise placed under public control, no evidence has been brought to show that ELSI was accorded less favourable treatment than any other enterprise.

In conclusion, it appears to me that some arguments employed in this case which has been brought to the Court by the Applicant in an espousal of the cause of Raytheon and Machlett are, unfortunately, based upon a misconception of the provisions of the 1948 FCN Treaty.

Even if the present proceedings had been brought in an espousal of ELSI's cause, by applying the proper provisions which guaranteed ELSI the most-favoured-nation treatment or national treatment, the Applicant would have had to provide sufficient evidence to show that ELSI had been denied justice in the Italian courts. It has failed to do so.

DISSENTING OPINION OF JUDGE SCHWEBEL * * *

The Chamber's Judgment concludes that "the possibility" of an orderly liquidation by ELSI "is purely a matter of speculation." I agree that an orderly liquidation would have been beset with uncertainties, but those uncertainties go not so much to ELSI's ability and entitlement to liquidate its assets as to the calculability of the damages which may be found to flow from the denial of that ability and entitlement by the requisition imposed upon ELSI.

In my view, it is unpersuasive for the Chamber to say, in effect, that ELSI would have gone into bankruptcy later if not sooner, and accordingly that the requisition did not matter. It is in this respect that I believe that the Chamber muddles what it finds to be the facts with time factors. At the time the requisition took place, it did matter, it did have the economic effects, or some of the economic effects, just described; and at the time it took place, it deprived Raytheon and Machlett of their right to control and manage and hence liquidate ELSI and it deprived ELSI of its right to be liquidated by a management responsible to Raytheon and Machlett. Accordingly the requisition placed Italy in violation of its obligation under Article III of the Treaty to permit Raytheon and Machlett to "control and manage" ELSI.

This conclusion is the more compelling when the meaning of the Treaty is interpreted in the light of the provisions and ratification processes set out in this opinion. Can it be said that the requisition, imposed as it was when it was, comported with the "full rights" of Raytheon and Machlett to "organize, direct and control" ELSI, that it comported with their "unobstructed control" and "maximum freedom of choice"? Was it consistent with "the principles of equitable treatment" which the Preamble to the Supplementary Agreement describes the Treaty as containing? Was the requisition consonant with assuring to Raytheon "the most liberal treatment practicable" in respect of the repatriation of its invested capital? Did it respect "the guaranty against political risks" which the Treaty as a whole was designed to provide? Not in my view.

Notes and Questions

1. *The Decision to Use Chambers.* The United States brought the *ELSI Case* with Italy to the ICJ shortly after the U.S. backed away from participating in the Merits stage of the *Nicaragua Case* and after it withdrew its consent to the Court's Article 36(2) compulsory jurisdiction, events that are chronicled in Chapter 8. Previously, the United States and Italy had been planning to take the ELSI dispute to an arbitral tribunal. See W. Michael Reisman, *Systems of Control in International Adjudication and Arbitration* 43 (1992). Having decided to go to the International Court, why would the United States and Italy choose to employ a five-judge chamber? Why would the Court have agreed to proceedings by a chamber rather than by its full membership?

2. *Exhaustion of Local Remedies.* Judge Oda in his Separate Opinion stresses that the U.S.–Italy Friendship, Commerce and Navigation Treaty was not raised in municipal court proceedings. Should ELSI (or its U.S. shareholders, Raytheon and Matchlett) have to go to an Italian court before their international law claims are litigated at the International Court or in an international arbitral proceeding? If companies seek relief in municipal courts first, should they be sure to argue international legal issues there?

3. *Access to the International Court.* Note that Raytheon itself has no standing to bring suit in the ICJ. The Statute of the ICJ provides that "only states may be parties in cases before the Court." Why would the U.S. government be willing to forward Raytheon's case to The Hague Court? What would be objections the U.S. government might have to so "internationalizing" the ELSI dispute? Certainly, if private litigants like Raytheon could bring cases themselves to the ICJ, there would be far more cases for the ICJ. Is this an argument for or against a right of private parties to sue in the ICJ? Could there be a half-way house, where municipal courts could refer international legal issues to the ICJ? There is such a mechanism, called a Preliminary Ruling, already in European law: Article 177 of the EEC Treaty permits domestic judges to ask the European Court of Justice in Luxembourg for their advice relating to the Treaty.

Chapter 6

INDIVIDUALS AND INTERNATIONAL LAW

A. INDIVIDUALS AS OBJECTS OF INTERNATIONAL LAW

In the traditional positivistic international law of the nineteenth and early twentieth centuries, individuals were viewed as "objects" of international law. Although individuals were not deemed to be "subjects" of international law (and so had neither international legal rights or duties), they could be objects of state v. state litigation. So grew up doctrines of state protection of individuals and state responsibility for injuries done to individuals. However, the traditional doctrines of state protection and state responsibility have at least three significant limitations. First, as we see in *Nottebohm* below, individuals may only be protected by their national states, and national links may be elusive. Second, when the notion of national links is extended to corporations, even more confusion can result, as *Barcelona Traction* illustrates. Finally, the objective view of individuals leaves nationals open to abuse by their own states, since it is impractical to conceive of a state protecting its own national against itself in international law.

THE NOTTEBOHM CASE

Liechtenstein v. Guatemala, 1955 I.C.J. 4, 1955 WL 1.

[Nottebohm, born German, obtained Liechtenstein citizenship in 1939, but nonetheless was subject to Guatemalan penalties as a German enemy alien during the Second World War. Liechtenstein sued Guatemala on Nottebohm's behalf in the ICJ, but Guatemala objected that Liechtenstein was not a state that might legitimately protect Nottebohm before the Court.]

Nottebohm was born at Hamburg on September 16th, 1881. He was German by birth, and still possessed German nationality when, in October 1939, he applied for naturalization in Liechtenstein.

In 1905 he went to Guatemala. He took up residence there and made that country the headquarters of his business activities, which increased and prospered; these activities developed in the field of commerce, banking and plantations. Having been an employee in the firm of Nottebohm Hermanos, which had been founded by his brothers Juan and Arturo, he became their partner in 1912 and later, in 1937, he was made head of the firm. After 1905 he sometimes went to Germany on business and to other countries for holidays. He continued to have business connections in Germany. He paid a few visits to a brother who had lived in Liechtenstein since 1931. Some of his other brothers, relatives and friends were in Germany, others in Guatemala. He himself continued to have his fixed abode in Guatemala until 1943, that is to say, until the occurrence of the events which constitute the basis of the present dispute.

In 1939, after having provided for the safeguarding of his interests in Guatemala by a power of attorney given to the firm of Nottebohm Hermanos on March 22nd, he left that country at a date fixed by Counsel for Liechtenstein as at approximately the end of March or the beginning of April, when he seems to have gone to Hamburg, and later to have paid a few brief visits to Vaduz where he was at the beginning of October 1939. It was then, on October 9th, a little more than a month after the opening of the second World War marked by Germany's attack on Poland, that his attorney, Dr. Marxer, submitted an application for naturalization on behalf of Nottebohm.

The Liechtenstein Law of January 4th, 1934, lays down the conditions for the naturalization of foreigners, specifies the supporting documents to be submitted and the undertakings to be given and defines the competent organs for giving a decision and the procedure to be followed. The Law specifies certain mandatory requirements, namely, that the applicant for naturalization should prove: (1) "that the acceptance into the Home Corporation (*Heimatverband*) of a Liechtenstein commune has been promised to him in case of acquisition of the nationality of the State"; (2) that he will lose his former nationality as a result of naturalization, although this requirement may be waived under stated conditions. It further makes naturalization conditional upon compliance with the requirement of residence for at least three years in the territory of the Principality, although it is provided that "this requirement can be dispensed with in circumstances deserving special consideration and by way of exception." In addition, the applicant for naturalization is required to submit a number of documents, such as evidence of his residence in the territory of the Principality, a certificate of good conduct issued by the competent authority of the place of residence, documents relating to his property and income and, if he is not a resident in the Principality, proof that he has concluded an agreement with the Revenue authorities, "subsequent to the revenue commission of the presumptive home commune having been heard." The Law further provides for the payment by the applicant of a naturalization fee, which is fixed by the Princely Government and amounts to at least one half of the sum payable by the applicant for reception into the Home Corporation of a

Liechtenstein commune, the promise of such reception constituting a condition under the Law for the grant of naturalization. * * *

On October 9th, 1939, Nottebohm, "resident in Guatemala since 1905 (at present residing as a visitor with his brother, Hermann Nottebohm, in Vaduz)," applied for admission as a national of Liechtenstein and, at the same time, for the previous conferment of citizenship in the Commune of Mauren. He sought dispensation from the condition of three years' residence as prescribed by law, without indicating the special circumstances warranting such waiver. He submitted a statement of the *Crédit Suisse* in Zurich concerning his assets, and undertook to pay 25,000 Swiss francs to the Commune of Mauren, 12,500 Swiss francs to the State, to which was to be added the payment of dues in connection with the proceedings. He further stated that he had made "arrangements with the Revenue Authorities of the Government of Liechtenstein for the conclusion of a formal agreement to the effect that he will pay an annual tax of naturalization amounting to Swiss francs 1,000 of which Swiss francs 600 are payable to the Commune of Mauren and Swiss francs 400 are payable to the Principality of Liechtenstein, subject to the proviso that the payments of these taxes will be set off against ordinary taxes which will fall due if the applicant takes up residence in one of the Communes of the Principality." He further undertook to deposit as security a sum of 30,000 Swiss francs. He also gave certain general information as to his financial position and indicated that he would never become a burden to the Commune whose citizenship he was seeking.

Lastly, he requested "that naturalization proceedings be initiated and concluded before the Government of the Principality and before the Commune of Mauren without delay, that the application be then placed before the Diet with a favourable recommendation and, finally, that it be submitted with all necessary expedition to His Highness the Reigning Prince."

On the original typewritten application which has been produced in a photostatic copy, it can be seen that the name of the Commune of Mauren and the amounts to be paid were added by hand, a fact which gave rise to some argument on the part of Counsel for the Parties. There is also a reference to the "*Vorausverständnis*" of the Reigning Prince obtained on October 13th, 1939, which Liechtenstein interprets as showing the decision to grant naturalization, which interpretation has, however, been questioned. Finally, there is annexed to the application an otherwise blank sheet bearing the signature of the Reigning Prince, "Franz Josef," but without any date or other explanation.

A document dated October 15th, 1939, certifies that on that date the Commune of Mauren conferred the privilege of its citizenship upon Mr. Nottebohm and requested the Government to transmit it to the Diet for approval. A certificate of October 17th, 1939, evidences the payment of the taxes required to be paid by Mr. Nottebohm. On October 20th,

1939, Mr. Nottebohm took the oath of allegiance and a final arrangement concerning liability to taxation was concluded on October 23rd.

This was the procedure followed in the case of the naturalization of Nottebohm.

A certificate of nationality has also been produced, signed on behalf of the Government of the Principality and dated October 20th, 1939, to the effect that Nottebohm was naturalized by Supreme Resolution of the Reigning Prince dated October 13th, 1939.

Having obtained a Liechtenstein passport, Nottebohm had it visa-ed by the Consul General of Guatemala in Zurich on December 1st, 1939, and returned to Guatemala at the beginning of 1940, where he resumed his former business activities and in particular the management of the firm of Nottebohm Hermanos.

Relying on the nationality thus conferred on Nottebohm, Liechtenstein considers itself entitled to seize the Court of its claim on his behalf, and its Final Conclusions contain two submissions in this connection. Liechtenstein requests the Court to find and declare, first, "that the naturalization of Mr. Frederic Nottebohm in Liechtenstein on October 13th, 1939, was not contrary to international law," and secondly, "that Liechtenstein's claim on behalf of Mr. Nottebohm as a national of Liechtenstein is admissible before the Court."

The Final Conclusions of Guatemala, on the other hand, request the Court "to declare that the claim of the Principality of Liechtenstein is inadmissible," and set forth a number of grounds relating to the nationality of Liechtenstein granted to Nottebohm by naturalization.

Thus, the real issue before the Court is the admissibility of the claim of Liechtenstein in respect of Nottebohm. Liechtenstein's first submission referred to above is a reason advanced for a decision by the Court in favour of Liechtenstein, while the several grounds given by Guatemala on the question of nationality are intended as reasons for the inadmissibility of Liechtenstein's claim. The present task of the Court is limited to adjudicating upon the admissibility of the claim of Liechtenstein in the respect of Nottebohm on the basis of such reasons as it may itself consider relevant and proper.

In order to decide upon the admissibility of the Application, the Court must ascertain whether the nationality conferred on Nottebohm by Liechtenstein by means of a naturalization which took place in the circumstances which have been described, can be validly invoked as against Guatemala, whether it bestows upon Liechtenstein a sufficient title to the exercise of protection in respect of Nottebohm as against Guatemala and therefore entitles it to seize the Court of a claim relating to him. * * *

Since no proof has been adduced that Guatemala has recognized the title to the exercise of protection relied upon by Liechtenstein as being derived from the naturalization which it granted to Nottebohm, the Court must consider whether such an act of granting nationality by

Liechtenstein directly entails an obligation on the part of Guatemala to recognize its effect, namely, Liechtenstein's right to exercise its protection. In other words, it must be determined whether that unilateral act by Liechtenstein is one which can be relied upon against Guatemala in regard to the exercise of protection. The Court will deal with this question without considering that of the validity of Nottebohm's naturalization according to the law of Liechtenstein.

It is for Liechtenstein, as it is for every sovereign State, to settle by its own legislation the rules relating to the acquisition of its nationality, and to confer that nationality by naturalization granted by its own organs in accordance with that legislation. It is not necessary to determine whether international law imposes any limitations on its freedom of decision in this domain. Furthermore, nationality has its most immediate, its most far-reaching and, for most people, its only effects within the legal system of the State conferring it. Nationality serves above all to determine that the person upon whom it is conferred enjoys the rights and is bound by the obligations which the law of the State in question grants to or imposes on its nationals. This is implied in the wider concept that nationality is within the domestic jurisdiction of the State.

But the issue which the Court must decide is not one which pertains to the legal system of Liechtenstein. It does not depend on the law or on the decision of Liechtenstein whether that State is entitled to exercise its protection, in the case under consideration. To exercise protection, to apply to the Court, is to place oneself on the plane of international law. It is international law which determines whether a State is entitled to exercise protection and to seize the Court.

The naturalization of Nottebohm was an act performed by Liechtenstein in the exercise of its domestic jurisdiction. The question to be decided is whether that act has the international effect here under consideration.

International practice provides many examples of acts performed by States in the exercise of their domestic jurisdiction which do not necessarily or automatically have international effect, which are not necessarily and automatically binding on other States or which are binding on them only subject to certain conditions: this is the case, for instance, of a judgment given by the competent court of a State which it is sought to invoke in another state.

In the present case it is necessary to determine whether the naturalization conferred on Nottebohm can be successfully invoked against Guatemala, whether, as has already been stated, it can be relied upon as against that State, so that Liechtenstein is thereby entitled to exercise its protection in favour of Nottebohm against Guatemala. * * *

International arbitrators have decided * * * numerous cases of dual nationality, where the question arose with regard to the exercise of protection. They have given their preference to the real and effective nationality, that which accorded with the facts, that based on stronger factual ties between the person concerned and one of the States whose nationality is involved. Different factors are taken into consideration, and their importance will vary from one case to the next: the habitual residence of the individual concerned is an important factor, but there are other factors such as the centre of his interests, his family ties, his participation in public life, attachment shown by him for a given country and inculcated in his children, etc.

Similarly, the courts of third States, when they have before them an individual whom two other States hold to be their national, seek to resolve the conflict by having recourse to international criteria and their prevailing tendency is to prefer the real and effective nationality.

The same tendency prevails in the writings of publicists and in practice. This notion is inherent in the provisions of Article 3, paragraph 2, of the Statute of the Court. National laws reflect this tendency when, *inter alia*, they make naturalization dependent on conditions indicating the existence of a link, which may vary in their purpose or in their nature but which are essentially concerned with this idea. The Liechtenstein Law of January 4th, 1934, is a good example.

The practice of certain States which refrain from exercising protection in favour of a naturalized person when the latter has in fact, by his prolonged absence, severed his links with what is no longer for him anything but his nominal country, manifests the view of these States that, in order to be capable of being invoked against another State, nationality must correspond with the factual situation. A similar view is manifested in the relevant provisions of the bilateral nationality treaties concluded between the United States of America and other States since 1868, such as those sometimes referred to as the Bancroft Treaties, and in the Pan-American Convention, signed at Rio de Janeiro on August 13th, 1906, on the status of naturalized citizens who resume residence in their country of origin.

The character thus recognized on the international level as pertaining to nationality is in no way inconsistent with the fact that international law leaves it to each State to lay down the rules governing the grant of its own nationality. The reason for this is that the diversity of demographic conditions has thus far made it impossible for any general agreement to be reached on the rules relating to nationality, although the latter by its very nature affects international relations. It has been considered that the best way of making such rules accord with the varying demographic conditions in different countries is to leave the fixing of such rules to the competence of each State. On the other hand, a State cannot claim that the rules it has thus laid down are entitled to recognition by another State unless it has acted in conformity with this general aim of making the legal bond of nationality accord with the individual's genuine connection with the State which assumes the defence of its citizens by means of protection as against other States. * * *

According to the practice of States, to arbitral and judicial decisions and to the opinions of writers, nationality is a legal bond having as its basis a social fact of attachment, a genuine connection of existence, interests and sentiments, together with the existence of reciprocal rights and duties. It may be said to constitute the juridical expression of the fact that the individual upon whom it is conferred, either directly by the law or as the result of an act of the authorities, is in fact more closely connected with the population of the State conferring nationality than with that of any other State. Conferred by a State, it only entitles that State to exercise protection vis-à-vis another State, if it constitutes a translation into juridical terms of the individual's connection with the State which has made him its national.

Diplomatic protection and protection by means of international judicial proceedings constitute measures for the defence of the rights of the State. As the Permanent Court of International Justice has said and has repeated, "by taking up the case of one of its subjects and by resorting to diplomatic action or international judicial proceedings on his behalf, a State is in reality asserting its own rights—its right to ensure, in the person of its subjects, respect for the rules of international law" (P.C.I.J., Series A, No. 2, p. 12, and Series A/B, Nos. 20–21, p. 17).

Since this is the character which nationality must present when it is invoked to furnish the State which has granted it with a title to the exercise of protection and to the institution of international judicial proceedings, the Court must ascertain whether the nationality granted to Nottebohm by means of naturalization is of this character or, in other words, whether the factual connection between Nottebohm and Liechtenstein in the period preceding, contemporaneous with and following his naturalization appears to be sufficiently close, so preponderant in relation to any connection which may have existed between him and any other State, that it is possible to regard the nationality conferred upon him as real and effective, as the exact juridical expression of a social fact of a connection which existed previously or came into existence thereafter.

Naturalization is not a matter to be taken lightly. To seek and to obtain it is not something that happens frequently in the life of a human being. It involves his breaking a bond of allegiance and his establishment of a new bond of allegiance. It may have far-reaching consequences and involve profound changes in the destiny of the individual who obtains it. It concerns him personally, and to consider it only from the point of view of its repercussions with regard to his property would be to misunderstand its profound significance. In order to appraise its international effect, it is impossible to disregard the circumstances in which it was conferred, the serious character which attaches to it, the real and effective, and not merely the verbal preference of the individual seeking it for the country which grants it to him.

At the time of his naturalization does Nottebohm appear to have been more closely attached by his tradition, his establishment, his interests, his activities, his family ties, his intentions for the near future to Liechtenstein than to any other State?

The essential facts appear with sufficient clarity from the record. The Court considers it unnecessary to have regard to the documents purporting to show that Nottebohm had or had not retained his interests in Germany, or to have regard to the alternative submission of Guatemala relating to a request to Liechtenstein to produce further documents. It would further point out that the Government of Liechtenstein, in asking in its Final Conclusions for an adjournment of the oral proceedings and an opportunity to present further documents, did so only for the eventuality of the Application being held to be admissible and not for the purpose of throwing further light upon the question of the admissibility of the Application.

The essential facts are as follows:

At the date when he applied for naturalization Nottebohm had been a German national from the time of his birth. He had always retained his connections with members of his family who had remained in Germany and he had always had business connections with that country. His country had been at war for more than a month, and there is nothing to indicate that the application for naturalization then made by Nottebohm was motivated by any desire to dissociate himself from the Government of his country.

He had been settled in Guatemala for 34 years. He had carried on his activities there. It was the main seat of his interests. He returned there shortly after his naturalization, and it remained the centre of his interests and of his business activities. He stayed there until his removal as a result of war measures in 1943. He subsequently attempted to return there, and he now complains of Guatemala's refusal to admit him. There, too, were several members of his family who sought to safeguard his interests.

In contrast, his actual connections with Liechtenstein were extremely tenuous. No settled abode, no prolonged residence in that country at the time of his application for naturalization: the application indicates that he was paying a visit there and confirms the transient character of this visit by its request that the naturalization proceedings should be initiated and concluded without delay. No intention of settling there was shown at that time or realized in the ensuing weeks, months or years—on the contrary, he returned to Guatemala very shortly after his naturalization and showed every intention of remaining there. If Nottebohm went to Liechtenstein in 1946, this was because of the refusal of Guatemala to admit him. No indication is given of the grounds warranting the waiver of the condition of residence, required by the 1934 Nationality Law, which waiver was implicitly granted to him. There is no allegation of any economic interests or of any activities exercised or to be exercised in Liechtenstein, and no manifestation of any intention whatsoever to transfer all or some of his interests and his business activities to Liechtenstein. It is unnecessary in this connection to attribute much importance to the promise to pay the taxes levied at the time of his naturalization. the only links to be discovered between the Principality and Nottebohm are the short sojourns already referred to and the presence in Vaduz of one of his brothers: but his brother's presence is referred to in his application for naturalization only as a reference to his good conduct. Furthermore, other members of his family have asserted Nottebohm's desire to spend his old age in Guatemala.

These facts clearly establish, on the one hand, the absence of any bond of attachment between Nottebohm and Liechtenstein and, on the other hand, the existence of a long-standing and close connection between him and Guatemala, a link which his naturalization in no way weakened. That naturalization was not based on any real prior connection with Liechtenstein, nor did it in any way alter the manner of life of the person upon whom it was conferred in exceptional circumstances of speed and accommodation. In both respects, it was lacking in the genuineness requisite to an act of such importance, if it is to be entitled to be respected by a State in the position of Guatemala. It was granted without regard to the concept of nationality adopted in international relations.

Naturalization was asked for not so much for the purpose of obtaining a legal recognition of Nottebohm's membership in fact in the population of Liechtenstein, as it was to enable him to substitute for his status as a national of a belligerent State that of a national of a neutral State, with the sole aim of thus coming within the protection of Liechtenstein but not of becoming wedded to its traditions, its interests, its way of life or of assuming the obligations—other than fiscal obligations—and exercising the rights pertaining to the status thus acquired.

Guatemala is under no obligation to recognize a nationality granted in such circumstances. Liechtenstein consequently is not entitled to extend its protection to Nottebohm vis-à-vis Guatemala and its claim must, for this reason, be held to be inadmissible.

The Court is not therefore called upon to deal with the other pleas in bar put forward by Guatemala or the Conclusions of the Parties other than those on which it is adjudicating in accordance with the reasons indicated above.

For these reasons,

THE COURT,

by eleven votes to three,

Holds that the claim submitted by the Government of the Principality of Liechtenstein is inadmissible.

Notes and Questions

1. *State Responsibility.* The doctrine of state responsibility provides that a state is responsible for illegal injuries done to a national of a foreign state. In the *Mavrommatis Palestine Concessions Case*, 1924 P.C.I.J., Ser.

A, No. 2, the Greek government sued the United Kingdom for denial of contractual rights of a Greek national to operate public works in Jerusalem and Jaffa in the British mandate of Palestine. Answering the British objection that Mavrommatis was merely a private person, the Permanent Court of International Justice held:

> [I]t is true that the dispute was at first between a private person and a State—i.e. between M. Mavrommatis and Great Britain. Subsequently the Greek Government took up the case. The dispute then entered upon a new phase; it entered into the domain of international law, and became a dispute between two States.

Id. at 12.

2. *State Protection.* The counterpart of state responsibility is state protection, a doctrine permitting a state to protect its nationals. However, a state like Liechtenstein in the *Nottebohm Case* is under no legal obligation to protect Nottebohm. What reasons would there have been for Liechtenstein to go to the trouble and expense of suing Guatemala in the International Court? Was it because of the government's concern for Nottebohm? Because of the threat to Liechtenstein's reputation as a safe haven?

If Liechtenstein had refused to pursue Nottebohm's claim, how else could Nottebohm have sought redress? What were his chances for real success in Guatemala's courts? Liechtenstein's courts? Diplomatic negotiations? International arbitration?

3. *Nationality of Claims.* The ICJ is careful to state that Nottebohm's Liechtenstein nationality is not "opposable" to Guatemala, and that Liechtenstein cannot "extend its protection to Nottebohm vis-à-vis Guatemala." Does this leave open the possibility that Liechtenstein might effectively espouse Nottebohm's claims against other states?

Should the principle of "nationality of claims" and the associated notion that a state is "in reality asserting its own right" extend to issues other than standing? For example, do you think a successful claimant state should have to turn over proceeds obtained from a responsible state to the injured private citizen?

4. *Stateless Persons.* Do stateless people have rights? How can stateless individuals pursue claims against states for violating their rights? In Trop v. Dulles, 356 U.S. 86, 78 S.Ct. 590, 2 L.Ed.2d 630 (1958), the U.S. Supreme Court found that depriving a military deserter of his U.S. citizenship was a violation of the Eighth Amendment's protection against cruel and unusual punishment:

> There may be involved no physical mistreatment, no primitive torture. There is instead the total destruction of the individual's status in organized society. It is a form of punishment more primitive than torture, for it destroys for the individual the political existence that was centuries in the development. The punishment strips the citizen of his status in the national and international political community. His very existence is at the sufferance of the country in which he happens to find himself. * * * In short, the expatriate has lost the right to have rights.
>
> This punishment * * * subjects the individual to a fate of ever-increasing fear and distress. He knows not what discriminations may

be established against him, what proscriptions may be directed against him, and when and for what cause his existence in his native land may be terminated. He may be subject to banishment, a fate universally decried by civilized people. He is stateless, a condition deplored in the international community of democracies. * * *

The civilized nations of the world are in virtual unanimity that statelessness is not to be imposed as punishment for crime.

Id. at 101–02, 78 S.Ct. at 598–99, 2 L.Ed.2d at 642–43.

5. *Attribution*. For whose acts is a state liable? The case law illustrates the considerable reach of the state responsibility doctrine. In the *Janes Case*, Janes (U.S.A.) v. United Mexican States (1925), 4 U.N.R.I.A.A. 82, an international arbitral tribunal attributed responsibility to Mexico for the failure of Mexican authorities to exercise due diligence in their efforts to apprehend a mine company employee who in 1918 shot and killed Byron Janes, a U.S. citizen who was a superintendent of mines. The United Kingdom was held responsible in the Union Bridge Co. Case (1924), 6 U.N.R.I.A.A. 138, for the acts of a low-level railway official in South Africa who wrongly interfered with property belonging to a U.S. citizen in 1900 when the U.S. was a neutral during the Anglo–Boer War. The International Law Commission, after surveying state practice, judicial decisions, and the writings of publicists, has concluded that a state may be held responsible for the acts of all of its organs—executive, legislative, and judicial. International Law Commission, 2 *Yearbook of the International Law Commission* 194–95 (1973). Some cases also pose difficult questions about whether the actions of individuals or groups may be attributed to a state. In Yeager v. Iran, 17 Iran–U.S. Claims Tribunal Reports 92 (1987), Iran was held responsible for the actions of Revolutionary Guards when they harassed U.S. citizens out of their employment in the country.

THE BARCELONA TRACTION CASE

Case Concerning the Barcelona Traction, Light and Power Co., Limited, Second Phase, Belgium v. Spain, 1970 I.C.J. 3, 1970 WL 1.

8. The Barcelona Traction, Light and Power Company, Limited, is a holding company incorporated in 1911 in Toronto (Canada), where it has its head office. For the purpose of creating and developing an electric power production and distribution system in Catalonia (Spain), it formed a number of operating, financing, and concession-holding subsidiary companies. Three of these companies, whose shares it owned wholly or almost wholly, were incorporated under Canadian law and had their registered offices in Canada (Ebro Irrigation and Power Company, Limited, Catalonian Land Company, Limited and International Utilities Finance Corporation, Limited); the others were incorporated under Spanish law and had their registered offices in Spain. At the time of the outbreak of the Spanish Civil War the group, through its operating subsidiaries, supplied the major part of Catalonia's electricity requirements.

9. According to the Belgian Government, some years after the First World War Barcelona Traction's share capital came to be very largely

held by Belgian nationals—natural or juristic persons—and a very high percentage of the shares has since then continuously belonged to Belgian nationals, particularly the Société Internationale d'Energie Hydro–Electrique (Sidro), whose principal shareholder, the Société Financière de Transports et D'Entreprises Industrieles (Sofina), is itself a company in which Belgian interests are preponderant. The fact that large blocks of shares were for certain periods transferred to American nominees, to protect these securities in the event of invasion of Belgian territory during the Second World War, is not, according to the Belgian contention, of any relevance in this connection, as it was Belgian nationals, particularly Sidro, who continued to be the real owners. For a time the shares were vested in a trustee, but the Belgian Government maintains that the trust terminated in 1946. The Spanish Government contends, on the contrary, that the Belgian nationality of the shareholders is not proven and that the trustee or the nominees must be regarded as the true shareholders in the case of the shares concerned.

[Barcelona Traction issued bonds, most of which were in pounds sterling. It serviced the bonds through funds transferred to it from its subsidiaries operating in Spain. Interest payments were disrupted in 1936 by the Spanish Civil War. The Spanish Government refused to allow transfers of foreign currency, and interest payments on the sterling bonds were never resumed. Three Spanish holders of Barcelona Traction bonds obtained a bankruptcy declaration against Barcelona Traction in Spanish court because of its failure to pay interest on the bonds. The bankruptcy receiver seized the assets of Barcelona Traction, Ebro, and a Spanish subsidiary. Barcelona Traction, which did not receive proper notice of the proceedings, failed to enter a plea opposing the bankruptcy judgment, as was required under Spanish law, within the requisite time period. In 1949, trustees in bankruptcy created new shares of the subsidiaries, cancelled the shares located outside Spain, and decreed that the head offices of Ebro and Catalonian Land were in Barcelona rather than Toronto. In 1952, the trustees, operating under court authorization, sold all the shares of the subsidiaries at public auction.]

20. The British Government made representations to the Spanish Government on 23 February 1948 concerning the bankruptcy of Barcelona Traction and the seizure of its assets as well as those of Ebro and Barcelonesa, stating its interest in the situation of the bondholders resident in United Kingdom. It subsequently supported the representations made by the Canadian Government.

21. The Canadian Government made representations to the Spanish Government in a series of diplomatic notes, the first being dated 27 March 1948 and the last 21 April 1952; in addition, approaches were made on a less official level in July 1954 and March 1955. The Canadian Government first complained of the denials of justice said to have been committed in Spain towards Barcelona Traction, Ebro and National Trust, but it subsequently based its complaints more particularly on conduct towards the Ebro company said to be in breach of

certain treaty provisions applicable between Spain and Canada. The Spanish Government did not respond to a Canadian proposal for the submission of the dispute to arbitration and the Canadian Government subsequently confined itself, until the time when its interposition entirely ceased, to endeavoring to promote a settlement by agreement between the private groups concerned.

22. The United States Government made representations to the Spanish Government on behalf of Barcelona Traction in a note of 22 July 1949, in support of a note submitted by the Canadian Government the previous day. It subsequently continued its interposition through the diplomatic channel and by other means. Since references were made by the United States Government in these representations to the presence of American interests in Barcelona Traction, the Spanish Government draws the conclusion that, in the light of the customary practice of the United States Government to protect only substantial American investments abroad, the existence must be presumed of such large American interests as to rule out a preponderance of Belgian interests. The Belgian Government considers that the United States Government was motivated by a more general concern to secure equitable treatment of foreign investments in Spain, and in this context cites, *inter alia*, a note of 5 June 1967 from the United States Government.

23. The Spanish Government having stated in a note of 26 September 1949 that Ebro had not furnished proof as to the origin and genuineness of the bond debts, which justified the refusal of foreign currency transfers, the Belgian and Canadian Governments considered proposing to the Spanish Government the establishment of a tripartite committee to study the question. Before this proposal was made, the Spanish Government suggested in March 1950 the creation of a committee on which, in addition to Spain, only Canada and the United Kingdom would be represented. This proposal was accepted by the United Kingdom and Canadian Governments. The work of the committee led to a joint statement of 11 June 1951 by the three Governments to the effect, *inter alia*, that the attitude of the Spanish administration in not authorizing the transfers of foreign currency was fully justified. The Belgian Government protested against the fact that it had not been invited to nominate an expert to take part in the enquiry, and reserved its rights; in the proceedings before the Court it contended that the joint statement of 1951, which was based on the work of the committee, could not be set up against it, being *res inter alios acta*.

24. The Belgian Government made representations to the Spanish Government on the same day as the Canadian Government, in a note of 27 March 1948. It continued its diplomatic intervention until the rejection by the Spanish Government of a Belgian proposal for submission to arbitration (end of 1951). After the admission of Spain to membership in the United Nations (1955), which, as found by the Court in 1964, rendered operative again the clause of compulsory jurisdiction contained in the 1927 Hispano–Belgian Treaty of Conciliation, Judicial Settlement and Arbitration, the Belgian Government attempted further

representations. After the rejection of a proposal for a special agreement, it decided to refer the dispute unilaterally to this Court.

[The Spanish Government objected, *inter alia*, that the Belgian Government "lacked capacity to submit any claim in respect of wrongs done to a Canadian company, even if the shareholders were Belgian." The Court joins that objection to the merits.]

28. * * * The claim is presented on behalf of natural and juristic persons, alleged to be Belgian nationals and shareholders in the Barcelona Traction, Light and Power Company, Limited. The submissions of the Belgian Government make it clear that the object of its Application is reparation for damage allegedly caused to these persons by the conduct, said to be contrary to international law, of various organs of the Spanish State towards that company and various other companies in the same group. * * *

30. The States which the present case principally concerns are Belgium, the national State of the alleged shareholders, Spain, the State whose organs are alleged to have committed the unlawful acts complained of, and Canada, the State under whose law Barcelona Traction was incorporated and in whose territory it has its registered office ("head office" in the terms of the by-laws of Barcelona Traction). * * *

32. In these circumstances it is logical that the Court should first address itself to what was originally presented as the subject-matter of the third preliminary objection: namely the question of the right of Belgium to exercise diplomatic protection of Belgian shareholders in a company which is a juristic entity incorporated in Canada, the measures complained of having been taken in relation not to any Belgian national but to the company itself.

33. When a State admits into its territory foreign investments or foreign nationals, whether natural or juristic persons, it is bound to extend to them the protection of the law and assumes obligations concerning the treatment to be afforded them. These obligations, however, are neither absolute nor unqualified. In particular, an essential distinction should be drawn between the obligations of a State towards the international community as a whole, and those arising vis-à-vis another State in the field of diplomatic protection. By their very nature the former are the concern of all States. In view of the importance of the rights involved, all States can be held to have a legal interest in their protection; they are obligations *erga omnes*.

34. Such obligations derive, for example, in contemporary international law, from the outlawing of acts of aggression, and of genocide, as also from the principles and rules concerning the basic rights of the human person, including protection from slavery and racial discrimination. Some of the corresponding rights of protection have entered into the body of general international law (*Reservations to the Convention on the Prevention and Punishment of the Crime of Genocide, Advisory Opinion, I.C.J. Reports 1951*, p. 23); others are conferred by international instruments of a universal or quasi-universal character.

35. Obligations the performance of which is the subject of diplomatic protection are not of the same category. It cannot be held, when one such obligation in particular is in question, in a specific case, that all States have a legal interest in its observance. * * * In the present case it is therefore essential to establish whether the losses allegedly suffered by Belgian shareholders in Barcelona Traction were the consequence of the violation of obligations of which they were the beneficiaries. In other words: has a right of Belgium been violated on account of its nationals' having suffered infringement of their rights as share-holders in a company not of Belgian nationality?

36. Thus it is the existence or absence of a right, belonging to Belgium and recognized as such by international law, which is decisive for the problem of Belgium's capacity.

> "This right is necessarily limited to intervention [by a State] on behalf of its own nationals because, in the absence of a special agreement, it is the bond of nationality between the State and the individual which alone confers upon the State the right of diplomatic protection, and it is as a part of the function of diplomatic protection that the right to take up a claim and to ensure respect for the rules of international law must be envisaged." (*Panevezys-Saldutiskis Railway, Judgment, 1939, P.C.I.J., Series A/B, No. 76,* p. 16.)

It follows that the same question is determinant in respect of Spain's responsibility towards Belgium. Responsibility is the necessary corollary of a right. In the absence of any treaty on the subject between the Parties, this essential issue has to be decided in the light of the general rules of diplomatic protection. * * *

38. In this field international law is called upon to recognize institutions of municipal law that have an important and extensive role in the international field. This does not necessarily imply drawing any analogy between its own institutions and those of municipal law, nor does it amount to making rules of international law dependent upon categories of municipal law. All it means is that international law has had to recognize the corporate entity as an institution created by States in a domain essentially within their domestic jurisdiction. This in turn requires that, whenever legal issues arise concerning the rights of States with regard to the treatment of companies and shareholders, as to which rights international law has not established its own rules, it has to refer to the relevant rules of municipal law. Consequently, in view of the relevance to the present case of the rights of the corporate entity and its shareholders under municipal law, the Court must devote attention to the nature and interrelation of those rights.

39. Seen in historical perspective, the corporate personality represents a development brought about by new and expanding requirements in the economic field, an entity which in particular allows of operation in circumstances which exceed the normal capacity of individuals. As such it has become a powerful factor in the economic life of nations. Of this, municipal law has had to take due account, whence the increasing

volume of rules governing the creation and operation of corporate entities, endowed with a specific status. These entities have rights and obligations peculiar to themselves.

40. There is, however, no need to investigate the many different forms of legal entity provided for by the municipal laws of States, because the Court is concerned only with that exemplified by the company involved in the present case: Barcelona Traction—a limited liability company whose capital is represented by shares. * * *

41. Municipal law determines the legal situation not only of such limited liability companies but also of those persons who hold shares in them. Separated from the company by numerous barriers, the shareholder cannot be identified with it. The concept and structure of the company are founded on and determined by a firm distinction between the separate entity of the company and that of the shareholder, each with a distinct set of rights. The separation of property rights as between company and shareholder is an important manifestation of this distinction. So long as the company is in existence the shareholder has no right to the corporate assets.

42. It is a basic characteristic of the corporate structure that the company alone, through its directors or management acting in its name, can take action in respect of matters that are of a corporate character. The underlying justification for this is that, in seeking to serve its own best interests, the company will serve those of the shareholder too. Ordinarily, no individual shareholder can take legal steps, either in the name of the company or in his own name. If the shareholders disagree with the decisions taken on behalf of the company they may, in accordance with its articles or the relevant provisions of the law, change them or replace its officers, or take such action as is provided by law. Thus to protect the company against abuse by its management or the majority of shareholders, several municipal legal systems have vested in shareholders (sometimes a particular number is specified) the right to bring an action for the defence of the company, and conferred upon the minority of shareholders certain rights to guard against decisions affecting the rights of the company vis-à-vis its management or controlling shareholders. Nonetheless the shareholders' rights in relation to the company and its assets remain limited, this being, moreover, a corollary of the limited nature of their liability. * * *

44. Notwithstanding the separate corporate personality, a wrong done to the company frequently causes prejudice to its shareholders. But the mere fact that damage is sustained by both company and shareholder does not imply that both are entitled to claim compensation. * * * Thus whenever a shareholder's interests are harmed by an act done to the company, it is to the latter that he must look to institute appropriate action; for although two separate entities may have suffered from the same wrong, it is only one entity whose rights have been infringed. * * *

47. The situation is different if the act complained of is aimed at the direct rights of the shareholder as such. It is well known that there are rights which municipal law confers upon the latter distinct from those of the company, including the right to any declared dividend, the right to attend and vote at general meetings, the right to share in the residual assets of the company on liquidation. Whenever one of his direct rights is infringed, the shareholder has an independent right of action. * * *

48. The Belgian Government claims that shareholders of Belgian nationality suffered damage in consequence of unlawful acts of the Spanish authorities and, in particular, that the Barcelona Traction shares, though they did not cease to exist, were emptied of all real economic content. It accordingly contends that the shareholders had an independent right to redress, notwithstanding the fact that the acts complained of were directed against the company as such. Thus the legal issue is reducible to the question of whether it is legitimate to identify an attack on company rights, resulting in damage to shareholders, with the violation of their direct rights. * * *

50. In turning now to the international legal aspects of the case, the Court must, as already indicated, start from the fact that the present case essentially involves factors derived from municipal law—the distinction and the community between the company and the shareholder—which the Parties, however widely their interpretations may differ, each take as the point of departure of their reasoning. If the Court were to decide the case in disregard of the relevant institutions of municipal law it would, without justification, invite serious legal difficulties. It would lose touch with reality, for there are no corresponding institutions of international law to which the Court could resort. Thus the Court has, as indicated, not only to take cognizance of municipal law but also to refer to it. It is to rules generally accepted by municipal legal systems which recognize the limited company whose capital is represented by shares, and not to the municipal law of a particular State, that international law refers. * * *

52. International law may not, in some fields, provide specific rules in particular cases. In the concrete situation, the company against which allegedly unlawful acts were directed is expressly vested with a right, whereas no such right is specifically provided for the shareholder in respect of those acts. Thus the position of the company rests on a positive rule of both municipal and international law. As to the shareholder, while he has certain rights expressly provided for him by municipal law * * *, appeal can, in the circumstances of the present case, only be made to the silence of international law. Such silence scarcely admits of interpretation in favour of the shareholder. * * *

56. * * * [Municipal] law, confronted with economic realities, has had to provide protective measures and remedies in the interests of those within the corporate entity as well as of those outside who have dealings with it: the law has recognized that the independent existence of the

legal entity cannot be treated as an absolute. It is in this context that the process of "lifting the corporate veil" or "disregarding the legal entity" has been found justified and equitable in certain circumstances. * * *

64. * * * In this connection two particular situations must be studied: the case of the company having ceased to exist and the case of the company's national State lacking capacity to take action on its behalf.

65. As regards the first of these possibilities the Court observes that * * * Barcelona Traction has lost all its assets in Spain, and was placed in receivership in Canada, a receiver and manager having been appointed. * * * [F]rom the economic viewpoint the company has been entirely paralyzed. It has been deprived of all its Spanish sources of income, and the Belgian Government has asserted that the company could no longer find the funds for its legal defence, so that these had to be supplied by the shareholders.

66. It cannot however, be contended that the corporate entity of the company has ceased to exist, or that it has lost its capacity to take corporate action. * * * [A] precarious financial situation cannot be equated with the demise of the corporate entity, which is the hypothesis under consideration: the company's status in law is alone relevant, and not its economic condition * * *. Only in the event of the legal demise of the company are the shareholders deprived of the possibility of a remedy available through the company; it is only if they became deprived of all such possibility that an independent right of action for them and their government could arise.

67. In the present case, Barcelona Traction is in receivership in the country of incorporation. Far from implying the demise of the entity or of its rights, this much rather denotes that those rights are preserved for so long as no liquidation has ensued. Though in receivership, the company continues to exist. Moreover, it is a matter of public record that the company's shares were quoted on the stock-market at a recent date.

68. * * * [E]ven if the company is limited in its activity after being placed in receivership, there can be no doubt that it has retained its legal capacity and that the power to exercise it is vested in the manager appointed by the Canadian courts. The Court is thus not confronted with the first hypothesis contemplated in paragraph 64, and need not pronounce upon it.

69. The Court will now turn to the second possibility, that of the lack of capacity of the company's national State to act on its behalf. The first question which must be asked here is whether Canada—the third apex of the triangular relationship—is, in law, the national State of Barcelona Traction.

70. In allocating corporate entities to States for purposes of diplomatic protection, international law is based, but only to a limited extent,

on an analogy with the rules governing the nationality of individuals. The traditional rule attributes the right of diplomatic protection of a corporate entity to the State under the laws of which it is incorporated and in whose territory it has its registered office. These two criteria have been confirmed by long practice and by numerous international instruments. This notwithstanding, further or different links are at times said to be required in order that a right of diplomatic protection should exist. Indeed, it has been the practice of some States to give a company incorporated under their law diplomatic protection solely when it has its seat (*siège social*) or management or centre of control in their territory, or when a majority or a substantial proportion of the shares has been owned by nationals of the State concerned. Only then, it has been held, does there exist between the corporation and the State in question a genuine connection of the kind familiar from other branches of international law. However, in the particular field of the diplomatic protection of corporate entities, no absolute test of the "genuine connection" has found general acceptance. Such tests as have been applied are of a relative nature, and sometimes links with one State have had to be weighed against those with another. In this connection reference has been made to the *Nottebohm* case. * * * However, given both the legal and factual aspects of protection in the present case the Court is of the opinion that there can be no analogy with the issues raised or the decision given in that case.

71. In the present case, it is not disputed that the company was incorporated in Canada and has its registered office in that country. The incorporation of the company under the law of Canada was an act of free choice. Not only did the founders of the company seek its incorporation under Canadian law but it has remained under that law for a period of over 50 years. It has maintained in Canada its registered office, its accounts and its share registers. Board meetings were held there for many years; it has been listed in the records of the Canadian tax authorities. Thus a close and permanent connection has been established, fortified by the passage of over half a century. This connection is in no way weakened by the fact that the company engaged from the very outset in commercial activities outside Canada, for that was its declared object. Barcelona Traction's links with Canada are thus manifold.

72. Furthermore, the Canadian nationality of the company has received general recognition. Prior to the institution of proceedings before the Court, three other governments apart from that of Canada (those of the United Kingdom, the United States and Belgium) made representations concerning the treatment accorded to Barcelona Traction by the Spanish authorities. The United Kingdom Government intervened on behalf of bondholders and of shareholders. Several representations were also made by the United States Government, but not on behalf of the Barcelona Traction company as such. * * *

74. * * * The Belgian Government admitted the Canadian character of the company in the course of the present proceedings. It explicitly

stated that Barcelona Traction was a company of neither Spanish nor Belgian nationality but a Canadian company incorporated in Canada. The Belgian Government has even conceded that it was not concerned with the injury suffered by Barcelona Traction itself, since that was Canada's affair.

76. * * * [F]rom 1948 onwards the Canadian Government made to the Spanish Government numerous representations which cannot be viewed otherwise than as the exercise of diplomatic protection in respect of the Barcelona Traction company. Therefore this was not a case where diplomatic protection was refused or remained in the sphere of fiction. It is also clear that over the whole period of its diplomatic activity the Canadian Government proceeded in full knowledge of the Belgian attitude and activity.

77. It is true that at a certain point the Canadian Government ceased to act on behalf of Barcelona Traction, for reasons which have not been fully revealed, though a statement made in a letter of 19 July 1955 by the Canadian Secretary of State for External Affairs suggests that it felt the matter should be settled by means of private negotiations. The Canadian Government has nonetheless retained its capacity to exercise diplomatic protection; no legal impediment has prevented it from doing so: no fact has arisen to render this protection impossible. It has discontinued its action of its own free will.

78. The Court would here observe that, within the limits prescribed by international law, a State may exercise diplomatic protection by whatever means and to whatever extent it thinks fit, for it is its own right that the State is asserting. Should the natural or legal persons on whose behalf it is acting consider that their rights are not adequately protected, they have no remedy in international law. All they can do is to resort to municipal law, if means are available, with a view to furthering their cause or obtaining redress. The municipal legislator may lay upon the State an obligation to protect its citizens abroad, and may also confer upon the national a right to demand the performance of that obligation, and clothe the right with corresponding sanctions. However, all these questions remain within the province of municipal law and do not affect the position internationally.

79. The State must be viewed as the sole judge to decide whether its protection will be granted, to what extent it is granted, and when it will cease. It retains in this respect a discretionary power the exercise of which may be determined by considerations of a political or other nature, unrelated to the particular case. Since the claim of the State is not identical with that of the individual or corporate person whose cause is espoused, the State enjoys complete freedom of action. Whatever the reasons for any change of attitude, the fact cannot in itself constitute a justification for the exercise of diplomatic protection by another government, unless there is some independent and otherwise valid ground for that.

80. This cannot be regarded as amounting to a situation where a violation of law remains without remedy: in short, a legal vacuum. There is no obligation upon the possessors of rights to exercise them. Sometimes no remedy is sought, though rights are infringed. To equate this with the creation of a vacuum would be to equate a right with an obligation. * * *

92. Since the general rule on the subject does not entitle the Belgian Government to put forward a claim in this case, the question remains to be considered whether nonetheless, as the Belgian Government has contended during the proceedings, considerations of equity do not require that it be held to possess a right of protection. * * * [A] theory has been developed to the effect that the State of the shareholders has a right of diplomatic protection when the State whose responsibility is invoked is the national State of the company. Whatever the validity of this theory may be, it is certainly not applicable to the present case, since Spain is not the national State of Barcelona Traction.

93. On the other hand, the Court considers that, in the field of diplomatic protection as in all other fields of international law, it is necessary that the law be applied reasonably. It has been suggested that if in a given case it is not possible to apply the general rule that the right of diplomatic protection of a company belongs to its national State, considerations of equity might call for the possibility of protection of the shareholders in question by their own national State. This hypothesis does not correspond to the circumstances of the present case.

94. In view, however, of the discretionary nature of diplomatic protection, considerations of equity cannot require more than the possibility for some protector State to intervene, whether it be the national State of the company, by virtue of the general rule mentioned above, or, in a secondary capacity, the national State of the shareholders who claim protection. In this connection, account should also be taken of the practical effects of deducing from considerations of equity any broader right of protection for the national State of the shareholders. It must first of all be observed that it would be difficult on an equitable basis to make distinctions according to any quantitative test: it would seem that the owner of 1 per cent. and the owner of 90 per cent. of the share-capital should have the same possibility of enjoying the benefit of diplomatic protection. The protector State may, of course, be disinclined to take up the case of the single small shareholder, but it could scarcely be denied the right to do so in the name of equitable considerations. In that field, protection by the national State of the shareholders can hardly be graduated according to the absolute or relative size of the shareholding involved.

95. The Belgian Government, it is true, has also contended that as high a proportion as 88 per cent. of the shares in Barcelona traction belonged to natural or juristic persons of Belgian nationality, and it has used this as an argument for the purpose not only of determining the amount of the damages which it claims, but also of establishing its right

of action on behalf of the Belgian shareholders. Nevertheless, this does not alter the Belgian Government's position * * * which implies, in the last analysis, that it might be sufficient for one single share to belong to a national of a given State for the latter to be entitled to exercise its diplomatic protection.

96. The Court considers that the adoption of the theory of diplomatic protection of shareholders as such, by opening the door to competing diplomatic claims, could create an atmosphere of confusion and insecurity in international economic relations. The danger would be all the greater inasmuch as the shares of companies whose activity is international are widely scattered and frequently change hands. It might perhaps be claimed that, if the right of protection belonging to the national States of the shareholders were considered as only secondary to that of the national State of the company, there would be less danger of difficulties of the kind contemplated. However, the Court must state that the essence of a secondary right is that it only comes into existence at the time when the original right ceases to exist. As the right of protection vested in the national State of the company cannot be regarded as extinguished because it is not exercised, it is not possible to accept the proposition that in case of its non-exercise the national States of the shareholders have a right of protection secondary to that of the national State of the company. Furthermore, study of factual situations in which this theory might possibly be applied gives rise to the following observations.

97. The situations in which foreign shareholders in a company wish to have recourse to diplomatic protection by their own national State may vary. It may happen that the national State of the company simply refuses to grant it its diplomatic protection, or that it begins to exercise it (as in the present case) but does not pursue its action to the end. It may also happen that the national State of the company and the State which has committed a violation of international law with regard to the company arrive at a settlement of the matter, by agreeing on compensation for the company, but that the foreign shareholders find the compensation insufficient. Now, as a matter of principle, it would be difficult to draw a distinction between these three cases so far as the protection of foreign shareholders by their national State is concerned, since in each case they may have suffered real damage. Furthermore, the national State of the company is perfectly free to decide how far it is appropriate for it to protect the company, and is not bound to make public the reasons for its decision. To reconcile this discretionary power of the company's national State with a right of protection falling to the shareholders' national State would be particularly difficult when the former State has concluded, with the State which has contravened international law with regard to the company, an agreement granting the company compensation which the foreign shareholders find inadequate. If, after such a settlement, the national State of the foreign shareholders could in its turn put forward a claim based on the same facts, this would be likely to introduce into the negotiation of this kind of

agreement a lack of security which would be contrary to the stability which it is the object of international law to establish in international relations. * * *

99. * * * [T]he promoters of a company whose operations will be international must take into account the fact that States have, with regard to their nationals, a discretionary power to grant diplomatic protection or to refuse it. When establishing a company in a foreign country, its promoters are normally impelled by particular considerations; it is often a question of tax or other advantages offered by the host State. It does not seem to be in any way inequitable that the advantages thus obtained should be balanced by the risks arising from the fact that the protection of the company and hence of its shareholders is thus entrusted to a State other than the national State of the shareholders.

100. In the present case, it is clear from what has been said above that Barcelona Traction was never reduced to a position of impotence such that it could not have approached its national State, Canada, to ask for its diplomatic protection, and that, as far as appeared to the Court, there was nothing to prevent Canada from continuing to grant its diplomatic protection to Barcelona Traction if it had considered that it should do so.

101. For the above reasons, the Court is not of the opinion that, in the particular circumstances of the present case, *jus standi* is conferred on the Belgian Government by considerations of equity. * * *

102. * * * The Court fully appreciates the importance of the legal problems raised by the allegation, which is at the root of the Belgian claim for reparation, concerning the denials of justice allegedly committed by organs of the Spanish State. However, the possession by the Belgian Government of a right of protection is a prerequisite for the examination of these problems. Since no *jus standi* before the Court has been established, it is not for the Court in its Judgment to pronounce upon any other aspect of the case, on which it should take a decision only if the Belgian Government had a right of protection in respect of its nationals, shareholders in Barcelona Traction.

103. Accordingly,

THE COURT

rejects the Belgian Government's claim by fifteen votes to one, twelve votes of the majority being based on the reasons set out in the present Judgment.

Notes and Questions

1. *Expropriation. Barcelona Traction* illustrates some of the problems involved in protecting a foreign branch or subsidiary from discriminatory treatment by the host country, even from out-right expropriation. A foreign expropriation can be blatant, for example, the expropriation by Cuba of United States sugar interests in Banco Nacional de Cuba v. Sabbatino, 376

U.S. 398, 84 S.Ct. 923, 11 L.Ed.2d 804 (1964), which we explore in the materials about the act of state doctrine in Chapter 10. Foreign expropriations, however, can also be rather more subtle.

In his two-part tale of *Barcelona Traction* in *The New Yorker*, John Brooks puts a face to the expropriation, that of "Juan March—the former smuggler who in the nineteen-twenties had become one of the richest men in Spain and in the nineteen-thirties had been the chief private financier of the counter-revolution that had put Francisco Franco in power." John Brooks, "Annals of Finance: Privateer—II," *The New Yorker*, May 28, 1979, at 42, 42. Juan March's maneuvers led a court in a small town in Spain to declare the Barcelona Traction Company bankrupt. The 1948 bankruptcy decree was issued despite the fact that the company had shown net profits of $3.7 million in the previous year and had sufficient cash on hand to pay off its debts. "[L]ater evidence strongly suggested [that] the complainants, the trustees in bankruptcy, and the judge himself were all allies of the man seeking to seize the company, Juan March." John Brooks, "Annals of Finance: Privateer—I," *The New Yorker*, May 21, 1979, at 42, 42–43.

2. *Diplomatic Protection*. The Barcelona Traction, Light and Power Co., Limited, was incorporated in Canada, as were some, though not all, of its subsidiaries. Its operating assets were, however, virtually all in Spain. What would be the advantages and disadvantages of Canadian incorporation for foreign investors? Certainly, one advantage would be the possibility of triggering the diplomatic intercession of the Canadian government in any investment dispute with Spain. How did Canada actually come to the aid of the expropriated company?

3. *The Jurisdiction of the ICJ*. Unlike Belgium, which had a treaty with Spain providing for the possible submission of disputes to the International Court of Justice, Canada had no way to bring Spain before the ICJ. Is it any wonder that Spain would not agree to an *ad hoc* case between it and Canada? Can the Belgian suit in the ICJ be viewed as a way to circumvent the obstacle posed by Spain's unwillingness to go to court with Canada? Does the ICJ's judgment take this obstacle of non-consent at all into account?

4. *Obtaining Justice for Barcelona Traction*. Is it equitable for Spain to, first, prevent a solvent Spanish company from paying its obligations denominated in foreign currency, second, through its judicial process declare the company bankrupt, and, third, sell the company's assets to domestic purchasers, thereby depriving the foreign shareholders of their stake in the company? Besides going to the ICJ, how did the foreign shareholders complain both inside and outside Spain? What other avenues of protest, legal or political, might they have followed?

5. *Genuine Link*. Should the ICJ adopt a *Nottebohm* genuine link requirement with respect to corporations? Some corporations are only technically incorporated in one state. They may have their headquarters and many operations in a second state, with shareholders and managers domiciled there. Which state should be able to pursue an international claim on the corporation's behalf for injury caused by a third state? Judge Jessup, who wrote a concurring opinion in *Barcelona Traction*, accepts the genuine link theory, and rejects Great Britain, the United States, and

Canada as claimants because their connections with Barcelona Traction are transitory and nominal. Belgium, he finds, might have a "genuine link" with the company because Belgian nationals beneficially own 88 per cent of the company's shares. Nevertheless, Belgium's claim fails because there was no continuous Belgian interest between the time injury was inflicted and the date Belgium "espoused" the claim. See 1970 I.C.J. at 200, 203. Judge Jessup finds that on the date of injury—which he deems to be February 12, 1948, the date of the bankruptcy decree—the Belgian shares are still held in trust by a U.S. corporation, which has legal title to and full control of the shares. Thus, he concludes, the claim is not Belgian in character at the critical date of injury. Does this suggest a flaw in the use of a "genuine link" approach? Are the problems with allowing all interested states—the state of incorporation and the states of any shareholders—to exercise rights of protection before the Court in fact insoluble?

B. INDIVIDUALS AS SUBJECTS OF INTERNATIONAL LAW

MARK W. JANIS, "INDIVIDUALS AS SUBJECTS OF INTERNATIONAL LAW"

17 *Cornell International Law Journal* 61 (1984).

Legal positivism has long provided the usual theory for comprehending international law. The typical positivist definition of international law is grounded on a subject-based differentiation between international and municipal rules. Positivism views international law as a set of rules with states as its subjects. Municipal law is thought of as pertaining to individuals who are subjects of a single state. * * *

Before positivism, there was no theoretical insistence that the rules of the law of nations applied only to states. William Blackstone reflected the sentiment of the middle eighteenth century. For Blackstone, individuals and states were both proper subjects of the law of nations. He drew no dividing line between what later came to be called public and private international law. Blackstone distinguished his law of nations from other sorts of law not on the basis of its subjects but because of its sources. He saw the rules of the law of nations as universal, emanating either from natural justice or from the practice of many states. Municipal legal rules, however, emanated from a single state.

In 1789, Jeremy Bentham created the term "international law" in his *Introduction to the Principles of Morals and Legislation*. Bentham defined the new concept as the law which relates to "the mutual transactions between sovereigns as such." He thought that "as to any transactions which may take place between individuals who are subjects of different states, these are regulated by the internal laws, and decided upon by the internal tribunals" of individual sovereign states. Categorizing laws on the basis of "the persons whose conduct is the object of the law," Bentham concluded that international law had only states as its subjects. While categorizing rules on the basis of the subjects to be governed is logical enough, it plainly was wrong for Bentham to assume that international law so defined was equivalent to the traditional law of nations.[8] There were significant differences between the two.

Two early nineteenth century positivists promoted the notion that the individual was not a proper subject of international law. Joseph Story, complaining that no treatises existed on the subject, crafted "private" international law to parallel Bentham's "public" international law. Public international law went to international matters affecting states, while private international law concerned international matters between individuals. John Austin argued that because public international law claimed to regulate matters between sovereign states which as sovereigns could not be regulated by any outside authority, international law was just a form of "positive morality" and not really law at all.

Legal positivism had taken the eighteenth century law of nations, a law common to individuals and states, and transformed it into public and private international law. The former was deemed to apply to states, the latter to individuals. Positivists scorned both sides of the discipline. Public international law was "international" but not really "law." Private international law was "law" but not really "international." Even so insightful a modern positivist as H.L.A. Hart assumed that the essence of international law was that it addressed states. Although Hart saw persuasive similarities between international and municipal law, he accepted uncritically Bentham's subject-based approach to the field.

The positivist definition of international law has had an enormous impact on modern perceptions concerning the individual and international law.[14] With few exceptions, the theory rejects the notion that

8. Bentham knew that he was creating a new term, but he thought that he was simply substituting one term for another without changing the scope of the field:

> The word *international*, it must be acknowledged, is a new one; though, it is hoped, sufficiently analogous and intelligible. It is calculated to express, in a more significant way, the branch of law which goes commonly under the name of the *law of nations*: an appellation so uncharacteristic, that, were it not for the force of custom, it would seem rather to refer to internal jurisprudence.

J. BENTHAM, AN INTRODUCTION TO THE PRINCIPLES OF MORALS AND LEGISLATION 296 (J. Burns & H.L.A. Hart eds. 1970).

14. The following are but a few examples: "[In international law] the whole social body is united into one sovereign independent state, and only its relations with other such bodies are the subject of its investigations." J.T. ABDY, in KENT'S COMMENTARY ON INTERNATIONAL LAW 7 (1866); "International law may be defined as *the rules which determine* the conduct of the general body of civilized states in their mutual dealings." T.J. LAWRENCE, THE PRINCIPLES OF INTERNATIONAL LAW 1 (4th ed. 1910); "The exclusive business of International Law is to define the Rights and Duties of each State with reference to the rest." T.E. HOLLAND, LECTURES ON INTERNATIONAL LAW 53 (1933); "International law consists of a body of rules governing the relations between states." 1 G. HACKWORTH, DIGEST OF INTERNATIONAL LAW 1 (1940); "The term international law may be fairly employed to designate the principles and rules of conduct declaratory thereof which States feel themselves bound to observe, and therefore, do commonly observe in their relations with each other." C.C. HYDE, 1 INTERNATIONAL LAW CHIEFLY AS INTERPRETED AND APPLIED BY UNITED STATES 1 (2d ed. 1947); "The Law of Nations, or International Law, may be defined as the body of rules and principles of action which are binding upon civilized states in their relations with one another." J.L. BRIERLY, individuals are proper subjects of public international law. Originally, the subject-based approach was merely Bentham's attempt to provide a rational way of explaining that law may have different subjects: individuals and states. While law can be categorized on the basis of its subjects, in practice the law of nations and international law have concerned more than the legal rights of states. * * *

A prominent example of the failure of positivism to describe adequately the reality of the individual as a subject of international law comes from the time of Bentham himself. In *Respublica v. De Longchamps*, an American municipal court indicted the defendant for assaulting the Consul General of France to the new United States. It was held that the case "must be determined on the principles of the laws of nations." There was, following Blackstone, no doubt that an individual could be guilty of an infraction of the law of nations. De Longchamps, for his violation of the law of nations, was ordered to pay a fine of one hundred French crowns to the Commonwealth of Pennsylvania and to be imprisoned for "a little more" than two years.

Even during the high tide of positivism, the United States Supreme Court had no difficulty seeing individuals as subjects of international law. In *The Paquete Habana*, the United States Navy had seized two Cuban fishing smacks in the opening days of the Spanish–American War. A lower federal court condemned the boats as prizes of war. The masters for themselves, their crews, and their owners, argued before the Supreme Court that peaceful fishing craft were exempt from seizure under the rules of international law. In perhaps the most famous statement ever made about international law by a United States court, the Supreme Court held that "[i]nternational law is part of our law, and must be ascertained and administered by the courts of justice of appropriate jurisdiction, as often as questions of right depending upon it are duly presented for their determination." The Court held that:

> By an ancient usage among civilized nations, beginning centuries ago, and gradually ripening into a rule of international law, coast fishing vessels, pursuing their vocation of catching and bringing in fresh fish, have been recognized as exempt, with their cargoes and crews, from capture as prize of war.

Individuals had a right to rely on this rule as against the United States. The Court ordered the government to pay over the proceeds of the sale of the vessels and their cargoes to the individual claimants.

THE LAW OF NATIONS 1 (6th ed. 1963). Brierly accepts Bentham's equation of the law of nations and international law.

> International law has been defined as the body of "rules which are considered legally binding by states with each other," or "the principles which are in force between all independent nations." While some would see law as much more than—or even something different from—"rules" or "principles," there is common acceptance that international law is that law which governs relations between states, the basic units in the world political system during more than 300 years.

L. HENKIN, R.C. PUGH, O. SCHACHTER & H. SMIT, INTERNATIONAL LAW CASES AND MATERIALS LVII (1980).

However inadequately subject-based theory accounted for individual rights and obligations in international law in the eighteenth and nineteenth centuries, positivism has done an even poorer job in explaining the practices of the twentieth century. The trials of Nazi war criminals after the Second World War highlighted the limitations of positivism. Faced with the excesses of a seemingly "civilized" state, those formulating and applying international law discarded any pretense that international rules applied only to state behavior.

The Charter of the International Military Tribunal at Nuremberg explicitly made individuals subject to international rules relating to crimes against peace, war crimes, and crimes against humanity. At Nuremberg and in other war trials, thousands of individuals were tried and convicted; hundreds were executed. Nuremberg re-established plainly and forcefully that the rules of international law should and do apply to individuals. The Nuremberg Tribunal held that "[c]rimes against international law are committed by men, not by abstract entities, and only by punishing individuals who commit such crimes can the provisions of international law be enforced." * * *

All of these examples—*De Longchamps*, *Paquete Habana*, the Nuremberg trials, the European and American human rights systems, the European Economic Community, and *Filartiga*—demonstrate that a large and important part of international law practice establishes individual rights and obligations and provides international and municipal procedures for enforcing these rights and obligations. The reality of practice contradicts the positivist insistence that international law applies only to relations among states. Insofar as the purpose of theory is to describe reality, the positivist, subject-based theory is inadequate.

Furthermore, restricting international law to states fails a second test by which positivism may be measured—its prescriptive worth. Surely, it is counter to the proper values of international law to prescribe that individuals may not be the subjects of international law. It was, at the time of the Nuremberg trials, politically and morally unacceptable to say that individuals within the German State between 1933 and 1945 were subjects only of German law to whom international rights and obligations could not pertain. In light of the atrocities of Nazi Germany, it would have been reprehensible to leave victims without legal rights and perpetrators without legal obligations. The lesson of Nuremberg is that there are individual international rights and obligations that transcend state boundaries.

Similar considerations pertain to international communities such as the Council of Europe and the European Economic Community. These groups have recognized the need to extend certain basic human and economic rights and obligations directly to individuals even though these rights and obligations emanate not from municipal law but from international law. Given the difficulty of addressing some issues, such as human rights and economic development, through municipal legal systems alone, such an extension of international law rules to individuals makes sense. It is impressive that, with the European Human Rights system and the legal system of the E.E.C., the Europeans have begun to open international legal processes to individuals.

It is wrong, both in terms of describing reality and in terms of preferential expression, for the theory of international law to hold that individuals are outside the ambit of international law rules. Individuals are and should be within this realm. The positivist notion that individuals are not fit subjects for international law springs not from a description of reality, but from a jurisprudential philosophy most concerned with a subject-based categorization of types of law. In so categorizing international law, the positivist theorists simply discarded the more inclusive notions of the law of nations. Whatever the impact of positivist theory, it never absolutely represented the practice of any time. Today, reality and preference have so revealed the weakness and obsolescence of subject-based theory that the sooner we rid ourselves of it the better. * * *

If we reject the positivist's subject-based definition of international law, then what should be our new concept of the nature of international law? What are the objections to reverting to Blackstone's understanding that the discipline should be characterized by its reliance on universal and multinational sources?

One might say that, so characterized, international law is not properly "inter-national," but this is a rather superficial problem. Bentham supposed international law to be the equivalent of the law of nations, but it was not. So, the fault, if any, in matching the term and the content of international law must rest with its creator. We could easily use the old term, law of nations, and eliminate the linguistic quibble. But the term "international law" is too much in use to abandon it now. I suggest that we continue using the word international but understand "nation" to mean not only the national state but also the individuals who are the nationals of state. This meaning is both true to the word "nation" and finally makes sense of Bentham's equivalence between the law of nations and international law.

Note: The Protection of Human Rights in Municipal Law

The principle that law should protect the rights of individuals against the abuses of governments can at least be dated back to John Locke's *Two Treatises of Government* published in 1690. Locke believed that human rights, not governments, came first in the natural order of things:

> If Man in the State of Nature be so free, as has been said; If he be absolute Lord of his own Person and Possessions, equal to the greatest, and subject to no Body, why will he part with his Freedom? Why will he give up this Empire, and subject himself to the Dominion and Controul of any other Power? To which 'tis obvious to Answer, that though in the state of Nature he hath such a right, yet the Enjoyment of it is very uncertain, and constantly exposed to the Invasion of others. For all being Kings as much as he, every Man his Equal, and the greater part no strict Observers of Equity and Justice, the enjoyment of the

> property he has in this state is very unsafe, very unsecure. This makes him willing to quit a Condition, which however free, is full of fears and continual dangers: And 'tis not without reason, that he seeks out, and is willing to joyn in Society with others who are already united, or have a mind to unite for the mutual *Preservation* of their Lives, Liberties and Estates.

John Locke, *Two Treatises of Government*, Book II, Chapter IX, section 123, at 395 (Peter Laslett rev.ed. 1963).

Locke's prose celebrated the rights to life, liberty, and property of the English under the limited government won by the Glorious Revolution of 1688. The particular advantages of England's unwritten constitution in the 18th century, especially the separation and balance of powers among the executive, legislative and judicial branches of government, were elaborated and popularized by the French political philosopher, Montesquieu, in the *Spirit of the Laws* in 1748. In 1762, the revolutionary potential of human rights—"Man is born free; and everywhere he is in chains"—was proclaimed by Jean Jacques Rousseau. Democratic revolutions soon followed in America and throughout Europe.

On July 4, 1776, the American Declaration of Independence issued from Philadelphia. The intellectual influences of Locke, Montesquieu, and Rousseau on Thomas Jefferson's document were plain to see. In a ringing affirmation of human rights and the duty of governments to protect them, the delegates of the thirteen United States of America proclaimed:

> We hold these truths to be self-evident, that all men are created equal, that they are endowed by their Creator with certain unalienable Rights, that among these are Life, Liberty and the pursuit of Happiness. That to secure these rights, Governments are instituted among Men, deriving their just powers from the consent of the governed. That whenever any Form of Government becomes destructive of these ends, it is the Right of the People to alter or to abolish it, and to institute new Government, laying its foundation on such principles and organizing its powers in such form, as to them shall seem most likely to effect their Safety and Happiness.

The last decades of the 18th century were a good time for political affirmations of human rights. As the constitutions of the newly independent American states were drafted in 1776, bills of rights enumerating specific rights were directly incorporated therein, even, as for Virginia, making up its first part. The fashion of bills of rights spread to Europe. Jefferson wrote James Madison from Paris on January 12, 1789: "Everybody here is trying their hands at forming declarations of rights." Thomas Jefferson, Letter of Jan. 12, 1789, 14 *The Papers of Thomas Jefferson* 436, 437 (Julian P. Boyd ed. 1958). Jefferson continued to play his part, reading and critiquing Lafayette's draft of what on August 27, 1789, a few weeks after the fall of the Bastille, would become the National Assembly's Declaration of the Rights of Man and Citizen. Thomas Jefferson, Letter of June 3, 1789, to Rabaut de St. Etienne, 15 *id.* at 166. The French Declaration's indebtedness to Rousseau's philosophy and Philadelphia's practice was widely acknowledged.

The French Declaration of the Rights of Man and Citizen recognized and proclaimed "in the presence and under the auspices of the Supreme Being, the following rights":

1. Men are born and remain free and equal in rights; social distinctions may be based only upon general usefulness.

2. The aim of every political association is the preservation of the natural and inalienable rights of man; these rights are liberty, property, security, and resistance to oppression.

3. The source of all sovereignty resides essentially in the nation; no group, no individual may exercise authority not emanating expressly therefrom.

4. Liberty consists of the power to do whatever is not injurious to others; thus the enjoyment of the natural rights of every man has for its limits only those that assure other members of society the enjoyment of those same rights; such limits may be determined only by law.

5. The law has the right to forbid only actions which are injurious to society. Whatever is not forbidden by law may not be prevented, and no one may be constrained to do what it does not prescribe.

6. Law is the expression of the general will; all citizens have the right to concur personally, or through their representatives, in its formation; it must be the same for all, whether it protects or punishes. All citizens, being equal before it, are equally admissible to all public offices, positions, and employments, according to their capacity, and without other distinction than that of virtues and talents.

7. No man may be accused, arrested, or detained except in the cases determined by law, and according to the forms prescribed thereby. Whoever solicit, expedite, or execute arbitrary orders, or have them executed, must be punished; but every citizen summoned or apprehended in pursuance of the law must obey immediately; he renders himself culpable by resistance.

8. The law is to establish only penalties that are absolutely and obviously necessary; and no one may be punished except by virtue of a law established and promulgated prior to the offence and legally applied.

9. Since every man is presumed innocent until declared guilty, if arrest be deemed indispensable, all unnecessary severity for securing the person of the accused must be severely repressed by law.

10. No one is to be disquieted because of his opinions, even religious, provided their manifestation does not disturb the public order established by law.

11. Free communication of ideas and opinions is one of the most precious of the rights of man. Consequently, every citizen may speak, write, and print freely, subject to responsibility for the abuse of such liberty in the cases determined by law.

12. The guarantee of the rights of man and citizen necessitates a public force; such a force, therefore, is instituted for the advantage of all and not for the particular benefit of those to whom it is entrusted.

> 13. For the maintenance of the public force and for the expenses of administration a common tax is indispensable; it must be assessed equally on all citizens in proportion to their means.
>
> 14. Citizens have the right to ascertain, by themselves or through their representatives, the necessity of the public tax, to consent to it freely, to supervise its use, and to determine its quota, assessment, payment, and duration.
>
> 15. Society has the right to require of every public agent an accounting of his administration.
>
> 16. Every society in which the guarantee of rights is not assured or the separation of powers not determined has no constitution at all.
>
> 17. Since property is a sacred and inviolable right, no one may be deprived thereof unless a legally established public necessity obviously requires it, and upon condition of a just and previous indemnity.

On September 25, 1789, less than a month after the promulgation of the French Declaration, the first Congress of the new Federal Government of the United States of America proposed the first ten amendments to the United States Constitution. These came into force following the tenth state ratification (Virginia's) on December 15, 1791:

> 1. Congress shall make no law respecting an establishment of religion, or prohibiting the free exercise thereof; or abridging the freedom of speech, or of the press; or the right of the people peaceably to assemble, and to petition the Government for a redress of grievances.
>
> 2. A well regulated Militia, being necessary to the security of a free State, the right of the people to keep and bear Arms, shall not be infringed.
>
> 3. No Soldier shall, in time of peace be quartered in any house, without the consent of the Owner, nor in time of war, but in a manner to be prescribed by law.
>
> 4. The right of the people to be secure in their persons, houses, papers, and effects, against unreasonable searches and seizures, shall not be violated, and no Warrants shall issue, but upon probable cause, supported by Oath or affirmation, and particularly describing the place to be searched, and the persons or things to be seized.
>
> 5. No person shall be held to answer for a capital, or otherwise infamous crime, unless on a presentment or indictment of a Grand Jury, except in cases arising in the land or naval forces, or in the Militia, when in actual service in time of War or public danger; nor shall any person be subject for the same offence to be twice put in jeopardy of life or limb, nor shall be compelled in any criminal case to be a witness against himself, nor be deprived of life, liberty, or property, without due process of law; nor shall private property be taken for public use, without just compensation.
>
> 6. In all criminal prosecutions, the accused shall enjoy the right to a speedy and public trial, by an impartial jury of the State and district wherein the crime shall have been committed, which district shall have been previously ascertained by law, and to be informed of the nature

and cause of the accusation; to be confronted with the witnesses against him; to have compulsory process for obtaining Witnesses in his favor, and to have the Assistance of Counsel for his defence.

7. In Suits at common law, where the value in controversy shall exceed twenty dollars, the right of trial by jury shall be preserved, and no fact tried by a jury, shall be otherwise re-examined in any Court of the United States, than according to the rules of the common law.

8. Excessive bail shall not be required, nor excessive fines imposed, nor cruel and unusual punishments inflicted.

9. The enumeration in the Constitution, of certain rights, shall not be construed to deny or disparage others retained by the people.

10. The powers not delegated to the United States by the Constitution, nor prohibited by it to the States, are reserved to the States respectively, or to the people.

Close in kinship, the American Declaration of Independence, the French Declaration of the Rights of Man and Citizen, and the U.S. Bill of Rights make up the eighteenth-century documentary foundation on which two centuries of legal protection of human rights in municipal law have been built. Constitutional guarantees of human rights are now widespread. One study showed that 82 per cent of the national constitutions drafted between 1788 and 1948, and 93 per cent of the constitutions drafted between 1949 and 1975, included protection for at least some human rights and fundamental freedoms. Henc van Maarseveen & Ger van der Tang, *Written Constitutions: A Computerized Comparative Study* 191–95 (1978). Though the record of observing these guarantees has varied from country to country and from time to time, domestic constitutional protections of human rights have become in two hundred years a legal commonplace. In some countries, such as the United Kingdom, the principal responsibility for protecting human rights rests with the democratically elected legislature. In others, such as the United States, that role has been assumed by the courts.

C. INTERNATIONAL HUMAN RIGHTS LAW

The idea that human rights could be protected by international, as well as municipal law, developed slowly. Throughout the 19th and early 20th centuries, the doctrine of state sovereignty proved a stumbling block to efforts to impose international legal obligations upon states to protect individuals. Instead, the doctrine of state responsibility examined above provided partial protection, but only so long as a foreign national injured by a state was effectively protected at the international level by that individual's national state. However, neither the doctrine of state sovereignty nor its counterpart, the doctrine of state protection, could shield individuals from abuses committed by their own governments. In practice, this fault excluded most instances of violations of human rights.

The turning point for this traditional approach in international law came in the 1940's in the midst of the extreme human rights abuses in war-torn Europe. In the Moscow Declaration of German Atrocities of

October 30, 1943, the United States, the United Kingdom, France, and the Soviet Union declared that individual Germans would be held responsible for their violations of international law. U.N. Doc. A/CN.4/5, at 87–88 (1949). In the August 8, 1945, Charter of the International Military Tribunal, the same four Allies established the Nuremberg Tribunal.

THE NUREMBURG TRIBUNAL

Charter of the International Military Tribunal, Annex to Agreement for the Prosecution and Punishment of the Major War Criminals of the European Axis, Aug. 8, 1945, 59 Stat. 1544 (1945).

Article 6.

(a) CRIMES AGAINST PEACE: namely, planning, preparation, initiation or waging of a war of aggression, or a war in violation of international treaties, agreements or assurances, or participation in a common plan or conspiracy for the accomplishment of any of the foregoing;

(b) WAR CRIMES: namely, violations of the laws or customs of war. Such violations shall include, but not be limited to, murder, ill-treatment or deportation to slave labor or for any other purpose of civilian population of or in occupied territory, murder or ill-treatment of prisoners of war or persons on the seas, killing of hostages, plunder of public or private property, wanton destruction of cities, towns or villages, or devastation not justified by military necessity;

(c) CRIMES AGAINST HUMANITY: namely, murder, extermination, enslavement, deportation, and other inhumane acts committed against any civilian population, before or during the war, or persecutions on political, racial or religious grounds in execution of or in connection with any crime within the jurisdiction of the Tribunal, whether or not in violation of the domestic law of the country where perpetrated.

Leaders, organizers, instigators and accomplices participating in the formulation or execution of a common plan or conspiracy to commit any of the foregoing crimes are responsible for all acts performed by an persons in execution of such plan.

Article 7.

The official position of defendants, whether as Heads of State or responsible officials in Government Departments, shall not be considered as freeing them from responsibility or mitigating punishment.

Article 8.

The fact that the Defendant acted pursuant to order of his Government or of a superior shall not free him from responsibility, but may be considered in mitigation of punishment if the Tribunal determines that justice so requires. * * *

Article 27.

The Tribunal shall have the right to impose upon a Defendant, on conviction, death or such other punishment as shall be determined by it to be just.

Notes and Questions

1. *The Nuremburg Judgment.* The 1946 judgment of the Nuremberg Tribunal confirmed the new norm that individuals, as well as states, were proper subjects of international law:

> It was submitted that international law is concerned with the actions of sovereign states, and provides no punishment for individuals; and further, that where the act in question is an act of state, those who carry it out are not personally responsible, but are protected by the doctrine of the sovereignty of the State. In the opinion of the Tribunal, both these submissions must be rejected. * * *
>
> * * * Crimes against international law are committed by men, not by abstract entities, and only by punishing individuals who commit such crimes can the provisions of international law be enforced.

"The Nuremberg Trial 1946," 6 F.R.D. 69, 110 (1946). The Nuremberg judgment has come to stand not only for the moral and political imperative that individuals be made legally responsible for violations of international law but also for the proposition that individual human rights ought to be protected at the level of international law.

2. *Human Rights and the U.N. Charter.* In the Preamble of the 1945 Charter of the United Nations, the People of the United Nations reaffirm their "faith in fundamental human rights." Charter Article 55 calls on the organization to promote "universal respect for, and observance of, human rights and fundamental freedoms for all without distinction as to race, sex, language, or religion."

The transformation of the substantive norms of human rights law from national to international law was made complete in 1948 in the Universal Declaration of Human Rights, where the United Nations General Assembly followed in the footsteps of Jefferson and the drafters of the French Declaration of the Rights of Man and Citizen and the U.S. Bill of Rights. The Universal Declaration, parts of which appear below, enumerates human rights norms at the level of international law.

THE UNIVERSAL DECLARATION OF HUMAN RIGHTS

G.A. Resolution 217A (III), U.N. Doc. A/810, at 71 (1948).

Article 3

Everyone has the right to life, liberty and the security of person.

Article 4

No one shall be held in slavery or servitude; slavery and the slave trade shall be prohibited in all their forms.

Article 5

No one shall be subjected to torture or to cruel, inhuman or degrading treatment or punishment.

Article 6

Everyone has the right to recognition everywhere as a person before the law.

Article 7

All are equal before the law and are entitled without any discrimination to equal protection of the law. All are entitled to equal protection against any discrimination in violation of this Declaration and against any incitement to such discrimination.

Article 8

Everyone has the right to an effective remedy by the competent national tribunals for acts violating the fundamental rights granted him by the constitution or by law.

Article 9

No one shall be subjected to arbitrary arrest, detention or exile.

Article 10

Everyone is entitled in full equality to a fair and public hearing by an independent and impartial tribunal, in the determination of his rights and obligations and of any criminal charge against him.

Article 11

1. Everyone charged with a penal offence has the right to be presumed innocent until proved guilty according to law in a public trial at which he has had all the guarantees necessary for his defence.

2. No one shall be held guilty of any penal offence on account of any act or omission which did not constitute a penal offence, under national or international law, at the time when it was committed. Nor shall a heavier penalty be imposed than the one that was applicable at the time the penal offence was committed.

Article 12

No one shall be subjected to arbitrary interference with his privacy, family, home or correspondence, nor to attacks upon his honour and reputation. Everyone has the right to the protection of the law against such interference or attacks.

Article 13

1. Everyone has the right to freedom of movement and residence within the borders of each State.

2. Everyone has the right to leave any country, including his own, and to return to his country.

Article 14

1. Everyone has the right to seek and to enjoy in other countries asylum from persecution.

2. This right may not be invoked in the case of prosecutions genuinely arising from nonpolitical crimes or from acts contrary to the purposes and principles of the United Nations.

Article 15

1. Everyone has the right to a nationality.

2. No one shall be arbitrarily deprived of his nationality nor denied the right to change his nationality.

Article 16

1. Men and women of full age, without any limitation due to race, nationality or religion, have the right to marry and to found a family. They are entitled to equal rights as to marriage, during marriage and at its dissolution.

2. Marriage shall be entered into only with the free and full consent of the intending spouses.

3. The family is the natural and fundamental group unit of society and is entitled to protection by society and the State.

Article 17

1. Everyone has the right to own property alone as well as in association with others.

2. No one shall be arbitrarily deprived of his property.

Article 18

Everyone has the right to freedom of thought, conscience and religion; this right includes freedom to change his religion or belief, and freedom, either alone or in community with others and in public or private, to manifest his religion or belief in teaching, practice, worship and observance.

Article 19

Everyone has the right to freedom of opinion and expression; this right includes freedom to hold opinions without interference and to seek, receive and impart information and ideas through any media and regardless of frontiers.

Notes and Questions

1. *State Sovereignty.* The emergence of international human rights law in the mid twentieth century has been described as the most "radical

development in the whole history of international law" since it so speedily established individuals as well as states as subjects of international law. John P. Humphrey, "The Revolution in the International Law of Human Rights," 4 *Human Rights* 205, 208 (1975). Why did it take so long for international law to protect human rights? Certainly, part of the answer lies in the idea of state sovereignty, one of the fundamental principles of international law since its modern emergence in the seventeenth century. Insofar as international law is meant to protect states from the interference of other states, international human rights law still poses a real conflict. When does a state's treatment of individuals within its own boundaries go so far wrong as to permit the interference of other states? Is it any surprise that it was the experience of Nazi-occupied Europe that destroyed the moral foundations of the positivist theory that international law and legal process should not be available to individuals?

2. *International Legal Machinery*. However rapid the emergence of the rules of international human rights law, the development of effective international human rights legal process has been much more gradual. Need there necessarily be a greater political consensus to create effective legal machinery than to promulgate rules of substantive law? Without formal international legal process, *i.e.*, with no court or executive to enforce international human rights law, how is international human rights law to be made efficacious? What is the influence of public pronouncements by critical governments or private groups? How can such pronouncements be made more forceful, *e.g.*, by economic or political sanctions?

Note: The United Nations and Human Rights Law

The Universal Declaration of Human Rights was followed by two U.N. treaties that address a wide range of individual rights, the International Covenant on Civil and Political Rights, Dec. 19, 1966, 999 U.N.T.S. 171, 1057 U.N.T.S. 407, and the International Covenant on Economic and Social Rights, Dec. 19, 1966, 993 U.N.T.S. 3. Other U.N. treaties concerning many specific human rights topics—including slavery, genocide, torture, racial discrimination, rights during armed conflicts, and the rights of women, children, refugees, and stateless persons—also have been widely accepted.

The United Nations has created some machinery directed at reporting human rights abuses and implementing human rights norms. For example, the U.N. Economic and Social Council in 1970 adopted Resolution 1503, titled "Procedure for Dealing with Communications Relating to Violations of Human Rights and Fundamental Freedoms." Resolution 1503 allows individuals to petition the U.N. Commission on Human Rights and its Subcommission on the Prevention of Discrimination and Protection of Minorities. Between 1972 and 1988 the Subcommission's Working Group on Communications considered over 350,000 Resolution 1503 petitions alleging human rights violations, but only 50 or so were referred all the way up through the Subcommission to the Human Rights Commission. The Resolution 1503 procedure has been criticized on the grounds that neither petitioners nor their lawyers can even attend, much less participate in, meetings, that the process involves undue delays, and that no notification is made as to the disposition of petitions. Furthermore, the vast majority of the relatively few petitions that are referred to the full Commission for investigation are discussed in secret, and observers have questioned how thoroughly the Commission has been able to investigate and monitor alleged human right abuses. For discussion of Resolution 1503 and other U.N. human rights procedures, see Richard Lillich & Hurst Hannum, *International Human Rights* 341–80 (3d ed. 1995), and Frank Newman & David Weissbrodt, *International Human Rights: Law, Policy, and Process* 173–216 (2d ed. 1996).

Of recent note is the establishment of the post of U.N. High Commissioner of Human Rights. Although there have been calls for such a post since the 1940's, the General Assembly resolved to create it only in December 1993. The first Commissioner, Jose Ayala Lasso of Ecuador, took office in April 1994. His first months in office have been plagued by underfunding, and according to Professor Philip Alston, a long-time observer of U.N. human rights activities, "it remains to be seen whether [the U.N. High Commissioner of Human Rights] has a clear vision of the role he can play and whether he will be able to give effect to it." Philip Alston, "ASIL Insight No 8: The United Nations High Commissioner for Human Rights," in *Newsletter of the American Society of International Law*, Sept.–Oct. 1995. For discussion of the U.N. High Commissioner and other possible steps to improve the effectiveness of U.N. human rights efforts, see American Bar Association Working Group on Improving the Effectiveness of the United Nations, "Recommendation and Report on the International Protection of Human Rights," in *The United Nations at 50: Proposals for Improving Its Effectiveness* 63 (John E. Noyes ed. 1997).

D. EUROPEAN HUMAN RIGHTS LAW

The proceedings at Nuremberg had special meaning for those who had witnessed the awful abuses of human rights in Nazi-occupied Europe. For the Europeans pressing for political union, human rights became an important priority. On May 5, 1949, the act creating the Council of Europe was signed by ten nations in London. It was widely expected that one of the early tasks of the Council would be to craft and implement a human rights treaty for Europe. The European Convention for the Protection of Human Rights and Fundamental Freedoms was signed on November 4, 1950, and came into force on September 3, 1953.

Merely as a European bill of rights, the Convention provides little exceptional on the international scene. The heart of the Convention rests in its two optional clauses, the crucial aspects of the system's enforcement machinery: Article 25 gives individuals as well as states the right to petition the European Commission of Human Rights, and Article 46 gives the European Court of Human Rights jurisdiction to hear and try cases already reported on by the Commission.

Historically, the Europeans were familiar with bills of rights, but they were unfamiliar with judicial enforcement of those rights. Domestically, they trusted the legislative and executive branches of government rather than the judiciary to protect fundamental freedoms. Would they now be willing to empower an international commission and a court to safeguard the Convention's rights?

Looking at the history of the system, it can be said that each of the five decades of the European Convention on Human Rights has told its own distinctive tale. The 1950's spoke of institutional development but had little actual case law about which to boast. The Convention was signed in 1950 and, ratified by eight states, came into force in 1953. In 1955 the Commission was granted the right to hear individual petitions against consenting states. The Court was constituted in 1958. Only on June 2, 1956 was an application declared admissible by the Commission (by Greece against the United Kingdom respecting Cyprus). Altogether only five applications (two government, three individual) were deemed admissible in the 1950's. No case was heard by the Court.

The 1960's saw both modest triumph and disquieting disobedience. There were some 54 applications admitted by the Commissions (five government and 49 individual), and the Court rendered its first ten decisions in seven cases. However, in 1969, following adverse reports by the Commission, Greece withdrew from the Council of Europe and denounced the European Convention on Human Rights. This reduced the total membership in the system from 16 to 15 at the end of the decade. The number of states accepting the right of individual petition had grown to 11. The same number (though not always the same states) accepted the jurisdiction of the Court.

The 1970's showed a solid maturation of the system. Greece rejoined the Convention in 1974. By the end of the decade some 20 countries belonged, 14 accepting individual petition and 17 consenting to the jurisdiction of the Court. One hundred sixty-eight applications (five government, 163 individual) were deemed admissible by the Commission. Twenty-four cases were decided by the Court.

The 1980's witnessed an explosion of activity under the Convention. As of December 31, 1989, 22 states were parties to the Convention. All had accepted the right of individual petition and the jurisdiction of the Court. Four hundred and fifty-five applications were deemed admissible by the Commission. One hundred and sixty-nine cases were decided by the Court.

The 1990's have evidenced the continuing growth of the system. As of July 31, 1996, 33 countries have ratified the European Human Rights Convention and accepted both Article 25 and Article 46. The member states now include many nations from the former Communist bloc: Hungary, Poland, Bulgaria, Estonia, Lithuania, Slovenia, the Czech Republic, Slovakia, and Romania. In the first three years of the decade (1990–1992), the Commission admitted 557 applications. Between 1990 and 1993, the Court delivered 243 judgments, more in those four years than in the previous four decades.

The story of the success of the European Human Rights Law system is the story of the two optional clauses. In 1950, it may have seemed that opponents had "gutted" the Convention by making the right of individual petition and the jurisdiction of the Court optional, but, over time, the nations "opted into" both procedures. What strategies did the Commission and the Court use to induce states to accept the optional clauses and to maintain their acceptances? Did the example of some European governments accepting the optional clauses make it difficult for other European governments to opt out? Were European governments influenced by human rights abuses in other parts of the world, and did they seek to underline their own commitments to human rights? See Mark W. Janis, Richard S. Kay & Anthony W. Bradley, *European Human Rights Law* 18–29 (2d ed. 1995).

THE SUNDAY TIMES CASE

European Court of Human Rights
Judgment of 26 April 1979, Ser. A: Vol. 30.

8. Between 1958 and 1961 Distillers Company (Biochemicals) Limited ("Distillers") manufactured and marketed under license in the United Kingdom drugs containing an ingredient initially developed in the Federal Republic of Germany and known as thalidomide. The drugs were prescribed as sedatives for, in particular, expectant mothers. In 1961 a number of women who had taken the drugs during pregnancy gave birth to children suffering from severe deformities; in the course of time there were some 250 such births in all. Distillers withdrew all drugs containing thalidomide from the British market in November of the same year. * * *

10. * * * [B]y 1971, three hundred and eighty-nine claims in all were pending against Distillers. Apart from a statement of claim in one case and a defence delivered in 1969, no further steps were taken in those actions where writs had been issued. Distillers had announced in February 1968 that they would provide a substantial sum for the benefit of the remaining three hundred and eighty-nine claimants and both sides were anxious to arrive at a settlement out of court. The case in fact raised legal issues of considerable difficulty under English law. Had any of the actions come on for trial, they would have been heard by a professional judge sitting without a jury.

In 1971 negotiations began on a proposal by Distillers to establish a charitable trust fund for all the deformed children other than those covered by the 1968 settlement. The proposal was made subject to the condition that all parents accepted but five refused, one, at least, because payments out of the fund would have been based on need. An application, on behalf of the parents who would have accepted, to replace those five by the Official Solicitor as next friend was refused by the Court of Appeal in April 1972. During subsequent negotiations, the original condition was replaced by a requirement that "a substantial majority" of the parents consented. By September 1972 a settlement involving the setting-up of a £3,250,000 trust fund had been worked out and was expected to be submitted in October to the court for approval.

11. Reports concerning the deformed children had appeared regularly in *The Sunday Times* since 1967 and in 1968 it had ventured some criticism of the settlement concluded in that year. There had also been comment on the children's circumstances in other newspapers and on television. In particular, in December 1971, the *Daily Mail* published an article which prompted complaints from parents that it might jeopardize the settlement negotiations in hand; the *Daily Mail* was "warned off" by the Attorney–General in a formal letter threatening sanctions under the law of contempt of court but contempt proceedings were not actually instituted. On 24 September 1972, *The Sunday Times* carried an article entitled "Our Thalidomide Children: A Cause for National Shame": this examined the settlement proposals then under consideration, describing them as "grotesquely out of proportion to the injuries suffered," criticized various aspects of English law on the recovery and assessment of damages in personal injury cases, complained of the delay that had elapsed since the births and appealed to Distillers to make a more generous offer. The article contained the following passage:

> "... the thalidomide children shame Distillers ... there are times when to insist on the letter of the law is as exposed to criticism as infringement of another's legal rights. The figure in the proposed settlement is to be £3.25 million, spread over 10 years. This does not shine as a beacon against pre-tax profits last year of £64.8 million and company assets worth £421 million. Without in any way surrendering on negligence, Distillers could and should think again."

A footnote in the article announced that "in a future article *The Sunday Times* [would] trace how the tragedy occurred." On 17 November 1972, the Divisional Court of the Queen's Bench Division granted the Attorney–General's application for an injunction restraining publication of this future article on the ground that it would constitute contempt of court * * *. * * *

17. The unpublished article which was the subject of the injunction opened with a suggestion that the manner of marketing thalidomide in Britain left a lot to be desired. It stated that Distillers:

"— relied heavily on the German tests and had not completed full trials of its own *before* marketing the drug;

— failed to uncover in its research into medical and scientific literature the fact that a drug related to thalidomide could cause monster births;

— before marketing the drug did no animal tests to determine the drug's effect on the foetus;

— accelerated the marketing of the drug for commercial reasons. Were not deflected by a warning from one of its own staff that thalidomide was far more dangerous than had been supposed;

— were not deflected by the discovery that thalidomide could damage the nervous system, in itself a hint that it might damage the foetus;

— continued to advertise the drug as safe for pregnant women up to a month from when it was withdrawn."

The body of the article described how, after their apparently disappointing initial ventures into pharmaceutics, Distillers learned in 1956 that the German firm of *Chemie Gruenenthal* had developed a sedative considered harmless and unique—thalidomide. The very large market existing at the time for sedatives was becoming overcrowded and Distillers thought it necessary to act quickly. Their decision to market the drug was taken before they had seen technical information, other than the transcript of a German symposium, and before carrying out independent tests. Indeed, they seemed to believe that thalidomide would not need elaborate tests. Distillers put in hand a search of scientific literature but failed to discover the results of research in 1950 by a Dr. Thiersch showing that a chemical related to thalidomide could cause monster births; opinions differed as to whether his work should have been found.

Sales of thalidomide began in Germany in October 1957 and Distillers were committed under their licensing agreement to commence marketing in April 1958. They put the programme for the drug's launch in hand even though clinical trials were behind. Results of the first British trials were published in January 1958: it had been found that thalidomide suppressed the work of the thyroid gland and that its method of action was unknown; the researcher warned that more tests were needed. Distillers did not rely on this advice, basing their decision on "flimsy" evidence, namely other trials in the United Kingdom and assurances concerning the results of research in Germany. The warning about anti-thyroid effects was particularly relevant since it was known that drugs affecting the thyroid could affect unborn children; it was reasonable to argue that Distillers should have delayed launching the drug pending further tests.

On 14 April 1958, continued the article, thalidomide went on sale in Britain, advertised as "completely safe." At the end of 1959, Distillers' pharmacologist discovered that thalidomide in liquid form was highly poisonous and that an overdose might be lethal, but his report was never published and the liquid product went on sale in July 1961. In December 1960, it was reported that patients who had taken thalidomide in the tablet form in which it had firstly been on sale showed symptoms of peripheral neuritis; this news had the result of holding up an application to market thalidomide in the United States of America where it was, in fact, never sold. Further cases of peripheral neuritis were reported in 1961 but Distillers' advertising continued to stress the drug's safety.

Early in 1961 children were born in the United Kingdom with deformities, but there was at the time nothing to connect them with thalidomide. However, between May and October, a doctor in Australia discovered that the common factor in a number of monster births was that the mothers had taken thalidomide during pregnancy. This was reported to *Chemie Gruenenthal* on 24 November who withdrew the drug two days later following newspaper disclosures. Distillers ended the public sale of thalidomide immediately afterwards. Tests on animals, published in April 1962, confirmed that thalidomide caused deformities, but sales to hospitals were not ended until December 1962.

The draft article concluded as follows:

> "So the burden of making certain that thalidomide was safe fell squarely on [Distillers]. How did the company measure up to this heavy responsibility? It can be argued that:
>
> 1. [Distillers] should have found all the scientific literature about drugs related to thalidomide. It did not.
> 2. It should have read Thiersch's work on the effects on the nervous system of drugs related to thalidomide, have suspected the possible action on unborn babies and therefore have done tests on animals for teratogenic effect. It did not.
> 3. It should have done further tests when it discovered that the drug had anti-thyroid activity and unsuspected toxicity. It did not.
> 4. It should have had proof before advertising the drug as safe for pregnant women that this was in fact so. It did not.
>
> For [Distillers] it could be argued that it sincerely believed that thalidomide was free from any toxicity at the time it was first put on the market in Britain; that peripheral neuritis did not emerge as a side effect until the drug had been on sale in Britain for two years; that testing for teratogenic effects was not general in 1958; that if tests had been done on the usual laboratory animals nothing would have shown because it is only in the New Zealand white rabbit that thalidomide produces the same effects as in human beings; and, finally, that in the one clinical report of thalidomide being given to pregnant women no serious results followed (because thalidomide is dangerous only during the first 12 weeks of pregnancy). * * *
>
> There appears to be no neat set of answers...." * * *

21. Distillers made a formal complaint to the Attorney–General that the *Sunday Times* article of 24 September 1972 constituted contempt of court in view of the litigation still outstanding and, on 27 September, the Solicitor–General, in the absence of the Attorney–General, wrote to the editor of *The Sunday Times* to ask him for his observations. The editor, in his reply, justified that article and also submitted the draft of the proposed future article for which he claimed complete factual accuracy. The Solicitor–General enquired whether the draft had been seen by any of the parties to the litigation, as a consequence of which a copy of the draft was sent by *The Sunday Times* to Distillers on 10 October. On the previous day, *The Sunday Times*

had been advised that the Attorney–General had decided to take no action in respect of the matter already published in September and October; Distillers also took no action. On 11 October, the Attorney–General's Office informed *The Sunday Times* that, following representations by Distillers, the Attorney–General had decided to apply to the High Court in order to obtain a judicial decision on the legality of the publication of the proposed article. On the following day, he issued a writ against Times Newspapers Ltd. in which he claimed an injunction "to restrain the defendants ... by themselves, their servants or agents or otherwise, from publishing or causing or authorizing to be published or printed an article in draft dealing, *inter alia*, with the development, distribution and use of the drug thalidomide, a copy of which article had been supplied to the Attorney–General by the defendants."

22. The Attorney–General's application was heard by three judges of the Queen's Bench Division from 7 to 9 November 1972; on 17 November the court granted the injunction.

In its judgment the court remarked:

> "the article does not purport to express any views as to the legal responsibility of Distillers ... but ... is in many respects critical of Distillers and charges them with neglect in regard to their own failure to test the product, or their failure to react sufficiently sharply to warning signs obtained from the tests by others. No one reading the article could ... fail to gain the impression that the case against Distillers on the footing of negligence was a substantial one."

The editor of the *Sunday Times* had indicated that any libel proceedings following publication would be defended by a plea that the contents of the article were true and the court approached the article on the footing that it was factually accurate.

23. The reasoning in the court's judgment may be summarised as follows. The objection to unilateral comment, prior to conclusion of the court hearing, was that it might prevent the due and impartial administration of justice by affecting and prejudicing the mind of the tribunal itself, by affecting witnesses who were to be called or by prejudicing the free choice and conduct of a party to the litigation. It was the third form of prejudice that was relevant to the present case. * * *

24. An appeal by Times Newspapers Ltd. against the Divisional Court's decision was heard by the Court of Appeal from 30 January to 2 February 1973. The court had before it an affidavit by the editor of the Sunday Times setting out developments in the intervening period both in the case itself and in public discussion thereof. With the leave of the court, counsel for Distillers made submissions on the contents of the proposed article, pointing to errors he said it contained. On 16 February, the Court of Appeal discharged the injunction. * * *

25. Lord Denning said that the proposed article:

> "... contains a detailed analysis of the evidence against Distillers. It marshals forcibly the arguments for saying that Distillers did not measure up to their responsibility. Though, to be fair, it does summarize the arguments which could be made for Distillers." * * *

"Trial by newspaper," continued Lord Denning, must not be allowed. However, the public interest in a matter of national concern had to be balanced against the interest of the parties in a fair trial or settlement; in the present case the public interest in discussion outweighed the potential prejudice to a party. The law did not prevent comment when litigation was dormant and not being actively pursued. * * *

28. Following the Court of Appeal's decision, the *Sunday Times* refrained from publishing the proposed article so as to enable the Attorney–General to appeal. The Court of Appeal refused him leave to appeal but this was granted by the House of Lords on 1 March 1973. The hearing before the House of Lords was held in May 1973. On 18 July 1973, the House gave judgment unanimously allowing the appeal and subsequently directed the Divisional Court to grant an injunction in the terms set out in paragraph 34 below. * * *

29. Lord Reid said that the House must try to remove the uncertainty which was the main objection to the present law. The law of contempt had to be founded entirely on public policy; it was not there to protect the rights of parties to a litigation but to prevent interference with the administration of justice and should be limited to what was reasonably necessary for the purpose. Freedom of speech should not be limited more than was necessary but it could not be allowed where there would be real prejudice to the administration of justice. * * *

The Court of Appeal had wrongly described the actions as "dormant" since settlement negotiations were in hand and improper pressure on a litigant to settle could constitute contempt. As for the Court of Appeal's balancing of competing interests, Lord Reid said:

> "... contempt of court has nothing to do with the private interests of litigants. I have already indicated the way in which I think that a balance must be struck between the public interest in freedom of speech and the public interest in protecting the administration of justice from interference. I do not see why there should be any difference in principle between a case which is thought to have news value and one which is not. Protection of the administration of justice is equally important whether or not the case involves important general issues."

Lord Reid concluded that publication of the article should be postponed for the time being in the light of the circumstances then prevailing; however, if things dragged on indefinitely, there would have to be a reassessment of the public interest in a unique situation.

[A summary of the concurring opinion of Lord Morris of Booth-y-Gest in the English House of Lords is omitted.]

31. Lord Diplock said that contempt of court was punishable because it undermined the confidence of the parties and of the public in the due administration of justice. The due administration of justice required that all citizens should have unhindered access to the courts; that they should be able to rely on an unbiased decision based only on facts proved in accordance with the rules of evidence; that, once a case was submitted to a court, they should be able to rely upon there being no usurpation by any other person, for example in the form of "trial by newspaper," of the function of the court. Conduct calculated to prejudice any of these requirements or to undermine public confidence that they would be observed was contempt of court.

[Summaries of the concurring opinions of Lord Simon of Glaisdale and Lord Cross of Chelsea in the English House of Lords are omitted.]

34. On 25 July 1973, the House of Lords ordered that the cause be remitted to the Divisional Court with a direction to grant the following injunction:

> "That ... Times Newspapers Ltd., by themselves, their servants, agents or otherwise, be restrained from publishing, or causing or authorising or procuring to be published or printed, any article or matter which prejudges the issues of negligence, breach of contract or breach of duty, or deals with the evidence relating to any of the said issues arising in any actions pending or imminent against Distillers ... in respect of the development, distribution or use of the drug 'thalidomide.' "

The defendants were granted liberty to apply to the Divisional Court for discharge of the injunction.

The Divisional Court implemented the above direction on 24 August 1973.

35. On 23 June 1976, the Divisional Court heard an application by the Attorney–General for the discharge of the injunction. It was said on behalf of the Attorney–General that the need for the injunction no longer arose: most of the claims against Distillers had been settled and there were only four extant actions which could by then have been brought before the courts if they had been pursued diligently. As there was a conflicting public interest in the *Sunday Times* being allowed to publish "at the earliest possible date," the Attorney–General submitted the matter to the court as one where the public interest no longer required the restraint. The court, considering that the possibility of pressure on Distillers had completely evaporated, granted the application.

[A discussion of the Phillimore Report on the Law of Contempt, issued in December 1974, is omitted.]

38. In their application, lodged with the Commission on 19 January 1974, the applicants claimed that the injunction, issued by the High

Court and upheld by the House of Lords, to restrain them from publishing an article in the *Sunday Times* dealing with thalidomide children and the settlement of their compensation claims in the United Kingdom constituted a breach of Article 10 of the Convention. They further alleged that the principles upon which the decision of the House of Lords was founded amounted to a violation of Article 10 and asked the Commission to direct or, alternatively, to request the Government to introduce legislation overruling the decision of the House of Lords and bringing the law of contempt of court into line with the Convention.

39. In its decision of 21 March 1975, the Commission, after describing the question before it as "whether the rules of contempt of court as applied in the decision of the House of Lords granting the injunction are a ground justifying the restriction under Article 10 § 2," declared admissible and accepted the application.

[Additional allegations were made by the applicant under Articles 14 and 18 of the Convention; though considered by the Commission and by the Court, neither additional allegation is held by either body to have demonstrated a violation of the Convention.]

41. In its report of 18 May 1977, the Commission * * * expressed the opinion:

—by eight votes to five, that the restriction imposed on the applicant's right to freedom of expression was in breach of Article 10 of the Convention * * *. * * *

42. The applicants claim to be the victims of a violation of Article 10 of the Convention which provides:

> "1. Everyone has the right to freedom of expression. This right shall include freedom to hold opinions and to receive and impart information and ideas without interference by public authority and regardless of frontiers. This Article shall not prevent States from requiring the licensing of broadcasting, television or cinema enterprises.
>
> 2. The exercise of these freedoms, since it carries with it duties and responsibilities, may be subject to such formalities, conditions, restrictions or penalties as are prescribed by law and are necessary in a democratic society, in the interests of national security, territorial integrity or public safety, for the prevention of disorder or crime, for the protection of health or morals, for the protection of the reputation or rights of others, for preventing the disclosure of information received in confidence, or for maintaining the authority and impartiality of the judiciary." * * *

45. It is clear that there was an "interference by public authority" in the exercise of the applicants' freedom of expression which is guaranteed by paragraph 1 of Article 10. Such an interference entails a "violation" of Article 10 if it does not fall within one of the exceptions provided for in paragraph 2. The Court, therefore, has to examine in turn whether the interference in the present case was "prescribed by

law," whether it had an aim or aims that is or are legitimate under Article 10 § 2 and whether it was "necessary in a democratic society" for the aforesaid aim or aims.

[In parts of the European Court's opinion omitted here it is held that there had been an "interference with the applicants' freedom of expression," that it was "prescribed by law," and that "the interference with the applicants' freedom of expression had an aim that is legitimate under Article 10 § 2." The crucial part of the case then follows: "Was the interference 'necessary in a democratic society' for maintaining the authority of the judiciary?"]

65. * * * As the Court remarked in its Handyside judgment, freedom of expression constitutes one of the essential foundations of a democratic society; subject to paragraph 2 of Article 10, it is applicable not only to information or ideas that are favourably received or regarded as inoffensive or as a matter of indifference, but also to those that offend, shock or disturb the State or any sector of the population.

These principles are of particular importance as far as the press is concerned. They are equally applicable to the field of the administration of justice, which serves the interests of the community at large and requires the co-operation of an enlightened public. There is general recognition of the fact that the courts cannot operate in a vacuum. Whilst they are the forum for the settlement of disputes, this does not mean that there can be no prior discussion of disputes elsewhere, be it in specialized journals, in the general press or amongst the public at large. Furthermore, whilst the mass media must not overstep the bounds imposed in the interests of the proper administration of justice, it is incumbent on them to impart information and ideas concerning matters that come before the courts just as in other areas of public interest. Not only do the media have the task of imparting such information and ideas: the public also has a right to receive them (see, *mutatis mutandis*, the Kjeldsen, Busk Madsen and Pedersen judgment of 7 December 1976, Series A no. 23, p. 26, § 52).

To assess whether the interference complained of was based on "sufficient" reasons which rendered it "necessary in a democratic society," account must thus be taken of any public interest aspect of the case. The Court observes in this connection that, following a balancing of the conflicting interests involved, an absolute rule was formulated by certain of the Law Lords to the effect that it was not permissible to prejudge issues in pending cases: it was considered that the law would be too uncertain if the balance were to be struck anew in each case (see paragraphs 29, 32 and 33 above). Whilst emphasising that it is not its function to pronounce itself on an interpretation of English law adopted in the House of Lords, the Court points out that it has to take a different approach. The Court is faced not with a choice between two conflicting principles but with a principle of freedom of expression that is subject to a number of exceptions which must be narrowly interpreted. In the second place, the Court's supervision under Article 10 covers not only the basic legislation but also the decision applying it. It is not sufficient that the interference involved belongs to that class of the exceptions listed in Article 10 § 2 which has been invoked; neither is it sufficient that the interference was imposed because its subject-matter fell within a particular category or was caught by a legal rule formulated in general or absolute terms: the Court has to be satisfied that the interference was necessary having regard to the facts and circumstances prevailing in the specific case before it.

66. The thalidomide disaster was a matter of undisputed public concern. It posed the question whether the powerful company which had marketed the drug bore legal or moral responsibility towards hundreds of individuals experiencing an appalling personal tragedy or whether the victims could demand or hope for indemnification only from the community as a whole; fundamental issues concerning protection against and compensation for injuries resulting from scientific developments were raised and many facets of the existing law on these subjects were called in question.

As the court has already observed, Article 10 guarantees not only the freedom of the press to inform the public but also the right of the public to be properly informed * * *.

In the present case, the families of numerous victims of the tragedy, who were unaware of the legal difficulties involved, had a vital interest in knowing all the underlying facts and the various possible solutions. They could be deprived of this information, which was crucially important for them, only if it appeared absolutely certain that its diffusion would have presented a threat to the "authority of the judiciary."

Being called upon to weigh the interests involved and assess their respective force, the Court makes the following observations:

In September 1972, the case had, in the words of the applicants, been in a "legal cocoon" for several years and it was, at the very least, far from certain that the parents' actions would have come on for trial. There had also been no public enquiry * * *.

The Government and the minority of the Commission point out that there was no prohibition on discussion of the "wider issues," such as the principles of the English law of negligence, and indeed it is true that there had been extensive discussion in various circles especially after, but also before, the Divisional Court's initial decision * * *. However, the Court considers it rather artificial to attempt to divide the "wider issues" and the negligence issue. The question of where responsibility for a tragedy of this kind actually lies is also a matter of public interest.

It is true that, if the *Sunday Times* article had appeared at the intended time, Distillers might have felt obliged to develop in public, and in advance of any trial, their arguments on the facts of the case * * *; however, those facts did not cease to be a matter of public interest merely because they formed the background to pending litigation. By bringing to light certain facts, the article might have served as a brake on speculative and unenlightened discussion.

67. Having regard to all the circumstances of the case on the basis of the approach described in paragraph 65 above, the Court concludes that the interference complained of did not correspond to a social need sufficiently pressing to outweigh the public interest in freedom of expression within the meaning of the Convention. The Court therefore finds the reasons for the restraint imposed on the applicants not to be sufficient under Article 10 § 2. That restraint proves not to be proportionate to the legitimate aim pursued; it was not necessary in a democratic society for maintaining the authority of the judiciary.

68. There has accordingly been a violation of Article 10. * * *

FOR THESE REASONS, THE COURT

1. *holds* by eleven votes to nine that there has been a breach of Article 10 of the Convention * * *.

Notes and Questions

1. *Balancing the Issues.* In *Sunday Times*, there was no doubt that the balancing of the legal issues—weighing the public's right to know and the Sunday Times right to freedom of expression against Distiller's right to a trial by the courts, not by the media, and the interest of the English government in the integrity of the judicial process—was a very close one. Eight English judges (three at the trial level and five in the House of Lords), five European Human Rights Commissioners, and nine European Human Rights Judges felt that the scales tilted toward granting an injunction against the *Sunday Times*. Three English judges (in the Court of Appeal), eight European Human Rights Commissioners, and eleven European Human Rights Judges felt that the balance went for permitting the *Sunday Times* to publish the thalidomide article. Of forty-four judges and commissioners who considered the case, half went one way and half the other. Reasonable men and women could and did differ. Was this really a case demanding international supervision?

2. *The Boldness of the Court.* A distinguished British international lawyer, F.A. Mann, felt that the European Court of Human Rights had gone too far:

> However uncertain its definition and scope may be in some respects, contempt of court is undoubtedly one of the great contributions the common law has made to the civilized behavior of a large part of the world beyond the continent of Europe where the institution is unknown. * * * Yet it is that very branch of the law which the European Court of Human Rights has seriously undermined by, in effect, overturning the unanimous decision of the House of Lords in the *Sunday Times* case—a unique event in the history of English law. In fact it is probably no exaggeration to say that the gravest blow to the fabric of English law has been dealt by the majority of eleven judges coming from Cyprus, Denmark, Eire, France, Germany, Greece, Italy, Portugal, Spain, Sweden and Turkey, who, over the dissent of nine judges from Austria,

> Belgium, Holland, Iceland, Luxembourg, Malta, Norway, Switzerland and the United Kingdom, decided in favor of the *Sunday Times*. * * *
>
> The reader will have to make up his or her own mind * * * whether the Strasbourg Court arrogated to itself powers of factual appreciation which it cannot possibly exercise convincingly * * * and ask whether according to the standards and traditions of English law and English public life it is the decision of the House of Lords or that of the European Court of Human Rights which more correctly assesses the "social need" and "the legitimate aim" of a civilized society * * * and whether the level of judicial reasoning is higher in London or Strasbourg.

F.A. Mann, "Contempt of Court in the House of Lords and the European Court of Human Rights," 95 *Law Quarterly Review* 348, 348–49, 352 (1979).

One can understand Mann's discomfort with the "overturning" of the House of Lords by the Strasbourg Court, but did *Sunday Times* really raise the question of which court's "judicial reasoning" was "higher"? As another observer remarked about another judgment against the U.K., the *Golder Case* above (see Chapter 1):

> Membership of a European institution, and submission to the jurisdiction of its organs, means the acceptance of a European way of thinking. The European Commission and Court of Human Rights are likely to construe texts in the "continental," not the common law, manner.

William Dale, "Human Rights in the United Kingdom—International Standards," 25 *International & Comparative Law Quarterly* 292, 302 (1976).

3. *Continued Acceptance of the Optional Clauses.* The United Kingdom was and is not obliged to forever accept "a European way of thinking." However, states have continued to accept both Article 25 and Article 46. At the time of the *Sunday Times Case* 14 of the 21 Council of Europe States had already accepted Article 25 individual petition, and 16 had consented to Article 46 jurisdiction of the Court. Not only has the United Kingdom continued to renew its pledges to both Article 25 and Article 46, but so have the other then consenting states. Furthermore, 19 more states have acceded to Article 25 and 17 more to Article 46. Far from discouraging governments, the *Sunday Times* judgment and cases like it have not slowed the accession of states to the legal machinery of European human rights law.

4. *The Efficacy of the Court.* How far can the Court and the Commission go without upsetting the apple cart of state consent? Writing just after the *Sunday Times* case, Ralph Beddard remarked on the caution exercised by the system's institutions up to that time:

> It is, and always has been, obvious that winning the confidence of the parties and the public was a first step in any attempt to establish judicial determination of the protection of human rights. The last 27 years have not been free of difficulties, however, and the confidence of the parties was won, particularly in the early days, by very careful treading on the part of the Commission. There are cases which, if presented to the Commission today, would probably make greater progress than they did at the time of application. However, a Commission

leaning heavily in favor of governments would have lost the confidence of the public.

Ralph Beddard, *Human Rights and Europe* 4 (1980).

Such caution has paid off. In 1980, Sir Humphrey Waldock, then President of the International Court of Justice but previously President of both the European Commission and the European Court of Human Rights, could conclude that "the system set up by the European Convention on Human Rights is, in general, effective is not, I believe, today open to serious question." Humphrey Waldock, "The Effectiveness of the System Set Up by the European Convention on Human Rights," 1 *Human Rights Law Journal* 1, 1 (1980).

5. *The Efficacy of International Law.* Regional international law, like European human rights law or European Community law, can become so effective that some commentators unused to a really efficacious system of international law think it has become a form of municipal law. Some, for example, view the law of the European Union as "federal" law. See John Bridge, "American Analogues in the Law of the European Community," 11 *Anglo-American Law Review* 130 (1982). Others feel European Union law is still fundamentally international law. See Derrick Wyatt, "New Legal Order or Old," 7 *European Law Review* 147 (1982). Does it really matter whether a legal system is denominated "federal law" or "regional international law"? Does one or the other have a more impressive connotation?

THE SOERING CASE

European Court of Human Rights
Judgment of 7 July 1989, Ser. A: Vol. 161.

As to the Facts

I. Particular circumstances of the case

11. The applicant, Mr. Jens Soering, was born on 1 August 1966 and is a German national. He is currently detained in prison in England pending extradition to the United States of America to face charges of murder in the Commonwealth of Virginia.

12. The homicides in question were committed in Bedford County, Virginia, in March 1985. The victims, William Reginald Haysom (aged 72) and Nancy Astor Haysom (aged 53), were the parents of the applicant's girlfriend, Elizabeth Haysom, who is a Canadian national. Death in each case was the result of multiple and massive stab and slash wounds to the neck, throat and body. At the time the applicant and Elizabeth Haysom, aged 18 and 20 respectively, were students at the University of Virginia. They disappeared together from Virginia in October 1985, but were arrested in England in April 1986 in connection with cheque fraud.

13. The applicant was interviewed in England between 5 and 8 June 1986 by a police investigator from the Sheriff's Department of Bedford County. In a sworn affidavit dated 24 July 1986 the investigator recorded the applicant as having admitted to killings in his presence

and in that of two United Kingdom police officers. The applicant had stated that he was in love with Miss Haysom but that her parents were opposed to the relationship. He and Miss Haysom had therefore planned to kill them. They rented a car in Charlottesville and traveled to Washington where they set up an alibi. The applicant then went to the parents' house, discussed the relationship with them and, when they told him they would do anything to prevent it, a row developed during which he killed them with a knife.

On 13 June 1986 a grand jury of the Circuit Court of Bedford County indicted him on charges of murdering the Haysom parents. The charges alleged capital murder of both of them and the separate non-capital murders of each.

14. On 11 August 1986 the Government of the United States of America requested the applicant's and Miss Haysom's extradition under the terms of the Extradition Treaty of 1972 between the United States and the United Kingdom * * *. On 12 September a Magistrate at Bow Street Magistrates' Court was required by the Secretary of State for Home Affairs to issue a warrant for the applicant's arrest under the provisions of section 8 of the Extradition Act 1870 * * *. The applicant was subsequently arrested on 30 December at HM Prison Chelmsford after serving a prison sentence for cheque fraud.

15. On 29 October 1986 the British Embassy in Washington addressed a request to the United States' authorities in the following terms:

> "Because the death penalty has been abolished in Great Britain, the Embassy has been instructed to seek an assurance, in accordance with the terms of ... the Extradition Treaty, that, in the event of Mr. Soering being surrendered and being convicted of the crimes for which he has been indicted ..., the death penalty, if imposed, will not be carried out.
>
> Should it not be possible on constitutional grounds for the United States Government to give such an assurance, the United Kingdom authorities ask that the United States Government undertake to recommend to the appropriate authorities that the death penalty should not be imposed or, if imposed, should not be executed."

16. On 30 December 1986 the applicant was interviewed in prison by a German prosecutor (*Staatsanwalt*) from Bonn. In a sworn witness statement the prosecutor recorded the applicant as having said, *inter alia*, that "he had never had the intention of killing Mr. and Mrs. Haysom and ... he could only remember having inflicted wounds at the neck on Mr. and Mrs. Haysom which must have had something to do with their dying later"; and that in the immediately preceding days "there had been no talk whatsoever [between him and Elizabeth Haysom] about killing Elizabeth's parents." The prosecutor also referred to documents which had been put at his disposal, for example the statements made by the applicant to the American police investigator, the

autopsy reports and two psychiatric reports on the applicant (see paragraph 21 below).

On 11 February 1987 the local court in Bonn issued a warrant for the applicant's arrest in respect of the alleged murders. On 11 March the Government of the Federal Republic of Germany requested his extradition to the Federal Republic under the Extradition Treaty of 1872 between the Federal Republic and the United Kingdom * * *. The Secretary of State was then advised by the Director of Public Prosecutions that, although the German request contained proof that German courts had jurisdiction to try the applicant, the evidence submitted, since it consisted solely of the admissions made by the applicant to the Bonn prosecutor in the absence of a caution, did not amount to a *prima facie* case against him and that a magistrate would not be able under the Extradition Act 1870 * * * to commit him to await extradition to Germany on the strength of admissions obtained in such circumstances.

17. In a letter dated 20 April 1987 to the Director of the Office of International Affairs, Criminal Division, United States Department of Justice, the Attorney for Bedford County, Virginia (Mr. James W. Updike, Jr.) stated that, on the assumption that the applicant could not be tried in Germany on the basis of admissions alone, there was no means of compelling witnesses from the United States to appear in a criminal court in Germany. On 23 April the United States, by diplomatic note, requested the applicant's extradition to the United States in preference to the Federal Republic of Germany.

18. On 8 May 1987 Elizabeth Haysom was surrendered for extradition to the United States. After pleading guilty on 22 August as an accessory to the murder of her parents, she was sentenced on 6 October to 90 years' imprisonment (45 years on each count of murder).

19. On 20 May 1987 the Government of the United Kingdom informed the Federal Republic of Germany that the United States had earlier "submitted a request, supported by *prima facie* evidence, for the extradition of Mr. Soering." The United Kingdom Government notified the Federal Republic that they had "concluded that, having regard to all the circumstances of the case, the court should continue to consider in the normal way the United States' request." They further indicated that they had sought an assurance from the United States' authorities on the question of the death penalty and that "in the event that the court commits Mr. Soering, his surrender to the United States' authorities would be subject to the receipt of satisfactory assurances on this matter."

20. On 1 June 1987 Mr. Updike swore an affidavit in his capacity as Attorney for Bedford County, in which he certified as follows:

> "I hereby certify that should Jens Soering be convicted of the offence of capital murder as charged in Bedford County, Virginia ... a representation will be made in the name of the United Kingdom to the judge at the time of sentencing that it is the wish of the United

Kingdom that the death penalty should not be imposed or carried out."

This assurance was transmitted to the United Kingdom Government under cover of a diplomatic note on 8 June. It was repeated in the same terms in a further affidavit from Mr. Updike sworn on 16 February 1988 and forwarded to the United Kingdom by diplomatic note on 17 May 1988. In the same note the Federal Government of the United States undertook to ensure that the commitment of the appropriate authorities of the Commonwealth of Virginia to make representations on behalf of the United Kingdom would be honored.

During the course of the present proceedings the Virginia authorities have informed the United Kingdom Government that Mr. Updike was not planning to provide any further assurances and intended to seek the death penalty in Mr. Soering's case because the evidence, in his determination, supported such action.

21. On 16 June 1987 at the Bow Street Magistrates' Court committal proceedings took place before the Chief Stipendiary Magistrate.

The Government of the United States adduced evidence that on the night of 30 March 1985 the applicant killed William and Nancy Haysom at their home in Bedford County, Virginia. In particular, evidence was given of the applicant's own admissions as recorded in the affidavit of the Bedford County police investigator (see paragraph 13 above).

On behalf of the applicant psychiatric evidence was adduced from a consultant forensic psychiatrist (report dated 15 December 1986 by Dr. Henrietta Bullard) that he was immature and inexperienced and had lost his personal identity in a symbiotic relationship with his girlfriend—a powerful, persuasive and disturbed young woman. The psychiatric report concluded:

> "There existed between Miss Haysom and Soering a '*folie à deux*,' in which the most disturbed partner was Miss Haysom ...
>
> At the time of the offence, it is my opinion that Jens Soering was suffering from [such] an abnormality of mind due to inherent causes as substantially impaired his mental responsibility for his acts. The psychiatric syndrome referred to as '*folie à deux*' is a well-recognized state of mind where one partner is suggestible to the extent that he or she believes in the psychotic delusions of the other. The degree of disturbance of Miss Haysom borders on the psychotic and, over the course of many months, she was able to persuade Soering that he might have to kill her parents for she and him to survive as a couple.... Miss Haysom had a stupefying and mesmeric effect on Soering which led to an abnormal psychological state in which he became unable to think rationally or question the absurdities in Miss Haysom's view of her life and the influence of her parents....
>
> In conclusion, it is my opinion that, at the time of the offences, Soering was suffering from an abnormality of mind which, in this

country, would constitute a defence of 'not guilty to murder but guilty of manslaughter.' "

Dr. Bullard's conclusions were substantially the same as those contained in an earlier psychiatric report (dated 11 December 1986 by Dr. John R. Hamilton, Medical Director of Broadmoor Hospital), which was not however put before the Magistrates' Court.

The Chief Magistrate found that the evidence of Dr. Bullard was not relevant to any issue that he had to decide and committed the applicant to await the Secretary of State's order for his return to the United States.

22. On 29 June 1987 Mr. Soering applied to the Divisional Court for a writ of habeas corpus in respect of his committal and for leave to apply for judicial review. On 11 December both applications were refused by the Divisional Court (Lord Justice Lloyd and Mr. Justice Macpherson).

In support of his application for leave to apply for judicial review, Mr. Soering had submitted that the assurance received from the United States' authorities was so worthless that no reasonable Secretary of State could regard it as satisfactory under Article IV of the Extradition Treaty between the United Kingdom and the United States * * *. In his judgment Lord Justice Lloyd agreed that "the assurance leaves something to be desired":

> "Article IV of the Treaty contemplates an assurance that the death penalty will not be carried out. That must presumably mean an assurance by or on behalf of the Executive Branch of Government, which in this case would be the Governor of the Commonwealth of Virginia. The certificate sworn by Mr. Updike, far from being an assurance on behalf of the Executive, is nothing more than an undertaking to make representations on behalf of the United Kingdom to the judge. I cannot believe that this is what was intended when the Treaty was signed. But I can understand that there may well be difficulties in obtaining more by way of assurance in view of the federal nature of the United States Constitution."

Leave to apply for judicial review was refused because the claim was premature. Lord Justice Lloyd stated:

> "The Secretary of State has not yet decided whether to accept the assurance as satisfactory and he has certainly not yet decided whether or not to issue a warrant for Soering's surrender. Other factors may well intervene between now and then. This court will never allow itself to be put in the position of reviewing an administrative decision before the decision has been made."

As a supplementary reason, he added:

> "Secondly, even if a decision to regard the assurance as satisfactory had already been made by the Secretary of State, then on the evidence currently before us I am far from being persuaded that

such a decision would have been irrational in the *Wednesday* sense." * * *

23. On 30 June 1988 the House of Lords rejected the applicant's petition for leave to appeal against the decision of the Divisional Court.

24. On 14 July 1988 the applicant petitioned the Secretary of State, requesting him to exercise his discretion not to make an order for the applicant's surrender under section 11 of the Extradition Act 1870 * * *.

This request was rejected, and on 3 August 1988 the Secretary of State signed a warrant ordering the applicant's surrender to the United States' authorities. However, the applicant has not been transferred to the United States by virtue of the interim measures indicated in the present proceedings firstly by the European Commission and then by the European Court * * *.

[The European Court of Human Rights reviews the laws relating to murder in England and Virginia and then turns to the prison conditions in Virginia for someone like Soering.]

61. There are currently 40 people under sentence of death in Virginia. The majority are detained in Mecklenburg Correctional Center, which is a modern maximum security institution with a total capacity of 335 inmates. Institutional Operating Procedures (IOP 821.1) establish uniform operating procedures for the administration, security, control and delivery of necessary services to death row in Mecklenburg. In addition conditions of confinement are governed by a comprehensive consent decree handed down by the United States District Court in Richmond in the case of *Alan Brown et al. v. Allyn R. Sielaff et al.* (5 April 1985). Both the Virginia Department of Corrections and the American Civil Liberties Union monitor compliance with the terms of the consent decree. The United States District Court also retains jurisdiction to enforce compliance with the decree. * * *

63. The size of a death row inmate's cell is 3m by 2.2m. Prisoners have an opportunity for approximately 7 1/2 hours' recreation per week in summer and approximately 6 hours' per week, weather permitting, in winter. The death row area has two recreation yards, both of which are equipped with basketball courts and one of which is equipped with weights and weight benches. Inmates are also permitted to leave their cells on other occasions, such as to receive visits, to visit the law library or to attend the prison infirmary. In addition, death row inmates are given one hour out-of-cell time in the morning in a common area. Each death row inmate is eligible for work assignments, such as cleaning duties. When prisoners move around the prison they are handcuffed with special shackles around the waist.

When not in their cells, death row inmates are housed in a common area called "the pod." The guards are not within this area and remain in a box outside. In the event of disturbance or inter-inmate assault, the guards are not allowed to intervene until instructed to do so by the ranking officer present.

64. The applicant adduced much evidence of extreme stress, psychological deterioration and risk of homosexual abuse and physical attack undergone by prisoners on death row, including Mecklenburg Correctional Center. This evidence was strongly contested by the United Kingdom Government on the basis of affidavits sworn by administrators from the Virginia Department of Corrections. * * *

68. A death row prisoner is moved to the death house 15 days before he is due to be executed. The death house is next to the death chamber where the electric chair is situated. Whilst a prisoner is in the death house he is watched 24 hours a day. He is isolated and has no light in his cell. The lights outside are permanently lit. A prisoner who utilizes the appeals process can be placed in the death house several times. * * *

AS TO THE LAW

I. Alleged Breach of Article 3

80. The applicant alleged that the decision by the Secretary of State for the Home Department to surrender him to the authorities of the United States of America would, if implemented, give rise to a breach by the United Kingdom of Article 3 of the Convention, which provides:

> "No one shall be subjected to torture or to inhuman or degrading treatment or punishment."

A. Applicability of Article 3 in cases of extradition

81. The alleged breach derives from the applicant's exposure to the so-called "death row phenomenon." This phenomenon may be described as consisting in a combination of circumstances to which the applicant would be exposed if, after having been extradited to Virginia to face a capital murder charge, he was sentenced to death.

82. In its report (at paragraph 94) the Commission reaffirmed "its case-law that a person's deportation or extradition may give rise to an issue under Article 3 of the Convention where there are serious reasons to believe that the individual will be subjected, in the receiving State, to treatment contrary to that Article."

The Government of the Federal Republic of Germany supported the approach of the Commission, pointing to a similar approach in the case-law of the German courts.

The applicant likewise submitted that Article 3 not only prohibits the Contracting States from causing inhuman or degrading treatment or punishment to occur within their jurisdiction but also embodies an associated obligation not to put a person in a position where he will or may suffer such treatment or punishment at the hands of other States. For the applicant, at least as far as Article 3 is concerned, an individual may not be surrendered out of the protective zone of the Convention without the certainty that the safeguards which he would enjoy are as effective as the Convention standard.

83. The United Kingdom Government, on the other hand, contended that Article 3 should not be interpreted so as to impose responsibility on a Contracting State for acts which occur outside its jurisdiction. In particular, in their submission, extradition does not involve the responsibility of the extraditing State for inhuman or degrading treatment or punishment which the extradited person may suffer outside the State's jurisdiction. To begin with, they maintained, it would be straining the language of Article 3 intolerably to hold that by surrendering a fugitive criminal the extraditing State has "subjected" him to any treatment or punishment that he will receive following conviction and sentence in the receiving State. Further arguments advanced against the approach of the Commission were that it interferes with international treaty rights; it leads to a conflict with the norms of international judicial process, in that it in effect involves adjudication on the internal affairs of foreign States not Parties to the Convention or to the proceedings before the Convention institutions; it entails grave difficulties of evaluation and proof in requiring the examination of alien systems of law and of conditions in foreign States; the practice of national courts and the international community cannot reasonably be invoked to support it; it causes a serious risk of harm in the Contracting State which is obliged to harbour the protected person, and leaves criminals untried, at large and unpunished.

In the alternative, the United Kingdom Government submitted that the application of Article 3 in extradition cases should be limited to those occasions in which the treatment or punishment abroad is certain, imminent and serious. In their view, the fact that by definition the matters complained of are only anticipated, together with the common and legitimate interest of all States in bringing fugitive criminals to justice, requires a very high degree of risk, proved beyond reasonable doubt, that ill-treatment will actually occur.

84. The Court will approach the matter on the basis of the following considerations.

85. As results from Article 5 § 1(f), which permits "the lawful ... detention of a person against whom action is being taken with a view to ... extradition," no right not to be extradited is as such protected by the Convention. Nevertheless, in so far as a measure of extradition has consequences adversely affecting the enjoyment of a Convention right, it may, assuming that the consequences are not too remote, attract the obligations of a Contracting State under the relevant Convention guarantee (see, *mutatis mutandis*, the Abdulaziz, Cabales and Balkandali judgment of 25 May 1985, Series A no. 94, pp. 31–32, §§ 59–60—in relation to rights in the field of immigration). What is at issue in the present case is whether Article 3 can be applicable when the adverse consequences of extradition are, or may be, suffered outside the jurisdic-

tion of the extraditing State as a result of treatment or punishment administered in the receiving State.

86. Article 1 of the Convention, which provides that "the High Contracting Parties shall secure to everyone within their jurisdiction the rights and freedoms defined in Section I," sets a limit, notably territorial, on the reach of the Convention. In particular, the engagement undertaken by a Contracting State is confined to "securing" ("*reconnaître*" in the French text) the listed rights and freedoms to persons within its own "jurisdiction." Further, the Convention does not govern the actions of States not Parties to it, nor does it purport to be a means of requiring the Contracting States to impose Convention standards on other States. Article 1 cannot be read as justifying a general principle to the effect that, notwithstanding its extradition obligations, a Contracting State may not surrender an individual unless satisfied that the conditions awaiting him in the country of destination are in full accord with each of the safeguards of the Convention. Indeed, as the United Kingdom Government stressed, the beneficial purpose of extradition in preventing fugitive offenders from evading justice cannot be ignored in determining the scope of application of the Convention and of Article 3 in particular.

In the instant case it is common ground that the United Kingdom has no power over the practices and arrangements of the Virginia authorities which are the subject of the applicant's complaints. It is also true that in other international instruments cited by the United Kingdom Government—for example the 1951 United Nations Convention relating to the Status of Refugees (Article 33), the 1957 European Convention on Extradition (Article 11) and the 1984 United Nations Convention against Torture and Other Cruel, Inhuman and Degrading Treatment or Punishment (Article 3)—the problems of removing a person to another jurisdiction where unwanted consequences may follow are addressed expressly and specifically.

These considerations cannot, however, absolve the Contracting Parties from responsibility under Article 3 for all and any foreseeable consequences of extradition suffered outside their jurisdiction.

87. In interpreting the Convention regard must be had to its special character as a treaty for the collective enforcement of human rights and fundamental freedoms. Thus, the object and purpose of the Convention as an instrument for the protection of individual human beings require that its provisions be interpreted and applied so as to make its safeguards practical and effective. In addition, any interpretation of the rights and freedoms guaranteed has to be consistent with "the general spirit of the Convention, an instrument designed to maintain and promote the ideals and values of a democratic society" (see the Kjeldsen, Busk Madsen and Pedersen judgment of 7 December 1976, Series A no. 23, p. 27, § 53).

88. Article 3 makes no provision for exceptions and no derogation from it is permissible under Article 15 in time of war or other national

emergency. This absolute prohibition of torture and of inhuman or degrading treatment or punishment under the terms of the Convention shows that Article 3 enshrines one of the fundamental values of the democratic societies making up the Council of Europe. It is also to be found in similar terms in other international instruments such as the 1966 International Covenant on Civil and Political Rights and the 1969 American Convention on Human Rights and is generally recognised as an internationally accepted standard.

The question remains whether the extradition of a fugitive to another State where he would be subjected or be likely to be subjected to torture or to inhuman or degrading treatment or punishment would itself engage the responsibility of a Contracting State under Article 3. That the abhorrence of torture has such implications is recognised in Article 3 of the United Nations Convention Against Torture and Other Cruel, Inhuman or Degrading Treatment or Punishment, which provides that "no State Party shall ... extradite a person where there are substantial grounds for believing that he would be in danger of being subjected to torture." The fact that a specialised treaty should spell out in detail a specific obligation attaching to the prohibition is not already inherent in the general terms of Article 3 of the European Convention. It would hardly be compatible with the underlying values of the Convention, that "common heritage of political traditions, ideals, freedom and the rule of law" to which the Preamble refers, were a Contracting State knowingly to surrender a fugitive to another State where there were substantial grounds for believing that he would be in danger of being subjected to torture, however heinous the crime allegedly committed. Extradition in such circumstances, while not explicitly referred to in the brief and general wording of Article 3, would plainly be contrary to the spirit and intendment of the Article, and in the Court's view this inherent obligation not to extradite also extends to cases in which the fugitive would be faced in the receiving State by a real risk of exposure to inhuman or degrading treatment or punishment proscribed by that Article.

89. What amounts to "inhuman or degrading treatment or punishment" depends on all the circumstances of the case (see paragraph 100 below). Furthermore, inherent in the whole of the Convention is a search for a fair balance between the demands of the general interest of the community and the requirements of the protection of the individual's fundamental rights. As movement about the world becomes easier and crime takes on a larger international dimension, it is increasingly in the interest of all nations that suspected offenders who flee abroad should be brought to justice. Conversely, the establishment of safe havens for fugitives would not only result in danger for the State obliged to harbour the protected person but also tend to undermine the foundations of extradition. These considerations must also be included among the factors to be taken into account in the interpretation and application of the notions of inhuman and degrading treatment or punishment in extradition cases.

90. It is not normally for the Convention institutions to pronounce on the existence or otherwise of potential violations of the Convention. However, where an applicant claims that a decision to extradite him would, if implemented, be contrary to Article 3 by reason of its foreseeable consequences in the requesting country, a departure from this principle is necessary, in view of the serious and irreparable nature of the alleged suffering risked, in order to ensure the effectiveness of the safeguard provided by that Article (see paragraph 87 above).

91. In sum, the decision by a Contracting State to extradite a fugitive may give rise to an issue under Article 3, and hence engage the responsibility of that State under the Convention, where substantial grounds have been shown for believing that the person concerned, if extradited, faces a real risk of being subjected to torture or to inhuman or degrading treatment or punishment in the requesting country. The establishment of such responsibility inevitably involves an assessment of conditions in the requesting country against the standards of Article 3 of the Convention. Nonetheless, there is no question of adjudicating on or establishing the responsibility of the receiving country, whether under general international law, under the Convention or otherwise. In so far as any liability under the Convention is or may be incurred, it is liability incurred by the extraditing Contracting State by reason of its having taken action which has as a direct consequence the exposure of an individual to proscribed ill-treatment.

B. Application of Article 3 in the particular circumstances of the present case

[The Court first determines that it was not unlikely that Soering would be charged with and convicted of a crime that would expose him to the "death row phenomenon."]

2. Whether in the circumstances the risk of exposure to the "death row phenomenon" would make extradition a breach of Article 3

(a) General considerations

100. As is established in the Court's case-law, ill-treatment, including punishment, must attain a minimum level of severity if it is to fall within the scope of Article 3. The assessment of this minimum is, in the nature of things, relative; it depends on all the circumstances of the case, such as the nature and context of the treatment or punishment, the manner and method of its execution, its duration, its physical or mental effects and, in some instances, the sex, age and state of health of the victim (see the above-mentioned Ireland v. the United Kingdom judgment, Series A no. 25, p. 65, § 162; and the Tyrer judgment of 25 April 1978, Series A no. 26, pp. 14–15, §§ 29 and 30).

Treatment has been held by the Court to be both "inhuman" because it was premeditated, was applied for hours at a stretch and "caused, if not actual bodily injury, at least intense physical and mental suffering," and also, "degrading" because it was "such as to arouse in [its] victims feelings of fear, anguish and inferiority capable of humiliating and debasing them and possibly breaking their physical or moral resistance" (see the above-mentioned Ireland v. the United Kingdom judgment, p. 66, § 167). In order for a punishment or treatment associated with it to be "inhuman" or "degrading," the suffering or humiliation involved must in any event go beyond that inevitable element of suffering or humiliation connected with a given form of legitimate punishment (see the Tyrer judgment, *loc. cit.*). In this connection, account is to be taken not only of the physical pain experienced but also, where there is a considerable delay before execution of the punishment, of the sentenced person's mental anguish of anticipating the violence he is to have inflicted on him.

101. Capital punishment is permitted under certain conditions by Article 2 § 1 of the Convention, which reads:

> "Everyone's right to life shall be protected by law. No one shall be deprived of his life intentionally save in the execution of a sentence of a court following his conviction of a crime for which this penalty is provided by law."

In view of this wording, the applicant did not suggest that the death penalty *per se* violated Article 3. He, like the two Government Parties, agreed with the Commission that the extradition of a person to a country where he risks the death penalty does not in itself raise an issue under either Article 2 or Article 3. On the other hand, Amnesty International in their written comments * * * argued that the evolving standards in Western Europe regarding the existence and use of the death penalty required that the death penalty should now be considered as an inhuman and degrading punishment within the meaning of Article 3.

102. Certainly, "the Convention is a living instrument which ... must be interpreted in the light of present-day conditions"; and, in assessing whether a given treatment or punishment is to be regarded as inhuman or degrading for the purposes of Article 3, "the Court cannot but be influenced by the developments and commonly accepted standards in the penal policy of the member States of the Council of Europe in this field" (see the above-mentioned Tyrer judgment, Series A no. 26, pp. 15–16, § 31). *De facto* the death penalty no longer exists in time of peace in the Contracting States to the Convention. In the few Contracting States which retain the death penalty in law for some peacetime offences, death sentences, if ever imposed, are nowadays not carried out. This "virtual consensus in Western European legal systems that the death penalty is, under current circumstances, no longer consistent with regional standards of justice," to use the words of Amnesty International, is reflected in Protocol No. 6 to the Convention, which provides for the abolition of the death penalty in time of peace. Protocol No. 6 was opened for signature in April 1983, which in the practice of the Council of Europe indicates the absence of objection on the part of any of the Member States of the Organization; it came into force in March 1985 and to date has been ratified by thirteen Contracting States to the Convention, not however including the United Kingdom.

Whether these marked changes have the effect of bringing the death penalty *per se* within the prohibition of ill-treatment under Article 3 must be determined on the principles governing the interpretation of the Convention.

103. The Convention is to be read as a whole and Article 3 should therefore be construed in harmony with the provisions of Article 2. On this basis Article 3 evidently cannot have been intended by the drafters of the Convention to include a general prohibition of the death penalty since that would nullify the clear wording of Article 2 § 1.

Subsequent practice in national penal policy, in the form of a generalized abolition of capital punishment, could be taken as establishing the agreement of the Contracting States to abrogate the exception provided for under Article 2 § 1 and hence to remove a textual limit on the scope for evolutive interpretation of Article 3. However, Protocol No. 6, as a subsequent written agreement, shows that the intention of the Contracting Parties as recently as 1983 was to adopt the normal method of amendment of the text in order to introduce a new obligation to abolish capital punishment in time of peace and, what is more, to do so by an optional instrument allowing each State to choose the moment when to undertake such an engagement. In these conditions, notwithstanding the special character of the Convention (see paragraph 87 above), Article 3 cannot be interpreted as generally prohibiting the death penalty.

104. That does not mean however that circumstances relating to a death sentence can never give rise to an issue under Article 3. The manner in which it is imposed or executed, the personal circumstances of the condemned person and a disproportionality to the gravity of the crime committed, as well as the conditions of detention awaiting execution, are examples of factors capable of bringing the treatment or punishment received by the condemned person within the proscription under Article 3. Present-day attitudes in the Contracting States to capital punishment are relevant for the assessment whether the acceptable threshold of suffering or degradation has been exceeded.

(b) The particular circumstances

105. The applicant submitted that the circumstances to which he would be exposed as a consequence of the implementation of the Secretary of State's decision to return him to the United States, namely the "death row phenomenon," cumulatively constitute such serious treatment that his extradition would be contrary to Article 3. He cited in particular the delays in the appeal and review procedures following a death sentence, during which time he would be subject to increasing tension and psychological trauma; the fact, so he said, that the judge or jury in determining sentence is not obliged to take into account the defendant's age and mental state at the time of the offence; the extreme conditions of his future detention on "death row" in Mecklenburg Correctional Center, where he expects to be the victim of violence and sexual abuse because of his age, color and nationality; and the constant

spectre of the execution itself, including the ritual of execution. He also relied on the possibility of extradition or deportation, which he would not oppose, to the Federal Republic of Germany as accentuating the disproportionality of the Secretary of State's decision.

The Government of the Federal Republic of Germany took the view that, taking all the circumstances together, the treatment awaiting the applicant in Virginia would go so far beyond treatment inevitably connected with the imposition and execution of a death penalty as to be "inhuman" within the meaning of Article 3.

On the other hand, the conclusion expressed by the Commission was that the degree of severity contemplated by Article 3 would not be attained.

The United Kingdom Government shared this opinion. In particular, they disputed many of the applicant's factual allegations as to the conditions on death row in Mecklenburg and his expected fate there.

i. Length of detention prior to execution

106. The period that a condemned prisoner can expect to spend on death row in Virginia before being executed is on average six to eight years * * *. This length of time awaiting death is, as the Commission and the United Kingdom Government noted, in a sense largely of the prisoner's own making in that he takes advantage of all avenues of appeal which are offered to him by Virginia law. The automatic appeal to the Supreme Court of Virginia normally takes no more than six months * * *. The remaining time is accounted for by collateral attacks mounted by the prisoner himself in habeas corpus proceedings before both the State and Federal courts and in applications to the Supreme Court of the United States for certiorari review, the prisoner at each stage being able to seek a stay of execution * * *. The remedies available under Virginia law serve the purpose of ensuring that the ultimate sanction of death is not unlawfully or arbitrarily imposed.

Nevertheless, just as some lapse of time between sentence and execution is inevitable if appeal safeguards are to be provided to the condemned person, so it is equally part of human nature that the person will cling to life by exploiting those safeguards to the full. However well-intentioned and even potentially beneficial is the provision of the complex of post-sentence procedures in Virginia, the consequence is that the condemned prisoner has to endure for many years the conditions on death row and the anguish and mounting tension of living in the ever-present shadow of death.

ii. Conditions on death row

107. As to conditions in Mecklenburg Correctional Center, where the applicant could expect to be held if sentenced to death, the Court bases itself on the facts which were uncontested by the United Kingdom Government, without finding it necessary to determine the reliability of the additional evidence adduced by the applicant, notably as to the risk

of homosexual abuse and physical attack undergone by prisoners on death row (see paragraph 64 above).

The stringency of the custodial regime in Mecklenburg, as well as the services (medical, legal and social) and the controls (legislative, judicial and administrative) provided for inmates, are described in some detail above (see paragraphs 61–63 and 65–68). In this connection, the United Kingdom Government drew attention to the necessary requirement of extra security for the safe custody of prisoners condemned to death for murder. Whilst it might thus well be justifiable in principle, the severity of a special regime such as that operated on death row in Mecklenburg is compounded by the fact of inmates being subject to it for a protracted period lasting on average six to eight years.

iii. The applicant's age and mental state

108. At the time of the killings, the applicant was only 18 years old and there is some psychiatric evidence, which was not contested as such, that he "was suffering from [such] an abnormality of mind ... as substantially impaired his mental responsibility for his acts" (see paragraphs 11, 12 and 21 above).

Unlike Article 2 of the Convention, Article 6 of the 1966 International Covenant on Civil and Political Rights and Article 4 of the 1969 American Convention on Human Rights expressly prohibit the death penalty from being imposed on persons aged less than 18 at the time of commission of the offence. Whether or not such a prohibition be inherent in the brief and general language of Article 2 of the European Convention, its explicit enunciation in other, later international instruments, the former of which has been ratified by a large number of States Parties to the European Convention, at the very least indicates that as a general principle the youth of the person concerned is a circumstance which is liable, with others, to put in question the compatibility with Article 3 of measures connected with a death sentence.

It is in line with the Court's case-law (as summarized above at paragraph 100) to treat disturbed mental health as having the same effect for the application of Article 3.

109. Virginia law, as the United Kingdom Government and the Commission emphasized, certainly does not ignore these two factors. Under the Virginia Code account has to be taken of mental disturbance in a defendant, either as an absolute bar to conviction if it is judged to be sufficient to amount to insanity or, like age, as a fact in mitigation at the sentencing stage * * *. Additionally, indigent capital murder defendants are entitled to the appointment of a qualified mental health expert to assist in the preparation of their submissions at the separate sentencing proceedings * * *. These provisions in the Virginia Code undoubtedly serve, as the American courts have stated, to prevent the arbitrary or capricious imposition of the death penalty and narrowly to channel the sentencer's discretion * * *. They do not however remove the relevance of age and mental condition in relation to the acceptability,

under Article 3, of the "death row phenomenon" for a given individual once condemned to death.

Although it is not for this Court to prejudge issues of criminal responsibility and appropriate sentence, the applicant's youth at the time of the offence and his then mental state, on the psychiatric evidence as it stands, are therefore to be taken into consideration as contributory factors tending, in his case, to bring the treatment on death row within the terms of Article 3.

iv. Possibility of extradition to the Federal Republic of Germany

110. For the United Kingdom Government and the majority of the Commission, the possibility of extraditing or deporting the applicant to face trial in the Federal Republic of Germany (see paragraphs 16, 19, 26, 38 and 71–74 above), where the death penalty has been abolished under the Constitution * * *, is not material for the present purposes. Any other approach, the United Kingdom Government submitted, would lead to a "dual standard" affording the protection of the Convention to extraditable persons fortunate enough to have such an alternative destination available but refusing it to others not so fortunate.

This argument is not without weight. Furthermore, the Court cannot overlook either the horrible nature of the murders with which Mr. Soering is charged or the legitimate and beneficial role of extradition arrangements in combating crime. The purpose for which his removal to the United States was sought, in accordance with the Extradition Treaty between the United Kingdom and the United States, is undoubtedly a legitimate one. However, sending Mr. Soering to be tried in his own country would remove the danger of a fugitive criminal going unpunished as well as the risk of intense and protracted suffering on death row. It is therefore a circumstance of relevance for the overall assessment under Article 3 in that it goes to the search for the requisite fair balance of interests and to the proportionality of the contested extradition decision in the particular case (see paragraphs 89 and 104 above).

(c) Conclusion

111. For any prisoner condemned to death, some element of delay between imposition and execution of the sentence and the experience of severe stress in conditions necessary for strict incarceration are inevitable. The democratic character of the Virginia legal system in general and the positive features of Virginia trial, sentencing and appeal procedures in particular are beyond doubt. The Court agrees with the Commission that the machinery of justice to which the applicant would be subject in the United States is in itself neither arbitrary nor unreasonable, but, rather, respects the rule of law and affords not inconsiderable procedural safeguards to the defendant in a capital trial. Facilities are available on death row for the assistance of inmates, notably through provision of psychological and psychiatric services * * *.

However, in the Court's view, having regard to the very long period of time spent on death row in such extreme conditions, with the ever present and mounting anguish of awaiting execution of the death penalty, and to the personal circumstances of the applicant, especially his age and mental state at the time of the offence, the applicant's extradition to the United States would expose him to a real risk of treatment going beyond the threshold set by Article 3. A further consideration of relevance is that in the particular instance the legitimate purpose of extradition could be achieved by another means which would not involve suffering of such exceptional intensity or duration.

Accordingly, the Secretary of State's decision to extradite the applicant to the United States would, if implemented, give rise to a breach of Article 3.

This finding in no way puts in question the good faith of the United Kingdom Government, who have from the outset of the present proceedings demonstrated their desire to abide by their Convention obligations, firstly by staying the applicant's surrender to the United States authorities in accord with the interim measures indicated by the Convention institutions and secondly by themselves referring the case to the Court for a judicial ruling (see paragraphs 1, 4, 24 and 77 above). * * *

FOR THESE REASONS, THE COURT UNANIMOUSLY

1. *Holds* that, in the event of the Secretary of State's decision to extradite the applicant to the United States of America being implemented, there would be a violation of Article 3 * * *.

Notes and Questions

1. *Soering's Fate.* Soon after the judgment of the Court, the United States represented to the United Kingdom that Soering would not be tried for a crime where the death penalty could be imposed. Soering was extradited to the United States, tried in Virginia, and found guilty on two counts of first-degree murder; it was recommended by the jury that he serve two life terms. Richard Lillich & Hurst Hannum, *International Human Rights* 768 (3d ed. 1995). Might the Court have differed from the Commission because it thought that Virginia might be willing to reduce the charge only if the United Kingdom were ordered *not* to extradite Soering otherwise?

2. *The United Kingdom's Predicament.* Note that if Virginia had refused to try Soering for a charge where the death penalty could not be imposed, then the United Kingdom would have been caught between a rock and a hard place in international law. By the terms of the U.K.–U.S. extradition treaty it seemed clear that the United Kingdom was bound to extradite Soering, but by the terms of the European Convention for the Protection of Human Rights and Fundamental Freedoms, the United Kingdom was obligated to follow the judgment of the European Court of Human Rights. If the conflict had persisted in practice, what should the United Kingdom have done? Should the U.K. government follow the extradition treaty because it is the international agreement later in time? Should the U.K. government follow the European Human Rights Convention because the Convention concerns more fundamental rights? Is the answer linked to

notions about *jus cogens*? See Chapter 3 and look back to *Filartiga* in Chapter 1. As it turned out, Virginia gets the United Kingdom off the hook. There is more about international conflict of laws in general in Chapter 10 and about the specific conflict in *Soering* in Stephan Breitenmoser & Gunter Wilms, "Human Rights v. Extradition: The *Soering* Case," 11 *Michigan Journal of International Law* 845 (1990).

3. *The Extraterritorial Effect of the* Soering *Judgment*. Is it fair to impose the human rights obligations of the European Convention on a non-party such as the United States? See Christine van den Wyngaert, "Applying the European Convention on Human Rights to Extradition: Opening Pandora's Box?" 39 *International & Comparative Law Quarterly* 757 (1990). Why should U.S. death row conditions be a fit topic for consideration by the Strasbourg Court?

Chapter 7

STATES AND INTERNATIONAL LAW

Although individuals and a variety of non-state entities shape and are affected by international law, states have been central actors in the international legal system, at least since the Peace of Westphalia in 1648. But just what is a "state"? In this chapter, we examine the ways in which international law helps define the sovereign state, including the importance of recognition for states.

We also address legal questions involving the transformation of states and governments, questions that have attracted much attention in recent years. For example, between 1990 and 1993, East and West Germany united, as did North and South Yemen; Eritrea seceded from Ethiopia; and the Soviet Union, Yugoslavia, and Czechoslovakia broke apart into new states. During this period, Namibia also gained full independence, and the United Nations' Trusteeship over the Marshall Islands ended. Just in the 46th session of the United Nations (1991–1992), 16 states were admitted as new U.N. members. New governments are even more common than new states. The new governments may be radically different from their predecessors, as new constitutions are adopted or governments fall in coups. What are the legal effects of the succession of states or governments? Do the legal obligations of a state continue when the state breaks apart, or when its government changes radically? What is the significance, in municipal legal systems, of the recognition of a new state or government?

Finally, in Part B of this chapter, we look at the international law relating to self-determination. To what groups of peoples should the concept apply? When it does apply, what have been the consequences? Discussion of self-determination is important both in its own right and because it can contribute to our understanding of the nature of the sovereign state.

A. THE RECOGNITION AND SUCCESSION OF STATES AND GOVERNMENTS

KADIC v. KARADZIC

70 F.3d 232 (2d Cir.1995).

JON O. NEWMAN, CHIEF JUDGE:

Most Americans would probably be surprised to learn that victims of atrocities committed in Bosnia are suing the leader of the insurgent Bosnia–Serb forces in a United States District Court in Manhattan. Their claims seek to build upon the foundation of this Court's decision in *Filartiga v. Pena–Irala*, 630 F.2d 876 (2d Cir.1980), which recognized the important principle that the venerable Alien Tort Act, 28 U.S.C. § 1350 (1988), enacted in 1789 but rarely invoked since then, validly creates federal court jurisdiction for suits alleging torts committed anywhere in the world against aliens in violation of the law of nations. * * *

These issues arise on appeals by two groups of plaintiffs-appellants from the November 19, 1994, judgment of the United States District Court for the Southern District of New York (Peter K. Leisure, Judge), dismissing, for lack of subject matter jurisdiction, their suits against defendant-appellee Radovan Karadžić, President of the self-proclaimed Bosnian–Serb republic of "Srpska." *Doe v. Karadzic*, 866 F.Supp. 734 (S.D.N.Y.1994)("*Doe*"). For reasons set forth below, we hold that subject matter jurisdiction exists, that Karadžić may be found liable for genocide, war crimes, and crimes against humanity in his private capacity and for other violations in his capacity as a state actor, and that he is not immune from service of process. We therefore reverse and remand.

BACKGROUND

The plaintiffs-appellants are Croat and Muslim citizens of the internationally recognized nation of Bosnia–Herzegovina, formerly a republic of Yugoslavia. Their complaints, which we accept as true for purposes of this appeal, allege that they are victims, and representatives of victims, of various atrocities, including brutal acts of rape, forced prostitution, forced impregnation, torture, and summary execution, carried out by Bosnian–Serb military forces as part of a genocidal campaign conducted in the course of the Bosnian civil war. Karadžić, formerly a citizen of Yugoslavia and now a citizen of Bosnia–Herzegovina, is the President of a three-man presidency of the self-proclaimed Bosnian–Serb republic within Bosnia–Herzegovina, sometimes referred to as "Srpska," which claims to exercise lawful authority, and does in fact exercise actual control, over large parts of the territory of Bosnia–Herzegovina. In his capacity as President, Karadžić possesses ultimate command authority over the Bosnian–Serb military forces, and the injuries perpetrated upon plaintiffs were committed as part of a pattern of systematic human rights violations that was directed by Karadžić and carried out by the military forces under his command. The complaints allege that Karadžić acted in an official capacity either as the titular head of Srpska or in collaboration with the government of the recognized nation of the former Yugoslavia and its dominant constituent republic, Serbia.

The two groups of plaintiffs asserted causes of action for genocide, rape, forced prostitution and impregnation, torture and other cruel, inhuman, and degrading treatment, assault and battery, sex and ethnic inequality, summary execution, and wrongful death. They sought compensatory and punitive damages, attorney's fees, and, in one of the cases, injunctive relief. Plaintiffs grounded subject-matter jurisdiction in the Alien Tort Act, the Torture Victim Protection Act of 1991 ("Torture Victim Act"), Pub.L.No. 102–256, 106 Stat. 73 (1992), *codified at* 28 U.S.C. § 1350 note (Supp.V 1993), the general federal-question jurisdictional statute, 28 U.S.C. § 1331 (1988), and principles of supplemental jurisdiction, 28 U.S.C. § 1367 (Supp.V 1993). * * *

Without notice or a hearing, the District Court by-passed the issues briefed by the parties and dismissed both actions for lack of subject-matter jurisdiction. * * *

Turning to the issue of subject-matter jurisdiction under the Alien Tort Act, the Court concluded that "acts committed by non-state actors do not violate the law of nations." Finding that "the current Bosnian–Serb warring military faction does not constitute a recognized state," and that "the members of Karadžić's faction do not act under the color of any recognized state law," the Court concluded that "the acts alleged in the instant actions, while grossly repugnant, cannot be remedied through [the Alien Tort Act]." The Court did not consider the plaintiffs' alternative claim that Karadžić acted under color of law by acting in concert with the Serbian Republic of the former Yugoslavia, a recognized nation. * * *

Discussion * * *

I. Subject–Matter Jurisdiction

Appellants allege three statutory bases for the subject matter jurisdiction of the District Court—the Alien Tort Act, the Torture Victim Act, and the general federal-question jurisdictional statute.

A. The Alien Tort Act

1. General Application to Appellants' Claims

The Alien Tort Act provides:

> The district courts shall have original jurisdiction of any civil action by an alien for a tort only, committed in violation of the law of nations or a treaty of the United States.

28 U.S.C. § 1350 (1988). Our decision in *Filartiga* established that this statute offers federal subject-matter jurisdiction when the following three conditions are satisfied: (1) an alien sues (2) for a tort (3) committed in violation of the law of nations (*i.e.*, international law). 630 F.2d at 878; *see also Amerada Hess Shipping Corp. v. Argentine Republic*, 830 F.2d 421, 425 (2d Cir.1987), *rev'd on other grounds*, 488 U.S.

428, 102 L.Ed.2d 818, 109 S.Ct. 683 (1989). The first two requirements are plainly satisfied here, and the only disputed issue is whether plaintiffs have pleaded violations of international law. * * *

Karadžić contends that appellants have not alleged violations of the norms of international law because such norms bind only states and persons acting under color of a state's law, not private individuals. In making this contention, Karadžić advances the contradictory positions that he is not a state actor, even as he asserts that he is the President of the self-proclaimed Republic of Srpska. For their part, the Kadic appellants also take somewhat inconsistent positions in pleading defendant's role as President of Srpska, and also contending that "Karadžić is not an official of any government."

Judge Leisure accepted Karadžić's contention that "acts committed by non-state actors do not violate the law of nations," and considered him to be a non-state actor. The Judge appears to have deemed state action required primarily on the basis of cases determining the need for state action as to claims of official torture, *see, e.g., Carmichael v. United Technologies Corp.*, 835 F.2d 109 (5th Cir.1988), without consideration of the substantial body of law, discussed below, that renders private individuals liable for some international law violations.

We do not agree that the law of nations, as understood in the modern era, confines its reach to state action. Instead, we hold that certain forms of conduct violate the law of nations whether undertaken by those acting under the auspices of a state or only as private individuals. * * *

Karadžić also contends that Congress intended the state-action requirement of the Torture Victim Act to apply to actions under the Alien Tort Act. We disagree. Congress enacted the Torture Victim Act to codify the cause of action recognized by this Circuit in *Filartiga*, and to further extend that cause of action to plaintiffs who are U.S. citizens. At the same time, Congress indicated that the Alien Tort Act "has other important uses and should not be replaced," because

> Claims based on torture and summary executions do not exhaust the list of actions that may appropriately be covered [by the Alien Tort Act]. That statute should remain intact to permit suits based on other norms that already exist or may ripen in the future into rules of customary international law.

The scope of the Alien Tort Act remains undiminished by enactment of the Torture Victim Act.

2. Specific Application of Alien Tort Act to Appellants' Claims

[The court concludes that genocide and war crimes are violations of international law that may be committed by individuals and may be the subject of Alien Tort Act claims against an individual.]

Torture and summary execution. In *Filartiga* we held that *official* torture is prohibited by universally accepted norms of international law, and the Torture Victim Act confirms this holding and extends it to cover summary execution. Torture Victim Act §§ 2(a), 3(a). However, torture and summary execution—when not perpetrated in the course of genocide or war crimes—are proscribed by international law only when committed by state officials or under color of law. *See* Declaration on Torture art. 1 (defining torture as being "inflicted by or at the instigation of a public official"); Convention Against Torture and Other Cruel, Inhuman, or Degrading Treatment or Punishment pt. I, art. 1, 23 I.L.M. 1027 (1984), *as modified*, 24 I.L.M. 535 (1985), *entered into force* June 26, 1987, *ratified by United States* Oct. 21, 1994, 34 I.L.M. 590, 591 (1995)(defining torture as "inflicted by or at the instigation of or with the consent or acquiescence of a public official or other person acting in an official capacity"); Torture Victim Act § 2(a)(imposing liability on individuals acting "under actual or apparent authority, or color of law, of any foreign nation").

* * * It suffices to hold at this stage that the alleged atrocities are actionable under the Alien Tort Act, without regard to state action, to the extent that they were committed in pursuit of genocide or war crimes, and otherwise may be pursued against Karadžić to the extent that he is shown to be state actor. Since the meaning of the state action requirement for purposes of international law violations will likely arise on remand and has already been considered by the District Court, we turn next to that requirement.

3. The State Action Requirement for International Law Violations

In dismissing plaintiffs' complaints for lack of subject-matter jurisdiction, the District Court concluded that the alleged violations required state action and that the "Bosnian–Serb entity" headed by Karadžić does not meet the definition of a state. Appellants contend that they are entitled to prove that Srpska satisfies the definition of a state for purposes of international law violations and, alternatively, that Karadžić acted in concert with the recognized state of the former Yugoslavia and its constituent republic, Serbia.

(a) *Definition of a state in international law.* The definition of a state is well established in international law:

> Under international law, a state is an entity that has a defined territory and permanent population, under the control of its own government, and that engages in, or has the capacity to engage in, formal relations with other such entities.

Restatement (Third) [*of the Foreign Relations Law of the United States*] § 201. * * *

Although the Restatement's definition of statehood requires the *capacity* to engage in formal relations with other states, it does not require recognition by other states. *See Restatement (Third)* § 202 cmt. b ("An entity that satisfies the requirements of § 201 is a state whether or not its statehood is formally recognized by other states.") * * *

The customary international law of human rights, such as the proscription of official torture, applies to states without distinction between recognized and unrecognized states. *See Restatement (Third)* §§ 207, 702. It would be anomalous indeed if non-recognition by the United States, which typically reflects disfavor with a foreign regime—sometimes due to human rights abuses—had the perverse effect of shielding officials of the unrecognized regime from liability for those violations of international law norms that apply only to state actors.

Appellants' allegations entitle them to prove that Karadžić's regime satisfies the criteria for a state, for purposes of those international law violations requiring state action. Srpska is alleged to control defined territory, control populations within its power, and to have entered into agreements with other governments. It has a president, a legislature, and its own currency. These circumstances readily appear to satisfy the criteria for a state in all aspects of international law. Moreover, it is likely that the state action concept, where applicable for some violations like "official" torture, requires merely the semblance of official authority. The inquiry, after all, is whether a person purporting to wield official power has exceeded internationally recognized standards of civilized conduct, not whether statehood in all its formal aspects exists.

(b) *Acting in concert with a foreign state.* Appellants also sufficiently alleged that Karadžić acted under color of law insofar as they claimed that he acted in concert with the former Yugoslavia, the statehood of which is not disputed. The "color of law" jurisprudence of 42 U.S.C. § 1983 is a relevant guide to whether a defendant has engaged in official action for purposes of jurisdiction under the Alien Tort Act. A private individual acts under color of law within the meaning of section 1983 when he acts together with state officials or with significant state aid. The appellants are entitled to prove their allegations that Karadžić acted under color of law of Yugoslavia by acting in concert with Yugoslav officials or with significant Yugoslavian aid.

[The court further concludes that the Torture Victim Protection Act permits "the appellants to pursue their claims of official torture under the jurisdiction conferred by the Alien Tort Act and also under the general federal question jurisdiction of section 1331," that the defendant was properly served with process, and that he is subject to the personal jurisdiction of the federal district court. The court also rejects the defendant's contention that the case presents a nonjusticiable political question.]

THE MONTEVIDEO CONVENTION

Convention on Rights and Duties of States
Dec. 26, 1933, 49 Stat. 3097, 165 L.N.T.S. 19.

Article 1

The state as a person of international law should possess the following qualifications: *a*) a permanent population; *b*) a defined territory; *c*) government; and *d*) capacity to enter into relations with the other states.

ARTICLE 2

The federal state shall constitute a sole person in the eyes of international law.

ARTICLE 3

The political existence of the state is independent of recognition by the other states. Even before recognition the state has the right to defend its integrity and independence, to provide for its conservation and prosperity, and consequently to organize itself as it sees fit, to legislate upon its interests, administer its services, and to define the jurisdiction and competence of its courts.

The exercise of these rights has no other limitation than the exercise of the rights of other states according to international law.

ARTICLE 4

States are juridically equal, enjoy the same rights, and have equal capacity in their exercise. The rights of each one do not depend upon the power which it possesses to assure its exercise, but upon the simple fact of its existence as a person under international law.

ARTICLE 5

The fundamental rights of states are not susceptible of being affected in any manner whatsoever.

ARTICLE 6

The recognition of a state merely signifies that the state which recognizes it accepts the personality of the other with all the rights and duties determined by international law. Recognition is unconditional and irrevocable.

ARTICLE 7

The recognition of a state may be express or tacit. The latter results from any act which implies the intention of recognizing the new state.

ARTICLE 8

No state has the right to intervene in the internal or external affairs of another.

Notes and Questions

1. *The Breakup of Yugoslavia. Kadic v. Karadzic,* which serves as a reminder that municipal courts may decide international human rights cases, involves allegations that the leader of the Bosnian Serbs was responsible for numerous international human rights violations during ethnic fighting that followed the breakup of Yugoslavia. Yugoslavia, which was originally known as the "Serb–Croat–Slovene State," was recognized as independent in treaties following World War I. It was composed of Macedonia, Croatia, Slovenia, and Bosnia and Herzegovina, all of which had been under the control of the Austrian–Hungarian Empire, and of independent Serbia and nominally independent Montenegro. Following World War II, the govern-

ment of Marshall Tito headed the Socialist Federal Republic of Yugoslavia (SFRY) for many years. During 1991–1992, the SFRY broke up into what are now generally recognized as Croatia, Bosnia–Herzegovina, Slovenia, and the Former Yugoslav Republic of Macedonia; two other components of the SFRY, Serbia and Montenegro, form the Federal Republic of Yugoslavia. Since 1991–1992, fighting among ethnic groups has plagued the region, Croatia and Bosnia–Herzegovina in particular. We revisit the situation in the Former Yugoslavia later in this chapter, when we consider state succession and self-determination, and in Chapter 8, when we examine the role of the United Nations in efforts to settle the conflict in the region. Our concern at this point is with the basic concept of the sovereign state.

2. *Defining the "State."* The *Kadic* court relies on the *Restatement (Third) of Foreign Relations Law* to define a "state." The definition in Article 1 of the Montevideo Convention is virtually identical to that in the *Restatement*, and is widely accepted. Should international lawyers rely on particular parts of the Montevideo Convention's definition more than on other parts? Is it more important, for example, for a state to have the "capacity to enter into relations" with other states than to have a defined territory?

Note that the question of what constitutes a state arises in a variety of contexts. For example, international lawyers are concerned with how and whether "states" may participate in international or municipal arbitral or judicial proceedings, be admitted to international organizations, allocate responsibilities to other entities, be affected by municipal statutes, and enter into treaties or other agreements. Why is it important for the *Kadic* court to analyze whether Srpska is a state? Is it likely that Srpska would be regarded as a state for other purposes, such as admission to the United Nations in accordance with Article 4 of the U.N. Charter? Why is it an entity can be considered a state for some purposes, but not others?

3. *States and International Decision Makers.* Who determines whether an entity is a "state"? As *Kadic v. Karadzic* illustrates, sometimes the answer is municipal courts. The same variety of decision makers that address other issues of international law—including, very often, foreign affairs offices of states—may grapple with whether a particular entity is a "state."

4. *The Constitutive and Declaratory Theories of Recognition.* Should recognition by already existing states be required as a condition of statehood? At times in history, the question has seemed to be of only abstract interest, for most recognitions of states have been routine. But when the Former Yugoslav Republic of Macedonia declared its independence during the breakup of Yugoslavia, only a very few states initially recognized it. This reluctance partly reflected Greece's complaints over Macedonia's use of the name of Greece's northern region. See Paul C. Szasz, "Introductory Note," 34 I.L.M. 1461 (1995). Is formal recognition by other states a legal prerequisite for statehood? Would this "constitutive" view mean, for example, that an established state would be entitled to invade an unrecognized "state" without its invasion being subject to scrutiny under international law? How many existing states need to recognize an entity before it legally becomes a state? One alternative to the constitutive view is to consider

recognition as merely "declaratory" of statehood, a position reflected in Articles 3 and 6 of the Montevideo Convention.

5. *Recognition and the Montevideo Convention.* What explains the treatment of recognition in the Montevideo Convention? The Montevideo Convention, which has been accepted by 15 Latin American states and by the United States, was adopted in 1933 at the 7th International Conference of American States. This Conference followed the 1930 pronouncement of the "Estrada Doctrine" by Mexico's Secretary of Foreign Relations, Don Genaro Estrada. Estrada called for an end to the practice of recognizing new governments. He stated:

> that the Mexican Government is issuing no declarations in the sense of grants of recognition, since that nation considers that such a course is an insulting practice and one which, in addition to the fact that it offends the sovereignty of other nations, implies that judgment of some sort may be passed upon the internal affairs of those nations by other governments, inasmuch as the latter assume, in effect, an attitude of criticism, when they decide, favorably or unfavorably, as to the legal qualifications of foreign regimes.

2 Marjorie Whiteman, *Digest of International Law* 85–86 (1963). Estrada's evident concern with intervention by major powers in the internal and external affairs of weaker Latin American states is reflected in the Montevideo Convention.

6. *Recognition and Positivist Conceptions of International Law.* Lassa Oppenheim, writing in Great Britain in the early twentieth century, held another view of the role of recognition. He thought the existence of a state required a people, a territory, a government, and sovereignty, but he went on to specify a role for recognition:

> As the basis of the Law of Nations is the common consent of the civilised States, statehood alone does not include membership of the Family of Nations. There are States in existence, although their number decreases gradually, which are not, or not fully, members of that family because their civilisation, if any, does not enable them and their subjects to act in conformity with the principles of International Law. Those States which are members are either original members because the Law of Nations grew up gradually between them through custom and treaties, or they are members which have been recognised by the body of members already in existence when they were born. For every State that is not already, but wants to be, a member, recognition is therefore necessary. * * *
>
> * * * It is generally agreed that a new State before its recognition cannot claim any right which a member of the Family of Nations has towards other members. * * * Through recognition only and exclusively a State becomes an International Person and a subject of International Law.

1 Lassa Oppenheim, *International Law* § 71 (1st ed. 1905). What accounts for Oppenheim's view of the role of recognition? Why is Oppenheim's view discredited today?

7. *The Importance of Recognition.* Does rejection of Oppenheim's view of recognition mean that recognition in some sense is not essential? Even if formal recognition is not a prerequisite of statehood, why might a new state—even one whose government appears stable and in control of the population—care about recognition? How well can a new state function if other states refuse to acknowledge its existence or enter into relations with it? Consider in this regard Professor D'Amato's definition of a "state:"

> As a construct of international law, a [state] is nothing more nor less than a bundle of entitlements, of which the most important ones define and secure its boundaries on a map, while others define its jurisdictional competency and the rights of its citizens when they travel outside its borders. * * *
>
> * * * [A state's] identity * * *, its "bundle of entitlements," is dependent upon the acquiescence of all the other states in the system. Since every state has the same bundle of entitlements—otherwise there would be legal inequality among states, a proposition that has never seriously been advocated—the other states in the system have an obvious interest in acquiescing in the entitlements of any given state.

Anthony D'Amato, *International Law: Process and Prospect* 19, 21 (2d ed. 1995).

8. *The Variety of "States."* Consider whether, and in what circumstances, the following entities should be regarded as "states":

a. The Republic of Nauru, an eight-square-mile South Pacific island with a population of 8000? Nauru is not a member of the United Nations, but is a party to the Statute of the International Court of Justice.

b. The Principality of Liechtenstein, which has delegated to Switzerland much responsibility for its defense, customs affairs, and diplomatic relations with other states? Liechtenstein was admitted to the United Nations in 1990.

c. Kuwait, after it was overrun by Iraq in 1990? In Chapter 8 we examine Article 2(4) of the United Nations Charter, which proscribes resort to the threat or use of force against the territorial integrity or political independence of any state. The U.N. General Assembly's Declaration of Principles of International Law Concerning Friendly Relations and Cooperation among States, G.A. Res. 2625 (1970), also provides that territorial acquisition resulting from the use of force will not be recognized as legal. More particularly with respect to Kuwait, the U.N. Security Council condemned Iraq's invasion as illegal and called on "all States, international organizations and specialized agencies not to recognize" the annexation. S.C. Res. 662 (1990). But what if the Iraqi occupation had continued for many years?

d. The Navajo Nation, which is comprised of approximately 200,000 Navajos living within a large, clearly bounded territory in the southwestern United States? In 1849, the Navajos acknowledged that, by virtue of an 1848 U.S.–Mexican treaty, the tribe "was lawfully placed under the exclusive jurisdiction and protection" of the United States.

Treaty between the United States of America and the Navajo Tribe of Indians, Sept. 9, 1849, art. I, 9 Stat. 974. An 1868 treaty set reservation boundaries and specified additional details of U.S.–Navajo relations. Treaty Between the United States of America and the Navajo Tribe of Indians, June 1, 1868, 15 Stat. 667. The Navajo Nation has its own constitution and exercises domestic self-governance. The United States has recognized the Navajos' right to a constitution to "provide for the exercise by the Navajo Tribe of any powers vested in the tribe * * * together with such additional powers as the members of the tribe may, with the approval of the Secretary of the Interior, deem proper to include therein." Pub. L. No. 81–474, § 6, 64 Stat. 44 (1950).

e. Canada? That Canada is now a state is, of course, certain, but when did it become one? Canada's status as a British colony was replaced initially with Dominion status within the British Commonwealth, which was short of full, formal independence. In 1931 the Statute of Westminster, 22 Geo. V, c. 4, recognized the autonomy of Canada and other Dominions by declaring that a Dominion's laws made after the effective date of the Statute were not inoperative because contrary to British laws. The Statute of Westminster also stated that acts of the British Parliament would not be considered applicable as law in a Dominion without the Dominion's consent. In 1937 the Imperial Conference recognized that each member of the British Commonwealth participated "in a multilateral treaty as an individual entity" and generally was "in no way responsible for the obligations undertaken by any other member." But Canadian representatives had participated in commercial treaty negotiations in the nineteenth century and had separately signed the Treaty of Versailles concluding World War I. Canada also joined the League of Nations. Finally, note that until 1982, when the United Kingdom passed the Canada Act, Canada could not amend its Constitution without approval of the Parliament of Great Britain.

f. The Byelorussian S.S.R. and the Ukrainian S.S.R., before the break-up of the Soviet Union? These entities were Union Republics within the Soviet Union and were referred to as "sovereign states" in the Soviet Constitution. The two Union Republics were members of the United Nations. Article 80 of the 1977 Soviet Constitution, which was virtually identical to Article 18a of the 1936 Constitution (as amended in 1944), gave Union Republics "the right to enter into relations with foreign states, conclude treaties with them, exchange diplomatic and consular representatives, and to be part in the work of international organizations." John N. Hazard, *Constitutions of the Countries of the World: Union of Soviet Socialist Republics* 33 (1978). See Henn–Jüri Uibopuu, "International Legal Personality of Union Republics of U.S.S.R.," 24 *International & Comparative Law Quarterly* 811 (1975).

g. The Commonwealth of Independent States? The C.I.S. was formed by the Alma Alta Declaration of December 21, 1991, which proclaims that with the establishment of the C.I.S., "the Union of Soviet Socialist Republics ceases to exist." The Declaration was signed on behalf of the Republic of Azerbaijan, the Republic of Armenia, the Republic of Belarus, the Republic of Kazakhstan, the Republic of Kyrgystan, the Republic of Moldova, the Russian Federation, the Republic of

Tajikistan, Turkmenistan, the Republic of Uzbekistan, and Ukraine, and was later acceded to by the Republic of Georgia. The Declaration provides: "Cooperation between the parties in the Commonwealth shall be conducted in accordance with the principle of equality through coordinating bodies constituted on a basis of parity and operating under * * * agreements between the parties in the Commonwealth, which is neither a State nor a supra-State entity." 31 I.L.M. 138, 148 (1992).

h. The Republic of Belarus, after it joined the Commonwealth of Independent States? According to the Alma Alta Declaration, "unified command of strategic military forces and joint control over nuclear weapons will be maintained," and Belarus has signed the collective security pact of the C.I.S. Its government has also supported close political and economic ties with the Russian Federation, including a merger of the monetary systems of the two entities. In May 1995, Russia and Belarus accepted a customs union and agreed to the removal of border posts. See Steven Erlanger, "Yeltsin Finds Success in Tiny Belarus," *New York Times*, May 27, 1995, at 5.

i. The Republic of Tatarstan, which is one of the 21 component republics of the Russian Federation? Tatarstan has an area of over 26,000 miles and is home to a approximately 3,750,000 people. In March 1992, over 60 per cent of voters in a referendum in Tatarstan agreed "that the Republic of Tatarstan is a sovereign state, a subject of international law, developing its relations with the Russian federation and other republics and states on the basis of equal treaties." *The Economist*, Mar. 28, 1992, at 49. Why do you think Tatarstan declared itself a sovereign state? Under a February 1994 treaty between Russia and Tatarstan, Tatarstan retained its own constitution, but acknowledged it was "united" with Russia. *The Economist*, Jan. 14, 1995, at 43–44.

Do these examples suggest that a state's sovereignty is a variable bundle of rights and duties, with some states being "more sovereign" than others? Or does every state possess some inviolable set of identical sovereign rights?

9. *Challenges to the Central Role of the Sovereign State in International Law.* The institution of the sovereign state has been subject to attacks on many fronts. Some, for example, stress the importance of economics in the modern world and see states as imposing artificial boundaries that impede the efficient operation of markets. Others argue that states are either too large or too small to respond well to current challenges; management problems may require structures larger than the state, while entities smaller than the state can most effectively produce political legitimacy. Still others criticize the state as standing in the way of a full realization of human rights and individual freedoms. In light of such criticisms of the state, what justifies its continuing role as a central actor in international law? See "Theoretical Perspectives on the Transformation of Sovereignty," 1994 *American Society of International Law Proceedings* 1.

10. *The Succession of States and Governments.* When new states or governments emerge, what is to become of the treaty commitments, debts, and liabilities of their predecessors? The next reading is an opinion from the Arbitration Commission of the Conference for Peace in Yugoslavia that

concerns succession issues following the breakup of Yugoslavia. The arbitrator in the *Tinoco Arbitration*, which follows the Arbitration Commission's opinion, elaborates widely accepted principles about the legal effects of succession and nonrecognition. Judges in municipal cases also often decide cases involving new states or governments. If the court's own government has not recognized a new "state," should it have access to the municipal court proceedings? What effect should be given to the official acts of an unrecognized entity? The U.S. court in the *Goldberg Case,* the last reading in this Part A, addresses these issues in the context of a dispute over stolen Byzantine mosaics.

CONFERENCE FOR PEACE IN YUGOSLAVIA ARBITRATION COMMISSION OPINION NO. 9

31 *International Legal Materials* 1523 (1992).

On 18 May 1992 the Chairman of the Arbitration Commission received a letter from Lord Carrington, Chairman of the Conference for Peace in Yugoslavia, asking for the Commission's opinion on the following question:

> If this is the case, (is the dissolution of the SFRY now complete?) on what basis and by what means should the problems of the succession of states arising between the different states emerging from the SFRY be settled? * * *

1. * * * In Opinion No. 8, the Arbitration Commission concluded that the dissolution of the Socialist Federal Republic of Yugoslavia (SFRY) had been completed and that the state no longer existed.

New states have been created on the territory of the former SFRY and replaced it. All are successor states to the former SFRY.

2. As the Arbitration Commission pointed out in its first Opinion, the succession of states is governed by the principles of international law embodied in the Vienna Convention of 23 August 1978 and 8 April 1983, which all Republics have agreed should be the foundation for discussions between them on the succession of states at the Conference for Peace in Yugoslavia.

The chief concern is that the solution adopted should lead to an equitable outcome, with the states concerned agreeing [on] procedures subject to compliance with the imperatives of general international law and, more particularly, the fundamental rights of the individual and of peoples and minorities.

3. In the declaration on former Yugoslavia adopted in Lisbon on 27 June 1992, the European Council stated that:

> "the Community will not recognize the new federal entity comprising Serbia and Montenegro as the successor State of the former Yugoslavia until the moment that decision has been taken by the qualified international institutions. They have decided to demand

the suspension of the delegation of Yugoslavia at the CSCE and other international fora and organizations."

The Council thereby demonstrated its conviction that the Federal Republic of Yugoslavia (Serbia and Montenegro) has no right to consider itself the SFRY's sole successor.

4. The Arbitration Commission is therefore of the opinion that:

— the successor states to the SFRY must together settle all aspects of the succession by agreement;

— in the resulting negotiations, the successor states must try to achieve an equitable solution by drawing on the principles embodied in the 1978 and 1983 Vienna Conventions and where appropriate, general international law;

— furthermore full account must be taken of the principle of equality of rights and duties between states in respect to international law;

— the SFRY's membership of international organizations must be terminated according to their statutes and that none of the successor states may thereupon claim for itself alone the membership rights previously enjoyed by the former SFRY;

— property of the SFRY located in third countries must be divided equitably between the successor states;

— the SFRY's assets and debts must likewise be shared equitably between the successor states;

— the states concerned must peacefully settle all disputes relating to succession to the SFRY which could not be resolved by agreement in line with the principle laid down in the United Nations Charter;

— they must moreover seek a solution by means of inquiry, mediation, conciliation, arbitration or judicial settlement;

— since, however, no specific question has been put to it, the Commission cannot at this stage venture an opinion on the difficulties that could arise from the very real problems associated with the succession to the former Yugoslavia.

Notes and Questions

1. *The European Union and the Breakup of Yugoslavia.* The European Community, now known as the European Union, and its member states convened a Yugoslav peace conference in 1991. As part of its peace efforts, the EC established an Arbitration Commission to engage in fact-finding and render legal opinions concerning aspects of the Yugoslav crisis. Beginning in August 1992, the Conference on the Former Yugoslavia, co-chaired by the Secretary–General of the United Nations and the head of the state holding the Presidency of the EC Council of Ministers, served as a forum for discussions and proposals concerning sanctions, cessation of violence, transit, humanitarian aid, and compliance with United Nations resolutions. See International Conference on the Former Yugoslavia: Documents Adopted at the London Conference, 31 I.L.M. 1488 (1992). The Conference structure

was terminated in January 1996, and efforts toward peace in the Former Yugoslavia have been pursued through an initiative involving the United Nations and the North Atlantic Treaty Organization. That initiative is discussed in Chapter 8.

2. *Succession to Treaties.* Agreements among successor and predecessor states often address what is to become of treaty obligations when new states emerge as a result of secession, the disintegration of existing states, or independence from a colonial power. Sometimes, however, as in the break-up of Yugoslavia, successor states have made no agreements concerning preexisting treaties. Should new states then be entitled to begin life with a "clean slate," under no obligation to continue to be bound by its predecessor's treaties? That is the general position of the Vienna Convention on Succession of States in Respect of Treaties, arts. 2(f), 16, Aug. 23, 1978, U.N. Doc. A/CONF.80/31 (1978), 17 I.L.M. 1488, 1490, 1496 (not yet in force), for "newly independent" states, defined as previously dependent territories "for the international relations of which the predecessor state was responsible." When parts of the territory of an existing state separate to form one or more new states, however, many treaties are said to continue in force. See *id.* art. 34, 17 I.L.M. at 1509. Is it sensible to distinguish among types of new states for the purpose of succession of treaty obligations? What practical reasons support a general presumption that treaties should continue in force for all successor states?

Should distinctions be made among types of treaties for the purpose of succession? For example, should Croatia be able to disregard historical agreements that establish boundaries with a neighboring state? Should the same presumptions concerning succession apply to bilateral and multilateral treaties? Note that an exchange of notes between a new state and its predecessor's treaty partners may specify which bilateral treaties are considered as continuing in effect. See, *e.g.,* Marian Nash (Leich), "Contemporary Practice of the United States Relating to International Law: Succession of States," 89 *American Journal of International Law* 761 (1995).

3. *Succession to Liabilities and Debts.* What should happen to the Former Yugoslavia's liabilities and debts, absent an agreement accepted by the successor states? In the Redward Claim (Hawaiian Claims)(Great Britain v. United States), 6 U.N.R.I.A.A. 157 (1925), the arbitral tribunal held that legal liability for wrongful imprisonment by the Hawaiian Republic had been extinguished when the Republic was annexed by the United States. Why should this be? Should state debts also be extinguished? Article 41 of the 1983 Vienna Convention on the Succession of States in Respect of State Property, Archives and Debts, Apr. 8, 1983, U.N. Doc. A/CONF.117/14 (1983), 22 I.L.M. 306, 324, which has not entered into force, provides for the succession of debt in equitable proportions when a state dissolves and the parts of its territory form two or more successor states. Arbitration Commission Opinion No. 9 also refers to equity. What does equity mean in this context? See Chapter 3 for discussion of the various meanings of equity in international law.

4. *Succession to Membership in International Organizations.* What should happen to the Former Yugoslavia's membership in international organizations? In Resolution 47/1 (1992), the U.N. General Assembly voted

that the Federal Republic of Yugoslavia (Serbia and Montenegro) could not continue automatically the membership of the Former Yugoslavia in the United Nations. The General Assembly decided that the Federal Republic "should apply for membership in the United Nations and that it shall not participate in the work of the General Assembly." What explains the U.N. action, given that Russia was allowed to retain the U.N. membership of the Soviet Union when it broke apart, and India was permitted to keep the U.N. membership of British India when Pakistan and India separated in 1947? Note that the Federal Republic of Yugoslavia was the subject of U.N. Security Council sanctions for its aggressive actions in Croatia and Bosnia–Herzegovina. See S.C. Res. 757 (1992). Also, unlike the cases of Russia and India, no devolution agreement specified the entity entitled to continuing U.N. membership. Furthermore, Russia and India, unlike the Federal Republic of Yugoslavia, each had a majority of the predecessor state's territory, population, and resources. See Michael P. Scharf, "Musical Chairs: The Dissolution of States and Membership in the United Nations," 28 *Cornell International Law Journal* 29 (1995). Croatia, Bosnia–Herzegovina, Slovenia, and the Former Yugoslav Republic of Macedonia have all been admitted as new members of the United Nations.

5. *New States and Customary International Law.* Should decision makers consider a new state to be bound by customary international law? The nature of customary international law is considered in Chapter 3.

THE TINOCO ARBITRATION

Arbitration Between Great Britain and Costa Rica, Opinion and Award of William H. Taft, Sole Arbitrator, Washington, D.C., Oct. 18, 1923, 18 *American Journal of International Law* 147 (1924), 1 U.N.R.I.A.A. 369 (1923).

This is a proceeding under a treaty of arbitration between Great Britain and Costa Rica. * * *

In January, 1917, the Government of Costa Rica, under President Alfredo Gonzalez, was overthrown by Frederico Tinoco, the Secretary of War. Gonzalez fled. Tinoco assumed power, called an election, and established a new constitution in June, 1917. His government continued until August, 1919, when Tinoco retired, and left the country. His government fell in September following. After a provisional government under one Barquero, the old constitution was restored and elections held under it. The restored government is a signatory to this treaty of arbitration.

On the 22nd of August, 1922, the Constitutional Congress of the restored Costa Rican Government passed a law known as Law of Nullities No. 41. It invalidated all contracts between the executive power and private persons, made with or without approval of the legislative power between January 27, 1917 and September 2, 1919, covering the period of the Tinoco government. It also nullified the legislative decree No. 12 of the Tinoco government, dated June 28, 1919, authorizing the issue of the 15 million colones currency notes. The colon is a Costa Rican gold coin or standard nominally equal to 46$\frac{1}{12}$

cents of an American dollar, but it is uncoined and the exchange value of the paper colon actually in circulation is much less. The Nullities Law also invalidated the legislative decree of the Tinoco government of July 8, 1919, authorizing the circulation of notes of the nomination of 1000 colones, and annulled all transactions with such colones bills between holders and the state, directly or indirectly, by means of negotiation or contract, if thereby the holders received value as if they were ordinary bills of current issue.

The claim of Great Britain is that the Royal Bank of Canada and the Central Costa Rica Petroleum Company are Britain corporations whose shares are owned by British subjects; that the Banco Internacional of Costa Rica and the Government of Costa Rica are both indebted to the Royal Bank in the sum of 998,000 colones, evidenced by 998 one thousand colones bills held by the Bank; that the Central Costa Rica Petroleum Company owns, by due assignment, a grant by the Tinoco government in 1918 of the right to explore for and exploit oil deposits in Costa Rica, and that both the indebtedness and the concession have been annulled without right by the Law of Nullities and should be excepted from its operation. She asks an award that she is entitled on behalf of her subjects to have the claim of the bank paid, and the concession recognized and given effect by the Costa Rican Government.

The Government of Costa Rica denies its liability for the acts or obligations of the Tinoco government and maintains that the Law of Nullities was a legitimate exercise of its legislative governing power. It further denies the validity of such claims on the merits, unaffected by the Law of Nullities.

It is convenient to consider first the general objections to both claims of Great Britain, urged by Costa Rica, and then if such general objections cannot prevail, to consider the merits of each claim and Costa Rica's special defenses to it.

Coming now to the general issues applicable to both claims, Great Britain contends, first, that the Tinoco government was the only government of Costa Rica *de facto* and *de jure* for two years and nine months; that during that time there is no other government disputing its sovereignty, that it was in peaceful administration of the whole country, with the acquiescence of its people.

Second, that the succeeding government could not by legislative decree avoid responsibility for acts of that government affecting British subjects, or appropriate or confiscate rights and property by that government except in violation of international law; that the act of Nullities is as to British interests, therefore itself a nullity, and is to be disregarded, with the consequence that the contracts validly made with the Tinoco government must be performed by the present Costa Rican Government, and that the property which has been invaded or the rights nullified must be restored.

To these contentions the Costa Rican Government answers: First, that the Tinoco government was not a *de facto* or *de jure* government according to the rules of international law. This raises an issue of fact.

Second, that the contracts and obligations of the Tinoco government, set up by Great Britain on behalf of its subjects, are void, and do not create a legal obligation, because the government of Tinoco and its acts were in violation of the constitution of Costa Rica of 1871.

Third, that Great Britain is stopped by the fact that it did not recognize the Tinoco government during its incumbency, to claim on behalf of its subjects that Tinoco's was a government which could confer rights binding on its successor.

Fourth, that the subjects of Great Britain, whose claims are here in controversy, were either by contract or the law of Costa Rica bound to pursue their remedies before the courts of Costa Rica and not to seek diplomatic interference on the part of their home government.

Dr. John Bassett Moore, now a member of the Permanent Court of International Justice, in his *Digest of International Law,* Volume I, p. 249, announces the general principle which has had such universal acquiescence as to become well settled international law:

> Changes in the government or the international policy of a state do not as a rule affect its position in international law. A monarchy may be transformed into a republic or a republic into a monarchy; absolute principles may be substituted for constitutional, or the reverse; but though the government changes, the nation remains, with rights and obligations unimpaired....
>
> The principle of the continuity of states has important results. The state is bound by engagements entered into by governments that have ceased to exist; the restored government is generally liable for the acts of the usurper. The governments of Louis XVIII and Louis Philippe so far as practicable indemnified the citizens of foreign states for losses caused by the government of Napoleon; and the King of the Two Cicilies made compensation to citizens of the United States for the wrongful acts of Murat.

Again Dr. Moore says:

> The origin and organization of government are questions generally of internal discussion and decision. Foreign powers deal with the existing *de facto* government, when sufficiently established to give reasonable assurance of its permanence, and of the acquiescence of those who constitute the state in its ability to maintain itself, and discharge its internal duties and its external obligations. * * *

First, what are the facts to be gathered from the documents and evidence submitted by the two parties as to the *de facto* character of the Tinoco government?

In January, 1917, Frederico A. Tinoco was Secretary of War under Alfredo Gonzalez, the then President of Costa Rica. On the ground that Gonzalez was seeking reelection as President in violation of a constitutional limitation, Tinoco used the army and navy to seize the government, assume the provisional headship of the Republic and become Commander-in-Chief of the army. Gonzalez took refuge in the American Legation, thence escaping to the United States. Tinoco constituted a provisional government at once and summoned the people to an election for deputies to a constituent assembly on the first of May, 1917. At the same time he directed an election to take place for the Presidency and himself became a candidate. An election was held. Some 61,000 votes were cast for Tinoco and 259 for another candidate. Tinoco then was inaugurated as the President to administer his powers under the former constitution until the creation of a new one. A new constitution was adopted June 8, 1917, supplanting the constitution of 1871. For a full two years Tinoco and the legislative assembly under him peaceably administered the affairs of the Government of Costa Rica, and there was no disorder of a revolutionary character during that interval. No other government of any kind asserted power in the country. The courts sat, Congress legislated, and the government was duly administered. Its power was fully established and peaceably exercised. The people seemed to have accepted Tinoco's government with great good will when it came in, and to have welcomed the change. * * * [T]hroughout the record as made by the case and counter case, there is no substantial evidence that Tinoco was not in actual and peaceable administration without resistance or conflict or contest by anyone until a few months before the time when he retired and resigned.

Speaking of the resumption of the present government, this passage occurs in the argument on behalf of Costa Rica:

> Powerful forces in Costa Rica were opposed to Tinoco from the outset, but his overthrow by ballot or unarmed opposition was impossible and it was equally impossible to organize armed opposition against him in Costa Rican territory.

It is true that action of the supporters of those seeking to restore the former government was somewhat delayed by the influence of the United States with Gonzalez and his friends against armed action, on the ground that military disturbances in Central America during the World War would be prejudicial to the interests of the Allied Powers. It is not important, however, what were the causes that enabled Tinoco to carry on his government effectively and peaceably. The question is, must his government be considered a link in the continuity of the Government of Costa Rica? I must hold that from the evidence that the Tinoco government was an actual sovereign government.

But it is urged that many leading Powers refused to recognize the Tinoco government, and that recognition by other nations is the chief and best evidence of the birth, existence and continuity of succession of a government. Undoubtedly recognition by other Powers is an important evidential factor in establishing proof of the existence of a government in the society of nations. What are the facts as to this? The Tinoco government was recognized by Bolivia on May 17, 1917; by Argentina on May 22, 1917; by Chile on May 22, 1917; by Haiti on May 22, 1917; by Guatemala on May 28, 1917; by Switzerland on June 1, 1917; by Germany on June 10, 1917; by Denmark on June 18, 1917; by Spain on June 18, 1917; by Mexico on July 1, 1917; by Holland on July 11, 1917; by the Vatican on June 9, 1917; by Colombia on August 9, 1917; by Austria on August 10, 1917; by Portugal on August 14, 1917; by El Salvador on September 12, 1917; by Romania on November 15, 1917; by Brazil on November 28, 1917; by Peru on December 15, 1917; and by Ecuador on April 23, 1917.

What were the circumstances as to the other nations?

The United States, on February 9, 1917, two weeks after Tinoco had assumed power, took this action:

> The Government of the United States has viewed the recent overthrow of the established government in Costa Rica with the gravest concern and considers that illegal acts of this character tend to disturb the peace of Central America and to disrupt the unity of the American continent. In view of its policy in regard to the assumption of power through illegal methods, clearly enunciated by it on several occasions during the past four years, the Government of the United States desires to set forth in an emphatic and distinct manner its present position in regard to the actual situation in Costa Rica which is that it will not give recognition or support to any government which may be established unless it is clearly proven that it is elected by legal and constitutional means.

And again on February 24, 1917:

> In order that citizens of the United States may have definite information as to the position of this Government in regard to any financial aid which they may give to, or any business transaction which they may have with those persons who overthrew the constitutional Government of Costa Rica by an act of armed rebellion, the Government of the United States desires to advise them that it will not consider any claims which may in the future arise from such dealings, worthy of its diplomatic support.

[The U.S. State Department reaffirmed its nonrecognition of the Tinoco regime in April 1918.]

Probably because of the leadership of the United States in respect to a matter of this kind, her then Allies in the war, Great Britain, France and Italy, declined to recognize the Tinoco government. Costa Rica was, therefore, not permitted to sign the Treaty of Peace at Versailles, although the Tinoco government had declared war against Germany.

The merits of the policy of the United States in this non-recognition it is not for the arbitrator to discuss, for the reason that in his consideration of this case, he is necessarily controlled by principles of international law, and however justified as a national policy non-recognition on such a ground may be, it certainly has not been acquiesced in by all the nations of the world, which is a condition precedent to considering it as a postulate of international law.

The non-recognition by other nations of a government claiming to be a national personality, is usually appropriate evidence that it has not attained the independence and control entitling it by international law to be classed as such. But when recognition *vel non* of a government is by such nations determined by inquiry, not into its *de facto* sovereignty and complete governmental control, but into its illegitimacy or irregularity of origin, their non-recognition loses something of evidential weight on the issue with which those applying the rules of international law are alone concerned. What is true of the non-recognition of the United States in its bearing upon the existence of a *de facto* government under Tinoco for thirty months is probably in a measure true of the non-recognition by her Allies in the European War. Such non-recognition for any reason, however, cannot outweigh the evidence disclosed by this record before me as to the *de facto* character of Tinoco's government, according to the standard set by international law.

Second. It is ably and earnestly argued on behalf of Costa Rica that the Tinoco government cannot be considered a *de facto* government, because it was not established and maintained in accord with the constitution of Costa Rica of 1871. To hold that a government which establishes itself and maintains a peaceful administration, with the acquiescence of the people for a substantial period of time, does not become a *de facto* government unless it conforms to a previous constitution would be to hold that within the rules of international law a revolution contrary to the fundamental law of the existing government cannot establish a new government. This cannot be, and is not, true. The change by revolution upsets the rule of the authorities in power under the then existing fundamental law, and sets aside the fundamental law in so far as the change of rule makes it necessary. To speak of a revolution creating a *de facto* government, which conforms to the limitations of the old constitution is to use a contradiction in terms. The same government continues internationally, but not the internal law of its being. The issue is not whether the new government assumes power or conducts its administration under constitutional limitations established by the people during the incumbency of the government it has overthrown. The question is, has it really established itself in such a way that all within its influence recognize its control, and that there is no opposing force assuming to be a government in its place? Is it discharging its functions as a government usually does, respected within its own jurisdiction? * * *

Third. It is further objected by Costa Rica that Great Britain by her failure to recognize the Tinoco government is estopped now to urge claims of her subjects dependent upon the acts and contracts of the Tinoco government. The evidential weight of such non-recognition against the claim of its *de facto* character I have already considered and admitted. The contention here goes further and precludes a government which did not recognize a *de facto* government from appearing in an international tribunal in behalf of its nationals to claim any rights based on the acts of such government.

To sustain this view a great number of decisions in English and American courts are cited to the point that a municipal court cannot, in litigation before it, recognize or assume the *de facto* character of a foreign government which the executive department of foreign affairs of the government of which the court is a branch has not recognized. This is clearly true. It is for the executive to decide questions of foreign policy and not courts. It would be most unseemly to have a conflict of opinion in respect to foreign relations of a nation between its department charged with the conduct of its foreign affairs and its judicial branch. But such cases have no bearing on the point before us. Here the executive of Great Britain takes the position that the Tinoco government which it did not recognize, was nevertheless a *de facto* government that could create rights in British subjects which it now seeks to protect. Of course, as already emphasized, its failure to recognize the *de facto* government can be used against it as evidence to disprove the character it now attributes to that government, but this does not bar it from changing its position. Should a case arise in one of its own courts after it has changed its position, doubtless that court would feel it incumbent upon it to note the change in its further rulings.

Precedents in American arbitrations are cited to show that an estoppel like the one urged does arise. They are Schultz's case (Moore, *International Arbitrations*, Vol. 3, 2973), Janson's case (*ibidem*, 2902), and Jarvis's case (Ralston, *Venezuela Arbitrations*, 150). In the opinions of these cases delivered by American commissioners, there are expressions sustaining the view that the bar of an estoppel exists, but an examination shows that no authorities are cited and no arguments are made in support of the view. Moreover, the array of facts in the cases was conclusive against the existence of a *de facto* government, and the expressions were unnecessary to the conclusion. In Schultz's case the claim of an American citizen was against the Juarez government for loss of goods by fire between the lines of battle waged by Miramon's forces against Juarez's government. The claim against Juarez's government was plainly not sustainable, first because it occurred in the train of war and, second, because the Miramon forces never had in fact constituted a *de facto* government. The Janson case before the same tribunal was for the value of an American bark seized by Miramon's soldiers to escape out of the country from the victorious army of Juarez. The commissioner devotes many pages to a résumé of evidence to show that neither Miramon nor Maximilian, with whom he acted, had ever had a *de facto* government; that Juarez was always in control of the greater part of Mexico and always resisting. The truth is that the language of the decisions should be more properly construed to emphasize the great and overwhelming weight to be given to the recognition of Juarez by the United States and its non-recognition of Miramon as evidence against the *de facto* character of the government of the latter, than to uphold the theory of bar by estoppel.

In Jarvis's case the facts were that Paez, a Venezuelan citizen, was an insurgent against the existing government of Venezuela in 1849, and enlisted in his conspiracy Jarvis, the American claimant, who furnished him a ship and arms and ammunition. This was a crime against the United States on Jarvis's part, because the United States was on terms of amity with Venezuela. The expedition failed. In 1861, thirteen years later, however, when Paez was in Venezuela, a sudden outbreak placed him in power. In 1863, just as he was about to retire with the collapse of his government, he issued bonds to Jarvis to repay him for his outlay in the unsuccessful insurrection of 1849, twelve years before. The commissioner held that there was no lawful consideration for the bonds. Certainly this was a righteous conclusion. It was a personal obligation of Paez, if it was an obligation at all. It was not a debt of Venezuela. It was invalid and unlawful because of its vicious origin, both by the laws of the United States and the laws of Venezuela. The commissioner also by way of additional but unnecessary support to his conclusion said the United States was estopped to urge the claim. * * *

I do not understand the arguments on which an equitable estoppel in such case can rest. The failure to recognize the *de facto* government did not lead the succeeding government to change its position in any way upon the faith of it. Non-recognition may have aided the succeeding government to come into power; but subsequent presentation of claims based on the *de facto* existence of the previous government and its dealings does not work an injury to the succeeding government in the nature of a fraud or breach of faith. An equitable estoppel to prove the truth must rest on previous conduct of the person to be estopped, which has led the person claiming the estoppel into a position in which the truth will injure him. There is no such case here.

* * * It may be urged that it would be in the interest of the stability of governments and the orderly adjustment of international relations, and so a proper rule of international law, that a government in recognizing or refusing to recognize a government claiming admission to the society of nations should thereafter be held to an attitude consistent with its deliberate conclusion on this issue. Arguments for and against such a rule occur to me; but it suffices to say that I have not been cited to text writers of authority or to decisions of significance indicating a general acquiescence of nations in such a rule. Without this, it cannot be applied here as a principle of international law.

It is urged that the subjects of Great Britain knew of the policy of their home government in refusing to recognize the Tinoco régime and cannot now rely on protection by Great Britain. This is a question solely between the home government and its subjects. That government may take the course which the United States had done and refuse to use any diplomatic offices to promote such claims and thus to leave its nationals to depend upon the sense of justice of the existing Costa Rican

Government, as they were warned in advance would be its policy, or it may change its conclusion as to the *de facto* existence of the Tinoco government and offer its subjects the protection of its diplomatic intervention. It is entirely a question between the claimants and their own government. It should be noted that Great Britain issued no such warning to its subjects as did the United States to its citizens in this matter.

The fourth point made on behalf of Costa Rica against the claims here pressed is that both claimants are bound either by their own contractual obligation entered into with the Government of Costa Rica, or by the laws of Costa Rica, to which they subscribed, not to present their claims by way of diplomatic intervention of their home government, but to submit their claims to the courts of Costa Rica. [The arbitrator concludes that Costa Rica's claim of failure to exhaust local remedies was not well founded.]

A consideration of the issues before us, therefore, recurs to the merits of the two claims. The decision of them must be governed by the answer to the question whether the claims would have been good against the Tinoco government as a government, unaffected by the Law of Nullities, and unaffected by the Costa Rican Constitution of 1871. [The arbitrator examines the complex banking arrangements related to the claim of the Royal Bank of Canada, and finds in favor of Great Britain on behalf of the Royal Bank. With respect to the issue of the petroleum concession, however, the arbitrator disallows recovery because the concession violated Costa Rica's 1917 constitution. Because of this violation, even Tinoco's government could have defeated the concession. Thus, when the Law of Nullities deemed the concession to be invalid, it worked no injury to the British companies of which Great Britain could complain.]

Notes and Questions

1. *The Arbitrator in the* Tinoco Case. William Howard Taft, the sole arbitrator in the *Tinoco Case*, was President of the United States during 1909–1913 and Chief Justice of the U.S. Supreme Court during 1921–1930. As President, he, along with other leading public figures, supported treaties of general arbitration, applicable even to questions of "vital interests" and "national honor." See Henry F. Pringle, 2 *The Life and Times of William Howard Taft* 737–39 (1939).

2. *Government Succession to Obligations*. Taft holds that by international law, a new government is bound by the legal commitments of an old government. Could there be any practical alternative to this rule? It is difficult to see how there could be any legally binding commitments of states if international obligations could be repudiated simply by forming or declaring a new government. Should an exception be made to permit the repudiation of national commitments when there has been a radical change in government? If so, who determines whether the change is radical enough?

3. De Facto *Governments*. Taft is concerned to establish that the Tinoco regime was the actual government of Costa Rica when it entered into

the banking and oil concession arrangements with the British companies. He discusses the categories of *de facto* and *de jure* governments. What is the difference between them? Taft seems to look most at the factor of popular acquiescence to determine whether the Tinoco regime was the *de facto* government of Costa Rica. What evidences would a judge or lawyer consider in evaluating the popular support for a government? If Taft had found that the Tinoco regime lacked popular support, would he necessarily have concluded it was not the *de facto* government?

4. De Jure *Governments*. The Tinoco regime was recognized by 20 foreign governments in 1917. There were about 50 governments world-wide then. Was this number of recognitions enough to establish Tinoco as the *de jure* government of Costa Rica? Would the answer depend on the degree to which the nonrecognizing foreign governments did not support the Tinoco regime and still supported the old Gonzalez regime?

5. *The Relative Importance of* De Facto *Control and* De Jure *Recognition*. What if the evidences of *de facto* control conflict with the evidences of *de jure* recognition? Which should control in determining the legitimate government of a state? Could there be different answers to this question depending on the forum and depending on whether the forum looks to an answer in international law or one or another municipal law?

6. *Estoppel*. How persuasive is Taft in his estoppel argument? Should Great Britain have been permitted to insist that the Tinoco regime was the *de facto* and *de jure* government of Costa Rica when it had failed to recognize the Tinoco regime? The Tinoco regime probably could not have availed itself of the British courts because it was unrecognized. See 1 *Oppenheim's International Law* § 47, at 158 (9th ed. by Robert Jennings & Arthur Watts, 1992). Should there be one answer as to the status of the Tinoco regime vis-à-vis Great Britain in British municipal courts and another in an international tribunal?

7. *Comparing the Succession of States and the Succession of Governments*. Is it always easy to distinguish changes in states from changes in governments? Should different consequences attach to changes in governments and changes in states? In the view of Professor O'Connell,

> the solution of the problem raised by political change cannot be left to the hazard of characterizing the event as a succession of States or a succession of governments. There is evident at the present time a developing pressure in the direction of assimilating these two categories of events, and as the nineteenth-century theory of the State, with its concomitant metaphysics of political personality, loses its cogency, legal theory will tend more and more to return to its eighteenth-century position.

1 D.P. O'Connell, *State Succession in Municipal Law and International Law* 7 (1967). This eighteenth-century position called for a succession to commitments without drawing a distinction between states and governments.

AUTOCEPHALOUS GREEK-ORTHODOX CHURCH OF CYPRUS v. GOLDBERG & FELDMAN FINE ARTS, INC.

917 F.2d 278 (7th Cir.1990), *cert. denied*,
502 U.S. 941, 112 S.Ct. 377, 116 L.Ed.2d 329 (1991).

BAUER, Chief Judge. * * *

* * * In this appeal, we consider the fate of several tangible victims of Cyprus' turbulent history: specifically, four Byzantine mosaics created over 1400 years ago. The district court awarded possession of these extremely valuable mosaics to plaintiff-appellee, the Autocephalous Greek–Orthodox Church of Cyprus ("Church of Cyprus" or "Church"). *Autocephalous Greek–Orthodox Church of Cyprus v. Goldberg & Feldman Fine Arts, Inc.*, 717 F.Supp. 1374 (S.D.Ind.1989). Defendants-appellants, Peg Goldberg and Goldberg & Feldman Fine Arts, Inc. (collectively "Goldberg"), claim that in so doing, the court committed various reversible errors. We affirm.

I. Background

In the early sixth century, A.D., a large mosaic was affixed to the apse of the Church of the Panagia Kanakaria ("Kanakaria Church") in the village of Lythrankomi, Cyprus. The mosaic, made of small bits of colored glass, depicted Jesus Christ as a young boy in the lap of his mother, the Virgin Mary, who was seated on a throne. Jesus and Mary were attended by two archangels and surrounded by a frieze depicting the twelve apostles. The mosaic was displayed in the Kanakaria Church for centuries, where it became, under the practices of Eastern Orthodox Christianity, sanctified as a holy relic. It survived both the vicissitudes of history, *see Autocephalous*, 717 F.Supp. at 1377 (discussing the period of Iconoclasm during which many religious artifacts were destroyed), and, thanks to restoration efforts, the ravages of time.

Testimony before Judge Noland established that the Kanakaria mosaic was one of only a handful of such holy Byzantine relics to survive into the twentieth century. Sadly, however, war came to Cyprus in the 1970s, from which the mosaic could not be spared.

The Cypriot people have long been a divided people, approximately three-fourths being of Greek descent and Greek–Orthodox faith, the other quarter of Turkish descent and Muslem [*sic*] faith. No sooner had Cyprus gained independence from British rule in 1960 than this bitter division surfaced. Civil disturbances erupted between Greek and Turkish Cypriots, necessitating the introduction of United Nations peacekeeping forces in 1964. (U.N. forces still remain in Cyprus.) Through the 1960s, the Greek Cypriots, concentrated in the southern part of the island, became increasingly estranged from the Turkish Cypriots, concentrated in the north.

The tensions erupted again in 1974, this time with more violent results. In July, 1974, the civil government of the Republic of Cyprus was replaced by a government controlled by the Greek Cypriot military. In apparent response, on July 20, 1974, Turkey invaded Cyprus from the north. By late August, the Turkish military forces had advanced to occupy approximately the northern third of the island. The point at which the invading forces stopped is called the "Green Line." To this day, the heavily-guarded Green Line bisects Nicosia, the capital of the Republic, and splits the island from east to west.

The Turkish forces quickly established their own "government" north of the Green Line. In 1975, they formed what they called the "Turkish Federated State of Cyprus" ("TFSC"). In 1983, that administration was dissolved, and the "Turkish Republic of Northern Cyprus" ("TRNC") was formed. These "governments" were recognized immediately by Turkey, but all other nations in the world—including the United States—have never recognized them, and continue to recognize the Republic of Cyprus ("Republic"), plaintiff-appellee in this action, as the only legitimate government for all Cypriot people.

The Turkish invasion led to the forced southern exodus of over 100,000 Greek Cypriots who lived in northern Cyprus. Turkish Cypriots living in southern Cyprus (and tens of thousands of settlers from mainland Turkey) likewise flooded into northern Cyprus, resulting in a massive exchange of populations.

Lythrankomi is in the northern portion of Cyprus that came under Turkish rule. Although the village and the Kanakaria Church were untouched by the invading forces in 1974, the villagers of Greek ancestry were soon thereafter "enclaved" by the Turkish military. Despite the hostile environment, the pastor and priests of the Kanakaria Church continued for two years to conduct religious services for the Greek Cypriots who remained in Lythrankomi. Hardy as they must have been, these clerics, and virtually all remaining Greek Cypriots, were forced to flee to southern Cyprus in the summer of 1976. Church of Cyprus officials testified that they intend to re-establish the congregation at the Kanakaria Church as soon as Greek Cypriots are permitted to return safely to Lythrankomi. (Thirty-five thousand Turkish troops remain in northern Cyprus.)

When the priests evacuated the Kanakaria Church in 1976, the mosaic was still intact. In the late 1970s, however, Church of Cyprus officials received increasing reports that Greek Cypriot churches and monuments in northern Cyprus were being attacked and vandalized, their contents stolen or destroyed. * * * In November, 1979, a resident of northern Cyprus brought word to the Republic's Department of Antiquities that this fate had also befallen the Kanakaria Church and its mosaic. Vandals had plundered the church, removing anything of value from its interior. The mosaic, or at least its most recognizable and valuable parts, had been forcibly ripped from the apse of the church. Once a place of worship, the Kanakaria Church had been reduced to a stable for farm animals.

Upon learning of the looting of the Kanakaria Church and the loss of its mosaics (made plural by the vandals' axes), the Republic of Cyprus took immediate steps to recover them. As discussed in greater detail in Judge Noland's opinion, these efforts took the form of contacting and seeking assistance from many organizations and individuals, including the United Nations Educational, Scientific and Cultural Organization ("UNESCO"); the International Council of Museums; the International Council of Museums and Sites; Europa Nostra (an organization devoted to the conservation of the architectural heritage of Europe); the Council of Europe; international auction houses such as Christie's and Sotheby's; Harvard University's Dumbarton Oaks Institute for Byzantine Studies; and the foremost museums, curators and Byzantine scholars throughout the world. The Republic's United States Embassy also routinely disseminated information about lost cultural properties to journalists, U.S. officials and scores of scholars, architects and collectors in this country, asking for assistance in recovering the mosaics. The overall strategy behind these efforts was to get word to the experts and scholars who would probably be involved in any ultimate sale of the mosaics. These individuals, it was hoped, would be the most likely (only?) actors in the chain of custody of stolen cultural properties who would be interested in helping the Republic and Church of Cyprus recover them.

The Republic's efforts have paid off. In recent years, the Republic has recovered and returned to the Church of Cyprus several stolen relics and antiquities. The Republic has even located frescoes and other works taken from the Kanakaria Church, including the four mosaics at issue here. These four mosaics, each measuring about two feet square, depict the figure of Jesus, the busts of one of the attending archangels, the apostle Matthew and the apostle James.

To understand how these pieces of the Kanakaria mosaic resurfaced, we must trace the actions of appellant Peg Goldberg and the other principals through whose hands they passed in 1988.

Peg Goldberg is an art dealer and gallery operator. Goldberg and Feldman Fine Arts, Inc., is the Indiana corporation that owns her gallery in Carmel, Indiana. In the summer of 1988, Peg Goldberg went to Europe to shop for works for her gallery. Although her main interest is 20th century paintings, etchings and sculptures, Goldberg was enticed while in The Netherlands by Robert Fitzgerald, another Indiana art dealer and "casual friend" of hers, to consider the purchase of "four early Christian mosaics." [The court details Goldberg's efforts to buy the mosaics. The sale was concluded by the exchange of the mosaics for $1,080,000 in $100 bills at the airport in Geneva, Switzerland.]

After their request for the return of the mosaics was refused by Goldberg, the Republic of Cyprus and the Church of Cyprus (collectively "Cyprus") brought this suit in the Southern District of Indiana for the recovery of the mosaics. * * * Judge Noland awarded possession of the mosaics to the Church of Cyprus. Goldberg filed a timely appeal.

II. Analysis * * *

[The court concludes that there is no statute of limitations bar to the action, and that applicable rules of replevin allow the plaintiff Church to recover the mosaics.]

Finally, Goldberg argues that several decrees of the TFSC (the entity established in northern Cyprus by the Turkish military immediately after the 1974 invasion) divested the Church of title to the mosaics. Goldberg asks us to honor these decrees under the notion that in some instances courts in the United States can give effect to the acts of nonrecognized but "*de facto*" regimes if the acts relate to purely local matters. *See Restatement (Third) of the Foreign Relations Law of the United States ("Third Restatement")* § 205(3)(1987);[15] *Salimoff v. Standard Oil Co.*, 262 N.Y. 220, 186 N.E. 679 (1933)(under Soviet law, U.S.S.R. nationalization decree effective to pass title to oil within Russia despite fact that U.S.S.R. was not yet recognized by the U.S.). The TFSC decrees at issue, all propagated in 1975, are principally these: 1) the "Abandoned Movable Property Law," which provided that all movable property within the boundaries of the TFSC abandoned by its owner because of the owner's "departure" from northern Cyprus "as a result of the situation after 20th July 1974" now belongs to the TFSC "in the name of the Turkish Community" and that the TFSC "is responsible for the possession and control of such property"; and 2) the "Antiquities Ordinance," which provided that all religious buildings and antiquities, including specifically "synagogues, basilicas, churches, monasteries and the like," located north of the Green Line, as well as any and all "movable antiquities" contained therein, are now the property of the TFSC.[16] Because these decrees were enacted before the Kanakaria Church was looted and its mosaics stolen, the argument concludes, the Church cannot here claim to hold title to the mosaics.

It is helpful to note at the outset what is *not* being claimed here. First, Goldberg does not (and cannot) suggest that this court should pass on the validity of the Turkish administration in northern Cyprus. We repeat here precepts that are well-established in the law of this country:

> [T]he conduct of foreign relations was committed by the Constitution to the political departments of the government, and the propriety of what may be done in the exercise of this political power [is] not subject to judicial inquiry or decision, ... [and] who is the sovereign of a territory is not a judicial question, but one the

15. This Restatement section provides:

> [C]ourts in the United States ordinarily give effect to acts of a regime representing an entity not recognized as a state, or of a regime not recognized as the government of a state, if those acts apply to territory under the control of that regime and relate to domestic matters only.

16. We note that Cyprus has raised arguments that cast substantial doubt on the actual meaning and effect of these and other TFSC decrees, even should we decide to apply them. For the purposes of disposing of Goldberg's argument, however, we will assume that the TFSC decrees actually mean what Goldberg represents them to mean.

determination of which by the political departments conclusively binds the courts[.]

United States v. Belmont, 301 U.S. 324, 328, 57 S.Ct. 758, 759–60, 81 L.Ed. 1134 (1937)(*citing Oetjen v. Central Leather Co.*, 246 U.S. 297, 38 S.Ct. 309, 62 L.Ed. 726 (1918)). Indeed, Goldberg herself supports the district court's decision to deny the TRNC's motion to intervene in this case, which decision was based on the TRNC's continued status as a nonrecognized entity. *See Third Restatement* § 205(1)(entity not recognized as a state ordinarily denied access to U.S. courts); *Republic of Vietnam v. Pfizer, Inc.*, 556 F.2d 892 (8th Cir.1977).

Second, this is not a case in which one party is claiming title under the laws of a state that has been entirely displaced, and the other is claiming title under the laws of the new, displacing regime. All Goldberg can hope to gain from the invocation of these TFSC edicts is a finding that the Church's claim of title is defective; she has no plausible claim of valid title in herself based on these edicts. This fact sets this case apart from the cases cited by Goldberg, including *Salimoff*, 186 N.E. 679 (plaintiff Russian nationals claimed title to property under laws of the old Russian Empire and defendant U.S. companies claimed title due to purchase from Soviet government, which seized the property pursuant to nationalization decree); and *The Denny*, 127 F.2d 404 (3d Cir.1942)(dispute between Lithuanian citizens wherein both claimed right to possess property as agents under Lithuanian law, one relying on the effect of nationalization decrees of the Lithuanian Soviet Socialist Republic, the other on pre-nationalization law).

What Goldberg is claiming is that the TFSC's confiscatory decrees, adopted only one year after the Turkish invasion, should be given effect by this court because the TFSC and its successor TRNC should now be viewed as the "*de facto*" government north of the Green Line. This we are unwilling to do. We draw on two lines of precedent as support for our decision. First, we note that, contrary to the New York court's decision in *Salimoff*, several courts of the same era refused to give effect to the nationalization decrees of the as-yet-unrecognized Soviet Republics. These courts relied on a variety of grounds, including especially the fact that the political branches of our government still refused to recognize these entities. *See, e.g., Latvian State Cargo & Passenger S.S. Line v. McGrath*, 188 F.2d 1000, 1002–04 (D.C.Cir.1951)(also stating as a possible alternative ground the following view: "since the nationalization decrees here involved were confiscatory and thus contrary to the public policy of this country, our courts would in no event give them effect," and citing cases); *The Maret*, 145 F.2d 431, 442 (3d Cir. 1944)("[N]o valid distinction can be drawn between the political or diplomatic act of nonrecognition of a sovereign and nonrecognition of the decrees or acts of that sovereign.... Nonrecognition of a foreign sovereign and nonrecognition of its decrees are to be deemed to be as essential a part of the power confided by the Constitution to the Executive for the conduct of foreign affairs as recognition."). Similarly, as regards the Turkish administration in northern Cyprus, the United

States government (like the rest of the non-Turkish world) has not recognized its legitimacy, nor does our government "recognize that [the Turkish administration] has functioned as a de facto or quasi government ..., ruling within its own borders."

Second, we are guided in part by the post-Civil War cases in which courts refused to give effect to property-affecting acts of the Confederate state legislatures. In one such case, *Williams v. Bruffy*, 96 U.S. 176, 24 L.Ed. 716 (1878), the Supreme Court drew a helpful distinction between two kinds of "*de facto*" governments. The first kind "is such as exists after it has expelled the regularly constituted authorities from the seats of power and the public offices, and established its own functionaries in their places, so as to represent in fact the sovereignty of the nation." This kind of *de facto* government, the Court explained, "is treated as in most respects possessing rightful authority, ... [and] its legislation is in general recognized." The second kind of *de facto* government "is such as exists where a portion of the inhabitants of a country have separated themselves from the parent State and established an independent government. The validity of its acts, both against the parent State and its citizens or subjects, depends entirely upon its ultimate success.... If it succeed, and become recognized, its acts from the commencement of its existence are upheld as those of an independent nation." (The Court held that the Confederacy was a government of the second type that ultimately failed.) Goldberg argues that the TFSC and its successor TRNC have achieved the level of "ultimate success" contemplated by this standard, because they have maintained control of the territory north of the Green Line for over fifteen years. We will not thus equate simple longevity of control with "ultimate success." The Turkish forces, despite their best efforts, did not completely supplant the Republic nor its officers. Instead, the TFSC and the TRNC, neither of which has ever been recognized by the non-Turkish world, only acceded to the control of the northern portion of Cyprus. The Republic of Cyprus remains the only recognized Cypriot government, the sovereign nation for the entire island. * * * [W]e conclude that the confiscatory decrees proffered by Goldberg do not divest the Church of its claim of title.

III. Conclusion

* * * Those who plundered the churches and monuments of war-torn Cyprus, hoarded their relics away, and are now smuggling and selling them for large sums, are * * * blackguards. The Republic of Cyprus, with diligent effort and the help of friends like Dr. True, has been able to locate several of these stolen antiquities; items of vast cultural, religious (and, as this case demonstrates, monetary) value. Among such finds are the pieces of the Kanakaria mosaic at issue in this case. Unfortunately, when these mosaics surfaced they were in the hands not of the most guilty parties, but of Peg Goldberg and her gallery. Correctly applying Indiana law, the district court determined that Goldberg must return the mosaics to their rightful owner: the Church of Cyprus. Goldberg's tireless attacks have not established

reversible error in that determination, and thus, for the reasons discussed above, the district court's judgment is AFFIRMED.

Lest this result seem too harsh, we should note that those who wish to purchase art work on the international market, undoubtedly a ticklish business, are not without means by which to protect themselves. Especially when circumstances are as suspicious as those that faced Peg Goldberg, prospective purchasers would do best to do more than make a few last-minute phone calls. * * * In such cases, dealers can (and probably should) take steps such as a formal IFAR [International Foundation for Art Research] search; a documented authenticity check by disinterested experts; a full background search of the seller and his claim of title; insurance protection and a contingency sales contract; and the like. If Goldberg would have pursued such methods, perhaps she would have discovered in time what she has now discovered too late: the Church has a valid, superior and enforceable claim to these Byzantine treasures, which therefore must be returned to it.

CUDAHY, CIRCUIT JUDGE, concurring * * *

A second * * * aspect of this case involves the treatment of the cultural heritage of foreign nations under international and United States law. The United States has both acceded to international agreements and enacted its own statutes regarding the importation of cultural property. These regulatory efforts have encompassed transfers of property during both wartime and peacetime and apply whether the property was originally stolen or "merely" illegally exported from the country of origin. The two most significant international agreements that attempt to protect cultural property are the 1954 Convention on the Protection of Cultural Property in the Event of Armed Conflict (the "1954 Hague Convention"), 249 U.N.T.S. 215 (1956), and the UNESCO Convention on the Means of Prohibiting and Preventing the Illicit Transport, Export and Transfer of Ownership of Cultural Property (the "UNESCO Convention"), 823 U.N.T.S. 231 (1972). Under both these multinational treaties, as well as under the United States' Convention on Cultural Property Implementation Act, 19 U.S.C. § 2601 *et seq.* (1983), the Cypriot mosaics would be considered cultural property warranting international protection. * * *

The 1954 Hague Convention may be applicable to the case before us given the incursion of Turkish armed forces into Cyprus in 1974 and our ongoing refusal to recognize the government established in the northern part of Cyprus. The 1954 Hague Convention, which is but the most recent multilateral agreement in a 200–year history of international attempts to protect cultural property during wartime, prohibits the destruction or seizure of cultural property during armed conflict, whether international or civil in nature, and during periods of belligerent occupation. The Hague Convention also applies to international trafficking during peacetime in cultural property unlawfully seized during an armed conflict. The attempt of the government established in northern Cyprus by the Turkish military to divest the Greek Cypriot church of ownership of the mosaics might be viewed as an interference of the sort contemplated by the 1954 Hague Convention. If this were the case, the acts and decrees of the northern Cyprus government divesting title to this cultural property would not demand the deference of American courts.

The second international agreement, the UNESCO Convention, focuses on private conduct, primarily during peacetime, and thus is also applicable to the theft and removal of the mosaics from Cyprus. Article 7 of that Convention requires signatory nations:

> (a) To take the necessary measures, consistent with national legislation, to prevent museums and similar institutions within their territories from acquiring cultural property originating in another State Party which has been illegally exported....;
>
> (b)(i) to prohibit the import of cultural property stolen from a museum or a religious or secular public monument or similar institution in another State Party ..., provided that such property is documented as appertaining to the inventory of that institution;
>
> (ii) at the request of the State Party of origin, to take appropriate steps to recover and return any such cultural property ..., provided, however, that the requesting State shall pay just compensation to an innocent purchaser or to a person who has valid title to that property....

It is clear that the mosaics in the case before us were stolen (under any reasonable definition of that word) from a religious institution and that the mosaics were extensively documented by the Dumbarton Oaks publication as belonging to the Kanakaria Church. While the UNESCO Convention seems to contemplate primarily measures to be implemented by the executive branch of a government through its import and export rules and policies, the judicial branch should certainly attempt to reflect in its decisionmaking the spirit as well as the letter of an international agreement to which the United States is a party.

Notes and Questions

1. *International Law and the Protection of Cultural Property.* The *Goldberg* opinions address international legal efforts to protect cultural property as well as recognition issues. Illegal trade in art and antiquities is big business; in dollar terms, it is larger than every area of international crime except the arms trade and narcotics trafficking. 1993 estimates of annual international art crime ranged from $3 billion to $6 billion. Only approximately 12 per cent of stolen art is recovered, and those who steal antiquities often destroy archaeological information. See Note, Lisa J. Borodkin, "The Economics of Antiquities Looting and a Proposed Legal Alternative," 95 *Columbia Law Review* 377, 377–78 (1995). The *Goldberg Case* and international trade in cultural property are explored in Dan Hofstadter, *Goldberg's Angel* (1994).

2. *Nonrecognition and the Use of Force.* The widespread refusal of states to recognize the Turkish Federated State of Cyprus (TFSC) or the

Turkish Republic of Northern Cyprus (TRNC) has been explained as a reaction to Turkey's unlawful use of force in Northern Cyprus. See Ian Brownlie, "The United Nations Charter and the Use of Force, 1945–1985," in *The Current Legal Regulation of the Use of Force* 491, 492 (A. Cassese ed. 1986). We consider international law and the use of force in Chapter 8.

3. *Giving Effect to the Laws of Unrecognized States and Governments.* In the *Goldberg Case* a U.S. court refuses to give effect to a law of an entity that the United States has not recognized as a state. If the TFSC and the TRNC had been recognized by many states, but not by the United States, would the court have scrutinized the decrees concerning the mosaics, because made by a *de jure* government? Does the *Goldberg* court refuse to consider the TFSC's decrees concerning the mosaics because the court finds the decrees objectionable? Should acts taken under *un*objectionable laws of an unrecognized state—such as laws setting procedures for marriages and divorces—be denied effect in U.S. courts?

4. *Access of Unrecognized States and Governments to U.S. Courts.* The *Goldberg* district court also refused to allow the TRNC to intervene directly in the case, stating that to do so "would create the incongruous result of having the Judicial Branch implicitly recognize that entity as a legitimate government in the face of explicit nonrecognition by the Executive Branch." Autocephalous Greek–Orthodox Church of Cyprus v. Goldberg & Feldman Fine Arts, Inc., No. IP 89–304–C (S.D.Ind. May 31, 1989), *quoted in* 86 *American Journal of International Law* 128, 129 (1992). Other decisions also have denied unrecognized states or governments access to U.S. courts. In one well-known case, Russian Socialist Federated Soviet Republic v. Cibrario, 235 N.Y. 255, 139 N.E. 259 (1923), the court concluded that foreign powers appeared in U.S. courts only as a matter of comity. The court defined comity as "that reciprocal courtesy which one member of the family of nations owes to the others," a concept that presupposed friendship. No comity was due a foreign government appearing as a plaintiff in U.S. court, the *Cibrario* court found, unless the United States had recognized that government. For a critique of the role of comity in U.S. law, see Joel Paul, "Comity in International Law," 32 *Harvard International Law Journal* 1 (1991).

The approach of the *Goldberg* and *Cibrario* courts, denying unrecognized entities the right to bring claims to U.S. court, has not been universally followed. In National Petrochemical Co. v. M/T Stolt Sheaf, 860 F.2d 551 (2d Cir.1988), *cert. denied*, 489 U.S. 1081, 109 S.Ct. 1535, 103 L.Ed.2d 840 (1989), the Second Circuit reversed the district court's dismissal of a suit brought by a corporation wholly owned by the government of Iran. The United States did not recognize Iran at the time. The court, relying on an *amicus curiae* brief filed by the U.S. Justice and State Departments, agreed that the plaintiff should have access to U.S. courts:

> Two reasons support this holding. First, as this century draws to a close, the practice of extending formal recognition to new governments has altered: The United States Department of State has sometimes refrained from announcing recognition of a new government because grants of recognition have been misinterpreted as pronouncements of approval. *See* 77 *State Dep't Bull.* 462–63 (Oct. 10, 1977)("In recent

years, U.S. practice has been to deemphasize and avoid the use of recognition in cases of changes of governments. . . ."); Restatement 3d § 203, reporter's note 1 (commenting on recent deemphasis of formal recognition). As a result, the absence of formal recognition cannot serve as the touchstone for determining whether the Executive Branch has "recognized" a foreign nation for the purpose of granting that government access to United States courts.

Second, the power to deal with foreign nations outside the bounds of formal recognition is essential to a president's implied power to maintain international relations. *Cf. United States v. Curtiss-Wright Export Corp.*, 299 U.S. 304, 318–20, 57 S.Ct. 216, 220–21, 81 L.Ed. 255 (1936). As part of this power, the Executive Branch must have the latitude to permit a foreign nation access to U.S. courts, even if that nation is not formally recognized by the U.S. government.

Id. at 554–55. Would it be preferable to allow unrecognized governments access to U.S. courts unless the executive branch expressly objects?

5. *U.S. Recognition Policy.* The *National Petrochemical Co.* court noted that U.S. recognition practice has changed in the late twentieth century. Earlier U.S. recognition policy placed considerable weight on whether a new government was in effective control in a state. Secretary of State Daniel Webster declared in 1852 that U.S. recognition policy "[f]rom President Washington's time down to the present day" reflected the view that "every nation possesses a right to govern itself according to its own will, to change its institutions at discretion, and to transact its business through whatever agents it may think proper to employ." *Quoted in* 1 Charles Cheney Hyde, *International Law Chiefly as Interpreted and Applied by the United States* § 43, at 159 (2d rev.ed. 1945). In the early twentieth century, however, President Woodrow Wilson thought it appropriate to withhold recognition from regimes that obtained power extraconstitutionally. See 1 Green Haywood Hackworth, *Digest of International Law* 180–81 (1940). When a government was recognized, the U.S. executive branch would traditionally proclaim the new government's authority, announce the U.S. decision to establish relations with the new government, or have its representative at the foreign capital send a note to that government.

6. *Comparing Recognition and the Establishment of Diplomatic Relations.* Recognition is ordinarily a prerequisite for the establishment of diplomatic relations. The U.S. Supreme Court has held that, unlike the traditional rule that an unrecognized government cannot sue in U.S. court, the lack of diplomatic relations has no such effect:

Respondents, pointing to the severance of diplomatic relations, commercial embargo, and freezing of Cuban assets in this country, contend that relations between the United States and Cuba manifest such animosity that unfriendliness is clear, and that the courts should be closed to the Cuban Government. We do not agree. This Court would hardly be competent to undertake assessments of varying degrees of friendliness or its absence, and, lacking some definite touchstone for determination, we are constrained to consider any relationship, short of war, with a recognized sovereign power as embracing the privilege of resorting to United States courts. Although the severance of diplomatic relations is an overt act with objective significance in the dealings of sovereign states, we are unwilling to say that it should inevitably result in the withdrawal of the privilege of bringing suit. Severance may take place for any number of political reasons, its duration is unpredictable, and whatever expression of animosity it may imply does not approach that implicit in a declaration of war.

Banco Nacional de Cuba v. Sabbatino, 376 U.S. 398, 410, 84 S.Ct. 923, 930–31, 11 L.Ed.2d 804, 819 (1964). Is this distinction between the effects of nonrecognition and severance of diplomatic relations sensible? Do recognition and the establishment of diplomatic relations serve different functions?

B. SELF-DETERMINATION

The meaning of "self-determination" is much debated in international law. Although it is clear that the concept of self-determination relates to group rather than individual rights, what groups comprise the relevant "self"? And once consensus develops that some group is entitled to self-determination, what legal consequences follow? How should international law determine and implement the wishes of a group that is entitled to self-determination?

President Woodrow Wilson, who helped shape the peace settlement after World War I, believed that the concept of national self-determination was important in maintaining a peaceful international society. For Wilson, self-determination had both an "external" aspect (freedom from alien rule) and an "internal" aspect (promotion of democratic institutions):

> No peace can last, or ought to last, which does not recognize and accept the principle that governments derive all their just powers from the consent of the governed, and that no right anywhere exists to hand peoples about from sovereignty to sovereignty as if they were property. I take it for granted, for instance, if I may venture upon a single example, that statesmen everywhere are agreed that there should be a united, independent, and autonomous Poland * * *.

Address of the President of the United States, Delivered Before the United States Senate on January 22, 1917, Submitting Certain Conditions Upon Which This Government Would Feel Justified in Approving Its Formal and Solemn Adherence to a League for Peace, Sen.Doc. No. 685, 64th Cong., 2d Sess. 6. Critics objected that Wilson's view of self-determination was indeterminate and that arguments over self-determination would destabilize the post-war settlement.

The Soviet leader at the time, Nikolai Lenin, also forcefully espoused, at least on the international level, a right of self-determination. Lenin's view of self-determination contained an anti-colonial emphasis. He argued that peoples under colonial rule had the right to gain their independence, a position that was closely tied to his more fundamental goal of achieving socialism on a global basis. While Wilson also thought that self-determination should be taken into account in settling colonial claims, he sought to balance self-determination concerns and the interests of the colonial powers, and to implement self-determination claims in an orderly, nonviolent manner.

Self-determination was particularly debated as a principle to regulate the break-up of the Austro–Hungarian and Ottoman Empires after World War I. Some populations were allowed to hold plebiscites to determine border changes. Talk of self-determination contributed to the inclusion of formal guarantees for minority rights in peace treaties between the victorious powers and new states. Nevertheless, the economic, strategic, and geopolitical interests of the Allies ultimately proved to be more important factors in determining the shape of the post-war world.

This section examines changing conceptions of self-determination in international law. We start with a decision of the League of Nations' Committee of Jurists, which concluded that self-determination did pose an international legal question in the particular context of the claims of the Aaland Islanders following World War I. The next set of readings concerns the United Nations' use of self-determination in its efforts to promote the independence of former colonies of European powers. Nowadays, claims for self-determination remain important as ethnic, cultural, linguistic, and religious groups seek to break away from existing states or to conclude special autonomy relationships with states. As an example, the last readings in this section examine some of the self-determination claims made during the dissolution of Yugoslavia in the early 1990s.

REPORT OF THE INTERNATIONAL COMMITTEE OF JURISTS ON THE LEGAL ASPECTS OF THE AALAND ISLANDS QUESTION

League of Nations Official Journal, Special Supp. No. 3 (1920).

At a meeting held on the 12th July, 1920, the Council of the League of Nations, assembled at London, unanimously adopted with the assent of Finland and Sweden, the opposing parties in a dispute as to whether the inhabitants of the Aaland Islands should "be authorized to determine forthwith by plebiscite whether the archipelago should remain under Finnish sovereignty or be incorporated in the kingdom of Sweden," the following resolution:

"An International Commission of three jurists shall be appointed for the purpose of submitting to the Council, with the least possible delay, their opinion on the following points:

(1) Whether, within the meaning of paragraph 8 of Article 15 of the Covenant, the case presented by Sweden to the Council with reference to the Aaland Islands deals with a question that should, according to International Law, be entirely left to the domestic jurisdiction of Finland. * * *"

SWEDEN'S CLAIM.

2. The question really takes this form: can the inhabitants of the Aaland Islands, as at present situated, and taking as a basis the principle that peoples must have the right of self-determination, request to be united to Sweden? Can Sweden, on her side, claim that a plebiscite should take place in order to give the inhabitants of the Islands the opportunity of recording their wish with regard to their union with Sweden or continuance under Finnish rule?

THE PRINCIPLE OF SELF-DETERMINATION AND THE RIGHTS OF PEOPLE.

Although the principle of self-determination of peoples plays an important part in modern political thought, especially since the Great War, it must be pointed out that there is no mention of it in the Covenant of the League of Nations. The recognition of this principle in a certain number of international treaties cannot be considered as sufficient to put it upon the same footing as a positive rule of the Law of Nations.

On the contrary, in the absence of express provisions in international treaties, the right of disposing of national territory is essentially an attribute of the sovereignty of every State. Positive International Law does not recognize the right of national groups, as such, to separate themselves from the State of which they form part by the simple expression of a wish, any more than it recognizes the right of other States to claim such a separation. Generally speaking, the grant or refusal of the right to a portion of its population of determining its own political fate by plebiscite or by some other method, is, exclusively, an attribute of the sovereignty of every State which is definitively constituted. A dispute between two States concerning such a question, under normal conditions therefore, bears upon a question which International Law leaves entirely to the domestic jurisdiction of one of the States concerned. Any other solution would amount to an infringement of sovereign rights of a State and would involve the risk of creating difficulties and a lack of stability which would not only be contrary to the very idea embodied in term "State," but would also endanger the interests of the international community. If this right is not possessed by a large or small section of a nation, neither can it be held by the State to which the National group wishes to be attached, nor by any other State.

The Commission, in affirming these principles, does not give an opinion concerning the question as to whether a manifest and continued abuse of sovereign power, to the detriment of a section of the population of a State, would, if such circumstances arose, give to an international dispute, arising therefrom, such a character that its object should be considered as one which is not confined to the domestic jurisdiction of the State concerned, but comes within the sphere of action of the League of Nations. Such a supposition certainly does not apply to the case under consideration, and has not been put forward by either of the parties to the dispute.

De facto and *de jure* Considerations. Their International Character.

3. It must, however, be observed that all that has been said concerning the attributes of the sovereignty of a State, generally speaking, only applies to a nation which is definitively constituted as a sovereign State and an independent member of the international community, and so long as it continues to possess these characteristics. From the point of view of both domestic and international law, the formation, transformation and dismemberment of States as a result of revolutions and wars create situations of fact which, to a large extent, cannot be met by the application of the normal rules of positive law. This amounts to a statement that if the essential basis of these rules, that is to say, territorial sovereignty, is lacking, either because the State is not yet fully formed or because it is undergoing transformation or dissolution, the situation is obscure and uncertain from a legal point of view, and will not become clear until the period of development is completed and a definite new situation, which is normal in respect to territorial sovereignty, has been established.

This transition from a *de facto* situation to a normal situation *de jure* cannot be considered as one confined entirely within the domestic jurisdiction of a State. It tends to lead to readjustments between the members of the international community and to alterations in their territorial and legal status; consequently, this transition interests the community of States very deeply both from political and legal standpoints.

Self-Determination as Applied to *de facto* Situations. Its Forms.

Under such circumstances, the principle of self-determination of peoples may be called into play. New aspirations of certain sections of a nation, which are sometimes based on old traditions or on a common language and civilisation, may come to the surface and produce effects which must be taken into account in the interests of the internal and external peace of nations.

The principle recognising the rights of peoples to determine their political fate may be applied in various ways; the most important of these are, on the one hand the formation of an independent State, and on the other hand the right of choice between two existing States. This principle, however, must be brought into line with that of the protection of minorities; both have a common object—to assure to some national Group the maintenance and free development of its social, ethnical or religious characteristics.

The protection of minorities is already provided for, to a very varying extent, in a fairly large number of constitutions. This principle appears to be one of the essential characteristics of liberty at the present time. Under certain circumstances, however, it has been thought necessary to go further, and to guarantee, by international treaties, some particular situation to certain racial or religious minorities. Thus, in some recent treaties a special legal régime, under the control and guarantee of the League of Nations, has been established for certain sections of the population of a State.

The fact must, however, not be lost sight of that the principle that nations must have the right of self-determination is not the only one to be taken into account. Even though it be regarded as the most important of the principles governing the formation of States, geographical, economic and other similar considerations may put obstacles in the way of its complete recognition. Under such circumstances, a solution in the nature of a compromise, based on an extensive grant of liberty to minorities, may appear necessary according to international legal conception and may even be dictated by the interests of peace.

HISTORICAL DEVELOPMENT OF FINLAND.

4. In the light of the foregoing, the question has to be decided as to whether, from the standpoint of territorial sovereignty, the situation of the Aaland Islands in the independent State of Finland is of a definite and normal character, or whether it is a transitory or not fully developed situation. * * *

Even if * * * the view most favorable to the Finnish theory be adopted * * * it remains true, nevertheless, that the State of Finland, which since 1899 was in fact treated by the Russian Government as an ordinary province, had not and also never claimed to have an independent legal existence in external affairs and was indissolubly bound to Russia. * * *

DECLARATION OF INDEPENDENCE.

At the same time, the Finnish Diet, on the 15th November, 1917, assumed the supreme power and constituted a national Government which, on the 4th December, 1917, sent forth an appeal to the Finnish people exhorting them to make every effort to enable Finland to take her place as an independent nation among the other nations. During the events which followed, this object was ultimately attained. * * *

INTERNAL SITUATION OF FINLAND.

In addition to these facts which bear upon the external relations of Finland, the very abnormal character of her internal situation must be brought out. This situation was such that, for a considerable time, the conditions required for the formation of a sovereign State did not exist.

In the midst of revolution and anarchy, certain elements essential to the existence of a State, even some elements of fact, were lacking for a fairly considerable period. Political and social life was disorganized; the authorities were not strong enough to assert themselves; civil war was rife; further, the Diet, the legality of which had been disputed by a large section of the people, had been dispersed by the revolutionary party, and the Government had been chased from the capital and forcibly prevented from carrying out its duties; the armed camps and the police were divided into two opposing forces, and Russian troops, and after a time

Germans also, took part in the civil war between the inhabitants and between the Red and White Finnish troops.

It is, therefore, difficult to say at what exact date the Finnish Republic, in the legal sense of the term, actually became a definitely constituted sovereign State. This certainly did not take place until a stable political organization had been created, and until the public authorities had become strong enough to assert themselves throughout the territories of the State without the assistance of foreign troops. It would appear that it was in May, 1918, that the civil war ended and that the foreign troops began to leave the country, so that from that time onwards it was possible to re-establish order and normal political and social life, little by little.

It follows from all these facts that the formation of an independent State of Finland in 1917 and 1918, whatever may have been the legal status of Finland formerly under the Russian Empire, must be considered, at any rate in several aspects, as a new political phenomenon and not as a mere continuation of a previously existing political entity. * * *

THE PURPORT OF THE FINNISH DECLARATION OF INDEPENDENCE.

The Aaland Islands were undoubtedly part of Finland during the period of Russian rule. Must they, for this reason alone, be considered as definitely incorporated *de jure* in the State of Finland which was formed as a result of the events described above?

The Commission finds it impossible to admit this. The extent and nature of the political changes, which take place as facts and outside the domain of law, are necessarily limited by the results actually produced. These results alone form the basis of the new legal entity which is about to be formed, and it is they which will determine its essential characteristics. If one part of a State actually separates itself from that State, the separation is necessarily limited in its effect to the population of the territory which has taken part in the act of separation. Though the political projects leading to the separation may be manifested in different ways in different parts of the territory, nevertheless these projects all have an equal value as a foundation for the new legal order, though of course only in so far as those who adopt them are able to maintain them. It may even be said that if a separation occurs from a political organism which is more or less autonomous, and which is itself *de facto* in process of political transformation, this organism cannot at the very moment when it transforms itself outside the domain of positive law invoke the principles of this law in order to force upon a national group a political status which the latter refuses to accept. * * *

COMPARISON BETWEEN THE POLITICAL ATTITUDE ON THE MAINLAND OF FINLAND AND ON THE ISLANDS. * * *

* * * The Aaland Islands agitation originated at a time when Finland was undergoing a process of transformation. The fact that Finland was eventually reconstituted as an independent State is not

sufficient to efface the conditions which gave rise to the aspirations of the Aaland Islanders and to cause these conditions to be regarded as if they had never arisen. These arguments are emphasized by the fact that the population of the Islands, which is very homogeneous, inhabits a territory which is more or less geographically distinct; further, the population is united by ties of race, language and traditions to the Swedish race, from which it was only separated by force, whereas the population of the Finnish mainland is, for the most part, of Finnish origin, and the small portion of Swedish which has become mingled with it to a large extent shares the ideal of the majority with regard to an independent State of Finland. It must be added that the population of the Islands had no means of asserting its nationalist aspirations during the period of Russian rule. * * *

CONCLUSIONS.

The Commission, after consideration of the arguments set out and developed in the preceding report, have arrived at the following conclusions:—

(1) The dispute between Sweden and Finland does not refer to a definitive established political situation, depending exclusively upon the territorial sovereignty of a State.

(2) On the contrary, the dispute arose from a *de facto* situation caused by the political transformation of the Aaland Islands, which transformation was caused by and originated in the separatist movement among the inhabitants, who quoted the principle of national self-determination, and certain military events which accompanied and followed the separation of Finland from the Russian Empire at a time when Finland had not yet acquired the character of a definitively constituted State.

(3) It follows from the above that the dispute does not refer to a question which is left by International Law to the domestic jurisdiction of Finland.

(4) The Council of the League of Nations, therefore, is competent, under paragraph 4 of Article 15, to make any recommendations which it deems just and proper in the case.

Notes and Questions

1. *The Aaland Islands Question.* The Aaland Islands question occupied delegates to the Paris Peace Conference at the end of World War I. The evident desire of the Aaland Islanders to unite with Sweden struck a chord in tune with President Woodrow Wilson's emphasis on self-determination. Sweden stressed the Aaland Islanders' racial, linguistic, and historical ties to Sweden. Yet, Britain wondered whether Swedish or Finnish control of the Islands would be the greater deterrent to their occupation by a great power, and France thought Finland a better buffer between Bolshevist Russia and Europe than historically neutral Sweden. See James Barros, *The Aaland Islands Question: Its Settlement by the League of Nations* 163, 215 (1968).

The problem was not resolved at the Paris Peace Conference, and eventually the League of Nations took it up. The Council of the League of Nations referred the politically sensitive question to a Committee of Jurists. At least one diplomat hoped that the Committee would conclude that the Council legally could not address the Aaland Islands question because it was an internal Finnish problem. "The Council could then have easily unshouldered the burden by declaring its noncompetence, an action for which they could never have been criticized." *Id.* at 281–82. The Committee's report, however, made it inevitable that the League would have to address the Aaland Islands question. This the League did by establishing a new Commission of Inquiry, which favored continuing Finnish control over the Aaland Islands, citing the Islands' geographical ties to the Finnish mainland and a range of Finnish and international political considerations. League of Nations, *The Aaland Islands Question: Report Submitted to the Council of the League of Nations by the Commission of Rapporteurs* (Doc. B 7.21/68/106)(1921). The Council of the League of Nations ultimately accepted Finnish sovereignty over the Aaland Islands in June 1921, but also sought guarantees concerning demilitarization of the Islands and autonomy for its residents. Finland agreed to support Swedish language schools for the Aaland Islanders, a preemptive right for the Islanders when outsiders sought to buy land, restrictions on the voting rights of immigrants to the Islands, and a say for the citizens of Aaland in the appointment of their governor. See Barros, *supra*, at 330–33.

2. *The Committee of Jurists and the International Legal Right to Self-determination.* The opinion of the Committee of Jurists touches on several issues related to the concept of statehood, including the importance of an independent government. Note particularly the Committee's treatment of the law concerning self-determination. In the Committee's view, the self-determination claim of the Aaland Islanders is not, under international law, reserved to Finland's domestic jurisdiction. Why is this so?

3. *Self-determination and the Protection of Minorities.* How does the Committee of Jurists regard the relationship between the principle of self-determination and the principle of protection of minorities?

4. *Autonomy Arrangements and the Right to Self-determination.* In many ways, the situation of the Aaland Islanders is conducive to arrangements for autonomy. Aaland Island is geographically separate from the rest of Finland; its boundaries are definite. The Islanders are homogeneous, overwhelmingly viewing themselves as Swedish. If a distinct group of peoples is not confined within clear territorial borders, or if a population within such borders is not homogeneous, should that preclude a legal right to self-determination?

5. *The League of Nations and "Internationalized" Territory.* The League of Nations itself was directly involved in governing certain "internationalized" territory. For example, the League, by virtue of Article 102 of the Versailles Peace Treaty, exercised protection over the Free City of Danzig. Poland conducted Danzig's foreign relations, and Polish customs regulations applied there; Poland also, jointly with Danzig, administered Danzig's port and waterways. The League, however, appointed a High Commissioner who was in residence in Danzig, and who was charged with

deciding all disputes with respect to the Treaty of Versailles. Appeals could be taken to the League's Council, whose decisions were binding on Danzig and Poland. The High Commissioner also could veto any Polish treaty applying to Danzig that he regarded as inconsistent with its "Free City" status, and revisions to Danzig's constitution could enter into force only when the League of Nations declared that it had no objections to them. For discussion of Danzig, other "internationalized" territories, and intellectual conceptions of these new international legal forms, see Nathaniel Berman, "'But the Alternative is Despair': Nationalism and the Modernist Renewal of International Law," 106 *Harvard Law Review* 1792, 1874–98 (1993).

Note: The United Nations and Decolonization

The Charter of the United Nations, unlike the Covenant of the League of Nations, specifically refers to self-determination. Article 1(2) of the Charter states that one of the purposes of the Organization is "to develop friendly relations among nations based on respect for the principle of equal rights and self-determination of peoples, and to take other appropriate measures to strengthen universal peace." Article 1(2) is phrased as a general goal, seemingly linked to the more fundamental goal of furthering friendly, peaceful relations among states. Neither Article 1(2) nor Article 56, which also invokes the principle of self-determination, indicates that states must take any immediate action.

The principle of self-determination has also been developed in subsequent treaty law. The International Covenant on Economic, Social and Cultural Rights, Dec. 16, 1966, 993 U.N.T.S. 3, 6 I.L.M. 360 (1967), and the International Covenant on Civil and Political Rights, Dec. 16, 1966, 999 U.N.T.S. 171, 6 I.L.M. 368 (1967), each widely accepted, contain an identically worded Article 1(1): "All peoples have the right of self-determination. By virtue of that right they freely determine their political status and freely pursue their economic, social and cultural development." Article 1(3) of each Covenant recognizes the importance of the principle of self-determination in the colonial context.

Decolonization was largely responsible for the increase in the number of states during the mid-twentieth century. In Africa in 1950, only South Africa, Liberia, Ethiopia, and Egypt were not colonies of European powers; by 1965, there were more than 35 independent African states. Worldwide, 70 territories gained independence between 1945 and 1979, and a few more territories have become independent since then. The next three readings explore the relationship between decolonization and the principle of self-determination.

U.N. DECLARATION ON THE GRANTING OF INDEPENDENCE TO COLONIAL COUNTRIES AND PEOPLES

U.N.G.A. Res. 1514(XV), Dec. 14, 1960.

The General Assembly,

Mindful of the determination proclaimed by the peoples of the world in the Charter of the United Nations to reaffirm faith in fundamental human rights, in the dignity and worth of the human person, in the equal rights of men and women and of nations large and small and to promote social progress and better standards of life in larger freedom,

Conscious of the need for the creation of conditions of stability and well-being and peaceful and friendly relations based on respect for the principles of equal rights and self-determination of all peoples, and of universal respect for, and observance of human rights and fundamental freedoms for all without distinction as to race, sex, language or religion,

Recognizing the passionate yearning for freedom in all dependent peoples and the decisive role of such peoples in the attainment of their independence, * * *

Convinced that all peoples have an inalienable right to complete freedom, the exercise of their sovereignty and the integrity of their national territory,

Solemnly proclaims the necessity of bringing to a speedy and unconditional end colonialism in all its forms and manifestations;

And to this end

Declares that:

1. The subjection of peoples to alien subjugation, domination and exploitation constitutes a denial of fundamental human rights, is contrary to the Charter of the United Nations and is an impediment to the promotion of world peace and co-operation.

2. All peoples have the right to self-determination; by virtue of that right they freely determine their political status and freely pursue their economic, social and cultural development.

3. Inadequacy of political, economic, social or educational preparedness should never serve as a pretext for delaying independence.

4. All armed action or repressive measures of all kinds directed against dependent peoples shall cease in order to enable them to exercise peacefully and freely their right to complete independence, and the integrity of their national territory shall be respected.

5. Immediate steps shall be taken, in Trust and Non–Self–Governing Territories or all other territories which have not yet attained independence, to transfer all powers to the peoples of those territories, without any conditions or reservations, in accordance with their freely expressed will and desire, without any distinction as to race, creed or color, in order to enable them to enjoy complete independence and freedom.

6. Any attempt aimed at the partial or total disruption of the national unity and the territorial integrity of a country is incompatible with the purposes and principles of the Charter of the United Nations.

7. All States shall observe faithfully and strictly the provisions of the Charter of the United Nations, the Universal Declaration of Human Rights and the present Declaration on the basis of equality, non-

interference in the internal affairs of all States, and respect for the sovereign rights of all peoples and their territorial integrity.

DECLARATION ON PRINCIPLES OF INTERNATIONAL LAW CONCERNING FRIENDLY RELATIONS AND CO-OPERATION AMONG STATES IN ACCORDANCE WITH THE CHARTER OF THE UNITED NATIONS

U.N.G.A. Res. 2625 (XXV), Oct. 24, 1970.

The General Assembly, * * *

Having considered the principles of international law relating to friendly relations and co-operation among States,

1. *Solemnly proclaims* the following principles: * * *

The principle of equal rights and self-determination of peoples

By virtue of the principle of equal rights and self-determination of peoples enshrined in the Charter of the United Nations, all peoples have the right freely to determine, without external interference, their political status and to pursue their economic, social and cultural development, and every State has the duty to respect this right in accordance with the provisions of the Charter.

Every State has the duty to promote, through joint and separate action, realization of the principle of equal rights and self-determination of peoples, in accordance with the provisions of the Charter, and to render assistance to the United Nations in carrying out the responsibilities entrusted to it by the Charter regarding the implementation of the principle, in order:

(*a*) To promote friendly relations and co-operation among States; and

(*b*) To bring a speedy end to colonialism, having due regard to the freely expressed will of the peoples concerned;

and bearing in mind that subjection of peoples to alien subjugation, domination and exploitation constitutes a violation of the principle, as well as a denial of fundamental human rights, and is contrary to the Charter.

Every State has the duty to promote through joint and separate action universal respect for and observance of human rights and fundamental freedoms in accordance with the Charter.

The establishment of a sovereign and independent State, the free association or integration with an independent State or the emergence into any other political status freely determined by a people constitute modes of implementing the right of self-determination by that people.

Every State has the duty to refrain from any forcible action which deprives peoples referred to above in the elaboration of the present principle of their right to self-determination and freedom and independence. In their actions against, and resistance to, such forcible action in pursuit of the exercise of their right to self-determination, such peoples are entitled to seek and to receive support in accordance with the purpose and principles of the Charter.

The territory of a colony or other Non-Self-Governing Territory has, under the Charter, a status separate and distinct from the territory of the State administering it; and such separate and distinct status under the Charter shall exist until the people of the colony or Non-Self-Governing Territory have exercised their right of self-determination in accordance with the Charter, and particularly its purpose and principles.

Nothing in the foregoing paragraphs shall be construed as authorizing or encouraging any action which would dismember or impair, totally or in part, the territorial integrity or political unity of sovereign and independent States conducting themselves in compliance with the principle of equal rights and self-determination of peoples as described above and thus possessed of government representing the whole people belonging to the territory without distinction as to race, creed or colour.

Every State shall refrain from any action aimed at the partial or total disruption of the national unity and territorial integrity of any other State or country.

THE NAMIBIA ADVISORY OPINION

Legal Consequences for States of the Continued Presence of South Africa in Namibia (South West Africa) Notwithstanding Security Council Resolution 276 (1970), 1971 I.C.J. 16, 1971 WL 8.

[This advisory opinion of the International Court of Justice follows a series of U.N. General Assembly and Security Council resolutions condemning apartheid South Africa's lack of compliance with its responsibilities as an administering power for Namibia (South West Africa). South Africa's authority as an administering power had originally been established under the League of Nations' mandates system. In 1966, the U.N. General Assembly decided that South Africa's Mandate to administer Namibia was terminated. G.A. Res. 2145 (XXI)(1966). Of central importance in the advisory opinion was Security Council Resolution 276, adopted in 1970. Paragraph 2 of Resolution 276 declares that "the continued presence of the South African authorities in Namibia is illegal" and thus that all acts taken by South Africa "on behalf of or concerning Namibia after the termination of the Mandate are illegal and invalid." Paragraph 5 of the same Resolution calls on "all States, particularly those which have economic and other interests in Namibia, to refrain from any dealings with Government of South Africa which are inconsistent with operative paragraph 2 of this resolution."]

45. * * * Article 22 of the Covenant [of the League of Nations], paragraph 1 * * * declares:

> "1. To those colonies and territories which as a consequence of the late war have ceased to be under the sovereignty of the States which formerly governed them and which are inhabited by peoples

> not yet able to stand by themselves under the strenuous conditions of the modern world, there should be applied the principle that the well-being and development of such peoples form a sacred trust of civilization and that securities for the performance of this trust should be embodied in this Covenant."

As the Court recalled in its 1950 Advisory Opinion on the *International Status of South–West Africa*, in the setting-up of the mandates system "two principles were considered to be of paramount importance: the principle of non-annexation and the principle that the well-being and development of such peoples form 'a sacred trust of civilization.' " * * *

52. Furthermore, the subsequent development of international law in regard to non-self-governing territories, as enshrined in the Charter of the United Nations, made the principle of self-determination applicable to all of them. The concept of the sacred trust was confirmed and expanded to all "territories whose peoples have not yet attained a full measure of self-government" (Art. 73). Thus it clearly embraced territories under a colonial regime. Obviously the sacred trust continued to apply to League of Nations mandated territories on which an international status had been conferred earlier. A further important stage in this development was the Declaration on the Granting of Independence to Colonial Countries and Peoples (General Assembly resolution 1514 (XV) of 14 December 1960), which embraces all peoples and territories which "have not yet attained independence." Nor is it possible to leave out of account the political history of mandated territories in general. All those which did not acquire independence, excluding Namibia, were placed under trusteeship. Today, only two out of fifteen, excluding Namibia, remain under United Nations tutelage. This is but a manifestation of the general development which has led to the birth of so many new States.

53. * * * [T]he ultimate objective of the sacred trust was the self-determination and independence of the peoples concerned. * * *

115. * * * The Court has * * * reached the conclusion that the decisions made by the Security Council in paragraphs 2 and 5 of resolution[] 276 (1970) * * * were adopted in conformity with the purposes and principles of the Charter and in accordance with its Articles 24 and 25. The decisions are consequently binding on all States Members of the United Nations, which are thus under obligation to accept and carry them out. * * *

121. The Court will * * * confine itself to giving advice on those dealings with the Government of South Africa which, under the Charter of the United Nations and general international law, should be considered as inconsistent with the declaration of illegality and invalidity made in paragraph 2 of resolution 276 (1970), because they may imply a recognition that South Africa's presence in Namibia is legal.

122. For the reasons given above, and subject to the observations contained in paragraph 125 below, member States are under obligation to abstain from entering into treaty relations with South Africa in all

cases in which the Government of South Africa purports to act on behalf of or concerning Namibia. With respect to existing bilateral treaties, member States must abstain from invoking or applying those treaties or provisions of treaties concluded by South Africa on behalf of or concerning Namibia which involve active intergovernmental co-operation. With respect to multilateral treaties, however, the same rule cannot be applied to certain general conventions such as those of a humanitarian character, the non-performance of which may adversely affect the people of Namibia. It will be for the competent international organs to take specific measures in this respect.

123. Member States, in compliance with the duty of non-recognition imposed by paragraphs 2 and 5 of resolution 276 (1970), are under obligation to abstain from sending diplomatic or special missions to South Africa including in their jurisdiction the Territory of Namibia, to abstain from sending consular agents to Namibia, and to withdraw any such agents already there. They should also make it clear to the South African authorities that the maintenance of diplomatic or consular relations with South Africa does not imply any recognition of its authority with regard to Namibia.

124. The restraints which are implicit in the non-recognition of South Africa's presence in Namibia and the explicit provisions of paragraph 5 of resolution 276 (1970) impose upon member States the obligation to abstain from entering into economic and other forms of relationship or dealings with South Africa on behalf of or concerning Namibia which may entrench its authority over the Territory.

125. In general, the non-recognition of South Africa's administration of the Territory should not result in depriving the people of Namibia of any advantages derived from international co-operation. In particular, while official acts performed by the Government of South Africa on behalf of or concerning Namibia after the termination of the Mandate are illegal and invalid, this invalidity cannot be extended to those acts, such as, for instance, the registration of births, deaths and marriages, the effects of which can be ignored only to the detriment of the inhabitants of the Territory.

126. As to non-member States, although not bound by Articles 24 and 25 of the Charter, they have been called upon in paragraphs 2 and 5 of resolution 276 (1970) to give assistance in the action which has been taken by the United Nations with regard to Namibia. In the view of the Court, the termination of the Mandate and the declaration of the illegality of South Africa's presence in Namibia are opposable to all States in the sense of barring *erga omnes* the legality of a situation which is maintained in violation of international law: in particular, no State which enters into relations with South Africa concerning Namibia may expect the United Nations or its Members to recognize the validity or effects of such relationship, or of the consequences thereof. The Mandate having been terminated by decision of the international organization in which the supervisory authority over its administration was

vested, and South Africa's continued presence in Namibia having been declared illegal, it is for non-member States to act in accordance with those decisions.

127. As to the general consequences resulting from the illegal presence of South Africa in Namibia, all States should bear in mind that the injured entity is a people which must look to the international community for assistance in its progress towards the goals for which the sacred trust was instituted. * * *

133. For these reasons,

THE COURT IS OF OPINION

in reply to the question:

> "What are the legal consequences for States of the continued presence of South Africa in Namibia, notwithstanding Security Council resolution 276 (1970)?"

by 13 votes to 2,

(1) that, the continued presence of South Africa in Namibia being illegal, South Africa is under obligation to withdraw its administration from Namibia immediately and thus put an end to its occupation of the Territory;

by 11 votes to 4,

(2) that States Members of the United Nations are under obligation to recognize the illegality of South Africa's presence in Namibia and the invalidity of its acts on behalf of or concerning Namibia, and to refrain from any acts and in particular any dealings with the Government of South Africa implying recognition of the legality of, or lending support or assistance to, such presence and administration;

(3) that it is incumbent upon States which are not Members of the United Nations to give assistance, within the scope of subparagraph (2) above, in the action which has been taken by the United Nations with regard to Namibia.

Notes and Questions

1. *Support for Self-determination in the United Nations.* General Assembly Resolutions 1514 and 1625 are two of the most important U.N. statements concerning self-determination. Resolution 1514 was adopted by a vote of 89 to 0, with Australia, Belgium, the Dominican Republic, France, Portugal, South Africa, Spain, the United Kingdom, and the United States abstaining. Resolution 1625 was adopted without a vote.

In 1970, the International Court of Justice concludes in the *Namibia Case* that the notion of a "sacred trust," the ultimate objective of which was self-determination and independence of peoples, applied not only to territories that had been the subject of a League of Nations mandate, but also to colonies. More recently, the Court has stressed that "the right of peoples to self-determination, as it evolved from the Charter and from United Nations practice, has an *erga omnes* character." Case Concerning East Timor (Portugal v. Australia), 1995 I.C.J. 90, 102, 1995 WL 688255. An obligation *erga omnes* is one, as the Court noted in the *Barcelona Traction Case,* reproduced in Chapter 6, that a state owes toward all other international actors, and whose fulfillment is not conditioned on what other states do in the same field. Obligations *erga omnes* are also discussed in Chapter 3.

2. *Construing the General Assembly Resolutions.* The two U.N. General Assembly resolutions are phrased in general terms. Nevertheless, the statements of broad principle reveal much about the shared perspectives of states toward a right to self-determination. Do the resolutions refer to "external" or "internal" self-determination? What peoples are entitled to self-determination? Certainly, peoples in non-self-governing territories are among those regarded as legally entitled to self-determination. The result of applying the principle to them was most often their independence, although some non-self-governing territories chose to associate with or integrate into another state. Do such peoples continue to enjoy a right to external self-determination once their former colony has attained independence? What peoples other than those in non-self-governing territories would generally be regarded as having a right to self-determination? For example, would a minority group be the beneficiary of the principle of self-determination as it has developed in the United Nations?

3. *Implementing the Right to Self-determination.* How should the will of peoples in non-self-governing territories with respect to external self-determination be ascertained? Since 1954, the United Nations has often organized and supervised plebiscites or elections in such territories.

4. *Self-determination and the Boundaries of States.* Almost all non-self-governing territories that achieved independence did so without any changes in their territorial boundaries. This has meant that several groups with different ethnic backgrounds have found themselves in the same state. Tensions among ethnic groups have sometimes contributed to horrific violence. Should the United Nations have sought changes in existing international boundaries in conjunction with its promotion of self-determination? After all, many of these boundaries were drawn by European powers in the late nineteenth century. Or, should the United Nations have more actively promoted autonomy relationships within newly independent states? Why were such steps generally not pursued?

5. *Violation of the Principle of Self-determination: Implications for the Use of Force.* What have been the responses when a state has violated the principle of self-determination with respect to non-self-governing territories? When a colony did not gain its independence peacefully, the colonial power could be condemned for illegally using force against liberation forces—despite what had been the widely accepted view that a state's decision to use force inside its own borders was a matter reserved to the domestic jurisdiction of that state. For example, when local liberation forces in Portuguese Guinea declared independence in September 1973 in the face of continued Portuguese opposition, the U.N. General Assembly invoked the right of self-determination, welcomed the independence of "the sovereign State of the Republic of Guinea–Bissau," and strongly condemned Portugal for its "illegal occupation of certain sectors of the Republic of Guinea–Bissau and the

repeated acts of aggression committed by its armed forces against the people of Guinea–Bissau." G.A. Res. 3061 (XXVIII). Many states recognized Guinea–Bissau even before this General Assembly resolution. Portugal itself formally recognized the independence of Guinea–Bissau on September 10, 1974, after a new government had taken power in Portugal, 13 I.L.M. 1244 (1974), and Guinea–Bissau was admitted as a member of the United Nations on September 17, 1974. G.A. Res. 3205 (XXIX). The General Assembly also referred to the duty of every state "to refrain from any forcible action which deprives peoples * * * of their right to self-determination and freedom and independence" in the 1970 Declaration on Friendly Relations. We take up the international law on the use of force in Chapter 8.

6. *Violation of the Principle of Self-determination: Nonrecognition of the Consequences of a Violation.* According to the *Namibia Case,* a state that breaches the right to self-determination may be subject to the countermeasure of refusal of legal recognition to the breaching situation. The ICJ outlines the types of relationships states legally may not enter with South Africa, because those relationships might imply recognition of the legality of South Africa's presence and administration in Namibia. What are the likely effects of the Court's decision?

7. *The U.N. Trusteeship Council.* The U.N. Trusteeship Council (made up of the five permanent members of the U.N. Security Council and the administering powers of the trust territories) helped promote self-government or independence for territories previously administered under League of Nations mandates, as well as for some former Italian and Japanese colonies. Ghana, the United Republic of Tanzania, Somalia, Togo, Cameroon, Rwanda, Burundi, Nauru, Papua New Guinea, the Federated States of Micronesia, the Northern Mariana Islands, and the Republic of the Marshall Islands were once trust territories, or are composed of parts of former trust territories. When Palau became self-governing in 1994, the last U.N. Trusteeship was dissolved. The U.N. Trusteeship Council is now dormant.

THE HELSINKI ACCORDS

Conference on Security and Co-operation in Europe, Final Act
14 *International Legal Materials* 1292 (1975).

Declaration on Principles Guiding Relations Between Participating States * * *

VIII. Equal Rights and Self-Determination of Peoples

The participating States will respect the equal rights of peoples and their right to self-determination, acting at all times in conformity with the purposes and principles of the Charter of the United Nations and with the relevant norms of international law, including those relating to territorial integrity of States.

By virtue of the principle of equal rights and self-determination of peoples, all peoples always have the right, in full freedom, to determine, when and as they wish, their internal and external political status, without external interference, and to pursue as they wish their political, economic, social and cultural development.

The participating States reaffirm the universal significance of respect for and effective exercise of equal rights and self-determination of peoples for the development of friendly relations among themselves as among all States; they also recall the importance of the elimination of any form of violation of this principle.

Notes and Questions

1. *The Conference on Security and Co-operation in Europe.* The Conference on Security and Co-operation in Europe (CSCE) opened in Helsinki on July 3, 1973, and was concluded on August 1, 1975. Leaders of the United States, Canada, the Soviet Union, and 32 other states in Eastern and Western Europe signed the Conference's Final Act. The Final Act did not only concern self-determination. It also addressed human rights, a particular concern of Western European states, and acknowledged the need to respect the territorial integrity of states, a politically important point for Eastern European states whose legitimacy had been challenged by the West. Coming as they did during the Cold War, the Helsinki Accords represented a significant political bargain. For more on human rights in Europe, see Chapter 6.

2. *The Legal Significance of the Helsinki Accords.* The states that signed the Helsinki Accords did not regard the instrument as legally binding. What, then, is its legal significance?

3. *Construing the Helsinki Accords.* How does the principle of self-determination articulated in Principle VIII of the Helsinki Accords compare to the principle as articulated in U.N. General Assembly resolutions? Does Principle VIII place more emphasis on internal self-determination than do the General Assembly resolutions? The debates leading up to the adoption of Principle VIII suggest concern with specifying a right to internal self-determination free from oppression by an authoritarian government. Is this intent reflected in the text? To what "peoples" were the signatories of the Helsinki Final Act willing to accord a right of external self-determination? Debates at the CSCE suggest complete agreement that national minorities were not covered, and the Accords include a separate Principle VII on minority individual rights. To what "peoples" does Principle VIII then refer? See Antonio Cassese, *Self-determination of Peoples* 278–92 (1995).

4. *Self-determination and the Breakup of Yugoslavia.* Arguments about self-determination have been prominent in recent controversies that are not tied to colonial territories, U.N. trust territories, or areas subject to foreign military occupation. During the breakup of Yugoslavia in the early 1990s, for example, different groups asserted a right of self-determination. The December 1991 Guidelines of the European Community and its Member States on Recognition of New States and the January 1992 opinion of the Conference on Yugoslavia Arbitration Commission, both reproduced below, had importance for the self-determination claims of the Serb populations of Croatia and Bosnia–Herzegovina.

DECLARATION ON YUGOSLAVIA, AND ON THE GUIDELINES ON THE RECOGNITION OF NEW STATES

European Community, Dec. 16, 1991
31 *International Legal Materials* 1485 (1992).

DECLARATION ON YUGOSLAVIA * * *

The Community and its member States agree to recognise the independence of all the Yugoslav Republics fulfilling all the conditions set out below. The implementation of this decision will take place on January 15, 1992.

They are therefore inviting all Yugoslav Republics to state by 23 December whether:

— they wish to be recognised as independent States;

— they accept the commitments contained in the above-mentioned guidelines;

— they accept the provisions laid down in the draft Convention—especially those in Chapter II on human rights and rights of national or ethnic groups—under consideration by the Conference on Yugoslavia,

— they continue to support

— the efforts of the Secretary General and the Security Council of the United Nations, and

— the continuation of the Conference on Yugoslavia.

The applications of those Republics which reply positively will be submitted through the Chair of the Conference to the Arbitration Commission for advice before the implementation date. * * *

The Community and its member States also require a Yugoslav Republic to commit itself, prior to recognition, to adopt constitutional and political guarantees ensuring that it has no territorial claims towards a neighboring Community State and that it will conduct no hostile propaganda activities versus a neighbouring Community State, including the use of a denomination which implies territorial claims.

DECLARATION ON THE "GUIDELINES ON THE RECOGNITION OF NEW STATES IN EASTERN EUROPE AND IN THE SOVIET UNION" * * *

The Community and its member States confirm their attachment to the principles of the Helsinki Final Act and the Charter of Paris,[1] in particular the principle of self-determination. They affirm their readiness to recognise, subject to the normal standards of international practice and the political realities in each case, those new States which, following the historic changes in the region, have constituted themselves

1. Conference on Security and Co-operation in Europe, Charter of Paris for a New Europe, Nov. 21, 1991, 30 I.L.M. 193 (1991)—ed.

on a democratic basis, have accepted the appropriate international obligations and have committed themselves in good faith to a peaceful process and to negotiations.

Therefore, they adopt a common position on the process of recognition of these new states, which requires:

— respect for the provisions of the Charter of the United Nations and the commitments subscribed to in the Final Act of Helsinki and in the Charter of Paris, especially with regard to the rule of law, democracy and human rights;

— guarantees for the rights of ethnic and national groups and minorities in accordance with the commitments subscribed to in the framework of the CSCE [Conference on Security and Cooperation in Europe];

— respect for the inviolability of all frontiers which can only be changed by peaceful means and by common agreement;

— acceptance of all relevant commitments with regard to disarmament and nuclear non-proliferation as well as to security and regional stability;

— commitment to settle by agreement, including where appropriate by recourse to arbitration, all questions concerning state succession and regional disputes.

The Community and its Member States will not recognise entities which are the result of aggression. They would take account of the effects of recognition on neighbouring States.

The commitments to these principles opens [*sic*] the way to recognition by the Community and its Member States and to the establishment of diplomatic relations. It could be laid down in agreements.

CONFERENCE ON YUGOSLAVIA ARBITRATION COMMISSION OPINION 2

31 *International Legal Materials* 1497 (1992).

On 20 November 1991 the Chairman of the Arbitration Commission received a letter from Lord Carrington, Chairman of the Conference on Yugoslavia, requesting the Commission's opinion on the following question put by the Republic of Serbia:

"Does the Serbian population in Croatia and Bosnia–Hercegovina, as one of the constituent peoples of Yugoslavia, have the right to self-determination?"

The Commission took note of the aide-mémoires, observations and other materials submitted by the Republics of Bosnia–Hercegovina, Croatia, Macedonia, Montenegro, Slovenia and Serbia, by the Presidency of the Socialist Federal Republic of Yugoslavia (SFRY) and by the "Assembly of the Serbian People of Bosnia–Hercegovina."

1. The Commission considers that international law as it currently stands does not spell out all the implications of the right to self-determination.

However, it is well established that, whatever the circumstances, the right to self-determination must not involve changes to existing frontiers at the time of independence (*uti possidetis juris*) except where the States concerned agree otherwise.

2. Where there are one or more groups within a State constituting one or more ethnic, religious or language communities, they have the right to recognition of their identity under international law.

As the Commission emphasized in its Opinion No 1 of 29 November 1991, published on 7 December, the—now peremptory—norms of international law require States to ensure respect for the rights of minorities. This requirement applies to all the Republics vis-à-vis the minorities on their territory.

The Serbian population in Bosnia–Hercegovina and Croatia must therefore be afforded every right accorded to minorities under international conventions as well as national and international guarantees consistent with the principles of international law and the provisions of Chapter II of the draft Convention of 4 November 1991, which has been accepted by these Republics.

3. Article 1 of the two 1966 International Covenants on human rights establishes that the principle of the right to self-determination serves to safeguard human rights. By virtue of that right every individual may choose to belong to whatever ethnic, religious or language community he or she wishes.

In the Commission's view one possible consequence of this principle might be for the members of the Serbian population in Bosnia–Hercegovina and Croatia to be recognized under agreements between the Republics as having the nationality of their choice, with all the rights and obligations which that entails with respect to the States concerned.

4. The Arbitration Commission is therefore of the opinion:

(i) that the Serbian population in Bosnia–Hercegovina and Croatia is entitled to all the rights accorded to minorities and ethnic groups under international law and under the provisions of the draft Convention of the Conference on Yugoslavia of 4 November 1991, to which the Republics of Bosnia–Hercegovina and Croatia have undertaken to give effect; and

(ii) that the Republics must afford the members of those minorities and ethnic groups all the human rights and fundamental freedoms recognized in international law, including, where appropriate, the right to choose their nationality.

Notes and Questions

1. *Self-determination and Secession from Existing States.* Claims that the legal principle of self-determination supports the secession of parts of an existing state have generally been rejected. In 1970 U.N. Secretary–General U Thant stated:

> So, as far as the question of secession of a particular section of a Member State is concerned, the United Nations' attitude is unequivocable. As an international organization, the United Nations has never accepted and does not accept and I do not believe it will ever accept the principle of secession of a part of its Member State.

"Secretary-General's Press Conferences," *UN Monthly Chronicle* 34, 36 (Feb. 1970). The same theme was sounded in the 1970 U.N. Declaration on Friendly Relations. What explains this position? The Serb-dominated Federal Republic of Yugoslavia initially invoked the lack of legal support for secession. It argued that parts of the SFRY had impermissibly seceded from it and that the Federal Republic was the continuation of the SFRY. An alternative conception, of course, is that the SFRY dissolved into entirely new states. In fact, Croatia, Bosnia-Herzegovina, Solvenia, the Former Yugoslav Republic of Macedonia, and the Federal Republic of Yugoslavia (Serbia and Montenegro)—formerly constituent republics of the federal state of Yugoslavia—have come to be regarded as separate new states.

2. *Self-determination in the Former Yugoslavia.* In its Opinion No. 3, the Arbitration Commission decided that the former internal Yugoslav boundaries between Croatia and Serbia and between Bosnia-Herzegovina and Serbia, "[e]xcept where otherwise agreed, * * * become frontiers protected by international law." 31 I.L.M. 1499, 1500 (1992). Should the Serb populations of Croatia and Bosnia—contrary to the conclusion of the Arbitration Commission in its Opinion No. 2—also have been accorded a legal right to decide whether they wished to develop as separate states, with international borders? Would a right to "self-determination" for those populations necessarily imply a right to separate statehood? In Croatia, the independence of Serb Krajina, its union with Serbia, its operation as an autonomous unit within Croatia with control over many governmental functions, and its complete integration into Croatia were all discussed as possible futures for Serb Krajina. One can envision an even broader menu of self-determination remedies. See Paul H. Brietzke, "Self-Determination, or Jurisprudential Confusion: Exacerbating Political Conflict," 14 *Wisconsin International Law Journal* 69, 122–23 (1995). During August 1995, however, Croatia's army invaded and took control of most of Serb Krajina. See "Croatia's Blitzkrieg," *The Economist*, Aug. 12, 1995, at 41.

3. *Recognition by the European Community.* The European Community did acknowledge the principle of self-determination in the preamble of its Recognition Guidelines, and emphasized the need for the breakaway Yugoslav republics to respect democracy and to guarantee "the rights of ethnic and national groups and minorities in accordance with the commitments subscribed to in the framework of the CSCE." The EC thus effectively declared its recognition of new states contingent on a form of internal self-determination. The EC's Arbitration Commission in fact attempted to monitor whether each republic had held referendums on independence and to ascertain whether each republic had implemented measures to respect individual, group, and minority rights. See Arbitration Commission Opinions Nos. 4–7, 31 I.L.M. 1501, 1503, 1507, 1511 (1992).

Decisions to recognize new states in Eastern Europe and the Balkans were politically charged, and one may question how strictly the European

Community followed its own Recognition Guidelines. For example, the EC decided to recognize Croatia in January 1992, despite an Arbitration Commission opinion stating that Croatia had not taken sufficient steps to protect its minority Serb population. See Arbitration Commission Opinion No. 5, 31 I.L.M. 1503 (1992). Should the guidelines not have been issued? Or were they appropriate in order to provide some minimal resistance on the part of the international community to unlawful behavior? See Roland Bieber, "European Community Recognition of Eastern European States: A New Perspective for International Law?," 1992 *American Society of International Law Proceedings* 374.

4. *Self-determination and the Rights of Indigenous Peoples.* Another important self-determination issue concerns the international status and rights of indigenous peoples. These have been the subject of negotiations in the U.N. Human Rights Commission and other international organizations. The Draft U.N. Declaration on the Rights of Indigenous Peoples, Oct. 28, 1994, 34 I.L.M 541 (1995), is significant as the first attempt to develop a body of group rights in international law for indigenous peoples. Drafts of the Declaration were circulated annually to the governing bodies of indigenous groups and to human rights experts, and nongovernmental organizations and representatives of indigenous peoples openly participated as observers at sessions of the Working Group on Indigenous Populations of the U.N. Subcommission on the Prevention of Discrimination and Protection of Minorities. The Declaration was adopted by the Subcommission, which is an expert body within the United Nations system, in April 1994. It was submitted to the U.N. Commission on Human Rights in 1995 for further action. See also International Labour Organization: Convention Concerning Indigenous and Tribal Peoples in Independent Countries, June 27, 1989, 28 I.L.M. 1382 (1989).

Note: International Personality

The documents reproduced above that define self-determination have been concluded by states. Do states alone have the legal authority to define the contours of a right to self-determination? Do certain peoples themselves have "international personality"?

Thus far, we have met a variety of entities other than states that influence international law and process: individuals, multinational corporations, loose associations of states (for example, the Commonwealth of Independent States), intergovernmental organizations, colonies, trusteeships and mandated territories, indigenous peoples, and nongovernmental organizations (such as Greenpeace, referred to in the *Rainbow Warrior Case* in Chapter 5). Other entities act in the international arena as well: economic unions, components of federal states that retain or obtain some degree of autonomy, governments-in-exile, protectorates, and revolutionary and insurgent movements. Furthermore, not all the entities that may be grouped under one heading share exact characteristics. The Permanent Court of International Justice, in its *Advisory Opinion of February 7, 1923, on Nationality Decrees in Tunis and Morocco*, while noting some common features of protectorates under international law, also stressed that "they have individual legal characteristics resulting from the special conditions under which they were created, and the stage of their development." 1923 P.C.I.J., Ser. B, No. 4, at 27.

One of the fundamental challenges facing international lawyers today is how to reconceptualize international law as a universal discipline that takes into account all the actors and processes that shape world events. Is it sensible to maintain that all the various entities just noted have international legal rights and obligations only if such rights and obligations are specified or authorized by states? Can an entity that possesses limited rights, duties, and powers under international law still have "international personality"? What does it mean for an entity to have "international personality"? In a 1949 advisory opinion, the International Court of Justice found that the United Nations Organization "is an international person," concluding "that it is a subject of international law and capable of possessing international rights and duties, and that it has capacity to maintain its rights by bringing international claims." Reparation for Injuries Suffered in the Service of the United Nations, 1949 I.C.J. 174, 179. "[T]he rights and duties of an entity such as the Organization," the Court continued, "must depend on its purposes and functions as specified or implied in its constituent documents and developed in practice." *Id.* at 180. We explore the *Reparation Case* and the nature of the United Nations in the next chapter.

Chapter 8

WAR, PEACE, AND THE UNITED NATIONS

A. THE USE OF FORCE AND ARTICLE 2(4)

From the advent of the modern state system in the Peace of Westphalia in 1648, through the early twentieth century, one state's unilateral use of force against another state was, for most commentators, a legitimate exercise of sovereign power. "It always lies within the power of a State to endeavor to obtain redress for wrongs, or to gain political or other advantages over another, not merely by the employment of force, but also by direct recourse to war." 2 Charles Cheney Hyde, *International Law Chiefly as Interpreted and Applied by the United States* § 597, at 189 (1922). Indeed, a traditional way for a state to acquire territory was by conquest followed by occupation and effective control, a method consistent with discretionary unilateral use of force.

Yet, the broad assertion that recourse to force was for many centuries "legal" deserves qualification. Rules of the law of nations have long suggested some limitations on the use of force. "War" was a formal legal status that depended on the intention of one of the parties. Serious political commitment was generally necessary before a state had recourse to war. Legal doctrine suggested limits on the use of lower levels of coercion, including reprisals (acts of self-help by an injured state that can involve the use of force), pacific blockades, and interventions to protect nationals and their property abroad. For example, reprisals were found to be legal only when the other state had previously violated international law, when a demand for amends had been unsuccessful, and when the reprisals were reasonably proportionate to the injury suffered. See Naulilaa Case, Port. v. Ger., 2 R.I.A.A. 1012 (1928). Treaties relating to specific situations also constrained states in their use of force. For example, some agreements limited the size of armed forces that could be placed along borders.

Furthermore, a *jus in bello* developed that included constraints on the conduct of hostilities (in contrast to the *jus ad bellum*, which concerned the decision to resort to force in the first place). Before the twentieth century, customary rules called for armies to protect civilian populations. Conventions proscribing certain conduct during hostilities were also negotiated and adopted. Many conventions specifying protections both for civilians and for enemy combatants were products of the Hague Peace Conferences of 1899 and 1906.

The early twentieth century saw new attempts to impose formal legal constraints applicable to decisions about warfare. Parties to the 1907 Hague Convention No. II agreed "not to have recourse to armed force for the recovery of contract debts claimed from the Government of one country by the Government of another country as being due to its nationals," although the limitation was not applicable if the debtor state refused to submit to arbitration or to comply with a resulting arbitral award. Following World War I, the Kellogg–Briand Pact, which is reproduced in Chapter 2, condemned "recourse to war for the solution of international controversies" and renounced war "as an instrument of national policy." The Covenant of the League of Nations also contained procedural mechanisms to encourage a cooling off period before hostilities could commence. Members of the League agreed to submit "any dispute likely to lead to a rupture" to arbitration or judicial settlement, or to the League's Council for inquiry. Members also agreed "in no case to resort to war until three months after the award by the arbitrators or the judicial decision or the report by the Council."

Following the carnage of World War II, the United Nations Charter in 1945 introduced the notion of a general prohibition on the unilateral use of force by states. Complementing Article 2(3) of the U.N. Charter, which calls for the peaceful settlement of disputes, Article 2(4) provides:

> All Members shall refrain in their international relations from the threat or use of force against the territorial integrity or political independence of any state, or in any other manner inconsistent with the Purposes of the United Nations.

The Charter does, however, explicitly accept the use of force by states in self-defense. Article 51 of the Charter reads in part:

> Nothing in the present Charter shall impair the inherent right of individual or collective self-defense if an armed attack occurs against a Member of the United Nations, until the Security Council has taken the measures necessary to maintain international peace and security.

The Charter also contemplates that the U.N. Security Council may authorize the use of force as a last resort to help maintain international peace and security. We explore the Security Council's role in Parts C and D of this chapter.

It is no secret that, despite Article 2(4), states have still often resorted to force. The first two readings in this section present differing views of the meaning of Article 2(4) and its importance in a world now armed with weapons of mass destruction. The third excerpt is from the International Court of Justice's opinion in *Nicaragua v. United States*, an important judicial analysis of the international law concerning the use of force.

LOUIS HENKIN, "THE USE OF FORCE: LAW AND U.S. POLICY"

In *Right v. Might: International Law and the Use of Force* 37 (Council on Foreign Relations, 1989).

* * * The Charter remains the authoritative statement of the law on the use of force. It is the principal norm of international law of this century.

The crucial norm is set forth in article 2(4). * * *

The Charter reflected universal agreement that the status quo prevailing at the end of World War II was not to be changed by force. Even justified grievances and a sincere concern for "national security" or other "vital interests" would not warrant any nation's initiating war. Peace was the paramount value. The Charter and the organization were dedicated to realizing other values as well—self-determination, respect for human rights, economic and social development, justice, and a just international order. But those purposes could not justify the use of force between states to achieve them; they would have to be pursued by other means. Peace was more important than progress and more important than justice. The purposes of the United Nations could not in fact be achieved by war. War inflicted the greatest injustice, the most serious violations of human rights, and the most violence to self-determination and to economic and social development. War was inherently unjust. In the future, the only "just war" would be war against an aggressor—in self-defense by the victim, in collective defense of the victim by others, or by all. Nations would be assured independence, the undisturbed enjoyment of autonomy within their territory, and their right to be let alone. Change—other than internal change through internal forces—would have to be achieved peacefully by international agreement. Henceforth there would be order so that international society could concentrate on meeting better the needs of justice and human welfare.

Efforts to Reconstrue the Charter

During the early postwar years there was general agreement as to what the prescriptions of article 2(4) meant. Clearly, the article outlaws war and other acts of armed aggression by one state against another; it also forbids lesser forms of intervention by force by one state in the territory of another. Apart from collective action under the auspices of the United Nations to enforce the peace, the only lawful use of force by a state is that contemplated under the limited exception in article 51 permitting the use of force in self-defense against an armed attack. In time, the language of article 2(4) proved to be not without ambiguities and not invulnerable to claims that intervention by force is permitted for certain "benign" purposes.

One initial ambiguity appears on the face of article 2(4). Does the prohibition of the use of force against "the territorial integrity" of another state forbid only a use of force designed to deprive that state of territory, or does it also prohibit force that violates the territorial borders of that state, however temporarily and for whatever purpose? Does the prohibition of the use of force against "the political independence" of another state outlaw only a use of force that aims to end that state's political independence by annexing it or rendering it a puppet, or does it also prohibit force designed to coerce that state to follow a particular policy or take a particular decisions? In what other circumstances would a use or threat of force be "inconsistent with the purposes of the United Nations"? Another debate concerned whether economic pressure—an oil embargo, a boycott, or other sanctions—designed to derogate from a state's territorial integrity or political independence is a "use of force" prohibited by article 2(4).

An effective United Nations system, or a court with comprehensive jurisdiction and recognized authority, might have answered these and other questions by developing the law of the Charter through construction and case-by-case application. In the absence of such authoritative interpretation, the meaning of the Charter has been shaped by the actions and reactions of states and by the opinions of publicists and scholars. Scholars have debated the ambiguities of the Charter that I have cited and other questions of interpretation; a government occasionally has sought to shape the law to justify an action it has taken. But governments generally have insisted on the interpretations most restrictive of the use of force: the Charter outlaws war for any reason; it prohibits the use of armed force by one state on the territory of another or against the forces, vessels, or other public property of another state located anywhere, for any purpose, in any circumstances. Virtually every use of force in the years since the Charter was signed has been clearly condemned by virtually all states. Virtually every putative justification of a use of force has been rejected. Over the years since the Charter's adoption, even states that have perpetrated acts of force, when seeking to justify their acts, have not commonly urged a relaxed interpretation of the prohibition. Rather, they have asserted facts and circumstances that might have rendered their actions not unlawful. For example, in 1950, North Korea claimed that the South Korean army had initiated hostilities, permitting North Korea to act in self-defense; in Czechoslovakia in 1948 and 1968, and in Hungary in 1956, the USSR claimed that its troops had been invited by the legitimate authorities to help preserve order.

Indeed, the community of states has acted formally to tighten the Charter's restrictions. The Declaration on Principles of International Law concerning Friendly Relations and Cooperation among States in Accordance with the Charter of the United Nations, adopted by consensus in the General Assembly in 1970, and the Definition of Aggression, adopted by consensus in 1974, have restated and expanded the law of the Charter as prohibiting armed intervention and aggression, broadly conceived. The resolution defining aggression made it clear that prohibited forms of aggression include not only invasion, but also attack or military occupation, however temporary; sending armed bands or mercenaries that carry out grave acts of armed force; bombarding a state's territory; blocking its ports; and attacking the forces of another state (wherever they are).

Suggested Exceptions to the Prohibitions of Article 2(4)

In time, however, some states claimed exceptions to the absolute prohibitions of article 2(4), as permitting intervention by force for certain "benign" purposes (in addition to the self-defense exception under article 51). None of the "benign exceptions" has been formally accepted; only one has brought wide acquiescence.

Humanitarian intervention. On several occasions states have claimed the right to use force in "humanitarian intervention." The paradigmatic case was the action of Israel in 1976 to extricate hostages held on a hijacked plane at Entebbe (Uganda). The United States claimed its unsuccessful attempt in 1980 to liberate the diplomatic hostages held in Teheran also came within the exception. States have been reluctant to adopt this exception to article 2(4) formally, but the legal community has widely accepted that the Charter does not prohibit humanitarian intervention by use of force strictly limited to what is necessary to save lives.

The exception, I believe, is not restricted to actions by a state on behalf of its own nationals. But it is a right to liberate hostages if the territorial state cannot or will not do so. It has not been accepted, however, that a state has a right to intervene by force to topple a government or occupy its territory even if that were necessary to terminate atrocities or to liberate detainees. Entebbe was acceptable, but the occupation of Cambodia by Vietnam was not. The U.S. invasion and occupation of Grenada, even if in fact designed to protect the lives of U.S. nationals, also was widely challenged.

Intervention to support self-determination. The suggestion that a state may intervene by force to help a people achieve "self-determination" in some circumstances has received some support.

Self-determination is a powerful political dogma that has been accepted as a principle of international law. It is incorporated in widely accepted treaties, including both the International Covenant on Civil and Political Rights and the International Covenant on Economic, Social and Cultural Rights. The concept of self-determination cries for definition, and few agree on its content, but all agree that it includes at least the right of peoples in Asia and Africa to be free from colonial domination, Western style.

Neither article 2(4) of the Charter nor any other provision of international law forbids authentic revolution and wars of independence. Indeed, there is a strong case that it is now unlawful for a state to maintain an unwilling people in colonial status, and such unlawfulness is compounded if a colony is maintained by force. A very different question, however, is whether an external power is permitted to intervene by force to help expel the colonial power or hasten its departure.

On various theories, many states have supported the right to intervene by force to help an entity achieve independence from colonial rule. The United States has firmly rejected any such right. In addressing India's invasion and occupation of Goa (Portuguese India) in 1961, Ambassador Adlai Stevenson said:

> What is at stake today is not colonialism; it is a bold violation of one of the most basic principles in the United Nations Charter.... But if our Charter means anything, it means that states are obligated to renounce the use of force, are obligated to seek a solution of their differences by peaceful means.

India used force to end Portuguese control in Goa and claimed the territory for itself; later, other states asserted a general right to intervene by force to help a people achieve independence. In a famous statement, attributed to Leonid Brezhnev, defending the Soviet invasion of Czechoslovakia in 1968, the USSR decried those who "regard the notion of sovereignty as prohibiting support for the struggle of progressive forces." He added: "Genuine revolutionaries, being internationalists, cannot but support progressive forces in their just struggle for national and social liberation."

The world rejected Brezhnev's invasion of Czechoslovakia; even the Third World was not persuaded by the "national liberation" justification. General Assembly resolutions, however, have confirmed the right of colonial peoples to achieve independence by force if necessary and included ambiguous declarations that suggested a right of other states to intervene to help them.

With colonialism no longer an important concern, the pressure for a "self-determination exception" to the law of the Charter has subsided, and the potential significance of such an exception, if recognized, is sharply reduced.

Intervention for socialism: *The Brezhnev Doctrine*. The Brezhnev regime also asserted generally the right of any socialist state to intervene in another when socialism there is threatened. It said:

> Just as, in Lenin's words, a man living in a society cannot be free from the society, a particular socialist state, staying in a system of other states composing the socialist community, cannot be free from the common interests of that community.
>
> The sovereignty of each socialist country cannot be opposed to the interests of the world of socialism, of the world revolutionary movement....
>
> Discharging their internationalist duty toward the fraternal peoples of Czechoslovakia and defending their own socialist gains, the U.S.S.R. and other socialist states had to act decisively and they did act against the antisocialist forces in Czechoslovakia.

The Brezhnev Doctrine has been generally condemned. The USSR itself appears to have disavowed it in the Helsinki accords.

Intervention for democracy. Self-determination as a justification for the use of force to end colonialism has lost its raison d'être, but some have invoked a people's right to "internal self-determination" to support the use of force by one state to preserve or impose democracy in another. One suggestion, for example, is that article 2(4) permits the use of force to "enhance opportunities of ongoing self-determination ... to increase the probability of the free choice of peoples about their government and political structure." Some see this view as the foundation of the so-called Reagan Doctrine, construed as including a claim of the right to intervene by force in another state to preserve or impose democracy.

The claim has received no support by any other government. Like the use of force to impose or maintain socialism or any other ideology, the use of force for democracy clearly would be contrary to the language of article 2(4), to the intent of its framers, and to the construction long given to that article by the United States.

At bottom, all suggestions for exceptions to article 2(4) imply that, contrary to the assumptions of the Charter's framers, there are universally recognized values higher than peace and the autonomy of states. In general, the claims of peace and state autonomy have prevailed.

Self-defense under the Charter * * *

The original intent of article 51 seems clear: despite the prohibition on the unilateral use of force in article 2(4), a victim of an armed attack may use force to defend itself, and others may join to use force in collective self-defense of the victim, pending action by the Security Council. No one has doubted that the right of individual or collective self-defense against armed attack continues to apply if the Security Council does not act, or if—as later proved to be the case—the Security Council becomes generally incapable of acting. It has also been accepted that the right of self-defense, individual or collective, is subject to limitations of "necessity" and "proportionality," but that self-defense includes a right both to repel the armed attack and to take the war to the aggressor state in order effectively to terminate the attack and prevent a recurrence. It is generally accepted, too, that states are permitted to organize themselves in advance in bona fide collective self-defense arrangements (such as the North Atlantic Treaty Organization) for possible response if one of the members should become the victim of an armed attack.

The right of self-defense is available "if an armed attack occurs." In the wake of Suez–Sinai (1956), however, some publicists began to argue that the "inherent right of self-defense" recognized by article 51 is the traditional right of self-defense, predating the Charter, which was not limited to defense against "armed attack." They argued that the right of self-defense "if an armed attack occurs" does not mean "only if an armed attack occurs." The only limitation on self-defense, they said, was that implied in the famous *Caroline* dictum: that the right of self-defense was available only when "the necessity of that self-defense is instant, overwhelming, and leaving no choice of means, and no moment for deliberation."

This more permissive interpretation of article 51 found favor with some commentators, but little with governments. The United States rejected it when its allies in effect invoked it at Suez (1956). During the Cuban missile crisis (1962), the United States, though eager to justify its blockade of Cuba, pointedly refrained from adopting the "loose" construction of article 51 and did not claim as justification a right to act in "inherent self-defense." To this day, the United States has not claimed a right to act in self-defense where no armed attack has occurred. In 1985, however, the United States interpreted the concept of armed attack to include certain terrorist activities. Declaring the Libyan government responsible for terrorist acts in Europe, including the bombing of a Berlin nightclub frequented by U.S. servicemen in which one was killed and many wounded, the United States launched a bomb attack on targets in Libyan territory. President Reagan described the attack as "fully consistent with Article 51 of the UN Charter," presumably because, in the American view, the terrorist act was an "armed attack" justifying the bombing as a use of force in self-defense.

In that case, the United States also referred to its attack as a "preemptive action." The legal implication of that phrase was not elaborated. Publicists have debated whether, under article 51, a state may use force in "preemptive," or "anticipatory," self-defense, particularly in the context of nuclear strategy. Some have suggested that if a state has strong reasons to believe it is about to be the target of a nuclear strike, the "armed attack has occurred" and the victim need not wait but may "respond" in "anticipatory self-defense." Fortunately, that issue has remained academic. The justification for the attack on Libya, however, apparently was using "preemptive action" in a different sense. The action was not designed to "beat Libya to the punch," but, President Reagan said, it "will not only diminish Colonel Quadhafi's capacity to export terror, it will provide him with incentives and reasons to alter his criminal behavior."

The bombing of Libya by the United States was widely condemned and the claimed justification widely rejected.

Intervention and Counterintervention

Before the UN Charter, the law seemed to be that a state may provide military assistance to the government of another state, even to help it suppress rebellion, but a state could not assist rebels against the incumbent government of another state. If rebellion succeeded sufficiently to achieve the status of "belligerent" and constitute a civil war, the law probably forbade assistance to either side. That law, confirmed by special Non–Intervention Agreements in the 1930s, was battered during the Spanish Civil War as states intervened on both sides. The

United States, however, honored the principle of nonintervention, helping neither side.

The United Nations Charter did not expressly address intervention in civil wars. Nothing in article 2(4) forbids sending military assistance to an incumbent government, but the use of force in support of rebels against an incumbent government would be a use of force against the territorial integrity of the state and, presumably, against its political independence. Under the Charter, a state probably may not send troops into the territory of another state to support either side in a civil war, since that too would violate the latter's territorial integrity and compromise its political independence. Assistance not involving the use of force, however—for example, providing advice, selling arms, or giving financial assistance to one (or both) sides in a civil war—seems not to be covered by article 2(4), but may violate norms against nonintervention that predate the Charter and have been strongly restated in numerous General Assembly resolutions.

W. MICHAEL REISMAN, "CRITERIA FOR THE LAWFUL USE OF FORCE IN INTERNATIONAL LAW"

10 *Yale Journal of International Law* 279 (1985).

Law includes a system of authorized coercion in which force is used to maintain and enhance public order objectives and in which unauthorized coercions are prohibited. * * * Law acknowledges the utility and the inescapability of the use of coercion in social processes, but seeks to organize, monopolize, and economize it.

The international legal system diverges from these general legal features only in terms of degree of organization and centralization of the use of coercion. In national systems, coercion is organized, relatively centralized, and, for the most part, monopolized by the apparatus of the state. In the international system, it is not. Individual actors historically have reserved the right to use force unilaterally to protect and vindicate legal entitlements.

Political and jurisprudential principles such as these must be kept in mind in an examination and rational interpretation of Article 2(4) of the United Nations Charter. Its sweeping prohibition of the threat or use of force in international politics was not an autonomous ethical affirmation of nonviolence * * *. Article 2(4) was embedded in and made initially plausible by a complex security scheme, established and spelled out in the United Nations Charter. If the scheme had operated, it would have obviated the need for the unilateral use of force. States with a grievance could have repaired to the Security Council, which could then apply the appropriate quantum and form of authoritative coercion and thereby vindicate collectively the rights it found had been violated. Under these circumstances, the need for and justification of a unilateral resort to force ceased. Even then, * * * the Charter acknowledged the inherent limits of its structures in the prevailing international politics by reserving to states the right of self-defense.

But the security system of the United Nations was premised on a consensus between the permanent members of the Security Council. Lamentably, that consensus dissolved early in the history of the organization. Thereafter, for almost all cases but those in which there was a short-term interest in collaboration, the Security Council could not operate as originally planned. Part of the systemic justification for the theory of Article 2(4) disappeared. At the same time, the Soviet Union announced, in effect, that it did not accept Article 2(4): "Wars of national liberation," an open-textured conception essentially meaning wars the Soviets supported, were not, in the Soviet conception, violations of Article 2(4). * * *

The international political system has largely accommodated itself to the indispensability of coercion in a legal system, on the one hand, and the deterioration of the Charter system, on the other, by developing a nuanced code for appraising the lawfulness of individual unilateral uses of force. The net result is not the value sterility of nineteenth century international legal conceptions of coercion, but neither is it Article 2(4). Some sense of the complexity of the code can be gained by examining, in a single time period, 1979, forceful unilateral interventions without the prior authorization of the United Nations.

In 1979, forces of Tanzania invaded Uganda, expelled the government of Idi Amin, and ultimately restored the government of Milton Obote. In the same year, French forces, in a quick and bloodless coup, expelled the government of Jean–Bedel Bokassa from the Central African Republic and installed a different president. In the same year, forces of the government of Vietnam entered Cambodia and sought to unseat the Pol Pot government and to replace it with a Vietnamese-backed government led by Heng Samrin. And in the same year, Soviet forces entered Afghanistan to support a government which, it seemed, would not have survived had it not been for the timely intervention and continued presence and operation of a foreign military force. * * *

Although efforts were made to arouse the United Nations to criticize the first two of these interventions, the organization resisted. But the organization condemned the latter two. Since all of these interventions, like all unilateral actions, were motivated in key part by the self-interest of the actors concerned, we must assume that there were some additional ingredients that rendered some of them internationally acceptable. I submit that it is in the identification of those factors that one can begin to describe the contemporary international law on the use of force.

The deterioration of the Charter security regime has stimulated a partial revival of a type of unilateral *jus ad bellum*. But in sharp contrast to the nineteenth century conception, which was value-neutral and ultimately power-based, the contemporary doctrine relates only to the vindication of rights which the international community recognizes but has, in general or in a particular case, demonstrated an inability to secure or guarantee. Hence, appraisals of state resort to coercion can no longer simply condemn them by invoking Article 2(4), but must test permissibility or lawfulness by reference to a number of factors, including the objective and the contingency for which coercion is being applied.

Nine basic categories appear to have emerged in which one finds varying support for unilateral uses of force. They are self-defense, which has been construed quite broadly; self-determination and decolonization; humanitarian intervention by the military instrument to replace an elite in another state; uses of the military instrument within spheres of influence and critical defense zones; treaty-sanctioned interventions within the territory of another state; use of the military instrument for the gathering of evidence in international proceedings; use of the military instrument to enforce international judgments; and countermeasures such as reprisals and retorsions. The categories themselves, however, are not determinative.

Merely locating an individual use of force in a particular category does not mean that it is lawful. * * *

In the determination of any action, a key and constant factor—less a criterion of lawfulness and more a sine qua non of survival—is the need for the maintenance of minimum order in a precarious international system. Will a particular use of force, whatever its justification otherwise, enhance or undermine world order?

When this requirement is met, attention may be directed to the fundamental principle of political legitimacy in contemporary international politics. It is, as anyone familiar with the UN Charter and with such key constitutive decisions as *Namibia* and *Western Sahara* knows, the enhancement of the ongoing right of peoples to determine their own political destinies. That obvious point bears renewed emphasis, for it is, in my view, the main purpose of contemporary international law: Article 2(4) is the means. The basic policy of contemporary international law has been to maintain the political independence of territorial communities so that they can continue to be able to express their ongoing desire for political organization in a form appropriate to them. Article 2(4), like so much in the Charter and in contemporary international politics, supports and must be interpreted in terms of this key postulate. Each application of Article 2(4) must enhance opportunities for ongoing self-determination. Though all interventions are lamentable, the fact is that some may serve, in terms of aggregate consequences, to increase the probability of the free choice of peoples about their government and political structure. Others have the manifest objective and consequence of doing exactly the opposite.

There is, thus, neither need nor justification for treating in a mechanically equal fashion, Tanzania's intervention in Uganda to overthrow the Amin despotism, on the one hand, and Soviet intervention in Hungary or Czechoslovakia to overthrow popular governments and to impose an undesired regime on a coerced population, on the other. Nor should the different appraisal of these cases by the international legal system occasion any surprise.

It is important to remember that norms are instruments devised by human beings to precipitate desired social consequences. One should not seek a point-for-point conformity to a rule without constant regard for the policy or principle that animated its prescription, with appropriate regard for the factual constellation in the minds of the drafters. Legal statements, like all others, are made in a context whose features are part of the expectations of speaker and audience. The expression of Article 2(4), in the form of a rule, is premised, I submit, on a political context and a technological environment which has been changing inexorably since the end of the nineteenth century. The rule assumes that the only threat to or usurpation of the right of political independence of a people within a particular territorial community is from external and overt invasion. It makes a historicist assumption as well: internal changes are deemed to be personnel changes in the composition of an elite which do not bring about basic changes in systems of public order within the country or in its external political alignments; governments come and go but the life of the people continues in its traditional fashion. Most important, it does not presuppose division, maintained by a precarious nuclear equipoise, between two contending public order systems, either of which might find itself substantially disadvantaged and pressed to intense coercion by the defection of a particular community from its own critical defense zone.

The rule-formulation of Article 2(4) is oblivious to these factors. * * *

The net effect of a mechanical interpretation of Article 2(4) may be to superimpose on an unwilling polity an elite, an ideology, and an external alignment alien to its wishes. This may entail far-reaching social and economic changes and grave deprivations of human rights for substantial numbers and strata of the population. * * *

Notes and Questions

1. *Contrasting Views of Article 2(4).* Contrast the views of Professors Henkin and Reisman concerning the international law governing the use of force. What for each is the role of Article 2(4)? What are the permissible exceptions to 2(4)? What instances of the use of force would both regard as illegal? How does each explain the fact that the world has seen many examples of the use of force involving territorial incursions since World War II?

The excerpts from Henkin and Reisman were both written during the Cold War. The United Nations Security Council has become more directly involved in authorizing or employing the use of force since 1989. Recent developments in the United Nations are addressed in Parts C and D of this chapter.

2. *The Relevance of International Law.* When is the international law relating to the use of force really taken into account? Debates over the use of force are often carried out in diplomatic or political fora, with states making opposing assertions about the legality of each other's recourse to armed force. In such highly political contexts, is the law on the use of force

irrelevant? Are the legal rules too indeterminate to matter? Do they sometimes provide at least a framework for debate and perhaps a structure for the formulation of policy positions?

How else might the international law relating to the use of force be relevant? As suggested in the Notes and Questions following the *Goldberg Case* in Chapter 7, states sometimes have refused to recognize a government that they believe has come into existence because of an illegal use of force. Furthermore, as we will see in Part C of this chapter, a state's illegal use of force also may affect measures that the U.N. Security Council takes against the state. Professor Brownlie believes that the international law on the use of force has influenced such varied matters as the law of treaties, the content of treaties, rules of engagement written by states for their armed forces, and the content of municipal laws and constitutions. See Ian Brownlie, "The United Nations Charter and the Use of Force, 1945–1985," in *The Current Legal Regulation of the Use of Force* 491 (A. Cassese ed. 1986).

3. *International Judicial Pronouncements.* On occasion, an international judicial tribunal has pronounced on the legality of some use of force. See the Corfu Channel Case (U.K. v. Albania), 1949 I.C.J. 4, 1949 WL 1. In the excerpt from the *Nicaragua Case* that follows, the International Court of Justice squarely faces arguments about the legality of one state's use of force against another.

THE NICARAGUA CASE

Case Concerning Military and Paramilitary Activities In and Against Nicaragua
Nicaragua v. United States, 1986 I.C.J. 14, 1986 WL 522 (Merits).

[The International Court of Justice faced difficult questions about its jurisdiction in the *Nicaragua Case*. In 1946 the United States accepted the Court's jurisdiction under Article 36(2) of the ICJ Statute, albeit with several reservations. When the United States learned that Nicaragua was about to file its claim in the International Court of Justice, the United States attempted to withdraw its acceptance of Article 36(2) jurisdiction with respect to disputes related to events in Central America, an attempt occurring just three days before the claim was filed. The Court ruled that the purported withdrawal was invalid because the United States had not provided six months' notice as specified in its 1946 declaration. In response to a U.S. argument that mutual consent to jurisdiction was lacking because Nicaragua itself had not accepted the Court's jurisdiction, the ICJ ruled that Nicaragua had accepted the jurisdiction of the Permanent Court of International Justice. This acceptance continued to apply to the ICJ by virtue of Article 36(5) of the ICJ Statute. The United States unsuccessfully raised other jurisdictional objections in a preliminary phase of the case. Case Concerning Military and Paramilitary Activities In and Against Nicaragua (Nicaragua v. United States), 1984 I.C.J. 392, 1984 WL 501 (Jurisdiction of the Court and Admissibility of the Application). See D.W. Greig, "Nicaragua and the United States: Confrontation Over the Jurisdiction of the International Court," 62 *British Yearbook of International Law* 119 (1991). Having lost its jurisdictional objections, the United States refused to appear in the merits phase of the *Nicaragua Case*. Subsequently, it withdrew its Article 36(2) acceptance of the Court's jurisdiction altogether.

The International Court of Justice decided that it could not rely directly on Article 2(4) of the U.N. Charter or on the Charter of the Organization of American States as legal authority in the merits phase of the *Nicaragua Case*, because of a U.S. multilateral treaty reservation to its 1946 acceptance of the Court's jurisdiction. For this reason, the excerpts from the opinion reproduced here address customary international law. In portions of the *Nicaragua* opinion not included here, the Court also finds the United States in breach of its obligations under a bilateral U.S.–Nicaragua Friendship, Commerce and Navigation Treaty.]

176. * * * [T]he Court observes that the United Nations Charter * * * by no means covers the whole area of the regulation of the use of force in international relations. On one essential point, this treaty itself refers to pre-existing customary international law; this reference to customary law is contained in the actual text of Article 51, which mentions the "inherent right" * * * of individual or collective self-defence, which "nothing in the present Charter shall impair" and which applies in the event of an armed attack. The Court therefore finds that Article 51 of the Charter is only meaningful on the basis that there is a "natural" or "inherent" right of self-defence, and it is hard to see how this can be other than of a customary nature, even if its present content has been confirmed and influenced by the Charter. Moreover, the Charter having itself recognized the existence of this right, does not go on to regulate directly all aspects of its content. For example, it does not contain any specific rule whereby self-defence would warrant only measures which are proportional to the armed attack and necessary to respond to it, a rule well established in customary international law. Moreover, a definition of the "armed attack" which, if found to exist, authorizes the exercise of the "inherent right" of self-defence, is not provided in the Charter, and is not part of treaty law. * * *

183. * * * Although the Court has no jurisdiction to determine whether the conduct of the United States constitutes a breach of those conventions, it can and must take them into account in ascertaining the content of the customary international law which the United States is also alleged to have infringed. * * *

186. It is not to be expected that in the practice of States the application of the rules in question should have been perfect, in the sense that States should have refrained, with complete consistency, from the use of force or from intervention in each other's internal affairs. The Court does not consider that, for a rule to be established as customary, the corresponding practice must be in absolutely rigorous conformity with the rule. In order to deduce the existence of customary rules, the Court deems it sufficient that the conduct of States should, in general, be consistent with such rules, and that instances of State conduct inconsistent with a given rule should generally have been

treated as breaches of that rule, not as indications of the recognition of a new rule. If a State acts in a way prima facie incompatible with a recognized rule, but defends its conduct by appealing to exceptions or justifications contained within the rule itself, then whether or not the State's conduct is in fact justifiable on that basis, the significance of that attitude is to confirm rather than to weaken the rule.

187. The Court must therefore determine, first, the substance of the customary rules relating to the use of force in international relations, applicable to the dispute submitted to it. * * *

188. The Court thus finds that both Parties take the view that the principles as to the use of force incorporated in the United Nations Charter correspond, in essentials, to those found in customary international law. The Parties thus both take the view that the fundamental principle in this area is expressed in the terms employed in Article 2, paragraph 4, of the United Nations Charter. They therefore accept a treaty-law obligation to refrain in their international relations from the threat or use of force against the territorial integrity or political independence of any State, or in any other manner inconsistent with the purposes of the United Nations. The Court has however to be satisfied that there exists in customary international law an *opinio juris* as to the binding character of such abstention. This *opinio juris* may, though with all due caution, be deduced from, *inter alia*, the attitude of the Parties and the attitude of States towards certain General Assembly resolutions, and particularly resolution 2625 (XXV) entitled "Declaration on Principles of International Law concerning Friendly Relations and Co-operation among States in accordance with the Charter of the United Nations." The effect of consent to the text of such resolutions cannot be understood as merely that of a "reiteration or elucidation" of the treaty commitment undertaken in the Charter. On the contrary, it may be understood as an acceptance of the validity of the rule or set of rules declared by the resolution by themselves. The principle of non-use of force, for example, may thus be regarded as a principle of customary international law * * *. * * *

189. As regards the United States in particular, the weight of an expression of *opinio juris* can similarly be attached to its support of the resolution of the Sixth International Conference of American States condemning aggression (18 February 1928) and ratification of the Montevideo Convention on Rights and Duties of States (26 December 1933), Article 11 of which imposes the obligation not to recognize territorial acquisitions or special advantages which have been obtained by force. Also significant is United States acceptance of the principle of the prohibition of the use of force which is contained in the declaration on principles governing the mutual relations of States participating in the Conference on Security and Co-operation in Europe (Helsinki, 1 August 1975), whereby the participating States undertake to "refrain in their mutual relations, *as well as in their international relations in general,*" (emphasis added) from the threat or use of force. Acceptance of a text in

these terms confirms the existence of an *opinio juris* of the participating States prohibiting the use of force in international relations.

190. A further confirmation of the validity as customary international law of the principle of the prohibition of the use of force expressed in Article 2, paragraph 4, of the Charter of the United Nations may be found in the fact that it is frequently referred to in statements by State representatives as being not only a principle of customary international law but also a fundamental or cardinal principle of such law. The International Law Commission, in the course of its work on the codification of the law of treaties, expressed the view that "the law of the Charter concerning the prohibition of the use of force in itself constitutes a conspicuous example of a rule in international law having the character of *jus cogens*." Nicaragua in its Memorial on the Merits submitted in the present case states that the principle prohibiting the use of force embodied in Article 2, paragraph 4, of the Charter of the United Nations "has come to be recognized as *jus cogens*." The United States, in its Counter–Memorial on the questions of jurisdiction and admissibility, found it material to quote the views of scholars that this principle is a "universal norm," a "universal international law," a "universally recognized principle of international law," and a "principle of *jus cogens*."

191. As regards certain particular aspects of the principle in question, it will be necessary to distinguish the most grave forms of the use of force (those constituting an armed attack) from other less grave forms. In determining the legal rule which applies to these latter forms, the Court can again draw on the formulations contained in the Declaration on Principles of International Law concerning Friendly Relations and Co-operation among States in accordance with the Charter of the United Nations (General Assembly resolution 2625 (XXV), referred to above). As already observed, the adoption by States of this text affords an indication of their *opinio juris* as to customary international law on the question. Alongside certain descriptions which may refer to aggression, this text includes others which refer only to less grave forms of the use of force. In particular, according to this resolution:

> "Every State has the duty to refrain from the threat or use of force to violate the existing international boundaries of another State or as a means of solving international disputes, including territorial disputes and problems concerning frontiers of States....
>
> States have a duty to refrain from acts of reprisal involving the use of force....
>
> Every State has the duty to refrain from any forcible action which deprives peoples referred to in the elaboration of the principle of equal rights and self-determination of that right to self-determination and freedom and independence.
>
> Every State has the duty to refrain from organizing or encouraging the organization of irregular forces or armed bands, including mercenaries, for incursion into the territory of another State.

> Every State has the duty to refrain from organizing, instigating, assisting or participating in acts of civil strife or terrorist acts in another State or acquiescing in organized activities within its territory directed towards the commission of such acts, when the acts referred to in the present paragraph involve a threat or use of force." * * *

193. The general rule prohibiting force allows for certain exceptions. In view of the arguments advanced by the United States to justify the acts of which it is accused by Nicaragua, the Court must express a view on the content of the right of self-defence, and more particularly the right of collective self-defence. First, with regard to the existence of this right, it notes that in the language of Article 51 of the United Nations Charter, the inherent right (or "droit naturel") which any State possesses in the event of an armed attack, covers both collective and individual self-defence. Thus, the Charter itself testifies to the existence of the right of collective self-defence in customary international law. Moreover, just as the wording of certain General Assembly declarations adopted by States demonstrates their recognition of the principle of prohibition of force as definitely a matter of customary international law, some of the wording in those declarations operates similarly in respect of the right of self-defence (both collective and individual). * * *

194. With regard to the characteristics governing the right of self-defence, since the Parties consider the existence of this right to be established as a matter of customary international law, they have concentrated on the conditions governing its use. In view of the circumstances in which the dispute has arisen, reliance is placed by the Parties only on the right of self-defence in the case of an armed attack which has already occurred, and the issue of the lawfulness of a response to the imminent threat of armed attack has not been raised. Accordingly the Court expresses no view on that issue. The Parties also agree in holding that whether the response to the attack is lawful depends on observance of the criteria of the necessity and the proportionality of the measures taken in self-defence. Since the existence of the right of collective self-defence is established in customary international law, the Court must define the specific conditions which may have to be met for its exercise, in addition to the conditions of necessity and proportionality to which the Parties have referred.

195. In the case of individual self-defence, the exercise of this right is subject to the State concerned having been the victim of an armed attack. Reliance on collective self-defence of course does not remove the need for this. There appears now to be general agreement on the nature of the acts which can be treated as constituting armed attacks. In particular, it may be considered to be agreed that an armed attack must be understood as including not merely action by regular armed forces across an international border, but also "the sending by or on behalf of a State of armed bands, groups, irregulars or mercenaries, which carry out acts of armed force against another State of such gravity as to amount to" (*inter alia*) an actual armed attack conducted by regular forces, "or

its substantial involvement therein." This description contained in Article 3, paragraph (g), of the Definition of Aggression annexed to General Assembly resolution 3314 (XXIX), may be taken to reflect customary international law. The Court sees no reason to deny that, in customary law, the prohibition of armed attacks may apply to the sending by a State of armed bands to the territory of another State, if such an operation, because of its scale and effects, would have been classified as an armed attack rather than as a mere frontier incident had it been carried out by regular armed forces. But the Court does not believe that the concept of "armed attack" includes not only acts by armed bands where such acts occur on a significant scale but also assistance to rebels in the form of the provision of weapons or logistical or other support. Such assistance may be regarded as a threat or use of force, or amount to intervention in the internal or external affairs of other States. It is also clear that it is the State which is the victim of an armed attack which must form and declare the view that it has been so attacked. There is no rule in customary international law permitting another State to exercise the right of collective self-defence on the basis of its own assessment of the situation. Where collective self-defence is invoked, it is to be expected that the State for whose benefit this right is used will have declared itself to be the victim of an armed attack. * * *

199. * * * [T]he Court finds that in customary international law, whether of a general kind or that particular to the inter–American legal system, there is no rule permitting the exercise of collective self-defence in the absence of a request by the State which regards itself as the victim of an armed attack. The Court concludes that the requirement of a request by the State which is the victim of the alleged attack is additional to the requirement that such a State should have declared itself to have been attacked.

[The Court next explores the principles of nonintervention and respect for state sovereignty.]

226. The Court, having outlined both the facts of the case as proved by the evidence before it, and the general rules of international law which appear to it to be in issue as a result of these facts, * * * has now to appraise the facts in relation to the legal rules applicable. In so far as acts of the Respondent may appear to constitute violations of the relevant rules of law, the Court will then have to determine whether there are present any circumstances excluding unlawfulness, or whether such acts may be justified upon any other ground.

227. The Court will first appraise the facts in the light of the principle of the non-use of force, examined in paragraphs 187 to 200 above. What is unlawful, in accordance with that principle, is recourse to either the threat or the use of force against the territorial integrity or political independence of any State. For the most part, the complaints by Nicaragua are of the actual use of force against it by the United States. Of the acts which the Court has found imputable to the

Government of the United States, the following are relevant in this respect:

— the laying of mines in Nicaraguan internal or territorial waters in early 1984 * * *;

— certain attacks on Nicaraguan ports, oil installations and a naval base * * *.

These activities constitute infringements of the principle of the prohibition of the use of force, defined earlier, unless they are justified by circumstances which exclude their unlawfulness, a question now to be examined. The Court has also found * * * the existence of military manoeuvres held by the United States near the Nicaraguan borders; and Nicaragua has made some suggestion that this constituted a "threat of force," which is equally forbidden by the principle of non-use of force. The Court is however not satisfied that the manoeuvres complained of, in the circumstances in which they were held, constituted on the part of the United States a breach, as against Nicaragua, of the principle forbidding recourse to the threat or use of force.

228. Nicaragua has also claimed that the United States has violated Article 2, paragraph 4, of the Charter, and has used force against Nicaragua in breach of its obligation under customary international law in as much as it has engaged in

> "recruiting, training, arming, equipping, financing, supplying and otherwise encouraging, supporting, aiding, and directing military and paramilitary actions in and against Nicaragua" * * *.

So far as the claim concerns breach of the Charter, it is excluded from the Court's jurisdiction by the multilateral treaty reservation. As to the claim that United States activities in relation to the *contras* constitute a breach of the customary international law principle of the non-use of force, the Court finds that, subject to the question whether the action of the United States might be justified as an exercise of the right of self-defence, the United States has committed a prima facie violation of that principle by its assistance to the *contras* in Nicaragua, by "organizing or encouraging the organization of irregular forces or armed bands ... for the incursion into the territory of another State," and "participating in acts of civil strife ... in another State," in the terms of General Assembly resolution 2625 (XXV). According to that resolution, participation of this kind is contrary to the principle of the prohibition of the use of force when the acts of civil strife referred to "involve a threat or use of force." In the view of the Court, while the arming and training of the *contras* can certainly be said to involve the threat or use of force against Nicaragua, this is not necessarily so in respect of all the assistance given by the United States Government. In particular, the Court considers that the mere supply of funds to the *contras*, while undoubtedly an act of intervention in the internal affairs of Nicaragua, as will be explained below, does not in itself amount to a use of force.

229. The Court must thus consider whether, as the Respondent claims, the acts in question of the United States are justified by the exercise of its right of collective self-defence against an armed attack. * * * For the Court to conclude that the United States was lawfully exercising its right of collective self-defence, it must first find that Nicaragua engaged in an armed attack against El Salvador, Honduras or Costa Rica.

230. As regards El Salvador, the Court has found * * * that it is satisfied that between July 1979 and the early months of 1981, an intermittent flow of arms was routed via the territory of Nicaragua to the armed opposition in that country. The Court was not however satisfied that assistance has reached the Salvadorian armed opposition, on a scale of any significance, since the early months of 1981, or that the Government of Nicaragua was responsible for any flow of arms at either period. Even assuming that the supply of arms to the opposition in El Salvador could be treated as imputable to the Government of Nicaragua, to justify invocation of the right of collective self-defence in customary international law, it would have to be equated with an armed attack by Nicaragua on El Salvador. As stated above, the Court is unable to consider that, in customary international law, the provision of arms to the opposition in another State constitutes an armed attack on that State. Even at a time when the arms flow was at its peak, and again assuming the participation of the Nicaraguan Government, that would not constitute such armed attack.

231. Turning to Honduras and Costa Rica, the Court has also stated * * * that it should find established that certain trans-border incursions into the territory of those two States, in 1982, 1983 and 1984, were imputable to the Government of Nicaragua. Very little information is however available to the Court as to the circumstances of these incursions or their possible motivations, which renders it difficult to decide whether they may be treated for legal purposes as amounting, singly or collectively, to an "armed attack" by Nicaragua on either or both States. The Court notes that during the Security Council debate in March/April 1984, the representative of Costa Rica made no accusation of an armed attack, emphasizing merely his country's neutrality and support for the Contadora process; the representative of Honduras however stated that

> "my country is the object of aggression made manifest through a number of incidents by Nicaragua against our territorial integrity and civilian population."

There are however other considerations which justify the Court in finding that neither these incursions, nor the alleged supply of arms to the opposition in El Salvador, may be relied on as justifying the exercise of the right of collective self-defence.

232. The exercise of the right of collective self-defence presupposes that an armed attack has occurred; and it is evident that it is the victim State, being the most directly aware of that fact, which is likely to draw

general attention to its plight. It is also evident that if the victim State wishes another State to come to its help in the exercise of the right of collective self-defence, it will normally make an express request to that effect. Thus in the present instance, the Court is entitled to take account, in judging the asserted justification of the exercise of collective self-defence by the United States, of the actual conduct of El Salvador, Honduras and Costa Rica at the relevant time, as indicative of a belief by the State in question that it was the victim of an armed attack by Nicaragua, and of the making of a request by the victim State to the United States for help in the exercise of collective self-defence.

233. The Court has seen no evidence that the conduct of those States was consistent with such a situation, either at the time when the United States first embarked on the activities which were allegedly justified by self-defence, or indeed for a long period subsequently. So far as El Salvador is concerned, it appears to the Court that while El Salvador did in fact officially declare itself the victim of an armed attack, and did ask for the United States to exercise its right of collective self-defence, this occurred only on a date much later than the commencement of the United States activities which were allegedly justified by this request. The Court notes that on 3 April 1984, the representative of El Salvador before the United Nations Security Council, while complaining of the "open foreign intervention practiced by Nicaragua in our internal affairs," refrained from stating that El Salvador had been subjected to armed attack, and made no mention of the right of collective self-defence which it had supposedly asked the United States to exercise. Nor was this mentioned when El Salvador addressed a letter to the Court in April 1984, in connection with Nicaragua's complaint against the United States. It was only in its Declaration of Intervention filed on 15 August 1984, that El Salvador referred to requests addressed at various dates to the United States for the latter to exercise its right of collective self-defence, asserting on this occasion that it had been the victim of aggression from Nicaragua "since at least 1980." In that Declaration, El Salvador affirmed that initially it had "not wanted to present any accusation or allegation [against Nicaragua] to any of the jurisdictions to which we have a right to apply," since it sought "a solution of understanding and mutual respect."

234. As to Honduras and Costa Rica, they also were prompted by the institution of proceedings in this case to address communications to the Court; in neither of these is there mention of armed attack or collective self-defence. * * *

235. There is also an aspect of the conduct of the United States which the Court is entitled to take into account as indicative of the view of that State on the question of the existence of an armed attack. At no time, up to the present, has the United States Government addressed to the Security Council, in connection with the matters the subject of the present case, the report which is required by Article 51 of the United Nations Charter in respect of measures which a State believes itself bound to take when it exercises the right of individual or collective self-

defence. The Court, whose decision has to be made on the basis of customary international law, has already observed that in the context of that law, the reporting obligation enshrined in Article 51 of the Charter of the United Nations does not exist. It does not therefore treat the absence of a report on the part of the United States as the breach of an undertaking forming part of the customary international law applicable to the present dispute. But the Court is justified in observing that this conduct of the United States hardly conforms with the latter's avowed conviction that it was acting in the context of collective self-defence as consecrated by Article 51 of the Charter. This fact is all the more noteworthy because, in the Security Council, the United States has itself taken the view that failure to observe the requirement to make a report contradicted a State's claim to be acting on the basis of collective self-defence. * * *

237. Since the Court has found that the condition *sine qua non* required for the exercise of the right of collective self-defence by the United States is not fulfilled in this case, the appraisal of the United States activities in relation to the criteria of necessity and proportionality takes on a different significance. * * * [E]ven if the United States activities in question had been carried on in strict compliance with the canons of necessity and proportionality, they would not thereby become lawful. If however they were not, it may constitute an additional ground of wrongfulness. On the question of necessity, the Court observes that the United States measures taken in December 1981 (or, at the earliest, March of that year * * *) cannot be said to correspond to a "necessity" justifying the United States action against Nicaragua on the basis of assistance given by Nicaragua to the armed opposition in El Salvador. First, these measures were only taken, and began to produce their effects, several months after the major offensive of the armed opposition against the Government of El Salvador had been completely repulsed (January 1981), and the actions of the opposition considerably reduced in consequence. Thus it was possible to eliminate the main danger to the Salvadorian Government without the United States embarking on activities in and against Nicaragua. Accordingly, it cannot be held that these activities were undertaken in the light of necessity. Whether or not the assistance to the *contras* might meet the criterion of proportionality, the Court cannot regard the United States activities * * * relating to the mining of the Nicaraguan ports and the attacks on ports, oil installations, etc., as satisfying that criterion. Whatever uncertainty may exist as to the exact scale of the aid received by the Salvadorian armed opposition from Nicaragua, it is clear that these latter United States activities in question could not have been proportionate to that aid. Finally on this point, the Court must also observe that the reaction of the United States in the context of what it regarded as self-defence was continued long after the period in which any presumed armed attack by Nicaragua could reasonably be contemplated.

238. Accordingly, the Court concludes that the plea of collective self-defence against an alleged armed attack on El Salvador, Honduras or

Costa Rica, advanced by the United States to justify its conduct toward Nicaragua, cannot be upheld; and accordingly that the United States has violated the principle prohibiting recourse to the threat or use of force by the acts listed in paragraph 227 above, and by its assistance to the *contras* to the extent that this assistance "involve[s] a threat or use of force" (paragraph 228 above).

[The Court also finds that U.S. activities in relation to the *contras* in Nicaragua are prima facie acts of intervention.]

249. * * * While an armed attack would give rise to an entitlement to collective self-defence, a use of force of a lesser degree of gravity cannot produce any entitlement to take collective counter-measures involving the use of force. The acts of which Nicaragua is accused, even assuming them to have been established and imputable to that State, could only have proportionate counter-measures on the part of the State which had been the victim of these acts, namely El Salvador, Honduras or Costa Rica. They could not justify counter-measures taken by a third State, the United States, and particularly could not justify intervention involving the use of force.

[The Court next concludes that U.S. assistance to the *contras* and the direct U.S. attacks on Nicaraguan ports and oil installations also infringed on the territorial sovereignty of Nicaragua.]

263. The finding of the United States Congress also expressed the view that the Nicaraguan Government had taken "significant steps towards establishing a totalitarian Communist dictatorship." However the régime in Nicaragua be defined, adherence by a State to any particular doctrine does not constitute a violation of customary international law; to hold otherwise would make nonsense of the fundamental principle of State sovereignty, on which the whole of international law rests, and the freedom of choice of the political, social, economic and cultural system of a State. Consequently, Nicaragua's domestic policy options, even assuming that they correspond to the description given of them by the Congress finding, cannot justify on the legal plane the various actions of the Respondent complained of. The Court cannot contemplate the creation of a new rule opening up a right of intervention by one State against another on the ground that the latter has opted for some particular ideology or political system. * * *

267. The Court also notes that Nicaragua is accused by the 1985 finding of the United States Congress of violating human rights. * * *

268. In any event, while the United States might form its own appraisal of the situation as to respect for human rights in Nicaragua, the use of force could not be the appropriate method to monitor or ensure such respect. With regard to the steps, actually taken, the protection of human rights, a strictly humanitarian objective, cannot be compatible with the mining of ports, the destruction of oil installations, or again with the training, arming and equipping of the *contras*. The Court concludes that the argument derived from the preservation of

human rights in Nicaragua cannot afford a legal justification for the conduct of the United States * * *.

269. The Court now turns to * * * the militarization of Nicaragua, which the United States deems excessive and such as to prove its aggressive intent, and in which it finds another argument to justify its activities with regard to Nicaragua. It is irrelevant and inappropriate, in the Court's opinion, to pass upon this allegation of the United States, since in international law there are no rules, other than such rules as may be accepted by the State concerned, by treaty or otherwise, whereby the level of armaments of a sovereign State can be limited, and this principle is valid for all States without exception. * * *

290. * * * The Court has * * * also to recall the principle that the parties to any dispute particularly any dispute the continuance of which is likely to endanger the maintenance of international peace and security, should seek a solution by peaceful means. Enshrined in Article 33 of the United Nations Charter, which also indicates a number of peaceful means which are available, this principle has also the status of customary law. * * *

292. For these reasons:

THE COURT * * *

(2) By twelve votes to three,

Rejects the justification of collective self-defence maintained by the United States of America in connection with the military and paramilitary activities in and against Nicaragua the subject of this case; * * *

(3) By twelve votes to three,

Decides that the United States of America, by training, arming, equipping, financing and supplying the *contra* forces or otherwise encouraging, supporting and aiding military and paramilitary activities in and against Nicaragua, has acted, against the Republic of Nicaragua, in breach of its obligation under customary international law not to intervene in the affairs of another State; * * *

(4) By twelve votes to three,

Decides that the United States of America, by certain attacks on Nicaraguan territory in 1983–1984, * * * and further by those acts of intervention referred to in subparagraph (3) hereof which involve the use of force, has acted, against the Republic of Nicaragua, in breach of its obligation under customary international law not to use force against another State; * * *

(5) By twelve votes to three,

Decides that the United States of America, by directing or authorizing overflights of Nicaraguan territory, and by the acts imputable to the United States referred to in subparagraph (4) hereof, has acted, against the Republic of Nicaragua, in breach of its obligation under customary international law not to violate the sovereignty of another State; * * *

(6) By twelve votes to three,

Decides that, by laying mines in the internal or territorial waters of the Republic of Nicaragua during the first months of 1984, the United States of America has acted, against the Republic of Nicaragua, in breach of its obligations under customary international law not to use force against another State, not to intervene in its affairs, not to violate its sovereignty, and not to interrupt peaceful maritime commerce; * * *

(12) By twelve votes to three,

Decides that the United States of America is under a duty immediately to cease and to refrain from all such acts as may constitute breaches of the foregoing legal obligations;

(13) By twelve votes to three,

Decides that the United States of America is under an obligation to make reparation to the Republic of Nicaragua for all injury caused to Nicaragua by the breaches of obligations under customary international law enumerated above; * * *

(15) By fourteen votes to one,

Decides that the form and amount of such reparation, failing agreement between the Parties, will be settled by the Court, and reserves for this purpose the subsequent procedure in the case; * * *

(16) Unanimously,

Recalls to both Parties their obligation to seek a solution to their disputes by peaceful means in accordance with international law.

Notes and Questions

1. *The International Court of Justice and Use of Force.* What are the advantages and disadvantages of the International Court of Justice hearing and deciding cases involving the use of force and intervention? Compare the *Nicaragua Case* with the ICJ decisions in Chapter 5. For reactions to the ICJ's decision, see "Appraisals of the ICJ's Decision: Nicaragua vs. United States," 81 *American Journal of International Law* 77 (1987).

2. *Nonappearance of the United States.* The United States did not appear at the merits stage of the *Nicaragua Case*. Was it wise not to appear and argue? What arguments could the United States have made, had it appeared? The United States had at least raised the right of collective self-defense during the proceedings on the Court's jurisdiction. The Court, however, raises on its own other issues, in order to satisfy itself that Nicaragua's claim was "well founded in fact and law." See Article 53(2) of the ICJ's Statute, reproduced in the Appendix.

3. *Customary International Law and Charter Norms.* In the *Nicaragua Case,* the Court discusses whether the customary international law relating to the use of force is coextensive with U.N. Charter law, a comparison made necessary by the multilateral treaty reservation to the U.S. acceptance of ICJ jurisdiction. How does the Court explain the existence of customary rules when states so often use force against other states? If state practice generally proscribes the use of force against the territorial integrity

of other states, why does that practice not indicate state compliance with a treaty obligation (the U.N. Charter) rather than with a customary legal obligation? If the content of customary and multilateral treaty norms were identical, why would an international lawyer need to distinguish them?

4. *Dissenting Opinions.* Judges Oda of Japan, Jennings of the United Kingdom, and Schwebel of the United States dissent from most of the Court's particular decisions; Judge Schwebel is the sole dissenter to the decision in paragraph 15 above. The tenor of Judge Schwebel's view of the *Nicaragua Case* is suggested by the first paragraph of his 136–page opinion, which is accompanied by a 133–page appendix:

> To say that I dissent from the Court's Judgment is to understate the depth of my differences with it. I agree with the Court's finding that the United States, by failing to make known the existence and location of the mines laid by it, acted in violation of customary international law (in relation to the shipping of third States); I agree that the CIA's causing publication of a manual advocating acts in violation of the law of war is indefensible; and I agree with some other elements of the Judgment as well. Nevertheless, in my view the Judgment misperceives and misconstrues essential facts—not so much the facts concerning the actions of the United States of which Nicaragua complains as the facts concerning the actions of Nicaragua of which the United States complains. It misconceives and misapplies the law—not in all respects, on some of which the whole Court is agreed, but in paramount respects: particularly in its interpretation of what is an "armed attack" within the meaning of the United Nations Charter and customary international law; * * * and in nearly all of its holdings as to which Party to this case has acted in violation of its international responsibilities and which, because it has acted defensively, has not. * * * [T]his Judgment asserts a jurisdiction which in my view the Court properly lacks, and it adjudges a vital question which, I believe, is not justiciable. And, I am profoundly pained to say, I dissent from this Judgment because I believe that, in effect, it adopts the false testimony of representatives of the Government of the Republic of Nicaragua on a matter which, in my view, is essential to the disposition of this case and which, on any view, is material to its disposition.

1986 I.C.J. at 249, 256.

5. *Nonintervention in Customary International Law.* The ICJ's conclusion that the use of force by the United States in Nicaragua could not be justified as collective self-defense under customary international law does not exhaust the Court's discussion of possible justifications for U.S. actions. The Court also addresses the international law relating to intervention and the right of third states to take countermeasures in response to intervention that did not amount to an armed attack. In particular, the Court considers the argument that U.S. actions were legitimate responses to Nicaragua's own acts in support of insurgents in El Salvador, when Nicaragua's acts did not amount to armed attacks.

The Court first defines the principle of non-intervention. This principle

> forbids all States or groups of States to intervene directly or indirectly in internal or external affairs of other States. A prohibited intervention

> must accordingly be one bearing on matters in which each State is permitted, by the principle of State sovereignty, to decide freely. One of these is the choice of a political, economic, social and cultural system, and the formulation of foreign policy. Intervention is wrongful when it uses methods of coercion in regard to such choices, which must remain free ones. The element of coercion, which defines, and indeed forms the very essence of, prohibited intervention, is particularly obvious in the case of an intervention which uses force, either in the direct form of military action, or in the indirect form of support for subversive or terrorist armed activities within another State.

1986 I.C.J. at 108. The principle of non-intervention, the Court concludes, is established as a matter of customary international law. The Court finds no exception in favor of a right of intervention to support "an internal opposition in another State, whose cause appear[s] particularly worthy by reason of the political and moral values with which it was identified." *Id.*

Applying the principle of non-intervention to the facts of the case, the Court concludes that U.S. support for "the military and paramilitary activities of the *contras* in Nicaragua by financial support, training, supply of weapons, intelligence and logistic support, constitutes a clear breach of the principle of non-intervention." *Id.* at 124. Not all U.S. actions, however, ran afoul of the rule against intervention. For example, the Court rejects Nicaragua's arguments that U.S. economic measures—stopping economic aid, reducing the sugar quota for U.S. imports from Nicaragua, and imposing a trade embargo—breached the customary international law principle of non-intervention. U.S. use of funds for "humanitarian assistance"—provided such assistance was to relieve human suffering or to protect life and health, and was "given without discrimination to all in need in Nicaragua, not merely to the *contras* and their dependents," *id.* at 125—also "cannot be regarded as unlawful intervention, or as in any other way contrary to international law." *Id.*

Having found that U.S. activities in relation to the *contras* constituted prima facie acts of intervention, the Court next considers possible justifications for the U.S. actions. A request for assistance from an opposing group in Nicaragua—assuming such a request had been made—would provide no justification: "[I]t is difficult to see what would remain of the principle of non-intervention in international law if intervention, which is already allowable at the request of a government of a State, were also to be allowed at the request of the opposition." *Id.* at 126. More controversial is the Court's treatment of the argument that Nicaragua's alleged intervention in El Salvador by supplying arms and other support to armed bands there (which the Court found did not constitute an "armed attack") might justify a response by the United States. Use of force amounting to less than an armed attack, the ICJ concludes, "cannot * * * produce any entitlement to take collective counter-measures involving the use of force." *Id.* at 127. Proportionate counter-measures by victim states, *e.g.*, El Salvador, would be appropriate, but counter-measures by a third state such as the United States were not. Judge Schwebel, in dissent, criticizes this conclusion, arguing that the limits that the ICJ specifies on collective response to intervention leave a victim state inappropriately exposed to a loss of its political independence. *Id.* at 350–51.

Perhaps because Central American states other than Nicaragua were not parties to the *Nicaragua Case*, the Court does not explore in any detail some aspects of the law governing intervention, such as the means a victim state may use to respond to interventions that are less than an armed attack.

If you find that legal standards relating to use of force, intervention, and counter-measures are inappropriately vague or are simply inappropriate, should they be clarified or changed? How? Is it desirable for states to act unilaterally in this area, thus providing examples of "state practice"? What are the prospects for bilateral agreements restricting intervention or the use of force? For steps by the United Nations?

6. *Reparations.* The ICJ decides, in paragraph 15, to leave the issue of reparations for a subsequent procedure, "failing agreement between the Parties." Nicaragua presented a claim for $12 billion to the ICJ in September 1987. Following a change in government in Nicaragua, however, Nicaragua opted, in September 1991, to discontinue the ICJ proceedings. See "International Court of Justice: Order on the Discontinuance and Removal from the List in the Case Concerning Military and Paramilitary Activities in and Against Nicaragua (Nicaragua v. United States)," 31 I.L.M. 103 (1992). The United States reportedly made it clear that trade and foreign aid packages to Nicaragua depended on Nicaragua's dropping its ICJ reparations claim. Tim Coone, "Nicaragua Renews Drive to Unblock Credit Pipeline," *Financial Times*, Dec. 5, 1990, at 6; Mark A. Uhlig, "U.S. Urges Nicaragua to Forgive Legal Claim," *New York Times*, Sept. 26, 1990, at 18. Had Nicaragua pursued its claim for reparations to a successful conclusion at the ICJ, how could the award have been enforced? See Mary Ellen O'Connell, "The Prospect of Enforcing Monetary Judgments of the International Court of Justice: A Study of Nicaragua's Judgment Against the United States," 30 *Virginia Journal of International Law* 891 (1990).

B. THE UNITED NATIONS

There are hundreds of international organizations, but most are either regional (such as the European Union and the Organization of African Unity) or devoted to specific subject matters (such as the World Bank and the International Monetary Fund). The United Nations, however, is both virtually universal in membership, counting almost all states among its members, and, by way of its principal organs, commissions, expert bodies, committees, and specialized agencies, generally wide-ranging in its ambitions. We have already seen something of the United Nations' roles concerning the making of international law in Chapter 3, human rights in Chapter 6, and decolonization in Chapter 7. In Chapter 9 we explore U.N. activities relating to areas beyond any national jurisdiction, such as the oceans.

The United Nations, formed by the Allied powers in reaction to World War II, was principally designed to control the actual and potential use of force by states. The first aim of the United Nations, set forth in the Preamble to the U.N. Charter, is to "save succeeding generations from the scourge of war"; the first purpose listed in Article I is "to maintain international peace and security."

The U.N. Security Council, one of the principal organs of the United Nations, has significant responsibilities relating to war and peace. Under Chapter VII of the U.N. Charter, the Security Council can take action with respect to threats to the peace, breaches of the peace, and acts of aggression. The Security Council is made up of five permanent members (the United States, France, Great Britain, Russia, and the People's Republic of China) and ten other members, whose seats rotate. Any permanent member can veto a Security Council resolution taken under Chapter VII, a feature that limited the Security Council's ability to act on sensitive matters during the Cold War from 1945 to 1989. Articles 25 and 48 of the Charter provide, however, that when the Security Council does reach a decision, U.N. Member States are obligated to accept it and carry it out.

Three other principal organs of the United Nations—the General Assembly, the International Court of Justice, and the Secretary–General—also play important roles concerning the use of force. The General Assembly was designed to be largely a deliberative body, but it also supervises numerous specialized agencies and has authority over budgetary matters. In practice, the General Assembly has adopted important resolutions relating to the use of force such as the Definition of Aggression considered in the *Nicaragua Case,* above. For its part, the International Court of Justice has jurisdiction in some contentious cases such as the *Nicaragua Case*, and it may also be asked to render advisory opinions concerning the use of force. Finally, the Secretary–General of the United Nations has authority under Article 99 of the Charter to "bring to the attention of the Security Council any matter which in his opinion may threaten the maintenance of international peace and security." The U.N. Secretariat, administered by the Secretary–General, helps to organize and supervise peace-keeping operations. The Secretary–General from time to time also has engaged in extensive mediation, attempting to resolve international disputes.

We take a closer look at U.N. "peace-keeping" and "Chapter VII enforcement" in Part C of this chapter. In this Part B, however, we pause to explore some fundamental questions about the nature of the United Nations. Does the Organization have "international personality" of its own? Or are its powers limited to those expressly delegated by Member States in the U.N. Charter? The International Court of Justice considers those questions in its advisory opinion in the *Reparations Case* which follows. That case specifically concerns the capacity of the Organization to bring an international claim for reparations when a U.N. agent is injured due to the responsibility of a state. May the United Nations itself bring such a claim? Or must such a claim be pursued, if at all, in traditional fashion by the state of the agent's nationality?

THE REPARATION CASE

Reparation for Injuries Suffered in the Service of the United Nations
1949 I.C.J. 174, 1949 WL 3.

On December 3rd, 1948, the General Assembly of the United Nations adopted the following Resolution:

> "Whereas the series of tragic events which have lately befallen agents of the United Nations engaged in the performance of their duties raises, with greater urgency than ever, the question of the arrangements to be made by the United Nations with a view to ensuring to its agents the fullest measure of protection in the future and ensuring that reparation be made for the injuries suffered; and
>
> Whereas it is highly desirable that the Secretary–General should be able to act without question as efficaciously as possible with a view to obtaining any reparation due; therefore
>
> The General Assembly
>
> Decides to submit the following legal questions to the International Court of Justice for an advisory opinion:
>
> I. In the event of an agent of the United Nations in the performance of his duties suffering injury in circumstances involving the responsibility of a State, has the United Nations, as an Organization, the capacity to bring an international claim against the responsible *de jure* or *de facto* government with a view to obtaining the reparation due in respect of the damage caused (a) to the United Nations, (b) to the victim or to persons entitled through him? * * *." * * *

Competence to bring an international claim is, for those possessing it, the capacity to resort to the customary methods recognized by international law for the establishment, the presentation and the settlement of claims. Among these methods may be mentioned protest, request for an enquiry, negotiation, and request for submission to an arbitral tribunal or to the Court in so far as this may be authorized by the Statute. * * *

But, in the international sphere, has the Organization such a nature as involves the capacity to bring an international claim? In order to answer this question, the Court must first enquire whether the Charter has given the Organization such a position that it possesses, in regard to its Members, rights which it is entitled to ask them to respect. In other words, does the Organization possess international personality? This is no doubt a doctrinal expression, which has sometimes given rise to controversy. But it will be used here to mean that if the Organization is recognized as having that personality, it is an entity capable of availing itself of obligations incumbent upon its Members.

To answer this question, which is not settled by the actual terms of the Charter, we must consider what characteristics it was intended thereby to give to the Organization.

The subjects of law in any legal system are not necessarily identical in their nature or in the extent of their rights, and their nature depends upon the needs of the community. Throughout its history, the development of international law has been influenced by the requirements of international life, and the progressive increase in the collective activities of States has already given rise to instances of action upon the international plane by certain entities which are not States. This development culminated in the establishment in June 1945 of an international organization whose purposes and principles are specified in the Charter of the United Nations. But to achieve these ends the attribution of international personality is indispensable.

The Charter has not been content to make the Organization created by it merely a centre "for harmonizing the actions of nations in the attainment of these common ends" (Article I, para. 4). It has equipped that centre with organs, and has given it special tasks. It has defined the position of the Members in relation to the Organization by requiring them to give it every assistance in any action undertaken by it (Article 2, para. 5), and to accept and carry out the decisions of the Security Council; by authorizing the General Assembly to make recommendations to the Members; by giving the Organization legal capacity and privileges and immunities in the territory of each of its Members; and by providing for the conclusion of agreements between the Organization and its Members. Practice—in particular the conclusion of conventions to which the Organization is a party—has confirmed this character of the Organization, which occupies a position in certain respects in detachment from its Members, and which is under a duty to remind them, if need be, of certain obligations. It must be added that the Organization is a political body, charged with political tasks of an important character, and covering a wide field namely, the maintenance of international peace and security, the development of friendly relations among nations, and the achievement of international co-operation in the solution of problems of an economic, social, cultural or humanitarian character (Article I); and in dealing with its Members it employs political means. The "Convention on the Privileges and Immunities of the United Nations" of 1946 creates rights and duties between each of the signatories and the Organization (see, in particular, Section 35). It is difficult to see how such a convention could operate except upon the international plane and as between parties possessing international personality.

In the opinion of the Court, the Organization was intended to exercise and enjoy, and is in fact exercising and enjoying, functions and rights which can only be explained on the basis of the possession of a large measure of international personality and the capacity to operate upon an international plane. It is at present the supreme type of international organization, and it could not carry out the intentions of its founders if it was devoid of international personality. It must be acknowledged that its Members, by entrusting certain functions to it, with the attendant duties and responsibilities, have clothed it with the competence required to enable those functions to be effectively discharged.

Accordingly, the Court has come to the conclusion that the Organization is an international person. That is not the same thing as saying that it is a State, which it certainly is not, or that its legal personality and rights and duties are the same as those of a State. Still less is it the same thing as saying that it is "a super-State," whatever that expression may mean. It does not even imply that all its rights and duties must be upon the international plane, any more than all the rights and duties of a State must be upon that plane. What it does mean is that it is a subject of international law and capable of possessing international rights and duties, and that it has capacity to maintain its rights by bringing international claims.

The next question is whether the sum of the international rights of the Organization comprises the right to bring the kind of international claim described in the Request for this Opinion. That is a claim against a State to obtain reparation in respect of the damage caused by the injury of an agent of the Organization in the course of the performance of his duties. Whereas a State possesses the totality of international rights and duties recognized by international law, the rights and duties of an entity such as the Organization must depend upon its purposes and functions as specified or implied in its constituent documents and developed in practice. The functions of the Organization are of such a character that they could not be effectively discharged if they involved the concurrent action, on the international plane, of fifty-eight or more Foreign Offices, and the Court concludes that the Members have endowed the Organization with capacity to bring international claims when necessitated by the discharge of its functions.

What is the position as regards the claims mentioned in the request for an opinion? Question I is divided into two points, which must be considered in turn. * * *

* * * It cannot be doubted that the Organization has the capacity to bring an international claim against one of its Members which has caused injury to it by a breach of its international obligations towards it. The damage specified in Question I (*a*) means exclusively damage caused to the interests of the Organization itself, to its administrative machine, to its property and assets, and to the interests of which it is the guardian. It is clear that the Organization has the capacity to bring a claim for this damage. As the claim is based on the breach of an international obligation on the part of the Member held responsible by the Organization, the Member cannot contend that this obligation is governed by municipal law, and the Organization is justified in giving its claim the character of an international claim.

When the Organization has sustained damage resulting from a breach by a Member of its international obligations, it is impossible to see how it can obtain reparation unless it possesses capacity to bring an international claim. It cannot be supposed that in such an event all the

Members of the Organization, save the defendant State, must combine to bring a claim against the defendant for the damage suffered by the Organization. * * *

Question I (*b*) is as follows:

> ... "has the United Nations, as an Organization, the capacity to bring an international claim ... in respect of the damage caused ... (*b*) to the victim or to persons entitled through him?" * * *

The traditional rule that diplomatic protection is exercised by the national State does not involve the giving of a negative answer to Question I (*b*). * * *

The Court is here faced with a new situation. The questions to which it gives rise can only be solved by realizing that the situation is dominated by the provisions of the Charter considered in the light of the principles of international law.

The question lies within the limits already established; that is to say it presupposes that the injury for which the reparation is demanded arises from a breach of an obligation designed to help an agent of the Organization in the performance of his duties. It is not a case in which the wrongful act or omission would merely constitute a breach of the general obligations of a State concerning the position of aliens; claims made under this head would be within the competence of the national State and not, as a general rule, within that of the Organization.

The Charter does not expressly confer upon the Organization the capacity to include, in its claim for reparation, damage caused to the victim or to persons entitled through him. The Court must therefore begin by enquiring whether the provisions of the Charter concerning the functions of the Organization, and the part played by its agents in the performance of those functions, imply for the Organization power to afford its agents the limited protection that would consist in the bringing of a claim on their behalf for reparation for damage suffered in such circumstances. Under international law, the Organization must be deemed to have those powers which, though not expressly provided in the Charter, are conferred upon it by necessary implication as being essential to the performance of its duties. This principle of law was applied by the Permanent Court of International Justice to the International Labour Organization in its Advisory Opinion No. 13 of July 23rd, 1926, and must be applied to the United Nations.

Having regard to its purposes and functions already referred to, the Organization may find it necessary, and has in fact found it necessary, to entrust its agents with important missions to be performed in disturbed parts of the world. Many missions, from their very nature, involve the agents in unusual dangers to which ordinary persons are not exposed. For the same reason, the injuries suffered by its agents in these circumstances will sometimes have occurred in such a manner that their national State would not be justified in bringing a claim for reparation on the ground of diplomatic protection, or, at any rate, would not feel disposed to do so. Both to ensure the efficient and independent performance of these missions and to afford effective support to its agents, the Organization must provide them with adequate protection. * * *

For this purpose, the Members of the Organization have entered into certain undertakings, some of which are in the Charter and others in complementary agreements. The content of these undertakings need not be described here; but the Court must stress the importance of the duty to render to the Organization "every assistance" which is accepted by the Members in Article 2, paragraph 5, of the Charter. It must be noted that the effective working of the Organization—the accomplishment of its task, and the independence and effectiveness of the work of its agents—require that these undertakings should be strictly observed. For that purpose, it is necessary that, when an infringement occurs, the Organization should be able to call upon the responsible State to remedy its default, and, in particular, to obtain from the State reparation for the damage that the default may have caused to its agent.

In order that the agent may perform his duties satisfactorily, he must feel that this protection is assured to him by the Organization, and that he may count on it. To ensure the independence of the agent, and, consequently, the independent action of the Organization itself, it is essential that in performing his duties he need not have to rely on any other protection than that of the Organization (save of course for the more direct and immediate protection due from the State in whose territory he may be). In particular, he should not have to rely on the protection of his own State. If he had to rely on that State, his independence might well be compromised, contrary to the principle applied by Article 100 of the Charter. And lastly, it is essential that—whether the agent belongs to a powerful or to a weak State; to one more affected or less affected by the complications of international life; to one in sympathy or not in sympathy with the mission of the agent—he should know that in the performance of his duties he is under the protection of the Organization. This assurance is even more necessary when the agent is stateless.

Upon examination of the character of the functions entrusted to the Organization and of the nature of the missions of its agents, it becomes clear that the capacity of the Organization to exercise a measure of functional protection of its agents arises by necessary intendment out of the Charter.

The obligations entered into by States to enable the agents of the Organization to perform their duties are undertaken not in the interest of the agents, but in that of the Organization. When it claims redress for a breach of these obligations, the Organization is invoking its own right, the right that the obligations due to it should be respected. On this ground, it asks for reparation of the injury suffered, for "it is a principle of international law that the breach of an engagement involves an obligation to make reparation in an adequate form"; as was stated by the Permanent Court in its Judgment No. 8 of July 26th, 1927. In claiming reparation based on the injury suffered by its agent, the Organization does not represent the agent, but is asserting its own right, the right to secure respect for undertakings entered into towards the Organization.

Having regard to the foregoing considerations, and to the undeniable right of the Organization to demand that its Members shall fulfill the obligations entered into by them in the interest of the good working of the Organization, the Court is of the opinion that, in the case of a breach of these obligations, the Organization has the capacity to claim adequate reparation, and that in assessing this reparation it is authorized to include the damage suffered by the victim or by persons entitled through him.

The question remains whether the Organization has "the capacity to bring an international claim against the responsible *de jure* or *de facto* government with a view to obtaining the reparation due in respect of the damage caused (*a*) to the United Nations, (*b*) to the victim or to persons entitled through him" when the defendant State is not a member of the Organization.

In considering this aspect of Question I (*a*) and (*b*), it is necessary to keep in mind the reasons which have led the Court to given an affirmative answer to it when the defendant State is a Member of the Organization. It has now been established that the Organization has capacity to bring claims on the international plane, and that it possesses a right of functional protection in respect of its agents. Here again the Court is authorized to assume that the damage suffered involves the responsibility of a State, and it is not called upon to express an opinion upon the various ways in which that responsibility might be engaged. Accordingly the question is whether the Organization has capacity to bring a claim against the defendant State to recover reparation in respect of that damage or whether, on the contrary, the defendant State, not being a member, is justified in raising the objection that the Organization lacks the capacity to bring an international claim. On this point, the Court's opinion is that fifty States, representing the vast majority of the members of the international community, had the power, in conformity with international law, to bring into being an entity possessing objective international personality, and not merely personality recognized by them alone, together with capacity to bring international claims.

Accordingly, the Court arrives at the conclusion that an affirmative answer should be given to Question I (*a*) and (*b*) whether or not the defendant State is a Member of the United Nations. * * *

FOR THESE REASONS,

The Court is of opinion

*On Question I (*a*):*

(i) unanimously,

That, in the event of an agent of the United Nations in the performance of his duties suffering injury in circumstances involving the responsibility of a Member State, the United Nations as an Organization has the capacity to bring an international claim against the responsible *de jure* or *de facto* government with a view to obtaining the reparation due in respect of the damage caused to the United Nations.

(ii) unanimously,

That, in the event of an agent of the United Nations in the performance of his duties suffering injury in circumstances involving the responsibility of a State which is not a member, the United Nations as an Organization has the capacity to bring an international claim against the responsible *de jure* or *de facto* government with a view to obtaining the reparation due in respect of the damage caused to the United Nations.

*On Question I (*b*):*

(i) by eleven votes against four,

That, in the event of an agent of the United Nations in the performance of his duties suffering injury in circumstances involving the responsibility of a Member State, the United Nations as an Organization has the capacity to bring an international claim against the responsible *de jure* or *de facto* government with a view to obtaining the reparation due in respect of the damage caused to the victim or to persons entitled through him.

(ii) by eleven votes against four,

That, in the event of an agent of the United Nations in the performance of his duties suffering injury in circumstances involving the responsibility of a State which is not a member, the United Nations as an Organization has the capacity to bring an international claim against the responsible *de jure* or *de facto* government with a view to obtaining the reparation due in respect of the damage caused to the victim or to persons entitled through him.

Notes and Questions

1. *Background.* The events leading the General Assembly to request an advisory opinion in the *Reparation Case* stemmed from the United Nations' involvement in Palestine. In April 1947, Great Britain, which had administered a League of Nations Mandate over Palestine, asked the U.N. General Assembly to consider the Palestine situation. Following a report by a U.N. Special Committee, the General Assembly approved a plan recommending that Palestine be divided into independent Arab and Jewish states; Jerusalem was to be administered under international control. Resulting skirmishes led the U.N. Security Council, in April 1948, to call for a truce in Palestine, S.C. Res. S/723, and to establish a Truce Commission. S.C. Res. S/727. The U.N. General Assembly appointed Count Folke Bernadotte, a Swedish national, to be U.N. Mediator in Palestine. On September 17, 1948, several months after the Provisional Government of Israel proclaimed Israel to be a state, Count Bernadotte and another U.N. observer, Colonel Serot of France, were assassinated in the Israeli-held zone of Jerusalem by men in Israeli uniform. 1 *Public Papers of the Secretaries–General of the United*

Nations 163 (1969). The General Assembly was concerned with whether the United Nations could seek reparations with respect to these assassinations.

2. *International Personality.* Why does the Court find that the United Nations has "international personality"? What are the implications of this finding? A variety of particular consequences may follow if the United Nations is accorded international personality, such as its capacity to enter into treaties. According to Professor Bederman, the *Reparation Case* has even more fundamental significance:

> The Court's opinion conclusively ushered in a new era of international law, fully diversified with multiple subjects and objects. Indeed, what the *Reparation* opinion achieved was a fusion between the subjects and objects of international law. Any entity, thing or person bound by international legal rules was an international legal person. The distinction between active subjects and passive objects of the law was no longer relevant.

David J. Bederman, "The Souls of International Organizations: Legal Personality and the Lighthouse at Cape Spartel," 36 *Virginia Journal of International Law* 275, 367 (1996).

3. *Capacity of the United Nations to Bring International Claims.* In the *Reparation Case*, the capacity of the United Nations to bring a claim for the death of Count Bernadotte does not follow automatically once the Court concludes the Organization has international personality. The Court separately finds that the United Nations may bring an international claim against the responsible government to obtain reparations on behalf of a U.N. employee or his survivors. Why does the Court reach this result? Is the Court persuasive in arguing that the intention of Article 100 of the U.N. Charter (see Appendix) would be compromised if the employee must rely only on protection from his own state?

Judge Hackworth dissents from the part of the Court's opinion finding that the United Nations has the capacity to sponsor an international claim on behalf of one of its agents. He says in part:

> [T]he Organization is one of delegated and enumerated powers. It is to be presumed that such powers as the Member States desired to confer upon it are stated either in the Charter or in complementary agreements concluded by them. Powers not expressed cannot freely be implied. Implied powers flow from a grant of expressed powers, and are limited to those that are "necessary" to the exercise of powers expressly granted. No necessity for the exercise of the power here in question has been shown to exist. There is no impelling reason, if any at all, why the Organization should become the sponsor of claims on behalf of its employees, even though limited to those arising while the employee is in line of duty. These employees are still nationals of their respective countries, and the customary methods of handling such claims are still available in full vigour.

1949 I.C.J. at 196, 198. Should the Court have required that the U.N. Charter be amended to authorize the United Nations to espouse claims on behalf of nationals of Member States in service of the Organization?

4. *Reparations Following the* Reparation Case. Following the decision in the *Reparation Case*, the U.N. General Assembly authorized the Secretary-General to bring a claim for reparations against allegedly responsible states for injuries incurred in the service of the United Nations. Arbitration was called for if negotiation did not lead to a settlement. G.A. Res. 365(IV)(1949). Israel paid $50,000 in reparations for the deaths of Count Bernadotte and Colonel Serot. 1 *Public Papers of the Secretaries-General of the United Nations* 228 (1969); Ralph Hewins, *Count Folke Bernadotte: His Life and Work* 239 (1950).

C. UNITED NATIONS PEACE-KEEPING AND CHAPTER VII ENFORCEMENT ACTIONS

According to Article 24 of the U.N. Charter, the Security Council is to have "primary responsibility for the maintenance of international peace and security." Under Chapter VII of the Charter, the Security Council is charged with taking action with respect to threats to the peace, breaches of the peace, and acts of aggression.

Cold War politics, however, often led one of the Security Council's permanent members to veto Security Council action. During the Korean War, the Soviet Union's veto power prompted the United States to propose, and the U.N. General Assembly to adopt, the Uniting for Peace Resolution, G.A. Res. 377(V)(1950). According to this Resolution, "failure of the Security Council to discharge its responsibilities * * * does not relieve * * * the United Nations of its responsibility under the Charter to maintain international peace and security." The Resolution then provides that:

> if the Security Council, because of lack of unanimity of the permanent members, fails to exercise its primary responsibility for the maintenance of international peace and security in any case where there appears to be a threat to the peace, breach of the peace, or act of aggression, the General Assembly shall consider the matter immediately with a view to making appropriate recommendations to Members for collective measures, including in the case of a breach of the peace or act of aggression the use of armed force when necessary, to maintain or restore international peace and security.

The U.S. Ambassador to the United Nations, Benjamin Cohen, drew parallels to U.S. constitutional law precedents in urging the General Assembly to pass the Uniting for Peace Resolution. He argued that the United Nations need not first amend its Charter and should construe the Charter flexibly. See Thomas M. Franck, *Nation Against Nation* 39 (1985).

The relative powers of the General Assembly and the Security Council with respect to maintaining international peace and security were at issue in a 1962 International Court of Justice advisory opinion, Certain Expenses of the United Nations (Article 17, Paragraph 2, of the Charter), 1962 I.C.J. 151, 1962 WL 4. The case arose after the General

Assembly authorized the United Nations Emergency Force (UNEF) in the Middle East in 1956, following Egypt's nationalization of the Suez Canal, and after the General Assembly assumed a role in the United Nations Operation in the Congo (ONUC), which the Security Council had initially authorized in 1960. When the General Assembly voted to treat UNEF and ONUC expenses as U.N. expenses, apportioned among Member States under Article 17 of the Charter, France and the Soviet Union refused to pay. They argued that only the Security Council could authorize or supervise peace-keeping activities, and that the only way to finance peace-keeping was through agreements under Article 43 of the U.N. Charter.

In the *Certain Expenses Case,* the ICJ disagreed with the French and Soviet arguments. The Court found that the General Assembly, and not just the Security Council, had a role with respect to international peace and security. Certainly, there were limits on the General Assembly's authority. In light of Article 12 of the Charter, "the Assembly should not recommend measures while the Security Council is dealing with the same matter unless the Council requests it to do so." 1962 I.C.J. at 163. Furthermore, the Court noted, only the Security Council "may order coercive action." *Id.* The Court found, however, that these limits did not invalidate the General Assembly's "measures" concerning UNEF and ONUC; UNEF and ONUC were not "coercive or enforcement actions" over which the Security Council had exclusive authority under Chapter VII of the Charter.

In practice, the United Nations has approved many "peace-keeping operations" that do not qualify as Chapter VII enforcement actions. Although the General Assembly early on authorized the creation and deployment of some peace-keeping forces, which are contributed by Member States, the Security Council now exercises this authority. The first reading in this Part, taken from a report of the U.N. Secretary–General, examines the changing nature of peace-keeping.

Resolutions of the U.N. Security Council relating to Iraq's 1990 invasion of Kuwait provide the background for a look at the nature of Chapter VII enforcement actions. Other readings and notes explore the relationship of such actions to the exercise of collective self-defense under Article 51 of the U.N. Charter. This Part of the chapter ends with a look at the nature of the U.N.'s role in attempts to resolve the 1990s crisis in the Former Yugoslavia.

As you read through these materials, consider how the functions of the United Nations with respect to international peace and security have developed over time. It seems undeniable that international organizations and the interpretation of their constitutive instruments constantly evolve.

1. U.N. PEACE-KEEPING

SUPPLEMENT TO AN AGENDA FOR PEACE

Position Paper of the Secretary-General on the Occasion of the Fiftieth Anniversary of the United Nations A/50/60-S/1995/1, 3 January 1995, in *An Agenda for Peace 1995*, at 5 (2d ed. 1995)(U.N. Sales No. E.95.I.15).

[Since the end of the Cold War, U.N. activities related to the maintenance of peace and security have increased dramatically. The Secretary-General cites several statistics on U.N. activities from 1988 to 1994 related to peace and security. For example, as at January 31, 1988, the Security Council had adopted 15 resolutions in the preceding 12 months, and as at December 31, 1994, it had adopted 78 in the preceding 12 months. As at January 31, 1988, the United Nations had been actively involved in preventive diplomacy or peacemaking in 11 disputes and conflicts during the preceding 12 months, and as at December 16, 1994, the number was 28 for the preceding 12 months. The number of military personnel deployed increased from 9,570 to 73,393 between January 31, 1988, and December 16, 1994, and the number of civilian police increased from 35 to 2,130. Over the same period, the number of states contributing military and police personnel increased from 26 to 76, and the U.N. annual budget for peace-keeping increased from $230.4 million to a projected $3.61 billion.]

II. Quantitative and Qualitative Changes * * *

9. This increased volume of activity would have strained the Organization even if the nature of the activity had remained unchanged. It has not remained unchanged, however: there have been qualitative changes even more significant than the quantitative ones.

10. One is the fact that so many of today's conflicts are within States rather than between States. The end of the Cold War removed constraints that had inhibited conflict in the former Soviet Union and elsewhere. As a result there has been a rash of wars within newly independent States, often of a religious or ethnic character and often involving unusual violence and cruelty. The end of the cold war seems also to have contributed to an outbreak of such wars in Africa. In addition, some of the proxy wars fueled by the cold war within States remain unresolved. Inter-State wars, by contrast, have become infrequent.

11. Of the five peace-keeping operations that existed in early 1988, four related to inter-State wars and only one (20 per cent of the total) to an intra-State conflict. Of the 21 operations established since then, only 8 have related to inter-State wars, whereas 13 (62 per cent) have related to intra-State conflicts, though some of them, especially those in former Yugoslavia, have some inter-State dimensions also. Of the 11 operations established since January 1992, all but 2 (82 per cent) related to intra-State conflicts.

12. The new breed of intra–State conflicts * * * are usually fought not only by regular armies but also by militias and armed civilians with little discipline and with ill-defined chains of command. They are often guerrilla wars without clear front lines. Civilians are the main victims and often the main targets. Humanitarian emergencies are commonplace and the combatant authorities, in so far as they can be called authorities, lack the capacity to cope with them. The number of refugees registered with the Office of the United Nations High Commissioner for Refugees (UNHCR) has increased from 13 million at the end of 1987 to 26 million at the end of 1994. The number of internally displaced persons has increased even more dramatically.

13. Another feature of such conflicts is the collapse of State institutions, especially the police and judiciary, with resulting paralysis of governance, a breakdown of law and order, and general banditry and chaos. Not only are the functions of government suspended, its assets are destroyed or looted and experienced officials are killed or flee the country. This is rarely the case in inter–State wars. It means that international intervention must extend beyond military and humanitarian tasks and must include the promotion of national reconciliation and the re-establishment of effective government. * * *

15. Peace-keeping in such contexts is far more complex and more expensive than when its tasks were mainly to monitor cease-fires and control buffer zones with the consent of the States involved in the conflict. * * *

18. A second qualitative change is the use of United Nations forces to protect humanitarian operations. Humanitarian agencies endeavour to provide succor to civilian victims of war wherever they may be. Too often the warring parties make it difficult or impossible for them to do so. This is sometimes because of the exigencies of war but more often because the relief of a particular population is contrary to the war aims of one or other of the parties. There is also a growing tendency for the combatants to divert relief supplies for their own purposes. Because the wars are intra–State conflicts, the humanitarian agencies often have to undertake their tasks in the chaotic and lawless conditions described above. * * *

20. A third change has been in the nature of the United Nations operations in the field. During the cold war United Nations peace-keeping operations were largely military in character and were usually deployed after a cease-fire but before a settlement of the conflict in question had been negotiated. Indeed one of their main purposes was to create conditions in which negotiations for a settlement could take place. In the late 1980s a new kind of peace-keeping operation evolved. It was established after negotiations had succeeded, with the mandate of helping the parties implement the comprehensive settlement they had negotiated. Such operations have been deployed in Namibia, Angola, El Salvador, Cambodia and Mozambique. In most cases they have been conspicuously successful.

21. The negotiated settlements involved not only military arrangements but also a wide range of civilian matters. As a result, the United Nations found itself asked to undertake an unprecedented variety of functions: the supervision of cease-fires, the regroupment and demobilization of forces, their reintegration into civilian life and the destruction of their weapons; the design and implementation of de-mining programmes; the return of refugees and displaced persons; the provision of humanitarian assistance; the supervision of existing administrative structures; the establishment of new police forces; the verification of respect for human rights; the design and supervision of constitutional, judicial and electoral reforms; the observation, supervision and even organization and conduct of elections; and the coordination of support for economic rehabilitation and reconstruction.

22. Fourthly, these multifunctional peace-keeping operations have highlighted the role the United Nations can play after a negotiated settlement has been implemented. It is now recognized that implementation of the settlement in the time prescribed may not be enough to guarantee that the conflict will not revive. Coordinated programmes are required, over a number of years and in various fields, to ensure that the original causes of war are eradicated. This involves the building up of national institutions, the promotion of human rights, the creation of civilian police forces and other actions in the political field. As I pointed out in *An Agenda for Development*, only sustained efforts to resolve underlying socio-economic, cultural and humanitarian problems can place an achieved peace on a durable foundation.

III. Instruments for Peace and Security

23. The United Nations has developed a range of instruments for controlling and resolving conflicts between and within States. The most important of them are preventive diplomacy and peacemaking; peace-keeping; peace-building; disarmament; sanctions; and peace enforcement. The first three can be employed only with the consent of the parties to the conflict. Sanctions and enforcement, on the other hand, are coercive measures and thus, by definition, do not require the consent of the party concerned. Disarmament can take place on an agreed basis or in the context of coercive action under Chapter VII. * * *

B. Peace-keeping * * *

43. As regards the availability of troops and equipment, problems have become steadily more serious. Availability has palpably declined as measured against the Organization's requirements. A considerable effort has been made to expand and refine stand-by arrangements, but these provide no guarantee that troops will be provided for a specific operation. For example, when in May 1994 the Security Council decided to expand the United Nations Assistance Mission for Rwanda (UNAMIR), not one of the 19 Governments that at that time had undertaken to have troops on stand-by agreed to contribute.

44. In these circumstances, I have come to the conclusion that the United Nations does need to give serious thought to the idea of a rapid reaction force. Such a force would be the Security Council's strategic reserve for deployment when there was an emergency need for peace-keeping troops. It might comprise battalion-sized units from a number of countries. These units would be trained to the same standards, use the same operating procedures, be equipped with integrated communications equipment and take part in joint exercises at regular intervals. They would be stationed in their home countries but maintained at a high state of readiness. * * *

V. Financial Resources

97. None of the instruments discussed in the present paper can be used unless Governments provide the necessary financial resources. There is no other source of funds. The failure of Member States to pay their assessed contributions for activities they themselves have voted into being makes it impossible to carry out those activities to the standard expected. It also calls in question the credibility of those who have willed the ends but not the means—and who then criticize the United Nations for its failures. * * *

98. The financial crisis is particularly debilitating as regards peace-keeping. The shortage of funds, in particular for reconnaissance and planning, for the start-up of operations and for the recruitment and training of personnel imposes severe constraints on the Organization's ability to deploy, with the desired speed, newly approved operations. Peace-keeping is also afflicted by Member States' difficulties in providing troops, police and equipment on the scale required by the current volume of peace-keeping activity.

Notes and Questions

1. *Traditional Peace-keeping.* Between 1948 and 1978, the United Nations authorized 13 peace-keeping bodies. Peace-keeping operations utilize forces contributed by U.N. Member States; there is no standing U.N. army. Early peace-keeping operations followed a traditional pattern: U.N. peace-keepers were stationed along a cease-fire line, interposed between belligerents, or assigned to observe boundaries; they could use force only to defend themselves or to remain in positions taken in accordance with U.N. authorization; they operated under U.N. command; and they included no representatives from any of the permanent members of the Security Council. Furthermore, peace-keeping operations traditionally have been established only with the consent of the states in which they were to be deployed. Why is such consent important?

2. *Peace-keeping and Peacemaking Since the End of the Cold War.* As Secretary–General Boutros–Ghali notes, some of the peace-keeping and preventive diplomacy (also known as "peacemaking") operations approved by the U.N. Security Council since the end of the Cold War have involved the Organization in functions far different from monitoring cease-fires or observing boundary lines. Perhaps the most extensive such operation was the United Nations Transitional Authority in Cambodia. UNTAC was contem-

plated by the 1991 Agreements on a Comprehensive Political Settlement of the Cambodian Conflict (the Paris Agreements), a pact entered into by warring factions in Cambodia and supported by the five permanent members of the U.N. Security Council. In addition to undertaking traditional peace-keeping functions, UNTAC coordinated with the U.N. High Commissioner for Refugees the repatriation of more than 360,000 refugees living in camps in Thailand. UNTAC also was charged with controlling the civil administration of Cambodia's government (in particular in the areas of defense, public security, finance, information, and foreign affairs), developing a civilian police force, and organizing and monitoring free elections. With respect to military issues, UNTAC's mandate included the demobilization and disarming of the armed forces of the various Cambodian factions. Over its 18 months of operation, UNTAC required about 22,000 international personnel and cost about $1.7 billion. For assessments of UNTAC's successes and failures, see Michael W. Doyle, *UN Peacekeeping in Cambodia: UNTAC's Civil Mandate* (1995), and Steven R. Ratner, *The New UN Peacekeeping* 135–206 (1995).

3. *Authority for Peace-keeping Operations*. The International Court of Justice effectively approved peace-keeping operations in the 1962 *Certain Expenses Case*, described in the introduction to this Part of the chapter. That case related to the scope of the General Assembly's authority with respect to international peace and security. In practice, the Security Council has exercised firm control over peace-keeping operations since the 1970s. Does the U.N. Charter clearly authorize the Security Council, if not the General Assembly, to establish peace-keeping operations? According to a former U.N. Under–Secretary–General for Political Affairs, "The technique of peacekeeping is a distinctive innovation by the United Nations. The Charter does not mention it. It was discovered, like penicillin. We came across it, while looking for something else, during an investigation of the guerrilla fighting in northern Greece in 1947." Brian Urquhart, "The United Nations, Collective Security, and International Peacekeeping," in *Negotiating World Order: The Artisanship and Architecture of Global Diplomacy* 59, 62 (Alan K. Henrikson ed. 1986), *quoted in* Frederic L. Kirgis, Jr., "The Security Council's First Fifty Years," 89 *American Journal of International Law* 506, 532 (1995). Some observers find sufficient Charter authority for peace-keeping operations in Chapter VII's Article 40, under which the Security Council may call on states to comply with "provisional measures." Others analogize peace-keeping to "peace-making" and point to Charter provisions in Chapter VI, which concerns the pacific settlement of disputes. See John F. Murphy, "Force and Arms," in 1 *United Nations Legal Order* 247, 294 (Oscar Schachter & Christopher C. Joyner eds. 1995). U.N. Secretary–General Dag Hammerskjold said that, in truth, peace-keeping derived from a Chapter "six-and-a-half" of the Charter, since it bridged Chapter VII, dealing with enforcement measures, and Chapter VI. Is it important to identify specific authority for peace-keeping in the text of the Charter?

4. *Funding for Peace-keeping Operations*. Following the 1962 *Certain Expenses Case*, in which the ICJ concluded that the General Assembly could assess Member States for UNEF and ONUC expenses, France and the Soviet Union still refused to pay their shares of peace-keeping assessments. What

steps can the United Nations possibly take when Member States are seriously in arrears in their payments? The delinquency of France and the Soviet Union eventually reached the point that some states argued that those states should be prohibited from voting under Article 19 of the U.N. Charter (see Appendix). The General Assembly went through its 1964–1965 session by dealing only with matters that could be acted on by consensus. Proponents of the view that voting rights of delinquent states should be suspended relented in 1965, however, and Article 19 was not enforced. France paid the amounts it had withheld several years later, and the Soviet Union made substantial payments beginning in the late 1980s.

Most peace-keeping operations have been funded either from the regular U.N. budget or from special assessments, and funding for such operations has become a major problem. As of December 31, 1995, the United Nations was owed $2.3 billion in peace-keeping costs and regular dues. In early 1996, the United States was the state most seriously in arrears, owing about $1.5 billion. See Barbara Crosette, "U.N., Facing Bankruptcy, Plans to Cut Payroll by 10%," *New York Times*, Feb. 6, 1996, at A3.

5. *Article 43 Agreements*. The drafters of the U.N. Charter did not envision the current practice of Member States voluntarily contributing their national forces to peace-keeping operations on an *ad hoc* basis. The drafters did, however, contemplate special agreements relating to the use of forces as a part of the "collective security" regime of Part VII of the Charter. According to Article 43 of the Charter, U.N. Member States would "make available to the Security Council, on its call and in accordance with a special agreement or agreements, armed forces, assistance, and facilities * * * necessary for the purpose of maintaining international peace and security." No such special agreements have ever been concluded, either for the purposes of Chapter VII enforcement actions or to assist with peace-keeping operations.

U.N. Secretary–General Boutros–Ghali suggested the possibility of concluding Article 43 agreements in 1992. He thought military force might be necessary as a last resort to enable the United Nations to carry out "peacemaking" responsibilities, and that Article 43 agreements could help to insure peace between hostile parties:

> It is the essence of the concept of collective security as contained in the Charter that if peaceful means fail, the measures provided in Chapter VII should be used on the decision of the Security Council, to maintain or restore international peace and security in the face of a "threat to the peace, breach of the peace, or act of aggression." * * *
>
> Under Article 42 of the Charter, the Security Council has the authority to take military action to maintain or restore international peace and security. While such action should only be taken when all peaceful means have failed, the option of taking it is essential to the credibility of the United Nations as a guarantor of international security. This will require bringing into being, through negotiations, the special agreements foreseen in Article 43 of the Charter, whereby Member States undertake to make armed forces, assistance and facilities available to the Security Council for the purposes stated in Article 42, not only on an ad hoc basis but on a permanent basis. * * * I

recommend that the Security Council initiate negotiations in accordance with Article 43, supported by the Military Staff Committee * * *.

"An Agenda for Peace: Preventive diplomacy, peacemaking and peace-keeping," Report of the Secretary-General pursuant to the statement adopted by the Summit Meeting of the Security Council on 31 January 1992, A/47/277-S/24111, 17 June 1992, in *An Agenda for Peace 1995*, at 39, 55-56 (2d ed. 1995)(U.N. Sales No. E.95.I.15). The Secretary-General did not repeat this call for negotiation of Article 43 agreements in his 1995 position paper, portions of which are reprinted above. Why have states been so reluctant to accept Article 43 agreements to make forces permanently available to the United Nations? What alternatives to Article 43 arrangements could make some forces available to the United Nations for use in crises?

2. CHAPTER VII OF THE UNITED NATIONS CHARTER AND IRAQ'S INVASION OF KUWAIT

On August 2, 1990, over 100,000 Iraqi troops attacked neighboring Kuwait. The greatly outnumbered Kuwaiti forces were routed, and the Emir of Kuwait fled the country. At various times, Iraq had charged that Kuwait's government was corrupt and had violated the rights of the Kuwaiti peoples; that Kuwait had violated the production quota of the Organization of Petroleum Exporting Countries; that Kuwait had been taking more than its share of oil from a huge oil field that straddled the Iraq-Kuwait border; and that Iraq had never agreed to its border with Kuwait, which the British had set in 1922. The invasion followed the collapse of talks in which Iraq had asserted financial and territorial claims.

The U.N. Security Council responded quickly. On the same day as the invasion, it voted 14-0, with Yemen abstaining, to condemn the invasion and to demand immediate and unconditional withdrawal of all Iraq forces. S.C. Res. 660 (1990). One week later, the Security Council voted unanimously to declare Iraq's "annexation" of Kuwait—a step Iraq had announced the day before—as null and void. S.C. Res. 662 (1990).

The readings in this section illustrate the nature and scope of Security Council action under Chapter VII of the U.N. Charter. We begin with two of the Security Council's resolutions responding to Iraq's invasion of Kuwait. First, Security Council Resolution 661 of August 6, 1990, passed by a vote of 13-0 (Yemen and Cuba abstaining), ordered a trade and financial boycott against Iraq and occupied Kuwait. (Later, Resolution 665 called on Member States to halt shipping in the area "in order to inspect and verify their cargoes and destinations and to ensure strict implementation of" the provisions of Resolution 661, and Resolution 670 directed states to make sure that their aircraft, or aircraft flying over their territories, were in compliance with Resolution 661.)

Second, Resolution 678, which passed on November 29, 1990, authorized Member States to use "all necessary means" to implement previous Security Council resolutions. Resolution 678 passed by a vote of 12-

2; Cuba and Yemen were opposed, and China abstained. Resolution 678 followed a massive buildup of U.S. military forces in Saudi Arabia and the region, and the deployment of many other non-U.S. troops as well. Beginning on January 16, 1991, following Iraq's noncompliance with a U.S. ultimatum to withdraw from Kuwait by January 15th, the air strikes and ground assault of "Operation Desert Storm" began. These led, by the end of February, to the restoration of Kuwaiti sovereignty within the territory of Kuwait. The U.N. Security Council has continued its involvement with Iraq, however, as indicated by Resolution 687, which is reproduced later in this Section.

SECURITY COUNCIL RESOLUTION 661

S/RES/661 (1990), Aug. 6, 1990, 29 *International Legal Materials* 1325 (1990).

The Security Council

Reaffirming its resolution 660 (1990) of 2 August 1990,

Deeply concerned that resolution has not been implemented and that the invasion by Iraq of Kuwait continues with further loss of human life and material destruction,

Determined to bring the invasion and occupation of Kuwait by Iraq to an end and to restore the sovereignty, independence and territorial integrity of Kuwait, * * *

Mindful of its responsibilities under the Charter of the United Nations for the maintenance of international peace and security,

Affirming the inherent right of individual or collective self-defense, in response to the armed attack by Iraq against Kuwait, in accordance with Article 51 of the Charter,

Acting under Chapter VII of the Charter of the United Nations, * * *

3. *Decides* that all States shall prevent:

(a) The import into their territories of all commodities and products originating in Iraq or Kuwait exported therefrom after the date of the present resolution;

(b) Any activities by their nationals or in their territories which would promote or are calculated to promote the export or trans-shipment of any commodities or products from Iraq or Kuwait; and any dealings by their flag vessels or in their territories in any commodities or products originating in Iraq or Kuwait and exported therefrom after the date of the present resolution, including in particular any transfer of funds to Iraq or Kuwait for the purposes of such activities or dealings;

(c) The sale or supply by their nationals or from their territories or using their flag vessels of any commodities or products, including weapons or any other military equipment, whether or not originating in their territories but not including supplies intended strictly for medical purposes, and, humanitarian circumstances, foodstuffs, to any person or body in Iraq or Kuwait or to any person or body for the purposes of any business carried on or operated from Iraq or Kuwait, and any activities by their nationals or in their territories which promote or are calculated to promote such sale or supply of such commodities or products;

4. *Decides* that all States shall not make available to the Government of Iraq or to any commercial, industrial or public utility undertaking in Iraq or Kuwait, any funds or any other financial or economic resources and shall prevent their nationals and any persons within their territories from removing from their territories or otherwise making available to that Government or to any such undertaking any such funds or resources and from remitting any other funds to persons or bodies within Iraq or Kuwait, except payments exclusively for strictly medical or humanitarian purposes and, in humanitarian circumstances, foodstuffs;

5. *Calls upon* all States, including States non-members of the United Nations, to act strictly in accordance with the provisions of the present resolution notwithstanding any contract entered into or license granted before the date of the present resolution;

6. *Decides* to establish, in accordance with rule 28 of the provisional rules of procedure of the Security Council, a Committee of the Security Council consisting of all the members of the Council, to undertake the following tasks and to report on its work to the Council with its observations and recommendations:

(a) To examine the reports on the progress of the implementation of the present resolution which will be submitted by the Secretary–General;

(b) To seek from all States further information regarding the action taken by them concerning the effective implementation of the provisions laid down in the present resolution;

7. *Calls upon* all States to co-operate fully with the Committee in the fulfillment of its task, including supplying such information as may be sought by the Committee in pursuance of the present resolution; * * *

9. *Decides* that, notwithstanding paragraphs 4 through 8 above, nothing in the present resolution shall prohibit assistance to the legitimate Government of Kuwait, and *calls upon* all States:

(a) To take appropriate measures to protect assets of the legitimate Government of Kuwait and its agencies;

(b) Not to recognize any régime set up by the occupying Power; * * *.

SECURITY COUNCIL RESOLUTION 678

S/RES/678 (1990), Nov. 28, 1990, 29 *International Legal Materials* 1565 (1990).

The Security Council,

Recalling, and reaffirming its resolutions 660 (1990) of 2 August 1990, 661 (1990) of 6 August 1990, 662 (1990) of 9 August 1990, 664

(1990) of 18 August 1990, 665 (1990) of 25 August, 1990, 666 (1990) of 13 September 1990, 667 (1990) of 16 September 1990, 669 (1990) of 24 September 1990, 670 (1990) of 25 September 1990, 674 (1990) of 29 October 1990 and 677 (1990) of 28 November 1990,

Noting that, despite all efforts by the United Nations, Iraq refuses to comply with its obligation to implement resolution 660 (1990) and the above mentioned subsequent relevant resolutions, in flagrant contempt of the Security Council,

Mindful of its duties and responsibilities under the Charter of the United Nations for the maintenance and preservation of international peace and security,

Determined to secure full compliance with its decisions,

Acting under Chapter VII of the Charter,

1. *Demands* that Iraq comply fully with resolution 660 (1990) and all subsequent relevant resolutions, and decides, while maintaining all its decisions, to allow Iraq one final opportunity, as a pause of goodwill, to do so;

2. *Authorizes* Member States co-operating with the government of Kuwait, unless Iraq on or before 15 January 1991 fully implements, as set forth in paragraph 1 above, the foregoing resolutions, to use all necessary means to uphold and implement resolution 660 (1990) and all subsequent relevant resolutions and to restore international peace and security in the area;

3. *Requests* all States to provide appropriate support for the actions undertaken in pursuance of paragraph 2 of the present resolution; * * *.

THOMAS M. FRANCK & FAIZA PATEL, "UN POLICE ACTION IN LIEU OF WAR: 'THE OLD ORDER CHANGETH' "

85 *American Journal of International Law* 63 (1991).

The United Nations system is an elegant, carefully crafted instrument to make war illegal and unnecessary. To this end, in Article 2(4) of the UN Charter, members are required to "refrain ... from the threat or use of force against the territorial integrity or political independence of any state." * * *

The new alternative to traditional wars of self-defense is collective police actions by the members of the international community. Exceptionally, these could be implemented by regional organizations. Usually, they would take the form of global action. Either way, the police action must be authorized specifically by the Security Council under Article 53 (for regional action) or Article 42 (for global action).

If states use armed force under the self-defense rubric of Article 51, their individual activities are subsumed by, or incorporated into, the global police response once it is activated. That is, the old way is licensed only until the new way begins to work: "until," in the words of Article 51, "the Security Council has taken the necessary measures to maintain international peace and security." * * *

* * * [T]he argument that the *war* power of member states was not intended to be restricted, but only augmented, by the Charter's creation of a new *police* power [is erroneous]. This interpretation flies in the face of common sense and the literal text. A new-style, UN-authorized police action functioning alongside a traditional sovereign exercise of war powers is conceptually and operationally untenable, the more so when states seeking the freedom to act unilaterally have forces committed alongside others in a Security Council police action. As a textual matter, it is obvious on its face that the Charter, in creating the new police power, intended to establish an exclusive alternative to the old war system. The old system was retained only as a fallback, available when the new system could not be made to work; not as an equal alternative, to be chosen at the sole discretion of the members. * * *

The delegates to the San Francisco Conference recognized that the enforcement provisions of chapter VII of the Charter provided "the teeth of the United Nations." The committee considering its military enforcement measures adopted Article 42 unanimously. In so doing, delegates intended to give the Security Council "the power, when diplomatic, economic, or other measures are considered by the Council to be inadequate, to undertake such aerial, naval, or other operations as may be necessary to maintain or restore international peace and security." This article was thought to remedy the principal defect of the League Covenant and the committee's rapporteur observed that "this unanimous vote ... renders sacred the obligation of all states to participate in the operations." Thus, "[m]ilitary assistance, in case of aggression, ceases to be a *recommendation* made to member states; it becomes for us an *obligation* which none can shirk."

This record is entirely inconsistent with the notion that, once the Security Council has taken measures, individual members are supposed to remain free to design their own military responses. * * *

Any effort to ascertain the intent of the drafters is somewhat clouded by the large amount of attention given by the drafters and ratifiers of the Charter to one provision pertaining to police action, which, historically, has proven to be something of a red herring. Just as Congress nowadays does not grant letters of marque and reprisal (Constitution, Article I, section 8(11)) or establish post roads (Article I, section 8(7)), so the Security Council has not made use of Article 43 of the Charter, which authorizes it to negotiate agreements with consenting member states that, preemptively, would have placed designated national military contingents at the Council's disposal. That no such agreements were made, owing to the Cold War, does not signify a lapse in the Organization's general police power, set out in Article 42, any more than the abstinence by Congress in matters of post roads signifies a lapse in its power to legislate on other matters pertaining to the Postal Service. Rather, the practice of the Security Council has evolved other means for taking coercive measures, including the use of police forces raised ad hoc in response to a specific threat to the peace. Both the Korean and the Kuwaiti situations are examples. What emerges from the institutional history of the years of stasis is not evidence that the Council's policing functions have fallen into desuetude but, on the contrary, that the central idea of a globally sanctioned police action was never abandoned; that the failure to implement Article 43 merely led to organic growth and the alternative creation of police action through invocation of Article 42, which does not require special agreements.

This is as one would expect. The UN Charter is not merely a treaty, but also the constitutive instrument of a living global organization. Its organs were designed both to implement important tasks and to interpret their own authority. Such organic growth is desirable and inevitable.

EUGENE V. ROSTOW, "UNTIL WHAT? ENFORCEMENT ACTION OR COLLECTIVE SELF-DEFENSE?"

85 *American Journal of International Law* 506 (1991).

Should the Persian Gulf war of 1990–1991 be characterized as an "international enforcement action" of the United Nations Security Council or as a campaign of collective self-defense approved, encouraged, and blessed by the Security Council?

This is not simply a nice and rather metaphysical legal issue, but an extremely practical one. The question it presents is whether the control and direction of hostilities in the gulf, their termination, and the substance of the settlement they produce were handled by the Council as the Korean War was handled, that is, as a campaign of collective self-defense, or as the United Nations' first "international enforcement action." * * *

On paper, the powers of the UN Security Council go beyond those possessed by the League of Nations. The Council can call on the members to apply measures not involving the use of armed force in order to deal with situations of aggression, and, if such measures are deemed inadequate, it "may take such action by air, sea, or land forces as may be necessary to maintain or restore international peace and security." Provision was made for the formation of a standing United Nations force, and of a Military Staff Committee to advise and assist the Security Council on these and cognate questions. The Military Staff Committee exists in a state of suspended animation at the present time, although it may be revived. Military actions to restore peace taken under Article 42 and 43 of the Charter are called "international enforcement actions."

Finally, after the Charter outlined the peacekeeping procedures of the Security Council under chapter VII in Articles 39–50, it provided in

Article 51 that "[n]othing in the present Charter shall impair the inherent right of individual or collective self-defense if an armed attack occurs ... until the Security Council has taken measures necessary to maintain international peace and security." In the narrowest sense, the present controversy is about the meaning of the word "until" in Article 51.

The coercive powers conferred on the Security Council have not yet become a working part of the process for managing the state system. The fate of these coercive powers thus far reflects the nature of the United Nations as a hybrid political entity superimposed on the system of sovereign states: not a superpower or a world government, but an instrumentality for achieving cooperation among the nations in the interest of peace; an instrumentality, a catalyst, to which certain powers have been tentatively delegated by those nations. Diplomacy and conciliation are the normal methods of the Security Council. * * *

While some eminent authorities consider the Korean War to have been a Security Council "enforcement action," they press the term too hard. In the Korean episode, the Security Council was able to function for two months because the Soviet Union was boycotting the Organization at the time. Even under those circumstances, however, the Council did not use the language of "decision" which would have activated Article 25. The Council's resolutions simply recommended that the members refrain from helping North Korea and urged them to "furnish such assistance to the Republic of Korea as may be necessary to repel the armed attack and to restore international peace and security in the area." For all their symbolic panoply of the United Nations flag and other emblems, the forces which finally prevailed in Korea were national forces carrying out a mission of collective self-defense under American direction, not a Security Council enforcement action. * * *

In the Persian Gulf crisis, Security Council Resolution 678 "[*a*]*uthorizes* Member States co-operating with the Government of Kuwait ... to use all necessary means to uphold [the earlier resolutions] and to restore international peace and security in the area." Except for the word "authorizes," the resolution is clearly one designed to encourage and support a campaign of collective self-defense, and therefore not a Security Council enforcement action. Instead of attempting to direct such an operation itself, the Council "requests the States concerned" to keep it regularly informed about their progress. The Security Council held no meetings on the gulf crisis between November 29, 1990, when Resolution 678 was adopted, and February 14, 1991, when it met in secret session to discuss the political aspects of the end of the war. And the initial cease-fire in the gulf war was achieved as a practical matter not by an agreed Security Council resolution but by President Bush's ultimatum of February 28, 1991. * * *

During the period of active hostilities, neither the Secretary–General nor any other part of the United Nations Secretariat attempted to exercise control over military operations, although a committee of the Council actively supervised the program of economic sanctions.

Thus, the practice followed in implementing Resolution 678 and in terminating hostilities has been that of an allied military campaign in defense of Kuwait directed by officers of the United States and the associated nations. Does the word "authorized" in Resolution 678 mean that the member states which cooperated with Kuwait in driving Iraq out of that country could not have done so without the Council's "authority"? As Professor Glennon points out, Resolution 678 is in fact permissive, like Resolution 83 of June 27, 1950, adopted by the Security Council during the Korean War. It imposes no legally binding obligation under Article 25 of the Charter. In Glennon's words, it "merely exhorts, authorizes or recommends," leaving to the member states the decision whether to cooperate in the effort of the allied coalition to liberate Kuwait. The word "authorizes" in Resolution 678 should not therefore be considered to transform a military campaign of self-defense into an enforcement action.

Thus far, the nominal authority of the Security Council to engage in military "enforcement actions" has not been tested. This is not a state of affairs to be deplored. Political relations among the members of the Council—permanent and temporary alike—are not sufficiently stable to make so radical a step politically feasible or desirable. Although the diplomacy of the gulf crisis in 1990 and 1991 has shown some movement in a promising direction, it remains to be seen whether these hints of progress are followed by more substantial changes.

Notes and Questions

1. *The Structure of Chapter VII.* What are the legal grounds for the Security Council's resolutions related to the Gulf War? Resolution 661 states the Security Council was acting generally under Chapter VII of the United Nations Charter. Under Chapter VII (see Appendix), Article 39 requires the Security Council to determine that a "threat to the peace, breach of the peace, or act of aggression" exists. It may then make recommendations or decide on measures to "be taken in accordance with Articles 41 or 42, to maintain or restore international peace and security." Article 41 contemplates the use of economic sanctions and other measures not involving the use of armed force. Read literally, Chapter VII does not require a state to have violated international law before Article 41 sanctions are applied, but in practice the Security Council has applied such sanctions only against states failing to comply with the Charter or some other important legal obligation. See Oscar Schachter, "United Nations Law," 88 *American Journal of International Law* 1, 12 (1995). The Security Council may take action under Article 42, which contemplates the use of force, if it considers Article 41 measures inadequate. Article 106 of the Charter suggests Article 42 was meant to have a dependent relationship with Article 43, which calls for Member States to conclude special agreements with the U.N. to make armed forces and other assistance available to the Security Council. According to Articles 46 and 47, the Security Council itself, with the advice and assistance of a Military Staff Committee, would plan for and

control the application of armed force. Note also the Security Council's roles under Chapter VI of the Charter, on the "Pacific Settlement of Disputes."

In practice, the Charter design with respect to the use of force under Chapter VII has not been followed. Since no Article 43 agreements have ever been concluded, some observers contend the Security Council's authorization of the use of force in Resolution 678 falls within some penumbra of powers that the Council has assumed under Chapter VII—an "Article 42½" power.

2. *Collective Self-defense v. Chapter VII Enforcement Action.* Did Security Council Resolution 678 authorize a type of Chapter VII enforcement action, as Franck and Patel suggest? Or was the use of force against Iraq an exercise of collective self-defense in accordance with Article 51 of the U.N. Charter? If the use of force against Iraq was an exercise of collective self-defense, why did the United States and other members of the Security Council find it necessary to pass Resolution 678?

3. *Suspending the Right of Self-defense in Light of Security Council Action.* According to Article 51 of the U.N. Charter, the right of self-defense is preserved "until the Security Council has taken measures necessary to maintain international peace and security." When is the right of states to use force in self-defense suspended? When the Security Council passes any resolutions under Chapter VII? When the Security Council decides U.N. Member States should impose comprehensive mandatory sanctions against a state that has used force? Note that the Security Council in Resolution 661 explicitly "affirms the inherent right of individual or collective self-defense, in response to the armed attack by Iraq against Kuwait, in accordance with Article 51 of the Charter," and in paragraph 9 decides that "assistance to the legitimate Government of Kuwait" is not prohibited. But what if references to Article 51 were absent in a comprehensive sanctions resolution? May the Security Council explicitly prohibit all military action by a state, including defensive action? Who decides whether any Security Council measures satisfy the "necessary to maintain international peace and security" clause of Article 51?

4. *The Binding Effect of Security Council Decisions.* Note the different phrasings of the operative provisions of Security Council Resolutions 661 and 678. Resolution 678 "authorizes" Member State action. Resolution 661, however, includes "decisions" of the Security Council. Member States are legally bound to carry out such decisions under Articles 25 and 48 of the U.N. Charter.

SECURITY COUNCIL RESOLUTION 687

S/RES/687 (1991), Apr. 3, 1991, 30 *International Legal Materials* 846 (1991).

The Security Council,

Recalling its resolutions 660 (1990) of 2 August 1990, 661 (1990) of 6 August 1990, 662 (1990) of 9 August 1990, 664 (1990) of 18 August 1990, 665 (1990) of 25 August 1990, 666 (1990) of 13 September 1990, 667 (1990) of 16 September 1990, 669 (1990) of 24 September 1990, 670

(1990) of 25 September 1990, 674 (1990) of 29 October 1990, 677 (1990) of 28 November 1990, 678 (1990) of 29 November 1990 and 686 (1991) of 2 March 1991,

Welcoming the restoration to Kuwait of its sovereignty, independence and territorial integrity and the return of its legitimate Government, * * *

Noting that Iraq and Kuwait, as independent sovereign States, signed at Baghdad on 4 October 1963 "Agreed Minutes Between the State of Kuwait and the Republic of Iraq Regarding the Restoration of Friendly Relations, Recognition and Related Matters," thereby recognizing formally the boundary between Iraq and Kuwait and the allocation of islands, which were registered with the United Nations in accordance with Article 102 of the Charter of the United Nations and in which Iraq recognized the independence and complete sovereignty of the State of Kuwait within its borders as specified and accepted in the letter of the Prime Minister of Iraq dated 21 July 1932, and as accepted by the Ruler of Kuwait in his letter dated 10 August 1932,

Conscious of the need for demarcation of the said boundary,

Conscious also of the statements by Iraq threatening to use weapons in violation of its obligations under the Geneva Protocol for the Prohibition of the Use in War of Asphyxiating, Poisonous or Other Gases, and of Bacteriological Methods of Warfare, signed at Geneva on 17 June 1925 [14 I.L.M. 49 (1975)], and of its prior use of chemical weapons and affirming that grave consequences would follow any further use by Iraq of such weapons,

Recalling that Iraq has subscribed to the Declaration adopted by all States participating in the Conference of States Parties to the 1925 Geneva Protocol and Other Interested States, held in Paris from 7 to 11 January 1989, establishing the objective of universal elimination of chemical and biological weapons,

Recalling also that Iraq has signed the Convention on the Prohibition of the Development, Production and Stockpiling of Bacteriological (Biological) and Toxin Weapons and on Their Destruction, of 10 April 1972 [11 I.L.M. 309 (1972)], * * *

Aware of the use by Iraq of ballistic missiles in unprovoked attacks and therefore of the need to take specific measures in regard to such missiles located in Iraq,

Concerned by the reports in the hands of Member States that Iraq has attempted to acquire materials for a nuclear-weapons programme contrary to its obligations under the Treaty on the Non–Proliferation of Nuclear Weapons of 1 July 1968 [7 I.L.M. 809 (1968)], * * *

Noting that despite the progress being made in fulfilling the obligations of resolution 686 (1991), many Kuwaiti and third country nationals are still not accounted for and property remains unreturned,

Recalling the International Convention against the Taking of Hostages [18 I.L.M. 1460 (1979)] opened for signature at New York on 18 December 1979, which categorizes all acts of taking hostages as manifestations of international terrorism,

Deploring threats made by Iraq during the recent conflict to make use of terrorism against targets outside Iraq and the taking of hostages by Iraq,

Taking note with grave concern of the reports of the Secretary–General of 20 March 1991 and 28 March 1991, and conscious of the necessity to meet urgently the humanitarian needs in Kuwait and Iraq,

Bearing in mind its objective of restoring international peace and security in the area as set out in recent resolutions of the Security Council,

Conscious of the need to take the following measures acting under Chapter VII of the Charter,

1. *Affirms* all 13 resolutions noted above, except as expressly changed below to achieve the goals of this resolution, including a formal cease-fire;

A

2. *Demands* that Iraq and Kuwait respect the inviolability of the international boundary and the allocation of islands set out in the "Agreed Minutes Between the State of Kuwait and the Republic of Iraq Regarding the Restoration of Friendly Relations, Recognition and Related Matters," signed by them in the exercise of their sovereignty at Baghdad on 4 October 1963 and registered with the United Nations and published by the United Nations in document 7063, United Nations, *Treaty Series*, 1964;

3. *Calls upon* the Secretary–General to lend his assistance to make arrangements with Iraq and Kuwait to demarcate the boundary between Iraq and Kuwait, drawing on appropriate material, including the map transmitted by Security Council document S/22412 and to report back to the Security Council within one month;

4. *Decides* to guarantee the inviolability of the above-mentioned international boundary and to take as appropriate all necessary measures to that end in accordance with the Charter of the United Nations;

B

5. *Requests* the Secretary–General, after consulting with Iraq and Kuwait, to submit within three days to the Security Council for its approval a plan for the immediate deployment of a United Nations observer unit to monitor the Khor Abdullah and a demilitarized zone, which is hereby established, extending ten kilometers into Iraq and five kilometers into Kuwait from the boundary referred to in the "Agreed Minutes Between the State of Kuwait and the Republic of Iraq Regarding the Restoration of Friendly Relations, Recognition and Related Matters" of 4 October 1963; to deter violations of the boundary through

its presence in and surveillance of the demilitarized zone; to observe any hostile or potentially hostile action mounted from the territory of one State to the other; and for the Secretary–General to report regularly to the Security Council on the operations of the unit, and immediately if there are serious violations of the zone or potential threats to peace;

6. *Notes* that as soon as the Secretary–General notifies the Security Council of the completion of the deployment of the United Nations observer unit, the conditions will be established for the Member States cooperating with Kuwait in accordance with resolution 678 (1990) to bring their military presence in Iraq to an end consistent with resolution 686 (1991);

C

[The Security Council decides Iraq will accept the destruction or removal of certain weapons, submit to on-site inspections of its weapons systems, and take other steps related to its military capabilities. The Council also calls on the U.N. Secretary–General and the International Atomic Energy Agency to carry out measures concerning Iraqi weapons, nuclear material, and nuclear facilities.]

D

15. *Requests* the Secretary–General to report to the Security Council on the steps taken to facilitate the return of all Kuwaiti property seized by Iraq, including a list of any property that Kuwait claims has not been returned or which has not been returned intact;

E

16. *Reaffirms* that Iraq, without prejudice to the debts and obligations of Iraq arising prior to 2 August 1990, which will be addressed through the normal mechanisms, is liable under international law for any direct loss, damage, including environmental damage and the depletion of natural resources, or injury to foreign Governments, nationals and corporations, as a result of Iraq's unlawful invasion and occupation of Kuwait;

17. *Decides* that all Iraqi statements made since 2 August 1990 repudiating its foreign debt are null and void, and demands that Iraq scrupulously adhere to all of its obligations concerning servicing and repayment of its foreign debt;

18. *Decides also* to create a fund to pay compensation for claims that fall within paragraph 16 above and to establish a Commission that will administer the fund;

19. *Directs* the Secretary–General to develop and present to the Council for decision, no later than 30 days following the adoption of the present resolution, recommendations for the fund to meet the requirement for the payment of claims established in accordance with paragraph 18 above and for a programme to implement the decisions in paragraphs 16, 17 and 18 above, including: administration of the fund; mechanisms for determining the appropriate level of Iraq's contribution

to the fund based on a percentage of the value of the exports of petroleum and petroleum products from Iraq not to exceed a figure to be suggested to the Council by the Secretary–General, taking into account the requirements of the people of Iraq, Iraq's payment capacity as assessed in conjunction with the international financial institutions taking into consideration external debt service, and the needs of the Iraqi economy; arrangements for ensuring that payments are made to the fund; the process by which funds will be allocated and claims paid; appropriate procedures for evaluating losses, listing claims and verifying their validity and resolving disputed claims in respect of Iraq's liability as specified in paragraph 16 above; and the composition of the Commission designated above;

F

20. *Decides*, effective immediately, that the prohibitions against the sale or supply to Iraq of commodities or products other than medicine and health supplies, and prohibitions against financial transactions related thereto contained in resolution 661 (1990) shall not apply to foodstuffs notified to the Security Council Committee established by resolution 661 (1990) concerning the situation between Iraq and Kuwait or, with the approval of that Committee, under the simplified and accelerated "no-objection" procedure, to materials and supplies for essential civilian needs as identified in the report of the Secretary–General dated 20 March 1991, and in any further findings of humanitarian need by the Committee;

21. *Decides* that the Council shall review the provisions of paragraph 20 above every 60 days in the light of the policies and practices of the Government of Iraq, including the implementation of all relevant resolutions of the Security Council, for the purpose of determining whether to reduce or lift the prohibitions referred to therein;

22. *Decides* that upon the approval by the Security Council of the programme called for in paragraph 19 above and upon Council agreement that Iraq has completed all actions contemplated in paragraphs 8, 9, 10, 11, 12 and 13 above, the prohibitions against the import of commodities and products originating in Iraq and the prohibitions against financial transactions related thereto contained in resolution 661 (1990) shall have no further force or effect;

23. *Decides* that, pending action by the Security Council under paragraph 22 above, the Security Council Committee established by resolution 661 (1990) shall be empowered to approve, when required to assure adequate financial resources on the part of Iraq to carry out the activities under paragraph 20 above, exceptions to the prohibition against the import of commodities and products originating in Iraq;

24. *Decides* that, in accordance with resolution 661 (1990) and subsequent related resolutions and until a further decision is taken by the Security Council, all States shall continue to prevent the sale or supply, or the promotion or facilitation of such sale or supply, to Iraq by

their nationals, or from their territories or using their flag vessels or aircraft, of:

(a) Arms and related *matériel* of all types, specifically including the sale or transfer through other means of all forms of conventional military equipment, including for paramilitary forces, and spare parts and components and their means of production, for such equipment;

(b) Items specified and defined in paragraphs 8 and 12 above not otherwise covered above;

(c) Technology under licensing or other transfer arrangements used in the production, utilization or stockpiling of items specified in subparagraphs (a) and (b) above;

(d) Personnel or materials for training or technical support services relating to the design, development, manufacture, use, maintenance or support of items specified in subparagraphs (a) and (b) above;

25. *Calls upon* all States and international organizations to act strictly in accordance with paragraph 24 above, notwithstanding the existence of any contracts, agreements, licenses, or any other arrangements;

26. *Requests* the Secretary–General, in consultation with appropriate Governments, to develop within 60 days, for the approval of the Security Council, guidelines to facilitate full international implementation of paragraphs 24 and 25 above and paragraph 27 below, and to make them available to all States and to establish a procedure for updating these guidelines periodically;

27. *Calls upon* all States to maintain such national controls and procedures and to take such other actions consistent with the guidelines to be established by the Security Council under paragraph 26 above as may be necessary to ensure compliance with the terms of paragraph 24 above, and calls upon international organizations to take all appropriate steps to assist in ensuring such full compliance;

28. *Agrees* to review its decisions in paragraphs 22, 23, 24 and 25 above, except for the items specified and defined in paragraphs 8 and 12 above, on a regular basis and in any case 120 days following passage of the present resolution, taking into account Iraq's compliance with the resolution and general progress towards the control of armaments in the region;

29. *Decides* that all States, including Iraq, shall take the necessary measures to ensure that no claim shall lie at the instance of the Government of Iraq, or of any person or body in Iraq, or of any person claiming through or for the benefit of any such person or body, in connection with any contract or other transaction where its performance was affected by reason of the measures taken by the Security Council in resolution 661 (1990) and related resolutions;

G

30. *Decides* that, in furtherance of its commitment to facilitate the repatriation of all Kuwaiti and third country nationals, Iraq shall extend all necessary cooperation to the International Committee of the Red Cross, providing lists of such persons, facilitating the access of the International Committee of the Red Cross to all such persons wherever located or detained and facilitating the search by the International Committee of the Red Cross for those Kuwaiti and third country nationals still unaccounted for; * * *

H

32. *Requires* Iraq to inform the Security Council that it will not commit or support any act of international terrorism or allow any organizations directed towards commission of such acts to operate within its territory and to condemn unequivocally and renounce all acts, methods and practices of terrorism;

I

33. *Declares* that, upon official notification by Iraq to the Secretary-General and to the Security Council of its acceptance of the provisions above, a formal cease-fire is effective between Iraq and Kuwait and the Member States cooperating with Kuwait in accordance with resolution 678 (1990);

34. *Decides* to remain seized of the matter and to take such further steps as may be required for the implementation of the present resolution and to secure peace and security in the area.

Notes and Questions

1. *Article 2(7) of the Charter.* In Resolution 687 the Security Council takes steps, some continuing well after the end of the Iraq–Kuwait war, that affect a wide range of Iraqi governmental functions. Iraq and some other states believe these steps illegitimately interfere with Iraqi sovereignty. As a matter of doctrine, the objection that Resolution 687 violates Article 2(7) of the U.N. Charter, which establishes the principle that the United Nations shall not intervene in matters essentially within the domestic jurisdiction of states, meets a significant obstacle. Article 2(7) is expressly subject to the limitation that the principle of nonintervention "shall not prejudice the application of enforcement measures under Chapter VII."

2. *The Legal Consequences of Security Council Resolutions.* What legal function does Resolution 687 serve? Is it fair to say that the Security Council, although a political institution, is providing "institutionalized countermeasures" as a means of enforcing international law? Vera Gowlland–Debbas, "Security Council Enforcement Action and Issues of State Responsibility," 43 *International & Comparative Law Quarterly* 55, 73 (1994).

What legal consequences flow from a Security Council determination under Article 39 of the U.N. Charter that there has been a "threat to the peace, breach of the peace, or act of aggression"? In Resolution 662 (1990), the Security Council declared Iraq's annexation of Kuwait to be a legal nullity. The imposition of sanctions may also be a consequence of Security Council action, as we saw in Resolution 661, above. What are the purposes and legal consequences of Resolution 687? The following notes examine the variety of measures in Resolution 687.

3. *The Security Council and International Boundaries*. Iraq has contested the validity of the 1963 Iraq–Kuwait Agreed Minutes setting out the international boundary between them. The drawing of international boundaries is a sensitive matter; states normally set them by agreement or by authorizing a tribunal to decide. But in paragraph 4 of Resolution 687, the Security Council itself seems to impose a settlement to an international boundary dispute. In Resolution 833 of May 1993, the Security Council "reaffirmed" its guarantee of the inviolability of the Iraq–Kuwait border and "welcomed" the decisions of the Demarcation Commission established pursuant to paragraph 3 of Resolution 687. Is it appropriate for the Security Council to exercise such authority?

4. *The Security Council and Compensation for War Damage*. Paragraphs 18 and 19 of Resolution 687 contemplate a compensation commission to assess Iraq's liability for losses suffered because of its invasion of Kuwait. In May 1991 the Security Council formally created the U.N. Compensation Commission, a subsidiary organ of the Security Council under Article 29 of the U.N. Charter (see Appendix). S.C. Res. 692 (1991). The Compensation Commission, whose procedures are supervised by a Governing Council composed of Security Council members' representatives acting in their governmental capacities, can resolve disputed claims, assess damages, and review damage assessments through an appellate mechanism. Successful claimants are to be compensated from a fund created by taking certain proceeds of Iraq's sales of its oil exports. See S.C. Res. 705 (1991), 706 (1991), 778 (1992). The Legal Adviser to the U.S. State Department has estimated that the Compensation Commission will eventually process over $200 billion in claims. Conrad K. Harper, "Protecting the Environment During Armed Conflict: The International Community's Effort to Enforce Norms, Remedy Harms, and Impose Accountability," Symposium on the Protection of the Environment During Armed Conflict and Other Military Operations, U.S. Naval War College, Sept. 20, 1995, at 7. Does the Security Council overstep its bounds by creating and supervising an adjudicatory commission, determining who is to receive compensation, and sequestering the natural resource wealth of a state to insure that the Commission's awards are paid?

5. *The Security Council and Claims in Municipal Courts*. Consider paragraph 29 of Resolution 687, which effectively requires all states to apply a *force majeure* defense to Iraqi claims in connection with otherwise valid transactions that were not carried out because of the Security Council's economic sanctions against Iraq. Should the Security Council legislate on *force majeure* in municipal courts?

6. *The Security Council and Humanitarian Measures*. Paragraphs 20 and 30 of Resolution 687 refer to humanitarian measures. Security Council Resolution 688 of April 1991, which condemned Iraq's repression of Kurds in northern Iraq, also related to humanitarian measures. Resolution 688 characterized the flow of Kurdish refugees "towards and across international

frontiers" as a threat to international peace and security, "insisted" that Iraq allow international humanitarian organizations immediate access to those in need of aid, requested the U.N. Secretary–General to pursue humanitarian efforts in Iraq, and demanded Iraqi cooperation with the Secretary–General on humanitarian measures. Was Security Council involvement justified? See Jane E. Stromseth, "Iraq's Repression of Its Civilian Population: Collective Responses and Continuing Challenges," in *Enforcing Restraint* 77 (Lori Fisler Damrosch ed. 1993). Iraq did consent to a U.N. humanitarian presence within Iraq in April 1991, and eventually asked the United Nations to take responsibility for Kurdish relief efforts.

7. *The Expiration of Security Council Sanctions.* Paragraph 24 of Security Council Resolution 687 provides that some sanctions the Security Council had imposed against Iraq are to continue in effect "until a further decision is taken by the Security Council." Given the possibility that one of the Security Council's permanent members could veto any proposal to lift sanctions, should the Security Council require that any sanctions it imposes expire if they are not renewed by some date certain? Or require that an initial sanctions resolution include a modified voting procedure to determine when the sanctions can be lifted? See David D. Caron, "The Legitimacy of the Collective Authority of the Security Council," 87 *American Journal of International Law* 552, 577–88 (1994).

3. THE UNITED NATIONS AND BOSNIA

The dividing line between "international" and "internal" conflicts is not always a sharp one. A range of factors—including intervention by outside states, the size and intensity of a purportedly domestic conflict, a flow of refugees across international borders, and the occurrence of significant human rights violations—may convince members of the Security Council that a particular conflict is sufficiently internationalized to warrant Security Council measures.

The Security Council, concluding that the crisis in the Former Yugoslavia had an international dimension, adopted many measures related to the region. Before the 1995 General Framework Agreement for Peace in Bosnia and Herzegovina (the Dayton Accords), the Security Council imposed an arms embargo on Bosnia, restricted flights over Bosnian airspace, imposed economic sanctions against the Federal Republic of Yugoslavia (Serbia and Montenegro), and froze overseas assets of the Federal Republic. The Council, in a step unprecedented under Chapter VII of the Charter, created a judicial organ, the International Criminal Tribunal for the Former Yugoslavia, to try individuals for violating international criminal law. The Security Council also authorized a peace-keeping operation, the U.N. Protection Forces (UNPROFOR), whose mandate included facilitating the delivery of humanitarian aid to civilians, protecting U.N.–declared "safe areas," and engaging in "preventive diplomacy" functions before the outbreak of conflict in particular areas. Other U.N. bodies have been involved in

Bosnia as well, including the U.N. Human Rights Commission, the U.N. High Commissioner for Refugees, other U.N. agencies that have provided aid to some of Bosnia's two million displaced persons, and the U.N. Secretary–General, who was involved in mediation efforts.

The crisis in the Former Yugoslavia also shows that the United Nations may rely on regional organizations in efforts to maintain peace and security. At the request of the U.N. Security Council, the North Atlantic Treaty Organization (NATO) was actively involved in enforcing the U.N. arms embargo, ensuring the ban on flights in Bosnian airspace, and carrying out air operations to support UNPROFOR safe areas. As the following excerpt suggests, NATO has assumed a significant role in implementing the Dayton Accords.

The Dayton Accords are complex, and the General Framework Agreement itself is at the center of other intricate arrangements involving international organizations and states. The state of Bosnia and Herzegovina, the Federation of Bosnia and Herzegovina (which is the product of an agreement between Bosnian Croats and Bosnian Muslims), and the Respublika Srpska (the Bosnian Serb entity) have concluded Annexes to the General Framework Agreement that relate to military matters, monitoring of the peace settlement, boundaries between entities within Bosnia and Herzegovina, a complex constitution for Bosnia and Herzegovina, elections, human rights, refugees, and binding arbitration of disputes. The Annexes contemplate, and constitute the parties' consent to, numerous roles for international organizations. See Bosnia and Herzegovina–Croatia–Yugoslavia: General Framework Agreement for Peace in Bosnia and Herzegovina with Annexes, Dec. 14, 1995, 35 I.L.M. 75 (1996). The following excerpt from a report of the U.N. Secretary–General addresses primarily the creation of a new Implementation Force (IFOR), which was designed to monitor and, if necessary, use force to enforce the peace settlement.

REPORT OF THE SECRETARY–GENERAL PURSUANT TO SECURITY COUNCIL RESOLUTION 1026

S/1995/1031, Dec. 13, 1995, 35 *International Legal Materials* 237 (1996).

5. The present report addresses the following aspects of implementation of the Peace Agreement that affect the United Nations:

(a) The transition from UNPROFOR to the Implementation Force (IFOR) provided for in annex 1–A to the Peace Agreement;

(b) Coordination of the United Nations contribution to implementation of the Peace Agreement:

(c) The United Nations role as regards:

(i) Humanitarian relief and refugees;

(ii) Demining;

(iii) Civilian police;

(iv) Human rights;

(v) Elections;

(vi) Rehabilitation of infrastructure and economic reconstruction.

* * *

6. The report will also deal with the future of certain existing United Nations activities, which will either be discontinued or be transferred to other agencies during implementation of the Peace Agreement, namely:

(a) The International Conference on the Former Yugoslavia, which was established, under the co-chairmanship of the Secretary-General of the United Nations and the President-in-Office of the European Community (as it then was), in London in August 1992;

(b) The functions of the United Nations Special Coordinator for Sarajevo, who was appointed pursuant to Security Council resolution 900 (1994);

(c) Monitoring of the no-fly zone and operation of Sarajevo airport;

(d) The functions of the United Nations Peace Forces headquarters (UNPF-HQ) in Zagreb.

II. Transition From UNPROFOR to IFOR

7. In paragraph 1 (a) of article I of the Agreement on the Military Aspects of the Peace Settlement (annex 1-A to the Peace Agreement), the Security Council is invited to authorize Member States or regional organizations or arrangements to establish a multinational military Implementation Force (IFOR), which will be composed of ground, air and maritime units from the members of the North Atlantic Treaty Organization (NATO) and from non-NATO States. The parties to the Agreement understand and agree that IFOR will begin implementation of the military aspects of the Peace Agreement upon the transfer of authority for the forces deployed in Bosnia and Herzegovina from the UNPROFOR Commander to the IFOR Commander. In paragraph 1(b) of that annex, the parties understand and agree that NATO may establish such a force, which will operate under the authority and subject to the direction and political control of the North Atlantic Council through the NATO chain of command. The modalities of the participation of non-NATO States in IFOR are to be agreed between those States and NATO.

8. An authorization by the Security Council and the subsequent establishment of IFOR will have a number of far-reaching implications for the United Nations presence in Bosina and Herzegovina and the mandate of UNPROFOR, which, in so far as they can be identified at the present stage, are outlined below. It should be stressed that a number of decisions can be taken only after authorization by the Security Council of the implementation arrangements envisaged in the Peace Agreement and the London conclusions.

9. One of the matters yet to be finalized is the composition of IFOR. * * * On the basis of consultations with troop-contributing countries, it can be assumed that the larger part of the UNPROFOR units will transfer to IFOR.

10. Following authorization by the Security Council, arrangements will be made without delay to effect the transfer of authority from UNPROFOR to IFOR, a process that could occur within 96 hours of the Council's decision. The UNPF Force Commander will become the Deputy Commander of IFOR but will retain his UNPF authority during the transitional period and will thus continue to exercise operational control over those UNPROFOR units that do not transfer to IFOR, until their withdrawal from the theatre. The arrangement of having the UNPF Force Commander serve simultaneously as Deputy Commander of IFOR will, *inter alia*, facilitate the coordination of the withdrawal of UNPROFOR contingents with the arrival of IFOR elements. The repatriation of United Nations military personnel not required by IFOR, including all United Nations military observers, will begin immediately after the transfer of authority. * * *

VI. Observations * * *

47. I welcome these * * * agreements because, if the parties will allow them to be implemented, they will end the terrible suffering inflicted on the people of those two Member States for so many years and a major source of instability in Europe will be removed. I also welcome them because of their implications for the United Nations. It is widely held that the United Nations' involvement in the former Yugoslavia has not been a success. I strongly dispute that allegation. The original and primary purpose in deploying United Nations peace-keepers in Bosnia and Herzegovina after war broke out there was to protect humanitarian activities. That mission has been successfully carried out, thanks to the courage and dedication of the civilian workers concerned but also thanks to the protection, logistics support and other services afforded to them by UNPROFOR. UNPROFOR also deserves credit for its successes in negotiating and helping to implement cease-fires and other military arrangements, often of a local nature, without which many people alive today would be dead and material destruction would have been even greater. I also count it a gain that the United Nations, Member States and Secretariat alike, have learnt many lessons in Bosnia and Herzegovina whose benefit will become apparent in our future peacemaking and peace-keeping endeavours.

48. The price for the United Nations has, however, been high. Too many United Nations personnel have been killed or suffered crippling injuries. The conflicts in the former Yugoslavia have dominated the Organization's agenda in the peace and security field in recent years and have distorted its peacemaking and peace-keeping efforts at the expense of other parts of the world. At the time of peak deployment, in August 1995, the former Yugoslavia accounted for nearly 70 per cent of peacekeepers world wide and over two thirds of peace-keeping cost. I therefore welcome the fact the Member States have decided that the vast task of helping to implement the Peace Agreement in Bosnia and Herzegovina should not be entrusted to the United Nations alone. Only a cooperative effort between many international organizations and Mem-

ber States can generate the skills and resources and, above all, the political will required to end the fighting and start building the peace in Bosnia and Herzegovina.

49. In the present report, as requested by the Security Council, I have set out proposals concerning a variety of ways in which the United Nations can make its contribution to this common effort. The most important of them are in the fields of humanitarian relief and return of refugees, where UNHCR is well placed to continue and develop the work it has been doing from the outset, and civilian police, where the parties have asked the United Nations to deploy a United Nations civilian police force greater than any previously seen. In both cases, I am confident that the United Nations has the ability to perform the tasks assigned to it, provided that the parties cooperate and provided that Member States make available the resources that will be necessary. In the case of UNHCR, that will primarily mean financial resources, voluntarily contributed. In case of the International Police Task Force, it will mean not only financial resources, which will have to be obtained through assessed contributions if the Force is to be deployed in time, but also human resources in the form of trained and experienced police officers. I urge Member States to respond promptly and generously to these requirements.

Notes and Questions

1. *International Involvement in Bosnia.* One is struck by the variety of states and international organizations involved in Bosnia with what might be regarded primarily as a tragic domestic civil war. In addition to the United Nations and its various agencies, NATO, the International Conference on the Former Yugoslavia, the Organization for Security and Cooperation in Europe, the European Union, the Council of Europe, the European Bank for Reconstruction and Development, and the World Bank all have played roles in the Bosnian conflict. Diplomats from several states also have been involved in mediation efforts, and approximately two dozen states from different parts of the world contributed troops to UNPROFOR.

2. *After the Dayton Accords.* As the Secretary–General notes, the United Nations will continue to be involved in Bosnia, particularly providing humanitarian assistance. The "international police task force" called for in one of the Dayton Accord annexes involves the United Nations in traditional peace-keeping functions, such as monitoring, observing, and giving advice. Why, however, was the United Nations itself not given the military role that IFOR has assumed, a role that was considered necessary as part of the peace accords? Some observers have criticized the U.N.'s and Europe's pre-Dayton "attempt at limited but impartial involvement," believing that it delayed or complicated efforts to resolve the fighting in Bosnia. See Richard K. Betts, "The Delusion of Impartial Intervention," *Foreign Affairs*, Vol. 73, No. 6, at 20 (Nov./Dec. 1994). Does a lack of assertiveness by U.N. officials in previous peace-keeping operations explain, in part, the decision to utilize NATO and IFOR? For analyses of various aspects of the Dayton Accords, see "Symposium: The Dayton Agreements: A Breakthrough for Peace and Justice?" 7 *European Journal of International Law* 147 (1996).

3. *Security Council Authorization of IFOR.* Annex 1–A of the General Framework Agreement for Peace in Bosnia and Herzegovina "invited" the U.N. Security Council to adopt a resolution authorizing Member States to establish IFOR. This the Security Council did in Resolution 1031, when it authorized Member States to cooperate with NATO "to establish a multinational implementation force (IFOR) under unified command and control," to "take all necessary measures" to implement and insure compliance with the Annex, and to "take all necessary measures, at the request of IFOR, either in defense of IFOR or to assist the force in carrying out its mission." S.C. Res. 1031 (1995), 35 I.L.M. 251, 253 (1996). Why was Security Council authorization of IFOR deemed necessary?

4. *The Role of Regional Organizations in Maintaining International Peace and Security.* Article 53 of the U.N. Charter, which is reproduced in the Appendix, contemplates that the Security Council, "where appropriate," may use regional arrangements or agencies for dealing with matters relating to the maintenance of international peace and security. For NATO itself, involvement in Bosnia represents a change from its original mandate. NATO was originally intended as a vehicle for collective self-defense against the Soviet Union and the Warsaw Pact. With the end of the Cold War, NATO has sought new tasks. See Dick A. Leurdijk, *The United Nations and NATO in Former Yugoslavia: Partners in International Cooperation* (1994); Robert B. McCalla, "NATO's Persistence After the Cold War," 50 *International Organization* 445 (1996).

D. LEGITIMACY AND CONSTITUTIONAL REFORM OF THE SECURITY COUNCIL

The Security Council has become increasingly active and innovative since the end of the Cold War. Relying on Chapter VII of the U.N. Charter, the Council has, as noted in Part C, taken such unprecedented actions as creating a Compensation Commission to determine losses stemming from Iraq's invasion of Kuwait and constituting an International Criminal Tribunal for the Former Yugoslavia. Should Security Council actions be subject to judicial review by the International Court of Justice? Would such review help to enhance the legitimacy of Security Council actions? What else could be done to increase the Security Council's legitimacy, making its measures more acceptable to states that are not permanent members of the Council? We explore such questions in this Part.

THE LOCKERBIE CASE

Case Concerning Questions of Interpretation and Application of the 1971 Montreal Convention Arising From the Aerial Incident at Lockerbie, Libya v. United States, 1992 I.C.J. 114, 1992 WL 190214 (Request for Provisional Measures).

ORDER * * *

Having regard to the Application by the Socialist People's Libyan Arab Jamahiriya (hereinafter called "Libya") filed in the Registry of the

Court on 3 March 1992, instituting proceedings against the United States of America (hereinafter called "the United States") in respect of "a dispute ... between Libya and the United States over the interpretation or application of the Montreal Convention" of 23 September 1971, a dispute arising from acts resulting in the aerial incident that occurred over Lockerbie, Scotland, on 21 December 1988,

Makes the following Order:

1. Whereas by its above-mentioned Application Libya founds the jurisdiction of the Court on Article 36, paragraph 1, of the Statute of the Court and Article 14, paragraph 1, of the Convention for the Suppression of Unlawful Acts Against the Safety of Civil Aviation done at Montreal on 23 September 1971 (referred to hereinafter as the "Montreal Convention"), instruments to which Libya and the United States are both parties;

2. Whereas in its Application Libya refers to the destruction of Pan Am flight 103 on 21 December 1988 over Lockerbie, in Scotland; whereas in its Application Libya further states that

> "On 14 November 1991, a Grand Jury of the United States District Court for the District of Columbia, United States of America, indicted two Libyan nationals (the 'accused') charging, *inter alia*, that they had caused a bomb to be placed aboard [that flight] ... which bomb had exploded causing the aeroplane to crash";

and whereas Libya also refers, in this connection, to Article 1 of the Montreal Convention, contending that the acts alleged by the indictment constitute an offence within the meaning of that provision;

3. Whereas, in its Application, Libya claims that the Montreal Convention is the only appropriate convention in force between the Parties dealing with such offences, and that the United States is bound by its legal obligations under the Montreal Convention, which require it to act in accordance with the Convention, and only in accordance with the Convention, with respect to the matter involving Pan Am flight 103 and the accused;

4. Whereas, in its Application, Libya submits that, while it has itself fully complied with all of its own obligations under the Montreal Convention, the United States has breached and is continuing to breach its obligations to Libya under Article 5, paragraph 2, Article 5, paragraph 3, Article 7, Article 8, paragraph 2, and Article 11 of the Convention which provide as follows:

> "*Article 5*....
>
> 2. Each Contracting State shall likewise take such measures as may be necessary to establish its jurisdiction over the offences mentioned in Article 1, paragraph 1 *(a), (b)* and *(c)*, and in Article 1, paragraph 2, in so far as that paragraph relates to those offences, in the case where the alleged offender is present in its territory and it does not extradite him pursuant to Article 8 to any of the States mentioned in paragraph 1 of this Article.

3. This Convention does not exclude any criminal jurisdiction exercised in accordance with national law."

"*Article 7.* The Contracting State in the territory of which the alleged offender is found shall, if it does not extradite him, be obliged, without exception whatsoever and whether or not the offence was committed in its territory, to submit the case to its competent authorities for the purpose of prosecution. Those authorities shall take their decision in the same manner as in the case of any ordinary offence of a serious nature under the law of that State."

"*Article 8*. . . .

2. If a Contracting State which makes extradition conditional on the existence of a treaty receives a request for extradition from another Contracting State with which it has no extradition treaty, it may at its option consider this Convention as the legal basis for extradition in respect of the offences. Extradition shall be subject to the other conditions provided by the law of the requested State. * * *"

"*Article 11.* 1. Contracting States shall afford one another the greatest measure of assistance in connection with criminal proceedings brought in respect of the offences. The law of the State requested shall apply in all cases.

2. The provisions of paragraph 1 of this Article shall not affect obligations under any other treaty, bilateral or multilateral, which governs or will govern, in whole or in part, mutual assistance in criminal matters";

5. Whereas it is stated in the Application that at the time the charge was communicated to Libya, or shortly thereafter, the accused were present in the territory of Libya; that after being apprised of the charge, Libya took such measures as were necessary to establish its jurisdiction over the offences charged, pursuant to Article 5, paragraph 2, of the Montreal Convention; that Libya also took measures to ensure the presence of the accused in Libya in order to enable criminal proceedings to be instituted, that it initiated a preliminary enquiry into the facts and that it submitted the case to its competent authorities for the purpose of prosecution; that Libya has not extradited the accused, there being no extradition treaty in force between it and the United States, and no basis for the extradition of the accused under Article 8, paragraph 2, of the Montreal Convention, since this provision subjects extradition to the law of the requested State and Libyan law prohibits the extradition of Libyan nationals; and that, pursuant to Article 11, paragraph 1, of the Montreal Convention, Libya has sought judicial assistance from the United States in connection with the criminal proceedings instituted by Libya, with the competent Libyan authorities offering to co-operate with the investigations in the United States or in other countries, but that the United States together with its law enforce-

ment officials have refused to co-operate in any respect with the Libyan investigations;

6. Whereas it is further alleged in the Application of the Libyan Government that the United States has clearly shown that it is not interested in proceeding within the framework of the Montreal Convention but on the contrary is intent on compelling the surrender to it of the accused, in violation of the provisions of that Convention; * * *

11. Whereas Libya, considering that the Court's jurisdiction in the case was prima facie established under the Montreal Convention, submitted that there were no impediments to indicating provisional measures and accordingly requested the Court to indicate forthwith provisional measures:

"*(a)* to enjoin the United States from taking any action against Libya calculated to coerce or compel Libya to surrender the accused individuals to any jurisdiction outside of Libya; and

(b) to ensure that no steps are taken that would prejudice in any way the rights of Libya with respect to the legal proceedings that are the subject of Libya's Application;" * * *

28. Whereas the United States * * * contended that the Security Council was actively seised of the situation which was the subject of the Application and that therefore the Court should not indicate provisional measures;

29. Whereas the United States further contended that the requested provisional measures were improperly directed to restraining action in the Security Council, including participation by Member States;

30. Whereas, following on the charges brought by a Grand Jury of the United States District Court for the District of Columbia against the two Libyan nationals in connection with the destruction of Pan Am flight 103, the United States and the United Kingdom issued on 27 November 1991 the following joint declaration:

"The British and American Governments today declare that the Government of Libya must:

— surrender for trial all those charged with the crime; and accept responsibility for the actions of Libyan officials;

— disclose all it knows of this crime, including the names of all those responsible, and allow full access to all witnesses, documents and other material evidence, including all the remaining timers;

— pay appropriate compensation.

We expect Libya to comply promptly and in full";

31. Whereas the subject of that declaration was subsequently considered by the United Nations Security Council, which on 21 January 1992 adopted resolution 731 (1992), of which the paragraphs here material read as follows:

"*The Security Council,*

Deeply disturbed by the world-wide persistence of acts of international terrorism in all its forms, including those in which States are directly or indirectly involved, which endanger or take innocent lives, have a deleterious effect on international relations and jeopardize the security of States,

Deeply concerned by all illegal activities directed against international civil aviation, and affirming the right of all States, in accordance with the Charter of the United Nations and relevant principles of international law, to protect their nationals from acts of international terrorism that constitute threats to international peace and security, . . .

Deeply concerned over the results of investigations, which implicate officials of the Libyan Government and which are contained in Security Council documents that include the requests addressed to the Libyan authorities by France, the United Kingdom of Great Britain and Northern Ireland and the United States of America in connection with the legal procedures related to the attacks carried out against Pan American flight 103 and Union de transports aériens flight 772; . . .

2. *Strongly deplores* the fact that the Libyan Government has not yet responded effectively to the above requests to cooperate fully in establishing responsibility for the terrorist acts referred to above against Pan American flight 103 and Union de transports aériens flight 772;

3. *Urges* the Libyan Government immediately to provide a full and effective response to those requests so as to contribute to the elimination of international terrorism;

32. Whereas in the course of the oral proceedings reference was made by both sides to the possibility of sanctions being imminently imposed by the Security Council on Libya in order to require it, *inter alia*, to surrender the accused to the United States or the United Kingdom;

33. Whereas Libya contended that provisional measures were urgently required in order to cause the United States to abstain from any action capable of having a prejudicial effect on the Court's decision in the case, and more specifically to refrain from taking any initiative within the Security Council for the purpose of impairing that right to exercise jurisdiction, which Libya asks the Court to recognize;

34. Whereas on 31 March 1992 (three days after the close of the hearings) the Security Council adopted resolution 748 (1992) stating *inter alia* that the Security Council:

" . . . *Deeply concerned* that the Libyan Government has still not provided a full and effective response to the requests in its resolution 731 (1992) of 21 January 1992,

Convinced that the suppression of acts of international terrorism, including those in which States are directly or indirectly involved, is essential for the maintenance of international peace and security, . . .

Determining, in this context, that the failure by the Libyan Government to demonstrate by concrete actions its renunciation of terrorism and in particular its continued failure to respond fully and effectively to the requests in resolution 731 (1992) constitute a threat to international peace and security, . . .

Acting under Chapter VII of the Charter,

1. *Decides* that the Libyan Government must now comply without any further delay with paragraph 3 of resolution 731 (1992) regarding the requests contained in documents S/23306, S/23308 and S/23309;

2. *Decides also* that the Libyan Government must commit itself definitively to cease all forms of terrorist action and all assistance to terrorist groups and that it must promptly, by concrete actions, demonstrate its renunciation of terrorism;

3. *Decides* that, on 15 April 1992 all States shall adopt the measures set out below, which shall apply until the Security Council decides that the Libyan Government has complied with paragraphs 1 and 2 above; . . .

7. *Calls upon* all States, including States not members of the United Nations, and all international organizations, to act strictly in accordance with the provisions of the present resolution, notwithstanding the existence of any rights or obligations conferred or imposed by any international agreement or any contract entered into or any license or permit granted prior to 15 April 1992";

35. Whereas, by a letter of 2 April 1992, a copy of which was transmitted to Libya by the Registrar, the Agent of the United States drew the Court's attention to the adoption of Security Council resolution 748 (1992) the text of which he enclosed; and whereas, in that letter, the Agent stated:

"That resolution, adopted pursuant to Chapter VII of the United Nations Charter, 'decides that the Libyan Government must now comply without any further delay with paragraph 3 of resolution 731 (1992) of 21 January 1992 regarding the requests contained in documents S/23306, S/23308 and S/23309.' It will be recalled that the referenced requests include the request that Libya surrender the two Libyan suspects in the bombing of Pan Am flight 103 to the United States or to the United Kingdom. For this additional reason, the United States maintains its submission of 28 March 1992 that the request of the Government of the Great Socialist People's Libyan Arab Jamahiriya for the indication of provisional measures of protection should be denied, and that no such measures should be indicated"; * * *

38. Whereas in its observations on Security Council resolution 748 (1992) presented in response to the Court's invitation, Libya contends as follows: first, that that resolution does not prejudice the rights of Libya to request the Court to indicate provisional measures, inasmuch as by deciding, in effect, that Libya must surrender its nationals to the United States and the United Kingdom, the Security Council infringes, or threatens to infringe, the enjoyment and the exercise of the rights conferred on Libya by the Montreal Convention and its economic, commercial and diplomatic rights; whereas Libya therefore claims that the United States and the United Kingdom should so act as not to infringe Libya's rights, for example by seeking a suspension of the relevant part of resolution 748 (1992);

39. Whereas Libya in its observations contends, secondly, that the risk of contradiction between the resolution and the provisional measures requested of the Court by Libya does not render the Libyan request inadmissible, since there is in law no competition or hierarchy between the Court and the Security Council, each exercising its own competence; whereas Libya recalls in this connection that it regards the decision of the Security Council as contrary to international law, and considers that the Council has employed its power to characterize the situation for purposes of Chapter VII simply as a pretext to avoid applying the Montreal Convention.

40. Whereas in its observations on Security Council resolution 748 (1992), presented in response to the Court's invitation, the United States observes that resolution was adopted under Chapter VII rather than Chapter VI of the Charter and was framed as a "decision" and contended that, given that binding decision, no object would be served by provisional measures; that, irrespective of the right claimed by Libya under the Montreal Convention, Libya has a Charter-based duty to accept and carry out the decisions in the resolution, and other States have a Charter-based duty to seek Libya's compliance; that any indication of provisional measures would run a serious risk of conflicting with the work of the Security Council; that the Council had rejected (*inter alia*) Libya's contention that the matter should be addressed on the basis of the right claimed by Libya under the Montreal Convention, which Libya asks the Court to protect through provisional measures; and that the Court should therefore decline the request;

41. Whereas the Court, in the context of the present proceedings on a request for provisional measures, has in accordance with Article 41 of the Statute, to consider the circumstances drawn to its attention as requiring the indication of such measures, but cannot make definitive findings either of fact or of law on the issues relating to the merits, and the right of the Parties to contest such issues at the stage of the merits must remain unaffected by the Court's decision;

42. Whereas both Libya and the United States, as Members of the United Nations, are obliged to accept and carry out the decisions of the Security Council in accordance with Article 25 of the Charter; whereas

the Court, which is at the stage of proceedings on provisional measures, considers that prima facie this obligation extends to the decision contained in resolution 748 (1992); and whereas, in accordance with Article 103 of the Charter, the obligations of the Parties in that respect prevail over their obligations under any other international agreement, including the Montreal Convention;

43. Whereas the Court, while thus not at this stage called upon to determine definitively the legal effect of Security Council resolution 748 (1992), considers that, whatever the situation previous to the adoption of that resolution, the rights claimed by Libya under the Montreal Convention cannot now be regarded as appropriate for protection by the indication of provisional measures;

44. Whereas, furthermore, an indication of the measures requested by Libya would be likely to impair the rights which appear prima facie to be enjoyed by the United States by virtue of Security Council resolution 748 (1992);

45. Whereas, in order to pronounce on the present request for provisional measures, the Court is not called upon to determine any of the other questions which have been raised before it in the present proceedings, including the question of its jurisdiction to entertain the merits of the case; and whereas the decision given in these proceedings in no way prejudges any such question, and leaves unaffected the rights of the Government of Libya and the Government of the United States to submit arguments in respect of any of these questions;

46. For these reasons,

THE COURT,

By eleven votes to five,

Finds that the circumstances of the case are not such as to require the exercise of its power under Article 41 of the Statute to indicate provisional measures.

IN FAVOUR: *Vice President* Oda, *Acting President*; *President* Sir Robert Jennings; *Judges* Lachs, Ago, Schwebel, Ni, Evensen, Tarassov, Guillaume, Shahabuddeen, Aguilar Mawdsley;

AGAINST: *Judges* Bedjaoui, Weeramantry, Ranjeva, Ajibola; *Judge* ad hoc El-Kosheri. * * *

SEPARATE OPINION OF JUDGE LACHS

While concurring in the Court's decision I consider it my duty to place on record certain considerations in respect of the circumstances in which it fell to be taken. Clouded as the circumstances may have been, some legal implications may be ascertained.

In the normal course of events, the request made to the Court in proceedings instituted on the basis of the Montreal Convention would have faced the Court with the necessity of deciding whether a genuine case existed for granting interim measures. However Libya's Application and request were placed before the Court when the Lockerbie catastrophe and the wider problem of international terrorism, which merits condemnation in all its manifestations, were already on the agenda of the Security Council, which had brought them together under the terms of resolution 731 (1992). The Council, by moving onto the terrain of Chapter VII of the Charter, decided certain issues pertaining to the Lockerbie disaster with binding force. Hence problems of jurisdiction and the operation of the *sub judice* principle came into the foreground as never before.

While the Court has the vocation of applying international law as a universal law, operating both within and outside the United Nations, it is bound to respect, as part of that law, the binding decisions of the Security Council. This of course, in the present circumstances, raises issues of concurrent jurisdiction as between the Court and a fellow main organ of the United Nations.

The framers of the Charter, in providing for the existence of several main organs, did not effect a complete separation of powers, nor indeed is one to suppose that such was their aim. Although each organ has been allotted its own Chapter or Chapters, the functions of two of them, namely the General Assembly and the Security Council, also pervade other Chapters than their own. Even the International Court of Justice receives, outside its own Chapter, a number of mentions which tend to confirm its role as the general guardian of legality within the system. In fact the Court is the guardian of legality for the international community as a whole, both within and without the United Nations. One may therefore legitimately suppose that the intention of the founders was not to encourage a blinkered parallelism of functions but a fruitful interaction.

Two of the main organs of the United Nations have the delivery of binding decisions explicitly included in their powers under the Charter: the Security Council and the International Court of Justice. There is no doubt that the Court's task is "to ensure respect for international law ..." It is its principal guardian. Now, it has become clear that the dividing line between political and legal disputes is blurred, as law becomes ever more frequently an integral element of international controversies. The Court, for reasons well known so frequently shunned in the past, is thus called upon to play an ever greater role. Hence it is important for the purposes and principles of the United Nations that the two main organs with specific powers of binding decision act in harmony—though not, of course, in concert—and that each should perform its functions with respect to a situation or dispute, different aspects of which appear on the agenda of each, without prejudicing the exercise of the other's powers. In the present case the Court was faced with a new situation which allowed no room for further analysis nor the indication of effective interim measures. The Order made should not, therefore, be seen as an abdication of the Court's powers; it is rather a reflection of the system within which the Court is called upon to render justice.

Whether or not the sanctions ordered by resolution 748 (1992) have eventually to be applied, it is in any event to be hoped that the two principal organs concerned will be able to operate with due consideration for their mutual involvement in the preservation of the rule of law.

SEPARATE OPINION OF JUDGE SHAHABUDDEEN

The Court's Order is based solely on Security Council resolution 748 (1992). That also is the ground of my concurrence with it. But for that resolution, I should have thought that Libya had presented an arguable case for an indication of interim measures. The resolution now makes it unnecessary to explore the legal elements of Libya's request for such measures. * * *

(i) THE LEGAL BASIS OF THE COURT'S ORDER

Whatever might have been the previous position, resolution 748 (1992) of the Security Council leaves the Court with no conclusion other than that to which it has come. This is the result not of imposition of superior authority—there is none—but of the fact that, in finding the applicable law, the Court must take account of the resolution in so far as it affects the enforceability of the rights for the protection of which Libya is seeking interim measures. The validity of the resolution, though contested by Libya, has, at this stage, to be presumed. Article 25 of the Charter of the United Nations obliges Libya to comply with the decision set out in the resolution. By virtue of Article 103 of the Charter, that obligation prevails over any conflicting treaty obligation which Libya may have. * * *

Several cases demonstrate, in one way or another, that the Court is not precluded from acting by the mere circumstance that the matter in contest is also under consideration by another organ of the United Nations (see, *inter alia, United States Diplomatic and Consular Staff in Tehran, I.C.J. Reports 1980*, p. 22, para. 40). In this case, it happens that the decision which the Court is asked to give is one which would directly conflict with a decision of the Security Council. That is not an aspect which can be overlooked. Yet, it is not the juridical ground of today's Order. This results not from any collision between the competence of the Security Council and that of the Court, but from a collision between the obligations of Libya under the decision of the Security Council and any obligations which it may have under the Montreal Convention. The Charter says that the former prevail. * * *

(iii) IMPLICATIONS OF THE COURT'S ORDER * * *

The question now raised by Libya's challenge to the validity of resolution 748 (1992) is whether a decision of the Security Council may override the legal rights of States, and if so, whether there are any limitations on the power of a decision entailing such consequences. Are there any limits to the Council's powers of appreciation? In the equilibrium of forces underpinning the structure of the United Nations within the evolving international order, is there any conceivable point beyond which a legal issue may properly arise as to the competence of the

Security Council to produce such overriding results? If there are any limits, what are those limits and what body, if other than the Security Council, is competent to say what those limits are?

If the answers to these delicate and complex questions are all in the negative, the position is potentially curious. It would not, on that account, be necessarily unsustainable in law; and how far the Court can enter the field is another matter. The issues are however important, even though they cannot be examined now.

DISSENTING OPINION OF JUDGE WEERAMANTRY * * *

B. THE COURT AND THE SECURITY COUNCIL * * *

General Observations

Created by the same Charter to fulfil in common the Purposes and Principles of the United Nations, the Security Council and the Court are complementary to each other, each performing the special role allotted to it by their common instrument of creation. Both owe loyalty alike to the same instrument which provides their authority and prescribes their goals. As with the great branches of government within a domestic jurisdiction such as the executive and the judiciary, they perform their mission for the common benefit of the greater system of which they are a part. * * *

An important difference must also be noted between the division of powers in municipal systems and the distribution of powers between the principal organs of the United Nations, for there is not among the United Nations organizations the same strict principle of separation of powers one sometimes finds in municipal systems. * * * Nor is there a hierarchical arrangement of the organs of the United Nations * * *.

* * * The Court by virtue of its nature and constitution applies to the matter before it the concepts, the criteria and the methodology of the judicial process which other organs of the United Nations are naturally not obliged to do. The concepts it uses are juridical concepts, its criteria are standards of legality, its method is that of legal proof. Its tests of validity and the bases of its decisions are naturally not the same as they would be before a political or executive organ of the United Nations.

Yet this much they have in common—that all organs alike exercise their authority under and in terms of the Charter. There can never truly be a question of opposition of one organ to another but rather a common subjection of all organs to the Charter. The interpretation of Charter provisions is primarily a matter of law, and such questions of law may in appropriate circumstances come before the Court for judicial determination. When this does occur, the Court acts as guardian of the Charter and of international law for, in the international arena, there is no higher body charged with judicial functions and with the determination of questions of interpretation and application of international law. Anchored to the Charter in particular and to international law in general, the Court considers such legal matters as are properly brought before it and the fact that its judicial decision based upon the law may have political consequences is not a factor that would deflect it from discharging its duties under the Charter of the United Nations and the Statute of the Court.

The Court's Autonomy * * *

* * * [I]t by no means follows * * * that the Court when properly seised of a legal dispute should co-operate with the Security Council to the extent of desisting from exercising its independent judgment on matters of law properly before it. * * *

* * * [T]he fact of Security Council action is only one of the circumstances the Court would take into account and is by no means conclusive. Since the Court and the Security Council may properly exercise their respective functions with regard to an international dispute or situation, each must in the exercise of the undoubted authority conferred on it exercise its independent judgment in accordance with the Charter. It follows that their assessment of a given situation will not always be in complete coincidence. Especially where matters of legal interpretation are involved, the Court will naturally zealously preserve its independence of judgment, for to do any less would not be a proper compliance with the requirements of the Charter. * * *

The Powers of the Security Council

The submission before us relating to the exercise of Security Council powers in adopting resolution 731 (1992) calls for a brief examination of those powers from a strictly legal point of view. * * *

[The Security Council] is charged under Article 24 with the primary responsibility for the maintenance of international peace and security and has a mandate from all Member States to act on their behalf in this regard. By Article 25, all Members agree to accept and carry out its decisions.

Chapter VI entrusts it with powers and responsibilities in regard to settlement of disputes, and Chapter VII gives it very special powers when it determines the existence of any threat to the peace, breach of the peace or act of aggression. Such determination is a matter entirely within its discretion.

With these provisions should be read Article 103 of the Charter which states that in the event of a conflict between the obligations of the Members of the United Nations under the Charter and their obligations under any international agreement, their obligations under the Charter shall prevail. Seeing that Security Council decisions are to be accepted and carried out by all Member States, the obligations thus created are given priority by Article 103 over obligations under any other agreement.

All this amounts to enormous power indeed and international law as embodied in the Charter requires all States to recognize this power and act according to the directions issuing from it.

But does this mean that the Security Council discharges its variegated functions free of all limitations, or is there a circumscribing boundary of norms or principles within which its responsibilities are to be discharged?

Article 24 itself offers us an immediate signpost to such a circumscribing boundary when it provides in Article 24(2) that the Security Council, in discharging its duties under Article 24(1), "*shall* act in accordance with the Purposes and Principles of the United Nations." The duty is imperative and the limits are categorically stated. The Preamble stresses *inter alia* the determination of the peoples of the United Nations to establish conditions under which respect for the obligations arising from treaties and other sources of international law can be maintained. * * *

Chapters VI and VII of the Charter * * *

* * * It is not for this Court to sit in review on a given resolution of the Security Council but it is within the competence of the Court and indeed its very function to determine any matters properly brought before it in accordance with international law. Consequently, the Court will determine what the law is that is applicable to the case in hand and would not be deflected from this course by a resolution under Chapter VI.

However, once we enter the sphere of Chapter VII, the matter takes on a different complexion, for the determination under Article 39 of the existence of any threat to the peace, breach of the peace or act of aggression, is one entirely within the discretion of the Council. It would appear that the Council and no other is the judge of the existence of the state of affairs which brings Chapter VII into operation. That decision is taken by the Security Council in its own judgment and in the exercise of the full discretion given to it by Article 39. Once taken, the door is opened to the various decisions the Council may make under that Chapter.

Thus, any matter which is the subject of a valid Security Council decision under Chapter VII does not appear, prima facie, to be one with which the Court can properly deal. * * *

Resolution 748 (1992) * * *

However, in my respectful view, it does not necessarily follow that the binding nature of resolution 748 (1992) renders it inappropriate for the Court to indicate provisional measures. I arrive at this conclusion after a careful perusal of all the provisions of resolution 748 (1992). There still seems to be room, while preserving full respect for resolution 748 (1992) in all its integrity, for the Court to frame an appropriate measure *propio motu* which in no way contradicts resolution 748 (1992), Article 25 or Article 103 of the Charter.

Notes and Questions

1. *International Litigation and the Crash of Pan Am Flight 103.* The 1988 crash of Pan Am flight 103, which killed 259 passengers and 11 people on the ground in Lockerbie, Scotland, led to a spate of litigation in addition to the proceedings before the ICJ. The two Libyans suspected of planting the bomb on the aircraft were indicted on criminal charges in the United States and Great Britain. The estates of the passengers filed civil suits in the United States against Pan Am and other defendants, alleging negligent and willful failure to provide adequate security services on flight 103. Trials, appeals, and settlement negotiations have been protracted. See Andrew Blum, "Court Chides Insurers in Pan Am Bomb Case; Federal Judge Says He's Been 'Fooled Too Often,' Suggests Bad Faith Delays Settlement," *National Law Journal,* Nov. 28, 1994, at A7. Pan Am and the estates of some of the passengers also filed separate civil suits against Libya in the United States and Scotland. Andrew Blum, "Pan Am, Insurer Sue Libya for $375 Million," *National Law Journal*, Dec. 27, 1993, at 6. Proceedings in municipal courts often raise international legal issues concerning the scope of a country's judicial jurisdiction, how attorneys can obtain evidence from abroad, whether one country's laws apply to events that do not take place entirely within that country, and whether foreign sovereigns may be sued in another country's courts. We take up such issues in Chapter 10.

2. *Security Council Action Against Libya.* In Resolution 748, the Security Council adopted requests from France, the United Kingdom, and the United States, and decided that Libya was obliged to extradite two of its nationals to the United States or the United Kingdom. Was this action legitimate? Libya claimed that its obligations with respect to any extradition request were governed by the 1971 Montreal Convention for the Suppression of Unlawful Acts against the Safety of Civil Aviation, which, Libya argued, did not mandate extradition in this situation. Commentators have observed that a state has no legal duty to extradite, unless it has accepted such a duty by treaty. See 1 *Oppenheim's International Law* §§ 415–424 (9th ed. by Robert Jennings & Arthur Watts, 1992).

The Security Council has tightened its sanctions against Libya. In November 1993, it adopted Resolution 883, which required a ban on sales to Libya of petroleum refining and exporting equipment, a freeze on Libya's overseas financial assets, and additional restrictions on flights to and from Libya. The Security Council reviews the sanctions against Libya every four months. As of December 1996, the sanctions had not been lifted.

3. *ICJ Provisional Judgments.* Note that the International Court of Justice in the *Lockerbie Case* issues only a provisional judgment, in accordance with Article 41 of the Court's Statute (see Appendix). The fact that the decision is a preliminary one does not dissuade the judges from writing numerous separate and dissenting opinions. Four years after this provisional decision, the ICJ had not yet reached a decision on the merits of the case brought by Libya.

4. *Judicial Review of Security Council Decisions?* Do the ICJ judges in the *Lockerbie Case* endorse the supremacy of Security Council decisions over all treaty and other international legal rights? Do they instead establish

that the ICJ would, in an appropriate case, declare Security Council decisions illegal? Or are the judges trying to signal the Security Council to exercise more self-restraint itself?

Dissenting Judge ad hoc El–Kosheri goes so far as to describe paragraph 1 of Security Council Resolution 748 as *ultra vires*. 1992 I.C.J. at 210. Other judges, however, have been reluctant to define specifically the Court's role in supervising the legality of Security Council action. See Mohammed Bedjaoui, *The New World Order and the Security Council: Testing the Legality of its Acts* (1994). What explains this reluctance? A belief that "judicial review" would give "unrepresentative" ICJ judges too much power? That either articles in the U.N. Charter or *jus cogens* norms are too indeterminate to enable the Court to review an act of another U.N. organ? That the Court lacks the stature to be sure that a decision that challenged the legality of Security Council acts would be respected? That the process of determining the nature and effects of "judicial review" is a long, evolutionary one? See Jose E. Alvarez, "Judging the Security Council," 90 *American Journal of International Law* 1 (1996).

Two provisions in the Court's Statute may limit the Court's role in interpreting or reviewing the validity of Security Council resolutions in contentious cases. First, the Court must have grounds for jurisdiction under Article 36. Second, according to Article 59 the decision in a contentious case binds only the parties; a Security Council decision, on the other hand, may bind all Member States. See Articles 25, 48, and 103 of the U.N. Charter. What are the possibilities for review of the legality of Security Council actions in advisory opinions?

5. *The Legitimacy of Security Council Decisions*. Apart from possible ICJ decisions construing Security Council actions, what limits the Security Council's power to take action against a Member State? What restrictions are suggested in the text of the U.N. Charter? What limits are built into the way the Security Council operates?

These questions relate to a broader inquiry into the legitimacy of Security Council actions. It is possible to think about the relationship between the ICJ and the Security Council, for example, by asking how the ICJ can contribute to the legitimacy of Security Council actions. Certainly, a perception of illegitimacy can have practical consequences. If states regard Security Council sanctions toward Libya as illegitimate, for example, they may ignore them. The last reading in this chapter addresses current concerns about the Security Council, and the last set of Notes and Questions asks what steps could assuage concerns about the legitimacy of Security Council actions.

JOSE E. ALVAREZ, "THE ONCE AND FUTURE SECURITY COUNCIL"

18 *The Washington Quarterly*, No. 2, at 3 (Spring 1995).

The post-cold war revival of the United Nations (UN) Security Council has come with a price: many UN members are questioning the Council's legitimacy and calling for its restructuring. * * *

IS THE COUNCIL OUT OF CONTROL? * * *

The [UN Charter] scheme has *never* worked precisely as intended. When, in the absence of the then Soviet Union, the Council managed to authorize force in Korea and delegated that authority to forces under the command of the United States, legal purists questioned whether the invasion by North Korea of the South was truly an instance of interstate aggression or was in reality an intervention in a civil war. Others demurred on the grounds that use of the UN flag was too easily delegated to the United States, without special agreements committing troops to the UN and without real supervision by the Military Staff Committee. Similarly, when the Council imposed sanctions on Rhodesia in 1966 and 1968, Dean Acheson, among others, demurred on the grounds that controversy over the legitimacy of the then Rhodesian government did not constitute a threat to the "international peace" and that therefore the Council's action was an illegal intervention in a state's domestic affairs.

But the cold war exercise of the veto meant that few had to worry about these legal qualms. Today the almost defunct organ largely unable to react to the most direct breaches of the international peace during the Cold War has become an entity capable of finding an "international threat to the peace" or "breach of the peace" in unexpected, not to say strange, places: in the context of conflicts *within* states (e.g., Somalia and, some would say, at least initially in the former Yugoslavia); because of ostensible threats to the human rights of a state's own citizens (e.g., the Kurds in Iraq); because of a state's refusal to surrender its own nationals accused of terrorism (Libya); or because a military elite has failed to respect the results of a UN-supervised election (Haiti). Further, the entity that had only rarely in 45 years authorized the use of force, has now, in the few years since the end of the Cold War, managed to delegate away the authority to use force in its name on several occasions—explicitly in Haiti and on the occasion of the Persian Gulf War—and implicitly in Somalia, post-Gulf war Iraq, and the former Yugoslavia. Yet, despite the increasing resort to force and its variants (such as the use of "peacekeepers" to track down a warlord in Somalia), articles 43 to 45 in the Charter remain effectively unimplemented: special agreements to allocate forces to the organization are not in place and neither is there an effective Military Staff Committee to oversee UN use of force. * * *

THE UN'S EMERGING DEMOCRATIC DEFICIT

Joseph Weiler has suggested that the making of law by international bodies, as in the European Union, appears to follow a peculiar dynamic: successful international organizations evolve into effective lawmaking institutions when members forgo their sovereign option to "exit" (either totally or selectively) and opt instead to correct the organization's inadequacies by exercising a greater "voice" in that organization's decision-making processes. Weiler argues that the more an international organization successfully "legislates," in the sense of the promulgation of rules that are binding both on and within states, the more members become conscious of the need to assert themselves in the organization's ways of making law, for instance, by keeping tighter "democratic" control over their executive branch representatives to that organization.

Although the UN is a long way from becoming the effective lawmaking institution that the European Union now is, the Council is issuing purportedly binding edicts on a regular basis and other parts of the UN are also showing signs of waking up from their cold war quiescence. And the more the organization "legislates," the more its members, particularly those without the veto, see possible threats to their "sovereignty." Recent claims within the UN for greater "democratic accountability" replicate, at a modest level, Weiler's exit and voice dynamic. Such demands, like those from states whose economies are dramatically affected by the UN's penchant for economic sanctions targeting their trading partners, stem from an increased realization that what the organization, and especially the Council, is doing *matters* to them.

Such demands also originate from pressures internal to governments—from nongovernmental interest groups and others affected by UN action. Council decisions are beginning to have a direct impact on individuals and corporations and not merely on their governments. An individual charged with a crime before an international tribunal created by the Council, the business whose contract for exports of goods to Iraq or Libya is breached at the Council's direction, the consumer who cannot get an imported product because of a decision by a sanctions committee, or the corporation whose claim against Iraq is dismissed because of a decision by the Compensation Commission, all have an interest in the Council's decisions and are beginning to articulate those interests * * *.
* * *

Amelioration of the emerging democratic deficit problems will, over the long term, require something more than the addition of two or three members to the Council. * * * General Assembly * * * proposals for greater coordination and consultation with the Assembly both prior to and after significant Council action * * * have a respectable lineage.
* * *

One approach, suggested by Michael Reisman, would be the formation of a "Chapter VII Consultation Committee" of 21 members of the Assembly. Under Reisman's proposal, the Council would immediately notify this committee whenever it planned to move into a chapter VII mode. The secretary general and the president of the Council would promptly meet with the committee to share information and solicit its views. Throughout the crisis, the Council and committee would remain in constant contact in the best tradition of "consultation" as understood in international law and practice. The Assembly would not have a veto over Council action, but at the same time its participation would extend beyond a right to mere notification. Such institutionalized give-and-take would facilitate a greater sense of participation and endow final Council decisions with the imprimatur, the legitimacy, of the larger world community. * * *

Less radical but no less useful may be more modest changes to the Council's now overly secretive "informal consultations." The Council, which did not hold a single meeting during the first four weeks of the 1991 air war over Iraq, needs to consider, as do all public bodies, the need for public accountability. Although much that goes on within the Council may need to remain confidential, especially in the midst of an ongoing crisis, at a minimum, states particularly affected by the imposition of economic sanctions or states that would be expected to contribute troops to a contemplated mission should be invited to Council deliberations before decisions are made—as is anticipated in articles 44 and 50 of the Charter. The Council also needs to take more seriously its duty to report to the Assembly; such reports should be more timely and include substantive discussions of the issues. They should not merely list Council decisions. After a crisis is over, the Council could seek the advice of others as to controversial issues likely to arise again.

THE SECURITY COUNCIL'S NORMATIVE DEFICITS

But the Security Council and the United States need to address not only *how* the Council undertakes decisions, but *what* decisions it undertakes. What is in doubt is the substance of its decisions, not only the procedures behind them.

The purported legal justifications offered for the Council's involvement in the Haiti situation suggest one major substantive issue: the Council has not come up with an alternative to interstate aggression as a raison d'etre likely to be coherent over the long term. To date it has given no principled answer—apart from realpolitik—to those who would ask why the Council chose to act in some cases falling short of manifest interstate aggression but not in other cases of arguable violation of the Charter. Why Libya and Haiti but not Israel, Cuba, or North Korea? Particularly to those unable to exercise a veto over these decisions, these Council actions—not to mention cases of Council inaction—pose increasingly difficult issues of normative justification.

The scope of recent peace operations suggests another set of normative gaps. * * * As the second stage of UN operations in Somalia showed, increasingly today "peacekeepers" are being sent where there is no peace to keep, where there is no host state to give consent to their presence, and where the rules of engagement anticipate the use of force in instances other than self-defense.

* * * [T]he Council is a lawmaking institution * * *. When it acts under chapter VII, the Council is authorized to make binding law that can be invoked against members of the UN and even non-members. In the cases discussed above and in others the Council purports to act to enforce the rule of law and purports to be subject to the rule of law. It also purports to act in a judicial manner. Council decisions "determine" that Iraq, Libya, Serbia, and Montenegro have violated international law in specific ways, invoke treaty authority to render judgment, and invite

the international community to judge the Council as if it were a court or legislature. States are encouraged to judge the Council's actions—which after all constitute precedents for the interpretation of the Charter—in the same way all laws are judged: by their textual clarity, consonance with other rules of general application, the match between deed and sanction, and the impartiality of application. When on close examination the Council's actions fail to meet these requisites, when no rule emerges to explain what the Council is doing or how its action comports with the Charter, including its principles, states are entitled to legalistic doubts. * * *

Today the Council sometimes goes beyond the immediate need to defuse a threat to international peace and security. At times it is attempting to adjudicate legal disputes and impose long-term legal solutions (as with Iraq on weapons, financial liability, and boundaries); trying to alter (or progressively develop) established law (as with the regime to "extradite or prosecute" terrorists and possibly with respect to war crimes); or trying itself to apply (or create) principles of international law (as through its delegated body to adjudicate claims against Iraq). Arguably nothing in the Charter precludes these actions. Indeed, back in 1945, the United States argued that the Council had two functions: the "political function" of taking enforcement action and a "quasi-judicial" function of settling disputes. It argued that the veto applied only to the first type of action and that every nation "large or small" should abstain from voting on disputes to which it was a party. Although the United States' promise not to deploy its veto and to abstain from voting all but died with the Cold War, the premise that the Council can successfully carry out this dual role is with us yet again.

Revival of the no-veto/abstention promise might yet make the Council's claim to "quasi-judicial" status credible, but this is dubious. The Council is preeminently a reactive, political forum apt to act on the basis of short-term needs, not long-term judicious (or judicial) perspective. Council representatives do not necessarily consider the broader legal consequences of what they do. This is probably as it must and should be, because the enforcer of the international peace must be political. A decision to act or to refuse to act in a case like Bosnia needs to consider factors other than the establishment of legal precedents pleasing to law professors. Council decisions are often the product of political horse-trading and compromise. No amount of tinkering in its membership is likely to turn the Council into an impartial court or a deliberative "lawmaking" body like the International Law Commission.

Yet, if at least some of the doubts now entertained about the Council are due to its tendency to assume a greater quasi-judicial role than is warranted by the existing threat to the peace, there are ways to defuse these doubts. The Council cannot and should not avoid taking legally binding decisions. The Council's legal determination that Iraq's purported annexation of Kuwait is "null and void," for instance, is part of its job. It can, however, consciously exercise some restraint and leave to more appropriate bodies the task of defining and applying the law. In other instances, when the Council has either no or only a dubious normative justification for doing what it is doing, it should reconsider the wisdom of doing it. * * *

CONCLUSION

UN Security Council decisions, like all of international law, are ultimately made effective by collective legitimation. Council sanctions have not always been faithfully enforced, and unless measures are taken to expand the sense of participation there may well be a progressive deterioration in the effectiveness of these and other Council decisions or, at a minimum, direct conflict between institutional organs—as is suggested by General Assembly resolutions that have criticized the Council's continued arms embargo for Bosnia. To avoid the fate of its illustrious but failed predecessor, the League of Nations, the UN needs to shore up its floundering legitimacy. Restructuring the Council is part of that task, but such restructuring must be pursued with a broader vision of the final goal.

From a Western lawyer's perspective, the Council's current dilemma is predictable. A Charter that puts at the helm unreviewable political authority with no competing political or judicial check may indeed be the basis of a workable system but it is not, as has been suggested, a constitution worthy of the name. Yet if there is to be a "new world order" based on the rule of law, it is difficult to see how that world can come about except through some approximation of such a constitutional system.

In its stead, the Council is flexing its legal muscles, and no other entity—certainly not the General Assembly and not the ICJ—has yet emerged as an acceptable check or balance on Council action.

Notes and Questions

1. *Changes Affecting the Security Council.* World politics has changed dramatically since 1945, when the United Nations was formed with the United States, Great Britain, France, China, and the Soviet Union as permanent members of the Security Council. Japan and Germany, in ruins after World War II, have emerged as major economic powers. Many new states have gained independence; the United Nations began with 51 Member States, but as of December 1996, membership stood at 185.

Since 1945, however, only a few changes have affected the structure and composition of the Security Council. In 1971, the government of the People's Republic of China replaced that of the government of the Republic of China (Taiwan) in the United Nations, and the PRC took the "Chinese seat" on the Security Council. The Russian Federation took over the seat of the Soviet Union in 1991, following the breakup of the Soviet Union. The U.N. Charter was amended in 1965, so that the membership of the Security Council now totals 15 states, rather than the original 11; nine votes are now required to adopt resolutions, rather than seven. There have been no changes, however, in the permanent member veto system.

2. *Enhancing the Legitimacy of the Security Council.* What changes in the composition of the Security Council, if any, would enhance its legitimacy? Should the veto power be changed? Should more states become members of the Security Council? If so, how many? Should any new members, say Germany and Japan, be made permanent members, with or without a veto?

One of the criticisms of the Security Council has been that too many of its deliberations are carried out in secret, and that Security Council decision making should become more "transparent." What are the prospects for enhancing the legitimacy of Security Council actions through greater transparency, more consultations with the General Assembly or with states affected by Security Council actions, or other nonstructural changes? See Michael C. Wood, "Security Council Working Methods and Procedure: Recent Developments," 45 *International & Comparative Law Quarterly* 150 (1996).

3. *Enhancing the Effectiveness of the Security Council.* Would changes that enhance the legitimacy of the Security Council allow it to act more or less effectively than it now does in order to help maintain international peace and security?

Chapter 9

INTERNATIONAL REGIMES AND COMMON SPACES

Common spaces are jurisdictions regulated by many or all states, in which all states have similar rights and duties. Arrangements said to be "international regimes" cover common spaces. An international regime encompasses the various rules, policies, and international institutions related to an international area.[1] More particularly, international regimes relating to a common space typically involve treaty-based settlements that define the common space's status for treaty parties, and have implications for other international actors as well. International organizations often have roles in regimes concerning international common spaces. This chapter examines international legal arrangements respecting Antarctica, outer space, the seas, and the environment.

A. ANTARCTICA

Ice-covered Antarctica, with its harsh and bitterly cold climate, has no indigenous human population. Some states have made territorial claims to portions of the continent, but other states have not generally recognized them.

What then is the nature of the legal regime governing Antarctica? The basic structure of the regime for Antarctica was laid out in the 1959 Antarctic Treaty. Additional treaties that regulate activities in Antarctica also have been negotiated, and the Treaty's Consultative Parties have issued approximately 200 Recommendations on such topics as meteorology, the environment, natural resources, tourism, and telecommunications. The readings that follow explore the evolution of the regime governing Antarctica, its effectiveness, and potential alternatives to it.

1. One standard source defines "regimes" as "sets of implicit or explicit principles, norms, rules, and decision-making procedures around which actors' expectations converge in a given area of international relations." Stephen D. Krasner, "Structural Causes and Regime Consequences: Regimes as Intervening Variables," in *International Regimes* 1, 2 (Stephen D. Krasner ed. 1992).

1. CLAIMS OF SOVEREIGNTY IN ANTARCTICA AND THE ANTARCTIC TREATY

In the nineteenth and early twentieth centuries, European explorers laid claim to parts of Antarctica on behalf of their states. For example, a 1929 royal commission by Great Britain's King George to the explorer Douglas Mawson authorized him "to take possession in Our name, during the course of the expedition presently to be conducted to the Antarctic regions * * * of such territories now unknown as may be discovered in the course of the aforesaid expedition, and further of certain territories not under the sovereignty of any other State which have been discovered in the past by subjects of Our Royal Predecessors or of Ourself * * *." Mawson's sailing instructions required him to conduct surveys and scientific investigations. In addition, Mawson was instructed to "plant the British flag wherever you find it practicable to do so, and in doing so you will read the proclamation of annexation * * *, attach a copy of the proclamation to the flagstaff, and place a second copy of the proclamation in a tin at the foot of the flagstaff. You will keep a record of each such act of annexation * * *." Reprinted in A. Grenfell Price, *The Winning of Australian Antarctica: Mawson's B.A.N.Z.A.R.E. Voyages 1929–31*, at 22–24 (1962).

After states laid claim to portions of Antarctica, they occasionally debated the nature and validity of their asserted sovereignty in diplomatic exchanges. For example, the British ambassador in Washington and the U.S. Secretary of State exchanged notes on the issue in 1934. In the British note, the ambassador expressed concern about U.S. airplane flights over, and the establishment of a wireless station and postal facilities in, the Ross Dependency, which is now the area of Antarctica claimed by New Zealand. If the United States were to establish a post office in this area or to sanction the use of U.S. postage stamps there without permission, the British ambassador claimed, "such acts could not be regarded otherwise than as infringing the British sovereignty and New Zealand administrative rights in the dependency as well as the laws there in force." The following excerpt picks up the story.

GREEN HAYWOOD HACKWORTH, *DIGEST OF INTERNATIONAL LAW*

Vol. I, at 457–59 (1940).

On November 14, 1934 the following informal note was sent to the British Ambassador:

> Referring to your recent inquiry, I beg to inform you that so far as I am advised the only action taken by my Government relative to the Byrd Expedition to the Antarctic since your note of January 29, 1934, and my reply thereto of February 24, 1934, consists in the Postmaster General of my Government having instructed a representative of his Department to proceed to Little America, Admiral Byrd's base, "for the purpose of assuming charge of the handling of the mail at that place."

> It is understood that His Majesty's Government in New Zealand bases its claim of sovereignty on the discovery of a portion of the region in question. While it is unnecessary to enter into any detailed discussion of the subject at this time, nevertheless, in order to avoid misapprehension, it is proper for me to say, in the light of long established principles of international law, that I can not admit that sovereignty accrues from mere discovery unaccompanied by occupancy and use.

In reply, the following note, dated December 27, was handed to the Secretary of State by the British Ambassador on December 29:

> With reference to the letter which you were so good as to address to me on November 14th last, I have the honour, under instructions from His Majesty's Principal Secretary of State for Foreign Affairs, at the instance of His Majesty's Government in New Zealand to inform you that the supposition that the British claim to sovereignty over the Ross Dependency is based on discovery alone, and, moreover, on the discovery of only a portion of the region, is based on a misapprehension of the facts of the situation.
>
> 2. The Dependency was established and placed under New Zealand Administration by an Order in Council of 1923 in which the Dependency's geographical limits were precisely defined. Regulations have been made by the Governor General of New Zealand in respect of the Dependency and the British title has been kept up by the exercise in respect of the Dependency of administrative and governmental powers, e.g. as regards the issue of whaling licenses and the appointment of a special officer to act as magistrate for the Dependency.
>
> 3. As I had the honour to state in my Note No. 33 of January 29th last, His Majesty's Government in New Zealand recognize the absence of ordinary postal facilities in the Dependency and desire therefore to facilitate as far as possible the carriage of mail by United States authorities to and from the Byrd Expedition. As regards Mr. Anderson's present mission, they understand that he is carrying letters to which are, or will be, affixed special stamps printed in the United States and that these stamps are to be cancelled and date-stamped on board the Expedition's vessel. They also understand that these stamps are intended to be commemorative of the Byrd Expedition and have been issued as a matter of philatelic interest.
>
> 4. In the above circumstances His Majesty's Government in New Zealand have no objection to the proposed visit of Mr. Anderson. They must, however, place it on record that, had his mission appeared to them to be designed as an assertion of United States sovereignty over any part of the Ross Dependency or as a challenge to British sovereignty therein, they would have been compelled to make a protest.

On February 7, 1935, the following note was addressed to the British Ambassador by the Secretary of State:

> I have received your note No. 402 dated December 27, 1934, concerning the British claim to sovereignty over the Ross Dependency. It is noted that His Majesty's Government in New Zealand have no objection to the proposed visit of Mr. Anderson.
>
> The Government of the United States considers that no useful purpose would be served by a discussion at this time of the questions raised in your note. In the circumstances, I consider it desirable merely to reaffirm the statement contained in my note of February 24, 1934, to the effect that the United States reserves all rights which this country or its citizens may have with respect to the matter.

Notes and Questions

1. *Acquisition of Territory.* One generally accepted way for states to acquire new territory is by discovery and occupation of *terra nullius*. The label is used to describe uninhabited territory, including new islands. Writers in the early twentieth century considered that discovery alone provided only an "inchoate" title, which in order to become effective against other states had to be followed by occupation and concrete acts exercising authority. See, *e.g.*, T.J. Lawrence, *The Principles of International Law* § 74 (1915). In light of the practical difficulties of establishing permanent settlements in Antarctica, should discovery alone have sufficed to establish sovereignty?

More controversial than discovery plus effective occupation as grounds for asserting sovereignty over portions of Antarctica are the contiguity theory, put forth by several states that are geographically close to Antarctica, and the sector theory. Under the sector theory, Antarctic territorial boundaries correspond to longitudinal lines that converge on the South Pole. The longitudinal lines either are extensions of the mainland boundaries of a nearby claimant state, or are drawn from the ends of a stretch of coast claimed by the state.

Other, traditionally accepted ways for a state to acquire territory are not applicable to Antarctica. These methods include cession from another state, accretion (the increase of land, as through new geological formations), prescription (a continuous, uncontested display of control), or subjugation (conquest followed by annexation, the legality of which as a way to acquire territory today runs afoul of the proscriptions on the use of force in the United Nations Charter). See 1 *Oppenheim's International Law* §§ 241–275 (9th ed. by Robert Jennings & Arthur Watts, 1992).

2. *Disputes Over Territorial Claims in Antarctica.* How does the exchange between the U.S. Secretary of State and the British ambassador about the Ross Dependency affect its legal status? Is this exchange part of the claim-counterclaim process used in the formation of customary international law?

Some disputes over territory in Antarctica led to tense incidents. The claims of Argentina, Chile, and the United Kingdom overlap, and in the areas of overlapping claims there were occasional displays of naval power and even the firing of shots by military personnel.

3. *Territorial Claims in Antarctica Before the Antarctic Treaty.* By the 1950s, Argentina, Australia, Chile, France, New Zealand, Norway, and the United Kingdom exercised or claimed territorial sovereignty over "pie slice" sectors of Antarctica that meet at the South Pole. The United States and the Soviet Union made no claims to territory in Antarctica but reserved their right to assert claims in the future. These "nonclaimant states" also refused to recognize the territorial claims of other states. As shown in Figure 9.1, one area of Antarctica was (and still is) unclaimed.

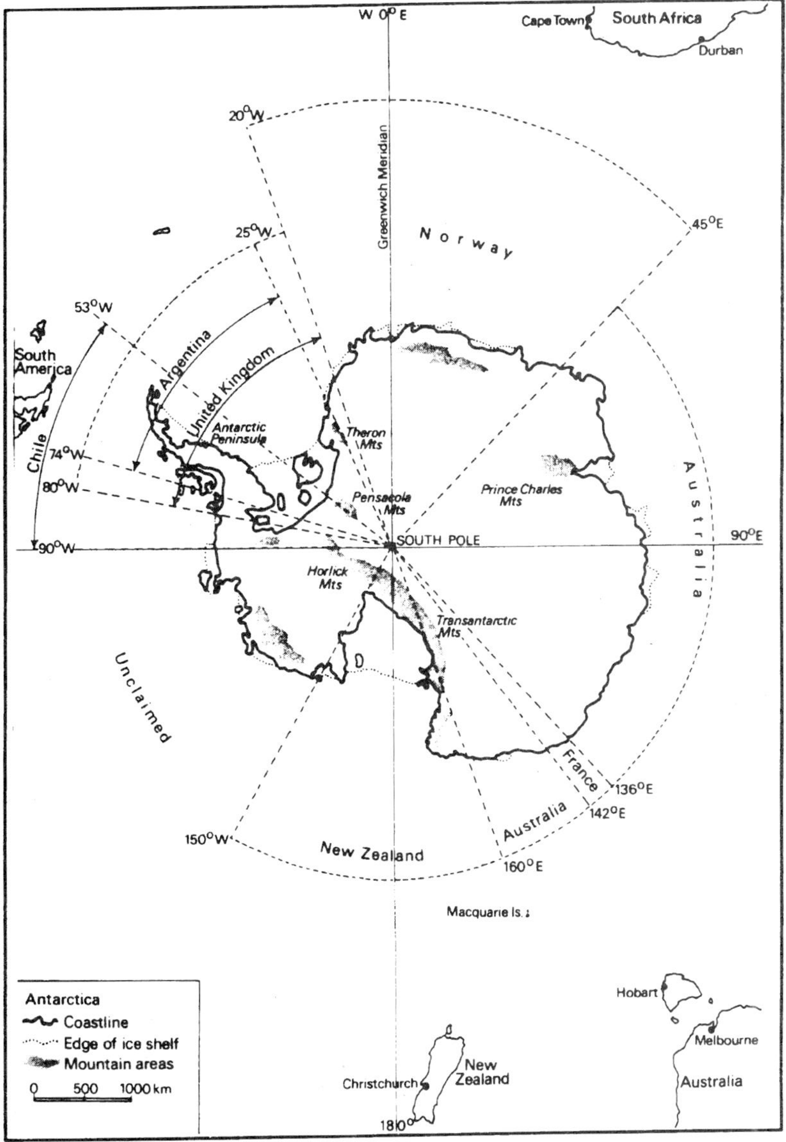

Figure 9.1. Map of national claims in Antarctica

THE ANTARCTIC TREATY

Dec. 1, 1959, 12 U.S.T. 794, 402 U.N.T.S. 71
19 *International Legal Materials* 860.

The Governments of Argentina, Australia, Belgium, Chile, the French Republic, Japan, New Zealand, Norway, the Union of South Africa, the Union of Soviet Socialist Republics, the United Kingdom of Great Britain and Northern Ireland, and the United States of America,

Recognizing that it is in the best interest of all mankind that Antarctica shall continue forever to be used exclusively for peaceful purposes and shall not become the scene or object of international discord;

Acknowledging the substantial contributions to scientific knowledge resulting from international cooperation in scientific investigation in Antarctica;

Convinced that the establishment of a firm foundation for the continuation and development of such cooperation on the basis of freedom of scientific investigation in Antarctica as applied during the International Geophysical Year accords with the interests of science and progress of all mankind;

Convinced also that a treaty ensuring the use of Antarctica for peaceful purposes only and the continuance of international harmony in Antarctica will further the purposes and principles embodied in the Charter of the United Nations;

Have agreed as follows:

Article I

1. Antarctica shall be used for peaceful purposes only. There shall be prohibited, *inter alia*, any measures of a military nature, such as the establishment of military bases and fortifications, the carrying out of military maneuvers, as well as the testing of any type of weapons.

2. The present Treaty shall not prevent the use of military personnel or equipment for scientific research or for any other peaceful purpose.

Article II

Freedom of scientific investigation in Antarctica and cooperation toward that end, as applied during the International Geophysical Year, shall continue, subject to the provisions of the present Treaty.

Article III

In order to promote international cooperation in scientific investigation in Antarctica, as provided for in Article II of the present Treaty, the Contracting Parties agree that, to the greatest extent feasible and practicable:

(a) information regarding plans for scientific programs in Antarctica shall be exchanged to permit maximum economy and efficiency of operations;

(b) scientific personnel shall be exchanged in Antarctica between expeditions and stations;

(c) scientific observations and results from Antarctica shall be exchanged and made freely available.

2. In implementing this Article, every encouragement shall be given to the establishment of cooperative working relations with those Specialized Agencies of the United Nations and other international organizations having a scientific or technical interest in Antarctica.

Article IV

1. Nothing contained in the present Treaty shall be interpreted as:

(a) a renunciation by any Contracting Party of previously asserted rights of or claims to territorial sovereignty in Antarctica;

(b) a renunciation or diminution by any Contracting Party of any basis of claim to territorial sovereignty in Antarctica which it may have whether as a result of its activities or those of its nationals in Antarctica, or otherwise;

(c) prejudicing the position of any Contracting Party as regards its recognition or nonrecognition of any other State's right of or claim or basis of claim to territorial sovereignty in Antarctica.

2. No acts or activities taking place while the present Treaty is in force shall constitute a basis for asserting, supporting or denying a claim to territorial sovereignty in Antarctica or create any rights of sovereignty in Antarctica. No new claim, or enlargement of an existing claim, to territorial sovereignty in Antarctica shall be asserted while the present Treaty is in force.

Article V

1. Any nuclear explosions in Antarctica and the disposal there of radioactive waste material shall be prohibited.

2. In the event of the conclusion of international agreements concerning the use of nuclear energy, including nuclear explosions and the disposal of radioactive waste material, to which all of the Contracting Parties whose representatives are entitled to participate in the meetings provided for under Article IX are parties, the rules established under such agreements shall apply in Antarctica.

Article VI

The provisions of the present Treaty shall apply to the area south of 60° South Latitude, including all ice shelves, but nothing in the present Treaty shall prejudice or in any way affect the rights, or the exercise of the rights, of any State under international law with regard to the high seas within that area.

ARTICLE VII

1. In order to promote the objectives and ensure the observance of the provisions of the present Treaty, each Contracting Party whose representatives are entitled to participate in the meetings referred to in Article IX of the Treaty shall have the right to designate observers to carry out any inspection provided for by the present Article. Observers shall be nationals of the Contracting Parties which designate them. The names of observers shall be communicated to every other Contracting Party having the right to designate observers, and like notice shall be given of the termination of their appointment.

2. Each observer designated in accordance with the provisions of paragraph 1 of this Article shall have complete freedom of access at any time to any or all areas of Antarctica.

3. All areas of Antarctica, including all stations, installations and equipment within those areas, and all ships and aircraft at points of discharging or embarking cargoes or personnel in Antarctica, shall be open at all times to inspection by any observers designated in accordance with paragraph 1 of this Article.

4. Aerial observation may be carried out at any time over any or all areas of Antarctica by any of the Contracting Parties having the right to designate observers.

5. Each Contracting Party shall, at the time when the present Treaty enters into force for it, inform the other Contracting Parties, and thereafter shall give them notice in advance, of

(a) all expeditions to and within Antarctica, on the part of its ships or nationals, and all expeditions to Antarctica organized in or proceeding from its territory;

(b) all stations in Antarctica occupied by its nationals; and

(c) any military personnel or equipment intended to be introduced by it into Antarctica subject to the conditions prescribed in paragraph 2 of Article I of the present Treaty.

ARTICLE VIII

1. In order to facilitate the exercise of their functions under the present Treaty, and without prejudice to the respective positions of the Contracting Parties relating to jurisdiction over all other persons in Antarctica, observers designated under paragraph 1 of Article VII and scientific personnel exchanged under subparagraph 1(b) of Article III of the Treaty, and members of the staffs accompanying any such persons, shall be subject only to the jurisdiction of the Contracting Party of which they are nationals in respect of all acts or omissions occurring while they are in Antarctica for the purpose of exercising their functions.

2. Without prejudice to the provisions of paragraph 1 of this Article, and pending the adoption of measures in pursuance of subparagraph 1(e) of Article IX, the Contracting Parties concerned in any

case of dispute with regard to the exercise of jurisdiction in Antarctica shall immediately consult together with a view to reaching a mutually acceptable solution.

ARTICLE IX

1. Representatives of the Contracting Parties named in the preamble to the present Treaty shall meet at the City of Canberra within two months after the date of entry into force of the Treaty, and thereafter at suitable intervals and places, for the purpose of exchanging information, consulting together on matters of common interest pertaining to Antarctica, and formulating and considering, and recommending to their Governments, measures in furtherance of the principles and objectives of the Treaty, including measures regarding:

(a) use of Antarctica for peaceful purposes only;

(b) facilitation of scientific research in Antarctica;

(c) facilitation of international scientific cooperation in Antarctica;

(d) facilitation of the exercise of the rights of inspection provided for in Article VII of the Treaty;

(e) questions relating to the exercise of jurisdiction in Antarctica;

(f) preservation and conservation of living resources in Antarctica.

2. Each Contracting Party which has become a party to the present Treaty by accession under Article XIII shall be entitled to appoint representatives to participate in the meetings referred to in paragraph 1 of the present Article, during such time as that Contracting Party demonstrates its interest in Antarctica by conducting substantial scientific research activity there, such as the establishment of a scientific station or the despatch of a scientific expedition.

3. Reports from the observers referred to in Article VII of the present Treaty shall be transmitted to the representatives of the Contracting Parties participating in the meetings referred to in paragraph 1 of the present Article.

4. The measures referred to in paragraph 1 of this Article shall become effective when approved by all the Contracting Parties whose representatives were entitled to participate in the meetings held to consider those measures. * * *

ARTICLE X

Each of the Contracting Parties undertakes to exert appropriate efforts, consistent with the Charter of the United Nations, to the end that no one engages in any activity in Antarctica contrary to the principles or purposes of the present Treaty.

ARTICLE XI

1. If any dispute arises between two or more of the Contracting Parties concerning the interpretation or application of the present Treaty, those Contracting Parties shall consult among themselves with a view to having the dispute resolved by negotiation, inquiry, mediation, conciliation, arbitration, judicial settlement or other peaceful means of their own choice.

2. Any dispute of this character not so resolved shall, with the consent, in each case, of all parties to the dispute, be referred to the International Court of Justice for settlement; but failure to reach agreement on reference to the International Court shall not absolve parties to the dispute from the responsibility of continuing to seek to resolve it by any of the various peaceful means referred to in paragraph 1 of this Article. * * *

ARTICLE XIII

1. The present Treaty shall be subject to ratification by the signatory States. It shall be open for accession by any State which is a Member of the United Nations, or by any other State which may be invited to accede to the Treaty with the consent of all the Contracting Parties whose representatives are entitled to participate in the meetings provided for under Article IX of the Treaty.

Notes and Questions

1. *The International Geophysical Year.* The shape of the current legal regime governing Antarctica was influenced by the 1957 International Geophysical Year (IGY). The IGY was a cooperative effort by 66 states including all the major powers except the People's Republic of China. One of the IGY's scientific projects involved Antarctica. Scientists meeting during the IGY allocated scientific stations in Antarctica to states and arranged cooperative ventures concerning mapping, collection of weather data, and exchanges of scientific personnel. The entry of the Soviet Union into Antarctic activities beginning in 1955 contributed to efforts to specify an international arrangement for Antarctica that would help to preserve the continent as a laboratory for cooperative scientific research and as a region used only for peaceful purposes.

Following the IGY, representatives of the 12 states active in the Antarctic work of the IGY met regularly in Washington, D.C., for preparatory treaty talks and a formal negotiating conference. The Antarctic Treaty was signed in Washington on December 1, 1959, and entered into force June 23, 1961. See Christopher C. Joyner, "U.S.–Soviet Cooperative Diplomacy: The Case of Antarctica," in *U.S.–Soviet Cooperation* 39 (Nish Jamgotch ed. 1989); Walter Sullivan, "Antarctica," in *The International Geophysical Year* 318 (International Conciliation No. 521, Jan. 1959).

2. *Freezing Territorial Claims.* Article IV of the Antarctic Treaty is said to "freeze" territorial and sovereignty claims. Why have states found this arrangement acceptable? Does the Article IV arrangement help to

explain why the Antarctic Treaty does not provide for an international organization to coordinate all Antarctic activities?

3. *Effect on Nonparties.* Does the Antarctic Treaty create legal obligations for nonparties? Does the Treaty thus create international obligations *erga omnes*? What would be the reaction if a nonparty to the Antarctic Treaty were to claim sovereignty over the "unclaimed sector" or some other portion of Antarctica? To dispose of radioactive waste anywhere on the continent? See Article X of the Treaty.

4. *Jurisdiction Over Activities in Antarctica.* What laws govern individuals' activities in Antarctica? Article VIII of the Antarctic Treaty provides at best a partial answer. Some of the issues relating to the assertion of "legislative jurisdiction" over crimes and torts in Antarctica are explored in Beverly May Carl, "The Need for a Private International Law Regime in Antarctica," in *The Antarctic Legal Regime* 65 (Christopher C. Joyner & Sudhir K. Chopra eds. 1988), and in Comment, Jonathan Blum, "The Deep Freeze: Torts, Choice of Law, and the Antarctic Treaty Regime," 8 *Emory International Law Review* 667 (1994).

5. *Classes of Parties to the Antarctic Treaty.* The Antarctic Treaty distinguishes between Consultative Parties and other parties. The 12 original parties to the Antarctic Treaty joined as Consultative Parties, entitled to decision-making roles in periodic international meetings. As of December 31, 1995, 42 states were parties to the Antarctic Treaty, but only 26 of them were Consultative Parties. What justifies the Treaty's two-tiered system? Among the Consultative Parties, should some special status be accorded those states that have asserted territorial claims? The following excerpt addresses some of these concerns.

2. ANTARCTICA AND THE COMMON HERITAGE OF MANKIND

UNITED NATIONS GENERAL ASSEMBLY DEBATES ON ANTARCTICA

A/C.1/38/PV.42 (1983), Thirty–Eighth Session, First Committee, Summary Record of the 42nd Meeting, Nov. 28, 1983; A/C.1/38/PV.44 (1983), Thirty–Eighth Session, First Committee, Summary Record of the 44th Meeting, Nov. 29, 1983; A/C.1/38/PV.5 (1984), Thirty–Eighth Session, First Committee, Verbatim Record of the 45th Meeting, Nov. 30, 1983; A/C.1/39/PV.54 (1984), Thirty–Ninth Session, First Committee, Verbatim Record of the 54th Meeting, Nov. 30, 1984.

MR. ZAINAL ABIDIN (Malaysia) * * *

* * * The [Antarctic] Treaty at its inception could have been considered as an unusually enlightened experiment in international cooperation.

In our view, however, the Treaty and its system have become mired in the obsession to maintain a *status quo* régime advantageous to the privileged few. * * * My delegation would like to draw the attention of the Committee to two crucial areas in which the Treaty has not kept pace with current international reality.

My delegation would like first to address the obvious structural flaw inherent in the Treaty system. The Treaty provides for a two-tier membership structure, characterized by gross inequality. This is evident from the relevant Treaty articles pertaining to membership [Articles XIII(1) and IX(2)]. * * *

This means that while every State is welcome and encouraged to accede to the Treaty only the original 12 can participate in decision-making, along with such other States as, in the unanimous judgement of the original Contracting Parties, have demonstrated significant interest in Antarctica by conducting substantial scientific research activity there. Thus, a State acceding to the Treaty formalizes its willingness to abide by the Treaty provisions without any role to play whatsoever, as voting and regulatory control are reserved for the full—or "consultative"—members only. States are, in actual fact, called upon to accede to the Treaty without any right to participate in the decision-making process. It is clear that this undemocratic arrangement which the Treaty perpetuates goes against the grain of current international reality. Most States would find accession without representation extremely difficult to accept, while the representation requirement of a significant capacity for research would be beyond their means. They are thus effectively frozen out of meaningful participation in the Antarctic Treaty system.

The second major flaw of the Treaty system, in the view of my delegation, pertains to the limitations on its efficacy. The Treaty purports to be an international régime that serves the interests of all mankind, yet it benefits only the few. * * * [Despite Article III(2) of the Antarctic Treaty, which encourages cooperative working relations with international organizations,] the Consultative Parties have actually rejected co-operation with the Food and Agriculture Organization of the United Nations (FAO), the United Nations Environment Programme (UNEP), the Committee on Natural Resources and other international organizations. Furthermore, the * * * flow of information about Antarctica * * * is very much limited to the Consultative Parties and is not even made available to ordinary parties of the Treaty, let alone the international community at large.

The efficacy of the Treaty system is especially questionable with regard to environmental and ecological management. * * * [T]o forestall any destruction of Antarctica's invaluable and irreplaceable endowments, environmentalists world-wide have advocated the designation of Antarctica as a world park. * * * [Because international nongovernmental organizations are denied access,] even as observers, to ATCP [Antarctic Treaty Consultative Party] meetings * * *, the world community is entitled to entertain serious doubts on the effective management of Antarctica's present and future environment, especially as the Treaty system lacks a centralized environmental review body and enforcement is left to individual States. * * *

We note that several closed-door meetings have been held to devise a new and exclusive minerals régime in Antarctica among the few parties enjoying consultative status within the Antarctic Treaty framework. * * *

* * * [S]afeguarding of the interests of all mankind * * * requires the creation of international mechanisms that are not only truly representative in membership but also truly committed to serving all of its constituents. The philosophy that guides those mechanisms must be such as to command unquestioned moral authority amongst the nations of the world. In this respect the concepts of common benefit and common heritage come to mind.

The common heritage approach * * * should be considered in a future international design for Antarctica. The elements of the common heritage concept—peaceful use, non-appropriation, preservation for future generations, including environmental protection and conservation of resources, international management and benefit-sharing—are of great relevance to Antarctica. * * *

In conclusion, may I be permitted to sum up the conviction of my delegation as follows. First, the world is in a process of evolution and there is an urgent need for all to display the necessary political will to make adaptations and adjustments to rapidly changing circumstances in order to build a structure of international peace and a just international order.

Secondly, the world of 1959, when the Antarctic Treaty was first formulated, is different from that of 1983. There are now 158 States Members of the United Nations, most of which are categorized as developing countries. Their rights, interests, aspirations and, not least, their views have to be accommodated by any purportedly international régime on Antarctica.

Thirdly, there is a growing and an inexorable demand by this articulate and growing majority for greater involvement in international decision-making. No longer can a handful of countries arrogate unto themselves the prerogative of representing humanity in matters of common concern when the majority of humanity is not directly involved.

Fourthly, the movement for a just and a balanced world order for the cause of mankind is irresistible. Significant areas of the world beyond national jurisdiction, and the celestial bodies in outer space, must be viewed in the context of the common heritage of mankind, and for the benefit of mankind as a whole.

And, fifth, Antarctica constitutes one such significant and vital area, because what happens in this region will have a direct effect on the rest of the world. * * * It is time that a proper and representative international régime beyond the Antarctic Treaty be explored within the framework of the United Nations.

Mr. Heap (United Kingdom) * * *

* * * [T]he Antarctic Treaty system was an exercise in prudent forethought. * * * [A] number of notable "firsts" * * * have been achieved by agreement between States within the Treaty system. The Antarctic Treaty was the first international agreement to demilitarize a whole continent, to provide for on-site inspection of all activities on a

continent, to outlaw nuclear explosions or the dumping of radioactive waste, to ensure freedom of scientific investigation and require that the results be freely available and to set aside, in favour of co-operation, conflicting views about the legal basis which should underlie the management of affairs over a whole continent.

* * * [T]hese firsts * * * are totally consistent with the Charter of the United Nations.

Since the Antarctic Treaty came into force in 1961 the development of a large number of agreements through its consultative mechanism has given rise to a number of other "firsts," among which are: the Agreed Measures for the Conservation of Antarctic Fauna and Flora, the first international agreement to prohibit the killing of any native mammal or native bird in Antarctica without a permit and to arrange for details on the permits issued to be internationally exchanged; the Convention for the Conservation of Antarctic Seals, the first and, I believe, so far the only international agreement to regulate the utilization of a living resource before any industry has developed to exploit it; the Convention for the Conservation of Antarctic Marine Living Resources, the first international agreement to require that regulation of the utilization of target species shall have regard to the effect that utilization has on the ecosystem as a whole. More generally, certain pioneering recommendations of the Treaty's consultative procedures require that the first consideration to be applied to a new activity in Antarctica is not whether it is profitable or in the interests of one or more Governments. Instead, prior consideration has to be given to whether or not it will be adverse effects on the Antarctic environment. This test, itself a notable first, is unparalleled anywhere else in the world.

* * * [A]ll these "firsts," and note especially those measures taken to protect Antarctic marine living resources, are in marked contrast to what happened before the Treaty system came into being. * * *

None of these "firsts" give substantive rights to the parties to the agreements. They all circumscribe the freedom of action of all parties. Overwhelmingly, they consist of obligations and not of rights. This record of achievement should go far to put right the misconception that the Antarctic Treaty Consultative Parties are carving up Antarctica for their own benefit.

MR. WOOLCOTT (Australia) * * *

* * * There seems to be a desire, at least on the part of some delegations, to have Antarctic resources, whatever these are or may be, declared the common heritage of mankind, like those of outer space and the deep sea-bed, beyond national jurisdiction. Australia is, of course, in favour of this principle in the Law-of-the-Sea context, but we do not consider it relevant or appropriate in Antarctica. First, for Australia and six other countries that maintain national territorial claims and, let me add, national settlements, Antarctica is not beyond national jurisdiction. Antarctica has instead been the subject of exploration, settlement and claims to sovereignty by a number of countries over many years. So

there can be no international consensus that a common-heritage approach to Antarctica is acceptable.

Secondly, the common-heritage concept embodies a developmental purpose, which is not now, and we hope will never be, dominant in Antarctica, where the environment is, as some of the sponsors of this draft resolution have stressed, extremely vulnerable to the activity of man and must be safeguarded by those pursuing activity there in the interest of all mankind. * * *

* * * The Treaty is not exclusive. Any State may join, and 28 countries with diverse economic and political interests have already done so. In 1983, two new members, China and India, joined the Treaty, and Finland only yesterday signified its intention to do so. * * *

What about the status of Consultative Parties? Claims have been made here which reveal a misunderstanding of the operation of the Treaty. Any State carrying out substantial scientific activities may become a Consultative Party to the Treaty. In 1983 Brazil and India took this step. There are now 16 Treaty members that are also Consultative Parties.

It is not unnatural that those heavily involved in scientific research should wish to consult together and then to make available to the international community the fruits of their consultations.

Claims that the deliberations of the Consultative Parties are conducted in secret and that consultative Parties meet as a cabal to take secret decisions, sometimes contrary to the interest of the acceding parties and the international community are quite simply untrue. Acceding parties, for their own good reasons, have presumably wished to limit their commitment to the Antarctic, short of that implied by consultative status. * * *

It is relevant that at the last meeting of the Consultative Parties in Canberra as recently as in September of this year, all members of the Antarctic Treaty, acceding as well as Consultative, participated in the deliberations. The results of the discussions at the meeting are before the Committee today, in the Final Report of the Twelfth Antarctic Treaty Consultative Meeting. * * *

Australia, when it determines its approach to a regional question, invariably gives weight to the views of the regional countries closest to, and most directly concerned with, the particular issue under consideration. * * * A glance at the map will show that Antarctica lies to Australia's immediate south. This is the basis of our own clear and legitimate concern that the present satisfactory situation there should not be disturbed. * * *

In current international circumstances it would simply, in the view of my delegation, not be realistic to expect that a new instrument could have the same provisions for total demilitarization of the region, verified by on-site inspection, for the setting aside of potential disputes over territorial sovereignty and for harmonious international co-operation in scientific research and environmental protection. In short, any new instrument would not as effectively protect important international interests in the Antarctic as does the current Treaty, and any attempt to revise this situation would, in our view, risk reopening the very contention and competition which the Treaty was created to do away with.

MR. JESUS (Cape Verde) * * *

* * * During this debate I have not heard anybody question the principles established in the Antarctic Treaty relating to the peaceful use of Antarctica, the preservation of flora, fauna and the environment in general or its declaration as an area free from military activities, or even the freedom of scientific research. In this respect, it seems to my delegation that we are all in agreement with one another. What therefore, we, the majority of members of the international community, are in disagreement with is the fact that a few countries which have consultative status, however powerful they might be, can ascribe to themselves the right to decide what is right or wrong for the whole of mankind. * * *

* * * [O]nly a party to the Treaty which demonstrates its interest in Antarctica by conducting substantial scientific research activity there, such as the establishment of a scientific station or the dispatch of a scientific expedition, is entitled to become a Consultative Party.

In other words, the majority of third world countries, even if they became parties to the Antarctic Treaty, would not be able to participate fully on an equal footing with any other State Consultative Party in establishing the policies for the activities of Antarctica for the simple reason that they cannot afford to send a scientific expedition to Antarctica or to establish a scientific station there. It is evident that the principle of equality of States established in the Charter, upon which the Antarctic Treaty is said to be based, cannot allow that its observance be limited with regard to co-operation on Antarctica merely because of lack of resources of third world countries.

The Antarctic Treaty can become a basis for universal co-operation in Antarctica, subject to the following provisos: the extension of the right of equal treatment to all States parties, irrespective of their conduct of substantial scientific research activity in Antarctica; that in all activities related to Antarctica decisions be taken by all States parties on the basis of one State, one vote; that provision be made to make it plain that Antarctica is free from national appropriation and therefore no territorial claim there should ever be recognized.

Notes and Questions

1. *The Common Heritage of Mankind.* Mr. Abidin of Malaysia lists in summary fashion several features typically associated with the common heritage of mankind principle, which we revisit later in this chapter when we examine the international law governing outer space and the deep sea bed. According to typical formulations, the common heritage principle requires: that no state appropriate an area or its resources; a common management

system with universal participation; equitable sharing of economic benefits, with particular attention to the needs of states with developing economies; the conservation of the area and its resources, a feature which requires that regard be given to environmental protection and the interests of future generations; and the peaceful use of the area. See Sudhir K. Chopra, "Antarctica as a Commons Regime: A Conceptual Framework for Cooperation and Coexistence," in *The Antarctic Legal Regime* 163, 172–74 (Christopher C. Joyner & Sudhir K. Chopra eds. 1988); Christopher C. Joyner, "Legal Implications of the Concept of the Common Heritage of Mankind," 35 *International & Comparative Law Quarterly* 190 (1986). Should a U.N. General Assembly resolution declare Antarctica to be the "common heritage of mankind"? What would be the implications of such a resolution? Would it be effective?

2. *The United Nations and Antarctica.* The issue of U.N. involvement with Antarctica was first posed shortly after World War II. India raised the question again in 1956, and Malaysia brought the issue before the U.N. General Assembly in 1982. The General Assembly has called on the Antarctic Treaty Consultative Parties to invite the U.N. Secretary–General to ATCP meetings, has expressed the conviction that regimes to protect the Antarctic environment "must be negotiated with the full participation of all members of the international community," has urged bans on prospecting and mining in Antarctica, and has urged all members of the international community to ensure that activities in Antarctica "are for the benefit of all mankind." G.A. Res. 44/124 (1989)(adopted by a vote of 108 states in favor, 0 opposed, and 6 abstaining).

3. *Possible Alternative Regimes.* One can envision a number of alternatives to either the current system or to an international administration of Antarctica as a common heritage. What would be the advantages and disadvantages of a territorial regime, for example, in which claimant states asserted absolute control over their sector-shaped claims? Of a condominium regime, under which the Antarctic Treaty parties established a system of joint sovereignty over the continent?

4. *Responding to Increased Interest in Antarctica Under the Antarctic Treaty.* What steps might be taken within the framework established by the Antarctic Treaty to respond to increased international interest in Antarctica?

Note: The Antarctic Environment and Mineral Resources

States, scientists, and nongovernmental organizations have been concerned about protecting the fragile Antarctic environment. The Antarctic Treaty itself contains several provisions relating to the environment, notably Article V's prohibition on nuclear explosions and the disposal of radioactive waste and Article IX(1)(f)'s call for consultations on the preservation and conservation of living resources. Approximately half of the many Recommendations adopted by the Antarctic Treaty Consultative Parties, which become formally effective once the ATCPs ratify them, have related to protection of the environment. Notable environmental instruments include the Agreed Measures for the Conservation of Antarctic Flora and Fauna, June 13, 1964, 17 U.S.T. 441, the Convention for the Conservation of

Antarctic Seals, Feb. 11, 1972, 29 U.S.T. 441, 11 I.L.M. 251 (1972), and the Convention for the Conservation of Antarctic Marine Living Resources (CCAMLR), May 20, 1980, 33 U.S.T. 3476, 19 I.L.M. 841 (1980).

The CCAMLR has as its goal a comprehensive management scheme that will maintain ecological relationships among all populations of Antarctic living resources. Whereas many fisheries treaties seek to insure the maximum sustainable yield of a particular species, the CCAMLR (which applies to birds and other organisms as well as to fish) follows an "ecosystem approach." Under the CCAMLR, a Commission composed of Contracting States to the Convention is to gather data, study environmental issues, and formulate and adopt conservation measures "on the basis of the best scientific evidence available." Reviews of the contributions of the CCAMLR to protecting the environment have been mixed. See Stuart B. Kaye, "Legal Approaches to Polar Fisheries Regimes: A Comparative Analysis of the Convention for the Conservation of Antarctic Marine Living Resources and the Bering Sea Doughnut Hole Convention," 26 *California Western International Law Journal* 75, 87–97 (1995); Deborah H. Overholt, "Environmental Protection in the Antarctic: Past, Present, and Future," 1992 *Canadian Yearbook of International Law* 227, 238–45, 250–52. Cutting against the adoption and implementation of strong environmental measures have been the requirement that the CCAMLR Commission must adopt conservation measures by consensus, the fact that the CCAMLR leaves it up to each Contracting State to "take appropriate measures within its competence to ensure compliance," and the possibility that nonparties to the CCAMLR may take detrimental actions.

Environmental considerations have also been important in negotiations relating to the use of mineral resources in Antarctica. Between 1982 and 1988—not coincidentally, a period of great interest in Antarctica at the United Nations—the ATCPs negotiated a regime to regulate mineral exploration and exploitation. The product of these negotiations, the Convention on the Regulation of Antarctic Mineral Resource Activities (CRAMRA), June 2, 1988, 27 I.L.M. 859 (1988), called for a regulatory framework to govern minerals activities. It provided for inspection, monitoring, reporting, obligatory dispute settlement, and the suspension of any activities that caused unacceptable damage to the environment. A new international institution, the Antarctic Minerals Resources Commission, was to decide whether to open an area for minerals exploration and development, and any activities were to be overseen by a Regulatory Committee.

In the summer of 1989, however, Australia and France announced they would not sign the CRAMRA, and it has not entered into force. Contributing to the demise of the CRAMRA were the efforts of international nongovernmental organizations concerned about the environment. They argued the Convention would promote prospecting and eventual exploitation, criticized the fact that enforcement ultimately remained with individual governments, and objected to the structure and powers of some of the proposed new institutions. Also contributing to the CRAMRA's demise were sovereignty concerns:

> Another prominent consideration influencing the Australian government hinged on the negative implications that CRAMRA would pose for

the status of Australia's territorial claim to Antarctica. * * * By agreeing that a treaty-based minerals arrangement on the continent was necessary and proper, Australia would be admitting that its claim to sovereignty was soft and could be compromised. No less important for Paul Keating, the Hawke government's head of the Exchequer, was that CRAMRA failed to provide any royalties to claimant states for other states' exploration or exploitation activities in claimed sectors. This premeditated failure to compensate claimant states with privileged payments for mining operations in claimed sectors could be read as tacit admission that claimant states were willing to give up full administrative control over *their* territory.

Christopher C. Joyner, "Antarctic Treaty Diplomacy: Problems, Prospects, and Policy Implications," in *The Diplomatic Record 1989–1990*, at 155, 163 (David D. Newsom ed. 1991).

Following the adverse reactions to CRAMRA, states negotiated the Madrid Protocol on Environmental Protection, Oct. 4, 1991, 30 I.L.M. 1455 (1991), a protocol to the Antarctic Treaty. The Madrid Protocol prohibits "[a]ny activity relating to mineral resources, other than scientific research," for at least 50 years. The focus of the Madrid Protocol is thus on preventing environmental harm by banning mining, rather than, as under the CRAMRA, on permitting activities but protecting against harm. Annexes to the Madrid Protocol also address other environmental issues: environmental impact assessments, the protection of flora and fauna, waste disposal, marine pollution, and management plans for specially protected areas. The Madrid Protocol, however, has not yet gained the ratifications necessary for it to enter into force.

Environmental and mineral resource issues lead one to wonder how adaptable the Antarctic legal regime will prove to be. Is it possible to achieve a satisfactory system of environmental protection in Antarctica by leaving so much control with states, some of which claim sovereignty over portions of the continent? Can states effectively regulate the Antarctic environment and mineral resources without a significant restructuring of the existing Antarctic Treaty regime?

B. OUTER SPACE

The United Nations and its specialized and associated agencies have played dominant roles in developing the international law of outer space. In 1959—two years after the launch of Sputnik I, the first satellite to orbit Earth—the United Nations General Assembly established the Committee for Peaceful Uses of Outer Space. The Committee's work led to the Treaty on Principles Governing the Activities of States in the Exploration and Use of Outer Space, Including the Moon and Other Celestial Bodies, which is set forth below. The notes that follow the Outer Space Treaty point to several other treaties and recent developments, and raise questions about the nature of legal regimes and lawmaking process concerning outer space.

1. THE OUTER SPACE TREATY

TREATY OF PRINCIPLES GOVERNING THE ACTIVITIES OF STATES IN THE EXPLORATION AND USE OF OUTER SPACE, INCLUDING THE MOON AND OTHER CELESTIAL BODIES

Jan. 27, 1967, 18 U.S.T. 2410, 610 U.N.T.S. 205
6 *International Legal Materials* 386 (1967).

ARTICLE I

The exploration and use of outer space, including the moon and other celestial bodies, shall be carried out for the benefit and in the interests of all countries, irrespective of their degree of economic or scientific development, and shall be the province of all mankind.

Outer space, including the moon and other celestial bodies, shall be free for exploration and use by all States without discrimination of any kind, on a basis of equality and in accordance with international law, and there shall be free access to all areas of celestial bodies.

There shall be freedom of scientific investigation in outer space, including the moon and other celestial bodies, and States shall facilitate and encourage international co-operation in such investigation.

ARTICLE II

Outer space, including the moon and other celestial bodies, is not subject to national appropriation by claim of sovereignty, by means of use of occupation, or by any other means.

ARTICLE III

States Parties to the Treaty shall carry on activities in the exploration and use of outer space, including the moon and other celestial bodies, in accordance with international law, including the Charter of the United Nations, in the interest of maintaining international peace and security and promoting international co-operation and understanding.

ARTICLE IV

States Parties to the Treaty undertake not to place in orbit around the Earth any objects carrying nuclear weapons or any other kinds of weapons of mass destruction, install such weapons on celestial bodies, or station such weapons in outer space in any other manner.

The moon and other celestial bodies shall be used by all States Parties to the Treaty exclusively for peaceful purposes. The establishment of military bases, installations and fortifications, the testing of any type of weapons and the conduct of military maneuvers on celestial bodies shall be forbidden. The use of military personnel for any other peaceful purposes shall not be prohibited. The use of any equipment or facility necessary for peaceful exploration of the moon and other celestial bodies shall also not be prohibited. * * *

Article VI

States Parties to the Treaty shall bear international responsibility for national activities in outer space, including the moon and other celestial bodies, whether such activities are carried on by governmental agencies or by non-governmental entities, and for assuring that national activities are carried out in conformity with the provisions set forth in the present Treaty. The activities of non-governmental entities in outer space, including the moon and other celestial bodies, shall require authorization and continuing supervision by the appropriate State Party to the Treaty. When activities are carried on in outer space, including the moon and other celestial bodies, by an international organization, responsibility for compliance with this Treaty shall be borne both by the international organization and by the States Parties to the Treaty participating in such organization.

Article VII

Each State Party to the Treaty that launches or procures the launching of an object into outer space, including the moon and other celestial bodies, and each State Party from whose territory or facility an object is launched, is internationally liable for damage to another State Party to the Treaty or to its natural or juridical persons by such object or its component parts on the Earth, in air space or in outer space, including the moon and other celestial bodies.

Article VIII

A State Party to the Treaty on whose registry an object launched into outer space is carried shall retain jurisdiction and control over such object, and over any personnel thereof, while in outer space or on a celestial body. Ownership of objects launched into outer space, including objects landed or constructed on a celestial body, and of their component parts, is not affected by their presence in outer space or on a celestial body or by their return to Earth. Such objects or component parts found beyond the limits of the State Party to the Treaty on whose registry they are carried shall be returned to that State Party, which shall, upon request, furnish identifying data prior to their return.

Article IX

In the exploration and use of outer space, including the moon and other celestial bodies, States Parties to the Treaty shall be guided by the principle of co-operation and mutual assistance and shall conduct all their activities in outer space, including the moon and other celestial bodies, with due regard to the corresponding interests of all other States Parties to the Treaty. States Parties to the Treaty shall pursue studies of outer space, including the moon and other celestial bodies, and conduct exploration of them so as to avoid their harmful contamination and also adverse changes in the environment of the Earth resulting from the introduction of extraterrestrial matter and, where necessary, shall adopt appropriate measures for this purpose. If a State Party to the Treaty has reason to believe that an activity or experiment planned by it or its nationals in outer space, including the moon and other celestial bodies, would cause potentially harmful interference with activities of other States Parties in the peaceful exploration and use of outer space, including the moon and other celestial bodies, it shall undertake appropriate international consultations before proceeding with any such activity or experiment. A State Party to the Treaty which has reason to believe that an activity or experiment planned by another State Party in outer space, including the moon and other celestial bodies, would cause potentially harmful interference with activities in the peaceful exploration and use of outer space, including the moon and other celestial bodies, may request consultation concerning the activity or experiment. * * *

Notes and Questions

1. *Legal Regimes and the Outer Space Treaty.* What types of regimes are revealed, albeit in broad outline, in the Outer Space Treaty? Is the Outer Space Treaty so full of ambiguities and platitudes that it should at most be regarded as a statement of general aspirations? Or does it set some helpful guidelines to govern specific uses of outer space?

2. *Territorial Sovereignty and Airspace.* The legal regime governing airspace below outer space is premised on notions of territorial sovereignty. For example, Article 1 of the Convention on International Civil Aviation, Dec. 7, 1944, T.I.A.S. No. 1591, 15 U.N.T.S. 295, to which over 185 states are parties, provides that "every State has complete and exclusive sovereignty over the airspace above its territory." Thus, the subjacent state has the right to enact and implement air traffic regulations and exercise police powers. International aviation has developed under treaties among states, rather than on the basis of a general principle of freedom of the air. Why were principles of state territorial sovereignty not extended skyward into outer space?

3. *Outer Space and the Common Heritage of Mankind.* Does the Outer Space Treaty articulate the notion that outer space and various bodies and resources found there are the common heritage of mankind, an issue raised in the United Nations debates over Antarctica? The common heritage of mankind is expressly mentioned in Article 11 of the Agreement Governing the Activities of States on the Moon and Other Celestial Bodies, Dec. 18, 1979, U.N. Doc. A/RES/34/68 ("Moon Treaty"). Article 11 calls for "equitable sharing by all States Parties" of benefits derived from the moon's resources, and the Treaty authorizes states parties to establish an international regime governing exploitation of the moon's resources when exploitation is about to become feasible. Although the Moon Treaty entered into force July 11, 1984, the United States and Russia, which have traditionally carried on most space activities, are not parties. As of September 1996, only nine states had accepted the Moon Treaty. By contrast, over 100 states, including the major powers, have ratified the Outer Space Treaty.

4. *The United Nations and Development of the International Law of Outer Space.* How has international law concerning outer space been developed? The U.N. Committee on the Peaceful Uses of Outer Space (COPUOS) is the primary forum for discussing international space law

issues. COPUOS has drafted treaties that have added specific content to some of the issues covered in the Outer Space Treaty. Article V of the Outer Space Treaty, which deals with rendering assistance to astronauts, was elaborated on in the Agreement on the Rescue of Astronauts, the Return of Astronauts and the Return of Objects Launched into Outer Space, Apr. 22, 1968, 19 U.S.T. 7570, 672 U.N.T.S. 119. Articles VI, VII, and VIII of the Outer Space Treaty, containing rules on liability for damage and jurisdiction, were expanded on in the Convention on International Liability for Damage Caused by Space Objects, Mar. 29, 1972, 24 U.S.T. 2389, 961 U.N.T.S. 187, and the Convention on Registration of Objects Launched into Outer Space, Jan. 14, 1975, 28 U.S.T. 695, 1023 U.N.T.S. 15. COPUOS has also from time to time proposed draft principles or guidelines, not intended to lead to treaties.

5. *Proceeding by Consensus*. COPUOS has usually proceeded by consensus, which means general agreement without a vote, in developing treaties. A proposed treaty will be negotiated and revised until all negotiating parties agree on the text, although such agreement does not necessarily mean that a state will become a party. If, during negotiations, a state abstains or sets out a unilateral interpretation of a particular provision, consensus will not be defeated. What are the advantages and disadvantages of proceeding by consensus?

2. THE BOGOTÁ DECLARATION AND ACCESS TO GEOSTATIONARY ORBIT

One currently important issue regarding the use of outer space is access to geostationary orbit, the circular orbit at approximately 22,300 miles above the Earth's equator. A satellite placed in this orbit will rotate at the same speed as the Earth and appears stationary from a spot on the Earth below. Thus, transmitting and receiving equipment can remain directed at the same spot in outer space, making satellite operations simpler and cheaper than if the equipment had to be continually redirected. Geostationary orbits can be considered a finite resource, their number limited by the fact that electronic signals from satellites whose orbits are too close together can interfere with each other. As the space powers began to occupy the geostationary orbit with their satellites, developing states became concerned that no room would be left in the geostationary orbit by the time they acquired space technology. The Bogotá Declaration, signed in 1976 by eight equatorial states, expresses the concerns of developing states. The Notes that follow explore the international regime that has evolved with respect to access to the geostationary orbit.

THE BOGOTÁ DECLARATION

ITU Broadcasting Satellite Conference, Doc. No. 81–E (Jan. 17, 1977), Annex 4, reprinted in 2 *Manual on Space Law* 383 (Nandasiri Jasentuliyan & Roy S.K. Lee eds. 1979).

1. THE GEOSTATIONARY ORBIT AS A NATURAL RESOURCE * * *

Equatorial counties declare that the geostationary synchronous orbit is a physical fact linked to the reality of our planet because its existence depends exclusively on its relation to gravitational phenomena generated by the earth, and that is why it must not be considered part of the outer space. Therefore, the segments of geostationary synchronous orbit are part of the territory over which Equatorial states exercise their national sovereignty. The geostationary orbit is a scarce natural resource, whose importance and value increase rapidly together with the development of space technology and with the growing need for communication; therefore, the Equatorial countries meeting in Bogota have decided to proclaim and defend on behalf of their peoples, the existence of their sovereignty over this natural resource. The geostationary orbit represents a unique facility that it alone can offer for telecommunication services and other uses which require geostationary satellites.

The frequencies and orbit of geostationary satellites are limited natural resources, fully accepted as such by current standards of the International Telecommunications Union. Technological advancement has caused a continuous increase in the number of satellites that use this orbit, which could result in a saturation in the near future.

The solutions proposed by the International Telecommunications Union and the relevant documents that attempt to achieve a better use of the geostationary orbit that shall prevent its imminent saturation, are at present impracticable and unfair and would considerably increase the exploitation costs of this resource especially for developing countries that do not have equal technological and financial resources as compared to industrialized countries, who enjoy an apparent monopoly in the exploitation and use of its geostationary synchronous orbit. In spite of the principle established by Article 33, sub-paragraph 2 of the International Telecommunications Convention of 1973, that in the use of frequency bands for space radio communications, the members shall take into account that the frequencies and the orbit for geostationary satellites are limited natural resources and must be used efficiently and economically to allow the equitable access to this orbit and to its frequencies, we can see that both the geostationary orbit and the frequencies have been used in a way that does not allow the equitable access of the developing countries * * *. * * *

2. Sovereignty of Equatorial States over the Corresponding Segments of the Geostationary Orbit

In qualifying this orbit as a natural resource, equatorial states reaffirm "the right of the peoples and of nations to permanent sovereignty over their wealth and natural resources that must be exercised in the interest of their national development and of the welfare of the people of the nation concerned," as it is set forth in Resolution 2692 (XXV) of the United Nations General Assembly entitled "permanent sovereignty over the natural resources of developing countries and expansion of internal accumulation sources for economic developments."

Furthermore, the charter on economic rights and duties of states solemnly adopted by the United Nations General Assembly through Resolution 3281 (XXIX) * * *, in Article 2 subparagraph i, * * * reads:

"All states have and freely exercise full and permanent sovereignty, including possession, use and disposal of all their wealth, natural resources and economic activities."

Consequently, the above-mentioned provisions lead the equatorial states to affirm that the synchronous geostationary orbit, being a natural resource, is under the sovereignty of the equatorial states.

3. Legal Status of the Geostationary Orbit

Bearing in mind the existence of sovereign rights over segments of the geostationary orbit, the equatorial countries consider that the applicable legal consultations in this area must take into account the following:

(a) The sovereign rights put forward by the equatorial countries are directed towards rendering real benefits to their respective people and for the universal community, which is completely different from the present reality when the orbit is used to the greater benefit of the most developed countries.

(b) The segments of the orbit corresponding to the open sea * * * beyond the national jurisdiction of states will be considered as common heritage of mankind. Consequently, the competent international agencies should regulate its use and exploitation for the benefit of mankind.

(c) The equatorial states do not object to the free orbital transit of satellites approved and authorized by the International Telecommunications Convention, when these satellites pass through their outer space in their gravitational flight outside their geostationary orbit.

(d) The devices to be placed permanently on the segment of a geostationary orbit of an equatorial state shall require previous and expressed authorization on the part of the concerned state, and the operation of the device should conform with the national law of that territorial country over which it is placed. * * *

4. Treaty of 1967

The Treaty of 1967 on "The Principles Governing the Activities of States in the Exploration and Use of Outer Space, including the Moon and Other Celestial Bodies," signed on 27 January, 1967, cannot be considered as a final answer to the problem of the exploration and use of outer space, even less when the international community is questioning all the terms of international law which were elaborated when the developing countries could not count on adequate scientific advice and were thus not able to observe and evaluate the omissions, contradictions and consequences of the proposals which were prepared with great ability by the industrialized powers for their own benefit. * * *

The lack of a definition of outer space in the Treaty of 1967 * * * implies that Article II should not apply to geostationary orbit and therefore does not affect the right of the equatorial states that have already ratified the Treaty. * * *

Notes and Questions

1. *The Bogotá Declaration.* Is the Bogotá Declaration consistent with the Outer Space Treaty? The Declaration has never been generally accepted. What is its legal significance? Is it simply a claim in customary international law?

2. *The Boundaries of Outer Space.* States could reasonably assert that the sovereignty regime governing airspace, outlined in the previous set of Notes and Questions, applied to the geostationary orbit if that orbit is not in outer space. The definition of "outer space" is not clear. Although states have made a variety of proposals for a demarcation line between airspace and outer space drawing on scientific or functional criteria, they have not agreed on such a line. See I.H. Ph. Diederiks–Verschoor, *An Introduction to Space Law* 15–19 (1993).

3. *The International Telecommunication Union.* The International Telecommunication Union (ITU) is one of the several dozen regional and global international organizations directly involved with outer space activities. The ITU, which helps promote common technical and operating standards for telegraph, telephone, radio, and satellite communications, supplanted the International Telegraph Union, one of the oldest international organizations, formed in 1865. Virtually all states are members of the ITU, which now is one of the specialized agencies of the United Nations. One of the permanent organs of the ITU is the International Frequency Registration Board (IFRB), which records radio frequency assignments made by member states and recommends solutions when coordination with other assignments is needed. The IFRB also helps prepare World Administrative Radio Conferences (WARCs). According to the ITU Convention, regulations adopted by WARCs have the same legal status as the ITU Convention itself. See Francis Lyall, "Posts and Telecommunications," in 2 *United Nations Legal Order* 789, 796–822 (Oscar Schachter & Christopher C. Joyner eds. 1995).

4. *Allocating Orbital Positions.* Traditionally, access to the geostationary orbit has been governed by a "first come, first served" principle. Thus, with respect to proposed satellite services (which use the radio spectrum), the IFRB engaged in its normal recording, notification, and coordination functions. To what entities should orbital positions be allocated? Should they be allocated to states, to industries, or to international organizations? The IFRB currently registers frequencies and coordinates orbital positions only for states. An international organization such as INTELSAT, which provides a commercial telecommunications satellite system, can engage in the IFRB notification and coordination process only when one of its member states acts on its behalf; groups or corporations designated by states to represent them in INTELSAT cannot participate directly in the IFRB process.

5. *Equitable Access to the Geostationary Orbit.* The concerns of developing states were acknowledged in a 1982 revision of the ITU Convention. Article 33(2) of the 1973 ITU Convention provided that states had access to

frequencies and to the geostationary orbit equitably in conformity with the ITU's regulations and "according to their needs and the technical facilities at their disposal." International Telecommunication Convention, Oct. 25, 1973, art. 33(2), 28 U.S.T. 2495, 2530, 1209 U.N.T.S. 32, 268. Article 33(2) was revised in 1982 to take into account "the special needs of the developing countries and the special geographical situation of particular countries." Developing states also influenced a 1985–1988 WARC, known as WARC–ORB, which modified procedures for the notification and coordination of satellite systems using the geostationary orbit. The 1988 WARC–ORB Final Act refers to the "special needs" of developing states, and an allotment plan adopted at the conference effectively guarantees each state at least one geostationary orbital position, regardless of national ability to place a satellite into orbit. Orbital positions not allocated under this plan, and allocated positions not yet claimed, remain available for use through the IFRB's normal notification and coordination procedures. See Milton L. Smith, "The Space WARC Concludes," 83 *American Journal of International Law* 596 (1989).

6. *Balancing Efficiency, Equity, and Entrepreneurial Efforts.* How successfully does the current regime for allocating geostationary orbital positions implement the goals of Article I of the Outer Space Treaty? Article I states that outer space "shall be free for exploration and use by all States without discrimination of any kind, on a basis of equality." Article I also requires that the use of outer space "be carried out for the benefit and in the interests of all countries, irrespective of their degree of economic or scientific development." Consider the challenges posed to the current geostationary orbital regime by the Kingdom of Tonga. In 1990 Tonga, complying with the IFRB's standard procedures, indicated its intent to reserve positions for 31 satellite networks on behalf of TONGASAT, an entity owned by members of Tonga's ruling family and a U.S. entrepreneur. INTELSAT protested, although Tonga was not a party to INTELSAT and thus not bound by the INTELSAT requirement not to cause "significant economic harm" to INTELSAT's global satellite system. The IFRB, although lacking explicit authority to do so, responded to INTELSAT's concern by asking Tonga to cancel any notifications that it was not actually likely to require. Tonga revised its claims, reserving only six orbital positions; it has subsequently leased some of these to commercial enterprises.

C. THE LAW OF THE SEA

From at least the eighteenth century, vast areas of the oceans—the high seas—have been generally regarded as common spaces, not subject to the sovereignty or exclusive control of any state. On the high seas, the flag state of a vessel has the right to regulate a vessel's activities. By contrast, in internal waters, such as ports, and in a narrow band of oceans near the coast known as the territorial sea, coastal states exercise sovereign rights. Rights of flag states are limited in these zones.

In the mid-twentieth century, what had been a relatively stable legal regime for the oceans began to disintegrate. Some states made claims over broad coastal zones. These assertions of jurisdiction related in large part to changes in technology, permitting mining or drilling for oil on the continental shelf. The ability of foreign trawlers and factory ships to capture and process huge quantities of fish near the shores of coastal states also contributed to proclamations of broad coastal fisheries zones. Assertions of coastal state control over broad coastal zones concerned maritime powers, which feared infringements on traditional navigational freedoms.

The modern law of the sea has been fundamentally shaped by the Third United Nations Conference on the Law of the Sea (UNCLOS III). UNCLOS III formally convened in 1973, following six years of studies and preparatory work by United Nations bodies. The Conference itself required 11 full sessions totalling 585 days, as well as numerous intersessional meetings of negotiating groups and lengthy consultations among delegates and lawyers within their own governments. It culminated in the 1982 United Nations Convention on the Law of the Sea, which entered into force in November 1994. The 1982 Convention codifies many principles that had previously been generally accepted in customary and treaty law. It also introduces or affirms new concepts, concerning the exclusive economic zone, fishing rights, the continental shelf, marine scientific research, pollution, transit passage through straits, the breadth of the territorial sea, and rights of landlocked states.

Part XI of the 1982 Convention, which establishes institutions to govern the mining of the deep sea bed beyond national jurisdiction, has proved particularly controversial. United Nations resolutions preceding UNCLOS III, and the Convention itself, declared the mineral resources of the deep sea bed to be the "common heritage of mankind." When the Convention finally received its sixtieth ratification in November 1993—necessary for its entry into force a year later—no major developed state had accepted it, with the United States leading the opposition to Part XI. Consultations at the United Nations eventually led to a July 1994 compromise agreement concerning sea-bed mining. Several developed states have now accepted the Convention, as modified by the 1994 agreement, and over 110 states are now parties.

International lawyers have debated whether the various new provisions in the 1982 Convention amount to customary international law, or whether they can only be binding as treaty law. Some argue that the Convention is a "package deal," the product of numerous compromises and trade-offs, and that a state cannot claim particular rights concerning the oceans while rejecting certain obligations. Others argue that acceptance of provisions at UNCLOS III, coupled with state practice, provide the necessary consensus for the bulk of the Convention to be considered customary international law.

International lawyers do not usually speak of one regime governing the oceans, for law of the sea issues are so diverse. It probably is more helpful to think about a regime governing warships, for example, and another governing sea-bed mining. The 1982 Convention, customary international law, other treaties, and regulations of international organizations such as the International Maritime Organization shape the law in many issue areas. Numerous other regional and global bodies, including the Intergovernmental Oceanographic Commission, the Food and Agriculture Organization, and the United Nations Environment Program, also have significant responsibilities for marine-related issues.

This Part begins with a look at two traditional law of the sea issues—the high seas and the nationality of vessels. It then explores assertions of coastal state jurisdiction over parts of the commons and over resources on the continental shelf, in exclusive economic zones, and in coastal fisheries zones. The last two sections address, respectively, changes affecting navigation rights (especially in the territorial sea) and the regime governing deep sea-bed mining. The various articles of the 1982 U.N. Convention that are cited throughout this Part are reproduced in the Appendix.

1. THE HIGH SEAS

HUGO GROTIUS, THE FREEDOM OF THE SEAS (1633)

Ralph van Deman Magoffin trans. & James Brown Scott ed. 1916.

CHAPTER I * * *

My intention is to demonstrate briefly and clearly that the Dutch—that is to say, the subjects of the United Netherlands—have the right to sail to the East Indies, as they are now doing, and to engage in trade with the people there. I shall base my argument on the following most specific and unimpeachable axiom of the Law of Nations, called a primary rule or first principle, the spirit of which is self-evident and immutable, to wit; Every nation is free to travel to every other nation, and to trade with it.

God Himself says this speaking through the voice of nature; and inasmuch as it is not His will to have Nature supply every place with all the necessaries of life, He ordains that some nations excel in one art and others in another. Why is this His will, except it be that He wished human friendships to be engendered by mutual needs and resources, lest individuals deeming themselves entirely sufficient unto themselves should for that very reason be rendered unsociable? * * * Those therefore who deny this law, destroy this most praiseworthy bond of human fellowship, remove the opportunities for doing mutual service, in a word do violence to Nature herself. For do not the ocean[s], navigable in every direction with which God has encompassed all the earth, and the regular and the occasional winds which blow now from one quarter and now from another, offer sufficient proof that Nature has given to all peoples a right of access to all other peoples? * * *

CHAPTER V * * *

If therefore the Portuguese have acquired no legal right over the nations of the East Indies, and their territory and sovereignty, let us consider whether they have been able to obtain exclusive jurisdiction over the sea and its navigation or over trade. Let us first consider the case of the sea.

Now, in the legal phraseology of the Law of Nations, the sea is called indifferently the property of no one (*res nullius*), or a common possession (*res communis*), or public property (*res publica*). It will be most convenient to explain the signification of these terms if we follow the practice of all the poets since Hesiod, of the philosophers and jurists of the past, and distinguish certain epochs, the divisions of which are marked off perhaps not so much by intervals of time as by obvious logic and essential character. And we ought not to be criticized if in our explanation of a law deriving from nature, we use the authority and definition of those whose natural judgment admittedly is held in the highest esteem. * * *

* * * [C]ommon possession relates to use, as is seen from a quotation from Seneca:

> "Every path was free, All things were used in common."

According to his reasoning there was a kind of sovereignty, but it was universal and unlimited. For God had not given all things to this individual or to that, but to the entire human race, and thus a number of persons, as it were *en masse*, were not debarred from being substantially sovereigns or owners of the same thing, which is quite contradictory to our modern meaning of sovereignty. For it now implies particular or private ownership, a thing which no one then had. * * *

It seems certain that the transition to the present distinction of ownerships did not come violently, but gradually, nature herself pointing out the way. For since there are some things, the use of which consists in their being used up, either because having become part of the very substance of the user they can never be used again, or because by use they become less fit for future use, it has become apparent, especially in dealing with the first category, such things as food and drink for example, that a certain kind of ownership is inseparable from use. For 'own' implies that a thing belongs to some one person, in such a way that it cannot belong to any other person. By the process of reasoning this was next extended to things of the second category, such as clothes and movables and some living things. * * *

This occupation or possession, however, in the case of things which resist seizure, like wild animals for example, must be uninterrupted or perpetually maintained, but in the case of other things it is sufficient if after physical possession is once taken the intention to possess is maintained. Possession of movables implies seizure, and possession of immovables either the erection of buildings or some determination of boundaries, such as fencing in. * * *

Two conclusions may be drawn from what has thus far been said. The first is, that which cannot be occupied, or which never has been occupied, cannot be the property of any one, because all property has arisen from occupation. The second is, that all that which has been so constituted by nature that although serving some one person it still suffices for the common use of all other persons, is today and ought in perpetuity to remain in the same condition as when it was first created by nature. * * *

The air * * * is not susceptible of occupation; and * * * its common use is destined for all men. For the same reasons the sea is common to all, because it is so limitless that it cannot become a possession of any one, and because it is adapted for the use of all, whether we consider it from the point of view of navigation or of fisheries. * * *

These things therefore are what the Romans call "common" to all men by natural law, or as we have said, "public" according to the law of nations; and indeed they call their use sometimes common, sometimes public. Nevertheless, although those things are with reason said to be *res nullius*, so far as private ownership is concerned, still they differ very much from those things which, though also *res nullius*, have not been marked out for common use, such for example as wild animals, fish, and birds. For if any one seizes those things and assumes possession of them, they can become objects of private ownership, but the things in the former category by the consensus of opinion of all mankind are forever exempt from such private ownership on account of their susceptibility to universal use; and as they belong to all they cannot be taken away from all by any one person any more than what is mine can be taken away from me by you. * * *

The nature of the sea * * * differs from that of the shore, because the sea, except for a very restricted space, can neither easily be built upon, nor inclosed; if the contrary were true yet this could hardly happen without hindrance to the general use. Nevertheless, if any small portion of the sea can be thus occupied, the occupation is recognized. * * *

Now Celsus holds that piles driven into the sea belong to the man who drove them. But such an act is not permissible if the use of the sea be thereby impaired. * * * Labeo * * * holds that in case any * * * construction should be made in the sea, the following injunction is to be enforced: "Nothing may be built in the sea whereby the harbor, the roadstead, or the channel be rendered less safe for navigation."

Now the same principle which applies to navigation applies also to fishing, namely, that it remains free and open to all. Nevertheless there shall be no prejudice if any one shall by fencing off with stakes an inlet of the sea make a fish pond for himself, and so establish a private preserve. * * *

* * * But outside of an inlet this will not hold, for then the common use of the sea might be hindered. * * *

* * * The Portuguese claim as their own the whole expanse of the sea which separates two parts of the world so far distant the one from the other, that in all the preceding centuries neither one has so much as

heard of the other. Indeed, if we take into account the share of the Spaniards, whose claim is the same as that of the Portuguese, only a little less than the whole ocean is found to be subject to two nations, while all the rest of the peoples in the world are restricted to the narrow bounds of the northern seas. * * * If in a thing so vast as the sea a man were to reserve to himself from general use nothing more than mere sovereignty, still he would be considered a seeker after unreasonable power. If a man were to enjoin other people from fishing, he would not escape the reproach of monstrous greed. But the man who even prevents navigation, a thing which means no loss to himself, what are we to say of him? * * *

* * * For it is most outrageous for you to appropriate a thing, which both by ordinance of nature and by common consent is as much mine as yours, so exclusively that you will not grant me a right of use in it which leaves it no less yours than it was before. * * *

CHAPTER VII * * *

The last defense of injustice is usually a claim or plea based on prescription or on custom. To this defense therefore the Portuguese have resorted. But the best established reasoning of the law precludes them from enjoying the protection of either plea. * * *

* * * [I]t is impossible to acquire by usucaption or prescription things which cannot become property, that is, which are not susceptible of possession or of quasi-possession, and which cannot be alienated. All of which is true of the sea and its use. * * *

* * * [S]ince the law of nature arises out of Divine Providence, it is immutable; but a part of this natural law is the primary or primitive law of nations, differing from the secondary or positive law of nations, which is mutable. For if there are customs incompatible with the primary law of nations, then, according to the judgment of Vasquez, they are not customs belonging to men, but to wild beasts, customs which are corruptions and abuses, not laws and usages. Therefore those customs cannot become prescriptions by mere lapse of time, cannot be justified by the passage of any law, cannot be established by the consent, the protection, or the practice even of many nations. * * *

The conclusion of the whole matter therefore is that the Portuguese are in possession of no right whereby they may interdict to any nation whatsoever the navigation of the Ocean to the East Indies.

UNITED NATIONS CONVENTION ON THE LAW OF THE SEA, ARTICLES 86–90, 301

Dec. 10, 1982, U.N. Doc. A/CONF.62.122.

Part VII

High Seas

Article 86

Application of the provisions of this Part

The provisions of this Part apply to all parts of the sea that are not included in the exclusive economic zone, in the territorial sea or in the internal waters of a State, or in the archipelagic waters of an archipelagic State. This article does not entail any abridgement of the freedoms enjoyed by all States in the exclusive economic zone in accordance with article 58.

Article 87

Freedom of the high seas

1. The high seas are open to all States, whether coastal or land-locked. Freedom of the high seas is exercised under the conditions laid down by this Convention and by other rules of international law. It comprises, *inter alia,* both for coastal and land-locked States:

(a) freedom of navigation;

(b) freedom of overflight;

(c) freedom to lay submarine cables and pipelines, subject to Part VI;

(d) freedom to construct artificial islands and other installations permitted under international law, subject to Part VI;

(e) freedom of fishing, subject to the conditions laid down in section 2;

(f) freedom of scientific research, subject to Parts VI and XIII.

2. These freedoms shall be exercised by all States with due regard for the interests of other States in their exercise of the freedom of the high seas, and also with due regard for the rights under this Convention with respect to activities in the Area.

Article 88

Reservation of the high seas for peaceful purposes

The high seas shall be reserved for peaceful purposes.

Article 89

Invalidity of claims of sovereignty over the high seas

No State may validly purport to subject any part of the high seas to its sovereignty.

Article 90

Right of navigation

Every State, whether coastal or land-locked, has the right to sail ships flying its flag on the high seas. * * *

PART XVI

General Provisions * * *

Article 301

Peaceful uses of the seas

In exercising their rights and performing their duties under this Convention, States Parties shall refrain from any threat or use of force against the territorial integrity or political independence of any State, or in any other manner inconsistent with the principles of international law embodied in the Charter of the United Nations.

Notes and Questions

1. *Hugo Grotius.* Hugo Grotius was a prodigy. He knew Latin and Greek by age 8, entered university at age 11, edited an encyclopedia at 15, was a lawyer pleading cases in the highest court of the Netherlands at 16, and became Attorney General of the Netherlands by the time he was 24. Grotius gained fame not only as a lawyer, but as a diplomat and political and legal theorist. He is one of the most important figures in the history of international law. *De Mare Liberum* was originally a chapter of *De Iure Praeda* (*Commentary on the Law of Prize and Booty*), a work written in 1604–1605. Grotius's most famous work, *De Jure Belli ac Pacis* (*On the Law of War and Peace*), was published in 1625.

2. *Grotius and High Seas Freedoms.* Grotius wrote *De Iure Praeda* to support Dutch access to the East Indian trade and to dispute Portugal's claims over the high seas. *De Mare Liberum* was separately published in 1609, probably in anticipation of a proclamation by King James I of England which prohibited foreigners from fishing in "British seas" unless they obtained a British license. How does Grotius envision the legal regime of the high seas? How does he support his position?

3. *John Selden and Closed Seas.* Grotius's views did not go unchallenged. The best-known response is that of the Englishman John Selden, who published *Mare Clausum sive De Domino Maris* in 1635. Selden argued that the seas could be appropriated, and that various uses of the oceans could diminish the owner's rights. Selden's work supported such British practices as requiring foreigners to obtain fishing licenses, demanding that foreign ships strike their flags in salute to British ships in "British seas," stopping hostilities by foreign ships in those seas, and imposing certain tolls on the passage of foreign vessels. See Ruth Lapidoth, "Freedom of Navigation—Its Legal History and Its Normative Basis," 6 *Journal of Maritime Law & Commerce* 259 (1975).

4. *British Sea Power and High Seas Freedoms.* Grotius's notion of the high seas as not subject to exclusive sovereignty came to be generally accepted:

> During the 19th century, British sea power, then supreme, helped consolidate an international maritime regime based on the freedoms of the high seas, freedoms to travel and to fish without coastal state regulation outside a 3–mile territorial sea. This was a customary legal regime, not written in any convention or treaty. It was, however, remarkably effective, respected by most states in times of peace from the end of the Napoleonic Wars in 1815 to the end of World War II in 1945. As a result, for over a century, navies and other users of the oceans could sail freely on seas covering some 70 percent of the earth's surface. Only within a narrow band of 3 miles, the territorial sea, did coastal states put some legal limits on the mobility of naval forces.

Mark W. Janis, *Sea Power and the Law of the Sea* xiii-xiv (1976).

5. *Twentieth-century Conceptions of High Seas Freedoms.* Article 2 of the 1958 Geneva Convention on the High Seas explicitly named navigation, fishing, overflight, and the laying of submarine cables and pipelines as high seas freedoms. These are repeated in Article 87 of the 1982 Convention on the Law of the Sea, which adds the freedom of scientific research and the freedom to build artificial islands and other installations permitted under international law to the list of high seas freedoms. Are other, unenumerated uses legitimate? For example, states have, from time to time, used the high seas for military purposes. Would it be legitimate for a state to declare a military test site in the oceans? To place weapons or military detection devices on the sea bed, invoking traditional high seas freedoms? What do you make of Articles 88 and 301 of the 1982 Convention? Overall, what modifications of the Grotian conception of *mare liberum* do Articles 86–90 of the 1982 United Nations Convention on the Law of the Sea reflect?

6. *Controlling Activities on the High Seas.* If the high seas are generally open to ships for a variety of purposes, who is responsible for maintaining order there? What if a ship engages in such egregious practices as slave trading, piracy, or the dumping of dangerous chemicals? The next two readings address the system of control over activities on the high seas.

2. VESSELS

CASE OF THE MUSCAT DHOWS

France–Great Britain, 1905, in *The Hague Arbitration Cases* 64 (George G. Wilson ed. 1915).

The Tribunal of Arbitration constituted in virtue of the Compromis concluded at London on October 13, 1904 between Great Britain and France;

Whereas the Government of His Britannic Majesty and that of the French Republic have thought it right by the Declaration of March 10, 1862 "to engage reciprocally to respect the independence" of His Highness the Sultan of Muscat,

Whereas difficulties as to the scope of that Declaration have arisen in relation to the issue, by the French Republic, to certain subjects of His Highness the Sultan of Muscat of papers authorizing them to fly the

French flag, and also as to the nature of the privileges and immunities claimed by subjects of His Highness who are owners or masters of dhows and in possession of such papers or are members of the crew of such dhows and their families, especially as to the manner in which such privileges and immunities affect the jurisdiction of His Highness the Sultan over his said subjects,

Whereas the two Governments have agreed by the Compromis of October 13, 1904 that these questions shall be determined by reference to arbitration * * *;

As to the First Question:

Whereas generally speaking it belongs to every Sovereign to decide to whom he will accord the right to fly his flag and to prescribe the rules governing such grants, and whereas therefore the granting of the French flag to subjects of His Highness the Sultan of Muscat in itself constitutes no attack on the independence of the Sultan,

Whereas nevertheless a Sovereign may be limited by treaties in the exercise of this right, and * * * whereas therefore the question arises, under what conditions Powers which have acceded to the General Act of the Brussels Conference of July 2, 1890 relative to the African Slave Trade, especially to article 32 of this Act, are entitled to authorize native vessels to fly their flags,

Whereas by article 32 of this Act the faculty of the Signatory Powers to grant their flag to native vessels has been limited for the purpose of suppressing slave trading and in the general interests of humanity, irrespective of whether the applicant for the flag may belong to a state signatory of this Act or not, and whereas at any rate France is in relation to Great Britain bound to grant her flag only under the conditions prescribed by this Act,

Whereas in order to attain the above mentioned purpose, the Signatory Powers of the Brussels Act have agreed in its article 32 that the authority to fly the flag of one of the Signatory Powers shall in future only be granted to such native vessels, which shall satisfy all the three following conditions:

I. Their fitters-out or owners must be either subjects of or persons protected by [protégés] the Power whose flag they claim to fly,

2. They must furnish proof that they possess real estate situated in the district of the authority to whom their application is addressed, or supply a solvent security as a guarantee for any fines to which they may eventually become liable,

3. Such fitters-out or owners, as well as the captain of the vessel, must furnish proof that they enjoy a good reputation, and especially that they have never been condemned for acts of slave trade,

Whereas in default of a definition of the term "protégé" in the General Act of the Brussels Conference this term must be understood in the sense which corresponds best as well to the elevated aims of the Conference and its Final Act, as to the principles of the law of nations, as they have been expressed in treaties existing at that time, in internationally recognized legislation and in international practice,

Whereas the aim of the said article 32 is to admit to navigation in the seas infested by slave trade only those native vessels which are under the strictest surveillance of the Signatory Powers, a condition which can only be secured if the owners, fitters-out and crews of such vessels are exclusively subjected to the sovereignty and jurisdiction of the State, under whose flag they are sailing, * * *

[The tribunal examines the meaning of the term "protégé." It reviews several instruments, including an 1863 French treaty and an 1863 municipal statute that limited France's rights to create new "protégés."]

Whereas the fact of having granted before the ratification of the Brussels Act on January 2, 1892 authorizations to fly the French flag to native vessels not satisfying the conditions prescribed by article 32 of this Act was not in contradiction with any international obligation of France,

For These Reasons,

decides and pronounces as follows:

1. before the 2nd of January 1892 France was entitled to authorize vessels belonging to subjects of His Highness the Sultan of Muscat to fly the French flag, only bound by her own legislation and administrative rules;

2. owners of dhows, who before 1892 have been authorized by France to fly the French flag, retain this authorization as long as France renews it to the grantee;

3. after January 2, 1892 France was not entitled to authorize vessels belonging to subjects of His Highness the Sultan of Muscat to fly the French flag, except on condition that their owners or fitters-out had established or should establish that they had been considered and treated by France as her "protégés" before the year 1863;

As to the 2nd Question:

Whereas the legal situation of vessels flying foreign flags and of the owners of such vessels in the territorial waters of an Oriental State is determined by the general principles of jurisdiction, by the capitulations or other treaties and by the practice resulting therefrom,

Whereas the terms of the Treaty of Friendship and Commerce between France and the Iman of Muscat of November 17, 1844 are [comprehensive enough to preclude visits by the authorities of the Sultan to French vessels without the consent of such vessels],

Whereas, although it cannot be denied that by admitting the right of France to grant under certain circumstances her flag to native vessels and to have these vessels exempted from visitation by the authorities of the Sultan or in his name, slave trade is facilitated, because slave traders may easily abuse the French flag, for the purpose of escaping from search, the possibility of this abuse, which can be entirely suppressed by the accession of all Powers to article 42 of the Brussels Convention, cannot affect the decision of this case, which must only rest on juridical grounds, * * *

FOR THESE REASONS,

decides and pronounces as follows:

1. dhows of Muscat authorized as aforesaid to fly the French flag are entitled in the territorial waters of Muscat to the inviolability provided by the French–Muscat Treaty of November 17, 1844; * * *.

Done at The Hague, in the Permanent Court of Arbitration, August 8, 1905.

SAFER SHIPS, CLEANER SEAS

Report of Lord Donaldson's Inquiry Into the Prevention of Pollution From Merchant Shipping, Cm. 2560 (1994).

1.1 On 5 January 1993 one of the Shetland Islanders' worst nightmares became a reality. The MV *BRAER* went onto the rocks at Garths Ness. She was fully laden with 84,700 tonnes of Norwegian Gullfaks crude oil and some 1,600 tonnes of heavy fuel oil bunkers. The weather was atrocious—storm force winds and mountainous seas. There were all the makings of a major economic and ecological disaster for the local community.

1.2 In the event the consequences were serious but miraculously less catastrophic than might have been expected. * * *

1.29 * * * [T]he *BRAER* was registered in Liberia * * *. * * *

1.31 It must not be forgotten that on 3 December 1992, only a month before the *BRAER* was wrecked off Shetland, the tanker *AEGEAN SEA* was wrecked off La Coruña in northern Spain. * * *

6.1 In an ideal world Flag States, whose flags are worn by the world's shipping, would lay down, and enforce upon their own shipowners, standards of design, maintenance and operation which would ensure a very high standard of safety at sea. Coastal States, along whose coasts shipping passes, and Port States, at whose ports or anchorages shipping calls, would have no cause to concern themselves with the maintenance of such standards.

6.2 The present system of Flag State Control falls well short of this ideal. At any one time the fleet of any Flag State will be scattered throughout the world. No Flag State has the resources to police its fleet on a continuous and all-embracing basis. The most that it can do is to insist upon periodic surveys and to undertake *ad hoc* inspection if it learns that a ship has suffered a casualty or, for some other reason such as a Port State Control inspection, it suspects that its ship no longer complies with internationally agreed standards. Good shipowners will maintain the seaworthiness of their ships regardless of whether a Flag State periodical survey is imminent. Regrettably, bad shipowners regard the imminence of such a survey as the only reason for spending money on maintenance or repairs and then only if satisfied that the survey will be thorough.

6.3 In this situation, even if Flag States were to comply to the full with their responsibilities, Coastal and Port States would have a part to play. They would, in their own interests, be concerned to detect the few unseaworthy ships which had escaped the Flag State net. Their role would be to supplement and support Flag State Control, but not to substitute for it.

6.4 Regrettably it is beyond argument that not all Flag States live up to their responsibilities. Figures for deficiencies and detections revealed by Port State Control inspections show that, for example, of 61 Indian registered ships inspected over one in four were so seriously deficient that they had to be detained in port. Over 85 per cent of the inspections of Indian registered ships uncovered deficiencies. India, although a striking example, is by no means alone and a number of other Flag States also have a poor record. * * *

6.5 In 1992 6,500 different foreign flag vessels called at UK ports. Excluding short-sea ferries and fishing vessels, there were 82,600 arrivals of which 61,100, or 74 per cent, were foreign flagged. These figures demonstrate two interrelated facts of crucial importance.

6.6 First, that the proportion of the world's shipping which still flies the Red Ensign and which is thus directly or indirectly subject to UK Flag State Control has steadily declined. In 1970 the UK registered merchant fleet was the third largest in the world, amounting to over 11 percent of the world's gross tonnage. By 1979, despite UK tonnage remaining at a similar level to that in 1970, this had fallen to under 7 per cent because of the overall increase in world tonnage. Since then the tonnage of the UK fleet has declined significantly as world tonnage has increased, to the extent that by June 1992 the tonnage of UK registered merchant vessels was less than a quarter of that in 1979 and amounted to just 1.35 per cent of the total.

6.7 Second, the UK, as a major trading nation wholly surrounded by sea, is heavily dependent upon foreign flagged shipping for the movement of its goods. * * *

6.8 A State which confers its nationality upon a ship, and thus authorizes it to fly its flag, has an unfettered right to subject that ship to its laws. This enables it to impose and maintain standards of design, construction, equipment, maintenance and operation. Whilst there is no upper limit to these standards, there are lower limits. These stem from the various international Conventions to which Flag States are parties, such as the SOLAS, MARPOL 73/78 and Load Line Conventions, under which Flag States are required to establish that ships flying their flags comply with the provisions of those Conventions and to issue the necessary certificates of compliance. * * *

6.9 Economic and competitive considerations effectively prevent Flag States from imposing standards which are higher than those internationally agreed and any improvement in standards is thus only achievable by international agreement. The machinery for such agreement is provided by the International Maritime Organization (IMO). * * *

6.12 It is for Flag States individually to decide how to give effect to their international obligations. In some cases the international Conventions specify precise requirements. SOLAS, for example, requires minimum pressures at fire hydrants and MARPOL includes precise formulae for the calculation of positions of ballast tanks. But in other cases, the Conventions merely specify that equipment must be "approved" by the Flag State or be "to the satisfaction of the Flag State." Sometimes such lack of precision is necessary for technical reasons or to allow for innovation. Regrettably in others it is merely designed to conceal differences of view between the members of IMO. * * *

6.18 When the international Conventions were originally drafted, most of the world's merchant fleet was owned by, and flew the flags of, the world's major maritime and trading powers. These States had already established survey and inspection of their ships as a matter of public policy aimed at protecting the safety of crews and passengers. While the setting of such standards was not immune from commercial pressures from shipowning interests, their enforcement was not subject to such pressures. This was presumably in reflection of the fact that in the UK, for example, there had been a long history of regulation through the Board of Trade and the fact that most UK trade was carried in UK ships which were subject to the same standards and accordingly competed fairly with one another. States had little or no direct financial interest in shipping and could apply and enforce standards in the interests of public policy without feeling any pressure to maintain or enhance their merchant fleets.

6.19 All that has changed. Today few States regard it as consistent with their national status and dignity to be without a register of national shipping of as large a size as possible. Some also regard such a register as a useful source of income. In seeking to achieve this aim, some see no need to limit eligibility to ships whose owners or operators have any connection with the State. They maintain what are called "open" registers. A few such States are landlocked and have no connection with the sea. Rather more include ships which are never likely to call at a national port. Perhaps in recognition of this fact one of the largest and, it has to be said, one of the most efficient, Liberia, maintains its register and discharges its responsibilities from an office in the USA. Relatively few Liberian ships ever call at Monrovia, their usual port of registry. Another example is Vanuatu, which has few foreign exports and whose register is run from the USA and London.

6.20 All this might be unobjectionable if, despite the very considerable difficulties in enforcing standards on ships (and shipowners) which have no real connection with the State whose flag the ships fly, agreed international standards were universally enforced. However they are not. The vice of "open" registers is twofold. First, in practice they lead to varying standards of safety. This is easily demonstrated by [statistics on] the incidence of total losses by flag. Second, the existence of "open" registers and the consequent ease with which ships can be transferred to a different register and flag has led to some shipowners shopping around for the registers which have the lowest standards of enforcement and which, in consequence, involve them in the least expense. This is positively encouraged by some of the Flag States concerned which have even been known to advertise competitive "prices" for their survey and certification work.

Notes and Questions

1. *The* Muscat Dhows *Arbitration.* The *Muscat Dhows Case* arose after the British captured, at the request of the Sultan of Oman, five Omani subjects holding French papers. Britain agreed to advise the Sultan to release the men if France agreed to arbitrate the question of the rights of French flag holders in the area. The arbitration was set against the backdrop of competing French and British efforts to assert authority in the Persian Gulf, with French influence on the wane. Also in the background were a series of French–British treaties the British had relied on to exercise limited rights with respect to vessels flying the French flag that were suspected of engaging in the slave trade.

Note that Muscat (Oman) was not a party to the arbitration. The Sultan was reportedly dissuaded from sending an Omani representative to The Hague because of the cost involved, and he asked Britain to act on Oman's behalf. France was not willing to accept this arrangement, however, and Oman was left out of the case. Following the arbitral decision, it took France and Britain over three years to agree on which particular French protégés and dhows were "grandfathered" under the French flag. For accounts of the arbitration and events leading up to it, see Briton Cooper Busch, *Britain and the Persian Gulf, 1894–1914*, at 154–86 (1967), and Charles Brunet–Millon, *Les Boutriers de la Mer des Indes* (1910).

2. *The Nationality of Ships.* During the *Muscat Dhows* arbitration, Great Britain argued that "Frenchifying" the dhows infringed upon the independence of the Sultan of Muscat, because dhows owned by Muscat nationals were "thereby withdrawn from their natural jurisdiction" and could not be searched by Muscat warships. *The Times (London)*, July 25, 1905, at 5. The arbitral tribunal, however, affirmed the general rule that a state may authorize any vessel to fly its flag. The flag that a ship is entitled to fly is a symbol of its nationality. See Article 91(1) of the 1982 U.N. Convention on the Law of the Sea.

3. *Flag State Authority and the Nationality of Ships.* Why is it important for ships to have nationality? Consider the following passage from United States v. Marino–Garcia, 679 F.2d 1373, 1382 (11th Cir.1982), in which the court addresses the nature of stateless vessels:

> * * * Vessels without nationality are international pariahs. They have no internationally recognized right to navigate freely on the high seas. Moreover, flagless vessels are frequently not subject to the laws of a flag-state. As such they represent "floating sanctuaries from authority" and constitute a potential threat to the order and stability of navigation on the high seas.
>
> The absence of any right to navigate freely on the high seas coupled with the potential threat to order on international waterways has led various courts to conclude that international law places no restrictions upon a nation's right to subject stateless vessels to its jurisdiction.

Is it important that ships have only one nationality? Article 92(2) of the 1982 Convention assimilates a ship flying the flags of more than one state, and using them according to convenience, to a stateless ship. On the high seas, a ship is generally immune from the exercise of jurisdiction except by the authorities of the ship's flag state. See Article 92(1) of the U.N. Convention on the Law of the Sea. Articles 105, 109, 110, and 111 of the Convention reflect limited exceptions to the principle of exclusive flag state jurisdiction and control on the high seas.

4. *Open Registry.* A system of flag state control poses difficulties if a flag state cannot or will not control its ships. The *Muscat Dhows* tribunal expresses concern that "slavetraders may easily abuse the French flag, for the purpose of escaping from search." Almost 90 years later the Liberian-flag *Braer* spilled huge quantities of crude oil when it ran aground off the Shetlands. The Braer's largely Filipino crew told the International Transport Workers' Federation in 1992 that the aging ship was undermanned. Jason Benetto, "The Cut-price Recipe for Catastrophe," *Independent on Sunday*, Jan. 10, 1993, at 22. Although vessels registered in "open registry" (also known as "flag of convenience") states certainly are not responsible for all vessel safety and pollution problems—the *Exxon Valdez*, which caused a massive oil spill off Alaska in 1989, was registered in the United States—the safety record of many such vessels has been questionable.

A 1970 British committee headed by Lord Rochdale identified six features common to open registry:

(i) The country of registry allows ownership and/or control of its merchant vessels by non-citizens;

(ii) Access to the registry is easy. A ship may usually be registered at a consul's office abroad. Equally important, transfer from the registry at the owner's option is not restricted;

(iii) Taxes on the income from the ships are not levied locally or are low. A registry fee and an annual fee, based on tonnage, are normally the only charges made. A guarantee or acceptable understanding regarding future freedom from taxation may also be given;

(iv) The country of registry is a small power with no national requirement under any foreseeable circumstances for all the shipping registered, but receipts from very small charges on a large tonnage may produce a substantial effect on its national income and balance of payments;

(v) Manning of ships by non-nationals is freely permitted; and

(vi) The country of registry has neither the power nor the administrative machinery effectively to impose any government or international regulations; nor has the country the wish or the power to control the companies themselves.

Committee of Inquiry into Shipping, *Report* 51 (London: HMSO, Cmnd. 4337, 1970). Approximately one-third of the world's tanker fleet flies Liberian or Panamanian flags, and the Bahamas, Malta, and Vanuatu also maintain large ship registers.

5. *Limiting Flag State Grants of Nationality.* In the *Muscat Dhows Case*, should France have had an unqualified right to determine the conditions under which a vessel was entitled to fly the French flag? Would conditions such as those set forth in Article 32 of the General Act of the Brussels Conference of 1890 make sense today?

States generally have not accepted significant limitations on their right to grant nationality to vessels. One limited response to open registry is the "genuine link" requirement, reflected in the International Law Commission's preparatory work for the 1958 United Nations Conference on the Law of the Sea. This requirement found its way into Article 5 of the 1958 Convention on the High Seas and Article 91(1) of the 1982 Convention on the Law of the Sea. What does this requirement mean? If one state were to determine that an open registry state had granted nationality to a ship with which a "genuine link" were absent, what would be the effect of that determination? Compare the *Nottebohm Case* in Chapter 6. Is a "genuine link" requirement for the nationality of ships sensible?

6. *Specifying the Responsibilities of Flag States.* States have accepted treaty provisions insisting that each flag state exercise administrative and supervisory responsibilities with respect to ships flying its flag. In this regard, do Articles 94 and 217 of the 1982 Convention on the Law of the Sea provide a reasonable approach to the challenges posed by open registry states? Would a system of inspections and approvals of ship safety by an international regulatory body be preferable?

7. *Coastal State Control of Foreign Flag Vessels.* The second question discussed in the *Muscat Dhows Case* suggests that a coastal state may visit foreign flag vessels while they are in the territorial sea, a zone of coastal state sovereignty that today may extend up to 12 miles from a state's coastal baselines. The coastal state may by treaty limit its rights in this regard, as Muscat had done in this case. Today, the exercise of jurisdiction by a coastal state over foreign flag merchant ships passing through the territorial sea and over people on board is addressed in Articles 27–28 of the U.N. Convention on the Law of the Sea. The right of a foreign flag vessel to "innocent passage" through a coastal state's territorial sea is discussed in Section 4 of this Part.

With respect to pollution issues, coastal states have considerable rights to set standards and to take enforcement measures in their offshore zones.

These measures can affect foreign flag ships. Should coastal states ever have rights with respect to pollution from foreign flag ships on the high seas? See Articles 220–221 of the U.N. Convention on the Law of the Sea.

8. *Port State Control of Foreign Flag Vessels.* What are the advantages and disadvantages of port state control over foreign flag vessels? Articles 218 and 219 of the 1982 U.N. Convention on the Law of the Sea authorize port states to take some enforcement measures with respect to marine pollution by foreign flag vessels that are voluntarily in port. Are there functions other than enforcement measures that a port state should undertake with respect to foreign flag ships?

9. *Multiple Treaty Obligations.* Besides the 1982 U.N. Convention on the Law of the Sea, other treaties set substantive and jurisdictional rules with respect to ships and shipboard activities. The 1958 Geneva Convention on the High Seas contains articles that are very similar to the high seas articles of the 1982 Convention. Some treaties address specific activities. See, *e.g.*, International Convention for the Suppression of Unlawful Acts against the Safety of Maritime Navigation, Mar. 10, 1988, 27 I.L.M. 668 (1988); Vienna Convention Against Illicit Traffic in Narcotic Drugs and Psychotropic Substances, Dec. 20, 1988, 28 I.L.M. 497 (1989); Narcotic Drugs: Interdiction of Vessels, U.S.-U.K., Nov. 13, 1981, 33 U.S.T. 4224.

Many of the 1982 Law of the Sea Convention's articles concerning maritime safety and protection of the marine environment are broadly worded. Other conventions, often drafted by the International Maritime Organization (IMO), contain specific substantive standards. Lord Donaldson's Report mentions a few examples: the Convention on Safety of Life at Sea, Nov. 1, 1974, 1184 U.N.T.S. 2, 32 U.S.T. 47 (SOLAS); the International Convention on the Prevention of Pollution from Ships, Nov. 2 1973, 13 I.L.M. 605 (1974), and its 1978 Protocol, Feb. 17, 1978, 17 I.L.M. 548 (1978)(MARPOL 73/78); and the International Convention on Load Lines, Apr. 5, 1966, 640 U.N.T.S. 133, 18 U.S.T. 1857. The 1982 Convention also, in places, requires municipal laws to have at least the same effect as "generally accepted international rules and standards" adopted by "the competent international organization," a reference to the IMO. See, *e.g.*, Article 211(2). This means that each State Party to the 1982 Convention may be legally obliged to apply detailed standards developed by the IMO, such as those found in MARPOL 73/78, even if that state is not a party to the specific treaty that sets the standards.

3. THE CONTINENTAL SHELF, FISHERIES ZONES, AND THE EXCLUSIVE ECONOMIC ZONE

In the middle of the twentieth century, coastal states began to make claims with respect to zones of the oceans beyond the narrow "territorial sea" over which states traditionally had asserted sovereignty. In this section, we first examine the regime of the continental shelf, developed as treaty law in the Convention on the Continental Shelf, Apr. 29, 1958, 15 U.S.T. 471, 499 U.N.T.S. 311, and in Part VI of the 1982 U.N. Convention on the Law of the Sea. We then look at coastal state claims to fisheries zones. These claims contributed to acceptance of preferential coastal state rights over fisheries in the exclusive economic zone (EEZ), a legal construct now set out in Part V of the 1982 Convention.

The seaward extension of national jurisdiction affects both access to and management of ocean resources. Some of the materials in this section explore attempts to devise international legal regimes to manage resources that range beyond particular national zones of authority.

THE TRUMAN PROCLAMATION

Proclamation 2667, Policy of the United States With Respect to the Natural Resources of the Subsoil and Sea Bed of the Continental Shelf
Sept. 28, 1945 3 C.F.R. 67 (1943–1948 Compilation).

WHEREAS the Government of the United States of America, aware of the long range world-wide need for new sources of petroleum and other minerals, holds the view that efforts to discover and make available new supplies of these sources should be encouraged; and

WHEREAS its competent experts are of the opinion that such resources underlie many parts of the continental shelf off the coasts of the United States of America, and that with modern technological progress their utilization is already practicable or will become so at an early date; and

WHEREAS recognized jurisdiction over these resources is required in the interest of their conservation and prudent utilization when and as development is undertaken; and

WHEREAS it is the view of the Government of the United States that the exercise of jurisdiction over the natural resources of the subsoil and sea bed of the continental shelf by the contiguous nation is reasonable and just, since the effectiveness of measures to utilize or conserve those resources would be contingent upon cooperation and protection from the shore, since the continental shelf may be regarded as an extension of the land-mass of the coastal nation and thus naturally appurtenant to it, since these resources frequently form a seaward extension of a pool or deposit lying within the territory, and since self-protection compels the coastal nation to keep close watch over activities off its shores which are of the nature necessary for utilization of these resources;

NOW, THEREFORE, I, HARRY S. TRUMAN, President of the United States of America, do hereby proclaim the following policy of the United States of America with respect to the natural resources of the subsoil and sea bed of the continental shelf.

Having concern for the urgency of conserving and prudently utilizing its natural resources, the Government of the United States regards the natural resources of the subsoil and sea bed of the continental shelf beneath the high seas but contiguous to the coasts of the United States as appertaining to the United States, subject to its jurisdiction and control. In cases where the continental shelf extends to the shores of another State, or is shared with an adjacent State, the boundary shall be determined by the United States and the State concerned in accordance with equitable principles. The character as high seas of the waters above the continental shelf and the right to their free and unimpeded navigation are in no way thus affected.

UNITED NATIONS CONVENTION ON THE LAW OF THE SEA, ARTICLES 77–78

Dec. 10, 1982, U.N. Doc. A/CONF.62.122.

Part VI

Continental Shelf * * *

Article 77

Rights of the coastal State over the continental shelf

1. The coastal State exercises over the continental shelf sovereign rights for the purpose of exploring it and exploiting its natural resources.

2. The rights referred to in paragraph 1 are exclusive in the sense that if the coastal State does not explore the continental shelf or exploit its natural resources, no one may undertake these activities without the express consent of the coastal State.

3. The rights of the coastal State over the continental shelf do not depend on occupation, effective or notional, or on any express proclamation.

4. The natural resources referred to in this Part consist of the mineral and other non-living resources of the sea-bed and subsoil together with living organisms belonging to sedentary species, that is to say, organisms which, at the harvestable stage, either are immobile on or under the sea-bed or are unable to move except in constant physical contact with the sea-bed or the subsoil.

Article 78

Legal status of the superjacent waters and airspace and the rights and freedoms of other States

1. The rights of the coastal State over the continental shelf do not affect the legal status of the superjacent waters or of the air space above those waters.

2. The exercise of the rights of the coastal State over the continental shelf must not infringe or result in any unjustifiable interference with navigation and other rights and freedoms of other States as provided for in this Convention.

Notes and Questions

1. *The Truman Proclamation on the Continental Shelf.* The Truman Proclamation on the continental shelf was a significant event in the twentieth-century movement toward extended coastal state jurisdiction. In June

1943, U.S. Secretary of the Interior Harold Ickes wrote to President Franklin Roosevelt, stating:

> The war has impressed us with the necessity for an augmented supply of natural resources. In this connection I draw your attention to the importance of the Continental Shelf not only to the defence of our country, but more particularly as a storehouse of natural resources. The extent of these resources can only be guessed at and needs careful investigation.
>
> The Continental Shelf extending some 100 or 150 miles from our shores forms a fine breeding place for fish of all kinds; it is an excellent hiding-place for submarines; and since it is a continuation of our continent, it probably contains oil and other resources similar to those found in our States.
>
> I suggest the advisability of laying the ground work now for availing ourselves fully of the riches in this submerged land and in the waters over them. The legal and policy problems involved, both international and domestic, are many and complex. In the international field, it may be necessary to evolve new concepts of maritime territorial limits beyond three miles, and of rights to occupy and exploit the surface and the subsoil of the open sea.

Quoted in Donald Cameron Watt, "First steps in enclosure of the oceans: The origins of Truman's proclamation on the resources of the continental shelf, 28 September 1945," 3 *Marine Policy* 211, 212 (1979). Ickes referred to "maritime territorial limits beyond three miles," because the United States, like many other states, already claimed sovereignty over a three-mile territorial sea. In 1988 the United States extended its territorial sea to 12 miles, a step consistent with Article 3 of the 1982 U.N. Convention on the Law of the Sea. See John E. Noyes, "United States of America Presidential Proclamation No. 5298: A 12–Mile U.S. Territorial Sea," 4 *International Journal of Estuarine & Coastal Law* 142 (1989).

President Roosevelt reacted favorably to Ickes's suggestion regarding the continental shelf when he forwarded Ickes's letter to Secretary of State Cordell Hull:

> I think Harold Ickes has the right slant on this. For many years I have felt that the old three-mile limit . . . should be superseded by a rule of common sense. For instance the Gulf of Mexico is bounded on the South by Mexico and on the North by the United States. In parts of the Gulf, shallow water extends very many miles offshore. It seems to me that the Mexican Government should be entitled to drill for oil in the Southern half of the Gulf and we in the Northern half of the Gulf. That would be far more sensible than allowing some European nation, for example, to come in there and drill.

Quoted in Watt, *supra,* at 213. The State Department's Office of Economic Affairs, reviewing Ickes's proposal and another proposal to establish U.S. fisheries conservation zones, argued that the proposals "constituted 'so significant a departure from past practices under the law of nations' that 'if proper precautions were not taken' they could lead to 'misunderstanding, suspicions and opposition on the part of many nations.' " *Id.* at 214. The

Office argued for international consultation with, and the "concurrence" of, various states. The U.S. proposals were in fact informally communicated to Canada, Cuba, Mexico, Newfoundland, the Soviet Union, and the United Kingdom. Some states raised the possibility of negotiating international agreements concerning resources outside the territorial sea, but the United States proceeded unilaterally. Was it appropriate for the United States unilaterally to extend its authority over the continental shelf?

2. *Latin American Coastal Zones.* Following the Truman Proclamation, Mexico issued a proclamation claiming the adjacent continental shelf and its superjacent resources. Several other Latin American states, including Argentina, Chile, Costa Rica, El Salvador, and Peru, soon claimed sovereign rights up to 200 miles from their coasts. Although other states cited U.S. action as precedent for their assertions of authority over broad coastal zones, each responded to its own set of national goals. Chile, for example, was particularly concerned to protect its new offshore whaling industry when it issued its proclamation, and Peru sought primarily to reserve rich offshore fisheries for its own citizens. See Ann Hollick, "The Origins of 200–Mile Offshore Zones," 71 *American Journal of International Law* 994 (1977). The states making these various claims typically disavowed any intention of interfering with freedom of navigation. After the Truman Proclamation, how could the United States best object to assertions by other coastal states of extensive authority over coastal zones?

3. *Evolution of the Legal Concept of the Continental Shelf.* The several unilateral proclamations contributed to a process by which the regime of the continental shelf came ultimately to be considered customary international law. In *Petroleum Dev't Ltd. v. Abu Dhabi*, 18 Int'l L. Rep. 144, 155 (1951), the arbitrator concluded "that in no form can the doctrine [of the continental shelf] claim as yet to have assumed * * * the hard lineaments or the definitive status of an established rule of International Law." Also in 1951, however, the International Law Commission adopted draft articles on the continental shelf, work that contributed significantly to the 1958 Geneva Convention on the Continental Shelf, Apr. 29, 1958, 15 U.S.T. 471, 499 U.N.T.S. 311. The contribution of the 1958 Convention to the crystallization of customary international law was addressed by the International Court of Justice in the 1969 *North Sea Continental Shelf Cases*, which appear in Chapter 3. The ICJ's decision also emphasized that the continental shelf was to be considered the "natural prolongation" of the land territory of a state. The legal status of the continental shelf was one of many issues addressed during the Third United Nations Conference on the Law of the Sea, which led to the 1982 U.N. Convention on the Law of the Sea.

4. *The Continental Shelf and the U.N. Convention on the Law of the Sea.* Under Part VI of the 1982 U.N. Convention on the Law of the Sea, what is the balance struck between coastal state rights and the rights of other states with regard to the continental shelf and activities on and above it?

5. *The Definition of the Continental Shelf.* What exactly is the continental shelf, and how far from shore does it extend? A White House press release accompanying President Truman's Proclamation No. 2667 stated

that "[g]enerally, submerged land which is contiguous to the continent and which is covered by no more than 100 fathoms (600 feet) of water is considered as the continental shelf." Article 1 of the 1958 Convention on the Continental Shelf refers to the continental shelf as

> the seabed and subsoil of the submarine areas adjacent to the coast but outside the area of the territorial sea, to a depth of 200 metres or, beyond that limit, to where the depth of the superjacent waters admits of the exploitation of the natural resources of the said areas * * *.

Compare the definition in Article 76 of the 1982 U.N. Convention on the Law of the Sea. Article 76 uses a complex geographical formula to determine the outer limit of a state's continental shelf, but every state is guaranteed a continental shelf of at least 200 nautical miles from its baselines. Why the changes in definition?

6. *Baselines.* The lines from which the breadth of a state's continental shelf and its other coastal zones is measured are known as "baselines." In general, the baseline follows the low-water line along the coast. See Article 3 of the 1958 Convention on the Territorial Sea and Contiguous Zone; Article 5 of the 1982 Convention on the Law of the Sea.

Some states have proclaimed lengthy straight baselines rather than baselines that closely follow the low water marks of the coastline. In 1951 the International Court of Justice approved Norway's decision to draw a straight baseline along a fringe of islands and rocks, known as the skjærgaard, that generally followed the direction of the coast. "Where a coast is deeply indented and cut into, as is that of Eastern Finnmark," the Court stated, "or where it is bordered by an archipelago such as in the 'skjærgaard' * * *, the base line becomes independent of the low-water mark, and can only be determined by means of a geometric construction." Anglo–Norwegian Fisheries Case, 1951 I.C.J. 116, 128–29, 1951 WL 12. The Court also suggested that important economic interests in a region, "clearly evidenced by a long usage," were a relevant consideration supporting straight baselines, in addition to geographical factors. *Id.* at 133. Article 7 of the 1982 U.N. Convention on the Law of the Sea describes conditions under which a state may draw straight baselines.

Approximately 80 states have drawn straight baselines along all or part of their coasts since 1951. Some of these baselines are many miles distant from the coast. See W. Michael Reisman & Gayle S. Westerman, *Straight Baselines in International Maritime Boundary Delimitation* (1992). What are the implications of the practice of drawing straight baselines? What mechanisms are available to challenge assertions of straight baselines?

7. *United States Fisheries Zones.* A companion to President Truman's continental shelf proclamation was Proclamation No. 2668, Policy of the United States With Respect to Coastal Fisheries in Certain Areas of the High Seas, Sept. 28, 1945, 3 C.F.R. 68 (1943–1948 Compilation). The fisheries proclamation asserted sole U.S. authority to conserve and manage fisheries in areas where U.S. nationals historically had fished exclusively, and called for joint arrangements in areas where both U.S. and foreign nationals had fished. The United States, however, never established conservation zones under this proclamation. The Exclusive Fisheries Zone Act of 1966, 16 U.S.C. §§ 1091–1094, established a 12–mile exclusive U.S. fisheries zone.

That statute was repealed by the 1976 Fishery Conservation and Management Act, 16 U.S.C. §§ 1801–1882, which established a 200–mile fisheries conservation zone. The American Fisheries Promotion Act of 1980, 16 U.S.C. § 1821(e), phased out foreign fishing in this 200–mile zone.

THE FISHERIES JURISDICTION CASE

United Kingdom v. Iceland, 1974 I.C.J. 3, 1974 WL 1 (Merits).

[In 1948, Iceland's Parliament passed a law authorizing the Ministry of Fisheries to set "conservation zones within the limits of the continental shelf of Iceland; wherein all fisheries shall be subject to Icelandic rules and control." In 1952, Iceland established a fisheries zone extending four miles from straight baselines and prohibiting foreign fishing within the zone. In 1958, Iceland proclaimed a 12–mile fisheries zone, again prohibiting foreign fishing within the new limit. British efforts to continue fishing in the 12–mile zone led to "incidents on the fishing grounds" and a 1959 Icelandic parliamentary resolution emphasizing Iceland's objective to extend a fisheries zone "over the whole of the continental shelf area." In a 1960 exchange of notes, the United Kingdom acknowledged Iceland's dependence on coastal fisheries for its livelihood and economic development and agreed not to object to the 12–mile zone. Iceland, for its part, agreed to give the United Kingdom six months' notice of any further extension of Icelandic fisheries jurisdiction and agreed to refer any dispute over such an extension to the International Court of Justice. When Iceland extended its fisheries jurisdiction to 50 miles in 1972, the United Kingdom brought a claim to the Court. Iceland refused to appear before the Court.]

11. In the course of the written proceedings, the following submissions were presented on behalf of the Government of the United Kingdom:

in the Application:

"The United Kingdom asks the Court to adjudge and declare:

(a) That there is no foundation in international law for the claim by Iceland to be entitled to extend its fisheries jurisdiction by establishing a zone of exclusive fisheries jurisdiction extending to 50 nautical miles from the baselines * * *; and that its claim is therefore invalid; and

(b) that questions concerning the conservation of fish stocks in the waters around Iceland are not susceptible in international law to regulation by the unilateral extension by Iceland of its exclusive fisheries jurisdiction to 50 nautical miles from the aforesaid baselines but are matters that may be regulated, as between Iceland and the United Kingdom, by arrangements agreed between those two countries * * *." * * *

50. The Geneva Convention on the High Seas of 1958, which was adopted "as generally declaratory of established principles of international law," defines in Article 1 the term "high seas" as "all parts of the

sea that are not included in the territorial sea or in the internal waters of a State." Article 2 then declares that "The high seas being open to all nations, no State may validly purport to subject any part of them to its sovereignty" and goes on to provide that the freedom of the high seas comprises, *inter alia*, both for coastal and non-coastal States, freedom of navigation and freedom of fishing. The freedoms of the high seas are however made subject to the consideration that they "shall be exercised by all States with reasonable regard to the interests of other States in their exercise of the freedom of the high seas."

51. * * * At the 1958 Conference, the main differences on the breadth of the territorial sea were limited at the time to disagreements as to what limit, not exceeding 12 miles, was the appropriate one. The question of the breadth of the territorial sea and that of the extent of the coastal State's fishery jurisdiction were left unsettled at the 1958 conference. These questions were referred to the Second Conference on the Law of the Sea, held in 1960. Furthermore, the question of the extent of the fisheries jurisdiction of the coastal State, which had constituted a serious obstacle to the reaching of an agreement at the 1958 Conference, became gradually separated from the notion of the territorial sea. This was a development which reflected the increasing importance of fishery resources for all States.

52. The 1960 Conference failed by one vote to adopt a text governing the two questions of the breadth of the territorial sea and the extent of fishery rights. However, after that Conference the law evolved through the practice of States on the basis of the debates and near-agreements at the Conference. Two concepts have crystallized as customary law in recent years arising out of the general consensus revealed at that Conference. The first is the concept of the fishery zone, the area in which a State may claim exclusive fishery jurisdiction independently of its territorial sea; the extension of that fishery zone up to a 12–mile limit from the baselines appears now to be generally accepted. The second is the concept of preferential rights of fishing in adjacent waters in favour of the coastal State in a situation of special dependence on its coastal fisheries, this preference operating in regard to other States concerned in the exploitation of the same fisheries, and to be implemented in the way indicated in paragraph 57 below.

53. In recent years the question of extending the coastal State's fisheries jurisdiction has come increasingly to the forefront. The Court is aware that a number of States has asserted an extension of fishery limits. The Court is also aware of present endeavours, pursued under the auspices of the United Nations, to achieve in a third Conference on the Law of the Sea the further codification and progressive development of this branch of the law, as it is of various proposals and preparatory documents produced in this framework, which must be regarded as manifestations of the views and opinions of individual States and as vehicles of their aspirations, rather than as expressing principles of existing law. The very fact of convening the third Conference on the Law of the Sea evidences a manifest desire on the part of all States to

proceed to the codification of that law on a universal basis, including the question of fisheries and conservation of the living resources of the sea. * * * In the circumstances, the Court, as a court of law, cannot render judgment *sub specie legis ferendae*, or anticipate the law before the legislator has laid it down.

54. The concept of a 12–mile fishery zone * * * has been accepted with regard to Iceland in the substantive provisions of the 1961 Exchange of Notes, and the United Kingdom has also applied the same fishery limit to its own coastal waters since 1964; therefore this matter is no longer in dispute between the Parties. At the same time, * * * the Applicant has expressly recognized Iceland's preferential rights in the disputed waters and at the same time has invoked its own historic fishing rights in these same waters, on the ground that reasonable regard must be had to such traditional rights by the coastal State, in accordance with the generally recognized principles embodied in Article 2 of the High Seas Convention. * * *

57. * * * The contemporary practice of States leads to the conclusion that the preferential rights of the coastal State in a special situation are to be implemented by agreement between the States concerned, either bilateral or multilateral, and, in case of disagreement, through the means for the peaceful settlement of disputes provided for in Article 33 of the Charter of the United Nations. * * *

58. State practice on the subject of fisheries reveals an increasing and widespread acceptance of the concept of preferential rights for coastal States, particularly in favour of countries or territories in a situation of special dependence on coastal fisheries. Both [a resolution at the 1958 conference] and [a] 1960 joint amendment concerning preferential rights were approved by a large majority of the Conferences, thus showing overwhelming support for the idea that in certain special situations it was fair to recognize that the coastal State had preferential fishing rights. After these Conferences, the preferential rights of the coastal State were recognized in various bilateral and multilateral international agreements. * * *

59. There can be no doubt of the exceptional dependence of Iceland on its fisheries. That exceptional dependence was explicitly recognized by the Applicant in the Exchange of Notes of 11 March 1961, and the Court has also taken judicial notice of such recognition, by declaring that it is "necessary to bear in mind the exceptional dependence of the Icelandic nation upon coastal fisheries for its livelihood and economic development" (*I.C.J. Reports* 1972, p. 16, para. 23).

60. The preferential rights of the coastal State come into play only at the moment when an intensification in the exploitation of fishery resources makes it imperative to introduce some system of catch-limitation and sharing of those resources, to preserve the fish stocks in the interests of their rational and economic exploitation. This situation appears to have been reached in the present case. * * *

61. The Icelandic regulations challenged before the Court have been issued and applied by the Icelandic authorities as a claim to exclusive rights thus going beyond the concept of preferential rights. Article 2 of the Icelandic Regulations of 14 July 1972 states:

> "Within the fishery limits all fishing activities by foreign vessels shall be prohibited in accordance with the provisions of Law No. 33 of 19 June 1922, concerning Fishing inside the Fishery Limits."

Article 1 of the 1922 Law provides: "Only Icelandic citizens may engage in fishing in the territorial waters of Iceland, and only Icelandic boats or ships may be used for such fishing." * * *

62. The concept of preferential rights is not compatible with the exclusion of all fishing activities of other States. A coastal State entitled to preferential rights is not free, unilaterally and according to its own uncontrolled discretion, to determine the extent of those rights. The characterization of the coastal State's rights as preferential implies a certain priority, but cannot imply the extinction of the concurrent rights of other States, and particularly of a State which, like the Applicant, has for many years been engaged in fishing in the waters in question, such fishing activity being important to the economy of the country concerned. * * *

63. In this case, the Applicant has pointed out that its vessels have been fishing in Icelandic waters for centuries and that they have done so in a manner comparable with their present activities for upwards of 50 years. Published statistics indicate that from 1920 onwards, fishing of demersal species by United Kingdom vessels in the disputed area has taken place on a continuous basis from year to year, and that, except for the period of the Second World War, the total catch of those vessels has been remarkably steady. Similar statistics indicate that the waters in question constitute the most important of the Applicant's distant-water fishing grounds for demersal species.

64. The Applicant further states that in view of the present situation of fisheries in the North Atlantic, which has demanded the establishment of agreed catch-limitations of cod and haddock in various areas, it would not be possible for the fishing effort of United Kingdom vessels displaced from the Icelandic area to be diverted at economic levels to other fishing grounds in the North Atlantic. Given the lack of alternative fishing opportunity, it is further contended, the exclusion of British fishing vessels from the Icelandic area would have very serious adverse consequences, with immediate results for the affected vessels and with damage extending over a wide range of supporting and related industries. It is pointed out in particular that wide-spread unemployment would be caused among all sections of the British fishing industry and in ancillary industries and that certain ports—Hull, Grimsby and Fleetwood—specially reliant on fishing in the Icelandic area, would be seriously affected. * * *

67. The provisions of the Icelandic Regulations of 14 July 1972 and the manner of their implementation disregard the fishing rights of the

Applicant. Iceland's unilateral action thus constitutes an infringement of the principle enshrined in Article 2 of the 1958 Geneva Convention on the High Seas which requires that all States, including coastal States, in exercising their freedom of fishing, pay reasonable regard to the interests of other States. It also disregards the rights of the Applicant as they result from the Exchange of Notes of 1961. The Applicant is therefore justified in asking the Court to give all necessary protection to its own rights, while at the same time agreeing to recognize Iceland's preferential position. Accordingly, the Court is bound to conclude that the Icelandic Regulations of 14 July 1972 establishing a zone of exclusive fisheries jurisdiction extending to 50 nautical miles from baselines around the coast of Iceland, are not opposable to the United Kingdom, and the latter is under no obligation to accept the unilateral termination by Iceland of United Kingdom fishery rights in the area. * * *

71. * * * Due recognition must be given to the rights of both Parties, namely the rights of the United Kingdom to fish in the waters in dispute, and the preferential rights of Iceland. Neither right is an absolute one: the preferential rights of a coastal State are limited according to the extent of its special dependence on the fisheries and by its obligation to take account of the rights of other States and the needs of conservation; the established rights of other fishing States are in turn limited by reason of the coastal State's special dependence on the fisheries and its own obligation to take account of the rights of other States, including the coastal State, and of the needs of conservation.

72. It follows that even if the court holds that Iceland's extension of its fishery limits is not opposable to the Applicant, this does not mean that the Applicant is under no obligation to Iceland with respect to fishing in the disputed waters in the 12–mile to 50–mile zone. On the contrary, both States have an obligation to take full account of each other's rights and of any fishery conservation measures the necessity of which is shown to exist in those waters. It is one of the advances in maritime international law, resulting from the intensification of fishing, that the former *laissez-faire* treatment of the living resources of the sea in the high seas has been replaced by a recognition of a duty to have due regard to the rights of other States and the needs of conservation for the benefit of all. Consequently, both Parties have the obligation to keep under review the fishery resources in the disputed waters and to examine together, in the light of scientific and other available information, the measures required for the conservation and development, and equitable exploitation, of those resources, taking into account any international agreement in force between them, such as the North–East Atlantic Fisheries Convention of 24 January 1959, as well as such other agreements as may be reached in the matter in the course of further negotiation.

73. The most appropriate method for the solution of the dispute is clearly that of negotiation. Its objectives should be the delimitation of the rights and interests of the Parties, the preferential rights of the coastal State on the one hand and the rights of the Applicant on the

other, to balance and regulate equitably questions such as those of catch-limitation, share allocations and "related restrictions concerning areas closed to fishing, number and type of vessels allowed and forms of control of the agreed provisions" (*Fisheries Jurisdiction (United Kingdom v. Iceland), Interim Measures, Order of 12 July 1973, I.C.J. Reports 1973*, p. 303, para. 7). This necessitates detailed scientific knowledge of the fishing grounds. It is obvious that the relevant information and expertise would be mainly in the possession of the Parties. The Court would, for this reason, meet with difficulties if it were itself to attempt to lay down a precise scheme for an equitable adjustment of the rights involved. * * *

78. In the fresh negotiations which are to take place on the basis of the present Judgment, the Parties will have the benefit of the above appraisal of their respective rights, and of certain guidelines defining their scope. The task before them will be to conduct their negotiations on the basis that each must in good faith pay reasonable regard to the legal rights of the other in the waters around Iceland outside the 12–mile limit, thus bringing about an equitable apportionment of the fishing resources based on the facts of the particular situation, and having regard to the interests of other States which have established fishing rights in the area. It is not a matter of finding simply an equitable solution, but an equitable solution derived from the applicable law. * * *

79. For these reasons,

THE COURT,

by ten votes to four,

(1) finds that the Regulations concerning the Fishery Limits off Iceland * * * promulgated by the Government of Iceland on 14 July 1972 and constituting a unilateral extension of the exclusive fishing rights of Iceland to 50 nautical miles from the baselines specified therein are not opposable to the Government of the United Kingdom;

(2) finds that, in consequence, the Government of Iceland is not entitled unilaterally to exclude United Kingdom fishing vessels from areas between the fishery limits agreed to in the Exchange of Notes of 11 March 1961 and the limits specified in the Icelandic Regulations of 14 July 1972, or unilaterally to impose restrictions on the activities of those vessels in such areas;

by ten votes to four,

(3) holds that the Government of Iceland and the Government of the United Kingdom are under mutual obligations to undertake negotiations in good faith for the equitable solution of their differences concerning their respective fishery rights in the areas specified in subparagraph 2;

(4) holds that in these negotiations the Parties are to take into account, *inter alia*:

(a) that in the distribution of the fishing resources in the areas specified in subparagraph 2 Iceland is entitled to a preferential share to the extent of the special dependence of its people upon the fisheries in the seas around its coasts for their livelihood and economic development;

(b) that by reason of its fishing activities in the areas specified in subparagraph 2, the United Kingdom also has established rights in the fishery resources of the said areas on which elements of its people depend for their livelihood and economic well-being;

(c) the obligation to pay due regard to the interests of other States in the conservation and equitable exploitation of these resources;

(d) that the above-mentioned rights of Iceland and of the United Kingdom should each be given effect to the extent compatible with the conservation and development of the fishery resources in the areas specified in subparagraph 2 and with the interests of other States in their conservation and equitable exploitation;

(e) their obligation to keep under review those resources and to examine together, in the light of scientific and other available information, such measures as may be required for the conservation and development, and equitable exploitation, of those resources, making use of the machinery established by the North–East Atlantic Fisheries Convention or such other means as may be agreed upon as a result of international negotiations.

Notes and Questions

1. *The Cod Wars.* During the "Cod Wars," Iceland boarded British vessels, arrested British fishermen, and cut the nets of British trawlers. The British sent frigates to escort and protect British trawlers off Iceland. There were shooting and ramming incidents. Tensions were particularly high during 1958–1961, after Iceland extended its fisheries zone from four to 12 miles, and during 1972–1973, after Iceland declared a 50–mile fisheries zone. Iceland's 1972 decisions to extend its fisheries zone and to denounce its 1961 agreement with Great Britain followed the 1971 Icelandic election, in which the Agrarian Progressive Party, which had made fisheries jurisdiction a major campaign issue, emerged as the head of a new coalition government.

Rejecting the decision in the *Fisheries Jurisdiction Case*, Iceland extended its fishing limits from 50 to 200 miles in 1975. Regulations Concerning the Fishery Limits off Iceland, July 15, 1975, 14 I.L.M. 1282 (1975). This extension resulted in further clashes involving British and Icelandic naval units. Other states became concerned the controversy might lead Iceland to withdraw from the North Atlantic Treaty Organization and to shut down a NATO military base in Iceland that was used to monitor Soviet vessels. In June 1976, Iceland and the United Kingdom finally reached an agreement allowing British fishing within the 200–mile limit, but at a substantially reduced level. Iceland–United Kingdom: Agreement Concerning British Fishing in Icelandic Waters, June 1, 1976, 15 I.L.M. 878 (1976). Iceland also concluded bilateral fishing agreements with Belgium, the Federal Republic of Germany, and Norway. Fisheries Agreement, Nov. 28, 1975, Ice.-Belg., 15 I.L.M. 1 (1976); Fisheries Agreement, Nov. 28, 1975, Ice.-F.R.G., 15 I.L.M. 43 (1976); Fisheries Agreement, Mar. 10, 1976, Ice.-Nor., 15 I.L.M. 875 (1976).

2. *The ICJ's View of Rights to Fisheries.* The ICJ concludes Iceland has disregarded British fishing rights, but does the ICJ grant the relief the British sought? What supports the existence of the rights that the Court finds in this case? The Court also concludes that Iceland and the United Kingdom should negotiate a settlement of their differences over rights to fisheries. Does this recourse to procedure as a way to deal with conflict suggest that, at base, the international law on this issue lacks consensus concerning substantive values?

3. *Customary International Law and Coastal State Fisheries Jurisdiction.* Judges Forster, Bengzon, Jimenez de Arechaga, Nagendra Singh, and Ruda concur separately in the *Fisheries Jurisdiction Case.* Although the judges agree with the result in the majority opinion and find a 12–mile fisheries zone is generally accepted in international law, they argue that no general rule of customary international law establishes 12 miles as the obligatory maximum limit. The judges argue that 30 to 35 coastal states had extended their fisheries jurisdiction beyond 12 miles, and note the general lack of protests to such extensions and the existence of public pronouncements inconsistent with making any protest. The concurring judges also cite declarations and proposals made at the then-ongoing Third United Nations Conference on the Law of the Sea. They question whether, on "a subject where practice is contradictory and lacks precision," it is "reasonable to discard entirely as irrelevant the evidence of what States are prepared to claim and to acquiesce in, as gathered from the positions taken by them in view of or in preparation for a conference for the codification and progressive development of the law on the subject." 1974 I.C.J. at 48. Finally, the judges lament the legal uncertainty at the time regarding the maximum limit of coastal state fisheries jurisdiction, and express the hope that the matter will be clarified at UNCLOS III.

4. *Multilateral Efforts to Codify the Law of the Sea.* The *Fisheries Jurisdiction* decision notes multilateral efforts prior to UNCLOS III to codify the international law of the sea. The excerpt above refers specifically to two of the four 1958 Geneva Conventions concluded at the First United Nations Conference on the Law of the Sea: the Convention on the High Seas, Apr. 29, 1958, 13 U.S.T. 2312, 450 U.N.T.S. 82, and the Convention on the Territorial Sea and the Contiguous Zone, Apr. 29, 1958, 15 U.S.T. 1606, 516 U.N.T.S. 205. The other two 1958 conventions are the Convention on the Continental Shelf, Apr. 29, 1958, 15 U.S.T. 471, 499 U.N.T.S. 311, and the Convention on Fishing and Conservation of the Living Resources of the High Seas, Apr. 29, 1958, 17 U.S.T. 138, 559 U.N.T.S. 285. The United Kingdom, but not Iceland, was party to those four conventions.

Note: UNCLOS III Negotiations Concerning the Exclusive Economic Zone

At the 1974 Caracas session of UNCLOS III, over 100 states spoke in favor of a 200–mile coastal state exclusive economic zone (EEZ). That is not to say that all issues relating to the EEZ were resolved early in the Conference. With regard to many such issues—concerning the legal status of the EEZ, the applicability of the EEZ to archipelagic states and small islands, the relationship between the EEZ and the continental shelf, boundary delimitation, dispute settlement, and coastal state responsibilities concerning fish in their EEZs—it took years to negotiate the language eventually contained in the 1982 United Nations Convention on the Law of the Sea.

The 1974 debates in the Second Committee of UNCLOS III reveal considerable variety in the positions of states. To pick just a few examples: Honduras's delegate claimed "inherent rights" over resources in its adjacent zones, and argued that foreign states had no competence there absent agreement with the coastal state. UNCLOS III, 2nd Sess., 2nd Comm., 22nd Mtg., July 31, 1974, in 2 *UNCLOS III Official Records* 171 (U.N. Sales No. E.75.V.4). The delegates of Kenya and Ecuador were among the many developing states that favored complete coastal state sovereignty in the EEZ, and suggested the desirability of 200–mile territorial seas. Somalia's delegate thought that the traditional law of the sea favored the major maritime powers, and that developing coastal states should not "sign away their territorial sovereignty in exchange for lesser rights." *Id.* at 210 (26th Mtg., Aug. 5, 1974).

Island states and archipelagic states had particular interests in fisheries. New Zealand's delegate criticized a suggestion that the economic zone of islands should be restricted. Archipelagic states also strongly supported the concept of an EEZ, but did not necessarily favor complete coastal state "sovereignty" over the EEZ.

For other states, the EEZ concept represented a significant concession. Mr. Ogiso, Japan's delegate, argued that "[f]reedom of access to fishery resources, if it was retained only beyond 200 miles, would become practically meaningless." *Id.* at 217 (28th Mtg., Aug. 6, 1974). He urged respect for traditional distant water fishing states whose economies were dependent on fishing. Maritime states, including states in the Soviet bloc, also stressed the importance of coastal states not exercising rights in their EEZs that would interfere with navigational freedoms. The concern was that extensive coastal state EEZ rights or 200–mile territorial seas might well allow coastal states to interfere with navigational freedoms by exercising control over pollution, scientific research, or customs, fiscal, immigration, and health matters. The delegate of the Ukrainian Soviet Socialist Republic stated that "[u]nder the pretext of exercising such controls, a coastal State might at any time detain a foreign vessel and reduce to nothing the freedom of navigation in the zone." *Id.* at 201 (25th Mtg., Aug. 5, 1974).

Land-locked and geographically disadvantaged states also voiced concerns. Upper Volta's delegate argued for assured access to the sea by land-locked countries and for their right to participate in the exploitation of EEZ resources. Mr. Ballah, the delegate from Trinidad and Tobago, said his state "conditioned its acceptance of the concept of the 200–mile exclusive economic zone on recognition by the Conference of preferential or equal rights for every State within a region or subregion to the living resources of the economic zones of the other States of the region." *Id.* at 179 (22nd Mtg., July 31, 1974). Turkey noted that, although it was surrounded on three sides by seas, those seas were semi-enclosed and not well stocked with fish. The delegate of the Federal Republic of Germany stressed dual needs: for effective conservation of fisheries and for equitable allocation of those resources, finding "no justification for the reallocation of available resources for the benefit of a limited number of geographically advantaged States." *Id.* at 192 (24th Mtg., Aug. 1, 1974). Germany was one of several states stressing the importance of an obligatory dispute settlement mechanism to review the actions of coastal states.

UNITED NATIONS CONVENTION ON THE LAW OF THE SEA, ARTICLES 55–58, 121

Dec. 10, 1982, U.N. Doc. A/CONF.62.122.

Part V

Exclusive Economic Zone

Article 55

Specific legal régime of the exclusive economic zone

The exclusive economic zone is an area beyond and adjacent to the territorial sea, subject to the specific legal regime established in this Part, under which the rights and jurisdiction of the coastal State and the rights and freedoms of other States are governed by the relevant provisions of this Convention.

Article 56

Rights, jurisdiction and duties of the coastal State in the exclusive economic zone

1. In the exclusive economic zone, the coastal State has:

(a) sovereign rights for the purpose of exploring and exploiting, conserving and managing the natural resources, whether living or non-living, of the waters superjacent to the sea-bed and of the sea-bed and its subsoil, and with regard to other activities for the economic exploitation and exploration of the zone, such as the production of energy from the water, currents and winds;

(b) jurisdiction as provided for in the relevant provisions of this Convention with regard to:

(i) the establishment and use of artificial islands, installations and structures;

(ii) marine scientific research;

(iii) the protection and preservation of the marine environment;

(c) other rights and duties provided for in this Convention.

2. In exercising its rights and performing its duties under this Convention in the exclusive economic zone, the coastal State shall have due regard to the rights and duties of other States and shall act in a manner compatible with the provisions of this Convention.

3. The rights set out in this article with respect to the sea-bed and subsoil shall be exercised in accordance with Part VI.

Article 57

Breadth of the exclusive economic zone

The exclusive economic zone shall not extend beyond 200 nautical miles from the baselines from which the breadth of the territorial sea is measured.

Article 58

Rights and duties of other States in the exclusive economic zone

1. In the exclusive economic zone, all States, whether coastal or land-locked, enjoy, subject to the relevant provisions of this Convention, the freedoms referred to in article 87 of navigation and overflight and of the laying of submarine cables and pipelines, and other internationally lawful uses of the sea related to these freedoms, such as those associated with the operation of ships, aircraft and submarine cables and pipelines, and compatible with the other provisions of this Convention.

2. Articles 88 to 115 and other pertinent rules of international law apply to the exclusive economic zone in so far as they are not incompatible with this Part.

3. In exercising their rights and performing their duties under this Convention in the exclusive economic zone, States shall have due regard to the rights and duties of the coastal State and shall comply with the laws and regulations adopted by the coastal State in accordance with the provisions of this Convention and other rules of international law in so far as they are not incompatible with this Part. * * *

PART VIII

Regime of Islands

Article 121

Régime of islands

1. An island is a naturally formed area of land, surrounded by water, which is above water at high tide.

2. Except as provided for in paragraph 3, the territorial sea, the contiguous zone, the exclusive economic zone and the continental shelf of an island are determined in accordance with the provisions of this Convention applicable to other land territory.

3. Rocks which cannot sustain human habitation or economic life of their own shall have no exclusive economic zone or continental shelf.

Notes and Questions

1. *Acceptance of the EEZ as Customary International Law.* As of January 1993, according to the United Nations Division for Ocean Affairs and Law of the Sea Office of Legal Affairs, 89 states had claimed a 200–mile exclusive economic zone (or one up to a median line with opposite states), and an additional 17 states had claimed a 200–mile fisheries zone (or one up to a median line with opposite states). Eleven states claimed a 200–mile territorial sea. In 1985 the International Court of Justice found it "incontestable that * * * the institution of the exclusive economic zone * * * is shown by the practice of states to have become part of customary law." Continental Shelf (Libya v. Malta) Case, 1985 I.C.J. 13, 33. Had the 1982 Convention's EEZ regime gained general acceptance as customary international law even before the Convention entered into force in November 1994? What additional information, if any, is needed to answer the question?

2. *High Seas Freedoms in the EEZ.* How does the Convention resolve the Grotius/Selden *mare liberum/mare clausum* debate with regard to the 200–mile EEZ? In light of Article 58, is the EEZ really still a part of the high seas?

3. *Conflicting Interests in the EEZ.* Access to and control over coastal fisheries was an issue of tremendous importance in the debate over the EEZ. Does the 1982 Convention follow the same conception of rights concerning fisheries that the ICJ articulated in the *Fisheries Jurisdiction Case*? Under the Convention, is a coastal state's role better described as that of a steward, to protect fisheries resources, or a proprietor? See Articles 61 and 62.

How satisfied do you think each of the states whose position on the EEZ is outlined in the Note above entitled "UNCLOS III Negotiations Concerning the Exclusive Economic Zone" was with the final text of Part V of the 1982 U.N. Convention on the Law of the Sea? To the extent some states' concerns were not satisfied, why would those states accept the Convention? With regard to land-locked states, note that their concerns with a right of access to the sea were separately addressed in another Part of the Convention. Separate Parts of the Convention also concern protection of the marine environment in the EEZ and elsewhere, and marine scientific research in the EEZ and on the continental shelf.

4. *Obligatory Third-party Dispute Resolution.* Part XV of the Convention on the Law of the Sea provides for obligatory reference of certain disputes to third-party tribunals if negotiated settlements fail. Parties may choose among different fora, including a new International Tribunal for the Law of the Sea; if they do not agree on the same forum or fail to indicate a preferred forum, the dispute will be submitted to arbitration. Among the few categories of disputes excluded from obligatory third-party arbitration or adjudication, however, are disputes relating to a coastal state's "sovereign rights with respect to the living resources in the exclusive economic zone or their exercise, including its discretionary powers for determining allowable catch, its harvesting capacity, the allocation of surpluses to other States and the terms and conditions established in its conservation and management laws and regulations." Article 297(3). Certain categories of EEZ fisheries disputes may be referred to a compulsory conciliation procedure. Why did states seek provisions for obligatory binding procedures in the Convention,

and why did they exclude certain fisheries disputes? What are the implications of the Article 297(3) exclusion for the balance of rights and obligations set out in Part V? For more on obligatory dispute settlement, see John E. Noyes, "Compulsory Third–Party Adjudication and the 1982 United Nations Convention on the Law of the Sea," 4 *Connecticut Journal of International Law* 675 (1989).

5. *Comparing the EEZ and the Continental Shelf.* Article 56 of the 1982 Convention, which is contained in Part V on the EEZ, refers to sovereign rights of coastal states to explore, exploit, conserve, and manage non-living, as well as living, natural resources. Why, then, does the Convention include a separate Part VI on the continental shelf?

6. *Straddling Stocks and Highly Migratory Species.* Some species of fish do not live exclusively in the EEZs of just one state. They swim into neighboring states' EEZs or into the high seas beyond the EEZ. What sort of international legal regime regulates the exploitation of such species? Is further extension of coastal state authority beyond the EEZ necessary to promote the effective management of straddling stocks? The next two readings and accompanying notes examine these questions.

UNITED NATIONS CONVENTION ON THE LAW OF THE SEA, ARTICLES 63(2), 116–119

Dec. 10, 1982, U.N. Doc. A/CONF.62.122.

Part V

Exclusive Economic Zone * * *

Article 63

Stocks occurring within the exclusive economic zones of two or more coastal States or both within the exclusive economic zone and in an area beyond and adjacent to it * * *

2. Where the same stock or stocks of associated species occur both within the exclusive economic zone and in an area beyond and adjacent to the zone, the coastal State and the States fishing for such stocks in the adjacent area shall seek, either directly or through appropriate subregional or regional organizations, to agree upon the measures necessary for the conservation of these stocks in the adjacent area.

Part VII

High Seas * * *

Section 2. Conservation and Management of the Living Resources of the High Seas

Article 116

Right to fish on the high seas

All States have the right for their nationals to engage in fishing on the high seas subject to:

(a) their treaty obligations;

(b) the rights and duties as well as the interests of coastal States provided for, *inter alia*, in article 63, paragraph 2, and articles 64 to 67; and

(c) the provisions of this section.

Article 117

Duty of States to adopt with respect to their nationals measures for the conservation of the living resources of the high seas

All States have the duty to take, or to co-operate with other States in taking, such measures for their respective nationals as may be necessary for the conservation of the living resources of the high seas.

Article 118

Co-operation of States in the conservation and management of living resources

States shall co-operate with each other in the conservation and management of living resources in the areas of the high seas. States whose nationals exploit identical living resources, or different living resources in the same area, shall enter into negotiations with a view to taking the measures necessary for the conservation of the living resources concerned. They shall, as appropriate, cooperate to establish subregional or regional fisheries organizations to this end.

Article 119

Conservation of the living resources of the high seas

1. In determining the allowable catch and establishing other conservation measures for the living resources in the high seas, States shall:

(a) take measures which are designed, on the best scientific evidence available to the state concerned, to maintain or restore populations of harvested species at levels which can produce the maximum sustainable yield, as qualified by relevant environmental and economic factors, including the special requirements of developing States, and taking into account fishing patterns, the interdependence of stocks and any generally recommended international minimum standards, whether subregional, regional or global;

(b) take into consideration the effects on species associated with or dependent upon harvested species with a view to maintaining or restoring populations of such associated or dependent species above levels at which their reproduction may become seriously threatened.

2. Available scientific information, catch and fishing effort statistics, and other data relevant to the conservation of fish stocks shall be contributed and exchanged on a regular basis through competent international organizations, whether subregional, regional or global, where appropriate and with participation by all States concerned.

3. States concerned shall ensure that conservation measures and their implementation do not discriminate in form or in fact against the fishermen of any State.

"GLOBAL SOLUTION MUST BE FOUND TO PROBLEMS OF MANAGEMENT, CONSERVATION, CHAIRMAN TELLS STRADDLING AND HIGHLY MIGRATORY FISH STOCKS CONFERENCE"

Conference on Straddling and Highly Migratory Fish Stocks
58th Meeting (AM), SEA/1475, 27 March 1995.

[The United Nations Conference on Environment and Development, held in Rio de Janiero in 1992, called for U.N. negotiations to implement the general provisions of the 1982 Convention on the Law of the Sea concerning straddling stocks and highly migratory species. This excerpt suggests some of the difficulties in the negotiations, which resulted in the U.N. Agreement Relating to the Conservation and Management of Straddling Fish Stocks and Highly Migratory Fish Stocks.]

The United Nations Conference on Straddling Fish Stocks and Highly Migratory Fish Stocks, which began its fifth session this morning, is expected to discuss a draft agreement * * * which could lead to a global treaty on the long-term conservation and sustainable use of those stocks. * * *

SATYA N. NANDAN (Fiji), Chairman of the Conference, said that a recent report by the Food and Agriculture Organization (FAO) indicated that the volume of marine and fresh water fish catches has continued to decline since its peak in 1989. Since the beginning of the 1990s, about 70 per cent of the world's conventional species of fish were fully exploited, over-exploited, depleted, or were in the process of being regenerated following depletion.

He said action was needed in the following areas: control of fishing effort and the reduction in the fishing industry's over-capacity; resource-allocation decisions and improved decision-making on resource use; and the adoption of precautionary approaches to fisheries conservation and management, among others. * * * The Conference must establish a sound legal framework consistent with the 1982 United Nations Convention on the Law of the Sea, in order to promote effective conservation and management measures so that fisheries resources could be utilized in a sustainable manner.

The problem concerned the international community, he continued; therefore, the solutions must be global, whose effect would be to bring order to oceans and to promote cooperation among States and reflect the balance of interests of States in matters relating to fisheries. He added that recent incidents involving fishing vessels underscored the urgency of the task ahead, but must not become an impediment in the negotiations.

BRIAN TOBIN, Minister for Fisheries of Canada, said the conditions of the world's fisheries had worsened in the last year. Despite the large number of distant-water vessels still operating, their catches on the high seas had continued to fall from 9.1 million metric tons in 1989 to 4.7 million tons in 1993. Some countries, like Japan, had made the necessary transition and operated reasonable distant-water fleets, which were not a threat to straddling and highly migratory stocks. "Other distant-water vessels were not operating in the same responsible manner." They had become increasingly desperate, fishing whatever, wherever and however they could, heedless of the consequences. "These fleets, from countries like Spain, fish today and forget tomorrow," he said. Such ecological disaster could not continue. It could have only one outcome—depletion and, in some cases, destruction of fish stocks.

Spanish vessels were not the only ones taking 10 or 20 times their cod and flounder quotas, under the terms of the North–West Atlantic Fisheries Organization. Canadians also took too much fish in the 1970s and 1980s, but it had faced up to those mistakes and implemented strong conservation and enforcement measures to protect the commercial extinction of straddling stocks. However, sacrifices made by fishermen in Atlantic Canada and their communities would all be in vain unless there was effective conservation and enforcement outside the 200–mile exclusive economic zones.

He stressed that an effective system of international control of high-seas fisheries included these elements: a legally binding United Nations treaty; a precautionary approach to conservation; compatibility between conservation measures inside and outside the 200–mile economic zones; binding and compulsory dispute settlement; and high-seas enforcement. While some progress had been made in the first four elements, work must still be done during the Conference in the area of high-seas enforcement. Everything accomplished by the Conference, the Law of the Sea Convention and the 1992 United Nations Conference on the Environment and Development (UNCED) would be rendered meaningless without effective high-seas enforcement.

* * * He stressed that Canada was not seeking an extension of the jurisdiction of the 200–mile exclusive economic zone, nor was it seeking authority for the kind of measures it had taken recently against a Spanish vessel. Canada wanted to work with others towards a convention which would ensure that no other country would ever again face the terrible situation that Canada faced. It wished to help prevent overfishing and avoid the kind of conflict that Canada was now involved in against Spain.

EMMA BONINO, Commissioner for Fisheries of the European Community, said * * * [e]ffective conservation could only be achieved by ensuring compatibility between measures taken on the high seas and inside national waters. Measures which were taken under different legal regimes should not undermine each other. When dealing with fish stocks which involved the rights of more than one State, sound and effective conservation could only be achieved through effective cooperation between those States. That implied due regard to the rights and obligations of others and must rest on transparent and objective procedures and criteria.

She stressed that if States asserted unilateral jurisdiction on the high seas, it would seriously undermine the Law of the Sea Convention and would have adverse repercussions on other issues governed by the Convention, not only fisheries. * * * Coastal States were much to blame for the problems of the migratory and straddling fish stocks, as the larger part of those fish stocks lived within the exclusive economic zones of coastal States. Distant-water-fishing States must assume their responsibilities, but could not be made "the scapegoat for the management faults committed by others."

The only remaining disagreement concerning fishing in the northwest Atlantic concerned the sharing of the total allowable catch among the fleets operating in the region, she continued. "It is inconceivable to pretend that where the coastal State catches the main portion of a stock, this is to be viewed as a responsible and ecological fishing activity, whereas if others claim to have the right to fish a part of that stock in the high seas, they plunder the seas." Claims of a purely economic interest could not be concealed behind a veil of ecological and humanitarian appearance.

Once the necessary conservation rules had been agreed on, there were two possibilities to accommodate economic interest at the international level: negotiations within a bilateral or multilateral framework could be held with a view to arriving at equitable solutions, while taking into account the interests of others; if negotiations failed to yield satisfactory results, any responsible party would be bound to accept international arbitration. She regretted that some chose to withdraw from international arbitration in the field of fisheries while knowing perfectly well that, in accordance with the procedures of international law, the lawlessness of their actions would have been established.

Notes and Questions

1. *The Depletion of Fisheries and the Case for International Management Regimes.* Grotius considered the supply of fish to be inexhaustible. "Freedoms of the high seas" implied open access to fisheries. Today, however, the depletion of fisheries to which Ambassador Nandan refers has been well documented. Why has the operation of market forces not served to protect fisheries? If a fisheries management regime is necessary, how should it be structured? Between 85 and 90 per cent of the world's commercial fisheries are found in states' coastal zones, and each state decides how to manage fish in its own EEZ. The case for international management regimes becomes stronger, however, when one considers species of fish that swim between the EEZs of two or more coastal states, or that divide their lives inside and outside EEZs. See William T. Burke, *The New International Law of Fisheries* (1994).

2. *Unilateral Coastal State Action to Conserve Straddling Stocks.* Greenland halibut is a "straddling stock" in the northwest Atlantic that lives both within Canada's EEZ and on the Grand Banks just outside the EEZ. Depletion of Greenland halibut led Canada to impose severe catch restrictions on Canadians; Canada also, in May 1994, enacted unilateral legislation authorizing conservation and management measures, as well as enforcement measures, with respect to non-Canadian ships fishing for straddling stocks outside Canada's 200–mile EEZ. Coastal Fisheries Protection Act, *entered into force* May 25, 1994, 33 I.L.M. 1383 (1994). Canada initially directed its attention to stateless and flag-of-convenience vessels, several of which were fishing in the high seas area affected by the legislation. In March 1995, Canada extended its regulations to prohibit Spanish and Portuguese vessels from fishing for Greenland halibut on the Grand Banks outside Canada's 200–mile EEZ. On March 9, 1995, Canada boarded and seized the Spanish trawler *Estai,* and, a few weeks later, used a giant scissors-like device to cut the nets of another Spanish trawler fishing on the Grand Banks. The European Union called Canadian officials "pirates"; Canada accused EU fishermen of being "conservation criminals." Lisa Anderson, "Depleted Fish Stocks Spark Canada's Turbot War with Spain," *Chicago Tribune*, Mar. 19, 1995, at 4.

Canada could not point to clear support in international practice for its high seas measures. Chile had announced a *mar presencial* in 1991 and used the boundaries of this broad area beyond its EEZ in a fisheries law, but the exact contours of Chile's presumed authority in its *mar presencial* were rather vague. See Francisco Orrego Vicuña, "Toward an Effective Management of High Seas Fisheries and the Settlement of the Pending Issues of the Law of the Sea," 24 *Ocean Development & International Law* 81, 87–89 (1993). No other states had claimed Canadian-style unilateral authority with respect to high seas fisheries. Was Canada's action consistent with the 1982 U.N. Convention on the Law of the Sea? What are the problems with unilateral assertions of coastal state jurisdiction beyond the 200–mile EEZ?

3. *The Role of Regional Organizations.* Article 63 of the 1982 U.N. Convention on the Law of the Sea refers to a role for regional organizations with regard to straddling stocks. The Northwest Atlantic Fisheries Organization (NAFO), established by the Convention on Future Multilateral Cooperation in the Northwest Atlantic Fisheries, Oct. 24, 1978, Sen. Exec. Doc. T, 96th Cong., 1st Sess, has regulatory powers in the Northwest Atlantic outside coastal states' EEZs. From Canada's perspective, NAFO's conservation and management efforts have been largely ineffective. Although NAFO's Fisheries Commission does have the authority to set catch quotas in its Regulatory Area, the Convention authorizes parties to veto these quotas. The European Union, one of the parties to the Convention, rejected a 12 per cent share of a 27,000–ton Greenland halibut catch quota that NAFO set for 1995—not the first time the EU had rejected a NAFO quota. NAFO also leaves enforcement of catch quotas and other conservation measures to flag states, and fishing vessels registered in states that are not members of NAFO are not bound by its regulations.

The crisis over Canada's seizure of Spanish vessels was defused when Canada and the EU agreed to propose to NAFO a reallocation of fishing quotas for Greenland halibut. Agreed Minute on the Conservation and

Management of Fish Stocks, Can.–Eur. Community, Apr. 20, 1995, 34 I.L.M. 1260 (1995). The Agreed Minute also provides for independent onboard observers, improved NAFO inspection procedures, and increased satellite surveillance of fishing vessels, and it allows Canada to inspect fishing vessels that call at Canadian ports.

4. *Multilateral Agreement on Conservation and Enforcement Measures.* The 1995 Agreement Relating to the Conservation and Management of Straddling Fish Stocks and Highly Migratory Fish Stocks, Sept. 8, 1995, A/CONF.167/37, 34 I.L.M. 1542 (1995), which will enter into force after 30 states accept it, requires that conservation and management regimes applicable to areas under national jurisdiction and to the high seas be coordinated. The Agreement calls for the collection, compilation, and exchange of data related to covered fish stocks; it also mandates use of the "precautionary principle" in an effort to insure lack of firm scientific data does not preclude conservation efforts.

What should be done to insure that fishing vessels flying the flag of a state that is not a member of a regional organization such as NAFO do not undermine its conservation measures? The Straddling Stocks Agreement requires States Parties to cooperate in regional conservation and management measures even if they are not members of the regional organization. Under Article 8(4), furthermore, only members of regional organizations or states agreeing to apply regional conservation and management measures are to have access to the fisheries to which the measures apply. The Agreement also contains innovative enforcement mechanisms. A State Party that also is a member of a regional fisheries organization may board and inspect vessels flying the flag of another State Party, even if the latter is not a member of the regional organization, in order to check whether the vessels comply with regional conservation and management measures. Should the flag state fail to respond when notified of a violation or fail to take enforcement action with respect to its vessel, the boarding state may secure evidence, bring the vessel into port, or take other steps proportionate to the seriousness of the violation. See also Agreement to Promote Compliance with International Conservation and Management Measures by Fishing Vessels on the High Seas, Nov. 24, 1993, 33 I.L.M. 968 (1994), a treaty directed at flag state obligations.

5. *Third-party Adjudication of Straddling Stocks Disputes.* What are the prospects for international adjudication of disputes over straddling stocks or highly migratory species? When Canada enacted its Coastal Fisheries Protection Act in June 1994, it amended its acceptance of the compulsory jurisdiction of the International Court of Justice to exclude the Court's jurisdiction over disputes arising from Canadian management, conservation, and enforcement measures concerning fishing in the NAFO Regulatory Area. Spain nevertheless instituted proceedings in the ICJ in March 1995, challenging the legality of the Canadian legislation and of Canada's boarding Spanish vessels on the high seas. If Canada and Spain were both parties to the 1982 U.N. Convention on the Law of the Sea, the provisions in Part XV of the Convention concerning the obligatory submission of disputes to a third-party tribunal would apply. The 1995 Straddling Stocks Agreement also incorporates the 1982 Conventions's third-party dispute settle-

ment mechanisms; these apply to parties to the Straddling Stocks Agreement even if they are not parties to the 1982 Convention.

4. THE TERRITORIAL SEA, STRAITS, AND NAVIGATIONAL FREEDOM

International law has long considered a coastal state to have sovereignty over a narrow band of waters adjacent to its coastline, known as the territorial sea. Every coastal state has interests in preserving a zone in which exclusive access to fish is assured. The need to prevent military incursions and threats from violations of fiscal and customs laws also helps to make the case for coastal state sovereignty over the territorial sea compelling.

The permissible breadth of the territorial sea, however, has been the subject of disagreement. Some have argued that, historically, the territorial sea extended as far as a cannon shot could reach. Many maritime states, including the United States, long maintained a three-mile territorial sea. In the mid-twentieth century, several Latin American states argued that coastal states should alone be able to determine the extent of their territorial seas, and the delegates to the 1958 First United Nations Conference on the Law of the Sea could reach no agreement on the permissible breadth of the territorial sea. In 1960, the Second United Nations Conference on the Law of the Sea failed by one vote to adopt a proposal for a six-mile territorial sea and an additional six-mile fisheries zone. Now, almost all states accept that the territorial sea may extend only up to 12 miles from a state's baselines, which is the breadth specified in Article 3 of the 1982 Convention; states favoring very broad territorial seas in order to protect their access to living resources were largely satisfied by the acceptance of a 200–mile EEZ in the 1982 United Nations Convention on the Law of the Sea. Furthermore, Article 33 of the 1982 Convention provides for a 24–mile contiguous zone, where coastal states are authorized to apply their customs, fiscal, immigration, and sanitary laws and regulations.

The sovereign rights of a coastal state in its territorial sea are not unlimited. Ships flying the flag of another state have a right of "innocent passage" in the territorial sea. Article 14(4) of the 1958 Geneva Convention on the Territorial Sea and the Contiguous Zone defines innocent passage as passage that "is not prejudicial to the peace, good order or security of the coastal state." Article 19(2) of the 1982 Convention on the Law of the Sea is more specific, enumerating activities that would render passage by foreign flag vessels noninnocent. Very controversial has been the issue of whether warships possess a right of innocent passage without having to notify the coastal state in advance or receive authorization from it. In 1989, the United States and the former Soviet Union concluded a bilateral agreement providing that "neither prior notification or authorization" is a precondition to warships' enjoying the right of innocent passage. Uniform Interpretation of Norms of International Law Governing Innocent Passage, Sept. 23, 1989, 28 I.L.M. 1444 (1989). However, several states maintain passage of warships through the territorial sea requires the prior consent of the coastal state. See 1 E.D. Brown, *The International Law of the Sea* 66–71 (1994).

Providing for navigational rights through straits was a particularly important issue for the United States, the Soviet Union, and other maritime powers during the negotiation of the 1982 United Nations Convention on the Law of the Sea. These powers were especially concerned to insure that submarines had the right to pass submerged through straits. Coastal state extensions of their territorial seas beyond three miles would eliminate a strip of high seas in many strategic straits. Altogether, some 116 straits that in the early 1970s contained a strip of high seas would become entirely territorial sea if states generally accepted 12 miles as the breadth of the territorial sea. Allowing commercial vessels to have free passage through straits was quite uncontroversial, assuming safe transit could be assured, since all states share an interest in allowing the shipment of goods by sea without burdensome regulations. The controversy centered on the rights of warships to pass through straits.

Prior to UNCLOS III, a primary authority on passage through straits was the Corfu Channel Case, 1949 I.C.J. 4, 1949 WL 1. In that case, the International Court of Justice found Albania responsible for damage to British warships caused by mines in the Corfu Strait, a strait 31 miles long between Albania and the Greek island of Corfu. The Court held:

> * * * States in time of peace have a right to send their warships through straits used for international navigation between two parts of the high seas without the previous authorization of a coastal State, provided that the passage is *innocent*. Unless otherwise prescribed in an international convention, there is no right for a coastal State to prohibit such passage through straits in time of peace. * * *
>
> On the other hand, it is a fact that the two coastal States did not maintain normal relations, that Greece had made territorial claims precisely with regard to a part of Albanian territory bordering on the Channel, that Greece had declared that she considered herself technically in a state of war with Albania, and that Albania, invoking the danger of Greek incursions, had considered it necessary to take certain measures of vigilance in this region. The Court is of opinion that Albania, in view of these exceptional circumstances, would have been justified in issuing regulations in respect of the passage of warships through the Strait, but not in prohibiting such passage or in subjecting it to the requirement of special authorization.

Id. at 28–29. Negotiation of a regime for passage through straits was contentious at UNCLOS III. The maritime powers took the position that "all ships and aircraft in transit shall enjoy the same freedom of navigation and overflight, for the purpose of transit through and over such straits, as they have on the high seas." A/AC.138/SC.IIL.4, 10

I.L.M. 1018 (1971). Many states bordering straits, on the other hand, thought passage through straits that were parts of the territorial sea should only be subject to innocent passage. See A/AC.138/SC.II/L.18 (1973), GAOR, 28th Sess., Supp. No. 21, Vol. III, p. 3. One reason why maritime powers were opposed to a regime of innocent passage through straits was because innocent passage required submarines to navigate on the surface.

The compromise that emerged at UNCLOS III provides for a right of transit passage through straits, applicable to most "straits which are used for international navigation between one part of the high seas or an exclusive economic zone and another part of the high seas or an exclusive economic zone." Convention on the Law of the Sea, Article 37. How does the right of transit passage through straits, set out in Part III of the Convention, differ from the right of innocent passage in Part II? How, with respect to the issue of transit passage through straits, does the Convention strike a balance between coastal states' claims of sovereignty and maritime powers' claims of high seas freedoms?

Many observers conclude that the maritime powers satisfied their freedom of navigation objectives in the articles on transit passage through straits. UNCLOS III negotiations concerning straits were not, however, carried out in isolation from negotiations on other issues. Some maritime powers, whose interests were well-served by the outcome of the negotiations on transit passage through straits, were less pleased by other negotiated compromises. In particular, some developed states criticized the regime for mining the deep sea bed that evolved at UNCLOS III. This regime is explored in the next section.

5. THE DEEP SEA BED

The contours of a legal regime to govern the sea bed beyond the limits of national jurisdiction have taken shape only in recent decades. In 1967, Arvid Pardo, Malta's Ambassador to the United Nations, addressed the uses and resources of the sea bed. In his speech, he touched on such varied matters as underseas archaeological treasures, offshore natural gas and petroleum, mineral deposits, ocean floor sediments, oceanographic research, missile systems and other fixed military installations, and pollution. He stirred much interest, in particular, when he "conservatively" projected net annual revenues of at least $5 billion from the exploitation of nonliving resources on the ocean floor beyond the boundaries of national jurisdiction. Pardo assumed these boundaries would be set at approximately the 200–meter isobath or 12 miles from the nearest coast. U.N. Doc. A/C.1/PV1515 (1967)(speech by Dr. Pardo in U.N. General Assembly, First Committee, Nov. 1, 1967). Though Pardo greatly underestimated the extent of national jurisdiction over the continental shelf that came to be accepted, during the negotiations at UNCLOS III many states shared a vision of great deep sea-bed wealth. Much attention focused on nodules rich in manganese, nickel, copper, and cobalt that are scattered over about 15 per cent of the sea bed at depths of 3000 to 6000 meters. Current technology allows recovery of these nodules, although such recovery has to date not been economically viable.

Pardo referred to the sea bed beyond the limits of national jurisdiction as the "common heritage of mankind" which "should be used and exploited for peaceful purposes and for the exclusive benefit of mankind as a whole." Pardo argued that developing states, "representing that part of mankind which is most in need of assistance, should receive preferential consideration" in the distribution of revenues derived from the exploitation of the sea bed. The following U.N. General Assembly resolution sets out one influential vision of the international legal regime for the deep sea bed, and the notes that follow highlight recent developments.

THE DECLARATION OF PRINCIPLES GOVERNING THE SEA-BED AND THE OCEAN FLOOR, AND THE SUBSOIL THEREOF, BEYOND THE LIMITS OF NATIONAL JURISDICTION

G.A. Res. 2749 (XXV), 25 U.N. GAOR Supp. (No. 28), at 24, U.N. Doc. A/8028 (1970).

The General Assembly,

Recalling its resolutions 2340 (XXII) of 18 December 1967, 2467 (XXIII) of 21 December 1968 and 2574 (XXIV) of 15 December 1969, * * *,

Affirming that there is an area of the sea-bed and the ocean floor, and the subsoil thereof, beyond the limits of national jurisdiction, the precise limits of which are yet to be determined,

Recognizing that the existing legal régime of the high seas does not provide substantive rules for regulating the exploration of the aforesaid area and the exploitation of its resources,

Convinced that the area shall be reserved exclusively for peaceful purposes and that the exploration of the area and the exploitation of its resources shall be carried out for the benefit of mankind as a whole,

Believing it essential that an international régime applying to the area and its resources and including appropriate international machinery should be established as soon as possible,

Bearing in mind that the development and use of the area and its resources shall be undertaken in such a manner as to foster the healthy development of the world economy and balanced growth of international trade, and to minimize any adverse economic effects caused by fluctuation of prices of raw materials resulting from such activities,

Solemnly declares that:

1. The sea-bed and ocean floor, and the subsoil thereof, beyond the limits of national jurisdiction (hereinafter referred to as the area), as well as the resources of the area, are the common heritage of mankind.

2. The area shall not be subject to appropriation by any means by States or persons, natural or juridical, and no State shall claim or exercise sovereignty or sovereign rights over any part thereof.

3. No State or person, natural or juridical, shall claim, exercise or acquire rights with respect to the area or its resources incompatible with the international régime to be established and the principles of this Declaration.

4. All activities regarding the exploration and exploitation of the resources of the area and other related activities shall be governed by the international régime to be established.

5. The area shall be open to use exclusively for peaceful purposes by all States, whether coastal or land-locked, without discrimination, in accordance with the international régime to be established.

6. States shall act in the area in accordance with the applicable principles and rules of international law, including the Charter of the United Nations and the Declaration on Principles of International Law concerning Friendly Relations and Co-operation among States in accordance with the Charter of the United Nations, adopted by the General Assembly on 24 October 1970, in the interests of maintaining international peace and security and promoting international co-operation and mutual understanding.

7. The exploration of the area and the exploitation of its resources shall be carried out for the benefit of mankind as a whole, irrespective of the geographical location of States, whether land-locked or coastal, and taking into particular consideration the interests and needs of the developing countries.

8. The area shall be reserved exclusively for peaceful purposes, without prejudice to any measures which have been or may be agreed upon in the context of international negotiations undertaken in the field of disarmament and which may be applicable to a broader area. One or more international agreements shall be concluded as soon as possible in order to implement effectively this principle and to constitute a step towards the exclusion of the sea-bed, the ocean floor and the subsoil thereof from the arms race.

9. On the basis of the principles of this Declaration, an international régime applying to the area and its resources and including appropriate international machinery to give effect to its provisions shall be established by an international treaty of a universal character, generally agreed upon. The régime shall, *inter alia*, provide for the orderly and safe development and rational management of the area and its resources and for expanding opportunities in the use thereof, and ensure the equitable sharing by States in the benefits derived therefrom, taking into particular consideration the interests and needs of the developing countries, whether land-locked or coastal.

10. States shall promote international co-operation in scientific research exclusively for peaceful purposes:

(*a*) By participation in international programmes and by encouraging co-operation in scientific research by personnel of different countries;

(*b*) Through effective publication of research programmes and dissemination of the results of research through international channels;

(*c*) By co-operation in measures to strengthen research capabilities of developing countries, including the participation of their nationals in research programmes.

No such activity shall form the legal basis for any claims with respect to any part of the area or its resources.

11. With respect to activities in the area and acting in conformity with the international régime to be established, States shall take appropriate measures for and shall co-operate in the adoption and implementation of international rules, standards and procedures for, *inter alia*:

(*a*) The prevention of pollution and contamination, and other hazards to the marine environment, including the coastline, and of interference with the ecological balance of the marine environment;

(*b*) The protection and conservation of the natural resources of the area and prevention of damage to the flora and fauna of the marine environment.

12. In their activities in the area, including those relating to its resources, States shall pay due regard to the rights and legitimate interests of coastal States in the region of such activities, as well as of all other States which may be affected by such activities. Consultations shall be maintained with the coastal States concerned with respect to activities relating to the exploration of the area and the exploitation of its resources with a view to avoiding infringement of such rights and interests.

13. Nothing herein shall affect:

(*a*) The legal status of the waters superjacent to the area or that of the air space above those waters;

(*b*) The rights of coastal States with respect to measures to prevent, mitigate or eliminate grave and imminent danger to their coastline or related interests from pollution or threat thereof or from other hazardous occurrences resulting from or caused by any activities in the area, subject to the international régime to be established.

14. Every State shall have the responsibility to ensure that activities in the area, including those relating to its resources, whether undertaken by governmental agencies, or non-governmental entities or persons under its jurisdiction, or acting on its behalf, shall be carried out in conformity with the international régime to be established. The same responsibility applies to international organizations and their members for activities undertaken by such organizations or on their behalf. Damage caused by such activities shall entail liability.

15. The parties to any dispute relating to activities in the area and its resources shall resolve such dispute by the measures mentioned in

Article 33 of the Charter of the United Nations and such procedures for settling disputes as may be agreed upon in the international régime to be established.

Notes and Questions

1. *The Legal Effect of U.N. General Assembly Resolutions.* The 1970 Declaration of Principles was adopted without opposition. What legal effect should be given to it? Also important was the Moratorium Resolution, G.A. Res. 2574–D (XXIV), Dec. 15, 1969. Pending the establishment of an international regime, the Moratorium Resolution declared that no state or person was to exploit the resources of the sea bed beyond the limits of national jurisdiction, and that no claim to the deep sea bed or its resources would be recognized.

2. *Differing Legal Conceptions of the Deep Sea Bed.* Before UNCLOS III, views of the legal nature of the deep sea bed differed widely. Some argued that the sea bed beyond the limits of national jurisdiction was *res nullius,* a conception that would allow unilateral claims of title or sovereignty. Others termed the deep sea bed *res communis* and thus not subject to expropriation. The General Assembly's 1970 Declaration of Principles proclaimed the deep sea bed and its resources to be the common heritage of mankind. In response to a 1974 claim by Deepsea Ventures, Inc. seeking U.S. recognition of "exclusive rights to develop, evaluate and mine" a claim in the deep sea bed, the U.S. State Department stated that it did not grant or recognize exclusive mining rights in the deep sea bed, but that "the mining of the seabed beyond the limits of national jurisdiction may proceed as a freedom of the high seas under existing international law." *Digest of U.S. Practice in International Law* § 5, at 342–43 (1974). Diplomats generally agreed UNCLOS III was the appropriate forum to develop a legal regime to govern the deep sea bed.

3. *International Institutions for the Deep Sea Bed.* Even before UNCLOS III was formally convened, debate centered on the appropriate structure of an international sea-bed authority. Some favored an authority that itself would engage in exploitation, others proposed an authority that would license private claims to blocks of the sea bed, and still others conceived of the authority as a supervisory and consultative body. Many developing states favored a body that would be able to profit from mining and redistribute the wealth to the developing states. The call for an international regime providing economic assistance to developing states was not restricted to developing states. President Richard Nixon endorsed that goal in his statement on U.S. sea-bed policy on May 23, 1970. Nixon proposed

> that all nations adopt as soon as possible a treaty under which they would renounce all national claims over the natural resources of the seabed beyond the point where the high seas reach a depth of 200 meters (218.8 yards) and would agree to regard these resources as the common heritage of mankind.
>
> The treaty should establish an international regime for the exploitation of seabed resources beyond this limit. The regime should include the collection of substantial mineral royalties to be used for internation-

al community purposes, particularly economic assistance to developing countries. * * *

* * * [A]greed international machinery would authorize and regulate exploration and use of seabed resources beyond the continental margins.

"United States Oceans Policy: Statement by the President," 6 *Weekly Compilation of Presidential Documents* 667, 667–68.

4. *The Sea-bed Mining Regime of the U.N. Convention on the Law of the Sea.* Part XI of the 1982 U.N. Convention on the Law of the Sea contains detailed rules and procedures concerning sea-bed mining beyond the limits of national jurisdiction. Article 136 of the Convention sets out the basic principle that the sea bed beyond the limits of national jurisdiction and its resources are the "common heritage of mankind." Part XI also provides for new international institutions. These include the Authority, which is to regulate and govern sea-bed mining primarily through rules, regulations, and procedures adopted by an Assembly and Council. The Enterprise is the mining arm of the Authority, and a Sea–Bed Disputes Chamber of the new International Tribunal for the Law of the Sea is available for compulsory third-party adjudication. Part XI contemplates a "parallel system," under which both the Enterprise and other actors (states and commercial entities) that pay fees and royalties to, and register with, the Authority will mine for sea-bed minerals; the benefits received by the Authority from activities in the deep sea bed are to be equitably shared. See Convention on the Law of the Sea, Article 140. Part XI also contains production limits, included to assuage the concerns of land-based producers of minerals that feared the economic impact of an influx of sea-bed minerals onto world markets. Was it wise to provide such detail in the Convention?

5. *U.S. Objections to the U.N. Convention's Sea-bed Mining Regime.* In 1981, near the end of the UNCLOS III negotiations, the United States under the Reagan Administration announced that it would not support the U.N. Convention on the Law of the Sea, objecting only to certain provisions in Part XI. Articles requiring payments from miners, limits on production, and the transfer of technology to the Enterprise were seen as incompatible with the operation of market forces. The United States also sought a greater role in the decision-making bodies of the Authority, and objected to provisions for a Review Conference, which could adopt amendments to Part XI binding on all states regardless of their concurrence. The United States, the Federal Republic of Germany, and the United Kingdom did not sign the Convention; other developed states signed but did not ratify it. On November 16, 1993, when the Convention received its sixtieth acceptance—the number necessary for its entry into force a year later—virtually all of the acceptances were by developing states.

6. *Unilateral Sea-bed Mining Legislation and "Reciprocating States" Treaties.* Efforts to provide for a regime to govern sea-bed mining have followed different tracks outside of UNCLOS III. One track involved municipal legislation. Legislation authorizing unilateral licensing of certain deep sea-bed mining activities was enacted in the United States. Deep Seabed Hard Minerals Resource Act of 1980, 30 U.S.C. §§ 1401–1473 (1994). By 1985, the Federal Republic of Germany, the United Kingdom, France, the

Soviet Union, Japan, and Italy also had adopted unilateral legislation. Each piece of legislation proclaimed that deep sea-bed mining conducted with due regard for the interests of other states was a high seas freedom. The legislation did not claim sovereignty or sovereign rights over any portion of the deep sea bed or its resources, and the governments of the states enacting the legislation claimed that it was interim in nature, to be in effect pending agreement on a satisfactory Convention text. Developed states also entered into "reciprocating states" treaties designed to respect licenses issued under national laws and to avoid overlaps in mining claims. See Agreement Concerning Interim Arrangements Relating to Polymetallic Nodules of the Deep Sea Bed, Sept. 2, 1982, 21 I.L.M. 950 (1982). The prospect of unilateral legislation had provoked debate at UNCLOS III, with developing states arguing that unilateral exploitation would be contrary to the Declaration of Principles and "a clear violation of international law." See UNCLOS III, Resumed 7th Sess., Plenary, 109th Mtg., Sept. 15, 1978, in 9 *UNCLOS III Official Records* 103–08 (U.N. Sales No. E.79.V.3).

7. *The Preparatory Commission.* A second track involved the Preparatory Commission for the International Sea–Bed Authority and for the International Tribunal for the Law of the Sea (Prepcom), established pursuant to Resolution I of UNCLOS III. Prepcom had two broad mandates. First, it was to plan for the international institutions and arrangements that would operate under Part XI when the 1982 Convention entered into force, making budget and agenda recommendations and preparing draft rules, regulations, and procedures for the Authority. Second, Prepcom exercised significant administrative power of its own, in regards to registering the deep sea-bed exploration activities of certain states and multinational mining consortia as "pioneer investors." While condemning as "wholly illegal" any mining-related activities incompatible with the 1982 Convention, U.N. Doc. LOS/PCN/72 (1985), Prepcom also displayed a flexible attitude with regard to the "reciprocating states" regime discussed in Note 6. In particular, Prepcom supported agreements to resolve overlapping claims to mine sites in the Pacific as a precondition to the registration of four pioneer investor states; these included agreements with the United States and other nonsignatories of the Convention. See Statement on the Implementation of Resolution II, Aug. 11–Sept. 5, 1986, 25 I.L.M. 1326 (1986).

8. *The 1994 Agreement Modifying the Law of the Sea Convention's Seabed Mining Regime.* A third track eventually resulted in a compromise agreement on sea-bed mining. Proposals to modify or set aside Part XI of the 1982 Convention were discussed in a series of informal meetings beginning in July 1990, undertaken at the initiative of the U.N. Secretary–General. The result of these meetings was the detailed Agreement Relating to the Implementation of Part XI, 33 I.L.M. 1309 (1994), which was opened for signature on July 29, 1994, less than four months before the Law of the Sea Convention entered into force. This Agreement dispenses with large annual fees for miners, production limitations, and the requirement that States Parties fund the Enterprise's mining operations. Part XI requirements concerning the transfer of private technology are not implemented; a mandate that the Enterprise and developing states "seek to obtain such technology on fair and reasonable commercial terms and conditions on the open market, or through joint venture arrangements" applies instead.

Multinational consortia previously licensed under municipal legislation are guaranteed access to sea-bed mining on terms "no less favorable than" terms given to entities whose mine site claims had been registered by Prepcom. With respect to several other issues, general principles, to guide the formulation of more specific rules, regulations, and procedures the Authority is to adopt when commercial production is imminent, will be used in place of detailed provisions of Part XI.

The 1994 Agreement also revises procedural aspects of Part XI. The Agreement provides the United States with a greater role in the decision-making process by effectively guaranteeing it a seat in the Council, and by allowing it to block decisions on important financial and budgetary matters in the Finance Committee. Under the Agreement, any of four chambers—including a chamber representing the industrialized states—may block important substantive decisions of the Council, including decisions on the sharing of benefits derived from sea-bed mining. Furthermore, provisions relating to the Review Conference "shall not apply," so no amendments to the sea-bed mining regime can apply to any state that does not accept them.

The 1994 Agreement contains provisions to help insure that the 1982 Convention is implemented along with the Agreement. States accepting the 1982 Convention after July 29, 1994, must also accept the Agreement, which is to be interpreted and applied together with the Convention as a single instrument. In addition, no state may accept the Part XI Agreement without also accepting the Convention. States that accepted the Convention prior to July 29, 1994, can become bound by the Agreement merely by signing it, unless they take affirmative steps to indicate their intent not to be bound. The Part XI Agreement entered into force on July 28, 1996.

9. *The Impact of International Law on Deep Sea-bed Mining*. Suppose a company or consortium were authorized under national legislation to exploit manganese nodules on the deep sea bed beyond the limits of national jurisdiction, and suppose the authorizing state is not a party to the U.N. Convention on the Law of the Sea. How would international law affect any decision to exploit nodules pursuant to such legislation? Are the 1982 Convention's deep sea-bed mining provisions an international legal obligation *erga omnes*?

10. *Equitable Sharing of Revenues From Mining the Continental Shelf.* Under Article 82 of the U.N. Convention on the Law of the Sea, each coastal state (with the exception of certain developing states) must pay a portion of its revenues from its exploitation of the nonliving resources of the continental shelf beyond 200 miles from its baselines. The Authority, established to regulate deep sea-bed mining, is to receive such payments. The Authority will then distribute them to parties to the Convention "on the basis of equitable sharing criteria, taking into account the interests and needs of developing States, particularly the least developed and the land-locked among them." Does the reference to "equitable sharing" have a definite meaning, or is it merely a grant of discretion to the Authority? See Chapter 3.

D. ATMOSPHERE AND THE ENVIRONMENT

Damage to the environment has been a concern for many years, and the subject of international arbitrations and treaties. During the 1980's, environmental disasters in Bhopal, Chernobyl, and Basel, and confirmation of the ozone hole over Antarctica, helped to make the international environment a more significant world political and legal issue than it had been in the past.

As in other sections in this chapter, our major concern is with international common spaces. We start, however, with an influential arbitral decision in which the claim concerned environmental damage within the borders of one state. The *Trail Smelter Case* raises questions about one way—a liability regime based on notions of state responsibility—international law and process might address damage to the environment. The materials following the *Trail Smelter Case* suggest other avenues.

1. STATE RESPONSIBILITY AND LIABILITY FOR TRANS-BORDER POLLUTION

THE TRAIL SMELTER CASE

United States v. Canada, 1941, U.N. Rep. Int'l Arb. Awards 1905 (1949).

CONVENTION FOR SETTLEMENT OF DIFFICULTIES ARISING FROM OPERATION OF SMELTER AT TRAIL, B.C. * * *

Signed at Ottawa, April 15, 1935; ratifications exchanged Aug. 3, 1935. * * *

ARTICLE I.

The Government of Canada will cause to be paid to the Secretary of State of the United States, to be deposited in the United States Treasury, within three months after ratifications of this convention have been exchanged, the sum of three hundred and fifty thousand dollars, United States currency, in payment of all damage which occurred in the United States, prior to the first day of January, 1932, as a result of the operation of the Trail Smelter. * * *

ARTICLE III.

The Tribunal shall finally decide the questions, hereinafter referred to as "the Questions," set forth hereunder, namely:

(1) Whether damage caused by the Trail Smelter in the State of Washington has occurred since the first day of January, 1932, and, if so, what indemnity should be paid therefore?

(2) In the event of the answer to the first part of the preceding Question being in the affirmative, whether the Trail Smelter should be required to refrain from causing damage in the State of Washington in the future and, if so, to what extent?

(3) In the light of the answer to the preceding Question, what measures or régime, if any, should be adopted or maintained by the Trail Smelter?

(4) What indemnity or compensation, if any, should be paid on account of any decision or decisions rendered by the Tribunal pursuant to the next two preceding Questions?

ARTICLE IV.

The Tribunal shall apply the law and practice followed in dealing with cognate questions in the United States of America as well as international law and practice, and shall give consideration to the desire of the high contracting parties to reach a solution just to all parties concerned. * * *

DECISION

REPORTED ON MARCH 11, 1941, TO THE GOVERNMENT OF THE UNITED STATES OF AMERICA AND TO THE GOVERNMENT OF THE DOMINION OF CANADA, UNDER THE CONVENTION SIGNED APRIL 15, 1935.

This Tribunal is constituted under, and its powers are derived from and limited by, the Convention between the United States of America and the Dominion of Canada signed at Ottawa, April 15 1935, duly ratified by the two parties, and ratifications exchanged at Ottawa, August 3, 1935 (hereinafter termed "the Convention"). * * *

The Tribunal herewith reports its final decisions.

The controversy is between two Governments involving damage occurring or having occurred, in the territory of one of them (the United States of America) and alleged to be due to an agency situated in the territory of the other (the Dominion of Canada). In this controversy, the Tribunal did not sit and is not sitting to pass upon claims presented by individuals or on behalf of one or more individuals by their Government, although individuals may come within the meaning of "parties concerned," in Article IV * * * of the Convention and although the damage suffered by individuals did, in part, "afford a convenient scale for the calculation of the reparation due to the State." * * *

As between the two countries involved, each has an equal interest that if a nuisance is proved, the indemnity to damaged parties for proven damage shall be just and adequate and each has also an equal interest that unproven or unwarranted claims shall not be allowed. For, while the United States' interests may now be claimed to be injured by the operations of a Canadian corporation, it is equally possible that at some time in the future Canadian interests might be claimed to be injured by an American corporation. As has well been said: "It would not be to the advantage of the two countries concerned that industrial effort should be prevented by exaggerating the interests of the agricultural community. Equally, it would not be to the advantage of the two countries that the agricultural community should be oppressed to advance the interest of industry."

Considerations like the above are reflected in the provisions of the Convention in Article IV, that "the desire of the high contracting parties" is "to reach a solution just to all parties concerned." And the phraseology of the questions submitted to the Tribunal clearly evinces a desire and an intention that, to some extent, in making its answers to the questions, the Tribunal should endeavor to adjust the conflicting interests by some "just solution" which would allow the continuance of the operation of the Trail Smelter but under such restrictions and limitations as would, as far as foreseeable, prevent damage in the United States, and as would enable indemnity to be obtained, if in spite of such restrictions and limitations, damage should occur in the future in the United States.

In arriving at its decision, the Tribunal has had always to bear in mind the further fact that in the preamble to the Convention, it is stated that it is concluded with the recognition of "the desirability and necessity of effecting a permanent settlement." * * *

On April 16, 1938, the Tribunal reported its "final decision" on Question No. 1, as well as its temporary decisions on Questions No. 2 and No. 3, and provided for a temporary régime thereunder. The decision reported on April 16, 1938, will be referred to hereinafter as the "previous decision." * * *

In conclusion (end of Part Two of the previous decision), the Tribunal answered Question No. 1 as follows:

> Damage caused by the Trail Smelter in the State of Washington has occurred since the first day of January, 1932, and up to October 1, 1937, and the indemnity to be paid therefore is seventy-eight thousand dollars ($78,000), and is to be complete and final indemnity and compensation for all damage which occurred between such dates. * * *

Answering Questions No. 2 and No. 3, the Tribunal decided that, until a final decision should be made, the Trail Smelter should be subject to a temporary régime (described more in detail in Part Four of the present decision) and a trial period was established to a date not later than October 1, 1940, in order to enable the Tribunal to establish a permanent régime based on a "more adequate and intensive study," since the Tribunal felt that the information that had been placed before it did not enable it to determine at that time with sufficient certainty upon a permanent régime. * * *

The period within which the Tribunal shall report its final decisions was extended by agreement of the two Governments until March 12, 1941. * * *

In 1896, a smelter was started under American auspices near the locality known as Trail, B.C. In 1906, the Consolidated Mining and Smelting Company of Canada, Limited, obtained a charter of incorporation from the Canadian authorities, and that company acquired the smelter plant at Trail as it then existed. Since that time, the Canadian company, without interruption, has operated the Smelter, and from time to time has greatly added to the plant until it has become one of the best and largest equipped smelting plants on the American continent. In 1925 and 1927, two stacks of the plant were erected to 409 feet in height and the Smelter greatly increased its daily smelting of zinc and lead ores. This increased production resulted in more sulphur dioxide fumes and higher concentrations being emitted into the air. In 1916, about 5,000 tons of sulphur per month were emitted; in 1924, about 4,700 tons; in 1926, about 9,000 tons—an amount which rose near to 10,000 tons per month in 1930. In other words, about 300–350 tons of sulphur were being emitted daily in 1930. (It is to be noted that one ton of sulphur is substantially the equivalent of two tons of sulphur dioxide or SO_2.)

From 1925, at least, to 1937, damage occurred in the State of Washington, resulting from the sulphur dioxide emitted from the Trail Smelter * * *.

The subject of fumigations and damage claimed to result from them was referred by the two Governments on August 7, 1928, to the International Joint Commission, United States and Canada, under Article IX of the Convention of January 11, 1909, between the United States and Great Britain, providing that the high contracting parties might agree that "any other question or matters of difference arising between them involving the rights, obligations or interests of either in relation to the other, or to the inhabitants of the other, along the common frontier between the United States and the Dominion of Canada shall be referred from time to time to the International Joint Commission for examination and report. Such reports shall not be regarded as decisions of the question or matters so submitted either on the facts or on the law, and shall not, in any way, have the character of an arbitral award."

[The Joint Commission's 1931 report recommended that steps be taken to reduce sulphur dioxide fumes from the Trail Smelter "to a point where it will do no damage in the United States." The Commission also found that damages to the United States caused by pollution from the Trail Smelter through January 1, 1932 amounted to $350,000.]

This report failed to secure the acceptance of both Governments. A sum of $350,000 has, however, been paid by the Dominion of Canada to the United States.

Two years after the filing of the above report, the United States Government, on February 17, 1933, made representations to the Canadian Government that existing conditions were entirely unsatisfactory and that damage was still occurring and diplomatic negotiations were entered into which resulted in the signing of the present Convention.

The Consolidated Mining and Smelting Company of Canada, Limited, proceeded after 1930 to make certain changes and additions in its plant, with the intention and purpose of lessening the sulphur contents of the fumes, and in an attempt to lessen injurious fumigations, a new system of control over the emission of fumes during the crop growing season came into operation about 1934. * * *

The tons of sulphur emitted into the air from the Trail Smelter fell from about 10,000 tons per month in 1930 to about 7,200 tons in 1931 and 3,400 tons in 1932 as a result both of sulphur dioxide beginning to be absorbed and of depressed business conditions. As depression receded, this monthly average rose in 1933 to 4,000 tons, in 1934 to nearly 6,300 tons and in 1935 to 6,800 tons. In 1936, however, it had fallen to 5,600 tons; in 1937, if further fell to 4,850 tons; in 1938, still further to 4,230 tons to reach 3,250 tons in 1939. It rose again, however, to 3,875 tons in 1940. * * *

PART TWO. * * *

Since the Tribunal has, in its previous decision, answered Question No. 1 with respect to the period from the first day of January, 1932, to the first day of October, 1937, it now answers Question No. 1 with respect to the period from the first day of October, 1937, to the first day of October, 1940, as follows:

(1) No damage caused by the Trail Smelter in the State of Washington has occurred since the first day of October, 1937, and prior to the first day of October, 1940, and hence no indemnity shall be paid therefor.

PART THREE.

The second question under Article III of the Convention is as follows:

> In the event of the answer to the first part of the preceding question being in the affirmative, whether the Trail Smelter should be required to refrain from causing damage in the State of Washington in the future and, if so, to what extent?

Damage has occurred since January 1, 1932, as fully set forth in the previous decision. To that extent, the first part of the preceding question has thus been answered in the affirmative. * * *

The first problem which arises is whether the question should be answered on the basis of the law followed in the United States or on the basis of international law. The Tribunal, however, finds that this problem need not be solved here as the law followed in the United States in dealing with the quasi-sovereign rights of the States of the Union, in the matter of air pollution, whilst more definite, is in conformity with the general rules of international law.

Particularly in reaching its conclusions as regards this question as well as the next, the Tribunal has given consideration to the desire of the high contracting parties "to reach a solution just to all parties concerned."

As Professor Eagleton puts it (*Responsibility of States in International Law*, 1928, p.80): "A State owes at all times a duty to protect other States against injurious acts by individuals from within its jurisdiction." A great number of such general pronouncements by leading authorities concerning the duty of a State to respect other States and their territory have been presented to the Tribunal. These and many others have been carefully examined. International decisions, in various matters, from the Alabama case onward, and also earlier ones, are based on the same general principle, and, indeed, this principle, as such, has not been questioned by Canada. But the real difficulty often arises rather when it comes to determine what, *pro subjecta materie*, is deemed to constitute an injurious act. * * *

No case of air pollution dealt with by an international tribunal has been brought to the attention of the Tribunal nor does the Tribunal know of any such case. The nearest analogy is that of water pollution. But, here also, no decision of an international tribunal has been cited or has been found.

There are, however, as regards both air pollution and water pollution, certain decisions of the Supreme Court of the United States which may legitimately be taken as a guide in this field of international law, for it is reasonable to follow by analogy, in international cases, precedents established by that court in dealing with controversies between States of the Union or with other controversies concerning the quasi-sovereign rights of such States, where no contrary rule prevails in international law and no reason for rejecting such precedents can be adduced from the limitations of sovereignty inherent in the Constitution of the United States.

In the suit of the State of Missouri *v.* State of Illinois (200 U.S. 496, 521) concerning the pollution, within the boundaries of Illinois, of the Illinois River, an affluent of the Mississippi flowing into the latter where it forms the boundary between that State and Missouri, an injunction was refused. "Before this court ought to intervene," said the court, "the case should be of serious magnitude, clearly and fully proved, and the principle to be applied should be one which the court is prepared deliberately to maintain against all considerations on the other side. (See Kansas *v.* Colorado, 185 U.S. 125.)" The court found that the practice complained of was general along the shores of the Mississippi River at that time, that it was followed by Missouri itself and that thus a standard was set up by the defendant which the claimant was entitled to invoke. * * *

In the more recent suit of the State of New York against the State of New Jersey (256 U.S. 296, 309), concerning the pollution of New York Bay, the injunction was also refused for lack of proof * * *. The court, referring to Missouri *v.* Illinois, said: "... the burden on the State of New York of sustaining the allegations of its bill is much greater than that imposed upon a complainant in an ordinary suit between private parties. Before this court can be moved to exercise its extraordinary power under the Constitution to control the conduct of one State at the suit of another, the threatened invasion of rights must be of serious magnitude and it must be established by clear and convincing evidence."

What the Supreme Court says there of its power under the Constitution equally applies to the extraordinary power granted this Tribunal under the Convention. What is true between States of the Union is, at least, equally true concerning the relations between the United States and the Dominion of Canada.

[The Tribunal summarizes other U.S. Supreme Court decisions.]

On the question whether an injunction should be granted or not [in *Georgia v. Tennessee Copper Co.*], the court said (206 U.S. 230):

> It (the State) has the last word as to whether its mountains shall be stripped of their forests and its inhabitants shall breathe pure air.... It is not lightly to be presumed to give up quasi-sovereign rights for pay and ... if that be its choice, it may insist that an infraction of them shall be stopped. This court has not quite the same freedom to balance the harm that will be done by an injunction against that of which the plaintiff complains, that it would have in deciding between two subjects of a single political power. Without excluding the considerations that equity always takes into account ... it is a fair and reasonable demand on the part of a sovereign that the air over its territory should not be polluted on a great scale by sulfurous acid gas, that the forests on its mountains, be they better or worse, and whatever domestic destruction they may have suffered, should not be further destroyed or threatened by the act of persons beyond its control, that the crops and orchards on its hills should not be endangered from the same source.... Whether Georgia, by insisting upon this claim, is doing more harm than good to her own citizens, is for her to determine. The possible disaster to those outside the State must be accepted as a consequence of her standing upon her extreme rights.

Later on, however, when the court actually framed an injunction, in the case of the Ducktown Company (237 U.S. 474, 477)(an agreement on the basis of an annual compensation was reached with the most important of the two smelters, the Tennessee Copper Company), they did not go beyond a decree "adequate to diminish materially the present probability of damage to its (Georgia's) citizens." * * *

The Tribunal, therefore, finds that the above decisions, taken as a whole, constitute an adequate basis for its conclusions, namely, that, under the principles of international law, as well as of the law of the United States, no State has the right to use or permit the use of its territory in such a manner as to cause injury by fumes in or to the territory of another or the properties or persons therein, when the case is of serious consequence and the injury is established by clear and convincing evidence.

The decisions of the Supreme Court of the United States which are the basis of these conclusions are decisions in equity and a solution inspired by them, together with the régime hereinafter prescribed, will, in the opinion of the Tribunal, be "just to all parties concerned," as long, at least, as the present conditions in the Columbia River Valley continue to prevail.

Considering the circumstances of the case, the Tribunal holds that the Dominion of Canada is responsible in international law for the conduct of the Trail Smelter. Apart from the undertakings in the Convention, it is, therefore, the duty of the Government of the Dominion of Canada to see to it that this conduct should be in conformity with the obligation of the Dominion under international law as herein determined.

The Tribunal, therefore, answers Question No. 2 as follows: (2) So long as the present conditions in the Columbia River Valley prevail, the Trail Smelter shall be required to refrain from causing any damage through fumes in the State of Washington; the damage herein referred to and its extent being such as would be recoverable under the decisions of the courts of the United States in suits between private individuals. The indemnity for such damage should be fixed in such manner as the Governments * * * should agree upon.

PART FOUR.

The third question under Article III of the Convention is as follows: "In the light of the answer to the preceding question, what measures or régime, if any, should be adopted and maintained by the Trail Smelter?"

Answering this question in the light of the preceding one, since the Tribunal has, in its previous decision, found that damage caused by the Trail Smelter has occurred in the State of Washington since January 1, 1932, and since the Tribunal is of opinion that damage may occur in the future unless the operations of the Smelter shall be subject to some control, in order to avoid damage occurring, the Tribunal now decides that a régime or measure of control shall be applied to the operations of the Smelter and shall remain in full force unless and until modified in accordance with the provisions hereinafter set forth * * *.

[The Tribunal establishes a highly technical regime of pollution abatement. In response to Question 4, concerning additional compensation or indemnity, the Tribunal states that "the prescribed regime * * * will probably result in preventing any damage of a material nature occurring in the State of Washington in the future." The Tribunal nevertheless calls for the payment of certain indemnities and costs if the Trail Smelter were to cause damage in the state of Washington in the future.]

Notes and Questions

1. *The Use of Interstate Arbitration to Resolve Environmental Disputes.* Does international arbitration based on principles of state responsibility recommend itself as an efficacious way to deter and remedy instances of transboundary environmental harm? The *Trail Smelter Case* was a lengthy and expensive process, requiring six years of fact-finding. The Tribunal not only heard detailed oral and documentary evidence, but its three members personally examined many damaged farms and orchards in Washington. In

addition, each government, in accordance with the Tribunal's 1935 constitution, appointed a scientist to assist in the process. The scientists heard all the witnesses and arguments, examined all the documents, consulted with the Tribunal, inspected the Trail Smelter and areas of alleged injury, and administered a trial regime for the operation of the smelter. Would it be better to hear such cases under some simplified procedure, or with some relaxation in required burdens of proof?

2. *Compliance with the Arbitral Decision.* It cost Consolidated Mining and Smelting Co., the company responsible for operating the Trail Smelter, approximately $20 million to comply with the Tribunal's pollution abatement regime. The Company's willingness to bear these costs may, at least in part, have been due to the fact that it was involved in all stages of the arbitration. The Company participated with the Government of Canada in negotiating the 1935 Convention, and both Company and Canadian Government lawyers were actively involved in all aspects of the proceedings. See John E. Read, "The Trail Smelter Dispute," 1 *Canadian Yearbook of International Law* 213, 227–28 (1963).

3. *The Governing Law.* Why did the parties to the 1935 Convention authorize the Tribunal, an international institution, to apply the law of the United States? Was it appropriate for the Tribunal to use the law of the United States in deciding the issues before it?

4. *Alternative Fora.* Could Washington landowners who claimed damage have pursued Consolidated Mining and Smelting Co. directly? Washington landowners would have faced hurdles had they sued Consolidated in British Columbia, not the least of which was the likelihood that a court in British Columbia would find it could not exercise jurisdiction in a suit based on damage to land located outside the province. See British South Africa Co. v. Companhia de Moçambique, [1893] A.C. 602. A plausible solution under the laws of Washington would have led Consolidated to purchase smoke easements from landowners threatened or affected by fumes, but Washington's constitution prohibited any alien person or corporation from holding interests in land in the state. Should individual landowners have access to an international tribunal to pursue their claims? Should nongovernmental environmental organizations be able to pursue claims in an international tribunal? As you read the following materials, consider what mechanisms, other than attempts to impose state responsibility through lawsuits or arbitral proceedings, should be used to address international environmental degradation.

STOCKHOLM DECLARATION OF THE UNITED NATIONS CONFERENCE ON THE HUMAN ENVIRONMENT

Adopted by the U.N. Conference on the Human Environment at Stockholm, 16 June 1972, U.N. Doc. A/CONF.48/14/Rev.1 at 3 (1973), U.N. Doc. A/CONF.48/14 at 2–65, and Corr.1 (1972), 11 *International Legal Materials* 1416 (1972).

Principle 6

The discharge of toxic substances or of other substances and the release of heat, in such quantities or concentrations as to exceed the capacity of the environment to render them harmless, must be halted in order to ensure that serious or irreversible damage is not inflicted upon ecosystems. The just struggle of the peoples of all countries against pollution should be supported. * * *

PRINCIPLE 21

States have, in accordance with the Charter of the United Nations and the principles of international law, the sovereign right to exploit their own resources pursuant to their own environmental policies, and the responsibility to ensure that activities within their jurisdiction or control do not cause damage to the environment of other States or of areas beyond the limits of national jurisdiction.

PRINCIPLE 22

States shall co-operate to develop further the international law regarding liability and compensation for the victims of pollution and other environmental damage caused by activities within the jurisdiction or control of such States to areas beyond their jurisdiction.

RIO DECLARATION ON ENVIRONMENT AND DEVELOPMENT

Adopted by the United Nations Conference on Environment and Development, June 14, 1992, UNCED Doc. A/CONF.151/5/Rev.1, 31 *International Legal Materials* 874 (1992).

PRINCIPLE 1

Human beings are at the centre of concerns for sustainable development. They are entitled to a healthy and productive life in harmony with nature.

PRINCIPLE 2

States have, in accordance with the Charter of the United Nations and the principles of international law, the sovereign right to exploit their own resources pursuant to their own environmental and developmental policies, and the responsibility to ensure that activities within their jurisdiction or control do not cause damage to the environment of other States or of areas beyond the limits of national jurisdiction.

PRINCIPLE 3

The right to development must be fulfilled so as to equitably meet developmental and environmental needs of present and future generations.

PRINCIPLE 4

In order to achieve sustainable development, environmental protection shall constitute an integral part of the development process and cannot be considered in isolation from it.

PRINCIPLE 5

All States and all people shall cooperate in the essential task of eradicating poverty as an indispensable requirement for sustainable development, in order to decrease the disparities in standards of living and better meet the needs of the majority of the people of the world.

PRINCIPLE 6

The special situation and needs of developing countries, particularly the least developed and those most environmentally vulnerable, shall be given special priority. International actions in the field of environment and development should also address the interests and needs of all countries.

PRINCIPLE 7

States shall cooperate in a spirit of global partnership to conserve, protect and restore the health and integrity of the Earth's ecosystem. In view of the different contributions to global environmental degradation, States have common but differentiated responsibilities. The developed countries acknowledge the responsibility that they bear in the international pursuit of sustainable development in view of the pressures their societies place on the global environment and of the technologies and financial resources they command.

PRINCIPLE 8

To achieve sustainable development and a higher quality of life for all people, States should reduce and eliminate unsustainable patterns of production and consumption and promote appropriate demographic policies.

PRINCIPLE 9

States should cooperate to strengthen endogenous capacity-building for sustainable development by improving scientific understanding through exchanges of scientific and technological knowledge, and by enhancing the development, adaptation, diffusion and transfer of technologies, including new and innovative technologies.

PRINCIPLE 10

Environmental issues are best handled with the participation of all concerned citizens, at the relevant level. At the national level, each individual shall have appropriate access to information concerning the environment that is held by public authorities, including information on hazardous materials and activities in their communities, and the opportunity to participate in decision-making processes. States shall facilitate and encourage public awareness and participation by making information widely available. Effective access to judicial and administrative proceedings, including redress and remedy, shall be provided.

PRINCIPLE 11

States shall enact effective environmental legislation. Environmental standards, management objectives and priorities should reflect the environmental and developmental context to which they apply. Standards applied by some countries may be inappropriate and of unwarranted economic and social costs to other countries, in particular developing countries.

PRINCIPLE 12

States should cooperate to promote a supportive and open international economic system that would lead to economic growth and sustainable development in all countries, to better address the problems of environmental degradation. Trade policy measures for environmental purposes should not constitute a means of arbitrary or unjustifiable discrimination or a disguised restriction on international trade. Unilateral actions to deal with environmental challenges outside the jurisdiction of the importing country should be avoided. Environmental measures addressing transboundary or global environmental problems should, as far as possible, be based on an international consensus.

PRINCIPLE 13

States shall develop national law regarding liability and compensation for the victims of pollution and other environmental damage. States shall also cooperate in an expeditious and more determined manner to develop further international law regarding liability and compensation for adverse effects of environmental damage caused by activities within their jurisdiction or control to areas beyond their jurisdiction.

PRINCIPLE 14

States should effectively cooperate to discourage or prevent the relocation and transfer to other States of any activities and substances that cause severe environmental degradation or are found to be harmful to human health.

PRINCIPLE 15

In order to protect the environment, the precautionary approach shall be widely applied by States according to their capabilities. Where there are threats of serious or irreversible damage, lack of full scientific certainty shall not be used as a reason for postponing cost-effective measures to prevent environmental degradation.

PRINCIPLE 16

National authorities should endeavor to promote the internalization of environmental costs and the use of economic instruments, taking into account the approach that the polluter should, in principle, bear the cost of pollution, with due regard to the public interest and without distorting international trade and investment.

PRINCIPLE 17

Environmental impact assessment, as a national instrument, shall be undertaken for proposed activities that are likely to have a significant adverse impact on the environment and are subject to a decision of a competent national authority.

PRINCIPLE 18

States shall immediately notify other States of any natural disasters or other emergencies that are likely to produce sudden harmful effects on the environment of those States. Every effort shall be made by the international community to help States so afflicted.

PRINCIPLE 19

States shall provide prior and timely notification and relevant information to potentially affected States on activities that may have a significant adverse transboundary environmental effect and shall consult with those States at an early stage and in good faith. * * *

PRINCIPLE 24

Warfare is inherently destructive of sustainable development. States shall therefore respect international law providing protection for the environment in times of armed conflict and cooperate in its further development, as necessary.

Notes and Questions

1. *The Stockholm and Rio Declarations.* The Stockholm Declaration and the Rio Declaration are examples of "soft law," declarations that the adopting states do not regard as creating legally binding obligations at international law. The Stockholm Declaration emerged from the 1972 Stockholm Conference on the Human Environment, the first major intergovernmental conference to address environmental issues in a comprehensive fashion. The Rio Declaration was adopted at the United Nations Conference on Environment and Development, the "Earth Summit," in Rio de Janeiro, Brazil in June 1992. It was attended by approximately 4000 representatives of over 170 states, as well as by 30,000 unofficial negotiators, and followed numerous preparatory committee meetings held over a two-year period. If states do not generally regard such instruments as the Stockholm Declaration and the Rio Declaration as legally binding, what is their significance for international law?

2. *Rules of State Responsibility for Environmental Harm.* International lawyers look for evidence of the content of principles of state responsibility for environmental harm in a variety of declarations and instances of state practice. Some commentators suggest that Principle 21 of the Stockholm Declaration deserves acceptance as a rule of customary law. How do Principle 21 of the Stockholm Declaration and Principle 2 of the Rio Declaration differ from the rules of state responsibility for environmental harm stated in the *Trail Smelter Case*?

3. *Obligations* Erga Omnes. If one state has polluted the international commons, do international legal norms suggest that the polluter should be legally responsible? The International Law Commission has endorsed the idea that obligations *erga omnes*, which we consider in Chapter 3, include obligations "of essential importance for the safeguarding and preservation of the human environment, such as those prohibiting massive pollution of the atmosphere or of the sea." U.N. GAOR, 31st Sess., Supp. No. 10, at 170, U.N. Doc. A/31/10 (1976), art. 19(3), *reprinted in* 2 *Yearbook of the Interna-*

tional Law Commission 73, U.N. Doc. A/CN.4/Ser.A/1976/Add.1 (1976). Does the concept of obligations *erga omnes*, proscribing massive pollution of the global commons, suggest that any state should be allowed to pursue a claim before a tribunal against the state or entity responsible?

4. *Multiple State Responsibility*. Several states may act in concert or independently to cause environmental harm in a neighboring state or in the global commons. State responsibility doctrine holds that the breach of any international obligation gives rise to a duty to make reparation. When reparation takes the form of compensation, should multiple responsible states be jointly and severally liable? In what circumstances?

> * * * Even in the simple case [in which the actions of a few states violate their international obligations with regard to indivisible injury], the nature of international legal process, including the difficulty of insuring contribution among wrongdoing states, explains why joint and several liability is not currently widespread in international practice. The absence of an international legislative authority also impedes the widespread adoption of such a rule. A legislative authority could more easily make the difficult policy choices necessary to formulate a detailed comprehensive legal regime in this area. * * *
>
> Despite procedural and political reasons that may impede the acceptance or limit the scope of application of joint and several liability, many considerations support its recognition as an international law rule governing the consequences of multiple state responsibility. The international community's concern with deterring wrongful conduct by channeling the cost of an injury to its author and with making an injured party whole through pecuniary compensation for loss is well reflected in international law rules of reparation. Municipal analogies, viewed either as general principles of law or as tools in the progressive development of international law, suggest that joint and several liability is the most appropriate method to achieve these objectives. Finally, state practice, although limited, evidences that joint and several liability has achieved a measure of acceptance in international law, demonstrates that tribunals deciding international cases have the requisite will and capacity to allocate the burden of compensation among multiple responsible states, and points toward favorable international reception of a principle of joint and several liability.

John E. Noyes & Brian D. Smith, "State Responsibility and the Principle of Joint and Several Liability," 13 *Yale Journal of International Law* 225, 266–67 (1988).

5. *Contributions of the Stockholm and Rio Conferences to International Regulatory Regimes*. States have created international information-gathering and regulatory regimes as alternatives or supplements to processes designed to hold states responsible for environmental harm. The Stockholm and Rio Conferences, in addition to contributing the declarations excerpted above, also produced new institutions and legal instruments relating to the international environment. The United Nations Environment Programme (UNEP) was established at the Stockholm Conference to coordinate efforts to protect the international environment. UNEP has initiated workshops and multilateral treaty negotiations, leading, for example, to the 1985

Convention for the Protection of the Ozone Layer (considered below) and the 1989 Basel Convention on the Control of Transboundary Movements of Hazardous Wastes and their Disposal. The Rio Earth Summit produced a Framework Convention on Climate Change, a Convention on Biological Diversity, and a statement of principles on forest conservation. The Rio Conference also produced Agenda 21, an approximately 800–page document that sets priorities and details steps for achieving sustainable growth, protecting human health, promoting urban habitability, encouraging efficient resource use, protecting the atmosphere and the oceans, and managing chemicals and hazardous and nuclear wastes.

2. A TREATY REGIME TO PROTECT THE OZONE LAYER

Scientists have concluded that the release of chlorofluorocarbons (CFCs), often found in refrigerants, air conditioners, and aerosol cans, and halons, used in fire extinguishers, results in the destruction of ozone in the stratosphere. Ozone in the stratosphere filters out shortwave ultraviolet radiation, so when the amount of ozone diminishes, more ultraviolet radiation reaches the earth. Increased ultraviolet radiation may lead to, among other things, increased incidence of skin cancer, cataracts, general suppression of the immune system, stunted crop growth, and a drop in the productivity of phytoplankton, an important marine food source.

Scientists first postulated the process of ozone depletion in 1974. Huge losses in the ozone layer over Antarctica were documented in 1985. In addition to the "ozone hole" over Antarctica, ozone depletion now affects the middle and high latitudes of both hemispheres.

The following excerpt explores the negotiation of the 1985 Vienna Convention for the Protection of the Ozone Layer, Mar. 22, 1985, 26 I.L.M. 1529 (1987), and subsequent protocols designed to limit the production and consumption of CFCs and other ozone-depleting substances. The Convention and its protocols have been accepted by most states, developed and developing alike.

DAVID D. CARON, "PROTECTION OF THE STRATOSPHERIC OZONE LAYER AND THE STRUCTURE OF INTERNATIONAL ENVIRONMENTAL LAWMAKING"

14 *Hastings International & Comparative Law Review* 755 (1991).

II. STRATOSPHERIC OZONE DEPLETION: THE PROBLEM AND A BRIEF HISTORY OF THE INTERNATIONAL RESPONSE * * *

C. UNEP and the 1985 Vienna Framework Convention

Even as the national debates proceeded, the groundwork for an international approach was laid. The United Nations Environmental Programme (UNEP) in 1977 convened a meeting to begin the international process. The meeting resulted in the adoption of the "World Plan of Action on the Ozone Layer" and the establishment of a Global Coordinating Committee on the Ozone Layer.

* * * In 1981 UNEP established an Ad Hoc Working Group of Legal and Technical Experts charged with the task of drafting a framework convention for the protection of the ozone layer. A framework convention is a document that aims not at substantive norms, but rather at establishment of the institutional framework that will result in such norms. * * * [S]everal * * * drafts were produced prior to the Vienna Conference in March 1985, which ultimately adopted a framework convention.

Adoption of the Vienna Convention was bittersweet, however, because several states had sought more from the Conference. * * * Ultimately a compromise was reached in the form of a Resolution of the Conference calling for the states to reassemble for the purpose of concluding a protocol regulating CFCs.

D. A Growing Sense of Urgency and the 1987 Montreal Protocol

Even as work proceeded in anticipation of a second meeting to adopt a protocol, two important trends were occurring. First, a British research group in May 1985 announced that huge losses in Antarctic ozone had occurred in the springs of 1982, 1983, and 1984. By late summer 1985 American satellite measurements, free of certain previous interpretational errors, confirmed the British findings. * * * [T]he Antarctic hole was significant because, even before the scientific community could confirm that chlorine was responsible for the hole, the public had what in its view was tangible and comprehensible evidence that humanity could fundamentally alter the Earth's atmosphere. As the public increasingly voiced its concern, the states participating in the international negotiations became increasingly receptive not only to a ban on aerosol use, but, more generally, to across the board phased reductions in CFC and halon consumption and production.

The second trend also facilitated the inclination to adopt across the board phased reductions. Specifically, the major producers of CFCs had come to believe that environmentally safe substitutes for CFSs existed, and that it was for each of them in their individual interest to be the first to develop and offer such substitutes. Although it was thought that such substitutes would be several times more expensive than CFCs, it was also thought that there would be a market for them in a world that called for limits on the use of CFCs. Simultaneously, numerous large users of CFCs moved to eliminate their reliance on such substances.

For these reasons, the Montreal meeting was quite different from the one held only two years earlier in Vienna in that virtually all of the interested parties were now in agreement that some amount of phased reductions was appropriate. Thus, even though the final report of the international study of the Antarctic hole was not yet released, a Protocol to the Vienna Convention calling for a 50 percent reduction in the production and consumption of specified CFCs over an approximately ten year period was adopted in Montreal in September 1987.

E. The Antarctic Ozone Hole and the Race to 1990 London Adjustments and Amendments

But even as states adopted the Montreal Protocol in September 1987, two major concerns were present regarding the instrument. First, the startling findings regarding the Antarctic ozone hole, officially confirmed only after the meeting in Montreal, had not been taken fully into account in the Protocol. The negotiators were frustrated by their apparent inability to draft regimes that kept up with the revelations emerging from the scientific community. They had taken a step forward in Montreal, but they felt that they were always two steps behind in their own understanding of the problem, and at least two steps behind in their response to the problem. Thus, there was a widespread feeling that the Protocol was inadequate and would require revision.

Second, the early indications by China and India, representing over one-third of humanity, that they would not become parties to the Protocol because of its failure to provide adequate assistance to developing countries, suggested that the international community might not be sufficiently cohesive to comprehensively regulate the matter. * * * It was apparent that any regime relating to protection of the ozone layer must include highly populated states, whether or not they presently were significant consumers or producers of ozone-depleting substances. This development was particularly important because it marked one of the few times that the industrialized world needed the cooperation and participation of the Third World. This need allowed the Third World to raise development and international equity concerns they believed had been unaddressed for too long.

As to the adequacy of the Montreal Protocol, planning for its adjustment and amendment began almost immediately. The political focus on the global environment in general, and on the protection of the ozone layer in particular, was intense from the 1987 Montreal Conference of Parties to the 1990 London Meeting of the Parties to the Montreal Protocol. Of particular importance at this time, although less publicly dramatic than the Antarctic ozone hole, was the release of a study by the U.S. Environmental Protection Agency asserting that even assuming 100 percent global participation in the Protocol, the presence of chlorine in the stratosphere would, by the year 2075, increase by a factor of three.

Amidst these new revelations, the entry into force of the Montreal Protocol on January 1, 1989, was anticlimactic and hardly noticed. At that time, one nation after another was calling for swifter and deeper cuts in the production and consumption of ozone-depleting substances, and in some cases unilaterally adopting such measures. By the opening of the London Meeting in June 1990, the negotiating parties were in agreement not merely on accelerating the phased reductions, but on phasing out entirely the substances specified by the Montreal Protocol. The primary issue was whether this phase out should be accomplished by the year 1997 or the year 2000, the latter representing the adjustment ultimately made to the Montreal schedules. Simultaneously, evolving scientific knowledge regarding the threat posed by other substances led to the consensus to amend the Protocol so that it would require phase outs of other fully halogenated CFCs and carbon tetrachloride by the year 2000, and a phaseout of methyl chloroform by the year 2005. Increased understanding that the substitutes thought to exist at the time of the Montreal Protocol might also be ozone-depleting and significant contributors to the greenhouse effect, resulted in the designation of these substitutes as "transitional ozone-depleting substances," and in the conclusion that the transitional substances should be phased out by the year 2040, or, if possible, by the year 2020.

The apparent willingness of nonparticipating countries such as China and India to operate outside of what they perceived to be an unjust regime, was pitted against the reluctance of some developed countries such as the United States, to construct new international structures, to recognize a right of such countries to assistance and technology transfer, and to encourage linkages between participation in regimes like the Protocol and recognition of the special situation of developing countries. This reluctance was particularly strong since, at this same time, the developing world was making analogous demands for a global climate change fund. * * * Ultimately, the London meeting adopted amendments to the Protocol that provided for technology transfer, and established a fund under the supervision of a fourteen member committee drawn from the developed and developing world. At the conclusion of the London Meeting, the representatives of China and India indicated their countries would sign the Protocol in 1992. * * *

F. The Task Ahead

* * * Although the list of controlled substances has been increased and, for the most part, total phaseouts have been called for, an observer group at the London Meeting noted that the phaseout periods—generally of ten years—will allow the production of another 17 million tons of ozone-depleting substances. Such arguments arise amidst continued findings by the scientific community that the ozone layer continues to deteriorate over Antarctica, the Arctic, and generally, and increasing evidence that the same substances that deplete ozone are major contributors to global warming. * * *

III. A RESTATEMENT OF THE REGIME

A. The Organization of the Regime

There are two main strands to the international organizational scheme created by the Vienna Convention and the Montreal Protocol, as amended and adjusted. First, there are state parties (to the Convention, to the Protocol, and to the Protocol as amended) who meet on a regular basis and who in smaller groups meet more regularly for particular tasks. Second, there is a Secretariat which fulfills a number of duties, occasionally through ad hoc working groups, assigned to it by the state parties in the Convention and Protocol.

* * * Inasmuch as a party to the [Montreal] Protocol or the Protocol as amended must also be a party to the Convention, the parties to the Protocol or the Protocol as amended are subgroups of the "Conference of the Parties" to the Convention.

* * * [O]nly Parties to the Protocol, and not those who are solely members of the Conference of the Parties to the Convention, can vote on amendments to the Protocol. Similarly, membership on the Executive Committee, which is responsible for the Multilateral Fund established by the London Amendments to the Protocol is limited to Parties to the Protocol as amended. * * *

Finally, the organizational structure created by the Convention and Protocol necessarily has extensive relations with two other organizational clusters. First, in order to provide a better foundation for the timely making of policy, there are relations with the public international scientific community (namely, the World Meteorological Organization and the World Health Organization), leading national scientific agencies, and private international scientific organizations. Second, in order to provide financial and technical assistance, there are relations with organizations such as the World Bank.

B. The Lawmaking Process

A number of innovative steps in lawmaking are contained in the Montreal Protocol. * * *

The Protocol anticipates that continued revision may be necessary, and calls for the Parties periodically to assess the adequacy of the measures taken in the Protocol. The Protocol provides that the parties, on the basis of such an assessment, may decide to adjust the reductions called for in the controlled substances, and if the parties are unable to reach agreement on such adjustments, two-thirds majority adoption of adjustments shall be binding upon all Parties to the Protocol. Thus, the Parties to the Protocol have limited legislative power in this area with an objector's recourse being withdrawal generally from the Protocol. Some of the actions taken at the London Meeting were adjustments.

In contrast to this legislative-like adjustment process, there is also the more commonly encountered amendment process that becomes binding only upon those states who accept such amendments. In this regard, it is particularly important to see that although the parties may make adjustments to the controlled substances already designated, they cannot use an adjustment to designate a new controlled substance. As a consequence, the actions taken at the London Meeting were in part also amendments. Many of the amendments relate to the creation of a financial mechanism, but many others relate to the addition of new controlled substances. The crucial implication, however, is that since amendments must be consented to in order to have application to any particular party, a confusing array of regimes may arise.

C. *The Normative Scheme*

1. The Obligation to Phase Out Designated Ozone–Depleting Chemicals

The basic regulatory approach of the Montreal Protocol in 1987 was to require the Parties to the Protocol to reduce their production and consumption of five chlorofluorocarbons specified in Group I to Annex A of the Protocol, and three halons specified in Group II to Annex A of the Protocol. The London Adjustments to the Protocol accelerated this timetable and deepened the cuts by requiring the parties to phase out production and consumption entirely by the year 2000. * * *

The London Amendments to the Protocol added new chemicals to the regulatory scheme, specifying them in a new Annex B. * * *

* * * [T]he scheduled reductions, leading ultimately to phaseouts, are expressed in terms of percentages of calculated national levels of consumption and production in either 1986, in the case of the substances originally regulated by the Protocol, or in 1989, for the substances added to the scope of the Protocol by the London Amendments. * * *

The use of national calculated levels is * * * significant because it inherently gives value to historical usage and avoids the difficult issue of equitably allocating between states a limited resource, the right to emit ozone-depleting substances. Thus, the United States could be viewed as particularly advantaged under the Montreal Protocol since a fifty percent reduction in its production and consumption would still leave it with a disproportionate per capita share of such use. This significance of course diminished greatly when the Protocol was adjusted and amended so as to require phaseouts rather than mere reductions. * * *

2. Recognition of the Special Situation of Developing Countries

The special situation of certain developing countries is recognized through the possibility of a delayed phaseout schedule for such countries. These special provisions apply to any party "that is a developing country and whose annual calculated level of consumption ... is less than 0.3 kilograms per capita...." The delay works in two ways. First, these parties are allowed to exceed the target percentage reduction at any point in the schedule by a specified percentage of their initial calculated level if such action is necessary in order to satisfy "basic domestic needs." Second, such developing countries, in order to meet basic domestic needs, also are entitled to delay at every point their compliance with the schedule of reductions leading to phase outs by a period of ten years.

3. The Resolution of States to Act Beyond the Requirements of the Protocol as Adjusted and Amended

It is important to recognize that the reduction schedule set forth in the Protocol as adjusted and amended represents only the baseline. A number of states have accepted greater obligations, and the Protocol urges the parties to act with greater dispatch when possible. * * *

D. Encouraging Participation and Facilitating Implementation

From the beginning, it was recognized that the shared nature of the ozone-depletion problem required widespread participation in the regime to be established by the Convention and Protocol. Encouragement of participation by developing countries, in particular India and China, required mechanisms to aid implementation of the regime by those countries. Thus, encouragement of participation and facilitation of implementation were and remain linked.

The regime encourages participation in a number of ways. First, because the reduction schedules are tied to either 1986 or 1989 levels of consumption and production, there is no advantage to waiting to join the regime. Second, although the parties to the regime during the phaseout periods may trade the controlled substances with one another, the Protocol, as adjusted and amended, progressively restricts trade involving controlled substances between parties and nonparties. Thus, for example, by January 1, 1993, the parties, having agreed upon a list of products containing the controlled substances specified in the Montreal Protocol, shall bar the import of those products from any state not party to the Protocol.

Third, the Protocol not only attempts to limit the advantages of remaining outside, but for developing countries, also provides incentives to join. The Montreal Protocol originally was vague on this point, providing that the parties, recognizing the particular needs of developing countries, "shall ... cooperate in promoting technical assistance to facilitate participation in and implementation of this Protocol." In response to the positions of India and China in particular, more specific and detailed provisions for financial assistance and technology transfer were adopted at the London Meeting.

E. Noncompliance, Enforcement, and Dispute Settlement

Thus far, the Parties to the Convention and the Protocol have been concerned primarily with elaboration of and formal participation in the regime. As a result, enforcement procedures at this point are not particularly developed.

The key monitoring and enforcement device at present is the requirement for parties to provide to the Secretariat statistics on production, on imports and exports to parties and nonparties, and on amounts destroyed or recycled as feedstocks. Such reports will aid Secretariat and party monitoring, and will also further nongovernmental organization involvement since such data is not regarded as confidential. Unfortunately, not all parties have made such reports, or have submitted incomplete reports. The London meeting of the parties, noting these reporting difficulties, established an ad hoc group of experts to consider the reasons for the difficulties and to recommend solutions.

Investigatory and dispute settlement provisions are quite limited. The Convention, with application to the Protocol, provides that in the event of a dispute concerning interpretation or application of a provision, the parties (1) shall negotiate; (2) failing that, seek the good offices of, or request mediation by, a third party; and (3) failing that, submit the dispute to conciliation. The parties, in accepting the Convention also may declare that they accept as a means of dispute settlement either arbitration or submission to the International Court of Justice, or both. Against that backdrop, the Parties to the Protocol have been considering procedures and institutional mechanisms for determining noncompliance and for treatment of parties found to be in noncompliance. Interim noncompliance provisions adopted at the London Meeting essentially provide for parties with reservations regarding implementation by other parties to report such concerns in writing to the Secretariat. The Secretariat shall transmit the submission to a Implementation Committee established by these same interim procedures, and that Committee shall consider the record with a view to securing an amicable resolution. The Committee shall report on its work to the Meeting of the Parties and the parties "may ... decide upon and call for steps to bring about full compliance ... including measures to assist the Party's compliance ...."

IV. THE EVOLVING STRUCTURE OF INTERNATIONAL ENVIRONMENTAL LAWMAKING

Reflection on the international effort to protect the stratospheric ozone layer illuminates the emerging structure of international environmental lawmaking. * * *

A. Lawmaking Amidst Uncertainty: The Process as the Solution

We ordinarily might expect that states seeking to address an international problem would work towards a diplomatic conference where a treaty addressing an issue could be negotiated. Without in any way implying that this "ordinary" situation is easy, the international environmental context can be far more difficult because the views of the parties as to the nature of the environmental problem not only can be quite different, but moreover, the knowledge of all environmental problems is likely incomplete even though evolving. In the "ordinary" context a central task in the lawmaking effort is to improve communication between the parties so that they may better understand each other's objectives and concerns. In negotiations concerning environmental matters, however, there is the added and quite different task of the parties seeking to discover precisely what the environment requires. In this sense, the environment is an unobtrusive, but central presence in the negotiations. It is a party that does not volunteer information, but may answer questions if asked correctly. It is also a party that refuses to negotiate.

In the case of stratospheric ozone depletion, the international community initially confronted great debate as to whether there was a problem at all, followed by debate regarding the extent of the problem. * * * [T]he nature of many environmental problems requires action by the relevant community before it has proof of the theory. In other words, the international community, despite uncertainty about the theory, must act to confront the danger indicated by the theory. Moreover, it must act knowing that its knowledge will continue to evolve and suggest further actions. These aspects of uncertainty and evolving knowledge lead to two major differences in international environmental lawmaking efforts from lawmaking efforts generally. Both of these differences evidence an emphasis on an ongoing process of lawmaking rather than, as ordinarily the case, the one time negotiation of a treaty at a particular conference.

The first difference is the explicit incorporation of scientific inquiry into the lawmaking process. Dealing with the uncertainty necessarily present in environmental problems requires that the process not only increase the shared knowledge of the parties, but that such knowledge also accurately reflect the state of scientific understanding of the problem. This requires much greater cooperation between the lawmaking community attempting to draft a response and the scientific community seeking to understand the phenomena. Imbedding this scientific effort in an international organizational structure or in international efforts that coordinate national efforts increases the perceived legitimacy, and hence shared nature, of the resulting description of the problem. Making the scientific inquiry an integral part of an ongoing lawmaking process serves both to educate the lawmakers and to speed up the incorporation of such knowledge into the process. In the case of the ozone regime, the Protocol institutionalizes this cooperation by requiring the convening of "appropriate panels of experts" (scientific, environmental, technical, and economic) at least one year before the parties meet to reassess the sufficiency of the Protocol's controls on ozone-depleting substances.

The second major difference is that the lawmaking effort that accommodates evolving knowledge through the establishment of an ongoing process of lawmaking continuously incorporates new knowledge and revises previous responses. In this sense, the Protocol calls for the parties to periodically "assess the control measures provided for in Article 2 on the basis of available scientific, environmental, technical, and economic information." Thus, we see a transition from a one-conference effort to an ongoing process, and from "two steps behind" to action on the basis of evolving knowledge. In this sense, cooperation and education are recognized as important aspects of the lawmaking process in the environmental area. For all these reasons, the solution to a threat such as ozone depletion is not the particular requirements of the Montreal Protocol of the London Adjustments and Amendments to the Protocol. Rather, the solution is the process which yielded the Protocol and which already looks ahead to the next adjustments and amendments.

B. Consensual Lawmaking on Transcendent Problems

International environmental lawmaking is also distinct in that the nature of many environmental problems requires that at least those countries primarily contributing, or potentially contributing, to the problem participate in the regime. * * *

In encouraging participation, the tools of the lawmaker are sticks and carrots. In other words, states either may be penalized for not joining the regime or rewarded for doing so. In the ozone protection regime, developing countries were encouraged to join through the recognition of their special needs. Moreover, although there are no sticks per se, the treaty does attempt to prevent those who remain outside from benefitting by doing so. First, there is no advantage in waiting to join the treaty since the baseline calculation from which reductions are to be made is fixed. Second, there is no trade advantage in remaining outside the convention since it restricts members from trading in areas involving the regulated substances with those outside the regime.

The more subtle implication of needing widespread participation, as discussed above, was the demand by China, India, and others for a linkage between their agreement to participate in the regime and satisfaction of other concerns, particularly, development assistance for the Third World. In the case of stratospheric ozone protection, linkage ultimately was made in the London amendments. The amendments provide for technology transfer and establish a fund to aid implementation of the Protocol by facilitating nonozone-depleting paths for growth in developing countries. * * *

C. The Tension Between Manageability of Negotiations and Systemic Thinking

One of the first lessons of environmental studies is the need to approach the environment as a system, an indivisible process. The lawmaker, however, can not approach the development of an environmentally sound relationship between humanity and the world all at once. Rather, negotiations must be limited so that the number of issues and interests involved remain at a manageable level. The danger with the slicing off of what appears to be a somewhat separable and manageable problem, however, is that systemic thinking may be lost. The question thus becomes how to best reconcile the need for manageable negotiations with the need for holistic thinking.

Notes and Questions

1. *The Framework Convention–Protocol Approach.* The Vienna Convention on Substances that Deplete the Ozone Layer and its 1987 Montreal Protocol are an example of a framework convention-protocol approach to regulate behavior affecting the environment. What are the advantages and disadvantages of such an approach compared to negotiating a single comprehensive convention? As of September 1996, 159 states had ratified the Vienna Convention and 157 the Montreal Protocol. Over 100 states also have accepted the 1990 London Amendment to the Montreal Protocol, June 29, 1990, 30 I.L.M. 537 (1991). Additional changes to the Montreal Protocol were approved in Copenhagen in November 1992, 32 I.L.M. 874 (1993), and in Vienna in December 1995. Is the distinction between "adjustments" and "amendments" in the ozone regime sensible? Would it be desirable to

increase the scope of the decisions that parties to the Montreal Protocol can, by majority or supermajority vote, make binding on all parties? See Geoffrey Palmer, "New Ways to Make International Environmental Law," 86 *American Journal of International Law* 259 (1992).

2. *Environmental Lawmaking in Areas of Scientific Uncertainty.* The Vienna Convention is intended to regulate behavior in order to prevent environmental harm, rather than simply to undo harm. Scientific evidence helped in this instance to galvanize international action; evidence of a hole in the ozone layer over Antarctica was unequivocal, and the dangers of ozone depletion were also well-documented. Yet with respect to many issues—such as global warming—scientific evidence of the extent, rate, or effects of environmental degradation is not so clear. How should states make use of scientists and equivocal scientific evidence? This issue was addressed in general terms in Principle 15 of the Rio Declaration, which sets out the "precautionary principle." Would any variation in the framework convention-protocol approach better take account of uncertain scientific evidence?

3. *Encouraging Widespread Participation in the Ozone Regime.* Note the various incentives that the Vienna Convention and its Protocols provide to encourage participation by many states. What other techniques could be used to prevent states from becoming "free riders," benefitting from widespread implementation of the Convention and the Protocols without themselves becoming parties?

4. *Developing States and the Ozone Regime.* What is the nature of the "special status" accorded developing states in the Vienna Convention and its protocols? Significant amendments to the Montreal Protocol adopted at the 1990 London review conference reflect the concerns of developing states. First, the procedure for approving adjustments in the permitted production or consumption of controlled substances listed in the Annex to the Montreal Protocol and in specified ozone-depleting potentials was changed. As amended in London, Article 2(9)(c) of the Montreal Protocol provides that, if it proves impossible to reach consensus decisions on such adjustments, decisions shall "be adopted by a two-thirds majority vote of the Parties present and voting representing a majority of the Parties operating under paragraph 1 of Article 5 [*i.e.*, developing states] present and voting and a majority of the Parties not so operating present and voting." 30 I.L.M. at 543. Previously, such decisions, which are binding on all parties, could be taken if approved by a two-thirds vote representing at least 50 per cent of the total consumption of controlled substances of the parties—a formulation that allowed a few large CFC-producing states to block adjustments.

Second, states agreed at the London conference to establish a Multilateral Fund, to be funded by developed states, to help developing states meet the cost of using substances and technologies that do not deplete the ozone layer. The Fund is administered by an Executive Committee on which developing and developed states are equally represented. *Id.* at 549–51. Establishing this Fund helped persuade China and India to accept the Vienna Convention and the Montreal Protocol. Would compensation to developing states for damage caused by CFC emissions, in accordance with the "polluter pays" principle (see Principle 16 of the Rio Declaration), be more equitable than payments relating to substitute technologies?

5. *The Role of International Organizations.* Note the range of roles that international intergovernmental institutions play in the ozone regime. UNEP helped in negotiating the regime, and the United Nations and its specialized agencies may participate as observers at meetings of the Conference of the Parties. Vienna Convention, art. 6(5), 26 I.L.M. at 1532. As Professor Caron notes, there are links with international scientific organizations such as the World Health Organization and international financial organizations such as the World Bank. The Vienna Convention itself creates an institution, the Secretariat, to carry out reporting and notification functions. How well could the ozone regime function if the only entities involved were states?

6. *The Role of Nongovernmental Organizations.* Nongovernmental organizations have provided scientific advice and gathered information important in the negotiation of environmental treaties. What other roles do and should NGOs play with regard to international environmental treaties? Article 6(5) of the Vienna Convention allows nongovernmental organizations "qualified in fields relating to the protection of the ozone layer" to sit as observers at a meeting of the Conference of the Parties "unless at least one-third of the Parties present object." 26 I.L.M. at 1532.

7. *Encouraging Compliance with the Ozone Regime.* What mechanisms should be used to promote compliance with the Protocols to the Vienna Convention? States at the 1990 London review conference established an Implementation Committee to issue reports and recommendations concerning reservations about a party's implementation of the Protocol. Non–Compliance Procedure, Annex III, U.N. Doc. UNEP/OzL.Pro.2/3, P.40 (1990). Should a monitoring system be set up to determine instances of noncompliance? Monitoring was discussed at the London conference, but was not implemented. Are there other benefits monitoring could bring, in addition to promoting compliance?

8. *Negotiations on Other Issues Affecting the Atmosphere.* Depletion of the ozone layer is only one of many environmental concerns related to the atmosphere. Debate surrounds how best to address acid rain, global warming, and the risk of nuclear pollution. Threats to the environment are interrelated. For example, as Professor Caron notes, certain substitutes for CFCs are also greenhouse gases that may contribute to global warming. More broadly, atmospheric pollution affects the oceans and land resources, and these in turn affect the atmosphere. Should a comprehensive treaty-making conference, along the lines of the Third United Nations Conference on the Law of the Sea, be convened to address all issues relating to use and pollution of the atmosphere?

Chapter 10

INTERNATIONAL CONFLICT OF LAWS

The resolution of international, as opposed to garden variety domestic, private legal disputes is often made more complex by the fundamental contradictions that exist between the realities of international transactions and the artifices of politics and law. A basic fact of international relations is that private transactions abound which overleap national boundaries. No such overleapings, however, characterize the ordinary allocation and exercise of political and legal authority. These remain predominately vested in sovereign states. Hence, a dispute involving a single international private transaction typically triggers responses from two or more national political and legal systems.

The intellectual discipline concerning the international interface between municipal political and legal systems has no satisfactory denomination. In civil law nations the field is usually called *private international law*, even though what is largely at issue is the international relations of national courts, legislatures, and administrations, surely a matter of public concern. In the United States and some other common law countries, the subject's customary appellation is *conflict of laws*, even though the relevant laws and processes have much more to do with conflict-avoidance and international judicial cooperation. What is agreed is that the substance of the discipline includes topics such as jurisdiction, foreign sovereign immunity, and act of state. All three are examined below. In practical terms, anticipating and solving problems of international conflict of laws constitute a large fraction of the work of most international lawyers.

A. JURISDICTION

1. PRINCIPLES OF JURISDICTION

In studying the complex world of international conflict of laws, a reasonable point of first contact is the description and analysis of the authority, power, or competence of different states to determine and affect the legal relationships of private parties. This topic is usually denoted by the term "jurisdiction." Legislative jurisdiction, adjudicatory jurisdiction, and executive jurisdiction are terms used to describe the power of states to make laws, to have their courts render authoritative judgments, and to enforce laws and the decisions of courts. Almost invariably in international private transactions, any one nation's exercise of any sort of jurisdiction conflicts, at least in principle and often in practice, with the jurisdictional realm of another state. The problems of jurisdiction, be they legislative, judicial, or executive, usually involve both describing and analyzing the permissible forms of national legal authority and explicating the means, municipal and international, of reconciling conflicts among such permissible assertions of legal competence.

a. The Territorial Principle

AMERICAN BANANA CO. v. UNITED FRUIT CO.

213 U.S. 347, 29 S.Ct. 511, 53 L.Ed. 826 (1909).

MR. JUSTICE HOLMES delivered the opinion of the Court.

The allegations of the complaint may be summed up as follows: The plaintiff is an Alabama corporation, organized in 1904. The defendant is a New Jersey corporation, organized in 1899. Long before the plaintiff was formed, the defendant, with intent to prevent competition and to control and monopolize the banana trade, bought the property and business of several of its previous competitors, with provision against their resuming the trade, made contracts with others, including a majority of the most important, regulating the quantity to be purchased and the price to be paid, and acquired a controlling amount of stock in still others. For the same purpose it organized a selling company, of which it held the stock, that by agreement sold at fixed prices all the bananas of the bringing parties. By this and other means it did monopolize and restrain the trade and maintained unreasonable prices. The defendant being in this ominous attitude, one McConnell in 1903 started a banana plantation in Panama, then part of the United States of Colombia, and began to build a railway (which would afford his only means of export), both in accordance with the laws of the United States of Columbia. He was notified by the defendant that he must either combine or stop. Two months later, it is believed at the defendant's instigation, the governor of Panama recommended to his national government that Costa Rica be allowed to administer the territory through which the railroad was to run, and this although that territory had been awarded to Colombia under an arbitration agreed to by treaty. The defendant, and afterwards, in September, the government of Costa Rica, it is believed by the inducement of the defendant, interfered with McConnell. In November, 1903, Panama revolted and became an independent republic, declaring its boundary to be settled by the award. In June, 1904, the plaintiff bought out McConnell and went on with the work, as it had a right to do under the laws of Panama. But in July, Costa Rican soldiers and officials, instigated by the defendant, seized a part of the plantation and a cargo of supplies and have held them ever since, and stopped the construction and operation of the plantation and railway. In August one Astua, by *ex parte* proceedings, got a judgment from a Costa Rican court, declaring the plantation to be his, although, it is alleged, the proceedings were not within the jurisdiction of Costa Rica, and were contrary to its laws and void. Agents of the defendant then bought the lands from Astua. The plaintiff has tried to induce the government of Costa Rica to withdraw its soldiers and also has tried to persuade the United States to interfere, but has been thwarted in both by the defendant and has failed. The government of Costa Rica remained in possession down to the bringing of the suit.

As a result of the defendant's acts the plaintiff has been deprived of the use of the plantation, and the railway, the plantation and supplies have been injured. The defendant also, by outbidding, has driven purchasers out of the market and has compelled producers to come to its terms, and it has prevented the plaintiff from buying for export and sale. This is the substantial damage alleged. * * *

It is obvious that, however stated, the plaintiff's case depended on several rather startling propositions. In the first place the acts causing the damage were done, so far as appears, outside the jurisdiction of the United States and within that of other states. It is surprising to hear it argued that they were governed by the act of Congress.

No doubt in regions subject to no sovereign, like the high seas, or to no law that civilized countries would recognize as adequate, such countries may treat some relations between their citizens as governed by their own law, and keep to some extent the old notion of personal sovereignty alive. They go further, at times, and declare that they will punish any one, subject or not, who shall do certain things, if they can catch him, as in the case of pirates on the high seas. In cases immediately affecting national interests they may go further still and may make, and, if they get the chance, execute similar threats as to acts done within another recognized jurisdiction. An illustration from our statutes is found with regard to criminal correspondence with foreign governments. And the notion that English statutes bind British subjects everywhere has found expression in modern times and has had some startling applications. But the general and almost universal rule is that the character of an act as lawful or unlawful must be determined wholly by the law of the country where the act is done. * * * For another jurisdiction, if it should happen to lay hold of the actor, to treat him according to its own notions rather than those of the place where he did the acts, not only would be unjust, but would be an interference with the authority of another sovereign, contrary to the comity of nations, which the other state concerned justly might resent.

Law is a statement of the circumstances in which the public force will be brought to bear upon men through the courts. But the word commonly is confined to such prophecies or threats when addressed to persons living with the power of the courts. A threat that depends upon the choice of the party affected to bring himself within that power hardly would be called law in the ordinary sense. We do not speak of blockade running by neutrals as unlawful. And the usages of speech correspond to the limit of the attempts of the lawmaker, except in extraordinary cases. It is true that domestic corporations remain always with the power of the domestic law, but in the present case, at least, there is not ground for distinguishing between corporations and men.

The foregoing considerations would lead in case of doubt to a construction of any statute as intended to be confined in its operation and effect to the territorial limits over which the lawmaker has general and legitimate power. "All legislation is *prima facie* territorial." Words having universal scope, such as "Every contract in restraint of trade," "Every person who shall monopolize." etc., will be taken as a matter of course to mean only every one subject to such legislation, not all that the legislator subsequently may be able to catch. In the case of the present statute the improbability of the United States attempting to make acts done in Panama or Costa Rica criminal is obvious, yet the law begins by making criminal the acts for which it gives a right to sue. We think it entirely plain that what the defendant did in Panama or Costa Rica is not within the scope of the statute so far as the present suit is concerned. Other objections of a serious nature are urged but need not be discussed.

For again, not only were the acts of the defendant in Panama or Costa Rica not within the Sherman Act, but they were not torts by the law of the place and therefore were not torts at all, however contrary to the ethical and economic postulates of the statute. * * * Giving to this complaint every reasonable latitude of interpretation we are of opinion that it alleges no case under the act of Congress and discloses nothing that we can suppose to have been a tort where it was done. A conspiracy in this country to do acts in another jurisdiction does not draw to itself those acts and make them unlawful, if they are permitted by the local law.

Notes and Questions

1. *The Territorial Principle.* In *American Banana* Justice Holmes maintains that "the general and almost universal rule is that the character of an act as lawful or unlawful must be determined wholly by the law of the country where the act is done." Does he explain if this is a jurisdictional rule based on U.S. law, Panamanian or Costa Rican law, or international law? What if the Court had found that Congress indeed had intended to prohibit U.S. companies from conspiring in the United States to restrain imports to the U.S.? Could international law or the law of Panama or that of Costa Rica have limited the extraterritorial reach of the U.S. statute? If so, in what court(s) could those limiting laws have been applied? If acts facilitating a restraint of trade had been done in the United States, *e.g.*, by

corporate officers of United Fruit, would the Supreme Court necessarily have had to construe the statute as reaching outside U.S. territory?

2. *Holmes and Legal Realism.* Holmes's reasoning in *American Banana* reflects his well-known version of American legal realism: "Law is a statement of the circumstances in which the public force will be brought to bear upon men through the courts." Holmes employs his realism to argue that it would be unusual to use the term "law" to describe one nation's prescription of rules on another nation's territory: "But the word commonly is confined to such prophecies or threats when addressed to persons living within the power of the courts. A threat that depends upon the choice of the party affected to bring himself within that power hardly would be called law in the ordinary sense."

3. *Competing Principles of Jurisdiction.* Nowadays, U.S. courts ordinarily recognize forms of extraterritorial jurisdiction that severely limit *American Banana*. In the 1990 *Kirkpatrick* case, Justice Scalia, delivering the opinion of the Supreme Court, wrote that *American Banana* had been "substantially overruled," *e.g.*, by Continental Ore Co. v. Union Carbide & Carbon Corp., 370 U.S. 690, 704–05, 82 S.Ct. 1404, 1413–14, 8 L.Ed.2d 777, 787–88 (1962), on the proposition "that the antitrust laws had no extraterritorial application." W.S. Kirkpatrick & Co. v. Environmental Tectonics Corp., 493 U.S. 400, 407, 110 S.Ct. 701, 705–06, 107 L.Ed.2d 816, 824 (1990). For more on the "erosion" of the authority of *American Banana*, see the review of authority in Zenith Radio Corp. v. Matsushita Elec. Indus. Co., 494 F.Supp. 1161, 1181–86 (E.D.Pa.1980). Nonetheless, though *American Banana* may no longer be good law respecting the exclusive potency of the territorial principle, it still can be used to support the territorial principle as one basis, albeit among several, for a state's assertion of legislative, judicial, or executive jurisdiction.

4. *Choice-of-Law Considerations. American Banana* may also be seen to reflect policy preferences justifying the act of state doctrine, a topic explored in Part C below. That is, instead of viewing *American Banana* as a case about jurisdiction, why not see it as a case about choice of law? Holmes could be said to have to chosen to respect a foreign law that permitted the company's activities rather than a U.S. law that outlawed them.

5. *Statutory Interpretation.* One of the reasons why U.S. courts have treated cases like *American Banana* as jurisdiction cases rather than choice-of-law cases has been that U.S. judges have traditionally seen their role as construing a federal statute, *e.g.*, asking whether Congress "meant" to regulate the matter in controversy. Is this too artificial an inquiry? Does Congress ordinarily "mean" anything about the reach of a statute outside the U.S.? Would it not make more sense and lead to a fairer evaluation if U.S. courts simply acknowledged that they were choosing among possible laws, each of which had a valid claim to regulate the transaction? We see a more sophisticated analysis of conflicts of jurisdiction in *Timberlane* below.

That the courts have never totally abandoned *American Banana*'s statutory interpretation approach can be seen in E.E.O.C. v. Arabian American Oil Co., 499 U.S. 244, 111 S.Ct. 1227, 113 L.Ed.2d 274 (1991). In that case Chief Justice Rehnquist refuses to extend U.S. anti-discrimination legislation to protect a U.S. citizen employed by a U.S. oil company in Saudi

Arabia: "It is a longstanding principle of American law 'that legislation of Congress, unless a contrary intent appears, is meant to apply only within the territorial jurisdiction of the United States.'" *Id.* at 248, 111 S.Ct. at 1230, 113 L.Ed.2d at 282, *quoting* Foley Bros., Inc. v. Filardo, 336 U.S. 281, 285, 69 S.Ct. 575, 577, 93 L.Ed. 680, 683.

b. The Nationality Principle

BLACKMER v. UNITED STATES

284 U.S. 421, 52 S.Ct. 252, 76 L.Ed. 375 (1932).

MR. CHIEF JUSTICE HUGHES delivered the opinion of the Court.

The petitioner, Harry M. Blackmer, a citizen of the United States resident of Paris, France, was adjudged guilty of contempt of the Supreme Court of the District of Columbia for failure to respond to subpoenas served upon him in France and requiring him to appear as a witness on behalf of the United States at a criminal trial in that court. Two subpoenas were issued, for appearances at different times, and there was a separate proceeding with respect to each. The two cases were heard together, and a fine of $30,000 with costs was imposed in each case, to be satisfied out of the property of the petitioner which had been seized by order of the court. The decrees were affirmed by the Court of Appeals of the District, and this Court granted writs of certiorari. * * *

While it appears that the petitioner removed his residence to France in the year 1924, it is undisputed that he was, and continued to be, a citizen of the United States. He continued to owe allegiance to the United States. By virtue of the obligations of citizenship, the United States retained its authority over him, and he was bound by its laws made applicable to him in a foreign country. Thus, although resident abroad, the petitioner remained subject to the taxing power of the United States. For disobedience to its laws through conduct abroad he was subject to punishment in the courts of the United States. *United States v. Bowman*, 260 U.S. 94, 102. With respect to such an exercise of authority, there is no question of international law, but solely of the purport of the municipal law which establishes the duties of the citizen in relation to his own government. While the legislation of the Congress, unless the contrary intent appears, is construed to apply only with the territorial jurisdiction of the United States, the question of its application, so far as citizens of the United States in foreign countries are concerned, is one of construction, not of legislative power. *American Banana Co. v. United Fruit Co.*, 213 U.S. 347, 357; *United States* v. *Bowman, supra.* Nor can it be doubted that the United States possesses the power inherent in sovereignty to require the return to this country of a citizen, resident elsewhere, whenever the public interest requires it, and to penalize him in case of refusal. What in England was the prerogative of the sovereign in this respect, pertains under our constitutional system to the national authority which may be exercised by the

Congress by virtue of the legislative power to prescribe the duties of the citizens of the United States. It is also beyond controversy that one of the duties which the citizen owes to his government is to support the administration of justice by attending its courts and giving his testimony whenever he is properly summoned. And the Congress may provide for the performance of this duty and prescribe penalties for disobedience.

In the present instance, the question concerns only the method of enforcing the obligation. The jurisdiction of the United States over its absent citizen, so far as the binding effect of its legislation is concerned, is a jurisdiction *in personam*, as he is personally bound to take notice of the laws that are applicable to him and to obey them. *United States* v. *Bowman*, supra. But, for the exercise of judicial jurisdiction *in personam*, there must be due process, which requires appropriate notice of the judicial action and an opportunity to be heard. For this notice and opportunity the statute provides. The authority to require the absent citizen to return and testify necessarily implies the authority to give him notice of the requirement. As his attendance is needed in court, it is appropriate that the Congress should authorize the court to direct the notice to be given and that it should be in the customary form of a subpoena. Obviously, the requirement would be nugatory, if provision could not be made for its communication to the witness in the foreign country. The efficacy of an attempt to provide constructive service in this country would rest upon the presumption that the notice would be given in a manner calculated to reach the witness abroad. The question of the validity of the provision for actual service of the subpoena in a foreign country is one that arises solely between the Government of the United States and the citizen. The mere giving of such a notice to the citizen in the foreign country of the requirement of his government that he shall return is in no sense an invasion of any right of the foreign government; and the citizen has no standing to invoke any such supposed right. While consular privileges in foreign countries are the appropriate subjects of treaties, it does not follow that every act of a consul, as, *e.g.*, in communicating with citizens of his country, must be predicated upon a specific provision of a treaty. The intercourse of friendly nations, permitting travel and residence of the citizens of each in the territory of the other, presupposes and facilitates such communications. In selecting the consul for the service of the subpoena, the Congress merely prescribed a method deemed to assure the desired result but in no sense essential. The consul was not directed to perform any function involving consular privileges or depending upon any treaty relating to them, but simply to act as any designated person might act for the Government in conveying to the citizen the actual notice of the requirement of his attendance. The point raised by the petitioner with respect to the provision for the service of the subpoena abroad is without merit. * * *

Notes and Questions

1. *The Nationality Principle. Blackmer* is a classic example of jurisdiction based upon the principle of nationality, but does the *Blackmer* Court fail

to recognize that the case raises rather different questions, *i.e.*, about legislative and judicial jurisdiction on the one hand and executive jurisdiction on the other? Chief Justice Hughes thoroughly explains why Blackmer as a U.S. citizen is subject to the laws and courts of the United States, but how effectively does Hughes ever grapple with the question of whether the U.S. had jurisdiction to serve process on *Blackmer* in France and the related question about the reconciliation of U.S. executive jurisdiction with the executive jurisdiction of France?

2. *Executive Acts on Foreign Soil.* The United States employed the U.S. Consul in Paris to serve process on Blackmer. Should it instead have used the French courts or French administrative officers? What responses might any country, including the United States, have to the exercise of executive jurisdiction within its territorial boundaries by a foreign country, even against a foreign citizen? Remember the outrage in Mexico over the kidnapping of one of its citizens in Mexico by the United States in *Alvarez–Machain* in Chapter 4 above. If France was theoretically or actually offended by the exercise of U.S. jurisdiction in the case, should Blackmer himself have had standing to complain? How would the French government itself object?

Should U.S. courts use cases like *Blackmer* to limit assertions of U.S. governmental power in foreign countries, or would that be too politically risky? Should U.S. courts be more ready to limit their own judicial jurisdiction in cases of international conflicts than they ought to be to limit extraterritorial assertions of U.S. legislative or executive power? In *Blackmer* and *Alvarez–Machain* the Supreme Court chose not to restrain the extraterritorial reach of the U.S. executive branch.

3. *Other Bases of Jurisdiction.* While territory and nationality are the two most important traditional bases of jurisdiction, others have also appeared. Besides effects jurisdiction, explored in *Aluminum* immediately below, there are:

— the protective principle, guarding the security or the central interests of the state;

— the universality principle, giving any state the right to extend its jurisdiction to certain sorts of offenders, *e.g.*, pirates and war criminals; and

— the passive personality principle, protecting nationals even when abroad.

See Mark W. Janis, *An Introduction to International Law* 328–30 (2d ed. 1993).

It is important to remember that the various principles of jurisdiction do not constitute hard and fast discrete categories, but are often blended together in judicial discussions about jurisdiction in specific cases. For example, in United States v. Bowman, 260 U.S. 94, 43 S.Ct. 39, 67 L.Ed. 149 (1922), a case cited in *Blackmer*, the offense was defrauding the U.S. government by claiming payment for 1000 tons of fuel oil delivered to a U.S.–operated vessel when the ship had really taken on and paid for only 600 tons. Since three of the four malfeasors were U.S. citizens, *Bowman* could certainly be read as the *Blackmer* Court read it, *i.e.*, that a U.S. citizen "was subject to punishment in the courts of the United States" for "disobedience to its laws through conduct abroad." Yet, the actual language in *Bowman* seemed to mix nationality with protective principles. Respecting criminal statutes, at least, *Bowman* held that there is a "right of the Government to defend itself against obstruction, or fraud whenever perpetrated, especially if committed by its own citizens, officers or agents." 260 U.S. at 98, 43 S.Ct. at 41, 67 L.Ed. at 151.

c. *The Effects Principle*

UNITED STATES v. ALUMINUM CO. OF AMERICA

148 F.2d 416 (2d Cir.1945).

L. HAND, CIRCUIT JUDGE

[The case concerns the application of U.S. antitrust laws to "Limited," a Canadian company, spun off from "Alcoa," a U.S. company.]

"Limited" was incorporated in Canada on May 31, 1928, to take over those properties of "Alcoa" which were outside the United States. * * * [F]ormally at any rate, the separation between the two companies was complete. At the conclusion of the transfers a majority, though only a bare majority, of the common shares of "Alcoa" was in the hands of three persons: Andrew W. Mellon, Richard B. Mellon, his brother, and Arthur V. Davis. Richard Mellon died in 1933, and Andrew in 1937, and their shares passed to their families; but in January, 1939, the Davises, the officers and directors of "Alcoa" and the Mellon families—eleven individuals in all—collectively still held 48.9 per cent of "Alcoa's" shares, and 48.5 per cent of "Limited's"; and Arthur V. Davis was then the largest shareholder in both companies.

[The court finds that "Alcoa" had not been party to the "Alliance," a foreign cartel fixing the price of aluminum world-wide].

Whether "Limited" itself violated [Section 1 of the Sherman Act] depends upon the character of the "Alliance." It was a Swiss corporation, created in pursuance of an agreement entered into on July 3, 1931, the signatories to which were a French corporation, two German, one Swiss, a British, and "Limited." The original agreement, or "cartel," provided for the formation of a corporation in Switzerland which should issue shares, to be taken up by the signatories. This corporation was from time to time to fix a quota of production for each share, and each shareholder was to be limited to the quantity measured by the number of shares it held, but was free to sell at any price it chose. The corporation fixed a price every year at which it would take off any shareholder's hands any part of its quota which it did not sell. No shareholder was to "buy, borrow, fabricate or sell" aluminum produced by anyone not a shareholder except with the consent of the board of governors, but that must not be "unreasonably withheld." Nothing was said as to whether the arrangement extended to sales in the United States; but Article X, known as the "Conversion Clause," provided that any shareholder might exceed his quota to the extent that he converted into aluminum in the United States or Canada any ores delivered to him in either of those countries by persons situated in the United States. This was confessedly put in to allow "Limited" to receive bauxite or alumina from "Alcoa," to smelt it into aluminum and to deliver the aluminum to "Alcoa." * * *

The agreement of 1936 abandoned the system of unconditional quotas, and substituted a system of royalties. Each shareholder was to have a fixed free quota for every share it held, but as its production exceeded the sum of its quotas, it was to pay a royalty, graduated progressively in proportion to the excess; and these royalties the "Alliance" divided among the shareholders in proportion to their shares. * * * Although this agreement, like its predecessor, was silent as to imports into the United States, when that question arose during its preparation, as it did, all the shareholders agreed that such imports should be included in the quotas. * * *

Did either the agreement of 1931 or that of 1936 violate § 1 of the Act? The answer does not depend upon whether we shall recognize as a source of liability a liability imposed by another state. On the contrary we are concerned only with whether Congress chose to attach liability to the conduct outside the United States of persons not in allegiance to it. That being so, the only question open is whether Congress intended to impose the liability, and whether our own Constitution permitted it to do so: as a court of the United States, we cannot look beyond our own law. Nevertheless, it is quite true that we are not to read general words, such as those in this Act, without regard to the limitations customarily observed by nations upon the exercise of their powers; limitations which generally correspond to those fixed by the "Conflict of Laws." We should not impute to Congress an intent to punish all whom its courts can catch, for conduct which has no consequences within the United States. American Banana Co. v. United Fruit Co., 213 U.S. 347, 357, 29 S.Ct. 511, 53 L.Ed. 826, 16 Ann.Cas. 1047; United States v. Bowman, 260 U.S. 94, 98, 43 S.Ct. 39, 67, L.Ed. 149; Blackmer v. United States, 284 U.S. 421, 437, 52 S.Ct. 252, 76 L.Ed. 375. On the other hand, it is settled—as "Limited" itself agrees—that any state may impose liabilities, even upon persons not within its allegiance, for conduct outside its borders that has consequences within its borders which the state reprehends; and these liabilities other states will ordinarily recognize. Strassheim v. Daily, 221 U.S. 280, 284, 285, 31 S.Ct. 558, 55 L.Ed. 735; Lamar v. United States, 240 U.S. 60, 65, 66, 36 S.Ct. 255, 60 L.Ed. 526; Ford v. United States, 273 U.S. 593, 620, 621, 47 S.Ct. 531, 71 L.Ed. 793; Restatement of Conflict of Laws § 65. It may be argued that this Act extends further. Two situations are possible. There may be agreements made beyond our borders not intended to affect imports, which do affect them, or which affect exports. Almost any limitation of the supply of goods in Europe, for example, or in South America, may have repercussions in the United States if there is trade between the two. Yet when one considers the international complications likely to arise from an effort in this country to treat such agreement as unlawful, it is safe to assume that Congress certainly did not intend the Act to cover them. Such agreements may on the other hand intend to include imports into the United States, and yet it may appear that they have had no effect upon them. That situation might be thought to fall within the doctrine that intent may be a substitute for performance in the case of a contract made within the United States; or it might be thought to fall within the doctrine that a statute should not be interpreted to cover acts abroad which have no consequence here. We shall not choose between these alternatives; but for argument we shall assume that the Act does not cover agreements, even though intended to affect imports or exports, unless its performance is shown actually to have had some effect upon them.

Both agreements would clearly have been unlawful, had they been made within the United States; and it follows from what we have just said that both were unlawful, though made abroad, if they were intended to affect imports and did affect them. Since the shareholders almost at once agreed that the agreement of 1931 should not cover imports, we may ignore it and confine our discussion to that of 1936: indeed that we should have to do anyway, since it superseded the earlier agreement. The judge found that it was not the purpose of the agreement to "suppress or restrain the exportation of aluminum to the United States for sale in competition with["] "Alcoa." By that we understand that he meant that the agreement was not specifically directed to "Alcoa," because it only applied generally to the production of the shareholders. If he meant that it was not expected that the general restriction upon production would have an effect upon imports, we cannot agree, for the change made in 1936 was deliberate and was expressly made to accomplish just that. It would have been an idle gesture, unless the shareholders had supposed that it would, or at least might, have that effect. The first of the conditions which we mentioned was therefore satisfied; the intent was to set up a quota system for imports.

The judge also found that the 1936 agreement did not "materially affect the * * * foreign trade or commerce of the United States"; apparently because the imported ingot was greater in 1936 and 1937 than in earlier years. We cannot accept this finding, based as it was upon the fact that, in 1936, 1937 and the first quarter of 1938, the gross imports of ingot increased. It by no means follows from such an increase that the agreement did not restrict imports; and incidentally it so happens that in those years such inference as is possible at all, leads to the opposite conclusion. It is true that the average imports—including "Alcoa's"—for the years 1932–1935 inclusive were about 15 million pounds, and that for 1936, 1937 and one-fourth of 1938 they were about 33 million pounds; but the average domestic ingot manufacture in the first period was about 96 million and in the second about 262 million; so that the proportion of imports to domestic ingot was about 15.6 per cent for the first period and about 12.6 per cent for the second. We do not mean to infer from this that the quota system of 1936 did in fact restrain imports, as these figures might suggest; but we do mean that nothing is to be inferred from the gross increase of imports. We shall dispose of the matter therefore upon the assumption that, although the shareholders intended to restrict imports, it does not appear whether in fact they did so. Upon our hypothesis the plaintiff would therefore fail, if it carried the burden of proof upon this issue as upon others. We think, however, that, after the intent to affect imports was proved, the burden of proof shifted to "Limited." In the first place a depressant upon production which applies generally may be assumed, ceteris paribus, to distribute its effect evenly upon all markets. Again, when the parties took the trouble specifically to make the depressant apply to a given market, there is reason to suppose that they expected that it would have some effect, which it could have only by lessening what would otherwise have been imported. If the motive they introduced was overbalanced in all instances by motives which induced the shareholders to import, if the United States market became so attractive that the royalties did not count at all and their expectations were in fact defeated, they to whom the facts were more accessible than to the plaintiff ought to prove it, for a prima facie case had been made. Moreover, there is an especial propriety in demanding this of "Limited," because it was "Limited" which procured the inclusion in the agreement of 1936 imports in the quotas.

There remains only the question whether this assumed restriction had any influence upon prices. To that United States v. Socony–Vacuum Oil Co., 310 U.S. 150, 60 S.Ct. 811, 84 L.Ed. 1129, is an entire answer. It will be remembered that, when the defendants in that case protested that the prosecution had not proved that the "distress" gasoline had affected prices, the court answered that that was not necessary, because an agreement to withdraw any substantial part of the supply from a market would, if carried out, have some effect upon prices, and was as unlawful as an agreement expressly to fix prices. The underlying doctrine was that all factors which contribute to determine prices, must be kept free to operate unhampered by agreements. For these reasons we think that the agreement of 1936 violated § 1 of the Act.

Notes and Questions

1. *Determining Legislative Jurisdiction.* Albeit the *Aluminum* analysis of legislative jurisdiction over an international transaction is more sophisticated than that of *American Banana* or *Blackmer*, is it thorough enough? Learned Hand pronounces that he is "concerned only with whether Congress chose to attach liability to the conduct outside the United States of persons not in allegiance to it." This avowal to look only at the intent of Congress is remarkably narrow and probably fictitious. Interpreting congressional intent as to extraterritorial reach usually leaves courts a great deal of latitude. Happily, Hand quickly circumvents his self-imposed obstacle and pays attention to "limitations customarily observed by nations upon the exercise of their powers; limitations which generally correspond to those fixed by the 'Conflict of Laws.'" However, rather than simply elaborating how Limited's participation in the foreign cartel was justifiably within the

legislative jurisdiction of the United States, why does he not attempt to determine whether the U.S., or Switzerland, or some other country had the better right to regulate Limited's conduct? The explicit reason given is that "as a court of the United States, we cannot look beyond our own law." How can this be true, when for centuries common law courts in England and America have routinely reviewed, incorporated, and applied rules of both foreign and international law?

2. *The Effects Doctrine.* When anyone, even Learned Hand, calls the extraterritorial assertion of jurisdiction by the United States "settled" law, the reader should be just as much on guard as when a lawyer or a judge reassuringly calls facts or law "clear" or "plain." There was then and is now no "settled" law clearly or plainly establishing what is sometimes called "effects" or "objective territorial" jurisdiction. Does the *Aluminum* court demonstrate that it understands that U.S. jurisdiction based on the effects of foreign conduct on the U.S. would necessarily overlap and conflict with the territorial jurisdiction of foreign countries, *e.g.*, Canada, France, Germany, Great Britain, and Switzerland? Does Learned Hand really grapple with the problem identified by Justice Holmes in *American Banana*, that U.S. antitrust law may attempt to make illegal overseas acts that are legal by the law or the foreign place in which they take place?

3. *Jurisdiction and Choice of Forum.* The variety of bases for jurisdiction lead inevitably to jurisdictional conflicts, as well as to practical questions about where to bring suit. As Professor Detlev Vagts has pointed out, in "An Introduction to International Civil Practice," 17 *Vanderbilt Journal of Transnational Law* 1, 6 (1984):

> Counsel must recommend whether to bring a suit and where it should be brought. The latter decision can be a complex one. First, the question of in personam jurisdiction must be considered. The bases for jurisdiction in the United States (from doing business, to mere presence, to long-arm statutes) vary from those recognized in Europe. Each system has some type of jurisdictional claim that others regard as "exorbitant." France allows suit by virtue of a plaintiff's nationality. Germany sustains a suit if some of the defendant's property is present; in one case, a skier's underwear provided the necessary property. Other nations may find it strange that jurisdiction can arise under United States law merely because the sheriff was able to catch the defendant in transit within United States borders.

Does Hand in *Aluminum* give us any useful guidance about how clashes between U.S. and foreign law and process ought to be settled? See the discussion in *Timberlane* and *Hartford Fire* below.

4. *Jurisdiction Over Corporations.* Note how Alcoa used the formalities of corporate law to try to avoid having its cartel activities caught up by U.S. antitrust law. Could the court have better regulated Alcoa simply by piercing the corporate veil between Alcoa and Limited? After all, Hand finds as facts that "in January, 1939, the Davises, the officers and directors of 'Alcoa,' and the Mellon families—eleven individuals in all—collectively still held 48.9 per cent of 'Alcoa's' shares, and 48.5 per cent of Limited's; and Arthur V. Davis was then the largest shareholder in both countries." The shareholders in *Barcelona Traction*, reproduced in Chapter 6, asked the

International Court of Justice to disregard the corporate form and look at the real owners of the company. In *Aluminum*, the shareholders argued successfully that the corporate form should be respected. See Phillip I. Blumberg, *The Law of Corporate Groups: Procedural Problems in the Law of Parent and Subsidiary Corporations* (1983).

2. RESOLVING CONFLICTS OF JURISDICTION

Since the time of cases such as *American Banana, Blackmer,* and *Aluminum,* U.S. courts have attempted to develop more sophisticated approaches for recognizing and resolving conflicts of jurisdiction. The three cases below illustrate three different approaches to conflict resolution: the balancing test, international comity, and *forum non conveniens.* Two other doctrines, foreign sovereign immunity and act of state, are considered in Parts B and C of this chapter.

a. The Balancing Test

TIMBERLANE LUMBER CO. v. BANK OF AMERICA

549 F.2d 597 (9th Cir.1976).

CHOY, CIRCUIT JUDGE * * *

CAST OF CHARACTERS

There are three affiliated plaintiffs in the Timberlane action. Timberlane Lumber Company is an Oregon partnership principally involved in the purchase and distribution of lumber at wholesale in the United States and the importation of lumber into the United States for sale and use. Danli Industrial, S.A., and Maya Lumber Company, S. de R.L., are both Honduras corporations, incorporated and principally owned by the general partners of Timberlane. Danli held contracts to purchase timber in Honduras, and Maya was to conduct the milling operations to produce the lumber for export. (Timberlane, Danli, and Maya will be collectively referred to as "Timberlane.")

The primary defendants are Bank of America Corporation (Bank), a California corporation, and its wholly-owned subsidiary, Bank of America National Trust and Savings Association, which operates a branch in Tegucigalpa, Honduras. Several employees of the Bank have also been named and served as defendants. * * *

Other defendants have been named, but have not been served. * * * Also unserved are two Honduras corporations, Pedro Casanova e Hijos, S.A., and Importadore Mayorista, S. de R.L., and Michael Casanova, a citizen of Honduras (together referred to as "Casanova"), who together represent one of the two main competitors to Timberlane and its predecessor in the Honduran lumber business. * * *

The Timberlane complaint identified two co-conspirators not named as defendants. Jose Lamas, S. de R.L. (Lamas), a Honduran corporation, is the second major competitor in the lumber business. Jose

Caminals Galegro (Caminals), a citizen of Spain, is described as an agent or employee of the Bank of Tegucigalpa.

Facts as Alleged

The conspiracy sketched by Timberlane actually started before the plaintiffs entered the scene. The Lima family operated a lumber mill in Honduras, competing with Lamas and Casanova, in both of which the Bank had significant financial interests. The Lima enterprise was also indebted to the Bank. By 1971, however, the Lima business was in financial trouble. Timberlane alleges that driving Lima under was the first step in the conspiracy which eventually crippled Timberlane's efforts, but the particulars do not matter for this appeal. What does matter is that various interests in the Lima assets, including its milling plant, passed to Lima's creditors: Casanova, the Bank, and the group of Lima employees who had not been paid the wages and severance pay due them. Under Honduran law, the employees' claim had priority.

Enter Timberlane, with a long history in the lumber business, in search of alternative sources of lumber for delivery to its distribution system on the East Coast of the United States. After study, it decided to try Honduras. In 1971, Danli was formed, tracts of forest land were acquired, plans for a modern log-processing plant were prepared, and equipment was purchased and assembled for shipment from the United States to Danli in Honduras. Timberlane became aware that the Lima plant might be available and began negotiating for its acquisition. Maya was formed, purchased the Lima employees' interest in the machinery and equipment in January 1972, despite opposition from the conspirators, and re-activated and the Lima mill.

Realizing that they were faced with better-financed and more vigorous competition from Timberlane and its Honduran subsidiaries, the defendants and others extended the anti–Lima conspiracy to disrupt Timberlane's efforts. The primary weapons employed by the conspirators were the claim still held by the Bank in the remaining assets of the Lima enterprise under the all-inclusive mortgage Lima had been forced to sign and another claim held by Casanova. Maya made a substantial cash offer for the Bank's interest in an effort to clear its title, but the Bank refused to sell. Instead, the Bank surreptitiously conveyed the mortgage to Casanova for questionable consideration, Casanova paying nothing and agreeing only to pay the Bank a portion of what it collected. Casanova immediately assigned the Bank's claim and its own on similar terms to Caminals, who promptly set out to disrupt the Timberlane operation.

Caminals is characterized as the "front man" in the campaign to drive Timberlane out of Honduras, with the Bank and other defendants intending and carrying responsibility for his actions. Having acquired the claims of Casanova and the Bank, Caminals went to court to enforce them, ignoring throughout Timberlane's offers to purchase or settle them. Under the laws of Honduras, an "embargo" on property is a court-ordered attachment, registered with the Public Registry, which precludes the sale of that property without a court order. Honduran law provides, upon embargo, that the court appoint a judicial officer, called an "interventor" to ensure against any diminution in the value of the property. In order to paralyze the Timberlane operation, Caminals obtained embargoes against Maya and Danli. Acting through the interventor, since accused of being on the payroll of the Bank, guards and troops were used to cripple and, for a time, completely shut down Timberlane's milling operation. The harassment took other forms as well: the conspirators caused the manager of Timberlane's Honduras operations, Gordon Sloan Smith, to be falsely arrested and imprisoned and were responsible for the publication of several defamatory articles about Timberlane in the Honduran press.

As a result of the conspiracy, Timberlane's complaint claimed damages then estimated in excess of $5,000,000. Plaintiffs also allege that there has been a direct and substantial effect on United States foreign commerce, and that defendants intended the results of the conspiracy, including the impact on United States commerce.

[The court reviews and rejects the application of the act of state doctrine. The act of state doctrine is explored in Part C below.]

There is no doubt that American antitrust laws extend over some conduct in other nations. There was language in the first Supreme Court case in point, *American Banana Co. v. United Fruit Co.*, 213 U.S. 347, 29 S.Ct. 511, 53 L.Ed. 826 (1909), casting doubt on the extension of the Sherman Act to acts outside United States territory. But subsequent cases have limited *American Banana* to its particular facts, and the Sherman Act—and with it other antitrust laws—has been applied to extraterritorial conduct. *See, e.g., Continental Ore Co. v. Union Carbide & Carbon Corp.*, 370 U.S. 690, 82 S.Ct. 1404, 8 L.Ed.2d 777 (1962); *United States v. Sisal Sales Corp.*, 274 U.S. 268, 47 S.Ct. 592, 71 L.Ed. 1042 (1927); *United States v. Aluminum Co. of America* 148 F.2d 416 (2d Cir.1945)(the "*Alcoa*" case). The act may encompass the foreign activities of aliens as well as American citizens.

That American law covers some conduct beyond this nation's borders does not mean that it embraces all, however. Extraterritorial application is understandably a matter of concern for the other countries involved. Those nations have sometimes resented and protested, as excessive intrusions into their own spheres, broad assertions of authority by American courts. Our courts have recognized this concern and have, at times, responded to it, even if not always enough to satisfy all the foreign critics. In any event, it is evident that at some point the interests of the United States are too weak and the foreign harmony incentive for restraint too strong to justify an extraterritorial assertion of jurisdiction. * * *

A tripartite analysis seems to be indicated. As acknowledged above, the antitrust laws require in the first instance that there be *some* effect—actual or intended—on American foreign commerce before the federal courts may legitimately exercise subject matter jurisdiction under those statutes. Second, a greater showing of burden or restraint may be necessary to demonstrate that the effect is sufficiently large to present a cognizable injury to the plaintiffs and, therefore, a civil *violation* of the antitrust laws. Third, there is the additional question which is unique to the international setting of whether the interests of, and links to, the United States—including the magnitude of the effect on American foreign commerce—are sufficiently strong, vis-á-vis those of other nations, to justify an assertion of extraterritorial authority. * * *

What we prefer is an evaluation and balancing of the relevant considerations in each case—in the words of Kingman Brewster, a "jurisdictional rule of reason." Balancing of the foreign interests involved was the approach taken by the Supreme Court in *Continental Ore Co. v. Union Carbide & Carbon Corp.*, 370 U.S. 690, 82 S.Ct. 1404, 8 L.Ed.2d 777 (1962), where the involvement of the Canadian government in the alleged monopolization was held not to require dismissal. The Court stressed that there was no indication that the Canadian authorities approved or would have approved of the monopolization, meaning that the Canadian interest, if any, was slight and was outweighed by the American interest in condemning the restraint. Similarly, in *Lauritzen v. Larsen*, 345 U.S. 571, 73 S.Ct. 921, 97 L.Ed. 1254 (1953), the Court used a like approach in declining to apply the Jones Act to a Danish seaman, injured in Havana on a Danish ship, although he had signed on to the ship in New York.

The elements to be weighed include the degree of conflict with foreign law or policy, the nationality or allegiance of the parties and the locations or principal places of business of corporations, the extent to which enforcement by either state can be expected to achieve compliance, the relative significance of effects on the United States as compared with those elsewhere, the extent to which there is explicit purpose to harm or affect American commerce, the foreseeability of such effect, and the relative importance to the violations charged of conduct with the United States as compared with conduct abroad. A court evaluating these factors should identify the potential degree of conflict if American authority is asserted. A difference in law or policy is one likely sore spot, though one which may not always be present. Nationality is another; though foreign governments may have some concern for the treatment of American citizens and business residing there, they primarily care about their own nationals. Having assessed the conflict, the court should then determine whether in the face of it the contacts and interests of the United States are sufficient to support the exercise of extraterritorial jurisdiction. * * *

The Sherman Act is not limited to trade restraints which have both a direct and substantial effect on our foreign commerce. Timberlane has alleged that the complained of activities were intended to, and did, affect the export of lumber from Honduras to the United States—the flow of United States foreign commerce, and as such they are within the jurisdiction of the federal courts under the Sherman Act. Moreover, the magnitude of the effect alleged would appear to be sufficient to state a claim.

The comity question is more complicated. From Timberlane's complaint it is evident that there are grounds for concern as to at least a few of the defendants, for some are identified as foreign citizens: Laureano Gutierrez Falla, Michael Casanova and the Casanova firms of Honduras, and Patrick Byrne, of Canada. Moreover, it is clear that most of the activity took place in Honduras, though the conspiracy may have been directed from San Francisco, and that the most direct economic effect was probably on Honduras. However, there has been no indication of any conflict with the law or policy of the Honduran government, nor any comprehensive analysis of the relative connections and interests of Honduras and the United States. Under these circumstances, the dismissal by the district court cannot be sustained on jurisdictional grounds.

We, therefore, vacate the dismissal, and remand the Timberlane action.

Notes and Questions

1. Banana *Revisited*. Note how the *Timberlane* court returns to a premise of the much-derided *American Banana* case, albeit taking extraterritorial jurisdiction doctrine into account: "That American law covers some conduct beyond this nation's borders does not mean that it embraces all, however." *American Banana* simply restricts U.S. jurisdiction to the water's edge. *Blackmer* and *Aluminum* equally simplistically look only to the reach of U.S. law. *Timberlane*, like *American Banana*, is willing to limit U.S. jurisdiction, but it refuses to do so by holding that U.S. law is not meant to apply. Rather, *Timberlane* holds that U.S. law sometimes *ought* not to be employed even if it might apply. *Timberlane* reaches this result by acknowledging that, in many international cases, laws of two or more countries govern transactions concurrently. Hence, Judge Choy's working assumption: "[I]t is evident that at some point the interests of the United States are too weak and the foreign harmony incentive for restraint too strong to justify an extraterritorial assertion of jurisdiction." Should a court therefore have discretion to weigh U.S. and foreign interests to find a balance in each individual case? If the court finds the balance tilts toward the interests of the foreign state, should the result be deemed a denial of U.S. jurisdiction or simply a choice of foreign law?

2. *Balancing Factors*. Given the recurrent problem of concurrent jurisdiction in international transactions, how should courts structure their analyses to best balance and reconcile competing national interests? Professor Lea Brilmayer identifies five "considerations" U.S. courts have taken into account when deciding whether to apply U.S. law extraterritorially: the legislative intent of the Congress, the presumptive "reach" of the statute, the limits imposed by international law, judicial doctrines of discretion like comity, and the U.S. Constitution. Lea Brilmayer, "The Extraterritorial Application of American Law: A Methodological and Constitutional Approach," 50 *Law and Contemporary Problems*, Summer 1987, at 11, 14–16. In a rebuttal, Professor Friedrich Juenger argues that "the solution to the

problem of extraterritoriality will remain elusive as long as the clash of regulatory policies is analyzed in terms of legislative jurisdiction," a choice of law analysis which he feels masks real conflicts of substantive policy. Friedrich K. Juenger, "Constitutional Control of Extraterritoriality?: A Comment on Professor Brilmayer's Appraisal," 50 *Law and Contemporary Problems*, Summer 1987, at 39, 46. For other formulations of the balancing test, see *Restatement (Third) of Foreign Relations Law of the United States* § 403 and Mannington Mills, Inc. v. Congoleum Corp., 595 F.2d 1287 (3d Cir.1979).

3. *The Role of Case Law.* Granting that there may always be conflicts of substantive national policies in problems of transnational litigation, why should the courts not try to resolve such conflicts as clearly and fairly as possible? Can a consistent pattern of court decisions help bolster international comity and help develop rules of international law respecting jurisdiction? Should U.S. courts look not only to their own judgments, but also to judgments made by foreign and international courts to develop such rules?

b. International Comity

HARTFORD FIRE INSURANCE CO. v. CALIFORNIA

509 U.S. 764, 113 S.Ct. 2891, 125 L.Ed.2d 612 (1993).

Justice Souter announced the judgment of the Court and delivered the opinion of the Court with respect to Parts I, II(A), III, and IV, and an opinion with respect to Part II(B) in which Justice White, Justice Blackmun and Justice Stevens join.

The Sherman Act makes every contract, combination, or conspiracy in unreasonable restraint of interstate or foreign commerce illegal. 15 U.S.C. § 1. These consolidated cases present questions about the application of that Act to the insurance industry, both here and abroad. The plaintiffs (respondents here) allege that both domestic and foreign defendants (petitioners here) violated the Sherman Act by engaging in various conspiracies to affect the American insurance market. A group of domestic defendants argues that the McCarran–Ferguson Act, 15 U.S.C. § 1011 *et seq.*, precludes application of the Sherman Act to the conduct alleged; a group of foreign defendants argues that the principle of international comity requires the District Court to refrain from exercising jurisdiction over certain claims against it. We hold that most of the domestic defendants' alleged conduct is not immunized from antitrust liability by the McCarran–Ferguson Act, and that, even assuming it applies, the principle of international comity does not preclude District Court jurisdiction over the foreign conduct alleged.

I

The two petitions before us stem from consolidated litigation comprising the complaints of 19 States and many private plaintiffs alleging that the defendants, members of the insurance industry, conspired in violation of § 1 of the Sherman Act to restrict the terms of coverage of commercial general liability (CGL) insurance available in the United

States. Because the cases come to us on motions to dismiss, we take the allegations of the complaints as true.

A

According to the complaints, the object of the conspiracies was to force certain primary insurers (insurers who sell insurance directly to consumers) to change the terms of their standard CGL insurance policies to conform with the policies the defendant insurers wanted to sell. The defendants wanted four changes.

First, CGL insurance has traditionally been sold in the United States on an "occurrence" basis, through a policy obligating the insurer "to pay or defend claims, whenever made, resulting from an accident or 'injurious exposure to conditions' that occurred during the [specific time] period the policy was in effect." In place of this traditional "occurrence" trigger of coverage, the defendants wanted a "claims-made" trigger, obligating the insurer to pay or defend only those claims made during the policy period. Such a policy has the distinct advantage for the insurer that when the policy period ends without a claim having been made, the insurer can be certain that the policy will not expose it to any further liability. Second, the defendants wanted the "claims-made" policy to have a "retroactive date" provision, which would further restrict coverage to claims based on incidents that occurred after a certain date. Such a provision eliminates the risk that an insurer, by issuing a claims-made policy, would assume liability arising from incidents that occurred before the policy's effective date, but remained undiscovered or caused no immediate harm. Third, CGL insurance has traditionally covered "sudden and accidental" pollution; the defendants wanted to eliminate that coverage. Finally, CGL insurance has traditionally provided that the insurer would bear the legal costs of defending covered claims against the insured without regard to the policy's stated limits of coverage; the defendants wanted legal defense costs to be counted against the stated limits (providing a "legal defense cost cap"). * * *

III

Finally, we take up the question presented by No. 91–1128, whether certain claims against the London reinsurers should have been dismissed as improper applications of the Sherman Act to foreign conduct. The Fifth Claim for Relief of the California Complaint alleges a violation of § 1 of the Sherman Act by certain London reinsurers who conspired to coerce primary insurers in the United States to offer CGL coverage on a claims-made basis, thereby making "occurrence CGL coverage ... unavailable in the State of California for many risks." The Sixth Claim for Relief of the California Complaint alleges that the London reinsurers violated § 1 by a conspiracy to limit coverage of pollution risks in North America, thereby rendering "pollution liability coverage ... almost entirely unavailable for the vast majority of casualty insurance purchasers in the State of California." The Eighth Claim for Relief of the California Complaint alleges a further § 1 violation by the London reinsurers who, along with domestic retrocessional reinsurers, conspired to limit coverage of seepage, pollution, and property contamination risks in North America, thereby eliminating such coverage in the State of California.

At the outset, we note that the District Court undoubtedly had jurisdiction of these Sherman Act claims, as the London reinsurers apparently concede. ("Our position is not that the Sherman Act does not apply in the sense that a minimal basis for the exercise of jurisdiction doesn't exist here. Our position is that there are certain circumstances, and that this is one of them, in which the interests of another State are sufficient that the exercise of that jurisdiction should be restrained).'' Although the proposition was perhaps not always free from doubt, see *American Banana Co. v. United Fruit Co.*, 213 U.S. 347 (1909), it is well established by now that the Sherman Act applies to foreign conduct that was meant to produce and did in fact produce some substantial effect in the United States.[22] Such is the conduct alleged here: that the London reinsurers engaged in unlawful conspiracies to affect the market for insurance in the United States and that their conduct in fact produced substantial effect.

According to the London reinsurers, the District Court should have declined to exercise such jurisdiction under the principle of international comity.[24] The Court of Appeals agreed that courts should look to that principle in deciding whether to exercise jurisdiction under the Sherman Act. This availed the London reinsurers nothing, however. To be sure, the Court of Appeals believed that "application of [American] antitrust laws to the London reinsurance market 'would lead to significant conflict with English law and policy,''' and that "[s]uch a conflict, unless outweighed by other factors, would by itself be reason to decline exercise of jurisdiction.'' But other factors, in the court's view, including the London reinsurers' express purpose to affect United States commerce

22. Justice Scalia believes that what is at issue in this case is prescriptive, as opposed to subject-matter, jurisdiction. The parties do not question prescriptive jurisdiction, however, and for good reason: it is well established that Congress has exercised such jurisdiction under the Sherman Act. See G. Born & D. Westin, International Civil Litigation in United States Courts 542, n.5 (2d ed. 1992)(Sherman Act is a "prime exampl[e] of the simultaneous exercise of prescriptive jurisdiction and grant of subject matter jurisdiction'').

24. Justice Scalia contends that comity concerns figure into the prior analysis whether jurisdiction exists under the Sherman Act. This contention is inconsistent with the general understanding that the Sherman Act covers foreign conduct producing a substantial intended effect in the United States, and that concerns of comity come into play, if at all, only after a court has determined that the acts complained of are subject to Sherman Act jurisdiction. See *United States v. Aluminum Co. of America*, 148 F.2d 416, 444 (C.A.2 1945)("it follows from what we have ... said that [the agreements at issue] were unlawful [under the Sherman Act], though made abroad, if they were intended to affect imports and did affect them''); *Mannington Mills, Inc. v. Congoleum Corp.*, 595 F.2d 1287, 1294 (C.A.3 1979)(once court determines that jurisdiction exists under the Sherman Act, question remains whether comity precludes its exercise); H.R. Rep. No. 97–686, p. 13 (1982). But cf. *Timberlane Lumber Co. v. Bank of America, N. T. & S. A.*, 549 F.2d 597, 613 (C.A.9 1976). In any event, the parties conceded jurisdiction at oral argument, and we see no need to address this contention here.

and the substantial nature of the effect produced, outweighed the supposed conflict and required the exercise of jurisdiction in this case.

When it enacted the Foreign Trade Antitrust Improvements Act of 1982 (FTAIA), 15 U.S.C. § 6a, Congress expressed no view on the question whether a court with Sherman Act jurisdiction should ever decline to exercise such jurisdiction on grounds of international comity. See H.R. Rep. No. 97–686, p. 13 (1982)("If a court determines that the requirements for subject matter jurisdiction are met, [the FTAIA] would have no effect on the court['s] ability to employ notions of comity . . . or otherwise to take account of the international character of the transaction")(citing *Timberlane*). We need not decide that question here, however, for even assuming that in a proper case a court may decline to exercise Sherman Act jurisdiction over foreign conduct (or, as JUSTICE SCALIA would put it, may conclude by the employment of comity analysis in the first instance that there is no jurisdiction), international comity would not counsel against exercising jurisdiction in the circumstances alleged here.

The only substantial question in this case is whether "there is in fact a true conflict between domestic and foreign law." *Societe Nationale Industrielle Aerospatiale v. United States District Court*, 482 U.S. 522, 555 (1987)(BLACKMUN, J., concurring in part and dissenting in part). The London reinsurers contend that applying the Act to their conduct would conflict significantly with British law, and the British Government, appearing before us as *amicus curiae,* concurs. They assert that Parliament has established a comprehensive regulatory regime over the London reinsurance market and that the conduct alleged here was perfectly consistent with British law and policy. But this is not to state a conflict. "[T]he fact that conduct is lawful in the state in which it took place will not, of itself, bar application of the United States antitrust laws," even where the foreign state has a strong policy to permit or encourage such conduct. Restatement (Third) Foreign Relations Law § 415, Comment *j*; see *Continental Ore Co., supra*, at 706–707. No conflict exists, for these purposes, "where a person subject to regulation by two states can comply with the laws of both." Restatement (Third) Foreign Relations Law § 403, Comment *e*.[25] Since the London reinsurers do not argue that British law requires them to act in some fashion prohibited by the law of the United States, or claim that their compliance with the laws of both countries is otherwise impossible, we see no conflict with British law. We have no need in this case to address other considerations that might inform a decision to refrain from the exercise of jurisdiction on grounds of international comity. * * *

25. JUSTICE SCALIA says that we put the cart before the horse in citing this authority, for he argues it may be apposite only after a determination that jurisdiction over the foreign acts is reasonable. But whatever the order of cart and horse, conflict in this sense is the only substantial issue before the Court.

JUSTICE SCALIA * * * delivered a dissenting opinion with respect to Part II, in which JUSTICE O'CONNOR, JUSTICE KENNEDY, AND JUSTICE THOMAS have joined. * * *

II

The petitioners in No. 91–1128, various British corporations and other British subjects, argue that certain of the claims against them constitute an inappropriate extraterritorial application of the Sherman Act. It is important to distinguish two distinct questions raised by this petition: whether the District Court had jurisdiction, and whether the Sherman Act reaches the extraterritorial conduct alleged here. On the first question, I believe that the District Court had subject-matter jurisdiction over the Sherman Act claims against all the defendants (personal jurisdiction is not contested). The respondents asserted non-frivolous claims under the Sherman Act, and 28 U.S.C. § 1331 vests district courts with subject-matter jurisdiction over cases "arising under" federal statutes. As precedents such as *Lauritzen v. Larsen*, 345 U.S. 571 (1953), make clear, that is sufficient to establish the District Court's jurisdiction over these claims. *Lauritzen* involved a Jones Act claim brought by a foreign sailor against a foreign shipowner. The shipowner contested the District Court's jurisdiction, apparently on the grounds that the Jones Act did not govern the dispute between the foreign parties to the action. Though ultimately agreeing with the shipowner that the Jones Act did not apply, the Court held that the District Court had jurisdiction.

> "As frequently happens, a contention that there is some barrier to granting plaintiff's claim is cast in terms of an exception to jurisdiction of subject matter. A cause of action under our law was asserted here, and the court had power to determine whether it was or was not founded in law and in fact."

The second question—the extraterritorial reach of the Sherman Act—has nothing to do with the jurisdiction of the courts. It is a question of substantive law turning on whether, in enacting the Sherman Act, Congress asserted regulatory power over the challenged conduct. See *EEOC v. Arabian American Oil Co.*, 499 U.S. 244, ___ (1991)(*Aramco*) (slip op., at 2)("It is our task to determine whether Congress intended the protections of Title VII to apply to United States citizens employed by American employers outside of the United States"). If a plaintiff fails to prevail on this issue, the court does not dismiss the claim for want of subject-matter jurisdiction—want of power to adjudicate; rather, it decides the claim, ruling on the merits that the plaintiff has failed to state a cause of action under the relevant statute. See *American Banana Co. v. United Fruit Co.*, 213 U.S. 347, 359 (1909)(holding that complaint based upon foreign conduct "alleges no case under the [Sherman Act]").

There is, however, a type of "jurisdiction" relevant to determining the extraterritorial reach of a statute; it is known as "legislative jurisdiction" or "jurisdiction to prescribe." This refers to "the authority of a state to make its law applicable to persons or activities," and is quite a separate matter from "jurisdiction to adjudicate." There is no doubt, of course, that Congress possesses legislative jurisdiction over the acts alleged in this complaint: Congress has broad power under Article I, § 8, cl. 3 "[t]o regulate Commerce with foreign Nations," and this Court has repeatedly upheld its power to make laws applicable to persons or activities beyond our territorial boundaries where United States interests are affected. But the question in this case is whether, and to what extent, Congress *has* exercised that undoubted legislative jurisdiction in enacting the Sherman Act.

Two canons of statutory construction are relevant in this inquiry. The first is the "long-standing principle of American law 'that legislation of Congress, unless a contrary intent appears, is meant to apply only within the territorial jurisdiction of the United States.' " *Aramco, supra,* at ___ (slip op., at 3)(quoting *Foley Bros., Inc. v. Filardo*, 336 U.S. 281, 285 (1949)). Applying that canon in *Aramco,* we held that the version of Title VII of the Civil Rights Act of 1964 then in force did not extend outside the territory of the United States even though the statute contained broad provisions extending its prohibitions to, for example, " 'any activity, business, or industry in commerce.' " We held such "boilerplate language" to be an insufficient indication to override the presumption against extraterritoriality. The Sherman Act contains similar "boilerplate language," and if the question were not governed by precedent, it would be worth considering whether that presumption controls the outcome here. We, have, however, found the presumption to be overcome with respect to our antitrust laws; it is now well established that the Sherman Act applies extraterritorially.

But if the presumption against extraterritoriality has been overcome or is otherwise inapplicable, a second canon of statutory construction becomes relevant: "[A]n act of congress ought never to be construed to violate the law of nations if any other possible construction remains." *Murray v. The Charming Betsy*, 2 Cranch 64, 118 (1804)(Marshall, C. J.). This canon is "wholly independent" of the presumption against extraterritoriality. It is relevant to determining the substantive reach of a statute because "the law of nations," or customary international law, includes limitations on a nation's exercise of its jurisdiction to prescribe. Though it clearly has constitutional authority to do so, Congress is generally presumed not to have exceeded those customary international-law limits on jurisdiction to prescribe.

Consistent with that presumption, this and other courts have frequently recognized that, even where the presumption against extraterritoriality does not apply, statutes should not be interpreted to regulate foreign persons or conduct if that regulation would conflict with principles of international law. For example, in *Romero v. International Terminal Operating Co.*, 358 U.S. 354 (1959), the plaintiff, a Spanish sailor who had been injured while working aboard a Spanish-flag and Spanish-owned vessel, filed a Jones Act claim against his Spanish employer. The presumption against extraterritorial application of federal statutes was inapplicable to the case, as the actionable tort had occurred in American waters. The Court nonetheless stated that, "in the absence of contrary congressional direction," it would apply "principles of choice of law that are consonant with the needs of a general federal maritime law and with due recognition of our self-regarding respect for the relevant interests of foreign nations in the regulation of maritime commerce as part of the legitimate concern of the international community." "The controlling considerations" in this choice-of-law analysis were "the interacting interests of the United States and of foreign countries."

Romero referred to, and followed, the choice-of-law analysis set forth in *Lauritzen v. Larsen*, 345 U.S. 571 (1953). As previously mentioned, *Lauritzen* also involved a Jones Act claim brought by a foreign sailor against a foreign employer. The *Lauritzen* Court recognized the basic problem: "If [the Jones Act were] read literally, Congress has conferred an American right of action which requires nothing more than that plaintiff be 'any seaman who shall suffer personal injury in the course of his employment.' " The solution it adopted was to construe the statute "to apply only to areas and transactions in which *American law would be considered operative under prevalent doctrines of international law*." To support application of international law to limit the facial breadth of the statute, the Court relied upon—of course—Chief Justice Marshall's statement in *The Charming Betsy* quoted *supra*. See also *McCulloch v. Sociedad Nacional de Marineros de Honduras*, 372 U.S. 10, 21–22 (1963)(applying *The Charming Betsy* principle to restrict application of National Labor Relations Act to foreign-flag vessels).

Lauritzen, Romero, and *McCulloch* were maritime cases, but we have recognized the principle that the scope of generally worded statutes must be construed in light of international law in other areas as well. More specifically, the principle was expressed in *United States v. Aluminum Co. of America*, 148 F.2d 416 (C.A.2 1945), the decision that established the extraterritorial reach of the Sherman Act. In his opinion for the court, Judge Learned Hand cautioned "we are not to read general words, such as those in [the Sherman] Act, without regard to the limitations customarily observed by nations upon the exercise of their powers; limitations which generally correspond to those fixed by the 'Conflict of Laws.' "

More recent lower court precedent has also tempered the extraterritorial application of the Sherman Act with considerations of "international comity." See *Timberlane Lumber Co. v. Bank of America, N.T & S.A.*, 549 F.2d 597, 608–615 (C.A.9 1976); *Mannington Mills, Inc. v. Congoleum Corp.*, 595 F.2d 1287, 1294–1298 (C.A.3 1979). The "comity" they refer to is not the comity of courts, whereby judges decline to exercise jurisdiction over matters more appropriately adjudged elsewhere, but rather what might be termed "prescriptive comity": the respect sovereign nations afford each other by limiting the reach of their laws. That comity is exercised by legislatures when they enact laws, and courts assume it has been exercised when they come to interpreting the scope of laws their legislatures have enacted. It is a traditional component of choice-of-law theory. See J. Story, Commentaries on the Conflict of Laws § 38 (1834)(distinguishing between the "comity of the courts" and the "comity of nations," and defining the latter as "the true foundation and extent of the obligation of the laws of one nation within the territories of another"). Comity in this sense includes the choice-of-law principles that, "in the absence of contrary congressional direction," are assumed to be incorporated into our substantive laws having extraterritorial reach. Considering comity in this way is just part of determining whether the Sherman Act prohibits the conduct at issue.

In sum, the practice of using international law to limit the extraterritorial reach of statutes is firmly established in our jurisprudence. In proceeding to apply that practice to the present case, I shall rely on the Restatement (Third) of Foreign Relations Law for the relevant principles of international law. Its standards appear fairly supported in the decisions of this Court construing international choice-of-law principles (*Lauritzen, Romero*, and *McCulloch)* and in the decisions of other federal courts, especially *Timberlane*. Whether the Restatement precisely reflects international law in every detail matters little here, as I believe this case would be resolved the same way under virtually any conceivable test that takes account of foreign regulatory interests.

Under the Restatement, a nation having some "basis" for jurisdiction to prescribe law should nonetheless refrain from exercising that jurisdiction "with respect to a person or activity having connections with another state when the exercise of such jurisdiction is unreasonable." Restatement (Third) § 403(*l*). The "reasonableness" inquiry turns on a number of factors including, but not limited to: "the extent to which the activity takes place within the territory [of the regulating state]," *id.*, § 403(2)(a); "the connections, such as nationality, residence, or economic activity, between the regulating state and the person principally responsible for the activity to be regulated," *id.*, § 403(2)(b); "the character of the activity to be regulated, the importance of regulation to the regulating state, the extent to which other states regulate such activities, and the degree to which the desirability of such regulation is generally accepted," *id.*, § 403(2)(c); "the extent to which another state may have an interest in regulating the activity," *id.*, § 403(2)(g); and "the likelihood of conflict with regulation by another state," *id.*, 403(2)(h). Rarely would these factors point more clearly against application of United States law. The activity relevant to the counts at issue here took place primarily in the United Kingdom, and the defendants in these counts are British corporations and British subjects having their principal place of business or residence outside the United States. Great Britain has established a comprehensive regulatory scheme governing the London reinsurance markets, and clearly has a heavy "interest in regulating the activity." Finally, § 2(b) of the McCarran–Ferguson Act allows state regulatory statutes to override the Sherman Act in the insurance field, subject only to the narrow "boycott" exception set forth in § 3(b)—suggesting that "the importance of regulation to the [United

States]" is slight. Considering these factors, I think it unimaginable that an assertion of legislative jurisdiction by the United States would be considered reasonable, and therefore it is inappropriate to assume, in the absence of statutory indication to the contrary, that Congress has made such an assertion.

It is evident from what I have said that the Court's comity analysis, which proceeds as though the issue is whether the courts should "decline to exercise ... jurisdiction," rather than whether the Sherman Act covers this conduct, is simply misdirected. I do not at all agree, moreover, with the Court's conclusion that the issue of the substantive scope of the Sherman Act is not in the case. To be sure, the parties did not make a clear distinction between adjudicative jurisdiction and the scope of the statute. Parties often do not, as we have observed (and have declined to punish with procedural default) before. It is not realistic, and also not helpful, to pretend that the only really relevant issue in this case is not before us. In any event, if one erroneously chooses, as the Court does, to make adjudicative jurisdiction (or, more precisely, abstention) the vehicle for taking account of the needs of prescriptive comity, the Court still gets it wrong. It concludes that no "true conflict" counseling nonapplication of United States law (or rather, as it thinks, United States judicial jurisdiction) exists unless compliance with United States law would constitute a *violation* of another country's law. That breathtakingly broad proposition, which contradicts the many cases discussed earlier, will bring the Sherman Act and other laws into sharp and unnecessary conflict with the legitimate interests of other countries—particularly our closest trading partners.

In the sense in which the term "conflic[t]" was used in *Lauritzen,* and is generally understood in the field of conflicts of laws, there is clearly a conflict in this case. The petitioners here, like the defendant in *Lauritzen,* were not compelled by any foreign law to take their allegedly wrongful actions, but that no more precludes a conflict-of-laws analysis here than it did there. Where applicable foreign and domestic law provide different substantive rules of decision to govern the parties' dispute, a conflict-of-laws analysis is necessary.

Literally the *only* support that the Court adduces for its position is § 403 of the Restatement (Third) of Foreign Relations Law—or more precisely Comment *e* to that provision, which states:

> "Subsection (3) [which says that a state should defer to another state if that state's interest is clearly greater] applies only when one state requires what another prohibits, or where compliance with the regulations of two states exercising jurisdiction consistently with this section is otherwise impossible. It does not apply where a person subject to regulation by two states can comply with the laws of both...."

The Court has completely misinterpreted this provision. Subsection (3) of § 403 (requiring one State to defer to another in the limited circumstances just described) comes into play only after subsection (1) of § 403 has been complied with—*i.e.*, after it has been determined that the exercise of jurisdiction by *both* of the two states is not "unreasonable." That prior question is answered by applying the factors (*inter alia*) set forth in subsection (2) of § 403, that is, precisely the factors that I have discussed in text and that the Court rejects.

Notes and Questions

1. *International Comity.* In Laker Airways v. Sabena, Belgian World Airlines, 731 F.2d 909 (D.C.Cir.1984), the court refuses to restrain a U.S. antitrust suit filed by a British company, Laker, against foreign competitors even when British courts ordered Laker to stop proceeding in U.S. courts. In the context of having to decide whether to uphold or strike down a U.S. anti-suit injunction issued in response to the British anti-suit injunction, Judge Wilkey addresses arguments that the U.S. injunction "violates the crucial principles of comity that regulate and moderate the social and economic intercourse between independent nations":

> [C]omity serves our international system like the mortar which cements together a brick house. No one would willingly permit the mortar to crumble or be chipped away for fear of compromising the entire structure.
>
> "Comity" summarizes in a brief word a complex and elusive concept—the degree of deference that a domestic forum must pay to the act of a foreign government not otherwise binding on the forum. Since comity varies according to the factual circumstances surrounding each claim for its recognition, the absolute boundaries of the duties it imposes are inherently uncertain. However, the central precept of comity teaches that, when possible, the decisions of foreign tribunals should be given effect in domestic courts, since recognition fosters international cooperation and encourages reciprocity, thereby promoting predictability and stability through satisfaction of mutual expectations. The interests of both forums are advanced—the foreign court because its laws and policies have been vindicated; the domestic country because international cooperation and ties have been strengthened. The rule of law is also encouraged, which benefits all nations.
>
> Comity is a necessary outgrowth of our international system of politically independent, socio-economically interdependent nation states. As surely as people, products and problems move freely among adjoining countries, so national interests cross territorial borders. * * * Every nation must often rely on other countries to help it achieve its regulatory expectations. Thus, comity compels national courts to act at all times to increase the international legal ties that advance the rule of law within and among nations.
>
> However, there are limitations to the application of comity. When the foreign act is inherently inconsistent with the policies underlying comity, domestic recognition could tend either to legitimize the aberration or to encourage retaliation, undercutting the realization of the goals served by comity. No nation is under an unremitting obligation to enforce foreign interests which are fundamentally prejudicial to those of the domestic forum. Thus, from the earliest times, authorities have

> recognized that the obligation of comity expires when the strong public policies of the forum are vitiated by the foreign act.

Id. at 937. Is use of comity consistent with use of a balancing test, such as the one set out in *Timberlane*?

Note how Justice Souter's conception of comity in *Hartford Fire* differs from the more traditional notion set out in *Laker Airways*. Souter finds cause for application of "comity" only when U.S. law is directly confronted by a foreign law that makes the conduct required under U.S. law illegal. Professor Dam criticizes the majority opinion in *Hartford Fire* for "plung[ing] forward in applying the Sherman Act extraterritorially, whatever the foreign interests involved." Kenneth W. Dam, "Extraterritoriality in an Age of Globalization: The Hartford Fire Case," 1993 *Supreme Court Review* 289, 294. In essence, Souter makes what had been called the "foreign compulsion defense" the centerpiece of his comity inquiry.

Even U.S. courts that have limited the application of U.S. law have not often relied directly on a traditional comity approach when faced with foreign conflicts. Instead, U.S. courts have tended to look to some other kind of justification for limiting the application of U.S. law or legal process, *e.g.*, the choice-of-law limitations posed by territorialism in *American Banana* or the abstention doctrines of *forum non conveniens*, foreign sovereign immunity, or act of state, all explored below.

2. *Hartford Fire and the Balancing Test.* Does *Hartford Fire* mean that the balancing test of *Timberlane* has been repudiated? Demetriou and Robertson think so: "[T]he balancing test [is] meaningless. So long as the conduct concerned 'was meant to produce and did in fact produce some substantial effect in the United States,' then jurisdiction is established." Marie Demetriou & Aidan Robertson, "US Extra-territorial Jurisdiction in Anti–Trust Matters: Recent Developments," 8 *European Competition Law Review* 461, 465 (1995). Unlike Justice Souter's majority opinion, Justice Scalia's dissent explicitly relies on *Timberlane* and other formulations of the balancing test.

Will *Hartford Fire* be narrowly construed? In Sterling Drug, Inc. v. Bayer USA Inc., 14 F.3d 733 (2d Cir.1994), the Second Circuit considers the extraterritorial application of an injunction restraining violations of the Lanham Act's trademark protection provisions. The court finds that even after *Hartford Fire*, the traditional notion of international comity remains an appropriate concern: "[T]he [*Hartford Fire*] Court's approach to the comity issue ... is not automatically transferable to the trademark context, especially where the contending parties both hold rights in the same mark under the respective laws of their countries." *Id.* at 746. In the court's view, the extraterritorial aspects of a trademark infringement injunction need to be "carefully crafted to prohibit only those foreign uses of the mark * * * that are likely to have significant trademark-impairing effects on United States commerce." *Id.* at 747. The Ninth Circuit has also addressed the implications of *Hartford Fire*. In Metro Indus., Inc. v. Sammi Corp., 82 F.3d 839 (9th Cir.1996), the court upholds a summary judgment for the defendant, finding Metro had not presented evidence sufficient to allow a rational fact finder to decide in Metro's favor on its Sherman Act claim against a Korean exporting company and two of its U.S. subsidiaries. In the course of its opinion, the court finds a traditional comity analysis relevant in deciding it has jurisdiction to rule on Metro's antitrust suit. According to the Ninth Circuit, although *Hartford Fire* held "that a foreign government's encouragement of conduct which the United States prohibits [could not] amount to a conflict of law, it did not question the propriety of the jurisdictional rule of reason or the seven comity factors set forth in *Timberlane.*" *Id.* at 846 n.5.

3. Hartford Fire *and the Global Economy.* Does the U.S.-centric approach of *Hartford Fire* fail to respond to modern international economic needs? Professor Dam believes that the judgment "sounds a discordant note in an increasingly globalized economy in an era when the need for more outward-looking and cooperative economic policy measures has become increasingly obvious." Dam, *supra*, at 297.

4. *Reactions to* Hartford Fire. One British commentator calls the *Hartford Fire* decision a "staggeringly blinkered approach" that in effect means that the United States will respect

> only * * * the laws of those foreign States which actually legislate in favour of monopolistic, price-fixing or other anti-competitive practices. The sovereign interests of those States which actually share US free-market principles but do not regulate anti-competition with the aggression or exorbitant reach of the US can be ignored. Under this approach, greater consideration would be due to the laws of an old-style Soviet State than those of a European trading partner.

Julian Wilson, Editorial, "US exports in anti-trust: the primacy of economic muscle over international law," *International Litigation News*, July 1995, at 3, 4. Will Justice Souter's narrow definition of comity in fact encourage other states to take actions that more directly challenge the applicability of U.S. law? In *Hartford Fire*, Justice Souter finds the assertion "that Parliament has established a comprehensive regulatory regime over the London reinsurance market and that the conduct alleged here was perfectly consistent with British law and policy" does not "state a conflict" with U.S. law. Might some states be tempted to enact counter-measures, making it illegal under their laws to comply with U.S. laws, refusing enforcement of U.S. judgments, or providing a cause of action allowing the recovery of damages paid as a result of a U.S. court's finding of liability? For discussion of legislative responses abroad to what have been regarded as overbroad assertions of U.S. antitrust jurisdiction, see, *e.g.*, A.V. Lowe, "Blocking Extraterritorial Jurisdiction: The British Protection of Trading Interests Acts, 1980," 75 *American Journal of International Law* 257 (1981).

c. Forum Non Conveniens

PIPER AIRCRAFT CO. v. REYNO

454 U.S. 235, 102 S.Ct. 252, 70 L.Ed.2d 419 (1981).

JUSTICE MARSHALL delivered the opinion of the Court. * * *

I

A

In July 1976, a small commercial aircraft crashed in the Scottish highlands during the course of a charter flight from Blackpool to Perth.

The pilot and five passengers were killed instantly. The decedents were all Scottish subjects and residents, as are their heirs and next of kin. There were no eyewitnesses to the accident. At the time of the crash the plane was subject to Scottish air traffic control.

The aircraft, a twin-engine Piper Aztec, was manufactured in Pennsylvania by petitioner Piper Aircraft Co. (Piper). The propellers were manufactured in Ohio by petitioner Hartzell Propeller, Inc. (Hartzell). At the time of the crash the aircraft was registered in Great Britain and was owned and maintained by Air Navigation and Trading Co., Ltd. (Air Navigation). It was operated by McDonald Aviation, Ltd. (McDonald), a Scottish air taxi service. Both Air Navigation and McDonald were organized in the United Kingdom. The wreckage of the plane is now in a hanger in Farnsborough, England.

The British Department of Trade investigated the accident shortly after it occurred. A preliminary report found that the plane crashed after developing a spin, and suggested that mechanical failure in the plane or the propeller was responsible. At Hartzell's request, this report was reviewed by a three-member Review Board, which held a 9–day adversary hearing attended by all interested parties. The Review Board found no evidence of defective equipment and indicated that pilot error may have contributed to the accident. The pilot, who had obtained his commercial pilot's license only three months earlier, was flying over high ground at an altitude considerably lower than the minimum height required by his company's operations manual.

In July 1977, a California probate court appointed respondent Gaynell Reyno administratrix of the estates of the five passengers. Reyno is not related to and does not know any of the decedents or their survivors; she was a legal secretary to the attorney who filed this lawsuit. Several days after her appointment, Reyno commenced separate wrongful-death actions against Piper and Hartzell in the Superior Court of California, claiming negligence and strict liability. Air Navigation, McDonald, and the estate of the pilot are not parties to this litigation. The survivors of the five passengers whose estates are represented by Reyno filed a separate action in the United Kingdom against Air Navigation, McDonald, and the pilot's estate. Reyno candidly admits that the action against Piper and Hartzell was filed in the United States because its laws regarding liability, capacity to sue, and damages are more favorable to her position than are those of Scotland. Scottish law does not recognize strict liability in tort. Moreover, it permits wrongful-death actions only when brought by a decedent's relatives. The relatives may sue only for "loss of support and society."

On petitioners' motion, the suit was removed to the United States District Court for the Central District of California. Piper then moved for transfer to the United States District Court for the Middle District of Pennsylvania, pursuant to 28 U.S.C. § 1404(a). Hartzell moved to dismiss for lack of personal jurisdiction, or in the alternative, to transfer. In December 1977, the District Court quashed service on Hartzell and transferred the case to the Middle District of Pennsylvania. Respondent then properly served process on Hartzell.

B

In May 1978, after the suit had been transferred, both Hartzell and Piper moved to dismiss the action on the ground of *forum non conveniens.* The District Court granted these motions in October 1979. It relied on the balancing test set forth by this Court in *Gulf Oil Corp. v. Gilbert*, 330 U.S. 501 (1947), and its companion case, *Koster v. Lumbermens Mut. Cas. Co.*, 330 U.S. 518 (1947). In those decisions, the Court stated that a plaintiff's choice of forum should rarely be disturbed. However, when an alternative forum has jurisdiction to hear the case, and when trial in the chosen forum would "establish ... oppressiveness and vexation to a defendant ... out of all proportion to plaintiff's convenience," or when the "chosen forum [is] inappropriate because of considerations affecting the court's own administrative and legal problems," the court may, in the exercise of its sound discretion, dismiss the case. To guide trial court discretion, the Court provided a list of "private interest factors" affecting the convenience of the litigants, and a list of "public interest factors" affecting the convenience of the forum.[6]

On appeal, the United States Court of Appeals for the Third Circuit reversed and remanded for trial. The decision to reverse appears to be based on two alternative grounds. First, the Court held that the District Court abused its discretion in conducting the *Gilbert* analysis. Second, the Court held that dismissal is never appropriate where the law of the alternative forum is less favorable to the plaintiff. * * *

II

The Court of Appeals erred in holding that plaintiffs may defeat a motion to dismiss on the ground of *forum non conveniens* merely by showing that the substantive law that would be applied in the alternative forum is less favorable to the plaintiffs than that of the present forum. The possibility of a change in substantive law should ordinarily not be given conclusive or even substantial weight in the *forum non conveniens* inquiry.

We expressly rejected the position adopted by the Court of Appeals in our decision in *Canada Malting Co. v. Paterson Steamships, Ltd.*, 285 U.S. 413 (1932). That case arose out of a collision between two vessels in American waters. The Canadian owners of cargo lost in the accident

6. The factors pertaining to the private interests of the litigants included the "relative ease of access to sources of proof; availability of compulsory process for attendance of unwilling, and the cost of obtaining attendance of willing, witnesses; possibility of view of premises, if view would be appropriate to the action; and all other practical problems that make trial of a case easy, expeditious and inexpensive." *Gilbert*, 330 U.S., at 508. The public factors bearing on the question included the administrative difficulties flowing from court congestion; the "local interest in having localized controversies decided at home"; the interest in having the trial of a diversity case in a forum that is at home with the law that must govern the action; the avoidance of unnecessary problems in conflict of laws, or in the application of foreign law; and the unfairness of burdening citizens in an unrelated forum with jury duty. *Id.*, at 509.

sued the Canadian owners of one of the vessels in Federal District Court. The cargo owners chose an American court in large part because the relevant American liability rules were more favorable than the Canadian rules. The District Court dismissed on grounds of *forum non conveniens*. The plaintiffs argued that dismissal was inappropriate because Canadian laws were less favorable to them. This Court nonetheless affirmed:

> "We have no occasion to enquire by what law the rights of the parties are governed, as we are of the opinion that, under any view of that question, it lay within the discretion of the District Court to decline to assume jurisdiction over the controversy.... '[The] court will not take cognizance of the case if justice would be as well done by remitting the parties to their home forum.' "

The Court further stated that "[t]here was no basis for the contention that the District Court abused its discretion."

It is true that *Canada Malting* was decided before *Gilbert*, and that the doctrine of *forum non conveniens* was not fully crystallized until our decision in that case. However, *Gilbert* in no way affects the validity of *Canada Malting*. Indeed, by holding that the central focus of the *forum non conveniens* inquiry is convenience, *Gilbert* implicitly recognized that dismissal may not be barred solely because of the possibility of an unfavorable change in law. Under *Gilbert,* dismissal will ordinarily be appropriate where trial in the plaintiff's chosen forum imposes a heavy burden on the defendant or the court, and where the plaintiff is unable to offer any specific reasons of convenience supporting his choice. If substantial weight were given to the possibility of an unfavorable change in law, however, dismissal might be barred even where trial in the chosen forum was plainly inconvenient.

The Court of Appeals' decision is inconsistent with this Court's earlier *forum non conveniens* decisions in another respect. Those decisions have repeatedly emphasized the need to retain flexibility. In *Gilbert*, the Court refused to identify specific circumstances "which will justify or require either grant or denial of remedy." Similarly, in *Koster*, the Court rejected the contention that where a trial would involve inquiry into the internal affairs of a foreign corporation, dismissal was always appropriate. "That is one, but only one, factor which may show convenience." And in *Williams v. Green Bay & Western R. Co.*, 326 U.S. 549, 557 (1946), we stated that we would not lay down a rigid rule to govern discretion, and that "[e]ach case turns on its facts." If central emphasis were placed on any one factor, the *forum non conveniens* doctrine would lose much of the very flexibility that makes it so valuable.

In fact, if conclusive or substantial weight were given to the possibility of a change in law, the *forum non conveniens* doctrine would become virtually useless. Jurisdiction and venue requirements are often easily satisfied. As a result, many plaintiffs are able to choose from among several forums. Ordinarily, these plaintiffs will select that forum whose choice-of-law rules are most advantageous. Thus, if the possibility of an unfavorable change in substantive law is given substantial weight in the *forum non conveniens* inquiry, dismissal would rarely be proper. * * *

The Court of Appeals' approach is not only inconsistent with the purpose of the *forum non conveniens* doctrine, but also poses substantial practical problems. If the possibility of a change in law were given substantial weight, deciding motions to dismiss on the ground of *forum non conveniens* would become quite difficult. Choice-of-law analysis would become extremely important, and the courts would frequently be required to interpret the law of foreign jurisdictions. First, the trial court would have to determine what law would apply if the case were tried in the chosen forum, and what law would apply if the case were tried in the alternative forum. It would then have to compare the rights, remedies, and procedures available under the law that would be applied in each forum. Dismissal would be appropriate only if the court concluded that the law applied by the alternative forum is as favorable to the plaintiff as that of the chosen forum. The doctrine of *forum non conveniens*, however, is designed in part to help courts avoid conducting complex exercises in comparative law. As we stated in *Gilbert*, the public interest factors point towards dismissal where the court would be required to "untangle problems in conflict of laws, and in law foreign to itself."

Upholding the decision of the Court of Appeals would result in other practical problems. At least where the foreign plaintiff named an American manufacturer as defendant, a court could not dismiss the case on grounds of *forum non conveniens* where dismissal might lead to an unfavorable change in law. The American courts, which are already extremely attractive to foreign plaintiffs, would become even more attractive. The flow of litigation into the United States would increase and further congest already crowded courts.

The Court of Appeals based its decision, at least in part, on an analogy between dismissals on grounds of *forum non conveniens* and transfers between federal courts pursuant to § 1404(a). In *Van Dusen v. Barrack*, 376 U.S. 612 (1964), this Court ruled that a § 1404(a) transfer should not result in a change in the applicable law. Relying on dictum in an earlier Third Circuit opinion interpreting *Van Dusen*, the court below held that that principle is also applicable to a dismissal on *forum non conveniens* grounds. However, § 1404(a) transfers are different than dismissals on the ground of *forum non conveniens*.

Congress enacted § 1404(a) to permit change of venue between federal courts. Although the statute was drafted in accordance with the doctrine of *forum non conveniens*, it was intended to be a revision rather than a codification of the common law. District courts were given more discretion to transfer under § 1404(a) than they had to dismiss on grounds of *forum non conveniens*.

The reasoning employed in *Van Dusen v. Barrack* is simply inapplicable to dismissals on grounds of *forum non conveniens*. That case did not discuss the common-law doctrine. Rather, it focused on "the construction and application" of § 1404(a). Emphasizing the remedial purpose of the statute, *Barrack* concluded that Congress could not have intended a transfer to be accompanied by a change in law. The statute was designed as a "federal housekeeping measure," allowing easy change of venue within a unified federal system. The Court feared that if a change in venue were accompanied by a change in law, forum-shopping parties would take unfair advantage of the relaxed standards for transfer. The rule was necessary to ensure the just and efficient operation of the statute.

We do not hold that the possibility of an unfavorable change in law should *never* be a relevant consideration in a *forum non conveniens* inquiry. Of course, if the remedy provided by the alternative forum is so clearly inadequate or unsatisfactory that it is no remedy at all, the unfavorable change in law may be given substantial weight; the district court may conclude that dismissal would not be in the interest of justice.[22] In these cases, however, the remedies that would be provided by the Scottish courts do not fall within this category. Although the relatives of the decedents may not be able to rely on a strict liability theory, and although their potential damages award may be smaller, there is no danger that they will be deprived of any remedy or treated unfairly.

III

The Court of Appeals also erred in rejecting the District Court's *Gilbert* analysis. The Court of Appeals stated that more weight should have been given to the plaintiff's choice of forum, and criticized the District Court's analysis of the private and public interests. However, the District Court's decision regarding the deference due plaintiff's choice of forum was appropriate. Furthermore, we do not believe that the District Court abused its discretion in weighing the private and public interests.

A

The District Court acknowledged that there is ordinarily a strong presumption in favor of the plaintiff's choice of forum, which may be overcome only when the private and public interest factors clearly point towards trial in the alternative forum. It held, however, that the presumption applied with less force when the plaintiff or real parties in interest are foreign.

22. At the outset of any *forum non conveniens* inquiry, the court must determine whether there exists an alternative forum. Ordinarily, this requirement will be satisfied when the defendant is "amenable to process" in the other jurisdiction. *Gilbert*, 330 U.S., at 506–507. In rare circumstances, however, where the remedy offered by the other forum is clearly unsatisfactory, the other forum may not be an adequate alternative, and the initial requirement may not be satisfied. Thus, for example, dismissal would not be appropriate where the alternative forum does not permit litigation of the subject matter of the dispute. Cf. *Phoenix Canada Oil Co. Ltd. v. Texaco, Inc.*, 78 F.R.D. 445 (Del.1978)(court refuses to dismiss, where alternative forum is Ecuador, it is unclear whether Ecuadorean tribunal will hear the case, and there is no generally codified Ecuadorean legal remedy for the unjust enrichment and tort claims asserted).

The District Court's distinction between resident or citizen plaintiffs and foreign plaintiffs is fully justified. In *Koster*, the Court indicated that a plaintiff's choice of forum is entitled to greater deference when the plaintiff has chosen the home forum. When the home forum has been chosen, it is reasonable to assume that this choice is convenient. When the plaintiff is foreign, however, this assumption is much less reasonable. Because the central purpose of any *forum non conveniens* inquiry is to ensure that the trial is convenient, a foreign plaintiff's choice deserves less deference.

B

The *forum non conveniens* determination is committed to the sound discretion of the trial court. It may be reversed only when there has been a clear abuse of discretion; where the court has considered all relevant public and private interest factors, and where its balancing of these factors is reasonable, its decision deserves substantial deference. Here, the Court of Appeals expressly acknowledged that the standard of review was one of abuse of discretion. In examining the District Court's analysis of the public and private interest, however, the Court of Appeals seems to have lost sight of this rule, and substituted its own judgment for that of the District Court.

(1)

In analyzing the private interest factors, the District Court stated that the connections with Scotland are "overwhelming." This characterization may be somewhat exaggerated. Particularly with respect to the question of relative ease of access to sources of proof, the private interests point in both directions. As respondent emphasizes, records concerning the design, manufacture, and testing of the propeller and plane are located in the United States. She would have greater access to sources of proof relevant to her strict liability and negligence theories if trial were held here. However, the District Court did not act unreasonably in concluding that fewer evidentiary problems would be posed if the trial were held in Scotland. A large proportion of the relevant evidence is located in Great Britain.

The Court of Appeals found that the problems of proof could not be given any weight because Piper and Hartzell failed to describe with specificity the evidence they would not be able to obtain if trial were held in the United States. It suggested that defendants seeking *forum non conveniens* dismissal must submit affidavits identifying the witnesses they would call and the testimony these witnesses would provide if the trial were held in the alternative forum. Such detail is not necessary. Piper and Hartzell have moved for dismissal precisely because many crucial witnesses are located beyond the reach of compulsory process, and thus are difficult to identify or interview. Requiring extensive investigation would defeat the purpose of their motion. Of course, defendants must provide enough information to enable the District Court to balance the parties' interests. Our examination of the record convinces us that sufficient information was provided here. Both Piper and Hartzell submitted affidavits describing the evidentiary problems they would face if the trial were held in the United States.

The District Court correctly concluded that the problems posed by the inability to implead potential third-party defendants clearly supported holding the trial in Scotland. Joinder of the pilot's estate, Air Navigation, and McDonald is critical to the presentation of petitioners' defense. If Piper and Hartzell can show that the accident was caused not by a design defect, but rather by the negligence of the pilot, the plane's owners, or the charter company, they will be relieved of all liability. It is true, of course, that if Hartzell and Piper were found liable after a trial in the United States, they could institute an action for indemnity or contribution against these parties in Scotland. It would be far more convenient, however, to resolve all claims in one trial. The Court of Appeals rejected this argument. Forcing petitioners to rely on actions for indemnity or contributions would be "burdensome" but not "unfair." Finding that trial in the plaintiff's chosen forum would be burdensome, however, is sufficient to support dismissal on grounds of *forum non conveniens*.

(2)

The District Court's review of the factors relating to the public interest was also reasonable. On the basis of its choice-of-law analysis, it concluded that if the case were tried in the Middle District of Pennsylvania, Pennsylvania law would apply to Piper and Scottish law to Hartzell. It stated that a trial involving two sets of laws would be confusing to the jury. It also noted its own lack of familiarity with Scottish law. Consideration of these problems was clearly appropriate under *Gilbert*; in that case we explicitly held that the need to apply foreign law pointed towards dismissal. The Court of Appeals found that the District Court's choice-of-law analysis was incorrect, and that American law would apply to both Hartzell and Piper. Thus, lack of familiarity with foreign law would not be a problem. Even if the Court of Appeals' conclusion is correct, however, all other public interest factors favored trial in Scotland.

Scotland has a very strong interest in this litigation. The accident occurred in its airspace. All of the decedents were Scottish. Apart from Piper and Hartzell, all potential plaintiffs and defendants are either Scottish or English. As we stated in *Gilbert*, there is "a local interest in having localized controversies decided at home." Respondent argues that American citizens have an interest in ensuring that American manufacturers are deterred from producing defective products, and that additional deterrence must be obtained if Piper and Hartzell were tried in the United States, where they could be sued on the basis of both negligence and strict liability. However, the incremental deterrence that would be gained if this trial were held in an American court is likely to be insignificant. The American interest in this accident is simply not sufficient to justify the enormous commitment of judicial time and resources that would inevitably be required if the case were to be tried here.

IV

The Court of Appeals erred in holding that the possibility of an unfavorable change in law bars dismissal on the ground of *forum non conveniens*. It also erred in rejecting the District Court's *Gilbert* analysis. The District Court properly decided that the presumption in favor of the respondent's forum choice applied with less than maximum force because the real parties in interest are foreign. It did not act unreasonably in deciding that the private interests pointed towards trial in Scotland. Nor did it act unreasonably in deciding that the public interests favored trial in Scotland. Thus, the judgment of the Court of Appeals is

Reversed.

Notes and Questions

1. Forum Non Conveniens *and Reasonable Jurisdiction.* The *forum non conveniens* doctrine is an important tool for courts faced with problems of concurrent jurisdiction. Rather than employ the restrictive statutory analysis of *American Banana* or the jurisdictional balancing test of *Timberlane*, *Piper* uses *forum non conveniens* as a factually-oriented test to evaluate the reasonableness of one jurisdiction against another. Note that there is no doubt in *Piper* that the federal court in Pennsylvania has adjudicatory jurisdiction over both Piper and Hartzell. Piper and Hartzell (though apparently not the pilot's estate, A.V. Navigation, and McDonald) could be sued in Pennsylvania. The question in the case is whether, in the trial court's opinion, it is unreasonable to try them there.

2. Forum Non Conveniens *and Judicial Discretion. Piper* establishes how discretionary may be a trial court's power to dismiss on *forum non conveniens* grounds. In effect the Supreme Court asks a trial court to reasonably weigh public and private interests and to determine the existence of an adequate alternative forum. Under what circumstances may an appeals court review and reverse a trial court's decision which is so based on the fact-specific nature of a particular case? *In re* Disaster at Riyadh Airport, Saudi Arabia, 540 F.Supp. 1141 (D.D.C.1982), and Nai–Chao v. Boeing Co., 555 F.Supp. 9 (N.D.Cal.1982), show trial courts willing to dismiss cases involving foreign plaintiffs where an alternative forum is adequate and where no overwhelming U.S. forum interest outweighs the problems of federal court congestion and overrides local interests in the case at hand. However, in *In re* Air Disaster Near Bombay, India on January 1, 1978, 531 F.Supp. 1175 (W.D.Wash.1982), the trial court denies a motion for a *forum non conveniens* dismissal, ruling there is no adequate alternative forum.

3. *The Foreign Plaintiff. Forum non conveniens* cases are sometimes ironic. In a typical case, a "far-away" foreign plaintiff chooses voluntarily to bring an action in the United States. The U.S. defendant then asserts that the U.S. court is not a "convenient" site for the action, even though it is the

foreign plaintiff who chose the "inconvenient" forum otherwise apparently "home" to the defendant. Does the irony demonstrate the importance of public interest factors when a court decides a *forum non conveniens* request?

Piper holds that less deference should be granted to a plaintiff's choice of a U.S. forum when the plaintiff is foreign. However, does it matter that *Piper* "did not consider the jurisdictional provisions of various FCN [friendship, commerce, and navigation] treaties which grant foreign plaintiffs equal access to American courts and apply with the force of statutory law"? Note, Maria A. Mazzola, "*Forum Non Conveniens* and Foreign Plaintiffs: Addressing the Unanswered Questions of *Reyno*," 6 *Fordham Journal of International Law* 577, 604 (1983).

4. Forum Non Conveniens *and International Lawyering Tactics.* Look, too, at *Piper* as a good example of lawyering tactics in international litigation. Plaintiffs' lawyer makes the first move, using his secretary to commence the action in a California state court on her home turf far away from the accident, the families of the decedent, and most, if not all, possible defendants. From then on, the tactical moves are those of defendants' lawyers. First, the case is removed to federal court in California where service on Hartzell is quashed. Second, the case is transferred to federal court in Pennsylvania, nearer Piper and Hartzell and further from plaintiffs' attorney. Third, defendants persuade the trial court and the Supreme Court to dismiss the case on *forum non conveniens* grounds. What likelihood is there that the California lawyer who initiated the action in California state court will follow the case all the way back to Scotland? Could the California attorney even hope to litigate the case in the United Kingdom? From a lawyering point of view, can the *Piper* case be viewed as the attempt of a California lawyer to use liberal U.S. jurisdictional rules to "capture" a litigation with little California connection being blocked by lawyers for Piper and Hartzell who use removal, transfer, and *forum non conveniens* rules as a way to "return" the case to Scotland where the case is most intimately connected? How much more "advanced" is this procedure than what went on in *American Banana* 72 years before?

5. *The States and* Forum Non Conveniens. The Texas Supreme Court has held that the Texas legislature abolished the doctrine of *forum non conveniens* as long ago as 1913. Dow Chemical Co. v. Alfaro, 786 S.W.2d 674 (Tex.1990), *cert. denied*, 498 U.S. 1024, 111 S.Ct. 671, 112 L.Ed.2d 663 (1991). This curious judgment evoked four vigorous dissents, one by Justice Cook:

> Like turn-of-the century wildcatters, the plaintiffs in this case searched all across the nation for a place to make their claims. Through three courts they moved, filing their lawsuits on one coast and then on the other. By each of those courts the plaintiffs were rejected, and so they continued their search for a more willing forum. Their efforts are finally rewarded. Today they hit pay dirt in Texas.
>
> No reason exists, in law or in policy, to support their presence in this state. The legislature adopted within the statute the phrase "may be enforced" to permit plaintiffs to sue in Texas, irrespective of where

they live or where the cause of action arose. The legislature did not adopt this statute, however, to remove from our courts all discretion to dismiss. To use the statute to sweep away, completely and finally, a common law doctrine painstakingly developed over the years is to infuse the statute with a power not contained in the words. Properly read, the statute is asymmetrical. Although it confers upon the plaintiffs an absolute right to bring claims in our courts, it does not impose upon our courts an absolute responsibility to entertain those claims.

Even if the statute supported the court's interpretation, however, I would remain unwilling to join in the opinion. The decision places too great a burden on defendants who are citizens of our state because, by abolishing *forum non conveniens*, the decision exposes our citizens to the claims of any plaintiff, no matter how distant from Texas is that plaintiff's home or cause of action. The interest of Texas in these disputes is likely to be as slight as the relationship of the plaintiffs to Texas. The interest of other nations, on the other hand, is likely to be substantial. For these reasons, I fear the decision allows assertions of jurisdiction by Texas courts that are so unfair and unreasonable as to violate the due process clause of the federal constitution.

Id. at 697. The Texas legislature responded to *Dow Chemical* by enacting a limited *forum non conveniens* statute in 1993. See Louise Ellen Teitz, *Transnational Litigation* § 3–5, at 123–25 (1996).

Not only the due process clause, but also federal common law might pose a problem for the majority in *Dow Chemical*. As we see below in the *Sabbatino Case*, the federal courts are able to elaborate a federal common law in certain areas of special concern to national interests such as foreign affairs. See Gary Born, "Forum Non Conveniens Held Unavailable Under Texas Law," 18 *International Business Lawyer* 392 (1990). Moreover, in diversity cases, the federal courts will apply the federal *forum non conveniens* doctrine, even in Texas. See Villar v. Crowley Maritime Corp., 780 F.Supp. 1467, 1483–85 (S.D.Tex.1992). However, in American Dredging Co. v. Miller, 510 U.S. 443, 114 S.Ct. 981, 127 L.Ed.2d 285 (1994), the Supreme Court passed by an opportunity to help nationalize the doctrine, holding that in admiralty cases states acting under the Jones Act and the "savings to suiters clause," which gives concurrent jurisdiction to U.S. state courts in certain admiralty actions, do not have to apply the federal *forum non conveniens* doctrine. Justice Scalia's majority opinion concludes that "maritime commerce in general does not require a uniform rule of *forum non conveniens*." *Id.* at 456, 114 S.Ct. at 990, 127 L.Ed.2d at 299. In dissent, Justice Kennedy for himself and Justice Thomas disapprove, believing "that *forum non conveniens* is an established feature of the general maritime law." *Id.* at 466, 114 S.Ct. at 993, 127 L.Ed.2d at 305. *American Dredging* involves only U.S. actors, however, and the Supreme Court might reach "a different result if those who raise the *forum non conveniens* objection are of foreign nationality." *Id.* at 469, 114 S.Ct. at 996, 127 L.Ed.2d at 307.

MARK W. JANIS, "THE DOCTRINE OF FORUM NON CONVENIENS AND THE BHOPAL CASE"

34 *Netherlands International Law Review* 192 (1987).

1. THE DOCTRINE OF *FORUM NON CONVENIENS*

1.1 Origins of the doctrine

It is generally acknowledged that a law review article by Paxton Blair in 1929,[3] popularized the term *forum non conveniens* in American law. To what degree the term denominated an already extant practice is not an easy question. Characterizing the existing American cases, Blair referred to Moliere's M. Jourdain: "he had been speaking prose all his life without knowing it." Subsequent commentators have argued, however, that Blair overestimated the foundation laid by the early case law.[5]

Blair relied heavily on a 1926 Scottish case heard in the House of Lords, *Société du Gaz Paris v. Société Anonyme de Navigation "Les Armateurs Français."* There the court held:

> If in the whole circumstances of the case it be discovered that there is a real unfairness to one of the suitors in permitting the choice of a forum which is not the natural or proper forum, either on the ground of convenience of trial or the residence or domicile of parties, or of its being either the *locus contractus,* or the *locus solutionis,* then the doctrine of *forum non conveniens* is properly applied.

Despite the term's Latin rendering, it does not seem that Scots law borrowed the term from the Continent. It is possible that the ancestor of *forum non conveniens* may be the Scottish doctrine of *forum non competens*, a plea used as long ago as 1610, "which normally was directed to a lack of jurisdiction, [but which] was [also] sustained in cases where the jurisdiction seemed clear but the parties were non-residents and trial in Scotland would have been inconvenient." In any event, *forum non conveniens* appears to have first entered modern cases in 1873 in the Scots case, *Macadam v. Macadam*. Within a few years, the term was also to be seen, albeit infrequently, in English cases where it was viewed as a development in the procedural law concerning abuse of process.

There had been American cases as early as 1793 where judges had refused to hear cases between aliens involving foreign transactions. In 1804, Chief Justice John Marshall held that federal courts sitting in admiralty cases did not have to adjudicate disputes between aliens, a holding thereafter influential in American maritime law. However, these cases upholding the discretionary power of American courts to

3. P. Blair, "The Doctrine of Forum Non Conveniens in Anglo–American Law", 29 Columbia LR (1929) p. 1.

5. Almost two decades after Blair wrote his article, Barrett concluded that even though the term *forum non conveniens* had become popular, only a half dozen states and, in 1947, the federal courts, actually incorporated the doctrine. See E.L. Barrett, "The Doctrine of *Forum Non Conveniens,*" 35 California LR (1947) pp. 380, 388–389.

refuse to hear cases within their proper jurisdiction had not been molded into a coherent doctrinal framework until Blair's 1929 article.

Blair's purpose was to address the problems caused by a flood of litigation in state courts in the "larger centers of population." Blair suggested that an expanded use of the doctrine of *forum non conveniens*, as already elaborated in the English and Scottish law, could be a way of alleviating court congestion without needing to rely upon new statutory legislation. He admitted he could find only one use of the term in existing New York case law, but felt that *forum non conveniens* was not constitutionally impermissible, and that cases like *forum non conveniens* were already not uncommon in American law. Blair's lead was soon followed, not only in the legal literature, but in the case law.

1.2 Development of the doctrine in federal practice

The settled establishment of the doctrine of *forum non conveniens* in American law came in 1947, in a pair of United States Supreme Court decisions: *Gulf Oil Corp. v. Gilbert* and *Koster v. Lumbermens Mutual Casualty Co.* In *Gilbert*, in an opinion written by Justice Jackson, the Court asked "whether the United States District Court has inherent power to dismiss a suit pursuant to the doctrine of *forum non conveniens* and, if so, whether that power was abused in this case." Gilbert brought suit against Gulf Oil alleging that Gulf negligently delivered gasoline to his Virginia warehouse tanks and pumps causing an explosion and fire. The plaintiff was a resident of Virginia, and the defendant was incorporated in Pennsylvania and qualified to do business in Virginia and New York. Suit was brought in the federal district court in New York on the basis of diversity of citizenship; there was no federal question involved. The district court applied the doctrine of *forum non conveniens* so that the case could be tried in Virginia; the court of appeal reversed; the Supreme Court in turn reversed the court of appeal.

The Supreme Court held in *Gilbert* that although jurisdiction and venue were proper, *forum non conveniens* could still be applied. Indeed,

> [i]n all cases in which the doctrine of *forum non conveniens* comes into play, it presupposes at least two forums in which the defendant is amenable to process; the doctrine furnishes criteria for choice between them.

Citing cases and literature, *inter alia*, *Les Armateurs Français* and Blair, the Court held that the "doctrine leaves much to the discretion of the court," but listed the interests that the court needed to weigh. These the Court divided into private interest factors, e.g., access to sources of proof, availability of compulsory process for unwilling witnesses, and "all other practical problems that make trial of a case easy, expeditious, and inexpensive," and public interest factors, e.g., court congestion, "having localized controversies decided at home," and "having the trial of a diversity case in a forum that is at home with the state law that must govern the case." The Court ruled that the *forum non conveniens* presumption must be with the plaintiff: "unless the balance is strongly in favor of the defendants, the plaintiff's choice of forum should rarely be disturbed." However, in *Gilbert* the Court held that the district court could rightly dismiss on *forum non conveniens* grounds: the plaintiff was not a resident of New York, all the witnesses and evidence were to be found in Virginia, and the law likely to be applied was the law of Virginia, not New York.

In *Koster,* the Supreme Court dealt with a stockholders derivative suit where a New York shareholder sought to have a New York federal district court hear his case against Illinois corporate and individual defendants for breach of trust. Following in the wake of *Gilbert,* Mr. Justice Jackson wrote that in making a *forum non conveniens* determination "the ultimate inquiry is where trial will best serve the convenience of the parties and the ends of justice." The defendant argued that the bulk of evidence was in Illinois and that Illinois law would be applicable, but the plaintiff refused to support his claim that suit should be brought in New York. The Supreme Court held that the district court could, as it did in *Koster,* dismiss the case on *forum non conveniens* grounds when "in a derivative action ... a defendant shows much harassment and plaintiff's response not only discloses so little countervailing benefit to himself in the choice of forum as it does here, but indicates such disadvantage as to support the inference that the forum he chose would not ordinarily be thought a suitable one to decide the controversy."

The *forum non conveniens* doctrine was partly transformed into United States federal law not long after the *Gilbert* and *Koster* cases. In 1948 Congress enacted the federal transfer statute which provides: "For the convenience of parties and witnesses, in the interest of justice, a district court may transfer any civil action to any other district or division where it might have been brought." So, in cases on facts like *Gilbert* and *Koster* where suit has been brought in one federal district court and the defendant wishes to move the action to another federal district court, the federal transfer statute rather than the judicial doctrine of *forum non conveniens* ought to be employed.

However, the federal transfer statute applies only to the transfer of cases within the United States federal judicial system. So, when defendants seek to move from one state court to another state court, or from a United States state or federal court to the court of a foreign country, reliance upon the judicial doctrine of *forum non conveniens* is still appropriate. This was, for example, true in the most important United States Supreme Court case to be decided on *forum non conveniens* grounds since the *Gilbert/Koster* pair of cases in 1947, i.e., *Piper Aircraft Co. v. Reyno.* * * *

* * * It is against the background of *Gilbert* and *Koster* and, especially *Piper,* that the employment of *forum non conveniens* in *Bhopal* must be surveyed.

2. The Bhopal Case

2.1 The accident

The industrial accident at the Union Carbide plant in Bhopal, India on December 3, 1984, released methyl isocyanate gas which killed more than 2,000 people and injured about 200,000. Newspaper investigations of the tragedy indicated that there were numerous violations of the operating codes established both by the company operating the plant, Union Carbide India Limited, and its parent company, Union Carbide Corporation. There may well have been negligence not only by those engaged in making the lethal chemical used in pesticides but also by the Indian governmental bodies charged with setting and enforcing safety standards. The factual pattern of the disaster and the allocation of legal responsibility for it are incredibly tangled webs.

2.2 The commencement of the litigation

Immediately after the accident, some American lawyers made an unseemly rush to Bhopal. As the *New York Times* reported: "Right behind the stream of scientists, executives, officials, aid givers, and others who have come to this central Indian city after the gas leak last week are American lawyers, members of a breed of legal specialists seen by some as ambulance chasers and by others as champions of the individual against the corporation and of industrial safety and consumer protection." The lawyers sought to bring suit for the Bhopal victims in United States courts not only because of more favorable United States tort law and prospects for high jury damage awards, but because of the contingent fees (sometimes as high as 30%–40% of any award) which American lawyers may be assigned in tort cases. The mammoth sums possibly available to American lawyers representing Bhopal claimants raised serious ethical issues for the American bar.

However, not only American lawyers were interested in suing Union Carbide in American courts. On March 9, 1985, the *New York Times* reported that the Indian Government had also decided to sue on behalf of the Indian victims in United States courts in order "to secure higher compensation and also because Union Carbide has to share responsibility for the gas leak at its Indian subsidiary." On March 29, 1985, the Indian Government enacted the Bhopal Gas Leak Disaster (Processing of Claims) Act (21 of 1985), a statute which vested in the Indian Government the exclusive right to represent the Indian plaintiffs in the Bhopal case in India and elsewhere. On April 8, 1985, pursuant to the Act, the Indian Government filed its own claims against Union Carbide in the American courts.

The Indian Government claims, along with some 144 lawsuits brought privately, were all consolidated on June 28, 1985, in a consolidated complaint filed in the federal district court for the Southern District of New York. The trial court created a Plaintiffs' Executive Committee composed of lawyers representing both the Indian Government and the private claimants so as to coordinate the plaintiffs' side of the litigation. The court emphasized that none of the Plaintiffs' Executive Committee had participated in the rush to India to "sign up" Indian plaintiffs, a rush the Court characterized as doing "little to better the American image in the Third World—or anywhere else."

However, even the more respectable face of the plaintiffs' lawyers would do no good. In an opinion rendered on May 12, 1986, Judge John F. Keenan, the United States District Court judge hearing the *Bhopal* case, concluded, using a *forum non conveniens* analysis, that the United States action should be dismissed so that Indian courts could adjudicate the matter. Keenan's opinion was affirmed in a modified form even more deferential to India by a unanimous three judge panel of the United States Court of Appeals for the Second Circuit in an opinion announced on January 14, 1987, written by Judge Mansfield before his death on January 7, 1987.

2.3 The adequacy of the Indian legal system

With the filing of the Indian Government claims, the *Bhopal* case showed the peculiar circumstance of a government arguing that its own courts were less preferable than those of a foreign State for the resolution of disputes touching on both legal systems. When the defendant, Union Carbide, raised the *forum non conveniens* argument, the Indian Government was in the even more awkward posture of contending (as part of the Plaintiffs' Executive Committee) that the Indian courts were actually inadequate for handling the Bhopal claims. Although both the trial court and the appeals court recognized that their *forum non conveniens* analysis was to be conducted pursuant to the holdings in *Gilbert* and *Piper*, neither the 1947 cases nor the 1981 case faced the question of whether the arguably more convenient forum was up to the task of adequately adjudicating the dispute at hand. It had been assumed that the courts of Virginia (in *Gilbert*), Illinois (in *Koster*), and the United Kingdom (in *Piper)*, were just as sophisticated as the courts in which the *forum non conveniens* dismissal was sought.

In *Bhopal*, both the District Court and the Court of Appeals concluded that the Indian courts could properly adjudicate the accident cases. Moreover, while the District Court imposed certain United States procedural guarantees on the Indian litigation, the Court of Appeals, even more respectful towards the foreign proceedings, modified the trial court's order and imposed none.

In reviewing the competence of the Indian courts, the District Court weighed the testimony of an American law professor, Marc Galanter, an expert on Indian law opposing the adequacy of the Indian legal system against the testimony of two senior Indian advocates, N. A. Palkhivala, formerly Ambassador of India to the United States, and J. B. Dadachanji arguing in favor of the Indian system. The court thought the conclusions of Professor Galanter "far less persuasive than those of" the two Indian lawyers. The District Court's opinion was summarized and approved by the Court of Appeal:

> The Indian judiciary was found by the court to be a developed, independent and progressive one, which has demonstrated its capability of circumventing long delays and backlogs prevalent in the Indian courts' handling of ordinary cases by devising special expediting procedures in extraordinary cases, such as by directing its High

Court to hear them on a daily basis, appointing special tribunals to handle them, and assigning daily hearing duties to a single judge. [The District Court judge] found that Indian courts have competently dealt with complex technological issues. Since the Bhopal Act provides that the case may be treated speedily, effectively and to the best advantage of the claimants, and since the Union of India represents the claimants, the prosecution of the claims is expected to be adequately staffed by the Attorney General or Solicitor General of India.

The tort law of India, which is derived from common law and British precedent, was found to be suitable for resolution of legal issues arising in cases involving highly complex technology. Moreover, Indian courts would be in a superior position to construe and apply applicable Indian laws and standards than would courts of the United States. Third parties may be interpleaded under Order 1, Rule 10(2) of the Indian Code of Civil Procedure, and defendants may seek contribution from third parties. The absence in India of a class action procedure comparable to that in federal courts here was found not to deprive the plaintiffs of a remedy, in view of existing Indian legal authorization for "representative" suits under Order 1, Rule 8 of the Indian Code of Civil Procedure, which would permit an Indian court to create representative classes. Judge Keenan further found that the absence of juries and contingent fee arrangements in India would not deprive the claimants of an adequate remedy.

Despite the District Court judge's satisfaction that the Indian courts were capable of adequately trying the Bhopal cases, he hedged his *forum non conveniens* dismissal of the American causes of action with three conditions. Only the first of these, that "Union Carbide shall consent to submit to the jurisdiction of the courts of India, and shall continue to waive defenses based upon the statute of limitations," was accepted by the Court of Appeals. The second condition, that "Union Carbide shall agree to satisfy any judgment rendered by an Indian court, and if applicable, upheld by an appellate court in that country, where such judgment and affirmance comport with the minimal requirements of due process," was rejected by the Court of Appeals first because an Indian judgment would normally be enforceable in the United States if in accord with due process and second because the condition runs "the risk that it may also be interpreted as providing for a lesser standard than we would otherwise require." The third condition, that "Union Carbide shall be subject to discovery under the model of the United States Federal Rules of Civil Procedure after appropriate demand by plaintiffs," was also rejected: "Basic justice dictates that both sides be treated equally."

2.4 Private and public interest factors

Having determined that Indian courts were an acceptable alternative to American courts for the adjudication of the Bhopal suits, the District and Circuit Courts turned to the weighing of private and public interest factors at the heart of any *forum non conveniens* inquiry. Both courts follows *Piper* in holding that since the plaintiffs in *Bhopal* were foreign, their choice of an American court was due less deference than had they been United States citizens seeking to sue at home. Given the factual situation surrounding the Bhopal accident, the courts had little difficulty in deciding that the claims arising from it should be decided in India, not America.

Looking first at the private interest factors, the District Court compared *Bhopal* to *Piper* where private interests pointed in two ways: "By contrast, this Court finds that the private interests point strongly one way"—India. The Circuit Court agreed:

> In short, the plant has been constructed and managed by Indians in India. No Americans were employed at the plant at the time of the accident. In the five years from 1980 to 1984, although there were more than 1,000 Indians employed at the plant, only one American was employed there and he left in 1982. No Americans visited the plant for more than one year prior to the accident, and during the 5–year period before the accident the communications between the plant and the United States were almost non-existent.
>
> The vast majority of material witnesses and documentary proof bearing on causation of and liability for the accident is located in India, not the United States, and would be more accessible to an Indian court than to a United States court. The records are almost entirely in Hindi or other Indian languages, understandable to an Indian court without translation. The witnesses for the most part do not speak English but Indian languages, understood by an Indian court but not by an American court. These witnesses could be required to appear in an Indian court but not in a court of the United States. Although witnesses in the United States could not be subpoenaed to appear in India, they are comparatively few in number and most are employed by [Union Carbide Corporation] which, as a party would produce them in India, with lower overall transportation costs than if the parties were to attempt to bring hundreds of Indian witnesses to the United States. Lastly, Judge Keenan properly concluded that an Indian court would be in a better position to direct and supervise a viewing of the Bhopal plant, which was sealed after the accident. Such a viewing could be of help to a court in determining liability issues.

Similarly, both courts decided that public interest factors tilted towards trying the case in India. Endorsing the findings of the District Court, the Circuit Court ruled:

> After a thorough review, the district court concluded that the public interest concerns, like the private ones, also weigh heavily in favor of India as the situs for trial and disposition of the cases. The accident and all the relevant events occurred in India. The victims, over 200,000 in number, are citizens of India and located there. The witnesses are almost entirely Indian citizens. The Union of India has a greater interest than does the United States in facilitat-

ing the trial and adjudication of the victims' claims. Despite the contentions of plaintiffs and amici that it would be in the public interest to avoid a "double standard" by requiring an American parent corporation (UCC) to submit to the jurisdiction of American courts, India has a stronger countervailing interest in adjudicating the claims in its courts according to its standards rather than having American values and standards of care imposed upon it.

India's interest is increased by the fact that it has for years treated UCIL as an Indian national, subjecting it to intensive regulations and governmental supervision of the construction, development and operation of the Bhopal plant, its emissions, water and air pollution, and safety precautions. Numerous Indian government officials have regularly conducted on-site inspections of the plant and approved its machinery and equipment, including its facilities for storage of the lethal methyl isocyanate gas that escaped and caused the disaster giving rise to the claims. Thus India has considered the plant to be an Indian one and the disaster to be an Indian problem. It therefore has a deep interest in ensuring compliance with its safety standards. Moreover, plaintiffs have conceded that in view of India's strong interest and its greater contacts with the plant, its operation, its employees, and the victims of the accident, the law of India, as the place where the tort occurred, will undoubtedly govern. In contrast, the American interests are relatively minor. Indeed, a long trial of the 145 cases here would unduly burden an already overburdened court; involving both jury hardship and heavy expense. It would face the court with numerous practical difficulties, including the most impossible task of attempting to understand extensive relevant Indian regulations published in a foreign language and the slow process of receiving testimony of scores of witnesses through interpreters.

The incongruity of finding that the public interest of India called for trying the *Bhopal* case in India even when the Indian Government sought to have it tried in America was rectified between the District Court opinion and that of the Circuit Court. The Government of India decided to support the judgment of the District Court. The private plaintiffs, however, continued in their opposition to the *forum non conveniens* dismissal.

3. Conclusion

The *Bhopal* decisions of the two American courts were proper and valuable applications of the *forum non conveniens* doctrine. Given the jurisdictional rules standing alone, the defendant Union Carbide Corporation was plainly within the adjudicatory competence of the United States. The factual context of the Bhopal accident, however, was such that for reasons both of private interests in a fair and convenient trial and public interests in a trial in the jurisdiction most closely linked to the accident, it was right that the case be tried in India and not the United States. The doctrine of *forum non conveniens* gave the American courts the discretion they needed to avoid the strict jurisdiction rules giving them power to hear the case and to choose, in a flexible fashion, to dismiss the case so that it could be tried very much more properly in India.

Furthermore, the doctrine of *forum non conveniens* so employed enabled the American courts and, by extension, the United States itself to avoid infringing upon the judicial competence and even the sovereignty of India. Too often the courts of the United States are accused of extending too far the extraterritorial jurisdiction of the United States. If the American courts had not applied *forum non conveniens* in the Bhopal case, they would, it is submitted, have been all too open to the accusation of overreaching, save perhaps for the curious choice of the Indian Government to support trial in the United States, at least in the arguments before the District Court. Once the Indian Government had taken its more natural position in the arguments before the Circuit Court in favor of adjudication in India, the deferential decisions of the two United States courts became valuable contributions to a tradition of international comity.

In a world increasingly filled with transactions and, sadly, accidents touching on more than one country, the need to properly allocate international judicial business becomes even more pressing. In time perhaps, public international law will help provide more answers to questions about the allocation of judicial competence between nations by the framing and application of international conventions. Until then, and, of course, in some cases even thereafter, States will have to moderate their extensions of jurisdiction to matters involving foreign countries by employing notions of comity and good sense. *Forum non conveniens* is one such useful notion, and it was rightly applied in the United States in the case of *Bhopal.*

Notes and Questions

1. *The Aftermath of the* Bhopal Case. Bi v. Union Carbide Chemicals & Plastics Co., 984 F.2d 582 (2d Cir.1993), an action brought by individual Indian victims of the Bhopal tragedy who sought to supplement the relief they ultimately won in the Indian courts, contains an interesting account of the aftermath of the *Bhopal Case.* In 1989, the Indian Supreme Court approved a settlement between the government of India representing all the victims and Union Carbide for $470 million. The Indian Supreme Court in a related decision that year also "upheld the constitutional validity of the Bhopal Act and confirmed the Indian Government's exclusive authority to compromise all claims arising out of the Bhopal disaster." *Id.* at 584. In 1990, Bi and another, class representatives for some of the Indian victims, filed suits against Union Carbide in Texas state court, arguing that the Indian government had a conflict of interest in trying to represent victims and that the settlement in India was too low. Union Carbide removed the suits to U.S. federal court in Texas, and the suits were then transferred to U.S. federal court in New York. The Southern District dismissed both actions under *forum non conveniens,* and the Second Circuit affirmed: "We hold that when a recognized democracy determines that the interests of the

victims of a mass tort that occurred within its borders will be best served if the foreign government exclusively represents the victims in courts around the world, we will not pass judgment on that determination * * *." *Id.* at 586.

2. *Judge-made Procedural Law.* Note that in *Gilbert* the Supreme Court rested the doctrine of *forum non conveniens* on the foundations of a court's "inherent power." *Forum non conveniens* is an excellent example of a procedure-facilitating rule based on judge-made common law. Contrast the source of the *forum non conveniens* doctrine with the statutory source of a rule achieving similar goals: the 1948 federal transfer statute, 28 U.S.C. § 1404 (a). Would anything be gained (or lost) if *forum non conveniens* were codified? Is a judge-made rule more responsive to changing notions of comity, *e.g.*, able to respond more readily to the development of case law in other countries accommodating (or not) conflicts of jurisdiction?

3. Forum Non Conveniens *and* International Shoe. Note that in the United States *forum non conveniens* is considered only if the court already has personal and subject matter jurisdiction over the defendants and the transaction. It is no coincidence that *forum non conveniens* formally entered into federal law in 1947, two years after International Shoe Co. v. State of Washington, 326 U.S. 310, 66 S.Ct. 154, 90 L.Ed. 95 (1945), extended the jurisdictional reach of state courts. After *International Shoe* plaintiffs had more choice about their courts. *Forum non conveniens* and the federal transfer statute moderated the new power of plaintiffs over forum selection.

4. *The Adequacy of the Foreign Legal System.* The U.S. Supreme Court chose not to review *Bhopal*, Executive Committee Members v. Union of India, 484 U.S. 871, 108 S.Ct. 199, 98 L.Ed.2d 150 (1987), letting stand the opinion of the Second Circuit. Thus, it did not consider the adequacy of the Indian legal system, a consideration also left unaddressed in its two key *forum non conveniens* decisions, *Gilbert* and *Piper*. Looking at the opinions of the trial court and the appellate court in *Bhopal*, we can see that they at least used another weighing test to evaluate the plausibility of justice being done in a foreign court, weighing here the testimony of conflicting expert witnesses. Is this an example, once again, of the judicial discretion built into *forum non conveniens*? In Bhatnagar v. Surrendra Overseas Ltd., 52 F.3d 1220 (3d Cir.1995), the Third Circuit holds that the potential for long delay in the Indian legal system is a permissible ground for denying a motion of *forum non conveniens*.

5. *International Mechanisms for the Resolution of Jurisdictional Conflicts.* Could a treaty or even an international court or panel help reconcile conflicts of jurisdiction better than ad hoc national judicial decision making? How might such a treaty or court be fashioned?

B. FOREIGN SOVEREIGN IMMUNITY

A variety of legal rules shield foreign sovereigns and their acts from the scrutiny of national courts. Although less pervasive nowadays than before, these rules generally have been grounded on the principle or policy that to implead foreign sovereigns before local courts or to challenge the legality of foreign sovereign acts could upset friendly relations between states. It has been reckoned that questions relating to the jurisdictional immunities of foreign sovereigns figure more before national courts than do any other questions of international law. Leo J. Bouchez, "The Nature and Scope of State Immunity from Jurisdiction and Execution," 10 *Netherlands Yearbook of International Law* 3, 4 (1979). In 1989, "a fairly ordinary year" for foreign sovereign immunities litigation in the U.S., there were altogether one Supreme Court decision, 19 reported judgments of federal appeals courts, 20 reported and seven unpublished but computer-available federal district court decisions, and one published state appellate court judgment relating to questions of foreign sovereign immunity. ABA Section of International Law and Practice, *Suing Foreign States: Newsletter of the Committee on Foreign Sovereign Immunity*, Vol. 1, No. 1, at 1, 10–15 (Spring 1990). In the United States, both the doctrine of sovereign immunity and the act of state doctrine examined in Part C may be said to be grounded on the judgment in 1812 of Chief Justice John Marshall in the case of *The Schooner Exchange.*

THE SCHOONER EXCHANGE v. McFADDON

11 U.S. (7 Cranch) 116, 3 L.Ed. 287 (1812).

This being a cause in which the sovereign right claimed by Napoleon, the reigning emperor of the French, and the political relations between the United States and France, were involved, it was, upon the suggestion of the Attorney General, ordered to a hearing in preference to other causes which stood before it on the docket.

It was an appeal from the sentence of the Circuit Court of the United States, for the district of Pennsylvania, which reversed the sentence of the District Court, and ordered the vessel to be restored to the libellants.

The case was this—on the 24th of August, 1811, *John McFaddon & William Greetham*, of the State of Maryland, filed their libel in the District Court of the United States, for the District of Pennsylvania, against the *Schooner Exchange*, setting forth that they were her sole owners, on the 27th of October, 1809, when she sailed from Baltimore, bound to St. Sebastians, in Spain. That while lawfully and peaceably pursuing her voyage, she was on the 30th of December, 1810, violently and forcibly taken by certain persons, acting under the decrees and orders of Napoleon, *Emperor of the French*, out of the custody of the libellants, and of their captain and agent, and was disposed of by those persons, or some of them, in violation of the rights of the libellants, and of the law of nations in that behalf. That she had been brought into the port of Philadelphia, and was then in the jurisdiction of that court, in possession of a certain *Dennis M. Begon*, her reputed captain or master. That no sentence or decree of condemnation had been pronounced against her, by any court of competent jurisdiction; but that the property of the libellants in her, remained unchanged and in full force. They therefore prayed the usual process of the court, to attach the vessel, and that she might be restored to them.

MARSHALL, *Ch. J.* Delivered the opinion of the Court as follows:

This case involves the very delicate and important inquiry, whether an American citizen can assert, in an American court, a title to an armed national vessel found within the waters of the United States. * * *

The jurisdiction of *courts* is a branch of that which is possessed by the nation as an independent sovereign power.

The jurisdiction of the nation within its own territory is necessarily exclusive and absolute. It is susceptible of no limitation not imposed by itself. Any restriction upon it, deriving validity from an external source, would imply a diminution of its sovereignty to the extent of the restriction, and an investment of that sovereignty to the same extent in that power which could impose such restrictions.

All exceptions, therefore, to the full and complete power of a nation within its own territories, must be traced up to the consent of the nation itself. They can flow from no other legitimate source.

This consent may be either express or implied. In the latter case, it is less determinate, exposed more to the uncertainties of construction; but, if understood, not less obligatory.

The world being composed of distinct sovereignties, possessing equal rights and equal independence, whose mutual benefit is promoted by intercourse with each other, and by an interchange of those good offices which humanity dictates and its wants require, all sovereigns have consented to a relaxation in practice, in cases under certain peculiar circumstances, of that absolute and complete jurisdiction within their respective territories which sovereignty confers. * * *

A nation would justly be considered as violating its faith, although that faith might not be expressly plighted, which should suddenly and without previous notice, exercise its territorial powers in a manner not consonant to the usages and received obligations of the civilized world.

This full and absolute territorial jurisdiction being alike the attribute of every sovereign, and being incapable of conferring extra-territorial power, would not seem to contemplate foreign sovereigns nor their sovereign rights as its objects. One sovereign being in no respect amenable to another; and being bound by obligations of the highest character not to degrade the dignity of his nation, by placing himself or its sovereign rights within the jurisdiction of another, can be supposed to enter a foreign territory only under an express license, or in the confidence that the immunities belonging to his independent sovereign station, though not expressly stipulated, are reserved by implication and will be extended to him.

This perfect equality and absolute independence of sovereigns, and this common interest impelling them to mutual intercourse, and an interchange of good offices with each other, have given rise to a class of cases in which every sovereign is understood to waive the exercise of a part of that complete exclusive territorial jurisdiction, which has been stated to be the attribute of every nation. * * *

When private individuals of one nation spread themselves through another as business or caprice may direct, mingling indiscriminately with the inhabitants of that other, or when merchant vessels enter for the purposes of trade, it would be obviously inconvenient and dangerous to society, and would subject the laws to continual infraction, and the government to degradation, if such individuals or merchants did not owe temporary and local allegiance, and were not amenable to the jurisdiction of the country. Nor can the foreign sovereign have any motive for wishing such exemption. His subjects thus passing into foreign countries, are not employed by him, nor are they engaged in national pursuits. Consequently there are powerful motives for not exempting persons of this description from the jurisdiction of the country in which they are found, and no one motive for requiring it. The implied license, therefore, under which they enter can never be construed to grant such exemption.

But in all respects different is the situation of a public armed ship. She constitutes a part of the military force of her nation; acts under the immediate and direct command of the sovereign; is employed by him in national objects. He has many and powerful motives for preventing those objects from being defeated by the interference of a foreign state. Such interference cannot take place without affecting his power and his dignity. The implied license therefore under which such vessel enters a friendly port, may reasonably be construed, and it seems to the Court, ought to be construed, as containing an exemption from the jurisdiction of the sovereign, within whose territory she claims the rites of hospitality.

Upon these principles, by the unanimous consent of nations, a foreigner is amenable to the laws of the place; but certainly in practice, nations have not yet asserted their jurisdiction over the public armed ships of a foreign sovereign entering a port open for their reception. * * *

It seems then to the Court, to be a principle of public law, that national ships of war, entering the port of a friendly power open for their reception are to be considered as exempted by the consent of that power from its jurisdiction. * * *

If the preceding reasoning be correct, the Exchange, being a public armed ship, in the service of a foreign sovereign, with whom the government of the United States is at peace, having entered an American port open for her reception, on the terms on which ships of war are generally permitted to enter the ports of a friendly power, must be considered as having come into the American territory, under an implied promise, that while necessarily within it, and demeaning herself in a friendly manner, she should be exempt from the jurisdiction of the country.

Notes and Questions

1. *The Historical Context.* In 1812, how anxious would Marshall be to have the U.S. legal system seize a French warship for the benefit of a private litigant? This was the very year the United States would go to war with Great Britain, France's enemy in the Napoleonic Wars. France and England were blockading each other's ports, and American merchant shipping was reaping large profits (and incurring considerable risks) in blockade running. Is it the mission of Marshall both to protect the dignity of France and to bolster the sovereignty of the United States? Notice Marshall's insistence upon how "distinct sovereignties" have "equal rights and equal independence."

2. *Sovereigns and the Forms of Jurisdiction.* Note that Marshall distinguished between "the jurisdiction of the courts" and the general jurisdiction "possessed by the nation as an independent sovereign power." Is this distinction an early sign of the development of what we would now call adjudicatory jurisdiction? Is the French government being protected just from the jurisdiction of the courts? Is Marshall's judgment broad enough to encompass protection from U.S. legislative and executive jurisdiction as well?

How similar is Marshall's belief in the "full and absolute territorial jurisdiction" of "every sovereign" to Holmes's belief a century later, in *American Banana* above, that "all legislation is *prima facie* territorial"? Both approaches certainly appear to limit extraterritorial jurisdiction. But why does Marshall make the territorial case so strongly when he means to upset it with an exception for the warships of foreign sovereigns?

3. *Public Law, U.S. Law, and International Law.* When Marshall wrote that it seems "to be a principle of public law, that national ships of war, entering the port of a friendly power open for their reception, are to be considered as exempted by the consent of that power from its jurisdiction," is he referring to a "principle" of U.S. law or of international law or of both?

VICTORY TRANSPORT, INC. v. COMISARIA GENERAL

336 F.2d 354 (2d Cir.1964), *cert. denied*, 381 U.S. 934, 85 S.Ct. 1763, 14 L.Ed.2d 698 (1965).

J. Joseph Smith, Circuit Judge: * * *

The appellant, a branch of the Spanish Ministry of Commerce, voyage-chartered the S.S. Hudson from its owner, the appellee, to transport a cargo of surplus wheat, purchased pursuant to the Agricultural Trade Development and Assistance Act, 7 U.S.C. § 1691 et seq., from Mobile, Alabama to one or two safe Spanish ports. * * *

Sovereign Immunity

Appellant's primary contention is that as an arm of the sovereign Government of Spain, it cannot be sued in the courts of the United States without its consent, which it declines to accord in this case. There is certainly a great deal of impressive precedent to support this contention, for the doctrine of the immunity of foreign sovereigns from the jurisdiction of our courts was early entrenched in our law by Chief Justice Marshall's historic decision in The Schooner Exchange v. McFaddon, 7 Cranch 116, 3 L.Ed. 287 (U.S. 1812). The doctrine originated in an era of personal sovereignty, when kings could theoretically do no wrong and when the exercise of authority by one sovereign over another indicated hostility or superiority. With the passing of that era, sovereign immunity has been retained by the courts chiefly to avoid possible embarrassment to those responsible for the conduct of the nation's foreign relations. However, because of the dramatic changes in the nature and functioning of sovereigns, particularly in the last half century, the wisdom of retaining the doctrine has been cogently questioned. Growing concern for individual rights and public morality, coupled with the increasing entry of governments into what had previously been regarded as private pursuits, has led a substantial number of nations to abandon the absolute theory of sovereign immunity in favor of a restrictive theory.

Meeting in Brussels in 1926, representatives of twenty nations, including all the major powers except the United States and Russia, signed a convention limiting sovereign immunity in the area of maritime commerce to ships and cargoes employed exclusively for public and non-commercial purposes. After World War II the United States began to restrict immunity by negotiating treaties obligating each contracting party to waive its sovereign immunity for state-controlled enterprises engaged in business activities within the territory of the other party. Fourteen such treaties were negotiated by our State Department in the decade 1948 to 1958. And in 1952 our State Department, in a widely publicized letter from Acting Legal Adviser Jack B. Tate to the Acting Attorney General Philip B. Perlman, announced that the Department would generally adhere to the restrictive theory of sovereign immunity, recognizing immunity for a foreign state's public or sovereign acts (*jure imperii*) but denying immunity to a foreign state's private or commercial acts (*jure gestionis*). * * *

Through the "Tate letter" the State Department has made it clear that its policy is to decline immunity to friendly foreign sovereigns in suits arising from private or commercial activity. But the "Tate letter" offers no guide-lines or criteria for differentiating between a sovereign's private and public acts. Nor have the courts or commentators suggested any satisfactory test. Some have looked to the nature of the transaction, categorizing as sovereign acts only activity which could not be performed by individuals. While this criterion is relatively easy to apply, it ofttimes produces rather astonishing results, such as the holdings of some European courts that purchases of bullets or shoes for the army, the erection of fortifications for defense, or the rental of a house for an embassy, are private acts. Furthermore, this test merely postpones the difficulty, for particular contracts in some instances may be made only by states. Others have looked to the purpose of the transaction, categorizing as *jure imperii* all activities in which the object of performance is public in character. But this test is even more unsatisfactory, for conceptually the modern sovereign always acts for a public purpose. Functionally the criterion is purely arbitrary and necessarily involves the court in projecting personal notions about the proper realm of state functioning. * * *

The purpose of the restrictive theory of sovereign immunity is to try to accommodate the interest of individuals doing business with foreign governments in having their legal rights determined by the courts, with the interest of foreign governments in being free to perform certain political acts without undergoing the embarrassment or hindrance of defending the propriety of such acts before foreign courts. Sovereign immunity is a derogation from the normal exercise of jurisdiction by the courts and should be accorded only in clear cases. Since the State Department's failure or refusal to suggest immunity is significant, we are disposed to deny a claim of sovereign immunity that has not been "recognized and allowed" by the State Department unless it is plain that the activity in question falls within one of the categories of strictly political or public acts about which sovereigns have traditionally been quite sensitive. Such acts are generally limited to the following categories:

(1) internal administrative acts, such as expulsion of an alien.

(2) legislative acts, such as nationalization.

(3) acts concerning the armed forces.

(4) acts concerning diplomatic activity.

(5) public loans.

We do not think that the restrictive theory adopted by the State Department requires sacrificing the interests of private litigants to international comity in other than these limited categories. Should diplomacy require enlargement of these categories, the State Department can file a suggestion of immunity with the court. Should diplomacy require contraction of these categories, the State Department can issue a new or clarifying policy pronouncement.

The Comisaría General's chartering of the appellee's ship to transport a purchase of wheat is not a strictly public or political act. Indeed, it partakes far more of the character of a private commercial act than a public or political act.

The charter party has all the earmarks of a typical commercial transaction. It was executed for the Comisaría General by "El Jefe del Servicio Commercial," the head of its commercial division. The wheat was consigned to and shipped by a private commercial concern. And one of the most significant indicators of the private commercial nature of this charter is the inclusion of the arbitration clause. The French Court of Appeal, in dismissing a claim of sovereign immunity where the governmental charterer had agreed to arbitration, pointed out:

> A contract relating to maritime transport is a private contract where the owner merely puts his ship and the ship's crew at the

> disposal of the State and does not take a direct part in the performance of the public service undertaken by the State in the latter's capacity as a charterer. The charter party does not contain any clause peculiar to public law or unusual in private law. It provides for a time charter of the vessel which is put at the disposal of the State chartering it. The insertion of the arbitration clause underlines the intention of the parties to make their agreement subject to private law.

Maritime transport has been included among the commercial or business activities specifically mentioned in recent United States treaties restricting sovereign immunity. And the 1926 Brussels Convention, the first major international attempt to restrict sovereign immunity, which Spain signed but never ratified, denied immunity to all maritime governmental activities except vessels operated exclusively on non-commercial service, such as warships, patrol vessels, or hospital ships.

Even if we take a broader view of the transaction to encompass the purchase of wheat pursuant to the Surplus Agricultural Commodities Agreement to help feed the people of Spain, the activity of the Comisaría General remains more in the commercial than political realm. Appellant does not claim that the wheat will be used for the public services of Spain; presumptively the wheat will be resold to Spanish nationals. Whether the Comisaría General loses money or makes a profit on the sale, this purchasing activity has been conducted through private channels of trade. Except for United States financing, permitting payment in pesetas, the Comisaría General acted much like any private purchaser of wheat.

Our conclusion that the Comisaría General's activity is more properly labeled an act *jure gestionis* than *jure imperii* is supported by the practice of those countries which have adopted the restrictive theory of sovereign immunity. Thus the Commercial Tribunal of Alexandria declined to grant immunity to this same Spanish instrumentality in a more difficult case—a suit arising from the Comisaría's purchase of rice to help feed the people of neutral Spain during wartime.

> It is not contended in the present case that the rice in question was bought by the *Comisaría General* for the needs of the Spanish public services. On the contrary, it seems clearly established that the rice was bought for the feeding of the Spanish population during a difficult period. In negotiating this purchase herself, instead of leaving the matter to private enterprise, Spain proceeded in much the same manner as any other Spanish trader would have done who wanted to buy rice in Egypt; that is to say, she got it out of Egypt with the necessary permits and carried it to Spain in a Spanish ship in order to re-sell it on the usual commercial lines. This being so, the *Comisaría General* cannot claim immunity from jurisdiction, and the judgment entered against it must be confirmed.

Though there are a few inconsistencies, the courts in those countries which have adopted the restrictive theory have generally considered purchasing activity by a state instrumentality, particularly for resale to nationals, as commercial or private activity.

Finally, our conclusion that the Comisaría General's claim of sovereign immunity should be denied finds support in the State Department's communication to the court in New York and Cuba Mail S. S. Co. v. Republic of Korea, 132 F.Supp. 684, 685 (S.D.N.Y.1955). There the Republic of Korea was allegedly responsible for damaging a ship while assisting in the unloading of a cargo of rice for distribution without charge to its civilian and military personnel during the Korean War. Though suggesting that Korea's property was immune from attachment, the State Department refused to suggest immunity "inasmuch as the particular acts out of which the cause of action arose are not shown to be of a purely governmental character." If the wartime transportation of rice to civilian and military personnel is not an act *jure imperii, a fortiori* the peacetime transportation of wheat for presumptive resale is not an act *jure imperii*.

Notes and Questions

1. *The Origins of Absolute Sovereign Immunity.* The *Victory Transport* court dates Marshall's decision in *The Schooner Exchange* by observing that Marshall's "doctrine originated in an era of personal sovereignty, when kings could theoretically do no wrong and when the exercise of authority by one sovereign over another indicated hostility or superiority." Can *The Schooner Exchange* really be read so broadly? After all, Marshall carefully delineated his issue as involving only "the very delicate and important inquiry, whether an American citizen can assert, in an American court, a title to an armed national vessel, found within the waters of the United States." Presumably, the answer to this specific inquiry has remained "no" over two centuries of U.S. practice. Is the doctrine of absolute sovereign immunity properly attributable to *The Schooner Exchange*? How good a job does Marshall do in balancing the territorial sovereign authority of the United States against the sovereign prerequisites of France and its Navy? Does the case say anything at all about the commercial activities of states that would be helpful in deciding *Victory Transport*?

2. *The Tate Letter.* Whatever the theoretical or practical soundness of the old doctrine of absolute sovereign immunity, the Tate letter, 26 *Department of State Bulletin* 984 (1952), inaugurated the restrictive doctrine in U.S. law. What exactly was the authority of Acting Legal Adviser to the State Department Jack Tate to change U.S. common law by way of a letter to the Acting Attorney General? Does the real authority belong to the federal courts, which merely respond to the Executive Branch's "suggestion" and which then authoritatively reverse old and set new precedent?

3. *Sovereign Immunity and International Law.* How influential was international law theory and practice either on Acting Legal Adviser Tate or on the U.S. courts? Is the rule about restrictive sovereign immunity one of international custom which is followed or incorporated in U.S. law? Or are the rules of sovereign immunity, both absolute and restrictive, simply a form of U.S. case law?

4. *Sovereign Immunity and Foreign Law.* How does foreign practice, *e.g.*, the decisions of Austrian, French, and Egyptian courts, help the U.S. court determine what are and are not "commercial activities" of foreign governments? U.S. courts not only watch foreign courts, but they are also watched by foreign courts. Looking at judicial cross-fertilization, Professor Stefan Riesenfeld writes that *The Schooner Exchange* has been recognized as the "earliest judicial pronouncement of the doctrine of sovereign immunity by the highest court of a nation." Stefan A. Riesenfeld, "Sovereign Immunity in Perspective," 19 *Vanderbilt Journal of Transnational Law* 1, 2 (1986). *Exchange* was soon followed by lower French courts, though not confirmed by the Cour de Cassation (the highest French civil court) until 1849. *Id.* at 2–4. Riesenfeld dates other early lower court decisions on sovereign immunity to 1819 in Germany and the early 19th century in Italy. *Id.* at 8–12. Such borrowing of rules among municipal legal systems is an example of what might be thought of as "international common law."

5. *Codifying Sovereign Immunity.* U.S. judicial deference toward foreign governments, rooted in *The Schooner Exchange*, began to be turned back in the Tate letter in 1952. *Victory Transport* shows how exceptions to sovereign immunity were beginning to overwhelm the rule of deference. The exceptions were codified in the Foreign Sovereign Immunities Act of 1976.

THE FOREIGN SOVEREIGN IMMUNITIES ACT OF 1976

28 U.S.C. §§ 1602–1605.

CHAPTER 97. JURISDICTIONAL IMMUNITIES OF FOREIGN STATES

§ 1602. Findings and declaration of purpose

The Congress finds that the determination by the United States courts of the claims of foreign states to immunity from the jurisdiction of such courts would serve the interests of justice and would protect the rights of both foreign states and litigants in United States courts. Under international law, states are not immune from the jurisdiction of foreign courts insofar as their commercial activities are concerned, and their commercial property may be levied upon for the satisfaction of judgments rendered against them in connection with their commercial activities. Claims of foreign states to immunity should henceforth be decided by courts of the United States and of the States in conformity with the principles set forth in this chapter.

§ 1603. Definitions

For purposes of this chapter—

(a) A "foreign state" * * * includes a political subdivision of a foreign state or an agency or instrumentality of a foreign state as defined in subsection (b).

(b) An "agency or instrumentality of a foreign state" means any entity—

(1) which is a separate legal person, corporate or otherwise, and

(2) which is an organ of a foreign state or political subdivision thereof, or a majority of whose shares or other ownership interest is owned by a foreign state or political subdivision thereof, and

(3) which is neither a citizen of a State of the United States as defined in section 1332(c) and (d) of this title, nor created under the laws of any third country.

(c) The "United States" includes all territory and waters, continental or insular, subject to the jurisdiction of the United States.

(d) A "commercial activity" means either a regular course of commercial conduct or a particular commercial transaction or act. The commercial character of an activity shall be determined by reference to the nature of the course of conduct or particular transaction or act, rather than by reference to its purpose.

(e) A "commercial activity carried on in the United States by a foreign state" means commercial activity carried on by such state and having substantial contact with the United States.

§ 1604. Immunity of a foreign state from jurisdiction

Subject to existing international agreements to which the United States is a party at the time of enactment of this Act a foreign state shall be immune from the jurisdiction of the courts of the United States and of the States except as provided in sections 1605 to 1607 of this chapter.

§ 1605. General exceptions to the jurisdictional immunity of a foreign state

(a) A foreign state shall not be immune from the jurisdiction of courts of the United States or of the States in any case—

(1) in which the foreign state has waived its immunity either explicitly or by implication, notwithstanding any withdrawal of the waiver which the foreign state may purport to effect except in accordance with the terms of the waiver;

(2) in which the action is based upon a commercial activity carried on in the United States by the foreign state; or upon an act performed in the United States in connection with a commercial activity of the foreign state elsewhere; or upon an act outside the territory of the United States in connection with a commercial activity of the foreign state elsewhere and that act causes a direct effect in the United States;

(3) in which rights in property taken in violation of international law are in issue and that property or any property exchanged for such property is present in the United States in connection with a commercial activity carried on in the United States by the foreign state; or that property or any property exchanged for such property

is owned or operated by an agency or instrumentality of the foreign state and that agency or instrumentality is engaged in a commercial activity in the United States;

(4) in which rights in property in the United States acquired by succession or gift or rights in immovable property situated in the United States are in issue; or

(5) not otherwise encompassed in paragraph (2) above, in which money damages are sought against a foreign state for personal injury or death, or damage to or loss of property, occurring in the United States and caused by the tortious act or omission of that foreign state or of any official or employee of that foreign state while acting within the scope of his office or employment; except this paragraph shall not apply to—

(A) any claim based upon the exercise or performance or the failure to exercise or perform a discretionary function regardless of whether the discretion be abused, or

(B) any claim arising out of malicious prosecution, abuse of process, libel, slander, misrepresentation, deceit, or interference with contract rights.

Notes and Questions

1. *The Ambiguity of the Foreign Sovereign Immunities Act.* The FSIA is a good example of ambiguous draftsmanship. Statutes are not necessarily more precise than case law! Note how Section 1602, "Findings and declaration of purpose," mixes possible sources of law. The first sentence seems to entrust the courts with power to decide questions of foreign sovereign immunity. The second sentence appears to incorporate rules from international law. The third instructs that the courts decide "in conformity with the principles set forth in" the statute. The truth is that deciding cases involving claims of foreign sovereign immunity has come to mean using material evidences from all three sources: case law, international law, and statute.

2. *The Presumption of Immunity.* Note that a presumption in *Victory Transport* has been reversed in the FSIA. *Victory Transport* presumes to deny immunity unless the state proved it deserved to be protected. Section 1604, on the other hand, presumes to grant immunity unless a private plaintiff shows an exception. As we shall see in *Amerada Hess* below, this reversal can make a decisive effect in practice. If the main purpose of the FSIA was to codify the commercial activities exception, was it necessary to codify other exceptions as an exclusive list? Why not leave some flexibility for the courts to develop exceptions?

3. *1996 Amendment.* Not reproduced above is a 1996 amendment to the Foreign Sovereign Immunities Act, added by the Antiterrorism and Effective Death Penalty Act of 1996, Pub.L. No. 104–132, § 221, 110 Stat. 1214, 1241 (1996). The amendment adds a new exception to those listed in section 1605(a), applicable to cases "not otherwise covered by paragraph (2), in which money damages are sought against a foreign state for personal injury or death that was caused by an act of torture, extrajudicial killing,

aircraft sabotage, hostage taking, or the provision of material support or resources * * * for such an act * * *." This exception can apply to cases arising outside U.S. territory. The new exception has its own exceptions. It does not apply "if the foreign state was not designated as a state sponsor of terrorism" under the Export Administration Act of 1979, 50 U.S.C. App. § 2405(j) (1994), or under the Foreign Assistance Act of 1961, 22 U.S.C. § 2371 (1994). The exception also does not apply, even to foreign states having such a designation, if the claimant or victim was not a U.S. national at the time of the act, or if "the act occurred in the foreign state against which the claim has been brought and the claimant has not afforded the foreign state a reasonable opportunity to arbitrate the claim in accordance with accepted international rules of arbitration."

TEXAS TRADING & MILLING CORP. v. FEDERAL REPUBLIC OF NIGERIA

647 F.2d 300 (2d Cir.1981), *cert. denied*, 454 U.S. 1148, 102 S.Ct. 1012, 71 L.Ed.2d 301 (1982).

IRVING R. KAUFMAN, CIRCUIT JUDGE:

These four appeals grow out of one of the most enormous commercial disputes in history, and present questions which strike to the very heart of the modern international economic order. An African nation, developing at breakneck speed by virtue of huge exports of high-grade oil, contracted to buy huge quantities of Portland cement, a commodity crucial to the construction of its infrastructure. It overbought, and the country's docks and harbors became clogged with ships waiting to unload. Imports of other goods ground to a halt. More vessels carrying cement arrived daily; still others were steaming toward the port. Unable to accept delivery of the cement it had bought, the nation repudiated its contracts. In response to suits brought by disgruntled suppliers, it now seeks to invoke an ancient maxim of sovereign immunity—*par in parem imperium non habet*—to insulate itself from liability. But Latin phrases speak with a hoary simplicity inappropriate to the modern financial world. For the ruling principles here, we must look instead to a new and vaguely-worded statute, the Foreign Sovereign Immunities Act of 1976 ("FSIA" or "Act")—a law described by its draftsmen as providing only "very modest guidance" on issues of preeminent importance. For answers to those most difficult questions, the authors of the law "decided to put [their] faith in the U.S. courts." Guided by reason, precedent, and equity, we have attempted to give form and substance to the legislative intent. Accordingly, we find that the defense of sovereign immunity is not available in any of these four cases.

I.

The facts of the four appeals are remarkably parallel, and can be stated in somewhat consolidated form. Early in 1975, the Federal Military Government of the Federal Republic of Nigeria ("Nigeria") embarked on an ambitious program to purchase immense amounts of cement. We have already had occasion in another case to call the program "incredible," but the statistics speak for themselves. Nigeria executed 109 contracts, with 68 suppliers. It purchased, in all, over sixteen million metric tons of cement. The price was close to one billion dollars.

A.

Four of the 109 contracts were made with American companies that were plaintiffs below in the cases now before us: Texas Trading & Milling Corp. ("Texas Trading"), Decor by Nikkei International, Inc. ("Nikkei"), East Europe Import–Export, Inc. ("East Europe"), and Chenax Majesty, Inc. ("Chenax"). The four plaintiffs are not industrial corporations; they are, instead, "trading companies," which buy from one person and sell to another in hopes of making a profit on the differential. Each of the plaintiffs is a New York corporation.

The contracts at issue were signed early in 1975. Each is substantially similar; indeed, Nigeria seems to have mimeographed them in blank, and filled in details with individual suppliers. Overall, each contract called for the sale by the supplier to Nigeria of 240,000 metric tons of Portland cement. Specifically, the contracts required Nigeria, within a time certain after execution, to establish in the seller's favor "an Irrevocable, Transferable abroad, Divisible and Confirmed letter of credit" for the total amount due under the particular contract, slightly over $14 million in each case. The contract also named the bank through which the letter of credit was to be made payable. Nikkei and East Europe named First National City Bank in New York, and Texas Trading specified Fidelity International Bank, also in New York. Chenax denominated Schroeder, Muenchmeyer, Hengst & Co. of Hamburg, West Germany. Drafts under the letters of credit were to be "payable at sight, on presentation" of certain documents to the specified bank.

Within a time certain after establishment and receipt of the letter of credit, each seller was to start shipping cement to Nigeria. The cement was to be bagged, and was to meet certain chemical specifications. Shipments were to be from ports named in the contracts, mostly Spanish, and were to proceed at approximately 20,000 tons per month. Delivery was to the port of Lagos/Apapa, Nigeria, and the seller was obligated to insure the freight to the Nigerian quay. Each contract also provided for demurrage. The Nikkei and East Europe contracts provided they were to be governed by the laws of the United States. The Chenax contract specified the law of Switzerland, and the Texas Trading contract named the law of Nigeria. * * *

The actual financial arrangements differed from those set forth in the cement contracts. Instead of establishing "confirmed" letters of credit with the banks named, Nigeria established what it called "irrevocable" letters of credit with the Central Bank of Nigeria ("Central Bank"), an instrumentality of the Nigerian government, and advised those letters of credit through the Morgan Guaranty Trust Company ("Morgan") of New York. That is, under the letters of credit as established, each seller was to present appropriate documents not to the named bank, but to Morgan. And, since the letters were not "confirmed," Morgan did not promise to pay "on sight"; it assumed no independent liability. Each of the letters of credit provided it was to be governed by the Uniform Customs and Practice for Documentary Credits ("UCP")(1962 Revision), as set forth in Brochure No. 222 of the International Chamber of Commerce. * * *

After receiving notice that the letters of credit had been established, the suppliers set out to secure subcontracts to procure the cement, and shipping contracts to transport it. They, through their subcontractors, began to bag the cement and load it on ships, as suppliers across the globe were doing the same. Hundreds of ships arrived in Lagos/Apapa in the summer of 1975, and most were carrying cement. Nigeria's port facilities could accept only one to five million tons of cement per year; at any rate, they could not begin to unload the over sixteen million tons Nigeria had slated for delivery in eighteen short months. Based on prior experience, Nigeria had made the contracts expecting only twenty percent of the suppliers to be able to perform. By July, when the harbor held over 400 ships waiting to unload—260 of them carrying cement—Nigeria realized it had misjudged the market considerably.

C.

With demurrage piling up at astronomical rates, and suppliers, hiring, loading, and dispatching more ships daily, Nigeria decided to act. On August 9, 1975, Nigeria caused its Ports Authority to issue Government Notice No. 1434, a regulation which stated that, effective August 18, all ships destined for Lagos/Apapa would be required to convey to the Ports Authority, two months before sailing, certain information concerning their time of arrival in the port. The regulation also stated vaguely that the Ports Authority would "co-ordinate all sailing," and that it would "refuse[e] service" to vessels which did not comply with the regulation. Then, on August 18, Nigeria cabled its suppliers and asked them to stop sending cement, and to cease loading or even chartering ships. In late September, Nigeria took the crucial step: Central Bank instructed Morgan not to pay under the letters of credit unless the supplier submitted—in addition to the documents required by the letter of credit as written—a statement from Central Bank that payment ought to be made. Morgan notified each supplier of Nigeria's instructions, and Morgan commenced refusing to make payment under the letters of credit as written. Almost three months later, on December 19, 1975, Nigeria promulgated Decree No. 40, a law prohibiting entry into a Nigerian port to any ship which had not secured two months' prior approval, and imposing criminal penalties for unauthorized entry. * * *

II.

The law before us is complex and largely unconstrued, and has introduced sweeping changes in some areas of prior law. In structure, the FSIA is a marvel of compression. Within the bounds of a few tersely-worded sections, it purports to provide answers to three crucial questions in a suit against a foreign state: the availability of sovereign immunity as a defense, the presence of subject matter jurisdiction over the claim, and the propriety of personal jurisdiction over the defendant. Through a series of intricately coordinated provisions, the FSIA seems at first glance to make the answer to one of the questions, subject matter jurisdiction, dispositive of all three. * * *

A.

Turning to the specific provisions of the law, a description of the FSIA's analytic structure is helpful. The jurisdiction-conferring provision of the Act, 28 U.S.C. § 1330(a), creates in the district courts:

> original jurisdiction without regard to amount in controversy of any nonjury civil action against a foreign state as defined in section 1603(a) of this title as to any claim for relief in personam with respect to which the foreign state is not entitled to immunity either under sections 1605–1607 of this title or any applicable international agreement.

Although § 1330(a) refers to sections 1605–1607, the section most frequently relevant, and the one applicable here, is § 1605. It provides, in part:

> (a) A foreign state shall not be immune from the jurisdiction of courts of the United States or of the States in any case—* * *
>
> (2) in which the action is based upon a commercial activity carried on in the United States by the foreign state; or upon an act performed in the United States in connection with a commercial activity of the foreign state elsewhere; or upon an act outside the territory of the United States in connection with a commercial activity of the foreign state elsewhere and that act causes a direct effect in the United States.

Crucial to each of the three clauses of § 1605(a)(2) is the phrase "commercial activity." In it is lodged centuries of Anglo–American and civil law precedent construing the term "sovereign immunity." If the activity is not "commercial," but, rather, is "governmental," then the foreign state is entitled to immunity under section 1605, and "original jurisdiction" is not present under § 1330(a).

For the definition of "commercial activity," we turn to subsection 1603(d), which provides:

> (d) A "commercial activity" means either a regular course of commercial conduct or a particular commercial transaction or act. The commercial character of an activity shall be determined by reference to the nature of the course of conduct or particular transaction or act, rather than by references to its purpose.

If "commercial activity" under § 1603(d) is present, and if it bears the relation to the United States required by § 1605(a)(2), then the foreign state is "not entitled to immunity," and the district court has statutory subject matter jurisdiction over the claim through § 1330(a). And, if the exercise of that jurisdiction falls within the judicial power set forth by

Article III of the Constitution, subject matter jurisdiction over the claim exists. * * *

B. * * *

The determination of whether particular behavior is "commercial" is perhaps the most important decision a court faces in an FSIA suit. This problem is significant because the primary purpose of the Act is to "restrict" the immunity of a foreign state to suits involving a foreign state's public acts. If the activity is not "commercial," it satisfies none of the three clauses of § 1605(a)(2), and the foreign state is (at least under that subsection) immune from suit. Unfortunately, the definition of "commercial" is the one issue on which the Act provides almost no guidance at all. Subsection 1603(d) advances the inquiry somewhat, for it provides: "The commercial character of an activity shall be determined by reference to the nature of the course of conduct or particular transaction or act, rather than by reference to its purpose." No provision of the Act, however, defines "commercial." Congress deliberately left the meaning open and, as noted above, "put [its] faith in the U.S. courts to work out progressively, on a case-by-case basis ... the distinction between commercial and governmental." We are referred to no less than three separate sources of authority to resolve this fundamental definitional question.

The first source is statements contained in the legislative history itself. Perhaps the clearest of them was made by Bruno Ristau, then Chief of the Foreign Litigation Section of the Civil Division, Department of Justice. Ristau stated: "[I]f a government enters into a contract to purchase goods and services, that is considered a commercial activity. It avails itself of the ordinary contract machinery. It bargains and negotiates. It accepts an offer. It enters into a written contract and the contract is to be performed." The House Report seems to conclude that a contract or series of contracts for the purchase of goods would be *per se* a "commercial activity," and the illustrations cited by experts who testified on the bill—contracts, for example, for the sale of army boots or grain—support such a rule. Or, put another way, if the activity is one in which a private person could engage, it is not entitled to immunity.

The second source for interpreting the phrase "commercial activity" is the "very large body of case law which exist[ed]" in American law upon passage of the Act in 1976. Testifying on an earlier version of the bill, Charles N. Brower, then Legal Adviser of the Department of State, stated:

> [T]he restrictive theory of sovereign immunity from jurisdiction, which has been followed by the Department of State and the courts since it was articulated in the familiar letter of Acting Legal Adviser Jack B. Tate of May 29, 1952, would be incorporated into statutory law. This theory limits immunity to public acts, leaving so-called private acts subject to suit. The proposed legislation would make it clear that immunity cannot be claimed with respect to acts or

transactions that are commercial in nature, regardless of their underlying purpose.

Finally, current standards of international law concerning sovereign immunity add content to the "commercial activity" phrase of the FSIA. Section 1602 of the Act, entitled "Findings and declaration of purpose," contains a cryptic reference to international law, but fails wholly to adopt it. The legislative history states that the Act "incorporates standards recognized under international law," and the drafters seem to have intended rather generally to bring American sovereign immunity practice into line with that of other nations. At this point, there can be little doubt that international law follows the restrictive theory of sovereign immunity.

Under each of these three standards, Nigeria's cement contracts and letters of credit qualify as "commercial activity." Lord Denning, writing in *Trendtex Trading Corp. v. Central Bank of Nigeria*, [1977] 2 W.L.R. 356, 369, 1 All E.R. 881, with his usual erudition and clarity, stated: "If a government department goes into the market places of the world and buys boots or cement—as a commercial transaction—that government department should be subject to all the rules of the marketplace." Nigeria's activity here is in the nature of a private contract for the purchase of goods. Its purpose—to build roads, army barracks, whatever—is irrelevant. Accordingly, courts in other nations have uniformly held Nigeria's 1975 cement purchase program and appurtenant letters of credit to be "commercial activity," and have denied the defense of sovereign immunity. We find defendants' activity here to constitute "commercial activity" * * *.

[The Court finds there is jurisdiction over Nigeria.]

VERLINDEN B.V. v. CENTRAL BANK OF NIGERIA

461 U.S. 480, 103 S.Ct. 1962, 76 L.Ed.2d 81 (1983).

CHIEF JUSTICE BURGER delivered the opinion of the Court.

We granted certiorari to consider whether the Foreign Sovereign Immunities Act of 1976, by authorizing a foreign plaintiff to sue a foreign state in a United States district court on a nonfederal cause of action, violates Article III of the Constitution.

I

On April 21, 1975, the Federal Republic of Nigeria and petitioner Verlinden B. V., a Dutch corporation with its principal offices in Amsterdam, the Netherlands, entered into a contract providing for the purchase of 240,000 metric tons of cement by Nigeria. The parties agreed that the contract would be governed by the laws of the Netherlands and that disputes would be resolved by arbitration before the International Chamber of Commerce, Paris, France.

The contract provided that the Nigerian Government was to establish an irrevocable, confirmed letter of credit for the total purchase price through Slavenburg's Bank in Amsterdam. According to petitioner's amended complaint, however, respondent Central Bank of Nigeria, an instrumentality of Nigeria, improperly established an unconfirmed letter of credit payable through Morgan Guaranty Trust Co. in New York.

In August 1975, Verlinden subcontracted with a Liechtenstein corporation, Interbuco, to purchase the cement needed to fulfill the contract. Meanwhile, the ports of Nigeria had become clogged with hundreds of ships carrying cement, sent by numerous other cement suppliers with whom Nigeria also had entered into contracts. In mid-September, Central Bank unilaterally directed its correspondent banks, including Morgan Guaranty, to adopt a series of amendments to all letters of credit issued in connection with the cement contracts. Central Bank also directly notified the suppliers that payment would be made only for those shipments approved by Central Bank two months before their arrival in Nigerian waters.[3]

Verlinden then sued Central Bank in the United States District Court for the Southern District of New York, alleging that Central Bank's actions constituted an anticipatory breach of the letter of credit. Verlinden alleged jurisdiction under the Foreign Sovereign Immunities Act, 28 U.S.C. § 1330. Respondent moved to dismiss for, among other reasons, lack of subject-matter and personal jurisdiction.

The District Court first held that a federal court may exercise subject-matter jurisdiction over a suit brought by a foreign corporation against a foreign sovereign. Although the legislative history of the Foreign Sovereign Immunities Act does not clearly reveal whether Congress intended the Act to extend to actions brought by foreign plaintiffs, Judge Weinfeld reasoned that the language of the Act is "broad and embracing. It confers jurisdiction over 'any nonjury civil action' against a foreign state." Moreover, in the District Court's view, allowing *all* actions against foreign sovereigns, including those initiated by foreign plaintiffs, to be brought in federal court was necessary to effectuate "the Congressional purpose of concentrating litigation against sovereign states in the federal courts in order to aid the development of a uniform body of federal law governing assertions of sovereign immunity." The District Court also held that Art. III subject-matter jurisdiction extends to suits by foreign corporations against foreign sovereigns, stating:

> "[The Act] imposes a single, federal standard to be applied uniformly by both state and federal courts hearing claims brought against foreign states. In consequence, even though the plaintiff's claim is one grounded upon common law, the case is one that 'arises under' a federal law because the complaint compels the application of the uniform federal standard governing assertions of sovereign immuni-

3. The parties do not seriously dispute the fact that these unilateral amendments constituted violations of Article 3 of the Uniform Customs and Practice for Documentary Credits (Int'l Chamber of Commerce Brochure No.222)(1962 Revision), which, by stipulation of the parties, is applicable.

ty. In short, the Immunities Act injects an essential federal element into all suits brought against foreign states."

The District Court nevertheless dismissed the complaint, holding that a foreign instrumentality is entitled to sovereign immunity unless one of the exceptions specified in the Act applies. After carefully considering each of the exceptions upon which petitioner relied, the District Court concluded that none applied, and accordingly dismissed the action.

The Court of Appeals for the Second Circuit affirmed, but on different grounds. The court agreed with the District Court that the Act was properly construed to permit actions brought by foreign plaintiffs. The court held, however, that the Act exceeded the scope of Art. III of the Constitution. In the view of the Court of Appeals, neither the Diversity Clause nor the "Arising Under" Clause of Art. III is broad enough to support jurisdiction over actions by foreign plaintiffs against foreign sovereigns; accordingly it concluded that Congress was without power to grant federal courts jurisdiction in this case, and affirmed the District Court's dismissal of the action.

We granted certiorari, and we reverse and remand.

II

For more than a century and a half, the United States generally granted foreign sovereigns complete immunity from suit in the courts of this country. In *The Schooner Exchange v. M'Faddon*, 7 Cranch 116 (1812), Chief Justice Marshall concluded that, while the jurisdiction of a nation within its own territory "is susceptible of no limitation not imposed by itself," the United States had impliedly waived jurisdiction over certain activities of foreign sovereigns. Although the narrow holding of *The Schooner Exchange* was only that the courts of the United States lack jurisdiction over an armed ship of a foreign state found in our port, that opinion came to be regarded as extending virtually absolute immunity to foreign sovereigns.

As *The Schooner Exchange* made clear, however, foreign sovereign immunity is a matter of grace and comity on the part of the United States, and not a restriction imposed by the Constitution. Accordingly, this Court consistently has deferred to the decisions of the political branches—in particular, those of the Executive Branch—on whether to take jurisdiction over actions against foreign sovereigns and their instrumentalities.

Until 1952, the State Department ordinarily requested immunity in all actions against friendly foreign sovereigns. But in the so-called Tate Letter, the State Department announced its adoption of the "restrictive" theory of foreign sovereign immunity. Under this theory, immunity is confined to suits involving the foreign sovereign's public acts, and does not extend to cases arising out of a foreign state's strictly commercial acts.

The restrictive theory was not initially enacted into law, however, and its application proved troublesome. As in the past, initial responsibility for deciding questions of sovereign immunity fell primarily upon the Executive acting through the State Department, and the courts abided by "suggestions of immunity" from the State Department. As a consequence, foreign nations often placed diplomatic pressure on the State Department in seeking immunity. On occasion, political considerations led to suggestions of immunity in cases where immunity would not have been available under the restrictive theory.

An additional complication was posed by the fact that foreign nations did not always make requests to the State Department. In such cases, the responsibility fell to the courts to determine whether sovereign immunity existed, generally by reference to prior State Department decisions. Thus, sovereign immunity determinations were made in two different branches, subject to a variety of factors, sometimes including diplomatic considerations. Not surprisingly, the governing standards were neither clear nor uniformly applied.

In 1976, Congress passed the Foreign Sovereign Immunities Act in order to free the Government from the case-by-case diplomatic pressures, to clarify the governing standards, and to "assur[e] litigants that ... decisions are made on purely legal grounds and under procedures that insure due process." To accomplish these objectives, the Act contains a comprehensive set of legal standards governing claims of immunity in every civil action against a foreign state or its political subdivisions, agencies, or instrumentalities. * * *

III

The District Court and the Court of Appeals both held that the Foreign Sovereign Immunities Act purports to allow a foreign plaintiff to sue a foreign sovereign in the courts of the United States, provided the substantive requirements of the Act are satisfied. We agree.

On its face, the language of the statute is unambiguous. The statute grants jurisdiction over "any nonjury civil action against a foreign state ... with respect to which the foreign state is not entitled to immunity." The Act contains no indication of any limitation based on the citizenship of the plaintiff. * * *

IV

We now turn to the core question presented by this case: whether Congress exceeded the scope of Art. III of the Constitution by granting federal courts subject-matter jurisdiction over certain civil actions by foreign plaintiffs against foreign sovereigns where the rule of decision may be provided by state law.

This Court's cases firmly establish that Congress may not expand the jurisdiction of the federal courts beyond the bounds established by the Constitution. Within Art. III of the Constitution, we find two sources authorizing the grant of jurisdiction in the Foreign Sovereign Immunities Act: the Diversity Clause and the "Arising Under" Clause.

The Diversity Clause, which provides that the judicial power extends to controversies between "a State, or the Citizens thereof, and foreign States," covers actions by citizens of States. Yet diversity jurisdiction is not sufficiently broad to support a grant of jurisdiction over actions by foreign plaintiffs, since a foreign plaintiff is not "a State, or [a] Citize[n] thereof." We conclude, however, that the "Arising Under" Clause of Art. III provides an appropriate basis for the statutory grant of subject-matter jurisdiction to actions by foreign plaintiffs under the Act.

The controlling decision on the scope of Art. III "arising under" jurisdiction is Chief Justice Marshall's opinion for the Court in *Osborn* v. *Bank of United States*, 9 Wheat. 738 (1824). In *Osborn*, the Court upheld the constitutionality of a statute that granted the Bank of the United States the right to sue in federal court on causes of action based upon state law. There, the Court concluded that the "judicial department may receive ... the power of construing every ... law" that "the Legislature may constitutionally make." The rule was laid down that

> "it [is] a sufficient foundation for jurisdiction, that the title or right set up by the party, may be defeated by one construction of the constitution or law[s] of the United States, and sustained by the opposite construction." * * *

By reason of its authority over foreign commerce and foreign relations, Congress has the undisputed power to decide, as a matter of federal law, whether and under what circumstances foreign nations should be amenable to suit in the United States. Actions against foreign sovereigns in our courts raise sensitive issues concerning the foreign relations of the United States, and the primacy of federal concerns is evident.

To promote these federal interests, Congress exercised its Art. I powers by enacting a statute comprehensively regulating the amenability of foreign nations to suit in the United States. The statute must be applied by the district courts in every action against a foreign sovereign, since subject-matter jurisdiction in any such action depends on the existence of one of the specified exceptions to foreign sovereign immunity, 28 U.S.C. § 1330(a). At the threshold of every action in a district court against a foreign state, therefore, the court must satisfy itself that one of the exceptions applies—and in doing so it must apply the detailed federal law standards set forth in the Act. Accordingly, an action against a foreign sovereign arises under federal law, for purposes of Art. III jurisdiction. * * *

V

A conclusion that the grant of jurisdiction in the Foreign Sovereign Immunities Act is consistent with the Constitution does not end the case. An action must not only satisfy Art. III but must also be supported by a statutory grant of subject-matter jurisdiction. As we have made clear, deciding whether statutory subject-matter jurisdiction exists under the Foreign Sovereign Immunities Act entails an application of the substantive terms of the Act to determine whether one of the specified exceptions to immunity applies.

In the present case, the District Court, after satisfying itself as to the constitutionality of the Act, held that the present action does not fall within any specified exception. The Court of Appeals, reaching a contrary conclusion as to jurisdiction under the Constitution, did not find it necessary to address this statutory question.[23] Accordingly, on remand the Court of Appeals must consider whether jurisdiction exists under the Act itself. If the Court of Appeals agrees with the District Court on that issue, the case will be at an end. If, on the other hand, the Court of Appeals concludes that jurisdiction does exist under the statute, the action may then be remanded to the District Court for further proceedings.

It is so ordered.

Notes and Questions

1. *Proving "Commercial Activities."* Section 1602 of the FSIA refers to the commercial activities exception as being part of international law and also instructs courts to decide sovereign immunity cases in accordance with the statute. How well does the *Texas Trading* court use both international law and statutory analysis to decide whether Nigeria was protected by the commercial activities exception? Does the FSIA much change the exercise of line-drawing between "public" and "private" acts as done before 1976, *e.g.*, in *Victory Transport*?

2. *Direct Effect in the United States.* Note how the district court in *Verlinden* distinguishes between U.S. and foreign suppliers of concrete to Nigeria for purposes of determining "direct effect in the United States." The *Texas Trading* court finds "direct effect in the United States":

> [T]he financial loss in these cases occurred "in the United States" for two * * * simple[ ] reasons. First, the cement suppliers were to present documents and collect money in the United States, and the breaches precluded their doing so. Second, each of the plaintiffs is an American corporation. Whether a failure to pay a foreign corporation in the United States or to pay an American corporation overseas creates an effect "in the United States" under § 1605(a)(2) is not before us. Both factors are present here and the subsection is clearly satisfied.

647 F.2d at 312.

Is a U.S. court or the FSIA itself limited by jurisdictional rules of international law in determining whether an activity has "a direct effect in

23. In several related cases involving contracts between Nigeria and other cement suppliers, the Court of Appeals held that statutory subject-matter jurisdiction existed under the Act. In those cases, the court held that Nigeria's acts were commercial in nature and "cause[d] a direct effect in the United States," within the meaning of 28 U.S.C. § 1605(a). *Texas Trading & Milling Corp. v. Federal Republic of Nigeria*, 647 F.2d at 310–313. Each of those actions involved a contract with an *American* supplier operating *within the United States*, however. In the present case, the District Court found that exception inapplicable, concluding that the repudiation of the letter of credit "caused no direct, substantial, injurious effect in the United States."

the United States"? Should the jurisdictional practice of other countries be taken into account? As one observer noted: "[A]ll States have a strong incentive to make reasonable rules of immunity. They know that the rules applied to other States in their national courts can be applied to them in the courts of other countries." Mark B. Feldman, "The United States Foreign Sovereign Immunities Act of 1976 in Perspective: A Founder's View," 35 *International & Comparative Law Quarterly* 302, 303 (1986).

In Martin v. Republic of South Africa, 836 F.2d 91 (2d Cir.1987), the Second Circuit rules that an African American cannot sue the government of South Africa in U.S. courts for a delay in providing him with medical treatment following an automobile accident in South Africa. A member of a U.S. dance company performing in South Africa, Martin had to wait longer for care than did a white companion also in the car. Citing *Texas Trading*, *inter alia*, Martin argued that for the court to refuse to find "direct effect" in his case would create an "anomaly between the treatment of corporations and the treatment of individuals." How persuasive is the court's rejection of Martin's claim?:

> We do not believe that such a distinction exists, nor do we create one here. Appellant was not in the United States at the time of the accident. He was in South Africa. Indeed, he did not return to the United States until more than a year after the date of the accident. Application of the plain language of § 1605(a)(2) leads us to conclude that South Africa's conduct did not cause a direct effect in the United States.

Id. at 95.

In Republic of Argentina v. Weltover, Inc., 504 U.S. 607, 112 S.Ct. 2160, 119 L.Ed.2d 394 (1992), Justice Scalia, writing for a unanimous Supreme Court, holds that Argentina's reschedulings of debt payments had a "direct effect" in the United States since New York was the place where the debts had to be repaid. *Id.* at 617, 112 S.Ct. at 2168, 119 L.Ed.2d at 407.

3. *Sovereign Immunity and the Executive Branch*. What should be the role of the executive branch vis-à-vis the courts and the legislature in making sovereign immunity determinations? As Chief Justice Burger notes in *Verlinden*, before the Foreign Sovereign Immunity Act was enacted in 1976, the State Department recommended the position the courts should take on a case-by-case basis. An internal memo to the Legal Adviser of the State Department in 1966 commented on the "plainly unsatisfactory" state of the law of sovereign immunity:

> 1. The determination by the State Department, though generally considered conclusive by the courts, is made without clear guideline or procedures. It is in part a "legal" determination, though it is held not to be reviewable; and in part a political determination, though made by lawyers. The determination is sometimes made after a kind of hearing, sometimes not, and there is virtually never an articulation of the reasons for the determination.
>
> 2. The courts, when asked to rule in the absence of a State Department suggestion, have no satisfactory distinctions to follow, and reach inconsistent results.

3. There is no consistency between the policy of the United States Government in defending suits abroad and in recognition by the Executive Branch of claims of immunity of foreign governments in the United States.

Quoted in Andreas F. Lowenfeld, *International Litigation and Arbitration* 588 (1993). The Foreign Sovereign Immunities Act places the burden of determining sovereign immunity with the federal courts. Was the statutory solution necessary, or could the courts have accomplished the same result simply through case law? Or would it have been wiser to leave the development of sovereign immunity to periodic executive pronouncement?

ARGENTINE REPUBLIC v. AMERADA HESS SHIPPING CORP.

488 U.S. 428, 109 S.Ct. 683, 102 L.Ed.2d 818 (1989).

CHIEF JUSTICE REHNQUIST delivered the opinion of the Court.

Two Liberian corporations sued the Argentine Republic in a United States District Court to recover damages for a tort allegedly committed by its armed forces on the high seas in violation of international law. We hold that the District Court correctly dismissed the action, because the Foreign Sovereign Immunities Act of 1976 (FSIA), 29 U.S.C. § 1330 *et seq.*, does not authorize jurisdiction over a foreign state in this situation.

Respondents alleged the following facts in their complaints. Respondent United Carriers, Inc., a Liberian corporation, chartered one of its oil tankers, the Hercules, to respondent Amerada Hess Shipping Corporation, also a Liberian corporation. The contract was executed in New York City. Amerada Hess used the Hercules to transport crude oil from the southern terminus of the Trans–Alaska Pipeline in Valdez, Alaska, around Cape Horn in South America, to the Hess refinery in the United States Virgin Islands. On May 25, 1982, the Hercules began a return voyage, without cargo but fully fueled, from the Virgin Islands to Alaska. At that time, Great Britain and petitioner Argentine Republic were at war over an archipelago of some 200 islands—the Falkland Islands to the British, and the Islas Malvinas to the Argentineans—in the South Atlantic off the Argentine coast. On June 3, United States officials informed the two belligerents of the location of United States vessels and Liberian tankers owned by United States interests then traversing the South Atlantic, including the Hercules, to avoid any attacks on neutral shipping.

By June 8, 1982, after a stop in Brazil, the Hercules was in international waters about 600 nautical miles from Argentina and 500 miles from the Falklands; she was outside the "war zones" designated by Britain and Argentina. At 12:15 Greenwich mean time, the ship's master made a routine report by radio to Argentina officials, providing the ship's name, international call sign, registry, position, course, speed, and voyage description. About 45 minutes later, an Argentine military aircraft began to circle the Hercules. The ship's master repeated his earlier message by radio to Argentine officials, who acknowledged receiving it. Six minutes later, without provocation, another Argentine military plane began to bomb the Hercules; the master immediately hoisted a white flag. A second bombing soon followed, and a third attack came about two hours later, when an Argentine jet struck the ship with an air-to-surface rocket. Disabled but not destroyed, the Hercules reversed course and sailed to Rio de Janeiro, the nearest safe port. At Rio de Janeiro, respondent United Carriers determined that the ship had suffered extensive deck and hull damage, and that an undetonated bomb remained lodged in her No. 2 tank. After an investigation by the Brazilian Navy, United Carriers decided that it would be too hazardous to remove the undetonated bomb, and on July 20, 1978, the Hercules was scuttled 250 miles off the Brazilian coast.

Following unsuccessful attempts to obtain relief in Argentina, respondents commenced this action in the United States District Court for the Southern District of New York for the damage that they sustained from the attack. United Carriers sought $10 million in damages for the loss of the ship; Amerada Hess sought $1.9 million in damages for the fuel that went down with the ship. Respondents alleged that petitioner's attack on the neutral Hercules violated international law. They invoked the District Court's jurisdiction under the Alien Tort Statute, 28 U.S.C. § 1350, which provides that "[t]he district courts shall have original jurisdiction of any civil action by an alien for a tort only, committed in violation of the law of nations or a treaty of the United States." Amerada Hess also brought suit under the general admiralty and maritime jurisdiction, 28 U.S.C. § 1333, and "the principle of universal jurisdiction, recognized in customary international law." The District Court dismissed both complaints for lack of subject-matter jurisdiction, ruling that respondents' suits were barred by the FSIA.

A divided panel of the United States Court of Appeals for the Second Circuit reversed. * * *

We think that the text and structure of the FSIA demonstrate Congress' intention that the FSIA be the sole basis for obtaining jurisdiction over a foreign state in our courts. Section 1604 and § 1330(a) work in tandem; § 1604 bars federal and state courts from exercising jurisdiction when a foreign state is entitled to immunity, and § 1330(a) confers jurisdiction on district courts to hear suits brought by United States citizens and by aliens when a foreign state is *not* entitled to immunity. As we said in *Verlinden,* the FSIA "must be applied by the district courts in every action against a foreign sovereign, since subject-matter jurisdiction in any such action depends on the existence of one of the specified exceptions to foreign sovereign immunity." *Verlinden B.V. v. Central Bank of Nigeria*, 461 U.S. 480, 493 (1983).

The Court of Appeals acknowledged that the FSIA's language and legislative history support the "general rule" that the Act governs the immunity of foreign states in federal court. The Court of Appeals, however, thought that the FSIA's "focus on commercial concerns" and

Congress' failure to "repeal" the Alien Tort Statute indicated Congress' intention that federal courts continue to exercise jurisdiction over foreign states in suits alleging violations of international law outside the confines of the FSIA. The Court of Appeals also believed that to construe the FSIA to bar the instant suit would "fly in the face" of Congress' intention that the FSIA be interpreted pursuant to "standards recognized under international law."

Taking the last of these points first, Congress had violations of international law by foreign states in mind when it enacted the FSIA. For example, the FSIA specifically denies foreign states immunity in suits "in which rights in property taken in violation of international law are in issue." 28 U.S.C. § 1605(a)(3). Congress also rested the FSIA in part on its power under Art. I., § 8, cl. 10, of the Constitution "[t]o define and punish Piracies and Felonies committed on the high Seas, and Offenses against the Law of Nations." From Congress' decision to deny immunity to foreign states in the class of cases just mentioned, we draw the plain implication that immunity is granted in those cases involving alleged violations of international law that do not come within one of the FSIA's exceptions.

As to the other point made by the Court of Appeals, Congress' failure to enact a *pro tanto* repealer of the Alien Tort Statute when it passed the FSIA in 1976 may be explained at least in part by the lack of certainty as to whether the Alien Tort Statute conferred jurisdiction in suits against foreign states. Enacted by the First Congress in 1789, the Alien Tort Statute provides that "[t]he district courts shall have original jurisdiction of any civil action by an alien for a tort only, committed in violation of the law of nations or a treaty of the United States." 28 U.S.C. § 1350. The Court of Appeals did not cite any decision in which a United States court exercised jurisdiction over a foreign state under the Alien Tort Statute, and only one such case has come to our attention—one which was decided after the enactment of the FSIA. * * *

We think that Congress' failure in the FSIA to enact an express *pro tanto* repealer of the Alien Tort Statute speaks only faintly, if at all, to the issue involved in this case. In light of the comprehensiveness of the statutory scheme in the FSIA, we doubt that even the most meticulous draftsman would have concluded that Congress also needed to amend *pro tanto* the Alien Tort Statute and presumably such other grants of subject-matter jurisdiction in Title 28 as § 1331 (federal question), § 1333 (admiralty), § 1335 (interpleader), § 1337 (commerce and antitrust), and § 1338 (patents, copyrights, and trademarks). Congress provided in § 1602 of the FSIA that "[c]laims of foreign states to immunity should *henceforth* be decided by courts of the United States in conformity with the principles set forth in this chapter," and very likely it thought that should be sufficient. * * *

Having determined that the FSIA provides the sole basis for obtaining jurisdiction over a foreign state in federal court, we turn to whether any of the exceptions enumerated in the Act apply here. These exceptions include cases involving the waiver of immunity, commercial activities occurring in the United States or causing a direct effect in this country, property expropriated in violation of international law, real estate, inherited, or gift property located in the United States, noncommercial torts occurring in the United States, and maritime liens. We agree with the District Court that none of the FSIA's exceptions applies on these facts.

Respondents assert that FSIA exception for noncommercial torts, § 1605(a)(5), is most in point. This provision denies immunity in a case

> "in which money damages are sought against a foreign state for personal injury or death, or damage to or loss of property, occurring in the United States and caused by the tortious act or omission of that foreign state or of any official or employee of that foreign state while acting within the scope of his office or employment."

Section 1605(a)(5) is limited by its terms, however, to those cases in which the damage to or loss of property occurs *in the United States*. Congress' primary purpose in enacting § 1605(a)(5) was to eliminate a foreign state's immunity for traffic accidents and other torts committed in the United States, for which liability is imposed under domestic tort law.

In this case, the injury to respondents' ship occurred on the high seas some 5,000 miles off the nearest shores of the United States. Despite these telling facts, respondents nonetheless claim that the tortious attack on the Hercules occurred "in the United States." They point out that the FSIA defines "United States" as including all "territory and waters, continental and insular, subject to the jurisdiction of the United States," and that their injury occurred on the high seas, which is within the admiralty jurisdiction of the United States, see *The Plymouth*, 3 Wall. 20, 36 (1866). They reason, therefore, that "by statutory definition" petitioner's attack occurred in the United States.

We find this logic unpersuasive. We construe the modifying phrase "continental and insular" to restrict the definition of United States to the continental United States and those islands that are part of the United States or its possessions; any other reading would render this phrase nugatory. Likewise, the term "waters" in § 1603(c) cannot reasonably be read to cover all waters over which United States courts might exercise jurisdiction. When it desires to do so, Congress knows how to place the high seas within the jurisdiction reach of a statute. We thus apply "[t]he canon of construction which teaches that legislation of Congress, unless contrary intent appears, is meant to apply only within the territorial jurisdiction of the United States." Because respondents' injury unquestionably occurred well outside the 3–mile limit then in effect for the territorial waters of the United States, the exception for noncommercial torts cannot apply.

The result in this case is not altered by the fact that petitioner's alleged tort may have had effects in the United States. Respondents state, for example, that the Hercules was transporting oil intended for use in this country and that the loss of the ship disrupted contractual payments due in New York. Under the commercial activity exception to the FSIA, § 1605(a)(2), a foreign state may be liable for its commercial activities "outside the territory of the United States" having a "direct effect" inside the United States. But the noncommercial tort exception, § 1605(a)(5), upon which respondents rely, makes no mention of "territory outside the United States" or of "direct effects" in the United States. Congress' decision to use explicit language in § 1605(a)(2), and not to do so in § 1605(a)(5), indicates that the exception in § 1605(a)(5) covers only torts occurring within the territorial jurisdiction of the United States. Respondents do not claim that § 1605(a)(2) covers these facts.

We also disagree with respondents' claim that certain international agreements entered into by petitioner and by the United States create an exception to the FSIA here. As noted, the FSIA was adopted "[s]ubject to international agreements to which the United States [was] a party at the time of [its] enactment." This exception applies when international agreements "expressly conflic[t]" with the immunity provisions of the FSIA, hardly the circumstances in this case. Respondents point to the Geneva Convention on the High Seas, Apr. 29, 1958, [1962] 13 U.S.T. 2312, T.I.A.S. No. 5200, and the Pan–American Maritime Neutrality Convention, Feb. 20, 1928, 47 Stat. 1989, 1990–1991, T.S. No. 845. These conventions, however, only set forth substantive rules of conduct and state that compensation shall be paid for certain wrongs. They do not create private rights of action for foreign corporations to recover compensation from foreign states in United States courts. Nor do we see how a foreign state can waive its immunity under § 1605(a)(1) by signing an international agreement that contains no mention of a waiver of immunity to suit in United States courts or even the availability of a cause of action in the United States. We find similarly unpersuasive the argument of respondent and *Amicus Curiae* Republic of Liberia that the Treaty of Friendship, Commerce and Navigation, Aug. 8, 1938, United States–Liberia, 54 Stat. 1739, T.S. No. 956, carves out an exception to the FSIA. Article I of this Treaty provides, in pertinent part, that the nationals of the United States and Liberia "shall enjoy freedom of access to the courts of justice of the other on conforming to the local laws." The FSIA is clearly one of the "local laws" to which respondents must "conform" before bringing suit in United States courts.

We hold that the FSIA provides the sole basis for obtaining jurisdiction over a foreign state in the courts of this country, and that none of the enumerated exceptions to the Act applies to the facts of this case. The judgment of the Court of Appeals is therefore

Reversed.

Notes and Questions

1. *The Alleged Violation of International Law.* In *Amerada Hess* the Supreme Court does not reach the issue of Argentina's alleged violation of

international law. The Court of Appeals believed that "[t]he facts alleged by [Amerada Hess and United Carriers], if proven, would constitute a clear violation of international law." Amerada Hess Shipping Corp. v. Argentine Republic, 830 F.2d 421, 423 (2d Cir.1987). Looking to treaties dating from the Declaration of Paris of 1856 to the United Nations Law of the Sea Convention of 1982, the Second Circuit ruled that "it is beyond controversy that attacking a neutral ship in international waters, without proper cause for suspicion or investigation, violates international law." *Id.* at 424. The Second Circuit's opinion is excerpted in Chapter 4.

Whatever the possibility of an international law violation, the Supreme Court rules that the Liberian shipping companies could not sue the Argentine government in a U.S. court. Where can the companies go now for redress? What is the potential for other legal procedures, *e.g.*, litigation in Argentina or international arbitration? Are there political or economic avenues open to the companies, *e.g.*, diplomatic protest or economic reprisals?

2. *The Alien Tort Statute.* The Supreme Court in *Amerada Hess* is careful not to decide questions relating to the 1789 Alien Tort Statute and non-governmental defendants: "The Alien Tort Statute by its terms does not distinguish among classes of defendants, and it of course has the same effect after the passage of the FSIA as before with respect to defendants other than foreign states." With respect to government defendants, given the *Amerada Hess* decision, does the Alien Tort Statute add anything to the arsenal of a plaintiff's lawyer that is not already there courtesy of the Foreign Sovereign Immunity Act?

3. *Exceptions to Immunity.* After ruling that the FSIA provides the only way to sue foreign governments, the Supreme Court in *Amerada Hess* considers whether any section 1605 exceptions to immunity exist. Justices Blackmun and Marshall dissent from this part of the judgment, arguing that the question of the FSIA's exceptions had not been fully briefed in the case. They prefer to remand. However, Justice Rehnquist and the majority reject the possibility that there was a section 1605(a)(5) tort "occurring in the United States." Might it have been shown that Argentina had made some sort of implicit waiver in customary international law under section 1605(a)(1)?

Justice Rehnquist also observes that the companies did not make a claim under section 1605(a)(2) for an exception based on "an act outside the territory of the United States in connection with a commercial activity of the foreign state elsewhere and that act causes a direct effect in the United States." What sort of a "commercial activities" exception claim could be made in *Amerada Hess*? The courts have grappled with the definition of a "commercial activity." In Republic of Argentina v. Weltover, Inc., 504 U.S. 607, 112 S.Ct. 2160, 119 L.Ed.2d 394 (1992), the Supreme Court decides that the Argentine government's issuance of "Bonods," bonds to protect foreign creditors, does qualify as "commercial": "[T]hey are in almost all respects garden-variety debt instruments: They may be held by private parties; they are negotiable and may be traded on the international market (except in Argentina); and they promise a future stream of cash income." *Id.* at 615, 112 S.Ct. at 2166, 119 L.Ed.2d at 405. In Cicippio v. Islamic Republic of

Iran, 30 F.3d 164 (D.C.Cir.1994), however, the court holds that kidnapping even for monetary ransom cannot be characterized as "commercial" for the purpose of the FSIA. And in Saudi Arabia v. Nelson, 507 U.S. 349, 113 S.Ct. 1471, 123 L.Ed.2d 47 (1993), the Supreme Court considers whether a U.S. citizen's alleged detention and torture by the Saudi government were so intertwined with his recruitment and hiring to work in a Saudi hospital as to bring into play the "commercial activity" exception of section 1605(a)(2). The Court finds the exception to immunity inapplicable.

4. *The Presumption of Immunity.* Is the *Amerada Hess Case* a good example of the shift in presumption made, perhaps unwittingly, by the drafters of the FSIA? How might the Court's analysis in *Amerada Hess* have been changed if, as in *Victory Transport*, it was incumbent upon Argentina to prove that immunity ought to be granted rather than upon plaintiffs to show that an exception to immunity existed?

5. *International Codification of Sovereign Immunity.* Might sovereign immunity be ripe for international codification? At least six national sovereign immunity statutes have been enacted since the 1976 when the FSIA became law in the United States. Sovereign immunity legislation is now in place in Australia, Canada, Pakistan, Singapore, South Africa, and the United Kingdom. Whatever the virtues of domestic legislation, might not international legislation better suit this field? If possible, why should not there be a treaty providing common rules for different states? For information about efforts to draft an international sovereign immunity convention, see Virginia Morris, "The International Law Commission's Draft Convention on the Jurisdictional Immunities of States and Their Property," 17 *Denver Journal of International Law & Policy* 395 (1989).

C. THE ACT OF STATE DOCTRINE

Also rooted in *The Schooner Exchange*, the act of state doctrine can be easily confused with the doctrine of foreign sovereign immunity. To make an easy distinction, note that act of state does not provide a jurisdictional immunity. Rather, it serves as a principle of choice of law, instructing a court to apply the law of a foreign state respecting an act made by the foreign government in its own territory. The act of state doctrine does share with the doctrine of foreign sovereign immunity (and indeed with the doctrine of *forum non conveniens*) the notion of comity; all in one way or another defer to foreign governments.

There is antique support for the act of state doctrine. In Blad v. Bamfield, 3 Swans. 605 (Chancery, 1674), Blad, a Danish subject, sued Bamfield and others, English subjects, in Chancery for an injunction to stay several actions Bamfield had commenced in the English law courts. Blad had a monopoly for certain trade in Iceland, which was Danish territory, and had seized Bamfield's goods brought to Iceland in contravention of Blad's rights. In Law, Bamfield argued that the Danish royal grants to Blad violated the free-trading terms of an English–Danish treaty. In issuing a perpetual injunction against Bamfield's legal action, Lord Nottingham ruled in Chancery:

> [C]ertainly no case [Blad's] was ever better proved; for the Plaintiff hath proved letters patent from the King of Denmark for the sole trade of Iceland; a seizure by virtue of that patent; a sentence upon that seizure; a confirmation of that sentence by the Chancellor of Denmark; an execution of that sentence after confirmation; and a payment of two thirds to the King of Denmark after that execution. Now, after all this, to send it to a trial at law, where either the Court must pretend to judge of the validity of the King's letters patent in Denmark, or of the exposition and meaning of the articles of peace; or that a common jury should try whether the English have a right to trade in Iceland, is monstrous and absurd.

Id. at 606–07.

In the United States, the act of state doctrine is usually thought to have been first separately elaborated in 1897 in *Underhill v. Hernandez* and to have reached its pinnacle in 1964 in *Banco Nacional de Cuba v. Sabbatino*. Both cases and some of their progeny follow.

UNDERHILL v. HERNANDEZ

168 U.S. 250, 18 S.Ct. 83, 42 L.Ed. 456 (1897).

In the early part of 1892 a revolution was initiated in Venezuela against the administration thereof, which the revolutionists claimed had ceased to be the legitimate government. The principal parties to this conflict were those who recognized Palacio as their head and those who followed the leadership of Crespo. General Hernandez belonged to the anti-administration party, and commanded its forces in the vicinity of Ciudad Bolivar. On the 8th of August 1892, an engagement took place between the armies of the two parties at Buena Vista, some seven miles from Bolivar, in which the troops under Hernandez prevailed, and on the 13th of August, Hernandez entered Bolivar and assumed command of the city. All of the local officials had in the meantime left, and the vacant positions were filled by General Hernandez, who from that date and during the period of the transactions complained of was the civil and military chief of the city and district. In October the party in revolt had achieved success generally, taking possession of the capital of Venezuela, October 6, and on October 23, 1892, the Crespo government, so called, was formally recognized as the legitimate government of Venezuela by the United States.

George F. Underhill was a citizen of the United States, who had constructed a waterworks system for the city of Bolivar under a contract with the government, and was engaged in supplying the place with water, and he also carried on a machinery-repair business. Some time after the entry of General Hernandez, Underhill applied to him as the officer in command for a passport to leave the city. Hernandez refused this request, and requests made by others in Underhill's behalf, until October 18, when a passport was given and Underhill left the country.

This action was brought to recover damages for the detention caused by reason of the refusal to grant the passport; for the alleged confinement of Underhill to his own house; and for certain alleged assaults and affronts by the soldiers of Hernandez' army.

MR. CHIEF JUSTICE FULLER, after stating the case, delivered the opinion of the court.

Every sovereign State is bound to respect the independence of every other sovereign State, and the courts of one country will not sit in judgment on the acts of the government of another done within its own territory. Redress of grievances by reason of such acts must be obtained through the means open to be availed of by sovereign powers as between themselves.

Nor can the principle be confined to lawful or recognized governments, or to cases where redress can manifestly be had through public channels. The immunity of individuals from suits brought in foreign tribunals for acts done within their own States, in the exercise of governmental authority, whether as civil officers or as military commanders, must necessarily extend to the agents of governments ruling by paramount force as matter of fact. Where a civil war prevails, that is where the people of a country are divided into two hostile parties, who take up arms and oppose one another by military force, generally speaking foreign nations do not assume to judge of the merits of the quarrel. If the party seeking to dislodge the existing government succeeds, and the independence of the government it has set up is recognized, then the acts of such government from the commencement of its existence are regarded as those of an independent nation. If the political revolt fails of success, still if actual war has been waged, acts of legitimate warfare cannot be made the basis of individual liability. * * *

We entertain no doubt upon the evidence that Hernandez was carrying on military operations in support of the revolutionary party. It may be that adherents of the side of the controversy in the particular locality where Hernandez was the leader of the movement entertained a preference for him as the future executive head of the nation, but that is beside the question. The acts complained of were the acts of a military commander representing the authority of the revolutionary party as a government, which afterwards succeeded and was recognized by the United States. We think the Circuit Court of Appeals was justified in concluding "that the acts of the defendant were the acts of the government of Venezuela, and as such are not properly the subject of adjudication in the courts of another government."

The decisions cited on plaintiff's behalf are not in point. Cases respecting arrest by military authority in the absence of the prevalence of war; or the validity of contracts between individuals entered into in aid of insurrection; or the right of revolutionary bodies to vex the commerce of the world on its common highway without incurring the penalties denounced on piracy; and the like, do not involve the questions presented here.

We agree with Circuit Court of Appeals, that "the evidence upon the trial indicated that the purpose of the defendant in his treatment of the plaintiff was to coerce the plaintiff to operate his waterworks and his repair works for the benefit of the community and the revolutionary forces," and that "it was not sufficient to have warranted a finding by the jury that the defendant was actuated by malice or any personal or private motive"; and we concur in its disposition of the rulings below. The decree of the Circuit Court is

Affirmed.

BANCO NACIONAL DE CUBA v. SABBATINO

376 U.S. 398, 84 S.Ct. 923, 11 L.Ed.2d 804 (1964).

MR. JUSTICE HARLAN delivered the opinion of the Court.

The question which brought this case here, and is now found to be the dispositive issue, is whether the so-called act of state doctrine serves to sustain petitioner's claims in this litigation. Such claims are ultimately found on a decree of the Government of Cuba expropriating certain property, the right to the proceeds of which is here in controversy. The act of state doctrine in its traditional formulation precludes the courts of this country from inquiring into the validity of the public acts a recognized foreign sovereign power committed within its own territory.

I.

In February and July of 1960, respondent Farr, Whitlock & Co., an American commodity broker, contracted to purchase Cuban sugar, free alongside the streamer, from a wholly owned subsidiary of Compania Azucarera Vertientes–Camaguey de Cuba (C. A. V.), a corporation organized under Cuban law whose capital stock was owned principally by United States residents. Farr, Whitlock agreed to pay for the sugar in New York upon presentation of the shipping documents and a sight draft.

On July 6, 1960, the Congress of the United States amended the Sugar Act of 1948 to permit a presidentially directed reduction of the sugar quota for Cuba. On the same day President Eisenhower exercised the granted power. The day of the congressional enactment, the Cuban Council of Ministers adopted "Law No. 851," which characterized this reduction in the Cuban sugar quota as an act of "aggression, for political purposes" on the part of the United States, justifying the taking of countermeasures by Cuba. The law gave the Cuban President and Prime Minister discretionary power to nationalize by forced expropriation property or enterprises in which American nationals had an interest.[3] Although a system of compensation was formally provided, the

3. "WHEREAS, the attitude assumed by the government and the Legislative Power of the United States of North America, which constitutes an aggression, for political purposes, against the basic interests of the Cuban economy, as recently evidenced by the Amendment to the Sugar Act just enacted by the United States Congress at the request of the Chief Executive of that country, whereby exceptional powers are

possibility of payment under it may well be deemed illusory. Our State Department has described the Cuban law as "manifestly in violation of those principles of international law which have long been accepted by the free countries of the West. It is in its essence discriminatory, arbitrary and confiscatory."

Between August 6 and August 9, 1960, the sugar covered by the contract between Farr, Whitlock and C. A. V. was loaded, destined for Morocco, onto the S. S. *Hornfels*, which was standing offshore at the Cuban port of Jucaro (Santa Maria). On the day loading commenced, the Cuban President and Prime Minister, acting pursuant to Law No. 851, issued Executive Power Resolution No. 1. It provided for the compulsory expropriation of all property and enterprises, and of rights and interests arising therefrom, of certain listed companies, including C. A. V., wholly or principally owned by American nationals. The preamble reiterated the alleged injustice of the American reduction of the Cuban sugar quota and emphasized the importance of Cuba's serving as an example for other countries to follow "in their struggle to free themselves from the brutal claws of Imperialism."[7] In consequence of the

conferred upon the President of the United States to reduce the participation of Cuban sugars in the American sugar market as a threat of political action against Cuba, forces the Revolutionary Government to adopt, without hesitation, all and whatever measures it may deem appropriate or desirable for the due defense of the national sovereignty and protection of our economic development process.

. . .

"WHEREAS, it is advisable, with a view to the ends referred to in the first Whereas of this Law, to confer upon the President and Prime Minister of the Republic full authority to carry out the nationalization of the enterprises and property owned by physical and corporate persons who are nationals of the United States of North America, or of enterprises which have majority interest or participations in such enterprises, even though they be organized under the Cuban laws, so that the required measures may be adopted in future cases with a view to the ends pursued.

"NOW, THEREFORE: In pursuance of the powers vested in it, the Council of Ministers has resolved to enact and promulgate the following

"LAW NO. 851

"ARTICLE 1. Full authority is hereby conferred upon the President and the Prime Minister of the Republic in order that, acting jointly through appropriate resolutions whenever they shall deem it advisable or desirable for the protection of the national interests, they may proceed to nationalize, through forced expropriations, the properties or enterprises owned by physical and corporate persons who are nationals of the United States of North America, or of the enterprises in which such physical and corporate persons have an interest, even though they be organized under the Cuban laws."

7. "WHEREAS, the attitude assumed by the Government and the Legislative Power of the United States of North America of continued aggression, for political purposes, against the basic interests of Cuban economy, as evidenced by the amendment to the Sugar Act adopted by the Congress of said country, whereby exceptional powers were conferred upon the President of said nation to reduce the participation of Cuban sugars in the sugar market of said country, as a weapon of political action against Cuba, was considered as the fundamental justification of said law.

"WHEREAS, the Chief Executive of the Government of the United States of North America, making use of said exceptional powers, and assuming an obvious attitude of economic and political aggression against our country, has reduced the participation of Cuban sugars in the North American market with the unquestionable design to attack Cuba and its revolutionary process.

"WHEREAS, this action constitutes a reiteration of the continued conduct of the government of the United States of North America, intended to prevent the exercise of its sovereignty and its integral development by our people thereby serving the base in-resolution, the consent of the Cuban Government was necessary before a ship carrying sugar of a named company could leave Cuban waters. In order to obtain this consent, Farr, Whitlock, on August 11, entered into contracts, identical to those it had made with C. A. V., with the Banco Para el Comercio Exterior de Cuba, an instrumentality of the Cuban Government. The S. S. *Hornfels* sailed for Morocco on August 12.

Banco Exterior assigned the bills of lading to petitioner, also an instrumentality of the Cuban Government, which instructed its agent in New York, Société Génerale, to deliver the bills and a sight draft in the sum of $175,250.69 to Farr, Whitlock in return for payment. Société Génerale's initial tender of the documents was refused by Farr, Whitlock, which on the same day was notified of C. A. V.'s claim that as rightful owner of the sugar it was entitled to the proceeds. In return for a promise not to turn the funds over to petitioner or its agent, C. A. V. agreed to indemnify Farr, Whitlock for any loss. Farr, Whitlock subsequently accepted the shipping documents, negotiated the bills of lading to its customer, and received payment for the sugar. It refused, however, to hand over the proceeds to Société Génerale. Shortly thereafter, Farr, Whitlock was served with an order of the New York Supreme Court, which had appointed Sabbatino as Temporary Receiver of C. A. V.'s New York assets, enjoining it from taking any action in regard to the money claimed by C. A. V. that might result in its removal from the State. Following this, Farr, Whitlock, pursuant to court order, trans-

terests of the North American trusts, which have hindered the growth of our economy and the consolidation of our political freedom.

"WHEREAS, in the face of such developments the undersigned, being fully conscious of their great historical responsibility and in legitimate defense of the national economy are duty bound to adopt the measures deemed necessary to counteract the harm done by the aggression inflicted upon our nation.

. . .

"WHEREAS, it is the duty of the peoples of Latin America to strive for the recovery of their native wealth by wresting it from the hands of the foreign monopolies and interests which prevent their development, promote political interference, and impair the sovereignty of the underdeveloped countries of America.

"WHEREAS, the Cuban Revolution will not stop until it shall have totally and definitely liberated its fatherland.

"WHEREAS, Cuba must be a luminous and stimulating example for the sister nations of America and all the underdeveloped countries of the world to follow in their struggle to free themselves from the brutal claws of Imperialism.

"NOW, THEREFORE: In pursuance of the powers vested in us, in accordance with the provisions of Law No. 851, of July 6, 1960, we hereby,

"RESOLVE:

"FIRST. To order the nationalization, through compulsory expropriation, and, therefore, the adjudication in fee simple to the Cuban State, of all the property and enterprises located in the national territory, and the rights and interests resulting from the exploitation of such property and enterprises, owned by the juridical persons who are nationals of the United States of North America, or operators of enterprises in which nationals of said country have a predominating interest, as listed below, to wit:

. . .

"22. Compaña Azucarera Vertientes Camagüey de Cuba.

. . .

"SECOND. Consequently, the Cuban State is hereby subrogated in the place and stead of the juridical persons listed in the preceding section, in respect of the property, rights and interest aforesaid, and of the assets and liabilities constituting the capital of said enterprises."

ferred the funds to Sabbatino, to abide the event of a judicial determination as to their ownership.

[The Court decides that Cuba could still sue in the United States though it was an unfriendly power, rejects the contention that the case should be decided by New York law, then turns to the act of state doctrine.]

IV.

The classic American statement of the act of state doctrine, which appears to have taken root in England as early as 1674, *Blad v. Bamfield*, 3 Swans. 604, 36 Eng.Rep. 992, and began to emerge in the jurisprudence of this country in the late eighteenth and early nineteenth centuries, see *e.g., Ware v. Hylton*, 3 Dall, 199, 230; *The Schooner Exchange v. M'Faddon*, 7 Cranch 116, 135, 136, is found in *Underhill v. Hernandez*, where Chief Justice Fuller said for a unanimous Court:

> "Every sovereign State is bound to respect the independence of every other sovereign State, and the courts of one country will not sit in judgment on the acts of the government of another done within its own territory. Redress of grievances by reason of such acts must be obtained through the means open to be availed of by sovereign powers as between themselves."

Following this precept the Court in that case refused to inquire into acts of Hernandez, a revolutionary Venezuelan military commander whose government had been later recognized by the United States, which were made the basis of a damage action in this country by Underhill, an American citizen, who claimed that he had been unlawfully assaulted, coerced, and detained in Venezuela by Hernandez.

None of this Court's subsequent cases in which the act of state doctrine was directly or peripherally involved manifest any retreat from *Underhill*. * * *

V.

Preliminarily, we discuss the foundations on which we deem the act of state doctrine to rest, and more particularly the question of whether state or federal law governs its application in a federal diversity case.

We do not believe that this doctrine is compelled either by the inherent nature of sovereign authority, as some of the earlier decisions seem to imply, or by some principle of international law. If a transaction takes place in one jurisdiction and the forum is in another, the forum does not by dismissing an action or by applying its own law purport to divest the first jurisdiction of its territorial sovereignty; it merely declines to adjudicate or makes applicable its own law to parties or property before it. The refusal of one country to enforce the penal laws of another is a typical example of an instance when a court will not entertain a cause of action arising in another jurisdiction. While historic notions of sovereign authority do bear upon the wisdom of employing the act of state doctrine, they do not dictate its existence.

That international law does not require application of the doctrine is evidenced by the practice of nations. Most of the countries rendering decisions on the subject fail to follow the rule rigidly. No international arbitral or judicial decision discovered suggests that international law prescribes recognition of sovereign acts of foreign governments, and apparently no claim has ever been raised before an international tribunal that failure to apply the act of state doctrine constitutes a breach of international obligation. If international law does not prescribe use of the doctrine, neither does it forbid application of the rule even if it is claimed that the act of state in question violated international law. The traditional view of international law is that it establishes substantive principles for determining whether one country has wronged another. Because of its peculiar nation-to-nation character the usual method for an individual to seek relief is to exhaust local remedies and then repair to the executive authorities of his own state to persuade them to champion his claim in diplomacy or before an international tribunal. Although it is, of course, true that United States courts apply international law as a part of our own in appropriate circumstances, the public law of nations can hardly dictate to a country which is in theory wronged how to treat that wrong within its domestic borders.

Despite the broad statement in *Oetjen* [*v. Central Leather Co.*, 246 U.S. 297, 38 S.Ct. 309, 62 L.Ed. 726 (1918)] that "The conduct of the foreign relations of our Government is committed by the Constitution to the Executive and Legislative ... Departments," it cannot of course be thought that "every case or controversy which touches foreign relations lies beyond judicial cognizance." *Baker v. Carr*, 369 U.S. 186, 211. The text of the Constitution does not require the act of state doctrine; it does not irrevocably remove from the judiciary the capacity to review the validity of foreign acts of state.

The act of state doctrine does, however, have "constitutional" underpinnings. It arises out of the basic relationships between branches of government in a system of separation of powers. It concerns the competency of dissimilar institutions to make and implement particular kinds of decisions in the area of international relations. The doctrine as formulated in past decisions expresses the strong sense of the Judicial Branch that its engagement in the task of passing on the validity of foreign acts of state may hinder rather than further this country's pursuit of goals both for itself and for the community of nations as a whole in the international sphere. Many commentators disagree with this view; they have striven by means of distinguishing and limiting past decisions and by advancing various considerations of policy to stimulate a narrowing of the apparent scope of the rule. Whatever considerations are thought to predominate, it is plain that the problems involved are uniquely federal in nature. If federal authority, in this instance this Court, orders the field of judicial competence in this area for the federal courts, and the state courts are left free to formulate their own rules, the purposes behind the doctrine could be as effectively undermined as if there had been no federal pronouncement on the subject.

We could perhaps in this diversity action avoid the question of deciding whether federal or state law is applicable to this aspect of the litigation. New York has enunciated the act of state doctrine in terms that echo those of federal decisions decided during the reign of *Swift v. Tyson*, 16 Pet. 1. * * *

However, we are constrained to make it clear that an issue concerned with a basic choice regarding the competence and function of the Judiciary and the National Executive in ordering our relationships with other members of the international community must be treated exclusively as an aspect of federal law. It seems fair to assume that the Court did not have rules like the act of state doctrine in mind when it decided *Erie R. Co. v. Tompkins*. Soon thereafter, Professor Philip C. Jessup, now a judge of the International Court of Justice, recognized the potential dangers were *Erie* extended to legal problems affecting international relations. He cautioned that rules of international law should not be left to divergent and perhaps parochial state interpretations. His basic rationale is equally applicable to the act of state doctrine. * * *

VI.

If the act of state doctrine is a principle of decision binding on federal and state courts alike but compelled by neither international law nor the Constitution, its continuing vitality depends on its capacity to reflect the proper distribution of functions between the judicial and political branches of the Government on matters bearing upon foreign affairs. It should be apparent that the greater the degree of codification or consensus concerning a particular area of international law, the more appropriate it is for the judiciary to render decisions regarding it, since the courts can then focus on the application of an agreed principle to circumstances of fact rather than on the sensitive task of establishing a principle not inconsistent with the national interest or with international justice. It is also evident that some aspects of international law touch much more sharply on national nerves than do others; the less important the implications of an issue are for our foreign relations, the weaker the justification of exclusivity in the political branches. The balance of relevant considerations may also be shifted if the government which perpetrated the challenged act of state is no longer in existence, * * * for the political interest of this country may, as a result, be measurably altered. Therefore, rather than laying down or reaffirming an inflexible and all-encompassing rule in this case, we decide only that the Judicial Branch will not examine the validity of a taking of property within its own territory by a foreign sovereign government, extant and recognized by this country at the time of suit, in the absence of a treaty or other unambiguous agreement regarding controlling legal principles, even if the complaint alleges that the taking violates customary international law.

There are few if any issues in international law today on which opinion seems to be so divided as the limitations on a state's power to expropriate the property of aliens. There is, of course, authority, in international judicial and arbitral decisions, in the expressions of national governments, and among commentators for the view that a taking is improper under international law if it is not for a public purpose, is discriminatory, or is without provision for prompt, adequate, and effective compensation. However, Communist countries, although they have in fact provided a degree of compensation after diplomatic efforts, commonly recognize no obligation on the part of the taking country. Certain representatives of the newly independent and underdeveloped countries have questioned whether rules of state responsibility toward aliens can bind nations that have not consented to them and it is argued that the traditionally articulated standards governing expropriation of property reflect "imperialist" interests and are inappropriate to the circumstances of emergent states.

The disagreement as to relevant international law standards reflects an even more basic divergence between the national interests of capital importing and capital exporting nations and between the social ideologies of those countries that favor state control of a considerable portion of the means of production and those that adhere to a free enterprise system. It is difficult to imagine the courts of this country embarking on adjudication in an area which touches more sensitively the practical and ideological goals of the various members of the community of nations.

When we consider the prospect of the courts characterizing foreign expropriations, however justifiably, as invalid under international law and ineffective to pass title, the wisdom of the precedents is confirmed. * * *

The possible adverse consequences of a conclusion to the contrary of that implicit in these cases is highlighted by contrasting that practices of the political branch with the limitations of the judicial process in matters of this kind. Following an expropriation of any significance, the Executive engages in diplomacy aimed to assure that United States citizens who are harmed are compensated fairly. Representing all claimants of this country, it will often be able, either by bilateral or multilateral talks, by submission to the United Nations, or by the employment of economic and political sanctions, to achieve some degree of general redress. Judicial determinations of invalidity of title can, on the other hand, have only an occasional impact, since they depend on the fortuitous circumstance of the property in question being brought into this country. Such decisions would, if the acts involved were declared invalid, often be likely to give offense to the expropriating country; since the concept of territorial sovereignty is so deep seated, any state may resent the refusal of the courts of another sovereign to accord validity to acts within its territorial borders. Piecemeal dispositions of this sort involving the probability of affront to another state could seriously interfere with negotiations being carried on by the Executive Branch and might prevent or render less favorable the terms of an agreement that could otherwise be reached. Relations with third countries which have engaged in similar expropriations would not be immune from effect.

The dangers of such adjudication are present regardless of whether the State Department has, as it did in this case, asserted that the relevant act violated international law. If the Executive Branch has undertaken negotiations with an expropriating country, but has refrained from claims of violation of the law of nations, a determination to that effect by a court might be regarded as a serious insult, while a finding of compliance with international law would greatly strengthen the bargaining hand of the other state with consequent detriment to American interests.

Even if the State Department has proclaimed the impropriety of the expropriation, the stamp of approval of its view by a judicial tribunal, however impartial, might increase any affront and the judicial decision might occur at a time, almost always well after the taking, when such an impact would be contrary to our national interest. Considerably more serious and far-reaching consequences would flow from a judicial finding that international law standards had been met if that determination flew in the face of a State Department proclamation to the contrary. When articulating principles of international law in its relations with other states, the Executive Branch speaks not only as an interpreter of generally accepted and traditional rules, as would the courts, but also as an advocate of standards it believes desirable for the community of nations and protective of national concerns. In short, whatever way the matter is cut, the possibility of conflict between the Judicial and Executive Branches could hardly be avoided. * * *

However offensive to the public policy of this country and its constituent States an expropriation of this kind may be, we conclude that both the national interest and progress toward the goal of establishing the rule of law among nations are best served by maintaining intact the act of state doctrine in this realm of its application.

Notes and Questions

1. *The* Underhill *Doctrine.* The famous line in *Underhill*, even reaching the *New York Times* ("Underhill's Suit Dismissed: No Judicial Remedy for His Detention in Venezuela," *New York Times*, Nov. 30, 1897, at 10), is the first one in Chief Justice Fuller's opinion: "Every sovereign State is bound to respect the independence of every other sovereign State, and the courts of one country will not sit in judgment on the acts of the government done within its own territory." Though first enunciating the act of state doctrine, could *Underhill* have also been decided simply by treating General Hernandez as an agent of the Venezuelan government and then by protecting both from the jurisdiction of U.S. courts by way of the doctrine of sovereign immunity? After all, the opinion goes on to say: "The acts complained of were the acts of a military commander representing the authority of the revolutionary party as a government, which afterwards succeeded and was recognized by the United States."

2. *The Background to* Sabbatino. The political events leading to the *Sabbatino Case* were front-page news in the United States. On June 23, 1960, "Premier Fidel Castro threatened * * * to meet 'economic aggression'

by the United States with the seizure of all American-owned property and business interests in Cuba." "U.S. Holdings to Be Taken If Sugar Is Cut, Castro Says," *New York Times*, June 24, 1960, at 1. On July 6, 1960, President Eisenhower "virtually ended * * * Cuba's sugar sales to the United States for this year." Tad Szulc, "U.S. Cuts Cuba Sugar Sale By 95% for Rest of Year; President Cites Hostility," *New York Times*, July 7, 1960, at 1, 9. The next day, Premier Castro "whipped [a] crowd of several thousand into displays of frenzied anger against the United States." R. Hart Phillips, "Castro Attacks Sugar Quota as 'Imperialism'," *New York Times*, July 8, 1960, at 1. And on August 7, 1960, the Cuban Premier proclaimed the "forcible expropriation" of all U.S.-owned companies in his country. R. Hart Phillips, "Castro Decrees Seizure of Rest of U.S. Property; Cites Cut in Sugar Quota," *New York Times*, Aug. 7, 1960, at 1. The *Sabbatino* decision of the U.S. Supreme Court also took on a high political profile. The Court's reaffirmation of the act of state doctrine—"The courts of one country will not sit in judgment on the acts of the government of another done within its own territory"—itself achieved front-page status. Anthony Lewis, "High Court Bars Judging of Cuba on Expropriation," *New York Times*, Mar. 24, 1964, at 1.

3. *The Reaction to* Sabbatino. It should be no surprise that the *Sabbatino* judgment evoked an uproar in the U.S. Congress, which promptly passed what became known as the *Sabbatino* or Second Hickenlooper Amendment to the Foreign Assistance Act of 1964. The amendment includes the following language:

> Notwithstanding any other provision of law, no court in the United States shall decline on the ground of the federal act of state doctrine to make a determination on the merits giving effect to the principles of international law in a case in which a claim of title or other right to property is asserted by any party including a foreign state (or a party claiming through such state) based upon (or traced through) a confiscation or other taking after January 1, 1959, by an act of that state in violation of the principles of international law, including the principles of compensation and the other standards set out in this subsection: Provided, that this subparagraph shall not be applicable (1) in any case in which an act of a foreign state is not contrary to international law or with respect to a claim of title or other right acquired pursuant to an irrevocable letter of credit of not more than 180 days duration issued in good faith prior to the time of confiscation or other taking, or (2) in any case with respect to which the President determines the application of the act of state doctrine is required in that particular case by the foreign policy interests of the United States and a suggestion to this effect is filed on his behalf in that case with the court.

22 U.S.C. § 2370(e)(2).

On remand, the Southern District Court in New York followed the dictate of the *Sabbatino* Amendment and dismissed plaintiff's complaint. The Second Circuit affirmed, while the Supreme Court denied *certiorari*, effectively permitting itself to be reversed by Congress. Banco Nacional de Cuba v. Farr, 243 F.Supp. 957 (S.D.N.Y.1965), *aff'd*, 383 F.2d 166 (2d Cir.1967), *cert. denied*, 390 U.S. 956, 88 S.Ct. 1038, 19 L.Ed.2d 1151 (1968).

See Richard A. Falk, *The Aftermath of Sabbatino* (Lyman M. Tondel, Jr. ed. 1965). What is the authority of the *Sabbatino Case* as precedent following Congress's *Sabbatino* Amendment? Do the decisions in the follow-up case affect its precedential value?

4. Sabbatino *and the Role of the Courts.* Is the Supreme Court too deferential in principle to the legislative and executive branches in *Sabbatino*? After all, the Court is reluctant to decide a case involving an uncertain point of international law apparently for fear of reaching a conflicting opinion with that of the President or Congress. Is not the Court the branch of the U.S. government best positioned to discover and elaborate international law? Here the international law rule could be used to trump the rule of the foreign state in U.S. litigation. When should the Court turn to the executive or legislative branches for their advice as to whether such a trumping would upset U.S. foreign relations? Compare the reasoning of the Court in *Dames & Moore v. Regan* in Chapter 4.

ALFRED DUNHILL OF LONDON, INC. v. CUBA

425 U.S. 682, 96 S.Ct. 1854, 48 L.Ed.2d 301 (1976).

MR. JUSTICE WHITE delivered the opinion of the Court.†

The issue in this case is whether the failure of respondents to return to petitioner Alfred Dunhill of London, Inc. (Dunhill), funds mistakenly paid by Dunhill for cigars that had been sold to Dunhill by certain expropriated Cuban cigar businesses was an "act of state" by Cuba precluding an affirmative judgment against respondents.

I

The rather involved factual and legal context in which this litigation arises is fully set out in the District Court's opinion in this case, *Menendez v. Faber, Coe & Gregg, Inc.*, 345 F.Supp. 527 (S.D.N.Y.1972), and in closely related litigation, *F. Palicio y Compania, S. A. v. Brush*, 256 F.Supp. 481 (S.D.N.Y.1966), aff'd, 375 F.2d 1011 (CA2), cert. denied, 389 U.S. 830 (1967). For present purposes, the following recitation will suffice. In 1960, the Cuban Government confiscated the business and assets of the five leading manufacturers of Havana cigars. These companies, three corporations and two partnerships, were organized under Cuban law. Virtually all of their owners were Cuban nationals. None were American. These companies sold large quantities of cigars to customers in other countries, including the United States, where the three principal importers were Dunhill, Saks & Co. (Saks), and Faber, Coe & Gregg, Inc. (Faber). The Cuban Government named "interventors" to take possession of and operate the business of the seized Cuban concerns. Interventors continued to ship cigars to foreign purchasers, including the United States importers.

† Part III of this opinion is joined only by THE CHIEF JUSTICE, MR. JUSTICE POWELL, and MR. JUSTICE REHNQUIST.

This litigation began when the former owners of the Cuban companies, most of whom had fled to the United States, brought various actions against the three American importers for trademark infringement and for the purchase price of any cigars that had been shipped to importers from the seized Cuban plants and that bore United States trademarks claimed by the former owners to be their property. Following the conclusion of the related litigation in *F. Palicio y Compania, S. A. v. Brush*, the Cuban interventors and the Republic of Cuba were allowed to intervene in these actions, which were consolidated for trial. Both the former owners and the interventors had asserted their right to some $700,000 due from the three importers for postintervention shipments: Faber $582,588.86; Dunhill, $92,949.70; and Saks, $24,250. It also developed that as of the date of intervention, the three importers owed sums totaling $477,200 for cigars shipped prior to intervention: Faber, $322,000; Dunhill, $148,600; and Saks, $6,600. These latter sums the importers had paid to interventors subsequent to intervention on the assumption that interventors were entitled to collect the accounts receivable of the intervened businesses. The former owners claimed title to and demanded payment of these accounts. * * *

III

If we assume with the Court of Appeals that the Cuban Government itself had purported to exercise sovereign power to confiscate the mistaken payments belonging to three foreign creditors and to repudiate interventors' adjudicated obligation to return those funds, we are nevertheless persuaded by the arguments of petitioner and by those of the United States that the concept of an act of state should not be extended to include the repudiation of a purely commercial obligation owed by a foreign sovereign or by one of its commercial instrumentalities. Our cases have not yet gone so far, and we decline to expand their reach to the extent necessary to affirm the Court of Appeals. * * *

Of course, sovereign immunity has not been pleaded in this case; but it is beyond cavil that part of the foreign relations law recognized by the United States is that the commercial obligations of a foreign government may be adjudicated in those courts otherwise having jurisdiction to enter such judgments. Nothing in our national policy calls on us to recognize as an act of state a repudiation by Cuba of an obligation adjudicated in our courts and arising out of the operation of a commercial business by one of its instrumentalities. For all the reasons which led the Executive Branch to adopt the restrictive theory of sovereign immunity, we hold that the mere assertion of sovereignty as a defense to a claim arising out of purely commercial acts by a foreign sovereign is no more effective if given the label "Act of State" than if it is given the label "sovereign immunity." In describing the act of state doctrine in the past we have said that it "precludes the courts of this country from inquiring into the validity of the *public* acts a recognized foreign sovereign power committed within its own territory." *Banco Nacional de Cuba v. Sabbatino* (emphasis added), and that it applies to "acts done within their own States, in the exercise of *governmental* authority."

Underhill v. Hernandez (emphasis added). We decline to extend the act of state doctrine to acts committed by foreign sovereigns in the course of their purely commercial operations. Because the act relied on by respondents in this case was an act arising out of the conduct by Cuba's agents in the operation of cigar businesses for profit, the act was not an act of state.

Reversed.

W.S. KIRKPATRICK & CO. v. ENVIRONMENTAL TECTONICS CORP. INTERNATIONAL

493 U.S. 400, 110 S.Ct. 701, 107 L.Ed.2d 816 (1990).

JUSTICE SCALIA delivered the opinion of the Court.

In this case we must decide whether the act of state doctrine bars a court in the United States from entertaining a cause of action that does not rest upon the asserted invalidity of an official act of a foreign sovereign, but that does require imputing to foreign officials an unlawful motivation (the obtaining of bribes) in the performance of such an official act.

I

The facts as alleged in respondent's complaint are as follows: In 1981, Harry Carpenter, who was then Chairman of the Board and Chief Executive Officer of petitioner W. S. Kirkpatrick & Co., Inc. (Kirkpatrick), learned that the Republic of Nigeria was interested in contracting for the construction and equipment of an aeromedical center at Kaduna Air Force Base in Nigeria. He made arrangements with Benson "Tunde" Akindele, a Nigerian citizen whereby Akindele would endeavor to secure the contract for Kirkpatrick. It was agreed that, in the event the contract was awarded to Kirkpatrick, Kirkpatrick would pay to two Panamanian entities controlled by Akindele a "commission" equal to 20% of the contract price, which would in turn be given as a bribe to officials of the Nigerian Government. In accordance with this plan, the contract was awarded to petitioner W. S. Kirkpatrick & Co., International (Kirkpatrick International), a wholly owned subsidiary of Kirkpatrick; Kirkpatrick paid the promised "commission" to the appointed Panamanian entities; and those funds were disbursed as bribes. All parties agree that Nigerian law prohibits both the payment and the receipt of bribes in connection with the award of a government contract.

Respondent Environmental Tectonics Corporation, International, an unsuccessful bidder for the Kaduna contract, learned of the 20% "commission" and brought the matter to the attention of the Nigerian Air Force and the United States Embassy in Lagos. Following an investigation by the Federal Bureau of Investigation, the United States Attorney for the District of New Jersey brought charges against both Kirkpatrick and Carpenter for violations of the Foreign Corrupt Practices Act of 1977, 15 U.S.C. § 78dd–1 *et seq.*, and both pleaded guilty.

Respondent then brought this civil action in the United States District Court for District of New Jersey against Carpenter, Akindele, petitioners, and others, seeking damages under the Racketeer Influenced and Corrupt Organizations Act, 18 U.S.C. § 1961 *et seq.*, the Robinson–Patman Act, 15 U.S.C. § 13 *et seq.*, and the New Jersey Anti–Racketeering Act N.J. Stat. Ann. § 2C:41–2 *et seq.* (West 1982). The defendants moved to dismiss the complaint under Rule 12(b)(6) of the Federal Rules of Civil Procedure on the ground that the action was barred by the act of state doctrine.

The District Court, having requested and received a letter expressing the views of the legal adviser to the United States Department of State as to the applicability of the act of state doctrine, treated the motion as one for summary judgment under Rule 56 of the Federal Rules of Civil Procedure and granted the motion. The District Court concluded that the act of state doctrine applies "if the inquiry presented for judicial determination includes the motivation of a sovereign act which would result in embarrassment to the sovereign or constitute interference in the conduct of foreign policy of the United States." Applying that principle to the facts at hand, the court held that respondent's suit had to be dismissed because in order to prevail respondent would have to show that "the defendants or certain of them intended to wrongfully influence the decision to award the Nigerian Contract by payment of a bribe, that the Government of Nigeria, its officials or other representatives knew of the offered consideration for awarding the Nigerian Contract to Kirkpatrick, that the bribe was actually received or anticipated and that 'but for' the payment or anticipation of the payment of the bribe, ETC would have been awarded the Nigerian Contract."

The Court of Appeals for the Third Circuit reversed. Although agreeing with the District Court that "the award of a military procurement contract can be, in certain circumstances, a sufficiently formal expression of a government's public interests to trigger application" of the act of state doctrine, it found application of the doctrine unwarranted on the facts of this case. The Court of Appeals found particularly persuasive the letter to the District Court from the legal adviser to the Department of State, which had stated that in the opinion of the Department judicial inquiry into the purpose behind the act of a foreign sovereign would not produce the "unique embarrassment, and the particular interference with the conduct of foreign affairs, that may result from the judicial determination that a foreign sovereign's acts are invalid." In light of the Department's view that the interests of the Executive Branch would not be harmed by prosecution of the action, the Court of Appeals held that Kirkpatrick had not met its burden of showing that the case should not go forward; accordingly, it reversed the judgment of the District Court and remanded the case for trial. We granted certiorari.

II

This Court's description of the jurisprudential foundation for the act of state doctrine has undergone some evolution over the years. We once viewed the doctrine as an expression of international law, resting upon "the highest considerations of international comity and expediency," *Oetjen v. Central Leather Co.*, 246 U.S. 297, 303–304 (1918). We have more recently described it, however, as a consequence of domestic separation of powers, reflecting "the strong sense of the Judicial Branch that its engagement in the task of passing on the validity of foreign acts of state may hinder" the conduct of foreign affairs, *Banco Nacional de Cuba v. Sabbatino*, 376 U.S. 398, 423 (1964). Some Justices have suggested possible exceptions to application of the doctrine, where one or both of the foregoing policies would seemingly not be served: an exception, for example, for acts of state that consist of commercial transactions, since neither modern international comity nor the current position of our Executive Branch accorded sovereign immunity to such acts, see *Alfred Dunhill of London, Inc. v. Republic of Cuba*, 425 U.S. 682, 695–706 (1976)(opinion of WHITE, J.); or an exception for cases in which the Executive Branch has represented that it has no objection to denying validity to the foreign sovereign act, since then the courts would be impeding no foreign policy goals, see *First National City Bank v. Banco Nacional de Cuba*, 406 U.S. 759, 768–770 (1972)(opinion of REHNQUIST, J.).

The parties have argued at length about the applicability of these possible exceptions, and, more generally, about whether the purpose of the act of state doctrine would be furthered by its application in this case. We find it unnecessary, however, to pursue those inquiries, since the factual predicate for application of the act of state doctrine does not exist. Nothing in the present suit requires the Court to declare invalid, and thus ineffective as "a rule of decision for the courts of this country," *Ricaud v. American Metal Co.*, 246 U.S. 304, 310 (1918), the official act of a foreign sovereign.

In every case in which we have held the act of state doctrine applicable, the relief sought or the defense interposed would have required a court in the United States to declare invalid the official act of a foreign sovereign performed within its own territory. In *Underhill v. Hernandez*, 168 U.S. 250, 254 (1897), holding the defendant's detention of the plaintiff to be tortious would have required denying legal effect to "acts of a military commander representing the authority of the revolutionary party as government, which afterwards succeeded and was recognized by the United States." In *Oetjen v. Central Leather Co.* and in *Ricaud v. American Metal Co.*, denying title to the party who claimed through purchase from Mexico would have required declaring that government's prior seizure of the property, within its own territory, legally ineffective. In *Sabbatino*, upholding the defendant's claim to the funds would have required a holding that Cuba's expropriation of goods located in Havana was null and void. In the present case, by contrast, neither the claim nor any asserted defense requires a determination that Nigeria's contract with Kirkpatrick International was, or was not, effective.

Petitioners point out, however, that the facts necessary to establish respondent's claim will also establish that the contract was unlawful. Specifically, they note that in order to prevail respondent must prove that petitioner Kirkpatrick made, and Nigerian officials received, payments that violate Nigerian law, which would, they assert, support a finding that the contract is invalid under Nigerian law. Assuming that to be true, it still does not suffice. The act of state doctrine is not some vague doctrine of abstention but a "*principle of decision* binding on federal and state courts alike." *Sabbatino* (emphasis added). As we said in *Ricaud,* "the act within its own boundaries of one sovereign State ... becomes ... a rule of decision for the courts of this country." Act of state issues only arise when a court *must decide*—that is, when the outcome of the case turns upon—the effect of official action by a foreign sovereign. When that question is not the case, neither is the act of state doctrine. That is the situation here. Regardless of what the court's factual findings may suggest as to the legality of the Nigerian contract, its legality is simply not a question to be decided in the present suit, and there is thus no occasion to apply the rule of decision that the act of state doctrine requires.

In support of their position that the act of state doctrine bars any factual findings that may cast doubt upon the validity of foreign sovereign acts, petitioners cite Justice Holmes' opinion for the Court in *American Banana Co. v. United Fruit Co.*, 213 U.S. 347 (1909). That was a suit under the United States antitrust laws, alleging that Costa Rica's seizure of the plaintiff's property had been induced by an unlawful conspiracy. In the course of a lengthy opinion Justice Holmes observed, citing *Underhill,* that "a seizure by a state is not a thing that can be complained of elsewhere in the courts." The statement is concededly puzzling. *Underhill* does indeed stand for the proposition that a seizure by a state cannot be complained of elsewhere—in the sense of being sought to be declared *ineffective* elsewhere. The plaintiff in *American Banana*, however, like the plaintiff here, was not trying to undo or disregard the governmental action, but only to obtain damages from private parties who had procured it. Arguably, then, the statement did imply that suit would not lie if a foreign state's actions would be, though not invalidated, impugned.

Whatever Justice Holmes may have had in mind, his statement lends inadequate support to petitioners' position here, for two reasons. First, it was a brief aside, entirely unnecessary to the decision. *American Banana* was squarely decided on the ground (later substantially overruled, see *Continental Ore Co. v. Union Carbide & Carbon Corp.*, 370 U.S. 690, 704–705 (1962)) that the antitrust laws had no extraterritorial application, so that "what the defendant did in Panama or Costa Rica is not within the scope of the statute." Second, whatever support the dictum might provide for petitioners' position is more than overcome by our later holding in *United States v. Sisal Sales Corp.*, 274 U.S. 268 (1927). There we held that, *American Banana* notwithstanding, the defendant's actions in obtaining Mexico's enactment of "discriminating legislation" could form part of the basis for suit under the United States antitrust laws. Simply put, *American Banana* was not an act of state case; and whatever it said by way of dictum that might be relevant to the present case has not survived *Sisal Sales*.

Petitioners insist, however, that the policies underlying our act of state cases—international comity, respect for the sovereignty of foreign nations on their own territory, and the avoidance of embarrassment to the Executive Branch in its conduct of foreign relations—are implicated in the present case because, as the District Court found, a determination that Nigerian officials demanded and accepted a bribe "would impugn or question the nobility of a foreign nation's motivations," and would "result in embarrassment to the sovereign or constitute interference in the conduct of foreign policy of the United States." The United States, as *amicus curiae*, favors the same approach to the act of state doctrine, though disagreeing with petitioners as to the outcome it produces in the present case. We should not, the United States urges, "attach dispositive significance to the fact that this suit involves only the 'motivation' for, rather than the 'validity' of, a foreign sovereign act," and should eschew "any rigid formula for the resolution of act of state cases generally." In some future case, perhaps, "litigation ... based on alleged corruption in the award of contracts or other commercially oriented activities of foreign governments could sufficiently touch on 'national nerves' that the act of state doctrine or related principles of abstention would appropriately be found to bar the suit," and we should therefore resolve this case on the narrowest possible ground, viz., that the letter from the legal adviser to the District Court gives sufficient indication that, "in the setting of this case," the act of state doctrine poses no bar to adjudication.

These urgings are deceptively similar to what we said in *Sabbatino*, where we observed that sometimes, even though the validity of the act of a foreign sovereign within its own territory is called into question, the policies underlying the act of state doctrine may not justify its application. We suggested that a sort of balancing approach could be applied—the balance shifting against application of the doctrine, for example, if the government that committed the "challenged act of state" is no longer in existence. But what is appropriate in order to avoid unquestioning judicial acceptance of the acts of foreign sovereigns is not similarly appropriate for the quite opposite purpose of expanding judicial incapacities where such acts are not directly (or even indirectly) involved. It is one thing to suggest, as we have, that the policies underlying the act of state doctrine should be considered in deciding whether, despite the doctrine's technical availability, it should nonetheless not be invoked; it is something quite different to suggest that those underlying policies are a doctrine unto themselves, justifying expansion of the act of state doctrine (or, as the United States puts it, unspecified "related principles of abstention") into new and uncharted fields.

The short of the matter is this: Courts in the United States have the power, and ordinarily the obligation, to decide cases and controversies properly presented to them. The act of state doctrine does not establish an exception for cases and controversies that may embarrass foreign governments, but merely requires that, in the process of deciding, the acts of foreign sovereigns taken within their own jurisdictions shall be deemed valid. That doctrine has no application to the present case because the validity of no foreign sovereign act is at issue.

The judgment of the Court of Appeals for the Third Circuit is affirmed.

It is so ordered.

Notes and Questions

1. *Restricting the Act of State Doctrine.* Is Justice White's opinion in *Dunhill*, which is only a plurality opinion of four, an attempt to overrule, at least in part, *Sabbatino*? Professor Achebe argues that *Sabbatino*, not *Dunhill*, was rightly decided and would prefer that the act of state doctrine not have a commercial activity exception. Ifeanyi Achebe, "The Act of State Doctrine and Foreign Sovereign Immunities Act of 1976: Can They Coexist?" 13 *Maryland Journal of International Law & Trade* 247, 259 (1989). Achebe also attacks *Texas Trading*, reproduced above, for not taking Nigerian public laws into account and contends that the act of state doctrine should have shielded Nigeria in the case regardless of any interpretation of the Foreign Sovereign Immunities Act. *Id.* at 265–87. Monroe Leigh, formerly Legal Adviser to the U.S. Department of State, takes the opposite tack, believing, *inter alia*, that *Dunhill* properly recognizes the Congressional preference for restrictive sovereign immunity and that "the commercial activity exception can be viewed as one specific manifestation of a general exception for agreed principles of customary international law." Monroe Leigh, "*Sabbatino*'s Silver Anniversary and the Restatement: No Cause for Celebration," 24 *International Lawyer* 1, 13 (1990). Although Leigh does not feel the act of state doctrine should be abolished, he contends that "the doctrine needs to be properly defined and limited," a task not accomplished, in his view, by the 1987 *Restatement (Third) of the Foreign Relations Law of the United States*. *Id.* at 20. A somewhat more sympathetic account of the act of state doctrine concludes that the doctrine "is in great need of reform." Daniel C.K. Chow, "Rethinking the Act of State Doctrine: An Analysis in Terms of Jurisdiction to Prescribe," 62 *Washington Law Review* 397, 475 (1987).

2. *Extraterritorial Acts.* The act of state doctrine applies to acts of a foreign government taken within its own territory. As the Second Circuit points out, "[a]cts of foreign governments purporting to have extraterritorial effect—and consequently, by definition, falling outside the scope of the act of state doctrine—should be recognized by the courts only if they are consistent with the law and policy of the United States." Allied Bank International v. Banco Credito Agricola, 757 F.2d 516, 522 (2d Cir.1985).

3. *Repudiating the Act of State Doctrine.* Unlike *Dunhill*, *Kirkpatrick* is a unanimous opinion. Justice Scalia writes that the act of state doctrine "is not some vague doctrine of abstention but a *principle of decision* binding on federal and state courts alike." Does this then repudiate the separation of powers rationale of *Sabbatino* and move act of state more to the choice of

law rationale of the plurality in *Dunhill*? One observer notes that *Kirkpatrick* "has sharply circumscribed the reach of the doctrine." Mark Feldman, "Supreme Court Limits the Act of State Doctrine," ABA Section of International Law and Practice, *Suing Foreign States: Newsletter of the Committee on Foreign Sovereign Immunity*, Vol. 1, No. 1, at 1 (Spring 1990).

Should *Sabbatino* and the act of state doctrine simply be eliminated from the common law of the United States? The doctrine "is being referred to repeatedly in court decisions in the United States and is used in different ways by different courts." Donald W. Hoagland, "The Act of State Doctrine: Abandon It," 14 *Denver Journal of International Law & Policy* 317, 317 (1986). Hoagland, a former Assistant Administrator of the U.S. Agency for International Development, argues that there are by now so many exceptions to the doctrine and it has been applied so confusingly, that act of state has little "integrity" left. *Id.* at 333. Would it make more sense simply to use ordinary conflict of laws rules to determine whether foreign law, U.S. law, or international law applies in cases where the act of state doctrine might otherwise be employed? Could *Underhill*, *Sabbatino*, *Dunhill*, and *Kirkpatrick* all have been answered in more or less the way they were with choice-of-law techniques without employing the act of state doctrine? What does the doctrine really add? Is the act of state doctrine more trouble than it is worth? For further discussion, see Gregory H. Fox, "Reexamining the Act of State Doctrine: An Integrated Conflicts Analysis," 33 *Harvard International Law Journal* 521 (1992).

APPENDIX

CONSTITUTION OF THE UNITED STATES OF AMERICA

ARTICLE I * * *

SECTION 8. The Congress shall have Power * * *

To regulate Commerce with foreign Nations, and among the several States, and with the Indian Tribes;

To establish an uniform Rule of Naturalization, and uniform Laws on the subject of Bankruptcies throughout the United States; * * *

To constitute Tribunals inferior to the supreme Court;

To define and punish Piracies and Felonies committed on the high Seas, and Offences against the Law of Nations;

To declare War, grant Letters of Marque and Reprisal, and make Rules concerning Captures on Land and Water;

To raise and support Armies, but no Appropriation of Money to that Use shall be for a longer Term than two Years;

To provide and maintain a Navy;

To make Rules for the Government and Regulation of the land and naval Forces;

To provide for calling forth the Militia to execute the Laws of the Union, suppress Insurrections and repel Invasions;

To provide for organizing, arming, and disciplining, the Militia, and for governing such Part of them as may be employed in the Service of the United States, reserving to the States respectively, the Appointment of the Officers, and the Authority of training the Militia according to the discipline prescribed by Congress; * * *

To make all Laws which shall be necessary and proper for carrying into Execution the foregoing Powers, and all other Powers vested by this Constitution in the Government of the United States, or in any Department or Officer thereof. * * *

SECTION 10. No State shall enter into any Treaty, Alliance, or Confederation; grant Letters of Marque and Reprisal; coin Money; emit Bills of Credit; make any Thing but gold and silver Coin a Tender in Payment of Debts; pass any Bill of Attainder, ex post facto Law, or Law impairing the Obligation of Contracts, or grant any Title of Nobility.

No State shall, without the Consent of the Congress, lay any Imposts or Duties on Imports or Exports, except what may be absolutely necessary for executing its inspection Laws; and the net Produce of all Duties and Imposts, laid by any State on Imports or Exports, shall be for the Use of the Treasury of the United States; and all such Laws shall be subject to the Revision and Controul of the Congress.

No State shall, without the Consent of Congress, lay any Duty of Tonnage, keep Troops, or Ships of War in time of Peace, enter into any Agreement or Compact with another State, or with a foreign Power, or engage in War, unless actually invaded, or in such imminent Danger as will not admit of delay.

ARTICLE II

SECTION 1. The executive Power shall be vested in a President of the United States of America. * * *

SECTION 2. The President shall be Commander in Chief of the Army and Navy of the United States, and of the Militia of the several States, when called into the actual Service of the United States; * * *.

He shall have Power, by and with the Advice and Consent of the Senate, to make Treaties, provided two thirds of the Senators present concur; and he shall nominate, and by and with the Advice and Consent of the Senate, shall appoint Ambassadors, other public Ministers and Consuls * * *.

ARTICLE III

SECTION 1. The judicial Power of the United States, shall be vested in one supreme Court, and in such inferior Courts as the Congress may from time to time ordain and establish. * * *

SECTION 2. The judicial Power shall extend to all Cases, in Law and Equity, arising under this Constitution, the Laws of the United States, and Treaties made, or which shall be made, under their Authority;—to all Cases affecting Ambassadors, other public Ministers and Consuls;—to all Cases of admiralty and maritime Jurisdiction;—to Controversies to which the United States shall be a Party;—to Controversies between two or more States;—between a State and Citizens of another State;—between Citizens of different States;—between Citizens of the same State claiming Lands under Grants of different States, and between a State, or the Citizens thereof, and foreign States, Citizens or Subjects.

In all Cases affecting Ambassadors, other public Ministers and Consuls, and those in which a State shall be Party, the supreme Court shall have original Jurisdiction. In all the other Cases before mentioned, the supreme Court shall have appellate Jurisdiction, both as to Law and Fact, with such Exceptions, and under such Regulations as the Congress shall make. * * *

ARTICLE VI

All Debts contracted and Engagements entered into, before the Adoption of this Constitution, shall be as valid against the United States under this Constitution, as under the Confederation.

This Constitution, and the Laws of the United States which shall be made in Pursuance thereof; and all Treaties made, or which shall be made, under the Authority of the United States, shall be the supreme Law of the Land; and the Judges in every State shall be bound thereby, any Thing in the Constitution or Laws of any State to the Contrary notwithstanding. * * *

AMENDMENTS I–X

[Amendments I–X are reproduced in Chapter 6, at pages 320–21.]

AMENDMENT XIV

SECTION 1. All persons born or naturalized in the United States, and subject to the jurisdiction thereof, are citizens of the United States and of the State wherein they reside. No State shall make or enforce any law which shall abridge the privileges or immunities of citizens of the United States; nor shall any State deprive any person of life, liberty, or property, without due process of law; nor deny to any person within its jurisdiction the equal protection of the laws. * * *

CHARTER OF THE UNITED NATIONS

June 26, 1945, 59 Stat. 1031, T.S. No. 993, 3 Bevans 1153, 1976 Y.B.U.N. 1043

WE THE PEOPLES OF THE UNITED NATIONS DETERMINED

to save succeeding generations from the scourge of war, which twice in our lifetime has brought untold sorrow to mankind, and

to reaffirm faith in fundamental human rights, in the dignity and worth of the human person, in the equal rights of men and women and of nations large and small, and

to establish conditions under which justice and respect for the obligations arising from treaties and other sources of international law can be maintained, and

to promote social progress and better standards of life in larger freedom,

AND FOR THESE ENDS

to practice tolerance and live together in peace with one another as good neighbors, and

to unite our strength to maintain international peace and security, and

to ensure, by the acceptance of principles and the institution of methods, that armed force shall not be used, save in the common interest, and

to employ international machinery for the promotion of the economic and social advancement of all peoples,

HAVE RESOLVED TO COMBINE OUR EFFORTS TO ACCOMPLISH THESE AIMS.

Accordingly, our respective Governments, through representatives assembled in the city of San Francisco, who have exhibited their full powers found to be in good and due form, have agreed to the present Charter of the United Nations and do hereby establish an international organization to be known as the United Nations.

CHAPTER I

PURPOSES AND PRINCIPLES

Article 1

The Purposes of the United Nations are:

1. To maintain international peace and security, and to that end: to take effective collective measures for the prevention and removal of threats to the peace, and for the suppression of acts of aggression or other breaches of the peace, and to bring about by peaceful means, and in conformity with the principles of justice and international law, adjustment or settlement of international disputes or situations which might lead to a breach of the peace;

2. To develop friendly relations among nations based on respect for the principle of equal rights and self-determination of peoples, and to take other appropriate measures to strengthen universal peace;

3. To achieve international cooperation in solving international problems of economic, social, cultural, or humanitarian character, and in promoting and encouraging respect for human rights and for fundamental freedoms for all without distinction as to race, sex, language, or religion; and

4. To be a center for harmonizing the actions of nations in the attainment of these common ends.

Article 2

The Organization and its Members, in pursuit of the Purposes stated in Article 1, shall act in accordance with the following Principles.

1. The Organization is based on the principle of the sovereign equality of all its Members.

2. All Members, in order to ensure to all of them the rights and benefits resulting from membership, shall fulfil in good faith the obligations assumed by them in accordance with the present Charter.

3. All Members shall settle their international disputes by peaceful means in such a manner that international peace and security, and justice, are not endangered.

4. All Members shall refrain in their international relations from the threat or use of force against the territorial integrity or political independence of any state, or in any other manner inconsistent with the Purposes of the United Nations.

5. All Members shall give the United Nations every assistance in any action it takes in accordance with the present Charter, and shall refrain from giving assistance to any state against which the United Nations is taking preventive or enforcement action.

6. The Organization shall ensure that states which are not Members of the United Nations act in accordance with these Principles so far as may be necessary for the maintenance of international peace and security.

7. Nothing contained in the present Charter shall authorize the United Nations to intervene in matters which are essentially within the domestic jurisdiction of any state or shall require the Members to submit such matters to settlement under the present Charter; but this principle shall not prejudice the application of enforcement measures under Chapter VII.

CHAPTER II

MEMBERSHIP

Article 3

The original Members of the United Nations shall be the states which, having participated in the United Nations Conference on International Organization at San Francisco, or having previously signed the Declaration by United Nations of January 1, 1942, sign the present Charter and ratify it in accordance with Article 110.

Article 4

1. Membership in the United Nations is open to all other peace-loving states which accept the obligations contained in the present Charter and, in the judgment of the Organization, are able and willing to carry out these obligations.

2. The admission of any such state to membership in the United Nations will be effected by a decision of the General Assembly upon the recommendation of the Security Council.

Article 5

A Member of the United Nations against which preventive or enforcement action has been taken by the Security Council may be suspended from the exercise of the rights and privileges of membership by the General Assembly upon the recommendation of the Security Council. The exercise of these rights and privileges may be restored by the Security Council.

Article 6

A Member of the United Nations which has persistently violated the Principles contained in the present Charter may be expelled from the Organization by the General Assembly upon the recommendation of the Security Council.

CHAPTER III

ORGANS

Article 7

1. There are established as the principal organs of the United Nations: a General Assembly, a Security Council, an Economic and Social Council, a Trusteeship Council, an International Court of Justice, and a Secretariat.

2. Such subsidiary organs as may be found necessary may be established in accordance with the present Charter.

Article 8

The United Nations shall place no restrictions on the eligibility of men and women to participate in any capacity and under conditions of equality in its principal and subsidiary organs.

CHAPTER IV

THE GENERAL ASSEMBLY

Composition

Article 9

1. The General Assembly shall consist of all the Members of the United Nations.

2. Each Member shall have not more than five representatives in the General Assembly.

Functions and Powers

Article 10

The General Assembly may discuss any questions or any matters within the scope of the present Charter or relating to the powers and functions of any organs provided for in the present Charter, and, except as provided in Article 12, may make recommendations to the Members of the United Nations or to the Security Council or to both on any such questions or matters.

Article 11

1. The General Assembly may consider the general principles of cooperation in the maintenance of international peace and security, including the principles governing disarmament and the regulation of armaments, and may make recommendations with regard to such principles to the Members or to the Security Council or to both.

2. The General Assembly may discuss any questions relating to the maintenance of international peace and security brought before it by any Member of the United Nations, or by the Security Council, or by a state which is not a Member of the United Nations in accordance with Article 35, paragraph 2, and, except as provided in Article 12, may make recommendations with regard to any such questions to the state or states concerned or to the Security Council or to both. Any such question on which action is necessary shall be referred to the Security Council by the General Assembly either before or after discussion.

3. The General Assembly may call the attention of the Security Council to situations which are likely to endanger international peace and security.

4. The powers of the General Assembly set forth in this Article shall not limit the general scope of Article 10.

Article 12

1. While the Security Council is exercising in respect of any dispute or situation the functions assigned to it in the present Charter, the General Assembly shall not make any recommendation with regard to that dispute or situation unless the Security Council so requests.

2. The Secretary–General, with the consent of the Security Council, shall notify the General Assembly at each session of any matters relative to the maintenance of international peace and security which are being dealt with by the Security Council and shall similarly notify the General Assembly, or the Members of the United Nations if the General Assembly is not in session, immediately the Security Council ceases to deal with such matters.

Article 13

1. The General Assembly shall initiate studies and make recommendations for the purpose of:

a. promoting international cooperation in the political field and encouraging the progressive development of international law and its codification;

b. promoting international cooperation in the economic, social, cultural, educational, and health fields, and assisting in the realization of human rights and fundamental freedoms for all without distinction as to race, sex, language, or religion.

2. The further responsibilities, functions, and powers of the General Assembly with respect to matters mentioned in paragraph 1(b) above are set forth in Chapters IX and X.

Article 14

Subject to the provisions of Article 12, the General Assembly may recommend measures for the peaceful adjustment of any situation, regardless of origin, which it deems likely to impair the general welfare or friendly relations among nations, including situations resulting from a violation of the provisions of the present Charter setting forth the Purposes and Principles of the United Nations.

Article 15

1. The General Assembly shall receive and consider annual and special reports from the Security Council; these reports shall include an account of the measures that the Security Council has decided upon or taken to maintain international peace and security. * * *

Article 17

1. The General Assembly shall consider and approve the budget of the Organization.

2. The expenses of the Organization shall be borne by the Members as apportioned by the General Assembly.

3. The General Assembly shall consider and approve any financial and budgetary arrangements with specialized agencies referred to in Article 57 and shall examine the administrative budgets of such specialized agencies with a view to making recommendations to the agencies concerned.

Voting

Article 18

1. Each member of the General Assembly shall have one vote.

2. Decisions of the General Assembly on important questions shall be made by a two-thirds majority of the members present and voting. These questions shall include: recommendations with respect to the

maintenance of international peace and security, the election of the non-permanent members of the Security Council, the election of the members of the Economic and Social Council, the election of the members of the Trusteeship Council * * *, the admission of new Members to the United Nations, the suspension of the rights and privileges of membership, the expulsion of Members, questions relating to the operation of the trusteeship system, and budgetary questions.

3. Decisions on other questions, including the determination of additional categories of questions to be decided by a two-thirds majority, shall be made by a majority of the members present and voting.

Article 19

A Member of the United Nations which is in arrears in the payment of its financial contributions to the Organization shall have no vote in the General Assembly if the amount of its arrears equals or exceeds the amount of the contributions due from it for the preceding two full years. The General Assembly may, nevertheless, permit such a Member to vote if it is satisfied that the failure to pay is due to conditions beyond the control of the Member.

Procedure

Article 20

The General Assembly shall meet in regular annual sessions and in such special sessions as occasion may require. Special sessions shall be convoked by the Secretary–General at the request of the Security Council or of a majority of the Members of the United Nations. * * *

CHAPTER V
THE SECURITY COUNCIL

Composition

Article 23[a]

1. The Security Council shall consist of fifteen Members of the United Nations. The Republic of China, France, the Union of Soviet Socialist Republics, the United Kingdom of Great Britain and Northern Ireland, and the United States of America shall be permanent members of the Security Council. The General Assembly shall elect ten other Members of the United Nations to be non-permanent members of the Security Council, due regard being specially paid, in the first instance to the contribution of Members of the United Nations to the maintenance of international peace and security and to the other purposes of the Organization, and also to equitable geographical distribution.

2. The non-permanent members of the Security Council shall be elected for a term of two years. In the first election of the non-permanent members after the increase of the membership of the Security Council from eleven to fifteen, two of the four additional members

a. Amended text of Article 23 that came into force August 31, 1965.

shall be chosen for a term of one year. A retiring member shall not be eligible for immediate re-election.

3. Each member of the Security Council shall have one representative.

Functions and Powers

Article 24

1. In order to ensure prompt and effective action by the United Nations, its Members confer on the Security Council primary responsibility for the maintenance of international peace and security, and agree that in carrying out its duties under this responsibility the Security Council acts on their behalf.

2. In discharging these duties the Security Council shall act in accordance with the Purposes and Principles of the United Nations. The specific powers granted to the Security Council for the discharge of these duties are laid down in Chapters VI, VII, VIII, and XII.

3. The Security Council shall submit annual and, when necessary, special reports to the General Assembly for its consideration.

Article 25

The Members of the United Nations agree to accept and carry out the decisions of the Security Council in accordance with the present Charter.

Article 26

In order to promote the establishment and maintenance of international peace and security with the least diversion for armaments of the world's human and economic resources, the Security Council shall be responsible for formulating, with the assistance of the Military Staff Committee referred to in article 47, plans to be submitted to the Members of the United Nations for the establishment of a system for the regulation of armaments.

Voting

Article 27[b]

1. Each member of the Security Council shall have one vote.

2. Decisions of the Security Council on procedural matters shall be made by an affirmative vote of nine members.

3. Decisions of the Security Council on all other matters shall be made by an affirmative vote of nine members including the concurring votes of the permanent members; provided that, in decisions under Chapter VI, and under paragraph 3 of Article 52, a party to a dispute shall abstain from voting.

b. Amended text of Article 27 that came into force August 31, 1965.

Procedure

Article 28

1. The Security Council shall be so organized as to be able to function continuously. Each member of the Security Council shall for this purpose be represented at all times at the seat of the Organization.

2. The Security Council shall hold periodic meetings at which each of its members may, if it so desires, be represented by a member of the government or by some other specially designated representative.

3. The Security Council may hold meetings at such places other than the seat of the Organization as in its judgment will best facilitate its work.

Article 29

The Security Council may establish such subsidiary organs as it deems necessary for the performance of its functions.

Article 30

The Security Council shall adopt its own rules of procedure, including the method of selecting its President.

Article 31

Any Member of the United Nations which is not a member of the Security Council may participate, without vote, in the discussion of any question brought before the Security Council whenever the latter considers that the interests of that Member are specially affected.

Article 32

Any Member of the United Nations which is not a member of the Security Council or any state which is not a Member of the United Nations, if it is a party to a dispute under consideration by the Security Council, shall be invited to participate, without vote, in the discussion relating to the dispute. The Security Council shall lay down such conditions as it deems just for the participation of a state which is not a Member of the United Nations.

CHAPTER VI

PACIFIC SETTLEMENT OF DISPUTES

Article 33

1. The parties to any dispute, the continuance of which is likely to endanger the maintenance of international peace and security, shall, first of all, seek a solution by negotiation, enquiry, mediation, conciliation, arbitration, judicial settlement, resort to regional agencies or arrangements, or other peaceful means of their own choice.

2. The Security Council shall, when it deems necessary, call upon the parties to settle their dispute by such means.

Article 34

The Security Council may investigate any dispute, or any situation which might lead to international friction or give rise to a dispute, in order to determine whether the continuance of the dispute or situation is likely to endanger the maintenance of international peace and security.

Article 35

1. Any Member of the United Nations may bring any dispute, or any situation of the nature referred to in Article 34, to the attention of the Security Council or of the General Assembly.

2. A state which is not a Member of the United Nations may bring to the attention of the Security Council or of the General Assembly any dispute to which it is a party if it accepts in advance, for the purposes of the dispute, the obligations of pacific settlement provided in the present Charter.

3. The proceedings of the General Assembly in respect of matters brought to its attention under this Article will be subject to the provisions of Articles 11 and 12.

Article 36

1. The Security Council may, at any stage of a dispute of the nature referred to in Article 33 or of a situation of like nature, recommend appropriate procedures or methods of adjustment.

2. The Security Council should take into consideration any procedures for the settlement of the dispute which have already been adopted by the parties.

3. In making recommendations under this Article the Security Council should also take into consideration that legal disputes should as a general rule be referred by the parties to the International Court of Justice in accordance with the provisions of the Statute of the Court.

Article 37

1. Should the parties to a dispute of the nature referred to in Article 33 fail to settle it by the means indicated in that Article, they shall refer it to the Security Council.

2. If the Security Council deems that the continuance of the dispute is in fact likely to endanger the maintenance of international peace and security, it shall decide whether to take action under Article 36 or to recommend such terms of settlement as it may consider appropriate.

Article 38

Without prejudice to the provisions of Articles 33 to 37, the Security Council may, if all the parties to any dispute so request, make recommendations to the parties with a view to a pacific settlement of the dispute.

CHAPTER VII

ACTION WITH RESPECT TO THREATS TO THE PEACE, BREACHES OF THE PEACE, AND ACTS OF AGGRESSION

Article 39

The Security Council shall determine the existence of any threat to the peace, breach of the peace, or act of aggression and shall make recommendations, or decide what measures shall be taken in accordance with Articles 41 and 42, to maintain or restore international peace and security.

Article 40

In order to prevent an aggravation of the situation, the Security Council may, before making the recommendations or deciding upon the measures provided for in Article 39, call upon the parties concerned to comply with such provisional measures as it deems necessary or desirable. Such provisional measures shall be without prejudice to the rights, claims, or position of the parties concerned. The Security Council shall duly take account of failure to comply with such provisional measures.

Article 41

The Security Council may decide what measures not involving the use of armed force are to be employed to give effect to its decisions, and it may call upon the Members of the United Nations to apply such measures. These may include complete or partial interruption of economic relations and of rail, sea, air, postal, telegraphic, radio, and other means of communication, and the severance of diplomatic relations.

Article 42

Should the Security Council consider that measures provided for in Article 41 would be inadequate or have proved to be inadequate, it may take such action by air, sea, or land forces as may be necessary to maintain or restore international peace and security. Such action may include demonstrations, blockage, and other operations by air, sea, or land forces of Members of the United Nations.

Article 43

1. All Members of the United Nations, in order to contribute to the maintenance of international peace and security, undertake to make available to the Security Council, on its call and in accordance with a special agreement or agreements, armed forces, assistance, and facilities, including rights of passage, necessary for the purpose of maintaining international peace and security.

2. Such agreement or agreements shall govern the numbers and types of forces, their degree of readiness and general location, and the nature of the facilities and assistance to be provided.

3. The agreement or agreements shall be negotiated as soon as possible on the initiative of the Security Council. They shall be concluded between the Security Council and Members or between the Security Council and groups of Members and shall be subject to ratification by the signatory states in accordance with their respective constitutional processes.

Article 44

When the Security Council has decided to use force it shall, before calling upon a Member not represented on it to provide armed forces in fulfillment of the obligations assumed under Article 43, invite that Member, if the Member so desires, to participate in the decisions of the Security Council concerning the employment of contingents of that Member's armed forces.

Article 45

In order to enable the United Nations to take urgent military measures, Members shall hold immediately available national air-force contingents for combined international enforcement action. The strength and degree of readiness of these contingents and plans for their combined action shall be determined, within the limits laid down in the special agreement or agreements referred to in Article 43, by the Security Council with the assistance of the Military Staff Committee.

Article 46

Plans for the application of armed force shall be made by the Security Council with the assistance of the Military Staff Committee.

Article 47

1. There shall be established a Military Staff Committee to advise and assist the Security Council on all questions relating to the Security Council's military requirements for the maintenance of international peace and security, the employment and command of forces placed at its disposal, the regulation of armaments, and possible disarmament.

2. The Military Staff Committee shall consist of the Chiefs of Staff of the permanent members of the Security Council or their representatives. Any Member of the United Nations not permanently represented on the Committee shall be invited by the Committee to be associated with it when the efficient discharge of the Committee's responsibilities requires the participation of that Member in its work.

3. The Military Staff Committee shall be responsible under the Security Council for the strategic direction of any armed forces placed at the disposal of the Security Council. Questions relating to the command of such forces shall be worked out subsequently.

4. The Military Staff Committee, with the authorization of the Security Council and after consultation with appropriate regional agencies, may establish regional subcommittees.

Article 48

1. The action required to carry out the decisions of the Security Council for the maintenance of international peace and security shall be taken by all the Members of the United Nations or by some of them, as the Security Council may determine.

2. Such decisions shall be carried out by the Members of the United Nations directly and through their action in the appropriate international agencies of which they are members.

Article 49

The Members of the United Nations shall join in affording mutual assistance in carrying out the measures decided upon by the Security Council.

Article 50

If preventive or enforcement measures against any state are taken by the Security Council, any other state, whether a Member of the United Nations or not, which finds itself confronted with special economic problems arising from the carrying out of those measures shall have the right to consult the Security Council with regard to a solution of those problems.

Article 51

Nothing in the present Charter shall impair the inherent right of individual or collective self-defense if an armed attack occurs against a Member of the United Nations, until the Security Council has taken measures necessary to maintain international peace and security. Measures taken by Members in the exercise of this right of self-defense shall be immediately reported to the Security Council and shall not in any way affect the authority and responsibility of the Security Council under the present Charter to take at any time such action as it deems necessary in order to maintain or restore international peace and security.

CHAPTER VIII

REGIONAL ARRANGEMENTS

Article 52

1. Nothing in the present Charter precludes the existence of regional arrangements or agencies for dealing with such matters relating to the maintenance of international peace and security as are appropriate for regional action, provided that such arrangements or agencies and their activities are consistent with the Purposes and Principles of the United Nations.

2. The Members of the United Nations entering into such arrangements or constituting such agencies shall make every effort to achieve pacific settlement of local disputes through such regional arrangements

or by such regional agencies before referring them to the Security Council.

3. The Security Council shall encourage the development of pacific settlement of local disputes through such regional arrangements or by such regional agencies either on the initiative of the states concerned or by reference from the Security Council.

4. This Article in no way impairs the application of Articles 34 and 35.

Article 53

1. The Security Council shall, where appropriate, utilize such regional arrangements or agencies for enforcement action under its authority. But no enforcement action shall be taken under regional arrangements or by regional agencies without the authorization of the Security Council, with the exception of measures against any enemy state, as defined in paragraph 2 of this Article, provided for pursuant to Article 107 or in regional arrangements directed against renewal of aggressive policy on the part of any such state, until such time as the Organization may, on request of the Governments concerned, be charged with the responsibility for preventing further aggression by such a state.

2. The term enemy state as used in paragraph 1 of this Article applies to any state which during the Second World War has been an enemy of any signatory of the present Charter.

Article 54

The Security Council shall at all times be kept fully informed of activities undertaken or in contemplation under regional arrangements or by regional agencies for the maintenance of international peace and security.

CHAPTER IX

INTERNATIONAL ECONOMIC AND SOCIAL COOPERATION

Article 55

With a view to the creation of conditions of stability and well-being which are necessary for peaceful and friendly relations among nations based on respect for the principle of equal rights and self-determination of peoples, the United Nations shall promote:

a. higher standards of living, full employment, and conditions of economic and social progress and development;

b. solutions of international economic, social, health, and related problems; and international cultural and educational cooperation; and

c. universal respect for, and observance of, human rights and fundamental freedoms for all without distinction as to race, sex, language, or religion.

Article 56

All Members pledge themselves to take joint and separate action in cooperation with the Organization for the achievement of the purposes set forth in Article 55. * * *

CHAPTER X

THE ECONOMIC AND SOCIAL COUNCIL * * *

CHAPTER XI

DECLARATION REGARDING NON–SELF–GOVERNING TERRITORIES

Article 73

Members of the United Nations which have or assume responsibilities for the administration of territories whose peoples have not yet attained a full measure of self-government recognize the principle that the interests of the inhabitants of these territories are paramount, and accept as a sacred trust the obligation to promote to the utmost, within the system of international peace and security established by the present Charter, the well-being of the inhabitants of these territories, and, to this end:

a. to ensure, with due respect for the culture of the peoples concerned, their political, economic, social, and educational advancement, their just treatment, and their protection against abuses;

b. to develop self-government, to take due account of the political aspirations of the peoples, and to assist them in the progressive development of their free political institutions, according to the particular circumstances of each territory and its peoples and their varying stages of advancement;

c. to further international peace and security;

d. to promote constructive measures of development, to encourage research, and to cooperate with one another and, when and where appropriate, with specialized international bodies with a view to the practical achievement of the social, economic, and scientific purposes set forth in this Article; and

e. to transmit regularly to the Secretary–General for information purposes, subject to such limitation as security and constitutional considerations may require, statistical and other information of a technical nature relating to economic, social, and educational conditions in the territories for which they are respectively responsible other than those territories to which Chapters XII and XIII apply.

Article 74

Members of the United Nations also agree that their policy in respect of the territories to which this Chapter applies, no less than in respect of their metropolitan areas, must be based on the general principle of good-neighborliness, due account being taken of the interests and well-being of the rest of the world, in social, economic, and commercial matters.

CHAPTER XII

INTERNATIONAL TRUSTEESHIP SYSTEM * * *

CHAPTER XIII

THE TRUSTEESHIP COUNCIL * * *

CHAPTER XIV

THE INTERNATIONAL COURT OF JUSTICE

Article 92

The International Court of Justice shall be the principal judicial organ of the United Nations. It shall function in accordance with the annexed Statute, which is based upon the Statute of the Permanent Court of International Justice and forms an integral part of the present Charter.

Article 93

1. All Members of the United Nations are *ipso facto* parties to the Statute of the International Court of Justice.

2. A state which is not a Member of the United Nations may become a party to the Statute of the International Court of Justice on conditions to be determined in each case by the General Assembly upon the recommendation of the Security Council.

Article 94

1. Each Member of the United Nations undertakes to comply with the decision of the International Court of Justice in any case to which it is a party.

2. If any party to a case fails to perform the obligations incumbent upon it under a judgment rendered by the Court, the other party may have recourse to the Security Council, which may, if it deems necessary, make recommendations or decide upon measures to be taken to give effect to the judgment.

Article 95

Nothing in the present Charter shall prevent Members of the United Nations from entrusting the solution of their differences to other tribunals by virtue of agreements already in existence or which may be concluded in the future.

Article 96

1. The General Assembly or the Security Council may request the International Court of Justice to give an advisory opinion on any legal question.

2. Other organs of the United Nations and specialized agencies, which may at any time be so authorized by the General Assembly, may also request advisory opinions of the Court on legal questions arising within the scope of their activities.

CHAPTER XV

THE SECRETARIAT

Article 97

The Secretariat shall comprise a Secretary–General and such staff as the Organization may require. The Secretary–General shall be appointed by the General Assembly upon the recommendation of the Security Council. He shall be the chief administrative officer of the Organization.

Article 98

The Secretary–General shall act in that capacity in all meetings of the General Assembly, of the Security Council, of the Economic and Social Council, and of the Trusteeship Council, and shall perform such other functions as are entrusted to him by these organs. The Secretary–General shall make an annual report to the General Assembly on the work of the Organization.

Article 99

The Secretary–General may bring to the attention of the Security Council any matter which in his opinion may threaten the maintenance of international peace and security.

Article 100

1. In the performance of their duties the Secretary–General and the staff shall not seek or receive instructions from any government or from any other authority external to the Organization. They shall refrain from any action which might reflect on their position as international officials responsible only to the Organization.

2. Each Member of the United Nations undertakes to respect the exclusively international character of the responsibilities of the Secretary–General and the staff and not to seek to influence them in the discharge of their responsibilities.

Article 101

1. The staff shall be appointed by the Secretary–General under regulations established by the General Assembly.

2. Appropriate staffs shall be permanently assigned to the Economic and Social Council, the Trusteeship Council, and, as required, to other organs of the United Nations. These staffs shall form a part of the Secretariat.

3. The paramount consideration in the employment of the staff and in the determination of the conditions of service shall be the necessity of securing the highest standards of efficiency, competence, and integrity. Due regard shall be paid to the importance of recruiting the staff on as wide a geographical basis as possible.

CHAPTER XVI

MISCELLANEOUS PROVISIONS

Article 102

1. Every treaty and every international agreement entered into by any Member of the United Nations after the present Charter comes into force shall as soon as possible be registered with the Secretariat and published by it.

2. No party to any such treaty or international agreement which has not been registered in accordance with the provisions of paragraph 1 of this Article may invoke that treaty or agreement before any organ of the United Nations.

Article 103

In the event of a conflict between the obligations of the Members of the United Nations under the present Charter and their obligations under any other international agreement, their obligations under the present Charter shall prevail.

Article 104

The Organization shall enjoy in the territory of each of its Members such legal capacity as may be necessary for the exercise of its functions and the fulfillment of its purposes.

Article 105

1. The Organization shall enjoy in the territory of each of its Members such privileges and immunities as are necessary for the fulfillment of its purposes.

2. Representatives of the Members of the United Nations and officials of the Organization shall similarly enjoy such privileges and immunities as are necessary for the independent exercise of their functions in connection with the Organization.

3. The General Assembly may make recommendations with a view to determining the details of the application of paragraphs 1 and 2 of this Article or may propose conventions to the Members of the United Nations for this purpose.

CHAPTER XVII

TRANSITIONAL SECURITY ARRANGEMENTS

Article 106

Pending the coming into force of such special agreements referred to in Article 43 as in the opinion of the Security Council enable it to begin the exercise of its responsibilities under Article 42, the parties to the Four–Nation Declaration, signed at Moscow, October 30, 1943, and France, shall, in accordance with the provisions of paragraph 5 of that Declaration, consult with one another and as occasion requires with other Members of the United Nations with a view to such joint action on behalf of the Organization as may be necessary for the purpose of maintaining international peace and security. * * *

CHAPTER XVIII

AMENDMENTS

Article 108

Amendments to the present Charter shall come into force for all Members of the United Nations when they have been adopted by a vote of two thirds of the members of the General Assembly and ratified in accordance with their respective constitutional processes by two thirds of the Members of the United Nations, including all the permanent members of the Security Council.

Article 109[c]

1. A General Conference of the Members of the United Nations for the purpose of reviewing the present Charter may be held at a date and place to be fixed by a two-thirds vote of the members of the General Assembly and by a vote of any nine members of the Security Council. Each Member of the United Nations shall have one vote in the conference.

2. Any alteration of the present Charter recommended by a two-thirds vote of the conference shall take effect when ratified in accordance with their respective constitutional processes by two thirds of the Members of the United Nations including all the permanent members of the Security Council.

3. If such a conference has not been held before the tenth annual session of the General Assembly following the coming into force of the present Charter, the proposal to call such a conference shall be placed on the agenda of that session of the General Assembly, and the conference shall be held if so decided by a majority vote of the members of the General Assembly and by a vote of any seven members of the Security Council. * * *

c. Amended text of Article 109 that came into force June 12, 1968.

STATUTE OF THE INTERNATIONAL COURT OF JUSTICE

Article 1

THE INTERNATIONAL COURT OF JUSTICE established by the Charter of the United Nations as the principal judicial organ of the United Nations shall be constituted and shall function in accordance with the provisions of the present Statute.

CHAPTER I

ORGANIZATION OF THE COURT

Article 2

The Court shall be composed of a body of independent judges, elected regardless of their nationality from among persons of high moral character, who possess the qualifications required in their respective countries for appointment to the highest judicial offices, or are jurisconsults of recognized competence in international law.

Article 3

1. The Court shall consist of fifteen members, no two of whom may be nationals of the same state.

2. A person who for the purposes of membership in the Court could be regarded as a national of more than one state shall be deemed to be a national of the one in which he ordinarily exercises civil and political rights.

Article 4

1. The members of the Court shall be elected by the General Assembly and by the Security Council from a list of persons nominated by the national groups in the Permanent Court of Arbitration, in accordance with the following provisions.

2. In the case of Members of the United Nations not represented in the Permanent Court of Arbitration, candidates shall be nominated by national groups appointed for this purpose by their governments under the same conditions as those prescribed for members of the Permanent Court of Arbitration by Article 44 of the Convention of The Hague of 1907 for the pacific settlement of international disputes.

3. The conditions under which a state which is a party to the present Statute but is not a Member of the United Nations may participate in electing the members of the Court shall, in the absence of a special agreement, be laid down by the General Assembly upon recommendation of the Security Council. * * *

Article 8

The General Assembly and the Security Council shall proceed independently of one another to elect the members of the Court.

Article 9

At every election, the electors shall bear in mind not only that the persons to be elected should individually possess the qualifications required, but also that in the body as a whole the representation of the main forms of civilization and of the principal legal systems of the world should be assured.

Article 10

1. Those candidates who obtain an absolute majority of votes in the General Assembly and in the Security Council shall be considered as elected. * * *

Article 13

1. The members of the Court shall be elected for nine years and may be re-elected; provided, however, that of the judges elected at the first election, the terms of five judges shall expire at the end of three years and the terms of five more judges shall expire at the end of six years. * * *

Article 16

1. No member of the Court may exercise any political or administrative function, or engage in any other occupation of a professional nature.

2. Any doubt on this point shall be settled by the decision of the Court.

Article 17

1. No member of the Court may act as agent, counsel, or advocate in any case.

2. No member may participate in the decision of any case in which he has previously taken part as agent, counsel, or advocate for one of the parties, or as a member of a national or international court, or of a commission of enquiry, or in any other capacity.

3. Any doubt on this point shall be settled by the decision of the Court. * * *

Article 20

Every member of the Court shall, before taking up his duties, make a solemn declaration in open court that he will exercise his powers impartially and conscientiously. * * *

Article 22

1. The seat of the Court shall be established at The Hague. This, however, shall not prevent the Court from sitting and exercising its functions elsewhere whenever the Court considers it desirable. * * *

Article 25

1. The full Court shall sit except when it is expressly provided otherwise in the present Statute.

2. Subject to the condition that the number of judges available to constitute the Court is not thereby reduced below eleven, the Rules of the Court may provide for allowing one or more judges, according to circumstances and in rotation, to be dispensed from sitting.

3. A quorum of nine judges shall suffice to constitute the Court.

Article 26

1. The Court may from time to time form one or more chambers, composed of three or more judges as the Court may determine, for dealing with particular categories of cases; for example, labor cases and cases relating to transit and communications.

2. The Court may at any time form a chamber for dealing with a particular case. The number of judges to constitute such a chamber shall be determined by the Court with the approval of the parties.

3. Cases shall be heard and determined by the chambers provided for in this Article if the parties so request.

Article 27

A judgment given by any of the chambers provided for in Articles 26 and 29 shall be considered as rendered by the Court.

Article 28

The chambers provided for in Articles 26 and 29 may, with the consent of the parties, sit and exercise their functions elsewhere than at The Hague.

Article 29

With a view to the speedy dispatch of business, the Court shall form annually a chamber composed of five judges which, at the request of the parties, may hear and determine cases by summary procedure. In addition, two judges shall be selected for the purpose of replacing judges who find it impossible to sit.

Article 30

1. The Court shall frame rules for carrying out its functions. In particular, it shall lay down rules of procedure.

2. The Rules of the Court may provide for assessors to sit with the Court or with any of its chambers, without the right to vote.

Article 31

1. Judges of the nationality of each of the parties shall retain their right to sit in the case before the Court.

2. If the Court includes upon the Bench a judge of the nationality of one of the parties, any other party may choose a person to sit as judge. Such person shall be chosen preferably from among those persons who have been nominated as candidates as provided in Articles 4 and 5.

3. If the Court includes upon the Bench no judge of the nationality of the parties, each of those parties may proceed to choose a judge as provided in paragraph 2 of this Article.

4. The provisions of this Article shall apply to the case of Articles 26 and 29. In such cases, the President shall request one or, if necessary, two of the members of the Court forming the chamber to give place to the members of the Court of the nationality of the parties concerned, and failing such, or if they are unable to be present, to the judges specially chosen by the parties.

5. Should there be several parties in the same interest, they shall, for the purpose of the preceding provisions, be reckoned as one party only. Any doubt upon this point shall be settled by the decision of the Court.

6. Judges chosen as laid down in paragraphs 2, 3, and 4 of this Article shall fulfil the conditions required by Articles 2, 17 (paragraph 2), 20, and 24 of the present Statute. They shall take part in the decision on terms of complete equality with their colleagues. * * *

Article 33

The expenses of the Court shall be borne by the United Nations in such a manner as shall be decided by the General Assembly.

CHAPTER II

COMPETENCE OF THE COURT

Article 34

1. Only states may be parties in cases before the Court.

2. The Court, subject to and in conformity with its Rules, may request of public international organizations information relevant to cases before it, and shall receive such information presented by such organizations on their own initiative.

3. Whenever the construction of the constituent instrument of a public international organization or of an international convention adopted thereunder is in question in a case before the Court, the Registrar shall so notify the public international organization concerned and shall communicate to it copies of all the written proceedings.

Article 35

1. The Court shall be open to the states parties to the present Statute.

2. The conditions under which the Court shall be open to other states shall, subject to the special provisions contained in treaties in

force, be laid down by the Security Council, but in no case shall such conditions place the parties in a position of inequality before the Court.

3. When a state which is not a Member of the United Nations is a party to a case, the Court shall fix the amount which that party is to contribute towards the expenses of the Court. This provision shall not apply if such state is bearing a share of the expenses of the Court.

Article 36

1. The jurisdiction of the Court comprises all cases which the parties refer to it and all matters specially provided for in the Charter of the United Nations or in treaties and conventions in force.

2. The states parties to the present Statute may at any time declare that they recognize as compulsory *ipso facto* and without special agreement, in relation to any other state accepting the same obligation, the jurisdiction of the Court in all legal disputes concerning:

a. the interpretation of a treaty;

b. any question of international law;

c. the existence of any fact which, if established, would constitute a breach of an international obligation;

d. the nature or extent of the reparation to be made for the breach of an international obligation.

3. The declarations referred to above may be made unconditionally or on condition of reciprocity on the part of several or certain states, or for a certain time.

4. Such declarations shall be deposited with the Secretary–General of the United Nations, who shall transmit copies thereof to the parties to the Statute and to the Registrar of the Court.

5. Declarations made under Article 36 of the Statute of the Permanent Court of International Justice and which are still in force shall be deemed, as between the parties to the present Statute, to be acceptances of the compulsory jurisdiction of the International Court of Justice for the period which they still have to run and in accordance with their terms.

6. In the event of a dispute as to whether the Court has jurisdiction, the matter shall be settled by the decision of the Court.

Article 37

Whenever a treaty or convention in force provides for reference of a matter to a tribunal to have been instituted by the League of Nations, or to the Permanent Court of International Justice, the matter shall, as between the parties to the present Statute, be referred to the International Court of Justice.

Article 38

1. The Court, whose function is to decide in accordance with international law such disputes as are submitted to it, shall apply:

a. international conventions, whether general or particular, establishing rules expressly recognized by the contesting states;

b. international custom, as evidence of a general practice accepted as law;

c. the general principles of law recognized by civilized nations;

d. subject to the provisions of Article 59, judicial decisions and the teachings of the most highly qualified publicists of the various nations, as subsidiary means for the determination of rules of law.

2. This provision shall not prejudice the power of the Court to decide a case *ex aequo et bono,* if the parties agree thereto.

CHAPTER III

PROCEDURE

Article 39

1. The official languages of the Court shall be French and English. If the parties agree that the case shall be conducted in French, the judgment shall be delivered in French. If the parties agree that the case shall be conducted in English, the judgment shall be delivered in English. * * *

3. The Court shall, at the request of any party, authorize a language other than French or English to be used by that party.

Article 40

1. Cases are brought before the Court, as the case may be, either by the notification of the special agreement or by a written application addressed to the Registrar. In either case the subject of the dispute and the parties shall be indicated.

2. The Registrar shall forthwith communicate the application to all concerned.

3. He shall also notify the Members of the United Nations through the Secretary–General, and also any other states entitled to appear before the Court.

Article 41

1. The Court shall have the power to indicate, if it considers that circumstances so require, any provisional measures which ought to be taken to preserve the respective rights of either party.

2. Pending the final decision, notice of the measures suggested shall forthwith be given to the parties and to the Security Council.

Article 42

1. The parties shall be represented by agents.

2. They may have the assistance of counsel or advocates before the Court.

3. The agents, counsel, and advocates of parties before the Court shall enjoy the privileges and immunities necessary to the independent exercise of their duties.

Article 43

1. The procedure shall consist of two parts: written and oral.

2. The written proceedings shall consist of the communication to the Court and to the parties of memorials, counter-memorials and, if necessary, replies; also all papers and documents in support. * * *

5. The oral proceedings shall consist of the hearing by the Court of witnesses, experts, agents, counsel, and advocates. * * *

Article 46

The hearing in Court shall be public, unless the Court shall decide otherwise, or unless the parties demand that the public be not admitted. * * *

Article 48

The Court shall make orders for the conduct of the case, shall decide the form and time in which each party must conclude its arguments, and make all arrangements connected with the taking of evidence. * * *

Article 50

The Court may, at any time, entrust any individual, body, bureau, commission, or other organization that it may select, with the task of carrying out an enquiry or giving an expert opinion. * * *

Article 53

1. Whenever one of the parties does not appear before the Court, or fails to defend its case, the other party may call upon the Court to decide in favor of its claim.

2. The Court must, before doing so, satisfy itself, not only that it has jurisdiction in accordance with Articles 36 and 37, but also that the claim is well founded in fact and law.

Article 54

1. When, subject to the control of the Court, the agents, counsel, and advocates have completed their presentation of the case, the President shall declare the hearing closed.

2. The Court shall withdraw to consider the judgment.

3. The deliberations of the Court shall take place in private and remain secret.

Article 55

1. All questions shall be decided by a majority of the judges present.

2. In the event of an equality of votes, the President or the judge who acts in his place shall have a casting vote.

Article 56

1. The judgment shall state the reasons on which it is based.

2. It shall contain the names of the judges who have taken part in the decision.

Article 57

If the judgment does not represent in whole or in part the unanimous opinion of the judges, any judge shall be entitled to deliver a separate opinion.

Article 58

The judgment shall be signed by the President and by the Registrar. It shall be read in open court, due notice having been given to the agents.

Article 59

The decision of the Court has no binding force except between the parties and in respect of that particular case.

Article 60

The Judgment is final and without appeal. In the event of dispute as to the meaning or scope of the judgment, the Court shall construe it upon the request of any party.

Article 61

1. An application for revision of a judgment may be made only when it is based upon the discovery of some fact of such a nature as to be a decisive factor, which fact was, when the judgment was given, unknown to the Court and also the party claiming revision, always provided that such ignorance was not due to negligence.

2. The proceedings for revision shall be opened by a judgment of the Court expressly recording the existence of the new fact, recognizing that it has such a character as to lay the case open to revision, and declaring the application admissible on this ground.

3. The Court may require previous compliance with the terms of the judgment before it admits proceedings in revision.

4. The application for revision must be made at latest within six months of the discovery of the new fact.

5. No application for revision may be made after the lapse of ten years from the date of the judgment.

Article 62

1. Should a state consider that it has an interest of a legal nature which may be affected by the decision in the case, it may submit a request to the Court to be permitted to intervene.

2. It shall be for the Court to decide upon this request.

Article 63

1. Whenever the construction of a convention to which states other than those concerned in the case are parties is in question, the Registrar shall notify all such states forthwith.

2. Every state so notified has the right to intervene in the proceedings; but if it uses this right, the construction given by the judgment will be equally binding upon it.

Article 64

Unless otherwise decided by the Court, each party shall bear its own costs.

CHAPTER IV

ADVISORY OPINIONS

Article 65

1. The Court may give an advisory opinion on any legal question at the request of whatever body may be authorized by or in accordance with the Charter of the United Nations to make such a request.

2. Questions upon which the advisory opinion of the Court is asked shall be laid before the Court by means of a written request containing an exact statement of the question upon which an opinion is required, and accompanied by all documents likely to throw light upon the question.

Article 66

1. The Registrar shall forthwith give notice of the request for an advisory opinion to all states entitled to appear before the Court.

2. The Registrar shall also, by means of a special and direct communication, notify any state entitled to appear before the Court or international organization considered by the Court or, should it not be sitting, by the President, as likely to be able to furnish information on the question, that the Court will be prepared to receive, within a time limit to be fixed by the President, written statements, or to hear, at a public sitting to be held for the purpose, oral statements relating to the question.

3. Should any such state entitled to appear before the Court have failed to receive the special communication referred to in paragraph 2 of this Article, such state may express a desire to submit a written statement or to be heard; and the Court will decide.

4. States and organizations having presented written or oral statements or both shall be permitted to comment on the statements made by other states or organizations in the form, to the extent, and within the time limits which the Court, or, should it not be sitting, the President, shall decide in each particular case. Accordingly, the Registrar shall in due time communicate any such written statements to states and organizations having submitted similar statements.

Article 67

The Court shall deliver its advisory opinions in open court, notice having been given to the Secretary–General and to the representatives of Members of the United Nations, of other states and of international organizations immediately concerned.

Article 68

In the exercise of its advisory functions the Court shall further be guided by the provisions of the present Statute which apply in contentious cases to the extent to which it recognizes them to be applicable.

* * *

VIENNA CONVENTION ON THE LAW OF TREATIES

May 23, 1969, 1155 U.N.T.S. 331, 8 *International Legal Materials* 679 (1969)

PART I

INTRODUCTION

Article 1

Scope of the present Convention

The present Convention applies to treaties between States.

Article 2

Use of Terms

1. For the purposes of the present Convention:

(a) "treaty" means an international agreement concluded between States in written form and governed by international law, whether embodied in a single instrument or in two or more related instruments and whatever its particular designation;

(b) "ratification," "acceptance," "approval" and "accession" mean in each case the international act so named whereby a State establishes on the international plane its consent to be bound by a treaty;

(c) "full powers" means a document emanating from the competent authority of a State designating a person or persons to represent the State for negotiating, adopting or authenticating the text of a treaty, for expressing the consent of the State to be bound by a treaty, or for accomplishing any other act with respect to a treaty;

(d) "reservation" means a unilateral statement, however phrased or named, made by a State, when signing, ratifying, accepting, approving or acceding to a treaty, whereby it purports to exclude or to modify the legal effect of certain provisions of the treaty in their application to that State;

(e) "negotiating State" means a State which took part in the drawing up and adoption of the text of the treaty;

(f) "contracting State" means a State which has consented to be bound by the treaty, whether or not the treaty has entered into force;

(g) "party" means a State which has consented to be bound by the treaty and for which the treaty is in force;

(h) "third State" means a State not a party to the treaty;

(i) "international organization" means an intergovernmental organization.

2. The provisions of paragraph 1 regarding the use of terms in the present Convention are without prejudice to the use of those terms or to

the meanings which may be given to them in the internal law of any State.

Article 3

International agreements not within the scope of the present Convention

The fact that the present Convention does not apply to international agreements concluded between States and other subjects of international law or between such other subjects of international law, or to international agreements not in written form, shall not affect:

(a) the legal force of such agreements;

(b) the application to them of any of the rules set forth in the present Convention to which they would be subject under international law independently of the Convention;

(c) the application of the Convention to the relations of States as between themselves under international agreements to which other subjects of international law are also parties.

Article 4

Non-retroactivity of the present Convention

Without prejudice to the application of any rules set forth in the present Convention to which treaties would be subject under international law independently of the Convention, the Convention applies only to treaties which are concluded by States after the entry into force of the present Convention with regard to such States.

Article 5

Treaties constituting international organizations and treaties adopted within an international organization

The present Convention applies to any treaty which is the constituent instrument of an international organization and to any treaty adopted within an international organization without prejudice to any relevant rules of the organization.

PART II

CONCLUSION AND ENTRY INTO FORCE OF TREATIES

SECTION 1: CONCLUSION OF TREATIES

Article 6

Capacity of States to conclude treaties

Every State possesses capacity to conclude treaties.

Article 7

Full powers

1. A person is considered as representing a State for the purpose of adopting or authenticating the text of a treaty or for the purpose of expressing the consent of the State to be bound by a treaty if:

(a) he produces appropriate full powers; or

(b) it appears from the States concerned or from other circumstances that their intention was to consider that person as representing the State for such purposes and to dispense with full powers.

2. In virtue of their functions and without having to produce full powers, the following are considered as representing their State:

(a) Heads of State, Heads of Government and Ministers for Foreign Affairs, for the purpose of performing all acts relating to the conclusion of a treaty;

(b) heads of diplomatic missions, for the purpose of adopting the text of a treaty between the accrediting State and the State to which they are accredited;

(c) representatives accredited by States to an international conference or to an international organization or one of its organs, for the purpose of adopting the text of a treaty in that conference, organization or organ.

Article 8

Subsequent confirmation of an act performed without authorization

An act relating to the conclusion of a treaty performed by a person who cannot be considered under article 7 as authorized to represent a State for that purpose is without legal effect unless afterwards confirmed by that State. * * *

Article 11

Means of expressing consent to be bound by a treaty

The consent of a State to be bound by a treaty may be expressed by signature, exchange of instruments constituting a treaty, ratification, acceptance, approval or accession, or by any other means if so agreed.

Article 12

Consent to be bound by a treaty expressed by signature

1. The consent of a State to be bound by a treaty is expressed by the signature of its representative when:

(a) the treaty provides that signature shall have that effect;

(b) it is otherwise established that the negotiating States were agreed that signature should have that effect; or

(c) the intention of the State to give that effect to the signature appears from the full powers of its representative or was expressed during the negotiation. * * *

Article 13

Consent to be bound by a treaty expressed by an exchange of instruments constituting a treaty

The consent of States to be bound by a treaty constituted by instruments exchanged between them is expressed by that exchange when:

(a) the instruments provide that their exchange shall have that effect, or;

(b) it is otherwise established that those States were agreed that the exchange of instruments should have that effect.

Article 14

Consent to be bound by a treaty expressed by ratification, acceptance or approval

1. The consent of a State to be bound by a treaty is expressed by ratification when:

(a) the treaty provides for such consent to be expressed by means of ratification;

(b) it is otherwise established that the negotiating States were agreed that ratification should be required;

(c) the representative of the State has signed the treaty subject to ratification; or

(d) the intention of the State to sign the treaty subject to ratification appears from the full powers of its representative or was expressed during the negotiation.

2. The consent of a State to be bound by a treaty is expressed by acceptance or approval under conditions similar to those which apply to ratification.

Article 15

Consent to be bound by a treaty expressed by accession

The consent of a State to be bound by a treaty is expressed by accession when:

(a) the treaty provides that such consent may be expressed by that State by means of accession;

(b) it is otherwise established that the negotiating States were agreed that such consent may be expressed by that State by means of accession; or

(c) all the parties have subsequently agreed that such consent may be expressed by that State by means of accession.

Article 16

Exchange or deposit of instruments of ratification, acceptance, approval or accession

Unless the treaty otherwise provides, instruments of ratification, acceptance, approval or accession establish the consent of a State to be bound by a treaty upon:

(a) their exchange between the contracting States;

(b) their deposit with the depositary; or

(c) their notification to the contracting States or to the depositary, if so agreed. * * *

Article 18

Obligation not to defeat the object and purpose of a treaty prior to its entry into force

A State is obliged to refrain from acts which would defeat the object and purpose of a treaty when:

(a) it has signed the treaty or has exchanged instruments constituting the treaty subject to ratification, acceptance or approval, until it shall have made its intention clear not to become a party to the treaty; or

(b) it has expressed its consent to be bound by the treaty, pending the entry into force of the treaty and provided that such entry into force is not unduly delayed.

SECTION 2: RESERVATIONS

Article 19

Formulation of reservations

A State may, when signing, ratifying, accepting, approving or acceding to a treaty, formulate a reservation unless:

(a) the reservation is prohibited by the treaty;

(b) the treaty provides that only specified reservations, which do not include the reservation in question, may be made; or

(c) in cases not falling under sub-paragraphs (a) and (b), the reservation is incompatible with the object and purpose of the treaty.

Article 20

Acceptance of and objection to reservations

1. A reservation expressly authorized by a treaty does not require any subsequent acceptance by the other contracting States unless the treaty so provides.

2. When it appears from the limited number of the negotiating States and the object and purpose of a treaty that the application of the treaty in its entirety between all the parties is an essential condition of the consent of each one to be bound by the treaty, a reservation requires acceptance by all the parties.

3. When a treaty is a constituent instrument of an international organization and unless it otherwise provides, a reservation requires the acceptance of the competent organ of that organization.

4. In cases not falling under the preceding paragraphs and unless the treaty otherwise provides:

(a) acceptance by another contracting State of a reservation constitutes the reserving State a party to the treaty in relation to that other State if or when the treaty is in force for those States;

(b) an objection by another contracting State to a reservation does not preclude the entry into force of the treaty as between the objecting and reserving States unless a contrary intention is definitely expressed by the objecting State;

(c) an act expressing a State's consent to be bound by the treaty and containing a reservation is effective as soon as at least one other contracting State has accepted the reservation.

5. For the purposes of paragraphs 2 and 4 and unless the treaty otherwise provides, a reservation is considered to have been accepted by a State if it shall have raised no objection to the reservation by the end of a period of twelve months after it was notified of the reservation or by the date on which it expressed its consent to be bound by the treaty, whichever is later.

Article 21

Legal effects of reservations and of objections to reservations

1. A reservation established with regard to another party in accordance with articles 19, 20 and 23:

(a) modifies for the reserving State in its relations with that other party the provisions of the treaty to which the reservation relates to the extent of the reservation; and

(b) modifies those provisions to the same extent for that other party in its relations with the reserving State.

2. The reservation does not modify the provisions of the treaty for the other parties to the treaty *inter se.*

3. When a State objecting to a reservation has not opposed the entry into force of the treaty between itself and the reserving State, the provisions to which the reservation relates do not apply as between the two States to the extent of the reservation. * * *

SECTION 3: ENTRY INTO FORCE AND PROVISIONAL APPLICATION OF TREATIES

Article 24

Entry into force

1. A treaty enters into force in such manner and upon such date as it may provide or as the negotiating States may agree.

2. Failing any such provision or agreement, a treaty enters into force as soon as consent to be bound by the treaty has been established for all the negotiating States.

3. When the consent of a State to be bound by a treaty is established on a date after the treaty has come into force, the treaty enters

into force for that State on that date, unless the treaty otherwise provides.

4. The provisions of a treaty regulating the authentication of its text, the establishment of the consent of States to be bound by the treaty, the manner or date of its entry into force, reservations, the functions of the depositary and other matters arising necessarily before the entry into force of the treaty apply from the time of the adoption of this text.

Article 25

Provisional application

1. A treaty or a part of a treaty is applied provisionally pending its entry into force if:

(a) the treaty itself so provides; or

(b) the negotiating States have in some other manner so agreed.

2. Unless the treaty otherwise provides or the negotiating States have otherwise agreed, the provisional application of a treaty or a part of a treaty with respect to a State shall be terminated if that State notifies the other States between which the treaty is being applied provisionally of its intention not to become a party to the treaty.

PART III

OBSERVANCE, APPLICATION AND INTERPRETATION OF TREATIES

SECTION 1: OBSERVANCE OF TREATIES

Article 26

Pacta sunt servanda

Every treaty in force is binding upon the parties to it and must be performed by them in good faith.

Article 27

International law and observance of treaties

A party may not invoke the provisions of its internal law as justification for its failure to perform a treaty. This rule is without prejudice to Article 46.

SECTION 2: APPLICATION OF TREATIES

Article 28

Non-retroactivity of treaties

Unless a different intention appears from the treaty or is otherwise established, its provisions do not bind a party in relation to any act or fact which took place or any situation which ceased to exist before the date of the entry into force of the treaty with respect to that party.

Article 29

Territorial scope of treaties

Unless a different intention appears from the treaty or is otherwise established, a treaty is binding upon each party in respect of its entire territory.

Article 30

Application of successive treaties relating to the same subject-matter

1. Subject to Article 103 of the Charter of the United Nations, the rights and obligations of States parties to successive treaties relating to the same subject-matter shall be determined in accordance with the following paragraphs.

2. When a treaty specifies that it is subject to, or that is not to be considered as incompatible with, an earlier or later treaty, the provisions of that other treaty prevail.

3. When all the parties to the earlier treaty are parties also to the later treaty but the earlier treaty is not terminated or suspended in operation under article 59, the earlier treaty applies only to the extent that its provisions are compatible with those of the later treaty.

4. When the parties to the later treaty do not include all the parties to the earlier one:

(a) as between States parties to both treaties the same rule applies as in paragraph 3;

(b) as between a State party to both treaties and a State party to only one of the treaties, the treaty to which both States are parties governs their mutual rights and obligations.

5. Paragraph 4 is without prejudice to article 41, or to any question of the termination or suspension of the operation of a treaty under article 60 or to any question of responsibility which may arise for a State from the conclusion or application of a treaty the provisions of which are incompatible with its obligations towards another State under another treaty.

SECTION 3: INTERPRETATION OF TREATIES

Article 31

General rule of interpretation

1. A treaty shall be interpreted in good faith in accordance with the ordinary meaning to be given to the terms of the treaty in their context and in the light of its object and purpose.

2. The context for the purpose of the interpretation of a treaty shall comprise, in addition to the text, including its preamble and annexes:

(a) any agreement relating to the treaty which was made between all the parties in connexion with the conclusion of the treaty;

(b) any instrument which was made by one or more parties in connexion with the conclusion of the treaty and accepted by the other parties as an instrument related to the treaty.

3. There shall be taken into account, together with the context:

(a) any subsequent agreement between the parties regarding the interpretation of the treaty or the application of its provisions;

(b) any subsequent practice in the application of the treaty which establishes the agreement of the parties regarding its interpretation;

(c) any relevant rules of international law applicable in the relations between the parties.

4. A special meaning shall be given to a term if it is established that the parties so intended.

Article 32

Supplementary means of interpretation

Recourse may be had to supplementary means of interpretation, including the preparatory work of the treaty and the circumstances of its conclusion, in order to confirm the meaning resulting for the application of article 31, or to determine the meaning when the interpretation according to article 31:

(a) leaves the meaning ambiguous or obscure; or

(b) leads to a result which is manifestly absurd or unreasonable.

Article 33

Interpretation of treaties authenticated in two or more languages

1. When a treaty has been authenticated in two or more languages, the text is equally authoritative in each language, unless the treaty provides or the parties agree that, in case of divergence, a particular text shall prevail.

2. A version of the treaty in a language other than one of those in which the text was authenticated shall be considered an authentic text only if the treaty so provides or the parties so agree.

3. The terms of the treaty are presumed to have the same meaning in each authentic text.

4. Except where a particular text prevails in accordance with paragraph 1, when a comparison of the authentic texts discloses a difference of meaning which the application of articles 31 and 32 does not remove, the meaning which best reconciles the texts, having regard to the object and purpose of the treaty, shall be adopted.

SECTION 4: TREATIES AND THIRD STATES

Article 34

General rule regarding third States

A treaty does not create either obligations or rights for a third State without its consent.

Article 35

Treaties providing for obligations for third States

An obligation arises for a third State from a provision of a treaty if the parties to the treaty intend the provision to be the means of establishing the obligation and the third State expressly accepts that obligation in writing.

Article 36

Treaties providing for rights for third States

1. A right arises for a third State from a provision of a treaty if the parties to the treaty intend the provision to accord that right either to the third State, or to a group of States to which it belongs, or to all States, and the third State assents thereto. Its assent shall be presumed so long as the contrary is not indicated, unless the treaty otherwise provides.

2. A State exercising a right in accordance with paragraph 1 shall comply with the conditions for its exercise provided for in the treaty or established in conformity with the treaty.

Article 37

Revocation or modification of obligations or rights of third States

1. When an obligation has arisen for a third State in conformity with article 35, the obligation may be revoked or modified only with the consent of the parties to the treaty and of the third State, unless it is established that they had otherwise agreed.

2. When a right has arisen for a third State in conformity with article 36, the right may not be revoked or modified by the parties if it is established that the right was intended not to be revocable or subject to modification without the consent of the third State.

Article 38

Rules in a treaty becoming binding on third States through international custom

Nothing in articles 34 to 37 precludes a rule set forth in the treaty from becoming binding upon a third State as a customary rule of international law, recognized as such.

PART IV: AMENDMENT AND MODIFICATION OF TREATIES

Article 39

General rule regarding the amendment of treaties

A treaty may be amended by agreement between the parties. The rules laid down in Part II apply to such an agreement except in so far as the treaty may otherwise provide.

Article 40

Amendment of multilateral treaties

1. Unless the treaty otherwise provides, the amendment of multilateral treaties shall be governed by the following paragraphs.

2. Any proposal to amend a multilateral treaty as between all the parties must be notified to all the contracting States, each one of which shall have the right to take part in:

(a) the decision as to the action to be taken in regard to such proposal;

(b) the negotiation and conclusion of any agreement for the amendment of the treaty.

3. Every State entitled to become a party to the treaty shall also be entitled to become a party to the treaty as amended.

4. The amending agreement does not bind any State already a party to the treaty which does not become a party to the amending agreement; article 30, paragraph 4(b), applies in relation to such State.

5. Any State which becomes a party to the treaty after the entry into force of the amending agreement shall, failing an expression of a different intention by that State:

(a) be considered as a party to the treaty as amended; and

(b) be considered as a party to the unamended treaty in relation to any party to the treaty not bound by the amending agreement.

Article 41

Agreements to modify multilateral treaties between certain of the parties only

1. Two or more of the parties to a multilateral treaty may conclude an agreement to modify the treaty as between themselves alone if:

(a) the possibility of such a modification is provided for by the treaty; or

(b) the modification in question is not prohibited by the treaty and:

(i) does not affect the enjoyment by the parties of their rights under the treaty or the performance of their obligations;

(ii) does not relate to a provision, derogation from which is incompatible with the effective execution of the object and purpose of the treaty as a whole.

2. Unless in a case falling under paragraph 1(a) the treaty otherwise provides, the parties in question shall notify the other parties of their intention to conclude the agreement and of the modification to the treaty for which it provides.

PART V

INVALIDITY, TERMINATION AND SUSPENSION OF THE OPERATION OF TREATIES

SECTION 1: GENERAL PROVISIONS

Article 42

Validity and continuance in force of treaties

1. The validity of a treaty or of the consent of a State to be bound by a treaty may be impeached only through the application of the present Convention.

2. The termination of a treaty, its denunciation or the withdrawal of a party, may take place only as a result of the application of the provisions of the treaty or of the present Convention. The same rule applies to suspension of the operation of a treaty.

Article 43

Obligations imposed by international law independently of a treaty

The invalidity, termination or denunciation of a treaty, the withdrawal of a party from it, or the suspension of its operation, as a result of the application of the present Convention or of the provisions of the treaty, shall not in any way impair the duty of any State to fulfil any obligation embodied in the treaty to which it would be subject under international law independently of the treaty.

Article 44

Separability of treaty provisions

1. A right of a party, provided for in a treaty or arising under article 56, to denounce, withdraw from or suspend the operation of the treaty may be exercised only with respect to the whole treaty unless the treaty otherwise provides or the parties otherwise agree.

2. A ground for invalidating, terminating, withdrawing from or suspending the operation of a treaty recognized in the present Convention may be invoked only with respect to the whole treaty except as provided in the following paragraphs or in article 60.

3. If the ground relates solely to particular clauses, it may be invoked only with respect to those clauses where:

(a) the said clauses are separable from the remainder of the treaty with regard to their application;

(b) it appears from the treaty or is otherwise established that acceptance of those clauses was not an essential basis of the consent of the other party or parties to be bound by the treaty as a whole; and

(c) continued performance of the remainder of the treaty would not be unjust.

4. In cases falling under articles 49 and 50 the State entitled to invoke the fraud or corruption may do so with respect either to the whole treaty or, subject to paragraph 3, to the particular clauses alone.

5. In cases falling under articles 51, 52 and 53, no separation of the provisions of the treaty is permitted.

Article 45

Loss of a right to invoke a ground for invalidating, terminating, withdrawing from or suspending the operation of a treaty

A State may no longer invoke a ground for invalidating, terminating, withdrawing from or suspending the operation of a treaty under articles 46 to 50 or articles 60 and 62, if, after becoming aware of the facts:

(a) it shall have expressly agreed that the treaty is valid or remains in force or continues in operation, as the case may be; or

(b) it must by reason of its conduct be considered as having acquiesced in the validity of the treaty or in its maintenance in force or in operation, as the case may be.

SECTION 2: INVALIDITY OF TREATIES

Article 46

Provisions of internal law regarding competence to conclude treaties

1. A State may not invoke the fact that its consent to be bound by a treaty has been expressed in violation of a provision of its internal law regarding competence to conclude treaties as invalidating its consent unless that violation was manifest and concerned a rule of its internal law of fundamental importance.

2. A violation is manifest if it would be objectively evident to any State conducting itself in the matter in accordance with normal practice and in good faith.

Article 47

Specific restrictions on authority to express the consent of a State

If the authority of a representative to express the consent of a State to be bound by a particular treaty has been made subject to a specific restriction, his omission to observe that restriction may not be invoked as invalidating the consent expressed by him unless the restriction was notified to the other negotiating States prior to his expressing such consent.

Article 48

Error

1. A State may invoke an error in a treaty as invalidating its consent to be bound by the treaty if the error relates to a fact or situation which was assumed by that State to exist at the time when the

treaty was concluded and formed an essential basis of its consent to be bound by the treaty.

2. Paragraph 1 shall not apply if the State in question contributed by its own conduct to the error or if the circumstances were such as to put that State on notice of a possible error.

3. An error relating only to the wording of the text of a treaty does not affect its validity * * *.

Article 49

Fraud

If a State has been induced to conclude a treaty by the fraudulent conduct of another negotiating State, the State may invoke the fraud as invalidating its consent to be bound by the treaty.

Article 50

Corruption of a representative of a State

If the expression of a State's consent to be bound by a treaty has been procured through the corruption of its representative directly or indirectly by another negotiating State, the State may invoke such corruption as invalidating its consent to be bound by the treaty.

Article 51

Coercion of a representative of a State

The expression of a State's consent to be bound by a treaty which has been procured by the coercion of its representative through acts or threats directed against him shall be without any legal effect.

Article 52

Coercion of a State by the threat or use of force

A treaty is void if its conclusion has been procured by the threat or use of force in violation of the principles of international law embodied in the Charter of the United Nations.

Article 53

Treaties conflicting with a peremptory norm of general international law (jus cogens)

A treaty is void if, at the time of its conclusion, it conflicts with a peremptory norm of general international law. For the purposes of the present Convention, a peremptory norm of general international law is a norm accepted and recognized by the international community of States as a whole as a norm from which no derogation is permitted and which can be modified only by a subsequent norm of general international law having the same character.

SECTION 3: TERMINATION AND SUSPENSION OF THE OPERATION OF TREATIES

Article 54

Termination of or withdrawal from a treaty under its provisions or by consent of the parties

The termination of a treaty or the withdrawal of a party may take place:

(a) in conformity with the provisions of the treaty; or

(b) at any time by consent of all the parties after consultation with the other contracting States. * * *

Article 56

Denunciation of or withdrawal from a treaty containing no provision regarding termination, denunciation or withdrawal

1. A treaty which contains no provision regarding its termination and which does not provide for denunciation or withdrawal is not subject to denunciation or withdrawal unless:

(a) it is established that the parties intended to admit the possibility of denunciation or withdrawal; or

(b) a right of denunciation or withdrawal may be implied by the nature of the treaty.

2. A party shall give not less than twelve months' notice of its intention to denounce or withdraw from a treaty under paragraph 1. * * *

Article 59

Termination or suspension of the operation of a treaty implied by conclusion of a later treaty

1. A treaty shall be considered as terminated if all the parties to it conclude a later treaty relating to the same subject-matter and:

(a) it appears from the later treaty or is otherwise established that the parties intended that the matter should be governed by that treaty; or

(b) the provisions of the later treaty are so far incompatible with those of the earlier one that the two treaties are not capable of being applied at the same time.

2. The earlier treaty shall be considered as only suspended in operation if it appears from the later treaty or is otherwise established that such was the intention of the parties.

Article 60

Termination or suspension of the operation of a treaty as a consequence of its breach

1. A material breach of a bilateral treaty by one of the parties entitles the other to invoke the breach as a ground for terminating the treaty or suspending its operation in whole or in part.

2. A material breach of a multilateral treaty by one of the parties entitles:

(a) the other parties by unanimous agreement to suspend the operation of the treaty in whole or in part or to terminate it either:

(i) in the relations between themselves and the defaulting State, or

(ii) as between all the parties;

(b) a party specially affected by the breach to invoke it as a ground for suspending the operation of the treaty in whole or in part in the relations between itself and the defaulting State;

(c) any party other than the defaulting State to invoke the breach as a ground for suspending the operation of the treaty in whole or in part with respect to itself if the treaty is of such a character that a material breach of its provisions by one party radically changes the position of every party with respect to the further performance of its obligations under the treaty.

3. A material breach of a treaty, for the purposes of this article, consists in:

(a) a repudiation of the treaty not sanctioned by the present Convention; or

(b) the violation of a provision essential to the accomplishment of the object or purpose of the treaty.

4. The foregoing paragraphs are without prejudice to any provision in the treaty applicable in the event of a breach.

5. Paragraphs 1 to 3 do not apply to provisions relating to the protection of the human person contained in treaties of a humanitarian character, in particular to provisions prohibiting any form of reprisals against persons protected by such treaties.

Article 61

Supervening impossibility of performance

1. A party may invoke the impossibility of performing a treaty as a ground for terminating or withdrawing from it if the impossibility results from the permanent disappearance or destruction of an object indispensable for the execution of the treaty. If the impossibility is temporary, it may be invoked only as a ground for suspending the operation of the treaty.

2. Impossibility of performance may not be invoked by a party as a ground for terminating, withdrawing from or suspending the operation of a treaty if the impossibility is the result of a breach by that party either of an obligation under the treaty or of any other international obligation owed to any other party to the treaty.

Article 62

Fundamental change of circumstances

1. A fundamental change of circumstances which has occurred with regard to those existing at the time of the conclusion of a treaty, and which was not foreseen by the parties, may not be invoked as a ground for terminating or withdrawing from the treaty unless:

(a) the existence of those circumstances constituted an essential basis of the consent of the parties to be bound by the treaty; and

(b) the effect of the change is radically to transform the extent of obligations still to be performed under the treaty.

2. A fundamental change of circumstances may not be invoked as a ground for terminating or withdrawing from a treaty:

(a) if the treaty establishes a boundary; or

(b) if the fundamental change is the result of a breach by the party invoking it either of an obligation under the treaty or of any other international obligation owed to any other party to the treaty.

3. If, under the foregoing paragraphs, a party may invoke a fundamental change of circumstances as a ground for terminating or withdrawing from a treaty it may also invoke the change as a ground for suspending the operation of the treaty.

Article 63

Severance of diplomatic or consular relations

The severance of diplomatic or consular relations between parties to a treaty does not affect the legal relations established between them by the treaty except in so far as the existence of diplomatic or consular relations is indispensable for the application of the treaty.

Article 64

Emergence of a new peremptory norm of general international law (jus cogens)

If a new peremptory norm of general international law emerges, any existing treaty which is in conflict with that norm becomes void and terminates.

SECTION 4: PROCEDURE

Article 65

Procedure to be followed with respect to invalidity, termination, withdrawal from or suspension of the operation of a treaty

1. A party which, under the provisions of the present Convention, invokes either a defect in its consent to be bound by a treaty or a ground for impeaching the validity of a treaty, terminating it, withdrawing from it or suspending its operation, must notify the other parties of its claim.

The notification shall indicate the measure proposed to be taken with respect to the treaty and the reasons therefor.

2. If, after the expiry of a period which, except in cases of special urgency, shall not be less than three months after the receipt of the notification, no party has raised any objection, the party making the notification may carry out in the manner provided in article 67 the measure which it has proposed.

3. If, however, objection has been raised by any other party, the parties shall seek a solution through the means indicated in Article 33 of the Charter of the United Nations.

4. Nothing in the foregoing paragraphs shall affect the rights or obligations of the parties under any provisions in force binding the parties with regard to the settlement of disputes.

5. Without prejudice to article 45, the fact that a State has not previously made the notification prescribed in paragraph 1 shall not prevent it from making such notification in answer to another party claiming performance of the treaty or alleging its violation.

Article 66

Procedure for judicial settlement, arbitration and conciliation

If, under paragraph 3 of article 65, no solution has been reached within a period of 12 months following the date on which the objection was raised, the following procedures shall be followed:

(a) any one of the parties to a dispute concerning the application or the interpretation of article 53 or 64 may, by a written application, submit it to the International Court of Justice for a decision unless the parties by common consent agree to submit the dispute to arbitration;

(b) any one of the parties to a dispute concerning the application or the interpretation of any of the other articles in Part V of the present Convention may set in motion the procedure specified in the Annex to the Convention by submitting a request to that effect to the Secretary–General of the United Nations.

Article 67

Instruments for declaring invalid, terminating, withdrawing from or suspending the operation of a treaty

1. The notification provided for under article 65, paragraph 1 must be made in writing.

2. Any act declaring invalid, terminating, withdrawing from or suspending the operation of a treaty pursuant to the provisions of the treaty or of paragraphs 2 or 3 of article 65 shall be carried out through an instrument communicated to the other parties. If the instrument is not signed by the Head of State, Head of Government or Minister for

Foreign Affairs, the representative of the State communicating it may be called upon to produce full powers. * * *

SECTION 5: CONSEQUENCES OF THE INVALIDITY, TERMINATION OR SUSPENSION OF THE OPERATION OF A TREATY

Article 69

Consequences of the invalidity of a treaty

1. A treaty the invalidity of which is established under the present Convention is void. The provisions of a void treaty have no legal force.

2. If acts have nevertheless been performed in reliance on such a treaty:

(a) each party may require any other party to establish as far as possible in their mutual relations the position that would have existed if the acts had not been performed;

(b) acts performed in good faith before the invalidity was invoked are not rendered unlawful by reason only of the invalidity of the treaty.

3. In cases falling under articles 49, 50, 51 or 52, paragraph 2 does not apply with respect to the party to which the fraud, the act of corruption or the coercion is imputable.

4. In the case of the invalidity of a particular State's consent to be bound by a multilateral treaty, the foregoing rules apply in the relations between that State and the parties to the treaty.

Article 70

Consequences of the termination of a treaty

1. Unless the treaty otherwise provides or the parties otherwise agree, the termination of a treaty under its provisions or in accordance with the present Convention:

(a) releases the parties from any obligation further to perform the treaty;

(b) does not affect any right, obligation or legal situation of the parties created through the execution of the treaty prior to its termination.

2. If a State denounces or withdraws from a multilateral treaty, paragraph 1 applies in the relations between that State and each of the other parties to the treaty from the date when such denunciation or withdrawal takes effect.

Article 71

Consequences of the invalidity of a treaty which conflicts with a peremptory norm of general international law

1. In the case of a treaty which is void under article 53 the parties shall:

(a) eliminate as far as possible the consequences of any act performed in reliance on any provision which conflicts with the peremptory norm of general international law; and

(b) bring their mutual relations into conformity with the peremptory norm of general international law.

2. In the case of a treaty which becomes void and terminates under article 64, the termination of the treaty:

(a) releases the parties from any obligation further to perform the treaty;

(b) does not affect any right, obligation or legal situation of the parties created through the execution of the treaty prior to its termination; provided that those rights, obligations or situations may thereafter be maintained only to the extent that their maintenance is not in itself in conflict with the new peremptory norm of general international law.

Article 72

Consequences of the suspension of the operation of a treaty

1. Unless the treaty otherwise provides or the parties otherwise agree, the suspension of the operation of a treaty under its provisions or in accordance with the present Convention:

(a) releases the parties between which the operation of the treaty is suspended from the obligation to perform the treaty in their mutual relations during the period of the suspension;

(b) does not otherwise affect the legal relations between the parties established by the treaty.

2. During the period of the suspension the parties shall refrain from acts tending to obstruct the resumption of the operation of the treaty.

PART VI: MISCELLANEOUS PROVISIONS

Article 73

Cases of State succession, State responsibility and outbreak of hostilities

The provisions of the present Convention shall not prejudge any question that may arise in regard to a treaty from a succession of States or from the international responsibility of a State or from the outbreak of hostilities between States.

Article 74

Diplomatic and consular relations and the conclusion of treaties

The severance or absence of diplomatic or consular relations between two or more States does not prevent the conclusion of treaties between those States. The conclusion of a treaty does not in itself affect the situation in regard to diplomatic or consular relations.

Article 75

Case of an aggressor State

The provisions of the present Convention are without prejudice to any obligation in relation to a treaty which may arise for an aggressor State in consequence of measures taken in conformity with the Charter of the United Nations with reference to that State's aggression. * * *

Annex * * *

2. When a request has been made to the Secretary–General under article 66, the Secretary–General shall bring the dispute before a conciliation commission * * *. * * *

6. The Commission shall report within twelve months of its constitution. Its report shall be deposited with the Secretary–General and transmitted to the parties to the dispute. The report of the Commission, including any conclusions stated therein regarding the facts or questions of law, shall not be binding upon the parties and it shall have no other character than that of recommendations submitted for the consideration of the parties in order to facilitate an amicable settlement of the dispute.

UNITED NATIONS CONVENTION ON THE LAW OF THE SEA

Dec. 10, 1982, U.N. Doc. A/CONF.62.122

PART I

INTRODUCTION

Article 1

Use of terms and scope

1. For the purpose of this Convention:

(1) "Area" means the sea-bed and ocean floor and subsoil thereof, beyond the limits of national jurisdiction;

(2) "Authority" means the International Sea–Bed Authority;

(3) "activities in the Area" means all activities of exploration for, and exploitation of, the resources of the Area; * * *.

PART II

TERRITORIAL SEA AND CONTIGUOUS ZONE

SECTION 1. GENERAL PROVISIONS

Article 2

Legal status of the territorial sea, of the air space over the territorial sea and of its bed and subsoil

1. The sovereignty of a coastal State extends, beyond its land territory and internal waters and, in the case of an archipelagic State, its archipelagic waters, to an adjacent belt of sea, described as the territorial sea.

2. This sovereignty extends to the air space over the territorial sea as well as to its bed and subsoil.

3. The sovereignty over the territorial sea is exercised subject to this Convention and to other rules of international law.

SECTION 2. LIMITS OF THE TERRITORIAL SEA

Article 3

Breadth of the territorial sea

Every State has the right to establish the breadth of its territorial sea up to a limit not exceeding 12 nautical miles, measured from baselines determined in accordance with this Convention. * * *

Article 5

Normal baseline

Except where otherwise provided in this Convention, the normal baseline for measuring the breadth of the territorial sea is the low-water line along the coast as marked on large-scale charts officially recognized by the coastal State. * * *

Article 7

Straight baselines

1. In localities where the coastline is deeply indented and cut into, or if there is a fringe of islands along the coast in its immediate vicinity, the method of straight baselines joining appropriate points may be employed in drawing the baseline from which the breadth of the territorial sea is measured.

2. Where because of the presence of a delta and other natural conditions the coastline is highly unstable, the appropriate points may be selected along the furthest seaward extent of the low-water line and, notwithstanding subsequent regression of the low-water line, the straight baselines shall remain effective until changed by the coastal State in accordance with this Convention.

3. The drawing of straight baselines must not depart to any appreciable extent from the general direction of the coast, and the sea areas lying within the lines must be sufficiently closely linked to the land domain to be subject to the regime of internal waters.

4. Straight baselines shall not be drawn to and from low-tide elevations, unless lighthouses or similar installations which are permanently above sea level have been built on them or except in instances where the drawing of baselines to and from such elevations has received general international recognition.

5. Where the method of straight baselines is applicable under paragraph 1, account may be taken, in determining particular baselines, of economic interests peculiar to the region concerned, the reality and the importance of which are clearly evidenced by long usage.

6. The system of straight baselines may not be applied by a State in such a manner as to cut off the territorial sea of another State from the high seas or an exclusive economic zone.

Article 8

Internal waters

1. Except as provided in Part IV, waters on the landward side of the baseline of the territorial sea form part of the internal waters of the State. * * *

SECTION 3. INNOCENT PASSAGE IN THE TERRITORIAL SEA

SUBSECTION A. RULES APPLICABLE TO ALL SHIPS

Article 17

Right of innocent passage

Subject to this Convention, ships of all States, whether coastal or land-locked, enjoy the right of innocent passage through the territorial sea.

Article 18

Meaning of passage

1. Passage means navigation through the territorial sea for the purpose of:

(a) Traversing that sea without entering internal waters or calling at a roadstead or port facility outside internal waters; or

(b) proceeding to or from internal waters or a call at such roadstead or port facility.

2. Passage shall be continuous and expeditious. However, passage includes stopping and anchoring, but only in so far as the same are incidental to ordinary navigation or are rendered necessary by *force majeure* or distress or for the purpose of rendering assistance to persons, ships or aircraft in danger or distress.

Article 19

Meaning of innocent passage

1. Passage is innocent so long as it is not prejudicial to the peace, good order or security of the coastal State. Such passage shall take place in conformity with this Convention and with other rules of international law.

2. Passage of a foreign ship shall be considered to be prejudicial to the peace, good order or security of the coastal State if in the territorial sea it engages in any of the following activities:

(a) any threat or use of force against the sovereignty, territorial integrity or political independence of the coastal State, or in any other manner in violation of the principles of international law embodied in the Charter of the United Nations;

(b) any exercise or practice with weapons of any kind;

(c) any act aimed at collecting information to the prejudice of the defence or security of the coastal State;

(d) any act of propaganda aimed at affecting the defence or security of the coastal State;

(e) the launching, landing or taking on board of any aircraft;

(f) the launching, landing or taking on board of any military device;

(g) the loading or unloading of any commodity, currency or person contrary to the customs, fiscal, immigration or sanitary laws and regulations of the coastal State;

(h) any act of willful and serious pollution contrary to this Convention;

(i) any fishing activities;

(j) the carrying out of research or survey activities;

(k) any act aimed at interfering with any systems of communication or any other facilities or installations of the coastal State;

(*l*) Any other activity not having a direct bearing on passage.

Article 20

Submarines and other underwater vehicles

In the territorial sea, submarines and other underwater vehicles are required to navigate on the surface and to show their flag.

Article 21

Laws and regulations of the coastal State relating to innocent passage

1. The coastal State may adopt laws and regulations, in conformity with the provisions of this Convention and other rules of international law, relating to innocent passage through the territorial sea, in respect of all or any of the following:

(a) the safety of navigation and the regulation of maritime traffic;

(b) the protection of navigational aids and facilities and other facilities or installations;

(c) the protection of cables and pipelines;

(d) the conservation of the living resources of the sea;

(e) the prevention of infringement of the fisheries laws and regulations of the coastal State;

(f) the preservation of the environment of the coastal State and the prevention, reduction and control of pollution thereof,

(g) marine scientific research and hydrographic surveys;

(h) the prevention of infringement of the customs, fiscal, immigration or sanitary laws and regulations of the coastal State.

2. Such laws and regulations shall not apply to the design, construction, manning or equipment of foreign ships unless they are giving effect to generally accepted international rules or standards.

3. The coastal State shall give due publicity to all such laws and regulations.

4. Foreign ships exercising the right of innocent passage through the territorial sea shall comply with all such laws and regulations and all generally accepted international regulations relating to the prevention of collisions at sea. * * *

Article 25

Rights of protection of the coastal State

1. The coastal State may take the necessary steps in its territorial sea to prevent passage which is not innocent.

2. In the case of ships proceeding to internal waters or a call at a port facility outside internal waters, the coastal State also has the right to take the necessary steps to prevent any breach of the conditions to

which admission of those ships to internal waters or such a call is subject.

3. The coastal State may, without discrimination in form or in fact among foreign ships, suspend temporarily in specified areas of its territorial sea the innocent passage of foreign ships if such suspension is essential for the protection of its security, including weapons exercises. Such suspension shall take effect only after having been duly published.

* * *

SUBSECTION B. RULES APPLICABLE TO MERCHANT SHIPS AND GOVERNMENT SHIPS OPERATED FOR COMMERCIAL PURPOSES

Article 27

Criminal jurisdiction on board a foreign ship

1. The criminal jurisdiction of the coastal State should not be exercised on board a foreign ship passing through the territorial sea to arrest any person or to conduct any investigation in connection with any crime committed on board the ship during its passage, save only in the following cases:

(a) if the consequences of the crime extend to the coastal State;

(b) if the crime is of a kind to disturb the peace of the country or the good order of the territorial sea;

(c) if the assistance of the local authorities has been requested by the master of the ship or by a diplomatic agent or consular officer of the flag State; or

(d) if such measures are necessary for the suppression of illicit traffic in narcotic drugs or psychotropic substances.

2. The above provisions do not affect the right of the coastal State to take any steps authorized by its laws for the purpose of an arrest or investigation on board a foreign ship passing through the territorial sea after leaving internal waters.

3. In the cases provided for in paragraphs 1 and 2, the coastal State shall, if the master so requests, notify a diplomatic agent or consular officer of the flag State before taking any steps, and shall facilitate contact between such agent or officer and the ship's crew. In cases of emergency this notification may be communicated while the measures are being taken.

4. In considering whether or in what manner an arrest should be made, the local authorities shall have due regard to the interests of navigation.

5. Except as provided in Part XII or with respect to violations of laws and regulations adopted in accordance with Part V, the coastal State may not take any steps on board a foreign ship passing through the territorial sea to arrest any person or to conduct any investigation in connection with any crime committed before the ship entered the territo-

rial sea, if the ship, proceeding from a foreign port, is only passing through the territorial sea without entering internal waters.

Article 28

Civil jurisdiction in relation to foreign ships

1. The coastal State should not stop or divert a foreign ship passing through the territorial sea for the purpose of exercising civil jurisdiction in relation to a person on board the ship.

2. The coastal State may not levy execution against or arrest the ship for the purpose of any civil proceedings, save only in respect of obligations or liabilities assumed or incurred by the ship itself in the course or for the purpose of its voyage through the waters of the coastal State.

3. Paragraph 2 is without prejudice to the right of the coastal State, in accordance with its laws, to levy execution against or to arrest, for the purpose of any civil proceedings, a foreign ship lying in the territorial sea, or passing through the territorial sea after leaving internal waters.

SUBSECTION C. RULES APPLICABLE TO WARSHIPS AND OTHER GOVERNMENT SHIPS OPERATED FOR NON–COMMERCIAL PURPOSES

Article 29

Definition of warships

For the purposes of this Convention, "warship" means a ship belonging to the armed forces of a State bearing the external marks distinguishing such ships of its nationality, under the command of an officer duly commissioned by the government of the State and whose name appears in the appropriate service list or its equivalent, and manned by a crew which is under regular armed forces discipline.

Article 30

Non-compliance by warships with the laws and regulations of the coastal State

If any warship does not comply with the laws and regulations of the coastal State concerning passage through the territorial sea and disregards any request for compliance therewith which is made to it, the coastal State may require it to leave the territorial sea immediately.

Article 31

Responsibility of the flag State for damage caused by a warship or other government ship operated for non-commercial purposes

The flag State shall bear international responsibility for any loss or damage to the coastal State resulting from the non-compliance by a warship or other government ship operated for non-commercial purposes with the laws and regulations of the coastal State concerning passage through the territorial sea or with the provisions of this Convention or other rules of international law.

Article 32

Immunities of warships and other government ships operated for non-commercial purposes

With such exceptions as are contained in subsection A and in articles 30 and 31, nothing in this Convention affects the immunities of warships and other government ships operated for non-commercial purposes.

SECTION 4. CONTIGUOUS ZONE

Article 33

Contiguous zone

1. In a zone contiguous to its territorial sea, described as the contiguous zone, the coastal State may exercise the control necessary to:

(a) prevent infringement of its customs, fiscal, immigration or sanitary laws and regulations within its territory or territorial sea;

(b) punish infringement of the above laws and regulations committed within its territory or territorial sea.

2. The contiguous zone may not extend beyond 24 nautical miles from the baselines from which the breadth of the territorial sea is measured.

PART III

STRAITS USED FOR INTERNATIONAL NAVIGATION * * *

SECTION 2. TRANSIT PASSAGE

Article 37

Scope of this section

This section applies to straits which are used for international navigation between one part of the high seas or an exclusive economic zone and another part of the high seas or an exclusive economic zone.

Article 38

Right of transit passage

1. In straits referred to in article 37, all ships and aircraft enjoy the right of transit passage, which shall not be impeded; except that, if the strait is formed by an island of a State bordering the strait and its mainland, transit passage shall not apply if there exists seaward of the island a route through the high seas or through an exclusive economic zone of similar convenience with respect to navigational and hydrographical characteristics.

2. Transit passage means the exercise in accordance with this Part of the freedom of navigation and overflight solely for the purpose of

continuous and expeditious transit of the strait between one part of the high seas or an exclusive economic zone and another part of the high seas or an exclusive economic zone. However, the requirement of continuous and expeditious transit does not preclude passage through the strait for the purpose of entering, leaving or returning from a State bordering the strait, subject to the conditions of entry to that State.

3. Any activity which is not an exercise of the right of transit passage through a strait remains subject to the other applicable provisions of this Convention.

Article 39

Duties of ships and aircraft during transit passage

1. Ships and aircraft, while exercising the right of transit passage, shall:

(a) proceed without delay through or over the strait;

(b) refrain from any threat or use of force against the sovereignty, territorial integrity or political independence of States bordering the strait, or in any other manner in violation of the principles of international law embodied in the Charter of the United Nations;

(c) refrain from any activities other than those incident to their normal modes of continuous and expeditious transit unless rendered necessary by *force majeure* or by distress;

(d) comply with other relevant provisions of this Part.

2. Ships in transit passage shall:

(a) comply with generally accepted international regulations, procedures and practices for safety at sea, including the International Regulations for Preventing Collisions at Sea;

(b) Comply with generally accepted international regulations, procedures and practices for the prevention, reduction and control of pollution from ships.

3. Aircraft in transit passage shall:

(a) observe the Rules of the Air established by the International Civil Aviation Organization as they apply to civil aircraft; state aircraft will normally comply with such safety measures and will at all times operate with due regard for the safety of navigation;

(b) at all times monitor the radio frequency assigned by the competent internationally designated air traffic control authority or the appropriate international distress radio frequency.

Article 40

Research and survey activities

During transit passage, foreign ships, including marine scientific research and hydrographic survey ships, may not carry out any research or survey activities without the prior authorization of the States bordering straits. * * *

Article 42

Laws and regulations of States bordering straits relating to transit passage

1. Subject to the provisions of this section, States bordering straits may adopt laws and regulations relating to transit passage through straits, in respect of all or any of the following:

(a) the safety of navigation and the regulation of maritime traffic, as provided in article 41;

(b) the prevention, reduction and control of pollution, by giving effect to applicable international regulations regarding the discharge of oil, oily wastes and other noxious substances in the strait;

(c) with respect to fishing vessels, the prevention of fishing, including the stowage of fishing gear;

(d) the loading or unloading of any commodity, currency or person in contravention of the customs, fiscal, immigration or sanitary laws and regulations of States bordering straits. * * *

4. Foreign ships exercising the right of transit passage shall comply with such laws and regulations.

5. The flag State of a ship or the State of registry of an aircraft entitled to sovereign immunity which acts in a manner contrary to such laws and regulations or other provisions of this Part shall bear international responsibility for any loss or damage which results to States bordering straits.

Article 43

Navigational and safety aids and other improvements and the prevention, reduction and control of pollution

User States and States bordering a strait should by agreement cooperate:

(a) in the establishment and maintenance in a strait of necessary navigational and safety aids or other improvements in aid of international navigation; and

(b) for the prevention, reduction and control of pollution from ships.

Article 44

Duties of States bordering straits

States bordering straits shall not hamper transit passage and shall give appropriate publicity to any danger to navigation or overflight within or over the strait of which they have knowledge. There shall be no suspension of transit passage.

SECTION 3. INNOCENT PASSAGE

Article 45

Innocent passage

1. The régime of innocent passage, in accordance with Part II, section 3, shall apply in straits used for international navigation:

(a) excluded from the application of the regime of transit passage under article 38, paragraph 1; or

(b) between a part of the high seas or an exclusive economic zone and the territorial sea of a foreign State.

2. There shall be no suspension of innocent passage through such straits.

PART IV

ARCHIPELAGIC STATES * * *

PART V

EXCLUSIVE ECONOMIC ZONE

[Articles 55–58 are reproduced in Chapter 9, at pages 563–64.]

Article 59

Basis for the resolution of conflicts regarding the attribution of rights and jurisdiction in the exclusive economic zone

In cases where this Convention does not attribute rights or jurisdiction to the coastal State or to other States within the exclusive economic zone, and a conflict arises between the interests of the coastal State and any other State or States, the conflict should be resolved on the basis of equity and in the light of all the relevant circumstances, taking into account the respective importance of the interests involved to the parties as well as to the international community as a whole. * * *

Article 61

Conservation of the living resources

1. The coastal State shall determine the allowable catch of the living resources in its exclusive economic zone.

2. The coastal State, taking into account the best scientific evidence available to it, shall ensure through proper conservation and management measures that the maintenance of the living resources in the exclusive economic zone is not endangered by over-exploitation. As appropriate, the coastal State and competent international organizations, whether subregional, regional or global, shall co-operate to this end.

3. Such measures shall also be designed to maintain or restore populations of harvested species at levels which can produce the maximum sustainable yield, as qualified by relevant environmental and economic factors, including the economic needs of coastal fishing commu-

nities and the special requirements of developing States, and taking into account fishing patterns, the interdependence of stocks and any generally recommended international minimum standards, whether subregional, regional or global.

4. In taking such measures the coastal State shall take into consideration the effects on species associated with or dependent upon harvested species with a view to maintaining or restoring populations of such associated or dependent species above levels at which their reproduction may become seriously threatened.

5. Available scientific information, catch and fishing effort statistics, and other data relevant to the conservation of fish stocks shall be contributed and exchanged on a regular basis through competent international organizations, whether subregional, regional or global, where appropriate and with participation by all States concerned, including States whose nationals are allowed to fish in the exclusive economic zone.

Article 62

Utilization of the living resources

1. The coastal State shall promote the objective of optimum utilization of the living resources in the exclusive economic zone without prejudice to article 61.

2. The coastal State shall determine its capacity to harvest the living resources of the exclusive economic zone. Where the coastal State does not have the capacity to harvest the entire allowable catch, it shall, through agreements or other arrangements and pursuant to the terms, conditions, laws and regulations referred to in paragraph 4, give other States access to the surplus of the allowable catch, having particular regard to the provisions of articles 69 and 70, especially in relation to the developing States mentioned therein.

3. In giving access to other States to its exclusive economic zone under this article, the coastal State shall take into account all relevant factors, including, *inter alia,* the significance of the living resources of the area to the economy of the coastal State concerned and its other national interests, the provisions of articles 69 and 70, the requirements of developing States in the subregion or region in harvesting part of the surplus and the need to minimize economic dislocation in States whose nationals have habitually fished in the zone or which have made substantial efforts in research and identification of stocks.

4. Nationals of other States fishing in the exclusive economic zone shall comply with the conservation measures and with the other terms and conditions established in the laws and regulations of the coastal State. These laws and regulations shall be consistent with this Convention and may relate, *inter alia,* to the following:

(a) licensing of fishermen, fishing vessels and equipment, including payment of fees and other forms of remuneration, which, in the case of developing coastal States, may consist of adequate compensation in the field of financing, equipment and technology relating to the fishing industry;

(b) determining the species which may be caught, and fixing quotas of catch, whether in relation to particular stocks or groups of stocks or catch per vessel over a period of time or to the catch by nationals of any State during a specified period;

(c) regulating seasons and areas of fishing, the types, sizes and amount of gear, and the types, sizes and number of fishing vessels that may be used;

(d) fixing the age and size of fish and other species that may be caught;

(e) specifying information required of fishing vessels, including catch and effort statistics and vessel position reports;

(f) requiring, under the authorization and control of the coastal State, the conduct of specified fisheries research programmes and regulating the conduct of such research, including the sampling of catches, disposition of samples and reporting of associated scientific data;

(g) the placing of observers or trainees on board such vessels by the coastal State;

(h) the landing of all or any part of the catch by such vessels in the ports of the coastal State;

(i) terms and conditions relating to joint ventures or other co-operative arrangements;

(j) requirements for the training of personnel and the transfer of fisheries technology, including enhancement of the coastal State's capability of undertaking fisheries research;

(k) enforcement procedures.

5. Coastal States shall give due notice of conservation and management laws and regulations.

Article 63

Stocks occurring within the exclusive economic zones of two or more coastal States or both within the exclusive economic zone and in an area beyond and adjacent to it

1. Where the same stock or stocks of associated species occur within the exclusive economic zones of two or more coastal States, these States shall seek, either directly or through appropriate subregional or regional organizations, to agree upon the measures necessary to co-ordinate and ensure the conservation and development of such stocks without prejudice to the other provisions of this Part. * * *

[Article 63(2) is reproduced in Chapter 9, at page 566.]

Article 69

Right of land-locked States

1. Land-locked States shall have the right to participate, on an equitable basis, in the exploitation of an appropriate part of the surplus of the living resources of the exclusive economic zones of coastal States of the same subregion or region, taking into account the relevant economic and geographical circumstances of all the States concerned and in conformity with the provisions of this article and of articles 61 and 62.

2. The terms and modalities of such participation shall be established by the States concerned through bilateral, subregional or regional agreements * * *. * * *

Article 70

Right of geographically disadvantaged States

1. Geographically disadvantaged States shall have the right to participate, on an equitable basis, in the exploitation of an appropriate part of the surplus of the living resources of the exclusive economic zones of coastal States of the same subregion or region, taking into account the relevant economic and geographical circumstances of all the States concerned and in conformity with the provisions of this article and of articles 61 and 62.

2. For the purposes of this Part, "geographically disadvantaged States" means coastal States, including States bordering enclosed or semi-enclosed seas, whose geographical situation makes them dependent upon the exploitation of the living resources of the exclusive economic zones of other States in the subregion or region for adequate supplies of fish for the nutritional purposes of their populations or parts thereof, and coastal States which can claim no exclusive economic zones of their own.

3. The terms and modalities of such participation shall be established by the States concerned through bilateral, subregional or regional agreements * * *. * * *

Article 73

Enforcement of laws and regulations of the coastal State

1. The coastal State may in the exercise of its sovereign rights to explore, exploit, conserve and manage the living resources in the exclusive economic zone, take such measures, including boarding, inspection, arrest and judicial proceedings, as may be necessary to ensure compliance with the laws and regulations adopted by it in conformity with this Convention.

2. Arrested vessels and their crews shall be promptly released upon the posting of reasonable bond or other security.

3. Coastal State penalties for violations of fisheries laws and regulations in the exclusive economic zone may not include imprisonment, in

the absence of agreements to the contrary by the States concerned, or any other form of corporal punishment.

4. In cases of arrest or detention of foreign vessels the coastal State shall promptly notify the flag State, through appropriate channels, of the action taken and of any penalties subsequently imposed.

Article 74

Delimitation of the exclusive economic zone between States with opposite or adjacent coasts

1. The delimitation of the exclusive economic zone between States with opposite or adjacent coasts shall be effected by agreement on the basis of international law, as referred to in Article 38 of the Statute of the International Court of Justice, in order to achieve an equitable solution.

2. If no agreement can be reached within a reasonable period of time, the States concerned shall resort to the procedures provided for in Part XV.

3. Pending agreement as provided for in paragraph 1, the States concerned, in a spirit of understanding and co-operation, shall make every effort to enter into provisional arrangements of a practical nature and, during this transitional period, not to jeopardize or hamper the reaching of the final agreement. Such arrangements shall be without prejudice to the final delimitation.

4. Where there is an agreement in force between the States concerned, questions relating to the delimitation of the exclusive economic zone shall be determined in accordance with the provisions of that agreement. * * *

PART VI

CONTINENTAL SHELF

Article 76

Definition of the continental shelf

1. The continental shelf of a coastal State comprises the sea-bed and subsoil of the submarine areas that extend beyond its territorial sea throughout the natural prolongation of its land territory to the outer edge of the continental margin, or to a distance of 200 nautical miles from the baselines from which the breadth of the territorial sea is measured where the outer edge of the continental margin does not extend up to that distance.

2. The continental shelf of a coastal State shall not extend beyond the limits provided for in paragraphs 4 to 6.

3. The continental margin comprises the submerged prolongation of the land mass of the coastal State, and consists of the sea-bed and subsoil of the shelf, the slope and the rise. It does not include the deep ocean floor with its oceanic ridges or the subsoil thereof.

4. (a) For the purposes of this Convention, the coastal State shall establish the outer edge on the continental margin wherever the margin extends beyond 200 nautical miles from the baselines from which the breadth of the territorial sea is measured, by either:

(i) a line delineated in accordance with paragraph 7 by reference to the outermost fixed points at each of which the thickness of sedimentary rocks is at least 1 per cent of the shortest distance from such point to the foot of the continental slope; or

(ii) a line delineated in accordance with paragraph 7 by reference to fixed points not more than 60 nautical miles from the foot of the continental slope.

(b) In the absence of evidence to the contrary, the foot of the continental slope shall be determined as the point of maximum change in the gradient at its base.

5. The fixed points comprising the line of the outer limits of the continental shelf on the sea-bed, drawn in accordance with paragraph 4(a)(i) and (ii), either shall not exceed 350 nautical miles from the baselines from which the breadth of the territorial sea is measured or shall not exceed 100 nautical miles from the 2,500 metre isobath, which is a line connecting the depth of 2,500 metres.

6. Notwithstanding the provisions of paragraph 5, on submarine ridges, the outer limit of the continental shelf shall not exceed 350 nautical miles from the baselines from which the breadth of the territorial sea is measured. This paragraph does not apply to submarine elevations that are natural components of the continental margin, such as its plateaux, rises, caps, banks and spurs.

7. The coastal State shall delineate the outer limits of its continental shelf, where that shelf extends beyond 200 nautical miles from the baselines from which the breadth of the territorial sea is measured, by straight lines not exceeding 60 nautical miles in length, connecting fixed points, defined by coordinates of latitude and longitude.

8. Information on the limits of the continental shelf beyond 200 nautical miles from the baselines from which the breadth of the territorial sea is measured shall be submitted by the coastal State to the Commission on the Limits of the Continental Shelf set up under Annex II on the basis of equitable geographical representation. The Commission shall make recommendations to coastal States on matters related to the establishment of the outer limits of their continental shelf. The limits of the shelf established by a coastal State on the basis of these recommendations shall be final and binding.

9. The coastal State shall deposit with the Secretary–General of the United Nations charts and relevant information, including geodetic data, permanently describing the outer limits of its continental shelf. The Secretary–General shall give due publicity thereto.

10. The provisions of this article are without prejudice to the question of delimitation of the continental shelf between States with opposite or adjacent coasts.

[Articles 77 and 78 are reproduced in Chapter 9, at page 550.]

Article 79

Submarine cables and pipelines on the continental shelf

1. All States are entitled to lay submarine cables and pipelines on the continental shelf, in accordance with the provisions of this article.
* * *

Article 81

Drilling on the continental shelf

The coastal State shall have the exclusive right to authorize and regulate drilling on the continental shelf for all purposes.

Article 82

Payments and contributions with respect to the exploitation of the continental shelf beyond 200 nautical miles

1. The coastal State shall make payments or contributions in kind in respect of the exploitation of the non-living resources of the continental shelf beyond 200 nautical miles from the baselines from which the breadth of the territorial sea is measured.

2. The payments and contributions shall be made annually with respect to all production at a site after the first five years of production at that site. For the sixth year, the rate of payment or contribution shall be 1 per cent of the value or volume of production at the site. The rate shall increase by 1 per cent for each subsequent year until the twelfth year and shall remain at 7 per cent thereafter. Production does not include resources used in connection with exploitation.

3. A developing State which is a net importer of a mineral resource produced from its continental shelf is exempt from making such payments or contributions in respect of that mineral resource.

4. The payments or contributions shall be made through the Authority, which shall distribute them to States Parties to this Convention, on the basis of equitable sharing criteria, taking into account the interests and needs of developing States, particularly the least developed and the land-locked among them.

Article 83

Delimitation of the continental shelf between States with opposite or adjacent coasts

1. The delimitation of the continental shelf between States with opposite or adjacent coasts shall be effected by agreement on the basis of international law, as referred to in Article 38 of the Statute of the International Court of Justice, in order to achieve an equitable solution.

2. If no agreement can be reached within a reasonable period of time, the States concerned shall resort to the procedures provided for in Part XV.

3. Pending agreement as provided for in paragraph 1, the States concerned, in a spirit of understanding and co-operation, shall make every effort to enter into provisional arrangements of a practical nature and, during this transitional period, not to jeopardize or hamper the reaching of the final agreement. Such arrangements shall be without prejudice to the final delimitation.

4. Where there is an agreement in force between the States concerned, questions relating to the delimitation of the continental shelf shall be determined in accordance with the provisions of that agreement.
* * *

PART VII

HIGH SEAS

SECTION 1. GENERAL PROVISIONS

[Articles 86–90 are reproduced in Chapter 9, at pages 537–38.]

Article 91

Nationality of ships

1. Every State shall fix the conditions for the grant of its nationality to Ships, for the registration of ships in its territory, and for the right to fly its flag. Ships have the nationality of the State whose flag they are entitled to fly. There must exist a genuine link between the State and the ship.

2. Every State shall issue to ships to which it has granted the right to fly its flag documents to that effect.

Article 92

Status of ships

1. Ships shall sail under the flag of one State only and, save in exceptional cases expressly provided for in international treaties or in this Convention, shall be subject to its exclusive jurisdiction on the high seas. A ship may not change its flag during a voyage or while in a port of call, save in the case of a real transfer of ownership or change of registry.

2. A ship which sails under the flags of two or more States, according to convenience, may not claim any of the nationalities in question with respect to any other State, and may be assimilated to a ship without nationality. * * *

Article 94

Duties of the flag State

1. Every State shall effectively exercise its jurisdiction and control in administrative, technical and social matters over ships flying its flag.

2. In particular every State shall:

(a) maintain a register of ships containing the names and particulars of ships flying its flag, except those which are excluded from generally accepted international regulations on account of their small size; and

(b) assume jurisdiction under its internal law over each ship flying its flag and its master, officers and crew in respect of administrative, technical and social matters concerning the ship.

3. Every State shall take such measures for ships flying its flag as are necessary to ensure safety at sea with regard, *inter alia*, to:

(a) the construction, equipment and seaworthiness of ships;

(b) the manning of ships, labour conditions and the training of crews, taking into account the applicable international instruments;

(c) the use of signals, the maintenance of communications and the prevention of collisions.

4. Such measures shall include those necessary to ensure:

(a) that each ship, before registration and thereafter at appropriate intervals, is surveyed by a qualified surveyor of ships, and has on board such charts, nautical publications and navigational equipment and instruments as are appropriate for the safe navigation of the ship;

(b) that each ship is in the charge of a master and officers who possess appropriate qualifications, in particular in seamanship, navigation, communications and marine engineering, and that the crew is appropriate in qualification and numbers for the type, size, machinery and equipment of the ship;

(c) that the master, officers and, to the extent appropriate, the crew are fully conversant with and required to observe the applicable international regulations concerning the safety of life at sea, the prevention of collisions, the prevention, reduction and control of marine pollution, and the maintenance of communications by radio.

5. In taking the measures called for in paragraphs 3 and 4 each State is required to conform to generally accepted international regulations, procedures and practices and to take any steps which may be necessary to secure their observance.

6. A State which has clear grounds to believe that proper jurisdiction and control with respect to a ship have not been exercised may report the facts to the flag State. Upon receiving such a report, the flag State shall investigate the matter and, if appropriate, take any action necessary to remedy the situation.

7. Each State shall cause an inquiry to be held by or before a suitably qualified person or persons into every marine casualty or

incident of navigation on the high seas involving a ship flying its flag and causing loss of life or serious injury to nationals of another State or serious damage to ships or installations of another State or to the marine environment. The flag State and the other State shall co-operate in the conduct of any inquiry held by that other State into any such marine casualty or incident of navigation.

Article 95

Immunity of warships on the high seas

Warships on the high seas have complete immunity from the jurisdiction of any State other than the flag State.

Article 96

Immunity of ships used only on government non-commercial service

Ships owned or operated by a State and used only on government non-commercial service shall, on the high seas, have complete immunity from the jurisdiction of any State other than the flag State.

Article 97

Penal jurisdiction in matters of collision or any other incident of navigation

1. In the event of a collision or any other incident of navigation concerning a ship on the high seas, involving the penal or disciplinary responsibility of the master or of any other person in the service of the ship, no penal or disciplinary proceedings may be instituted against such person except before the judicial or administrative authorities either of the flag State or of the State of which such person is a national.

2. In disciplinary matters, the State which has issued a master's certificate or a certificate of competence or licence shall alone be competent, after due legal process, to pronounce the withdrawal of such certificates, even if the holder is not a national of the State which issued them.

3. No arrest or detention of the ship, even as a measure of investigation, shall be ordered by any authorities other than those of the flag State. * * *

Article 99

Prohibition of the transport of slaves

Every State shall take effective measures to prevent and punish the transport of slaves in ships authorized to fly its flag and to prevent the unlawful use of its flag for that purpose. Any slave taking refuge on board any ship, whatever its flag, shall *ipso facto* be free.

Article 100

Duty to co-operate in the repression of piracy

All States shall co-operate to the fullest possible extent in the repression of piracy on the high seas or in any other place outside the jurisdiction of any State.

Article 101

Definition of piracy

Piracy consists of any of the following acts:

(a) any illegal acts of violence or detention, or any act of depredation, committed for private ends by the crew or the passengers of a private ship or a private aircraft, and directed:

(i) on the high seas, against another ship or aircraft, or against persons or property on board such ship or aircraft;

(ii) against a ship, aircraft, persons or property in a place outside the jurisdiction of any State;

(b) any act of voluntary participation in the operation of a ship or of an aircraft with knowledge of facts making it a pirate ship or aircraft;

(c) any act of inciting or of intentionally facilitating an act described in subparagraph (a) or (b). * * *

Article 103

Definition of a pirate ship or aircraft

A ship or aircraft is considered a pirate ship or aircraft if it is intended by the persons in dominant control to be used for the purpose of committing one of the acts referred to in article 101. The same applies if the ship or aircraft has been used to commit any such act, so long as it remains under the control of the persons guilty of that act.

Article 105

Seizure of a pirate ship or aircraft

On the high seas, or in any other place outside the jurisdiction of any State, every State may seize a pirate ship or aircraft, or a ship or aircraft taken by piracy and under the control of pirates, and arrest the persons and seize the property on board. The courts of the State which carried out the seizure may decide upon the penalties to be imposed, and may also determine the action to be taken with regard to the ships, aircraft or property, subject to the rights of third parties acting in good faith. * * *

Article 108

Illicit traffic in narcotic drugs or psychotropic substances

1. All States shall co-operate in the suppression of illicit traffic in narcotic drugs and psychotropic substances engaged in by ships on the high seas contrary to international conventions.

2. Any State which has reasonable grounds for believing that a ship flying its flag is engaged in illicit traffic in narcotic drugs or psychotropic substances may request the co-operation of other States to suppress such traffic.

Article 109

Unauthorized broadcasting from the high seas

1. All States shall co-operate in the suppression of unauthorized broadcasting from the high seas.

2. For the purposes of this Convention, "unauthorized broadcasting" means the transmission of sound radio or television broadcasts from a ship or installation on the high seas intended for reception by the general public contrary to international regulations, but excluding the transmission of distress calls.

3. Any person engaged in unauthorized broadcasting may be prosecuted before the court of:

(a) the flag State of the ship;

(b) the State of registry of the installation;

(c) the State of which the person is a national;

(d) any State where the transmissions can be received; or

(e) any State where authorized radio communication is suffering interference.

4. On the high seas, a State having jurisdiction in accordance with paragraph 3 may, in conformity with article 110, arrest any person or ship engaged in unauthorized broadcasting and seize the broadcasting apparatus.

Article 110

Right of visit

1. Except where acts of interference derive from powers conferred by treaty, a warship which encounters on the high seas a foreign ship, other than a ship entitled to complete immunity in accordance with articles 95 and 96, is not justified in boarding it unless there is reasonable ground for suspecting that:

(a) the ship is engaged in piracy;

(b) the ship is engaged in the slave trade;

(c) the ship is engaged in unauthorized broadcasting and the flag State of the warship has jurisdiction under article 109;

(d) the ship is without nationality; or

(e) though flying a foreign flag or refusing to show its flag, the ship is, in reality, of the same nationality as the warship.

2. In the cases provided for in paragraph 1, the warship may proceed to verify the ship's right to fly its flag. To this end, it may send a boat under the command of an officer to the suspected ship. If suspicion remains after the documents have been checked, it may proceed to a further examination on board the ship, which must be carried out with all possible consideration.

3. If the suspicions prove to be unfounded, and provided that the ship boarded has not committed any act justifying them, it shall be compensated for any loss or damage that may have been sustained.

4. These provisions apply *mutatis mutandis* to military aircraft.

5. These provisions also apply to any other duly authorized ships or aircraft clearly marked and identifiable as being on government service.

Article 111

Right of hot pursuit

1. The hot pursuit of a foreign ship may be undertaken when the competent authorities of the coastal State have good reason to believe that the ship has violated the laws and regulations of that State. Such pursuit must be commenced when the foreign ship or one of its boats is within the internal waters, the archipelagic waters, the territorial sea or the contiguous zone of the pursuing State, and may only be continued outside the territorial sea or the contiguous zone if the pursuit has not been interrupted. It is not necessary that, at the time when the foreign ship within the territorial sea or the contiguous zone receives the order to stop, the ship giving the order should likewise be within the territorial sea or the contiguous zone. If the foreign ship is within a contiguous zone, as defined in article 33, the pursuit may only be undertaken if there has been a violation of the rights for the protection of which the zone was established.

2. The right of hot pursuit shall apply *mutatis mutandis* to violations in the exclusive economic zone or on the continental shelf, including safety zones around continental shelf installations, of the laws and regulations of the coastal State applicable in accordance with this Convention to the exclusive economic zone or the continental shelf, including such safety zones.

3. The right of hot pursuit ceases as soon as the ship pursued enters the territorial sea of its own State or of a third State.

4. Hot pursuit is not deemed to have begun unless the pursuing ship has satisfied itself by such practicable means as may be available that the ship pursued or one of its boats or other craft working as a team and using the ship pursued as a mother ship is within the limits of the territorial sea, or, as the case may be, within the contiguous zone or the exclusive economic zone or above the continental shelf. The pursuit may only be commenced after a visual or auditory signal to stop has been given at a distance which enables it to be seen or heard by the foreign ship.

5. The right of hot pursuit may be exercised only by warships or military aircraft, or other ships or aircraft clearly marked and identifiable as being on government service and authorized to that effect.

6. Where hot pursuit is effected by an aircraft:

(a) the provisions of paragraphs 1 to 4 shall apply *mutatis mutandis* * * *. * * *

Article 112

Right to lay submarine cables and pipelines

1. All States are entitled to lay submarine cables and pipelines on the bed of the high seas beyond the continental shelf. * * *

SECTION 2. CONSERVATION AND MANAGEMENT OF THE LIVING RESOURCES OF THE HIGH SEAS

[Articles 116–119 are reproduced in Chapter 9, at pages 566–68.]

PART VIII

RÉGIME OF ISLANDS

[Article 121 is reproduced in Chapter 9, at page 564.]

PART IX

ENCLOSED OR SEMI-ENCLOSED SEAS * * *

PART X

RIGHT OF ACCESS OF LAND-LOCKED STATES TO AND FROM THE SEA AND FREEDOM OF TRANSIT * * *

PART XI

THE AREA

SECTION 1. GENERAL PROVISIONS * * *

Article 134

Scope of this Part

1. This Part applies to the Area.

2. Activities in the Area shall be governed by the provisions of this Part.

3. The requirements concerning deposit of, and publicity to be given to, the charts or lists of geographical co-ordinates showing the limits referred to in article 1, paragraph 1(1), are set forth in Part VI.

4. Nothing in this article affects the establishment of the outer limits of the continental shelf in accordance with Part VI or the validity of agreements relating to delimitation between States with opposite or adjacent coasts.

Article 135

Legal status of the superjacent waters and air space

Neither this Part nor any rights granted or exercised pursuant thereto shall affect the legal status of the waters superjacent to the Area or that of the air space above those waters.

SECTION 2. PRINCIPLES GOVERNING THE AREA

Article 136

Common heritage of mankind

The Area and its resources are the common heritage of mankind.

Article 137

Legal status of the Area and its resources

1. No State shall claim or exercise sovereignty or sovereign rights over any part of the Area or its resources, nor shall any State or natural or juridical person appropriate any part thereof. No such claim or exercise of sovereignty or sovereign rights nor such appropriation shall be recognized.

2. All rights in the resources of the Area are vested in mankind as a whole, on whose behalf the Authority shall act. These resources are not subject to alienation. The minerals recovered from the Area, however, may only be alienated in accordance with this Part and the rules, regulations and procedures of the Authority.

3. No State or natural or juridical person shall claim, acquire or exercise rights with respect to the minerals recovered from the Area except in accordance with this Part. Otherwise, no such claim, acquisition or exercise of such rights shall be recognized.

Article 138

General conduct of States in relation to the Area

The general conduct of States in relation to the Area shall be in accordance with the provisions of this Part, the principles embodied in the Charter of the United Nations and other rules of international law in the interests of maintaining peace and security and promoting international co-operation and mutual understanding.

Article 139

Responsibility to ensure compliance and liability for damage

1. States Parties shall have the responsibility to ensure that activities in the Area, whether carried out by States Parties, or state enterprises or natural or juridical persons which possess the nationality of States Parties or are effectively controlled by them or their nationals, shall be carried out in conformity with this Part. The same responsibility applies to international organizations for activities in the Area carried out by such organizations. * * *

Article 140

Benefit of mankind

1. Activities in the Area shall, as specifically provided for in this Part, be carried out for the benefit of mankind as a whole, irrespective of the geographical location of States, whether coastal or land-locked, and

taking into particular consideration the interests and needs of developing States and of peoples who have not attained full independence or other self-governing status recognized by the United Nations in accordance with General Assembly resolution 1514(XV) and other relevant General Assembly resolutions.

2. The Authority shall provide for the equitable sharing of financial and other economic benefits derived from activities in the Area through any appropriate mechanism, on a non-discriminatory basis, in accordance with article 160, paragraph 2(f)(i).

Article 141

Use of the Area exclusively for peaceful purposes

The Area shall be open to use exclusively for peaceful purposes by all States, whether coastal or land-locked, without discrimination and without prejudice to the other provisions of this Part. * * *

SECTION 3. DEVELOPMENT OF RESOURCES OF THE AREA * * *

SECTION 4. THE AUTHORITY * * *

SECTION 5. SETTLEMENT OF DISPUTES AND ADVISORY OPINIONS * * *

PART XII

PROTECTION AND PRESERVATION OF THE MARINE ENVIRONMENT

SECTION 1. GENERAL PROVISIONS * * *

SECTION 2. GLOBAL AND REGIONAL CO-OPERATION * * *

SECTION 3. TECHNICAL ASSISTANCE * * *

SECTION 4. MONITORING AND ENVIRONMENTAL ASSESSMENT * * *

SECTION 5. INTERNATIONAL RULES AND NATIONAL LEGISLATION TO PREVENT, REDUCE AND CONTROL POLLUTION OF THE MARINE ENVIRONMENT * * *

Article 211

Pollution from vessels

1. States, acting through the competent international organization or general diplomatic conference, shall establish international rules and standards to prevent, reduce and control pollution of the marine environment from vessels and promote the adoption, in the same manner, wherever appropriate, of routeing systems designed to minimize the threat of accidents which might cause pollution of the marine environment, including the coastline, and pollution damage to the related interests of coastal States. Such rules and standards shall, in the same manner, be re-examined from time to time as necessary.

2. States shall adopt laws and regulations for the prevention, reduction and control of pollution of the marine environment from

vessels flying their flag or of their registry. Such laws and regulations shall at least have the same effect as that of generally accepted international rules and standards established through the competent international organization or general diplomatic conference. * * *

SECTION 6. ENFORCEMENT * * *

Article 217

Enforcement by flag States

1. States shall ensure compliance by vessels flying their flag or of their registry with applicable international rules and standards, established through the competent international organization or general diplomatic conference, and with their laws and regulations adopted in accordance with this Convention for the prevention, reduction and control of pollution of the marine environment from vessels and shall accordingly adopt laws and regulations and take other measures necessary for their implementation. Flag States shall provide for the effective enforcement of such rules, standards, laws and regulations, irrespective of where a violation occurs.

2. States shall, in particular, take appropriate measures in order to ensure that vessels flying their flag or of their registry are prohibited from sailing, until they can proceed to sea in compliance with the requirements of the international rules and standards referred to in paragraph 1, including requirements in respect of design, construction, equipment and manning of vessels.

3. States shall ensure that vessels flying their flag or of their registry carry on board certificates required by and issued pursuant to international rules and standards referred to in paragraph 1. States shall ensure that vessels flying their flag are periodically inspected in order to verify that such certificates are in conformity with the actual condition of the vessels. These certificates shall be accepted by other States as evidence of the condition of the vessels and shall be regarded as having the same force as certificates issued by them, unless there are clear grounds for believing that the condition of the vessel does not correspond substantially with the particulars of the certificates.

4. If a vessel commits a violation of rules and standards established through the competent international organization or general diplomatic conference, the flag State, without prejudice to articles 218, 220 and 228, shall provide for immediate investigation and where appropriate institute proceedings in respect of the alleged violation irrespective of where the violation occurred or where the pollution caused by such violation has occurred or has been spotted.

5. Flag States conducting an investigation of the violation may request the assistance of any other State whose co-operation could be useful in clarifying the circumstances of the case. States shall endeavour to meet appropriate requests of flag States.

6. States shall, at the written request of any State, investigate any violation alleged to have been committed by vessels flying their flag. If satisfied that sufficient evidence is available to enable proceedings to be brought in respect of the alleged violation, flag States shall without delay institute such proceedings in accordance with their laws.

7. Flag States shall promptly inform the requesting State and the competent international organization of the action taken and its outcome. Such information shall be available to all States.

8. Penalties provided for by the laws and regulations of States for vessels flying their flag shall be adequate in severity to discourage violations wherever they occur.

Article 218

Enforcement by port States

1. When a vessel is voluntarily within a port or at an off-shore terminal of a State, that State may undertake investigations and, where the evidence so warrants, institute proceedings in respect of any discharge from that vessel outside the internal waters, territorial sea or exclusive economic zone of that State in violation of applicable international rules and standards established through the competent international organization or general diplomatic conference.

2. No proceedings pursuant to paragraph 1 shall be instituted in respect of a discharge violation in the internal waters, territorial sea or exclusive economic zone of another State unless requested by that State, the flag State, or a State damaged or threatened by the discharge violation, or unless the violation has caused or is likely to cause pollution in the internal waters, territorial sea or exclusive economic zone of the State instituting the proceedings.

3. When a vessel is voluntarily within a port or at an off-shore terminal of a State, that State shall, as far as practicable, comply with requests from any State for investigation of a discharge violation referred to in paragraph 1, believed to have occurred in, caused, or threatened damage to the internal waters, territorial sea or exclusive economic zone of the requesting State. It shall likewise, as far as practicable, comply with requests from the flag State for investigation of such a violation, irrespective of where the violation occurred.

4. The records of the investigation carried out by a port State pursuant to this article shall be transmitted upon request to the flag State or to the coastal State. Any proceedings instituted by the port State on the basis of such an investigation may, subject to section 7, be suspended at the request of the coastal State when the violation has occurred within its internal waters, territorial sea or exclusive economic zone. The evidence and records of the case, together with any bond or other financial security posted with the authorities of the port State,

shall in that event be transmitted to the coastal State. Such transmittal shall preclude the continuation of proceedings in the port State.

Article 219

Measures relating to seaworthiness of vessels to avoid pollution

Subject to section 7, States which, upon request or on their own initiative, have ascertained that a vessel within one of their ports or at one of their offshore terminals is in violation of applicable international rules and standards relating to seaworthiness of vessels and thereby threatens damage to the marine environment shall, as far as practicable, take administrative measures to prevent the vessel from sailing. Such States may permit the vessel to proceed only to the nearest appropriate repair yard and, upon removal of the causes of the violation, shall permit the vessel to continue immediately.

Article 220

Enforcement by coastal States

1. When a vessel is voluntarily within a port or at an off-shore terminal of a State, that State may, subject to section 7, institute proceedings in respect of any violation of its laws and regulations adopted in accordance with this Convention or applicable international rules and standards for the prevention, reduction and control of pollution from vessels when the violation has occurred within the territorial sea or the exclusive economic zone of that State.

2. Where there are clear grounds for believing that a vessel navigating in the territorial sea of a State has, during its passage therein, violated laws and regulations of that State adopted in accordance with this Convention or applicable international rules and standards for the prevention, reduction and control of pollution from vessels, that State, without prejudice to the application of the relevant provisions of Part II, section 3, may undertake physical inspection of the vessel relating to the violation and may, where the evidence so warrants, institute proceedings, including detention of the vessel, in accordance with its laws, subject to the provisions of section 7.

3. Where there are clear grounds for believing that a vessel navigating in the exclusive economic zone or the territorial sea of a State has, in the exclusive economic zone, committed a violation of applicable international rules and standards for the prevention, reduction and control of pollution from vessels or laws and regulations of that State conforming and giving effect to such rules and standards, that State may require the vessel to give information regarding its identity and port of registry, its last and its next port of call and other relevant information required to establish whether a violation has occurred.

4. States shall adopt laws and regulations and take other measures so that vessels flying their flag comply with requests for information pursuant to paragraph 3.

5. Where there are clear grounds for believing that a vessel navigating in the exclusive economic zone or the territorial sea of a State has, in the exclusive economic zone, committed a violation referred to in paragraph 3 resulting in a substantial discharge causing or threatening significant pollution of the marine environment, that State may undertake physical inspection of the vessel for matters relating to the violation if the vessel has refused to give information or if the information supplied by the vessel is manifestly at variance with the evident factual situation and if the circumstances of the case justify such inspection.

6. Where there is clear objective evidence that a vessel navigating in the exclusive economic zone or the territorial sea of a State has, in the exclusive economic zone, committed a violation referred to in paragraph 3 resulting in a discharge causing major damage or threat of major damage to the coastline or related interests of the coastal State, or to any resources of its territorial sea or exclusive economic zone, that State may, subject to section 7, provided that the evidence so warrants, institute proceedings, including detention of the vessel, in accordance with its laws.

7. Notwithstanding the provisions of paragraph 6, whenever appropriate procedures have been established, either through the competent international organization or as otherwise agreed, whereby compliance with requirements for bonding or other appropriate financial security has been assured, the coastal State if bound by such procedures shall allow the vessel to proceed. * * *

Article 221

Measures to avoid pollution arising from maritime casualties

1. Nothing in this Part shall prejudice the right of States, pursuant to international law, both customary and conventional, to take and enforce measures beyond the territorial sea proportionate to the actual or threatened damage to protect their coastline or related interests, including fishing, from pollution or threat of pollution following upon a maritime casualty or acts relating to such a casualty, which may reasonably be expected to result in major harmful consequences.

2. For the purposes of this article, "maritime casualty" means a collision of vessels, stranding or other incident of navigation, or other occurrence on board a vessel or external to it resulting in material damage or imminent threat of material damage to a vessel or cargo.

SECTION 7. SAFEGUARDS * * *

SECTION 8. ICE–COVERED AREAS * * *

SECTION 9. RESPONSIBILITY AND LIABILITY * * *

SECTION 10. SOVEREIGN IMMUNITY * * *

SECTION 11. OBLIGATIONS UNDER OTHER CONVENTIONS ON THE PROTECTION AND PRESERVATION OF THE MARINE ENVIRONMENT * * *

PART XIII

MARINE SCIENTIFIC RESEARCH * * *

PART XIV

DEVELOPMENT AND TRANSFER OF MARINE TECHNOLOGY * * *

PART XV

SETTLEMENT OF DISPUTES

SECTION 1. GENERAL PROVISIONS

Article 279

Obligation to settle disputes by peaceful means

States Parties shall settle any dispute between them concerning the interpretation or application of this Convention by peaceful means in accordance with Article 2, paragraph 3, of the Charter of the United Nations and, to this end, shall seek a solution by the means indicated in Article 33, paragraph 1, of the Charter.

Article 280

Settlement of disputes by any peaceful means chosen by the parties

Nothing in this Part impairs the right of any States Parties to agree at any time to settle a dispute between them concerning the interpretation or application of this Convention by any peaceful means of their own choice.

Article 281

Procedure where no settlement has been reached by the parties

1. If the States Parties which are Parties to a dispute concerning the interpretation or application of this Convention have agreed to seek settlement of the dispute by a peaceful means of their own choice, the procedures provided for in this Part apply only where no settlement has been reached by recourse to such means and the agreement between the parties does not exclude any further procedure.

2. If the parties have also agreed on a time-limit, paragraph 1 applies only upon the expiration of that time-limit.

Article 282

Obligation under general, regional or bilateral agreements

If the States Parties which are parties to a dispute concerning the interpretation or application of this Convention have agreed, through a general, regional or bilateral agreement or otherwise, that such dispute shall, at the request of any party to the dispute, be submitted to a procedure that entails a binding decision, that procedure shall apply in lieu of the procedures provided for in this Part, unless the parties to the dispute otherwise agree.

Article 283

Obligation to exchange views

1. When a dispute arises between States Parties concerning the interpretation or application of this Convention, the parties to the dispute shall proceed expeditiously to an exchange of views regarding its settlement by negotiation or other peaceful means.

2. The parties shall also proceed expeditiously to an exchange of views where a procedure for the settlement of such a dispute has been terminated without or where a settlement has been reached and the circumstances require consultation regarding the manner of implementing the settlement.

Article 284

Conciliation

1. A State Party which is a party to a dispute concerning the interpretation or application of this Convention may invite the other party or parties to submit the dispute to conciliation in accordance with the procedure under Annex V, section 1, or another conciliation procedure.

2. If the invitation is accepted and if the parties agree upon the conciliation procedure to be applied, any party may submit the dispute to that procedure.

3. If the invitation is not accepted or the parties do not agree upon the procedure, the conciliation proceedings shall be deemed to be terminated.

4. Unless the parties otherwise agree, when a dispute has been submitted to conciliation, the proceedings may be terminated only in accordance with the agreed conciliation procedure.

Article 285

Application of this section to disputes submitted pursuant to Part XI

This section applies to any dispute which pursuant to Part XI, section 5, is to be settled in accordance with procedures provided for in this Part. If an entity other than a State Party is a party to such a dispute, this section applies *mutatis mutandis*.

SECTION 2. COMPULSORY PROCEDURES ENTAILING BINDING DECISIONS

Article 286

Application of procedures under this section

Subject to section 3, any dispute concerning the interpretation or application of this Convention shall, where no settlement has been reached by recourse to section 1, be submitted at the request of any party to the dispute to the court or tribunal having jurisdiction under this section.

Article 287

Choice of procedure

1. When signing, ratifying or acceding to this Convention or at any time thereafter, a State shall be free to choose, by means of a written declaration, one or more of the following means for the settlement of disputes concerning the interpretation or application of this Convention:

(a) the International Tribunal for the Law of the Sea established in accordance with Annex VI;

(b) the International Court of Justice;

(c) an arbitral tribunal constituted in accordance with Annex VII;

(d) a special arbitral tribunal constituted in accordance with Annex VIII for one or more of the categories of disputes specified therein.

2. A declaration made under paragraph 1 shall not affect or be affected by the obligation of a State Party to accept the jurisdiction of the Sea–Bed Disputes Chamber of the International Tribunal for the Law of the Sea to the extent and in the manner provided for in Part XI, section 5.

3. A State Party, which is a party to a dispute not covered by a declaration in force, shall be deemed to have accepted arbitration in accordance with Annex VII.

4. If the parties to a dispute have accepted the same procedure for the settlement of the dispute, it may be submitted only to that procedure, unless the parties otherwise agree.

5. If the parties to a dispute have not accepted the same procedure for the settlement of the dispute, it may be submitted only to arbitration in accordance with Annex VII, unless the parties otherwise agree.

6. A declaration made under paragraph 1 shall remain in force until three months after notice of revocation has been deposited with the Secretary–General of the United Nations.

7. A new declaration, a notice of revocation or the expiry of a declaration does not in any way affect proceedings pending before a court or tribunal having jurisdiction under this article, unless the parties otherwise agree.

8. Declarations and notices referred to in this article shall be deposited with the Secretary–General of the United Nations, who shall transmit copies thereof to the States Parties.

Article 288

Jurisdiction

1. A court or tribunal referred to in article 287 shall have jurisdiction over any dispute concerning the interpretation or application of this Convention which is submitted to it in accordance with this Part.

2. A court or tribunal referred to in article 287 shall also have jurisdiction over any dispute concerning the interpretation or application of an international agreement related to the purposes of this Convention, which is submitted to it in accordance with the agreement.

3. The Sea–Bed Disputes Chamber of the International Tribunal for the Law of the Sea established in accordance with Annex VI, and any other chamber or arbitral tribunal referred to in Part XI, section 5, shall have jurisdiction in any matter which is submitted to it in accordance therewith.

4. In the event of a dispute as to whether a court or tribunal has jurisdiction, the matter shall be settled by decision of that court or tribunal. * * *

Article 291

Access

1. All the dispute settlement procedures specified in this Part shall be open to States Parties.

2. The dispute settlement procedures specified in this Part shall be open to entities other than States Parties only as specifically provided for in this Convention.

Article 292

Prompt release of vessels and crews

1. Where the authorities of a State Party have detained a vessel flying the flag of another State Party and it is alleged that the detaining State has not complied with the provisions of this Convention for the prompt release of the vessel or its crew upon the posting of a reasonable bond or other financial security, the question of release from detention may be submitted to any court or tribunal agreed upon by the parties or, failing such agreement within 10 days from the time of detention, to a court or tribunal accepted by the detaining State under article 287 or to the International Tribunal for the Law of the Sea, unless the parties otherwise agree.

2. The application for release may be made only by or on behalf of the flag State of the vessel.

3. The court or tribunal shall deal without delay with the application for release and shall deal only with the question of release, without prejudice to the merits of any case before the appropriate domestic forum against the vessel, its owner or its crew. The authorities of the detaining State remain competent to release the vessel or its crew at any time.

4. Upon the posting of the bond or other financial security determined by the court or tribunal, the authorities of the detaining State shall comply promptly with the decision of the court or tribunal concerning the release of the vessel or its crew.

Article 293

Applicable law

1. A court or tribunal having jurisdiction under this section shall apply this Convention and other rules of international law not incompatible with this Convention.

2. Paragraph 1 does not prejudice the power of the court or tribunal having jurisdiction under this section to decide a case *ex aequo et bono*, if the parties so agree. * * *

Article 295

Exhaustion of local remedies

Any dispute between States Parties concerning the interpretation or application of this Convention may be submitted to the procedures provided for in this section only after local remedies have been exhausted where this is required by international law.

Article 296

Finality and binding force of decisions

1. Any decision rendered by a court or tribunal having jurisdiction under this section shall be final and shall be complied with by all the parties to the dispute.

2. Any such decision shall have no binding force except between the parties and in respect of that particular dispute.

SECTION 3. LIMITATIONS AND EXCEPTIONS TO APPLICABILITY OF SECTION 2

Article 297

Limitations on applicability of section 2

1. Disputes concerning the interpretation or application of this Convention with regard to the exercise by a coastal State of its sovereign rights or jurisdiction provided for in this Convention shall be subject to the procedures provided for in section 2 in the following cases:

(a) when it is alleged that a coastal State has acted in contravention of the provisions of this Convention in regard to the freedoms and rights of navigation, overflight or the laying of submarine cables and pipelines, or in regard to other internationally lawful uses of the sea specified in article 58;

(b) when it is alleged that a State in exercising the aforementioned freedoms, rights or uses has acted in contravention of this Convention or of laws or regulations adopted by the coastal State in conformity with this Convention and other rules of international law not incompatible with this Convention; or

(c) when it is alleged that a coastal State has acted in contravention of specified international rules and standards for the protection and preservation of the marine environment which are applicable to the coastal State and which have been established by this Convention or through a competent international organization or diplomatic conference in accordance with this Convention. * * *

3. (a) Disputes concerning the interpretation or application of the provisions of this Convention with regard to fisheries shall be settled in accordance with section 2, except that the coastal State shall not be obliged to accept the submission to such settlement of any dispute relating to its sovereign rights with respect to the living resources in the exclusive economic zone or their exercise, including its discretionary powers for determining the allowable catch, its harvesting capacity, the allocation of surpluses to other States and the terms and conditions established in its conservation and management laws and regulations.

(b) Where no settlement has been reached by recourse to section 1 of this Part, a dispute shall be submitted to conciliation under Annex V, section 2, at the request of any party to the dispute, when it is alleged that:

(i) a coastal State has manifestly failed to comply with its obligations to ensure through proper conservation and management measures that the maintenance of the living resources in the exclusive economic zone is not seriously endangered;

(ii) a coastal State has arbitrarily refused to determine, at the request of another State, the allowable catch and its capacity to harvest living resources with respect to stocks which that other State is interested in fishing; or

(iii) a coastal State has arbitrarily refused to allocate to any State, under articles 62, 69 and 70 and under the terms and conditions established by the coastal State consistent with this Convention, the whole or part of the surplus it has declared to exist.

(c) In no case shall the conciliation commission substitute its discretion for that of the coastal State.

(d) The report of the conciliation commission shall be communicated to the appropriate international organizations.

(e) In negotiating agreements pursuant to articles 69 and 70, States Parties, unless they otherwise agree, shall include a clause on measures which they shall take in order to minimize the possibility of a disagreement concerning the interpretation or application of the agreement, and on how they should proceed if a disagreement nevertheless arises.

Article 298

Optional exceptions to applicability of section 2 * * *

PART XVI

GENERAL PROVISIONS

Article 300

Good faith and abuse of rights

States Parties shall fulfil in good faith the obligations assumed under this Convention and shall exercise the rights, jurisdiction and freedoms recognized in this Convention in a manner which would not constitute an abuse of right.

[Article 301 is reproduced in Chapter 9, at page 538.]

PART XVII

FINAL PROVISIONS * * *

Article 308

Entry into force

1. This Convention shall enter into force 12 months after the date of deposit of the sixtieth instrument of ratification or accession. * * *

Article 309

Reservations and exceptions

No reservations or exceptions may be made to this Convention unless expressly permitted by other articles of this Convention. * * *

Index

References are to pages

A

References are to pages

References are to pages

D

H

References are to pages

I

References are to pages

References are to pages

References are to pages

†